MANAGEMENT

A Total Quality Perspective

Gregory M. Bounds
Queens College

Gregory H. Dobbins
University of Tennessee

Oscar S. Fowler
University of Tennessee

SOUTH-WESTERN College Publishing

An International Thomson Publishing Company

Acquisitions Editor:	Randy G. Haubner
Developmental Editor:	Cinci Stowell
Production Editor:	Sharon L. Smith
Production, Art, and Prepress:	PC&F, Inc.
Cover Design:	Tin Box Studio
Cover Illustration:	Bill Frampton
Internal Design:	Ellen Pettengell Design
Internal Illustration:	Photonics/Alan Brown
Marketing Manager:	Stephen E. Momper
Sponsoring Representatives:	Everett Crow
	Pamela M. Person

GC61AA
Copyright © 1995
by South-Western College Publishing
Cincinnati, Ohio

Library of Congress Cataloging-in-Publication Data

Bounds, Gregory M.
     Management: a total quality perspective / Gregory M. Bounds, Gregory H. Dobbins, Oscar S. Fowler.
          p.   cm.
     Includes index.
     ISBN 0-538-84344-6
     1. Total quality management.   2. Management.   I. Dobbins, Gregory H. II. Fowler, Oscar S., 1935–   .   III. Title.
     HD62.15.868   1994
     658.5'62—dc20
                                                                94-33898
                                                                CIP

1 2 3 4 5 6 7 KI 0 9 8 7 6 5 4
Printed in the United States of America

I(T)P

International Thomson Publishing

South-Western College Publishing is an ITP Company. The ITP trademark is used under license.

CONTENTS IN BRIEF

CONTENTS

P A R T   1

THE FIELD OF MANAGEMENT 1

6   DECISION MAKING AND TQM

P A R T   3

8   ORGANIZATIONAL STRUCTURE AND DESIGN

ORGANIZING TO
COMPETE
273

9 HUMAN RESOURCES MANAGEMENT 308

10 ORGANIZATIONAL CULTURE

P A R T   4

SOCIAL AND CULTURAL PROCESSES
385

13 COMMUNICATION 468

Foreword

In 1840, a train wreck on the Western Railroad brought about a re-examination of how the railroads should be run. It also brought about changes in the way *all* businesses would operate. It resulted in the emergence of a new role called the **manager.** It was the dawn of the Industrial Revolution.

For all practical purposes, the management approach begun in 1840 has been the prevailing premise of management in the United States; the source of problems is primarily operator error and dereliction of duty; therefore, managers' main responsibility is to control and motivate.

In 1950, however, a new premise of management emerged. The Japanese call it TQC for Total Quality Control. They learned the basics from Dr. W. Edwards Deming and Dr. Joseph Juran. The new approach emphasized customers, systems, and improvement. It worked against the 110-year-old management practice of "blame the worker."

American managers in the last few decades of this century have been thrust into the transition from old management to new management and from the focus on managers, culprits, and blame to the focus on customers, systems, and improvement. *Management: A Total Quality Perspective* is a contribution to this need for transition and those who must undergo it. It is a good effort for a noble cause.

Peter R. Scholtes

Peter R. Scholtes is the President of Scholtes Seminars and Consulting, a company specializing in teaching managers the new approaches to quality management. He is the author of The Team Handbook *which has sold over 600,000 copies. He has also written several articles on Quality-related topics.*

Albert Einstein, unquestionably one of the most successful and important people of the century, was once asked how he became so successful. His answer was profound. He said, "Try not to become a person of success, try rather to become a person of value."

Business success is measured by profits and return on investments. But the path to business success is through the value of the products and services provided to customers. After all, the customer is the final judge of quality, they have all the votes, and they vote with their dollars.

Management: A Total Quality Perspective is a text about how to be successful in business by creating value that wins customers' votes.

Total Quality is achieved only when customers are *completely satisfied*. No one person and no one business process can totally satisfy a customer's needs.

It requires the whole organization, working together in a systematic way toward a common purpose. Total Quality Management techniques help the people and processes that make up the firm accomplish together what they cannot achieve alone.

This book contains proven principles of management that harness the full power of an organization. By focusing that power on customer needs, value will be delivered to customers who, in turn, will create jobs for employees and profit for owners. Firms that completely meet the needs of its customers, employees, and shareholders are truly successful.

Raymond E. Kordupleski
AT&T Customer Satisfaction
Director

At Motorola, we believe our purpose is to deliver quality products and services to our customers. When we do a good job of this, we prosper. The challenge for today's managers is to keep that purpose in the center of their thoughts and use it to direct all their activities.

Over the past few decades, American businesspeople have seen the value of the systems view of organizations and the insights of TQM for successfully managing systems. That approach represents the heart and soul of Motorola's operating philosophy. We learned this from benchmarking the best practices of worldwide leading companies and from our own experiences. The ideas presented in this textbook are in agreement with the Motorola approach to managing.

In an intensely competitive, no-holds-barred global marketplace, committing to a TQM game plan that is customer-focused and results-oriented through a trained and empowered workforce is about the best way to make sure you will remain a player in this marketplace. I am glad to see textbooks like this one emphasizing this approach for students. They will soon be our next generation of managers, and they need to understand these principles and how to put them into action.

Richard C. Buetow
Senior Vice President
Director of Corporate Quality
Motorola, Inc.

Should we reengineer our delivery processes? Maybe if we organize in teams? A Total Quality approach? How can we effectively empower every group? We're all searching for a way to create the fast, flexible, adaptive, customer-focused organization needed to survive in today's rapidly changing marketplace. However, despite a wide variety of valuable tools, the reality is that we have been much better at describing the type of organization that we would like to create than we have been at building the skills and making the tough choices necessary to change significantly.

It's natural to wish for a clear road map—a tried-and-true process that, if followed, will result in the types of changes we know are required to achieve future success. If there were one, things would be more predictable and the payoff from the journey more certain. However, as much as we might wish otherwise, there is no universally applicable method that will work equally well in all circumstances. Although many organizations appear similar, even incremental differences in organizations can result in dramatic differences in the way organizations react to improvement attempts. The reality is that we must embrace complexity and customize a method that will be effective in a particular situation at a particular point in time. We must come to grips with the fact that uncertainty is a permanent condition.

When certainty fails us, experimentation is the only road to success. Given the pace of change and the unpredictable nature of the changes we face, every improvement attempt is necessarily an experiment and every experiment an opportunity to learn how to create more effective experiments in the future. At its best, experimentation teaches us which actions can produce a sought-for systematic change *in that particular system.* At its worst, experimentation takes us down blind alleys. Yet even the blind alley can lead us to greater insight, provided we have learned to learn and profit from our mistakes.

Unfortunately, few leaders have learned to learn from their implementation efforts. Too often we've adopted an improvement methodology and we've expected these methods, combined with minor changes in our behavior and organization structure, to yield dramatic differences. When the results were less than we had hoped for, we often set out in search of a better method. We conducted the experiment but we failed to analyze the results. Instead of systematically investigating the cause of our failures and addressing them systematically, we looked for the next experiment. It's no wonder that many people labeled our improvement efforts "management by best seller" or "flavor-of-the-month management."

Effective leaders of the future will reject the notion that they can "do it right the first time" when it comes to substantial organizational improvement efforts and will embrace the idea that looking less than brilliant comes with the territory. They will be comfortable with uncertainty, evangelical about the need to experiment and will surround themselves with people who incessantly question past practices. And maybe more importantly, they will have an insatiable appetite for learning. Whether they call it TQM or XYZ improvement methodology, they will view every interaction as a learning opportunity and they will ensure that every person shares a method for evaluating progress and sharing insights.

In this text, the authors have adopted a learning philosophy and have applied that philosophy to the tasks that have been considered management responsibilities in the past while questioning the relevancy of many traditional roles. Such a text is long overdue. It is imperative that we accept the fact that what we know about how to lead in the future pales in comparison to what we don't know. Only then will we be on the road to creating the fast, flexible, adaptive, customer-focused organization that may survive and prosper in the future.

Gary Heil

Gary Heil is President of Heil and Associates and founder of The Center for Innovative Leadership. He also serves as examiner for the Malcolm Baldrige Quality Awards. His new book Leadership and the Customer Revolution *can be found in bookstores across the country.*

PREFACE

There is revolution going on in management today. Old understandings are being questioned as never before. New insights are changing the way managers understand their responsibilities. Those running the most admired corporations view their companies in a new light—as systems made of interacting and interrelated parts. They understand that the primary purpose of their companies is meeting and exceeding customer needs and expectations. They know that this is what generates profits so they will be around tomorrow. This systems view has brought about a new attitude and approach for successfully serving customer needs. The emphasis is on bringing employees together as team members to execute organizational processes. This approach includes a variety of techniques for helping an organization continuously improve its productivity and the quality and value of its products and services. This new approach goes by the name Total Quality Management or TQM. It forms the foundation and theme of this text.

We provide instructors with a new rendering of many of the ideas they will find in other texts but filtered through the lens of Total Quality. While this new approach clearly differentiates us, we have not done this just to be different. We believe that TQM is a more realistic way to understand and execute management tasks. Students who understand the principles of teamwork, informed decision making, continuous improvement, and a relentless focus on customer value are more likely to prosper in today's job market. Indeed, because of the new demands of the globally competitive business environment that managers face today, such a fresh approach to educating our future managers is not just a good idea—it is imperative.

THE SYSTEMS VIEW AS THE FOUNDATION

For decades the field of management has been enamored of the "systems view" or "open system theory" of organizations. The systems view regards the organization as an integrated set of activities (or processes) for bringing together inputs from the outside environment, transforming them into products and services, and then releasing them as outputs back into the environment. Information feedback and other returns from the environment help to regenerate the system and sustain its activity.

Engaging metaphors from the systems view lead us to think of an organization as a living organism rather than a machine, and to see that people within the organization are vibrant social beings with feelings, hopes and dreams, and not just cogs in the machine. Like natural lifeforms, an organization is dependent on its environment for its survival and prosperity.

Until very recently, however, the systems view has been little more than an intriguing concept. It has not appealed to practicing managers who typically discount it as either too abstract or too commonsensical. With the advent of TQM as a way to operationalize the systems view, practicing managers are finally embracing it.

As a logical extension of the systems view, TQM emphasizes the importance of focusing on external customers who provide the lifeblood of a business organization by purchasing its goods and services. TQM also emphasizes the importance of learning about the interdependent processes of the organization and continuously improving those processes to ensure that the organization provides superior customer value. These inherent values of TQM translate into a new set of managerial roles.

TQM requires managers to be creative visionaries, leaders of change, facilitators of learning, and promoters of teamwork. This approach to management is required in today's intensely competitive global business environment. Managers are realizing that TQM is an approach to management that enhances their ability to achieve their organization's mission, and ultimately it determines their economic performance. This reality has captured their attention.

Traditionally, principles of management texts have not fully explored the rich implications of the systems view. They have treated TQM cautiously, not sure whether it is a passing fad or just another concoction by consultants. Other texts have, at best, relegated TQM to part of a single chapter, usually toward the end of the book, or mentioned it in special exhibits and boxed features. This is not the situation with this text. We take the systems view and TQM as the integrative framework and underpinning for the entire textbook.

We have taken this bold step for a number of reasons. First and foremost, we hold that since organizations are systems, this is the best way to manage them. Second, the customers in the principles of management market are demanding it. Third, leading organizations are demanding that students be educated on the concepts and methods of TQM. Finally, we were convinced that students need an integrative framework to help them make sense of the many concepts and methods that they will encounter in their first introduction to the field of management.

TQM and the systems view provide the best integrative framework currently available. They furnish us with a set of values and a purpose for management. They give students a sense of direction that will serve them well throughout their academic and professional careers.

While we are in transition to this new approach to management, the phrases "Total Quality Management" and "TQM" will likely be used to differentiate what managers are doing now from what they have done in the past. As the history of the field of management continues to march on, we may eventually drop this special terminology and simply refer to what we now call TQM as just "good management."

CONTENT

TQM forms the backdrop of every chapter in the text. While many of the chapters cover topics common to every text (and appropriately so), you will find the ideas often described in terms of systems, processes, and customer focus. Our text also offers two unique chapters on TQM (Chapters 3 and 16). Instructors who teach management from a quality perspective will find a lot to love in this text. Until now, they have been forced to rely upon a hodgepodge of books and articles that were not written explicitly for classroom use. If you are one of these instructors, you will be glad to learn that our text advocates TQM and provides all of the special features and ancillaries that you have come to expect in a major principles of management text.

Instructors who are just moving in this direction will find many familiar topics that they have been teaching from other texts. We recognize the importance of understanding the foundations of the field of management. To this end, we have covered all major areas of management as they have been traditionally covered in principles texts. We have also covered the basic theories of management that most instructors like to introduce in the principles course. However, we have either integrated discussion of these theories into a Total Quality perspective, or we have contrasted them with TQM, whichever seems appropriate.

We have carefully sought a balance between the traditional topics that form the foundation of the field of management and the cutting edge of Total Quality Management. And we have shown how this foundation gets reinterpreted in TQM. Instructors who are interested in teaching students from a Total Quality perspective but still want to ensure that the traditional topics of management are covered will find much to love here.

We provide an abundance of cases and examples to illustrate the concepts and demonstrate to students that what they are learning is not just theory but important perspectives on real world management practices. Students will perceive the relevance of the text to their professional lives, whether they concentrate on management, accounting, marketing, finance, logistics, or engineering. In any of these fields, students will eventually end up working in an organization, and this text will help them appreciate how they fit into the larger business context.

Although we cover the major theories of management, we do not approach the material from the perspective of a researcher or theory builder. The text is well grounded in established theories, but these are discussed in a reader-friendly way. We also show how managers use theory to accomplish the goals of their organizations.

PEDAGOGICAL FEATURES

As authors of this text, we have not forgotten that we are also teachers. We have carefully considered how we can help you, the instructor, give students a valuable and memorable learning experience. Our first obligation here is done through our writing: to conceive the field of management, introduce concepts and methods, and tie these together into an integrated approach to management. Beyond this basic responsibility, however, we have included a number of pedagogical features and a variety of ancillary materials that will help you teach the concepts and methods. Among the pedagogical elements, you will find:

- **Learning Objectives.** At the beginning of the chapter the learning objectives specify what the students should be able to do after reading the chapter. These objectives are specifically worded in behavioral terms to convey to students that we expect them to do more than just *understand* what they read.

They must also be able to do such things as "explain," "describe," "discuss," and "define" the concepts and methods that they have read about. Behaviorally defined learning objectives also tell the students that we intend for them to be *active learners,* not just passive recipients of information. This active learning is further reinforced through the other pedagogical features discussed below.

- **Chapter Outline.** The chapter outline provides students with an overview of the chapter prior to reading it. (Recall that your own English Composition professor may have advised you to use the following structure for papers and oral presentations: "Tell them what you are going to tell them, tell them, and then tell them what you told them.") We have included all first- and second-level headings in these outlines, which gives the student a detailed first glance of the chapter contents. Students can use this outline in studying for tests to learn how specific topics fit together. It also provides another means for students to glance through the text to find specific topics within chapters.

- **Case in Point as Chapter Introduction and Case in Point, Revisited at Chapter End.** Each chapter contains an opening *Case in Point,* a brief case on a real company that pertains to the topic or major themes of the chapter. While some companies profiled here are well-known, we have also sought out cases from small- and medium-size firms, the kind that most students are likely to work for. These cases foreshadow the chapter material, establish the importance of specific concepts or methods, or introduce a problem or issue that will be resolved later in the chapter. Sometimes we refer to the Case in Point company in the chapter to illustrate certain points or provide more information that fits in with what students have already read about the company. Toward the end of each chapter we revisit the Case in Point to provide additional information or insights about the events of the case. These may also raise more questions, in light of the foregoing chapter content. The Case in Point helps students see that the concepts and methods they are reading about are not just theories but relevant to real managers. This feature of *perceived relevance* is extremely important since one of the most difficult challenges we face as educators is to establish within students a *motivation to learn.*

- **A Look At Diversity, Ethics, Technology, The Global Environment, and TQM in Action.**

DIVERSITY   ETHICS   TECHNOLOGY   THE GLOBAL ENVIRONMENT   TQM IN ACTION

The *A Look At* boxes also help to accomplish "perceived relevance" by adding more cases and examples to the text. Several of these boxes are sprinkled throughout each chapter, positioned close to appropriate topics in the narrative. These boxes address what might be described as hot topics, as suggested by the American Assembly of Collegiate Schools of Business, including diversity, ethics, technology, global/international, and TQM/quality issues. They present students with real examples of companies applying the principles and techniques the text describes. In addition to bringing the chapter to life for students, these features also provide a mental break from grinding through the chapter content. It gives students a reason to relax for a moment and perhaps assimilate what they have been reading. These boxes can also be an integrative learning experience that promotes understanding of how several concepts fit together or helps students derive additional meaning from the chapter concepts.

- **A Look At Managers in Action.** Besides the *A Look At* boxes that describe hot topics, another important feature is *A Look At Managers in Action*. These are boxes written specifically for this text by real people who are experienced managers and practitioners of Total Quality Management. The organizations represented here are drawn from diverse industries, and the managers are drawn from diverse levels, ranging from the top levels of the executive boardroom to the front lines of management. The messages are tailored to the chapters that contain them, and they are addressed to the student. These boxes are another creative way to give life to the chapters, embody the concepts in practice, increase the perceived relevance of the text, and provide the students with a diverse set of role models.

A LOOK AT

MANAGERS
IN ACTION

We thank these people for taking the time to write these messages:

Mike Copeland *Procter & Gamble*	Louise Goeser *Whirlpool Corporation*
Alouise McNichols *AT&T*	Greg Conway *Watervliet Arsenal*
Robert S. Kincade *Westinghouse*	Edward J. Leroux *Xerox Corporation*
G. Robert Lea *Paul Revere Insurance Group*	Beth Hauser *Florida Power & Light*
Brian Boling *Phillips Consumer Electronics*	Danica M. Taurosa *Delta Airlines*
Paula Goodman *Citibank*	Dave Siefert *Hallmark Cards*
Christopher B. Galvin *Motorola*	Robert J. Dika *Chrysler Corporation*
Raul Cosio *IBM Latin America*	

- **Case Analysis and Application.** We provide students the opportunity to apply what they have learned through the Case Analysis and Application featured at the end of each chapter. Once again, these cases feature real managers and real organizations as they wrestle with the challenges of management that are addressed in the chapter. The discussion questions that accompany each case lead students in their analysis and help them apply the concepts and methods from the chapter. This feature actively involves students in the learning process.

- **Thinking Critically Questions.** At the end of each major section of a chapter, we include two to four questions that ask students to think critically about the issues and ideas that they just read about. These "thinking critically"

questions never ask students to recite what they just read or recall facts. Rather, they require students to consider and apply these ideas in light of their own experiences. Or they ask them to speculate on how these ideas might work in an organization they know something about. Our goal throughout has been to draw students in by having them reflect on the personal relevance of these ideas and how they might provide insight into their own experiences. We hope they prompt lively and useful discussion for the class as a whole or in small groups.

- **Margin Definitions.** In the margins of each chapter we list the definitions of key terms as these terms come up. Our purpose is to ensure that students take note of them as they are reading the chapter. These margin definitions are also useful to students as they review the material in preparation for tests.

- **Icons as Visual Aids Within the Text.** In addition to offering an attractive layout, with pictures, exhibits, and charts to illustrate and clarify the written ideas, we also include icons that visually point out many of the special features of the text that we just described. The icons indicate the location of critical thinking questions, the appropriate place to use specific videos, and the location of special boxes on Diversity, Ethics, Technology, Global Environment, TQM in Action, and Managers in Action. These icons are located in the Table of Contents and in the body of the chapters to help the instructor easily locate the special features of the text.

- **Chapter Summary.** At the end of the chapter we provide a summary (to "tell them what we told them"). We have sought to capture the key concepts in the chapter, presented in bulleted points under the major chapter headings. This provides another overview of the chapter in an accessible form to help students understand how the many specific topics fit together and to help them assimilate what they just read.

- **List of Key Terms with Page Numbers.** We have included a list of key terms from the chapter along with the page numbers where students can find the definitions. This feature is a convenient means for students to quickly find definitions as they review the chapter and study for tests. It also provides them with a checklist that they can use to ensure that they are able to define all key terms. If they are unsure about a definition, they can quickly refer to the page number listed and refresh their memory.

- **Review Questions.** Review questions test students' understanding of the most important ideas presented in the chapter. These questions simply ask students to recall definitions, ideas, or explanations. They do not ask students to generate new ideas or explanations, as did the critical thinking questions within the chapter. If students have trouble answering a review question, they can often find within the question a key term listed just above the review questions. They can then refer to the listed page number to get the answer.

- **Experiential Exercises.** The experiential exercises provide yet another means of promoting active learning by requiring students to apply what they have learned from the chapter. The experiential exercises at the end of each chapter offer a variety of formats, including individual and team activities, in-class and out-of-class activities, analyses, applications, discussions, and role-plays.

- **End-of-Part Integrative Cases.** At the end of each part of the book, we present an integrative case that pertains to the chapters contained in that part. These cases are extensive and offer an in-depth look at the practice of management by real managers in real organizations. Furthermore, the organizations represented in these cases are quite diverse, including service and manufacturing organizations. The companies featured in these cases are Ritz-Carlton, Alliant Health System, Sega, Nissan, and FedEx. Again, these cases contribute to the "perceived relevance" of the concepts and methods presented in the text. They also give students yet another opportunity for active learning through the questions listed at the end of the case which require analysis and application. These cases are also quite amenable to use in small-group activities.

ANCILLARIES

We know that teaching this course requires a variety of media and support materials for students and instructors. To that end, this text includes an exceptional array of ancillary materials to help instructors teach and students learn. Included in the text package:

- **Videos on Total Quality Management.** Visual and auditory images are often the most memorable experiences that we carry with us throughout our lives. To take advantage of this robust medium for learning, we have provided an exceptional collection of videos that are integrated with the concepts and methods presented in the text. These videos illustrate how Total Quality Management is implemented by real managers in real organizations. The organizations represented in our collection of videos are quite diverse in size and type of industry, as you see in the list below:

Motorola	Westinghouse
Cadillac	Cooperative Home Care Assoc.
FedEx	Stein & Company
Xerox	Cummins Engine
Milliken	Springfield ReManufacturing Corp.
IBM	Wallace Co.
Merck & Co.	Northern Telecom
Finast	Prudential Insurance
Easy Pay	Flex-N-Gate
DAKA International	Ames Rubber
Toyota	Graniterock
Eastman Chemical Co.	Ben & Jerry's Homemade
Hanna Andersson	Inland Steel
AT&T Transmission Systems	GE Plastics
Globe Metallurgical	

Every chapter has at least one and often several accompanying videos. Video icons, located in the chapter margins, identify for you where in your lectures you could appropriately show the videos. The videos either focus explicitly on Total Quality Management or on another topic that is growing in importance among academics and practicing managers alike—combining social responsibility and quality management.

- **Video Cases on Combining Social Responsibility and Quality Management.** Along with the business community, we have all lamented the failure of business schools to teach students about ethics and give them a sense of social responsibility. We are doing better at teaching these important topics now than in past decades. Some schools require special courses in this area, and most principles of management books include at least a chapter on the topic. In this text, we have gone even further by including cases and video documentaries that illustrate how managers can combine social responsibility and quality management. This material is spread throughout the text and is integrated with the themes of 13 of our chapters. These cases and video documentaries feature real people who provide students with role models and bring to life the concepts of social responsibility and quality management.

  These videos were contributed by the Business Enterprise Trust, a national nonprofit organization led by James Burke, Warren Buffett, Katherine Graham, Norman Lear, Robert Reich, and other prominent leaders in American business, academia, labor, and the media. Since its founding in 1989, the Trust has identified acts of courage, integrity, and social vision in business and, through its educational materials, has promoted these role models of practical, socially minded innovations. These bold, creative leaders are exactly the kinds of inspirational role models that our future managers need.

  This is the only principles of management text to offer the Business Enterprise Trust cases and video documentaries. This unique feature of our text vividly illustrates how managers of the future can combine sound management and social consciousness. The discussion questions that accompany each video case also provide students with yet another opportunity to analyze real events and apply what they have learned in the text chapters.

- **Videodisc and Videodisc Guide.** Excite your students with the color and variety of a multimedia presentation, using cutting-edge videodisc technology. The videodisc contains animated illustrations, transparencies, and videos for classroom projection. These can be viewed in any order you choose, and with an optional computer and South-Western software you can prepare a complete video "script" of your classroom presentation ahead of time. An accompanying *Videodisc Guide* describes how to integrate this technology into your classroom. A compatible "CAV-type" videodisc is required to use this ancillary.

- **Instructor's Resource Guide.** The Instructor's Resource Guide is one-stop shopping for everything you need to prepare lectures, implement student activities, and bring in additional materials. The heart of the resource guide is the *expanded outline* for each chapter. In addition to the key points of each section, these outlines offer additional *examples, teaching tips,* and *extra activities* not in the text. They also include cues to identify when to *show videos, discuss exhibits, use review questions,* and *show transparencies,* along with *discussion aids* to use with transparencies.

The resource guide also contains the *learning objectives* with summaries of their key points, and *complete solutions* to the thinking critically questions, review questions, cases, video cases, and integrative cases. For the experiential exercises, the resource guide provides guidance for implementing and evaluating these important student activities. For instructors switching from other texts, each chapter of the resource guide begins with a brief summary of key chapter features and correlations with chapters from your old text. All *videos are previewed* for you in the resource guide. The guide gives the running times, a brief summary of each video, solutions to questions posed, and additional discussion tips.

- **Test Bank and MicroExam 4.0.**   The Test Bank includes an abundance of *true-false, multiple-choice, scenario,* and *essay questions, with answers and page references* for where in the text the answers can be found. Each question is identified as "definition," "application," or "conceptual." You can use these type identifications to design tests that fit the abilities of your students. Most instructors feel that it is important for students to apply concepts, not just memorize them. Therefore, most questions in the test bank are of the application or conceptual type. The short scenarios present students with typical management problems and require them to solve them using chapter concepts.

  All items from the printed test bank are available on disk through South-Western's automated testing program, *MicroExam 4.0.* This program allows you to create exams by selecting questions as provided by the program, modifying existing questions, or adding questions. MicroExam 4.0 will run on MS–DOS computers with a minimum 640K memory, a 3½" disk drive, and a hard drive. MicroExam 4.0 is provided free of charge to instructors at educational institutions that adopt *Management: A Total Quality Perspective,* by Bounds, Dobbins, and Fowler.

- **Transparencies.**   To supplement your lectures, we have worked with the publisher to create 150 color transparencies to illustrate key concepts. Approximately 70 percent of the transparencies are new—they do not appear in the text. The other 30% are key text exhibits. The transparencies have been carefully designed to be easily readable from the back of a large lecture hall.

- **Study Guide.**   Our research has shown that students use study guides to help them prepare for exams. Therefore, our Study Guide has been specially designed to contain the same types of questions, including scenarios and essays, and the same level of difficulty as the questions in the test bank. Solutions appear at the back. If students do well on their study guide practice questions, they should do well on the exams. In addition to practice questions, the study guide contains chapter outlines, enhanced with key points and additional explanations to help students understand.

ACKNOWLEDGEMENTS

In writing this text we have enjoyed the support and assistance of many of our friends and colleagues and The University of Tennessee. We cannot possibly list all of the people who have helped us with this endeavor. However, we do want to acknowledge some very special people. We are indebted to a number of our colleagues who read the manuscript and made many suggestions for improvement, which, in the best tradition of TQM, we did our best to implement. We want to acknowledge those individuals here:

Melville W. Adams
University of Alabama–Huntsville

Gina Wilson Beckles
Bethune–Cookman College

Joseph E. Cantrell
DeAnza College

Roy A. Cook
Fort Lewis College

Dale Feinauer
University of Wisconsin Oshkosh

Barbara Hastings
The University of South Carolina Spartanburg

Steven E. Huntley
Florida Community College

Ulysses S. Knotts
Georgia Southern University

Vince Luchsinger
University of Baltimore

Jason Lunday
The Ethics Resource Center, Washington, DC

Mike McCullough
University of Tennessee at Martin

Herbert Moskowitz
Purdue University

Larry A. Pace
Louisiana State University in Shreveport

C. Richard Paulson
Mankato State University

Harry V. Roberts
The University of Chicago

Gregory K. Stephens
Texas Christian University

Romuald A. Stone
James Madison University

H. William Vroman
Morgan State University

H. Oliver Welch
Clark Atlanta University

Dale Young
Miami University

Thanks all!

We are particularly thankful to all of the managers and companies who contributed their time, ideas, information, illustrations, videos and other material to help us take this text to the cutting edge of management practices.

Several colleagues and students at the University of Tennessee made numerous contributions to several chapters: Dudley Dewhirst, Bob Maddox, Jeff Kudish, Aaron Fausz, Kyle Lundby, Harold Black, Al Cole, Tammy Allen, Lauren Baumann, and Bill Judge. Thanks to all of you.

We want to especially thank John Woods for his tireless efforts to contribute ideas, conduct additional research, and help us develop the final draft of the manuscript. John has an extensive background in publishing, writing, business, and quality management and is the editor of *The Quality Yearbook* (McGraw-Hill, published annually). Having him as part of our team made it possible for us to accomplish what must be record time for completing a project of this magnitude and importance.

The text and ancillaries were developed and produced using the team concept. We would like to thank South-Western's Management Team for applying their Total Quality concept so effectively to this project: Randy Haubner, Cinci Stowell, Sharon Smith, Sherie Lajti, Joe Devine, Steve Momper, Pam Person, Peggy Buskey, Tracy Megison, and Chris Sofranko.

We would also like to thank the excellent team of ancillary authors who prepared this comprehensive package in a very short time: Lauren Baumann and Bob Maddox, University of Tennessee: Instructor's Resource Guide and Transparencies; Mike McCullough, University of Tennessee at Martin: Study Guide; and Barbara Hastings, University of South Carolina-Spartanburg: Test Bank.

ABOUT THE AUTHORS

GREG BOUNDS

As a Research Associate with The University of Tennessee's Management Development Center, and as an instructor in other executive development programs, Dr. Bounds has helped to develop and disseminate the thought and practice of Total Quality Management (TQM) throughout American business and industry. Dr. Bounds began this work in 1986, before TQM was in vogue. By assisting with the Center's interventions and studying their outcomes, Dr. Bounds has learned firsthand about the failures and the conditions of success in implementing TQM. As an Adjunct Professor in the Management Department, also at The University of Tennessee, Dr. Bounds has brought this cutting-edge knowledge into the classroom and translated it into valuable learning experiences for students. Dr. Bounds has authored a number of journal articles on TQM and co-authored three advanced level texts on its themes, including *Competing Globally Through Customer Value* (Quorum, 1991), *Beyond Total Quality Management* (McGraw-Hill, 1994), and *Cases and Profiles in Quality* (Irwin, 1995). Dr. Bounds is also President and Senior Partner in Partners International, Inc., a consulting firm dedicated to developing effective business relationships between customers and suppliers using the concepts and methods of Total Quality Management.

GREG DOBBINS

Dr. Dobbins is Professor of Management and holds the William B. Stokely Chair of Management at The University of Tennessee in Knoxville. He teaches courses in personnel, leadership, performance appraisal, and organizational behavior. He teaches undergraduate, MBA, and Ph.D. level seminars and also frequently teaches in executive development programs. Dr. Dobbins has published over 60 articles on topics such as leadership, human resources management, decision making, and Total Quality Management, and is on the Editorial Review Board of the *Journal of Management*. His work has been published in the best scholarly journals and is frequently cited. He regularly serves as a consultant for several large organizations in the areas of leadership and human resources management. Dr. Dobbins is also the codirector of the Tennessee Assessment Center, a consulting organization that conducts supervisory and managerial assessments for industry.

OSCAR S. FOWLER

Dr. Fowler is Associate Professor and Head, Department of Management, University of Tennessee in Knoxville. He teaches Production and Operations Management at the Undergraduate and Graduate levels. He is a CPIM at the Fellow level, and continues to consult with numerous organizations in Latin America and the Caribbean Basin on organizational improvement. Most recently he has been involved with universities and newly privatized organizations in Central and Eastern Europe. He gained experience in procurement and inventory management in both the military and private sectors before entering academics.

THE FIELD OF MANAGEMENT

1. MANAGERS AND ORGANIZATIONS TODAY

MANAGEMENT AND THE QUALITY OF FOLDED CARTONS[1]

In the mid-1980s, CEO Larry Field, Chief Executive Officer of Field Container Company, received a call from a representative of a major packaged goods firm, one of his company's largest customers. This firm was inviting the CEO and one salesperson from each of its folding-carton suppliers to a two-day seminar on supplier certification. The representative told Field it was not mandatory that he come. With relief that he didn't have to bother with the inconvenience of attending, he went about his business of managing Chicago-based Field Container, the nation's largest manufacturer of folding cartons for cake mixes, dog food, ice cream, frozen dinners, spark plugs, and many other types of familiar consumer products.

Sometime in the middle of that night, Field woke up with a nagging feeling that maybe he should go to that session. He did attend, and this was where he heard for the first time about such ideas as statistical process control and continuous improvement. What he also heard about was that over the next two years, the company was going to reduce its suppliers of folding cartons from 13 to four, and two years after that to just two suppliers. As Field remarked, "That got my attention. And it made me very nervous."

When he returned to his office, Field immediately had all his managers in for an all-day meeting. The message of that meeting was delivering products of ever higher quality to their customers had to become a priority. It was not an idealistic goal. It was about the company's survival.

Up until that time, things had gone pretty well for the company, and it was experiencing reasonable growth. However, it was clear that if the company was going to be around in the future as a competitor, things had to improve, and that meant there had to be changes in the ways the company was managed. Field and his managers had to figure out how to become better at making and delivering their products to satisfy more finicky customers in a more competitive environment. The ideas that Field learned at the seminar hinted at the new management techniques they would have to adopt.

Initially the senior managers decided that all managers and supervisors would undergo training in quality improvement techniques. While people started out

Reprinted by permission of Field Container Corporation

3

enthusiastically, the message soon came up to Field that these techniques weren't going to work at this company. Why? His managers told him, "The feeling among us is that you'll give your money [to this training] but not your time. You have not gone to the training, and until such time as you make a commitment, it's not going to work."

This was Field's second wake-up call, and he got the message and attended the seminar. At the seminar, he became aware of just how crucially important it was for this new approach to be embraced by everyone in the company—from chairman on down. Since then, nearly every employee in the company has had at least one full day's training to understand how to improve their contribution to the quality of the company's products. Now Field employs full-time trainers at each of its manufacturing locations.

As the company has learned more and more about what is involved in working to improve the quality and value of its products, there have been many changes in how managers go about their jobs. One big change was the formation of employee teams to take on improvement projects. They were charged with figuring out how to make things work better and had the authority to make improvements.

For example, the company employs huge printing presses that cost $300 an hour to run. For every new job, they have to be stopped to change inks and plates. These are six-color presses, and this took about 1 1/2 hours per color—or sometimes up to nine hours to "make-ready" a new run. The teams decided to videotape the processes they used to do this. After thoroughly analyzing their own work, they came up with changes that reduced make-ready

time to four hours. Their goal is to further reduce the entire process to one hour, which has already been reached on some printing presses. This kind of change increases productivity dramatically and allows the company to reduce or hold prices steady.

This is just one example of many changes that have taken place at Field Container Company since that supplier seminar (Field survived the cut, by the way). All the changes have come as a result of the company's managers completely reevaluating their roles and work. As a result, all of them are focused on the never-ending process of "continuous improvement" to better serve their customers. Sales at the company have grown from $70 million in 1986 to over $400 million today. Their goal is to reach $1 billion by the year 2000.

We will learn more about the results at the Field Container Company at the end of this chapter. This case illustrates the kind of growth and improvement taking place in companies around the world. Managers are discovering better ways to understand and manage their organizations. You will read a lot about these principles and practices in this book.

What you read may differ from what you have been led to expect by your own work experience or from stereotypes of managers on TV and in the movies. You will see that managing effectively and efficiently includes (1) giving employees real power to make decisions about their work, (2) making the delivery of quality products and services that please and even delight customers the central goal of all work, (3) continuously improving how work gets done, (4) basing decisions more on the analysis of data than on hunches and prejudices, (5) using more employee teams to facilitate working together, . . . and many other related actions. To start our exploration of the challenges of management, we will look at some basic ideas about organizations, and how to manage them.

THE ROLE OF ORGANIZATIONS

We all spend a lot of our time either working in, dealing with or being influenced by organizations: restaurants, colleges, professional football teams, city orchestras, churches, grocery stores, auto makers, federal agencies, fraternities. Each of these is an **organization** or *a collection of people working together to achieve a common purpose*. Organizations vary in size, structure, and the kinds of activities they engage in. However, they all have certain things in common. All organizations bring people and resources together to fulfill some mission or purpose. They have a reason to exist. The church provides a means for people to fulfill their need for spiritual sustenance. A football team provides entertainment to its fans. An automobile maker provides customers with a means of personal transportation. Some of these organizations, like automobile makers, are for-profit commercial enterprises. Others, like churches, are not-for-profit organizations, providing various social services.

Organization A collection of people working together to achieve a common purpose.

Organizations also have an identity that endures over time. A crowd of people waiting for the arrival of an airplane has a common purpose, but they are not an organization because they are not working together in a coordinated way over time to achieve that purpose. They show up, and when the airplane arrives, they each collect their family, friends or colleagues, and they depart. Similarly, the crowd attending a football game cooperate by sitting in their assigned seats and obeying certain rules of game-time etiquette. However, they are not an organization because they do not exist beyond the length of the game. The teams they come to see play, such as the Giants, Vikings, Cowboys, or 49ers, are organizations. They have an identity that endures over time, and a purpose they are trying to fulfill. That purpose is to win games and entertain their fans.

Organizations play a key role in society by enabling people to collectively accomplish more working together than they could acting alone. Organizations allow us to divide up our labor, specialize, and become far more efficient at creating the goods, services, and knowledge that contribute to making life more interesting, comfortable, and fulfilling. People working together make it possible for us to design, produce, and deliver the vast array of products and services to satisfy our material and non-material needs and wants. Consumer electronics of every size and function, cruises in the Caribbean, copy machines, fast or gourmet food, clothing (available at the mall or by mail), university education, cellular phones, medical surgery, books on philosophy (and every other subject), Caffeine-free Diet Cherry Coke—these are just a few of the products and services (some frivolous, some vital) available to us every day. None of these items would be available without people working together in organizations. Besides allowing us to create all of these things, organizations also provide us with employment and funds to buy the goods and services provided by others.

The products and services listed above and thousands more are the fruits of our continually evolving technologies and knowledge. Our ancestors could not even dream of many of the things that are commonplace today. Similarly, we can hardly speculate on what the material world will be like 100 years from now. Organizations help to develop specialized knowledge that allows us to provide all of this material wealth. They play an equally important role in compiling and passing on that knowledge to successive generations. Organizations such as schools, universities, research foundations, churches, and the government provide a means of achieving continuity for the culture and the knowledge base of a civilization. The success of our organizations in doing this depends directly on how well they are managed.

MANAGEMENT: MAKING ORGANIZATIONS WORK

Management The organization that embraces the decisions and actions involved in bringing people and other resources together to achieve some purpose.

Management *embraces the decisions and actions involved in bringing people and other resources together to achieve some purpose.* Human beings are the most important resource of any organization. Why? Because, at their heart, organizations and the people that comprise them are the same thing. Further, all organizations exist to fulfill human needs of all kinds. It is by managing our human creativity and ingenuity that we ultimately bring together all other resources, including technology, information, money, materials, equipment, and facilities, to deal with these needs.

While the definition given above is simple, the execution is complex. Guiding the people of today's organizations in today's business and social environment is a multifaceted job. New understandings of the management challenge, such as those offered by *Total Quality Management* (TQM), are helping managers redefine their responsibilities and practices in ways that will help them better fulfill their organization's mission. TQM helps managers understand the importance of continuously improving every aspect of an organization to achieve excellence, remain competitive, and provide more value to customers. We'll talk more about TQM later in this chapter, and in every other chapter in this book. It is the key theme in this text. However, it is an idea that is easier to understand after you have some grounding in a few basic concepts of management. Let's start by looking at some classic descriptions of the manager's job and role in the organization.

DESCRIPTIONS OF THE MANAGER'S JOB

The traditional approach to management has emphasized a hierarchical approach, not unlike the military model, with departments and divisions, and people organized according to their functional responsibilities. Thus, a company like IBM would have its mainframe software division with people organized by functional area, such as programming, accounting, and marketing. The whole division would have a manager with a hierarchy of people reporting to him or her. TQM questions whether this approach is the best way to get people to work together to achieve organizational goals.

Despite the differences between traditional management practices and Total Quality Management, researchers and practitioners have identified a variety of responsibilities common to both approaches. The differences between these approaches reside in interpretation and application. Successful managers do not just make decisions, issue orders, and check to see if the orders are carried out. They *enable and empower* people to fulfill their roles by doing the following:

- Clarify and communicate the organization's mission and vision of its future
- Articulate a set of actions for achieving the mission and vision
- Identify and bring together the people and other resources needed
- Organize and coordinate these resources to perform required work
- Provide the systems, processes, operating methods, procedures, and information that enable people to perform their work
- Lead people to perform their work
- Measure and assess organizational performance in fulfilling the mission and progress in achieving the vision for the future
- Continuously improve every facet of the organization

Managers can do all of these activities by working with and through other people or teams of people consisting of other managers and employees. In fact, much of the management process depends upon facilitating teamwork among employees to fulfill the organization's mission. Getting people to work together can be a challenge. This is particularly true in corporate cultures characterized by adversarial relationships, distrust, lack of shared information, and just the complexity inherent in large traditional industrial organizations. Such organizations are usually composed of people with different functional responsibilities working in different departments and divisions who often do not have a sense of how their jobs fit in with those of others. The primary job of the manager is to build cooperation across functions and help all employees understand their job in relation to all the others. To understand how managers work to do this, let's look at their special roles in the organization.

Managerial Roles

Roles are *the expected behaviors and performance results associated with a particular position.* So, what defines a role is a set of behaviors associated with it. All of us play different roles depending on the situations in which we find ourselves. Our understanding of the relationship between ourselves and the situation drives our role behavior. For example, we behave one way as a student in class, another way as a brother or sister, yet another way as a son or daughter, and so on.

The managerial role consists of the behavior expectations we have for a "manager." Within traditional management study, there are two frameworks that researchers and practitioners use to describe the manager's job and role: one proposed by Henri Fayol, a French mining engineer and executive, and the other by Henry Mintzberg, a management professor and researcher. Let's explore these models briefly. They are useful for understanding how managers have defined their roles.

Roles The expected behaviors and performance results associated with a particular position.

Fayol's Description of the Manager's Roles

Henri Fayol suggested that it is the role of managers to *plan, organize, coordinate, direct, and control.*[2] The following describes each of these activities.

- **Planning.**   This involves determining in advance *what* the organization should accomplish and *how* to accomplish it. Planning requires managers to set strategies and goals and develop courses of action for implementing the strategies and achieving the goals in the short term and the long term.
- **Organizing.**   This prescribes the logical relationships between people and resources to successfully achieve the organization's goals.
- **Coordinating.**   This involves adjusting the activities of independent groups to ensure harmonious action. Effective coordination blends the independent work of various people to accomplish organizational goals and objectives.
- **Directing.**   This includes influencing or affecting the behavior of other members of the organization to work effectively together to accomplish the organization's goals.
- **Controlling.**   This involves comparing actual performance with standards, goals, or expected levels of performance and taking any necessary corrective action.

Fayol's framework has dominated management thought and education for decades. It provides a broad overview of managerial activities, but it is also very general and does not give us a sense of what managers do every day. Some writers have criticized Fayol's roles as being vague, inadequate, and not good descriptors of what managers really do. Henry Mintzberg has been particularly critical of Fayol's framework.

Mintzberg's Critique of Fayol's Classical Roles

Mintzberg suggests that, at best, Fayol's roles indicate some undefined objectives managers have when they work. Ask yourself the following question to see what Mintzberg meant: "When he is called and told that one of his factories has just burned down, and he advises the caller to see whether temporary arrangements can be made to supply customers through a foreign subsidiary, is he planning, organizing, directing, or controlling? How about when he presents a gold watch to a retiring employee? Or when he attends a conference to meet people in the trade? Or on returning from that conference, when he tells one of his employees about an interesting product idea he picked up there?"[3] Mintzberg suggests that specific behaviors may fulfill more than one of the classical roles.

To grasp what it is like to be a manager, Mintzberg says you have to understand managers' agendas: why they do what they do, their behaviors in various situations, and what they are trying to achieve. You must ask managers what they seek to accomplish by talking on the phone, running a meeting, or asking questions. When you get answers to these questions, then you start to understand how managers serve the organization.

Mintzberg's Managerial Roles

Besides criticizing Fayol, Mintzberg also studied managers and has proposed three sets of managerial roles (see Exhibit 1-1): (1) *Interpersonal roles* (figurehead, leader, liaison) arise from a manager's formal authority. (2) *Informational roles* (monitor, disseminator, and spokesman) derive from the information gathering

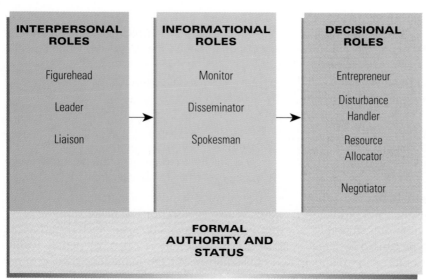

Source: Adapted from Henry Mintzberg, "The Manager's Job: Folklore and Fact," *Harvard Business Review*, July-August, 1975.

accomplished by the manager as a liaison. (3) *Decisional roles* (entrepreneur, disturbance handler, resource allocator, and negotiator) derive from both the authority bestowed on managers and their use of information which serves as an input to decision making.[4] Let's review these roles in more depth.

Interpersonal roles are those requiring managers to deal with people.

- **Figurehead.** As the head of an organizational unit, a manager often has to perform ceremonial duties, or "make appearances."
- **Leader.** As a leader, the manager inspires people to fulfill the unit's purpose. The leadership role is similar to Fayol's commanding, except that leadership involves more than just being a boss who issues commands. Leaders also provide vision and ensure employees' needs are met.
- **Liaison.** As a liaison, a manager contacts people outside the vertical chain of command. As a liaison, the manager builds up an information system and network of relationships that serve his or her agenda.

Informational roles are those through which a manager processes information and communicates it to others.

- **Monitor.** As monitor, a manager gathers information from a network of contacts, such as subordinates, peers, superiors, and people outside the organization. The information comes in various forms, ranging from gossip to formal written reports.
- **Disseminator.** By being in the center of information flows, the manager has access to more information than anyone else in the unit. As disseminator, the manager shares and distributes this information to subordinates who need it.

- **Spokesman.**   As spokesman, the manager sends information to people outside his or her work unit, including peers, customers, suppliers, business partners, and others. Managers impart information through various oral and written media.

Decisional roles are those through which a manager guides the strategy and courses of action of the unit.

- **Entrepreneur.**   As entrepreneur, a manager looks out for new ideas and makes decisions to improve the unit and adapt to changing conditions. The manager may propose new projects or initiatives to enhance the performance of the unit. As an entrepreneur the manager acts as a voluntary initiator of change.
- **Disturbance Handler.**   As a disturbance handler, a manager responds to pressures and problems. Despite the manager's efforts to make sure the organization runs smoothly, unexpected circumstances do arise. Such disturbances can be caused by larger systems of which the unit is a part, by people within the unit, or by unanticipated consequences of the manager's own actions. Whatever the source, the manager must handle the disturbance.
- **Resource Allocator.**   As resource allocator, the manager must decide who will get what. The manager must make short-term allocations, and determine long-term resource allocations, such as the structure of reporting relationships, division of responsibilities and authority, monetary resources, equipment, and other supplies. Managers must also clarify who can make what decisions about which resources.
- **Negotiator.**   Managers often have to balance individual needs by negotiating solutions between opposed parties. Sometimes managers act as intermediaries between other people, and sometimes they act on their own behalf.

Mintzberg offers a more refined description of managerial roles than does Fayol, but that does not mean Fayol's ideas are wrong. These two descriptions are just different ways of looking at management. The value of Fayol's descriptors of management responsibilities is that they focus us on the broad categories of effective management actions. They provide a broad context for understanding what management is about. Mintzberg's roles focus us more on the day-to-day behavior of managers as they go about their jobs.

Criticisms of Mintzberg's and Fayol's Managerial Roles

Mintzberg and Fayol slice real work into categories to help us think about how managers serve the organization. However, neither of them fully describe managerial roles because they do not provide real insight how a manager determines which actions will be productive or not. Managers do the things Fayol and Mintzberg suggest, but so what? By answering that question we get a lot closer to figuring out how managers really add value to an organization.

By not providing guidance on what managers should accomplish, Mintzberg and Fayol have proposed generic descriptions of managerial roles. They apply to almost all managers, regardless of the position, the organization, or the purpose. For example, according to Fayol, managers first plan by setting goals, objectives, and strategies and then organize, direct, and control to successfully implement the plans. However, Fayol does not suggest a focus for planning. For traditional managers who lack a customer focus, plans are often internally oriented, focused on financial indicators of short-term performance for immediate profitability. Such disregard for long-term performance puts companies in a competitive disadvantage in global markets.[5]

For example, providing additional services to customers could lead to greater customer satisfaction. However, these activities are often cut out, since the profit value of these activities is difficult to judge.[6] Such a short-term profit orientation may even tempt managers to actually decrease value for customers. Managers can increase short-term profits by deferring machine maintenance, worker training, process improvement, and new product development. The unfortunate results may be more defects, longer cycle time to deliver products to customers, and less customer satisfaction.

Furthermore, when managers are not required to make plans to continuously improve, planning often just establishes a roadmap and goals for administering existing strategies, systems, and policies. Managers may wrongly conclude that as long as they play their roles, and diligently attend to the job of being a manager, customers will automatically be served, and the organization will survive and prosper. These days, it usually does not work out this way. Instead, managers need to have a purpose that guides their behaviors and roles. Again, we must ask the question "Why?" "Why do managers play these roles?" "What purpose or agenda do they pursue?" Fayol and Mintzberg lay the groundwork for the further advancement of the theory and practice of management, but their suggestions are incomplete. Total Quality Management helps to make their suggestions complete.

TQM reminds us that managers must continuously improve the organization and its work processes to provide better customer value. Only Mintzberg's entrepreneur role comes close to this idea of improvement, but it still does not advocate customer value. In the competitive markets of the 1990s, managers have learned that pursuing purposes other than customer value may jeopardize the organization's long term survival and prosperity. The managerial agenda suggested by Total Quality Management suggests what managers should accomplish for the organization.[7]

❓ THINKING CRITICALLY

1. How does Fayol's description of the manager's job help us to better grasp what management is about? Do these ideas provide you with direction for managing goal-oriented activities, such as your education? Why or why not?
2. What makes Mintzberg's description of managerial work valuable in your opinion? Can you relate these activities to your everyday experiences?
3. How are the ideas of Mintzberg and Fayol incomplete? How does Total Quality Management help us to further refine and give direction to these roles?

TYPES OF MANAGERIAL POSITIONS

While the hierarchical approach, when applied in a traditional "command and control" manner, can lead to problems, hierarchies are still prevalent in organizations. As the word "hierarchy" implies, not every manager has full responsibility

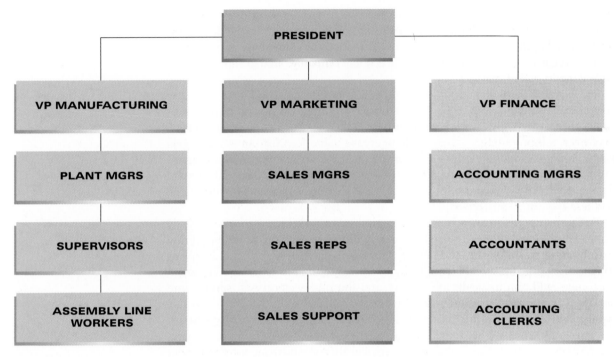

EXHIBIT 1-2
A simplified organizational chart showing the management hierarchy

Division of labor The dividing up of work into individual tasks that, when brought together in a coordinated fashion, help the organization achieve its overall goals.

Specialization The act of specifying work tasks when the organization puts into practice division of labor.

Departmentalization The organization of work groups according to some commonality, such as function or product group.

Hierarchy The structure of superior and subordinate reporting relationships in an organization.

for facilitating the performance of the entire organization. Most have responsibility for only a small part of it. The everyday work of managers will vary depending on their level. In most large organizations, there are several levels that make up a managerial hierarchy, and managerial positions vary in terms of the scope of activities for which a manager has responsibility.

Levels of Management

As organizations grow larger and more complex they typically divide into specialized units or groups of people who concentrate on particular activities. We refer to this characteristic of organizations as **division of labor, specialization, and departmentalization.** By doing this, people can come together, each contributing his or her own special skills to achieve an organizational purpose. This is an important idea that will help you better understand the logic and practices of TQM. So keep this in mind as we proceed through this book.

Large and complex organizations usually develop several levels of managerial positions that are arrayed in a **hierarchy,** which is *the structure of superior and subordinate reporting relationships.* At least three levels of a hierarchy can be identified: top, middle, and first-line. While their roles overlap to some degree, each of these levels of management take on different responsibilities in helping the organization achieve its mission. Exhibit 1-2 shows a chart with a simplified organizational hierarchy.

While this hierarchical approach to management is typical, it is also changing. New organizational structures are centered on processes (not tasks or functions), on using teams, and on rapid access to information. As background, though, let's review the traditional hierarchical management structure to understand the changes taking place.

Top Managers

Top managers sit at the top of the organization's hierarchy. All other managers report to them. They are usually given such titles as chairman of the board, chief executive officer, chief operating officer, or president. Besides these titles, **top managers** also include *senior executives with titles such as senior vice president, chief financial officer, and executive vice president. These people are responsible for the overall performance of the organization.* This responsibility includes such activities as scanning the business environment and marketplace to identify opportunities and threats that affect the organization's long-term well-being. Managers also shape the organizational culture, as they are key decision makers and role models for all the other employees.

Based on what they learn about the environment, top managers devise strategies and decide on long-term plans for executing these strategies. They make decisions about what new markets the company might enter and what products and services they will offer. They decide what new ventures the company might invest in, what companies they might acquire. They set internal policies and procedures. Top managers usually spend a lot of time in meetings, listening to briefings by other employees, and talking to people in person and on the telephone. In large companies, they usually do not have much contact with lower-level employees, while in medium and small companies, they may have regular contact with workers. The *A Look at TQM in Action* box on page 14 provides an overview of how one top manager has changed his style and the results of that change in the organization he leads.

Top managers have many challenges and responsibilities. They have significant influence on the fate of their organizations, for good or bad. Dealing with fickle markets, unions, inefficient processes, internal bureaucracies, culture problems—the buck on all these areas stops at the CEO's desk. It can seem bewildering. However, top managers do not accomplish their tasks alone. They must engage their subordinates in this work. Middle managers and lower level managers are instrumental in making the plans and visions of top managers happen. This is especially true at large organizations, with many products and divisions. While top managers may provide vision, leadership, resources, and approvals, the other levels of management must implement and execute these decisions.

Middle Managers

Middle managers make up the middle of the traditional organizational hierarchy, which can consist of several levels in large organizations. They often have titles such as regional manager, division manager, branch manager, director, plant manager, store manager, or superintendent. Middle managers report to managers above them, and they also have subordinate managers reporting to them. In this position, **middle managers** *serve as the "linking pins" between the strategic activities of the top managers and the operational activities at the bottom of the managerial hierarchy.* They are primarily responsible for implementing the strategies and policies devised by their superiors, and they may sometimes

Top managers The management group that includes the chairman, president, CEO, and COO as well as other senior executives who have responsibility for overall organizational performance.

Middle manager The level of management primarily responsible for implementing the strategies and policies devised by their superiors.

TQM IN ACTION

A LOOK AT TQM

A TTITUDE TRANSPLANT FOR A CEO[8]

When Jack Croushore was departmental superintendent of National Works, a specialty steel division of U.S. Steel, he had a reputation for being a hard-nosed, take-no-prisoners type boss. He did not think twice about handing out discipline slips to union employees and suspensions without pay. He was demanding and critical of everyone who worked for him and did not hesitate to let people know when he did not like their work.

In 1984, Jack Croushore was transferred to Christy Park Works, later spun off as CP Industries, which manufactures seamless pressure vessels for transporting gasses. This happened because, despite all his pushing and following of the rules, the plant was not efficient enough, and U.S. Steel shut it down. That experience was a watershed event in Croushore's life, and he made a conscious decision to change his management style and approach. He relates his change of heart in this way: "I had done everything I was asked to do at National Works, and, in the end, I couldn't keep the plant open. I followed all the rules. I did what they said would work. And in the end, they said, 'We're going to shut it down.' So when I came here [to CP Industries], I told the fellow who'd hired me, 'Look, I'm not going to do things the way I did down there—because they don't work. I'm going to try new things.' I walked up as this tough guy—and the next day I walked home as a . . . cream puff."

Croushore's new approach is based on a simple idea: the Golden Rule. He says, "Usually, when I get into a situation, I think how I would feel and how I would want to be treated if I were in that person's place." His new style is to encourage employees to take responsibility and give them as much authority as they need to get their work done. He realizes that a discipline slip only encourages a grievance procedure, which takes time to resolve, creates an adversarial culture, and undermines worker productivity. He had learned as well that "there is only so much energy in an organization. And when you use it in nonproductive ways—such as discipline—it's gone. Why waste the energy of the organization."

At the time Croushore arrived at Christy Park, it was a drag on U.S. Steel. Its products were labor-intensive, and productivity was a problem. With his humane approach to managing people, he was quickly able to improve yields from the work processes from 87 percent to 99.7 percent. Two years after his taking on Christy Park, it was profitable enough to attract a buyer, and in 1988, the new owners named Croushore president and CEO. After obtaining an agreement from the United Steel Workers union, he set up programs to cross-train workers to do several different jobs in the plant and began rotating job assignments and combining jobs as workers left or retired. Through attrition, the workforce decreased from 159 hourly employees in 1984 to just 89 employees in 1992, but at the same time sales increased by 20%, and productivity had soared.

Croushore's approach is not to blame or incriminate anyone if something goes wrong. He figured that if you take that approach, no one would ever admit to making a mistake. In a more open environment, the attitude was "If you screw up, tell us. Let us figure out how it happened and how we can prevent it from happening again."

Other changes have included training in hiring practices and then giving shop floor employees the authority and responsibility for hiring and orienting new employees. CP Industries is a small company, and its relationship with the United Steel Workers is not perfect. The union balked at Croushore's idea of instituting a gainsharing [a kind of bonus] program with workers. But the company is much more open and productive because of his transformed management style, one that affirms and involves all employees in an open and supportive environment.

participate in developing these strategies and policies. However, middle managers are more concerned with the events of the next few months or maybe a couple of years, rather than long term plans (over three years into the future). Middle managers also provide communication and coordination among the specialized units and departments of the organization.

First-Line Managers

First-line managers make up the base of the managerial hierarchy. They have titles such as office manager, team leader, facilitator, foreman, supervisor, and department head. **First-line managers** *facilitate the work of non-managerial people such as workers, laborers, operators, service representatives, technical representatives, sales personnel, technical specialists, or staff professionals.* First-line managers spend most of their time directly overseeing and assisting with the work of their subordinates. They act as coaches, providing hands-on training and guidance to their employees. Sometimes team leaders or supervisors actually perform the same work as their subordinates, but they take on additional duties such as scheduling daily work, measuring and reporting performance, and leading improvement activities. Workers who enter the managerial ranks usually do so through the position of first-line manager. Recent college graduates often start their managerial careers in this position also. Note that in all these descriptions managers oversee people, but their primary responsibility is always managing their units to help the organization meet its goals.

First-line manager The management level that facilitates the work of non-managerial people such as workers, laborers, operators, service representatives, technical representatives, sales personnel, technical specialists, or staff professionals.

General Versus Functional Managers

Managerial positions also vary in the scope of responsibility assigned to the manager. **Functional managers** *take responsibility for one type of specialized activity or function, such as marketing, finance, research and development, manufacturing, or distribution.* A **general manager** *takes responsibility for all or part of the organization, such as a division, a plant, a subsidiary, a hospital, or a government agency, and has authority over the specialized activities or functions.* In a manufacturing company, a plant manager oversees purchasing, accounting, manufacturing, warehousing, shipping, and personnel departments. The general manager of a division or a subsidiary may take responsibility for several plants as well as marketing and research and development activities.

Functional manager A classification for managers who take responsibility for one type of specialized activity or function, such as marketing, finance, research and development, manufacturing, or distribution.

Next we will look at a relatively new and valuable approach to defining what an organization is. This approach will take us beyond such classifications as functional and general manager and provides valuable insights about how to manage all functions within the organization.

General manager The classification for managers who take responsibility for all or part of the organization, such as a division, a plant, a subsidiary, a hospital, or a government agency and have top authority for most specialized activities or functions.

❓ THINKING CRITICALLY

1. What is the value of having different levels of management in an organization? Do you think this is a useful way to get people to work together to achieve organizational goals? Why or why not?
2. Based on your own experience and what you have read so far, do you think dividing a company into functional areas, such as accounting, marketing, and product development, is an efficient way to organize employees to get work done? Explain your reasoning.

THE ORGANIZATION AS A SYSTEM

System A way of understanding an organization (or anything) as a set of interacting components working together to sustain themselves and achieve various goals.

A useful concept for understanding how anything works is the idea of a **system.** This idea moves us away from seeing the parts of our world as isolated objects and toward understanding them *as sets of interacting components working together to sustain themselves and achieve various goals.* You have probably learned that your body is really an exceptionally complex and elegant system of interacting organs. When all the organs work well together, we thrive. When the interaction breaks down, we become sick or worse.

The natural world is much better understood as an ecological system rather than as a lot of independent elements. We know that in reality there is both diversity and deep interdependence among all the parts of an ecosystem. To preserve and take advantage of what an ecosystem may provide requires that we become aware of and deal with these interdependencies.

Ignorance of the relationships among the parts of an ecosystem (including the important role we play as a part of the system) can cause us to irreparably change it in ways that may destroy its ability to sustain life. Farmers cutting down the trees of the Brazilian rain forests, for example, may be ignorant of the fact that the trees are part of a complex ecosystem, and their actions are changing the planet's ability to replenish oxygen in the atmosphere. While these farmers may think cutting down trees is an isolated act with no consequences other than creating cleared land, we know that is not the case. Just as our bodies and the rain forests are systems, so too are organizations. And when we understand that, it affects our approach to management.

One of the most influential books of the 1990s in management is Peter Senge's *The Fifth Discipline: The Art and Practice of the Learning Organization.* This book helps readers understand organizations as systems. Senge describes "systems thinking" as: "a discipline for seeing wholes. It is a framework for seeing interrelationships rather than things, for seeing patterns of change rather than static 'snapshots.'"[9] Senge's premise is that the systems view helps us see that the intelligent management of organizations *only* happens through cooperative interaction among many different people. This view shows that each person's actions are dependent on and influenced by the actions of many others in and outside the organization and vice versa. The systems approach has profound consequences for understanding how to help an organization function effectively and efficiently to accomplish its goals. It moves management focus away from the actions and behaviors of individuals performing functional work and toward the smooth working of the processes by which the whole system operates.

As we proceed through this book, we will frequently refer to the work of W. Edwards Deming, a leading theorist in systems thinking. He is credited more than any other single person with teaching these techniques to Japanese managers after World War II and the leading award for management excellence in Japan is the Deming Award. Here is Deming on the idea of systems:

A key element of Profound Knowledge [as Deming calls his approach] is the concept and application of the theory of a system. A business is a complex system. All of the components—research and development, sales, manufacturing, etc.—are interdependent and must work together to produce products and services that accomplish the aim of the system. Optimization for accomplishing the aim of a system requires cooperation between the components of the system. Left to themselves, components become selfish, competitive, independent profit centers. An organization, accordingly, must be managed.[10]

There is more to a system than just cooperative interaction. Organizations are not just systems, they are *open* systems. This means they function within a larger environmental system, with which they interact. Using the open systems perspective, we can break the actions of an organization into three stages:

1. The *input* of material and energy from the larger environment
2. The *transformation* of inputs into outputs
3. The release of *outputs* back to the larger environment

Let's take a simple example. A single Domino's Pizza store is an open system. First it takes in special inputs from suppliers, such as ovens and other utensils from cooking equipment companies, pizza ingredients from restaurant food companies, soft drinks from the Coca Cola Company, and energy from the local utility. Second, employees, using carefully defined processes, combine and transform these inputs into pizza and drinks to fill the orders of customers. Third, the store boxes and delivers an output, the ordered pizzas, to customers in the larger environment. We could define any organization in terms of these steps. In fact, the open systems approach is the *best* way to make sense of what organizations do. It helps us understand in unambiguous terms that the responsibility of management is to help make the system operate efficiently and effectively to accomplish these activities, from the acquisition of inputs to the transformation processes to the delivery of the final output. Exhibit 1-3 illustrates Domino's from the systems view.

Efficient and Effective: A Systems Perspective

The terms "efficient" and "effective" will be used frequently in this book, so let's briefly review what they mean from the open systems perspective. **Efficient** *means minimizing waste in transforming inputs into outputs and in delivering them to customers.* In our Domino's example, the efficient store will always have the proper amount of fresh ingredients on hand (not more or less than it needs). Its processes for creating pizzas will minimize waste of these ingredients, using

Efficient Minimizing waste in transforming inputs into outputs and in delivering them to customers.

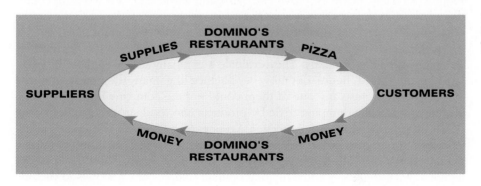

EXHIBIT 1-3
Domino's Pizza Restaurants viewed as an open system

neither more nor less than its processes call for. It will then have drivers who know the shortest routes to their destinations to minimize time and gasoline in delivering their products to customers. Efficiency is important because it helps keep down the cost of producing outputs. Lower costs translate into lower prices, making the output more attractive to customers. This allows the company to make a profit and continue in business. If a product's costs exceed its value to a customer, the company cannot make a profit, and it will cease to exist unless it makes some changes.

Effective The delivery of outputs that customers and others in the external environment will desire, value, and accept.

Effective is the other half of the management challenge. It means *providing outputs that customers and others in the external environment will desire, value, and accept.* In other words, effective means delivering outputs that customers need, want, can afford, and will purchase at a price high enough for the organization to make a profit. Further, it includes delivering these products or services without breaking the law, and generally behaving in ways that are ethical and in the best interests of the larger environment in which the organization functions. Domino's, for example, had to abandon its 30-minute delivery guarantee because some drivers, in their haste to meet the deadline, have caused car accidents. These accidents called into question the effectiveness of this guarantee for individuals in light of the needs of larger society for safe driving by all.

As a way to further think about the notions of efficient and effective, consider the definition from Peter Drucker, one of the most highly regarded management theorists of the twentieth century: "Effectiveness is the foundation of success—efficiency is a minimum condition for survival after success has been achieved. Efficiency is concerned with doing things right. Effectiveness is doing the right things."[11] Doing things right and doing the right things—these are the basic charges of successful managers.

Systems and Stakeholders

Stakeholders The individuals and organizations who have an interest in the performance of the organization.

There are a number of constituents or **stakeholders** who *have a vested interest in the performance of the organization.* The effective organization seeks to optimize its ability to satisfy all stakeholders. Among these stakeholders are the employees, including workers and managers, investors, stockholders, the neighbors and neighborhood in which the organization is located, government, and other social institutions. Each of these stakeholders has different needs and, therefore, will evaluate the effectiveness of the organization differently. Customers obviously want value in the products and services they purchase. Employees want secure employment, satisfying work, and safe working conditions. Investors and stockholders want returns on the money they invest with the company. Government agencies want compliance with laws and regulations.

The challenge managers face is that each of these stakeholders expects different things from the company. They evaluate a company's effectiveness differently. Managers must figure out how to balance the many demands of these stakeholders, because any one of them could put the company out of business. A company illegally dumping toxic by-products into local streams might be shut down by the Environmental Protection Agency. A company that offends a political action group may be boycotted. A company that abuses its employees may be shut down by a strike. A company that produces shoddy products may be avoided by customers. A company that operates inefficiently and fails to provide a reasonable return on investment will find it difficult to acquire the credit and

...eeds to stay in business. Balancing the diverse interests of these ... be a complex task. However, it is essential for the survival and ... organization.

...y engage in a variety of behaviors or managerial roles, such as ... by Fayol and Mintzberg—planning, organizing, leading, resource ...egotiating, and the rest. What is important, though, is to understand ...ke on these roles and perform these acts *to keep the processes within* ...*nization functioning efficiently and effectively to satisfy its stakeholders—* ...*t among them, its customers.* Notice that we focus on managing processes. ... is a reason for this. It reminds us that, from the systems perspective, what ...managed are the processes (or steps or interactions) by which work gets ...e. To make the most of Fayol's and Mintzberg's roles and behaviors, then, we ...eed to always think about them in the context of managing a system.

Total Quality Management and Systems Thinking

What characterizes the systems view of an organization are interrelationships and interactions among employees to achieve a goal. A process incorporates the steps that define those interactions. Earlier, we said that Total Quality Management emerges from the systems view of organizations. Thus, what TQM is about is the effective and efficient management of these processes. The concerns of TQM, from a focus on delivering value to customers, to continuous improvement of organizational processes to deliver that value, to facilitating teamwork, to the use of data to make better decisions, all start from the premise that an organization is an open system.

While traditional management looks at work in terms of functions and the performance of individuals, all with an eye to the bottom line, **Total Quality Management** *looks at processes—the interactions among people and organizational resources—and their continuous improvement to serve the needs of customers.* Of course there is a great deal for managers to do to effectively and efficiently manage for total quality. And this does not mean that TQM is not concerned with profit. It is, however, the recognition that while profit is important to attract investment, it should not just be a goal of business but a way to measure the value customers place on its offerings. Here is what Peter Drucker says about the place of profit in managing an organization: "The profit motive and its offspring maximization of profits are . . . irrelevant to the function of a business, the purpose of a business, and the job of managing a business." He then goes on to point out, "There is only one valid definition of business purpose: *to create a customer.*"[12] This idea is at the heart of TQM. It emerges from understanding that taking inputs from the larger system and adding value to them by various processes is the *only* way to attract the resources that will allow a company to continue in business.

Only in the last two decades have managers recognized the value of the systems perspective and TQM. TQM is at the heart of the management practices of our most admired corporations, including Xerox, Hewlett-Packard, Fidelity Investments, Motorola, Ritz-Carlton Hotels, as well as thousands of other businesses of all sizes. And for some of our largest corporations that have stumbled in the marketplace in the early 90s, including IBM and General Motors, TQM is at the heart of their efforts to turn around.

In the 1990s, the complexity of this task is growing because of the increasing rates of change in external environments. Managers must work to help their

Total Quality Management An approach to management that looks at processes—the interactions among people and organizational resources—and their continuous improvement to serve the needs of customers.

organizations continuously adapt to these changes to ensure tha
erly aligned with the demands and desires of their key stakeh
TQM is based on an open systems view, it keeps managers foc
ing the organization's alignment with the larger environment.

? THINKING CRITICALLY

1. Give an example from your own experience of how the systems view
   help an organization perform more effectively and efficiently.
2. Describe a business that you know of in terms of its inputs, what its trans
   mation processes are and how they add value to the inputs, and what
   final outputs are.
3. Put yourself in the place of your professor and list all the stakeholders to
   whom you think he or she is responsible.

TOTAL . . . QUALITY . . . MANAGEMENT

The field of management is one that is susceptible to fads, gimmicks, quick fixes,
techniques, and buzzwords that flare up in the popular consciousness and then
fade away. We have already mentioned Total Quality Management at various
points in this chapter. It has the feel of being just another buzzword or fad. In
fact, it would not be surprising if you have read about TQM as yesterday's fad.

There is a reason for these criticisms. If you just approach TQM as a set of
techniques for solving particular organizational problems, it will inevitably fail.
This is because if you apply techniques without grasping the effect they will
have on the entire system, you'll make mistakes that will cause more problems.
Let's go back to our example of the Brazilian farmers. There is no reason why
there shouldn't be some opportunity to develop farms in the Amazon basin of
Brazil. However, they must be developed in concert with the rain forest and with
a sensitivity to how these farms will affect the entire ecosystem. The same is true
of TQM. You need to understand and believe TQM's fundamental premise that
an organization is a system, and then analyze the processes that explain how
employees work together to deliver products and services to customers. By starting with those assumptions, you can then intelligently take advantage of TQM
tools and techniques to get better and better at this. To better appreciate just
what Total Quality Management is about, let's examine the term, word by word.

Total

Total means just that. You cannot apply TQM to a single part of the organization,
for example on the manufacturing plant floor, and continue to manage the rest of
the company using the standard command and control approach and expect to see
a positive difference. The success of TQM requires the adoption of continuous
improvement in the delivery of customer value and system/process management
throughout the organization, from the mailroom to the boardroom. Further, it suggests that you must focus on optimizing the entire organization, not just one part of it.

Quality

Armand V. Feigenbaum is one the founders of the Total Quality Management movement. Here is how he defines quality:

Quality *is a customer determination, not an engineer's determination, not a marketing determination, or a general management determination. It is based upon the customer's actual experience with the product or service, measured against his or her* requirements—*stated or unstated, conscious or merely sensed, technically operational or entirely subjective—and always representing a moving target in a competitive market.*[13]

When a company understands quality in terms of the customer's requirements and can create products or services that meet these requirements and deliver them to customers in an efficient and effective manner, it will succeed. Quality, thus, gives meaning to what everyone in the company does. Value and quality are what attract customers to purchase from one firm instead of another, which gives a company the funds it needs to continue in business. This is what everyone in the organization must focus on.

In a total quality managed company, we should be able to define every job in terms of how it adds value to customers. While the term "quality" applies to the outputs of the organization, it also implies excellence in people and processes to attain those outputs. As such, it is an attitude and approach to work, without which the organization's capabilities are compromised.

Management

The *management* part of TQM focuses our attention on the particular actions of everyone in the organization to bring about quality for customers. It helps us understand that we must *manage* the processes that define how people work together and that to compete successfully, we must continuously improve those processes. The tools, techniques, and methods of TQM center around how to do that so as to optimize all the parts of the system and to continuously improve its ability to deliver quality products or services that will satisfy and even delight customers.

Total Quality Management: A Summary

Let's bring these ideas together. **Total** reminds us that we are dealing with every part of the organization and that TQM only can work when it is the basis of all managerial action throughout the organization. **Quality** tells us the purpose of the company: To provide products and services that will meet the needs of customers, as they define those needs. Quality also defines an attitude and approach to work that brings out the best in everyone. **Management** is the actions we take to bring all the parts of the organization to deliver those quality products and services.

Another way to say this is that what we are really writing about here is *managing the total organization to deliver quality to customers.* How you do that is the essence of this textbook. We'll give you lots of details. If you remember this one italicized phrase two sentences above, everything in the book will take on more meaning for you.

MIKE COPELAND AT PROCTER & GAMBLE

In most chapters of this book, we will include a "Managers in Action" section. The purpose of these boxes is to give you a sense of what real managers in real companies have to say about the ideas in this book and their application in various situations. Here we have the observations of Mike Copeland, who is International Training and Development Manager at Procter & Gamble. Procter & Gamble has embraced Total Quality Management as standard management practice. It has trained all its employees in the principles and techniques of TQM because top management believes that this is the best way to make sure the company remains competitive. Here are Mike Copeland's thoughts on the value of Total Quality Management.

- Organizations today are being managed with a simple standard of performance: Do more with less, faster and cheaper. This is what TQM is about.
- TQM in many ways is the expression of what most employed people want to do: deliver their very best efforts in accomplishing the organization's mission and purpose—and provides them with a means to do so.
- TQM gives individuals a more realistic and useful perspective on how to manage an organization, how to understand its mission, and how their job is related to accomplishing this mission.
- TQM reminds us that every job and each task and meeting has a direct connection to the delivery of a product or service and should be in complete alignment with that purpose—otherwise it doesn't need to be done.
- Change is the tension between the next better idea and the way things are done now. TQM, with its emphasis on continuous improvement, provides direction for figuring out which changes make sense and which ones take our focus away from accomplishing the organization's mission.
- TQM helps you enhance your management skills by better understanding where the organization is going and how you can help it get there, and such skills will be the key measures to evaluate your progress.
- By understanding TQM, you have an opportunity to maximize your efforts early and to have the greatest positive effect on your area of work.
- Your understanding of TQM will be the "value added" to any organization you join. By your mastery of these ideas, you will be immediately ready to become a contributing member of any organization.

Teamwork

The focus on *systems and processes* is important because it gets managers to encourage teamwork throughout the organization. When managers understand they are working in a system with interrelated parts, they realize that they should not act as if their part were independent and isolated from the rest of the parts. Team formation allows people to work more closely and communicate with one another, and to use individual and mutual talents to solve problems, improve processes, and keep work moving ahead. An important part of the effective implementation of TQM is the use of teams, especially cross-functional teams that bring together people with different skills and expertise. For example, in publishing this book we had a team consisting of the authors, the sponsoring editor, the developmental editor, the designer, the marketing manager, the production supervisor, and the manufacturing supervisor. We all had to perform the specific steps in the publishing process. By setting ourselves up as a team, we were better able to work together to plan, write, produce, and print the final product.

When managers build teams in their organizations, they must take on new roles as facilitators and coaches. You will read more about teams and their affect on the role of managers in Chapter 3. The *A Look at TQM in Action* box below provides an example of the difference TQM and teamwork has made at one small company.

THINKING CRITICALLY

1. What are the implications of a systems view for managing an organization? How does this differ from the more traditional hierarchical approach?
2. What aspects of the managerial job are defined in Total Quality Management but not represented in the descriptions provided by Fayol and Mintzberg?

THE REVIVAL AT CLEARWATER[14]

A LOOK AT

TQM IN ACTION

In December, 1990, Kellie Dodson, president of Ace Clearwater Enterprises, a small sheet-metal-fabricating subcontractor to aerospace companies, was called to a meeting with the company's major customer, Boeing Company. Ace Clearwater, which had recently received a $5 million order from Boeing, was not performing well. The company was delivering 71 percent of orders late, and Boeing rejected 10 percent of the parts delivered because of defects. The procurement manager told Dodson that if her company did not shape up, it was history as a Boeing supplier.

Ace Clearwater had been started by Kellie Dodson's grandfather 30 years earlier as a welding shop and in 1990 was still being run by her father, Tim Dodson. The message from Boeing was clear; the company had to make some changes. Her father decided to turn over the reins to his daughter to make them. She immediately began to act. Up until then the company had been managed by the "seat of the pants" with no controls or documented processes in place. The first thing she did was to strengthen the management team, bringing in directors of manufacturing and of administration and sales, a financial controller, an accounting manager, a manager of manufacturing engineering, a new plant manager, and a materials manager to handle purchasing. The second action was to institute training throughout the company. Thirty-four hourly employees went through 154 hours of training on TQM and statistical process control (SPC) techniques. [SPC is a way to measure outputs and gather information from a process so you can improve it.] All management employees also took courses in TQM, SPC, and leadership.

They created nine production teams, and they were given the authority and resources to effectively self-manage their production processes. These teams, with the support of management and the use of their newly acquired TQM-oriented skills, have turned things around at Ace Clearwater. In fact, the company has been so successful, that on November 16, 1993, it won the supplier-of-the-year award from Boeing's Commercial Aircraft Group. By figuring out a way to get everyone working together using sound techniques for managing their work, a company that might easily have disappeared is alive, well, and growing.

3. Based on what you have read about Ace Clearwater Enterprises, why would you think that the training and creation of teams would be so important in the company's revival?

TQM AND THE NEW MANAGEMENT CHALLENGES AND TRENDS

As mentioned earlier, managers today face an increasingly complex and dynamic business environment. The managerial job will be molded by this environment; thus, it is important for managers to understand the factors that influence the environment. In the old days (before the 1980s), business was less competitive, media scrutiny was less intense, the workforce was less diverse, and change was not as rapid. This is no longer the case. There are now several major environmental challenges that can have direct consequences on a company's ability to compete. These challenges include: the globalization of markets, ethics and social responsibility, technology and innovation, and diversity in the workforce. Let's review each of these challenges in more detail and the TQM approach to handling them.

Globalization and International Management

A map of the world still shows national boundaries; however, economic boundaries are rapidly disappearing. Three regions of the world are emerging as centers of economic power in this borderless world: the Americas, Europe, and the Pacific Rim. Western European countries have joined together to establish the European Economic Community within which goods and money will flow freely. With the collapse of communism in Eastern Europe, other countries may soon join them or create their own community. The United States, Canada, and Mexico have embarked on a new era of free trade with the passage of the North American Free Trade Agreement (NAFTA). Inclusion of South American countries in the free trade zone may not be far behind. Japan is increasingly establishing economic ties with the newly industrialized countries of the Pacific rim, such as South Korea, Hong Kong, and Singapore. And China, the once sleeping giant, has the fastest growing economy in the world.

Economic developments within and among these three regions have increased the globalization of the business community. Many large companies even operate as multinational organizations. Recognizable companies such as Procter & Gamble, Toyota, General Motors, IBM, and McDonald's have operations in several countries as well as international partnerships. A company based in the United States may design and develop its products at home, manufacture them in Korea and Taiwan, and sell them throughout the world. Athletic shoes are a good example of this. Without such a global approach, it is doubtful we would have the range of choice or quality level among the offerings of such companies as Nike and Reebok. Such globalization of business organizations presents managers with the challenge of learning to operate in diverse cultural settings.

The globalization of business has also increased the competition that managers are facing. They will have to participate in global markets. Improvements in transportation and logistics have provided producers around the world with access to global markets. Customers now have wider choices and are becoming more sophisticated in selecting products and services. They expect new and improved product benefits, better service, and lower prices.

McDonald's is one of many U.S.-based companies that have operations abroad.

With increasing numbers of global competitors learning how to meet these demands, managers must continuously improve the value they offer customers or they will not succeed in the marketplace. Managers cannot think just of the domestic market and domestic competitors when devising business strategies. They must consider global opportunities and threats. For example, Coca-Cola saw market opportunities abroad, expanded its production and distribution around the world, and now derives more than half of its revenues from sales outside the United States. A cover story in *Business Week* proclaims "GE's Brave New World: CEO Jack Welch sees the future: It's in China, India, and Mexico."[15] TQM is at the forefront of helping managers figure out how to deal with this global challenge. This is because its focus on managing relationships among parts of a system, internal and external to the organization, along with a dedication to continuously improving the value of products and services, keeps managers asking the right questions about what to do next.

Ethics and Social Responsibility

We become aware of the ethical and social responsibilities of managers when environmental catastrophes, scandals, and corruption make the news headlines. However, ethics and social responsibility are important considerations for managers even in daily decisions that will never reach the news desk. For example, several years ago two days before a bid was due on a government contract, the Martin Marietta company received a brown paper bag with the bid of one of its competitors in it. The president of Martin Marietta didn't spend 10 minutes deciding what to do. They turned the information over to the U.S. government and did not change their bid. The company lost the contract, lost some money for its shareholders, and some employees lost their jobs. Should the company have used the information? Norman Augustine, the company's president, responded that the outcome was only unfavorable in the short term. "We helped establish our reputation that, in the long run, will draw business to us."[16]

This situation raises a question: Can a company be too ethical or too socially responsible? the answers are not always so clear. Consider the Johns Manville company placing warning labels on its fiberglass insulating product stating that it was a potential carcinogen. This was required in the U.S., but the company also included labels on the products it sells in Japan—something not required and not even considered a good idea by the Japanese. For Manville, the decision was not difficult to make. As the world's largest producer of asbestos, it was just emerging from bankruptcy after paying off over 150,000 lawsuits from individuals whose health was compromised from exposure to asbestos. The company initially lost about 40 percent of its Japanese sales as a result of the decision to include the labels, but it is now regaining that business.

Now consider the Control Data Corporation. In the 60s and 70s the company was considered a role model in its commitment to corporate social responsibility. It built factories in the inner city and spent heavily on hiring and educating minority employees. The company also spent over $900 million to develop computer-based education programs for schools. During this time, the company was greatly admired, but in 1985 it lost over $568 million and the chairman of the company was accused of spending too much time with these projects to the detriment of the company's overall health. While it may be true that a company should not compromise its ethics, it may also be true that to be so committed to socially responsible behavior that the company loses money is not sound management policy. In spending more than it could afford, it may be that Control Data did not properly balance its commitment to all of its stakeholders, including the community, its customers, shareholders, and employees.

We expect managers to do what is right and always avoid what is wrong. However, managers face decision situations that rarely have black or white answers. Ethical and socially responsible behavior is more than just obeying the laws of the land. The morality of most decisions is usually some shade of gray, with both good and bad associated with its outcomes. In these complex decision situations, managers need to understand how to use an ethical decision-making process.

TQM, with its focus on the importance of balancing the needs of stakeholders, helps provide guidelines for behavior that are ethical and socially responsible. For example, consider a situation in which a manager might think he should fudge financial data to make his boss look good to top management. Such an action may not be a lie but just a manipulation of the current financial results. While this is in the best interest of a department or particular group, it is not in the best interest of the entire organization. A company that takes the systems view will understand this, and managers are much less likely to be faced with dilemmas that call for a compromise of ethics in the first place.[17]

Technological Change

Technological advances have been explosive over the last two decades. These advances have two facets: (1) the development of many applications for this technology in our everyday lives and (2) a rapid change in the way we work (and play) brought about by having access to this new technology. Pagers,

be high performers and also tend to be more active in team problem-solving and are twice as likely to submit suggestions for improving products and processes.[19]

Aging Workers.   Another trend is the overall aging of the workforce. The population is not growing as rapidly as it once did, and the baby boomers (born in the two decades following World War II) are getting older. As a result, a greater proportion of the workforce will be people in their 40s, 50s, and even 60s. There will be relatively fewer young people available than before. One challenge this presents is the need to retrain older workers to use the emerging technologies and new ways of doing work. People throughout the organization will have to engage in lifelong learning to continue to be productive members of their organization.

TQM and Diversity in the Workforce.   TQM's approach to diversity is first to recognize the realities of the new workforce and how this affects the efficiency and effectiveness of the organization as a system. Unless people work in an atmosphere of dignity and trust, it will compromise their ability to cooperatively execute the processes by which work gets done. TQM suggests removing as many roadblocks as possible that hinder people from working together. If employees must be concerned with the welfare of their families during the day, then it makes sense for the company to make it easy to deal with this issue, not difficult. Further, its focus on continuous improvement of the system and its processes places a premium on training to help employees at all levels become more efficient and effective. One expert summarizes the situation in this way: "Managing diversity means enabling a heterogeneous workforce, which includes white men, to perform to its potential in an equitable work environment where no one group has an advantage or disadvantage."[20]

While workforce diversity does present managers with some challenges, TQM shows how managers can handle this as a source of strength. Diverse cultural perspectives, personalities, and educational backgrounds provide an organization with a wellspring of creativity to deal with our rapidly changing environments. To handle diversity a manager needs to be flexible. Some attitudes that emerge from Total Quality Management's approach are summarized in Exhibit 1-4. As we proceed through this book, we will come back to this issue of the diverse workforce. We will look at how the insights of TQM provide us with guidelines for bringing people together to achieve organizational goals.

EXHIBIT 1-4 Traditional Attitudes-vs-Flexible Manager

Traditional Attitudes	Flexible Manager
• Fairness means treating all employees the same	• Seeks equitable, not uniform, treatment
• Must sacrifice personal needs to get ahead	• People perform better free of personal pressures
• Flexibility is accommodation to specific employee	• Flexibility is competitive issue, and management tool
• Assesses performance largely based on hours at the office	• Measures performance based on value added, not hours worked

Source: Families and Work Institute, Work & Family Council, reported in *Business Week*, June 28, 1993, p. 82.

Manager meetings are a necessary reinforcement of TQM—they provide a forum for discussing workforce diversity and system improvement.

? THINKING CRITICALLY

1. Explain why the above challenges and trends make it important for managers to implement Total Quality Management.
2. Do you think a company can be too ethical? Why or why not? What about being too socially responsible? Does a company have any obligation to act altruistically to the benefit of society?
3. Why do you think diversity in the workplace has become such a hot topic? How does TQM help us understand and manage diversity effectively?

MANAGERIAL SKILLS

Being a successful manager in the environment described above is not easy. However, good managers are developed, not born. TQM provides us with the guidelines we need to develop managerial skills. It helps us direct management efforts toward optimizing the way systems function to serve and satisfy customers and other stakeholders. When people enter an organization they bring with them a foundation of innate abilities, knowledge, experience, and skills. However, the skills of managing, especially as described by TQM, are cultivated through further education, training, and developmental experiences on the job. To effectively manage organizations, there are three broad categories of skills you need: technical, human, and conceptual.

Technical Skills

Technical skills are those important in executing specific work or using particular technologies. For example, a marketing manager needs to understand and be able to perform such processes as customer research, advertising, publicity, and sales support. Without having these technical skills, the marketing manager will not do a very good job of overseeing and coordinating the processes by which marketing specialists work together to contribute to achieving organizational goals. Technical skills are particularly important for first-line managers who supervise workers on a daily basis.

Human Skills

Human skills help managers work successfully with people in both one-on-one situations as well as in groups and teams. Managers have to be able to communicate, coach, lead, help resolve conflicts, build harmony, achieve consensus, and develop esprit de corps among fellow employees. They need human skills in building relationships with other people, such as customers, suppliers, subordinates, superiors, and peers, which is what managers spend a lot of their time doing. Human skills are important at all levels of management. TQM, with its emphasis on teamwork and building an environment of trust so everyone can work well together, places a high value on human skills. We will spend much more time on this subject in parts three and four of this text.

Conceptual Skills

TQM not only relies on technical and human skills, it also requires that managers understand and use data to make decisions. It helps us appreciate the value of conceptual thinking and seeing the relationships among data and the environment, and how these are likely to affect organizational performance. Conceptual skills enable a manager to understand the big picture and the organization's place in it. Without conceptual skills managers will be unable to devise effective strategies for adapting and succeeding in the highly competitive environments that they face today. Managers must also have conceptual abilities to analyze problems, devise solutions and action plans, and anticipate the consequences of their decisions. Conceptual skills are particularly important at higher levels of management, where managers spend more of their time thinking and planning than overseeing the work of technical specialists.

Vision: The Extra Talent

In addition to technical, human, and conceptual skills, good managers need to have **vision,** which is *an ability and imagination to create the future.* Vision is a special subset of conceptual skills and is the extra talent that gives managers the leadership quality and makes them someone that others want to follow. Vision means that managers do not just react to the problems and demands that are placed upon them. Rather, they look ahead and anticipate opportunities and threats and envision strategies and new realities that go beyond the current state of affairs. Good managers are also able to get others to understand and commit to their vision. And using all of their skills, they engage others in transforming the vision into a reality. Vision is essential to good management. Without it managers do not have a focus for channeling their skills and leading others to future accomplishments. TQM, with its emphasis on systems and processes, helps managers develop vision. It keeps them fixed on asking the right questions about interrelationships and the organization's role in the larger environment.

Vision An ability and imagination to see the future of an organization and guide it to achieve this future.

❓ THINKING CRITICALLY

1. Imagine you are a manager of a small retail business. Describe how the four managerial skills would help you be more likely to succeed.
2. What is the relationship of these skills to Total Quality Management? How would they help you better implement TQM?
3. How would you go about attaining these skills besides by taking classes in college?

LOOKING AHEAD

Total Quality Management articulates new ways for effectively and efficiently directing the work of organizations. While the concerns of management have always been helping groups of people work well together to achieve goals, our understanding of how to do that is evolving (Chapter 2 goes into this in depth). This textbook will help you understand this new management approach. It is quite different from the traditional, hierarchical, "command and control" model that has been the accepted wisdom for a long time. We have discovered over the last few decades that that model is not the best way to manage a system with processes. It results in inefficiency and often focuses employees on pleasing the boss rather than pleasing the customer.

Total Quality Management is the term we use to distinguish this new approach from those that have preceded it. However, it is important to appreciate that this is a label of convenience. TQM has its share of naysayers, people suggesting that it is only the latest management fad. Those people have misunderstood TQM. In actuality, it is the best approach we have for understanding organizations as systems. In the future you will find the term "Total Quality Management" will disappear. This is because the TQM practices of today and the refinements we make to them over time will simply be the standard management practices of tomorrow, and there will be no reason to give them any special label.[21] W. Edwards Deming, one of the people most connected with the ideas of TQM, never used the term. For him, TQM did not exist. In fact, when asked by a management magazine to comment on the current state of TQM, this was his response: "The trouble with Total Quality Management is that there is no such thing. It is a buzzword. I have never used the term, as it carries no meaning."[22] He saw these ideas as the expression of the best, soundest approach anyone can take to managing organizations and did not want the term to get in the way of our understanding that.

To avoid confusion and to emphasize the differences of this approach to management from more traditional ideas, we will, despite Deming's objection, use the term Total Quality Management. This text will expose you to the wide variety of concepts and practices you need to understand how to manage well. There is no way to develop skills in all these areas in just one or even many courses. You need on-the-job experience as well. However, you will read here about basic management principles, and there will be plenty of examples. Our goal is to give you a solid foundation on which to build, once you take your place in the world of work.

GETTING BETTER AND BETTER AT FIELD CONTAINER COMPANY[23]

The managers at Field Container Company that we introduced at the beginning of this chapter have found that Total Quality Management means they must involve every employee in their efforts. For example, besides printing boxes, the company also die cuts and glues these boxes together. Before they implemented TQM and started thinking about continuous improvement, this process usually took about 45 minutes. However, after TQM, a process improvement team working in this area, using video cameras, taped themselves doing the job to figure out how it could be done easier and faster. They discovered that the job included loosening and tightening several bolts of different sizes using different wrenches. The team recommended shutting down the machine completely and retrofitting it with bolts that could be tightened by hand. This change reduced set-up time to 10 minutes with no wrenches required.

As the company became more efficient, you might think this means it could lay off workers no longer needed. However, that is not part of the company's culture or policy. With the training department in the lead, the company made plans to redeploy extra workers from one department to another with proper training. The result has been employee loyalty to the company based on the company being loyal to employees. Besides job retraining, the company also sponsors English as a second language for many of its hourly employees who speak Spanish, Russian, and even Chinese, and employees take this course on the job.

While Field has transformed itself, creating a culture that values employees and works to continuously improve its ability to deliver value to customers, they have found there is no precise formula for doing this. Once you have the principles, learning how to best make these principles work for a company requires trial and error, with the understanding that mistakes are learning opportunities. Larry Field comments, "I don't think we're an example of 'Boy, it's really working here!' The idea of continuously improving says you never reach perfection. We've got a long way to go, but I think we're getting successful at it." As a footnote, 10 years after that seminar that Fields attended, that same packaged goods company named Field Container "Supplier of the Year."

The company's next thrust is on more improvements in non-production areas, with measurement taken of the amount of training per employee, of customer satisfaction, and of on-time deliveries. The managers are well aware that the opportunities for improvement are endless, and their responsibility is to continue the search for those opportunities—relentlessly.

You will find that each chapter begins and ends with a "Case in Point" example describing a situation at a particular company. There will also be a variety of "A Look At . . . " boxes that incorporate such topics as ethics, the global environment, diversity, technology, and TQM. In some chapters, you will also find a "Manager in Action" feature, which profiles the views and actions of an actual manager who is putting the chapter's ideas to work in his or her organization. We have also included a short case at the end of each chapter and a longer integrative case at the end of each part to help you pull ideas together. We hope this text will provide you with a memorable introduction to the exciting field of management.

SUMMARY

The Role of Organizations

- Organizations are collections of people working together to achieve a common purpose.
- Organizations play a key role in society by enabling people to accomplish more working together than they could by acting individually. This is possible because organizations facilitate the division of labor and specialization necessary to efficiently create all the goods and services we now enjoy.

Management: Making Organizations Work

- The heart of management is guiding and coordinating the ingenuity and creativity of people and other resources to serve our human needs.

Descriptions of the Manager's Job

- Successful managers view their job as enabling people to fulfill their roles in performing the work by which the organization fulfills its mission.
- Two theorists, Henri Fayol and Henry Mintzberg, have proposed useful frameworks for understanding the work of managers. Fayol described the managerial task as consisting of *planning, organizing, commanding, coordinating,* and *controlling.* Mintzberg described it as consisting of (1) Interpersonal roles (figurehead, leader, liaison) (2) Informational roles (monitor, disseminator, and spokesman) and (3) Decisional roles (entrepreneur, disturbance handler, resource allocator, and negotiator).

Type of Managerial Positions

- Managerial work varies across the levels of the managerial hierarchy; top, middle, and lower. Middle and lower level managers are responsible for the accomplishing of specific tasks within a particular department or functional area. Top managers have global responsibility for accomplishing goals across functional or departmental lines.

The Organization as a System

- In recent years many managers have come to appreciate the idea of a system, composed of interdependent parts, as a better way to understand organizations and how to manage them.
- The systems perspective helps us appreciate that an organization must balance the needs of a variety of stakeholders to achieve its mission, including employees, investors, stockholders, lenders, government, and, most importantly, customers.
- Total Quality Management emerges from the systems view as a more efficient and effective approach to managing the processes of organizations to serve customers and other stakeholders.

Total . . . Quality . . . Management
- To best understand TQM, it is useful to look at the three words that make up the term, with the understanding that it has to do with *managing* the *total* organization to deliver superior *quality* to customers.
- TQM helps managers appreciate the value of teams and teamwork to better bring together all the interacting employees to facilitate their working together more efficiently and effectively.

TQM and the New Management Challenges and Trends
- The future challenges and trends that managers will face include: globalization and international management, ethics and social responsibility, technological change, and diversity in the workforce.
- To succeed in this environment managers need technical, human and conceptual skills. They must also have vision, which is an extra talent to perceive new possibilities, and they must be able to engage others in making the vision a reality.

Managerial Skills
- There are four skills that modern managers should master to deal with modern organizational challenges. These are: (1) technical skills, (2) human skills, (3) conceptual skills, and (4) vision, a special skill to see and create the future.
- TQM, with its emphasis on systems management, helps managers gain and use these skills intelligently to their own and their organizations' benefit.

KEY TERMS

Departmentalization 12	Organization 5
Division of labor 12	Roles 7
Effective 18	Specialization 12
Efficient 17	Stakeholders 18
First-line manager 15	System 16
Functional manager 15	Teams 22
General manager 15	Top manager 13
Hierarchy 12	Total Quality Management 19
Management 6	Vision 31
Middle manager 15	

REVIEW QUESTIONS

1. What is the difference between an organization and a crowd of people who have come together with the common purpose of watching a sporting event?

2. How do managers enable employees and the organizations of which they are a part to fulfill their mission?
3. What activities does Fayol say the job of management embraces? Why do some theorists criticize Fayol's ideas?
4. What managerial functions serve as the basis for Mintzberg's three managerial roles?
5. What are the three levels of management in an organization, and how are their responsibilities different? What is the difference between a functional manager and a general manager?
6. Why is the concept of a system a good way to understand an organization?
7. What is the difference between "effective" and "efficient"?
8. What and who are stakeholders and why must managers be concerned with them?
9. How does the term "Total Quality Management" help us to understand what managing a system consists of?
10. Why are teams and teamwork an important part of TQM?
11. What are the four challenges of management for the 1990s and beyond? How does TQM help us to deal with these challenges?
12. Based on what you have read in this chapter, what is the difference between ethics and social responsibility?
13. Why does W. Edwards Deming call Total Quality Management a "buzzword"?

EXPERIENTIAL EXERCISE

Throughout our lives we have all participated in organized activities in schools, clubs, churches, sports, and work. We have also encountered organizations in our daily lives as customers of industrial organizations or constituents of government organizations. All of these have some form of management. Our experiences with these organizations provide us with a background for appreciating the principles of management covered in this text.

Individually list three good experiences you have had with organizations. Then list three bad experiences. Assemble into groups of about five people each and share your experiences. List the common elements of your experiences and the differences. As a group, devise a list of principles of management that you think would universally apply to all organizations. These principles should be general statements or guideline of managerial action. For example, one principle might be "Managers should always ensure that employees are properly trained to perform their assigned duties."

After about 20 minutes of work in groups, reconvene as a class and share some of these principles.

CASE ANALYSIS AND APPLICATION
Eastman Chemical Company's Award-winning Style

Eastman: Baldrige Award Winner

Eastman Chemical Company, headquartered in Kingsport, Tennessee, has over 17,000 employees who work in plants in four other states, Canada, and the United Kingdom. Ranking as the 10th largest chemical company in the U.S., Eastman sales top $4 billion. Just as Kodak, its parent, was spinning off the firm as an independent and publicly traded company, Eastman was honored with state and national quality awards. The company had made many improvements in its operations, and in 1993 it became the first chemical company to win the Malcolm Baldrige National Quality Award. In an industry driven by engineers and technicians, Eastman was able to get in touch with the softer side of business and organize its people into teams committed to continuously improving its processes and satisfying its customers. Eastman's approach epitomizes what many people call Total Quality Management; however, Eastman managers prefer to think of it as just good management. What follows is a description of some of elements of the Eastman way of implementing TQM.

The company has a fully integrated planning process that systematically deploys business priorities to all employees and work groups. Each work group then develops its own vision and mission based on the company's vision, mission, values, and business objectives. Then these groups develop plans, set goals, and establish measurements for the their operations, administration, training needs, and customer value.

To empower employees to execute its business strategy, Eastman has reorganized into self-managed work teams in many of its operating units. These teams have the authority to make decisions for improving their work and how they will achieve their group's and the company's mission.

Eastman has also adopted a formal statement of values and principles, "The Eastman Way," including honesty, integrity, trust, teamwork, diversity, employee well-being, citizenship, and a winning attitude. All managers are required to live up to these values and principles as they execute their duties.

Eastman has overhauled its entire organizational structure. It recently replaced several of its senior vice presidents in charge of functional units (marketing, production, engineering, etc.) with cross-functional teams responsible for managing a whole business. Earnest Deavenport, Eastman's President and CEO, claims "It makes people take off their functional hats and put on their team hats. It gives people a much broader perspective and forces decision making down at least another level." Now, virtually all of the company's managers work on at least one cross-functional team addressing issues such as human resources, cellulose technology, and product support. The resulting organization chart now looks more like a pepperoni pizza than a traditional pyramid. Says Deavenport, "We did it in a circular form (pepperonis represent the cross-functional business teams) to show that everyone is equal in the organization. No one dominates the other and the white space (the cheese) between the circles is critical."

Eastman managers credit the Baldrige Award for many of the changes they have made. As Robert Joines, Vice President of Quality, explains, "It shows the importance of focusing on the total system, not just statistical measures or employee involvement or strategic planning." The Eastman approach is like a broad umbrella that encompasses a number of key components, including leadership, data analysis, planning, people issues, process management, results orientation, and customer satisfaction. Joines adds, "Quality is no longer a stand-alone objective, it is integrated into the objective of achieving operational results and meeting customer expectations." As evidence of its commitment to customers, Eastman is one of the only producers of plastic that offers a no-fault return policy.

Eastman's business results seem to confirm the success of its business strategy and approach to management. In an industry that is sometimes stagnant, Eastman thrives on innovation, particularly in new product development. Recently 22 percent of Eastman's sales came from new products that were commercialized within the last five years. This is twice the average of 11 percent for the 13 leading chemical companies in the U.S. From 1988 to 1992, more than 70 percent of its 7,000 customers have designated Eastman as their top supplier. The "Eastman Way" seems to be working.

Discussion Questions

1. Reread the case and identify examples of the managerial roles described by Fayol and Mintzberg. How does each of these examples either illustrate or not illustrate Total Quality Management?
2. What initiatives and changes have been undertaken at Eastman and how have each of these improved the efficiency and effectiveness of the company?

VIDEO CASE: COMBINING QUALITY MANAGEMENT AND SOCIAL RESPONSIBILITY
Gun Denhart-Hanna Andersson

In many of the following chapters we will feature people and organizations who have received awards from the Business Enterprise Trust, a national nonprofit organization that identifies bold, creative leadership in combining quality management and social responsibility. The words "quality management" are interpreted broadly to mean the application of sound principles of management to achieve important business objectives. The words "social responsibility" mean social consciousness in increasing the positive effect and reducing the negative effect of business on society.

Gun Denhart, Chief Executive Officer of Hanna Andersson, was honored with a Business Enterprise Award for creating the Hannadowns program, an innovative way to satisfy a major marketing objective while simultaneously filling a critical social need.

Hanna Andersson is a direct mail order marketer of 100% cotton clothing for children, established by Gun Denhart and her husband, Tom. Upon the birth of their son in 1980, the Denharts became aware of the scarce availability of durable and attractive cotton clothing for children—the type Gun wore as a girl in her native Sweden. Feeling there was an opportunity to capitalize on the second generation of the baby boom, the couple began in 1983 what would quickly become a successful mail order company.

Gun Denhart conceived of the "Hannadowns" program in 1986 during a conversation with a friend who had commented on the waste tolerated in the U.S. as compared to Sweden. For marketing purposes, Denhart wanted to emphasize the durability of the clothes—the idea that "Hannas" are made to last for more than one child. For social purposes, she wanted to somehow "give back" to the community that supports her business, particularly to those less fortunate. These multiple goals resulted in "Hannadowns," a program which encourages Hanna Andersson customers to return their used clothing for a 20 percent credit on future purchases. The company then donates the clothes to needy children, in particular those living in emergency shelters to escape abuse and those who are homeless. As of October 1993, the "Hannadowns" promotion has generated credits of over $700,000. The program continues to grow rapidly.

The "Hannadowns" program is a key feature of the marketing strategy which has grown the company to over 400,000 customers, 210 employees and annual sales of over $44 million. The company sends out over 15 million catalogues per year.

"Hannadowns" is the cornerstone of a broader commitment on the part of Gun Denhart to support programs specifically geared to disadvantaged women and children. Denhart, now that Hanna Andersson is a commercial success, is excited about the opportunity to continue to use the company as a vehicle for supporting social change while at the same time enhancing its business success.

Video Case Questions

1. Describe the managerial roles that Gun Denhart enacted as a manager of Hanna Anderson and the Hannadowns program.
2. What elements of the "systems view" of management and organizations does this case illustrate?

2.

THE EVOLUTION OF MANAGEMENT

LEARNING OBJECTIVES

When you finish this chapter you should be able to:

1. Describe the evolution of management theories and practice.

2. Describe the goals and management tasks of the classical school and discuss the criticisms of this approach.

3. Explain the importance of the behavioral school in building a more comprehensive theory of management and practices.

4. Describe and explain the various movements generated under the banner of the behavioral school.

5. Identify the strengths and weaknesses of management science and operations research.

6. Explain the goals of the practitioners of industrial statistics and the value of statistical process control in improving quality.

7. Explain the idea of an open system and its value in understanding an organization and its goals.

8. Describe how TQM evolves from the open systems idea and TQM's three basic elements.

9. Explain the criticisms of TQM and respond to these criticisms.

10. Explain the relationship of TQM and the contingency view of management.

XEROX: LEADERSHIP THROUGH QUALITY

A few years ago, Xerox proclaimed itself to be "The Document Company," reflecting its mission to provide customers with all the tools necessary to create, store, and reproduce documents. Xerox manufactures over 250 equipment products, with software, supplies, and accessories, and sells these products in over 130 countries through 15,000 sales representatives and a vast network of dealers, distributors, and agents. Xerox is certainly a big document company; however, to be *The* Document Company means they have to be judged *The* Best by customers.

During its first 15 years (when it had few competitors), Xerox was the best in an industry where copy machines are still synonymous with its name. However, in the mid-1970s, foreign and U.S. competitors surpassed Xerox in making machines of lower cost and higher quality. Xerox was not even second best with some products. David Kearns, former Chief Executive Officer of Xerox, knew he had to do something. Xerox was losing out in the market it had created. He sent a team of top executives to Japan to study the competition. In his book describing the turnaround of Xerox, *Prophets in the Dark*, he writes,

We learned that the Japanese were able to carry six to eight times less inventory than we were, they were so efficient in getting their products out. The quality of incoming parts at Xerox was 95 percent; at the Japanese firms it was 99.5 percent, a significant gap. Our overhead was twice theirs. We found that for every direct worker who put together a copier, painted it, or packed it into a box, there were 1.3 overhead workers who were clerks or managers. In Japanese firms, there was .6 overhead worker for every direct worker . . . In category after category, the difference wasn't 50 percent better or anything like that; it was almost always over 100 percent![1]

What they also discovered was the way the Japanese were achieving this kind of performance. It had to do with their approach to management—an unrelenting focus on delivering value and quality to their customers and on continuously improving the execution of every aspect of their business. In 1984, responding to these findings and lost market share, Kearns and his senior management team launched an ambitious initiative, "Leadership Through Quality," to completely revamp how they managed their company. Their new approach redefined the job of all Xerox employees, making the continuous improvement of quality and customer satisfaction everyone's primary responsibility. Since then, Xerox has been an American success story: winner of the 1989 Malcolm Baldrige National Quality Award (we'll talk more about this award later in the book) and one of the few U.S. companies to regain lost market share in an industry targeted by the Japanese for dominance.

How was Xerox managed before, and how did these changes make things

better? In the 1980s and before, Xerox was divided into groups that performed specific functions like marketing, finance, and manufacturing. There were many barriers to cooperation among these functions. Each area had its own concerns, often at cross purposes with other functional areas. "The Leadership Through Quality" initiative had resulted in everyone in each area becoming more efficient in how they did things. However, it had not addressed "cross-functional" issues involving more than one function. Xerox discovered this lack of coordination among departments was a major source of inefficiencies.

As the company began coming to terms with these cross-functional problems, Xerox leaders developed a new vision for the organization and the role of managers. They identified 14 basic business processes, which span all functions and geographies, and assigned each to an executive owner. For example, Dr. Fred Hewitt was named Vice President and owner of Inventory Management and Logistics (IM&L), the process responsible for "getting the right things, to the right place, at the right time." IM&L became the test case for this new vision. Fred was given resources to build an organization, Central Logistics and Asset Management, with more than 35 change agents whose roles were focused on accomplishing cross-functional improvements. In 1989, Xerox senior executives gave Fred a mandate to work with each of the functional groups to reduce inventory levels from 20% to 10%, reduce logistics cost from 11% to 7%, and achieve 100% customer satisfaction.

Under Fred Hewitt's leadership, a team of executives developed a vision of the *integrated supply chain* to achieve these results. The idea of the integrated supply chain was to make changes so everyone in the organization worked well together. To minimize waste and maximize customer satisfaction, Xerox had to change the way it did business. It had to refocus managerial roles. Why would a company be set up like the Xerox of the 1980s in the first place? How does Xerox or any company change its management culture and techniques? Those are the kinds of questions we will address in this chapter.

Xerox's current approach to management is state of the art for the 1990s. However, this approach has its roots in theories and practices that extend far back into history. This book describes principles of management from the perspective of Total Quality Management (TQM) which views organizations as systems with processes that provide value to customers. This approach represents our best understanding of how organizations work and how we can best manage them. But to grasp how we came to these insights and to put them into practice, it's useful to understand some management history.

Total quality perspective is based on what we have learned over many decades, indeed centuries, about management. Exploring this history can give you a better foundation for understanding the tasks and challenges of managers in today's global economy. It can also help you understand the management styles and actions of those organizations and managers who have not yet adopted TQM. As we proceed, there is one other thing to remember: *Management is a human enterprise*. It is about using our individual and collective talents and resources as we work together in organizations. This chapter explores how we have come to our current understanding of what that involves.

MANAGEMENT THEORY AND PRACTICE

We are going to look at some management theories, but we cannot understand the evolution of management only by examining theories. We must also look at how these theories work in practice to help organizations function well. In fact, theory and practice go hand in hand, since each influences the other. After all, a **theory** is *a set of beliefs about the relationship between observable events*. For example, in biology, genetic theory explains what traits offspring inherit from their parents and why. And in management our theories help us understand how people and organizations function to achieve various goals, and they provide direction for making sound decisions that will most likely get us the results we seek. We develop these theories by observing the practice of management and documenting relationships between organizational events. Our theories are our explanations for our experience, and they provide direction in how to deal with the situations we encounter.

Today, we have some very good theories about sound management practice. Unfortunately, many managers are ignorant of these theories and continue to manage using practices that are less efficient and less effective at getting things done—leaving their companies vulnerable to those taking a better approach. This was the state of affairs at Xerox before it began its transformation. The key to advancing effective management practice is to come up with theories that are based on a sound understanding of how organizations function best. Our best understanding today is contained in the insights and practices of Total Quality Management, which is the foundation of this book.

Theory A set of beliefs about the relationship between observable events.

A Management Revolution?

A **revolution** is a *disruptive turn of events that results in a dramatically different situation*. Revolution is often contrasted with **evolution,** which is *steady progress to alter a situation, often through small and undramatic changes*. The theories and practices of Total Quality Management seem revolutionary for managers who have primarily focused on the "bottom line," quarterly financial reports, and how well various individuals are performing. This is because Total Quality Management requires managers to:

Revolution A disruptive turn of events that results in a dramatically different situation.

Evolution Steady progress to alter a situation, often through small and undramatic changes.

- make customers a top priority
- relentlessly pursue continuous improvement of business processes
- manage the systems of the organization through teamwork, not individual accountability

As mentioned in Chapter 1, the leaders of many industrial organizations have realized that their old assumptions about management are causing their lack of competitiveness. These old assumptions and values required managers to:

- put a priority on short term profits
- reward those who were effective at internal politicking
- maintain the status quo, making improvements only occasionally
- manage the systems of the organization through a hierarchy of reporting relationships, whereby the superior controls his or her subordinates to meet individualized goals

Transforming an organization from the old assumptions and values to Total Quality Management requires tremendous energy, commitment, resources, and time. Former Chairman of Xerox, David T. Kearns, explains:

In the late 1970s, we realized that we had lost our customer focus and that to be a world class competitor in the eighties and nineties, we had to challenge everything we had done in the past. We had to change dramatically—from the way we develop and manufacture our products to the way we market and service them.

For us, that amounted to a major cultural change. We had to change the way we managed and worked. We had to train people in new processes. We had to change the way we rewarded people and the criteria we used to promote people. We had to communicate more with people and share information with them. We had to bring more discipline and teamwork to our corporate culture. And we had to make decisions that were based not on intuition and feel but on hard data and statistical analysis. . . . But our journey is far from over.

That's because as we improve, two highly dynamic forces are at work. First, as we get better, so does our competition. Second, as we meet the requirements of our customers, their expectations of Xerox also increase. What we see is an upward and never-ending spiral of increased competition and heightened customer expectations.

If you had told us that [in 1985], we would probably have been discouraged by the thought of running a marathon race with no finish line. Today, we find that prospect invigorating.[2]

Making the shift from traditional management to TQM can seem revolutionary to those doing the work. However, TQM actually evolved over many years.

The Evolution of Total Quality Management

We have all had teachers who turned history into the less than engaging task of memorizing names, dates, and events. However, the study of history can be exciting if we back away from the specific incidents, and view them in a larger context. By studying history from an evolutionary perspective, we start to see how earlier events contribute and are related, to later ones. When we do this we quickly discover that we are very much the products of our history. For example, only by reviewing the history of Northern Ireland or Bosnia can we understand why these areas remain in turmoil to this day.

Look more closely, and you see that the fabric of American society is woven from the various cultural values of our immigrant ancestors. Delve deeper, and you find ancient influences: British common law, the social order of the Roman empire, Greek democracy, the Judeo-Christian values of Palestine, and the code of laws established by the king of Babylon, Hammurabi, in the 18th century B.C. The study of history is not an intellectual exercise with no other purpose. It helps us understand what is going on today and improves our ability to shape future events. This is certainly true for management.

Every step in the evolution of any institution or process stems from those that precede it. Theories are developed to help explain and deal with the current environment. These theories are useful and bring about great improvements in the way organizations are managed. What happens after a while, though, is that people find inadequacies in a given approach. As circumstances change, they seek refinements and modifications to address those inadequacies. As we study how management thought has evolved to its current state, Total Quality Management, keep that point in mind. Each management school has emerged to deal with problems in those that preceded it. Exhibit 2-1 graphically displays the steps in the evolution of management that we will review in this chapter. As we

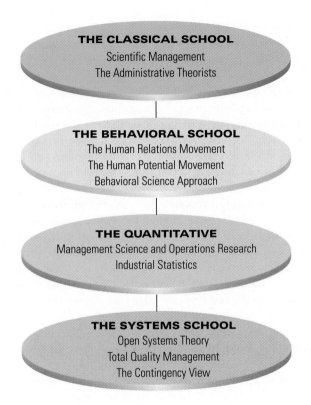

EXHIBIT 2-1
The Evolution of Management
Thought

proceed through this chapter you will see that management practices at companies like Xerox have emerged from four schools of management thought: the classical, behavioral, quantitative, and systems schools.

THINKING CRITICALLY

1. Why is it important to have a theory of management?
2. Think about the organizations you have been a member of. If you feel some were better led or managed than others, what was the difference between the well-managed and the poorly managed organizations?

MANAGEMENT BEFORE THE TWENTIETH CENTURY

Suggestions of how best to organize people date back at least to Biblical times. For example, Moses' father-in-law Jethro once visited Moses and observed him settling disputes among the people. He saw that Moses was kept busy from morning till night. Jethro advised Moses:

You are not doing this right. You will wear yourself out and these people as well. This is too much for you to do alone. Now let me give you some good advice. . . . You should choose some capable men and appoint them as leaders of the people: leaders of thousands, hundreds, fifties, and tens. They must be God-fearing men who can be trusted and who cannot be bribed. Let them serve as judges for the people on a permanent basis. They can bring all the difficult cases to you, but they themselves can decide all the smaller disputes.[3]

Ancient armies and religious organizations, such as the Catholic Church, fashioned similar approaches to manage large groups of people to accomplish their objectives, whether to destroy a neighbor or to save him. Archeological studies have revealed ancient societies that organized people to accomplish amazing feats: the road system built by the Roman empire, the Egyptian Pharaohs' pyramids, the Great Wall of China, and the temples and cities of Mayan and Incan civilizations.

While there are few written records, there is enough evidence to suggest that the overseers of these productions engaged in management, as we would call it today. They planned and organized by assembling human and material resources. They communicated with others to issue orders, and monitored and controlled their workers to make sure the work was completed. These ancient managers laid the foundation for contemporary management theory and practice. However, the events of the last few centuries have more directly influenced modern management.

The Family Business and Proprietorships

Up until the 1700s in the Western World, most business organizations were simple. They consisted of families whose members shared responsibilities. For example, the leather tanner and the blacksmith each had sons and daughters to help. It was natural for family members to cooperate in order to survive, so managing was also quite simple. Later, as artisans became *proprietors* who hired apprentices, managers' tasks grew a bit more complex, for they now had to select, train, oversee, and inspect the work of subordinates. With the industrial revolution, these proprietorships often grew much larger, and managing them became more complex.

The Quest for Efficiency

Between 1750 and the early part of the 1800s, the industrial revolution started in Great Britain. Opportunities existed for producers who could find more efficient ways to produce affordable goods for the unwealthy masses. Adam Smith (1723–1790) noted that *division of labor* and *specialization,* or dividing work into simple and focused tasks, improves efficiency. Business organizations confirmed the merits of this approach. Instead of building single products from hand-made parts, one at a time, workers mass-produced uniform parts that could be assembled interchangeably. Markets for industrial products opened up as distribution systems based on telegraph, shipping, railroads, and canals improved. This encouraged further industrialization. Demand for goods of all sorts grew, and industrial organizations increased in size as proprietors added workers.

By 1850 the quest for efficiency became rampant. The challenge for managers was to maintain affordability while increasing capacity, which promoted efficient mass production. From the simple arranging of a few family members, managers now had to organize hundreds if not thousands of employees. The era of the modern business organization had begun.[4]

? THINKING CRITICALLY

1. Why do you think efficiency in work would be the first thing that concerned management theorists?
2. How did the industrial revolution create a need for better management practices?

THE CLASSICAL SCHOOL

The **classical school** of management was the first significant effort to develop formal theories of management for modern industrial organizations. These theorists emphasized *specialization, division of labor, and the application of scientific principles to increase efficiency*. They thought there was "one best way" to do a specific task or "one best way" to manage an organization. Finding that "one best way" and putting it in place was the manager's job. They also thought of the organization as if it were a machine, and people were simply cogs in the machine. The classical school treated problems with productivity as engineering problems that they could fix through job or organizational redesign. They suggested that only monetary incentives would motivate employees. The prevailing model of **economic man** suggested that *people would work harder only for personal rewards*. The two branches of the classical school focused on different aspects of the organization. *Scientific management* focused on production work on the shop floor. *Administrative theory* focused on the bigger picture, the overall functioning of the organization.

Scientific Management

Frank Gilbreth (1868–1924) and Lillian Gilbreth (1878–1972), a husband and wife team, emphasized motion studies, and even used motion picture cameras to figure out how to eliminate wasted motion. Together, the Gilbreths developed methods for analyzing work and using work standards to improve productivity. They also introduced new ideas about personnel management, and Lillian, in particular, helped to establish the field of industrial psychology. However, Frederick Taylor (1856–1915) is generally considered the "father" of **scientific management,** which is *the application of scientific methods of observation, data collection and data analysis to improve managerial practice and worker productivity*.

Taylor conducted time and motion studies by carefully observing and timing workers' movements. Taylor developed many of his ideas while working as a foreman and studying the men who shoveled coal or loaded pig iron at Midvale Steel Company. Taylor noticed that each employee performed the work differently, and that some were more productive than others. He also noticed that management decisions were just as arbitrary as worker methods and were often based on opinions or even whims, not scientific data. For example, managers would assign work without considering a worker's abilities.

Convinced that scientific principles could make an organization more efficient, Taylor set out to determine the best way to do various jobs, such as shoveling coal. He considered variables that might affect the worker's productivity: the pounds of coal scooped up, the type of shovel used, and the techniques for scooping and unloading coal. He monitored worker fatigue and productivity

Classical school The first significant effort to develop formal theories of management for modern industrial organizations. These theorists emphasized specialization, division of labor, and the application of scientific principles to increase efficiency.

Economic man A view of human nature that suggests people will work harder only for personal rewards.

Scientific management The application of scientific methods of observation, data collection and data analysis to improve managerial practice and worker productivity.

Once a labor-intensive task, coal furnace stoking is now done quickly and efficiently by machine.

rates and he recommended changes in the work pace and ways to eliminate wasted motion. He introduced rest periods and developed tests of worker skills and abilities to select the most qualified applicants.

Taylor also developed a piece-rate wage method which pays the worker according to how much he or she produces. Taylor felt that allowing the workers to earn more money helped counter their fears that they would work themselves out of a job if they completed the work too quickly. Taylor recommended dividing responsibilities between workers and management. It was the job of management to analyze and improve work, and it was the job of labor to do the work in the prescribed manner. Taylor's methods resulted in substantially increased efficiency, and the managers of many organizations adopted his recommendations.

Criticisms of Scientific Management

Taylor intended for both management and workers to benefit from productivity gains. However, some companies abused workers by forcing them to speed up their work. They used scientific management as their excuse for doing this, though it was never Taylor's intent to take advantage of workers. Thus, scientific management is seen (not completely accurately) as a contributing factor to much labor unrest.

A more valid criticism is that scientific management wrongly assumed that managers can treat people as if they were machines and that economic incentives are their main motivation. Later schools of management point out that these are not valid assumptions. People are not machines that you can turn on and off at will. And with a better understanding of what motivates human beings on the job, managers can create a more satisfying and productive work life for everyone in the organization.

Many companies use time and motion studies today. For example, companies such as Toyota, Nissan, and Saturn work diligently to reduce wasted motion and reduce work time. A major difference, however, is that these companies *involve the employees in analyzing their own work,* rather than have an industrial engineer determine and dictate work standards. They also diffuse employee fears by offering job security. If they eliminate jobs, they reassign the employees or send them for more training until they find other jobs for them. These more humane practices make time and motion studies much more acceptable to employees.

The Administrative Theories

The **administrative theories** *developed ideal models of how to manage large organizations.* Two of the administrative theorists, Max Weber and Henri Fayol, helped to establish management as a field of study. The administrative theorists also focused on efficiency, getting the maximum output for the resources expended.

Administrative theories Management theories that attempt to develop ideal models of how to manage large organizations.

Max Weber's Bureaucracy.   Max Weber (pronounced vay-ber) (1864–1920) was a German sociologist and economist. He proposed **bureaucracy** as *a highly efficient model of organization and structure.* Weber was the first person who formally took a holistic perspective on organizations. He had observed many abuses by managers, including favoritism, capriciousness, and inefficiency. Weber sought to answer the question, "How might any large organization function more fairly and efficiently?" He answered this question with a model of the ideal organization, which he called a *bureaucracy*—a blueprint of structure, authority, activities, and relationships. As you read the characteristics of bureaucracy listed below, think about how it might apply in an organization you know about, for example, your college or university.

Bureaucracy An idealized model of an efficient organization which includes a blueprint of structure, authority, activities, and relationships.

1. **Division of Labor.**   Labor is divided into specialized tasks with clear lines of authority and responsibility.
2. **Rules and Regulations.**   A sense of duty and a set of rational rules and regulations guide the actions of members in a bureaucracy.
3. **Hierarchy of Authority.**   Each position is under the authority of a higher one.
4. **Formal Selection.**   All employees are selected and promoted based upon technical qualifications, experience, or merit, rather than favoritism or whim. Qualifications are objectively measured and career opportunities are mapped out in advance.
5. **Documentation.**   Managers record their decisions in writing to provide organizational memory and continuity over time.
6. **Professionalism.**   Managers are professionals, separate from the owners of the organization.
7. **Impersonality.**   Managers are subject to rules and controls regarding the conduct of their official duties. Rules are impersonal and uniformly applied to all employees.

The Drawbacks of Bureaucracy Today.   There is an intuitive appeal and logic to Weber's bureaucracy. However, the word has negative connotations today because excessive obedience to a fixed code of conduct breeds rigidity and inflexibility. In perpetuating the status quo, bureaucracies do not adapt well to rapidly changing environments. Furthermore, under pressures to meet high standards of performance and to compete for advancement, many managers display personal insecurities and engage in counterproductive, ritualistic, and aloof behavior to protect their authority and positions. Such practices will cause these organizations to self-destruct as more responsive organizations appear.[5]

Whether a bureaucracy that intelligently applied Weber's principles ever existed or not, it is true that complex organizations that resemble Weber's bureaucracy have replaced the small businesses of earlier times. In the period from 1900 to 1950, the bureaucratic model flourished. It made the most sense to managers as they sought to direct and control their growing companies. Although many of today's large organizations bear some resemblance to Weber's bureaucracy, they more closely adhere to the principles of another theorist, Henri Fayol.

Fayol's Principles of Management.   Perhaps the most influential of all classical theorists was Henri Fayol (1841–1925), the French industrialist. We introduced the ideas of Fayol in Chapter 1. Let's explore them further here. In 1916, Fayol described what managers do in their daily managerial activities. Rather than focusing on organizational structure, he looked at the functions managers perform. He came up with five categories of actions or processes: *planning, organizing, coordinating, directing,* and *controlling,* all of which we discussed in Chapter 1. Fayol also described 14 principles of management or guidelines for teaching others how to execute these actions.[6]

1. **Division of Labor.**   Simplified tasks allow people to specialize and more efficiently perform their work.
2. **Authority and Responsibility.**   Authority means "the right to give orders and the power to exact obedience." Responsibility means being accountable for the results achieved.
3. **Discipline.**   Discipline implies that members follow the rules and regulations that govern the organization and that managers are fair in rewarding employees for superior performance, and in penalizing employees promptly for breaking the rules.
4. **Unity of command.**   Each employee receives orders from only one superior. If an employee reported to more than one boss, the employee would be confused.
5. **Unity of direction.**   Those activities within the organization that have the same objective should be directed by only one manager using one plan in order to avoid confusing policies and procedures.
6. **Subordination of individual interest to the common good.**   The interest of one employee or group of employees should not prevail over that of the organization as a whole.
7. **Remuneration.**   Compensation should be fair to both employees and the organization.
8. **Centralization.**   Centralization lowers the importance of subordinates in decision making. Power and authority are concentrated with top managers. Managers delegate just enough authority to subordinates for them to do their jobs.
9. **Scalar chain.**   There should be a clear chain of command from the top to the bottom of an organization to insure the orderly flow of information.
10. **Order.**   Materials and people should be in the right place at the right time.

11. **Equity.** Managers should treat subordinates equally and fairly.
12. **Stability of tenure of personnel.** High turnover of employees should be avoided as it is not good for the efficient functioning of the organization.
13. **Initiative.** Managers should give subordinates the freedom to formulate and implement their plans.
14. **Esprit de Corps.** Management should encourage harmony, team spirit, and togetherness to give the organization a sense of unity.

Many of Fayol's principles are still useful today. Problems come, however, when people apply such principles as though they were *laws* rather than *guidelines* for effective performance (as we saw above when discussing bureaucracy).

Criticisms of the Administrative Theories

A rigid and formalized approach to management was important in the days of Weber and Fayol. Executives were struggling to provide order and direction to their organizations and having these principles to work from allowed them to do that. Many of the administrative theorists' principles explain and guide management practices today. However, they do not provide adequate direction for the current challenges: intense international competition, rapidly changing technology, resource depletion and pollution, and increasing customer demands. Dealing with these realities requires a greater flexibility and a deeper understanding of organizations and people.

The administrative theorists failed to deal adequately with the human side of organizations. The classical school tended to regard the employee as an expendable cog and the organization as a big machine. The behavioral school, which we will review next, arose partly in response to this inadequacy of the classical school. For example, although most organizations retain some degree of division of labor today, many organizations rotate workers through jobs and give them more diverse tasks to make the work more interesting and more effective in serving customers.

One of the most unfortunate outcomes of the administrative theories is the division of organizations into specialized functions. Although delivering the final product or service to customers usually requires cooperation across functions, the administrative theories encourage divisiveness and internal competition as each person seeks to fulfill individual goals and satisfy his or her superior. For example, if one functional department will look good by holding down inventory costs and does so, this could hurt another department, which finds itself short on needed supplies to do its work. This result undermines an organization's ability to compete. As we will see, the Total Quality approach to management suggests a more realistic set of principles for implementing cross-functional teamwork.

Today's challenges require that managers tailor an organization to the market that it is trying to serve. Under these circumstances, managers must not accept any principle or ideal model as an absolute truth. They must challenge everything about the organization in an effort to continuously improve. The *A Look at TQM in Action* box on p. 52, from Vice President Gore's report, *Creating a Government that Works Better and Costs Less,* provides a good example of what happens when organizations look inward, concerned more with their structures and rules than their customers.

A LOOK AT

TQM IN ACTION

FROM VICE PRESIDENT GORE'S NATIONAL PERFORMANCE REVIEW INDUSTRIAL-ERA BUREAUCRACIES IN AN INFORMATION AGE[7]

Is government inherently incompetent? Absolutely not. Are federal agencies filled with incompetent people? No. The problem is much deeper: Washington is filled with organizations designed for an environment that no longer exists—bureaucracies so big and wasteful they can no longer serve the American people. Consider this exchange between Vice President Gore and employees at the Department of Housing and Urban Development (HUD):

Participant: We had an article in our newsletter several months ago that said—the lead story was "I'd rather have a lobotomy than have another idea." And that was reflecting the problem of our Ideas Program here in HUD.

Many of the employees have wonderful ideas about how to save money and so on, but the way it works is that it has to be approved by the supervisor and the supervisor's supervisor and the supervisor's supervisor's supervisor before it ever gets to the Ideas Program . . .

Many of the supervisors feel threatened because they didn't think of this idea, and this money wasted in their office, and they didn't believe or didn't know it was happening, and didn't catch it. So they are threatened and feel it will make them look bad if they recognize the idea.

Vice President Gore: So they strangle the idea in the crib, don't they?

Participant: And then they strangle the person who had the idea.

It is important to appreciate in reading this material that no one intends to be inefficient in these kinds of absurd ways. Indeed, these government organizations were set up initially to be efficient and better serve their constituents, but somewhere along the way they lost sight of their goals, and they failed to adapt to a changing environment.

? THINKING CRITICALLY

1. Would you agree or disagree that there is always "one best way" to perform a task? Justify your answer. Why do you think the classical theorists were concerned with finding the one best way to perform different tasks?
2. Do you think a piece-rate pay system would help workers be more productive if managers did not use it to take advantage of them? Why or why not?
3. What are the strengths of Weber's bureaucracy? Why do you think bureaucracies do not work well as an efficient organizational structure?

THE BEHAVIORAL SCHOOL

Behavioral school An approach that emphasizes the importance of understanding human behaviors, needs, emotions, and attitudes in the workplace, as well as social interactions and group processes.

The **behavioral school** of management rose and flourished partly in reaction to the impersonal nature of scientific management and the machine-like nature of the administrative theories. The behavioral school emphasizes *the importance of understanding human behaviors, needs, emotions, and attitudes in the workplace, as well as social interactions and group processes.*

Three writers were notable in providing a transition between the classical and behavioral schools of thought. Hugo Munsterberg was a German psychologist who helped found the field of industrial psychology by applying psychology and behavioral analysis to improve selection, training, and motivation of employees.[8] Like the advocates of scientific management, Munsterberg believed that managers should try to achieve a better fit between the individual skills of workers and job demands. However, Munsterberg used psychological tests as well as observations of behavior to improve the selection of employees.

Chester Barnard was the President of New Jersey Bell Telephone Company. Barnard viewed organizations as social systems, not machine bureaucracies.[9] He suggested that the power to influence people really comes from their acceptance of authority rather than a formal right of the superior. This meant that it was more important for managers to obtain cooperation by establishing social relationships and communication.

Finally, Mary Parker Follett, a social philosopher, also rejected the idea that formal authority was the primary basis for leading people.[10] She emphasized the development of a group ethic, democratic participation in decision making, and cooperation among workers and managers. To manage this way, executives had to develop expertise and knowledge. Thus, Follett also emphasized adult education and career development. While Munsterberg, Barnard and Follett set the stage, the Hawthorne studies gave credibility to the behavioral school of management.

The Hawthorne Studies

The Hawthorne studies were a series of investigations conducted between 1924 and 1933 at the Hawthorne plant of the Western Electric Company just outside of Chicago. The original studies were devised by industrial engineers to investigate lighting conditions and worker productivity. A group of Harvard researchers, Elton Mayo, Fritz Roethlisberger, and William Dickson, conducted much of the research at Hawthorne.[11]

The researchers divided workers into test groups and control groups. The test groups worked under various conditions of lighting, while the control groups worked under unchanged conditions. Unexpectedly, the researchers noticed increased worker productivity in both the test groups and the control groups. In the test groups, worker productivity improved even when lighting was made worse. Only under conditions of near darkness did productivity decrease. The researchers concluded there must have been something other than lighting causing the productivity improvements.

Other investigations that introduced changes such as rest periods and shorter work days yielded similar results. The researchers concluded that the improvements resulted from the sense of pride that the work groups developed in participating in the experiments and the extra attention the workers were receiving. Ever since these experiments, *the extra motivation that results from paying attention to people* has been called the **Hawthorne effect.**

In another study at Hawthorne, the company paid a small group of workers on a piecework basis to produce telephone exchange assemblies. The more pieces these workers produced, the more money they could earn. Contrary to the economic man model, however, the workers did not exert maximum effort to earn as much money as possible. Instead, they conformed to social pressure from other workers in the group to produce a *socially acceptable* amount of work. People who overproduced were called "rate busters," and they were pressured to slow down because the workers feared the industrial engineers would raise the standard rates of production. People who underproduced were called "chiselers," and they were chastised for not keeping up.

Hawthorne effect The extra employee motivation that results from managers paying attention to them.

In experiments conducted at the Hawthorne Works of Western Electric, the intensity of illumination was increased and decreased and the effect of output was observed.

This study contradicted the traditional assumption that economic incentives were the best way to motivate extra effort. The researchers concluded that the social needs of people affect motivation, and that people respond well when they receive the attention and support of management.

The Human Relations and Human Potential Movements

Human relations movement An approach that assumes people are basically good and that they would make a positive contribution if treated with decency and respect.

The Hawthorne studies were broadly publicized and helped launch the **human relations movement,** which assumed that *people were basically good and that they would make a positive contribution if they were treated with decency and respect.* The human relations movement suggested that an employee is not just an "economic being" but also a "social being," with needs, feelings, and dignity. It encouraged managers to attend to their style of management and to develop an honest and open relationship with their subordinates.

Human potential movement A view of the employee as a "self-actualizing being" who seeks to reach fully his or her potential.

An offshoot of the human relations field in management is the human potential movement. The advocates of the **human potential movement** also regarded people as basically good. However, while the human relations movement viewed the employee as a "social being," the human potential movement viewed the employee as a *"self-actualizing being" who seeks to reach fully his or her potential.*

The most influential theorists of the human potential movement were Abraham Maslow and Douglas McGregor. Maslow advocated a hierarchy of human needs, ranging from very basic needs to higher order needs. These include physiological, safety/security, love, esteem, cognitive, aesthetic, and self-actualization needs.[12] Maslow argued that it was necessary to satisfy lower level needs before an individual could progress to higher order needs, which motivate more significant human accomplishments.

Douglas McGregor described two different sets of assumptions about the nature of people at work.[13] He labeled the negative set of assumptions as *Theory X,* and the positive set of assumptions as *Theory Y,* which expresses the sentiments of the human potential movement. For example, a Theory X assumption is that people do not like to work and they try to avoid it. By contrast, a Theory Y assumption is that people do not dislike work, and work is a natural part of our lives. Both Maslow's and McGregor's theories are more thoroughly discussed in a later chapter.

Criticisms of the Human Relations and Human Potential Movements

The basic premise of the human relations movement—that satisfied workers are more productive workers—does not always hold true.[14] In fact, the causal relationship (what caused what) between satisfaction and productivity, under some circumstances, may be the reverse of what the human relations movement suggests. Instead of satisfaction leading to productivity, people who are very productive may derive satisfaction from their accomplishments.[15] The main criticism of the human relations movement, though, is that the social environment is only one of many factors affecting employee motivation and productivity. It is clear that there are other things that drive human behavior besides social needs. Some of these were identified by the human potential movement. It is also clear that there is more to management than just getting along well with others.

The human potential movement shares one of the same deficiencies that plagues the human relations movement: there are many other factors that influence work motivation and performance besides individual human needs. The behavioral sciences and succeeding schools of management more thoroughly address these issues, including job design, communication, leadership, organizational culture and structures, group dynamics, information systems, and technology. Furthermore, the theories of the human potential movement were largely derived through observations and collections of anecdotes that support the writer's opinions. The theories were not developed on the basis of the scientific study of human behavior, and they are difficult to prove or disprove.

The Behavioral Sciences

The **behavioral sciences** sought *to overcome the deficiencies of the human relations and human potential approaches by developing theories about human behavior based on scientific methods and study.* Taylor had applied science to the study of job tasks, but the behavioral sciences take the scientific method one step further. Researchers set aside their personal opinions and study the behavioral processes of individuals and groups. The behavioral sciences retained the attitude that humans have great potential. Further, they suggest that people should be regarded as the organization's most valuable resource, but in order to unlock the vast human potential, managers must understand the causes of behavior.

Behavioral scientists have learned much about human behavior in organizations, including motivation, leadership, group dynamics, interpersonal communication, decision making, organizational culture, and organizational structure and design. We have devoted whole sections and several text chapters to these topics. For now, remember that the behavioral sciences have been vital in building a more complete and successful approach to managing people and organizations.

Behavioral sciences An attempt to overcome the deficiencies of previous theories of management by developing theories about human behavior based on scientific methods.

Criticisms of the Behavioral Sciences

The major criticism of the behavioral sciences is that a great deal of the research and theory is divorced from the practical concerns of everyday managers. As we mentioned earlier, the advancement of management depends on useful theory that helps explain and shape practice. However, for the first time in the history of management, many of the theorists and researchers are not also practicing managers, as were Taylor, Barnard, and Fayol. The research is conducted primarily by academicians in the fields of industrial psychology and organizational behavior, and much of it is so advanced that the practicing manager has a difficult time understanding it, much less making use of it.

Consider the following article title that was published in the *Journal of Applied Psychology:* "Statistical Power of Differential Validity and Differential Prediction Analyses for Detecting Measurement Nonequivalence." It requires a Ph.D. to think up these titles, much less to interpret the contents of the paper. For this reason, many managers are impatient with academicians. Obviously, this criticism does not apply to all academicians. Many researchers are making valuable contributions to the field of management. However, managers often think academic researchers and theorists are engaged in the delicate splitting of hairs when what a manager needs is a good barber who just knows how to use a pair of scissors to successfully shape the organization.

? THINKING CRITICALLY

1.   Thinking about the Hawthorne effect, what makes employees more productive when managers pay attention to them in a non-threatening manner?
2.   From your own experience as an employee or member of an organization, how do you think the quality of your relationships with others affects your performance and productivity?

Quantitative school An approach that advocates the use of quantifiable data and scientific methods to improve the decision making of managers.

THE QUANTITATIVE SCHOOL

The **quantitative school** *uses quantifiable data and scientific methods to improve the decision making of managers.* This approach includes *management science, operations research,* and *industrial statistics.* The goals and motivation for this school were to eliminate uncertainty and guesswork, using science and numbers to improve the precision and certainty of managerial decisions.

Management science The development of sophisticated techniques and mathematical models to understand complex situations.

Management Science and Operations Research

Management science is different from Taylor's scientific management. **Management science** employs *sophisticated techniques and mathematical models to understand complex situations and uses computers to overcome our limited human capacity to handle large amounts of information.* We use the term **operations research** to refer to *the application of management science to managerial problems, such as inventory control, transportation, and other issues that lend themselves to quantitative analysis.*

Operations research The application of management science to real managerial problems.

Management science and operations research were born out of necessity during World War II. The British and American armies had to make decisions about troop movements, how to deploy limited resources like aircraft, and how to increase hit rates with different types of munitions. The government assembled groups of scientists, including mathematicians, statisticians, and physicists to apply the scientific method and mathematics to maximize the use of available resources.

The *scientific method* is a universal process and involves the following steps:

- observe or collect data in the real situation (especially data that you can quantify)
- develop a model that simulates reality, make predictions based on the model
- test the predictions to validate the model
- make revisions to the model
- use the model for decision making

After the war, these same scientists went to work in industrial settings. They looked to apply operations research techniques throughout the company, from manufacturing to finance, marketing, and human resources, including resource allocation, acquisitions, the costs and benefits of investments, employee staffing, scheduling, inventory control, facilities location, and logistics and transportation decisions.

Operations research is often used today by managers who have to plan and control activities to provide products and services. For example, a Coors beer distributorship in Tucson, Arizona developed a computer program to forecast the monthly demands for its various beers. The operations researchers analyzed historical sales data and interviewed managers to get expert opinion regarding future sales. They discovered sales were up and were expected to continue rising. They also discovered fluctuations in sales that varied with the seasons. They built a model taking these factors into account in predicting monthly sales. Then they tested the model using historical data. This revealed that the model worked well except for the months of May, July, and September, each of which has a big beer-drinking holiday. The researchers adjusted the model to account for increased demand in these months. As a result, the managers of the distributorship can better predict demand for their beers. The model helps them make ordering, stocking, and shipping decisions, reduce their costs of carrying inventory, make sure beer is always available, and provide fresh beer to customers by reducing its shelf time.[16]

Criticisms of Management Science and Operations Research

The models of management science and operations research depend upon quantifiable data. Thus, managers use this approach when deciding about issues that involve numbers, such as sales dollars, costs, units shipped, or demand volume, as the beer example demonstrates. However, it is difficult to quantify every factor that goes into many decisions, and often the numbers available are not reliable. Further, mathematical models cannot easily predict human behavior because there are so many unknown and unmeasurable factors that affect what we do.

For a typical manager, there will be times when operations research will be useful. Unfortunately, it can take many years to learn how to conduct effective operations research in a particular firm. For most managers, their time is better spent mastering other knowledge and skills. When operations research seems appropriate, it is better to hire an expert to do the work. To understand and use an expert's advice, managers should appreciate the methods of operations research. For this reason, we devote one chapter to this topic, and we suggest that students take at least one course on this subject.

Industrial Statistics

Industrial statistics The study of variation in measured characteristics, to analyze and improve business results.

In the first half of this century managers started to use **industrial statistics.** This is *the study of variation in measured characteristics, to analyze and improve business results*. In other words, managers began to appreciate that they could take and record measurements, such as the time to complete a certain step in a manufacturing process or how many rings before a customer service representative answers the phone. Then, using *statistical process control (SPC),* they could analyze these data for variations that would help them figure out how well the process was working and identify factors for making improvements. Sound SPC analysis allows managers to make decisions based on real data, not hunches. It provides an understanding of the current capability of people working together in a system.

The methods of statistical process control and sampling techniques were developed at AT&T's Bell Laboratories in the 1930s. Specifically, in 1931 Walter A. Shewhart launched the field with the publication of his book *Economic Control of Quality of Manufactured Products*. Shewhart was one of a larger group at Bell Laboratories investigating problems of quality. What he showed is that it is possible to have standards for the quality you expect a product to have. Measuring variation from standards then becomes a way to measure quality.

Sampling Techniques. Two other people at Bell Labs, Harold Dodge and Harry Romig, made important advances in sampling techniques. These techniques allowed inspectors to check a certain number of items in a particular shipment of goods and count the number of defective items. If the number of defects in the sample was acceptable, you could assume the entire shipment was acceptable. These techniques helped the Bell System improve the quality of its telephone equipment and service for customers. However, neither the sampling techniques nor statistical process control had much impact outside the Bell System, until World War II created the need for large volumes of munitions.

The Impact of World War II. When faced with the problem of supplying the U.S. Army with large quantities of high quality arms and ammunition from multiple suppliers, the War Department turned to the AT&T Bell Lab statisticians. They focused on techniques for acceptance sampling. The techniques relieved the primary bottleneck in moving arms to the field, the understaffed inspection process. Suppliers whose arms satisfied acceptable quality levels were inspected less frequently, while those failing to meet these targets were scrutinized more extensively. Using these techniques, inspectors became more productive, and product quality levels improved. The War Department tried to disseminate these techniques to other industries through training courses and seminars for executives, engineers, inspectors, and other practitioners. The era after the war, however, was a time when quantity of production, not quality, was important, and most of these trainees did not use what they had learned. The role of industrial statistics in management was more fully developed in Japan, where "quality management" evolved along a somewhat different course than in the United States.

Developments in Post-War Japan.   The Japanese course of action was influenced by Americans like W. Edwards Deming, whom we introduced in Chapter 1 and who was a disciple of Walter Shewhart. Deming came to Japan at the invitation of the Japanese Union of Scientists and Engineers (JUSE). He taught executives and engineers to study and reduce variation through statistical control charts and scientific thinking. In contrast to acceptable quality levels (AQL) approach to quality, which tolerates a certain level of defects, Deming's approach required managers to continuously improve production systems to reduce the chances for any defects. Deming also taught the Japanese modern approaches to consumer research. While Americans discounted these approaches as wartime efforts that were not needed in a booming postwar economy, the Japanese saw them as the means of rebuilding their country. The efforts of Deming and JUSE succeeded in making statistical quality control fashionable in Japanese factories in the 1950s. Then the Japanese moved on to a more comprehensive approach, Total Quality Control, to improve every aspect of the company. These developments in Japan were largely ignored by Americans, until the Japanese started grabbing market share with high quality products in industries traditionally dominated by U.S. firms. Their efforts helped form the foundations of Total Quality Management.

Criticisms of Industrial Statistics

The acceptance sampling approach to quality has received a great deal of criticism in recent years. It relies on inspection and does not provide a means of learning about the causes of quality problems in order to continuously improve. By contrast, statistical process control grew in popularity in the 1980s. Many companies saw it as a panacea for all their quality problems. Many American companies in various industries, including General Motors and Campbell Soup, spent outrageous amounts of money training their people in statistical process control. Most of the applications were limited to manufacturing operations.

By the end of the 1980s, managers began to realize that accomplishing continuous improvement requires more than just the application of industrial statistics in manufacturing. There is nothing inherently wrong with statistical process control, but taken alone, it does not ensure management success. This is why many of the companies that started out with statistical process control eventually shifted to Total Quality Management, a more comprehensive approach to improvement. The *A Look at The Global Environment* box on page 60 provides a graphic example of how Harley-Davidson went beyond SPC, using the techniques of TQM to compete effectively against the Japanese.

❓ THINKING CRITICALLY

1. After reading the box about Harley-Davidson, how do you think statistical process control contributed to the turnaround at that company?
2. Which do you think is more important for success: the intelligent gathering and use of quantitative information to make management decisions or having an uncompromising concern for serving customers and basing decisions on how well the company does that? Are these two concerns compatible?

A LOOK AT

THE GLOBAL ENVIRONMENT

HARLEY-DAVIDSON REGAINS THE LEAD FROM THE JAPANESE

The Harley-Davidson motorcycle has epitomized the American desire for power, speed, and personal freedom. However, the 90-year-old company has been on an industrial roller-coaster ride. Harley-Davidson once dominated the super-heavyweight motorcycle market, then nearly went bankrupt, and finally regained its former dominance. The saga begins in 1903, when three brothers, William, Walter, and Arthur Davidson, built the first motorcycle that would eventually become known as the Harley-Davidson "Hog." Harley-Davidson survived two world wars and the Great Depression by building motorcycles better than any other company in the United States. By 1953, Harley-Davidson was the only domestic maker of motorcycles.

The company's good fortunes turned bad when recreational products company AMF acquired Harley-Davidson in 1968 with plans to invest and help it grow. AMF increased production dramatically but drove down quality while doing it. Harleys were failing final quality inspection more than 50% of the time, and some of the defective bikes were slipping through to the customers. At the same time Japanese motorcycle companies, like Honda, Suzuki, Yamaha, and Kawasaki, were invading the U.S. heavyweight motorcycle market with high-quality products. Because of their quality problems, Harley-Davidson's market share fell from more than three-fourths of the market in 1973 to less than one-fourth in 1983. Profits plummeted along with market share. In 1982, Harley-Davidson had a net loss of $25 million.

Forecasting a possible bankruptcy, Harley's executives bought the company from AMF. Citing their weakened market share and financial conditions, the executives lobbied for and received substantial tariff protection from the U.S. Congress for a period of five years. Without the government protection, Harley-Davidson would have had no chance to survive. However, they made the best of this second chance. Harley's executives were determined to rebuild the company by transforming its approach to management. They invested heavily to train suppliers, educate employees, gain union cooperation, improve teamwork, reduce the overblown bureaucracy, and revamp its approach to manufacturing.

Statistical process control was an important part of Harley-Davidson's improvement strategy, but it was not the only part. At the time he was Chairman and Chief Executive Officer, Vaughn L. Beals stated: "Statistics is only a single tool—not an entire tool box. To be competitive by international standards, industry needs statistical management techniques—and several other tools as well. . . . Statistical management techniques, employee involvement, just-in-time inventory, and operator responsibility for production, quality, and machine maintenance—all have to be implemented simultaneously."

Harley-Davidson executives were actively involved in the improvement efforts. They even traveled to Harley Owners Group (H.O.G.) rallies on weekends. They gathered information on customer preferences and customer satisfaction with current products and used the information to guide design decisions and to prioritize quality improvement efforts. For example, they discovered that Harley owners preferred that the bike's engines be exposed, with the motor parts not covered with sheet metal like the aerodynamic Japanese motorcycles. Harley-Davidson has indeed made the best of its second chance. In 1991, just eight years after being on the brink of bankruptcy, its market share had grown to 63% and it continues to climb.[17]

THE SYSTEMS SCHOOL

In Chapter 1 we introduced the systems view of organizations as a foundation for Total Quality Management. The systems school has flourished because the global environment has forced executives to continually re-examine their approach to management.

As a way to think about these changes in personal terms, consider the difference between high school and college. In high school, many bright students don't have to work too hard to get good grades. The reason for this is that the competition for good grades may be relatively low. When these students move on to colleges and universities, they begin to realize that most of the other students are equally bright or they wouldn't be there. Thus, the level of competition is much higher. This requires students to reevaluate their study techniques and how they manage their time. Similarly, managers reevaluated their approaches and discovered the value of viewing organizations as systems. The **systems school** *conceives management in terms of the relationships within the organization and with the environment in which it exists.* There are three areas of the systems school that we will review here: open systems theory, Total Quality Management, and. the contingency view of management.

Systems school A conception of management that focuses on the relationship of the organization to the larger environment.

Open Systems Theory

Ludwig von Bertalanffy, a theoretical biologist, launched open systems theory by using the living organism as an analogy to explain a systems view of the world.[18] It helped people appreciate how a system is a whole in which each part affects every other part. Further, a living organism exists as a part of a larger system. The living organism open system analogy opposes the classical mechanistic view. The mechanistic view treats an organization as a *closed system,* like a big mechanical clock, because it focuses on internal designs without considering the relationship to the environment.[19] If the environment is rapidly changing, ignoring it can be costly, if not deadly.

The **open systems model,** as shown in Exhibit 2-2, *assumes that an organization is open to its environment as it turns inputs (labor, energy, capital, raw materials) into outputs (products and services), through a series of transformation processes.* Accordingly, management focus shifts away from structure and hierarchy. Managers attend to the relationships between the linked and interdependent *processes* of taking in resources, transforming resources into outputs, and delivering these outputs to various "customers" who value them.[20]

Open systems model An approach that assumes an organization is open to its environment as it turns inputs (labor, energy, capital, raw materials) into outputs (products and services), through a series of transformation processes.

EXHIBIT 2-2
Open System Model of Organization

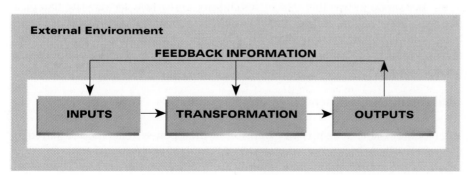

The open systems model sees customers as an important source of feedback about the performance of the organization and the value provided by its products and services. Similarly, the organization is a customer of its suppliers, so it also provides feedback and works cooperatively with suppliers to improve the value it receives. For example, the purchasing department of Honda Motor Company sends its own consultants to help improve the production processes of its suppliers to help guarantee it receives parts of the quality it requires. Thus, management responsibility extends beyond the traditional boundaries of the organization.

Open systems theory also suggests that an organization is composed of various *subsystems,* such as strategic, technical, structural, human/cultural, and managerial subsystems. Like an organ system in the body, each of these has its own processes by which things happen. These subsystems must be properly aligned in order to efficiently and effectively transform inputs into outputs.[21] From this perspective, an important responsibility of managers, in the managerial subsystem, is to accomplish alignment among the other subsystems. For example, the managers of TelePad Corporation of Reston Virginia have articulated a strategic vision based on their ability to identify customer needs, and rapidly develop new products, such as a new pen-based computer, to meet those needs. To implement their strategy, the managers have adopted a structure that is lean, with only 14 people, and they can make quick decisions. These people spend their time building alliances with other companies that can manufacture and deliver their products. TelePad has developed more than two dozen collaborative alliances: IBM does its manufacturing; another company, GVO, executes design and development; Intel does its engineering; and Automatic Data Processing prepares the paychecks for its 14 employees.[22] This works because Telepad managers have successfully aligned all these services to keep the company running smoothly.

A major difference between the open systems view and the mechanistic view is the importance each places on efficiency—translating input into output with little waste of time, labor, or materials. In the mechanistic view, efficiency is the driving force. In the systems view, efficiency is necessary, but it is not sufficient for survival and prosperity. Managers must also address effectiveness.

Criticisms of Open Systems Theory

It is difficult to refute open systems theory. However, when it is explained to managers, they often respond: "It seems like an overcomplicated statement of the obvious," or "That's just common sense." While this may seem like a condemnation of open systems theory, it is really quite flattering. It means this theory must reflect reality for these managers, even if they do not understand its full implications. The problem was that executives did not know how to translate this idea into managerial action. It was only after the emergence of Total Quality Management, with its emphasis on process management, a focus on the customer, and the importance of teamwork, that the full value of the open systems theory became apparent.

Total Quality Management

Quest for Excellence V

Total Quality Management is an extension of the open systems model, although the systems theorists did not develop TQM. It actually grew and blossomed in Japan as the best method for reestablishing industry after the devastation of

World War II. A universally accepted definition of TQM does not exist. However, the following definition was endorsed by the CEOs of nine major U.S. corporations, deans and professors of major universities, and eminent consultants in Total Quality Management:

Total Quality (TQ) is a people-focused management system that aims at continual increase in customer satisfaction at continually lower cost. TQ is a total system approach (not a separate area or program) and an integral part of high-level strategy. It works horizontally across functions and departments, involving all employees, top to bottom, and extends backwards and forwards to include the supply chain and the customer chain. TQ stresses learning and adaptation to continual changes as keys to organizational success.

The foundation of Total Quality is the scientific method. TQ includes systems, methods, and tools. The systems permit change; the philosophy stays the same. TQ is anchored in values and the power of community action. This definition of "Total Quality" suggests that customer satisfaction—even customer delight—is a useful definition of "quality."[23]

While this definition may not suit everyone, it is acceptable to most. There are lots of elements to this definition; however, it should be clear that Total Quality Management adds three critical elements to open systems view:

1. The customer is the top priority stakeholder.
2. Managers and all employees must take responsibility for managing cross-functional systems and processes.
3. Managers and all employees must continuously improve every aspect of the organization to provide better value to customers.

The Competitive Context.   During the era of the classical school, efficiency was the driving force. Managers tried to produce more, for less, and faster, in order to satisfy the voracious appetite of the growing number of customers. Before global competition became intense, managers and customers lacked comparisons from tough competitors. Even when companies began to feel competition, with markets opening up and growing quickly, they could simply abandon one market and move on to harvest a newer one just becoming ripe. Despite their stated customer orientation, even companies like General Electric have used investment strategies that require them to divest a division whose products were not number one or two in their market. Consulting companies like the Boston Consulting Group have made millions of dollars advising companies to do this sort of thing.

By the 1980s, global competitors began to move into U.S. markets in a big way with quality products and good prices. They took huge chunks of market share from American firms not prepared for such competitors. Even the biggest American companies such as General Motors and Xerox began to feel the strain. Executives finally came to realize that their traditional assumptions about how to manage were not getting the results they wanted. Look again at David Kearns' quote on page 41 about the state of affairs at Xerox in the face of Japanese competitors.

A fine example of a company that has gotten the message is Chrysler. Read what *The Wall Street Journal* said about the Neon and other models when introduced early in 1994:

TOTAL QUALITY CULTURE AT WESTINGHOUSE

Robert S. Kincade, Program Manager of Westinghouse's Unmanned Ground Vehicles Group in Huntsville, Alabama, describes his appproach to establishing a Total Quality Culture.

In my most recent management endeavor, I have had the privilege to participate in the development of a start-up organization, which was a "greenfield" opportunity to establish a total quality culture. In simplest terms, organizational culture can be defined as "the natural thing to do, once all rules have been defined." These rules are the invisible boundaries (rules) of culture. As I see it, there are three "P's" of organizational culture: Perception, Performance, and Perpetuation.

Perception plays a significant role in visualizing cultural boundaries. For example, when we established our new organization, we handpicked individuals whose personal philosophy and understanding of TQM fit our vision. Furthermore, we encourage people to do their jobs according to the rule "do it right the first time." We would rather the work take a little longer because an employee stops operations to fix a problem rather than quickly pass a defect on down the line.

Performance is the primary objective of our Total Quality Culture. Culture sets the context and defines the standards expected for individual performance. Our culture reinforces a sense of "duty" to perform not only for individual recognition, but also for the overall success of the organization in serving customers.

Finally, once the culture has been established, the organization must *Perpetuate* the culture. This is true not only for new employees, but also for current employees. We assign sponsors to each new employee once they are assigned to a work team. Every member of the organization has a sponsor whose primary job is to reinforce our Total Quality Culture through one-on-one communication.

Japanese auto makers, which are trying to sell Civics and Tercels in Neon's class for more than $11,000, aren't happy about the Neon [starting at $8,975] or its big sisters, the Chrysler Cirrus and the Dodge Stratus, two midsized compact sedans. Those two have sleek good looks and thoughtful interiors that are common to the best Japanese family sedans. Said one Nissan executive after sitting in the Cirrus: "Chrysler's got it." [24]

Using cross-functional teams, cooperating with suppliers, and focusing unrelentingly on customer value, Chrysler is now the leading innovator among the Big Three, and its automobile division is profitable.

The Spirit of Total Quality.   Fledgling proprietorships can more easily accomplish the integration for effectiveness than large organizations. The owner acts as a jack-of-all-trades, so the management of diverse work is not divided among different people. Communication and coordination problems are virtually non-existent. The owner designs the product, procures materials, produces and delivers goods, and accounts for revenues and expenses. The owner is not isolated from the work by layers of middle managers. Nor is the owner isolated from customers by specialized departments, such as customer service, marketing, sales, or warrantee claims. When necessary, the owner looks the customer in the eye and apologizes for making a shoddy product. The owner gets feedback directly from the customer. In large organizations, with many managers, these activities are divided into specialized departments, with hierarchical lines of communication and responsibility, which makes integration more difficult to achieve. The roles of managers in the Total Quality approach are designed to reproduce within larger organizations the spirit and integration of the smaller proprietorship. We need specialization and division of labor to make large organizations efficient, and TQM gives us a way to put it all together again so that the whole organization is effective.

The Future of Total Quality.   How widespread is this commitment to TQM? A growing number of business leaders argue that TQM is critical to U.S. competitiveness. As a measure of this commitment, the chief executives of American Express, Ford, IBM, Motorola, Procter & Gamble, and Xerox published an open letter on TQM in the *Harvard Business Review*. "We are absolutely convinced that TQM is a fundamentally better way to conduct business and is necessary for the economic well-being of America. TQM results in higher-quality, lower cost products and services that respond faster to the needs of the customer."[25] Students who aspire to be the future leaders and managers of these organizations will have to understand Total Quality Management.

Criticisms of Total Quality Management

As with open systems theory, the philosophy of Total Quality Management is difficult to refute. However, the primary criticism of Total Quality Management is that managers do not implement it well. The primary reason for this poor performance is that managers often try to do it according to a cookbook mentality. They look for the ingredients and the step by step instructions, which are readily provided by consultants or managers who have used these methods in other companies. They gather up the Total Quality tools and techniques, like statistical process control, and some others that will be discussed in later chapters. Then they attempt to duplicate the recipe by implementing a similar program in their organization. These managers are still looking for the one best way to manage, which is a misguided lesson taught to managers by the classical school.

This cookbook mentality has driven more than a few people to categorize TQM as just the latest management fad. And these critics would be correct if TQM was just a bunch of techniques. However, it is much more than techniques. It incorporates the open systems view as its foundation, and it logically builds its techniques based on this foundation.

Managers must realize that Total Quality Management is not a program that can be lifted from one organization and transplanted to another, nor does it suggest one best way to do things. Such simplistic approaches to transforming management do not and cannot work. Total Quality Management is, more than anything, an insight into organizations, what they are, and how they function. With those insights, we have direction for figuring out successful methods, actions, and decisions. As a way to summarize what we have been saying, here is what Rosabeth Moss Kanter, a respected author and professor at the Harvard Business School, says about TQM:

When TQM programs fail, it is because they are mounted as programs, unconnected to the business strategy, rigidly and narrowly applied, and are expected to bring about miraculous transformations in the short term without top management lifting a finger. Once companies in an industry jump on the bandwagon and adopt new practices, and once customers begin to see product or service perfection as a God-given right, rather than something some companies thoughtfully provide, then TQM-type practices become a baseline business necessity to stay in the game at all.[26]

TQM and the Contingency View

Contingency view An approach that suggests that the decisions managers make and methods they use should depend on the situation.

There is one other aspect of TQM useful to know about and appreciate, in light of modern management thought and practice. There is no one right TQM answer for dealing with every organizational opportunity or problem. TQM incorporates in its approach what some call a **contingency view** of management which *suggests that the decisions managers make and methods they use should depend on the situation*. While Total Quality Management helps us understand that an organization is a system with processes for serving customers, there are any number of ways to take advantage of this insight. TQM does not really provide answers. It helps managers ask the right questions:

1. How does this situation affect the organization's other processes?
2. What was inherent in our processes to cause this situation in the first place?
3. What is the short-term solution, and how can we change our processes to prevent this from happening again in the long-term?
4. What we can learn from this situation that we can improve on in the future?
5. How can we help the people involved to grow from this experience?
6. How well or poorly have we served our customers and how can we improve at this?

Notice that these questions focus on figuring out what happened *in the system* and how we can learn from it and improve it.

❓ THINKING CRITICALLY

1. How does the open systems view help explain the idea that an organization should focus on serving customers?
2. Assuming an organization is an open system, what do you think some of the concerns of a conscientious manager should be in making sure it is successful?
3. Based on what you have read here, what elements of the other management schools does TQM incorporate? What distinguishes TQM from these other approaches?

THE EVOLUTION OF MANAGEMENT: 20–20 HINDSIGHT

Now that we have reviewed the evolution of management, let's look back on the ground we covered. The first thing to consider is why people are interested in this subject in the first place. The answer we suggest is that organizations give us the ability to divide up our labor, specialize, and develop far more wealth than by working alone. So it makes sense to understand how we can make these organizations, made up of people like you and me, function well and achieve their purposes. That is the challenge of management.

Let's go back, though, to the late 19th century. Imagine you are Frederick Taylor, and as you observe the way work gets done, you see there are tremendous inefficiencies and inconsistencies in how employees go about their jobs. You and your colleagues, the Gilbreths, seek to use the scientific method to figure out how to make workers more efficient and productive. Your goal is to use science to make the world of work function better. And you succeed at this.

Now, change places with Max Weber, and as you look at organizations, you see that the way organizations are set up to administer large numbers of people is also quite inefficient. You propose a model that lays out an ideal organizational structure, again to make large organizations of all types more efficient. You are joined by another practitioner, Henri Fayol, who also has ideas about making organizations more efficient. Lots of organizations see the value of your work and they adopt your models and methods and become more efficient.

Now imagine you are Chester Barnard, and you observe that while organizations are more efficient, they are also exploiting workers and treating them just as another piece of replaceable machinery. You understand that workers are human beings, and that you must address their human needs as well as the needs of the organization for efficiency. Indeed, you discover that by not treating people humanely, you may be undermining the long-term efficiency of the organization as employees come and go. You introduce an approach to managing that focuses on better communication, and you work to help people relate better to one another and to create a positive work environment. You and those that follow you continue this trend, seeking to make the workplace more humane and thus to enhance employee motivation. This seems to be a real improvement over the cold scientific management approach of the early 20th century. However, as the marketplace becomes increasingly competitive, this approach does not seem to be enough to help companies gain a strategic advantage or further enhance productivity.

You are now Walter Shewhart and know a lot about the value of statistics to determine how well organizational processes are functioning and how they might be improved. You develop statistical methods to analyze and improve processes. At the same you are doing this, others are also starting to use quantitative methods to analyze large amounts of data to help managers make better decisions. As with the previous steps in the evolution of management, these tools helped organizations improve their productivity. Indeed, some people thought statistical methods would solve all their problems.

Finally, imagine you are a fairly enlightened modern manager and you hear about the open systems view of an organization. Compared with other approaches, which focused on management methods and organizational structures, this one started with a definition of what an organization is, an open system that interacts with and is dependent on the larger environment of which it is a part. You see how Total Quality Management, which stresses the improvement of processes to deliver goods and services to customers, seems the most sensible approach to managing efficiently and effectively. You see that TQM uses scientific methods to improve the processes of the organization. Then, by understanding that an organization is a system made up of interrelated parts, you see that it is your responsibility to help these parts work in harmony to maximize performance. You see that TQM is an open-minded and comprehensive approach that uses tools and methods developed in previous schools in a more intelligent and directed method.

IMPROVEMENTS THROUGHOUT THE SYSTEM

Just as the philosophy of TQM suggests, implementing improved strategies for customer value often requires continuous improvements throughout the organization. Here are some examples of improvements Xerox made in policies, motivation systems, work processes, technologies, and methods of executing work.

- **Policies.**   In the old Xerox, one policy charged financial responsibility for manufacturing variance (deviation from plan) to the marketing unit that caused the variance. If marketing canceled a product, and caused excessive manufacturing cost, it would be charged for it. Or if marketing requested a hedge (some extra inventory in case of market demand increases), it would be charged for it. The policy created internal competition and undermined cooperation and teamwork between marketing and manufacturing. So, if marketing ordered something from manufacturing, they had to take it even if market demand changed. The policy was not consistent with the demand-driven vision of the integrated supply chain, which says that you do not produce something unless there is demand for it. The policy was eliminated.

- **Goals.**   Manufacturing and marketing inventory levels were evaluated once a year. Manufacturing was responsible for work-in-process inventory, and marketing was responsible for finished goods inventories. Manufacturing would do better at the end of the year if it shipped as much inventory as possible across to the marketing company. And, of course, marketing would do better if several months before the end of the year it told manufacturing "I don't want to take what I ordered." To eliminate bickering and suboptimization, Xerox changed goals and established partnerships and congruent goals to reduce combined manufacturing and marketing inventory.

- **Production Processes.**   Production lines for various machines changed from traditional assembly lines to focused factories, with production cells, rather than long assembly lines. Multi-skilled workers capable of producing any product move from cell to cell. They work as a team, dividing tasks among themselves, to produce whatever is demanded. Flexible manufacturing allows Xerox to quickly meet changing demands. If Xerox needs to increase production, they simply add another cell and another production team. Using the old assembly line approach, they would change the content of many jobs and rebalance the work all the way down the assembly line.

- **Decision-Making Process.**   Xerox developed production planning process (P3) teams at each plant to make data-driven production decisions on the production floor. The P3 team includes four analysts: marketing, manufacturing, operations, and supplier materials managers. They monitor information and have the authority to shut down production and send workers home or off to training. Their only proviso is to ensure finished goods inventories stay within certain boundaries, and if so, the company required no further review by other layers of management.

- **Technology.**   To do the revised production planning process (P3), managers initially computed minimum and maximum inventory levels using calculators, with individuals on computers drawing data from diverse sources. Lack of technology constrained how quickly, and thus how frequently, managers could make inventory adjustments (every two or three weeks). With new software, analysts read information from diverse sources and languages, instantly compute inventory levels, and better achieve the integrated supply chain vision.

- **Methods of Executing Work.** Work methods improved at Xerox include calculating inventory levels, assembling copiers in the manufacturing cells, and calculating the inventories of spare parts held in their service engineers' trunks.[27]

Finally, you conclude that the evolution of management thought and practice to where we are now, like all human activities, is the result of trial and error experience. Each management school emerged as a response to new conditions in the environment and to internal organizational problems that the one that preceded it dealt with poorly. The appeal of TQM is that it acknowledges what went before, incorporates the best of those schools, and applies these to managing the organization as a system.

While it's easy to spot the fallacies of the earlier schools of management with 20–20 hindsight, you find it is also useful to reflect that we needed to go through those steps to get to where we are today. And further, you realize that our understanding of how to manage systems, especially those composed of people, will continue to evolve. You understand that this fact reflects another tenet of TQM: we must continuously improve on the products and services we deliver and how we produce them.

THINKING CRITICALLY

1. How do changes in the external environment influence the evolution of the schools of management?
2. What pieces of the various schools have been retained by the Total Quality Management?
3. Identify the influences of the various schools of management in the improvements made by Xerox.

SUMMARY

Management Theory and Practice
- By understanding theories of what organizations are and how they function, we can be more successful in managing them.
- Total Quality Management has evolved from several schools of management and represents our current best understanding of management theory and practice.

Management Before the Twentieth Century
- Management has been around as long as people have been organizing themselves into groups to achieve mutual goals.
- In commercial enterprises, management was initially relatively simple. Either a single proprietor took care of everything or an artisan directly oversaw the work of apprentices.
- With the industrial revolution and the growth of large organizations came the quest for more efficient ways to direct the work of employees.

The Classical School
- The classical school was the first modern effort to develop a formal theory of management. This school's goal was to enhance the efficiency of work in organizations.

- The scientific management theorists emphasized specialization and division of labor, and sought the "one best way" to perform organizational tasks, including managing them.

- The administrative theorists sought to develop ideal models of organizations to enhance efficiency.

The Behavioral School

- The behavioral school emerged in reaction to the impersonal nature of scientific management. It emphasizes understanding the complete human being—behaviors, needs, emotions, attitudes, motivation, and social interaction.

- The human relations movement suggested that managers needed to develop open and honest relationships with their employees.

- The human potential movement stressed the notion of helping individuals reach their full potential.

- The behavioral sciences sought to apply scientific methodologies to understanding human behavior to manage people better.

The Quantitative School

- The quantitative school includes management science, operations research, and industrial statistics.

- Management science seeks to use mathematical models to understand organizations and provide direction for decisions.

- Operations research refers to the application of management science to managerial problems.

- Industrial statistics studies variations in processes, such as in manufacturing, to identify sources of defects, and provide information for making improvements.

The Systems School

- The systems school conceives of management in terms of the relationship between an organization and its environment.

- The open systems approach sees the organization taking inputs from the external environment and transforming them into outputs to be delivered to those who need them.

- Total Quality Management is the management approach that integrates a variety of attitudes, techniques, and tools for most successfully managing a system.

The Evolution of Management: 20-20 Hindsight

- A review of the evolution of management shows how each school emerged in response to weaknesses in its predecessor.

- TQM, with its emphasis on managing system processes to continuously improve the organization's ability to deliver quality products to customers, is our current best understanding of the management task.

KEY TERMS

Administrative theories 49

Behavioral school 52

Behavioral sciences 55

Bureaucracy 49

Classical school 47

Contingency view 66

Economic man 47

Evolution 43

Hawthorne effect 53

Human potential movement 54

Human relations movement 54

Industrial statistics 58

Management science 56

Open systems model 61

Operations research 56

Quantitative school 56

Revolution 43

Scientific management 47

Systems school 61

Theory 43

REVIEW QUESTIONS

1. What is the importance of theory in becoming a successful manager?
2. Why was there little need for special management theories and practices before the industrial revolution?
3. Why was efficiency the initial focus of management theorists?
4. What is scientific management, and why do you think that was the first identifiable management school?
5. What was the goal of the administrative theorists? What are the strengths of their theories? What are the weaknesses?
6. What inadequacies in scientific management did the behavioral school seek to remedy?
7. How did the behavioral sciences attempt to overcome the deficiencies of the human relations movement? What are the strengths and weaknesses of the behavioral sciences approach?
8. What was the motivation for the quantitative school of management?
9. What is the goal of statistical process control?
10. What is the difference between an open system and a closed system?
11. How does the competitive environment motivate managers to adopt TQM?
12. What are the criticisms of TQM? Are they well-founded? Why does TQM sometimes seem to fail when managers try it?
13. What is the relationship of TQM with the contingency view of management?

EXPERIENTIAL EXERCISE

Divide into groups of 5 or 6 students. Read the passage below, which describes a mechanistic view and a systems view of a university. Pretend your group has been hired as consultants, and suggest what you would do to change the management of your university or college in accordance with the systems school of management.

A mechanistic thinker, in explaining a university, would begin by disassembling it until he reached its elements; for example, from university to college, from college to department, and from department to faculty, students, and subject matter. Then he would define faculty, student, and subject matter. Finally, he would aggregate these into a definition of a department, thence to college, and conclude with a definition of a university.

A systems thinker confronted with the same task would begin by identifying a system containing the university; for example, the educational system. Then such a thinker would define the objectives and functions of the educational system and do so with respect to the still larger social system that contains it. Finally, he or she would explain or define the university in terms of its roles and functions in the educational system.[28]

CASE ANALYSIS AND APPLICATION
Zebco Saving Time to Stay on Top[29]

Fishing-reel maker Zebco Corp., in Tulsa, Oklahoma, shows the indispensable value of close contact with customers. As part of a "value analysis" carried out in the company, Zebco asked its customers what they want most when having their fishing gear repaired. Time was their overriding concern. Zebco's customers asked for immediate service, quick repairs, instant answers to questions, and fast delivery of reel parts.

To satisfy its customers, Zebco instituted some "streamlining," says Leon Rademacher, customer-service chief. Competitors were taking about 21 days to complete repairs on equipment, he says. Although Zebco was completing repairs generally in five to seven days, the process was still hampered by bottlenecks and duplicated efforts. When they tracked down those problems and eliminated them, Zebco was able to finish repairs on warranty items in 48 hours and on non-warranty items in 72 hours.

Rademacher says Zebco usually does better than its promise. The average turnaround time on a repair is now about 20 hours. In addition, the company now gives each customer a card stating the times they received the item and when they fixed it. Zebco also promises to respond to inquiries within three days. "We went about increasing each customer's level of expectation," says Rademacher. In other words, they have set the bar higher for all their competitors and have a distinct advantage over those not as responsive.

By at least one account, the customers are judging Zebco favorably. Rademacher says that about 95 percent of the 500 letters the firm received from customers last year were compliments.

Discussion Questions

1. What elements of Total Quality Management does this case illustrate?
2. Explain how this case demonstrates the relationship of the ideas of efficiency and effectiveness to succeed in a competitive market.

VIDEO CASE: COMBINING QUALITY MANAGEMENT AND SOCIAL RESPONSIBILITY
Gail Mayville

To honor the initiative and vision of individual employees who help their companies serve society better, The Business Enterprise Trust in 1991 cited Gail Mayville, a clerical employee who became the environmental coordinator of Ben & Jerry's Homemade, Inc. of Waterbury, Vermont. Mayville helped Ben & Jerry's, a premium ice cream company known for its commitment to global social issues, realize that it could do much more to address environmental concerns at home.

Gail Mayville came to Ben & Jerry's in 1986 as administrative assistant to the company's president. Reared on a farm where "we recycled absolutely everything—but for economic reasons," Mayville became disappointed that Ben & Jerry's was not doing more to lessen its own impact on the environment. She soon found an opportunity to make improvements. Ben & Jerry's growing production had led it to violate a town permit from Waterbury for disposal of ice cream waste. Mayville offered to handle the dilemma and devised a creative and cost-effective solution. She arranged for a special truck to come each day and cart the ice cream waste to a Vermont farmer who fed it to his pigs.

Mayville's environmental commitment was further encouraged by a company mission statement adopted late in 1988. The statement invited individual employees to propose things the company could do to fulfill any aspect of its mission. "That was my ticket," says Mayville, who wrote a detailed memo suggesting dozens of ideas for improving the company's environmental performance. Over the next eighteen months, Mayville initiated a flurry of proposals for purchasing recycled materials, decreasing packaging, and changing waste disposal procedures. There was no available technology to recycle the plastic ingredient buckets which flooded landfills used by Ben & Jerry's, so she worked with a national container corporation to develop such a technology. Coordinating efforts with other Vermont companies, she created new collection systems for recyclable materials and a consortium with sufficient buying power to purchase recycled products at reasonable prices.

Along the way, Mayville, whose formal education was limited to two years of college, became an environmental expert, addressing national recycling gatherings and even a United Nations commission. She pioneered ways of introducing recycling to small companies and rural locations. In mid-1990, Mayville invited other Ben & Jerry's employees to form a "Green Team" to take responsibility for the many environmental initiatives now underway. Gail Mayville's individual initiative, commitment, and dogged persistence have lead her company to become a leader in environmental efficiency.

Video Case Questions

1. Which of the four major schools of management does Gail Mayville, and Ben & Jerry's Homemade, Inc., most closely resemble? Explain.
2. Identify elements of Total Quality Management in this case and explain how these elements contribute to Ben & Jerry's success as a business.

3. MANAGING SYSTEMS: THE PRINCIPLES OF TQM

LEARNING OBJECTIVES

When you finish this chapter you should be able to:

1. Explain the logic behind the TQM approach to managing systems.
2. Describe the connection between sound managerial decisions and a focus on delivering value to customers.
3. Discuss the importance of continuously improving all systems and processes to remain competitive.
4. Explain why TQM focuses on the management of processes rather than people.
5. Describe cause-and-effect diagrams and "five whys" as methods for identifying root causes.
6. Explain why finding root causes is important in continuous improvement.
7. Describe the importance of training and education to help organizations maintain their competitiveness.
8. Explain why TQM emphasizes teamwork and empowering employees to make organizations operate efficiently and effectively.

SOUTHERN PACIFIC TURNAROUND[1]

In 1990, the Southern Pacific Railroad, once the most important railroad in the West, was slowly dying. It was the victim of government deregulation and financial manipulation, and, yes, poor management. By the time it was purchased by Philip F. Anschutz in 1988, it was an amalgam of various companies and cultures, the result of various mergers, with offices in several different cities. It was functioning, but just barely. When Mr. Anschutz took stock of the company in 1990, this was the situation:

- It was losing money. Its assets and cash indicated the company could last five years at best as it currently operated.
- Because it was losing money, it could not borrow money from investors to help turn the company around.
- It had alienated many customers because of poor service and many of these customers were turning to trucks to transport their goods.

Those who remained did so because they had no alternative.

- The company had to deal with many different craft unions of its own and its subsidiaries, making labor relations complicated at best.
- The management of the different railroads under its ownership had little in common philosophically and culturally.
- The company had weak processes for getting work done. Decisions emerged from the bowels of a bureaucracy more concerned with its own rules and regulations than the needs of other employees or the company as a whole. Employees were very protective of their own turf and jobs. In this mode, the company was constantly dealing with crises, with management operating reactively rather than proactively.

With no money to invest in turning this situation around, Mr. Anschutz decided to take a gamble on Total Quality Management to return the company to profitability. There was clearly a lot of work to do. To help coordinate everyone's actions he brought in an expert, Kent Sterrett, as Vice President for Quality. Sterrett had been with Florida Power and Light, a company that had transformed itself using TQM techniques.

Sterrett saw that SP had to make changes "on the cheap" and do several things in parallel if they were going to succeed. He immediately initiated activities in the following areas:

- leadership, commitment, and involvement by top management
- information and benchmarking (learning from the best practices of others)
- developing action plans
- involving the unions
- involving middle managers in improving processes

The company set up a Quality Council consisting of the CEO, COO (Chief Operating Officer), and Vice Presidents of the company. This council's responsibility was to demonstrate the company's commitment to this new direction and provide the authority and resources needed to make changes happen. The Quality Council targeted four areas for improvement: *customer service, revenue expansion, productivity,* and *union involvement.*

In January 1991, 200 SP managers and 50 union officers came together for the annual management meeting. This was the first time union leaders had

ever come to such a meeting at any railroad. The company's poor financial state was presented to everyone, including the revelation that the productivity of management and professional workers was poor by industry comparisons. The company then began taking actions. These actions included the following:

- **Leadership.** The plan required total participation of top management to demonstrate their commitment. During the next six months, top managers introduced the new quality-driven approach to workers in 125 different meetings throughout the company and face-to-face meetings with other employees.

- **Training.** To help all employees understand the new approach, they hired a new Vice President for Human Resources (they formerly had only a Labor Relations Director). This new VP was responsible for developing in-house training programs for everyone in the company.

- **Quality Improvement Teams.** The operating units of the company have formed teams of all sorts. About 25 percent of these are cross-functional in nature. Each

of these teams is undertaking various improvement projects, and all are empowered to make the changes necessary to implement their plans.

- **Key Performance Indicators (KPI).** The managers of each operating unit identified the quantifiable measures of performance (KPIs) based on top management's four areas for improvement. The quality department also came up with external benchmarks (based on the performance of competitors). They then carefully charted the KPIs and distributed the information widely throughout the company so all employees knew how they were doing.

- **Integrated Planning.** The improvement priorities now became the basis for each unit's budget plan. Each unit manager had to show an understanding of how the planning process integrates strategy, quality, finance, marketing, and operations. The plans include goals stated in terms of KPIs.

Let's look at a specific example that illustrates the difference these changes have made at SP. One of the KPIs had to do with increasing the reliability of

cars and maintaining them in good running order. One problem they had been encountering was that cars the company interchanged with another line tended to break down, compromising the reliability of SP to its customers. A group of unionized carmen (the title of those responsible for car maintenance) formed a team to deal with this problem. Using the steps they learned in training, the carmen worked with employees from the other company to ensure cars were in good running order when released back to SP. They succeeded in markedly improving the KPI category covering this aspect of company performance. The team was flown back to San Francisco to give a report to senior management, and earned the respect of their colleagues in the train yard.

While this kind of action brought about a specific improvement in one KPI, it also has a ripple effect throughout the entire company. The increased efficiency and effectiveness in one part of the business affects the other parts by making it easier for others to do their work and by serving as an example for what is possible.

TOTAL QUALITY AND SYSTEMS MANAGEMENT

The Southern Pacific Railroad company is a system. Its purpose is to provide transportation services to freight shippers and passengers. When it does a good job of this, it succeeds and is profitable. When it does a poor job of this, it loses money and endangers its existence. By 1990, SP had a management structure in place that proved to be very inefficient and ineffective at managing the SP system. The processes did not work well. There was waste, and the system was breaking down. It seemed as if the employees had forgotten the company's purpose. Of course, its customers had not, and that's why they were abandoning SP for other companies that could better serve their transportation needs. Fortunately, top management at SP recognized that they had some deep problems and that there was an approach to managing that would help them solve these problems. That approach was Total Quality Management.

We have talked a lot about systems and TQM in Chapters 1 and 2. Now we are going to provide you with the basic principles for managing systems. These principles form the foundation of TQM. As we suggested in Chapter 2, TQM logically flows from the idea that an organization is a system. The systems view has been around for a long time, but no one had understood the special implications of that idea for managing more effectively. After people like W. Edwards Deming, Joseph M. Juran, Kaoru Ishikawa, and a few other pioneers articulated the principles of TQM, business people began to see the light. It is now clear that managing the total organization as a system to serve customers and other stakeholders (including employees, investors, and the community) is the best way for an organization to survive and thrive in an unforgiving global economy.

THE PRINCIPLES OF TOTAL QUALITY MANAGEMENT

Motorola: Baldrige Award Winner

We will cover seven principles for effectively and efficiently managing a system. All of these principles are interrelated. A manager cannot decide to implement one or two of them and expect positive results. We use these principles as the rationale and foundation for all the other ideas in this book. Here they are:

Principle 1: Focus on delivering customer value.
Principle 2: Continuously improve the system and its processes.
Principle 3: Manage processes, not just people.
Principle 4: Look for root causes to solve and prevent problems.
Principle 5: Collect data and use science for analysis.
Principle 6: People are the organization's primary resource.
Principle 7: Work in teams to execute processes efficiently and effectively.

There is an interdependency among these principles. For example, you cannot survive in a competitive environment without delivering more value to your customers. And you cannot do that without improving your system and its processes. To improve the system you have to look for root causes of problems and, working with people closest to the situation, find ways to prevent problems in the first place. You have to collect data and use sound scientific methods to analyze that data and make decisions about improving based on facts, not opinions. The work of organizations happens as interrelated processes, and thus only by managing processes can you help the organization improve its ability to provide value to customers. All work ultimately gets done by and for people, so understanding that and facilitating their ability to perform is the only way to get the system working better. Finally, because the execution of processes requires employees to work cooperatively, teams make it easier to do this efficiently and effectively. All of these ideas are part and parcel of each other and of TQM, not unlike the organ systems that make up our bodies. All have a role to play and are important for the entire organization to function properly. The *TQM in Action* box on product development at Thermos provides an example of the interdependency of these principles.

TQM IN ACTION

INVENTING A NEW BARBEQUE GRILL AT THERMOS[2]

When Monte Peterson took over as CEO of the Thermos Company, the company famous for inventing the vacuum bottle, he recognized, as stated in *Fortune* magazine, that "today's intelligent and demanding customers cannot be tricked by clever advertising or slick packaging into buying a so-so, me-too product. To survive in this brutal environment, companies must constantly innovate, creating goods that give customers high quality at the right price—in a word, value." Thermos was just drifting when Peterson came on board, living off the sales of its established products with lukewarm growth and a bureaucratic culture organized around functions, such as marketing, manufacturing, and engineering. It was hardly a company ready to compete for the business of those intelligent and demanding consumers mentioned above.

Peterson chose to make changes in Thermos and chose to start the change with the development of a new barbecue grill. The market for grills is about $1 billion annually, the competition is tough with Sunbeam, Char-Broil, and Weber all firmly entrenched. Here's the process he initiated to meet this challenge:

- He put together a product-development team of six middle managers and supervisors from different functional areas such as engineering, marketing, manufacturing, and finance with the goal of developing a new and innovative grill. This group gave itself the name the "Lifestyle" team to help it focus on customers and the benefits of the product and not the product itself. They then added some members from various suppliers to work with them, including an industrial design firm. The idea was to get everyone who would be involved in the final product working together from the beginning.

- The team's first challenge was to find out as much as possible about customers and how they use grills, and they did a lot of field research in this quest. Among other information, they discovered that people were getting tired of messy charcoal, and such grills are often banned in apartments.

- After they completed their research and analysis, they decided on an electric-powered grill that included the heating element in the grill itself instead of below the grill as in competing models. They built a prototype and again checked it out with the market. This resulted in refinements to the final design, such as a larger and stronger shelf.

- It is a common problem that when designers work independently, they come up with products that are complicated and costly to manufacture. By having a team of experts, Thermos avoided this problem and also developed a superior product.

- After more testing and tweaking, the final product was rolled out, on schedule, at the National Hardware Show, where it was a hit with retailers.

Monte Peterson had started a revolution at Thermos. This new grill was the main reason revenues at Thermos jumped 13% in 1993. Using cross-functional teams that involve getting people throughout the company to work together to improve customer value is the reason Thermos is now growing again.

The seven principles we reviewed above are now at work at Thermos. Management got everyone focusing their energy on serving customers. They understood the importance of improving their processes for developing products and getting employees from all areas involved in this. Peterson understood that the causes for problems at the company were not the fault of employees but the company's processes, and that only by changing those processes could the company start to come out of its doldrums. They did not work from hunches, but gathered data to make sure the product they were developing would satisfy customer needs. Finally, by creating a team to make this all happen, the product development process went much smoother. This is not a random success. It is the outcome of a more logical, efficient, and effective management approach that focuses on making the organization work better as a system. Now let's review these seven principles of Total Quality Management in more detail.

? THINKING CRITICALLY

1. Think about a business with which you have had some dealings either as a customer or an employee. Based on your intuitive sense of the seven principles of TQM, discuss how these principles might help explain how well or poorly this business is functioning.
2. Why do you think focus on the customer is the first principle?

PRINCIPLE 1: FOCUS ON DELIVERING CUSTOMER VALUE

Back in 1960 Theodore Levitt, a Harvard professor, wrote one of the most quoted articles ever to appear in the *Harvard Business Review:* "Marketing Myopia."[3] In this article, Professor Levitt explained why the railroads were losing ground in this country: They thought they were in the business of railroading, not the business of transporting goods from here to there. When alternatives to railroads offered shippers more benefits than the railroads, they switched. In Levitt's words: "The reason they defined their industry wrong was because they were railroad-oriented and not transportation-oriented; they were product-oriented instead of customer-oriented." In the Thermos example, remember the name the team chose for itself, the "Lifestyle" team, not "The New Grill" team.

What customers value, what they buy, is *never* the product itself. They *always* buy the benefit or service they expect to derive from that product. In the store, customers may purchase a Thermos grill, but as far as they are concerned, what they are actually buying is the benefit of a convenient way to barbecue food outdoors. That's what customers value and what motivates them to buy. From the open systems view, we can see the importance of delivering value to customers. It attracts the resources the company needs to continue in business— funds from customers as well as from investors and lenders to invest in people and capital to make barbecues, offer transportation services, publish textbooks, and everything else that is of value to us.

Customer Value and Management Decisions

When managers focus on customer value as a guiding principle for their efforts, they make better decisions. Why? Because it forces them to figure out the best use of people and allocation of resources to create goods and services consumers will want to buy, and thus keep the company viable. These are the kinds of decisions that lead to better strategies, a better deployed workforce, and better quality and productivity.

This focus on customers allows managers to better assess the long-term impact of their decisions. Otherwise, some decisions that seem to be in the best interest of a company, such as across-the-board budget cuts to immediately reduce costs, could actually reduce its ability to provide customer value and cause the company to lose customers (even though that was not the intention).

While Principle 1 reminds us of what must be the primary goal of the company, the other six principles guide us in achieving this goal. We will talk more about customer value and quality in Chapter 7 on strategic planning. You will find another perspective on this idea in the *A Look at The Global Environment* box on page 81, which talks about how the Japanese learned to focus on customers.

W. Edwards Deming and Quality for the Customer

We introduced W. Edwards Deming in Chapter 1. As we proceed in this book, we will frequently mention his ideas along with those of other pioneers. Deming was also in Japan during the late 1940s and early 1950s as a teacher and consultant to help get Japanese industry back on its feet. He also gave management courses, including a famous session in 1950, attended by many of the leading figures of Japanese industry. In that session, Deming presented what he called a chain reaction for succeeding in business. Exhibit 3-1 illustrates the chain reaction.

What this chain reaction demonstrates is the importance of focusing on quality as a starting point to make good things happen in an organization. All the goals we normally identify for businesses, including increased market share, higher productivity, and higher profits, all start with improving quality. This is because improving quality means figuring out what customers want and then figuring out how to build it with as few steps and resources as possible. Indeed, what it also demonstrates is that if managers, for example, try to reduce costs

EXHIBIT 3-1
Deming's Chain Reaction. This diagram demonstrates that to improve organizational performance, managers must start by improving the quality of products and services.

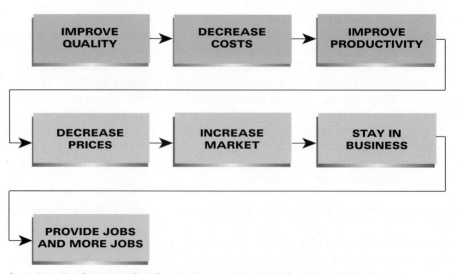

Source: Adapted from Brian L. Joiner, *Fourth Generation Management* (New York: McGraw-Hill, Inc., 1994) p. 23.

THE GLOBAL ENVIRONMENT

AMERICANS TEACH THE JAPANESE ABOUT CUSTOMER VALUE[4]

Some people assume this focus on the customer to be a Japanese concept because the Sonys and Toyotas of the world seem so good at it. However, the customer focus was actually introduced to the Japanese by Americans. We can credit General Douglas MacArthur, the commander of the U.S. Occupation forces in Japan, with initiating the industrial success enjoyed by many Japanese manufacturers. Just after World War II, MacArthur wanted to improve Japan's key industries, such as telephone and radio, to enable the military to communicate with all parts of Japan. At MacArthur's request, American engineers Homer Sarasohn and Charles Protzman developed and delivered a training course to help the Japanese organize to do this. They advocated the following message about quality:

- Every company needs a concise, complete statement of its purpose, one that provides a well-defined goal for the efforts of employees.
- Companies must put quality [value for customers] ahead of profit, pursuing it rigorously with techniques such as statistical quality control.

Sarasohn says of the Japanese in the 1940s, "They thought that quality meant making half of your products okay and throwing out the other half." However, leaders in the Japanese electronics industry learned the American lessons about quality. Sarasohn and Protzman's pupils included such figures as Matsushita Electric's Masaharu Matsushita; Mitsubishi Electric's Takeo Kato; Fujitsu's Hanzou Omi; Sumitomo Electric's Bunzaemon Inoue; and Akio Morita and Masaru Ibuka, the founders of what is now Sony Corporation. Masaharu Matsushita recalls: "Mentioned on the first page of this seminar's text was the title, 'The Objective of the Enterprise,' under which the philosophy of corporate management—the social mission of the enterprise—was clearly explained, and this made a deep impression on the participants of the seminar." The Japanese business leaders listened well, and we see the result today in Sony, Mitsubishi, Panasonic, and so many other Japanese products and services.

without improving quality, they will simply cause more problems for their organization.[5] For example, when a company like General Motors started losing money in the 1980s, what's the first thing they did? They started cutting costs— laying off workers, cutting corners on product quality, installing robots to assemble the cars that people were not buying in the first place. Meanwhile they did not address the problems that were ultimately the cause of costs—inefficient processes and ineffective strategies for determining what customers wanted. This resulted in poor quality cars that customers did not purchase in sufficient numbers.

Customer Value and Measurement Systems

One of the leading thinkers and participants in the Japanese rise to industrial power, Kaoru Ishikawa, puts his own slant on understanding customer focus. He suggests that "managers should adopt a system of 'market in' in which consumer requirements are to be of utmost concern . . . and take them into account when they design, produce, and sell their products."[6] To make "market in" real for all people in the organization, management must have a system of measurements to determine how well they are doing.

One way to do this is to use indicators of performance to evaluate work accomplishments. However, there is a problem in many organizations as their measures are not focused on quality and customer value. For example, engineers in the design function are often measured on the technical merits of their work and whether they meet a schedule or certain goals for cost containment. Because of this, engineers focus on meeting internal technical and numerical specifications that prescribe what constitutes "good" engineering design, independent of the needs of customers. Engineers may produce, on schedule, drawings for products that are technically correct, but the product designs may not match the needs of customers. As another example, quarterly reports used to evaluate manufacturing managers often concentrate on productivity and efficiency rather than customer value. As a result, manufacturing managers may efficiently produce the goods, but these goods may sit in a warehouse for months because there is little customer demand. This is an example of efficiency without effectiveness, still a chronic problem in American business.

To be customer driven (efficient and effective), people throughout the organization should focus on measures that encourage them to do *the right things to produce what customers value.* For example, FedEx has instituted what it calls Service Quality Indicators, 12 components they have found have the greatest impact on their ability to meet customers' needs. They track these SQIs daily and compile weekly reports and monthly summaries to learn how well they are doing. Their goal is 100 percent defect-free performance in delivering their customers' packages with an emphasis on finding root causes of problems to prevent these problems from recurring.[7] Once managers have these kinds of customer-focused measurements in place, they have a foundation for implementing the other six principles of TQM.

❓ THINKING CRITICALLY

1. Think about some purchase you have made recently. What benefits were you seeking from the item(s) purchased? Do you feel these items delivered full value to you or did you have reason to be disappointed with your purchase? What is the relevance of your feelings to managers?
2. Explain in your own words the logic of Deming's Chain Reaction.

PRINCIPLE 2: CONTINUOUSLY IMPROVE THE SYSTEM AND ITS PROCESSES

Kaoru Ishikawa suggests the connection between Principle 1: Focus on delivering customer value and Principle 2: Continuously improve the system and its processes. He states: "There are no standards—whether they be national, international, or company-wide—that are perfect. Usually standards contain some inherent defects. Customer requirements also change continuously, demanding higher quality year after year. Standards that were adequate when they were first established, quickly become obsolete. . . . Good control means allowing quality standards to be revised constantly to reflect the voices of consumers and their complaints."[8] The motto of Toyota Motor Company's luxury division, Lexus, captures this point with their motto: "The Relentless Pursuit of Perfection."

American Traditions

It has been difficult for many American managers to adopt this attitude of continuous improvement because of a long tradition of tolerating a certain level of imperfection. For example, in the decades following World War II, many companies computed an Acceptable Quality Level (AQL) to set the maximum percent defects allowable for a supplier to still be considered satisfactory. As long as defects do not rise above the AQL, managers take no action. Many companies even budget to cover losses due to defects and mistakes, and they make no plans to prevent recurrence. They just see this as a cost of doing business. This seemed all right in the post-World War II world when there was high demand and economic growth. Unfortunately for many companies, the world has changed, but their approach to management has not.

Some American managers pursue improvement half-heartedly; they reduce defects only to a certain level. They assume the costs of further reduction are not worth the benefits. They believe that continuing to improve quality is too expensive. However, what we now understand is that organizations should never stop improving. There are always areas where they can do things better.

Exhibit 3-2 illustrates the costs of failure to improve are like an iceberg. The immediately visible costs, such as reprocessing, dealing with returns, and warranties are fairly obvious and easily understood. However, they are literally just

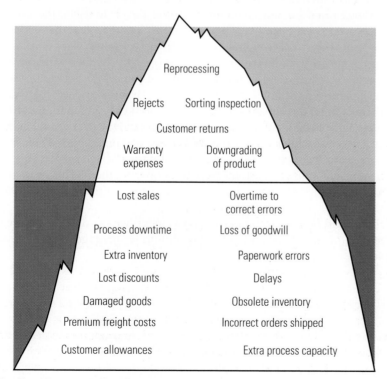

EXHIBIT 3-2
Most costs of poor quality are not immediately apparent.

Source: Adapted from J.M. Juran and Frank M. Gryna, *Quality Planning and Analysis, Third Edition* (New York: McGraw-Hill, Inc., 1993) p. 23.

the tip of that iceberg. There are many other costs that managers may not take into consideration, such as loss of future business, rework costs from doing paperwork over again, and costs involved in rushing replacement products to customers. Clearly there is an economic incentive for companies to continuously improve beyond some arbitrary AQL.

Differences in attitudes toward what is an acceptable quality level lead to very different approaches and results for management. The following story illustrates the different attitudes that existed between IBM and a Japanese supplier.[9] "Apparently the computer giant decided to have some parts manufactured in Japan as a trial project. In the specifications they set out that the limit of defective parts would be acceptable at three units per 10,000. When the delivery came in there was an accompanying letter. 'We Japanese have a hard time understanding North American business practices. But the three defective parts per 10,000 have been included and are wrapped separately. Hope this pleases.'"

Continuous Improvement and the Changing Environment

Organizations must improve to respond to the changing environment in which they exist. The problem is that many managers are not aware of the systems view and take the approach "if it ain't broke, don't fix it." The irony of this is that when organizations stand still as the world changes all around them, they may not be broke now, but they soon will be. They will lose their ability to compete with those companies that are improving business strategies and processes. IBM learned this lesson the hard way.

During the early 1990s IBM had to completely redefine itself. As the world turned to microcomputers, IBM had stuck with mainframes, the company's largest source of income for at least three decades. IBM and its stockholders paid a tremendous price for not changing with the times. In 1993, the company's stock price descended from over $100 a share to less than half that within a few weeks time. As this book is written, the stock has yet to recover.

Managers must be careful to ensure that proposed changes will add value to customers and not just result in waste because customers do not care. Sometimes even the Japanese have fallen victim to making "improvements" that added no value. For example, the Nissan Laurel, a model sold only in Japan, had 87 different steering wheel sizes, colors, and other variations. However, managers discovered that 80% of the sales came from 20% of the combinations.[10] Their response to this discovery has been to improve by cutting way back on features that do not add sufficient value to customers to keep offering them. This example illustrates the importance of combining the first and second principles of TQM, customer value and continuous improvement.

To understand how to accomplish improvement, we need to look more closely at the idea of processes and how they should be managed. This leads us to Principle 3: Manage processes, not people.

❓ THINKING CRITICALLY

1. What is the relationship between continuous improvement (or continuous decline), the changing environment, and remaining competitive?

2. Why is acceptable quality level no longer acceptable?
3. Using exhibit 3-2 as a starting point, why do you think it costs less to produce high quality products, and why do poor quality products actually cost more?

PRINCIPLE 3: MANAGE PROCESSES, NOT JUST PEOPLE

This principle is controversial to some, but it is critical to understanding TQM. It is an acknowledgment that in organizations work happens through processes, whether we know that or not. Traditional management has emphasized managing people, but people just execute organizational processes, based on their experiences, skills, understandings, and the tools and other resources organizations provide to help them do this. When a manager wants to improve the performance of employees, there is only one way for this to happen. That is to improve the processes that define and support their work.

Joseph M. Juran, along with W. Edwards Deming, both pioneers of the quality management movement, found that only 15 to 20 percent of all work problems in an organization were worker-controllable.[11] Worker-controllable means that employees clearly understand what they are supposed to be doing and have the means and authority to do it. When they fail to perform under such circumstances, it is appropriate to deal with the person as the cause of the problem. However, in 80 to 85 percent of the cases employees are doing what they are supposed to be doing when an organization has poor results. In those cases, the problems have to do with the organization's structure, its processes, policies, culture, and other organization-wide constraints. Indeed, Deming suggests that 96 percent of all problems can be blamed on the system and its processes. Blaming the person for process problems cannot and will not yield real solutions to such problems.

Deming as well as Juran and all the other early contributors to Total Quality Management theory understood the importance of process management. Since Deming provides a good review of this idea, let's explore what he has to say about it.

Deming's View of Systems and Process Management

In the same 1950 seminar that Deming developed his idea of a chain reaction, he also presented his view of an organizational system, suggesting the interrelationships among such processes as design, purchasing, manufacturing, and marketing. Deming describes a system as a horizontal flow from suppliers delivering inputs to the organization and the organization transforming these inputs and finally delivering them to end user customers. Exhibit 3-3 on page 86 shows Deming's representation of an organization as a system with processes for delivering quality goods and services to customers. Here's how Deming tells us he explained this diagram when he first presented it to the Japanese in 1950:

Materials and equipment come in at the left. It would be necessary, I explained, to improve incoming materials. Work with your vendor as a partner on a long-term relationship of loyalty and trust to improve the quality of incoming materials and to decrease costs. The consumer is the most important part of the production line.

EXHIBIT 3-3
The arrows all indicate
processes. Changes in any one
process affect all the others.

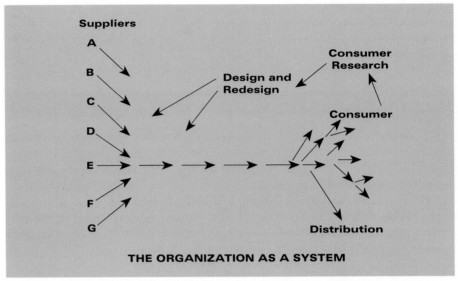

Source: Adapted from Brian L. Joiner, *Fourth Generation Management* (New York: McGraw-Hill, Inc., 1994) p. 26.

Quality should be aimed at the needs of the consumer, present and future. Quality begins with the intent, which is fixed by management. The intent must be translated by engineers and others into plans, specifications, tests, production. [12]

The arrows in Exhibit 3-3 remind us that when we change any one process, it affects all the others along the line. They also help demonstrate that managers must be concerned with the entire organization and that to achieve results they must optimize the processes of the entire system, not just a part of it.

In his book *Fourth Generation Management,* Brian Joiner uses a dramatic analogy to make this point. He writes about a crew team rowing a racing shell and the necessity for all members of the team to synchronize their strokes to achieve maximum speed. The actual oar speed each team member could achieve is not relevant. In fact, for a video presentation, Joiner had a crew team filmed, with each member rowing at his best. The result was chaos as the shell swung first one way and then the other, and some crew members lost control of their oars.[13] The point of this analogy was clear, you must get all parts of the organization aligned and working together to manage its processes effectively and efficiently to achieve desired results.

Traditional Management and Process Management

When managers move from managing people and functions in an organization to managing processes, it changes their entire perspective. They start to understand this job as one of facilitating the success of the entire organization rather than constantly monitoring individuals to find out which people are doing their jobs right and which are not. Managers understand that organizational structure and hierarchies are no longer the relevant issue. Instead, they focus on how work flows through the organization to deliver outputs customers will value. Exhibit 3-4 summarizes the difference between traditional management and process management.

The interesting thing about this approach to management, as noted in its characteristics listed in Exhibit 3-4, is that by focusing on processes, managers also do the things that create a positive work environment for people. When employees do not have to worry about being blamed when something goes wrong, they can concentrate on learning from the experience and working with other employees to improve the company. Process managers also understand the importance of using sound scientific principles for making improvements. Principles 4 and 5 look more deeply at this idea.

❓ THINKING CRITICALLY

1. Have you ever been in a job or other situation where something went wrong that seemed to be beyond your control? Describe the situation. How do you think that situation relates to the idea of "blame the process not the person"?
2. How do you think managing processes rather than people might create a better environment for people at their work?

PRINCIPLE 4: LOOK FOR ROOT CAUSES TO SOLVE AND PREVENT PROBLEMS

Perhaps an unfortunate aspect of the American culture is that we often seek short-term relief from the symptoms of a problem rather than eliminating the cause of that problem. Another aspect of our culture is an emphasis on rugged individualism. We believe that individuals are absolutely responsible for their success or failure independent of the world in which they exist. They control their own circumstances and destiny. In acknowledging these cultural characteristics, we

EXHIBIT 3-4   Differences Between Traditional and Process Managers

Traditional Manager	Process Manager
• Employees are the problem	• The process is the problem
• Doing my job	• Help to get things done
• Understanding my job	• Knowing how my job fits into the total process
• Measuring individuals	• Measuring the process
• Change the person	• Change the process
• Can always find a better employee	• Can always improve the process
• Controlling employees	• Developing people
• Don't trust anyone	• We are all in this together
• Who made the error	• What allowed the error to occur?
• Bottom line driven	• Customer driven

Source: Adapted from H. James Harrington, *Business Process Improvement* (New York: McGraw-Hill, Inc., 1991) p. 5.

should not be surprised that in a world fraught with uncertainties, managers easily get caught up in day-to-day firefighting as they do what's necessary to deal with the immediate symptoms of organizational problems.

The message in many organizations is: just make the numbers look good this month, and worry about next month when it comes. American managers are good at dealing with symptoms and crises. That is often what they are rewarded for doing. Perhaps nowhere is this orientation toward crisis management more on display than in American politics, but it is common in all our organizations as well.

Read about the activities of a typical manager as described by Henry Mintzberg in his 1973 classic book, *The Nature of Managerial Work*. It is still accurate for many companies today:

A subordinate calls to report a fire in one of the facilities; then the mail, much of it insignificant, is processed; a subordinate interrupts to tell of an impending crisis with a public group; a retiring employee is ushered in to receive a plaque; later there is a discussion of bidding on a multi-million-dollar contract; after that the manager complains that office space in one department is being wasted.[14]

And so on and on. The people who do these activities well are the ones who get recognized and promoted. They are able to come up with quick solutions to deal with the symptoms of today's problems, but they often do not realize that they are just solving the same problem over and over. They do not consider whether any of these actions will permanently solve a problem.

The Traditional Approach for Dealing with Problems

Traditional management practice focuses on setting goals and delegating to subordinates the responsibility for figuring out how to achieve these goals. This approach is called Management by Objectives (MBO). Once managers and employees agree on the goals, these managers use interpersonal skills and motivational programs to inspire or manipulate people to meet the goals. If the goals are not met, managers assume that somehow the performance of their employees is the reason for this—they messed up and did not meet their objectives. Usually, employees take the heat for this during their annual performance appraisal. However, in reality, the cause of the problem is often somewhere deep in the system itself.

A TQM Alternative for Discovering Causes

Root cause The initial flaw deep in a process that causes problems later in a process, often manifesting itself far down the line.

When we take the systems perspective to organizations, we can see that this traditional approach to discovering a problem's causes has flaws. We know that a system consists of interrelated parts and that work gets done by employees working together to accomplish the process steps that result in a final output. When something goes wrong in any step in the process, this is most likely an "effect" of a "cause" someplace else in the system. Or another way of saying this is that an immediate problem is the symptom of a deeper and more abiding problem someplace else in the system. Only by dealing with that cause can we permanently get rid of the symptom. Root cause analysis is a way to do this. A **root cause** is *the initial flaw deep in a process that causes problems later in a process, often manifesting itself far down the line.*

Total Quality Management reminds managers that to solve problems and to make improvements in the organization so it can achieve various goals, they must, as we saw above, "blame the process and not the person." TQM, because it focuses on processes and systems, has developed a set of tools for effectively analyzing the system to identify root causes to solve problems. Donald L. Dewar, a consultant and co-founder of the Association for Quality and Participation, tells of three lessons he learned about the importance of causes and continuous improvement:

Lesson One.   Pursue *kaizen* (continuous improvement), by making hundreds and even thousands of micro improvements to a system and its processes. In the end they add up to macro improvements in the efficiency and effectiveness of the entire system.

Lesson Two.   Don't simply deal with the symptoms as they arise. Shut down the process when any monitoring point indicates a problem. Then seek out the cause of the problem and fix it before starting the process up again.

Lesson Three.   Systems often have built-in redundancies in processes to take care of what doesn't go right the first time. Rather than rely on rework, managers should seek to get rid of such defects in the first place since they only add costs to the final product. The goal is to do it right the first time.

Dewar then goes on to describe a typical gold-plating process for bracelets with the following steps: (1) clean bracelet, (2) apply undercoating, (3) dip in gold plating tank, (4) error in plating? If the answer is no, send to shipping; if yes, remove gold and undercoating and start over. This process does not seek to understand the cause of an error in plating; it just assumes there will be such problems and accepts rework as part of the process. However, applying the lessons of kaizen, cause identification and eliminating rework, a revised and preferable process has these steps: (1) clean bracelet, (2) apply undercoating, (3) dip in gold plating tank, (4) error in plating? If no, send to shipping; if yes, stop! shut down the process. Find the root cause of the problem and make corrections before restarting the process. Finding those causes requires the use of various statistical and other tools of TQM, but it also eliminates rework, lowers costs, improves quality, and makes the organization more efficient, effective, and profitable.

Ishikawa's System of Cause and Effect Relationships

Kaoru Ishikawa has made many contributions to the management theory known as TQM, but what he is best known for is his discussion of causes and effects. He describes the processes of a system as "a collection of cause factors [that] must be controlled to obtain better products and effects."[15] What he means is that each step in a process affects the outcome or effect of the next step. For example, say you have a routine (or process) for getting up, dressing, having breakfast, studying, and going to class and doing other activities. If you fail to get up regularly when your alarm goes off, this can affect all the steps in your process, such as cutting back your study time with the eventual result (or effect) of doing poorly on an exam. The immediate cause for this result is that you didn't study enough, and the initial cause of this is that you were not getting up early enough to do this. By discovering and dealing with initial or root causes, you prevent similar problems from happening in the future.

Ishikawa developed a diagram for illustrating the relationships between causes and their effects. Generically this is called a cause-and-effect diagram, but it is also known as a "fishbone diagram" or an "Ishikawa diagram." The reason it is called a fishbone diagram is its appearance. Exhibit 3-5 shows one of these diagrams. It demonstrates that in a system, for any one effect there are relationships to various types of causes, especially those involving the 4 Ms: material, machines, methods, and manpower. In the diagram the effect is at the right hand end. The words at the tips of the "bones" are the branches that classify the various major causes. The lines emerging from the main bones are the minor causes for each of those areas. For an area like material for example, we can delve deeper and deeper into the system to discover what might cause a materials problem that eventually results in the effect we are exploring. There may be multiple causes, and this diagram helps us to identify those, prioritize, and then start dealing with each of them.

Ishikawa's cause and effect diagram makes graphic the message to managers that manpower is only one cause among many. To improve the effects managers should explore all possible causes of problems, not just manpower. Ishikawa understood that a system is made of interrelated and interdependent parts. Managers cannot simply exhort employees to work harder to achieve goals (or gain an effect). They must look deeply in the process, which Ishikawa calls a collection of cause factors. Only in this way can they deal with and shape causes to get the effects they desire.

"Five Whys"

Looking for root causes of problems is a logical part of being a process-oriented manager. Masaaki Imai, the author of *Kaizen,* further explains how to think in terms of processes to get at root causes of problems:

EXHIBIT 3-5
A generic cause-and-effect diagram. The large arrows indicate main categories of causes. The smaller arrows indicate deeper causes in the main categories.

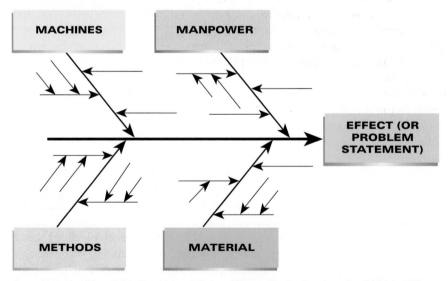

Source: Adapted from Warren H. Schmidt and Jerome P. Finnigan, *TQManager* (San Francisco: Jossey-Bass Publishers, 1993).

Because of its preoccupation with data and processes rather than results, [TQM] encourages people to go back to the previous process on the production line to seek out a problem's causes. Improvement requires that we always be aware of what comes from the previous process. In the factory, problem solvers are told to ask "why" not once but five times. Often the first answer to the problem is not the root cause. Asking why several times will dig out several causes, one of which is usually the root cause.[16]

The actual principle here is tied less to the number of times you ask "why" than to your asking it enough times to discover the actual cause of a particular problem. Taiichi Ohno, former Toyota Motor vice president, provides the following example of finding the real cause of a machine stoppage.[17]

Question 1: Why did the machine stop?
Answer 1: There was an overload and the fuse blew.
Question 2: Why was there an overload?
Answer 2: The bearing was not sufficiently lubricated.
Question 3: Why was it not lubricated sufficiently?
Answer 3: The lubrication pump was not pumping sufficiently.
Question 4: Why was it not pumping sufficiently?
Answer 4: The shaft of the pump was worn and rattling.
Question 5: Why was the shaft worn out?
Answer 5: There was no strainer attached and metal scrap got in.

By repeating "why" at least five times, the managers identify the real cause and hence the real solution: attaching a strainer to the lubricating pump. If they had not carried out the questioning, they might have settled with an intermediate countermeasure, such as replacing the fuse or changing the lubricating fluid. Asking "why" over and over uncovers the real cause of the problem, which is often hidden behind more obvious symptoms. Ishikawa further explains that "process does not refer merely to the manufacturing process. Work relating to design, purchasing, sales, personnel, and administration are all processes."[18] From this comment we can infer that there are various types of causes, including material, machines, methods, and manpower, in departments throughout the organization. And each of these causes potentially impacts customer value. Exhibit 3-6 on page 92 provides a graphic illustration of how to get at the root cause of a problem by asking why five times. Rather than the more conventional approach that asks "who?" when a problem arises, we can see that from a systems and processes view, asking "why?" just makes more sense.

❓ THINKING CRITICALLY

1. Consider a problem you have had to deal with, for example a problem with your car or your computer. Develop a cause-and-effect diagram with the four branches—machines, manpower, methods, and material—that explores the possible causes of that problem or effect. Explain how this might help to eliminate the problem for good.
2. Put yourself in the place of a manager of a supplier to automotive companies; an employee has just informed you that the company will be a month

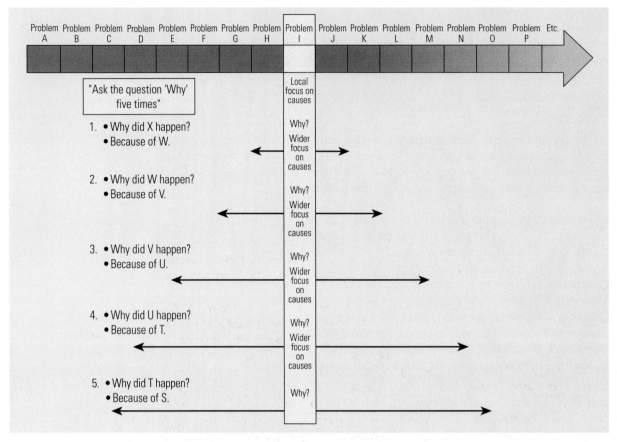

Source: Adapted from Joiner Associates Inc., "Performance Appraisal: Developing Management Alternatives," training course, 1989.

EXHIBIT 3-6
Asking "why?" five times. Each why gets the questioner deeper into the system and closer to the actual cause of a problem.

late in delivering an order of plastic ashtrays to an important client, Ford. Ask why five times to come up with a potential cause for why this might have happened. Start with "Why are we going to be a month late?" Then, after you come up with a hypothetical answer for this question, ask why again, and so on. From your hypothetical analysis, suggest a way to eliminate being late with an order in the future.

PRINCIPLE 5: COLLECT DATA AND USE SCIENCE FOR ANALYSIS

To effectively and efficiently manage a system, we need information about how well that system's processes are operating. When we have that information, we can make more informed decisions to make them work better. For this reason, one important principle of TQM is the careful collection and analysis of data. With such analysis in hand, managerial decisions and actions are much more likely to contribute to an organization's success. That data can be as simple as counting the number of cars coming off an assembly line during a shift, or tracking sales of a particular product, or as intricate as taking precise measurements of the thickness of microchip bases coming off a high-tech manufacturing process.

In gathering data and making measurements one thing we always discover is that there is variation in the things we track. From day to day, different numbers of cars will be manufactured each shift, and the thicknesses of microchip bases will vary from one to another. Understanding these variations helps us understand how well the processes are working and how to manage them better, including making improvements in our processes to reduce variation.

To better understand the idea of process variation, think back to Chapter 1 where we talked about the human body as a system. When doctors or researchers want to understand how well the body is functioning, they will perform tests, such as an electrocardiogram, to gather data that they can analyze. An electrocardiogram measures the regularity of our heart beat. When there is something wrong with the heart, the pattern of variations changes, sometimes becoming erratic. The data from the electrocardiogram provides doctors with information they need to understand and help patients get better and minimize heart problems in the future. Similarly, managers collect and analyze data to deal with the organization as a system.

In analyzing the jewelry gold-plating process discussed earlier, we might find many small variations in the final outputs that, while still acceptable, make one bracelet slightly different from another. Such variations could result from temperature differences in the gold-plating material from time to time, the amount of time the bracelet is left in the plating material, and for similar other reasons, all inherent in the plating process itself. Rather than just taking guesses, managers can collect data and use basic statistical techniques to analyze these data and figure out how to reduce variation and improve quality. Such data analysis helps managers understand just how well the system works in the first place. We discuss these statistical techniques at length in a later chapter.

The Importance of Data-Based Decisions

When managers and employees collect data on a process and understand variation, they then have real information on which they can make sound decisions for how to improve things. The importance of collecting and analyzing data using control charts, like the one in Exhibit 3-7 on page 94, is central to W. Edwards Deming's teachings about TQM. Deming died in December 1993, but in his last interview, given two months earlier, he was still talking about this. For example, read the following exchange:

Interviewer: *What about statistical variation?*
Deming: *That's a function of the control chart. The control chart is a gift from Dr. Walter A. Shewhart [see Chapter 2]. What happens within the control limits belongs to a system, a common cause. A point outside the limits would indicate a special cause. The usual procedure is that when anything happens, we suppose that somebody did it. Who did it? Pin a necklace on him. He's our culprit. He's the one who did it. That's wrong, entirely wrong. Chances are good, almost overwhelming, that what happened, happened as a consequence of the system that he works in, not from his own efforts. In other words, individual performance cannot be measured. You only can measure the combined effect of the system and his efforts as part of it. You cannot untangle the two.*[19]

EXHIBIT 3-7
This graph shows book sales plotted on a control chart. The dashed lines are the upper and lower control limits. All variations in sales inside the control limits are due to common causes inherent in the system. Variations outside the control limits are due to special causes.

BOOK SALES BY MONTH	
Jan	9,700
Feb	11,000
Mar	10,350
Apr	9,300
May	15,300
Jun	9,100
Jul	9,700
Aug	10,600
Sep	11,350
Oct	4,250
Nov	10,150
Dec	9,300

Deming's point was that managers often want to blame someone for variations in the system rather than blame the system and interacting processes that brought about a particular result.

Control Charts: An Analogy

Collecting data and creating control charts is a relatively mechanical activity, and managers often jump onto using this tool without implementing all the other principles of TQM. This is not the implementation of TQM. It must incorporate all the principles because they all support each other. As a way to conclude this section and explain the idea of a control chart further, let's return to the body as a system. The principle of common-cause and special-cause variation is the basis of the polygraph or lie detector machine. When people are wired up to this machine and asked questions to which they give truthful answers, the machine measures all the normal variations in pulse and blood pressure, and the needle swings back and forth staying within expected upper and lower control limits for most people. However, when people lie, this causes changes in the pulse and blood pressure, the needle swings outside the control limits, and they are suspected of lying. Without collecting such data on the system (a person's body), it would be more difficult to tell if a person is lying or not—it would be mostly guesswork by the listener. By collecting system data (from the body's processes), the listener can be more certain about whether a person is lying or not. The principle behind the polygraph machine is the same one at work in collecting and using data to understand and improve the processes of organizational systems. Furthermore, just like the polygraph is useful only in the hands of a skilled polygrapher, control charts are useless outside the context of TQM and skilled management. Control charts provide useful information only if management knows enough about the system to interpret the data.

TQM also recognizes that people are at the heart of these systems and that we must facilitate their working together for the system to function well, and this is what we will examine in the final two principles.

? THINKING CRITICALLY

1. Why do you think it is important to gather and analyze data to make decisions?
2. Based on what you have read here, how would a manager deal with common causes versus special causes of variation in a process when trying to reduce variation and improve the functioning of a system?

PRINCIPLE 6: PEOPLE ARE THE ORGANIZATION'S PRIMARY RESOURCE

If you were to visit an organization that has fully implemented TQM both in its procedures and its culture, it is likely that when employees are referred to, it will be by such titles as "associates," or "teammates," or "colleagues." There is a reason for this. It acknowledges a point indicated in Exhibit 3-4, "We're all in this together." People, not machines, execute the organization's processes. Machines are tools and contribute to the productivity of people. However, they have no meaning without people to figure out how to use them in concert with one another to create the company's outputs. There are three aspects to explore with regard to this idea. These are (1) training and education, (2) empowering employees, and (3) new roles for managers. Let's review these ideas, and, as you read, remember that these points are inseparable.

Training and Education

At a small company in Chicago, Gold Coast Dogs, a kind of upscale hot dog restaurant, the owner Barry Potekin believes in training for his employees. His training courses cover not only skills such as fast food and customer service but also such areas as personal finance and tenant-landlord law. Why would Potekin's training cover both personal and job-related topics? He understands that off-the-job concerns, such as family problems, affect on-the-job performance, and to maximize his employees' abilities at work, he needs to address the whole person.[20]

For organizations to get the most from their people, at all levels, they must institute regular training to help them upgrade skills. Continuously improving an organization's processes includes helping employees continuously improve their abilities to fulfill the job responsibilities of today and tomorrow. In the rapidly changing technological and competitive environment, managers must be concerned with continuously improving the capabilities of everyone in the company. In traditionally managed companies, this point is sometimes forgotten. Consider this quote from the great industrialist Andrew Carnegie, which captures this idea: "Leave my factories but take my people and soon grass will grow on my factory floors. Take my factories, but leave my people, and soon we will have new and better plants." Investing in improving the skills and abilities of employees pays big returns.

The Malcolm Baldrige National Quality Award, the United States' most prestigious award for management excellence, makes training and people development an important criteria when judging award applicants. The award criteria description says this about what training and education should entail:

Quality and related education and training address the knowledge and skills employees need to meet their objectives as part of the company's quality and operational performance improvement. This might include quality awareness, leadership, project management, communications, teamwork, problem solving, interpreting and using data, meeting customer requirements, process analysis, process simplification, waste reduction, cycle time reduction, error-proofing, and other training that affects employee effectiveness, efficiency, and safety. In many cases it might also include job enrichment skills and job rotation that enhance employees' career opportunities. It might also include basic skills such as reading, writing, language, arithmetic, and basic mathematics needed for quality and operational performance improvement.[21]

The Baldrige criteria do not stress training as just a nice idea to keep employees happy. It is vital if an organization wants to continuously improve and remain competitive. The list of items from the Baldrige criteria suggests many of the skills and techniques TQM requires.

The first large U.S. company to win a Baldrige award was Motorola, headquartered in Schaumberg, Illinois. This company has determined that to maintain its competitive edge, it must invest more and more in training to make its employees more responsive, adaptable, and creative. In 1994, every company employee received at least 40 hours of training per year, one of the heaviest commitments to training of any American company. Yet, they believe that by the year 2000 they need to have quadrupled this amount of time for employee training. The chairman and CEO of Motorola, Gary L. Tooker, says this about the importance of training: "If knowledge is becoming antiquated at a faster rate, we have no choice but to spend on education. How can that not be a competitive weapon?"[22]

Japanese companies are notorious for the large investment they make in education and training. Ishikawa suggests that a strategy that incorporates quality and continuous improvement "begins with education and ends with education." Ishikawa repeatedly emphasizes the importance of education and training in other statements, for example: "To promote [quality and continuous improvement] with participation by all, education must be given to all employees, from the President to assembly-line workers."[23]

Finally consider this story of a tiny German company (not really more than a corner garage), whose owner had made a substantial investment in employee training. When asked why he had spent so much on training, the owner appeared confused and after blinking a couple of times said, "Well, what would the alternative be?"[24] That idea captures the point of training as well as any other.

Organizations are only as good as their employees are at doing their jobs. The answer to the German proprietor's question is simple: the alternative is mediocrity, at best, and complete failure, at worst.

Empowering Employees

Empowerment is a buzzword in management and pop psychology these days. In TQM, though, it is more than a fad. It ensures *that employees know their roles in implementing the organization's mission, as well as have the resources, information, skills, and decision-making authority for those roles.* Further, empowerment recognizes that authority goes hand-in-hand with responsibility. Employees cannot be responsible for what they do without some authority to make decisions.

This does not mean that employees (including managers) can do their jobs any way they see fit. It does mean that they should have the responsibility and authority for dealing with problems as they occur without checking with their manager. It means being able to take care of a customer complaint on the spot without going through channels. Empowered employees understand they have the decision-making authority they need to make their maximum contribution for serving customers efficiently and effectively. For example, all Ritz-Carlton front desk employees have the authority to make adjustments of a customer's bill up to $2,000 on their own to guarantee customer satisfaction.[25] Empowerment recognizes that unexpected circumstances will arise, and that while they must offer guidelines, managers cannot spell out every contingency. How does management implement a program of empowerment? Exhibit 3-8 provides some useful guidelines for doing this.

Empowerment A principle that ensures that employees know their roles in implementing the organization's mission, as well as have the resources, information, skills, and decision-making authority for those roles.

Eastman Chemical Co.

EXHIBIT 3-8 Empowering Employees

- **Put senior management in the shoes of those to be empowered.**
  Let managers gain an empathy with employees. This exercise helps managers understand what employees need to do their jobs well.

- **Give employees authority.**
  Employees must actually have the authority to make decisions without managers second guessing or reviewing what they did. If they make mistakes, it is an opportunity to learn and improve.

- **Make employees feel comfortable with decision making.**
  Managers must support the decisions of their employees and provide them with feedback to help them improve their decision-making abilities.

- **Provide employees with the resources to solve problems.**
  Having the authority to make decisions will not do much good if employees do not have information and other resources to move ahead in an intelligent manner.

- **Help middle managers facilitate, not punish.**
  Because empowerment threatens middle managers who must relinquish authority, they must see that their jobs now involve managing employees' skill levels, not their decisions. Middle managers now serve as coaches, not bosses.

Source: Adapted from Harold Laurence Sirkin, "The Employee Empowerment Scam," *Industry Week*, October 18, 1993, p. 58.

The *A Look at TQM in Action* box on page 99, called "Empowerment at Ericsson General Electric," provides a clear example of what happened at one company when management saw the value of empowering employees.

New Roles for Managers

When a company understands that people are its primary resource and provides them with training and education and the authority to make decisions, this changes the role of line managers. As suggested in Exhibit 3-6, managers will become concerned with the overall processes, including documentation and measurement, and then work with employees to improve these processes. They will act more as team leaders, facilitating the success of team members, and interact with other team leaders to help coordinate the work of the teams. They will be more like coaches and resource facilitators than bosses. A coach is one who helps team members understand their jobs, get better at them, and provides the overall direction for a team. As Sam Hedrick of Ericsson GE suggested, this approach frees up their time from trying to monitor the work of individuals to take care of the coordination, communication, and support for employees. In other words, empowerment frees up managers to work on the broader system.

Here is a way to understand the Total Quality Manager's responsibility. Working on their own within a company system, empowered employees can make changes that can generally improve the company's productivity and quality about 15 percent. However, where the big opportunities come is often not from making small improvements to how the system currently operates but making big changes to the methods and processes of the entire system. That accounts for the other 85 percent of possible improvements. The responsibility for making those big changes to the whole system belongs to managers.[26] Exhibit 3-9 illustrates this idea.

By providing a vision of what the organization is attempting to accomplish, and by improving systems, managers enable employees to contribute. They are not frustrated by the lack of direction and deficiencies in the means of fulfilling their roles. Perhaps most importantly, by their actions, managers inspire employees to become full partners in the organization's quest to continuously improve its ability to provide value to customers.

EXHIBIT 3-9
Employees are responsible for improvements within the system. Managers are responsible for improvements of the entire system.

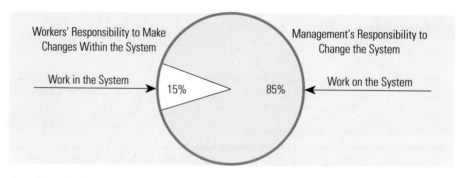

Source: Adapted from George L. Miller and LaRue L. Krumm, *The Whats, Whys, and Hows of Quality Improvement* (Milwaukee: ASQC Quality Press, 1992) p. 30.

EMPOWERMENT AT ERICSSON GENERAL ELECTRIC[27]

TQM IN ACTION

In 1984 Jack Welch (chairman of GE), told John Trani, then general manager of GE's Mobile Communications unit (police radios, cellular phones, and similar devices), which was losing money, to close it, fix it, or sell it. Trani decided to fix it. After laying off as many workers as he could and freezing salaries of everyone else in the company, he sought the help of an outside consultant for what to do to improve the performance of those who were left. The recommendation was to develop a gain-sharing program that would allow employees to be paid for improved productivity. They called the program "Winshare." The consultant told Trani there were three ways to set up a gain-sharing program: The first stresses paying employees a bonus when the company reaches a certain level of profitability, but with no employee involvement in figuring out how to do that; the second also includes a bonus and with some level of employee involvement; the third is built around extensive employee involvement and substantially changes the way employees are managed.

With some reluctance they decided, at the insistence of the consultant, to go with the third method. This was based on the assumption that the employees on the line know best how to do their jobs and they have good ideas about how to improve. The company set up voluntary "Win Teams," each led by an elected leader, that had both the power and budget to implement changes that would increase productivity. Initially the teams were given a budget of $250 per year to implement any changes the team agreed were appropriate. That budget is now $6,000 annually. Managers can belong to Win Teams, but only as resource people who help with interdepartmental legwork. Final authority lies with the team and its leader.

By 1989 the company had returned to profitability and gained the attention of Swedish electronics company Ericsson, which bought 60% of the company from GE. GE agreed to this because mobile communications was not a core GE business.

The Winshare program not only affected the bottom line, it has also transformed the company's culture. For example, consider the feelings of Jimmy Howerton, a veteran of the company. Before Winshare, he felt he was supposed to check his brain at the front gate and pick it up on his way home. Now he is excited to come to work. To Jimmy, this is no longer just Ericsson GE's company. He and the other employees feel they own it, because they know they have the responsibility and authority to make job-related decisions.

The improvements and gains in productivity that come from the Win Teams range from minor to significant. After training in statistical process control, one employee, Wilma Porter, looked around her workstation where she saw parts being wasted. She figured out a way to use those parts that saved the company $100,000 in 12 weeks. Other changes are small, like moving a trash can to where everyone can get to it faster, saving steps and time. In 1992, employees saw 4,900 of their ideas for improvement implemented, and in the first half of 1993, nearly 3,000 ideas had been adopted.

Many Win Team members have become what the company calls "Winshare ambassadors." In this role, they conduct customers on plant tours and occasionally give presentations on Winshare to employees at other companies.

What do middle managers and supervisors think about it? Gordon Campbell, one supervisor is glad to see this shift in responsibility. It has freed him to focus on the real work of supervisors, providing employees with feedback, scheduling, and helping employees as they need it. The coordinator of the Winshare program, Sam Hedrick, summed up the company's attitude about the program this way: "You cannot imagine the creativity of American workers. We have not given them credit for such a long time. Once you give them the space they need, they perform extremely well."

? THINKING CRITICALLY

1. Do you think it makes sense to call employees associates or teammates when an organization is seeking to implement TQM, or is it patronizing? Justify your answer.
2. Clarify the role of people in TQM by explaining how principles 3 and 6 really fit together and only appear contradictory.

PRINCIPLE 7: WORK IN TEAMS TO EXECUTE PROCESSES EFFICIENTLY AND EFFECTIVELY

The processes that result in organizations delivering quality products and services to customers are not confined to one functional department or work area. In an airline for example, getting customers safely and happily from one city to another is the joint effort of many departments and people, from plane maintenance to scheduling to ticketing to food preparation to luggage handling to the flight crew, and all of the less obvious work by top management and the accounting and finance, and marketing departments. TQM recognizes this fact of organizational life and emphasizes the importance of teams and teamwork to facilitate people working together.

Team A small group of people with complementary skills who are committed to a common purpose, set of performance goals, and approach for which they hold themselves mutually accountable.

We can define a **team** in this way: *It is a small group of people with complementary skills who are committed to a common purpose, set of performance goals, and approach for which they hold themselves mutually accountable.*[28] By this definition, the members of a team have individual roles and responsibilities, each of which is important to achieving the team's goal. While each team member has his or her own role, the success of any member is dependent on the success of all of them. Remember the rowing team example.

To effectively implement teams, employees must believe that management supports their use and will empower the teams to implement the improvements they suggest by providing them with the resources and time to do so. Further, to make the team approach work, it must be ingrained in the organizational culture. Everyone must understand that this is "the way we do things here." The culture of Ericsson GE not only supports the team approach but expects that this is how employees will work together.

Different Teams for Different Purposes

Quality circle An on-going voluntary membership team, often with people all from the same department, with the responsibility to develop specific suggestions for how to improve a process.

Though an organization may set up teams to facilitate any activity, through experience we have come to recognize four categories of teams for taking care of different kinds of projects and processes. These are: (1) Quality Circles, (2) Quality or Process Improvement Teams, (3) Special Task or Project Teams, (4) Self-Managed Work Teams. There is some overlap among these categories, but there are also differences.

- A **quality circle** is *an on-going voluntary membership team, often with people all from the same department, with the responsibility to develop specific sugges-*

tions for how to improve a process to make it more efficient and effective at delivering quality products and services.

- A **quality or process improvement team** has the responsibility *to improve a process, improve the quality of a process's output, decrease waste, or improve productivity in a process that crosses departmental lines.*[29]
- A **task force or project team** usually has *a specific problem to solve or a project to complete.*
- A **self-managed team** is *given responsibility for planning, controlling, improving a whole process and the authority to take appropriate measures to do so.*

While the formation of teams is an important characteristic of all organizations that seek to operate effectively and efficiently, there is a cultural aspect of this principle as well. Managers who consciously seek to implement TQM create a culture in their organizations that encourages employees across the organization to work together. There is a spirit of teamwork evident even when people are not on formal teams working together on some project. This spirit manifests itself as an understanding among employees that the success of any one individual and the company as a whole depends of everyone working well together and supporting each other. The *A Look at Managers in Action* box on page 102 gives one manager's description of the culture of quality and teams in a large insurance company.

The Horizontal Corporation

The principle of using teams and teamwork has led some to suggest that TQM creates a **horizontal corporation.** This means that *people are primarily concerned with how their work fits into a process flow across specialized functions to serve customers.* People communicate and cooperate with other co-workers in the process, so there is less need for a supervisor to look over their shoulder. The horizontal corporation eliminates levels of functional management that may no longer be necessary once a company moves to process teams and TQM and implements the principles covered in this chapter. In fact, the horizontal corporation is one of the natural outcomes of an organization moving to TQM as it seeks to become more efficient and effective at delivering value to customers. Exhibit 3-10 describes the seven key elements of the horizontal corporation.

? THINKING CRITICALLY

1. Why do you think teams might work better to bring about improvement in an organization than people working independently of one another in functional areas?
2. Why is the horizontal corporation the logical consequence of a company that implements TQM?

Quality or process improvement team A team charged with improving a process, improving the quality of a process's output, decreasing waste, or improving productivity in a process that crosses departmental lines.

Task force or project team A team set up with a specific problem to solve or a project to complete.

Self-managed team A team given responsibility for planning, controlling, and improving a whole process and the authority to take appropriate measures to do so.

Horizontal corporation People primarily concerned with how their work fits into a process flow across specialized functions to serve customers.

MANAGERS
IN ACTION

TEAMS AND QUALITY MAMAGEMENT AT THE PAUL REVERE INSURANCE GROUP

G. Robert Lea is Vice President of Quality and Corporate Services at the Paul Revere Insurance Group. The following is his description of some of the aspects of what this company calls its "Quality Has Value" approach to management.

The "Quality Has Value" process was established at Paul Revere to strengthen our corporate advantage in the marketplace. It has been part of the Paul Revere way of doing business since 1984. We view quality as a process, not a program, and it is ongoing. Our basic objective is to improve service in both fact and perception in the eyes of the customer.

From the start, the key to the success of our quality process has been 100% participation. Every employee at Paul Revere is on a quality team, from the top executive to the newest employee on the payroll. Teams generally consist of 8–10 employees within a natural work unit. Quality teams focus on ways to improve service to our customers, through process and other tools.

In the beginning, teams focused on short-term, goal-oriented projects. We looked inside the company to determine where opportunities for improvement existed, and teams developed ideas and implemented them. This type of structure gave employees the opportunity to take ownership of their job with full management support, and they seized the opportunity. In the first two years, quality teams generated more than 25,000 ideas and saved the company more than $16 million.

Since that time we have moved away from an annual goal-setting format that had a start/stop nature to a philosophy of continuous improvement that focuses on our customers and their needs. We've also moved the administration of the quality process into the management ranks, where it truly belongs.

All levels of management at Paul Revere are involved in communicating the quality message. This communication effort helps to build relationships and trust with our external customers. Management also works to ensure that employees who deal directly with our customers have the knowledge and training to solve problems quickly and effectively. These employees are kept involved in departmental goals and strategies as well as the overall goals of the company. These efforts work toward continuous improvement and ultimately bring the quality message to our customers through exceptional service and well-trained, empowered employees.

Recently, the company has adopted a key performance indicators (KPI) approach to quality, where each individual, team, department, and division has developed measurable KPIs that tie into corporate goals. These KPIs start at the corporate level and are developed, in part, through customer feedback. Division heads use the corporate KPIs to develop measurements necessary to achieve these corporate goals. Department heads determine their KPIs and then work with employees to develop KPIs at the individual level. These individual KPIs, again, relate back to the corporate level KPIs. If each individual achieves his or her KPIs, then the corporate goals are achieved as well.

The challenge of the KPI approach is that, once attained, the targets always move higher. Our customers expectations are constantly increasing, and we are constantly looking at ways to meet and exceed these expectations. For Paul Revere that's what quality and continuous improvement are all about.

EXHIBIT 3-10   The Elements of the Horizontal Corporation

1. Organize around process not task.
Instead of emphasizing functions or departments, the company identifies its core processes for delivery of final products and sets specific performance goals for these processes.

2. Flatten hierarchy.
By eliminating functional departments, this eliminates the need for supervisors and managers of these departments who no longer add value.

3. Use teams to manage everthing.
Self-managed teams become the building blocks of the organization. Give the team a common purpose and hold it accountable for measurable performance goals.

4. Let customers drive performance.
Customer satisfaction, not stock appreciation or profitability, becomes the primary driver and measure of performance. The understanding is that profits will come when customers are satisfied.

5. Reward team performance.
Change appraisal and pay systems to reward team results, not individual performance. In addition, reward employees for developing multiple skills that allow them to add more value to the organization.

6. Maximize supplier and customer contact.
Make suppliers and customers partners in the company and if possible bring them onto company teams. This acknowledges the interdependence of all parties and facilitates the cooperation and communication needed to improve processes and product or service quality.

7. Inform and train all employees.
Give employees complete information and train them in its use to make sound decisions.

Source: Adapted from John A. Byrne, "The Horizontal Corporation," *Business Week,* December 20, 1993, pp. 76-81.

INTEGRATION OF THE PRINCIPLES

It is important to appreciate that TQM is not the practice of these various principles in a kind of mechanical fashion any more than creating a great novel is writing one grammatically correct sentence after another. These principles are inherent in one another. While we talk about them individually, each is enfolded into the others in an inseparable way.

While TQM re-defines the role of managers, it in no way diminishes the important role of managers. They have ultimate responsibility for developing the strategic mission of the organization and shaping a culture that brings to life the principles described in this chapter. Managers, especially top managers, shape the work environment for all employees. Without management's enthusiastic and unflagging support of TQM, these principles will never be integrated to achieve their potentially profound effect.

As we proceed through this book, keep the seven principles of this chapter in mind. They provide the rationale for the rest of the ideas, techniques, and tools you will read about.

WHAT HAPPENED AT SOUTHERN PACIFIC?

What's the result of all the actions taken at SP? In the first year of the program, despite a recession in California, there was a $43 million improvement on the bottom line. Eventually, SP became profitable once again. Perhaps more importantly, the company was growing again. It was not cutting back as is usually the case when companies face profound financial problems.

There are several lessons Southern Pacific has claimed to have learned from its turnaround. As you read the following list of these lessons, think about the principles covered in this chapter.

- **A strong and clear leadership statement of the quality mission is essential.** All employees have to know what top managers have in mind, and there must be consistent behavior in implementing this mission.

- **There must be a strong emphasis on team building** Cross-functional teams are essential to get work done efficiently and effectively.

- **Develop data for key performance indicators as early as possible.** Without real data to figure out how they were doing, they would not have information for improving.

- **There must be union involvement.** All employees are in this together, and adversarial relationships with unions are destructive to the entire organization. This requires open and regular communication with all employees and union leaders.

- **Don't skimp on training.** For employees to function well in a new culture that is team-oriented and customer-focused requires employees trained in these new techniques.

- **A quality program is cost-effective.** Investing in the changes suggested by TQM will have the long-term effect of turning Southern Pacific into a very competitive and profitable railroad.

Bringing everyone at Southern Pacific on board, focusing on improvements through the use of teams and sound scientific methods, all with the goal of providing better and better service to customers has made a once-dying organization vital again.

SUMMARY

Total Quality and Systems Management
- The principles and techniques of TQM all center around the idea of an organization as a system.
- Though the idea that an organization is a system has been around for a long time, it is only since the emergence of TQM that we have understood the implications of that idea for managing.

The Principles of Total Quality Management
- There are seven key principles of TQM.
- All the principles of TQM are interdependent and must be taken all together to provide meaningful guidance for managers.

Principle 1: Focusing on Delivering Value to Customers
- Customers always buy the benefits they expect to derive from a product or service. TQM gives managers guidelines for making this idea the basis of sound management practice.
- Focus on customer value provides managers with a perspective for assessing their decisions based on how they affect the organization's ability to deliver quality.
- Deming's chain reaction demonstrates the importance of starting with quality to improve the organization's performance.
- It is useful for the organization to have a way to measure how well they are doing at delivering quality to customers to help them improve and remain competitive.

Principle 2: Continuously Improve the System and Its Processes
- Poor quality has costs associated in terms of rework and dealing with returns, and it also has many hidden costs in terms of lost customers and opportunities for organizational growth.
- The open systems view reminds us that the external environment is constantly changing, and only by an organization continuously improving in light of these changes can it remain competitive.

Principle 3: Manage Processes Not Just People
- Because processes define how work gets done in an organization, it is a manager's job to understand processes and how to improve them.
- Process managers focus on the whole organization and its interacting pieces rather than individuals and functional departments.

Principle 4: Look for Root Causes to Solve and Prevent Problems
- There is a great tendency to manage crises and deal with symptoms rather than their causes and prevention. TQM teaches that we should look for problem causes deep in the system and get rid of them to prevent problems.
- Ishikawa's cause-and-effect diagram can be a useful tool for discovering root causes of problems.
- Asking "why" at least five times can help you get to the base of a problem and prevent its recurrence rather than just dealing with the problem's symptom elsewhere in the process.

Principle 5: Collect Data and Use Science for Analysis
- All processes are subject to variation that affects quality and only by scientifically collecting and analyzing data using tools like a control chart can you understand these variations.
- All major theorists of TQM stress the importance of making decisions based on the analysis of data.

Principle 6: People Are the Organization's Primary Resource
- If the organization wants to improve, it must make sure its people improve through training and education.

- By empowering employees, managers unleash employees' creativity and commitment to continuously improve their productivity.

Principle 7: Work in Teams to Execute Processes Efficiently and Effectively

- Teams make it easier for employees to work together to execute organizational processes.
- The horizontal corporation emerges from the implementation of TQM and teams.

Integration of the Principles

- All the principles of TQM go together to facilitate the management of systems.

KEY TERMS

Empowerment 97

Horizontal corporation 101

Quality circle 100

Quality or process improvement
  team 101

Root cause 88

Self-managed team 101

Task force or project team 101

Team 100

REVIEW QUESTIONS

1. What is the relationship between the idea of the organization as a system and Total Quality Management?
2. How does TQM and the systems view help us understand a customer-focused strategy?
3. What does "acceptable quality level" mean for management practice, and how can this idea lead to problems for managers?
4. What is the relationship between continuous improvement and the constantly changing external environment?
5. Why is it important for managers to focus on organizational processes rather than the work of individual employees?
6. By managing processes effectively and efficiently, how does this also help make individual employees perform better?
7. What is the difference between dealing with the symptoms of a problem and dealing with the root causes of a problem?
8. How does an Ishikawa diagram help a manager understand and deal with root causes? What is the value of asking "why" five times?
9. Why is the collection and scientific analysis of data important for more effectively and efficiently managing a system?
10. What should managers do to ensure that people are treated as the organization's primary resource?
11. How does empowering employees help an organization operate more efficiently and effectively?

12. Why are teams and teamwork important to the successful implementation of TQM?

EXPERIENTIAL EXERCISES

1. Divide the class into groups of five or six people and complete the following task. As a customer of your university or college, identify a key process that provides you with a product or service, for example the class registration process or buying texts at the beginning of the term. Discuss among your group how the university administration could apply each of the seven principles of TQM to this process. Prepare a summary of your ideas and choose a member of your group to report to the entire class.

2. Contact a local business and get permission from the owner or person in charge to interview one or more managers and employees. Discuss each of the seven principles described in this chapter with these people and get them to explain how these principles apply to their work. Write down and report to class on at least one example for each principle. If you discover that employees and managers do not apply all these principles, find out why they do not.

3. What follows are seven common aspects of conventional management thought. Divide into groups of six or seven people. Using the TQM principles covered in this chapter, each group should select one item and discuss its flaws, with special emphasis on why it is flawed and what might happen in companies where managers believe such things. Then go around the class and have each group present its conclusions on the selected point to the entire class.
   1. Once we have good practices in place, stick with them.
   2. Solve problems as they occur.
   3. Make decisions based on the most current data.
   4. Focus on doing whatever is necessary to ensure short-term profitability.
   5. Focus on the performance of individuals and get rid of those who fail to meet their goals.
   6. Organize the company around functions and hold managers accountable only for meeting goals in their functional area.
   7. Don't invest in formal training; the results are too hard to measure. Rely on current employees to train new employees.

CASE ANALYSIS AND APPLICATION
Nuking Tradition at John Crane Belfab[30]

John Crane Belfab is a $20 million company that produces edge-welded bellows and bellow seals used by other large companies such as Allied Signal, Pratt and Whitney, and Rockwell International as components in their products. Over the past few years the President of the company, Doug Fockler, has been, as he calls it, "nuking" Belfab's functional departments.

Employees in the company, known as "colleagues," are organized around four semi-autonomous product-based groups, with each group having its own section of the company's 36,000 square foot headquarters. The company has scrapped its former five levels of management and 11 grades of hourly pay. It now has only two levels of management, and all employees are salaried. This has broken down a barrier between management and labor. Everyone receives the same benefits, sick leave, and time off. The product-based groups work in teams and have the authority and responsibility of setting their own work schedules for each customer order and determining exactly how the work will get done. Each colleague gets about 38 hours of formal training annually to make sure they have the skills they need to help the company continuously improve.

Two of Belfab's product groups are dedicated to single customers, and these customers' logos and colors dominate the work areas of these groups. In fact, some new employees became confused about whether they were working for Belfab or the customer. That is all right with Fockler. He believes that by working for the customer, colleagues are doing their best for Belfab.

Belfab has stiff standards for itself. They seek zero defects, 100 percent on time delivery, and a commitment to always be twice as good as the competition. About two-thirds of the colleagues voluntarily participate in SGIA (Small Group Improvement Activity) teams. These usually include members from across functions and address specific problems and make suggestions to management for improvement.

All these changes have resulted in reduction of customer order lead times by 75 percent, an on-time delivery rate of 99.67 percent, cut scrap to .5 percent of sales, and increased productivity by 67 percent in five years. The company has earned elite-supplier certification from customers Pratt & Whitney, Allied Signal, and Rockwell International.

Discussion Questions

1. From this description of Belfab, what principles of TQM can you identify at work in this company?
2. Based on what you have read in this chapter, speculate on why this company has had such dramatic improvements in performance by making the changes described in this case.

VIDEO CASE: COMBINING QUALITY MANAGEMENT AND SOCIAL RESPONSIBILITY
The Prudential Insurance Company of America

Prudential was honored by the Business Enterprise Trust for its sensitivity to the needs of its policyholders and its determination to change industry practice as demonstrated in its pioneering and championing the Living Needs Benefits program.

The aging of the population and increasing costs of terminal illness are placing intense new burdens on the nation's system of long-term health care. Nursing home costs are skyrocketing, and more than 10 percent of elderly Americans require such care today—a number certain to climb in the decades ahead. In January 1990, Prudential announced an innovative approach to coping with these spiraling costs: a new "Living Needs Benefit" option offered, at no additional charge, to their life insurance policyholders. The option, which allows the terminally ill and permanently confined to receive life insurance benefits *before* their death, creates a brand of life insurance that is both humane and cost-effective. By giving the terminally ill access to what is frequently their only major asset, the program can provide some dignity and control in the final months of life.

The concept of accelerated benefits was first considered by Prudential employees in both the United States and Canada in 1986. That year, Ron Barbaro, at the time President of Prudential's Canadian operation, visited a Toronto AIDS hospice. Moved by a patient's plea to "help us die with dignity" Barbaro charged his employees with developing a way in which terminally ill and permanently confined policyholders could gain earlier access to their benefits. Despite initial concerns that it was not feasible, the group eventually developed the product. Concurrently, Prudential attorneys and actuaries in the United States were discussing alternate designs for their own "accelerated benefit" rider and the substantial legal and regulatory hurdles such a program would encounter. While Barbaro had an easier time instituting the rider in Canada, Prudential employees in the U.S. labored through an excruciating year-and-a-half process of regulatory and legislative approval of the program in each of the fifty states.

The program pays approximately 90–95 percent of the face value of the policy. There is no upfront charge: rather, it is "paid" by applying a discount rate to the benefit, if and when the accelerated benefit is requested. Claims are processed within two weeks, and there are absolutely no restrictions on how the insured may use the benefit. As of October 1993, Prudential paid out more than $48 million to 588 policyholders, with an average payout of over $80,000.

Since Prudential took the lead, many other insurance companies have followed suit in offering some form of accelerated benefits. Prudential's business has benefited as well: increased sales of Prudential's permanent life policies is in part attributed to agent and customer interest in accelerated benefit riders. Prudential officials also report the program has significantly boosted company morale. Indeed, Living Needs Benefits is a victory on all counts—for the policyholders who benefit, for the company in terms of increase sales and boosted morale, and for the industry's reputation as a whole.

Video Case Questions

1. Describe how Prudential translated the TQM concept of "customer value" into an integral part of its business strategy.
2. What are the benefits of the "Living Needs Benefit" for society and for the business?

4. INTERNATIONAL MANAGEMENT

DISNEY LEARNS A LESSON ABOUT EUROPE[1]

The Walt Disney Company has adopted many of the practices of TQM, but that does not mean it or any other company always gets things right. This can be especially true when a company starts to expand into the global marketplace. Consider Euro Disney in France. This venture was started after the success of a similar theme park in Japan outside of Tokyo. Because of its success with parks in the U.S. and Japan, Disney thought it had the formula for creating a family recreation and vacation destination that could not miss. It knew how to deliver the goods to its customers. A full 30% of the company's 1991 movie and video revenues came from Europe. It thought it knew this market. However, the European tourists and especially the French have not reacted to the Magic Kingdom in exactly the same ways American and Japanese tourists have.

It seems that these tourists have found the parks to be too expensive for their thrifty tastes, and by early 1994, the park was losing nearly $1 million a day. As TQM reminds us, quality and value are judgments made by your customers. Disney and its partners in the venture had overestimated the value of their family entertainment center to its customers. When the park opened, the price of one-day's admission for an adult was $42.45, more than any of the other parks. And a night's stay at the Disneyland Hotel near the park entrance was about $340, the same as a top hotel in Paris. For the average European, these prices were simply too high.

In the planning stage, Disney tried to anticipate such problems and develop a sensitivity to the French culture and language. All signs were in French and the castle that is central in each park had the name *Le Chateau de la Belle au Bois Dormant* (Sleeping Beauty's Castle). Because it rains a lot in northern France, the company built special covered waiting areas for its rides, but in general the park featured all the familiar attractions of the other parks—a decidedly Disney kind of place with a Davy Crockett campground and the Big Thunder Mountain roller-coaster. However, they also included a special attraction, Discoveryland, inspired by the works of Jules Verne.

In addition, the designers of the park convinced Disney chairman Michael Eisner that a park in Europe, with its elaborate cathedrals and monuments, must be extra special, and the company spent lavishly on details that stand up to the scrutiny of presumably more critical Europeans. For example, the castle was larger and more elaborate than in any other park. However, this detail also added extra costs which inflated the final cost of the park to nearly $3 billion.

The Disney Company expected first-year attendance to be 11 million visitors with gross receipts of $1.12 billion. That

did not happen. By the time the park opened in 1992, Europe was in the midst of a recession and only about 9.5 million visitors passed through the gates. One miscue, for example, was that Disney assumed that parents would keep their children out of school for a few days' visit to the park, as often happens in the U.S. However, this is not the custom of the Europeans.

Another problem in attempting to import American cultural values and management to Europe is reflected in the initial banning of alcohol from the park. They have since reversed this in light of the standard glass of wine nearly all French people have with lunch. The company also anticipated that Monday would be a light day at the park and Friday a heavy one. What happened was the reverse. Further, under French labor laws, Disney cannot just tell an employee scheduled to work not to come in, as it does in Florida. Therefore, it must plan labor schedules much more carefully.

In its first year, the park lost $900 million. This has not been a financial disaster for Disney. It owns 49 percent of the park but only initially invested $160 million, with the rest being financed by loans and from a public offering of stock to the French public, which owns the other 51 percent of the park. Disney is, however, responsible for the park's management and for securing the financing to keep the park in business. At the beginning of 1994, Disney was working with French and other European banks to refinance its loans and make other management and operational changes to turn the company around. At the end of this chapter, we'll explore some of those changes.

The lesson has been clear from this venture into Europe by Disney: You have to know what your customers will value, and you have to be aware of the economic and political environment in which you are doing business. Even a juggernaut of success like Disney, where everything the company touches seems to turn into dollars, temporarily lost that touch by not knowing its customers and other stakeholders as well as it should have.

Like all organizations, the Walt Disney Company is an open system—in this case, a very large one—operating in a larger system, the global environment. Like all other organizations, it will survive and thrive in that environment, depending on how successfully it meets the needs of its stakeholders. In this chapter we review the challenges of managing in the global environment, and the facets of the global environment that managers need to understand to succeed there.

THE INTERNATIONAL MANAGER

International management The efficient and effective managing of organizational (or system) processes and resources across national borders to serve one or more customer groups.

Let's start with a definition: **International management** means *the efficient and effective managing of organizational (or system) processes and resources across national borders to serve one or more customer groups*. Two basic business activities that require international management skills are the processes involved in trading goods between countries and those involved in investing in other countries. Both of these involve the management and coordination of such standard business processes as sales, finance, distribution, and transportation, but with special insight into how to coordinate these activities in a variety of countries with different laws, customs, tastes, and levels of development.

Companies that engage in international trade and investment consist of virtually all major corporations, most medium-size firms, and many small companies. They range from Compaq and Dell computer companies selling their products in

Europe, Asia, and South America; Caterpillar selling heavy earth-moving equipment around the world; and small companies like Pasco Scientific selling educational laboratory equipment in Europe.

There are many opportunities in other countries, and one important way to take advantage of them is through **exporting,** *selling domestically created goods to customers in other countries* . Of course, large companies like Coca-Cola have sold their products around the world for decades. Exhibit 4-1 lists the 25 largest U.S. exporters. In reviewing this list, note the percentage of total sales made up by exports. The lower this percentage, the more opportunity there is for growth in the international marketplace.

Exporting Selling domestically created goods to customers in other countries.

All major Japanese companies depend on export sales, and they are particularly adept at this. Japanese companies sell so many automobiles to the United States that the nameplates of Toyota, Honda, and Nissan are almost as commonplace as the domestic nameplates of General Motors, Ford and Chrysler. Despite the success of many companies in countries around the world, caution is still required. For example, Japanese companies, though known for being export-oriented, still make mistakes about what will sell. The management of Isuzu decided in 1994 to withdraw their cars and sell only four-wheel drive sport vehicles in the U.S. Because Americans did not find their cars, such as the Impreza and the Impulse, attractive enough to buy when compared to the competition, Isuzu could not make money selling cars to U.S. consumers.

EXHIBIT 4-1   Top 25 U.S. exporters, 1992

COMPANY	EXPORTS $ MILLIONS	% TOTAL SALES
1. Boeing	17,486	57.8%
2. General Motors	14,045	10.6%
3. General Electric	8,200	13.2%
4. International Business Machines	7,524	11.6%
5. Ford Motor	7,220	7.2%
6. Chrysler	7,051	19.1%
7. McDonnell Douglasl	4,983l	28.5%
8. Philip Morris	3,797	7.6%
9. Hewlett-Packard	3,720	22.6%
10. E.I. DuPont De Nemoursi	3,509	9.4%
11. Motorola	3,460	25.9%
12. United Technologies	3,451	15.7%
13. Caterpillar	3,341	32.8%
14. Eastman Kodak	3,220	15.6%
15. Archer Daniels Midlandl	2,700l	28.9%
16. Intel	2,339	39.1%
17. Digital Equipment	1,900	13.5%
18. Allied Signal	1,810	15.0%
19. Unisys	1,796	21.3%
20. Sun Microsystems	1,783	49.2%
21. Raytheon	1,760	19.3%
22. Weyerhaeuser	1,500	16.2%
23. Merck	1,490	15.2%
24. Minnesota Mining & Mfg.	1,433	10.3%
25. Westinghouse Electric	1,360	11.2%

Source: Adapted from Therese Eiben, "U.S. Exporters Keep On Rolling," *Fortune,* June 14, 1993, pp. 130-131.

Often the products of "foreign" companies are not really foreign at all. Toyotas are recognized as Japanese automobiles, but many Toyotas are actually built in America, by Americans. Toyota Motor Manufacturing, Inc. in Georgetown, Kentucky not only builds many of the Camrys sold here, it even exports some of these back to Japan. Most Mazdas made in Flat Rock, Michigan, have a higher percentage of domestic parts than some American makes. Coca-Cola has bottling companies around the world in the markets that it serves. In each of these cases, global management involves investing abroad and creating subsidiaries. These investments allow a company to combine its skills and resources with those of the country in which it locates its plants to serve the needs of new groups of customers in diverse geographic and economic settings.

Domestic firms Firms that produce and sell goods and services in only one country.

When managers engage in international trade and international investment, their business activities clearly cut across national boundaries. However, even the managers of **domestic firms,** *those that produce and sell goods and services in only one country,* have to address global management issues. Economic and technological developments in other countries can and do affect the business activities of domestic firms. Fluctuations in the value of foreign currencies can make imported products seem more affordable and may increase competition for the domestic firm. A domestic company also may draw upon technological advances in other countries as a source for improving its product and process technologies. Indeed, the Japanese are masters of this, taking the technological advances in one country and applying them to commercial products. One example is fuzzy logic, a theoretical idea originating with U.S. scientists, which the Japanese have used to improve the automated qualities of such products as still and video cameras and several other consumer electronics products.

With increased communication and transportation capabilities, which give organizations access to markets around the world, it is difficult for any manager to remain isolated from the global business environment. All managers will be either directly or indirectly affected by international business activities. For example, the growth of China as an economic power and exporter of all kinds of inexpensive goods, from toys to small appliances to tools, clearly affects domestic competitors. It also offers them opportunities for setting up plants in China or importing Chinese goods to sell themselves.

To be effective in the global environment, managers must be able to relate to people in other countries, such as customers, suppliers, employees, or business partners. Further, managers must often integrate diverse people into a unified approach to accomplish their organization's mission. Finally, managers must compete with business organizations around the world. Local or domestic standards for products are no longer adequate indicators of performance. With the emergence of a global business community, managers must be concerned with meeting international standards for excellence to compete.

❓ THINKING CRITICALLY

1. What is the difference between managing a firm that only does business domestically and a firm that does business in the international marketplace?
2. Based on what you have read so far, what do you think caused some of the problems at Euro Disney?

INTERNATIONAL TRADE

We have already suggested that international trade is one important area to which managers must address their attention. Trade allows companies and customers to sell and buy goods and services from those who are best equipped to deliver them. Trade is simply a fact of economic life and, with enhanced communication and transportation, it will become ever more important.

Comparative Advantage

In economics, there is a concept called the **law of comparative advantage.** This law reminds us that *it is to our advantage for work of various types to be done by those who do it best for the least price.* Comparative advantage suggests that the Chinese should be making inexpensive plastic toys because this is low-skill, low-wage work to create goods that customers will only pay a small price for, and this is one area in which the Chinese now excel. At the same time, American firms excel in the development of software and microcomputers, which require high investment, high skills, and high wages to create products which have a value to customers commensurate with these costs.

Law of comparative advantage An economic concept that reminds us it is to our advantage for work of various types to be done by those who do it best for the least price.

Open international trade that emphasizes the law of comparative advantage is also consistent with the principles of TQM to make the best use of people and resources to serve customers. It allows consumers in countries around the planet to have a larger selection of goods and services for reasonable prices than would be possible if they tried to do it all themselves. From the perspective of a manager, international trade presents both challenges and opportunities. The challenges have to do with understanding the diverse cultural, legal, political, and economic differences among countries and keeping up with the international competitors who are relentlessly improving the value of their products. The opportunities have to do with the development of new markets for our goods and services. For example, free elections and the elimination of apartheid in South Africa has eliminated the moral and legal restrictions on trade and investment with that country. Many American firms are exploring opportunities there. The *A Look at The Global Environment* box on page 116 describes how Harley-Davidson has prospered by exporting motorcycles around the world.

The Centers of Trade Power

Every nation in the world engages in some form of international trade. However, the explosion of international business activity has been concentrated among three regions: The European Community (EC), North America, and the Pacific Rim. The EC is made up of European countries (Britain, Germany, France, Italy, the Netherlands, Belgium, Ireland, Spain, Denmark, Greece, Luxembourg, and Portugal), which united to create an economic market with annual purchasing power of $4 trillion. Another center of trading power is North America, particularly the United States. With the ratification of the North American Free Trade Agreement (NAFTA), the three nations of Canada, the United States, and Mexico have joined together to promote free trade among themselves. The North American approach resembles that of the EC, but it is not nearly as extensive. For example, the EC has plans to promote a common currency (though that is unlikely to happen for several years),

A LOOK AT

THE GLOBAL ENVIRONMENT

THE HARLEY MYSTIQUE TRANSLATES WELL[2]

Few products possess such a powerful image for people across the globe than the big Harley-Davidson motorcycles. In Chapter 1, we saw how Harley-Davidson, Inc. turned itself around by enthusiastically embracing TQM. The improved quality of its bikes helped it regain a majority of the U.S. market. But Harleys also carry a special appeal in Europe and Japan these days as well. In fact, the company's managers see the overseas market as a major opportunity to increase sales. The company had always exported some of its products, but it had never really made a big effort in these markets. Now it is.

The company has undertaken a big marketing push to sell its bikes round the globe. Managers have begun setting up international distribution, sponsoring Harley Owner Groups (HOGs), and advertising extensively. The company now publishes Harley magazines in several languages and stages rallies where owners can get together and swap stories. The company's managers realize that people don't just buy Harleys as a means of transportation. Harley owners everywhere have a special subculture and self-image that the company helps to nurture and perpetuate by selling biker clothes and other related products.

However, this does not mean that there are no differences from country to country. And to succeed in exporting Harleys, the company's managers have had to learn about these differences. For example, the company's advertising in the U.S. had the line "one steady constant in an increasingly screwed up world." This did not work so well in Japan. Toshifumi Okui, president of the Japan unit of H-D, got permission to run ads juxtaposing American images with traditional Japanese images, such as American riders passing a rickshaw. This contrast between things American and Japanese is designed to play up the Harley mystique to potential Japanese bikers.

The company has also had to adapt to other cultural differences, such as in France where people keep later hours than in the U.S. At one company-sponsored rally, managers had planned to shut off the beer and band at midnight. For the attendees, though, the party was just getting started, and they convinced the Harley representatives to keep the band and the beer going till around 3 or 4 in the morning.

Harley managers have come to understand that success is tied to staying close to the customer, no matter what country or culture that customer comes from. These managers attend rallies and ride motorcycles with their customers. They listen to them and, in the case of Harley-Davidson, respond to them. It is clear that Harley has figured out how to successfully export its product (which is much more than just a motorcycle). There are waiting lists several months long in all its international outlets.

and the North American countries have no such plans. In the Pacific Rim, Japan has become a global economic superpower, and the newly industrialized countries (South Korea, Taiwan, Singapore, and Hong Kong—known as the four tigers) are rapidly becoming superpowers as well. Trade among these three regions has grown steadily over the last few decades. Not far behind are Malaysia and Thailand. And China has the fastest growing economy in the world, much of this due to the creation of goods for export. China will also reclaim Hong Kong from Great Britain in 1997, which will further its presence as an economic power.

In the near future, these three regions may be joined by others that are rapidly improving their economic capabilities for global trade. Former communist block countries in Eastern Europe, such as Poland, Hungary, The Czech Republic, Slovakia, and Romania are moving toward market-based economies and are becoming more active in international trade. Other countries such as India, Israel, the Arab nations, and Brazil are also becoming more active international traders. The volume of international trade will grow even more in the future as the people of these regions earn greater purchasing power and acquire tastes for the goods and services offered by other countries.

From the perspective of customers, the increased competition will be beneficial as it brings more goods and services to the market with enhanced features and better prices. From the perspective of managers, this new world will require astute marshalling of resources to stay in the game. The insights and practices of TQM, with its focus on continuous improvement and customer value, provide the guidelines for successfully competing in this environment.

❓ THINKING CRITICALLY

1. In terms of the law of comparative advantage, what are some arguments against countries using tariffs and other trade restrictions?
2. Besides motorcycles, what else is Harley-Davidson exporting that makes their products so appealing in the international marketplace?

INTERNATIONAL INVESTMENT

In addition to international trade, companies can take advantage of global economic growth by investing in international operations. Companies like General Motors, Procter & Gamble, and RJR Nabisco are known as **multinational corporations** (MNCs) because they *maintain significant operations in more than one country.* Some big U.S. multinationals like Gillette, Colgate, IBM, NCR, Coca-Cola, Digital Equipment, Dow Chemical, and Xerox often get up to half of their gross revenues from foreign markets.[3]

Many of these MNCs are not simply setting up distribution centers to sell goods produced in America; they are also investing in manufacturing operations around the world. For example, in Europe, the Americas, and the Far East, Xerox manufactures over 250 equipment products that are supported by software, supplies, and accessories. (See Exhibit 4-2 on page 118, illustrating Xerox locations around the globe.) Xerox's document processing products range from desktop copiers to high performance integrated systems which handle every aspect of document creation, storage, and reproduction. The company markets and distributes these products through various geographically based marketing organizations. Responsible for the customer interface in sales and services, these marketing organizations offer the company's total range of products in over 130 countries by a direct sales force of 15,000 and a vast network of dealers, distributors, and agents. For the majority of its products and geographies, Xerox owns the supply chain right down to the after-sales service force of 30,000.

Going into the 1990s, companies and other investors in the United States had $1.2 trillion in assets abroad.[4] This number was expected to more than double by the middle of the decade. Most of the investment takes place in the three centers of trading power, the EC, North America, and the Pacific Rim. However, with the demise of communism in Eastern Europe and the former states of the Soviet Union, other opportunities for investment are attracting U.S. multinationals.

Multinational corporation (MNC) A company that maintains significant operations in more than one country.

EXHIBIT 4-2
Worldwide locations of Xerox manufacturing sites

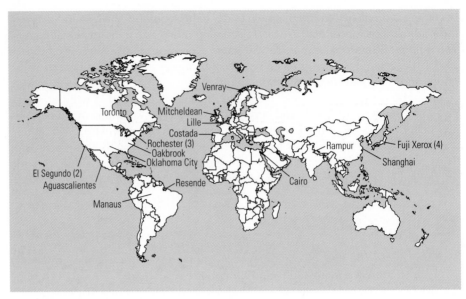

Source: Courtesy of Xerox Corporation.

MNCs are difficult business ventures to manage. As we discuss later, managers have to deal with diverse economic, political, technological, and cultural realities that are also compounded by language barriers. Why bother becoming an MNC? There are many reasons why companies make international investments, and there are different forms that these investments might take.

Reasons for International Investment

There are four primary reasons for international investment:

- to gain access to labor and resources
- to increase sales volume in foreign markets
- to reduce costs of exporting
- to take advantage of financial conditions

As we review each of these, note the connection between these reasons for investing and organizational improvement goals. In other words, the systems approach and TQM provide us with an insight into the rationale organizations have for their business investment decisions. Let's review these reasons in more detail.

To Gain Access to Labor and Resources.   One of the primary reasons companies invest in international operations is to gain access to resources that may otherwise be inaccessible or too costly. Many American companies go offshore with their manufacturing operations to get cheap labor. For example, a labor-intensive job like assembling wiring harnesses for automobiles may be located in a low-wage country like Mexico. The lower wage levels make labor-intensive work

MEXICO'S MAQUILADORAS[5]

A LOOK AT

ETHICS

There has been a great deal of discussion focused on U.S. firms exporting capital to lesser-developed countries to take advantage of cheap labor. Much discussion has centered around the Mexico maquiladoras. Maquiladoras are assembly plants operating along the Mexican border from Texas to California that supply cheap labor to assemble products for export. Through special tax arrangements with the Mexican Government, an American-owned company can bring U.S. components and equipment into Mexico duty-free; U.S. duties are assessed on only the Mexican value added (primarily labor) before reexport to the United States. Manufacturing labor compensation in Mexico is currently about 14% of U.S. levels.[6]

Even though the Mexican maquiladoras may be a special case, a similar argument would most likely apply to the export of capital for labor rate advantage to any lesser-developed country. While the exporting capital for labor rate advantage sounds like a good strategy, is it really? Let's take a look at what is involved.

The argument overlooks the many factors, other than labor rate advantage, that drive business decisions. U.S. firms are now forced to compete in a global economy and, to do so, they must be the best in the world, not just in the United States. They must provide their people with the best skills, knowledge, and technology in the industry. They must also hire and train people with skills, knowledge, technology, and experience supported by training and rewards. And most important of all, they must develop a team of managers that can put it all together so outputs will compete in world markets.

While the labor rate may be low in lesser-developed countries like Mexico, so are the skill levels of workers. Further, the infrastructure to support foreign industrial plants is also often lacking. To succeed may require a firm to invest large amounts of capital on infrastructure (schools, roads, health care, housing, etc.) and in training personnel (managers and employees). Once trained, managers and employees will have skills and greater opportunity for mobility and professional development. This will give rise to manager and employee demands for a higher standard of living, which in turn will drive up the salaries and wages producing a broader base of middle class consumers. Investing in people and infrastructure will be a major capital expenditure for all firms competing in a world class economy.

There is also a large underdeveloped class of workers and managers in the United States. By the year 2000, more than 65 percent of all U.S. jobs will require some education beyond high school; 23 million will be employed in professional and technical jobs, the largest single category that will require ongoing training. In addition, almost 50 million workers will need additional training just to perform their current jobs effectively. According to Labor Secretary Reich, "The American workforce is coming to be the American economy. That is the way you begin to define the American economy—in terms of skills and capacities of the people who are here."

Reich sees education and worker training as the key to raising U.S. productivity, economic growth, and living standards. According to Reich, "Untrained Americans are losing out. If not competing with low-wage earners abroad, they are competing with new technologies here at home."[7] If the U.S. becomes more efficient at producing domestic goods and services, U.S. standards of living will rise regardless of what happens on the world market. Conversely, if productivity does not increase for the goods the United States produces and uses, nothing that happens in the international economic markets can raise the U.S. standard of living.

The dilemma that is often faced by many U.S. companies is whether to take an immediate, but short-run labor rate advantage by relocating factories in underdeveloped countries or take a long run view that starts with the upgrading of American workers. What would you do?

more cost-effective. Companies also invest abroad to get access to raw materials. MNCs from abroad may invest in the United States to get access to the abundance of natural resources like natural gas, timber, and minerals, as well as our agricultural products.

To Increase Sales Volume in Foreign Markets. Companies often invest abroad in order to increase their sales in foreign markets. For example, McDonald's is now selling hamburgers in restaurants throughout Europe, the Far East, Australia, and even Russia. In order for a service organization like McDonald's to increase foreign sales, it obviously has to locate restaurants in foreign countries. But why would an MNC like Toyota decide to locate in a foreign country when it could just produce automobiles in Japan and ship them overseas? One reason is that the manufacturer may feel that it can better understand the needs of its consumers if it sets up business in the country. Further, consumers may have more positive feelings toward a company that resides in the community. In the early 1990s, when the general public and the news media fueled "Japan bashing," Honda of America, located in Marysville, Ohio, started running advertisements featuring American workers proudly reminding the viewer that the Honda Accord is "made in America." Toyota also runs such ads. Additionally, some markets will be closed to imports. The U.S. restricted the number of Japanese cars which could be brought into this country. To maintain their market share and grow, the Japanese had to manufacture here.

To Reduce Costs of Exporting. MNCs like Toyota have also increased investments abroad to reduce the costs of exporting. These costs include the administration and freight charges associated with shipping across the ocean, unloading, and port processing. Exporting also requires that a company maintain a larger stock of unsold automobiles, which can be quite costly. By producing in the markets in which they sell products, for example, in Georgetown Kentucky, Toyota also reduces the time it takes for them to adjust their production schedules to fluctuations in customer demand. Toyota can produce each day only automobiles that have been ordered by customers. This allows this company to hold little or no stock of finished but unsold automobiles.

Other costs of exporting include tariffs. A **tariff** is *a tax that a company must pay in order to bring its goods into another country*. For example, exporters of trucks from other countries have to pay a tariff that is proportionate to the value of the vehicle. In response, Toyota produces trucks that are not completely finished, leaving off the truck bed and other amenities like chrome bumpers, rollbars, stereo, and details, to reduce the amount of the tariff. The truck is finished by Toyota's port processing centers that install the domestically produced truck bed and other amenities. Another Japanese transplant, Nissan, avoids the tariff on trucks altogether by producing them in Smyrna, Tennessee.

Tariff A tax that a company must pay in order to bring its goods into another country.

To Take Advantage of Financial Conditions. There are times when foreign investments might offer managers greater financial returns. For example, during the 1980s when the value of the Japanese yen increased in comparison to the dollar, many Japanese investors bought millions of dollars worth of real estate in America. A strong yen made even high-priced American real estate, like Rockefeller Center in New York City, seem to be a bargain. Unfortunately, the bottom fell out

GE'S GLOBAL STRATEGY[8]

THE GLOBAL ENVIRONMENT

In 1992 and 1993, GE's sales grew at only a 3 percent rate, and the company's management feels that prospects for better growth in the U.S. are marginal at best. Since 1987, though, GE's annual sales from exports and operations outside the U.S. have grown at a rate of 30 percent annually, and in 1993 contributed 40 percent of the company's sales. The company's managers now see the greatest opportunities for growth in countries outside the U.S. They have especially targeted China, India, and Mexico, followed by Southeast Asia, countries with large populations and just now taking off in terms of their economic development. They have decided to systematically invest in these countries, carefully choosing their opportunities and working with local companies when necessary.

The company's strategy is to start slowly with investments of $20-$100 million, spent on both increasing its staff to support exports and developing international subsidiaries. The following provide some specific examples of GE's strategy:

- **Appliances.** The company is making inexpensive ovens in India in a joint venture with a local company. It is building gas ovens in Mexico with a local partner, and it has recently established a research center in Mexico.

- **Jet Engines.** The company sold $500 million worth of engines to China in 1993, and has opened service centers in 17 Chinese cities. It has established an engine repair facility in Indonesia.

- **Medical Systems.** They have started a joint venture in China to develop low-cost imaging equipment for the Chinese market and export. They have a similar deal in India and are developing ultrasound devices.

- **GE Capital.** The company has set up a $200 million fund to take equity positions in Asian power plants, and has a stake in $2.5 billion in Indonesia. It is working to establish the first commercial lending operation in China.

- **Plastics.** GE has purchased a commercial resin business in Mexico and is completing a plastics manufacturing plant in India.

- **Power Systems.** The company expects to get 50 percent of its orders for its giant electric generators from Asia through the year 2000. It is a leader in a consortium building a $600 million power plant in Mexico.

Each of these moves by GE allow it take advantage of its resources and expertise to serve market segments across the globe. GE's businesses are especially aimed at the development of infrastructure, such as transportation, financing, and electric power. The U.S. has mature markets for all these areas. We should not be surprised, therefore, at GE's direction. It is simply taking its strengths where the customers now are.

---

of the real estate market a few years later, and many Japanese have since sold off their American holdings at considerable financial losses.

Some companies will invest in international production operations to totally avoid such unfavorable and unpredictable fluctuations in exchange rates. Exchange rates can change the affordability of products overnight and immediately attract bargain hungry consumers. To stay on a financially level playing field with domestic producers like Procter & Gamble, the Japanese multinational Kao Corporation invested heavily in America by purchasing companies like Andrew Jergens, an American producer of beauty lotion and hand soap.

Forms of International Investment

Businesses often enter into international operations by exporting. Usually they start by contracting with established distributors in other countries. For example, Japanese producers of motorcycles, such as Honda and Kawasaki, launched their international operations by establishing a distribution network and local dealerships in foreign countries. Or, companies may devote salespeople to global territories, either with or without starting an export department. Both of these are steps GE has taken as explained in the *A Look at The Global Environment* box on page 121. These initial steps toward international operations do not require a great deal of investment. Other forms of investment, which require more financial and managerial resources, include:

- licensing
- franchising
- joint ventures/strategic alliances
- fully owned subsidiaries.

These forms of international investment vary in the extent of managerial involvement and control that is retained by the company making the investment. Exhibit 4-3 graphically displays these levels of involvement.

Licensing The selling of rights to manufacture or market brand name products or product specifications or to use copyrighted materials, patented production processes, or other assets, usually granted to a company for a fee or royalty based on sales.

Licensing.   **Licensing** means *selling the rights to manufacture or market brand name products or product specifications or to use copyrighted materials, patented production processes, or other assets. The license may be granted to a company for a fee or royalty which is based on sales.* Usually the license only grants the licensee rights to operate in a specific geographic region, continent, or country. For example, a company may license a Brazilian firm the right to manufacture and sell a patented motor in South America for 10 years. Publishers in one country frequently negotiate licenses to publish translated versions of books from other countries. The company granting the license usually has very little to do with the management of the licensee's operations. This lack of control is the

EXHIBIT 4-3
Forms of international investment that vary in their extent of managerial involvement and control

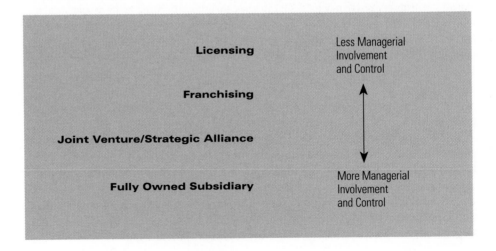

major risk of licensing, since the licensee might turn out to be either incompetent or unethical. The licensing company should carefully choose the licensee to avoid squandering market opportunities abroad.

When done right, licensing allows a company to extend the profitability of a proven product or process without the costs of dealing with government regulations, transporting the product, or starting up and managing global operations. Companies likely to issue licenses in international markets are those that (1) invest more heavily in research and development (R&D) than in manufacturing operations, (2) are small firms that lack resources for foreign investment, and (3) are established firms that have products on the downside of their life cycle curve and that want to move on to other things. By licensing others, such firms can still derive revenues from their products without further direct investment.

Franchising.   Franchising is a form of licensing, except the **franchise** is *a package deal, perhaps a combination of trademark, equipment, materials, managerial guidelines, consulting advice, and cooperative advertising.* The franchisee typically pays a fee up front and then a percentage of revenues to the parent company. The franchising firm may also require the franchisee to buy special ingredients or materials, which gives the firm another stream of revenue. The hotel and fast food industries use franchising extensively. McDonald's, Kentucky Fried Chicken, Pizza Hut, and Holiday Inn have been very successful in expanding operations around the world through franchising.

> **Franchise** A form of licensing in which the parent company offers a combination of trademark, equipment, materials, managerial guidelines, consulting advice, and cooperative advertising for a fee and a percentage of revenues.

As with licensing, the franchising company may play a very limited role in the management of foreign operations. Of course, the extent of managerial involvement depends on the terms of the franchising contract and the philosophy of the franchising company. Some companies retain the right to revoke a franchise agreement if certain standards for quality, service, and profitability are not maintained. Most franchisees welcome the advice of managers who have proven their methods of management.

However, franchising in foreign countries should be implemented with enough flexibility to allow local management to adapt to the customs and special needs of their customers. Most fast food operations, for example, allow for variations in the menu to suit local tastes. The same is true in promoting products. For example when marketing a product in Latin countries, managers may not want to focus too much on product guarantees or warranties as these are less valued than in the U.S. Appealing to the Latino's family motives creates a more positive response.[9]

Joint Ventures/Strategic Alliances.   A **joint venture, or strategic alliance** (which is a popular term today), is a *partnership to pursue mutual business objectives.*[10] International alliances are formed when two companies from different nations share the cost of developing new products or processes, building facilities, and managing and maintaining the operations. The partners may invest by providing cash or other assets such as raw materials. Strategic alliances are a powerful means of launching an international operation. It allows the investors to share the risk, although each must give up a share of control to their partner. If managed appropriately, with unselfish cooperation, each company can contribute their best assets, such as product and process technology, brand image, marketing expertise, distribution channels, or managerial prowess. A company weak in one or more of these areas can be compensated by the strengths of its partner.

> **Joint venture/strategic alliance** A partnership to pursue mutual business objectives.

The collective power of a strategic alliance can produce an operation that is much more competitive than what either of the partners could produce working alone. For the alliance to work, however, the partners have to adapt to one another, and they must be willing to settle for only a fair share, and not all of the financial benefits. We saw that this is a strategy of General Electric. The *A Look at The Global Environment* box on page 125 describes Anheuser-Busch's approach to international investment to expand into the market.

Fully-owned subsidiary

An international investment approach where the multi-national corporation directly invests capital and personnel by building a new operation abroad or by purchasing operating facilities from a foreign company.

Fully-Owned Subsidiaries.   Multinational corporations (MNCs) often prefer to *directly invest capital and personnel by building a new operation abroad or by purchasing operating facilities from a foreign company.* In either case, the operations become a **fully-owned subsidiary** of the corporation making the investment. Building a new operation from the ground up has the advantages of being built to the exact specifications of the owner. With a new operation, there are no existing cultural problems or liabilities that might undermine the owner's business strategy or corporate objectives. The owner retains full control of the operations. There are disadvantages to building from scratch. It can take longer to establish a successful business, especially if the MNC is also attempting to develop a new market for its products and services. Some companies simply move their manufacturing operations offshore to get cheaper labor and hold down the costs of production, and earn higher profits on the goods shipped back to domestic customers. This form of international investment is particularly offensive to domestic labor unions and the workers whose jobs are transferred abroad.

By purchasing an existing operation, with the people and other physical resources left intact, the MNC can move quickly into a new market. The buyout, if done tactfully, can preserve existing relationships with suppliers, customers, and other stakeholders. Over time the MNC can mold the culture and operating systems of the foreign subsidiary, and adapt itself, to ensure a good fit between the MNC and its subsidiary. This is another of GE's tactics. When it invests in a fully-owned subsidiary, an MNC retains managerial control and all the financial benefits for itself. However, it also bears all the risk. And it can be quite a challenge to take full responsibility for running an operation in a foreign country.

The Impact of International Investment

Each of these forms of investment impact the MNC's home and host countries in many ways. The MNC alters job opportunities, levels of technological advantage, availability of capital, import/export balances of trade, and levels of competition in the marketplace. The MNC may even impact the culture of the local community where it invests. For example, MNCs that invest in regions of the world where women are subservient to men may stir up social and familial controversy by placing women in positions of authority over men and by encouraging women to develop their fullest human potential and positive self-image.

Managers of MNCs have to be prepared for the fallout that results from their investments. They will create both opponents and proponents on all important issues. For example, one segment of the business community in a host country may object to a joint venture/strategic alliance because it drains local capital away from alternative investments that would solely benefit the local economy. Another segment of the business community may welcome the alliance because

SAYING BUDDD... WEISER IN MORE THAN ONE LANGUAGE[11]

Budweiser is by far the best-selling beer in the U.S. with nearly 43 percent of the market. Opportunities for growth are limited here, so Anheuser-Busch is looking for new places to make money selling beer. To do this, the company has set up several licensing agreements with overseas brewers to brew and sell Budweiser in markets like Japan and Russia. However, this approach has not generated the kind of revenue growth the company is now seeking. Their goal is to transform its international brewing operations into the company's second largest profit center.

Their strategy now is to invest in and create strategic alliances with foreign breweries around the world. For example the company has acquired a 5 percent stake in Tsingtao, the leading Chinese brewery, and a 17.7 percent stake in Grupo Modelo in Mexico, the maker of Corona. Busch expects to have Tsingtao brew and sell Budweiser in the fast-growing Chinese market, and to reap profits from eventually owning up to 50 percent of Grupo Modelo. Anheuser-Busch has also forged an alliance with Kirin Brewery of Japan, the world's fourth largest brewer, to market Budweiser in Japan. There is also speculation that Anheuser-Busch will buy a stake in Kirin and that they will collaborate in other Asian markets.

All this is a reasonably new activity and represents the initial steps in Anheuser-Busch's attempt to figure out the best ways to gain a larger presence in the world beer market. There are various ways companies might do this. For Anheuser-Busch, the world's largest brewer, the most effective and efficient method for now seems to be by investment and strategic alliance.

THE GLOBAL ENVIRONMENT

it provides opportunity for local purchasing of supplies and raw materials. Also, paychecks for employees help boost the local service and retail economy. One of the major impacts that international investment has on host business communities is the infusion of new ways of thinking and managing, and improved levels of competition, like Honda which serves consumers with improved products.

❓ THINKING CRITICALLY

1. How do you think a manager makes a decision about what type of international investment to make?
2. What are the pros and cons of relying on domestic production and exporting to reach foreign markets versus making international investments in production facilities in the markets where goods are sold?
3. Why has GE selected various developing countries as main targets for international investment?

THE GLOBAL BUSINESS ENVIRONMENT

Many factors influence and shape the environment in which organizations function. Going back to our definition of an organization as an open system, the **business environment** *sets the context for the system's operation and provides its inputs and accepts its outputs.* Management's ability to understand and adapt to the global environment has a significant impact on the efficiency and effectiveness of the business as it seeks to serve customers. This is true in the domestic

Business environment
The context for the system's operation that provides its inputs and accepts its outputs.

business environment, where we must be concerned with social, legal, techno-logical, economic, and other factors that shape and constrain what a business can and cannot do. It is equally true in the global business environment. The differ-ence is that in the domestic environment, we have a personal familiarity with all these factors as we have been a part of them all our lives. When organizations decide to expand beyond their borders, they must be especially aware of the environmental differences. A misunderstanding of the legal or social context for doing business can have disastrous effects on the success of international opera-tions. The Case in Point on Euro Disney at the beginning of this chapter is one example of a company that did not quite grasp the social dimensions.

The most important global business environment dimensions are political/legal, economic, technological, and social, and those are the ones we will review in this chapter. Exhibit 4-4 graphically illustrates these dimensions. While we deal with each one separately, as each has its own nuances, you should be aware that each is really just a perspective we use to help us make our decisions. They are not independent of each other. The social dimension influ-ences the political dimension, which influences the economic dimension. The technological dimension is dependent on the level of development in the coun-try. Nevertheless, breaking the environment into these dimensions is still useful for helping us make sense of and deal with it.

The Political/Legal Dimension

The political/legal dimension of a global business environment is perhaps the most important, for it sets the formal boundaries within which the other dimen-sions take shape. Important aspects of the political/legal dimension include polit-ical stability, and other factors such as policies and laws. There are also important historical events that have shaped the political climate of the global business environment.

EXHIBIT 4-4
Dimensions of the global business environment

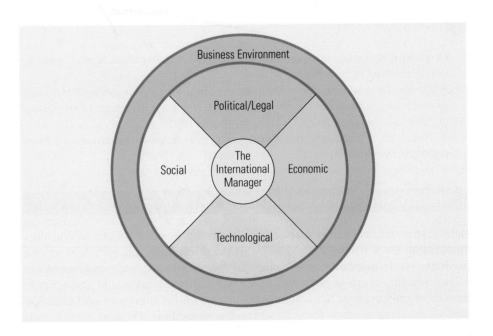

Political Stability.   The most obvious factor in the political environment is the political stability of a country. **Political stability** is *the likelihood that the current political system or policies will remain in place.* There are risks involved with making investments in countries that are on the edge of political instability. A multinational corporation could lose its entire investment if a dictatorial regime took over the government and seized all foreign assets as property of the state, as happened in Iran after the fall of the Shah and the rise of the Ayatollah Khomeini in the late 1970s.

China is one such country where the political winds have changed quickly and dangerously in the past, and it is still ruled by Communists, albeit much more pragmatic ones. Despite a penchant toward human rights abuse, an anathema to the U.S., it is the largest potential market in the world for the goods and services of developed countries. U.S., Japanese, and European companies are rushing quickly to sell everything from cosmetics to cars to telecommunications equipment to the Chinese. Companies such as Xerox, PPG Industries, Warner-Lambert, H.J. Heinz, Kodak, Motorola, AT&T, and many others are making deals in China. In doing this, they assume the U.S. will maintain its friendly relationships with the government, and that the politicians running the government of China will act rationally.[12] Nevertheless, carefully monitoring China's political stability is an important factor for managers undertaking operations in this country.

One of the reasons for less economic activity in the new democracies in Russia and central Europe is a remaining concern about their stability. It is ironic that Russia, which officially is more committed to strong ties with the West than China, is considered to be a much less attractive place to invest than China because of political instability. Part of this instability has to do with the cultural diversity of Russia and part with the jolt the country has undergone trying to change from a centrally planned economy to a free market economy. They do not know how to do this, and the deprivations suffered by the people have created an unsure environment for outside investors. Until things settle down politically in Russia, it is likely to remain a place that most multinational corporations deal with at arm's length. As managers move more and more into the global marketplace, they must separately gauge each country's political stability, as well as the stability of the entire region. For example, the presence of Saddam Hussein's regime in Iraq casts doubt over doing business in neighboring countries such as Jordan.

Other Political/Legal Factors.   Even when political stability can be assured, the political environment still presents a number of important factors that managers of MNCs must consider when investing and operating in foreign countries. These factors include the host country's foreign policies, laws and regulations governing international trade, taxes, import tariffs and quotas, copyrights, patents, and currency exchange. MNCs will make investment decisions based on these factors.

We noted earlier the concept of the *comparative advantage* of various nations in producing certain goods or services. For example, the United States has an advantage in producing specialty steels, whereas Taiwan and Korea have an advantage in producing crude steel. Each country will seek to export the goods and services for which it has an advantage. However, some countries may resist the importation of goods from other countries because they want to protect their domestic industries and give them an opportunity to grow and develop. Accordingly, Taiwan may protect its companies that produce specialty steels by restricting imports from the United States. There are several forms that this protection might take.

Political stablity
A concept suggesting the likelihood that a nation's political system or policies will remain in place.

Quota Limit on the quantity or monetary value of imported goods.

Many countries impose import tariffs, taxes on products transported across a nation's border, and import **quotas,** *limits on the quantity or monetary value of imported goods.* Tariffs and quotas raise the price of imported goods, making them less attractive to local buyers and thus help to protect domestic industries. For example, in response to the powerful Japanese farm lobby, Japan imposes strict trade restrictions on commodities such as rice, fruit, and beef in order to protect its domestic agricultural industry. Japan's farmers would otherwise find it difficult to compete with more efficient, lower cost foreign producers in the U.S., Asia, and Australia. It is unlikely that the Japanese can ever be more efficient in agriculture, and the restrictions here are more the result of political clout by farmers than any hope of competing on a level playing field with agricultural imports.

The tariffs and quotas on foreign automobiles imposed by the United States are part of the reason why foreign producers have decided to locate production facilities here. In addition to protecting the automobile industry and other industries such as semiconductors, the United States has frequently protected the defense industry from foreign competition to ensure that the U.S. retains the capability to provide for its own national defense. It has also restricted the types of defense-related products that may be exported. For example, before the break up of the Soviet Union, firms were forbidden from selling even microcomputers in the Soviet Union.

Historical Events.   Immediately after World War II, the United States stood alone as the only economic and military superpower unravaged by the horrors of war. Its industrial plants and infrastructure of roads and bridges didn't take a hit from a single bomb. By contrast, much of the infrastructure of Germany and Japan was destroyed. The same was true for other countries in Europe. However, these people did not stay down for long. Their managers began rebuilding and also rewriting the rules of international business and management. In the decades following World War II, the United States, and Western nations in general, were focused on another agenda: The Cold War. As an economic superpower, the U.S. could and did channel vast resources into the defense establishment as well as providing large amounts of military aid to our allies while the government of the Soviet Union was doing the same thing. No leader better epitomized the resolve of the U.S. to resist and defeat communism than President Ronald Reagan. One of his 1984 presidential campaign ads best summarized the rationale for expending vast resources on military deterrence and preparation for battle:

There is a bear in the woods. For some people, the bear is easy to see. Others don't see it at all. Some people say the bear is tame. Others say it is vicious and dangerous. Since no one can really be sure who's right, isn't it smart to be as strong as the bear—if there is a bear?

This appeal played on the fears of people. In the context of politics, the perceived threat was not unfounded, as history reveals with the Soviet launch of the world's first satellite, Sputnik; communist expansion beyond Eastern Europe, into the third world, into the Americas in Cuba and Nicaragua; Khrushchev's threats to bury capitalist democracies; the construction of the Berlin Wall; the Cuban Missile Crisis; and wars in Korea, Vietnam and Afghanistan. The Soviets seemed to be a threat, socially and militarily. Of course, the Soviet Union would argue that its actions were justified by U.S. behavior and policies, and actions of the Soviet Union helped justify U.S. policies. Each side was justifiably suspicious of the other.

However, with the dawning of the 1990s, as Lester Thurow puts it in his book *Head to Head,*[13]

Suddenly, the bear disappeared. The Berlin Wall came down, East Germany and West Germany were united, democracy and capitalism arrived in the formerly communist countries of Middle Europe, the Red Army withdrew to the east, the Warsaw Pact was abrogated, the Soviet Union split asunder, and communism ended in Europe, its birthplace. Democracy and capitalism had won. Together they had beaten dictatorship and communism.

The Cold War was over, but at what price to the victor?

The United States stands alone as the only military superpower in the 1990s. However, U.S. citizens are realizing that "winning" the cold war dims in light of the now obvious global economic contest. Indeed, one presidential candidate in 1992, Paul Tsongas, used the line, "The Cold War is over, and Japan won." During the decades that the U.S. was preoccupied with winning the Cold War, with military buildups and political maneuvering, Germany and Japan were emerging as new economic superpowers. The world gradually shifted from being a single polar economic world revolving around the United States to a tripolar world anchored in the United States, Japan, and the European Community.

Certainly, the U.S. was not oblivious to these economic developments. These were the result of programs such as the Marshall Plan and the post World War II rules governing international economic competition. These programs did exactly what they were designed to do—help war-torn and undeveloped countries return to economic viability. The assumption was that economic prosperity fosters democracy, and hence, world security; an assumption that has largely proven true. However, while others were catching up, the Cold War distracted the U.S. from its own development in two ways: (1) the diversion of monetary investments away from consumer and industrial goods to the military-industrial complex, and (2) not taking the rapid development of Japan and Germany seriously enough.

Americans have recently discovered that it is difficult to remain both a military superpower and an economic superpower, especially when others concentrate just on economics. Japan and Germany were constitutionally restricted from massive military buildups, while the U.S. channeled limited resources into the military and away from economic development. Unfortunately, while military spending did prop up the U.S. economy and produced some marketable R&D inventions, the trickle down of military spending really did not and cannot guarantee long term global competitiveness for U.S. firms.

Much of the U.S. has not kept pace with Germany, Japan and other new economic powers. With their unrelenting focus on customer satisfaction and more effective and efficient operations, they are taking business away from American and European firms. In the century to come, the U.S. will be just one among other powers engaged in an economic competition where the rules of engagement are determined by how much value and quality competitors deliver to customers—something practitioners of TQM can well relate to. Now global competitiveness and economic development depend less on the abundance of natural resources and being born rich, and more on human-made advantages, such as a deep understanding of customers and how to marshall resources to serve them. Revolutions in telecommunications, computers, transportation, and logistics permit global sourcing and a world capital market. Old approaches suitable to the bipolar world no longer work in a multipolar world.

The Economic Dimension

The political/legal dimension establishes boundaries for the economic dimension of a country's business environment. It sets the stage for business activities. Economic factors that managers of MNCs must consider are patterns of economic growth, inflation, currency exchange rates, stock market activity, and financial rates of return. Large MNCs typically have a staff of economists and financial planners to monitor these economic factors, make predictions, and recommend courses of action. For example, a company purchasing commodities from overseas may wait until exchange rates are more favorable before making a purchase. A fluctuation of a few percentage points can mean millions of dollars saved for very large purchases. As another example, managers also have access to capital markets around the world, which creates international flows of capital. If the capital market in the United States tightens up with higher interest rates, the financial managers may borrow money in Europe where rates may be lower. Such practices allow businesses to operate efficiently and keep down the costs of their investments.

The political and economic dimensions also overlap with the establishment of economic communities or free trade areas. The North American Free Trade Agreement (NAFTA) created a free trade area among Mexico, the United States, and Canada. The European Community (EC) created a unified and borderless economy through political agreements among many sovereign nations in Europe. There are both benefits and drawbacks to the use of free trade zones. On the positive side, free trade zones remove barriers between trading partners within the zone, which makes it easier and more efficient to conduct business. Consumers may enjoy the benefits of increased efficiency (lower costs) and greater access to an array of products and services.

On the negative side, people outside the free trade zones face stiff tariffs for importing their goods and services, which makes prices artificially high for consumers. In the short term, free trade zones do protect inside companies, but in the long term the reduced competition allows them to be less aggressive in making improvements. The danger is that protection within the trade zone can create complacency. Without making improvements in the efficiency and effectiveness of their strategies, these companies will not be prepared for global competition if they are ever forced to go head-to-head without protection. These companies may also be unable to expand their markets beyond the limits of the free trade zone because of their lack of global competitiveness.

The European Community.   The EC removed impediments to trade among its members, while stimulating broader economic growth. Further, Eastern European countries, such as The Czech Republic, Slovakia, Hungary, Poland, and even the nations of the former Soviet Union, are abandoning centrally planned and administered economies in favor of deregulated, market-based competitive economies. Perhaps one day these countries will join the EC. If the EC continues to expand and eventually includes Middle and Eastern Europe, it could create an European economy more than twice as large as Japan and the United States combined. These formerly communist countries certainly have a long way to go to catch up with Western standards for quality and customer value.[14] However, their potential should not be ignored.

Companies from the U.S., Japan, and other nations expanded investments in EC nations to maximize their "insider" status by the end of 1992, the time of EC integration. Such investments strengthened the EC's global competitiveness. The EC's local content rule requires companies to acquire 40 percent of their parts and components from local (EC) companies or pay a tax on all parts imported for assembly. This law dissuades foreign investors from setting up assembly shops fed by the free flow of imported parts, which would not be much different from importing the product in the first place. For example, to encourage the transfer of technology to Europe's semiconductor industry, and to provide better paying, high-skilled jobs for its workers, the EC imposes a high tariff on the imported silicon wafers, which form the base of most microchips, that are not produced within the EC.[15]

In the future, U.S. companies will face technologically capable European firms that are supported with the macroeconomic policies and labor force skills needed to be more competitive. While the Europeans are putting in place the macroeconomic infrastructure needed to support global competitiveness, the Japanese are going even further. At the micro level, within organizations, the Japanese are continuing to refine managerial approaches that optimally fit with macroeconomic strategies. Business practices within Japan will continue to present some challenging economic conditions for MNCs.

The Technological Dimension

The technological dimension of the global environment presents a number of challenges for MNC managers. The first challenge is to find a fit between the technology and the preparedness of the host community for it. Second, the global technological environment is changing rapidly, and managers will have to adopt suitable strategies, as illustrated by Japan's national technology strategy. Finally, trends in technological advancement will revolutionize many business practices and product markets.

Technological Preparedness.   There are obvious differences in levels of technological development across the business communities of the world. This variation presents several issues for managers. The first issue is that managers must be sensitive to the receptivity of local people to their company's technology. People fear that which they do not understand. In communities where the people are not educated and rely more on superstition than scientific thinking, it may be a mistake to introduce high technology production processes. A village in rural Germany probably would be more receptive to high technology than one in rural Brazil. Another critical issue is the level of preparedness of the human resources in terms of education and technical skills. Even though the local community may welcome a technology, they may not be prepared or even capable of learning how to work with the technology. When locating in educationally impoverished regions of the world, MNCs must carefully screen applicants to select capable employees. Initially, the MNC may have to bring in people from other operations. In these cases, the MNC should cooperate with local officials to develop schools that prepare people for fitting into its ways of operating.

Technology Strategies.   In the last two decades, the global technology environment has changed dramatically. Old approaches to management and ways of thinking no longer explain what is happening in dynamic world markets. In many industries, new process technologies have become relatively more important than new product technologies. Industries of the future increasingly rely on brainpower rather than endowments of natural resources and capital. These developments are important factors in determining the strategies that nations and business organizations will adopt in the future. Let's consider how the Japanese manage technology.

In addition to the Japanese institutional mechanisms used to plan the country's economy, the Japanese also promote a national technology strategy. They improve technology through investments to upgrade manufacturing facilities and improve quality because of severe inter-firm competition, short product life-cycles, and fast obsolescence of facilities. The development of technological skills emphasizes engineering, innovation, and technology assimilation. A world technology scanning system, technology-oriented information system, and networking arrangements are widely used.

The Japanese notoriously take products invented elsewhere and learn to produce them better and cheaper than anyone else through process improvements. For example, in the past two decades the Japanese have taken control of the markets for three leading new products, video cameras, VCRs, and fax machines, all invented by Americans, and the CD player, invented by the Dutch.

They are able to do so because they devote two thirds of their research and development (R&D) expenditures to new process technologies and only one third to new product technologies. With continuous improvements by a knowledgeable and skilled work force, they make the product better and cheaper and take the market away from the inventor. American firms do just the opposite, spending more on new product technologies, in hopes of getting monopoly power to set higher prices and earn higher profits on a new product. As low-cost, high-quality competitors enter the market, the American firms abandon the market in pursuit of new product markets.[16]

Japanese government organizations monitor, forecast, analyze, plan, and coordinate strategic industrial development. They encourage technology development and innovation, as well as the design and engineering that translates basic innovations into marketable products. They even administer national exams for engineering consultants. A number of factors combine to create a technology-oriented climate, such as a commitment to science, the importance of quality, and willingness to take risks.[17] These technology strategies are supported by the collective economic strategies discussed earlier.

Trends in Technological Advancement.   Trends in technological advancement will revolutionize business practices as well as create market opportunities. Consider the burgeoning field of laser chemistry. The potential value to be derived from the marriage of knowledge and tools in this field is astounding. Laser chemists use such exotic maneuvers as "laser traps" and "optical tweezers" to grab, slow, and manipulate bits of molecules of living cells. In the process, they are discovering better techniques for such diverse tasks as etching circuits on silicon and unraveling the inner workings of cells.[18] Future applications of this process technology can create entirely new markets and provide unforeseen value to customers.

Other advancements in technology promise to unify the global economy through computerization, telecommunications, and other forms of information technology. For example, if Motorola follows through with plans to circle the earth with dozens of telecommunications satellites, workers around the world will be able to share information instantaneously. MNCs will then be composed of interactive co-workers as close together as the next cubicle or the next country.[19]

The Social Dimension

The social dimension of the global business environment is made up of the human behaviors, interactions, and communications that occur while conducting business. Managers must attend to social behaviors that occur within the firm, such as the manager's interaction with local employees, and between international firms. Cultural differences and communication barriers are two important factors that determine the success of these social interactions.

Cultural Differences.   Culture is an integrated set of values, beliefs, and practices that are accepted by a society or group of people. If you have traveled abroad, or watched National Geographic specials on television, you have an idea how diverse the cultures of the world really are. However, you can fully appreciate these differences only when you interact with people from other nations and cultures. Managers of MNCs often blunder when conducting business because they do not understand the host's culture. For example, many countries do not have strict laws governing political bribery. In fact, in many countries, bribery is openly accepted as part of the costs of doing business. A salesman or company representative could come away empty handed if he refuses to "stoop" to bribery in such a country. However, as international commerce grows, such ethically questionable customs as bribery are increasingly viewed as an unacceptable way to get business in any country. The *A Look at Ethics* box on page 136 provides further exploration into the differences between ethics in U.S. business and in other countries.

There are many cultural differences that can undermine business relationships if the MNC manager does not adapt. For example, Latinos tend to stand much closer when talking and literally breathe the same air. A British manager who is more comfortable maintaining arms-length distance may offend the Latino by backing up. One of the most commonly cited cultural differences today is the emphasis on rugged individualism typical of Americans versus groupism and the value of consensus typical of the Japanese. These differences are manifested in many ways, such as in how managers treat employees, delegate authority, and conduct business negotiations. The following story illustrates how costly the lack of cultural understanding can be.

The managers of one American firm, believing that the Japanese reached agreements in the same way as Americans, arrived in Japan to negotiate a joint venture agreement with a contract already in hand. The contract, incidentally, had been worked on for days by the firm's legal department. In the first meeting with the potential joint venture partner, the American managers placed a

BRIAN BOLING AT PHILLIPS CONSUMER ELECTRONICS

Brian Boling, General Manager of Speaker Systems, Phillips Consumer Electronics, tells what he has learned about dealing with cross-cultural differences when conducting business around the world.

One of the remarkable aspects of working in a multinational company is the opportunity to share the experience of many work environments (cultures, styles, philosophies) all in one business. Over my 14 years of employment by Phillips I have seen five unique business environments—in four different countries—in three key regions of the world. Having so far survived this tour of duty there is a combination of a growing confidence in the idea of a "global village," with a deep respect for the cultural quicksand that can await the innocent!

As an American working overseas, I was pleasantly surprised to find that with my single language—Tennessee English—I could conduct business in every corner of the globe. After a short time, however, it became clear to me that *while a business conversation might be held in English, the translation could bring remarkable complexity.* A simple example in this case might be enlightening. During potential alliance or joint venture discussions I will often suggest a period of "dating" in order to assure we like each other enough before one of us "proposes." (O.K., so it's a rotten idea!) However, this is an analogy I felt best communicated my philosophy of building a win/win relationship. As you may have guessed, my example works pretty well in the U.S. and Europe, but can lose much of its message in the Far East where marriages have always been arranged—and liking someone has little to do with it! In these cases I found the interpretation was: "Yes, there is a commitment toward the proposal, but first there is this *ritual* required by the Tennessean." Unfortunately, I *really meant dating* and often would not propose. This certainly led to some conflict and inefficiency until I discovered the error of my ways.

Good leadership and management principles apply quite universally. Every team or group is looking for vision—based on information—backed by a deployment plan and lots of enthusiasm. *The real difference is in your deployment tactics.* To illustrate, I often compare three business units in three regions all in the process of going to the other side of a mountain. If on the same moment all teams concluded that it was in their interest to go to the other side of the mountain A.S.A.P., you would invariably see the following result: In Europe the team would spend the first days discussing with the unions and various agencies whether the objective that they had chosen was the right one. In the U.S. the first days would be spent on deciding on who would be on the climbing team, how it should be structured, and who would hold rank. In the Far East the first days would be spent in climbing the mountain. The Far East team will be over the mountain discussing the next objective, albeit with casualties, while the American team is only starting an organized climb, with the European team working on plans for a potential tunnel. The fact is that all three teams can move quickly and professionally to reach objectives, but they may use different tactics in doing so.

Over the past few years the academic and business community have been researching cultural aspects much more aggressively. This trend indicates that we are becoming more aware that proper management of cultural differences is a key success factor. The warning I would give is not to overreact to your newly discovered cultural behaviors! Some of the biggest misunderstandings I have witnessed were Asians trying to behave in a Western fashion and Westerners in an Asian fashion to show-off their cultural I.Q.s. Understanding and sensitivity leading to alteration of your delivery, or speed, etc. . . . is enough! In addition, since business is often like war, *you must always remember that cultural differences will as well be used in some negotiation tactics.* Some business people will be aware of your nationality and some of your norms and honor them and/or abuse them accordingly.

   These small lessons have turned into a great asset for me and my business ventures! With the experience and understanding of the different business environments you can start challenging your own people to reach beyond what they see as their limits. Most often their limits are self-imposed and when you provide them these insights at the right moment, breakthroughs are forever possible!

leather-bound, fifty-page contract before each of the twelve Japanese negotiators. During the meeting, which took up the entire afternoon, none of the bound contracts were opened and the Japanese negotiators steered the conversation to general business conditions in the two countries. After this first meeting, the Americans were unable to get the Japanese to the negotiating table again and, consequently, they went home empty-handed. The behavior of the Americans in presenting a legal contract at the beginning of the first meeting was seen as both extremely rude and inept by the Japanese managers, who decided that it would not be wise to enter into a business arrangement with such a firm.[20]

   Exhibit 4-5 on page 137 provides an overview of how managers can be more successful in the Japanese market.

Communication Barriers.   Managers of MNCs face obvious communication barriers when they conduct business in countries where a different language is spoken. The average U.S. manager is particularly inept at dealing with language differences. Most Americans speak only English. We may study a second language in high school or college, but we rarely become proficient at it. Part of the reason for this is our relative isolation, compared to the diversity of cultures and languages on the European continent, where there is a payoff for knowing more than one language. But this excuse is losing its validity. After all, the U.S. population today more than ever before consists of people from many nations speaking many languages. It is also bordered by Mexico, a Spanish speaking country, and French speaking Quebec in Canada. More accurately, people from other countries might point to our self-centered attitude as an underlying cause of our language deficiencies. We often don't stop to consider the perspective of others around the world, sometimes with costly consequences. For example, Ford introduced a low cost truck, the "Fiera," into some Hispanic countries without realizing that the name meant "ugly old woman" in Spanish. Similarly, General Motors several years ago introduced the Chevy "Nova," which means "it doesn't go" in Spanish. Sales for the Fiera and Nova were disappointing.

   Perhaps the primary reason we only speak one language is that we are pampered. Thanks to the historical influences of Britain and the U.S. in global politics and economics, English is the official business language of the world. People in Europe are often multilingual. It's not unusual for an Italian or German to speak two or three languages. Almost all Europeans start to learn English in primary school, as do the Japanese. People in host countries will often, by speaking English, be able to compensate for the basic language deficiencies of the American manager of an MNC.

ETHICS

ETHICS HERE AND ETHICS OVER THERE[21]

In an article in the magazine *Across the Board,* David Vogel observes, "During the past 15 years, more corporate officers and prominent businessmen have been jailed or fined in the United States than in all other capitalist nations combined. Likewise, the fines imposed on corporations in the United States have been substantially greater than in other capitalist nations." He goes on to catalog several differences in ethical standards and values between the U.S. and Europe and Japan. For example,

- Non-profit organizations in the U.S. regularly rank corporations in such areas as their behavior toward women, minority employment, military contracting (not desirable), concern about the environment, and animal testing. There are also awards for excellence in ethics. Such rankings and awards are unknown outside of the U.S.

- Many U.S. companies have been the targets of consumer boycotts for one perceived moral breach or another. Consumer boycotts in Europe and Japan are neither common nor popular.

- In the U.S., business organizations are considered to be social institutions with responsibility for the moral and physical character of the communities in which they invest. Historically, business responsibility has been more narrowly defined in Europe and Japan, such as providing jobs and material wealth for society.

- In the U.S., ethical values and behavior reside in and are the responsibility of the individual, while in Europe and Japan, managers tend to make decisions based on the shared values and responsibilities of the organization.

How do these differences manifest themselves? While whistle-blowing (i.e., informing the government of illegal acts by your employer) remains an act of courage in the U.S. and abroad, whistle-blowers are more likely to be protected and admired in the U.S. than elsewhere. Indeed, whistle-blowing is a very unlikely occurrence in most capitalist countries. And in the U.S., top managers often profess to make ethics a top priority, and most large and medium-sized companies have codes of ethics that employees must pledge to follow. Such codes are very rare elsewhere. Finally, American business places a high value on objective and fair consideration of each person and situation based on merit. The Japanese and to some extent Southern European countries place more priority on obligations to others based on long-standing and long-term relationships.

Vogel summarizes all these differences in business ethics in this way: The American approach "is about individuals making more judgments based on general rules that treat everyone the same. By contrast, business ethics in Europe and Japan have more to do with managers arriving at decisions that are based on shared values, often rooted in a peculiar corporate culture, applied according to specific circumstances, and strongly affected by the nature of one's social ties and obligations."

All these differences are rooted in the unique cultures of various countries. However, as Vogel points out, with increasing globalization of business, higher and more universal standards of ethical behavior are becoming the norm. Why? High ethical standards, along with trust and mutual understanding, make business relationships work better.

EXHIBIT 4-5   Doing Business in Japan

EXHIBIT 4-5
Some cultural and business
guidelines for dealing with the
Japanese

How to Boost Business in Japan

1. Provide products or services that match or exceed competing Japanese products.
2. Make zero defects your goal.
3. Provide local technical services, including training for customers.
4. Deliver products exactly when Japanese customers expect them.
5. Make brochures and other literature available in Japanese.
6. Hire and train local representatives.
7. Keep your Japanese representatives up to date about your company, its products and services, and its policies.
8. Make sure visitors from the U.S. have decision-making authority when dealing with Japanese customers.
9. Top management should visit Japan at least twice a year or even quarterly, to reinforce commitment to the market.
10. Develop a good working relationship with the commercial officers at the U.S. Embassy in Tokyo and the American Chamber of Commerce in Japan. Both of these can help in getting business established in Japan.

Dos and Don'ts When Dealing with the Japanese

1. Don't be late; the Japanese value punctuality.
2. Don't wear sunglasses; they have sinister connotations.
3. Do carry bilingual business cards (one side English, one side Japanese).
4. Do present your card with both hands and a slight bow; this indicates respect.
5. Do present gifts (American made and wrapped).
6. Don't present the same gift to everyone, unless all members are the same rank.
7. Don't knock competitors.
8. Do use chopsticks (or attempt to do so).
9. Don't offer to split the bill with a Japanese host.
10. Do avoid backslapping and other casual contact.

Source: "Inc. Magazine's Going Global: Japan," *Inc.*, January 1994.

Even when the American manager does learn to speak the language of the host country, there are other communication problems that arise. People of some regions, such as Germany, Switzerland, Scandinavia, and North America, are much more explicit in their communications, while others do not say exactly what they mean. By contrast, Arabs, Latin Americans and Japanese are much more implicit in their communications, allowing much of the meaning of their words to be inferred, but never openly acknowledged.[22] Such tendencies in communication are often reinforced with cultural norms. For example, the Japanese value the importance of "saving face" or preserving one's honor in an embarrassing situation rather than explicitly confronting and shaming a person. Experienced translators can help overcome some of these subtle barriers. However, managers of MNCs should learn as much as possible about the cultural and communication patterns of the host country. Many MNCs like Procter & Gamble and Xerox develop their people with cross-cultural educational programs designed to help their managers adapt abroad.

Managers may also employ the services of a "cultural integrator" to assist with communications and mutual understanding between the MNC and its host. To be most effective, the integrator must be familiar with the home, corporate, and host cultures. Otherwise, the ability to help integrate these often divergent orientations will be diminished. A good source might be a native of the host country who has either worked in the home country or was educated there. These people will likely have the communication skills as well as personal experience in adapting to another culture. Managers in need of a cultural integrator might contact universities or organizations like the Fulbright program, which has sponsored thousands of foreign scholars around the world.[23]

❓ THINKING CRITICALLY

1. From the perspective of systems management, how does understanding the global environment in which a company operates affect its efficiency and effectiveness?
2. Do you think managers should adapt to local ethical standards when doing business abroad? Why or why not?
3. Why is taking cultural differences into account so crucial to a company's success when selling in the global marketplace?

INTERNATIONAL MANAGEMENT CHALLENGES

The global business environment presents managers with a number of challenges. Managers' responses to these challenges will depend greatly on understanding how to bring together organizational resources to take advantage of international opportunities. Exhibit 4-6 shows the key factors that help determine the success of multinational firms as global competitors.

There is probably no one model or list of "success factors" that will guarantee success. However, the attitudes of managers in at least two key areas are likely to be critical to their ability to deliver quality to customers in the international business arena: (1) attitude toward cultural differences, and (2) attitude toward global cooperation.

Attitude toward Cultural Differences

We can describe a manager's attitude toward cultural differences as either ethnocentric, polycentric, or geocentric. These attitudes may express themselves in the organization through such things as corporate strategy, marketing approaches, organizational structure, decision-making processes, hiring policies, and management development.[24]

Ethnocentric An approach to management that assumes that one's own culture is superior to that of other nations where a company has operations.

Ethnocentric Attitude.   An **ethnocentric** manager *assumes that his own culture is superior to that of foreign countries that host its operations.* Accordingly, these managers attempt to transport their home organization's culture to the host country when establishing international operations. They assume that what has been successful at home will be successful abroad.

An ethnocentric company philosophy may not result from a negative attitude toward other cultures. A big successful firm operating in a big market (like the United States) may simply approach international expansion as just a natural extension of its current strategy. Such an ethnocentric U.S. firm may launch inter-

EXHIBIT 4-6   Key Factors for the Success of Multinational Firms

MULTINATIONAL FIRMS . . .

1. See themselves as multinational enterprises and are led by a management team that is comfortable in the world arena.
2. Develop integrated and innovative strategies that make it difficult and costly for other firms to compete.
3. Aggressively and effectively implement their world-wide strategy and back it with large investments.
4. Understand that technological innovation is no longer confined to the United States and develop methods for tapping technological innovation abroad.
5. Have organizational structures designed to handle their unique problems and challenges and thus provide them the greatest efficiency.
6. Develop a system that keeps them informed about political changes around the world and the implications of these changes on the firm.
7. Have management teams that are international in composition and thus better able to respond to the various demands of their respective markets.
8. Allow their outside directors to play an active role in the operation of the enterprise.
9. Are well-managed and tend to follow such important guidelines as sticking close to the customer, having lean organization structures, and encouraging autonomy and entrepreneurial activity among the personnel.

Source: Adapted from R.M. Hodgetts and F. Luthans, *International Management* (New York: McGraw-Hill, Inc., 1991) p. 21.

EXHIBIT 4-6
Notice that these points describe how an organization that is a system can most effectively and efficiently succeed in the global marketplace by understanding the environment and how to use its resources to best serve customers.

national operations in France in the same way that it would expand from a northeastern home base in New York to operations in the northwest, Seattle and Portland. Ethnocentric MNCs place managers from home in all of the key positions of its foreign operation. Strategy, policies, and products are simply transplanted with little concern for adapting to the host culture. This approach makes it easy for the new operation to start up and maintain communications with the home headquarters; with no culture clash within the MNC. However, the danger is that operations abroad may be out of touch with the needs and values of local employees, suppliers, and customers. The astute manager, as we saw in the Harley-Davidson example, will figure out if this is the case and do something about it.

Polycentric Attitude.   A **polycentric** manager *sees each country's culture and operating environment as unique and difficult to handle using only his home culture's perspective.* Polycentric managers feel that since local people best understand the needs and customs of their own country they are more capable of running local operations. Thus, local people fill the key positions in the MNCs operations abroad. Further, these locals are allowed to appoint and develop their own people. As long as operations are profitable and meeting corporate objectives, headquarters leaves them alone.

A polycentric business approach may result if an MNC operates as a holding company or if it is highly decentralized. Such a company may allow each of its operating units, at home and abroad, to independently exercise a lot of autonomy. A polycentric approach to international business certainly allows the MNC to adapt to local traditions, which can be a strength. However, it can also be a weakness, since local managers may not take advantage of knowledge and capabilities that reside elsewhere in the corporation. The polycentric MNC may fail to integrate global operations to enhance the performance of the whole company. A moderate form of polycentrism may be found in MNCs that organize operating units into

Polycentric An approach to management that sees each country's culture and operating environment as unique and difficult to handle from the perspective of the home culture.

regional divisions which handle all business activities (e.g., strategic planning, production, marketing) for one region, such as Europe, South America, or Africa. These firms may be referred to as regiocentric. Gillette takes this approach.

Geocentric An approach to management that appreciates cultural differences but takes an integrative international viewpoint.

Geocentric Attitude. A **geocentric** manager *appreciates cultural differences but has an international viewpoint.* As a compromise between the two extremes of ethnocentrism and polycentrism, a geocentric manager attempts to balance the needs of the local business environment with the global strategy and objectives of the firm. The geocentric MNC has a globally integrated business philosophy and attempts to integrate its operations around the world. It selects and assigns people to jobs based on professional qualifications rather than cultural background. It treats people as equals regardless of their national identity. In fact, in its most extreme form, the geocentric firm does not even recognize international divisions. Nothing is considered as foreign. The firm feels that it is dealing with one global market. Like the ethnocentric firm, it seeks to develop one corporate culture, strategy, and systems of operation. However, it takes on a global character and not just the character of one country. The drawbacks of this approach are that there is still a tremendous amount of cultural diversity and barriers to cultural integration. The world is not yet homogenized. Globally competitive organizations of the future may be more geocentric. However, it is likely that the MNC will have to adopt a mixture of these attitudes to fit its unique situation, depending on its mission and strategy.

Attitude toward Global Cooperation

MNCs headquartered around the world are starting to play by a new set of economic rules. They are rethinking their attitudes toward global cooperation among companies within an industry, and among industries and governments around the world. To function effectively in diverse business environments requires special efforts to work with local suppliers through alliances. For example, when Chrysler decided to start selling Jeep Cherokees in Japan, it struck an alliance with Honda Motor Company to distribute Jeeps. To appeal to the Japanese market, the company equipped these models with right-hand steering wheels to accommodate the Japanese who drive on the left side of the road, and performed special quality checks to meet the needs of discerning Japanese consumers. By working together with its partner Honda, the company, which in 1993 expected to sell about 1,000 Jeeps in Japan, ended up selling around 2,500, and there was a long list of customers waiting to take delivery.[25] In addition we saw how GE and Anheuser-Busch are setting up alliances with local companies to help gain footholds in different international markets.

THINKING CRITICALLY

1. Which of the four managerial attitudes discussed above do you think are most relevant for managing a diverse workforce in today's organization?
2. Which of the four managerial perspectives (ethnocentric, polycentric, regiocentric, or geocentric) do you think will be more effective in the global business environment described in this chapter? Explain your answer.

EUROPEAN ECONOMIC UNITY . . . AND DIVERSITY[26]

With the free flow of goods and services among all nations of the European Community, you might think it is easier to standardize products for the entire continent. Why should companies develop different brands and formulations for soap or mayonnaise for different countries now that they have easy access to the entire continent? The answer to this question reminds us that while we can legally eliminate economic restrictions among countries, cultural differences remain and may even be reinforced.

Companies selling across Europe have found that customers do not consider themselves "European," but Spanish, Italian, French, etc., each with their own particular tastes and expectations. While satellite networks like CNN, Sky TV, and MTV will help to break down differences among citizens of different countries, this is not going to happen soon. Indeed, the new unity seems to bring out a need for people in member countries to express their particular style of nationalism.

Companies that want to succeed in Europe need to create products and promotions aimed at consumers in each country. For example, Kraft General Foods has different versions of Philadelphia brand cream cheese for Germany (pear flavored) and Spain (salmon flavored). Managers of Allen Bradley, a seller of industrial automation equipment, found that in selling their products in different countries they must take very different approaches with their customers. In Germany, the sales emphasis must be on engineering, and the German purchaser expects to be told all about the engineering excellence that went into a product's development. In Italy and France, there is less concern with engineering and more with the product's ability to solve their problem. They are more interested in results than in how the product works. Allen Bradley has also found that training needs differ from country to country. For example, some prefer one-on-one sessions while others prefer group training. In each case the company adapts its approach to the customer.

There are products that are universally accepted across Europe and the world for that matter. Coca-Cola is one, and its advertising message remains pretty much the same from country to country. And the push is on by other companies to standardize across borders. Mars, for example, has changed the name of the French candy Bonitos to M&Ms, which is what it is called everywhere else. They also changed the name of their British candy bar Marathon to Snickers, its standard name in all other markets. Such consolidation of brands across international markets requires careful planning and promotion. And while the long-term trend is in this direction, there still remains a great deal of difference among European customers that managers from all countries must be sensitive to.

A LOOK AT

THE GLOBAL ENVIRONMENT

INTERNATIONAL MANAGEMENT AND TOTAL QUALITY MANAGEMENT

According to expert W.F. Cascio, one-third of the profits and one-sixth of the jobs in U.S. corporations are directly or indirectly related to international business. Further, more than 100,000 U.S. companies do business overseas, and there are more than 3,500 multinational corporations.[27] And this is where the growth is for many different companies. To compete in this changing, diverse, and intensely competitive market requires management excellence. Those who lead and execute business strategy have little room for error.

MAKING CHANGES TO TURN EURO DISNEY AROUND[28]

The question for Disney has been how to change the way the park is managed to make it more efficient and effective at delivering quality and value to Europe's vacationers. Starting in 1994, the company initiated "Challenge 94" with the goal of turning Euro Disney into a less expensive resort. The focus of all the changes has been to improve its processes by which "cast members" (employees) serve the park's guests (customers). These changes include more training for employees, employee-initiated improvement programs, and several other changes all designed to bring the costs of their offering into line with what customers are willing to pay.

Though investors in the $3 billion park have shouldered most of the loss, it is very important that these changes work and that Disney finds ways to refinance the park's debt. Among other things, there are 9,000 full-time employees whose jobs would be at risk if the park were to close. It seems clear that the company understands its problems and its obligations to all its stakeholders—investors, the French Government, employees, and customers and that it is making the right changes to turn things around. However, it is also clear that even a company as well-regarded and profitable as Disney needs to understand its mission and the environment when entering the international market. One Disney executive is quoted as saying, "We were arrogant. It was like we're building the Taj Mahal, and people will come—on our terms." Clearly Disney, like many other companies, has discovered that this is not the case.

Total Quality Management, with its focus on understanding customer needs and aligning organizational resources to meet these needs, keeps managers asking the right questions about how to do this. The principles and management actions we reviewed in Chapter 3 are directly relevant to an organization's success in the global marketplace. They remind managers that they must (1) adapt to different markets and customer needs, (2) figure out the best way to enter the market, be that by exports, licensing, or various forms of investment, and (3) get people working together to continuously improve the value of their offerings to remain competitive. The many examples we have cited throughout this chapter show how managers with a "quality consciousness" should and are approaching the challenge of international management. These managers understand that practicing quality principles is not an end but a means to survival in a completely unforgiving global economy.

? **THINKING CRITICALLY**

1. If you were a manager contemplating international opportunities for your firm, how would the principles of TQM help you figure out what to do to take advantage of these opportunities?

SUMMARY

The International Manager
- International management involves the efficient and effective marshalling of organizational resources to deliver goods and services to customers in other nations.
- Even managers of firms that only do business in the U.S. need to be aware of international management issues as their competitors may come from abroad or they may be influenced by international business events, such as currency fluctuations.

International Trade
- The law of comparative advantage suggests that it is to the advantage of all for various types of products and services to be created by those who do it best.
- International trade is conducted through importing and exporting among countries what each produces best and for the lowest cost.
- International trade agreements have created groups of trading partners, such as the European Community, and the North American Free Trade Agreement (NAFTA).

International Investment
- Multinational corporations (MNCs) are increasingly going beyond just import/export trading to reach global markets by investing in international operations.
- Through international investment managers gain access to resources, increase sales volume, reduce costs of exporting, and take advantage of financial conditions.
- The forms of international investment vary in the extent of managerial involvement and control by the MNC, and include licensing, franchising, joint ventures/strategic alliances, and fully owned subsidiaries.

The Global Business Environment
- In order to succeed in this new global economy, managers need to understand the global business environment—which sets the context for their operation and provides their inputs and accepts their outputs.
- Four important dimensions of this environment include the political/legal, economic, technological, and social dimensions. Each of these dimensions impacts on how managers do business in a particular country.

International Management Challenges
- Managers need to develop a global perspective with appropriate attitudes toward cultural differences and global cooperation.

International Management and Total Quality Management
- TQM, with its focus on developing and improving the efficiency of business

processes to deliver quality goods and services to customers, provides managers with the insights and guidelines necessary to survive and prosper in the international marketplace.

KEY TERMS

Business environment 125	Joint venture/strategic alliance 123
Culture 133	Law of comparative advantage 115
Domestic firms 114	Licensing 122
Ethnocentric 138	Multinational corporation (MNC) 117
Exporting 113	Political stability 127
Franchise 123	Polycentric 139
Fully-owned subsidiary 124	Quota 128
Geocentric 140	Tariff 120
International management 112	

REVIEW QUESTIONS

1. Why do managers need to be concerned with international management issues?
2. What is a primary reason for a manager to begin exporting goods to other countries?
3. What are the primary reasons that managers pursue international investment?
4. What forms does international investment typically take? How would the principles of TQM help a manager decide among these forms?
5. What are the four major dimensions of the global business environment and how are these interrelated?
6. Why is it so important for a manager to understand the cultural dimension when entering a market in another country?
7. What are the three attitudes a manager might take toward cultural differences in making management decisions? Explain the characteristics of each attitude.
8. How does TQM help managers ask the right questions as they move their companies into international markets?

EXPERIENTIAL EXERCISES

1. Go to the library and get a recent copy (no more than 3 months old) of a business magazine, such as *Business Week, Fortune, Inc.,* or *The Wall Street Journal,* and find a story on a multinational corporation that has recently launched (or is currently launching) an international investment. Describe the company's strategy (purpose and objectives) for its international investment. Describe the aspects of the international business environment that its managers seem to have already addressed. Describe those aspects that were not mentioned (or seem to have been ignored), but which might be crucial to the

MNCs success. What are the potentially positive and negative impacts that the MNC will have on its host country? How would you suggest the MNC deal with the negative impacts?

2. Divide the class into homogeneous groups based upon combinations of ethnicity, gender, religious affiliation, or other cultural factors. (For example, one group might be African-American, female, Protestants). Have each group describe itself in terms of values, beliefs, and cultural practices which might influence the way the group members conduct themselves at work. Have each group list the potential conflicts that they may encounter with other groups in the class. Then discuss solutions for overcoming these conflicts.

CASE ANALYSIS AND APPLICATION
Going International: A Software Company Learns the Hard Way[29]

Acme Corporation is a specialty software company now headquartered in California's Silicon Valley, and its products are doing quite well in the U.S., Europe, and Japan. However, the company's first attempt at moving into global markets was anything but smooth. In 1987, when Acme was barely four years old, Ian Greene, the company's founder, received a phone call from Ken Ahara in Japan, who told him Ahara's company wanted to work with Acme to distribute its products in Japan. Ahara invited Greene to Tokyo to talk about a deal. Greene went, and when he arrived he discovered that Ahara had already translated Acme brochures into Japanese and had even lined up potential customers like Mitsubishi and Matsushita.

Ahara ran a company he called SofTouch, and he talked Greene into giving his company an exclusive distributorship for Acme products. He did this for what he thought were two good reasons: nobody from the home office had to be sent over, and (2) the company could always get rid of a distributor. Initially everything went well, and SofTouch was contributing significant revenues to Acme. However, that did not last. Customers were buying evaluation units but were hesitant to purchase more from a company without a real presence in Japan.

Ahara proposed that his company, SofTouch, and Acme set up a joint venture in Japan with two other large corporate partners so Acme could better serve the Japanese market. These two large partners would invest $150,000 in the venture. Greene saw this as a good deal since setting up the company brought in cash he hadn't expected to see. It seemed like a win-win situation for all. However, the new company's charter granted each party veto rights, which paralyzed decision making when there was any disagreement.

Ahara set himself up as CEO of the new venture as well as SofTouch. What happened then was that most of the sales of Acme in Japan were to SofTouch, for resale to other customers. Sensing a problem with depending on one customer, Greene got Ahara and the other two partners to grant Acme 51% control of the joint venture and the ability to make decisions. Greene tried to run the business from the U.S., but Ahara was still in place at both Acme Japan and SofTouch. Four years into the venture, Greene sent an American to Tokyo to keep an eye on the place. This person soon discovered that SofTouch was in fiscal trouble and unable to pay for the products it had ordered and received from Acme.

About this time, Greene received a call from another Japanese software reseller, Modern Technologies, which was considering acquiring the assets of

SofTouch. They explained that SofTouch was deeply in debt and did not have the funds to pay them off. Modern Technologies wanted to know what Greene thought about this situation. What Greene thought was that he needed to collect the $900,000 owed the company by SofTouch and to do it quickly.

In the meantime, Modern Technologies found that SofTouch was in even worse shape than it thought, and decided not to go through with the acquisition. SofTouch also informed Greene that it was unable to pay its debt to Acme. Subsequently, Ahara and SofTouch were drummed out of the Acme Japanese joint venture. Acme then ran into an interesting Japanese law. A company cannot write off a bad debt unless the debtor goes bankrupt. SofTouch did not declare bankruptcy. So this meant that Acme simply lost all this money and could not write if off against its tax liability.

When all was said and done, Acme had lost its $900,000 plus $200,000 in legal fees. In 1992, Modern Technologies joined up with the Acme joint venture and purchased $4 million worth of its products to sell to its customers. Acme was finally on its feet in the Japanese market, but it didn't get there easily. Greene now reflects, "I look back and wonder how I could have done such idiotic things. But going international is something you learn by doing, so you might as well do it when you're small and mistakes are less costly."

Discussion Questions

1. What aspects of the Japanese business environment did Greene not know enough about in this case?
2. Why do you think the distributorship arrangement and subsequent joint venture with Ahara did not work out?

VIDEO CASE: COMBINING QUALITY MANAGEMENT AND SOCIAL RESPONSIBILITY
Merck and Company, Inc.

This Business Enterprise Trust Award recognizes a significant act of social conscience and business leadership: Merck & Co.'s open-ended commitment to donate a new wonder drug to millions of people in the Third World who desperately need but cannot afford it. Merck spent years developing the drug, despite its dismal commercial prospects, and then devised an ambitious system to distribute and administer it safely in remote villages throughout the Third World.

It is estimated that 18 million people in Africa and parts of Latin America and the Middle East carry parasitic worms that cause the painful, debilitating disease of onchocerciasis, commonly known as river blindness. Hordes of microfilariae swarm through the victims' skin and eyes, causing extremely severe itching, skin decay, lesions in the eyes, and eventual blindness. Some 350,000 of those afflicted are currently blind.

The first sign that there might be a preventive drug treatment for this ancient disease came in the late 1970s, when Merck researcher Will Campbell suggested that the river blindness parasite could be neutralized by a Merck veterinary drug, ivermectin. From the start, Merck realized that the potential commercial market for a treatment was dubious, given the poverty of the disease's victims. Nonetheless, the company, led by Dr. P. Roy Vagelos, the head of Merck's research division and now Chairman and CEO, gave the go-ahead for further research. By 1985, human clinical tests demonstrated that the drug, later named Mectizan, was safe for human use and remarkably effective at just a single dose per year. The French government approved Mectizan for use against onchocerciasis in October 1987.

Neither host governments nor international health organizations, however, could shoulder the costs of producing Mectizan. Furthermore, simply giving the drug away was not a solution because no distribution system existed to reach the millions of potential victims in isolated rural areas. Pressed by the realization that any delay would cost thousands of lives, Merck decided not only to donate an unlimited supply of Mectizan to the estimated 18 million at-risk individuals, but to help create a reliable international apparatus for distributing the drug.

Merck convened a five-member expert committee of world-class scientists and health officials to devise medical protocols for the safe distribution, record keeping and monitoring of Mectizan. The company has also played a major role in informing governments of the drug's existence and value, assigning a full-time "product manager" to oversee distribution, and creating a medical liaison with recipient African nations. Thanks to Merck's ongoing commitment, as of year-end 1993, over seven million persons have been treated in on-going programs in 34 countries.

Video Case Questions

1. Explain how Merck might have dealt with each dimension of the global business environment in providing the drug Mectizan to the people who needed it.
2. Describe Merck's attitude toward global cooperation in terms of the concepts presented in this chapter.

5. SOCIAL RESPONSIBILITY AND ETHICS

JOHNSON & JOHNSON'S TYLENOL NIGHTMARE

Johnson & Johnson was shaken by a health-care producer's nightmare in October 1982 when its products were apparently killing people. Seven people had died in Chicago after taking Extra-Strength Tylenol capsules to which lethal amounts of cyanide had been added. The company acted immediately and without hesitation. Within hours Johnson & Johnson announced a recall of an entire batch, 93,400 bottles of Extra-Strength Tylenol, despite the fact that tests indicated the poisoning probably did not occur during manufacturing. Then Johnson & Johnson warned physicians, hospitals, and wholesalers about the problem through nearly half a million Mailgrams. The company flew scientists and security people to Chicago to assist with the investigation. It even set up a laboratory with 30 chemists to help analyze samples of Extra-Strength Tylenol. Five hundred salespersons were devoted to recalling shipments of Tylenol. That evening Johnson & Johnson offered a $100,000 reward for information that would lead to the arrest and conviction of the person responsible for the deaths. The company stopped all advertising of Tylenol. When a death was traced to a capsule from another batch, in another manufacturing plant, Johnson & Johnson expanded the recall to include a batch of 171,000 bottles. When a strychnine-laced Tylenol capsule nearly killed a man in Oroville, California, Johnson & Johnson recalled all Tylenol capsules, regular and extra strength, and completely halted production. Johnson & Johnson managers did what was in the best interest of the public.

Tylenol accounted for 7 percent of Johnson & Johnson's 1981 sales of $5.4 billion and 17 percent of its $467.6 million in profits. In a similar situation, managers in other companies may have been tempted to keep the production running, minimize the publicity, and deny responsibility for the poisoning. Instead, Johnson & Johnson did everything it could to avoid more deaths. Johnson & Johnson Chairman James E. Burke said, "It's important that we demonstrate that we've taken every single step possible to protect the public, and that there's simply nothing else we can do."[1]

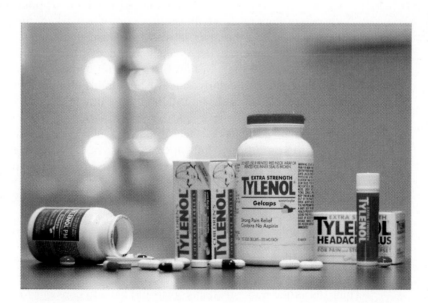

The authors thank the Ethics Resource Center in Washington, D.C., and particularly Jason Lunday, Senior Consultant, for contributing ideas, material, and advice for developing this chapter.

THE IMPORTANCE OF SOCIAL RESPONSIBILITY AND BUSINESS ETHICS

The Tylenol episode dramatically illustrates the effect of managerial decisions on the society in which a company operates and of which it is a part. Most managerial decisions are not nearly as sensational nor as closely watched as the Johnson & Johnson Tylenol incident. But each day, managers make decisions that affect the lives of people the manager will never see.

Managers face many difficult situations, and figuring out the right way to handle these is not always easy. Some situations can be quite vexing. Consider these examples.[2]

1. A large corporation has negotiated to purchase stock and take over a smaller one. In merging the two companies, top managers discover that many positions in one company are duplicated in the other. Is it right to fire or demote managers holding these duplicate positions when many of them have faithfully served their respective companies for years?
2. A manufacturer that grew rapidly in an expanding market was helped greatly during that growth by wholesale distributors that introduced its products to retail stores. Now the market is large enough to warrant direct distribution from the factory to the store in truckloads, and the market is competitive enough to make the cost savings from direct distribution very meaningful. Is it proper to change distribution channels?
3. A paper company in northern Maine can generate power and reduce its energy costs by building a large dam on land that it owns. However, the dam will block a river that canoeists and fishermen have used for years. Is it fair to ruin recreational opportunities for others to reduce energy costs?
4. A young staff assistant who has been working for a company for about six months discovers that it is common practice there to pour used solvents and cleaning solutions down the storm drain. When asked, the assistant's manager explained that the practice was legal in small amounts. The assistant does not think that the practice is legal, and does not think the amounts are that small. However, the assistant fears getting involved in a controversy at this career stage, particularly since it took nine months to find this job. Is it acceptable for the assistant to ignore the dumping?

Once a manager makes a decision about such issues, others may judge it as right or wrong, proper or improper, good or bad, acceptable or unacceptable. People judge such managerial decisions based on their own moral standards. How do managers make sure they do what is right, and avoid what is wrong? The answer to these questions is not obvious because there are no absolute standards on which to judge decisions.

Moral standards vary because people's values vary. These differences depend on family background, cultural heritage, religious affiliations, educational experiences, and personal life experiences. People vary in what they feel are appropriate tradeoffs between the economic benefits of a decision and social obligations.[3] Think about the tradeoffs that you would have to consider to answer the following questions:

- Should business only have to abide by the letter of the law? If the law does not cover questionable practices, does that make doing them OK?

- Should companies make products that could be harmful to consumers (tobacco, silicon implants, alcohol)?

- Should businesses refrain from laying off loyal employees? If not, to what extent should they go to make the layoffs easy on the employees?

- Should companies be expected to give a certain amount of their profits to charitable causes?

- To what extent should companies be responsible for the practices of their suppliers?

- To what extent should companies abide by environmental law or seek to exceed environmental legislation?

- Should business be used to further social causes such as AIDS education, banning smoking in the workplace, diversity education, and treatment for drug or alcohol abuse?

To answer questions like these, managers are increasingly seeking to learn more about the ideas of social responsibility and ethics. The terms social responsibility and ethics are often used interchangeably to mean doing what is right, good, or acceptable, and not doing what is wrong, bad, or unacceptable. Although the concepts do overlap, each term has a distinct meaning. **Social responsibility** is *the obligation a business assumes to increase its positive effect and reduce its negative effect on society as a whole.* The term **ethics** as applied to business is used in two ways to refer to: 1) *the moral principles and standards that guide behavior in the world of business,* and 2) *the individual actions of doing right in business when there is pressure to do otherwise.*

The two concepts of social responsibility and ethics both have to do with "goodness" or "morality." However, we can differentiate in terms of breadth. Ethics in business is a narrower concept that applies to *the morality of an individual's decisions and behaviors and ideas surrounding the making of decisions between right and wrong.* Social responsibility is a broader concept that applies to the *impact of an organization on society, beyond just doing what is morally "right."* Social responsibility is also frequently used to imply "going beyond the call of duty," or contributing to society more than just through the creation of jobs, profits, and valuable goods and services. For example, many business organizations engage in socially responsible acts of philanthropy by donating time or money to social causes, such as improving our educational systems, assisting impoverished people, or rebuilding communities in the wake of natural disasters.

The two concepts overlap since organizations are composed of employees who make decisions and adopt particular courses of action. An organization does not act by itself. It has no life without the people who run it. The combination of many individual decisions in an organization determines the impact that organization has on society. Therefore, business ethics help individuals take actions that ensure that an organization is socially responsible. A good place to start thinking about business ethics is to look at some of the moral principles that are used to understand how people make ethical decisions.

Social responsibility The obligation a business assumes to increase its positive effect and reduce its negative effect on society as a whole.

Business ethics The moral principles and standards that guide behavior in the world of business.

❓ THINKING CRITICALLY

1. Why do you think decisions involving ethical dilemmas are rarely black and white?
2. Evaluate the merit of the following statement: "Every decision that a manager makes involves social responsibility and/or ethics." Is it true? Why? What does it mean for managing successfully?

THE MORAL PRINCIPLES OF BUSINESS ETHICS

There are many moral principles that people might use to guide their decisions. The one commonality that seems to override all differences is the belief that the members of a society bear some responsibility for the well-being of other members. For most of us, this assertion makes sense and "feels" right. From a systems point of view, we can rationalize it further by noting that systems deal with relationships and processes. As a member of a system, it is logical to suggest that to look out for oneself means to look out for one's relationships, both within the organization and, from an organizational perspective, within the larger society of which the organization itself is a part.

This idea is captured in the Bible's Golden Rule: "Do unto others as you would have them do unto you." We usually think of this as an idealistic statement that we should try to achieve. However, there is another way to consider it if, in fact, we are all members of a system where relationships and interdependencies are primary defining characteristics. This other way is to assert that the Golden Rule simply reminds that we do, whether we are aware of it or not, treat others as we would like to be treated, be that for good or ill. What we do to others provides them with the information they need to guide their relationship with us in the future. If businesspeople cheat customers, they are saying that their relationship with their customers is based on cheating. This is the information that customers will need to deal with these businesspeople in the future. In other words, a person who cheats invites cheating in return. Conversely, people who go out of their way to be fair are likewise inviting fairness in return. Another way of saying this is that we teach others how we wish to be treated by how we treat them. The Golden Rule simply captures this premise in a more poetic tone. All this does not mean that it is easy or obvious to figure out what is the fair or right way to interrelate with others. However, it does a provide a sound rationale for taking ethical behavior very seriously. This is because behaving ethically has positive personal and business consequences.

Below, we discuss three principles or approaches that can help us gain a better sense of what is fair and what is ethical. These include the Utilitarian, Moral Rights, and Justice approaches. Each approach has strengths and weaknesses. In managing the organization as a system, managers can successfully combine these ideas to help them make better ethical decisions.

Utilitarian Approach

Utilitarian approach An approach that suggests managers should strive to provide the greatest degree of benefits (or utility) for the largest number of people for the least costs.

Grounded in the philosophies of Jeremy Bentham and J.S. Mill, the **utilitarian approach** suggests that *managers should strive to provide the greatest degree of benefits (or utility) for the largest number of people for the least costs.* Another way of saying this is that we must recognize and weigh the costs versus the benefits of our actions. The utilitarian approach recognizes that some harm or costs will always result from taking any particular action. However, these costs are acceptable as long as we seek to minimize them and deliver the greatest good for the most people, not just a privileged few.

Applying the utilitarian approach can be difficult because it is difficult for a manager to anticipate and compute benefits and costs. To overcome this limitation, managers may institute certain rules to embody the utilitarian approach. These rules are based on experience that costs of breaking such rules are nearly always greater than the benefits, even if that is not obvious at the time. For example, experience tells us that the rules "never tell a lie" and "always honor a contract" will help managers accomplish the greatest good for the greatest number and at the lowest cost if everyone acts in accordance with such rules.

Another potential problem with utilitarianism is that it can encourage people to focus on the potential benefits to themselves and their companies and assume that a cost, even if it means exploiting another person, is worth those benefits. This is another way of stating that the ends justify the means. Although we do occasionally exploit individuals for the good of society (e.g., draft young men and send them to die in war), we generally do not feel that it is right to take advantage of others just for the sake of profit or pleasure for a few people. To help managers decide where to draw the line on utilitarian approach, they should consider an approach that emphasizes the moral rights of individuals.

Moral Rights Approach

The **moral rights approach** emphasizes *the importance of preserving an* individual's *rights and liberties*. Individuals are given certain rights by the U.S. Constitution, Bill of Rights, and federal laws. Some of these rights are listed below.

Moral rights approach
An approach that emphasizes the importance of preserving an *individual's* rights and liberties.

1. Right to Life and Safety—to not have our lives and safety unknowingly endangered.
2. Right to Freedom of Conscience—to refuse to carry out orders that contradict our moral or religious beliefs.
3. Right to Free Consent—to be treated as we knowingly and freely consent to be treated.
4. Right to Privacy—to control access to and use of information about our private lives.
5. Right to Truthfulness—to not be intentionally deceived about matters about which we have a right to know.
6. Right to Free Speech—to speak openly and truthfully about the ethics or legality of the actions of others.
7. Right to Due Process—to an impartial hearing and fair treatment when accused.
8. Right to Own Private Property—to acquire, own, use and dispose of property.

Under the moral rights approach, even if a decision accomplishes the greatest good for the greatest number of people, it is unethical if it denies an individual any of these rights. The shortcoming of the moral rights approach is that it can lead to self-serving behavior, particularly if people act as though they have the right to do anything they want. It can also lead to gridlock when people's rights stand in the way of progress for society. Cooperative social actions require people to suppress their own desires at times so as to reach a mutually acceptable decision. Again, we may note that thinking of organizations and societies in terms of systems helps us think about the balance between individual and societal rights.

Justice Approach

Justice approach An approach that emphasizes the equitable treatment of people and relies on concepts of equity, fairness, and impartiality.

Procedural justice An approach that requires managers to clearly state and consistently administer the rules and established procedures of the organization, and not bend the rules to serve their own interests or to show favoritism.

Distributive justice An approach that requires managers not be arbitrary and use only relevant characteristics or evidence in deciding how to treat people.

The **justice approach** emphasizes *the equitable treatment of people and relies on concepts of equity, fairness, and impartiality*. The justice approach seeks to allocate resources and costs fairly.[4] **Procedural justice** requires that managers *clearly state and consistently administer the rules and established procedures of the organization, and not bend the rules to serve their own interest, or to show favoritism*. For example, disciplinary actions should be administered impartially. **Distributive justice** requires that managers *not be arbitrary and use only relevant characteristics or evidence to determine how to treat people*. Thus we should not judge people on such characteristics as race, gender, religious preference, or other irrelevant characteristics, but only on the actual facts of a situation. If people are similar in relevant characteristics, then they should be treated similarly, and if they are different in relevant characteristics, then they should be treated similarly in proportion to those differences. For example, people who vary in job skill should be paid differently, but there should not be differences in pay based on race or gender.

The justice approach embodies the democratic principle and protects the interest of those who might otherwise lack power. However, there are shortcomings. In general, it does not address the issue of individual rights, which may be denied some people in the interest of justice. It can also create a sense of entitlement and reduce risk taking, which may reduce overall benefits and increase costs to society. For example, part of the reason for the number of law suits in this country stems from different people feeling they were treated unjustly. Sometimes they are correct, and sometimes they are not.

Combining the Approaches

Ethical relativism A suggestion that the definition of what is right and wrong varies relative to cultural or regional standards.

Moral standards vary from one person to another, from one group of people to another, and from one country to another. Furthermore, these standards change over time. Managers face a world wherein **ethical relativism** seems to be the rule, that is, *the definition of what is right and wrong varies relative to cultural or regional standards*. Under these circumstances, managers will find it increasingly difficult to consistently apply any single set of moral principles to all groups in all cultures at all times. In other words, what is moral or just or of utility to one group will not be to another.

We have seen that each of these principles has influenced ethics in American society. As a manager, which do you use? Each seems equally plausible, yet also incomplete in some way. There is no single system of ethics that always applies. This means managers should combine the approaches so that the weaknesses in one approach are compensated by another approach. It may help to think through the consequences of your actions in terms of each approach. Does the decision result in greater benefits than costs for society, without inordinate costs to any minority group, or does the decision just serve an elite group? Does the decision deny any individuals their moral rights? Does the decision treat people fairly and give them the justice they deserve? Answers to these questions will not always ensure that the decision will be ethical in everyone's eyes. There will be conflicts and difficult choices. But at least the manager will make an informed and thoughtful decision. And if it does not work as expected, then he or she can learn from the experience to do better next time.

❓ THINKING CRITICALLY

1. Do you agree that the Golden Rule helps us to understand that we always treat others as we would have them treat us, even when we treat them poorly? Why or why not? What is the relationship of the Golden Rule to the systems view of organizations and society?
2. You have received a piece of proprietary information from a friend at a competitive company that will be useful to your organization. Make an argument for using or not using this information to your company's benefit based on the utilitarian, moral rights, and justice approaches to ethics.

MODERN BUSINESS ETHICS

While it has a rich history, business ethics has only recently emerged as a critical issue and it has evolved quickly in the last few decades.[5] Before 1960 ethical issues largely centered around workers' rights and wages. However, this changed as Americans joined "social causes" in the 1960s. For example, John F. Kennedy laid the foundation for the consumer rights movement and set the tone for the decade in 1962 when he delivered a "Special Message on Protecting the Consumer Interest." Kennedy advocated four basic consumer rights: the right to safety, the right to be informed, the right to choose, and the right to be heard.

The consumer movement shifted into high gear with the publication of Ralph Nader's 1965 book, *Unsafe At Any Speed.* Nader criticized the automobile industry, particularly General Motors, for putting profit and style ahead of lives and safety. Nader's lobbying eventually led to legislation that required automobile makers to equip cars with safety belts, padded dashboards, stronger door latches, head restraints, shatter-proof windshields, and collapsible steering columns. This concern with safety continues today with airbags and more rigid body construction.

In the 1970s, business ethics emerged as a field of study, as businesses became more concerned about public image, and social demands grew. Theologians, religious thinkers, philosophers, and businesspeople joined together at conferences to discuss issues such as bribery, deceptive advertising, price collusion, product safety, and environmental impact. Universities and foundations established centers to study business ethics. Academic researchers began to identify ethics issues and describe courses of action.

By the 1980s academics and practitioners acknowledged business ethics as a legitimate field of study, and the field flourished. Business ethics organizations started providing their growing membership with publications, courses, conferences, and seminars. And businesses such as General Electric, The Chase Manhattan Corporation, and General Motors formally established policies and committees to institutionalize business ethics. Business ethics courses enrolled thousands of college students. Exhibit 5-1 lists the forty ethical issues most frequently discussed in the ethics education programs of eighty-six accredited business schools.

The State of Business Ethics

All this attention on business ethics seems to have arrived just in the nick of time, since unethical behavior appears to be rampant in American society. The corporate world is awash with stories of corruption, graft, immoral behavior, and theft. The mass media report daily on such unethical activities in government, business, sports, religion, science, and medicine. Nightly news shows feature scandals related to alleged bribes, deceptive communications, and ecological disasters. A national survey found that more than 60 percent of senior business executives believe that people are at least occasionally unethical in their business activities.[6] Consider a sampling of several types of unethical activities:

Lack of management supervision:
- Salomon Bros., a big investment bank and brokerage, was found guilty of purchasing a larger percentage of certain treasury auction inventories than was permitted by regulation. The company's four top officers eventually left the company over the affair.
- A number of large brokerage houses in New York paid fines and/or had employees who went to jail after insider trading charges were filed. Many firms beefed up supervisory systems designed to catch insider trading.

EXHIBIT 5-1
This list contains the 40 most frequently discussed ethical issues in the undergraduate curricula of 86 accredited business schools. Issues are listed in decreasing order of frequency.

EXHIBIT 5-1 40 Business Ethics Issues

1. Honesty	22. Accuracy of books, records
2. Conflicts of interest	23. Privacy of employee records
3. Marketing/advertising issues	24. Political activities and contributions
4. Environmental isuues	25. Misuse of company assets
5. Discrimination by race, age, or sex	26. Corporate governance issues
6. Product liability and safety	27. Ethical theory
7. Codes of ethics and self-governance	28. Ethics in negotiation
8. Relations with customers	29. Relations with local communities
9. Bribery	30. Plant closing and layoffs
10. Rights of and responsibilities to shareholders	31. Employee discipline
11. Whistleblowing	32. Use of others' proprietary information
12. Kickbacks	33. Relations with U.S. Government representatives
13. Insider trading	
14. Antitrust issues	34. Relations with competitors
15. Issues facing multinationals	35. Employee benefits
16. Relations with foreign governments	36. Mergers and acquisition
17. Ethical foundations of capitalism	37. Drug and alcohol abuse
18. Workplace health and safety	38. Drug and alcohol testing
19. Managing an ethical environment	39. Intelligence gathering
20. Relations with suppliers and subcontractors	40. Leverage buyouts
21. Use of company proprietary information	

Source: Adapted from a report prepared by Lynn Sharp Paine, *Ethics Education in American Business Schools,* (Washington, DC: Ethics Resource Center, Inc., 1988), p.17.

- Prudential and Metropolitan Life insurance companies made headlines when their insurance agents were accused of selling insurance products disguised as other types of products.

Pattern of ignoring early company research as to possible dangers:
- Dow Corning had early research that silicon implants might pose a health risk to women, but they ignored the data.
- Johns Manville had records of early research that suggested the asbestos its workers were exposed to could be hazardous to their health.
- Ford investigated putting an inexpensive gas tank shield in its cars to prevent the tank from catching fire in the event of a rear-end collision, but a cost-benefit analysis convinced the company not to install the shield.

Corporate under-reaction to crisis:
- Exxon was criticized for its slow reaction to the Exxon *Valdez* oil spill, when faster action might have led to a better cleanup effort.
- During the wake of publicized product recalls, Gerber decided not to implement a substantial recall when glass shards were found it its baby food containers.
- A gas leak killed approximately 2,000 citizens in Bhopal, India, and Union Carbide at first rejected liability for hospitalization of the town's other citizens because it only owned 51% of the venture.

Faulty incentive systems:
- Sears Auto Center employees were accused of selling unneeded parts and services to customers to help make required quotas.
- Some financial houses have been charged with structuring incentive systems that led traders to create fictitious trades in order to award themselves higher bonuses.

If we look beyond the stories, we can see that questionable practices and misconduct are not simply the actions of one or two individuals. They often exist because corporate structures and strategies are poorly planned, break down, do not anticipate changes in the business environment, or lack ethical leadership. In essence, corporations—sometimes inadvertently, sometimes intentionally—create environments that foster unethical behaviors. They are not just "accidental." While one person may have "pulled the trigger," the organization's culture may have "loaded the weapon, pointed it, and given the order to fire." This is where business ethics and Total Quality Management (TQM) intersect. TQM helps managers improve the organizational culture and processes that influence managerial decision making. The systems view helps managers perceive the interconnections among all elements of the organization.

Public Awareness

The general public is more aware of socially irresponsible and unethical business practices today than ever before. But that does not necessarily mean there is more unethical behavior than there used to be. We could simply be more interested in it and more educated to detect it. The mass media seem to thrive on such controversial subjects. The public expects captivating stories of intrigue and deception, and news reporters fervently uncover dirt in all segments of society. The public has come to feel entitled to know about all of the wrongdoings of our leaders and managers.

The growing interest in social responsibility and ethics is good news for society. To deal with possible legal and ethical transgressions, more people must be aware of and work at preventing bad deeds that detract from society. On a more positive note, people also need to learn to initiate and expect good deeds that contribute to society. In simple terms, social responsibility and ethics boil down to reducing bad deeds and increasing good deeds in society. The challenge for managers, however, is to define good and bad. One way to define good and bad is to look at what the law says.

? THINKING CRITICALLY

1. Are people more aware of business ethics because there is more unethical behavior now than in the past? Or does the amount of unethical behavior remain stable, while the growing interest in ethics causes increased awareness and detection of it? Explain your answer.
2. Do you think that business ethics will help managers better compete in global markets? Why or why not?
3. Do you think the managers making the decisions listed under the head "The State of Business Ethics" were intentionally behaving in an unethical manner? Why or why not? In answering the question, think about whether "ends justify the means" might have been at work in these companies. Finally, from a business perspective, why do the ends not always justify the means?

THE LEGAL PROCESS

Legal process The laws and procedures for enforcing laws and regulating behavior.

Businesses exist in society because they deliver economic benefits, first to customers, and then to employees and society in general. State governments formally sanction and establish corporations and legally empower them to make contracts, own property, and to exist after the founders die. Once established, government regulates and controls businesses through the **legal process,** or *the laws and procedures for enforcing laws and regulating behavior.* City, county, state, and federal regulatory agencies and legislatures establish laws and guidelines, and issue executive orders and regulations. These laws, regulations, and orders set minimum standards for ethical behavior. These standards are then enforced through the courts, which interpret the standards and judge whether business has met them.

Ethics and the Law

A former supreme court justice once said, "The law floats in a sea of ethics." Although ethics and the law are not always the same, we can consider the law as society's attempt to codify some basic ethical norms. Any time people or groups regularly violate a shared ethical norm of society, government leaders will likely propose legislation to prevent future violations. For instance, during the early part of the century, the government became aware of the dangers and abuses of large companies that virtually controlled business and consumer markets as monopolies, and it enacted the Sherman Antitrust Act to prohibit monopolies.

Perhaps a good way of looking at the interrelationship between ethics and the law is understanding law as being a floor and ethics being at the same level or above the floor. When tax time comes around, most people do not feel an ethical imperative to pay anything beyond what the law requires. Many companies do not feel an ethical obligation to set their minimum wage level at anything beyond the legal standard, though they will pay some workers more to attract employees with higher skills. However, on other issues we may feel a responsibility to stay way above the law, such as in the areas of environmental protection and worker safety.

Government imposes legal standards on business quite simply because it does not trust business to always do what is right and good for society. However, it is easy to see how the legal process can sometimes be complex and bewildering for managers. Operating within the many state and local jurisdictions of the United States, a company may have to deal with hundreds of regulatory bodies. Multinational firms may have to deal with thousands of them.

Congressional Legislation

The U.S. Constitution provides the foundation for the legal standards of all governing bodies in the United States and for the legal process itself. Among other things, the constitution gives government the power to regulate interstate and foreign commercial activities and to promote the general welfare. Laws and regulations controlling business must be consistent with the fundamental rights and obligations outlined in the Constitution. In general, the legal standards set at broader levels of government (like the federal government) provide the framework for local government standards (in states, counties, and townships). Some of the most important Congressional legislation that affects business managers includes laws that address competition, consumers, the environment, and equity and safety for workers:

- **Competition.** Laws help promote competition to ensure that businesses continuously improve quality and reduce costs of goods and services. The Sherman Antitrust Act of 1890 prohibits organizations from maintaining monopolies in their industry and the Celler-Kefauver Act of 1950 prohibits one corporation from controlling another to reduce competition. Other acts deregulated the railroad, airline, and trucking industries to promote more competition.

- **Consumers.** A number of laws protect consumers by making sure that businesses provide accurate information about products and services and follow standards for safety and health. The first consumer protection law, the Pure Food and Drug Act of 1906, was passed partly in response to a novel by Upton Sinclair, *The Jungle,* which described the atrocities and unsanitary conditions of the meat-packing industry in Chicago and outraged the public. This act prohibits adulteration and mislabeling of foods and drugs. Since 1906 several laws have been passed to regulate the labeling of hazardous substances, disclosure of lending/credit terms, product warranties, pricing, disclosure of leasing terms, and toy safety.

- **Investors.** The collapse of financial markets during the Great Depression led to laws that protect investors and keep people from engaging in overly speculative trading with other people's money. The Securities Act of 1933 and the Securities and Exchange Act of 1934 require companies selling their securities in interstate commerce to file reports with the Securities and Exchange Commission and distribute public reports about their financial condition. The SEC determines what facts should be disclosed and polices the disclosure of information to catch errors and guard against insider trading.

- **Environment.** While looking out for their own financial well-being, businesses may ignore their impact on the environment since the costs of environmental damage for society are difficult to compute. So, congress has enacted laws protecting the environment from toxic waste and air, water, and noise pollution. For example, the Clean Air Act of 1970 established air quality standards and requires states to establish plans to implement the standards. The Environmental Protection Agency (EPA) monitors compliance and enforces these environmental protection laws.

- **Equity.** Laws promoting equity in the workplace protect the rights of older people, minorities, women, and persons with disabilities to ensure they are treated fairly. For example, a significant law is Title VII of the Civil Rights Act of 1964. It specifically prohibits discrimination in employment on the basis of race, color, sex, national origin, or religion. The Equal Employment Opportunity Commission (EEOC) enforces the provisions of Title VII and assists businesses with the development of action plans to accomplish its objectives. Government agencies and the courts continue to wrestle with the controversial aspects of this legislation, such as hiring quotas, to balance the interests of employers and the people protected by civil rights laws.

- **Safety.** Laws also promote the safety of workers in the workplace. The Occupational Safety and Health Act (OSHA) of 1970 requires employers to provide safe and healthy working conditions for all workers. The Occupational Safety and Health Administration enforces the act through reporting requirements, regular surprise inspections, and sanctions.

Ethical Shortcomings of Laws

While the terms "legal" and "ethical" are not synonymous, laws make some ethics decisions easier for managers. Managers must simply refer to the law to get an answer about what is appropriate and what is inappropriate. In many cases, illegal behavior is also clearly unethical. For example, during the period 1979–82 senior managers at General Dynamics added $63 million of improper overhead expenses to defense contracts, including country club memberships and dog kennel fees.[7] Their behavior was clearly illegal and unethical.

In other cases, a business may obey the law but still behave unethically. For example, the McCarran-Ferguson Act of 1944 exempts the insurance industry from antitrust laws and allows them to join together and set insurance premiums at specific industry wide levels. Many would argue that, while legal, this exemption is unethical because it can impose hardships on some individuals and extra costs to society. As a result of this law, competition was neutralized, prices no longer reflected the costs of insurance protection, and many insurance companies reduced their coverage and increased premiums to improve their profits. For example, the Texas Easter Seal Society had its coverage reduced and its premiums raised by 1,000 percent over just a three year period.[8] The perceived injustice and unethical practices of the insurance industry has prompted many law suits.

THE WRECK OF THE EXXON VALDEZ[9]

ETHICS

In 1989 Exxon Corporation and Alyeska Pipeline Service Company—an eight-company consortium that operates the Trans-Alaska pipeline and the shipping terminal in Valdez, Alaska—mishandled a major oil spill from an Exxon tanker. The Exxon *Valdez* ran aground near Valdez, Alaska, on March 24, 1989, and spilled 240,000 barrels—eleven million gallons—of crude oil that eventually covered 2,600 square miles of Prince William Sound and the Gulf of Alaska. The Exxon spill was not the largest in history. However, it was one of the worst in terms of environmental damage and disruption of the oil industry. It jeopardized the future of oil production in environmentally sensitive areas of Alaska.

The spill spread rapidly within a few days, killing thousands of sea birds, sea otters, and other wildlife. It covered the coastline with oil and closed the fishing season in the sound. The enormity of the accident is surpassed only by the lack of preparation, mismanagement, incompetence, and negligence that contributed to the disaster. There is plenty of blame to go around. While the whole story is not told below, consider how the captain, Alyeska, and Exxon all contributed to the disaster.

With approval from the Coast Guard, Captain Joseph Hazelwood set the automatic pilot to steer the ship southward into the inbound shipping lane and instructed Third Mate Gregory Cousins to maintain the course until after the ice chunks from the glaciers were past. While the captain was asleep below deck, the ship ran aground on Bligh Reef. Mr. Cousins was either not told or he forgot that the automatic pilot was on when he tried to steer clear of the Reef. Mr. Cousins reportedly was not licensed to pilot the vessel through the treacherous waters of Prince William Sound. Immediately after the accident, Captain Hazelwood tried for an hour to rock the tanker free from the reef, while he ignored Coast Guard warnings that rocking the ship would make the oil spill worse and could even sink the ship. Tests showed Captain Hazelwood had a blood alcohol content of 0.061, which exceeded the 0.04 limit for operating a ship.

The Alyeska Pipeline Service was responsible through a formal agreement to react promptly to oil spills. It was supposed to encircle any serious oil spill with floating containment booms within 5 hours of the first report of the occurrence and to recover 50 percent of the spill within 48 hours. However, Alyeska did not show up until the following afternoon, and did not have the equipment, the crew, or the training necessary to do the job. Alyeska's barge was out of service and undergoing repairs. It did not have the required number of tug boats and oil skimmers. It lacked enough booms and other important equipment. Its emergency crew had been disbanded to cut costs. Alyeska was fully aware of these inadequacies since it had conducted "spill drills," monitored by the state. Recent drills were bungled and considered unsuccessful.

As part of the eight-company consortium, Exxon shared responsibility for Alyeska's lack of preparedness. Exxon more directly bore responsibility for the practices that led to the wreck. For example, it was common practice to turn over the command of oil tankers to unlicensed officers. Exxon officials also later admitted they knew of Hazelwood's alcohol problems, yet they still gave him command of Exxon's largest tanker. Exxon even supplied beer to tanker crewmen, despite its own policy against drinking on board its ships. Further, in 1972, the company owners of the Alyeska Pipeline Service promised Alaskan officials and fishermen that the tanker fleet operating out of Valdez would incorporate safety features such as double hulls and protective ballast tanks to minimize the possibility of spills. However, by 1977, Alyeska convinced the Coast Guard that the safety features were unnecessary and only a few ships in the Valdez fleet incorporated them. The Exxon *Valdez* did not do so. You can read more about the Exxon *Valdez* incident on page 180, Case in Point, Revisited.

In other situations, disobeying the law might seem to be ethical. A simple example would be running a stop light to get a patient in cardiac arrest to the hospital. The positive result of saving a life clearly outweighs the negative act of traffic violation. In this simple case, the decision would seem obvious. For the business manager, decisions to violate laws to accomplish a good outcome are not always this simple. Business managers usually face more complex situations where the outcomes are not always so clearly anticipated. Consider how complex a driver's apparently simple decision could become if the traffic violation causes another driver to veer into another lane and strike a pedestrian. Would you still consider the traffic violation an ethical act?

Even with laws in place to guide them, business managers must make difficult and complex decisions. They still have to think through the ethical implications of their actions. In fact, managers most often make decisions in situations not covered by law. For example, should the duplicate managers be laid off after a merger of two companies? In these cases, managers need other guidelines to help them make ethical decisions.

? THINKING CRITICALLY

1. If the law is an expression of societal ethics, why do we need to study business ethics? Why can we not just adhere to the legal process?
2. Pick one of the laws discussed above and describe how it relates to each of the utilitarian, moral rights, and justice approaches to ethics.
3. Identify the elements of the Exxon *Valdez* crisis that seemed to be just legal matters and identify those that were just ethical matters.

SERVING MULTIPLE STAKEHOLDERS IN SOCIETY

Our definition of social responsibility suggests that managers and organizations are responsible for the impact of their decisions on society. But what is society? Society consists of a collection of people who are interdependent and living together as a community. The term society can be applied very broadly to encompass the global community or very narrowly to specify a small township. As we have stated earlier, society, by virtue of the interdependency of the people and organizations which make it up, can also be seen as a system.

At any level of application, the term society is so general that it would seem not to be very useful to managers who have to make specific decisions. For one thing, it wrongly implies that the interests and values of all people within the society are the same. It is more accurate and more useful for managers to think of society as consisting of many diverse groups of stakeholders, whose interests are interdependent but different at the same time. In Chapter 1, we defined "stakeholders" as the individuals and groups who have an interest in the performance of the organization. Thus stakeholders are people who will be affected by what an organization does. These stakeholders include: owners, stockholders, customers, competitors, creditors, government agencies (local, state, federal, foreign), courts, employees, unions, suppliers, business partners, media, special interest groups (trade associations, professional associations, protest groups, public interest groups), residents, community businesses, and the community, the nation, and beyond.

Each of these stakeholders may define social responsibility differently because they want different things from the organization. Each stakeholder has a different set of needs, interests, and goals. Consider some examples. Customers want valued products and services. Owners or stockholders want good financial returns. Courts want compliance with laws. Employees want a good standard of living through pay and benefits and high quality of work life through job safety, security, and satisfaction. Special interest groups may want any number of things, like environmental protection or less government regulation of an industry. Community businesses want continued economic growth. Residents want a livable environment and quality of life.

The stakeholder concept provides a basis for addressing the question: "Responsible to Whom?" Further, it can lead managers to more specific information about the impact of their decisions on society. For example, managers might ask themselves the following questions about their decisions:

- What is the likely outcome of each decision for each party (customers, employees, suppliers, community, etc.)?
- What responsibilities do I have and to whom?
- What rights do others have who may be impacted by my decision?
- What am I supposed to learn from this problem?
- How will my decision express my true concern for those affected?
- How does each stakeholder feel about the effects of the decision?
- Am I truly thinking about the concerns of those who may be affected?

Finding answers to these questions helps managers find a balance in fulfilling their responsibilities to their stakeholders.

Range of Social Responsibilities

The range of social responsibilities that managers might feel obligated to fulfill fall into four categories: economic, legal, ethical, and discretionary responsibilities. These categories are useful in describing the total social responsibilities of an organization (see Exhibit 5-2 on page 164).[10] **Economic responsibilities** *require the organization to provide valued goods and services to customers and profitable returns to owners or shareholders.* **Legal responsibilities** *require the organization to operate within the framework of laws and regulations.* **Ethical responsibilities** *require the organization to meet societal expectations for doing what is right, beyond meeting the minimal requirements of law.* **Discretionary responsibilities** are *those responsibilities left to the judgment and choice of the organization, which voluntarily contributes to society beyond its economic, legal, and ethical responsibilities.*

The order of the categories in Exhibit 5-2 implies that the economic and legal responsibilities are fundamental to the survival and prosperity of the organization. A business focuses on fulfilling these fundamental responsibilities, which provides a foundation for fulfilling ethical and discretionary responsibilities. Peter Drucker explains it this way: "The first 'social responsibility' of business is then to make enough profit to cover the costs of the future. If this 'social responsibility' is not met, no other 'social responsibility' can be met. Decaying businesses in a decaying economy are unlikely to be good neighbors, good employers, or

Economic responsibilities Responsibilities that require the organization to provide valued goods and services to customers and profitable returns to owners or shareholders.

Legal responsibilities Requirements that the organization operate within the framework of laws and regulations.

Ethical responsibilities Requirements that the organization meet societal expectations for doing what is right, beyond meeting the minimal requirements of law.

Discretionary responsibilities Those responsibilities left to the judgment and choice of the organization, in which it voluntarily contributes to society beyond its economic, legal, and ethical responsibilities.

EXHIBIT 5-2
The four areas of total corporate
social responsibility

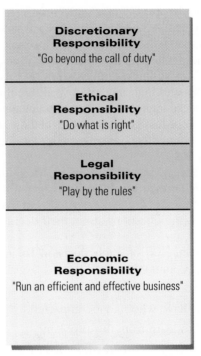

Source: Archie B. Carroll,"A Three-Dimensional Model of Corporate Performance," *Academy of Management Review,* 1979, Vol. 4, p. 499.

'socially responsible' in any way. When the demand for capital grows rapidly, surplus business revenues available for noneconomic purposes, especially for 'philanthropy,' cannot possibly go up. They are almost certain to shrink."[11] To put it briefly, economic performance is a prerequisite for the fulfillment of other social responsibilities. But if the organization then ignores its social responsibilities, it will undermine its foundation.

The Debate over the Definition of Social Responsibility

We defined social responsibility in terms of a range of options, including economic, legal, ethical, and discretionary responsibilities. However, not everyone agrees that each responsibility should be pursued. Some people define social responsibility only in terms of economic performance and meeting legal requirements. Nobel laureate Milton Friedman argues that any definition of social responsibility that includes voluntary actions by business is "a fundamentally subversive doctrine." Friedman argues that managers should make decisions that are in the best financial interest of the stockholders and within legal limits and should not consider other social costs or benefits unless they have direct bearing on the company's economic performance. Further, the costs of social programs must be passed on to consumers without their consent, and this confuses the roles of government and business because the costs of social programs are incorporated into market prices without the consent of consumers. He also warns that business can become too powerful if corporations are allowed to shape the social system for their own purposes.[12]

Many people would argue that managers must consider more than just the economic and legal implications of their decisions. For one thing, society expects it of organizations, so it helps create goodwill with the public. Furthermore, by taking initiative on social concerns, companies may avoid regulation, which increases the relative power of government, increases operating costs of complying with regulations, and constrains flexibility and freedom to make quick decisions in a competitive marketplace.

There is no right answer that resolves this debate. Each manager and each organization must decide for themselves what their ethical and social responsibilities are. The range of social responsibilities that might be chosen is certainly broad. Increasingly, however, managers and business organizations are attending to all four social responsibilities.

Compliance Versus Integrity Approaches to Social Responsibility and Ethics

One prominent writer in the area of business ethics, Lynn Sharp Paine of the Harvard Business School, has looked at the approaches of different companies to their social and ethical responsibilities. She has made the distinction between companies that develop a policy of *compliance* with the law and those that implement a policy of *integrity*. Paine contrasts the two approaches:

While compliance is rooted in avoiding legal sanctions, organizational integrity is based on the concept of self-governance in accordance with a set of guiding principles. From the perspective of integrity, the task of ethics management is to define and give life to an organization's guiding values, to create an environment that supports ethically sound behavior, and to instill a sense of shared accountability among employees. The need to obey the law is viewed as a positive aspect of organizational life, rather than an unwelcome constraint imposed by external authorities.[13]

In other words, in taking the **compliance approach,** *firms have a policy of telling employees what not to do—do not break the law, but there is no direction for what to do beyond that in terms of ethical or socially responsible behavior.* When taking the **integrity approach,** *firms proactively develop policies that direct employees to do what is legal, right, ethical, and socially responsible, for other employees, customers, and all stakeholders.* Exhibit 5-3 on page 166 provides an overview of the difference between compliance and integrity approaches to business ethics. In looking at this exhibit, consider the idea of ethical/legal/socially responsible behavior as a continuum, with the compliance end representing a minimum acceptable approach, and the integrity end as representing an approach to which well-managed organizations should strive. Most companies are somewhere in the middle. TQM, with its emphasis on serving customers (rather than taking advantage of them for the company's sole benefit), teamwork, and proactively preventing problems, is very consistent with the integrity approach to ethical management.

? THINKING CRITICALLY

1. Identify the primary stakeholders of a business that you are familiar with, and describe what each of them might say about Milton Friedman's view of social responsibility.

Compliance approach An approach to ethics in which firms have a policy of telling employees what not to do—do not break the law, but there is no direction for what to do beyond that.

Integrity approach An approach in which firms proactively develop policies that direct employees to do what is legal, right, ethical, and socially responsible for all stakeholders.

EXHIBIT 5-3 Continuum of Management Ethics

Minimum Acceptable Approach ←————————————————→ *Fully Acceptable Approach*

COMPLIANCE APPROACH TO ETHICS	*CHARACTERISTICS*	INTEGRITY APPROACH TO ETHICS
conformity with externally imposed standards	Ethos	self-governance according to chosen standards
prevent criminal misconduct	Objective	enable responsible conduct
lawyer driven	Leadership	management driven with aid of lawyers, HR, others
education, reduced discretion, auditing and controls, penalties	Methods	education, leadership, accountability, organizational systems and decision processes, auditing and controls, penalties
autonomous beings guided by material self-interesr	Behavioral Assumptions	social beings guided by material self-interest, values, ideals, peers
	IMPLEMENTATION	
criminal and regulatory law	Standards	company values and aspirations, social obligations, including law
lawyers	Staffing	executives and managers, with lawyers, others
develop compliance standards train and communicate handle reports of misconduct conduct investigations oversee compliance audits enforce standards	Activities	lead development of company values and standards, train and commmunicate, integrate into company systems, provide guidance and consultation, assess values performance, identify and resolve problems, oversee compliance activities
compliance standards	Education	decision making and values compliance standards

Source: Adapted from Lynn Sharp Paine, "Managing for Organizational Integrity," *Harvard Business Review*, March-April 1994, p.113.

2. Are the four categories of social responsibilities independent or interrelated? Explain your answer?
3. As a member of an organization, would you prefer a culture that promoted a compliance approach or an integrity approach to ethics and social responsibility? Explain your answer.

MANAGING ECONOMIC PERFORMANCE

We who occupy the developed world have advanced our standard of living to levels unmatched in history. There are more products available, to more people, from more places in the world now than ever before. Business organizations are key to achieving this economic abundance. They get people to pool their resources and work cooperatively to accomplish much more than they ever could working in isolation.

Managers are socially obligated to run an effective and efficient business. All other chapters of this text suggest how managers can do a better job of fulfilling this social responsibility with a special emphasis on techniques suggested by Total Quality Management. Gary Edwards, President of The Ethics Resource Center in Washington, DC, has suggested that there are a number of connections between TQM and business ethics, because TQM, the systems view, and an emphasis on continuously improving processes requires:

- honesty and forthrightness in communication
- an open environment where honesty and forthrightness in communication are encouraged and rewarded
- clearly stated policies and procedures related to ethical conduct by employees in their relationships with one another and with the company's customers, suppliers, local communities, regulators, and shareholders
- ethics policies and procedures that are actively monitored and enforced
- honest, realistic goalsetting and planning
- adequately informed and honest performance evaluations
- the maintenance of accurate financial books and records
- nondiscriminatory practices in hiring and promotion
- accountability, personal responsibility, and fair disciplinary practices
- credible and trustworthy leadership, rather than a management team that lies, speaks halftruths, or tries to "spin" information that it shares with employees[14]

The compatibility between the principles of TQM and successful systems management and the moral principles that underlie business ethics demonstrate that acting ethically is sound business policy. In the long term, such practices contribute to the organization's primary economic objectives for survival and prosperity. However, in the short term, managers must achieve a balance with the pressures to achieve short-term profits, which can undermine both TQM and business ethics, not to mention the actual long-term survival of the organization.

Beware of the Profit Motive

While Drucker suggests that socially responsible managers must do the things that will allow their organizations to be profitable, this does not mean managers should pull out all the stops to maximize short-term profit. When managers focus on profit maximization for stockholders in the short term, they tend to make bad decisions, such as to:

- delay investments in research and development, capital upgrades, market studies, and training and development for employees
- abuse other stakeholders
- reduce the wages and benefits of employees, which cuts costs immediately, but creates tensions and compromises the company's ability to attract and retain talented people

- buy from low-bid suppliers and negotiate deals that financially burden the suppliers, which over the long term may reduce material quality and erode the supply base
- skimp on the products and services provided customers, which undermines customer loyalty and taints the company's reputation

All of these practices may lead to short-term profits at the expense of long-term economic performance. In Chapter 1, we pointed out that organizations do not exist to make a profit. They exist to fulfill the needs of customers and their other stakeholders and society as a whole. Profit is a way of measuring how well they do that and gives them the resources to continue, but when managers make profit their goal, it focuses them on the wrong actions for fulfilling the organization's actual purpose as a social institution as well as threatening its long-term survival.

We should also consider that managers' personal and professional fortunes are often riding on the economic performance of their organization. Bonuses, salary increases, and promotions may all be tied to measurable figures such as budget variances, operating costs, sales, profits, and various financial returns. It is often difficult to walk the line between normal economic self-interest and greed. However, managers must remember that social responsibility and ethics often require choosing between personal benefits and the obligations that we all have to society. And in fact, by understanding and emphasizing that the organization and all its managers and employees are part of society, we can see that the interests of society and those of the organization coincide.

The history of American industry is sprinkled with people who loved money and took the profit motive to immoral extremes.[15] The so-called robber barons of the 19th and early 20th century made millions through their "anything goes" approach to business. The prevailing philosophy of Social Darwinism, "the strongest survive," provided rationale to their actions. Legendary men like John D. Rockefeller, Andrew Carnegie, Jay Gould, Cornelius Vanderbilt and John Pierpont (J.P.) Morgan made millions in industries like railroads, shipping, and oil. They regularly exploited workers, made a mockery of federal laws, misled and duped investors, and engaged in devious trade practices. The public seemed to expect it and the robber barons seemed to feel little remorse for it. J.P. Morgan once stated, "I owe the public nothing." This perspective, however, is not one based on an understanding of organizations or society as systems.

These businesspeople were not necessarily bad to the bone. Many of them conducted their personal lives uprightly. Consider historian Ida Tarbell's description of John D. Rockefeller: "Mr. Rockefeller was 'good.' There was no more faithful Baptist in Cleveland than he. Every enterprise of that church he had supported liberally from his youth. He gave to its poor. He visited its sick. He wept with its suffering. Moreover, he gave unostentatiously to many outside charities of whose worthiness he was satisfied. . . . Yet he was willing to strain every nerve to obtain for himself special and unjust privileges from the railroads which were bound to ruin every man in the oil business not sharing them with him."[16]

In the 19th century, employees were accustomed to being abused, competitors expected to be undercut, coal mines were assumed to be unsafe, and steel mills were expected to produce pollution as well as profits. Such abuses are not totally relics of the past. However, managers who may be inclined to abuse their stakeholders now face increased regulation and scrutiny. For example, Dennis B. Levine, a merger specialist at the investment banking firm Drexel Burnham Lambert Inc. gave confidential inside information (advance notice of mergers and takeovers) to arbitrageur Ivan F. Boesky in exchange for a share of the handsome profits. From such sources, Boesky made a profit of more than $28 million on advance information about Nestle's purchase of Carnation Company. When he got caught, Boesky paid a $100 million Securities and Exchange Commission penalty, the largest ever for insider trading, and he was sentenced to three years in prison.[17] The days of public tolerance and apathy are long gone. Society expects more of managers in the 1990s. Again, by viewing organizations as systems, we see this as a natural outcome as we come to appreciate the interconnection among all elements of society—individuals and organizations—and what they do.

❓ THINKING CRITICALLY

1. As an individual who sells your services to employers, do you choose the employer who will pay you the most money right now (maximize your personal profits), or would you take less money to work in a company that practices TQM and has high ethical standards? Provide a rationale for your answer.
2. Do you think that being ethical and practicing TQM means compromising on profitability? Why or why not? In answering this question, consider how ethical behavior and TQM focus managers on preventing problems.

MAKING ETHICAL DECISIONS

How do the leaders of an organization ensure their people make ethical decisions? First, managers must learn to recognize when decisions have ethical implications. In other words, they need to learn to recognize ethics situations. An ethics situation requires a manager to engage in thought, discussion, or investigation to determine the moral impact of a decision. Second, managers must learn to evaluate complex situations in terms of ethics. Both of these issues are discussed below.

Education on Recognizing Ethics Situations

Managers are more likely to recognize ethics situations when they are familiar with the kinds of situations that have ethical implications. The educational courses offered by colleges, universities, and many business organizations help to promote awareness of specific ethics situations, such as those listed earlier in Exhibit 5-1. Unfortunately, it is difficult to list all specific ethics situations that managers might face. If managers simply used a checklist of specific ethics situations, they might overlook those not listed. So, it might also be helpful for managers to recognize some general classifications of ethical issues that are relevant to all business organizations. Here are three:

- *Conflict of interest* exists when an individual must choose between his or her personal interest and those of the company or some other group. For example, a purchasing manager may experience a conflict of interest when offered bribes or kickbacks to induce the purchase of an inferior product.
- *Honesty* means truthfulness and integrity. Without honesty, it is difficult to maintain trusting business relationships with suppliers, customers, and employees.

For example, false or misleading advertising can destroy customers' trust in a company and lead customers to avoid the company in the future.

- *Fairness* means impartiality and equitable treatment. People resent being treated unfairly, and they generally avoid unfair treatment whenever possible. This avoidance can be costly, for example, when the company loses good employees who quit because of unfair treatment.[18]

Managers may recognize ethics situations better if they first assume that every managerial decision has potential ethical implications. Every decision can be evaluated in terms of its goodness or badness, or whether it avoids conflict of interest and embodies honesty and fairness. A manager might ask himself or herself whether the decision would be accepted or rejected by others. When a manager feels uncomfortable at the thought of discussing a decision with peers, subordinates, or superiors, he or she has likely identified an ethics situation that requires further evaluation.

Evaluating Complex Situations in Terms of Ethics

Many people believe that if the organization only hires good people with strong ethical values, then ethical decision making will be an automatic result. Certainly an individual's personal values and moral philosophies influence his or her decisions. Moral rules, like one of the Ten Commandments in the Bible, Thou shalt not lie, apply to a variety of situations in life, whether personal or business. In fact, Domino's Pizza, Inc. lists the Golden Rule first among its 15 Operating Principles. It would seem that good people equipped with moral rules will always make ethical decisions.

However, the business context offers more complex moral dilemmas than an individual typically faces in his or her personal life. The values learned from family, church, and school may not provide enough guidance for complex business decisions about such things as advertising, pricing, hiring practices, and pollution control. Many business decisions are close calls because it is often difficult to tell whether or not the good that comes out of a decision will outweigh the bad. So, managers have to use their judgment to apply moral and business standards to make ethics decisions. The following is a discussion of what makes business ethics decisions complex.

What Makes Business Ethics Decisions Complex

The fundamental cause of complexity in business ethics decisions is the existence of many stakeholders. Consider the difficulty managers face in positively (as opposed to negatively) applying the Golden Rule. To do it right, managers should find out what the stakeholders want done and should not just assume they already know. Different stakeholders with special interests will have different standards for judging decisions. Under these circumstances, it is hard to please all of the stakeholders of the organization, and managers are forced to make trade-offs. Other reasons for the complexity of business ethics decisions include:

- *Extended Consequences.* The results of managerial decisions and actions do not stop with the immediate outcomes of the decision. Rather, the results ripple through society and affect many stakeholders. Pollution can diminish the health of the environment (and we should note that the organization exists in that environment, so pollution also harms the polluter). In the case of fishing communities, it can even destroy an industry, put people out of work, contaminate the food supply, and lead to sickness and death. Unsafe products can lead to loss of life and injury, law suits, and astronomical insurance claims that ultimately affect the insurance premiums of everyone else.

- *Multiple Alternatives*. It would be easy to think that ethics decisions involve a simple yes or no choice. Should a factory pollute the environment or not? Should a manager bribe a government official or not? Should a company produce a slightly unsafe product or not? Ethics decisions may seem this simple to the outsider, however, managers, operating in environments filled with ambiguities, usually see many alternatives that are much less distinct.

- *Mixed Outcomes*. It might seem that ethics decisions involve a simple tradeoff between economic benefits and social costs. Pollute the environment and thus avoid the costs of pollution control devices. Pay a bribe and thus ensure the prompt delivery and sales of imported goods. Produce a slightly unsafe product and thus hold down material and labor costs. In reality, the tradeoffs between financial and social costs are not always so clear. Every alternative in an ethics decision involves both financial costs and benefits, and social costs and benefits. The more stakeholders that are involved, the more mixed the financial and social outcomes are likely to be. Further, if managers opt, for example, to put a slightly unsafe product on the market and someone is injured, the costs of taking care of the subsequent fallout from this injury (financial and in terms of lost business) may be even higher than the costs of preventing the problem in the first place.

- *Uncertain Consequences*. Another factor that complicates ethics decisions is that the consequences of any decision are not always known. For example, the company that pollutes the environment cannot be sure about the fines and cleanup costs, nor about whether or not the public would find out and how it would react if it did. Further, the company cannot know for certain that investment in pollution control equipment would yield promised results, such as emissions reduced by 20 percent at only 5 percent increase in operating costs. The outcomes are not always guaranteed. Extended consequences are even more uncertain. For example, how can the company assess the long term impact of pollution on forest habitat, animals, or future generations of people.

- *Personal Implications*. Managers are not free to make impersonal decisions that have consequences divorced from their own lives and careers. Not only must managers seek to balance the competing interests and needs of many stakeholders, they must consider their own interest. The personal implications of ethics decisions can create dilemmas for managers. What is good for other stakeholders may not necessarily be good for them, particularly if we only consider the short-term personal impact

Dealing with the Complexity

Because managers make decisions that affect other people, their decisions can become complex. These decisions can have extended consequences, multiple alternatives, mixed outcomes, uncertain consequences, and personal implications. These characteristics of complex ethics situations mean that managers must

A LOOK AT

TECHNOLOGY

THE ETHICS AND LEGALITY OF ELECTRONIC SURVEILLANCE OF EMPLOYEES[19]

With the advent of e-mail, voice mail, video cameras, and devices for tapping phones, organizations have the ability to use these devices to secretly monitor the actions of their employees. Managers can read e-mail messages, listen to voice mail, covertly videotape employees, and listen in on their phone conversations. All of these activities can either be legal or illegal depending on how they are done. Many employers have been sued for violating employee privacy or for not properly informing employees of the company's policy on surveillance.

For example, the owners of a liquor store in Camden, Arkansas suspected an employee of theft. They went about systematically recording her phone conversations without telling her directly they were going to do this. They discovered that she was going to sell a keg of beer at a discounted price to a male friend, with whom, it turned out, she was having an affair. She had several steamy conversations with this person, which the owners captured on tape. They later informed the employee's spouse of her affair and fired her. She and her boyfriend then sued the owners for violation of the Wiretap Act and won. The court held that the owners had only hinted to the employee that they were going to record conversations, and that the employee and her friend had a reasonable expectation that the calls were private and further that taping and disclosing the calls served no business purpose. The store had to pay her $40,000 plus legal expenses.

When using electronics to observe employees' use of company property, equipment, and time, managers must make sure employees have been properly informed, and it is a good idea to have them sign an agreement accepting this surveillance. Further, the listening-in and observation must be relevant to business activities. For example, many insurance and telemarketing managers listen to the calls of salespeople and customer service representatives. Companies may also check the invoices of employee phone lines to make sure they are not making excessive personal calls on company time and expense.

Electronic mail is easy enough for managers to monitor. This technology is not infrequently used for personal as well as business purposes by employees. If this is against company policy, management must tell employees and inform them that the company monitors e-mail. An employee-friendly organization may want to establish electronic bulletin boards for personal mail and give each employee their own password in order to access their mail.

The new technology requires that managers and employees understand its purpose to facilitate business and use it in this way. Otherwise, both might find themselves guilty of, at least, ethical transgressions or, worse, violation of the law as well.

not just engage in financial analysis to help them choose courses of action. Rather, they should openly address each of these factors. The following list of decision-making activities can help in doing a thorough analysis:

1. Investigate the extended consequences of their decisions by discussing the decision alternatives with many stakeholders.
2. Ask the stakeholders to propose other alternatives that have not been considered.
3. Clarify the outcomes of each decision alternative to openly weigh the benefits and costs of each.
4. Gather input from many stakeholders about the certainty of each consequence.
5. Openly discuss the personal implications of ethics decisions with others.

There are clearly limits to how much information managers can publicly dis-close in situations that seem to have ethical consequences. However, managers are more likely to arrive at ethically sound decisions if they discuss the situation with other stakeholders. For example, when managers face personal dilemmas, like whether or not to invest in pollution control equipment, they should talk to their superiors and peers within the organization. These people may be able to help reduce the personal constraints to free managers to make ethical decisions. A superior might relax the return on capital investment goals to encourage the investment in pollution control equipment.

The Benefits of Business Ethics and Social Responsibility

The obvious benefits of ethics and social responsibility are the feelings of having a clear conscience and self-respect as a "moral" manager. But do good ethics make good business? It stands to reason that over the long term, when managers do what is right for their primary stakeholders and faithfully try to balance all of their interests, they will be looking out for the business at the same time. How-ever, it is hard to back up this belief with facts. For example, numerous studies have been conducted to examine correlations between a company's reputation for ethics and its stock price performance, but the results are not conclusive. There may be many reasons for this, including the fact that ethical behavior and sound management in other aspects of the business do not necessarily coincide. Despite the lack of research results to demonstrate that good ethics make good business, there are some good reasons to promote business ethics:

- *Avoiding the Costs of Unethical Business Conduct.* Failure to attend to cus-tomer needs for safety and health can drive customers away and hurt the cor-porate image. In addition to these indirect losses in the marketplace, the recently-enacted U.S. Sentencing Guidelines for Organizations are designed to increase fines for companies that do not address criminal conduct and decrease fines for companies that do.

- *Long-term, Proactive Strategy to Foster Trust.* When Johnson & Johnson decid-ed to recall Tylenol, it ultimately cost them about $100 million. However, it sent a clear message to its consumers: "You can trust us to keep your best interest in mind." A similar message emerged from H.B. Fuller when the com-pany quickly changed the chemical formula for its glue upon discovering that children in Latin America were getting high on it.

- *Concerns Regarding Changes in Corporate Culture due to Growth and Diversi-fication.* To cope with an increasingly complex business environment, many companies are engaged in restructuring, reorganization, leveraged buy-outs, flattening corporate hierarchies, and making radical changes in organizational culture. Since these changes bring about uncertainty, confusion, and doubt among employees, many of these companies have undertaken ethics initiatives to ensure that, as the business changes, their ethical practices remain intact.

- *Desired Consistency Between Conscience and Business Conduct.* Levi Strauss & Co. has had a long-standing reputation regarding how it treats people in its business operations. In the early 1950s, it moved to desegregate its plants in the southern U.S. before civil rights legislation. In the late 1980s, Levi Strauss went further when it adopted a "Statement of Aspirations" to treat people with respect and consideration. Subsequent changes in company practices include a more liberal benefits package and other employee-directed programs to treat employees like they would individually like to be treated. In recent years, faced with downsizing its U.S. workforce to better compete with foreign producers, Levi Strauss implemented a progressive plant closing policy to minimize the impact of closings for the local community and to help re-employ laid-off workers. It has also led corporate America with its approach to AIDS education in the workplace. Most recently, Levi Strauss pulled its operations out of mainland China because it said it could not be confident of the country's labor practices. Levi Strauss feels good about aligning its social conscience with its business conduct. As a bonus, Levi Strauss also feels that these practices have led to lower turnover of current employees and a greater ability to attract good employees.

❓ THINKING CRITICALLY

1. Are business ethics decisions complex primarily because managers are dealing with a difficult topic, ethics, or because conducting business is just complex. Explain. In answering this question, consider the idea of balancing the interests of stakeholders.
2. Have you ever been in a situation where you had to make a decision that had ethical implications? In deciding what to do, what consequences did you take into account? What was the outcome of your decision?
3. Explain how TQM might help managers deal with complexity in ethical business decisions.

MAKING DISCRETIONARY CONTRIBUTIONS

Business organizations may contribute to society in ways that exceed the minimal requirements of law and even go beyond making ethical decisions to balance the interests of the stakeholders. This final area of social responsibility, making discretionary contributions, is totally voluntary on the part of the company. The company decides what to do with the profits gained from its economic performance. The word discretionary means it is up to the organization what social agenda to advance, how to advance it, and how much of its resources to devote to it.

Companies may simply give money to charities that actually do the work. For example, the Alcoa Foundation authorized two grants of $100,000 each to the American Red Cross, and The Salvation Army for disaster relief as a result of Hurricane Andrew. Or the company may actually conduct business in ways that are more socially responsible toward various stakeholders. Alcoa, for example, has also established a Minority Business Development program to increase the amount of purchases made from minority vendors. What follows are several more instances of discretionary contributions by different companies.

McDonald's Commitment to the Environment.   McDonald's Corporation produces an enormous amount of trash from food wrappers, beverage containers, and paper bags. To help cope with the environmental mess it helps to create, McDonald's has made a commitment to the environment by improving the way it handles solid waste. This Commitment to the Environment is reproduced in Exhibit 5-4.

EXHIBIT 5-4
McDonald's commitment to
the environment

McDONALD'S® CORPORATION
Our Commitment to the Environment

McDonald's believes it has a special responsibility to protect our environment for future generations. This responsibility is derived from our unique relationship with millions of consumers worldwide–whose quality of life tomorrow will be affected by our stewardship of the environment today. We share their belief that the right to exist in an environment of clean air, clean earth and clean water is fundamental and unwavering.

We realize that in today's world, a business leader must be an environmental leader, as well. Hence our determination to analyze every aspect of our business in terms of its impact on the environment, and to take actions beyond what is expected if they hold the prospect of leaving future generations an environmentally sound world. We will lead, both in word and in deed.

Our environmental commitment and behavior is guided by the following principles:

EFFECTIVELY MANAGING SOLID WASTE - We are committed to taking a "total lifecycle" approach to solid waste, examining ways of reducing materials used in production and packaging, as well as diverting as much waste as possible from the solid waste stream. In doing so, we will follow three courses of action: reduce, reuse and recycle.

REDUCE - We will take steps to reduce the weight and/or volume of packaging we use. This may mean eliminating packaging; adopting thinner and lighter packaging; changing manufacturing and distribution systems; adopting new technologies or using alternative materials. We will continually search for materials that are environmentally preferable.

REUSE - We will implement reusable materials whenever feasible within our operations and distribution systems as long as they do not compromise our safety and sanitation standards, customer service and expectations, nor are offset by other environmental or safety concerns.

RECYCLE - We are committed to the maximum use of recycled materials in the construction, equipping and operations of our restaurants. We are already the largest user of recycled paper in our industry, applying it to such items as tray liners, Happy Meal boxes, carry out bags, carry out trays and napkins.

Domino's Pizza Partners Foundation.   Domino's established a Partners Foundation as a charity that gives financial help to Domino's Pizza Team Members when there has been an accident, tragedy, or serious medical problem. To fund the Partners Foundation, franchise offices, regional offices, and individual team members hold all kinds of auctions, golf tournaments, and even donate speaker fees to support the Foundation. The two most popular and effective fund-raising programs are the Payroll-Deduction Employer-Match Program, which is exactly what it sounds like, and the Pennies Program, which collects change from employees in a jar at the store. Some stores encourage donations to the Pennies Program for policy or uniform infractions. If managers, supervisors, or franchisees are caught doing something they shouldn't, they are expected by the crew to make substantial donations to the jar. The Foundation keeps its office expenses to under 15.5% of what is donated to ensure more money is available to meet Team Members' needs.

IBM Concentrates on Education.   More than 50 years ago, Thomas J. Watson Sr. told IBM employees: "Take time off from your IBM duties to do a good job in your community because no country can ever be better than its communities make it. And, the local community has to depend on the people who live there." IBM CEOs since Mr. Watson have confirmed and expanded upon this commitment to good citizenship, corporate as well as individual. IBM recognizes that in the global marketplace, it is difficult to separate a company's economic goals from its larger responsibilities as a member of society. The company supports efforts to solve problems that are identified through studies as being of concern to its employees and other stakeholders. IBM contributions, which have averaged about $135 million annually over the last 10 years, are concentrated in the areas of education, the environment, health, the arts, employee involvement, people with disabilities, and the economically disadvantaged.

Since IBM feels that quality education is crucial to the success of individuals, companies, and countries alike, it devotes nearly half of its worldwide contributions each year to education, and about 22,000 employees in the United States alone volunteer their time. IBM programs that support education, particularly elementary and secondary education (K-12) include: Grants for Technology in Education, Summer Youth Work/Study Program, and Faculty Loan Program. IBM also makes regular contributions to the United Negro College Fund. As a high-technology company, IBM views education as an area of commitment for its own self interest. It needs educated employees and suppliers to develop, make, and sell its products, and it needs educated customers to make use of them.

Coors Promotes Responsible Use of Alcohol.   The abuse of alcohol certainly detracts from the welfare of society. Drunk drivers take lives. Alcoholism destroys families and wastes human potential. Drunkenness generally leads people to do stupid things that incur all kinds of social costs. What responsibility does Coors bear for how their products are used? Selling and using alcohol is perfectly legal. It would be easy for the producers to take the profits and forget about the abuses. After all, the more people drink, the more profits there are, but this is not the attitude at Adolph Coors Company.

To promote the responsible use of its alcoholic products, Coors supports educational programs aimed at preventing misuse of alcohol and encourages positive life-style decisions. The company formed the Alcohol Misuse and Abuse Prevention Task Force and created its own Alcohol Issues Department, which supports such programs as National Collegiate Alcohol Awareness Week, Partners in Prevention, Pharmacists Against Drug Abuse and the All STAR program. In 1988, Coors and its distributors were honored by the director of the National Highway Traffic Safety Administration for their support of the national program, "Alcohol, Drugs, Driving and You." Despite their obvious contribution to the use of alcohol, Coors seeks to make sure its product is not abused to the detriment of society.

Sometimes companies that go beyond the call of duty find that social responsibility is also good business. Consider the experiences of South Shore Bank of Chicago and 3M.

South Shore Bank of Chicago.   A few years ago, South Shore Bank of Chicago found that more and more banks were competing for business from customers with good credit risks, meaning less market share for each individual bank. The competitive conditions led to fewer lending options for people with higher credit risks. South Shore turned this problem into an opportunity. It went into a less wealthy section of Chicago's inner city and worked business by business through loan arrangements that would help develop the neighborhood's economic base

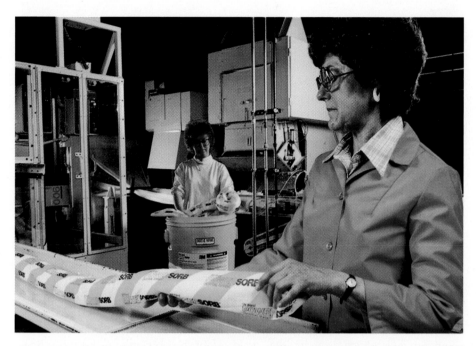

Waste at a 3M plant in Aberdeen, SD, was substantially reduced by reformulating a respirator mask product so that material left over after stamping out the masks could be used to make a new oil-absorbing product.

while improving the credit worthiness of the bank's portfolio. By "banking" on the overall reliability of the neighborhood's borrowers, South Shore increased its lending while helping to improve the area's economic base, thus lowering its credit risk over the long run.

Minnesota Mining and Manufacturing Company (3M).   3M has long been a proponent of innovation in the workplace. In recent years 3M has seen its manufacturing processes generate larger amounts of toxic chemicals as production increased. At the same time, increased competition led to greater financial pressures. To reduce pollution and keep down production costs, 3M began promoting innovative technologies through its "Pollution Prevention Pays," or 3P Program. In the program's first 19 years, 3M employees initiated 4200 3P projects involving product reformulations and process changes. As a result, 3M cut the output of air, land, and water toxins by 1.3 billion pounds and also saved over $720 million through increased efficiencies.

? THINKING CRITICALLY

1. Based on what you have read here, do you think discretionary contributions are just doing good for the community and society or do they have positive consequences for the organization as well? Why or why not?
2. Provide a rationalization for discretionary contributions by taking the systems view of organizations and society.

PROMOTING SOCIAL RESPONSIBILITY AND ETHICS

Managers face complex problems and decisions in business. It is not always easy to make decisions that meet society's standards for social responsibility and ethics. To help their managers make better decisions, many companies take active measures to promote social responsibility and ethics. These measures include entities, programs, and formal communications.

Entities

One of the most frequently used entities for promoting ethics and social responsibility is the ethics committee. The committee may be composed of executives and managers from throughout the organization. Committees may be used to promote discussion of the impact of company policies and practices on society. Sometimes these committees report directly to the board of directors. They may oversee corporate activities, make recommendations, set corporate policies, and assist in reviewing business operations from an "ethical" or "social" perspective.

Also, in the past few years, many companies have set up ethics offices. These offices are often multi-purposed: they hear accusations of misconduct in the company, give advice on gray areas, help establish corporate business practices, communicate standards throughout the company, act as a mediator in disputes, and write reports on the company's practices. Some companies have also added specialists in such areas as employee diversity, international regulations, and environmental issues to offer more complete assistance to the company when dealing with specific issues. These specialists can also assist executives in policy formulation.

Programs

Many companies have instituted specific programs to assist in the efforts of their committees, offices, and departments to promote ethics and social responsibility. They may conduct ethics audits to uncover opportunities for improving the routines and decisions of the company. Ethics education and training programs are also becoming popular as a means of imparting information, knowledge, and skill to employees. Citibank even developed a board game to make the training fun for employees, as the *A Look at Managers in Action* box on page 179 describes.

Formal Communications

Most companies have formal mission statements, credos, or value statements that address the purpose of the organization and broad principles by which it conducts its business. Companies also usually have policies and procedures that specifically spell out how employees are to carry out business operations. These formal communications often include statements about business ethics and social responsibility. The most popular means of promoting ethics and social responsibility still remains the use of written ethics codes. The Case in Point, Revisited at the end of this chapter provides an example.

PAULA GOODMAN PROMOTES ETHICS AT CITIBANK

MANAGERS IN ACTION

Paula Goodman is a Senior Recruiter for Global Management Associate Programs and directs recruiting for several Citibank businesses. She also delivers an educational game called The Work Ethic *at major MBA campuses around the country and conducts seminars for new recruits within Citibank. Paula explains how Citibank promotes business ethics using* The Work Ethic.

At Citibank, there exists a Code of Conduct and Ethical Policies that each employee receives. A cover letter from the Chairman of Citicorp, our parent corporation, begins by saying that "The principle that guides conduct at Citicorp is a simple one: do the right thing—certainly because it is the right thing to do, but also because it is the foundation for sustained business success. Our reputation for trustworthiness and service is at least as important to our customers as the products and services we offer." The letter goes on to say that "individually and as a corporation, we have to earn that reputation every day by demonstrating unquestionable integrity and good judgment, as well as superior products and services. We should never make compromises to achieve expedient solutions that could damage Citicorp's reputation and Franchise."

One of the ways that Citibank reinforces the need for ethical decision making is via an interactive group exercise called *The Work Ethic.* This exercise gives Citibank employees that chance to practice making ethical decisions in a risk-free environment. *The Work Ethic* was developed in 1985 by the Communications Unit and Corporate Human Resources as a way to introduce the topic of integrity into orientation sessions for new employees. Since its development, we have used it in a variety of settings in addition to orientation, including staff meetings, off-site conferences, and training sessions.

The purpose of *The Work Ethic* is to increase the awareness of the importance of integrity in the company by getting employees to talk about ethical issues. It serves as an introduction to policies, but it is not a replacement for policy manuals. The intent is not to teach people ethics but rather to point out a variety of techniques and resources to help make ethical decisions. It has been effectively used by Citibank businesses throughout Asia, Europe, South America, Africa, and North America. It has been translated into a number of languages, including Japanese, Spanish, French, German, Flemish, Italian, and Portuguese.

Originally produced as a board game, *The Work Ethic* first included nearly 100 cards, each with a brief description of an ethical dilemma and four possible courses of action. (You will find some of these dilemmas listed in an exercise at the end of this chapter.) Issues covered deal with conflict of interest, confidentiality, handling money, and people management skills. Today *The Work Ethic* is played using overheads or handouts instead of the format of a board game. Participants work together in groups to generate solutions. An Appeals Board of three senior managers helps to evaluate the solutions that participants generate. The Board members share their own experiences, stories, and anecdotes to reinforce the importance of integrity at Citibank.

At the end of the exercise, I conclude by pointing out that the entire group wins at the game by learning more about what Citibank expects of its people in terms of integrity and ethical decision making. Participants learn about their ability to influence others, why certain issues are extremely important to the bank, tips on making ethical decisions, and resources to help them when they face ethical dilemmas. Two points are reinforced: many real-life situations do not have easy answers and often the best solution to an ethical dilemma comes from discussions with a variety of people with varied experiences.

COMPARING EXXON AND JOHNSON & JOHNSON CODES OF ETHICS[20]

Many companies develop a written code of ethics to describe "the way we do business around here." The code of ethics is an attempt to set the moral standards for the company. It also suggests how everyone in the organization should approach decisions and actions that raise ethical and legal questions. The code of ethics reflects organizational culture and reinforces it by reminding people how they should contribute to society. Quite often the code of ethics really does reveal a lot about the way a company does business. Consider the contrast between the code of ethics for Exxon Company, U.S.A., the regional portion of Exxon Corporation responsible directly for Exxon Shipping Company and indirectly for Alyeska Pipeline Service Company, and that for Johnson & Johnson, the makers of Tylenol products. These codes of ethics are shown here.

The Exxon U.S.A. code of ethics suggests that employees be honest, truthful, obey the law, and avoid conflicts of interest. However, the code is directed at lower levels of the organization and focused on financial honesty and legal propriety. It is implicitly bent toward the interest of stockholders. The code makes no mention of worker safety, environmental protection, customer service, or distributor loyalty. This code represents a compliance approach to business ethics. Did Exxon's lack of a progressive stance in its ethics code contribute to the disastrous oil spill in Prince William Sound? That is a difficult question to answer. However, the contrast with the code of ethics of Johnson & Johnson is obvious because it makes no mention of financial honesty or legal propriety. Perhaps the company assumes those virtues. Instead, Johnson & Johnson lists, in order of priority, the accepted social responsibilities of the company. This represents an example of taking the integrity approach to business ethics.

During the Tylenol Nightmare, Johnson & Johnson executives were apparently willing to place the welfare of their customers, employees, and society above the profits of their stockholders. When people died from taking capsules laced with poison, the company spent over $100 million removing Tylenol from the shelves of

---

Summary Code of Ethics of Exxon Company, U.S.A.

Business Ethics

Our company policy is one of strict observance of all laws applicable to its business.

A reputation for scrupulous dealing is itself a priceless Company asset.

We do care how we get results.

We expect candor at all levels and compliance with accounting rules and controls.

Antitrust

It is the established policy of the Company to conduct its business in compliance with all state and federal antitrust laws.

Individual employees are responsible for seeing that they comply with the law.

Employees must avoid even the appearance of violation.

Conflict of Interest

Competing or conducting business with the Company is not permitted, except with the knowledge and consent of management.

Accepting and providing gifts, entertainment, and services must comply with specific requirements.

An employee may not use Company personnel, information, or other assets for personal benefit.

Participating in certain outside activities requires the prior approval of management.

Source: Exxon Company, U.S.A. Company document, December 1988.

every store in the United States. Mr. James Burke, chairman of Johnson & Johnson, credits the written code of ethics for providing guidance to the company during the ordeal. He states: "This document spells out our responsibilities to all of our constituencies: consumers, employees, community and stockholders. It served to guide all of us during the crisis, when hard decisions had to be made in what were often excruciatingly brief periods of time. All of our employees worldwide were able to watch the process of the Tylenol withdrawal and subsequent reintroduction in tamper-resistant packaging, confident of the way in which the decisions would be made. There was a great sense of shared pride in the knowledge that the Credo was being tested . . . and it worked."

OUR CREDO

We believe our first responsibility is to the doctors, nurses and patients,
to mothers and fathers and all others who use our products and services.
In meeting their needs everything we do must be of high quality.
We must constantly strive to reduce our costs
in order to maintain reasonable prices.
Customers' orders must be serviced promptly and accurately.
Our suppliers and distributors must have an opportunity
to make a fair profit.

We are responsible to our employees,
the men and women who work with us throughout the world.
Everyone must be considered as an individual.
We must respect their dignity and recognize their merit.
They must have a sense of security in their jobs.
Compensation must be fair and adequate,
and working conditions clean, orderly and safe.
We must be mindful of ways to help our employees fulfill
their family responsibilities.
Employees must feel free to make suggestions and complaints.
There must be equal opportunity for employment, development
and advancement for those qualified.
We must provide competent management,
and their actions must be just and ethical.

We are responsible to the communities in which we live and work
and to the world community as well.
We must be good citizens – support good works and charities
and bear our fair share of taxes.
We must encourage civic improvements and better health and education.
We must maintain in good order
the property we are privileged to use,
protecting the environment and natural resources.

Our final responsibility is to our stockholders.
Business must make a sound profit.
We must experiment with new ideas.
Research must be carried on, innovative programs developed
and mistakes paid for.
New equipment must be purchased, new facilities provided
and new products launched.
Reserves must be created to provide for adverse times.
When we operate according to these principles,
the stockholders should realize a fair return.

Johnson & Johnson

The Responsibilities of Management

The concepts of ethics and social responsibility offered in this chapter suggest that managers are servants of all organizational stakeholders, not just the owners, and not just themselves. While companies have installed certain support mechanisms to assist managers in business ethics and social responsibility, the responsibility ultimately falls to individual managers who have to make decisions on a daily basis.

Managers have to realize that each of their decisions can have far-reaching effects on many people inside and outside the company (as the systems view reminds us). Managers are responsible for exercising sound judgment in their decisions. When they recognize conditions that compel them or others to behave unethically, they are responsible to either correct the problem themselves or bring it to the attention of someone who can correct it. This is a challenging responsibility that will sometimes require managers to make difficult decisions.

Organizations that promote the values of Total Quality Management will find it easier to encourage business ethics and social responsibility. The systems view encourages managers to balance the long-term interests of all stakeholders by creating systems with processes that efficiently and effectively serve customers. This approach to management serves the best interest of society.

It offers people an opportunity to do meaningful work. It offers people a chance to gratify human needs that are too often neglected: the need for purpose in life, the need to feel important, the need to feel pride in one's work, the need to contribute to noble causes. Certainly we all share needs for self-gratification, and we all want to live the good life. However, focusing only on ourselves and greed leads to a hollow human existence. We are part of the world in which we exist, and only by looking out for that world can we look out for ourselves.

The ethical and quality approach to management does not rule out prosperity and riches for individuals. Indeed, those managers who are most adept at practicing this approach to management will likely be those who prosper the most in the future. Managers should view the ideas set forth in this text as offering them an opportunity to improve human conditions for themselves and for others. With customers and other stakeholders in society becoming more demanding of business organizations, there may be no alternative for organizations that intend to survive and prosper.

 THINKING CRITICALLY

1. Does ethics and social responsibility deserve special consideration by practicing managers, or are these just topics that are of academic interest? Explain.
2. If you were the CEO of a Fortune 500 company, how would you promote business ethics and social responsibility?

SUMMARY

The Importance of Social Responsibility and Business Ethics
- Social responsibility and business ethics are important concepts that help managers make decisions about right and wrong, and consider the impact of their decisions on society.

The Moral Principles of Business Ethics
- Three moral principles or approaches for understanding ethical business behavior are the utilitarian, moral rights, and justice approaches.
- Managers can combine these three approaches to help them make sound ethical decisions in an ambiguous business environment.

Modern Business Ethics
- While business ethics have foundations in ancient writings, only in the past few decades have organizations begun to feel concern about public image and the consequences of unethical behavior, and thus it is a much higher concern among today's managers.
- The general public, through education and the media, is much more aware of and intolerant of unethical behavior than in the past.

The Legal Process
- The law represents society's attempt to codify some basic ethical norms.
- Laws provide only minimal requirements for business ethics in a variety of areas, including: competition, consumers, investors, environment, equity, and safety.

Serving Multiple Stakeholders in Society
- The many stakeholders that make up society increasingly expect managers and organizations to be socially responsible and ethical.
- In making decisions with ethical implications, managers must be careful to balance the needs and expectations of all stakeholders.
- The range that managers might use for determining what is socially responsible behavior includes economic performance, legal compliance, ethical decision making, and discretionary contributions.
- Managers and organizations are increasingly coming to see the importance of all four areas when developing a policy for socially responsible behavior.
- Organizations that choose a compliance approach only seek to follow the law. Organizations that choose an integrity approach proactively develop policies for employees to do what is legal, right, ethical, and socially responsible.

Managing Economic Performance
- The most fundamental social responsibility managers have is to manage the successful economic performance of organizations.
- The principles of systems management and TQM demonstrate that ethical behavior is fully consistent and necessary in helping managers fulfill this responsibility.
- Managing for long-term economic viability means that managers must be careful not to let short-term profitability dominate their ethical and business decisions and actions.

Making Ethical Decisions
- Making ethical decisions first requires managers to recognize ethics situations. Common situations are those that involve conflict of interest, and those that may compromise a manager's honesty or fairness.

- Managers can deal with complex ethics decisions if they learn what makes them complex, including extended consequences, multiple alternatives, mixed outcomes, uncertain consequences, and personal implications.

Making Discretionary Contributions
- Organizations might make discretionary contributions to society by voluntarily donating time, money, and other resources to advance any social agenda that is important to them.

Promoting Social Responsibility
- Many organizations are actively promoting social responsibility and ethics through entities, programs, and formal communications.
- This trend is not only good for society, but also good for individual employees because it helps provide meaning and purpose to their work.
- Managers have the responsibility to not only make ethical decisions themselves, but also to foster a work environment that encourages others to do so.

KEY TERMS

Business ethics 151

Compliance approach 165

Discretionary responsibilities 163

Distributive justice 154

Economic responsibilities 163

Ethical relativism 154

Ethical responsibilities 163

Integrity approach 165

Justice approach 154

Legal process 158

Legal responsibilities 163

Moral rights approach 153

Procedural justice 154

Social responsibility 151

Utilitarian approach 152

REVIEW QUESTIONS

1. What are the differences between business ethics and social responsibility and why is each important to managers?
2. What are three moral principles managers can use to drive ethical decisions? How is each of these different from the others?
3. What are some reasons why managers have ethical lapses in today's organizations?
4. What is the relationship between business ethics and the laws governing business practice? What is the difference between ethics and the law?
5. What role do stakeholders play in business decisions involving ethics and social responsibility?
6. What are the levels of social responsibility that a manager may use to guide decisions and actions? How is each different from the others?
7. What is the difference between the compliance and integrity approaches to business ethics?
8. What is the relationship between basic principles of TQM, ethical behavior, and sound business decisions and action?

9. How can the profit motive undermine ethical behavior and long-term business success?
10. What makes ethics decisions complex? What are some techniques managers can use to improve the ethics of their decision making?
11. Why do managers have a responsibility to act ethically?

EXPERIENTIAL EXERCISE
The Citibank Work Ethic

Divide into groups of five or six people and discuss the following ethical dilemmas drawn from Citibank's game *The Work Ethic*. Decide what you would do in each dilemma and support your decision using the concepts presented in this chapter. (If you are short on time, you may choose to focus each group on only one or two dilemmas). Reconvene the class to discuss some of the solutions that the groups generated.

Dilemma 1: John, a vice president in your organization, asks you to help find a new job for a manager is his area. You know this manager is a poor performer, although John hasn't reflected any performance issues on the manager's performance reviews. John tells you he wants this manager out of his area within three months. Your rapport with John is critical to success in your job.

Dilemma 2: You're a manager of a systems area in a country with extremely high import duties on technological equipment. You want to import a large computer mainframe for your department. It would create 30 to 40 jobs in the local economy, which is very depressed. The problem: the import duty on the computer is about US $500,000. Colleagues advise you that local practice to avoid duty is to make a payment to government officials.

Dilemma 3: You attend a party on a weekend and notice that another manager—from another part of your business—is also a guest. You're surprised to see him use cocaine several times during the evening.

Dilemma 4: On occasion, you and your manager Pat travel together on business. After an evening of cocktails during one of these trips, Pat grabs you and kisses you in the hotel elevator. Pat has never made any kind of advance to you in the past.

Dilemma 5: You spot a situation with a customer account that you feel could be a potential threat to your company's reputation and might even expose the company legally. You tell your manager about it and he tells you there's nothing to worry about. You disagree and still think there's a problem.

CASE ANALYSIS AND APPLICATION
Joe Camel Says It's Cool[21]

R.J. Reynolds, a leading producer of tobacco products located in Winston-Salem, North Carolina, uses a cartoon character named Joe Camel to market its brand of Camel cigarettes. Joe Camel is a smartly dressed "bad-boy" who sports cool sunglasses, frequents pool halls and pickup bars, and smokes Camel cigarettes. This image is portrayed in magazines and on billboards to give the reader the feeling that he or she can have this cool lifestyle with the assistance of Camel cigarettes.

The Federal Trade Commission has recommended that the FTC ban the Joe Camel advertising campaign because it entices minors to smoke. This recommendation is supported by the U.S. Surgeon General, the American Medical Association, Attorneys General from most states, and the Coalition on Smoking or Health, which includes the American Cancer Society, American Heart Association, and American Lung Association. The recommendation is based on studies that have found that more than half the children between the ages of three and six were able to match the Joe Camel cartoon with a photo of a cigarette. Children six years old were almost as familiar with Joe Camel as they were with Mickey Mouse. This data is alarming when you consider that Camel's share of the underage market (people less than 18 years of age) has increased from 0.5 percent to more than 33 percent in the first five years of the Joe Camel campaign. This corresponds to an increase of sales to underage people from $6 million to $476 million.

R.J. Reynolds insists that "Old Joe" doesn't appeal to kids, and it invokes the First Amendment right of free speech to defend its advertising campaign. Company officials insist that advertising does not make anyone start smoking, but only causes people to switch brands. RJR admits that the Joe Camel ads appeal to younger smokers, but it argues that the ads are aimed at those of legal age. The campaign has nearly doubled sales in the market of people between 18 and 24 years of age. Joe Camel remains the focal point of Camel's advertising because of this huge success at a time when RJR is engaged in a price war with Philip Morris, its wealthier rival. To quote an RJR spokeperson, "If the campaign works among our adult target audience, why would we want to move away from it?" RJR strongly opposes any efforts to ban the Joe Camel ads.

Discussion Questions

1. Identify the various stakeholders who are affected by RJR's decision to continue its Joe Camel advertising campaign, and describe what their point of view might be. What are RJR's ethical responsibilities to each of these stakeholders?
2. Using the concepts presented in this chapter, evaluate the "ethics" of RJR's decision to continue Joe Camel advertising.

VIDEO CASE: COMBINING QUALITY MANAGEMENT AND SOCIAL RESPONSIBILITY
Rick Surpin—Cooperative Home Care Associates

Rick Surpin, President of Cooperative Home Care Associates, was honored with a Business Enterprise Award for creating a business designed not only to make a profit, but to serve a critical social need in underdeveloped areas and provide quality jobs for underemployed workers.

As director of community economic development at the Community Service Society of New York, Surpin believed that worker-owned businesses offered one of the most promising vehicles for achieving social objectives within a business context. Surpin searched for a new business that could employ over 100 people, enter a growing market, provide a needed product or service, employ people who otherwise had few job opportunities, and provide the potential for "decent jobs" (salaried positions of over $15,000 a year with benefits and a career ladder).

Despite a 60–70 percent annual turnover rate, low wages, and poor benefits, Surpin believed that a worker-owned home health care business, whose profits would be re-invested internally, could offer better wages and benefits, and full-time employment. Not only could the business provide good jobs for low-income individuals, it could give them a sense of dignity, respect, and ambition for career advancement. Surpin hoped such employment could give workers a greater sense of control over their lives and create a more stable workforce. Employees would be more satisfied, turnover would decline, and the quality of home care would improve.

With $400,000 in medium-term debt from a variety of alternative lenders, Cooperative Home Care Associates (CHCA) was born. Most of the company's employees are African-American and Hispanic women who live and work in the South Bronx and Harlem. Many are single heads of households, and nearly 80 percent were on public assistance before they began working at CHCA. Surpin deliberately fostered a sense of "organizational ownership" among the aides, and employees are treated with great dignity and respect.

Most of the company's 200+ aides have opted to become worker-owners, entitling them to vote for board members and on major policy issues. Worker-owners control 100 percent of the company and enjoy dividends. In addition, the majority CHCA's nine directors are home care aides.

Today, Cooperative Home Care Associates has eight contractors and revenues of $3 million. Employee turnover is at 15 percent, one-third that of the industry norm and the average wage per hour is $6.50, fifty cents greater than the industry norm. By restructuring the internal dynamics of a home health care company so that it is a genuine community, Rick Surpin has made Cooperative Home Care Associates a "yardstick corporation" whose achievements and reputation in a difficult field set new standards by which other companies in the industry are judged.

Video Case Questions

1. Identify the stakeholders and describe how each of them was served by Rick Surpin's creation of CHCA.
2. Do you think the workers at CHCA are more likely to behave ethically or exercise more social responsibility than their counterparts at a private, for-profit competitor? Explain your answer.

THE RITZ-CARLTON HOTEL COMPANY

In 1983, W. B. Johnson Properties set out to create a first—an American hotel group with products and services designed to appeal to and suit the demands of both the prestigious travel consumer and the corporate travel and meeting planner worldwide. Until that time, the U.S. luxury hotel industry was extremely fragmented and mostly limited to independently operated hotels that were not responsive to corporate and association meetings or multiple location requirements. Furthermore, because hotel service delivery depends on an individual's ability to properly execute various tasks, wide service variability existed, even in luxury hotels.

Because customers perceived uncertainty in selecting intangible hotel products and services and needed a reliable single supplier, our company made a clear commitment to quality. In 1983, we acquired the exclusive North American rights to the name Ritz-Carlton, the foremost name in luxury hotels for over 60 years. In order to broaden the appeal of The Ritz-Carlton, our company pioneered its own service quality approach.

By comparing the research of the travel industry against our own findings we identified the most important, yet least consistent, quality within hotels—highly personalized, genuinely caring service delivery. Today our customers are placing greater emphasis on reliability, timely delivery, and price value. Competition in the luxury segment of the hotel industry is worldwide and world class. We plan to increase our competitive advantage by becoming virtually defect free by 1996. We also plan to reach 100% customer retention. Our approach to reaching these goals is discussed below in terms of the Malcolm Baldrige National Quality Award criteria.

1.0 Leadership

At The Ritz-Carlton, the senior leadership group doubles as the senior quality committee. The senior leaders personally devised the two original quality strategies to broaden the quality leadership of The Ritz-Carlton. The first course of action was new hotel start-up quality assurance. Since 1984, the senior leadership has personally assured that each new hotel product and service provides the characteristics expected by our main customers. An important aspect of this quality practice takes place during the concentrated and intense "seven day countdown" when our senior leaders work side by side with our new employees. During these formative sessions, which all new employees must attend, the President, C. O. O. communicates our company's principles. He personally creates the employee-guest interface image and facilitates each work area's first vision statement. Throughout the entire process, the senior leaders monitor work areas for "start-up," instill our Gold Standards, model our relationship management, insist upon 100% compliance to customer's requirements, and recognize outstanding achievement.

The other initial course of action was the establishment of our Gold Standards (see Figure 1). The Gold Standards, in their simplicity, represent an easy-to-understand definition of service quality, which is aggressively communicated and internalized at all levels of the organization. The constant and continuous reinforcement techniques of our Gold Standards, led by senior leaders, include training, daily line-up meetings, pocket cards outlining our principles, bulletin board postings and other methods unique to each hotel. As a result, our employees have an exceptional understanding and devotion to our company's vision, values, quality goals, and methods.

A primary responsibility of senior leaders is the protection of the environment and society at large with respect to our business activities. Accordingly, life safety and security receive a very high priority at The Ritz-Carlton and are considered to be part of everyone's job. A three-factor security system is designed and implemented in the early stages of

Source: The authors want to thank Ritz-Carlton and Patrick Mene for providing the summary of their winning application for the Malcolm Baldrige National Quality Award as the basis for this case. Reprinted by permission of The Ritz-Carlton Hotel Company.

Three Steps of Service

1

A warm and sincere greeting. Use the guest name, if and when possible.

2

Anticipation and compliance with guest needs.

3

Fond farewell. Give them a warm good-bye and use their names, if and when possible.

"We Are Ladies and Gentlemen Serving Ladies and Gentlemen"

THE RITZ-CARLTON

CREDO

The Ritz-Carlton Hotel is a place where the genuine care and comfort of our guests is our highest mission.

We pledge to provide the finest personal service and facilities for our guests who will always enjoy a warm, relaxed yet refined ambience.

The Ritz-Carlton experience enlivens the senses, instills well-being, and fulfills even the unexpressed wishes and needs of our guests.

FIGURE 1

each new hotel and includes: (1) analysis of vulnerable areas; (2) establishment of security priorities; (3) organization of a comprehensive security system. Each new hotel also undergoes life safety risk analysis. This practice determines the proper combination of technology and procedures to achieve: (1) early detection and response to fire and other emergencies; (2) intelligent handling and evacuation of guests during emergencies; (3) minimization of property loss. At The Ritz-Carlton, senior leaders continue "going to school" on quality improvement concepts and strive to improve their effectiveness.

Lessons Learned: When senior leaders personally instill a strong vision and a set of principles in their employees and then give them the confidence, freedom and authority to act, people take responsibility for their jobs and do whatever is necessary to satisfy their customers.

2.0 Information and Analysis

Our approach to capture and use customer satisfaction and quality-related data is real time and proactive because of our intensive personalized service environment.

Systems for the collection and utilization of customer reaction and satisfaction are widely deployed and extensively used throughout the organization. Our efforts are centered on various customer segments and product lines.

Our approach is the use of systems which allow every employee to collect and utilize quality-related data on a daily basis. These systems provide critical, responsive data which includes: (1) on-line guest preference information; (2) quantity of error-free products and services; (3) opportunities for quality improvement.

Our automated property management systems enable the on-line access and utilization of guest preference information at the individual customer level. All employees collect and input this data, and use the data as part of their service delivery with individual guests.

Our quality production reporting system is a method of aggregating hotel level data from nearly two dozen sources into a summary format. It serves as an early warning system and facilitates analysis. The processes employees use to identify quality opportunities for improvement are standardized in a textbook, and available throughout our organization. Individuals and teams have access to eight improvement mechanisms. Team improvement methods are functional (within a work area) while others are cross functional (within a hotel). Some opportunities receive the attention of national cross functional teams (across hotels).

Systems for the collection and utilization of employee performance data are used exclusively to assess the capabilities of a prospective employee to meet specific job requirements. (Characteristic behaviors displayed by successful employees form the basis of a structured, empirical interview and selection process.)

Our "born at birth" benchmarking approach is focused entirely on hotel industry best practices and performances. Currently we study the best in any industry through the use of industry watchers and consultants.

Today, the goal of our business management system is to become more integrated, more proactive, and more preventive. Efforts are underway to continuously check our work to evaluate if we are providing what the customer wants most: on time every time. These test measures are then statistically charted to help teams determine when and where to act. The quality, marketing, and financial results of each hotel are aggregated and integrated to determine what quality factors are driving the financial outcome. These systems, combined with benchmarking, enable leaders and teams to better determine goals and justify expenditures.

Lessons Learned: We needed immediate responses from listening posts, combined with systems accessible to all, just to keep pace with everchanging individual customer demands.

3.0 Strategic Quality Planning

Our primary objective, during our genesis period, was opening new hotels that met the highest travel industry quality ratings by opening day. This required detailed planning and was achieved through our pre-opening control plan. This continuously improving plan synchronizes all steps leading up to opening day. A specially selected staff from other hotels throughout the company ensures all work areas, processes, and equipment are ready.

Today, the quality plan continues to be the business plan. The primary objectives are to improve the quality of our products and services, reduce cycle time and improve price value and customer retention. Through benchmarking studies within and outside of our industry, we have developed a disciplined, integrated planning system.

At each level of the company—from corporate leaders to managers and employees in the 720 individual work areas of our company—teams are charged with setting objectives and devising action plans, which are reviewed by the corporate steering committee. These teams enhance the quality and productivity of The Ritz-Carlton by: (1) aligning all levels around our common vision and objectives; (2) encouraging all of our people to think beyond the demands of day-to-day activities; (3) increasing communication among the diverse functions that make up The Ritz-Carlton; (4) simultaneous, integrated problem solving. In addition, each hotel has a quality leader who serves as a resource and advisor to teams and workers developing and implementing their quality plan. All plans center on directing the resources of The Ritz-Carlton—time, money, and people—to the wishes and needs of our guests and travel planners, as well as employees.

Lessons Learned: Action plans developed by each level of the organization must be screened to ensure they: (1) have been adequately researched; (2) have been adequately resourced; (3) contain no complexity before they are undertaken.

4.0 Human Resources Utilization

A most important resource in any organization is the people. This is especially true in a growing quality organization that provides highly personalized, genuinely caring service to a demanding prestigious travel consumer. Accordingly, the human resources function works in a closely coordinated effort with each function of our operations to unleash the potential of our workforce so they can completely and immediately satisfy the expectations of our guests.

All hotels have a director of human resources and a training manager on their staff. Both are assisted with their planning efforts by the hotel's quality leader. Each work area has a departmental trainer on staff who is charged with the training and certification of new employees in that unit.

Our commitment to planning and to realizing the full potential of our people begins with our selection process. We use a highly predictive instrument to determine the capability of a candidate to meet the requirements of each of our 120 job positions. This technology, known as "character trait recruiting," reduces service variability, acts as an aid to productivity, and has enabled us to reduce turnover by nearly 50% in the past three years.

Once a hotel is open, the training manager and the senior hotel executives work as an orientation team, over a period of two days, to personally demonstrate our Gold Standards and methods and to instill these values in all new employees. This orientation unit reconvenes three weeks later for a follow-up session to monitor the effectiveness of the instruction and to make necessary changes. At this stage the employee is considered a Lady or Gentleman at The Ritz-Carlton.

The next gate review is the responsibility of the work area leader and their departmental trainer. The new employees undergo a comprehensive training period to master the procedures of their respective position. At the end of the training period the employee must pass written and skill demonstration tests to become certified. Work area teams are responsible for setting the quality certification performance standards of each position.

Every day, in every work area, during every shift, a quality line-up meeting of employees occurs for a briefing session. During these sessions, employees receive instructions on becoming a certified quality engineer. Each employee becomes capable of identifying the wasteful complexity within their work. They are given examples of mistakes, rework, breakdowns, delays, inconsistencies, and variations.

A quality leader and her team in our Marina del Rey hotel were looking for an easy-to-remember method for communicating these types of complexities. They found the answer in a mischievous looking, animated character named Mr. Biv—the acronym of Mistakes, Rework, Breakdowns, Inefficiencies and Variations. This symbolic culprit of waste went on to serve as an inspiration to the entire workforce of our company.

Through these and other mechanisms, employees receive over 100 hours of quality education to foster premium service commitment, solve problems, set strategic quality plans and generate new ideas.

Effective involvement and empowerment grow in part from effective quality training. Each individual employee can: (1) move heaven and earth to satisfy a customer; (2) contact appropriate employees to help resolve a problem swiftly (lateral service concept); (3) spend up to $2,000 in order to satisfy a guest; (4) decide the acceptability of products and services; (5) decide the business terms of a sale (sales and marketing); (6) become involved in setting the plans of their work area; (7) speak with anyone regarding any problem.

There are many opportunities for employee recognition. A total of 39 awards are given to employees for excellence in a wide variety of areas. Performance appraisals are based upon the expectations explained during the orientation, training, and certification processes.

Individuals who consistently apply our performance standards receive verbal and written praise. Top performers receive the coveted new hotel start-up team assignment. Team-oriented awards include bonus pools when solutions they recommend to problems are successfully implemented and effective. In addition, employees of The Ritz-Carlton share in achievement through the gratuity system (money from customers for tasks performed), an immediate quality and productivity incentive program. The system of sharing gratuities is thoughtfully and purposefully integrated with our customer service goals in a manner that enhances an employee's performance against these goals.

The Ritz-Carlton safeguards the health, safety, and security of our employees and guests. Special project teams at new hotel start-ups and regular operating hotels decide the proper combination of technology and procedures in order to eliminate causes of safety and security problems. Safety, security, and health engineers conduct ongoing audits to identify any potential risks. The Ritz-Carlton has never had an industrial fatality or a major O.S.H.A. citation.

Personal security is also addressed at The Ritz-Carlton through preventive health plans, cross training, retirement plans, and the leadership principle: The genuine care and concern for each employee.

Employees are surveyed annually to ascertain their levels of satisfaction and understanding of our quality standards. Workers are keenly aware that excellence is a top hotel and personal priority. A full 96% of all employees surveyed in 1991 singled out this priority, although our company had added 3,000 new employees in the previous three years.

Lessons Learned: A collective quality commitment must be gained from the entire workforce. There is no substitute for selecting employees who believe in the organization's values.

5.0 Management of Process Quality
Our process for assuring the quality of the new hotel products and services has evolved over eight years of benchmarking, development, and improvement.

Our product management process has three integral parts: interactive team pyramid, basic product management process, and regional product management process. The entire process and its goals are supported by the senior leaders of our company who work as a binding agent with professional development planning experts, from several fields, to prevent and resolve new hotel development issues.

Several critical aspects contribute to the effectiveness of our product management process: (1) standard design team; (2) forced interface of all design, marketing, operations, and legal functions throughout each project to anticipate requirements and evaluate progress; (3) concentrated focus on basic, regional, and individual customer requirements; (4) synchronized start-up control plan that tests and evaluates the performance of facility construction, furnishings, equipment, systems, staffing, suppliers, food preparation, service delivery, and guest interface; (5) continuous emphasis on our principles and prevention of problems; (6) final assessment of products and services by senior leaders before opening day. All problems are resolved prior to initial customer occupancy while teams from operating hotels improve the entire process.

Customized hotel products and services, such as meetings and banquet events, receive the full attention of local hotel cross functional teams.

These teams are effective due to several aspects of their product management process: (1) all internal and external suppliers become involved as early as possible in the design of the event; (2) verification of production and delivery capabilities prior to each event; (3) samples are prepared, then critiqued by event planners; (4) "after event" assessments are conducted for continuous improvement; (5) all suppliers who come in contact with our customers must apply our principles, especially The Three Steps of Service, our method of guest interface (see Figure 2).

An important part of delivering quality in hotels after their initial launch is using systematic controls. We have three types of controls:

- Self control of the individual employee based upon their spontaneous and learned behavior, managed through our selection and development processes.

- Basic control mechanism which is carried out by every member of our workforce. The first person who detects a problem is empowered to break away from routine duties, investigate and correct the problem immediately, document the incident and then return to their routine. These incidents are aggregated on a daily quality production report and pattern problems are investigated and corrected permanently.

- Critical success factor control which is underway for critical processes. Process teams are using customer and organizational requirement mea-

THE RITZ-CARLTON HOTEL COMPANY
Three Steps of Service

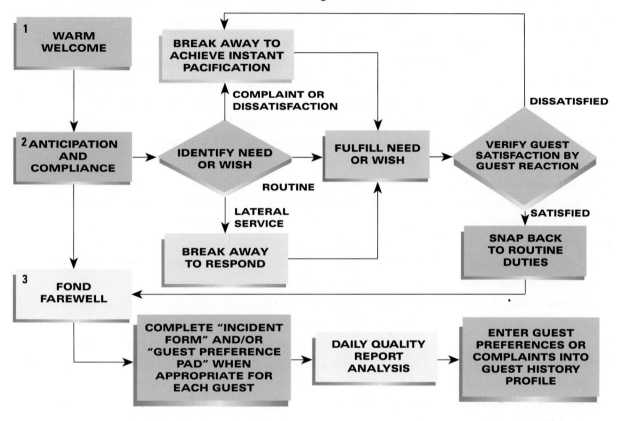

FIGURE 2

surements to determine quality, speed, and cost performance. These measurements are compared against benchmarks and customer satisfaction data to determine corrective action and resource allocation.

There are eight mechanisms used solely to improve the quality of our processes, products and services.

Method/Purpose

1. *New Hotel Start-up Improvement Process* A cross sectional team from the entire company that takes advantage of the time when our people are together to identify and correct problem areas.

2. *Comprehensive Performance Evaluation Process* The work area team mechanism that empowers the people who perform the job to develop the job procedures and performance standards. These standards drive our training certification, performance evaluation, and individual employee growth and development.

3. *Quality Network* A mechanism for the individual employee to advance a good idea through peer approval.

4. *Standing Problem Solving Team* A standing work area team that works on any problem they choose.

5. *Quality Improvement Teams* Special teams assembled to improve an assigned problem that was identified by an individual employee or leaders.

6. *Strategic Quality Planning Annual Work Area Teams* Teams that identify: (1) their missions; (2) primary supplier objectives and action

plans; (3) internal objectives and action plans; (4) progress reviews.

7. *Streamlining Process* The annual hotel evaluation of processes, products or services that are no longer valuable to the customer.

8. *Process Improvement* The team mechanism of corporate leaders, managers and employees to improve our most critical processes.

To make sure we deliver quality products and services, The Ritz-Carlton continually conducts both self audits and outside audits which are performed by independent travel and hospitality rating organizations. The means used to improve audit findings revolves around four points: (1) all audits must be documented by the person performing the audit; (2) any documented audit finding must be submitted to the senior leaders of the unit being audited; (3) senior leaders of the unit are responsible for action; (4) implementation and effectiveness of recommended corrective actions are assessed from the previous audit, using the same data.

Lessons Learned: New products and services that get off to a good start are most reliable and efficient. The major thrust of our quality effort is to prevent difficulties from ever reaching a customer.

6.0 Quality and Operational Results

The Ritz-Carlton compares its quality levels with the best competitive products and services in the U.S. and in the world. We subscribe to the ser-

vices of independent travel and hospitality professionals and rating organizations. The independent testing and consumer measurements of the American Automobile Association and the Mobil Travel Guide assess the key product and service qualities that lead to customer satisfaction and retention. These measurements cover what customers want the most: reliability and timely delivery of facilities, personalized service, genuinely caring staff, exceptional food and beverage, and value for the money spent. The quality performance criteria of these organizations includes over 100 specific quality measurements. Within the past six years, The Ritz-Carlton is the consistent benchmark for quality hotel products and services in the United States. We maintain a 10% performance gap over our best competitor (the former benchmark eight years ago). We also maintain a 95% performance gap over the industry average.

Within the past two years, The Ritz-Carlton has also been named the benchmark for quality hotel products and services in the United States by the Zagat Survey. The Ritz-Carlton was the only hotel group to receive their highest rating level (extraordinary to perfection) for all measured attributes.

Within the past two years, independent product analysis by travel industry experts has found our products and services to be competitive internationally and superior in human resources utilization. We have also achieved dramatic improvements in important

measures such as on time delivery of new hotel start-ups, rates of employee turnover, cooperation between departments, the amount of hours worked per guest room, and profits per guest room.

Lessons Learned: Never underestimate the value of even one idea or quality improvement effort.

7.0 Customer Satisfaction

Customer satisfaction is a deeply held belief at The Ritz-Carlton and begins with an absolute understanding of the needs and expectations of our customers. Customer information is gathered in a number of ways: (1) from the extensive research by the travel industry; (2) from focus groups of different market segments; (3) from preferences detected by all employees who come in contact with our customers daily; (4) from customers who have just used our products and services; (5) through our guest and travel planner satisfaction system; (6) from information collected at various points in our new hotel development.

There are five major means by which we integrate customer satisfaction and other quality related data into our business management system. They are: (1) Gold Standard leadership; (2) a cross-functional senior leadership group that also serves as the senior quality committee. This group also addresses relationship management and business simplification to make it easy for a customer to conduct business with The Ritz-Carlton (Customer relationship management is the central theme around which every employee activity is organized); (3) quality leaders at the corporate office and in the field working with supplier partners to aggregate, integrate, and analyze quality data for the senior leadership group; (4) fully utilizing the potential and expertise of the entire workforce through various mechanisms of involvement and empowerment; (5) customer driven marketing and sales efforts that determine the needs of various market segments and communicate our capabilities to these customers.

Customer contact employees are afforded excellent career opportunities. Former receptionists and servers can be found on the Executive Committee of any Ritz-Carlton Hotel.

We make it simple for our customers to voice their needs and expectations to The Ritz-Carlton. We design public spaces and employee work stations that facilitate employee-customer interface. Customer service managers are available in each hotel twenty-four hours a day. Guest comment cards, addressed to the President, C. O. O., are available in every guest room. We are accessible through 800 numbers and major airline systems. We have meeting planning services located at each hotel and in nine cities throughout the world. Employees are supported by technology, including automated systems, to provide on-line access to guest preference information for personalized service delivery. Our repeat guest system recognizes customers on the basis of their expecta-

tion that they will receive special personal recognition for their loyal patronage.

When customer standards need to be reset, problem solving teams or process improvement teams are frequently used. Standards for customer interface, such as our Gold Standards are set nationally to ensure uniformity of what customers want most. Each hotel then develops customized tasks and performance standards with employee teams to address their own unique situation. Our guest and travel planner measurement system verifies how well performance standards are met. Our standards are reset whenever customer needs and expectations change.

By acquiring the exclusive rights to The Ritz-Carlton trademark, we made a clear, unconditional commitment to our customers—expect the best. Within the past two years we have made two significant improvements in our commitment to customers. Our frequent guest program was the first nationwide hospitality program to recognize a customer's personal preferences. Our travel agent policies were the first in our industry to respond fully to the needs of travel agents in terms of commission payment, supplier partnerships and reservation practices.

Our customers tell us how well we are fulfilling our promises to them. In addition to maintaining our high standards, we actually exceed our customers' expectations in nine attributes: (1) suitability of room assignment;

(2) comfort of furnishings; (3) distinctiveness of facility; (4) genuinely caring attitude of staff members; (5) well-groomed and courteous staff members; (6) staff members are available for a service request; (7) staff members anticipate your needs; (8) staff members have on-the-spot hotel information; (9) staff members are familiar with your preferences. We are above the industry average by thirty-two points for genuinely caring employees.

When customers do have complaints, we use a customer management system that is largely driven by employees, not managers. Customer complaint management has been elevated to high levels at The Ritz-Carlton. Every customer complaint is considered important. Everyone in the organization is constantly testing, seeking out, observing and responding to customer complaints. The person who first becomes aware of a problem is the owner of that problem and is responsible for resolving it quickly and completely.

Our major method for assessing customer satisfaction has been our guest and travel planner satisfaction system. Each quarter, surveys are conducted asking guests and planners to rate their rational and emotional reactions to various aspects of our product and service delivery. The timely delivery of important attributes is not sufficient for most prestigious travel consumers; they seek a memorable experience (a feeling of elation from the overall experience). This emotional feeling cannot be captured by normal customer satisfaction survey systems and scales. We address this with supplemental measures.

The resulting customer satisfaction data is separated into major customer segments and product lines, then given comprehensive analysis with the assistance of our research partners. The individual hotels are responsible for their units' performance, while the senior leaders concentrate on the problems of the entire system. Direction for change is set on both the local and national levels. Annually, this data passes through our strategic planning process to establish objectives and action plans.

Customer satisfaction continues to achieve high levels, even in the face of our worldwide expansion. Customers are not merely satisfied; they have received a memorable experience. A full 97% of prestigious travel consumers had their expectations met and received a memorable experience. The satisfaction levels of customers who plan meetings were 97% on staff members; 97% with sales personnel; 95% with facilities, and 94% with pro-

cedures for two consecutive years. The Gallup Survey has found The Ritz-Carlton Hotel Company to be the first choice of our customers at 94% satisfaction rating compared to our closest competitor at 57% satisfaction rating, for the past two years. A nationwide study of frequent business travelers found we are the clear choice of customers who use our competitors— we outperformed our best competitor an average of 15 points on nine attributes.

While customer satisfaction has been increasing, adverse indicators of customer dissatisfaction, such as rebates and complaints, have declined.

Perhaps the best indicator of customer satisfaction is customer retention. Over the past three years our key national account retention has improved 20% toward our goal of 100% retention. During this time, we corrected the price/value concerns of our customers. Over the past three years, our business center hotels have retained 97.1% of their key local corporate accounts. At The Ritz-Carlton, the objective of our quality effort is: *never lose a single customer.*

 CASE QUESTIONS

1. Based on what you learned in the first five chapters, list what you think are the major challenges that managers face today. List at least one example of how The Ritz-Carlton managers have taken on roles and responsibilities to deal with each of these challenges.

2. Imagine that you have been retained as a consultant by a competitor of The Ritz-Carlton Hotel Company. It is your job to develop a set of management principles that will enable your hotel company to compete with The Ritz-Carlton. Drawing from the systems and approaches illustrated in this case, write this set of principles. Each principle should be only a sentence or two in length.

3. What elements of Total Quality Management did The Ritz-Carlton overlook? Based on your own experiences with hotels and what you have learned in this book so far, make some suggestions for improving The Ritz-Carlton's approach to management.

STRATEGIC MANAGEMENT

6. DECISION MAKING AND TQM

MAKING DECISIONS AT SAMSUNG AND AT NEXT[1]

I magine you are Lee Kun-Hee, chairman of Samsung Electronics Co. of Korea, a corporation with annual sales of over $54 billion. When Samsung was becoming a powerhouse in the electronics market (it is the world's largest manufacturer of computer memory chips, for example), the company was able to compete because of cheap labor and cheap Korean currency. However, as the 51-year-old chairman of Samsung, you know those days are past. The playing field is level, and your competition is every other world class company in the electronics industry.

In the past, your company's culture was conservative, and decisions were made at the top or only after consultation with top managers. You know that won't work anymore. It slows things down, and it doesn't foster creativity and problem-solving skills among your thousands of employees and managers. Because of your training at a top Japanese university and George Washington University, you understand that you have to make some radical changes in your company's culture and values if you are going to get people to take a new approach to their responsibilities and work. You want your employees to better understand the global business environment and make decisions that will help them make the company a strong competitor in its markets.

In Korea, the traditional hours for work are long, usually from about 9:00 A.M. to 8:00 P.M., with drinks with buddies afterward. However, you are trying to break tradition, so you change the work hours at Samsung from 7:00 A.M. to 4:00 P.M. Then, to make sure your employees get the message, you randomly call employees after 4:00 P.M., and if they are still at work, you chew them out. You want them to understand that you are not looking for long hours; you want your workers to be more productive. With the shorter work days, people have time for self-improvement off the job as well as time to take company sponsored training courses.

Once, on a trip to Frankfurt with several senior colleagues, one of your most trusted advisors tells you while you are on the plane that he believes the Samsung Design Center is poorly run. He also reports that nobody at the center would listen to his advice for improvement. You also hear that a piece of expensive testing equipment isn't being used because of a broken socket. When you land at Frankfurt you get on the phone, and about an hour later, when you are done telling the employees back in Seoul of your displeasure in terms they cannot mistake, you order that a tape you have made of the conversation be played for everyone at the center. You declare at the end of that call what comes to be known as the Frankfurt Declaration: "Quality first, no matter what."

As chairman, you have consciously decided to be dramatic time and time again because you know that is what is necessary to transform your company

into a world-class competitor. Your decisions about the company, its policies, its culture, its emphasis on quality products and well-trained employees, are all consistent with this goal.

Now, switch gears and imagine you are Steve Jobs, the co-founder of Apple Computer and the founder of Next, Inc. You are known as a visionary in the personal computer business and the force behind the development of the Macintosh computer in the early 1980s. After you left Apple, you started Next to create computer workstations for use in universities and then later for businesses as well.

However, despite your reputation as a near legend in this business, things don't go well for your new company. For example, you insist on including an optical disk drive in your new computer, a device that allows for hundreds of megabytes of memory on a single disk, but is very slow to access information and is expensive. Because yours is the only machine with this drive, software companies refuse to deliver their programs on these disks. You finally agree to put a floppy drive in the machine, but only after being forced into it. Your machine, while clever, has no clear advantages over competing products from companies like Apple, Sun, and others.

You also develop innovative systems software, called NextStep for your machine. This software is lauded as years ahead of the competition and that it makes applications programs like word processors much easier to develop. In 1989 you cut a deal with IBM for them to use NextStep as systems software for a new generation of their machines. However, the agreement gets bogged down when you insist on absolute control over how NextStep is used in IBM's products. You are afraid IBM machines using NextStep will undermine sales of your computer. IBM, frustrated with your attitude, withdraws from its deal with you and forms an alliance with Apple to develop an alternative to your program, which they call Taligent.

You continue to believe in your computer and in NextStep and keep making decisions to invest the company's dwindling resources in the refinement of the machine and the software. But it's slow going, and the machine is not catching on. Several times various advisors tell you that you need to go with your strength, NextStep, and abandon the hardware business. You just don't have the resources to compete against billion dollar companies, despite your reputation. You seem to listen, but you keep throwing more money into refinement of your computer, and this takes funds away from the development of a version of NextStep that would work on Intel microprocessors used in all IBM-compatible machines, a necessary action if you want to make NextStep a software standard.

Finally, in early 1993 you see the writing on the wall, and you make the decision to close down the hardware business—you are running out of money, and you really have no choice. Next, Inc. will now just be a software company, but it was unclear that, even with a good product, it could survive.

MANAGERS AND DECISIONS

By putting yourself in the place of these managers, perhaps you can begin to appreciate the importance and implications of management decisions. They can have a profound effect on an organization and its future. At Samsung and at Next, these CEOs were making decisions that have affected the future of their companies. In one case, the decisions were good ones and in the other not so good. This chapter is about how managers make decisions, large and small, important and routine, that give direction to an organization's processes and the people who execute them. As we have seen, since the decisions of managers determine the fate of an organization, it is critical that their decisions are good ones. For this to happen, it is very useful to understand exactly what sound decision making is all about.

Decision Making Defined

Decision making—deciding what to do next, figuring out which opportunity to pursue, or solving a problem—is an important part of any manager's responsibility. More formally, **decision making** is *a process for developing and selecting a course of action to address problems or opportunities*. A **problem** exists *when actual conditions differ from what is desired or when people need an answer to a question*. An **opportunity** is *an occasion to make an improvement or to create new possibilities*.

Managers make decisions every day. Some decisions are small, in terms of their consequences or importance, like deciding where to hold a department meeting. Others are large, like deciding whether to abandon or continue in a particular line of business. In fact, decision making is so pervasive in managerial activities, we can consider it to be the essence of management. In making decisions, managers are responsible for developing and selecting courses of action that enable the organization to accomplish its purpose, such as business strategy, the deployment of human resources, and how to manage technology.

Decisions in Everyday Life

Before launching into the details of managerial decision making, keep in mind that making decisions is not a unique activity. We all make decisions everyday as we go about our lives. As a student, you make decisions about things like where you live, what activities you will participate in, what topic you will write a paper on, where you will spend your next semester or quarter break, whether to buy a car or not, and lots more. How much fun you have, how well you do in school, how far your money goes are all dependent on the decisions you make.

Most of us make our decisions at least somewhat unconsciously. We are confronted with situations, and we are aware of alternatives; we choose one, and move ahead. It is part of our normal everyday experience, and we usually don't think much about the mental processes that go into this. If the consequences of the decision are positive or negative—you chose the wrong subject for your paper, for example, and cannot find enough references—you learn from that. And this experience will influence what you do when you are confronted with a similar situation in the future.

Mostly our everyday decisions concern minor problems or opportunities, and if we make a decision with results we don't like, the consequences are not dire. However, this is not always true for managers. Their decisions can and do affect many people throughout the organization who are dependent on what they decide and do. The failure or success of most businesses often hangs on the quality of decisions and their implementation by managers and others in the organization.

Decision making A process for developing and selecting a course of action to address problems or opportunities.

Problem A situation that exists when actual conditions differ from what is desired or when people need an answer to a question.

Opportunity An occasion to make an improvement or to create new possibilities.

THINKING CRITICALLY

1. Without looking at the book, write out your own definition of decision making. After you have done this, compare it to the definition above. Do they differ? In what ways?
2. Why do you think decision making is so crucial to what managers do?

DECISION MAKING, PROBLEM SOLVING, AND TQM

Role Models for Excellence

In the case in point at the opening of this chapter, we asked you to put yourself in the place of two managers making decisions with quite different consequences for their companies. We saw that in each case there was a consistency in their decisions, based on the personal goals they have for themselves and their companies. Normally when we reflect on decision making, we think about choices that we and others make among alternatives. That is one way to understand decisions.

However, there are other ways to make sense of this process that may shed more light on what is going on when we make decisions. *The decisions we make really reflect our best understanding of ourselves in relation to the situations in which we find ourselves at the time we make those decisions.* In other words, we don't make decisions exactly. What we do is understand situations. Steve Jobs' actions, for example, represent how he viewed or understood himself and his company in the business environment in which they operate. Given his understanding, he could not have done anything other than what he did. If you look at your own or the decisions of any other person, you will see that the choices we all make are *always* consistent with our best understanding of ourselves in relation to the circumstances *at the time*. This understanding and the subsequent actions we take reflect the information we have available and our experience and knowledge in similar situations.

Thus, the quality of our understanding of various situations will greatly influence the quality our decisions and the subsequent actions we take. What becomes significant in the decision-making process is not the decision, but the way we make sense of all the things that impinge on that decision. Once we understand a situation in a particular way, the decision becomes obvious and the most trivial part of the process. It is like working a math problem. Once you understand the elements of the problem and how they fit together, you can only come to one solution. If you have misunderstood these elements, your solution will not be correct. In matters less precise than mathematics, such as in managing organizations or most other human activities, there is never just one right answer or decision. However, this does not change the fact that our decision in any situation will still depend on how we understand and define the problem or situation we are dealing with.

Returning to the managers in the opening cases, Lee Kun-Hee had an understanding or vision for what he wanted his company to be like to remain competitive and grow. He also had an understanding of the core problems that were preventing the company from achieving that vision. This provided the context for his decisions on how to shake up the bureaucracy and non-responsiveness of Samsung employees to make them more aware of their obligation to help the company become more competitive. The decisions he made in each situation he encountered where employees were not changing can best be understood by knowing this vision. Steve Jobs also had a vision for his compa-

A LOOK AT

DIVERSITY

LEVI STRAUSS DECIDES ACCORDING TO ITS PRINCIPLES[2]
The Levi Strauss Company, under the leadership of CEO Robert Haas, is committed to developing a culture that is sensitive to the needs of its employees, its customers, and the community. This commitment reflects Haas' understanding that by caring about these groups, the company is looking out for itself. This has led to several management decisions regarding such issues as diversity training and the care of AIDS patients.

The company vision statement includes the concept "the corporation without boundaries." To Haas and the company's management, this means developing programs that promote employee awareness of cultural and ethnic diversity. Executing this vision has included making decisions to offer programs that educate its employees on minority, lifestyle, and gender issues, and achieving a balance between the need to meet organizational objectives and human concerns. The programs emphasize the importance of tolerance for and understanding of the value systems and behaviors of different ethnic and lifestyle groups.

As an example of its progressive social attitude, Levi Strauss developed an internal AIDS program that included an information desk, an AIDS education committee, an employee task force, and an AIDS training program to inform people about the epidemic. The company has made sure that its medical plan covers health care and hospice services for AIDS patients. As another example, Levi Strauss provides funding for "Project Change," which is dedicated to reducing racism and dismantling the institutional mechanisms that sustain its effects. Levi Strauss has not only helped employees to appreciate the personal differences among themselves, but also the importance of marketing merchandise to different cultures.

These changes have increased employee empowerment, morale, and commitment to the company. Robert Haas and all the employees at Levi Strauss understand that by making decisions that honor the diversity of its workforce and its customers, they also look out for the company at the same time.

While Levi Strauss's commitment to diversity has been a source of strength in developing its company culture and in reaching new markets, it sometimes gets into hot water. For example, the company recently cut its funding for Boy Scout activities because of the group's ban on homosexual troop leaders. This move led some Christian groups to call for a boycott of Levi Strauss and prompted a flood of complaints from the public. Even some of its own employees and retailers have complained. Despite the heat, Levi's executives argue that standing firm sends an important message to employees of all races and lifestyles. Do you think Levi Strauss made the right decision about cutting funding for Boy Scout activities?

ny and how it would be what some people called "the next great thing." So intensely did he believe this vision and so closed was he from marketplace realities, that his decisions, though consistent with his vision, were actually hurting his company. We can understand why he made his decisions only by knowing about his vision.

TQM and Systems as the Context for Sound Management Decisions

We have consistently stressed that TQM is the logical outcome of understanding an organization as a system. It provides guidelines, tools, and techniques for managing a system efficiently and effectively. TQM principles and the idea of an organization as a system also provide a context for understanding and dealing with the situations that managers confront routinely every day or situations that are special. These principles help managers understand those situations and guide their decisions in figuring how an organization might attain positive results for all its stakeholders.

For example, if Steve Jobs had better understood his company as a system with the purpose of delivering value to its customers and other stakeholders, the nature of his actions might have been different. He might have looked a little harder at how well the company was pleasing its customers in light of its resources and the competition and then understood better that the direction he was taking the company in was not good. He might have seen that customers did not value his offerings enough to bring in the funds necessary to succeed in the personal computer market. Or he might have seen that the company's processes needed to be more efficient to deliver a product at a low enough price to attract more customers. In retrospect, we can see how his misunderstanding of his company and its abilities to compete led to the current demise of the hardware part of Next. However, if Jobs had thought more about his company in terms suggested by TQM, his decisions might have been different, and the Next computer might have fared better in the marketplace.

Questions TQM Suggests to Help Managers Make Better Decisions

To understand a situation or problem and come to a conclusion about it that leads to a decision and action usually requires that managers get answers to various questions. Thus, asking the right questions about a situation is very important. This is like an attorney trying a case before a jury. The case will turn on the questions he or she asks the witnesses and the interpretation put on those answers. To draw out the evidence that will cause the jury to *decide* on the verdict desired, the right questions have to be asked. The same is true for managers except they are seeking information not for a jury but for themselves to help them decide what to do.

TQM suggests several questions a manager might ask to get information that will lead to the best decisions for the company and all its stakeholders. By getting answers to these questions, managers are more likely to have the information they need to correctly understand a situation and then take actions that are most likely to lead to organizational success (or minimize the risk of failure). What follows is a sampling of such questions. This list cannot be complete, as different problems and situations will suggest variations on this list. Many of these questions will derive from the principles of TQM that we reviewed in Chapter 3. As you read this list, think about how asking these questions and getting answers to them might have affected the managerial decisions and actions described in the two situations described in the case in point at the opening of this chapter.

1. What are the underlying conditions in the organization that current problems may be symptoms of? (This question will help get at the fundamental causes of a problem.)
2. What changes can we make in our processes to prevent this problem from happening again? (This question will help managers fix the fundamental causes of a problem and not simply alleviate a symptom.)
3. What factual data versus opinions do we have about this process and how well it works? (This question focuses all employees on gathering data rather than making guesses about a problem.)
4. Are these processes in statistical control? (By understanding if a process is in statistical control or not, managers can determine whether a problem has a special cause outside the system or is the result of a common cause within the system.)

GOOD MANAGERS . . . BAD ETHICAL DECISIONS[3]

A LOOK AT

ETHICS

In a Harvard Business Review article of a few years ago, Saul W. Gellerman sought to answer the question of why seemingly good managers would make unethical decisions. In this article he cites three examples of companies whose managers made bad ethical decisions:

• The Manville Corporation was the major U.S. producer of asbestos. Nearly 40 years ago the company started to hear about the health problems asbestos was creating for its employees. Manville managers suppressed this information and even chose not to tell the employees who had been checked by company doctors and found to be ill. Why did they do this? The managers found themselves caught up in an environment where they determined that it was cheaper to pay workman's compensation claims than to develop safer working conditions. While this seems terrible, the managers thought they were acting in the best interests of the company, never realizing the long-term implications of this decision. In the mid-1980s, a lawsuit against Manville brought by thousands of former employees resulted in the company turning over more than 80 percent of its equity to a trust to compensate those who had sued the company.

• The chairman of the Continental Illinois Bank declared in 1976 that he wanted his bank's lending to match that of the largest bank in the country. The bank achieved this goal but only by pursuing lending opportunities that were extremely risky. The company began to take over the loans of many smaller banks, and in particular got involved with poorly capitalized oil producers in Oklahoma. When oil prices fell, those who borrowed the money defaulted, and the bank lost a billion dollars. Even when a lower-level employee attempted to warn the chairman of the risky nature of the bank's lending policies, the chairman ignored him, so enamored was he with his goal of making big buck loans. Eventually the bank went under and over 80 percent of its assets were under control of the Federal Deposit Insurance Corporation.

• E.F. Hutton & Company ran a scheme for several years where branch managers would deposit clients' checks in one of its banks and write checks on those before the funds were collected by the bank, thus giving itself interest-free loans. Though everyone knew this was a shady practice, branch managers were routinely congratulated for their skill in doing this. When the government finally discovered what the company was doing, Hutton had to pay fines of nearly $3 million. Worse, though, was that for a company that asks customers to trust it with their money, Hutton had severely undermined its reputation.

Why do managers of companies like these make such poorly considered and unethical decisions? Gellerman suggests four rationalizations for their behavior, all of which are interrelated. They have to do with the overall managerial perception that nearly any behavior can be acceptable if it is in the short-term best interest of the company. These four are:

1. *Top managers come to believe that the questionable activity is within reasonable ethical limits and is not really illegal or unethical.* For a short-term gain, these managers are willing to push the definition of what is ethical to its limits. There is no specific ban on the activity, so they figure it is ok. In taking this attitude, they create an environment where lower-level managers lose their sense of what is ethical, believing that behaving in questionable ways is what they have to do to succeed, and things just progress from bad to worse. At some point they may even cross the line from the unethical to illegal, because they never really learned any limits.

2. *Top managers come to believe that the activity is in the individual's or the company's best interest and that the individual is somehow expected to undertake the activity.* This is a way

to get results, but it only looks at the world from the viewpoint of the company or the individual manager. These managers fail to understand the full implications of this attitude on others. Gellerman suggests that top managers who want to combat this kind of attitude must be concerned with more than just results; they have to look at how results are obtained.

3. *Top managers come to believe that the activity is "safe" because it will never be found out or publicized—as long as they won't get caught, it's fine.* This has long been a reason among managers to act unethically or even illegally. They believe there is no price to pay for their wrong behavior, so why not do it? To deal with this attitude, Gellerman suggests not more severe punishment for transgressors, but to heighten the perceived likelihood of being caught.

4. *Managers come to believe that because the activity helps the company, even if it is questionable ethically, the company will condone it and even protect the person who engages in it.* Like number 3, there seems to be a payoff for managers who engage in unethical behavior, and the company will protect them if they get caught. Unless top managers, by their words and deeds, discourage such behaviors, unethical behavior will become acceptable among the ambitious.

In thinking about these behaviors and the rationales for them, it is helpful to ponder how many managers assume their organizations are somehow separate from the larger society in which they function. The problem is this is always a false assumption. For those who believe they can prosper by taking advantage of their customers or society, they will learn the hard way this is not possible. One of the benefits of the open systems view of organizations and TQM is that it raises management consciousness that organizations are part of the larger society, and that to look out for the organization, they must also look out for that society—a sound and sensible foundation for highly ethical behavior.

5. How are our products and services designed to provide value to customers? How do our customers perceive the quality of our products and services compared to our competitors? (This question focuses managers on the benefits versus the costs of its offerings for customers. It also focuses them on asking whether customers will value these enough to pay for them compared to offerings from competitors.)

6. Are managers working to make sure our processes are aligned with and capable of providing offerings that customers value? (This question makes sure managers are fulfilling their responsibility to improve processes.)

7. Have we given our employees the resources, training, and authority to solve problems that arise from conditions or processes they control before they become big problems? (This question addresses whether the organization is using employees to their best advantage and what changes they might make to do this.)

8. Do we know how our employees throughout different parts of the organization are working together to accomplish our overall mission? (This question gets managers thinking about the cross-functional nature of most work and how to get employees working together most efficiently.)

9. Do we have methods in place that allow us to continually improve our processes and the quality of our offerings? (This question forces managers to focus on the continuous improvement of organizational processes to help the company remain competitive.)

In reviewing these questions, note how they all focus on organizational processes and serving customers. Asking such questions forces managers to understand business problems and opportunities in certain ways.

? THINKING CRITICALLY

1. What decisions have you made and acted on that, if you had understood the situation differently, would have resulted in a different action?
2. Why do you think TQM and the view of organizations as systems provide a sound context for understanding business situations, making decisions, and taking actions?

TYPES OF DECISION SITUATIONS

Managers and organizations face different types of decision situations. Many business situations are routine and familiar and require a standardized decision and action. For example, in response to a customer complaint about food quality, a restaurant manager or employee will routinely offer the customer another item for free. When these situations occur, managers have come to understand the best ways to handle them, and decisions require little time or thought. Other times managers will confront situations that are new or unusual and not clearly defined. An example would be whether or not to invest in research and development on a newly emerging technology. Here, a manager has to gather information and, using some set of assumptions, interpret it to decide whether to move ahead or not.

Those who study management have developed terms to describe these two general types of decision situations. They are called: **programmed decision situations,** which are *familiar situations for which standard decisions and actions have been developed,* and **nonprogrammed decision situations,** which are *new, novel, or poorly defined situations that require special analysis and actions to deal with.*

Programmed Decision Situations

Managers often have to face similar problems or situations over and over again. When this happens and they have defined and analyzed the components of a particular problem, they can usually develop a programmed solution or procedure for dealing with it. In such situations, managers or employees do not really have to make a decision, it is already programmed for them in terms of a rule, policy, or procedure. A **rule** provides *a proven solution and prescribes what a manager should or should not do.* For example, a company travel rule may dictate that everyone should travel economy class, and not first class. A **policy** only provides *guidelines to influence thinking, and unlike a rule, it requires some judgment.* For example, a human resource policy that states "we select and promote the most qualified people" requires some judgment to interpret what the term "most qualified" means. A **procedure** provides *a definite approach or sequence of steps to resolve a problem.* For example, a grocery store follows a procedure for determining when to restock its shelves and how much inventory to

Programmed decision situations Familiar situations for which standard decisions and actions have been developed.

Nonprogrammed decision situations New, novel, or poorly defined situations that require special analysis and actions to deal with.

Rule A proven solution or prescription for what a manager should or should not do.

Policy Guidelines to influence thinking and requiring the use of judgment.

Procedure A definite approach or sequence of steps to resolve a problem.

order from suppliers based on a formula that comes from an analysis of forecasts, past sales, and seasonal trends. In programmed decision situations, all managers or employees need to do is make sure they implement the rule, policy, or procedure properly.

Programmed decisions can be an important part of a company's strategy for improving how it operates, for example in its relations with customers. In the past, Compaq Computer had a reputation for being "standoffish." However, the company changed its policy for dealing with consumers of its products. Before the change, if a consumer called in and said he or she had bought a Compaq computer but had no documentation, Compaq would respond, "Call your dealer." Today Compaq will send the documents overnight upon request.[4]

Total Quality Management, as noted above, provides managers with guidelines for making the rules, policies, and procedures that govern programmed decision situations. These guidelines focus attention on actions that will enhance quality delivered to customers and the efficiency and improvement of organizational processes by which work gets done. Compaq's new way of being more responsive to consumers is an example of how TQM influenced one company policy. TQM also helps in nonprogrammed decision situations, though the proper action is not always immediately obvious.

Nonprogrammed Decision Situations

Nonprogrammed decision situations are those that are unusual or hard to define initially. Such situations do not have standard rules, policies, or procedures for generating appropriate decisions and actions. Managers have to treat these situations as unique and think through them to develop a particular response. For example, a management team hearing presentations from three advertising agencies seeking their account is not a situation where a programmed response is appropriate. This requires careful analysis and balancing of various factors based on the organization's needs, resources, customers' needs and other factors from which a final understanding will emerge pointing to their choice.

Dealing with nonprogrammed decision situations is an important responsibility for top managers, where their decisions will broadly affect the organization. For example, when Don Fites, chairman of Caterpillar, Inc., the heavy equipment manufacturer, was faced with a strike by the United Auto Workers, who insisted on negotiating an agreement similar to those with the John Deere Company, Fites decided this was not in Caterpillar's best interest. When the union employees struck and refused to compromise, he threatened dismissal of all who did not return and the hiring of replacement workers. Many members of the union gave in and returned to work.[5] This kind of decision certainly cannot be programmed, though it is consistent with Don Fites' view of what he believes are management prerogatives to act in the best interests of the company. Further, this is not the kind of decision that could have been made by managers at lower levels of the company.

Nonprogrammed decision situations that top of the organization most often deals with will include those dealing with areas like organizational strategy, restructuring, and labor relations. However, managers at all levels of an organization are becoming more involved with nonprogrammed decision situations. There is a trend toward increased participation and empowerment of employees to deal with various problems. This allows mid-level managers and supervisors to solve problems based on their experience and understanding of what is in the best interest of the organization, without having to follow specific rules, policies, or procedures. Lower-level managers usually deal with nonprogrammed decision-making situations that are narrow and affect only certain operations, such as problem solving to reduce product defects, selection of work tools, and revision of work methods.

Programmed decisions emerge over time as managers repeatedly encounter the same or similar problems. For example, a manager may repeatedly decide on requests for unpaid time off, treating each as a unique case, and then eventually establish a rule to formally handle all cases in the future. Managers have even devised procedures and formulas to help them make complex decisions, such as to evaluate corporate investment opportunities, for example, based on market growth potential and returns on investment.

Managers should be careful in trying to reduce complex situations to a handful of definable factors that they can quantify and plug into a formula. Such an approach may give managers comfort that they have objectively and scientifically come to a decision. But the feeling can be deceptive if there are significant issues left unaddressed by such analysis. Managers may often have to rely on other factors, such as their intuition, experience, and consensus among a team of people. Most of the important decision situations that managers face are going to be nonprogrammed in nature.

Empowerment and the Delegation of Decisions

In Chapter 3, we reviewed the idea of empowering employees by giving them the resources, training, and the authority to solve problems and continuously improve work processes. In earlier times, employees on the line had no real authority over their work; their bosses decided everything. However, today this is both inefficient and inappropriate. The management approach articulated by TQM recognizes this. It acknowledges that those doing the work are also the ones most qualified to solve problems that come up as they go about their jobs and figure out how to improve their work processes.

In the past, management basically laid out rules, policies, and procedures, and employees followed them. Any decision situation in which they were involved was either covered by these rules, policies, and procedures, or required checking with management before taking any action. Nonprogrammed decision situations were not the province of workers. But in organizations that seek to take full advantage of their employees' talents and abilities and make best use of everyone's time, it just makes more sense for those who best understand a particular problem or improvement opportunity to make decisions to deal with those. Allowing that to happen, of course, means that everyone has a clear sense of the organization's processes and mission and how their work fits in with that of others to execute processes and to achieve that mission.

In Chapter 14, we will see how employees at Edy's have authority for all the processes involved in making their ice cream products. As another example, Don Fites at Caterpillar has also been a champion of empowerment, turning over authority for pricing to district offices, where salespeople are closer to customers and understand their needs.[6]

Exhibit 6-1 on page 210 spells out the difference in attitudes toward empowerment between the traditional hierarchical management approach and the TQM approach. In the former, all control resides with management. In the latter, managers acknowledge the responsibility and authority workers should have to maximize their contribution to the organization.

EXHIBIT 6-1 Comparison of Traditional and TQM Approaches

	Traditional Management Approach	TQM Approach
Overall Perception of Employees	Some employees might be careless or sloppy. Some might be dishonest. The company must protect itself and cannot rely on its people.	All employees are to be trusted and respected. Loyalty drives everyone to safeguard company materials. Ethics and integrity unquestioned.
Financial Assets	Authorization for funds depends on level in management hierarchy. Multiple signatures required.	A person's job needs, not position, define authorization for handling funds.
Physical Assets	Passkeys provided only to managers and to designated employees.	Any employee can access any place (safety practices will be followed, if appropriate).
Business Information	Sensitive information is available only to managers and designated employees.	Any employee can access any information.
Level of Authority	Employees and managers can only make decisions or solve problems with the approval of their manager.	Employees have authority to solve problems and make improvements regarding their work in concert with company mission and processes.

Source: Adapted from Arthur R. Tenner and Irving J. DeToro, *Total Quality Management: Three Steps to Continuous Improvement* (Reading, MA: Addison-Wesley Publishing Co., Inc., 1992) p. 182.

Less and More Uncertainty

In business and in life, there are few if any sure things. Try as we might, and we do try hard, we cannot predict the future consequences of our actions or the actions of others with complete certainty. As individuals or as managers, we encounter various situations, we do our best to make sense of them, and based on our conclusions, decide what our next moves will be. Programmed decision situations have outcomes that, on a continuum with "less uncertain" at one end and "more uncertain" at the other, fall at the "less uncertain" end. Conversely, the outcomes in nonprogrammed decision situations will fall at the more uncertain end of the continuum. A goal of managers is to work at limiting the amount of uncertainty in the actions that result from their decisions. Exhibit 6-2 illustrates a continuum of uncertainty and how this relates to programmed and nonprogrammed decision situations.

Less Uncertainty.   Under conditions of less uncertainty, managers usually have accurate and reliable information on the outcomes of various actions they might take. Since they have a good idea what will happen, making the decision is generally straightforward. However, as we noted above, all decisions have some uncertainty about them, and we can never be completely sure of a particular outcome.

   For example, consider the purchase of new office furniture. If price is an important criteria, a manager may simply compare prices and select the least expensive. Even in this kind of situation, unexpected problems might occur when there are competing objectives. If the company decides that it will

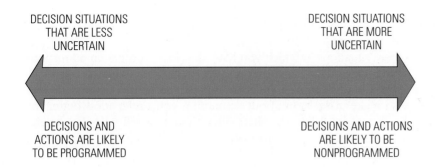

EXHIBIT 6-2
A continuum of decision uncertainty

uniformly supply all of its offices with one style of furniture, there may be conflict among office employees based on personal preferences. Some people may prefer ergonomically designed office furniture that provides back support, while others prefer another style that has a certain aesthetic appeal. In addition, the overall price of such office equipment can be uncertain because of the unpredicted costs associated with late delivery or poor warranty service. Such problems often require tradeoffs that can complicate even seemingly simple decisions. There is some degree of uncertainty in every managerial decision, especially in today's business environments that are complex and dynamic.

More Uncertainty.   Managers face more uncertainty in figuring out what to do when confronted with decision situations where outcomes are ambiguous. This happens when there is a reasonable chance that events will not turn out as planned, either because the conditions change or the information on which they base decisions is not good enough. Careful and thoughtful managers usually have enough information about a situation to understand and predict the probability or likelihood of various outcomes. Managers may be able to judge these probabilities based on intuition, past experience, expert advice, and analysis of past history. However, there is often a lot of risk involved, and even seemingly well-considered decisions, such as starring Arnold Schwarzenegger in *The Last Action Hero* movie can go bust.

Wallace Co.: Baldrige Award Winner

Managers may occasionally face decision situations where they feel almost complete uncertainty. Perhaps the business environment is beyond the control of the company, or managers may simply not understand it very well. The reactions of people affected by a decision, such as competitors or customers, may be completely unpredictable. For example, an acquisition manager at a publishing company may have to decide whether to sign a contract with an author to write a book without any well-defined idea of how the public will respond to the book. Most of the time, though, managers have at least some knowledge of the outcomes. Experienced acquisition managers, for instance, can usually spot a "bad" book when they see it; however, they usually cannot figure out which books are likely to make the bestseller lists.

Two factors that affect uncertainty concern the availability of accurate and reliable information about (1) customer needs and (2) what the competition is doing. Careful formulation of the decision problem or opportunity, thorough information gathering and analysis, and clear thinking all help to reduce the potential negative effects of a decision and increase the potential positive effects. This suggests using a rational process that employs the insights of TQM and the systems view for understanding situations and making decisions.

? THINKING CRITICALLY

1. Are there situations in which you have developed programmed responses for handling them? What are these? Are your responses effective?
2. Have you ever been in a situation where you had to depend on someone else to make a decision about something you understood better than the decision maker? What was that? What does that tell you about delegating decision making to the appropriate level in an organization?

A RATIONAL APPROACH TO DECISION MAKING

We have stressed that decision making has to do with *understanding a situation* and then taking action based on that understanding. We all use the word "understanding" frequently without thinking much about the definition of that word. For the purposes of reviewing a rational approach to decision making, it is useful to define what it means to *understand a situation.* When we use this phrase, we mean that a person comprehends how the components of a situation—people, equipment, money, suppliers, the business environment, customers, time, and other things—relate to each other in an ordered fashion. In other words, we see how everything fits together and what changes are likely to happen through time. A rational approach to decision making is about figuring out the order and relationships among a situation's relevant components so we are most likely to get things right and act successfully.

Such an approach requires managers to think through a number of issues to figure out what the situation's components are, the different ways they might relate to one another, and how they will react once the organization takes some action. The goal is to develop the most realistic course of action in light of the organization's objectives, the information available, and management's knowledge and experience. Once managers have done this, the decision and actions are simply the logical extension of this process. Doing this in a conscious and conscientious fashion is what we mean by using the word **rational.** We are *using sound procedures, carefully collected data, and sound analysis, all directed toward achieving established organizational goals and objectives.* This is not easy to do, and we never have enough information, but compared to decision by hunch and guesswork, it is much more likely to yield positive results.

Rational The use of sound procedures, carefully collected data, and sound analysis, all directed toward achieving established organizational goals and objectives.

The *rational decision-making* process involves six steps:

1. Recognize and define the problem or opportunity and its affected organizational components.
2. Gather information about the problem or opportunity.
3. Generate alternative courses of action and the effects of these on organizational processes.
4. Choose your action based on the outcomes that will get results most consistent with organizational goals and objectives.
5. Implement the action.
6. Assess the results.

We will now review each of these steps in depth.

1. Recognize and Define the Problem or Opportunity

The first step in the rational decision-making process is to recognize a problem or opportunity. To do so, the manager has to know the mission, vision, and goals of the organization, and then observe and listen to employees, customers, suppliers, competitors, and other sources of information in the business environment. Vigilant observation can reveal questions that need to be answered, perceived discrepancies between current or future performance and goals, undesirable situations that need correcting, and opportunities that could or should be pursued. For example, Phil Knight, chairman of Nike, has recognized that if he wants his company to continue to grow at the rate it has in the past, the company has to more aggressively pursue sales in the international marketplace. That is an opportunity he has recognized.[7]

Once managers have recognized a problem or opportunity, they then must clearly define it. At this point the manager should become an investigator to gather more information about the decision situation to help them better understand the problem or opportunity. Otherwise, they may simply react to the symptoms or attempt to solve only the easy and readily apparent aspects of the problem. Before a problem can be solved the manager must understand the causes. In the case of Nike, the company's managers have defined one aspect of the problem of poor growth in the international market as being related to ineffective distribution and unfocused advertising.

In addition to defining the problem or opportunity, the manager also needs to make sure that the situation really requires a new course of action. Is it important, relevant, expected, or worthy of managerial attention? What will be gained? What are the goals for the decision? What aspects of the problem should be addressed? Once managers define the problem or opportunity and decide that it needs to be addressed, they should proceed to the remaining steps in the decision-making process.

The insights of TQM and the systems view provide a valuable context for framing and defining organizational problems and opportunities. Nike's managers, for example, have discovered that a reason for their poor growth is that they have not worked well with international distributors nor do overseas consumers perceive the Nike brand to have as much value to them as it does to U.S. consumers. In other words, the company has a problem with its distribution processes and with its understanding of what *customers value,* two important focuses of TQM.

2. Gather Information About the Problem or Opportunity

The problem definition step depends on having access to information, from both outside and within the organization. The goal here is to systematically gather reliable data about the situation that will allow managers to formulate alternative actions and understand the consequences of these actions for the organization. In doing this, managers might need information that relates the problem or opportunity to customers, processes, employees affected, suppliers, and the competition.

When looking to solve a problem, managers need to explore not only the symptom but causes as well. It is only by dealing with causes, as we saw in Chapter 3, that problems can be solved in a permanent way. In gathering information about an opportunity, it is important to focus on the needs from which the opportunity emerges. Companies too often concentrate on building neat technology, such as we saw with Steve Jobs' Next computer, rather than on the needs such technology might fulfill. In the case of Next, there was not a strong need or demand for its product.

Often the information managers need is in the heads of their employees, but they need a system for accessing it. Recognizing this, in the mid-1980s AT&T launched an on-line computer service called AAA—Access to AT&T Analysts—to help managers learn from the tens of thousands of employees with specialized insight on various topics. AT&T invites its employees to fill out questionnaires identifying their areas of expertise, among other things. Users of AAA can log in key words and get a list of company experts on a particular topic along with their job titles and phone numbers. With AAA, a manager can quickly get information that might otherwise require weeks of research. The network also operates in the other direction: If an employee uncovers a tidbit about a competitor, for example, he or she can "broadcast" it on the AAA system to employees in long-distance operations.[8]

3. Generate Alternative Courses of Action and the Effects of These on Organizational Processes

The next step of decision making is to generate possible solutions or actions and their consequences to the organization. These components will include such things as the company's resources, culture, departments, and employees, along with its suppliers, its image in the market, the amount of investment required, potential competitive reaction, and many others. Managers also need to explore how solutions will fit in with the company's current processes. Can the current processes handle the proposed change, or will they have to be modified as well? Most potential actions, especially in a nonprogrammed decision situation, are going to involve and affect how all these components relate and interact, and managers should seek to optimize these interactions in the best interest of all the organization's stakeholders.

To evaluate each alternative, managers should list potential outcomes and estimate the likelihood of each happening. They ask the question, "If we do this . . . , what is the likelihood of . . . happening?" Then they can figure out how well each alternative will succeed in resolving the problem or taking advantage of the opportunity and what the consequences are likely to be for the organization and its stakeholders.

For example, Nike has in place a system it calls "Futures" that requires distributors to order its shoes up to eight months before delivery. This allows the company to predict demand and better control manufacturing by its Asian subcontractors and its inventory. The payoff for its distributors is reliable delivery and a discount of up to 10 percent for cooperating with the company. Any deviation from this approach could have profound consequences in Nike's dealings with suppliers, its financial systems, its distributors, and the processes by which it designs and delivers final products to the market. However, international distributors have been reluctant to order shoes far in advance of delivery because they say they cannot predict demand that far ahead. Nike's managers must look carefully at how to accommodate the needs of these distributors given its current way of operating. The company must generate various alternative scenarios for how all parts of the organization can work together to increase its sales internationally.

In this process, managers are often tempted to act quickly, accepting the first alternative they come up with and not necessarily fully appreciating the consequences of this on all the different parts of the organization and its processes. This tendency for quick action rather than examining various alternatives can be a mistake. For one thing, there are very few organization problems or opportunities that have only one solution. By taking time to list a number of scenarios and their potential consequences for the entire organization, managers can identify not only standard solutions but creative ones as well. As they go about this process, managers should avoid the tendency to evaluate and shoot down ideas as they are brought up. Nike, for example, could simply give its international distributors the right to order shoes only when they need them. However, there are probably better solutions that the company should consider.

4. Choose an Action Most Consistent with Organizational Goals and Objectives

Once all the alternative courses of action are listed, the next step is to choose the best one. At this point in the process, managers should have a good sense of the feasibility of each alternative in terms of its effect on the organization and its processes and the achievement of organizational goals. All the steps before this point are the "understanding the problem or opportunity" part of the process. Once managers have carefully gone through these steps in understanding, the best alternative will become apparent, and that is the one they will choose.

For example, in Nike's case, the Futures program is vital to the company's way of doing business, and managers agreed that they could not compromise that. After due consideration, the company's managers understood they needed to take a combination of actions. They began to buy up overseas distributors while at the same time better focusing their advertising to create continued demand for its products. It especially wants to get back to its roots, delivering shoes that are not only fashion statements but really meet the needs of athletes. The managers believe this will allow it to build enough consumer demand that the Futures system will work in all markets. To underscore its commitment to the international market, Phil Knight, in Nike's 1993 annual report, delivered the shareholder message in five languages (English, Spanish, French, German, and Japanese). The message: Nike has gone global.[9]

In thinking about this example, it is important to appreciate that once managers had framed their problem in a certain way and considered the implications of various solutions, this course of action was the one that logically emerged. It is difficult to overemphasize the importance of the steps a manager must go through in defining the problem or opportunity and figuring out the effects of various actions on the organization. The quality of organizational results will reflect the quality of thinking that goes into understanding the problem. And though managers are becoming better at this process, *The Wall Street Journal* and other publications regularly feature stories about managers who misunderstood their problems and took actions that caused severe damage to their companies. For example, in the same issue of *Business Week* that reported on Nike, there was also a story about the problems at Borland International Inc., a software company, which a few years earlier was prospering. The company sales were down, and its managers were struggling to turn the company around based on its decisions to develop new products, some for markets in which it has little experience. Most analysts were saying Borland's chances for survival were slim.

5. Implement the Action

Once managers select a course of action, they must implement it. The whole process is a waste of time unless something of value happens because of it. In implementing a decision, the organization may already have a set of processes in place. For example, if the decision is to move ahead with a new product, the company may have processes in place for doing this, and those kick into action. Alternatively, a decision may involve starting something entirely new, such as developing a company sales force instead of using independent commission representatives. In this case, managers must be sensitive to people's resistance to change and take time to educate them on the purpose of the change and build commitment to the implementation. They should also make sure that they have put in place the needed resources and established schedules for implementation.

6. Assess the Results

Managers should assess the results of their actions to find out whether or not they did the right things and did them well. What are the actual consequences of the decision? Have we met our goals? Are the discrepancies being eliminated? Managers should pay particular attention to areas that they identified as possible points of resistance by stakeholders. Any problems or opportunities that are discovered during assessment then become an occasion for another round of the decision-making process.

Exhibit 6-3 summarizes the steps of this process. Note that the process is never ending and builds on itself, an idea we will explore more in the next section.

EXHIBIT 6-3
The rational decision-making process as a continuous cycle

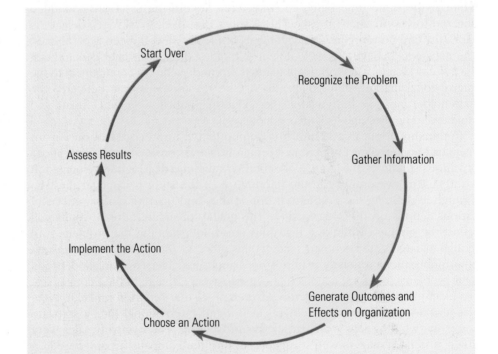

Escalation of investment in the turboprop Starship resulted in financial disaster for Beech Aircraft.

The Benefits of Rational Decision Making

The rational process can help managers guard against committing decision-making errors. For example, people often mistakenly assess the frequency or likelihood of an event's occurrence by how easily they can remember it.[10] Another common error is **escalation,** that is, *continuing to commit to a previous decision when a "rational" decision maker would withdraw.*[11] Escalation occurs because the decision maker focuses on "sunk" costs, or historical costs, and fails to focus on future costs and benefits. For example, in business, escalation occurs when a manager decides to invest even more money in a failing business on the slim chance that the infusion of more resources will revive it. You may think of personal examples: Do you put more money into the repair of an old car than it is worth? How long do you wait once you have been put on "hold" by a receptionist? By following a rational decision-making process a manager objectively faces the facts and avoids mental mistakes like escalation.

Escalation A situation where a manager continues to commit to a previous decision when a "rational" decision maker would withdraw.

A QUALITY CONTEXT FOR DECISION MAKING AT A WESTINGHOUSE DIVISION[12]

The Commercial Nuclear Fuel Division (CNFD) of Westinghouse Electric Corporation engineers and manufactures fuel assemblies for commercial nuclear power reactors. It is a leader in a market where mistakes cannot be tolerated. The division's managers attribute its success to its "Quality First" approach to management. The foundation of this approach was the creation of value for customers, employees, stockholders, and the community. All decisions and actions in the company were held to this standard. The Westinghouse Quality First model is built on four imperatives an organization must have: (1) quality management systems, (2) quality products, (3) quality technology, and (4) quality people. And then they combine these components with the goal of absolute customer satisfaction.

Quality First is thus the context for all decisions in this Westinghouse division. It causes managers to carefully consider all actions in terms of the goals of Quality First and has created an understanding that there must be a synergy among all the components of the organization. Managers know that Quality First has been the most important factor in the division's business strategy and helped make it a world leader in its business. However, the most important thing it has done is give employees a new way of thinking about situations by coming up with new ideas for solving problems and improving the division's ways of operating.

By 1988, the company had a 42 month record of on-time delivery of finished assemblies. It also delivers software to its customers, and it had a 98 percent rating on accuracy and on-time delivery of these products. Costs were reduced by 30 percent in the first four years after adopting Quality First. Further, the division has been able to measure increases in customer satisfaction, meaning customers attach more value to the division's offerings.

The managers of Westinghouse CNFD have articulated four lessons they have learned from Quality First:

1. An organization must have a common vision, and all people in that organization must embrace a common vision.
2. A framework of Quality First is absolutely crucial. This keeps everyone focused on satisfying customers and on continuous improvement.
3. Measure, measure, measure. Data is necessary to understand and improve the processes by which work gets done.
4. There must a long-term commitment to continuous quality improvement. Neither the culture nor the procedures can be built quickly, but the payoff of keeping at it is unquestioned.

As both a context for understanding problems and opportunities and for figuring out what to do, Quality First has worked exceptionally well at Westinghouse CNFD. In fact, this division was the recipient of the 1988 Malcolm Baldrige National Quality Award.

For example, Beech Aircraft's managers invested $350 million (perhaps much more) in its turboprop Starship executive aircraft.[13] Their original goal was to develop an all-composites aircraft, meaning it was made entirely of high-strength, low-weight, non-metal materials. However, they had trouble certifying the aircraft with the FCC, and as they continued to make modifications, the plane got heavier and heavier and eventually took six years to develop rather than two using far more funds than planned. By the time it hit the market in 1989, it was as heavy as other aircraft and, though it is a propeller plane, cost the same as executive jets that fly faster. It includes great technology, but the market does not like it.

In over five years since the plane was introduced, the company has sold only 15 of them at around $4 million each. While they have learned about composites and other technology, the plane has been a heavy drain on the company's resources and position in the market. The point is that while the managers' goals for a completely modern aircraft ran into government regulation problems and market resistance, they refused to give in, causing them to develop a product that elicits this comment from a *Fortune* magazine writer: "Trade magazines have hesitated to say how the Starship—as merchandise—has fared. Let me help: It's a dud. A fiasco. A Little Bighorn with wings."[14] Rational decision making tied to continuously improving the delivery of value might have helped Beech avoid the escalation that resulted in this disaster.

Rational Decision Making and Continuous Improvement

The rational decision-making process we have just reviewed is standard practice for many managers. It is how they create the future for the organization. By their understanding of problems and opportunities, they provide the direction their organization will take. Earlier we said that managers never have as much information as they need to predict with certainty exactly what will happen when they make a decision. There are two general things, though, that they can always learn from taking an action. One is how well things work out, and the other is what problems occur as a result of this action or what new opportunities open up because of it. Astute managers understand that every situation in which they become involved is a chance to learn about and to make the organization's processes work better and better. This principle is behind the TQM notion of continuous improvement.

Continuous improvement assumes continuous learning based on experience—the personal experience of managers, the experience of the entire company, and that of others, such as competitors. Managers can use these learning experiences to help their organization get better and better at delivering quality products and services to customers and at satisfying all stakeholders.

Exhibit 6-4 presents a graphical representation of what is sometimes called the **PDCA cycle** or the "Deming Cycle" for continuous improvement. (This is because W. Edwards Deming popularized it when he gave his lectures in Japan in 1950. He based this on the work of Walter Shewhart.) It *includes four elements: Plan, Do, Check, and Act or "PDCA.* (Sometimes the *Check* step is called *Study,* and the acronym becomes *PDSA.*") As shown, the cycle goes uphill, indicating continuously getting better at what one does. By using the PDCA cycle, everyone in the organization can learn from experience and help the company improve.

PDCA cycle An approach to improving decision making that includes four elements: plan, do, check, and act.

We can relate these four elements, PDCA, to the steps in the rational decision-making process that we just reviewed in this way:

- *Plan* incorporates steps 1-4—problem recognition, information gathering, outcome generation, and choosing the best course of action.
- *Do* incorporates the implementation of the chosen action.
- *Check* incorporates assessing or evaluating the results of an action.
- *Act* involves institutionalizing or modifying actions based on the assessment.

EXHIBIT 6-4
The Deming PDCA Cycle for continuous improvement

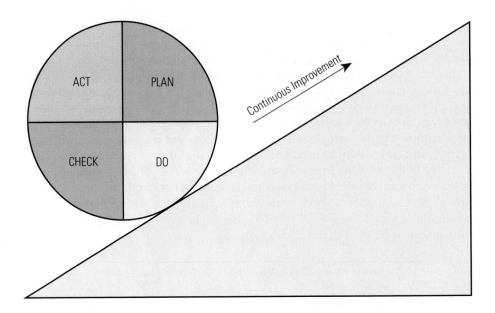

And then the process starts all over again in an endless cycle of improvement. TQM reminds us that this is necessary if an organization is to prosper in an ever more competitive business environment. It is a recognition of the dynamic changing nature of business, where organizations can either get better or they can decline. There is no standing still. While this idea of continuous improvement seems straightforward and logical, it is also true that a great many organizations are not good at it. They have not institutionalized learning from experience as part of their way of operating. Instead, there is a tendency to blame someone when something goes wrong. "Somebody didn't do their job," is the cry. And there is no review of the processes and relationships among organizational components to understand and learn and really get better.

? THINKING CRITICALLY

1. Why do you think "understanding the situation" is the key to decision making?
2. Why do you think managers such as those at Beech Aircraft or at Next might be prone to escalation? How might TQM help managers avoid escalation?
3. All of us have used steps like those in PDCA to learn and improve. What situation have you have been in that would illustrate these steps?
4. Based on the rational decision-making processes, why do you think the Quality First culture at Westinghouse CNFD worked to improve decisions and performance?

LESS THAN RATIONAL DECISION MAKING

While complete rationality is a great goal, we have seen that it is not possible to know with certainty the results of any decision we might make. This does not mean we should not strive for rationality, and the process described above can help us improve the quality of our decisions. We should realize it is very difficult for organizations to go through this process systematically and objectively. The steps in the process are more a kind of model to help us to understand what goes through any person's mind as he or she confronts a problem and goes about solving it. Whether we consciously seek information, generate alternatives, and select the best one, we nevertheless do something approximating these steps, at least subconsciously. This is how our minds work. By becoming aware of this, we can get better at problem solving and improve our decisions by making a more deliberate effort to go through the steps. However, no matter how well we do this, there will always be constraints of time, available data, and information, lack of experience, and bias. So, while we can improve our decisions, there will still always be uncertainty. We do the best we can and we learn from our experience.

Many organizations do not systematically implement this process. They make decisions in a less thoughtful, more haphazard and as-needed basis. Scholars have explored how companies go about making decisions as they seek to cope with the problems and opportunities all managers of organizations have to deal with. To understand how managers really act, rather than the idealized rational model, they have come up with the idea of bounded rationality, and two decision-making models, which they call logical incrementalism and "the garbage can model."

Bounded Rationality

The rational decision-making process described before seems to imply that managers conduct a careful and calculated evaluation of every alternative. However, managerial decision making often does not resemble this rational process because of the manager's **bounded rationality,** or *limitations to the human ability to be rational.*[15] To be completely rational a manager would need a complete list of all alternatives and knowledge of their outcomes in relation to all of the manager's goals. Of course, that is impossible. Thus all rationality is bounded in one way or another.

Bounded rationality
Limitations on the human ability to be rational.

Computers can help. Managers can use them to calculate costs and benefits of quantitative aspects of various situations. However, most situations have non-quantitative aspects as well. So, managers have to use their own heads to evaluate many decisions. In any case, it can be expensive and time consuming to conduct extensive analysis and evaluation.

Managers often avoid systematic analysis, because of time constraints and the amount of work it involves. Rather than conduct extensive evaluations to find the optimal solution, they will rely on intuition and past experience and seek a solution that, given the time and resources they want to give to it, will seem satisfactory. When managers do this, they are said to **satisfice** or *settle for an alternative that is acceptable or reasonable to all stakeholders.* They may consider only a few alternatives and choose the one that seems *good enough.* The extent to which managers carefully execute the steps of rational decision making may depend upon the extent of familiarity and the importance of the decision situation.

Satisfice A solution to a problem that involves settling for an alternative that is acceptable or reasonable to all stakeholders.

Exhibit 6-5 on page 222 illustrates that when a manager is very familiar with the decision situation and it is not very important, the manager may simply rely upon habit, or do what he has always done, as in a programmed decision situation, for example, when deciding to restock office supplies. In contrast, when the situation is unfamiliar and very important, the manager may engage in extensive analysis and evaluation, for example, when planning a new corporate strategy.

EXHIBIT 6-5
A classification of the extent of
deliberation in decision making

LEVEL OF IMPORTANCE

	HIGH	LOW
FAMILIARITY WITH THE SITUATION — HIGH	Limited Processing (Satisfice)	Choice by Habit
FAMILIARITY WITH THE SITUATION — LOW	Extensive Processing	Limited Processing (Satisfice)

At other times, such as a situation of high importance and high familiarity, the manager may simply satisfice. For example, Dick Yuengling, the head of D.G. Yuengling & Sons, the country's oldest brewery, has a problem with success. For years, Yuengling beer was mainly sold to coal miners in Western Pennsylvania. His success problem happened when the beers of small microbreweries started to get popular. Mr. Yuengling started to expand distribution to places like Philadelphia and other population centers in the Northeast, where the beer was positioned as a high-priced premium brew. However, after building up a following in these markets, he had to cut back his distribution to them when the company was unable to brew enough beer to meet demand at home. He felt he had to keep his hometown customers happy first even though for them the beer is not thought of as upscale, and the price is lower than in the new markets. Yuengling, in making this decision, was satisficing—doing the best thing he could to please his customers and keep the company viable given time and resources available.[16]

Logical Incrementalism: A Process of Muddling Through

The rational model of decision making implies that managers have a clear sense of where they are going, perhaps with a bold plan or specific set of goals in place to guide their decisions. This view of decision making conjures up an image of a band of crusaders who know they are going to the promised land for the explicit purpose of taking it from those who they consider unworthy inhabitants. By contrast, the decision making of most managers more often looks like a process of **muddling through,** wherein *managers find their way and develop a sense of direction as they undertake a sequence of individual decisions.*[17]

Professor James B. Quinn has elaborated on this idea to explain the process through which an organization often decides on its direction or chooses its strategy. Quinn called it **logical incrementalism,** which means that *individual decision processes stream together in a piecemeal fashion over time to form an*

Muddling through A method where managers find their way and develop a sense of direction as they undertake a sequence of individual decisions.

Logical incrementalism A term describing individual decision processes as streaming together in a piecemeal fashion over time to form an overall strategy for the organization without necessarily having a strong sense of direction ahead of time.

overall strategy for the organization without necessarily having a strong sense of direction ahead of time.[18] In other words, the strategy and direction of the organization emerges and incrementally (or gradually) changes over time as decisions are made in the organization.

In this view, decisions are not always consciously directed toward a grand vision or strategy of the organization. However, the process is called logical because these decisions are directed toward goals, although the goals are often short term or narrowly related only to a specific problem or opportunity that arises in the environment. In this view, decisions are also greatly affected by organizational politics and personal agendas of individuals within the organization. Unfortunately, the internal politics can lead to decisions that are not necessarily in the best interest of the organization. In thinking about this, we could understand it in terms of the PDCA cycle described above, except it is less a conscious effort at getting better in the long term than in surviving in the short term. Logical incrementalism will almost always catch up with an organization, making it vulnerable to more effective and efficient competitors.

This approach to management decision making is fairly common in U.S. corporations, even those that are highly regarded. After a long period of muddling through, we will see a new regime and a new, even revolutionary change of strategic direction, followed by more logical incrementalism. For example, General Motors got by muddling through for a long period of time until things got bad enough to bring in the new management group with a new set of ideas for managing the company. It is too early to tell whether this team will lapse again into logical incrementalism after a few years.

There are certain situations where logical incrementalism could make sense, such as in turbulent and rapidly changing business environments. For example, in the fast-paced field of bio-technology, an organization frequently has to adjust and adapt to emerging technologies. It is difficult for leaders to establish a long term vision and strategy that will remain unchanged for very long. Leaders have to be flexible and adapt to the inevitable and frequent changes in technology, and they have to quickly adjust their visions and strategies to respond to new problems and opportunities.

The Garbage Can Model of Decision Making

The **garbage can model** of decision making suggests that *the decision-making process in an organization is best described as "organized anarchy" which verges on randomness when dealing with nonprogrammed decision situations.* It states that managerial decision making can be the random combination of four independent streams that persist over time:

1. Problems
2. Potential solutions
3. Solution technologies (methods)
4. Decision makers who are seeking something useful to do

The analogy of a garbage can implies that these streams are all jumbled together in an organization and occasionally combine to create a decision situation.[19]

Garbage can model The decision-making process in an organization best described as "organized anarchy" that verges on randomness when dealing with nonprogrammed decision situations.

Like logical incrementalism, the garbage can model of decision making suggests that managerial decisions are not always so rational or purposefully directed toward organizational goals. In this view, managers tend to address only the problems for which they already have solutions or solution technologies. They somewhat randomly discover various combinations of problems, solutions, and solution technologies that lead to a decision situation. The old adage applies that if a person only has a hammer, then everything starts to look like a nail. This adage points out that, unfortunately, we are all prone to apply the skills that we currently have to all of our problems, whether or not these skills fully address the issue at hand.

Furthermore, the garbage can model questions the extent in many organizations to which decision making is orderly and flows from one stage to another. For example, the rational model suggests that the first step is to define the problem or opportunity before generating alternative outcomes, evaluating and figuring out which one will work best. In reality, the definition of the problem may evolve as a solution is devised. In other words, the problem may be recast to fit the solution that is available. Or, in another case, managers' understanding of the problem may change as they study and evaluate the available solutions.

This view is consistent with our suggestion that the rational decision-making process is related to organizational learning and continuous improvement and is an ongoing process. However, the garbage can model also reflects a kind of cultural malaise in many organizations that are riding on past successes. An example of this kind of company might be Southern Pacific Railroad (Case in Point, Chapter 3) before it adopted TQM. The garbage can model is not a conscious, customer-focused approach for continuously improving the organization's processes to help it survive and grow in today's competitive environment. TQM provides concrete direction for helping managers eliminate this malaise and transform their companies into efficient and effective competitors.

 THINKING CRITICALLY

1. Can you think of a situation where you "satisficed?" What were the circumstances? What do you think the differences between satisficing and optimizing are?
2. How do you think TQM can help managers stop muddling through or taking the garbage can approach to decision making?

TOTAL QUALITY MANAGEMENT AND SOUND DECISION MAKING

All managers' rationality is bounded and they seek to satisfice stakeholders as well as they can. "As well as they can," though, can mean different things to different managers. Sometimes managers make a decision quickly when they really should employ the process of rational decision making in a more conscientious fashion, and, as a result, this diminishes the overall quality of their decisions. Sometimes managers proceed to resolve a problem without a clear idea of their goals. Sometimes they go in search of a problem because they have a new tech-

PARTICIPATIVE DECISION MAKING AT AT&T

Aloise McNichols is the District Manager of the Process Support Team in AT&T's Human Resources Organization. This organization operates nationally to support AT&T's strategic direction and the success of its business units and divisions. It delivers human resource services, including internal and external recruiting, diversity consulting, assessment of motivation and employment training needs, and manages employee data. Aloise describes how decision making in her organization has changed in recent years.

Hierarchical, autocratic management styles were once the norm at AT&T. Important decisions were made only at the top and cascaded throughout the rest of the organization. However, the global business environment is forcing us to adopt novel and more effective decision-making processes. To adapt to rapid rates of change in the external environment and increased demands from external customers, we are constantly changing our organizational culture. This requires us to not only focus on external customers, but also on our employees as customers. We are flattening the traditional organizational pyramid and moving decision making to the lowest levels in the organization, to those closest to the work and closest to our customers.

We are striving to act more like a business and not just a support service organization. We are always looking for ways to improve our business processes, reduce costs, and provide competitive products and services to earn business from our customers. We require more from people now, and we are asking them to display skills and competencies, attitudes and behaviors, that in many cases they have not been prepared for. We are managing many priorities at the same time and many customers with varying expectations. To meet these challenges we have adopted a decision-making framework called *policy deployment,* which involves people at every level in developing and implementing new strategies and plans for improvement.

We began policy deployment with assessments of customer needs, markets, competition, capability, and core competencies. These six assessments, along with our formal statements of vision and values, provide the basis for developing the 3-5 year strategic guidelines, which are the critical areas where we continue to try to achieve breakthroughs. Then we ask each functional group to develop objectives and action plans, targeted for each strategic guideline. We then use what we call the performance management process to translate functional goals into individual goals and objectives in three areas: business results, people/supervisory results, and personal development.

These planning and decision-making processes are very participative, with the leaders and those they support striving to achieve consensus through repeated discussions and clarifications, a communication process we call "catch-ball." We provide training to teach employees about other important aspects of performance management, including feedback, coaching, and recognition as day-to-day management tools. Finally, we conduct appraisal and performance reviews to assess our progress toward strategic objectives.

Policy deployment has changed the way we conduct strategic planning and decision making. It has created a better alignment among all our people, across vertical levels of the hierarchy and across functional boundaries. Our people are now engaged and involved in our strategic decision-making processes. They are more aware and knowledgable of our overall business which makes them more capable of accepting authority and accountability to make decisions at lower levels. This fulfills our business strategy and allows us to better serve our customers.

A LOOK AT

MANAGERS IN ACTION

SAMSUNG GETS IT TOGETHER; FUTURE UNSURE AT NEXT

Think again of yourself as Lee Kun-Hee. You have made many radical changes in Samsung's culture. The head of Daewoo, Korea's other electronics giant, questions your moves. He asks, "Why is he doing this. It's a big risk. You can't make a good organization innovative in one day." He does not seem to get what you are trying to do, but the Japanese seem to. They take you very seriously; they know of your strength and success in semiconductors and believe you are showing real leadership at your company. Your former professor at George Washington University, Phillip D. Grub, has this to say about your actions: "With decentralization, they're gaining strength, and there is a greater sense of esprit because people feel they're part of decision-making." Grub notes that your company is now on the leading edge of areas like liquid-crystal display screens and digital VCRs, and highly computerized machinery. Your competitors seem aware that you are making the right moves to take your company into the 21st century.

Now change gears again and put yourself in the place of Steve Jobs. You have finally agreed to get out of the hardware business. But so much has happened since you were first advised to do this that you lost most of the momentum that built up when NextStep software was first introduced. Microsoft's Jim Allchin, who leads Microsoft's team, says, "We're doing a lot more than NextStep, and we'll have it finished a lot sooner than Jobs thinks." One of your developers who left Microsoft and came to Next in 1990 to help with NextStep leaves your company in November, 1992 because, he says, "I wanted to get out of businesses where you're directly competing with Goliaths."

You are dealt another blow in April, 1993 when IBM, Hewlett-Packard, Sun, Novell and other software concerns form an alliance to standardize important aspects of workstation software, and Next is not invited to join. Best friends, like Oracle Software's CEO, asserts that for Next to be successful, a company like Novell must take a large equity position and get involved in the further development of NextStep. Meantime, you don't give in and believe that everyone wants an alternative to Microsoft, and you have it. Will it matter? No one knows for sure, but at this point, a big player, Scott McNealy says, "I don't think a company the size of Next survives, no matter how impressive its technology." While we can't say what the future of Next is, we can say in retrospect that somehow your decisions have not always reflected solid rational analysis, and that McNealy may have called it right.

nology or method for solving problems. Managers also have emotions and personal and political agendas that seem logical to the individual but do not always seem rational to others. For a number of reasons, the quality of satisfaction generated by their decisions may be less than acceptable to various stakeholders.

While it is impossible to overcome all limitations to rationality, Total Quality Management provides some help to managers. For one thing, when managers develop a TQM culture, such as the Quality First culture at Westinghouse CNFD, they establish and clearly communicate a vision and purpose for the organization. A TQM culture gets the jobs and responsibilities of everyone aligned with an organization's processes and purpose. In TQM, people take a broader perspective on their individual decisions and avoid some of the limitations of logical incrementalism or, worse, the garbage can model. TQM also encourages people to base their decisions on scientific data rather than opinion and personal whim. In doing this it helps managers overcome the unhealthy reliance on political persuasion and personal politicking that is associated with logical incrementalism.

In traditional organizations that do not effectively practice Total Quality Management, managers are particularly prone to act according to the garbage can model, randomly mixing and matching problems, solutions, and technologies. By contrast, TQM encourages managers to develop a learning organization that continuously develops deeper insight into itself, acquires new knowledge, skills, and technologies, asks new questions, uncovers new problems, and seeks new opportunities.

TQM also gives managers a set of solution technologies and methods that they can use to gather and analyze data to solve problems and improve organization processes. Unfortunately, when managers do not fully appreciate TQM in the context of systems management, adopting its tools can create as many problems as they solve. In the 1980s when TQM was just becoming well known, many managers thought statistical process control, an important TQM tool, was the answer to all their problems. Unfortunately, these managers failed to appreciate the corresponding need for cultural and managerial role changes to create a context for the intelligent use of TQM tools. All managerial tools should be pulled into place only when needed and appropriate. For example, no matter how many TQM tools Westinghouse CNFD applied, there would have been no significant improvement without the cultural change that goes with them.

When used properly, the tools of TQM can help managers sort through information that could otherwise overwhelm them. These tools can help managers overcome some of their bounded rationality. These tools were developed as a means for gathering data about systems and processes so managers can understand situations and make better decisions to help the organization solve problems and take advantage of opportunities.

❓ THINKING CRITICALLY

1. Why do you think TQM enhances rational decision making?
2. Why do you think the tools of TQM work poorly without adopting a TQM culture?

SUMMARY

Managers and Decisions
- Decision making is an important managerial activity that pervades almost everything a manager does.
- Everyone is involved in decisions about their personal lives, and by becoming more conscious of how and what decisions we make, we can enhance the outcomes of those decisions.

Decision Making, Problem Solving, and TQM

- The decisions we make really reflect our best understanding of ourselves in relation to the situations in which we find ourselves at the time we make those decisions.

- TQM and the idea of an organization as a system assist managers to understand business situations and guide their decisions in figuring how an organization might attain positive results for all its stakeholders.

- TQM suggests several questions managers can ask themselves and others to better understand problems and opportunities and guide their thinking in deciding how to handle these.

Types of Decision Situations

- There are two types of decision situations managers face: programmed decision situations (familiar situations that require a standardized action) and nonprogrammed decision situations (novel situations that require new and unique actions).

- Sound management suggests that managers delegate decisions to those in the best position to handle problems. This allows the organization to take full advantage of employees' talents and abilities.

- The outcomes of decisions are never certain. A managerial goal, however, is to lessen uncertainty by using data, knowledge, and experience to better understand decision situations.

A Rational Approach to Decision Making

- A goal of the rational decision-making process is to help managers reduce the degree of uncertainty in their decisions by giving them a realistic perspective for understanding problems and opportunities and taking actions that will lead to organizational success.

- There are six steps in the rational decision-making process that include recognizing the problem, gathering information, assessing effects on the organization, making the choice, implementing the change, and checking the results.

- Rational decision making helps managers minimize the possibility of getting involved in situations where escalation might take place.

- The rational decision-making process facilitates continuous improvement in an organization and is analogous to the Deming Cycle for improvement: Plan, Do, Check, Act.

Less than Rational Decision Making

- Bounded rationality suggests that no one can be completely rational, and given the time, experience, knowledge, and resources, managers often seek to satisfice, doing the best thing for all concerned, under current circumstances.

- Logical incrementalism suggests that managers logically muddle through situations, learning as they go along, but with no stongly held strategy or vision to guide their actions.

- The garbage can model suggests that decisions are a combination of the problems, potential solutions, solution technologies (methods), and decision makers who are seeking something useful to do. Things happen, but the quality of thought that goes into decisions is lacking.

Total Quality Management and Sound Decision Making

- TQM helps managers create a culture that values rational decision making. It provides tools to help managers better achieve goals of improving processes and delivering ever higher quality products and services to customers.

KEY TERMS

Bounded rationality 221	PDCA cycle 219
Decision making 201	Policy 207
Escalation 217	Problem 201
Garbage can model 223	Procedure 207
Logical incrementalism 222	Programmed decision situations 207
Muddling through 222	Rational 212
Nonprogrammed decision situations 207	Rule 207
Opportunity 201	Satisfice 221

REVIEW QUESTIONS

1. What does it mean to say that decision making is mostly concerned with understanding situations?
2. What does it mean to say TQM provides a context for making better decisions?
3. What is a programmed decision situation? What is a nonprogrammed decision situation? Why do nonprogrammed decision situations require the attention of upper management?
4. Why does delegation of decision making make sense to get an organization operating most efficiently and effectively?
5. What is the relationship between less and more uncertainty and programmed and nonprogrammed decision situations?
6. What is the relationship between the six steps of the rational decision-making process and the Plan, Do, Check, Act cycle?
7. What does "escalation" mean in the context of decision making? How does TQM help managers avoid this problem?
8. What does it mean for a manager to satisfice when making decisions?
9. Why does the logical incrementalism style of decision making eventually cause problems for organizations?

EXPERIENTIAL EXERCISE

Reflect upon your decision-making process when you were deciding what to do and where to go after graduating from high school. List the factors that you considered. Describe your decision-making process. How similar was that process to the rational decision-making model presented in this chapter? What would you do now to improve that process? Would you make the same decision?

CASE ANALYSIS AND APPLICATION
Encyclopedic Mistakes at Britannica[20]

Encyclopedia Britannica is a 200-year-old publishing company with sales of $650 million dollars. It has a reputation as the most prestigious and authoritative encyclopedia in the world. Yet, in just four years, this company has become almost a has-been in the encyclopedia business. How did this happen? The answer is CD-ROM.

While in 1990, the CD-ROM drive on a home computer was rare, by 1994, both CD-drives and computers were common. Industry estimates were that 16 million homes would have this technology by the end of 1994. This large hardware base brings with it demand for software. And this has not gone unnoticed by the other big encyclopedia companies, most notably *Compton's, Grolier's,* and *Encarta,* a product from Microsoft based on *Funk & Wagnall's New Encyclopedia.* These products sell at prices that range from $99 to $399, take up no shelf space, and include moving pictures and sound. With Microsoft's *Encarta,* for example, the entry on Verdi includes 30 seconds of soprano Monika Krause singing "Sempre Libera" from *La Traviata.*

Contrast this with Britannica's multi-volume product that weighs 118 pounds, takes up 4 1/2 feet of book shelf space, and costs $1,500. In 1990, Britannica was doing well, earning more that $40 million after taxes. But in 1991, the company lost $12 million, and, being owned by a private foundation, it has decided not to report its losses in 1992 and 1993. In this same period, Britannica's sales force has collapsed from 2,300 active reps to fewer than 1,100. Therein lies the tale of Britannica's current problems.

Over the years, *Encyclopedia Britannica* has been sold by a commission sales force. A representative receives about $300 for each set of books sold. Management believed this sales force was the key to its success, and they could not risk offending these people by bringing out a low-priced product for which there would be minimum commission. Yet as CD-ROM started to make in-roads on Britannica's sales and it started to feel strapped for cash, management decided to sell Compton's Encyclopedia, which it had bought years ago for a low-end product. The irony of this decision is that Compton's published the first CD-ROM encyclopedia in 1989, and it was a hit. Unfortunately, Britannica's top managers, blinded by their perceived need to keep their sales force selling books, sold Compton's to the Chicago Tribune Company.

With business drying up among more affluent encyclopedia customers, who were buying CDs, Britannica's sales force has been forced to sell on the installment plan to less affluent customers, who often can just make the down payment. These are just the kind of customers who can least afford and probably have the least need for these books. As a result, defaults skyrocketed, further exacerbating the cash crunch.

In the meantime, all the other encyclopedia publishers were jumping on the CD bandwagon, even *World Book,* owned by billionaire Warren Buffet, which offers its product for $395 or $99, if it is purchased with the books. And though its book sales have dropped as well, it remains profitable. Britannica's managers are trying to stage a comeback. The company's managers announced early in 1994 that *Britannica* would be available via Internet to university students and faculty. However, that is likely to generate little revenue. The company also a version on disk, which it leases to corporate research departments, but it does not include sound and motion like its competitors.

In concluding his piece on *Encyclopedia Britannica* for *Forbes,* writer Gary Samuels says, "The best hope now for the *Britannica:* Sell it to Buffet, Gates [president of Microsoft], or some other smart person who understands that even the strongest franchise will wither unless they keep up with the times, no matter what the salespeople say."

Discussion Questions

1. What understanding of their situation forced Britannica's managers to stick with books rather than moving to a CD version of their product?
2. If you were consulting with Britannica's managers back in 1990–1994 and understood the ideas of TQM, what would you have advised them to do to maintain their position in the encyclopedia market?
3. Do you think the decisions of Britannica's management have doomed the company to be sold? Why or why not?
4. What lessons can you learn from this case about the importance of properly understanding a company's problems and opportunities and how this affects its decisions?

7. STRATEGIC MANAGEMENT

LEARNING OBJECTIVES

After you finish this chapter you should be able to:

1. Define and explain why strategic management is important.

2. Describe the steps of the strategic management process.

3. Explain how the steps of the strategic management process are interrelated.

4. Describe the levels of strategy within a corporation: the corporate, business, and functional levels.

5. Explain the different approaches to strategy at each of these levels.

6. Explain the importance of the concept of customer value in strategic management.

STRATEGY, QUALITY, AND PROCTER & GAMBLE[1]

Procter and Gamble's (P&G) managers first saw the value of the total quality approach to management in 1983. The company's quality journey began with lower-level managers, but it has made its way to the top to pervade all aspects of the company and influence the development of organizational strategy.

In 1983, some P&G engineers were exposed to the teachings of W. Edwards Deming and were intrigued by an approach to improvement called statistical process control (SPC). At that time, P&G's paper products managers had serious quality problems with disposable diapers. They used SPC to reduce variation and product defects in manufacturing. They learned a great deal about how to manufacture diapers with fewer steps and to achieve consistent quality standards. As a result, P&G was able to start up new diaper-making lines around the world in one-half the normal time. They also reduced the level of defects by 50 percent, an accomplishment that got the attention of senior managers.

By 1985, P&G's interest in continuous improvement had evolved beyond SPC in the manufacturing plants to focus on all the processes involved in delivering products to customers. They sought to align their suppliers' processes, their internal processes and their delivery of products to customers into one seamless flow. The effort initially emphasized improving raw material quality from suppliers. However, by 1987 it had evolved into a proactive and thorough approach to understanding the needs of consumers, the final users of its products, as well as retail trade customers like Kroger's and Wal-Mart, which delivered their products to consumers. By 1990 P&G had implemented a standardized measurement system around the world to monitor the level of consumer and customer satisfaction with P&G products. As a result, P&G has developed a comprehensive understanding of total quality as their operational approach throughout the company. P&G managers and employees understood that total quality is not a program to be implemented or some fad that applies only to certain functions within the organization.

Since TQM represents an emphasis on system and customers, a different way of operating than P&G was accustomed to, this has required a fundamental change in the P&G culture. To make these changes, P&G managers discovered that TQM had to be built into all its processes, including those for developing and deploying the company's long- and short-term strategies. Exhibit 7-1 on page 234 illustrates the process used for strategy development and deployment within the Soap Sector. It consists of three major phases: the long-term vision, the

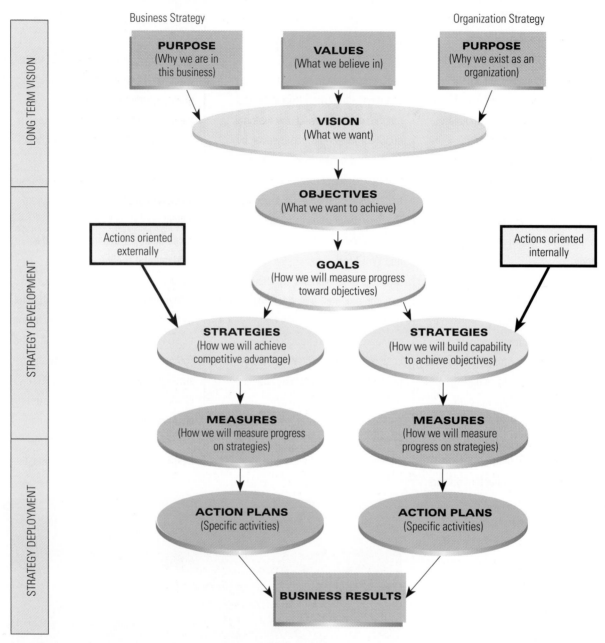

Business Strategy   Organization Strategy

PURPOSE
(Why we are in this business)

VALUES
(What we believe in)

PURPOSE
(Why we exist as an organization)

VISION
(What we want)

OBJECTIVES
(What we want to achieve)

Actions oriented externally

GOALS
(How we will measure progress toward objectives)

Actions oriented internally

STRATEGIES
(How we will achieve competitive advantage)

STRATEGIES
(How we will build capability to achieve objectives)

MEASURES
(How we will measure progress on strategies)

MEASURES
(How we will measure progress on strategies)

ACTION PLANS
(Specific activities)

ACTION PLANS
(Specific activities)

BUSINESS RESULTS

LONG TERM VISION

STRATEGY DEVELOPMENT

STRATEGY DEPLOYMENT

Source: M. J. Stahl and G. M. Bounds, *Competing Globally Through Customer Value,* Quorum, 1991, an imprint of Greenwood Publishing Group, Inc., Wesrport, CT. Reprintied by permission.

EXHIBIT 7-1   P&G Soap Company strategic planning model

strategy development itself, and finally, deploying the strategy.

The process begins with leaders clarifying the purpose of the organization. They ask the question, "Why is P&G's Soap Sector in business?" Many managers refer to this as a mission statement, but P&G prefers the term "purpose" because it conveys a sense of permanence. When TQM became the driving force of P&G's Soap Sector strategic development process, it prompted debate over what the purpose of the organization actually was. The debate centered on whether they were in business simply to make money for shareholders, which was the conventional wisdom in the company, or was the main purpose of their business to provide superior satisfaction to final consumers and their retailers.

After the dust settled, we should not be surprised to learn that they understood their purpose in terms of their customers. Further, they understood that they were more likely to make their company profitable by working as hard as they could to make their division efficient in its processes and effective at serving customers. They came up with the statement that the Soap Sector was in business to provide premium brands that achieve superior consumer and customer satisfaction, and that financial returns would result from increased market share and lower costs. P&G's Soap Sector managers recognized that any company needs financial returns to continue to survive and fairly serve its shareholders, but a single-minded focus on financial returns, particularly in the short term, may jeopardize a company's long-term survival. Bill Saxton, Vice President of P&G's Noxell Division, provides this analogy: "Everyone needs to eat in order to live, but very few of us would say that we live to eat."

UNDERSTANDING STRATEGIC MANAGEMENT

Strategic management is about defining and communicating an organization's purpose and facilitating efforts to fulfill that purpose. As Procter & Gamble's strategic planning model illustrates, making strategy real requires both planning and action. Strategic management is a specific application of the rational decision-making process that we explored in Chapter 6. When done well it provides the organization with a realistic sense of purpose and a way to align its resources and abilities with the needs of the market to create its future. Without strategic management, a company will lack purpose and direction, a prescription for failure in today's unrelentingly competitive business environment. To develop and deploy successful strategies, managers must understand strategy, the strategic management process, and how every level of the organization is involved in the development and implementation of strategy.

What Is Strategy?

The word strategy is familiar to those of us who grew up playing board games or sports. In a competitive game, strategy commonly means a scheme for achieving some purpose, namely, to win the game. The origin of the word "strategy" dates back to ancient times, to the Greek word *stratego,* meaning generals and the leadership they exert in battle. In business, **strategy** has come to mean *the organization's plan for achieving its mission and goals in the business environment.* A sound strategy spells out in detail what managers believe is the best use of the organization's resources and talents and how they will go about deploying these to the mutual benefit of the organization and its customers. A strategy is a kind of decision managers make. As with any other decision, it represents managers' best understanding of how to make the company succeed and grow in whatever business it is in.

There are three important elements that come together in the forming of a company's strategy, which we can call the "3 Cs."[2] These are Customers, Competitors, and Corporation. Exhibit 7-2 on page 236 illustrates the relationship among these three elements. All these elements are subsystems of, and interact with, the larger environment in which they exist and operate. As we move

Strategy The organization's plan for achieving its mission and goals in the business environment.

EXHIBIT 7-2
The 3 C's of strategy formulation

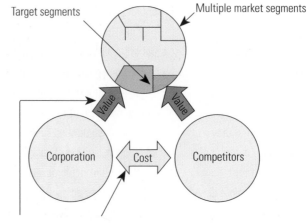

Source: Adapted from Kenichi Ohmae, *The Mind of a Strategist* (New York: McGraw-Hill, 1981) p.92. Reproduced with permission of McGraw-Hill.

through this chapter, we will review how managers formulate strategies and their different insights into those strategies.

The strategic goal of the organization is to deliver goods and services to customers that they will value and purchase, and to do it better than competitors. When successful, a company differentiates itself enough to attract a segment of customers and gain the sales and profits needed to continue in business.

Strategy is an important component of success. An organization that operates without a strategy will flounder in the marketplace and eventually go out of business when more focused competitors better meet the needs of customers. Without a strategy, managers are likely to misallocate resources and fail to coordinate their actions. When all employees understand the long- and short-term strategies, they generally know in which direction they are headed, what their goals are, and how they are going to get there. However, this does not mean that the strategy remains unchanged over time. In fact, during the course of conducting business, the strategy probably should change. This idea is like a game plan for football—the strategy changes as the coaches and team members adapt to changing circumstances.

The Nature of an Organization's Mission

Mission statement

A statement that identifies the organization's purpose and answers the question, "What business are we in?"

An organization's mission is often summed up in a formal **mission statement** that *identifies the organization's purpose and answers the question, "What business are we in?"* This statement, to form a sound basis for action, must relate the organization's abilities with the customer group it intends to serve. It should also state the mission in terms of the problem to be solved and the product or service delivered to help solve this problem. Remember, customers buy solutions and the utility they expect to derive from a product or service and not the thing itself. Recognizing this in the mission statement helps keep everyone's attention properly placed. This idea is completely consistent with the basic premise of TQM, which recognizes that serving customers can be the *only* purpose of an organization.

For example, the mission statement of a textbook publisher might read as follows: *Our mission is to be a leading supplier of high-quality media and services that help professors teach and students learn.* This statement relates the publisher's activities with how its two customer groups, professors and students like your-self, will use the outputs of its processes. Notice that the mission statement speaks of media and services, not books, leaving it open to figuring out the best configuration of items that will meet customer needs. A mission statement like this one provides a context and sets a direction for the organization's strategy and work.

The Nature of Business Competition

Although there are differences, the nature of business competition is similar to that in competitive games and warfare. What are the similarities? Once they have cho-sen a market to serve, business organizations nearly always have competitors that are trying to serve the same customer groups. General Motors competes with Ford and other automobile companies to sell cars to various customer segments. The Gap competes with The Limited to sell clothes to young women. This approach to competition suggests that for one company to win, another has to lose.

Viewing competition in this way encourages leaders to borrow competitive strategies from sports and warfare strategists. They focus their attention on com-petitors and may respond to each of their moves with a countermove. The object of strategy, in this competitor-focused approach, is to out-position your competition. USAir drops its fare prices, so do American and United and all the other airlines. Miller offers a light beer, so does Budweiser. In this tit-for-tat strategic positioning, each firm tries to outflank or to avoid getting outflanked by other firms.

Unfortunately, this competitor-focused approach sometimes distracts managers from the needs of their customers. Certainly, managers must watch competitors. However, they are more likely to come up with superior strategies if they are pri-marily customer focused, seeking to create their own futures, and not being obsessed with what competitors do. This is one of the keys of Japanese success.

THINKING CRITICALLY

1. Alfred D. Chandler defined strategy as "the determination of the basic long-term goals and objectives of an enterprise, and the adoption of courses of action and the allocation of resources necessary for carrying out these goals."[3] Do you think this is an adequate definition in light of the presentation above? For example, do you think this would focus managers more inward or outward in their thinking? What approach to management might this defi-nition encourage?
2. How do you think strategic management will change with the rising empha-sis on Total Quality Management?

THE STRATEGIC MANAGEMENT PROCESS

In the slower-moving times of the past, managers could work from informally-devised strategies that did not change much. They knew what business they were in intuitively, and they were succeeding, so going through some formal process did not seem necessary. Things worked on an ad hoc basis. However, the increasingly competitive global business environment has made a formally devised strategy more important to the survival and prosperity of business organizations. Managers now have to give more focused attention to the development of company strategy.

Trends in the business environment include quickening rates of technological change, shortened product life cycles, and increased international competition. Organizational trends include expansion of multinational corporations, increased organizational complexity and size, and growth in product offerings and markets served. These trends make it more necessary for managers to take a deliberate and systematic approach to strategy, which is called strategic management.[4]

Strategic management is *a systematic process of choosing a mission, conducting external and internal analyses, forming improvement plans, and taking action to achieve the organization's mission.*

Managers in most industries are affected by the trends mentioned above. Thus, strategic management has become important for managers in all kinds of businesses, including manufacturers of all sizes, service businesses, restaurants, hospitals, churches, and even volunteer organizations. All of these organizations have many stakeholders that they are trying to serve, including customers, investors, employees, suppliers, the community, and other business partners. Strategic management helps managers to establish a plan for balancing the interests of these stakeholders and sustaining itself over time.

Until recently, strategic management in large organizations has been an activity conducted by professional strategists. However, managers are now seeing the importance of getting deeply involved, as they are the ones who must finally decide on the whats and hows of the strategy and its implementation. They understand that it is an integrative activity that helps to link all specialized units, functions, and departments, and their common purpose in executing organizational processes. The more involved they are in the work of planning strategy, the more informed their decisions will be in its execution.

The strategic management process, especially in the context of TQM, is oriented more toward the *long-term* direction and growth of the organization than the planning activities of earlier decades. Those activities tended to focus on annual budgeting, setting objectives for functional departments, and meeting short-term financial goals.[5]

There are four major steps in managing the development of organizational strategy: 1) define the business, 2) gather data and conduct analyses, 3) decide on a plan, and 4) take action. Exhibit 7-3 illustrates these. In considering these steps, it is useful to relate them to the steps of the rational decision-making process. In reality, these steps are analogous to those a manager takes in exploring and understanding any situation and taking action in light of that understanding. It is just that in this case, the situation is the organization as a whole and what direction it will take in the future.

Although we discuss them in sequential order, in practice these steps are not always done sequentially. Managers may have to move back and forth between steps as they work to develop an effective strategy. For example, after conducting analyses, an organization may decide to refine or redefine its mission based on what it learns. So, what appears to be a very logical and sequential strategic management process flow is probably a lot more complicated in actual practice with lots of feedback and adjustments, not unlike most other human endeavors.

Strategic management
A systematic process of choosing a mission, conducting external and internal analyses, forming improvement plans, and taking action to achieve the organization's mission.

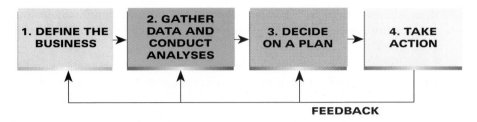

EXHIBIT 7-3   Steps in developing an organizational strategy

Step 1: Define the Business

As mentioned earlier, managers often write a *mission statement* to sum up what they see as their purpose or place in the world, products offered, or customers served. (You can often find the mission statement featured in the company's annual report.) For example, Hewlett-Packard's mission statement says: "Hewlett-Packard is a major designer and manufacturer of electronic products and systems for measurement and computation. HP's basic business purpose is to provide the capabilities and services needed to help customers worldwide improve their personal and business effectiveness." Notice the focus of this statement on helping customers become more effective using electronic devices for various purposes. It brings together what the company does with what customers need.

Sometimes the mission statement conveys the company's sense of vision for what the company sees itself becoming in the future, or its **strategic intent,** *an expression of a desired leadership position and the criterion by which the organization will chart its progress.*[6] For example, MCI Communications has stated "MCI's mission is leadership in the global telecommunications services industry." While they use the word "mission" in this statement, it is really a company "vision" of how they want to see themselves in their industry in the future. Vision statements usually focus on the future and what role the organization sees itself playing as an economic entity. To realize its vision to be a leader in telecommunications means that MCI must aggressively invest in technologies and markets. In Chapter 6 we wrote about Steve Jobs' vision for Next as a computer hardware company, which, though flawed, was what drove his daily, as well as strategic, decisions. Though vision statements often focus on the future, there can be overlap with mission statements that usually deal with the present, and we should not get too technical in trying to distinguish between them.

Another way that managers define their business is by stating long term **goals,** which are *aspirations defining various aspects of future business performance.* Managers can state goals in general terms or in very specific terms, with deadlines and targets. Either way, goals help managers to start converting their statements of mission and vision into courses of action. Managers may have goals for a number of areas, including: overall size and rank in the industry, annual growth in revenues and earnings, return on investment, annual dividend increases, market share, reputation for product quality, technological leadership, recognition as a "blue chip" company, ability to ride out ups and downs in the economy, degree of diversification, financial strength, customer service, overall customer value, and cost competitiveness. The strategic goals of some well-known corporations are listed below on page 239:

Strategic intent An expression of a desired leadership position and the criterion by which the organization will chart its progress.

Goals Aspirations defining various aspects of future business performance.

- Alcan Aluminum: To be the lowest-cost producer of aluminum; and to outperform the average return on equity of the Standard & Poor's Industrial Stock Index.
- General Electric: To become the most competitive enterprise in the world by being number one or number two in market share in every business the company is in.
- Black & Decker: To continue new product introductions and globalization.
- Quaker Oats Co.: To achieve return on equity at 20 percent or above, "real" earnings growth averaging 5 percent or better over time, be a leading marketer of strong consumer brands, and improve the profitability of low-return businesses or divest them.[7]

Sometimes managers write statements of mission or vision that are uninspiring and too long for employees to remember. To convey the organization's mission and self-image in a memorable way, many companies adopt a brief slogan, with just a few words: Xerox, "The Document Company;" Lexus, "The Relentless Pursuit of Perfection;" DuPont, "Better Things for Better Living." These concise phrases are often used internally with employees and in promotions to communicate the organization's sense of purpose and reinforce its image. Organizations that have a clear and simple purpose tend to be more successful in business than those which are less focused.[8] However, if the managers of these companies do not demonstrate a commitment to doing what these phrases suggest, they lose credibility with their employees and with their customers.

Step 2: Gather Data and Conduct Analyses

When managers state their company's mission, core competence, vision, strategic intent, or goals, they help to define the company's business. However, these statements remain useless hopes and prayers if managers do not take action to make the statements real. The purpose of gathering data and conducting internal and external analyses is to establish an information base from which strategic plans will emerge. Well-conceived plans ensure that the internal processes and capabilities of the organization match or align with the requirements, opportunities, and threats in the external environment. This match was formally summed up as **SWOT analysis,** *a review of the organization's strengths, weaknesses, opportunities and threats.* An organization's strategy will be more successful to the extent it has a favorable match between the internal strengths and weaknesses of the organization's processes and its external opportunities and threats.[9]

An **opportunity** is *an occasion to make an improvement or to create new possibilities* (see Chapter 6). Examples include customers unsatisfied by current offerings, new technology, availability of capital, and access to skilled employees. A **threat** is *anything, internally or externally, that might hurt the organization's ability to profitably serve customers.* Potential threats are competitors, government regulations, and shifts in customer value or demand. To take advantage of opportunities and deal with threats, managers must know the capabilities and limits, or strengths and weaknesses of their organization, which constrain their options. **Strengths** are *any resources or abilities to which the organization has access to take advantage of opportunities or to fight off threats.* Strengths may be a highly skilled work force, a reputation for high quality and

SWOT analysis A review of the organization's strengths, weaknesses, opportunities and threats.

Threat Anything, internally or externally, that might hurt the organization's ability to profitably serve customers.

Strength Any resource or ability to which the organization has access to take advantage of opportunities or to fight off threats.

low cost products, and patent protected products. **Weaknesses** are *deficiencies in the organization's resources and processes that make it vulnerable in the marketplace.* Weaknesses may include deficient research and development (R&D) capabilities, inflexible manufacturing processes, and inadequate information systems.

The Timex watch company provides a classic example of the importance of SWOT analysis to business strategy. The following excerpt illustrates than when internal strengths and weaknesses match external opportunities and threats, a business is much more likely to meet its strategic goals.

After World War II, during which the company produced timing devices for explosives, Timex began to search for new opportunities to employ its strength in designing and producing simple, cheap, and rugged mechanical timers. Wristwatches by leading designers were expensive, delicate objects sold through jewelry stores. Timex saw an opportunity to change this and established the goal of becoming a dominant competitor in the low end of the watch market. The firm successfully used its strengths to take advantage of the opportunity and soon reached its goal. At the height of the firm's success, one of every three watches sold in the world was a Timex.

However, the advent of digital electronic watches presented a threat. Initially, Timex ignored this threat, believing that digital technology would never be competitive with mechanical watches. Because of this, Timex failed to address its weakness in digital and electronics design and production. When the cost of digital technology fell to the point that highly reliable electronic watches were less expensive than an old-fashioned looking Timex, the company's position weakened. Electronics firms stormed the market, and Timex spent years struggling to build comparable strengths in digital technology just to survive. Based on a new analysis of the strategic situation, Timex realized that it would never again enjoy the industry domination that it once claimed, and the firm developed new goals that took it into a number of new markets such as personal computers. However, the firm has never repeated the near-perfect alignment among strategic goals, internal strengths, and external opportunities it once had in the wristwatch market.[10] (In 1993, the company started to do well in the digital market against competitors like Casio. Timex has its own new technology—indiglo—that makes it easy to see the watch in the dark.)

External Environment Analysis.   As the Timex example illustrates, managers need to analyze and understand the external environment to keep up with current events as well as to anticipate future trends. Managers can employ forecasting techniques to project trends in market growth, competitive behavior, costs of capital and labor, and so on, but such predictions always have some uncertainty. The farther into the future managers try to predict, the larger the uncertainty will be. For this reason, many companies concentrate on developing organizations able to respond quickly to environmental changes, including changes in such areas as: consumer tastes, the actions of competitors, the industry, and the business environment.

Managers can analyze the *business environment* from a number of perspectives, some of which we discussed in the earlier chapter on international management (political/legal, economic, social, and technological). Having a firm grip on the environment helps companies anticipate opportunities and threats. For

Weakness Any deficiency in the organization's resources and processes that make it vulnerable in the marketplace.

example, *social trends and attitudes,* such as toward health and physical fitness, leisure, and environmental protection, will influence customer demand for various foods and services, and other stakeholder expectations, such as not polluting. *Economic trends* like inflation, international exchange rates, interest rates, and consumer confidence will influence the attractiveness of business investments in terms of costs of doing business and anticipated returns on investment. *Political/legal factors* such as federal, state, and local regulations on taxes, labor rates, workplace safety, and environmental protection will create constraints on managerial decisions. *Technology trends* such as shorter product life cycles, miniaturization, automation, and computerization will affect the efficiency of organization processes and their products. Managers must also attend to *ecological trends* in global warming, population growth, deforestation, pollution, and general health, which can also affect how they operate.

Managers need to know how these environmental trends specifically affect their industry. For example, in the last decade, trends toward greater concern for health and physical fitness led to increased sales of exercise equipment, athletic shoes, and frozen yogurt as well as a trend away from beef and toward chicken. Managers can gather data about industry trends from sources such as customer/supplier meetings, trade publications, and industry conferences and exhibits. These sources provide managers with specific information about their competitors' new products and services, future offerings and information about internal operations and other things. In looking at this information, they should anticipate the long-term consequences of competitive actions. Failure to do so can be quite costly.

For example, during the 1980s IBM failed to pay close enough attention to the environment in which it operated. It did not fully appreciate the impact of microcomputers on the mainframe computer business, which it dominated and in which it had very high profit margins. Such margins insulated the company from problems and paying close attention to the competitive environment in which it operated, and it became bloated and bureaucratic. By the 1990s, though, with more and more powerful chips, such as the Intel 486 and Pentium microprocessors, it was clear that microcomputers, not mainframes, were the future, and that lots of companies could make and sell PCs as well as IBM could. The problem was that with IBM's huge overhead, the company could not price its machines competitively. This allowed companies with lower costs like Gateway 2000, Packard Bell, Dell, Compaq, and some others to grow into billion dollar microcomputer companies. By the early 1990s, IBM was in serious trouble, and the board of directors dismissed CEO John Akers and brought in Louis V. Gerstner to redirect company strategy. With huge layoffs, Gerstner is trying to seriously cut the fat from IBM and redirect its efforts toward microcomputers and their various uses and leveraging the company's size and technology expertise across markets in ways it has not done in the past. Time will tell if this works.[11]

The "Five Forces" Model. The "five forces" model, developed by Harvard professor Michael Porter, is the most frequently used analytical tool for understanding the competitiveness of an industry in traditional management approaches.[12] Exhibit 7-4 graphically illustrates this model. Porter suggests that five forces determine how competitive, and therefore how profitable, a particular industry will be. These forces include:

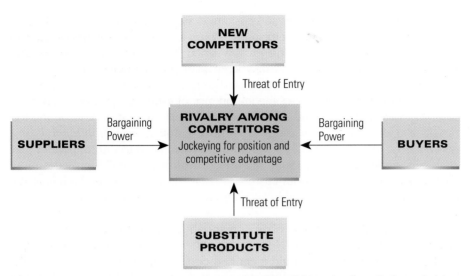

EXHIBIT 7-4
Michael Porter's five
force model

Source: Adapted and reprinted with permission of The Free Press, an imprint of Simon & Schuster from *Competitive Strategy: Techniques for Analyzing Industries and Competitors* by Michael E. Porter. Copyright © 1980 by The Free Press.

1. The threat of potential new competitors.
2. The bargaining power of suppliers.
3. The bargaining power of customers.
4. The threat of substitute products.
5. The intensity of rivalry among competitors.

The five forces model offers managers a useful tool for analyzing competition and provides a basis for developing and evaluating a strategy for competing within an industry. Porter suggests that a firm will be more profitable to the extent that it can reduce the threat of potential new competitors, reduce the bargaining power of suppliers and customers, eliminate the threat of substitute products, and reduce the intensity of rivalry. These factors thus become important as managers devise strategy.

Porter suggests that managers should anticipate changes in these five forces and what steps competitors might take. For example, in late 1988, Clorox entered the $4 billion-a-year laundry detergent market with a new product, Clorox Super Detergent. The entry triggered a double retaliation from Procter & Gamble (P&G), the industry leader which held fifty percent of the market. First, P&G offered a new product of its own, Tide with Bleach. Then P&G entered the $660 million-a-year bleach market, from which Clorox earned about half its net profits. P&G's retaliation eroded Clorox's competitive position and eventually drove it from the laundry detergent market in 1991.[13] The threat of entry and retaliation to entry are powerful forces that affect strategic decisions. However, these forces lead to defensive postures that do not help the company to come up with more creative strategies to compete.

TQM and Understanding Customers.   While the five forces model is a useful guide for strategists, the TQM approach suggests that managers take different courses of action for dealing with suppliers and customers than those Porter suggests.

Porter seems to regard suppliers and customers as adversaries in a game of nego-tiation over purchase price. For example, Porter's model suggests managers can make more profit by negotiating for low price from suppliers and frequently switching suppliers to make sure they keep their prices down (a practice called low-cost bidding).

By contrast, TQM emphasizes the importance of establishing partnerships with suppliers and customers, and most importantly, making customer value the top priority to guide business decisions. **Customer value** is *the combination of ben-efits received and costs paid by a user of a product or service.* An important way of understanding value is through the idea of *utility*. Exhibit 7-5 provides more background on this idea about customer value, the creation of which is at the heart of any successful strategy.

Customer value The combination of benefits received and costs paid by a user of a product or service.

Market Research.   A major goal of any organization should be to earn customers' loyalty by satisfying or even delighting them with high-value products and services. To do this well, managers should identify their interests with those of their cus-tomers and use market research techniques to learn as much as possible about their problems and needs. Learning about customers is perhaps the most important element of external environment analysis. Managers should not view customers as adversaries whose bargaining power they must reduce. They must accept that cus-tomers are going to purchase what they believe is in their best interest, not the company's. Even when an organization is the sole supplier of a product or service, its managers need to act as if this were not the case. This is the kind of attitude that will motivate managers to continuously improve customer value, which in turn attracts more customers and helps ensure any company's place in its market.

External analysis helps managers develop goals and understand how to align the capabilities with market needs. However, to do this well, they must under-stand their organization's capabilities before they start to devise strategies and processes to match these capabilities to the external environment. This under-standing comes from *internal analysis.*

Internal Analysis.   Internal analyses help managers understand the capabilities and limitations and strengths and weaknesses of their organization. One way to begin this analysis is by looking at a number of measures of results, such as costs of production, overhead rates, profit, return on investment, productivity, on-time-delivery performance, quality levels, and customer satisfaction. Then, to under-stand more deeply a company's strengths and weaknesses, managers need to analyze what caused these results. This requires an analysis of the current strate-gies, systems, and processes to figure out how an organization uses its resources to get certain results.

In Chapter 3 we talked about generic causes when using cause-and-effect dia-grams. These include 4 Ms: manpower, machines, materials, and methods. Now we will add a fifth M as well, measurements.[14] To understand the causes of results, managers should ask questions about each of these areas. The following list provides an overview of what the 5Ms suggest to managers as they undertake internal analysis:

- *Manpower* includes managerial and labor capabilities. What are the skills and education levels of employees? What are our managers capable of? What lev-els of technical knowledge do our staff experts have and are these relevant?

THE ASPECTS OF CUSTOMER VALUE

Happiness is the maximum agreement of reality with desire.
—Martin Cruz Smith, *Polar Star*

This quote from a popular novel captures one way of understanding customer value. Another is the idea of *utility*. Any successful company seeks to give customers as much utility for the cost as possible. Utility has four aspects:

1. *Form Utility.* This is the *physical form* the offering takes. It includes such things as how easy something is to use, how pleasing it looks, how well it fits, how carefully it is made, the quality of materials, and everything else that is incorporated into the physical product. In services, form utility can include the courtesy and competence of those delivering the services, and the cleanliness, comfort, and overall atmosphere of the place where the services are delivered.

2. *Place Utility.* This has to do with *where* the product is delivered. If the place you go to make a purchase is a retail store or if you go to a restaurant or barber shop, place utility means it is easy to get to. Mail order companies add place utility by allowing you to shop at home and then shipping your order to you. Companies that serve as suppliers to other companies deliver place utility by having sales people call at their customers' offices and then delivering the goods where the customer wants them.

3. *Time Utility.* This has to with delivering products *when* customers want them. This means that stores stock the items you are looking for when you want them. It means that when a customer orders from a supplier, they can expect the supplier to have what they want and have it delivered exactly when they expect it. Just-in-time delivery is a type of time utility. Christmas cards lose time utility the day after Christmas, and that is why they are marked down 50 percent or more.

4. *Possession Utility.* This has to with *payments and warranties*. Companies deliver possession utility by making it easy to buy something. Accepting credit cards, having special sales, allowing 30 or 60 days for payment, and guaranteeing satisfaction with a purchase are all ways companies make it easy for customers to gain possession of what they sell.

An effective strategy always seeks to combine these four forms of utility into a package that customers want and can afford and that positively differentiates one company's offerings from another.

EXHIBIT 7-5   Understanding customer value

Do employees need training? Based on population demographics, will the organization have access to an adequate labor force in the future?

- *Materials* include raw materials, parts, and supplies that are transformed into products and services. Are our suppliers low or high cost relative to customers' needs and competitors' suppliers? What is our approach to managing relationships with suppliers? Do we help suppliers make improvements in quality, cost, and delivery? Do our logistics and transportation processes ensure materials are available for workers when needed? Do we have access to needed materials?

- *Machinery* includes the equipment and tools needed to transform material inputs into products and services. What are our technical capabilities? Do we have access to the right machine tools? Is our information processing equipment adequate?

- *Methods* include the ways manpower uses machinery and materials to produce products and services. Are our work methods wasteful or inefficient? Do we do preventive maintenance to keep machinery in top shape and avoid breakdowns and quality problems? How can our operating practices be improved? What are our methods of problem solving and continuous improvement?

- *Measurement* includes the ways data are collected and communicated. Are our measurements customer focused? Do we measure key processes at key intervals and not just end of line results? Are our data reliable and accurate? Are our data interpretable? Do our data allow statistical analysis and understanding of the causes of variation?

Managers should use these 5M categories to better understand current strategies, the results they attained, and how well organizational processes are working to achieve results.

Once managers have established a tentative strategy, they will again have to reconsider these questions to reveal any gaps between what they want to do and their organization's resources and capabilities. In fact, this task of continuously analyzing and improving internal capabilities never ends. This is the key task in the ongoing formulation of strategy. This never-ending process is analogous to the PDCA improvement cycle we reviewed in Chapter 6, and is simply another example of PDCA at work in the management of organizations.

Managers need to undertake this 5M analysis for each functional area or department, such as research and development, design, engineering, marketing, sales, accounting, manufacturing, and finance. Managers seeking to implement TQM often come to realize that an organization can be strong on the 5M elements within each function, yet their overall capabilities are weak because the functions do not work well together. For this reason, many companies also assess their internal capabilities for achieving integration and cooperation across processes spanning functional units. Other important aspects of the internal environment include the organization's infrastructure, such as information systems to support decision making and communication. The extent of autonomy given to decision makers and freedom from bureaucracy can be important determiners of overall strengths and weaknesses of the organization. Some companies even analyze their culture and leadership to evaluate internal

USING THE MALCOLM BALDRIGE NATIONAL QUALITY AWARD CRITERIA FOR INTERNAL ANALYSIS

TQM IN ACTION

The Malcolm Baldrige National Quality Award was established by law in 1987 to enhance U.S. competitiveness by promoting quality excellence. The award program provides a conceptual model and means of assessing organizations in terms of the model. The award criteria are divided into seven categories:

1. Strong customer focus
2. Effective, hands-on leadership
3. Good systems for acquiring, analyzing, and using information
4. A strategic, long-range outlook toward quality
5. Focus on human resource development and excellence
6. Effective process management
7. Focus on a variety of measurements and results indicators

Many managers of organizations use the award criteria to do internal analysis of their capabilities and learn where to focus energies to improve. Since the award process generates scores for participants, it also provides managers a way of comparing their organization to other firms.

Most of the companies that have won the Baldrige award have been either large companies, like Xerox or Milliken, or divisions of large companies, like Westinghouse's nuclear fuels division or IBM Rochester in Rochester, Minnesota. However, a growing number of small- and medium-sized companies are competing in the small business category of the award. In 1993, one winner was a small $20 million company, Ames Rubber, that supplies precision rubber parts for use in copy machines and other devices. Award programs patterned after the Baldrige Award are sponsored by several states and at the local level as well.[16] Some large firms sponsor them for divisions within the company and have quality awards for suppliers as well.

For example, the Minnesota Council for Quality has had financial support from companies like 3M, Honeywell, and IBM for seminars, meetings, local councils, and annual competitions called "Baby Baldriges," patterned after the Baldrige Award. While the state competition usually requires less documentation than the national award, it can serve as a dress rehearsal for the big dance. For example, Zytec Corporation in Eden Prairie, Minnesota won the first state competition and won the Baldrige award the same year. The improvement efforts inspired by the competition can bring fortune to small companies. After failing to win the first year it applied for the Baldrige, Hutchinson Technology, Inc., a maker of components for computer disk drives, spent the next 12 months working on its deficiencies. Hutchinson's president, Wayne M. Fortun, credits these efforts for a 40% jump in annual earnings, to $13 million, on a revenue gain of 12%, to $160 million.

The real value of the Baldrige Award and the criteria set up for the award are as guidelines for helping managers assess their organizations. Curt W. Reimann and Harry Hertz, administrators of the award, have written, "Few organizations seek either awards or registration, but most wish to have non-costly means to learn how well they are doing and how they could get better. The most cost-effective means to achieve these purposes is through self-assessment" [using the Baldrige criteria.][17]

It is just as important for small organizations to conduct internal analysis as it is for large ones. Small companies are a vital part of the global economic community. Small and midsize companies account for about half of the total value added by U.S. manufacturing, produce nearly half of all U.S. exports, and employ more than half of all factory workers.[18]

strengths and weaknesses. Lou Gerstner found, for example, that some decisions at IBM required as many as 18 different signatures to implement.[15]

Gathering data and doing analyses is the part of the strategic management process by which managers come to understand, in decision-making terms, the current situation and possible alternative directions they might take. By assessing how these various alternative strategies might affect their success, one or some combination will emerge as the most logical approach to take. At that point, the next step is to formulate plans.

Step 3: Decide on a Plan

After analyzing the internal situation to identify strengths and weaknesses and the external environment to identify opportunities and threats, managers then have much of the information they need to build a strategic plan. In practice, managers do not always use a structured approach like SWOT analysis to help them develop an information base for strategic planning. But at some level, they have an understanding of these issues and how their firms fit into the competitive environment and how they might offer a unique combination of elements that will appeal to some market segment. They are primarily concerned about providing value to customers by addressing three general factors:

1. Quality, which helps to differentiate the product or service from other alternatives.
2. Cost, which helps keep purchase price low for customers and allows profit margins for the producer.
3. Time, which is important for speed of new product development and timely delivery of products to customers.

These three factors are what managers can manipulate to create the four utilities (form, time, place, and possession) that will ultimately comprise the value of what they put on the market.

Evaluating Strategic Alternatives.   Managers may come up with a number of strategy alternatives. Ultimately, they have to come to a conclusion about which of these is the one the company will go with. The following criteria can be useful in evaluating strategic alternatives:[19]

- *Internal Consistency*. The various parts of the action plan support each other.
- *Realistic*. The plan is achievable, even if it is challenging.
- *Focused on Strategic Problems*. The plan addresses the key problems revealed through earlier analyses.
- *Capable of Solving Key Subproblems*. The plan addresses minor problems and symptoms of company deficiencies.
- *Customer Benefit*. The plan improves value for customers.

Perhaps the most important principle for managers to remember in making their choice is that they are managing an open system. This principle provides a context for using all of the above criteria. The open systems view suggests that all parts of an organization need to be mutually reinforcing and aligned for everything to work well. Human resources must fit the technology and production processes, which in turn must fit the product design, which in turn must fit the needs of customers and other stakeholders. Without internal and external alignment, all actions that managers take to enact their strategy will be less than efficient or effective and may be done completely in vain.

The Adaptive Model.   When evaluating alternative strategies, managers may want to consider an **adaptive model** of strategy that *describes a strategy that changes and adapts to changes in the external environment.*[20] In other words, this is a strategy that suggests that companies, like people, be able to adapt and adjust to the changing environment. The model suggests three different adaptive strategies for doing this:

Adaptive model An approach that describes a strategy that changes and adapts to changes in the external environment.

- *Prospector Strategy.* If the environment in which a firm operates is dynamic and has big potential for growth, the prospector strategy makes sense. Prospectors are leaders, not followers. They take risks and pursue innovation to develop new products and market opportunities. FedEx has always been a prospector, blazing new trails in the package delivery market. Many software companies also pursue a prospector strategy seeking to deliver new computer applications that arise because of the increasing power and decreasing prices of PCs.
- *Defender Strategy.* In a slow growth or stable environment, the defender strategy makes sense. A defender avoids changing its current products and markets. It seeks to hold onto existing market share through improvements in efficiency or incremental quality improvement. WD-40 has pursued this strategy since the 1950s, offering only a single product, a petroleum-based lubricant. The company has pursued this so well that it still has no significant competitors.
- *Analyzer Strategy.* Analyzers are a combination of prospector and defender, and they seem best suited for moderately changing environments. They emphasize achieving more market share, efficiency, and economies of scale in current product lines. They will pursue change, but only as cautious followers. They usually innovate only after a leader, a prospector, has forged ahead and shown the way into new markets. Analyzers often imitate other products, in a "me too" strategy, but they will occasionally lead their industry with a new product. Procter & Gamble is an analyzer, with a number of established consumer products, like Pampers and Crest toothpaste, and occasional innovations, like Pampers Phases for different stages of child development. P&G has also entered the drug market with an innovative new analgesic, Aleve.

In considering the adaptive strategies, remember that these are approaches for figuring out what a company's strategy should be and how it might best use its resources given the environment in which it does business.

Step 4: Take Action

Once managers have figured out what strategy makes the most sense and have laid out their plans, the next step is to put it into action. We often refer to this step as implementation. It begins when managers communicate the strategic plan to the organization's employees. The strategy provides a means of integrating employee decisions and actions throughout the organization. It provides a common view of where the organization is going and how to get there.

The term "implementation" is deceptive because it sounds like it can be done instantly and separately from the foregoing steps of planning. Nothing could be further from the truth. As managers start to take action they will learn more about the business environment, internal and external to the firm. They will realize gaps between the plan and reality and make adjustments to the strategy while they are "implementing" it. In a sense, managers continue to engage in planning, refining their definition of the business (mission, vision, and goals), collecting and analyzing information, devising and choosing alternative plans, and again, taking further action.

While this fact of continuous strategy revision has long been a part of organizational life, with TQM we gain a perspective on this need for revision and a methodology for doing it. The PDCA cycle again fits here and helps us understand how to continuously improve strategy. Without this perspective, we find managers and companies often decide on a strategy, put it into action, and then not know what to do when things do not work as they expected. TQM acknowledges that there is always uncertainty about outcomes and that we are always learning how to improve.

Implementation does not occur instantly. It takes time to make the investments in people and organizational processes and develop the capabilities to execute the strategy, especially if it is a major departure from the past. The factors important to strategy implementation should have been revealed in earlier analyses. These may include decision making and reporting structures, human resources, information systems, control systems, or technology, or combinations of these.

For example, Microsoft Corporation has designs to be an important player in shaping and supplying software for the information highway. This is a new strategic direction for the company. Bill Gates, chairman of Microsoft, has had to set up a new division of the company, called the Advanced Technology Group (ATG), to research and develop software that consumers might use to navigate this highway. The company has devoted an initial investment of $100 million and 500 people to this effort. Gates is aware of the risk involved here, noting that the average ATG project will take three years to develop and has less than a 50 percent chance of success. Nevertheless, this is a major opportunity, and the company is committed to moving ahead and becoming a leader in this new area and has committed organizational resources and time to achieve this strategic goal.[21]

In implementing strategy, managers must make sure that the important factors are in place throughout the organization. They must also continue to measure and assess how things are working to determine whether the organization is on the right track to achieve its goals. If it gets off track, managers need to make quick adjustments to get it back on course or even change course if that seems appropriate. For example, Microsoft, in its ATG efforts, sought to set up a joint venture between TCI (a major cable company) and Time Warner to create an interactive TV system. This did not work out, and the company went with a less ambitious plan with TCI to develop systems for delivering movies and other programming on demand via interactive cable technology.[22]

? THINKING CRITICALLY

1. What are the similarities and differences between the strategic management process and the problem-solving/decision-making processes described in an earlier chapter?
2. Based on your own experience, why do you think the four utilities—form, time, place, and possession—provide a sound way to understand how you put a value on some large purchase you have recently made?
3. How does understanding customer value influence the development of a company's strategy?
4. Review the seven categories of criteria for the Malcolm Baldrige National Quality Award (*A Look at TQM In Action* box on page 247). Provide your own rationale for why each of these criteria would be useful in doing an internal analysis of an organization. What is the relationship of these criteria with sound strategic management and its execution?

LEVELS OF STRATEGY

Strategic management processes can be applied at several levels of the corporation. The three most common are: (1) corporate, (2) business unit, and (3) functional level strategy. **Corporate level strategy** pertains *to large corporations that operate in more than one business area and how they manage and allocate resources among them*. For example, RJR Nabisco produces tobacco products and food products. The key corporate question is how to allocate resources among each of the business units or separate companies that make up a diverse corporation. Then within these units the managers have to devise business level strategy.

Strategy at the business level also pertains to smaller companies or undiversified organizations doing business in only one area, such as Apple Computer in microcomputers. **Business level strategy** focuses on *understanding and meeting customer needs, and market positioning of products and services relative to competitors*. Within these business organizations, managers also have to address functional strategies, within areas such as manufacturing, finance, research and development. **Functional level strategy** is largely directed at *integrating functional department goals with those of the entire business*. We discuss each level of strategy in more detail below.

Corporate Strategy

Organizations made up of more than one business have to develop corporate level strategy to help them balance allocation of resources with market opportunities. For example, the primary businesses of Johnson & Johnson consists of its consumer products division, including wound care, toiletries, oral care, and skin care. However, a division of the company also produces and distributes pharmaceutical products, chemicals, food and beverage ingredients, and over-the-counter drugs. Some of these units operate in partnership with other Johnson & Johnson (J&J) companies, and some operate independently.

Corporate level strategy
A level of strategic management that large corporations use when operating in more than one business area and how they allocate resources among them.

Business level strategy A level of strategy that focuses on understanding and meeting customer needs, and market positioning of products and services relative to competitors.

Functional level strategy A level of strategy that deals with integrating functional department goals with those of the entire business.

Diversified companies like Johnson & Johnson have to decide what businesses they want to be in, how to allocate resources, what goals to set, and how to assess performance of these businesses. There are two general ways to describe corporate strategy: (1) portfolio management, and (2) grand strategies. Grand strategies help managers provide an overall direction for the organization and figure out the best direction for individual business units. Portfolio analysis is especially useful for figuring out how to allocate resources among units.

As we review each of these approaches, remember they simply represent ways managers understand the organization of resources and priorities to which their companies must attend to serve different markets effectively and efficiently. For each such approach the subsequent decisions and execution are what are most important. The alignment of corporate resources with market needs and the continuous improvement of processes will determine how well any company does.

Portfolio Management

Portfolio management
A strategy approach used by managers of diversified corporations to evaluate each business and define that business's roles and goals within the corporation.

When a company like General Electric owns businesses that are diverse, each business may have its own strategy, serve different markets, and operate somewhat autonomously. As a result, some businesses may perform very well, and others may perform poorly. From the corporate perspective, managers need a strategy for optimally allocating resources across all of these businesses. **Portfolio management** is *a strategy approach used by managers of diversified corporations to evaluate each business and define that business's roles and goals within the corporation.* There are a number of approaches to portfolio management that have been developed by companies like General Electric and Shell, and consulting firms like McKinsey and Company, Arthur D. Little, and the Boston Consulting Group.[23] We will review here the approach of the Boston Consulting Group (BCG), a popular and perhaps the most basic approach to portfolio management.

The BCG Matrix. The BCG approach suggests that the best way to manage diverse businesses is to view them together, as a portfolio of products, using a small number of fundamental criteria.[24] BCG suggests two criteria for evaluating business units: (1) *market growth* and (2) *relative market* share. BCG assumes that market growth reflects both the vitality of the market and the stage of a product in its life cycle. Relative market share, defined as the ratio of a business's sales to that of its largest competitor, is assumed to reveal the competitive position of the business.

BCG matrix A four-cell form used to categorize a business according to whether it is high or low on the two dimensions of market share and market growth.

The **BCG matrix** is a *four-cell form that can be used to categorize a business according to whether it is high or low on the two dimensions of market share and market growth.* Exhibit 7-6 illustrates this matrix. Managers try to place each business or product line on the BCG matrix and label it either a cash cow, a star, a question mark, or a dog, with corresponding implications for strategic decisions about their future.

- A cash *cow* is a business generating more resources than it needs, often with low growth but high market share. It is called a cash cow because it generates a lot of money and profit. However, because of low growth and relative ease in holding onto market share, not all the cash should be reinvested in the cash

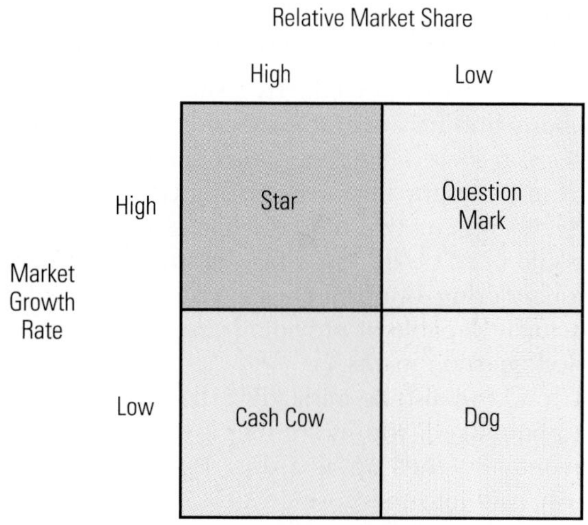

Relative Market Share

EXHIBIT 7-6
The Boston Consulting Group
(BCG) matrix for strategic
portfolio analysis

cow. Money spent on product development, advertising, promotion, or other marketing tactics for a cash cow would not yield as much return as it would if spent on a question-mark or star business.

- A *question mark* is a business with negative returns in a high growth market but with low market share. The question mark needs cash for investments from other businesses and fails to generate a positive cash flow. With proper investment to increase market share in a growing market, a question mark might become a star. Without these investments, a question mark could become a dog.

- A *star* is an emerging business in a high growth market that has high relative market share. Maintaining share in high growth markets requires more investment than for a cash cow. Cash flow may be small or negative initially; however, stars can generate handsome profits. Eventually, when market growth slows, stars become cash cows.

- A *dog* is a business with low returns in a low growth market and low relative market share. It does not require much cash, but it doesn't generate much either. Moving a dog to another category can require enormous resources. Alternatively, the corporation may choose to harvest the business by keeping it until it fails, sell the business, or abandon it completely. Dogs are often divested or liquidated because of their drain on cash. However, some well-managed dogs can generate large amounts of cash.

The BCG Matrix provides corporate managers with specific ideas about how to allocate cash and other resources among its businesses to improve the financial performance of the portfolio as a whole. In the simplest of terms, according to BCG, a corporation should strive to have the majority of its businesses positioned as cash cows since these provide the cash needed for the others. Only a few businesses should be question marks since they require significant investment to transform them into stars, and they can become dogs if something goes wrong. Relatively more businesses should be stars, since these have the potential to become cash cows. Finally, only a few businesses should be dogs since they eat up a lot of cash.

Criticisms of Portfolio Management

The BCG Matrix in particular can be criticized since the criteria for categorizing businesses are arbitrary and may lead to unsound advice for corporate strategy. The only businesses considered high on market share are those that are market leaders. This can result in many businesses being labeled dogs. The labeling is misleading because it suggests that these businesses are not worthy of further investment and should even be disposed of. Unfortunately, managers who take this advice are squandering opportunities because many of the companies labeled dogs are actually capable of providing cash that could be used to invest in businesses labeled question marks.[25]

The label "cash cow" can also be misleading, because it implies that the business is there just to be milked, with no further investment or creativity applied, so the business eventually ends up as a dog. By contrast, a creative strategy could launch a cash cow into the position of a star, as illustrated by Yamaha Piano in the *A Look at the Global Environment* box on page 260. This idea is related to the mistake of focusing on products rather than the utility people derive from the products. If organizations categorize their businesses without looking at the benefits these products deliver to customers, they can make mistakes that close them off to opportunities.

Another problem with portfolio management is that it focuses corporate managers on results, namely market growth and share, and distracts them from understanding the causes of these results, namely customer's needs and the improvement of an organization's internal processes and capabilities. To learn about the causes of these results, they should gather, analyze, and consider specific information about the internal and external environments, using the SWOT approach, for example.

Yet another problem with portfolio management at the corporate level is that executives tend to divorce themselves from the businesses they are "managing." They do not take an active interest in guiding business unit strategy. Rather, they make strategic decisions about buying and selling as if they were dealing with Monopoly money, divesting Illinois Avenue to invest in Park Place, because of how the two compare on paper.

In today's competitive environments, with increased consumer power and the growing importance of customer value, even high-level corporate managers cannot afford to be detached. Business unit strategy is increasingly important as a means to achieve long-term value for all stakeholders of the organization. Certainly, corporate managers must make tough decisions about how to allocate cash to diverse businesses. However, many companies are discovering that, in the long term, investors and stockholders are better served when the organization concentrates on developing successful business unit strategies. Corporate managers may use portfolio management to help them generally decide how to allocate cash investments. However, they must develop business level strategies to make specific plans for using those resources wisely within their respective business environments.

Grand Strategies

Grand strategy An overall approach to taking action at the corporate level.

A **grand strategy** is *an overall approach to taking action at the corporate level.* There are at least three grand strategies that managers can select: growth,

THE FOUNDATION OF SUCCESS AT MOTOROLA

Christopher B. Galvin is the President and Chief Operating Officer of the Motorola Corporation. His company is a Baldrige Award winner and one of the premier high technology companies in the world. He writes about the strategic mission of his company:

Motorola's organizational mission and the basis for all its strategy can be found on a small card that employees carry around in a wallet or purse. One side of this card simply reads,

MANAGERS IN ACTION

Our Fundamental Objective
(Everyone's Overriding Responsibility)
Total Customer Satisfaction.

That means that customers drive a strategy based on quality and bringing about continuous renewal, change, and improvement. It recognizes that the primary sources of competitive advantage are quality, cycle time, cost, and functionality.

On the other side of the card is a list of key beliefs, goals, and initiatives under which total customer satisfaction is carried out. Though our actions change, they are based on unchanging beliefs:

- Constant respect for people and
- Uncompromising integrity.

We have three basic goals that drive our actions:

- Best-in-class people, marketing, technology, product (software, hardware, and systems), manufacturing, and service.
- Increased global market share, and
- Superior financial results.

To reach these goals, we have five key operational initiatives:

- Six Sigma Quality
- Total cycle time reduction
- Product, manufacturing, and environmental leadership
- Profit improvement, and
- Empowerment for all, in a participative, cooperative, and creative workplace.

These beliefs, goals, and initiatives require that quality is rooted and institutionalized in the business process. It begins with each individual and business unit asking basic questions: What is my mission? What is my product or service? Who are my customers? Who are my suppliers? What do I need to satisfy my customers?

Then we map the process of serving the customer, record cycle times and defects, and analyze results. Finally, we institutionalize the solutions. We apply new procedures at each appropriate step of the process, and start all over again. It is an endless process of continuous learning and improvement. It leads to customer satisfaction through best-in-class quality, cycle time, cost, and functionality.

This approach has enabled Motorola to achieve leadership during a period of rapid technological change and a growing global customer base. Sales have grown from $4.3 billion in 1983 to $17.0 billion in 1994. The company is the world leader in cellular phones, paging, and two-way radio communications, and is one of the three largest semiconductor companies in the world. The company's beliefs, goals, and initiatives point toward continued growth and renewal driven by its attention to customer satisfaction.

retrenchment, and stability. Corporations may also pursue a combination of these across different divisions or businesses.[26] These three strategies are shown in Exhibit 7-7.

Growth strategy A strategic approach that seeks to increase an organization's overall size, by increasing its volume, market share, or number of markets served.

Growth Strategy. A **growth strategy** *seeks to increase an organization's overall size, by increasing its volume, market share, or number of markets served.* A business can achieve growth either through current or new products or through current or new markets.[27] Companies like General Motors, operating in highly competitive markets, may attempt to grow by improving the quality and value of current products. Other ways to grow include:

- *Acquisition.* For example, in the 1980s Chrysler grew by acquiring Jeep and creating Eagle as a new nameplate and Philip Morris grew through acquiring Miller Brewing, General Foods, and Kraft. Companies can grow through product development, such as when Pepsi added a clear cola to its product line to attract additional sales (however, that product has been a disappointment).

- *Diversification.* Tandy Corporation used this approach when its chain of Radio Shack stores added telephones, intercoms, calculators, clocks, electronic and scientific toys, personal computers, and peripheral computer equipment to its existing line of radio and stereo equipment.

- *Joint Ventures and Strategic Alliances.* These are partnerships with other corporations to develop products or to facilitate vertical integration (alliances with specific suppliers or customer groups). Examples include the partnership between Apple, IBM, and Motorola to develop the PowerPC microchip. An example of a vertical alliance would be Boeing Corporation which has developed long-term relationships with a core group of suppliers and has incorporated its customers in the design of its products.

- *Core Competence.* Some companies use their expertise in some field to leverage their growth. For example, in the 1980s, Honda's diverse line of products, including cars, garden tillers, motorcycles, lawnmowers, snowblowers, snowmobiles, power generators, and outboard motors, seems to be a growth strategy of unrelated diversification. However, Honda has simply exploited its core competence in small engine technology and manufacturing and its brand recognition to leverage growth into diverse power equipment markets.

Retrenchment An attempt to turn around a poorly performing company by reducing the size or number of operations.

Retrenchment Strategies. Growth strategies are not always what is best for the corporation. Strategies must fit the internal and external environments. Sometimes retrenchment is the best strategy. **Retrenchment** is *an attempt to turn around a*

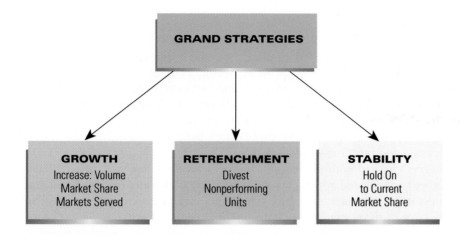

EXHIBIT 7-7
The three types of grand strategies

poorly performing company by reducing the size or number of operations. Retrenchment is the opposite of a growth strategy. It may be brought on by economic realities, like recession, downturns in market demand, new regulations, or internal financial problems (often brought on by poor strategic management).

Intense competition can also drive companies to retrench. For example, in the early 1980s, a number of producers of personal computers, like Xerox, withdrew from the increasingly competitive business. Companies may *divest* or sell off plants or whole divisions intact. The company may even *liquidate* some of its operations, such as older, inefficient plants, by closing them down and selling off the assets (inventory, equipment, furniture, buildings).

Stability Strategies.   The third grand strategy, **stability,** is *an attempt to maintain the status quo, to neither gain position nor retrench.* A stability strategy requires little investment but seeks to hold onto current market share and profitability by focusing managerial resources on current operations. (A firm may grow, however, if the market is growing). Budgets for marketing and research and development may be cut altogether or diverted to pay for maintaining and replacing worn equipment in existing production lines (or vice versa). A firm that is already quite successful, with large market share and profitability, may choose a stability strategy to enjoy the fruits of its labor. This could mean good cash flow, continued profitability, and handsome dividends for stockholders. In terms of the BCG matrix, we might think of this as the cash cow approach.

A firm that lacks resources for further investment may choose to maintain stability. Also, a firm that has just gone through a retrenchment may choose to pursue stability, taking no risks, just to establish a firm footing for the future. Some firms inadvertently pursue a stability strategy because of their complacency and failure to devise new strategies and failure to continuously improve existing operations.

Under any of these circumstances, a stability strategy may work for a few years. However, with increasing international competition, it will not last for long. Few companies enjoy long-term and total protection from new entrants, substitute products, or competitors who are determined to grow themselves. Companies that do not anticipate growing competition and fail to invest for the future, may not have a pleasant future.

Stability An attempt to maintain the status quo, to neither gain position nor retrench.

Business Level Strategy

Business level strategy is the broad plan a specific business unit (such as Philip Morris's Oscar Mayer division) has for achieving its mission, vision, and goals. Business level strategy involves understanding and meeting customer needs, and market positioning of products and services relative to competitors. Many of the concepts discussed above, such as SWOT analysis, the grand strategies of growth, retrenchment, and stability, and Porter's five forces model, can be useful for corporate and business level strategists.

Managers charged with developing business level strategy will benefit from some other concepts and approaches to strategy. Michael Porter has suggested that a business might achieve competitive advantage or carve out a niche for itself by pursuing one of three strategies: *differentiation, cost leadership, or focus.*[28] Managers may even pursue a combination of these strategies. Customer value, again, is the integrative concept for business level strategy. We discuss each of these below.

Differentiation strategy
A strategy that creates customer value by offering products or services that are somehow perceived as different from other alternatives by customers.

Differentiation Strategy.   A business adopting a **differentiation strategy** *attempts to offer a product that is somehow perceived by the customer as different from other alternatives.* Of course, at one level all competition comes from trying to differentiate your offerings from those of your competitors by using a combination of the four utilities discussed earlier. However, companies pursuing this strategy make special effort to distinguish themselves with some combination of form, time, or place utility, creating high value for consumers and justifying high prices. For example, Nordstrom's, a Seattle-based department store chain, differentiates itself on two factors, an upscale image and unmatched service. Nordstrom sales people are renowned for doing "whatever it takes" to please the customer. Such service might include personally going across town to pick up an out-of-stock item and delivering it to the customer's house, or staying after work to take up the hem in a dress when the customer absolutely needs it the next day. Volvo seeks to differentiate itself on the basis of automobile safety, and Mercedes on the basis of luxury and image. However, differentiation does not always equate to high price. For example, Toyota differentiated itself on the basis of product quality and reliability. But it also earned market share because of the affordability of its models.

Cost leadership strategy
A strategy that creates customer value by producing goods at low cost and competing on price to gain market share.

Cost Leadership Strategy.   A business pursuing a **cost leadership strategy** *attempts to produce a product inexpensively so it can lower its price and gain market share.* K-Mart originated this approach in discount merchandising, and Wal-Mart seems to have mastered it in recent years. These discounters have enormous buying power, with retail outlets all over the country, so they can bargain for cheaper prices on large quantities. Wal-Mart continues to revolutionize this industry by reducing its costs through efficient logistical operations and supplier management, eliminating massive inventories and warehouses.

Traditionally, companies attempted to achieve cost leadership by squeezing suppliers to reduce purchasing costs or implementing automation to reduce labor costs. Recently companies practicing TQM have discovered that quality improvement is a better way to achieve cost reduction. This means that cost leadership and differentiation on the basis of quality can go hand in hand, rather than be mutually exclusive strategies.

Focus Strategy. Businesses pursuing a **focus strategy** may emphasize differentiation or cost leadership or, more likely, a combination of the two, but *they target their products for a particular market segment.* They do this by segmenting customers into homogeneous groups with common needs and then targeting the segment or segments they are best equipped to serve. Typical segmenting dimensions include demographics (age, gender, education, income, life cycle stage, religion, and ethnicity), lifestyles (grouping by similarities in attitudes, interests, and opinions), and other dimensions for identifying commonalities. Examples of focus strategy include Johnson Publishing Company, which targets African Americans with *Ebony* and *Jet* magazines. Many small companies use this strategy, often targeting some group of enthusiasts, such as owners of cars like Porsches or Ford Mustangs from the 1960s. The Gap targeted its outlets to provide trendy fashions for young Americans. Various cable television networks target special groups, such as MTV or the Nashville Network.

Focus strategy A strategy that creates customer value by targeting products or services toward a particular market segment.

Functional Strategy

Functional level strategy refers to the specific plans that each function has for executing the business level strategy. Typical functions in a business include marketing, sales, research and development, engineering, purchasing, manufacturing, quality control, accounting, and human resources/personnel. Functional level strategy represents an extension of the implementation plan for business level strategy. Each function has a specific role to play in implementing the business strategy to serve a company's external customers. However, each may also have its own unique internal and external customers. For example, purchasing managers supply parts and material to manufacturing, and manufacturing in turn supplies finished goods to distributors and ultimately external retailers.

Many of the concepts discussed above still apply to this level of strategy. For example, it is important for functional managers to understand their internal strengths and weaknesses in relation to external opportunities and threats (SWOT). Other concepts, like portfolio management and grand strategy are not relevant to functional strategy. The most important issue for functional level strategy is to make sure that all of the respective strategies fit together to form a coherent whole and successfully implement the business strategy.

For example, a purchasing strategy of buying from low cost bidders and using many sources for a single part are incompatible with a just-in-time manufacturing strategy which requires high quality, on-time deliveries from suppliers and little variation in the parts delivered. *Sole sourcing* or purchasing a part from only one supplier, instead of several suppliers, ensures the part will be more consistent in quality. The way various functions fit together across the company to implement a business strategy largely depends on how they are organized, which is the topic of the next chapter.

❓ THINKING CRITICALLY

1. Based on what you have read here, what do you think the strengths of the BCG matrix are? What are its weaknesses? If you were developing strategy for a large corporation, would you use the BCG matrix? Why or why not?

THE GLOBAL ENVIRONMENT

THE JAPANESE FOCUS ON THE CUSTOMER

In a sense, business level strategy is head-to-head competition between companies. However, if managers approach strategic management with this mindset, rather than an intense focus on customers, they can miss many opportunities. This is a point where the typical U.S. approach to strategy differs from that of the Japanese. A leading Japanese theorist of management and economics, Kenichi Ohmae, explains:

To many western managers, the Japanese competitive achievement provides hard evidence that a hallmark of a successful strategy is the creation of sustainable competitive advantage by beating the competition. If it takes world-class manufacturing to win, you have to beat competitors with your factories. If it takes rapid product development, you have to beat them with your labs. If it takes mastery of distribution channels, you have to beat them with your logistics system. No matter what it takes, the goal of strategy is to beat the competition. After a decade of losing ground to the Japanese, managers in the U.S. and Europe have learned this lesson very well. As a guide to action, it is clear and compelling. As a metric of performance, it is unambiguous. It is also wrong.

Winning the manufacturing or product development or logistics battle is not a bad thing. But it is not really what strategy is—or should be—about. When the focus of attention is on ways to beat the competition, strategy inevitably gets defined primarily in terms of the competition. . . . When you go toe-to-toe with competitors, you cannot let them build up any kind of advantage. You must watch their every move. Or so the argument goes.

Of course, it is important to take the competition into account, but that should not come first in making strategy. First comes painstaking attention to the customer's needs and close analysis of a company's real degrees of freedom in responding to those needs. The willingness to rethink what products are and what they do, as well as how to organize the business system that designs, builds, and markets them, must follow. Competitive realities are what you test possible strategies against; you define them in terms of customers.

[Your strategy] should also encompass the determination to avoid competition whenever and wherever possible. As the great philosopher Sun Tzu observed five hundred years before Christ, the smartest strategy in war is the one that allows you to achieve your objectives without having to fight. Nintendo's "family computer" sold 12 million units in Japan alone, during which time it had virtually no competition at all. . . .

. . . in my experience, managers too often and too willingly launch themselves into old-fashioned competitive battles. It's familiar ground. They know how to fight. They have a much harder time seeing when an effective customer-oriented strategy could avoid the battle altogether."[29]

Kenichi writes of how a customer-oriented strategy based on customer value can translate into business success. Yamaha achieved a 40% share in the piano market after years of persistent work. But demand started to dwindle by 10% a year. The market was saturated, with 40 million pianos in dens, living rooms, and concert halls around the world, mostly just sitting idle. With low-cost producers entering the market (e.g., the Koreans), it would have been tempting for the Yamaha managers to label the piano division a potential "dog," and milk it dry while it was still a "cash cow," tenuously holding onto market share leadership. Or they could divest while the divesting was still good.

However, Yamaha didn't do these things. Nor did Yamaha just try the traditional approaches to retaining and gaining market share in head-to-head competition, such as proliferating new models, cutting costs, slicing overhead, or going upscale with luxury/specialty items. Yamaha managers decided they could not improve a product in an area where traditional piano technology had not changed for many years.

Rather, Yamaha thought about the value customers might derive from the use of a piano. They achieved a broader view of the market, and thought in "customer terms" of providing "musical entertainment" and not simply in "product terms" of providing pianos. They recognized that more people were listening to music than ever before, and most people do not have the time to learn to play a piano. Then they recalled the idea of the player piano and updated this idea with modern optical technology. This technology distinguishes 92 degrees of strength and speed of key touch, digitally records and reproduces keystrokes with great accuracy, and stores music on a 3.5 inch computer disk.

This enables people to invite great pianists into their homes, play their own instruments with piano accompaniment, transfer music over the phone lines, and remotely enjoy many concerts through a mail-order club. Since introducing the new technology in a line of pianos called the DiskLavier, new piano sales have increased significantly. (Introduced in 1987, the DiskLavier contributed about 19% of Yamaha's profitability by 1993.) Yamaha revitalized their piano business by capitalizing on their competencies in piano and electronic technologies to offer new products and services.[30]

2. What do you think would have happened to the Yamaha investment in pianos if they had done a BCG matrix analysis?
3. How do you think organizations should balance their focus on customers and their needs and what competitors are doing in developing a strategy? Which is more important? Why?

CUSTOMER VALUE, TQM AND STRATEGIC ADVANTAGE

Every strategy, when boiled down to its essence, is about how organizations employ their resources and abilities to generate something of value for someone else. When they do this well, which includes all the attendant internal processes and external marketing, finance, and distribution, they succeed. When they do it poorly, they lose money and can go out of business. This should not be news to you. We have made this point throughout this and other chapters in the book.

This point is also the foundation of TQM. Through creativity and the application of TQM tools and techniques, managers at thousands of companies in the U.S. and around the world are refining their abilities to develop strategic advantages for themselves. These managers understand their jobs in terms of system management and delivering some combination of the four types of utility to customers in their products and services. They are working to eliminate any tasks that do not add value to their processes for doing this. They understand that execution is never easy, and that business is a continuous learning experience. They believe that one of their primary responsibilities is to use this learning to improve the processes of their organizations. Everything you have read in this chapter is basically a commentary on these basic ideas, with some direction on how to go about implementing them when formulating strategy.

P&G ALIGNS EACH FUNCTION WITH CUSTOMER'S AND CONSUMER'S NEEDS[31]

Procter & Gamble's managers realized that to create value, a company must align its organizational units or functions with the needs of its customers (retailers like Kroger's and Wal-Mart) and the ultimate consumers (people in households who use its products). The first critical step in creating value is to understand the end-user's purchase criteria. P&G managers generally recognize that the following purchase criteria are important for P&G products:

1. *Performance*. What the product is designed to do; the benefits it provides.
2. *Dependability*. How well the product performs versus expectations time after time.
3. *Price*. What the consumer must pay for the benefits received.
4. *Availability*. The ease of obtaining the product and its in-stock status at the time of purchase.
5. *Awareness*. Awareness that the product exists and offers certain benefits to the consumer. Consumers can be disappointed that no product meets certain needs when, in fact, the product is simply not known to the potential consumer.
6. *Image*. The intangible benefits of a product that fill the emotional needs of consumers. Knowing that the product is "the best" for doing a particular function.

7. *Service*. In some industries, the after sale is extremely important in the purchase decision.

When managers in various functions of the organization agree on their approaches to achieving these outcomes for customers, it creates internal alignment. The Exhibit below illustrates how each of four functional organizations at P&G (sales, advertising, product supply, and product development) influence customers' and consumers' needs. Outside the dotted circle are those internal functional elements that have a direct effect on meeting or exceeding consumer needs shown inside the circle. We can say

they are the "causes" for the "effects" that bring about company success. For example, the product development function primarily influences the consumer's need for performance, image, and price. To satisfy those needs, the product development function works on product design, package design, product concept, and product cost. However, the product development function does not directly affect other factors, such as product availability or awareness, which are the responsibility of advertising and sales. Each function has a particular role to play in enhancing P&G's ability to deliver value and quality to customers.

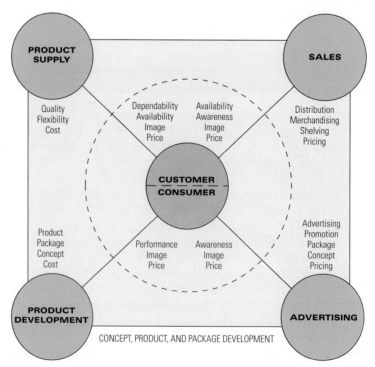

Source: M.J. Stahl and G.M. Bounds, *Competing Globally Through Customer Value*, Quorum, 1991, an imprint of Greenwood Publishing Group, Inc., Wesrport, CT. Reprinted by permission.

SUMMARY

Understanding Strategic Management

- Strategy spells out in detail what managers believe is the best use of the organization's resources and talents and how they will go about deploying these to the mutual benefit of the organization and its customers.

- Three important elements come together in forming a company's strategy: Customers, Competitors, and the Corporation.

- An intended strategy is the organization's plan for achieving its objectives; a realized strategy is what they actually do. The difference between the two often has to do with a process of continuous revision in light of changes in the environment and internal capabilities.

- Top managers develop mission and vision statements and goals to provide everyone inside and outside the organization with a strong sense of its purpose and direction.

- It is necessary and appropriate for managers to focus on the competition, but sometimes they spend more time doing this than examining customer needs, which can be a problem.

The Strategic Management Process

- Strategic management incorporates a process by which managers choose a mission, collect data and conduct analyses, decide on a plan, and take action to achieve the mission.

  —The first step in the process, defining the business, has to do with managers understanding their capabilities in relation to customer needs and problems.

  —The second step, gathering data and conducting analyses, includes understanding the strengths, weaknesses, opportunities, and threats (SWOT) that confront the organization. It includes examinations of the external and internal environments of the organization.

  —The third step, deciding on a plan, incorporates the actions for evaluating what the company must do in light of what it has discovered in step two. There are various criteria managers can use in making their decisions on strategy.

  —The fourth step, taking action, is the execution of the plan. In doing this, managers usually find that circumstances change and that they will be constantly revising the plan to handle these changes.

Levels of Strategy

- The strategic management process can be applied in three levels of the organization: the corporate level, the business level, and the functional level.

- The corporate level of strategy focuses managers of large corporations that operate in several business areas with direction on how to manage and allocate resources among them.

- The business level of strategy focuses a specific business on understanding and meeting the needs of customers relative to competitors.

- Functional level strategy focuses managers on integrating and aligning functional department goals with business and corporate goals.
- Devising corporate level strategy includes the use of portfolio management tools such as the Boston Consulting Group Matrix, a tool for figuring out where to allocate corporate resources to get the best return.
- Another approach to corporate level strategy is the use of grand strategies, which helps managers decide whether they should focus on growth, retrenchment, or stability.
- At the business level, managers may choose among strategies that emphasize differentiation (incorporating special high-value features and benefits), cost leadership (low price to the customer), or focus (specializing in serving unique market segments).
- The most important issue for functional level strategy is to make sure that all of the respective strategies fit together to form a coherent whole and successfully implement the business strategy.

Customer Value, TQM, and Strategic Advantage

- Delivering customer value is at the heart of strategy development. It is also at the heart of TQM. The foundation of TQM—systems management and customer focus—also provides managers with the tools and techniques for effectively and efficiently developing and executing organizational strategy.

KEY TERMS

Adaptive model 249

BCG matrix 252

Business level strategy 251

Corporate level strategy 251

Cost leadership strategy 258

Customer value 244

Differentiation strategy 258

Focus strategy 259

Functional level strategy 251

Goals 239

Grand strategy 254

Growth strategy 256

Mission statement 236

Opportunity 240

Portfolio management 252

Retrenchment 256

Stability 257

Strategic intent 239

Strategic management 238

Strategy 235

Strength 240

SWOT analysis 240

Threat 240

Weakness 241

REVIEW QUESTIONS

1. What are the "3Cs" and what is their relevance to understanding strategic management?

2. What is a mission statement and why is it important?
3. What is the difference between an organizational mission and organizational goals?
4. What part of the strategic management process is SWOT analysis? How does this analysis contribute to developing strategy?
5. What is the "five forces" model? How do these forces help managers understand strategic challenges?
6. What are the "5Ms?" What is their connection with internal analysis?
7. What are the three strategies suggested by the adaptive model? When should managers use each strategy?
8. What are the three levels of strategy and what is the relevance of each to strategic planning?
9. How does the BCG matrix help managers make strategic decisions?
10. What are the three types of grand strategies? When should managers use each type when developing corporate strategy?
11. How do each of Porter's three business strategies help a company deliver customer value?
12. How does TQM help guide managers in developing strategy?

EXPERIENTIAL EXERCISE 1

Using the concepts discussed in this chapter, develop a strategic plan for your professional life for the next ten years. In doing this, think about how others will value what you might do and how this will influence your plan. Create mission and vision statements to provide direction for your career. Do a brief SWOT analysis to help you better understand where you stand now in terms of your mission and abilities. Based on what you have learned, develop a plan for achieving your mission. This exercise can be conducted outside of class as a project which results in about a five-page paper. Alternatively, divide the class into groups of five or six people, and with each group focusing on one individual, help that person develop a personal strategic plan using the concepts in the chapter.

EXPERIENTIAL EXERCISE 2

Find a local small business (*not* a franchise like McDonald's or Pizza Hut) and make an appointment to talk with the owner or entrepreneur. In the interview, gather as much information as possible to complete the following task:

- Identify all of the stakeholders of the business (e.g., employees, customers, suppliers, managers, owners, investors). Try to imagine how each stakeholder views the business, and write a statement of company goals (short term and long term) from each stakeholder's perspective. If possible, also write some quantitative objectives that accompany each goal. After doing this preliminary work, reflect on your work and
  —Describe the balance or imbalance among the various goals. What would you do as a manager to achieve a better balance?
  —What is the company's particular combination of the four utilities that it brings together to deliver customer value?

—Using the concepts discussed in this chapter, identify the strategy that the business seems to be implementing, for example, growth, retrenchment, or stability or differentiation, price leadership, or focus?

CASE ANALYSIS AND APPLICATION
Strategic Makeover at Mattel[32]

Mattel, Inc. designs, develops, manufactures, markets, and distributes a variety of toys around the world. Its operations span from Penang, Malaysia to Monterrey, Mexico. Mattel is the second largest toy company in the world. Mattel outsources some of its basic functions. It purchases designs from independent toy designers and developers, and it contracts with independent manufacturers to produce some of its products.

Although they offer an array of products, large toy companies like Mattel tend to focus on a few core product lines that account for most of the company's revenues. Core product lines are those which the company expects to be selling for a long time and that have consistently grown in sales and profitability. Mattel's core product lines include Barbie fashion dolls, doll clothing and accessories, Hot Wheels toy vehicles and accessories, Disney toys and dolls, and Li'l Miss products. By focusing on core product lines for most of its business, a toy company can reduce its reliance on new products and the associated risks.

One way Mattel increases the likelihood of success with new products is through licensing agreements with companies that have established images. For example, Mattel purchased licenses to create lines of dolls based on Disney's animated films "Aladdin," "Beauty and the Beast," and "Snow White and The Seven Dwarfs." Mattel has other license agreements with DC Comics, Twentieth Century Fox, Hanna-Barbera, Viacom, and Nickelodeon. Mattel also distributes Nintendo products in Australia.

Despite its enormous success over the years, Mattel cannot rest. In the late 1980s and 1990s, the toy industry has experienced a great deal of consolidation, with many companies merging and acquiring smaller companies. In fact, Mattel recently acquired Fisher-Price, which gives it established product lines in the preschool and infant markets. Mattel's primary competitors, such as Hasbro and Tyco Toys, have made similar acquisitions. Toy companies are motivated to consolidate to offer a broader range of products.

The increased consolidation of retail distribution channels also affects the toy industry. The large specialty toy stores and discount retailers like Toys R Us, Wal-Mart, Kmart and Target have increased their share of the retail market. In turn, these retailers have increased their reliance on the large toy companies because of their financial stability and their ability to advertise, promote, and distribute products on a global scale.

These trends toward consolidation and growth fuel another trend for U.S. toy companies to increase expansion into global markets and global manufacturing operations. Mattel is particularly devoted to global expansion, since it believes that globalization provides it the opportunity to significantly increase the sales volume of core products and extend the life cycles of new products. Mattel has taken several actions to support its efforts to globalize.

As mentioned earlier, the company acquired Fisher-Price, another company with global marketing and manufacturing operations. The acquisition gave Mattel broader product lines and allowed the combined companies to reduce redundant international operating costs by $35 million and potentially another $31 million in redundant domestic operating costs. The acquisition provides better international distribution channels for Fisher-Price's line of products and allows Mattel to take advantage of Fisher-Price's ability to introduce new products.

Mattel lobbied strongly for the North American Free Trade Agreement (NAFTA), which would provide the toy company with more open markets and reduce its costs of doing business in Mexico and Canada. For example, Mattel would no longer have to pay Mexico's 20% duty on toys sold in Mexico. The elimination of tariffs and quotas will also greatly reduce Mattel's cost of production since Mattel's Mexican manufacturing plants in Tijuana and Monterrey purchase raw materials and components from some 45 U.S. suppliers, and Fisher-Price has large Mexican production operations that do the same.

Mattel has also made a breakthrough in reducing the costs of importing by going paperless. It's import transactions at major seaports are now being processed electronically. The paperless system allows Mattel to better comply with customs regulations and avoid costly penalties, as well as reduce filing errors and processing time to more quickly move toys from the vessels to store shelves. These improvements (which reduce Mattel's costs in money and time) are important to Mattel because the majority of its outsourced manufacturing suppliers are located overseas in China.

Mattel has also begun reengineering (i.e., substantially redesigning) key business processes. For example, it has established a team of company and outside people to work on a project called Reengineering the Order Management Process (ROMP). The aim of ROMP is to determine the specific amount of each product available to every customer. Toy companies like Mattel have to stay abreast of "what's hot and what's not." Joe Roth, director of the ROMP project, explains, "Having a fully integrated supply management is difficult in the fashion business—and this is a fashion business—because the turnaround time is not the same in the plant as it is on the shelf. . . . It's a real challenge to pull together the needs of manufacturing and the needs of the retailer's shelf."

In large part, ROMP is a matter of improving information flow. It sounds like a simple task, but Mattel's ROMP team faced a number of challenges. For one thing, sales in the toy industry are seasonal, with a majority of retail sales occurring in the last two quarters, from September to December. In anticipation of this seasonal increase in retail sales, Mattel has historically increased its production in advance of the peak selling period to build up inventories. Unfortunately, Mattel's old order management process does not cope well with demands of retailers in the 1990s. As Roths explains, "Retailers are demanding just-in-time delivery, quick response, and more information." In addition to wanting the product when they want it, in the quantities they've ordered, retailers increasingly demand changes in palletization, product packaging, and labeling.

It is difficult for toy companies to simply standardize the product because retailers each seem to want something about the product to be a little bit different. When it is completely installed sometime in the mid-1990s, Mattel's new order management process will greatly improve Mattel's ability to provide retailers exactly what they want. Mattel will also be able to closely monitor consumers' acceptance of particular products through electronic data interchange with large retailers like Wal-Mart. Re-engineering efforts like ROMP and the other improvements mentioned above will help Mattel improve its ability to operate globally in a very efficient and effective manner.

Discussion Questions

1. Identify the elements of Mattel's strategy for globalization that appear at the three levels discussed in the chapter, namely, the corporate, business, and functional levels of strategy.
2. How are the themes of Total Quality Management manifested in Mattel's strategy?

VIDEO CASE: COMBINING QUALITY MANAGEMENT AND SOCIAL RESPONSIBILITY
Finast

The decline of America's inner cities has been exacerbated by a lack of high-quality, reasonably priced supermarkets. For years, conventional wisdom in the supermarket industry has said that it makes no sense to serve distressed urban areas when profits in the serene suburbs come so much more easily. But, since 1986, Finast, Ohio, has demonstrated that a big business can operate profitably in the inner city, spurring new economic development in the process. Through resourceful management and active collaboration with local communities, Finast now runs six state-of-the-art "superstores" in the heart of Cleveland proper that offer the same wide variety and low prices as suburban stores.

The Business Enterprise Trust is honoring Finast for its vision in recognizing a neglected business opportunity and for serving a challenging market while enhancing overall profitability, operational skills, and market share.

Finast superstores are the reincarnation of the decades-old Pick-N-Pay grocery stores of inner-city Cleveland. Original owner Julius Kravitz was committed to remaining in urban areas, and his social and business ideals continue to be shared by Finast's current management team. Those managers, including succeeding CEOs Richard Bogomolny and John Shields, oversaw major upgrades to the Pick-N-Pay stores (renamed "Finast") and the building of new superstores in inner-city areas. Finast was not only capturing a market niche but also keeping abreast of the general trend in the retailing industry toward bigger stores with a wider selection of products. The Federal Government and the City of Cleveland encouraged this economic development with fiscal incentives.

Finast managers devised creative solutions to the unique problems of operating in the inner city. First, they enlisted the aid of churches, civic groups, and other key neighborhood institutions in winning community trust and support for their ventures. Second, they conducted exhaustive market research for each store to learn precisely what products and services were desired by customers of various ethnic backgrounds. Third, they dealt innovatively with operational issues:

installing calculators on the shopping carts so customers could stay within their budgets and minimize the number of surplus items at the check-out stand, and employing security guards in the stores and parking lots to alleviate customers' safety concerns.

While the urban stores are a social and economic benefit to previously underserved communities, they are also money-making vehicles. Indeed, the eleven Cleveland-proper locations are profitable as a group and contribute to the chain's overall market share. Beyond these bottom-line results, Finast has reaped a wealth of management lessons applicable to its suburban stores.

Video Case Questions

1. Discuss the elements of each level of strategy that Finast managers had to address.
2. Describe what Finanst might have done at each stage of the strategic management process in launching its strategy.

SEGA TAKES "COOL" TO A NEW LEVEL

Video-game powerhouse Sega Enterprises Ltd., which popularized such figures as Sonic the Hedgehog and Toejam & Earl, is based in Tokyo, but it was founded by an American, David Rosen. After doing a stint with the U.S. Air Force in Japan, Rosen, a 20-year-old from Brooklyn, returned to Tokyo in 1954. Running a one-man business called Rosen Enterprises, Rosen imported and exported art and other items. Soon Rosen introduced two-minute photo booths, which charged half as much as competing darkroom services and delivered services in minutes instead of hours or days.

Rosen's company started approaching its modern form in 1956 when he started importing mechanical coin-operated games which allowed players to hit baseballs or shoot moving targets with rifles. Not satisfied with the games provided by leading manufacturers in Chicago, Rosen started making his own in 1965. He acquired a factory with the purchase of a Tokyo jukebox and slot-machine maker. The company stamped "Sega" on its games, short for Service Games, and Rosen soon adopted it for the name of his company. The following year Sega produced Periscope, which let players torpedo ships by aiming through a periscope. The game became a world-wide hit and rejuvenated the industry. It even helped Rosen become a millionaire when he sold his company to Gulf & Western Industries, Inc. in 1971.

Although he sold his company, Rosen stayed on as CEO. By the early 1980s, Sega was riding high along with the rest of the industry. Sega's revenues rose to $214 million in 1982 before an industry crash was brought on by a flood of mediocre games. Both the arcades and the U.S. home entertainment markets fell. Eventually, Sega was forced to sell off its U.S. assets completely. Sega survived in Japan primarily because Rosen joined with a brilliant young Japanese entrepreneur, Nakayama, to buy back Sega's assets for $38 million. Nakayama became Sega's CEO and Rosen headed the U.S. subsidiary.

After getting the company back on its feet, Nakayama and Rosen took the company pulic, selling Sega stock in Japan in 1986. Sega survived. However, the near-death experience profoundly affected Rosen and Nakayama. It taught them not to stick with one thing too long. They learned that each generation of technology has a limited lifespan, and that they should seize opportunities as soon as they appear. In short, better technology wins markets.

In the late 1980s, Sega was still a minor player in an industry still dominated by Nintendo. Nintendo had singlehandedly revived the industry in the mid-1980s by building a better machine than the previous giant of the industry, Atari. Nintendo sold hardware at a price that barely covered its costs and made its profits selling software. It also drew 30% of its revenues by charging software makers heavy license fees to manufacture game cartridges for them. Sega began to overtake Nintendo in 1989 when it brought out a superior machine, the Genesis. With 16 bits of processing power (twice that of Nintendo), Genesis allowed for faster, and more lifelike action. Nintendo eventually matched Sega/Genesis with its Super Nintendo Entertainment System, but Sega had become a major player in the game.

Sega also enjoyed success in the marketplace because of several other advantages over Nintendo. Nintendo's relatively high licensing fees alienated many retailers and software developers. Also, Nintendo attempted to keep enthusiasm for its games high by limiting the supply. However, Nintendo found out that you walk a thin line when you try to control a product's supply. You can kill a product if retailers lose sales because the product is not

Sources: Brandt, Richard, "Sega!" *Business Week* (February 21,1994), 66–74.
Gross, Neil, "Watch Out—Those Game Boys are Growing Up," *Business Week* (November 22, 1993): 106
Coy, Peter, "There'll be a Heaven for Couch Potatoes, By and By," *Business Week* (November 1,1993): 38.

available. As a result, retailers will be more likely to look to someone else for products to sell.

Sega also started running comparative ads in 1990, which branded Nintendo as children's games. This "in your face" advertising slammed Nintendo and established Sega as the coolest machine. Its fast-paced, clever ads created instantly recognizable trademarks and memorable images, such as the "Sega scream," in which wild-eyed, fast-motion characters from Tyrannosaurus rex to Joe Montana finish the ad by yelling into the camera, "Sega." Nintendo failed to respond to the ad campaign, which turned out to be a terrible mistake. The financial results of these events were devastating for Nintendo, and remarkable for Sega. In 1992, Sega's revenue jumped 62%, and in 1993 Sega grabbed more market share away from Nintendo, as Nintendo's share of the 16-bit machine business plummeted from 60% to 37% in just one year.

However, this fast-growth period didn't last long for Sega and it had leveled off by 1994. After three years in which it increased revenues five fold and profits sixfold and swiped gobs of Nintendo's market share, Sega's profits started to shrink. A brutal price war with Nintendo in Europe was responsible for some of the shrinkage. But company officials sensed that their current generation of video games was losing steam, and that many customers were waiting for the new machines to hit the streets in late 1994. Also, customers

were already tired of the same racing and fighting tricks. The industry needed new story lines or something to rejuvenate enthusiasm.

Nintendo responded to these challenges by holding down expenses, cutting prices, and sticking to its strength—cartridge-based games. Nintendo prides itself on retaining a lean staff of proven and experienced managers, whereas Sega has twice as many employees, many of which are unseasoned, fresh and young. This brash approach to staffing extends into Sega's plans for new products and new markets.

Sega is taking some bold actions to reignite its earnings. To broaden the market for video games, Sega has teamed up with Hitachi, Ltd. to develop and market a new compact-disk (CD) machine, code-named Saturn, that will play more realistic games than the ones currently on CDs or cartridges. Saturn's computing power lets it create 3D illusions based on "polygon" images composed of triangles and four-sided figures called parallelograms. Computer chips work furiously to constantly recalculate the geometries as a player moves through the virtual 3-D space. Saturn will hit the streets in 1995—a year ahead of Nintendo's next machine.

Beyond video games, Sega has plans to use the profits and know-how garnered from video games to build an entertainment empire. To paraphrase its advertising slogan, Sega intends to take it to the next level by challenging Walt Disney Co. with virtual-reality

theme parks, taking on Hasbro Inc. with electronic toys, and luring viewers from TV networks with interactive entertainment on the Information Superhighway. These bold new initiatives will require Sega to converge the worlds of computers, communications, and entertainment. Sega seems uniquely poised to make the necessary connections since it has already successfully straddled these different worlds. Sega has proven that it can tinker with both hardware and software to make them work together at peak performance, create engaging new forms of entertainment, as well as coddle the Hollywood stars that play roles in its interactive games.

With its new virtual reality theme parks, Sega will try to exploit the efficiency of electronics over the iron and steel that Walt Disney uses to construct roller coasters and castles. With virtual reality, Sega will place visitors inside windowless, truck-size capsules and make them feel as though they're driving a race car or piloting a spaceship. Theme parks packed with these capsules will occupy maybe 3% of the land area of Florida's Disney World. They are not only much cheaper to build than Disney World, perhaps $20 to $40 million a piece, but they are also much easier to renovate, with just the change of software. This means Sega can place parks in densely populated areas. The bottom line for Sega is that the theme parks offer greater profit margins that Disney style parks (30% profit margins for Sega versus less than 25% for Disney).

After experimenting with Sega VirtuaLand at the Luxor Las Vegas hotel, Sega opened theme parks in Osaka and Yokohama. Sega has plans to open 50 more parks by 1997. Other applications of virtual reality may prove even more profitable for Sega. Architects could use virtual reality to allow you to walk through a building before it is built. Industrial trainers could use it to prepare people for operating dangerous machinery.

One of the keys to succeeding in these new markets is for Sega to collaborate with other companies that can provide needed technology and expertise. It is Sega's American style entrepreneurship that has enabled it to do just that. Its business partners include AT&T in communications, Hitachi in computer chips, Yamaha in sound, JVC in game machines, and Martin Marietta in the advanced computer graphics used for virtual reality. Sega is even negotiating with Microsoft Corp. to enable its machines to draw on multiple streams of data for source material, such as from cartridges, CDs, or cable systems. This capability could be key to taking advantage of the market potential of the Information Superhighway. AT&T has already provided Sega with a modem that lets Sega Genesis owners play games over phone lines. And Sega had teamed up with Time Warner and Tele-Communications to provide a cable channel to transmit game software. Sega's core capabilities in creating interactive software are the key to integrating these other business partners into its strategy for providing diverse forms of entertainment.

Sega's plans for entering new markets are bold and creative. However, they are also expensive. In addition to all of the start up expenses, Sega is spending more than $200 million a year on research and development. Sega needs a steady stream of attractive new games to keep its core business home entertainment systems vibrant and profitable. These profits provide the cash needed to fund its diversification strategy. Unfortunately, these profits are not guaranteed. In addition to price wars with major competitors like Nintendo, Sega will face other new competitors, such as Sony, Atari, and a U.S. startup called 3DO, who are entering the market with competitive products. Since the video-game players are very fickle, Sega could be deemed uncool as rapidly as it became cool.

? CASE QUESTIONS

1. What seems to be the driving vision of Sega's leaders? What business do the leaders perceive themselves to be in? What is Sega's strategic intent? What key principles seem to underlie Sega's long term strategy?

2. Identify all of the key points at which Sega has made strategic decisions. List what you think were the major factors considered in the decision and the rationale that the managers might have used to justify their decision.

3. Describe Sega's strategy at the corporate, business unit, and functional levels.

4. If you were the CEO of Sega, what would you now do to implement Sega's strategy?

ORGANIZING TO COMPETE

8. ORGANIZATIONAL STRUCTURE AND DESIGN

DEL NORTE REDESIGNS ITS ORGANIZATIONAL STRUCTURE[1]

Del Norte Technology, Inc., is a Euless, Texas manufacturer of precise electronic positioning systems and correctional facilities security systems. The company gets about 70 percent of its sales from abroad, and in the late 1980s those sales were declining. While the company's products were generally high quality, it seems that customers wanted more service out of the company than it could deliver. Management quickly saw that Del Norte's survival may depend on making some radical changes in the way it runs its business.

At this time, Del Norte had a traditional top-down organizational structure with orders from the top being fulfilled by workers at the bottom. Wendell Brooks, CEO, was astute enough to realize that the kinds of changes they needed to make required a revamping of this structure into one that facilitated more open communication and maximized the value added by each employee. After studying the situation, the top managers came up with a new three-tiered structure that was more like a network than a hierarchy. Exhibit 8-1 illustrates this new structure. In the center is what the company calls its quality steering committee. This committee has responsibility for corporate strategy, coordination, and communication. Surrounding the center are the middle managers and supervisors, organized into what is called the Corrective Action Team (CAT), charged with facilitating interdepartmental communication and the continuous improvement of the company's processes and the skills of its employees. Outside of the CAT are the work teams, formerly known as departments, that do the work of the company's processes. Besides these three permanent layers, there are also temporary task teams, with members from across functions, whose role is to solve specific problems as they arise and then disband.

One could say that this is just a new way of drawing the old tiers of organizational hierarchy, but that would be false. The whole reason for these changes was to open the company's channels of communication and make it easier for people to work together to deliver quality products and services to its customers. We'll look more at Del Norte at the end of this chapter and review some of the results of this new structure.

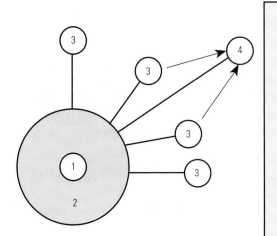

1. Quality Steering Committee	• Responsible for corporate direction
2. Corrective Action Team	• A team of middle managers and supervisors who provide resources to work teams and task teams
	• The team is the hub around which improved interdepartmental communication will continue to develop
	• The members also form task teams (4) to accomplish specific objectives
3. Work Teams	• Perform specific work activities and improve those activities through problem solving
4. Task Teams	• Usually a temporary team formed to accomplish specific objectives (often across department lines)
	• Team members are selected from the various work teams that have an interest in the objective

EXHIBIT 8-1

Source: Helen L. Schneider, Christopher Schneider, and Dean Riley, "Clearing a Hurdle to Quality," *Quality Progress*, September 1991, pp. 39–41. © 1991 American Society for Quality Control

ORGANIZATIONAL STRUCTURE AND PROCESSES

Organizational structure
The specific working relationships among people and their jobs to efficiently and effectively achieve organizational purpose.

In Chapter 1 we defined an organization as a collection of people working together to achieve a common purpose. That being the case, **organizational structure** then refers to *the specific working relationships among people and their jobs to efficiently and effectively achieve that purpose.* We can think of structure as defining those relationships in reasonably enduring patterns. Structure is important because it helps people understand their position and role in the organization's processes—who they work with, who works with them—to do the company's work. If processes are the "function" part of an organization, then structure is the "form" part. In well-managed organizations, structure and processes go together smoothly to facilitate delivery of value to customers.

Total quality management's emphasis on understanding and improving processes means that managers must also be concerned with structure. In this chapter we will look at a variety of organizational structures. As you read, remember that each one exists to help people work together efficiently to serve the organization's customers. Companies reorganize when managers believe they can improve current structures to help them serve customers better.

TQM, with its emphasis on teams, helps managers create structures that facilitate flexibility and openness among employees to get work done. This is opposed to more rigid structures that restrict and constrain what people can do. The key word here is flexibility. In today's highly competitive world, the goal is to develop those structures that help people maximize their added value to the organization and its processes. There is no one best structure for doing this. But this standard—maximizing added value to serve customers—is the best one for judging how well a structure is working.

Tom Peters, the famous management author and speaker, points out in no uncertain terms how structure has gotten in the way of accomplishment at many companies: "Today's structures were designed for controlling turn-of-the-century mass-production operations under stable conditions, with primitive technologies. They have become perverse, action-destroying devices, completely at odds with current competitive needs."[2] Not everyone is as critical as Peters, but his point is that structures must facilitate not hinder the ability of organizations to serve customers in a very unforgiving competitive environment. Too often, it seems, they do hinder.

Organizational design
The process of creating a structure that best fits a particular strategy and environment.

So, organizational structure provides a framework for how people will work together. Figuring out what that structure should be is what the **organizational design** is about or, more formally, it is *the process of creating a structure that best fits a particular strategy and environment.* By understanding their organization as a system and their purpose in terms of serving customers, managers can then use the organizational design process to come up a structure that best meets their needs. The design process includes the following elements:

1. *Divide* the work and design jobs to accomplish the organization's goals.
2. *Coordinate* the work to achieve a whole that is effective and efficient. Managers achieve coordination by taking the following actions:
   - Establish a *formal structure* through reporting relationships and delegation of authority.
   - Cultivate an *informal structure* through social and cultural processes.
   - Supplement the structure with *coordination mechanisms* as needed.

These elements are not listed in sequential order. Organization design is an ongoing process that requires managers to attend to each of these elements, but not in any particular order. In doing this, their goal is always to develop and improve organizational processes that work better to create and deliver high quality products and services to customers. We will discuss these elements in the rest of this chapter.

? THINKING CRITICALLY

1. Can you think of a personal experience you have had in an organization where the structure of defined relationships either inhibited or enhanced accomplishing goals? Some organizations you might consider include your church, school, a political organization, school organizations, or businesses you may have worked for.
2. Why do you think the structure of an organization might hinder action? How do you think organizational structure facilitates coordinated action?

DIVISION OF LABOR AND COORDINATION

Since ancient times societies have prospered using division of labor. People discovered that when they specialized in various trades, they could collectively improve their standard of living above that which they would enjoy if each person produced everything for himself or herself. With the industrial revolution and the growth of mass markets for products, division of labor was taken to its next logical step. The work of producing a particular product was broken into even smaller specialized tasks.

The Productivity Benefits of Division of Labor

Division of labor increases productivity and reduces the costs of production for a number of reasons. Most importantly, it allows for **job specialization,** *the breaking of work into smaller tasks that require less skill to perform.* This allows an employee to quickly master a task and become highly proficient in its execution, and this increases the overall productivity of the organization. Further, job specialization makes it easier to match individual skills with specific jobs so people do what they are best at. This also makes it easier to train a new employee. Job specialization eliminates the time that would be lost changing tasks if one person did all the work to produce something. Finally, by performing only a simple task, employees need less equipment to perform their special jobs.

Job specialization The breaking of work into smaller tasks that require less skill to perform.

The Problems of Division of Labor and Job Specialization

There are some problems to job specialization. When people repeatedly perform the same simple task, day after day, they get bored. The alienation and lack of challenge that can result may take its toll on the workforce in human terms. It may also cost the organization money through increased turnover and absenteeism, and the poor quality that results from employee inattention and lack of commitment. Managers concerned about providing employees with challenging and meaningful jobs must be careful not to go too far with division of labor. Again, the goal here is to create jobs where employees can best take advantage of their skills and experience to add value to the organization. Human beings are born problem solvers, and jobs requiring repetitive non-thinking behavior greatly reduce people's ability to use their full capabilities. (See the *A Look at TQM in Action* box on the IBM Credit Corporation on page 279.) There are ways to address this last problem through job enrichment. This will be discussed in Chapter 12, which covers motivation and work performance.

The Need for Coordination

Coordination The alignment of the work of employees into efficient and effective processes to achieve a common purpose.

Despite some disadvantages arising from division of labor, job specialization will always be necessary in organizations. Once work is divided and assigned to different people, the organization faces the challenge of achieving **coordination,** which means *aligning the work of different employees into efficient and effective processes to achieve a common purpose.* Without coordination employees may separately perform their tasks well, but they may fail to work together to achieve their common goals, and the overall performance of the organization will be compromised. This need to coordinate how employees work together is an important management responsibility. TQM, with its focus on process improvement, has developed tools and techniques for measuring the outputs of employees working together to help managers execute their responsibility for coordinating work.

The necessity to coordinate work helped to create the role of management in the early industrial organization. At the beginning of the 20th century, Henry Ford greatly refined the assembly line approach to mass production. This approach divided work into simple, specialized tasks and then coordinated those tasks through the structure of the assembly line which defined the flow and timing of the production work. Managers were the ones who performed this coordination work, were responsible for improvements, and solved problems as they arose.

Formal and Informal Organizational Structure

Formal structure An illustration of how the organization looks as planned out on paper, with specified relationships among employees.

Informal structure The patterns of relationships and communications that evolve as people interact to do their work on a daily basis.

Formal structure is *how the organization looks as planned out on paper, with specified relationships.* Like the architectural drawings of a house, formal structure is captured in organization charts and job descriptions. However, just as a house's floor plan does not fully describe the home life of a family, formal structure does not fully describe how an organization actually works. **Informal structure** consists of *the patterns of relationships and communications that evolve as people interact.* Informal structure is not always planned or sanctioned by management. It emerges spontaneously as employees interact to perform their jobs and keep current with information they need to know. Two managers resolve an interdepartmental conflict as they are playing golf on Saturday afternoon. An engineer needs some technical information so she telephones a friend in another division to get it. Some business acquaintances sharing a lunch table exchange rumors about the impending reorganization. These are examples of the informal relationships and communications that occur outside the formal structure.

Although informal structure is not formally sanctioned, it is not usually disapproved either. People can often get things done through informal means that otherwise might never happen. For example, rather than go up through the chain of command with a formal request to get a vital piece of information, a human

OVERSPECIALIZATION AT IBM CREDIT CORPORATION[3]

A LOOK AT

TQM IN ACTION

Division of labor and specialization can lead to inefficient process flows, like at IBM Credit Corp., a wholly owned subsidiary of IBM. IBM Credit finances the computers, software, and services that IBM corporation sells. IBM Credit has long been one of the most profitable of all IBM subsidiaries. However, just a few years ago, IBM Credit's operations were inefficient and poorly organized because of *overspecialization.*

Before IBM got a handle on the problem, when salespeople called to set up financing for a customer, they reached one of 14 people in an office in Old Greenwich, Connecticut, whose job was to log the request on a sheet of paper. That was the first of five steps in a process that moved through several departments as specialists on credit, pricing, interest rates, and others checked and then approved the request. This generally took from six days to two weeks to complete.

Meanwhile, the salespeople worried that this waiting period would give customers a chance to change their minds, find another lender, or perhaps another vendor. The salespeople would be calling in repeatedly to find out if the loan was approved. Usually there was no answer as the request was "in process."

One day two senior managers at IBM Credit had an idea. They decided to hand carry a request for financing manually through all five steps to find what was involved in the approval process and how long each step took. What they learned was that the actual work for the five steps took only about 90 minutes to complete. The rest of the time was spent passing paper around and waiting in line to be approved.

The upshot of this discovery was to replace four specialists with generalists, whose job it was to perform all the steps involved in approving finance requests. How could one generalist replace four specialists? The assumption behind having specialists was that each request was unique and required handling by trained experts. This was not in fact the case. Most requests were routine and easy to handle, using a computer system that gives the generalist all the data and tools needed. For nonroutine requests, there was still a small number of specialists who could take care of these.

The result of this change was that most requests were turned around in four hours, not six days. The volume of requests the company now handles has increased 100 times, with a slight decrease in the number of staff members. The point: While division of labor and job specialization is indeed important, sometimes managers overdo it. They have to make sure they understand job requirements and the role of any job in serving the company's customers.

resources planner may simply invite her colleague to lunch to discuss the issue. Technology has enhanced the informal aspects of organizational structure. Many companies have implemented electronic mail systems that allow employees to send and receive messages with anyone in the organization without "going through channels." More than anything else, technology such as e-mail and voice mail (the use of telephone answering technology to be in touch with other employees and broadcast messages) is playing an important role in enhancing the informal structure of organizations.

Informal structure can be the key to overcome the burdens and limitations that formal structure imposes on people. On the other hand, informal structure can have drawbacks, particularly if it undermines the formal strategy and goals of the organization. In fact, the purpose of formal structure is to align people with the strategy and goals of the organization. And while formal structure does not fully determine everything that happens in an organization, it does establish general patterns of activity and communications and helps to coordinate work among employees in the organization. In the remainder of the chapter, we discuss several ways that managers achieve coordination through formal structure and special coordination mechanisms.

? THINKING CRITICALLY

1. Explain in your own words the economic benefits of the division of labor and job specialization.
2. How does the division of labor help you to understand an important role of a manager? How do you think division of labor is related to process management?

TYPES OF FORMAL STRUCTURE

Simple structure A type of formal structure in which the owner/manager makes or approves most of the business decisions, provides coordination by directly overseeing work tasks, and performs many tasks that would be delegated to specialists in a larger organization.

Newly founded businesses often begin with a **simple structure.** *The owner/manager makes or approves most of the business decisions, provides coordination by directly overseeing the work tasks, and even performs many of the tasks that would be delegated to specialists in a larger organization.* As the business grows larger than 15 to 20 people, it becomes more complex and requires some specialization, division of labor, and thus, more coordination—in short there is a need for a structure that helps employees understand the roles in the company.

In a business organization that has a large number of employees, the owner or manager cannot possibly oversee and coordinate the activities of every employee. He or she may hire other managers to assist in providing coordination by placing each manager in charge of a group of employees. When these groups are formed and assigned to a manager, this is the beginning of formal structure.

Departmentalization and Coordination

To achieve coordination and reach the organization's business goals, groups of employees are not just randomly established. Rather, they are assembled in some logical way. Through departmentalization groups of employees that have some special relationship or interdependency are established as departments or work units. Departments can be formed on a number of bases, such as geography, task similarity, product similarity, or customer segment served. Whatever the basis, departmentalization is usually the first step toward providing a formal structure to coordinate the activities of an organization. Within a department, we then usually find employees with a variety of functional responsibilities from accounting to product development to marketing.

The Organization Chart

Responsibility assignments The specific work tasks different managers oversee and coordinate in a department.

The departmental structure is often illustrated in an organization chart. An organization chart reveals several things about formal structure. First, it shows the **responsibility assignments** of a manager, which are *the specific work tasks different managers oversee and coordinate in a department.* Second, it reveals the

chain of command, or *the hierarchical reporting relationships between superiors and subordinates*. These two aspects of formal structure, namely responsibility assignments and chain of command, help to define the **formal authority** of managers within the organization. Formal authority consists of *the official right to make decisions and take actions that go with a certain formal position*. For example, a sales manager may have the formal authority to make or approve prices for the products or services his or her group is trying to sell.

There are some other important features of formal structure revealed in the organization chart. The managerial **span of control,** or span of responsibility, is *the number of people that report directly to a manager*. For example, some managers may have only two or three people that report to them, and others may have 100 or more. In designing an organization, a manager should give careful thought to determining the span of control. Some factors to consider are listed below.[4]

- *Similarity of Work.* The more similar the work, the easier it is to have a wide span of control. This is because the problems of all employees engaged in the same kind of work will be similar, thus fewer managers are needed.

- *Geography:* The more that people are geographically close, the easier it is to have a wide span of control.

- *Complexity.* The more complex the work, the harder it is to have a wide span of control. This is because it requires more managerial time to deal with specific issues of each employee.

- *Coordination.* The more coordination required to integrate the work of subordinates, the harder it is to have a wide span of control. Again, this takes up more managerial time per employee.

- *Planning.* The more time the manager has to spend planning the systems and goals of the subordinates, the harder it is to have a wide span of control. Again, it is an issue of managerial time and responsibility.

TQM and Formal Structure

The formal organization chart and issues of chain of command and span of control are still visible elements of organizational structure. They are basic concepts that you need to be familiar with because they help you understand the structure of any company you might join. However, in today's competitive environment, these elements of structure are like window dressing in companies that have taken TQM to heart. TQM emphasizes the importance of aligning a system's parts to deliver value to customers as the coordinating mechanism. Rather than achieve coordination simply through the organization hierarchy by issuing directives from superior to subordinate, TQM leaders attempt to build a common vision and commitment to providing superior customer value. TQM also emphasizes the importance of managing business processes and systems that cut across organizational boundaries. In TQM organizations, managers achieve coordination more through information technology and open communications than through hierarchical relationships.

In this environment, the role of middle management becomes one of coaching, facilitating, and improving business processes and systems, with less emphasis on the command and control approach to management that has often been

Chain of command The hierarchical reporting relationships between superiors and subordinates.

Formal authority The official right to make decisions and take actions that go with a certain formal position in the organizational hierarchy.

Span of control The number of people that report directly to a manager.

an inherent part of management hierarchies. These elements of a TQM organization provide structure, guidance, and direction; however, they are not apparent on an organization chart. They are more a part of the social processes that make up the culture of the organization.

Tall Versus Flat Organization

Many TQM organizations that are eliminating unnecessary bureaucracy and streamlining their business processes are finding that some levels of their managerial hierarchies are not needed. When these levels are removed, the organization chart changes in ways that are easily described in the terms discussed above. For example, the span of control in an organization is directly related to another feature of formal structure, that is, the degree to which the organization is either tall or flat. A **tall organization** *has narrow spans of control and therefore more levels in the chain of command from top to bottom.* When a TQM organization eliminates levels of management from the hierarchy, it becomes flatter. A **flat organization** *has wider spans of control and therefore fewer levels in the chain of command from top to bottom.* Compare the two structures in Exhibit 8-2.

Flatter organization generally means managers make decisions quicker, because communications do not have to flow across so many levels of the chain of command. This speed allows the organization to respond to environmental changes and flexibly respond to problems or opportunities. It also reduces the costs of administration, with less paperwork and less need for middle managers (and more need for skilled, well-trained employees).

A possible drawback of a flat organization is that a wide span of control can sometimes overwhelm a manager. Considering the factors listed above, for example, if the work is complex and requires a lot of planning and coordination, it can be difficult for the manager to be personally involved or in touch with all the work of many directly reporting subordinates.

On the other hand, a taller organization may be easier to oversee because of the narrower span of control: the managers can be personally involved in a subordinate's work. However, a taller organization can be unwieldy because it requires more time to get decisions and communications to flow up and down the chain of command. It is certainly more costly in terms of middle manager salaries. Tall organizations with many layers of middle managers, are finding it increasingly difficult to operate in dynamic business environments. Many managers generally regard it as a positive result if they can eliminate middle managers and flatten the organization.

To achieve a flatter organization, the five guidelines listed on page 281 should not be taken as constants that are unchangeable, or fixed inputs to an equation that will give the right span of control. Rather they should be viewed as variables that can be changed through making improvements in the organization. The exception here may be the factor *similarity* of tasks, which may be dictated by the nature of the work and difficult to change. However, the other factors are clearly subject to change. Managers are increasingly able to overcome the limitations of *geography* with advancements in information technology and telecommunications. *Complexity* in the work can be reduced through work simplification and automation. The extent of managerial *planning* and *coordination* can be reduced through delegation of authority to subordinates and through self-managing teams (empowerment, which we discussed in Chapter 3). Less direct

Tall organization A structure in which managers have narrow spans of control and therefore more levels in the chain of command from top to bottom.

Flat organization A structure in which managers have wider spans of control and therefore fewer levels in the chain of command from top to bottom.

TALL STRUCTURE with five levels

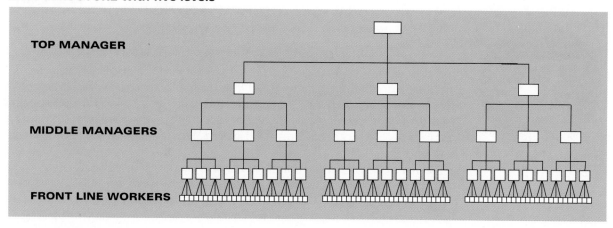

FLAT STRUCTURE with three levels

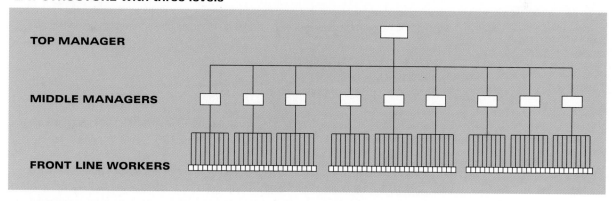

EXHIBIT 8-2   A tall structure with narrow spans of control versus a flat structure with broad spans of control

supervision is possible when managers place more emphasis on the importance of establishing a common vision and understanding through ongoing education and training. Through taking action on these factors, managers can achieve wider spans of control and thereby achieve a flatter organization with all the associated benefits.

Tom Peters, who we quoted earlier, has more to say about the benefits of flattening the organizational structure:

A meticulous 1985 study of forty-one large companies by management consultants A.T. Kearney contrasted winning and losing companies on the basis of long-term financial performance. Winners had 3.9 fewer layers of management than losers (7.2 versus 11.1) and 500 fewer central staff specialists per $1 billion in sales.[5]

When management restructures to achieve a flatter organization it often makes a number of other changes to support the structural change. Consider the changes that Marvin Runyon has embarked upon at the U.S. Postal Service in the *A Look at TQM in Action* box on page 284.

MARVIN RUNYON REVAMPING THE U.S. POSTAL SERVICE[6]

The U.S. Postal Service is a big business. It has more than 700,000 employees, plus many seasonal and temporary workers, and the contractors and vendors who transport mail, build post offices, and furnish supplies. It also has the largest customer base of any company in America, including over 250 million users. The Postal Service delivers to each and every American address, makes its rounds six-days-a-week, in all types of weather and conditions. It also helps all of America's businesses, from big corporations to mom-and-pop outfits, communicate with their customers.

Like any other business, the Postal Service is grappling with difficult economic issues and challenges. Mail volume has tapered off after the phenomenal growth in the 1980s, with back-to-back annual drops in mail volume in the early 1990s and only moderate growth since then. Regular rate increases have contributed to the problem of decreasing growth. Postal deficits caused significant postage hikes in the last two decades, averaging 11.1 percent per year. When the new Postmaster General, Marvin Runyon, arrived in 1992, the Postal Service was facing a potential deficit of $2 billion in 1993 and another significant deficit in 1994. To improve customer satisfaction, regain its business, and strengthen its financial standing, the Postal Service started changing the way it does business. It embarked on a three-point plan for change:

1. To reduce postal overhead and bureaucracy
2. To improve service quality
3. To stabilize postage rates through at least 1994

Marvin Runyon explained the plan in a November 16, 1992 speech to the Economic Club of Detroit, Michigan.

We began by building a new organizational structure, one that is simpler, flatter, less bureaucratic, and more responsive. We've finished putting the new structure in place. We've selected our key managers and professionals, and the new headquarters structure is up and running.

We've announced the field structure, and we're close to having field staffing in place. We've reduced the number of officers, the layers of management approval, and eliminated 30,000 overhead positions, without impacting the key resources necessary to serve customers. . . .

The second area where we're improving our performance is in service quality. When we began the restructuring process in August, many customers were concerned that service might suffer as a result of the retirements, especially during the upcoming holiday mailing season. We've taken a number of steps to protect the quality of mail service—by improving our monitoring systems, setting up trouble-shooting teams in major facilities, delaying some retirements, and stepping up our training.

The measures are working. So far, we've had no major problems. In fact, our most current information shows that we're meeting our operating plans for moving all classes of mail out of our facilities much better than we were this time last year. And we're doing it with over 46,000 fewer employees.

The Inverted Hierarchy and Servant Leadership

The hierarchy or chain of command in a typical organization chart looks like a triangle. It implies that the ultimate power and authority rests with one individual at the top of the organization, and all others are subordinate to this person and are supposed to do his or her bidding. Many top managers are rejecting this concept of the organization as unrealistic and unproductive. In doing so, they are inverting the triangle, symbolizing the role that top manager plays as a **servant leader.** In other words, *rather than command and control, managers should perceive their roles as primarily to support their employees and help them perform the work that provides value to customers.* William W. Arnold, CEO of Centennial Medical Center in Nashville, Tennessee says of the inverted pyramid, "I am the least important person here. The most important people in this organization are at the top—the associates, the patients, and the physicians. It is a myth that one person runs an organization."[7]

The concept of servant leadership is popular with service organizations, where the value delivered to customers is greatly determined by the front line employees. To ensure service quality, managers must supply employees with the education, skills, technologies, and support systems that they need. FedEx also conceives of its structure as an inverted pyramid (Exhibit 8-3). Notice that FedEx maintains a relatively flat organization for a company its size, with a total of only seven layers of the hierarchy.

FedEx's corps of more than 40,000 front-line customer contact people includes:

- Couriers, who pick up and deliver packages in vans or on foot
- Customer service agents who work in 24 "call centers" around the world, or

Servant leader A structure in which managers perceive their roles as primarily to support their employees and help them perform the work that provides value to customers.

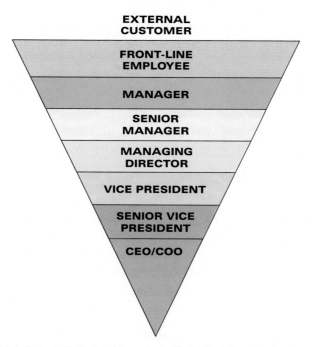

EXHIBIT 8-3
Servant leader structure at FedEx

behind the counters of retail service centers and handle customer's pick-up requests, queries, and complaints

- Billing agents, who assist customers in resolving invoice problems
- Sales people, who build relationships with customers

FedEx's philosophy tries to shorten the organizational distance between management and these front-line people. The triangle in Exhibit 8-3 on page 285 shows that there are only five layers of management between FedEx's executive management and its front-line service employees. This relatively shallow organizational hierarchy not only saves money, but it also ensures that corporate goals can filter through the organization easily and rapidly.[8]

? THINKING CRITICALLY

1. What do you think would be the major differences (for you personally) between working in a tall organization versus a flat organization?
2. How do you think the inverted hierarchy would affect the role of top managers? How do you think this structure affects the attitude and performance of employees?

HOW PEOPLE ARE ORGANIZED

As mentioned earlier, to achieve coordination and reach the organization's business goals, employees must be grouped together in some logical way. The way managers decide to group employees to develop reporting relationships and work interactions defines the formal structure of an organization. There are a number of bases for the departmentalization of employees and work. The most common are:

- **Functional.** For example, marketing, engineering, accounting, manufacturing, research and development.
- **Product.** For example, mainframe computers versus personal computers.
- **Customer.** For example, public utilities versus refineries.
- **Geography.** For example, northeast, southeast, midwest, etc.
- **Operational task.** For example, machining, sub-assembly, final assembly, testing.

The labels on organizational charts usually reveal how an organization is departmentalized. Exhibit 8-4 illustrates these different approaches to departmentalization. These bases are used to establish the formal structure of an organization. Functional, divisional, hybrid, and matrix forms of organization are discussed below.

Functional Structure

A **functional structure** is *built with groups of employees involved in similar or related activities or who belong to the same profession or occupational group. The jobs of these employees all revolve around the same function in the organization.*

Functional structure
A structure with groups of employees involved in similar or related functional activities or who belong to the same professional or occupational group.

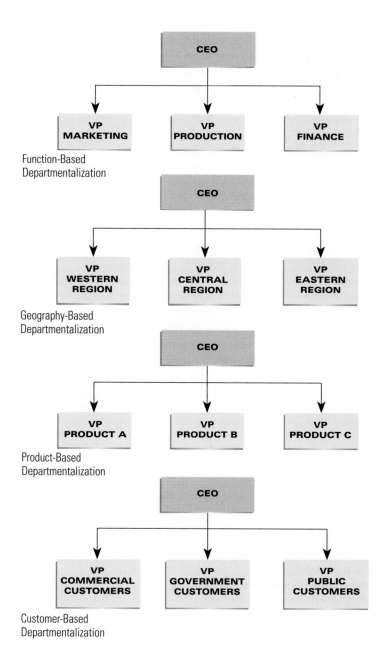

EXHIBIT 8-4
Different bases for
departmentalization

For example, an organization may have departments like marketing, accounting, production and operations, and research and development. The activities of people in each of these departments is overseen by a specialist who is technically competent in that particular area. This person will then report to a general manager, responsible for the entire company or division.

Benefits and Problems of Functional Departments.   At the organizational level, functional departments have the same productivity benefits that result from job specialization, such as economies of scale and minimal duplication of efforts across the organization. For example, in a company with several product lines, organizing by functional area means that a department of specialists will deal with marketing for all product lines. This in turn means that fewer employees may be required than if each line had its own marketing person. The manager of a functional department can focus on mastering a relatively narrow range of skills and technology and developing these skills in subordinates. Since the people in the department have similar educational and experiential backgrounds, they are likely to think alike and develop a shared culture within the department. This situation allows for problem-solving groups to work very efficiently to solve technical problems. The internal cohesion that can develop within functional departments means that coordination within those departments can be achieved with relative ease.

However, the major problems of functional structure is that coordination across departments can be difficult to achieve because they tend to become overspecialized. Functional departments tend to develop their own goals, priorities, and cultures in isolation from other departments. Communication problems are likely to emerge. People within the department may lack any connection to external customers or the needs of people in other departments who depend on their work and on whose work they may depend. Decision making within a functional structure can be slow and unresponsive to environmental changes because of the diverse perspectives and lack of coordination across departments.

As organizations grow larger, functional departments tend to become more isolated and myopically focused on their own concerns. Functional structures seem to work best with smaller organizations that offer only a few products or services, where the top manager may be able to oversee and coordinate all the functional departments, and communication among employees in different departments is easy.

Divisional Structure

Divisional structure

A structure which groups employees into work units that contain all of the functions necessary to conduct business.

As functional organizations grow large and complex they often reorganize into a **divisional structure.** *A division usually contains all of the functions necessary to conduct business.* By forming divisions an organization breaks itself into semi-autonomous units that act much like separate organizations. Each division usually designs, produces, and markets its own products and services. However, a division is not completely independent because it is a part of a larger organization composed of other divisions. In making decisions, a division manager should consider the impact of the decision on other divisions.

Divisions may be formed on several bases, each of which provide the division with a focus. Divisions may be formed based on *geography* to allow people in one region, such as Europe, North America, or Africa, to focus on responding to local needs and accomplish logistical efficiency. For example, Motorola has found that the Asian market for semiconductors offers the best opportunity for growth. Motorola headquarters in Tokyo used to serve Japan and the rest of Asia. However, in the 1980s Motorola split up its regional semiconductor headquarters and moved part of it to Hong Kong to serve the rest of Asia. The restructuring made it easier for Motorola to focus on the needs of already big markets in Taiwan, South Korea, and Hong Kong, as well as emerging markets in Indonesia, Thailand, and China. Now Motorola's Asia-Pacific division is one of Motorola's most profitable and fastest-growing semiconductor units.[9]

Divisions may be formed based on *customers,* as in the insurance industry, to provide the customer with access to people who really know their needs. Divisions may be formed on the basis of *products*. For example, General Motors is organized around its car divisions. Organizing a division around a product provides a common bond across all of the functions within the division, since each functional department focuses on that product and market in addition to focusing on its specialty.

The major advantage of a divisional structure is that decision making and coordination occur quicker and easier because its people are focused on a particular product and/or market. Also, accountability for business results, such as customer satisfaction, market share, and profitability, is much easier to determine. Corporate managers are also freed from the demands of daily operations so they can focus on long-term strategic plans. In other words, divisions create smaller entities that can focus on efficiently and effectively doing work to serve customers. This helps minimize waste and inefficiency that comes with larger structures and less customer-focused structures.

The divisional structure can create some duplication of function. For example, each division may have its own separate marketing, human resources, and accounting departments, with relatively higher costs of administration. In other words, if three divisions were lumped together into one, it would probably require fewer resources, money, and people, to administer the human resources function, for example, than to maintain three separate HR departments. However, the company may make up this extra cost by the overall increased efficiency and effectiveness in a division's ability to serve particular customer groups.

One variation of the divisional structure is a **strategic business unit** (SBU) structure which *combines related divisions into homogeneous groups*. For example, Westinghouse uses SBUs to manage its dozens of different divisions. SBUs make it even easier for corporate managers to oversee the divisions. Corporate managers get help from SBU managers in coordinating and controlling the divisions within the SBU. Furthermore, SBU managers are better able to achieve synergies among the related divisions. The potential drawbacks for SBU structure involve the difficulties achieving interdivisional synergies. The SBU structure just adds another layer of management and formal barriers that impede communication among divisions across SBUs.

An extreme form of divisional structure is the **holding company structure** in which *the corporation manages unrelated businesses as autonomous profit centers*. For example, ITT uses a holding company structure. Corporate managers do not get involved in the overall operations, but they may act as consultants to assist its businesses. Corporate managers primarily engage in portfolio management (as discussed in the last chapter) to decide which businesses to acquire and which to divest in the interest of maximizing profits for the corporation. The primary advantage of holding company structure is that autonomy allows divisional executives to respond quickly to market changes. Unfortunately, autonomy can also be a drawback since the corporate managers lack control over the operations and are almost totally dependent on divisional managers to make the right decisions.[10] On the other hand, they do get feedback because of profit center control systems.

Strategic business unit
A structure which combines related divisions in a large corporation into homogeneous groups.

Holding company structure A structure in which the corporation manages unrelated businesses as autonomous profit centers.

Matrix Structure

We have discussed two of the fundamental structural choices that managers have: functional structure, where people are grouped by specialty, and divisional structure, where people are grouped by product, market, region, or some other basis that puts functions together for a specific purpose or special project. Sometimes managers face a situation where they need the technological expertise that can be provided by a specialized function, but they also need the coordination across functions that is provided by divisional form. The matrix structure evolved to fulfill these two needs.

Matrix structure A structure that leaves the functional hierarchy in place but superimposes a horizontal structure based on products or projects to achieve some coordination and integration across the functional departments.

Matrix structure *leaves the functional hierarchy in place but superimposes a horizontal structure to achieve some coordination and integration across the functional departments*[11] (see Exhibit 8-5). We can define this structure in terms of products or projects. Product-based matrix structures tend to be more permanent, while project based matrix structures are only temporary and last only as long as the projects composing them. For example, Bechtel Corporation, a large engineering and construction firm, uses a matrix structure to manage its many construction and engineering projects. Functional managers in such departments as nuclear engineering, civil engineering, construction, and accounting serve as technical experts and personnel managers, while project managers pull together teams of experts to complete a project, such as the design and construction of a nuclear plant, dam, bridge, tunnel, or industrial complex.

Benefits of the Matrix Structure. In a matrix structure the product or project manager takes responsibility to coordinate and expedite work among the functional departments. This means that employees typically have two bosses, one in charge of the function and the other in charge of the project. Matrix structures vary in terms of the division of power and authority between functional managers and product or project managers. If most of the power resides with the functional managers, and they "call the shots," then the product or project managers are little more than "go-betweens" to facilitate communication and help

EXHIBIT 8-5
A matrix organization structure

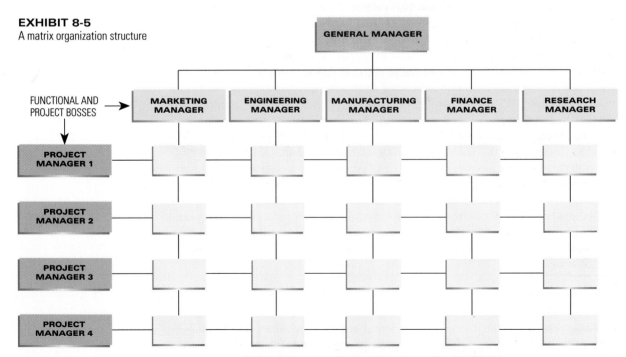

EMPLOYEES REPORTING TO TWO BOSSES

resolve problems. However, if most of the power resides with the product or project managers, then the functional managers serve primarily as human resource administrators and advisors on technical problems.

Some of the key benefits of matrix structures result from combining the strengths of functional specialization with product or project organization. Matrix structure efficiently uses human resources. People with similar specialties are put together into a function, but they are also shared across products or projects. Only the people necessary for completing a project are assigned to a team, and this avoids the duplication of resources common to the divisional structure. Additionally, by working on a project together, the team learns to appreciate the diverse perspectives of people in other functions. They develop common understanding and commitments based on their common allegiance to the project. The horizontal dimension of the matrix also clarifies the accountability for the project's performance in meeting quality, cost, and schedule targets.

While they had been used by the U.S. military, matrix structures were made widely popular by Aerospace firms in the early 1960s. Aerospace projects typically occurred in phases and needed different types of engineers and support personnel at each stage. But the projects also needed people flexible enough to remain with the project through all stages.[12] In the 1970s, matrix structures became quite popular in other industries, as health care organizations, construction companies, electronics companies, and banks believed the new approach would help them adapt to dynamic business environments.[13] In the 1980s, many companies abandoned the matrix structure for more simple traditional forms because of difficulties in implementing the matrix.

Problems of the Matrix Structure.   The typical matrix structure has several problems associated with it. To begin with, the purpose of the product/project managers is to either help administer or to circumvent existing systems, but they are not traditionally given the responsibility to improve processes for doing the work. They simply resolve problems as they arise among those working on the project or product and foster communication across functions. Thus, the complexity of the functional organization remains. Also, the bureaucracy and top-heavy nature of a dual command structure, with too many managers, can add excessive monetary costs to the organization as well as increase the delays in decision making. Matrix structures rarely work as they are designed; thus their potential advantages are seldom completely realized. However, they do point to the recognized importance of people from different functions working jointly to create and market a product or complete a special project, something TQM helps managers deal with more successfully.

Even when product or project managers have authority to make improvements in systems, the products or projects still share resources, facilities, equipment. Managers may compete with each other for resources. The resulting power struggles and noncooperation can lead managers to fail to optimize their performance for all customers.[14] Another problem with matrix structures is the dual reporting relationships, which can cause stress for an employee whose two bosses are pulling him in different directions. Not everyone adapts well to a matrix structure. The matrix structure can also be disruptive of social relationships since teams are reconfigured when one project ends and another begins. It requires flexibility and good interpersonal skills.

Some good advice on making a matrix structure comes from Floris Maljers, the co-chairman and CEO of Unilever, a transnational (Dutch-British) firm that has evolved into a matrix structure. Maljers states, "I like to use an analogy with a dance called the quadrille. This is an old-fashioned dance, in which four people change places regularly. This is also how a good matrix should work, with sometimes the regional partner, sometimes the product partner, sometimes the functional partner, and sometimes the labor-relations partner taking the lead. Flexibility rather than hierarchy should always be a transnational's motto—today and in the future."[15]

Hybrid Structure

Hybrid structure A combination of divisional, functional, and matrix structures.

As organizations grow they tend to add layers that contain several different bases of departmentalization. For example, a marketing department in a functional organization may be divided into marketing for mainframes and marketing for personal computers (product basis). Again, the marketing for mainframes may be further divided along a customer basis, such as government versus private sector. As organizations grow larger and more complex, their structures may be described as a mixture of various forms as discussed above. Such a structure might be called a **hybrid structure,** or *a combination of divisional, functional, and matrix structures.* In a hybrid structure, there may be functional departments and business divisions at the same level in the organizational hierarchy.

The Xerox Hybrid Structure.   An example of a company with a hybrid structure is Xerox. Before the company reorganized itself in 1992, its hybrid structure was defined by geography, function, and product type. This organization included geographically-based marketing divisions and separate functional departments for product development and manufacturing. It also included other functional departments as well. The management at Xerox came to realize that this structure was too complex and fragmented, and it kept Xerox from optimally using its assets to serve its customers. To simplify the company's structure and help all employees better focus on the customer rather than internal boundaries, Xerox Chairman and CEO Paul Allaire worked with other managers to come up with a new hybrid structure for the company.[16]

To accomplish these objectives, in 1992 Xerox reorganized into business divisions. (See Exhibit 8-6 for a simplified view of this new structure.) According to Xerox managers, a business division is a set of activities, people, and assets that approximate a complete "end to end" business with an income statement and a balance sheet. Each division has effective control over the complete value-added chain, including business planning, product planning, development, manufacturing, distribution, marketing, sales, and customer service and support. Each division has a clear set of product and service offerings, a set of primary markets towards which those offerings are targeted, and an identifiable set of competitors. Xerox created the following nine business divisions:

- Personal Document Products
- Office Document Systems
- Office Document Products
- X-Soft

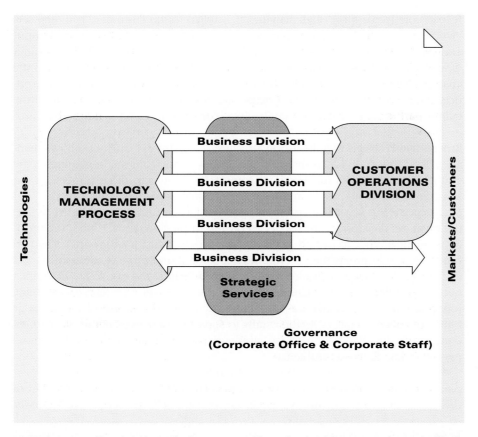

EXHIBIT 8-6   Xerox hybrid organization structure with two functional departments that work with all business divisions. The functional departments and business divisions are at the same level in the organizational structure of Xerox.

- Advanced Office Document Services
- Document Production Systems
- Printing Systems
- Xerox Engineering Systems
- Xerox Business Services

While the dominant feature of Xerox's new structure is the business division, its structure is also a hybrid. As shown in Exhibit 8-6, there are two functionally specialized units that serve all business divisions, the Technology Management Process and the Customer Operations Divisions. These functions help to make sure that Xerox forms an effective linkage between the most advanced technologies available and the customer needs in the marketplace.

The head of the Technology Management Process has responsibility for research and development of technology that provides the core competencies for all parts of the corporation. Customer Operations Division has people assigned to specific geographic regions. Their function is to help improve the customer interface for all Xerox business divisions and make sure that Xerox, as a whole company, is easy to do business with. The Customer Operations Division is responsible for support of all activities that relate to the customer, including service, administration, integration of major customer relationships, sales support, and local administration of the business division's sales forces. The Customer Operations Division helps to ensure that Xerox presents a consistent face to the customer, no matter from which business division the customer is buying products and services. Xerox has customized the design of its structure to support the culture and strategy that make up its vision for the future.

Benefits and Problems with the Hybrid Structure.   The hybrid structure allows managers to develop divisions that can align themselves from the beginning to the end of a process with the needs of some targeted group of customers. At the same time, it also allows them to create functional departments with certain specific expertise to serve the common needs of all the divisions. In Xerox's case, the business divisions were set up according to product lines. (Other organizations might do this according to geographic areas or customer groups). The two functional departments then served the needs of all the product divisions.

Potential problems with the hybrid structure include the possibility of conflict between the functional department and the division over who has responsibility for what work. It also includes the possibility of inefficient use of resources as functional departments build their staffs to serve the perceived needs of the company's divisions. Every time a new problem arises, it suggests the need for more people to handle these problems.

While the hybrid structure can be a sound way to deploy resources and people, it is mainly appropriate for organizations large enough to justify a number of divisions that have common needs that can be served by functional departments.

The Network Structure

Network structure A temporary network of independent companies linked by information technology to share skills, costs, and access to one another's markets.

Another type of structure growing in popularity is the **network structure** or what is sometimes called "the virtual corporation." This structure is *a temporary network of independent companies linked by information technology to share skills, costs, and access to one another's markets.* Calling it a virtual company implies that the pieces come together as needed and then separate when the job or project is over. Each company contributes what it regards as its "core competencies." A network company mixes and matches what it does best with the best of other companies and entrepreneurs. The group of collaborators quickly unite to exploit a specific opportunity. Once the opportunity is met, the network will usually disband. A network structure allows a small company to bring together a variety of resources to do a deal that it could not do on its own. It also allows large companies to call on outsiders to help them do deals as well without having to hire people permanently. Companies as diverse as the Japanese giant Matsushita Electric Industrial Co. and the tiny InterSolve Group Inc., a four partner Dallas-based management consulting firm, have boasted of the benefits of network structures. Exhibit 8-7 illustrates the structure and relationships of a network organization.

Network structures have long characterized several industries, such as movie making and construction, where companies come together for a few years for specific projects. However, in recent years large and small companies are using networks to gain access to new markets or technologies. For large companies,

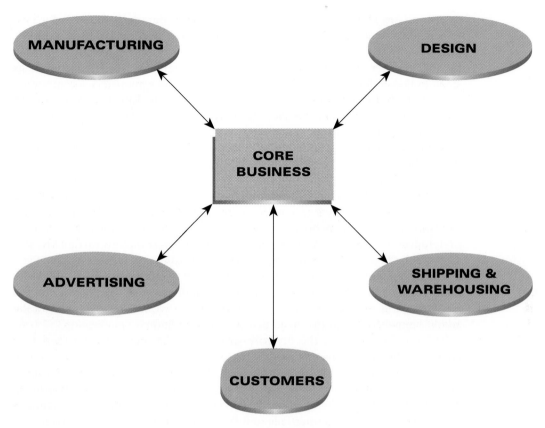

EXHIBIT 8-7   Network structure

the network structure is made up of strategic alliances and outsourcing agreements. For example, Apple Computer has always pursued a strategy of partnering. When it lacked the capacity to produce its entire line of PowerBook computers, Apple contracted with Sony Corp. in 1991 to manufacture the least-expensive version. The alliance was a nice fit; it brought together Apple's easy-to-use software with Sony's manufacturing skills in miniaturization. After selling 100,000 Sony-made models in the first year, Apple ended its agreement.

For small companies, the structure may consist of a handful of managers working in a central organization to plan and coordinate the activities of the corporation. They form strategic alliances with other companies which are contracted to provide services and perform essential functions like design, manufacturing, marketing, distribution and sales. The primary role of the network managers is to manage these external relationships.

For example, Kingston Technology of Fountain Valley, California has grown into one of the world's leading upgraders of personal computers, and *Inc.* magazine's fastest growing company in 1993. It meets the needs of customers with dated PCs who need more memory to run new Windows and other memory hogging programs. Though its sales are growing fast, Kingston creates its products and serves its customers through a set of established and close relationships with other companies, such as Express Manufacturing, a company which

Kingston uses to take its components to quickly upgrade computers for customers like computer retailers. When Computerland needed 100 upgraded PCs for Bank of America, it called Kingston and Kingston went to Express, which put the PCs together in a matter of hours. When its advertising needs outstripped its small in-house design and printing capacity, Kingston's managers set up a relationship with an outside printer, who moved closer to Kingston to handle its business. These arrangements allow Kingston to remain relatively small in terms of employees and focus on responding to customer needs, taking advantage of the skills of its partners to do this. These partners also prosper with the steady flow of business Kingston gives them.[17]

Benefits and Problems of the Network Structure.   The primary benefit of the network structure is the flexibility it gives a company to move quickly in dynamic markets like computers, where technology changes rapidly, and fashion, where consumer preferences change rapidly. The network allows a company to quickly pull together the best resources without the cost of starting up new operations. Even a small company can operate globally through the network structure. With improvements in telecommunications and computers, it is getting easier to link all of the partners in the network. As a result, the network can avoid many of the administrative costs and overhead that plague a traditional organization.

The main problem of the network structure is that network managers lack control of the operations that are critical to the execution of their strategy. They are almost completely dependent on their partners to perform essential functions. Network managers have to manage a complex system of relationships, which can be overwhelming at times. The performance of the whole system can be undermined if one partner fails to fulfill its responsibility. Network managers have to work closely with partners to improve the whole system. It is also difficult to maintain control of proprietary information, such as technological breakthroughs and strategic improvements. To operate within a network structure, managers have to be comfortable with openly sharing information. Exhibit 8-8 lists the suggestions of consultants Booz Allen & Hamilton, Inc. for creating a successful virtual corporation.

THINKING CRITICALLY

1. If you were running a large organization, make an argument for going with a divisional structure rather than one based on functions. How would you make a decision on the basis of divisions, such as choosing between geography or customer groups or product lines?
2. Do you think you would like to work as an employee in a matrix organization? Why or why not?

STRATEGY AND STRUCTURE

The most important factor for designing the structure of an organization is its strategy and how it will go about serving customers. The best organizational designs are those that bring about alignment of all the processes involved in get-

EXHIBIT 8-8   Making the Virtual Corporation Work

- *Marry Well*: Choose the right partners for the right reasons—because they are dependable, can be trusted, and offer the best products or services.

- *Play Fair*: Every link must offer a win-win opportunity for everyone, even if the outcome isn't always successful. Partnerships must serve the interests of all parties.

- *Offer the Best and Brightest*: Put your best people into these relationships. It's the easiest way to tell your partners your link with them is important.

- *Define Objectives*: When you ask the question, "what's in it for me?" you should have a quick and ready answer. Know what you and your partners will be getting out of the virtual enterprise.

- *Build a Common Infrastructure*: Until networks and standards let corporations talk to each other across the street or across the ocean, information systems must at least communicate with current and potential partners.

Source: Adapted from "The Virtual Corporation," *Business Week*, February 8, 1993, pp. 98-103.

ting high-quality low-cost products and services out the door to customers. And any changes in the strategic direction of the company will generally also bring corresponding changes in the organization's structure.[18] Just like any other elements in a system, for optimal performance, strategy and structure should support one another. In other words, organizational structure is a crucial enabling factor in the successful execution of an organization's strategy.

In his classic book *Strategy and Structure*, the Pulitzer Prize winner Alfred Chandler argued that structural changes follow changes in strategy.[19] Other scholars have elaborated on this relationship by presenting specific models regarding the fit which must exist between strategy, structure, and process and systems.[20]

A classic example of the relationship between strategy and structure is General Motors. For decades, GM pursued the strategy of differentiating its products to serve major market niches. Cadillac and Buick served the upper end, while Chevrolet and Pontiac served the lower end, and Oldsmobile served the middle of the market. Correspondingly, GM created autonomous divisions that would design, produce, and market these various nameplates. The strategy worked well for a number of years. However, GM got away from this strategy when it cut costs by eliminating duplications in design and development and production facilities. For example, the Fisher Body division was charged with producing many body styles for different GM makes, and part of their responsibility was to use similar components across car lines. This saved money, but by the mid-1980s, this structure resulted in cars with different nameplates that looked a lot alike. For example, the only difference between an Oldsmobile Calais and a Pontiac Grand-Am was the nameplate and a few amenities. Even more dramatic was that a distinctive car like the Cadillac Seville looked very much like similar models of Oldsmobile and Buick. People stopped distinguishing among the various models. By its structural changes, GM undermined its niche strategy. In the 1990s, GM has swung back toward allowing the divisions to be more autonomous and come up with their own models. The Oldsmobile Aurora is an example of this revised approach.

Although strategy tends to drive structure, structure can affect (or constrain) strategy. Existing structures tend to perpetuate themselves by limiting the vision of those who work in them and creating vested interests which resist change.[21] In some instances the relationship between strategy and structure may be clearly reversed, so strategy follows structure. In the extreme, the faddish imitation of other companies can lead to structure determining strategy, for example, as when a multidivisional structure is installed because everyone else is doing it, and then management pursues an acquisition strategy to make the structure viable.[22]

Another classic example of problems between strategy and structure is the trouble that IBM had in its early attempts to introduce the personal computer. IBM's organizational structure (along with its culture and technical capabilities) was conducive to building mainframe computers, and not for designing, building, and selling PCs. It was not until IBM established a separate division devoted only to personal computers that it successfully entered this market.

⚙ THINKING CRITICALLY

1. Why do you think structure and strategy are so closely related? How do you think structure might constrain the effective implementation of a strategy?

TOTAL QUALITY MANAGEMENT AND ORGANIZATIONAL STRUCTURE

Many companies, like Procter & Gamble (discussed in Chapter 7 on strategy), are formally integrating Total Quality Management into their strategic planning processes. An important part of their strategy is to continuously improve the value of their products to their customers (retailers) and consumers (the final users). P&G and other companies understand and have adopted TQM as the best method to do this. These companies seek to create structures that facilitate the efficient and effective execution of all processes across functions. They see this as the best way to make organizational form follow organizational function to achieve their strategic goals.

Companies pursuing Total Quality Management attempt to eliminate non-value-adding activities, simplify communication flows, speed up decision making, and encourage participation and employee involvement. The structural implications for these changes are to streamline and eliminate unnecessary layers of middle management, which creates a flatter organization.

Another trend for organizations pursuing continuous improvement is the extensive use of cross-functional teams in various forms, which creates even more reasons to flatten the hierarchy. Further, many organizations are implementing self-managing teams to increase employee participation in decision making, improvement activities, planning, and communication with other teams. These teams have less need for middle managers to act as supervisors and coordinators. Cross-functional teams are also increasingly used to provide an alternative to the hierarchical chain of command as a decision making and coordination mechanism. Exhibit 8-9 shows the kind of organizational structure suggested by TQM. It suggests functional teams, with substantial interaction and cooperation among teams, and with special project teams created and disbanded as needed. Top management usually will be a team as well, consisting of the CEO and other senior executives, responsible for business functions. We will talk more about teams in Chapter 14.

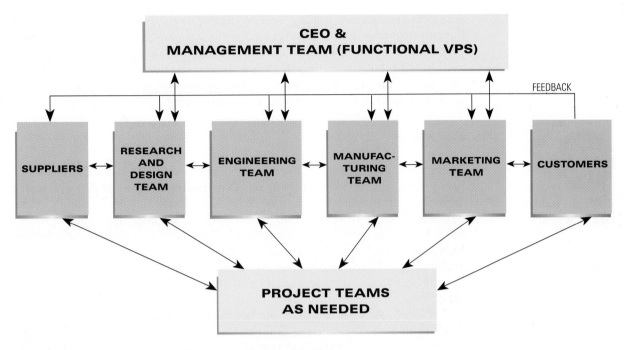

EXHIBIT 8-9   A potential organizational structure suggested by TQM

 **THINKING CRITICALLY**

1. What do you think the connection is between flattening an organization and seeking to eliminate non-value-adding positions?

DESIGN TRENDS

Global competition is moving managers to better understand the insights of the systems view of organizations and TQM and the implications of these for organizational design. We just wrote about the increased use of teams and the emphasis on cross-functional cooperation to manage and continuously improve organizational processes. This suggests innovative new structures, such as shown in exhibit 8-9. We also discussed the idea of a network or virtual organization that comes together to meet specific market needs. These structures allow companies to coordinate their activities and cooperate in ways that were unimagined in the past. As companies become more expert at managing these types of structures, the net result for customers and society in general will be positive. The best technology and managerial resources will be efficiently brought together to provide improved products and services for all of us.

Another way managers are attempting to be more competitive is by revamping old structures. They are flattening organizations by eliminating layers of middle management. This is made possible by improved technology that facilitates communication and by training employees better. Organizations are also using self-managing teams of employees who take on tasks that otherwise would be performed by a supervisor, such as planning, staffing, and problem solving. Such structural changes are leading to lean organizations that have less costs, less bureaucracy, and more involved employees. Companies are also reengineering processes, which means radical change in work flows, job design, responsibility, and authority, but not necessarily radical changes in other aspects of formal structure, like the hierarchy of reporting relationships and departmentalization. We discuss downsizing and reengineering in the next section.

Downsizing

Milliken: Baldrige Award Winner

Downsizing Restructuring that involves reducing organization size by laying off large numbers of employees to cut costs.

Restructuring can be good. However, a troubling trend is the love affair that companies have developed for downsizing. **Downsizing** involves *reducing organization size by laying off large numbers of employees to cut costs.* Certainly some belt-tightening and cost reduction is necessary to help companies survive recessions, like in the early 1990s. Under these circumstances, companies refer to this form of restructuring as "rightsizing." However, many top managers feel pressure to downsize just because everyone else is doing it. When they do this, they almost indiscriminately cut employees at all levels of the organization. This approach gets rid of levels of management and bureaucracy. However, because it is often not well-planned, the companies are not better off afterwards. Even companies that were highly profitable, such as Compaq Computer, General Electric, and Campbell Soup, laid off workers during the recession. In some cases layoffs are necessary to avoid future financial problems. However, indiscriminant layoffs can cut dangerously into a company's economic muscle long after the fat is gone. When a company loses experienced and skilled employees, it is hard to replace them once managers discover they were really needed for the company to grow.

Downsizing, done with proper planning to achieve the right size, can be an important part of an organization's restructuring efforts. In doing this, though, managers should be careful not to blame a seemingly overstaffed work force for bringing down profits when the real problem is the failure to respond to changing markets by redesigning products and processes to meet customers needs.[23] IBM and Sears are examples of companies that were both overstaffed and out of touch with their markets.

Reengineering

Reengineering The fundamental rethinking and radical redesign of business processes to achieve dramatic improvements in critical contemporary measures of performance such as cost, quality, service, and speed.

Reengineering has emerged as an important way of improving organizational structures and processes to be more efficient and effective. It means *"the fundamental rethinking and radical redesign of business processes to achieve dramatic improvements in critical contemporary measures of performance such as cost, quality, service, and speed".*[24] Reengineering is not another term for downsizing or restructuring, although it may result in these changes. Four words are key to understanding reengineering: fundamental, radical, dramatic, and process.

- *Fundamental* describes how companies must view the rules that govern the way they conduct business. They must ask fundamental questions such as "Why do we do this in the first place and why do we do it this way?"
- *Radical* means getting to the root of things, not making superficial changes or fiddling with what is already in place, but throwing away the old and inventing completely new ways of accomplishing work.

Pizzas, Shamrocks, and New Organizational Structures[25]

TQM IN ACTION

In discussing the kinds of organizational structures starting to appear in companies these days, *Business Week* writer John Byrne starts his article with these thoughts: "If the 21st century corporation goes horizontal, what will its organization chart look like? That's right, those dull, lifeless templates that reduce power relationships to a confusing mass of boxes and arrows. As a growing number of planners try to turn a management abstraction into a pragmatic reality, organization charts are beginning to look stranger and stranger."

At Eastman Chemical Company (a 1993 Baldrige Award winner), for example, CEO Earnest Deavenport describes his organizational structure as a pepperoni pizza, with top management as the center pepperoni. He says, "We did it in circular form to show that everyone is equal in the organization." Each pepperoni represents a cross-functional team responsible for managing a business, a geographic area, a function, or a core competence in a specific technology or field such as innovation. The space between the pepperonis represents where collaboration among the teams happens. The point of this chart: eliminate hierarchy and enhance cooperation and customer focus while eliminating bureaucracy and inefficiency. This is the goal with other proposed structures as well.

Charles Handy, a lecturer at the London School of Economics and the author of the highly regarded *The Age of Paradox,* suggests the shamrock or three-leaf clover as an appropriate structure. Its three leaves represent the joining forces of core employees, external contractors, and part-time staffers. This idea emerges from the notion of the virtual corporation, a business approach sure to become more popular. James Brian Quinn, a Dartmouth business school professor, has suggested the organizational chart as a star burst, with a widening network of circles representing interconnected groups working together to achieve organizational goals.

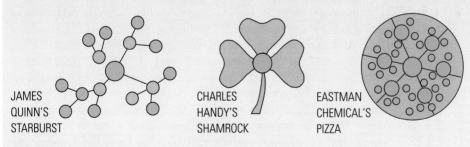

JAMES QUINN'S STARBURST   CHARLES HANDY'S SHAMROCK   EASTMAN CHEMICAL'S PIZZA

EXHIBIT 8-10   Some new organizational structures.

These structures are really just metaphors to move managers away from traditional thinking about hierarchies and power relationships. They help us understand how to set up and efficiently and effectively manage the cross-functional processes by which organizational employees actually deliver the goods to customers.

- *Dramatic* means quantum leaps in performance, not marginal or incremental improvements.

- *Process* is the most important word, but it also gives managers the most difficulty. Most managers are accustomed to thinking in terms of tasks, jobs, people, or organizational structures, and not processes, which are the flows of work that transform inputs into outputs for customers.[26]

The problems that many organizations face are due not to their organizational structures per se, but to inefficient processes. For example, in the early 1980s, Ford, like many other American corporations, was searching for ways to cut costs. It found an opportunity in its North American accounts payable department, the unit was staffed with 500 people to pay the bills submitted by Ford's suppliers. The reengineering is described below.

Under the old system, Ford's purchasing department would send a purchase order to a supplier with a copy going to accounts payable. When the supplier shipped the goods and they arrived at Ford, a clerk at the receiving dock would complete a form describing the goods and send it to accounts payable. The supplier, meanwhile, sent accounts payable an invoice. The system was Byzantine. Many of the 500 clerks spent most of their time straightening out the infrequent situations in which the documents—purchase order, receiving document, and invoice—did not match. Sometimes resolution required weeks of time and enormous amounts of work to trace and clarify discrepancies.

Ford's new accounts payable process looks radically different. Accounts payable clerks no longer match purchase order with receiving document, primarily because the new process eliminates the invoice entirely. The new process looks like this: When a buyer in the purchasing department issues a purchase order to a vendor, that buyer simultaneously enters the order into an on-line database. Suppliers, as before, send goods to the receiving dock. When they arrive, someone in receiving checks a computer terminal to see whether the received shipment corresponds to an outstanding purchase order in the database. Only two possibilities exist: It does, or it doesn't. If it does, the clerk at the dock accepts the goods and pushes a button on the terminal keyboard that tells the database that the goods have arrived. Receipt of the goods is now recorded in the database, and the computer will automatically issue and send a check to the supplier at the appropriate time. If, on the other hand, the goods do not correspond to an outstanding purchase order in the database, the clerk on the dock will refuse the shipment and send it back to the supplier.

The basic concept of the change at Ford is simple. Payment authorization, which used to be performed by accounts payable, is now accomplished at the receiving dock. The old process fostered enough complexity to keep 500 clerks and their managers doing lots of busywork. The new process comes close to eliminating the need for an accounts payable department altogether. The results have proved dramatic. Instead of 500 people, Ford now has just 125 people involved in supplier payment. In some parts of Ford, such as the Engine Division, the head count in accounts payable is now just 5% of its former size.[27]

Of course, with the simplification of processes and reduction in the number of people also comes the simplification of the organizational structure, with fewer layers of management and more delegation of authority and decision making to

WHAT HAPPENED AT DEL NORTE?

The idea of the Del Norte three-tier network-like structure was to make the company more flexible, efficient, and responsive to its customers. To orient employees to the new structure, the company started a Quality Education and Training (QET) program. To make sure the training met the needs of employees, the Corrective Action Team (CAT) set up cross-departmental teams. These teams were to decide their common training needs and suggest the best ways to implement QET throughout the company. The training program used real Del Norte on-the-job problems so employees could learn the value of the new structure for handling situations they would encounter every day.

When a department member discovers a problem or area for improvement, it is immediately brought before the CAT, which selects a facilitator to take ownership of the problem and forms a task team to come up with a suggested solution. These teams are also empowered to use resources at their disposal to solve the problem.

Another change has been the opening up of communication in the company. All employees are encouraged to speak up when they have problems or suggestions for improvement, with the assurance their concerns will be heard and acted on. A year after this new structure and the changes that went with it were implemented, the company had made lots of small improvements that resulted in $200,000 in savings. In an article about Del Norte, a consultant writes, "Continuous quality improvement, total quality management, and total customer satisfaction begin with the people who know their processes, equipment, and responsibilities best: the employees. The freedom to express ideas and see a timely reaction is one of the best vehicles for turning a corporate vision into a reality."[28] It is the change of the structure, along with the attitude and support of top management, that has brought these improvements about.

the employees doing the work. Rather than processes following organizational structure, with lots of busywork, reengineering properly reverses this so the structure of the organization facilitates processes, with a lot of flexibility built in to deal with problems.

Managers in various industries are achieving dramatic results through reengineering. It is a generic approach to analyzing and revamping organizational processes and structure that can be used in any type of organization. Some prominent applications of reengineering in government, for example, include: Napa County's public assistance system in California, the state of Alabama's financial management system, the Florida Department of Transportation, voter registration processes in Oklahoma and Minnesota, and the state of North Carolina's computer infrastructure.

THINKING CRITICALLY

1. Explain your understanding of the difference between downsizing and rightsizing.
2. How do you think reengineering organization processes affects organization structure?
3. Why do you think organizations are moving to metaphors like pizzas and starbursts to characterize organizational structures?

SUMMARY

Oganizational Structure and Processes

- Structure is the "form" part of organizations and processes are the "function" part. In well-managed organizations, structure and processes go together smoothly to facilitate delivery of value to customers.

- Organizational design includes the division of labor to facilitate organization processes and the coordination of that labor into a logical framework to take best advantage of organizational resources.

Division of Labor and Coordination

- Division of labor allows for job specialization, which helps employees to master work tasks and become more productive. However, this must be done with care so jobs do not become too mechanical and so employees use their human problem-solving abilities.

- After division of labor, a role of managers is to coordinate the work of employees to achieve organizational goals.

- While formal structure defines the official relationships among employees, informal structure defines the everyday patterns of interaction by which people work together.

Types of Formal Structure

- Departmentalization, based on geography, task similarity, product similarity, customer segments, or other commonality, are ways managers divide employees into groups so as to more efficiently coordinate their activities.

- The organization chart defines responsibilities and the chain of command in the organization.

- Span of control indicates the number of employees directly reporting to one manager. This may be wide (several people) or narrow (few people) depending on criteria concerning work complexity, similarity, geographic location, and coordination demands on the manager.

- TQM affects organizational structure by influencing managers in the alignment of processes and the empowerment of employees, thus flattening the organizational hierarchy.

- There are a number of factors that are moving organizations toward flatter structures, including enhanced information and communication technology, better trained employees, and the automation of many tasks.

- One structure gaining in popularity is the inverted hierarchy, with customers and line employees at the top and management at the bottom in support of the other levels.

How People are Organized

- A standard way to organize employees is by work function, such as marketing, accounting, engineering, and so on.

- Divisional structures allow organizations to group employees together to serve a common market, with all necessary business functions included within that division.

- A matrix structure includes both functional managers and product or project managers, and employees report to both managers to develop and market products or execute various projects.
- Hybrid structures include both functional and divisional aspects.
- The network structure creates temporary relationships among independent companies to use their mutual resources to serve some customer group.

Strategy and Structure
- Strategy is closely related to structure, and managers must make sure that structure does not undercut its ability to execute its strategy.

Total Quality Management and Organizational Structure
- TQM suggests structures that take more advantage of teams and extensive cross-functional interaction to efficiently and effectively meet organizational goals.

Design Trends
- Two design trends are downsizing and reengineering, which, when properly executed, allow organizations to better match processes with strategy implementation.

KEY TERMS

Chain of command 281

Coordination 278

Divisional structure 288

Downsizing 300

Flat organization 282

Formal authority 281

Formal structure 278

Functional structure 286

Holding company structure 289

Hybrid structure 292

Informal structure 278

Job specialization 277

Matrix structure 290

Network structure 294

Organizational design 276

Organizational structure 276

Reengineering 300

Responsibility assignments 280

Servant leader 285

Simple structure 280

Span of control 281

Strategic business unit 289

Tall organization 282

REVIEW QUESTIONS

1. What is the relationship between organizational processes and organizational structure?
2. Why is division of labor the first step in organizational design?
3. How has technology enhanced the importance of the informal structure of organizations?
4. How does TQM influence the creation of formal organizational structures?
5. Why does the inverted hierarchy make sense for service organizations?
6. Why would an organization choose a functional organizational structure? What are the problems with a functional structure?

7. What are the bases on which to develop a divisional structure? How does a manager choose which structure is best?
8. When is it good for an organization to adopt a matrix structure? Why does this structure often have problems?
9. What type of organization is most likely to have a hybrid structure? Why?
10. How does the network structure work to create a virtual company?
11. What is the relationship between strategy and structure?
12. What are some of the influences that are causing organizations to flatten their structures?
13. What is the difference between downsizing and rightsizing?
14. How does process reengineering affect organizational structure?

EXPERIENTIAL EXERCISE

In groups of 5 or 6 people, discuss and describe the structure of the university or college that you attend. Describe the structure in words and in graphic form (charts or diagrams). What are the elements of its structure that ensure that you are served well as a customer? What are the elements of its structure than interfere or keep you from being served well? What design changes would you propose to better serve your needs?

CASE ANALYSIS AND APPLICATION
J.C. Penney Goes Global[29]

J.C. Penney has often been regarded as a smaller version of Sears in the highly competitive retail industry serving the lower to middle income segment of the market. However, J.C. Penney has been able to avoid some of the woes that Sears has encountered, squeezed by discounters like Wal-Mart and Kmart at the lower end of the market. For example, J.C. Penney realized that its core customers (in the lower-to middle-income bracket) want fashion as well as affordability. In response, J.C. Penney developed its own private line of fashionable and affordable clothes. The new line was a great success. J.C. Penney has also grabbed the lion's share of ex-Sears catalogue customers through its catalogue sales. Despite these marketplace successes, J.C. Penney considers the U.S. market to be over-exposed to retail shopping and sees greater opportunity for growth in foreign markets.

The opportunities abroad are revealed in a number of ways. Research shows that in the U.S. stores that border Mexico, 60% of the shoppers are Mexican citizens crossing the border to shop. In Chile, many of the residents who have expendable income will fly to the United States just to shop. This eagerness of non-U.S. citizens to shop in the U.S. has convinced J.C. Penney that there is a ready market in many parts of the globe for U.S. style retailing.

Unfortunately, J.C. Penney's last foray into world markets in the late 1970s was a bad experience. For example, problems arose when they acquired chains in Italy and Belgium. Zoning laws prohibited them from locating in the choice spots, although the local competitors often received ideal locations to develop malls. When the stores lost money and attempted to lay off employees, local laws prohibited it. J.C. Penney soon sold the stores at a loss. J.C. Penney has not been the only U.S. retailer to fail in global expansion. Sears in South America and Federated in Spain have also failed.

Past failures made J.C. Penney leery but the lowering of trade restrictions through NAFTA and GATT made global expansion more attractive. J.C. Penney decided to investigate some foreign markets in a recent 21-day, seven-country tour. The touring managers discovered that they were far ahead of the foreign competition in their retailing capabilities. For example, in East Berlin they found shirts in display windows covered with dust, and in Istanbul they saw poorly arranged displays such as a display of women's lingerie next to plumbing equipment.

While confident in their merchandising abilities, J.C. Penney decided to proceed cautiously with a more prudent strategy for global expansion than it had pursued the last time. Rather than buy existing retail chains in foreign countries, J.C. Penney decided to link up with local partners. This way the local merchants would have a stake in the success of Penney and local governments would be less likely to instigate unfair laws against J.C. Penney. Perhaps most importantly, the local merchants would know the local culture, tastes, and traditions. This understanding would greatly help J.C. Penney tailor its offerings to meet local preferences, and prevent them from trying to sell to everyone as if they were Americans.

After deciding to go global, J.C. Penney then had to decide which countries to enter. After analyzing political and economic conditions, growth trends, demographics, and the ability to repatriate profits from various countries, J.C. Penney settled on a list of 20 countries. Surprisingly, the list excluded most of the Eastern European countries.

Realizing that a single game plan will not work the same in all countries, J.C. Penney crafted strategies that are adapted to regional differences as follows:

1. In countries favorable to buisness with affordable real estate and a lack of competing retail stores, J.C. Penney would open and operate the store itself. This is the case in Mexico. J.C. Penney feels that Mexican consumers are similar enough to U.S. consumers that the retail outlets there can be run much as they are in the U.S. In fact, the majority of J.C. Penney's global expansion will be in Mexico. By the end of the decade, J.C. Penney hopes to operate at least 15 stores in Mexico.
2. In more saturated markets, as in the advanced countries of Western Europe, or where regulations make it difficult to run its own stores, J.C. Penney would license local retailers to operate J.C. Penney collections stores and to sell its private labels.
3. In very difficult markets with high property costs and regulations making it nearly impossible to build, like Singapore and Japan, J.C. Penney would license other retailers to operate in-store shops selling J.C. Penney goods.
4. In areas with strong consumer demands and insurmountable barriers, like Iceland and Russia, J.C. Penney would sell through catalogs.[30]

Discussion Questions

1. What mistakes do you think J.C. Penney made in its first attempt to go global? How has it compensated for these mistakes and made plans to avoid them in its current attempt to go global?
2. Pretend that you are the CEO of J.C. Penney, and you have to devise an organizational structure that will support the company's strategy for global expansion. Using the concepts described in this chapter, devise an organizational structure, explain each of its elements, and justify why you chose those elements.

9. HUMAN RESOURCES MANAGEMENT

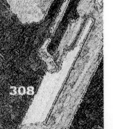

PEOPLE FIRST AT SCITOR[1]

oger Meade, founder and CEO of Scitor, a Sunnyvale, California company that provides products and services in program management, systems engineering, and customized computer information systems, sees his employees as assets, and he looks out for them.

He recognizes that people can get sick so he has instituted unlimited sick leave with no lost wages and no tracking of sick days taken, and there is a company-paid health care plan, along with a $1,400 fund for each employee for dental and vision care and unreimbursed medical expenses. He recognizes that his employees have children, so new mothers get 12 weeks of paid maternity leave and the option of full or part-time work when they return. Meade understands that job

sharing can make sense and that not everyone can be there between 8 A.M. and 5 P.M., so his company has job sharing and flextime and provides benefits to any employees who work at least 17.5 hours per week. He knows his employees like to have fun, so everybody gets tickets to one 49ers home game, and there are company-organized picnics, chili cook-offs, ski trips, fishing trips, wine-tasting trips, and road rallies. He knows people need to be excited about their company, so he holds an annual fiscal year kick-off meeting in a first-class resort that all employees attend. He pays for transportation, food, and lodging for each employee and his or her guest for the three day affair.

Why is Meade so seemingly lavish with his employees? He says, "Scitor is our people. Our success depends on

them. Knowledge resides in their minds and their feet. Too many companies fail to grasp that feet can walk out the door as easily as they walked in." Meade sees his programs as investments not costs. He further explains, "People are your resources. Taking care of people's needs is the key to productivity. [Every work-family program at Scitor] is based upon analysis, not emotion. Our benefits exist because they support our attract-and-retain objectives. It isn't being generous. And it certainly isn't being liberal. It's simple economics."

Scitor has found, for example, that a $2,400 investment to provide sick-care service for employees' children saves the company $17,000 in lost customer billings. Meade says, "Everything we do is driven toward increasing our competitiveness and productivity."

Scitor is a fairly unique company. Its policies and actions in managing its human resources reflect the perspective of a manager who has thought carefully about where the value lies in his organization and how he can enhance that value. He knows that doing right by his people is how he does right by his organization. Not all managers recognize this, but it is becoming more widely understood. TQM, with its emphasis on empowerment, training, teams, and allowing employees to maximize their contributions is helping to raise management consciousness that by looking out for their employees they look out for their company. In this chapter, we will review the formal aspects of human resources management. As you read this material, reflect on how Roger Meade has implemented these different aspects of human resources management in his company. At the end of the chapter we will look more at how the policies of Scitor have affected the success of this company.

HUMAN RESOURCES PLANNING

Human resources planning A process for developing alignment between the organization's strategy and the people it employs to execute this strategy.

Intelligent, sound human resources management (HRM) begins with planning. **Human resources planning** brings about *alignment between the organization's strategy and the people it employs to execute this strategy.* For planning to be effective and efficient, managers need to view it from the systems perspective, which helps them appreciate the interrelationships between people and organizational performance. The goal with this planning is to make sure that every member of the organization adds value rather than costs as people work together to serve the needs of customers.

Systems and the Environment of HR Management

In earlier chapters we have regularly referred to organizations as systems. One aspect of this systems perspective is the understanding that the organization is constantly interacting and exchanging resources and information with the larger environment of which it is a part. An organization does not and cannot operate in isolation. What happens in the environment affects people in the organization and vice versa. Thus to begin to get a handle on HR management, we need to appreciate some of the environmental forces that affect this planning. These forces include: globalization, competitiveness, unions, labor market trends, legal requirements, and technological advances.

Globalization.   American firms like Ford and Xerox have operated in other countries for many years. They purchase supplies, manufacture, and sell their products around the world. Japanese firms like Toyota and Sony, and European firms like Unilever and Siemens have set up subsidiaries in the United States. Increasingly, the national identity of a company is becoming less important, as companies buy and sell goods and services around the globe. Improved logistics and communication systems will ensure that these trends toward globalization continue. Firms operating in the global community will need people who are able to bridge the linguistic and cultural barriers that can interrupt business transactions.

Globalization often takes the form of joint ventures or partnerships. For example, NUMMI is a joint venture between Toyota and General Motors to build vehicles in California. The Fuji-Xerox joint venture builds copiers in Japan. Some of the unique HRM challenges faced by these international joint ventures include:

- Host country may demand staffing policies that seem to conflict with strategic goals.
- Interpersonal and communication problems may arise from geographical dispersion and cultural differences.
- There may be perceived and real compensation differences.
- There may be perceptions regarding the value of overseas assignments.
- There are differences in standards and measures of performance.[2]

Successful human resources management requires that organizations deal with these differences to achieve their strategic goals.

Competitiveness. One of the outcomes of globalization is increased competitiveness. As managers face more intense competition in the future, this will require the ever more efficient and effective management of organizational resources to remain a player. In terms of its human resources, managers must develop an organizational culture that encourages flexibility to respond quickly to market needs and competitive pressures. In addition, the organization needs to develop employees who value and work at the continuous improvement of work processes and the outputs delivered to customers.

Technological Advances. We are in an era of explosive technological development. Communications and information management systems are improved daily. New technology for products and services brings new market opportunities. Improved technology for production processes gives managers better ways of transforming raw materials into goods and services that customers will value. Robotics and numerically controlled machinery are growing more sophisticated. People at all levels of the organization will have to keep up with these technological advances to make the best use of technology in serving customers.

Strategic planners will have to understand how new product technologies fit customer needs in the marketplace. Middle managers will have to understand how new technology contributes to the efficiency and effectiveness of their work processes in order to make wise investment decisions. Operators will have to understand how to handle and maintain sophisticated new equipment to do their work. The most important aspect of the technological revolution concerns decisions about what work is best done by machines and what work is best done by people. Production line work that is tedious and repetitive should be done by machines. People are best at work that requires flexibility and judgment.

Education and Job Skills. By the year 2000, twenty-five percent of the work force will have completed a college education. This growing number of educated workers means that organizations will have people who demand more involvement in corporate decision making and who want to use their intellectual abilities to influence the organization.[3] These better-educated workers will also put more value on self development and personal growth. Again, organizations will have to develop programs to meet such demands.

Organizations that are flattening the hierarchy and removing middle management positions will have to come up with ways other than job promotions to provide employees with additional challenge. In today's organizations, there are fewer levels through which aspiring managers can rise. These organizations will be offering more lateral transfers to other divisions or departments and special assignments to provide challenge and opportunities for continuous learning and skill improvement. By offering employees opportunities for self-fulfillment and work satisfaction, managers keep people fresh, challenged, and committed to their work.

Lifestyles.   American workers are demanding more from their jobs than just good pay and promotional opportunities. They are becoming more concerned with how their job fits into their overall lifestyle, including leisure pursuits and family obligations. Increasingly, more and more organizations are implementing career development programs to meet the needs of special groups of employees. For example, some organizations offer job sharing, wherein two people work part time to share a job that would otherwise be full time for one person. Job sharing is an attractive alternative for parents who want to devote part of their work week to caring for their young children.

Diversity of Workers.   The demographics of the American work force are changing. Greater numbers of women, minorities, older workers, and disabled persons are entering the work force. Members of this diverse work force are taking positions, such as in management, that were previously dominated by white males. Such diversity should prove to be an asset in global competition. Organizations need all the talent they can get, regardless of the gender or ethnic background of employees. To make the best use of its human resources, organizations will need to make some changes to accommodate a diverse work force. They may need to develop courses in English and other skills for their employees. They may have to establish courses on communicating across multicultural lines to better integrate their work force and facilitate their working together. They may also need to improve facilities to give people equal access, develop more flexible work schedules, and offer child-care arrangements.

Legal Requirements.   In addition to all of these environmental and demographic forces, managers face increasingly complex legal requirements. They must understand federal laws like the Civil Rights Act of 1964 (revised in 1991), the 1990 Americans with Disabilities Act (ADA), the Age Discrimination in Employment Act (ADEA) of 1967 (amended in 1978 and 1986), and the Pregnancy Discrimination Act of 1978. In addition to federal laws, there are a number of state, and local laws, regulations, executive orders, and rules that address virtually every type of personnel decision. These legal requirements address HR decisions such as equal opportunity, health and safety, employee compensation and pensions, plant closures, mergers and acquisitions, and new immigration.

As if the legal requirements alone were not enough to overwhelm them, managers must keep up with the legal interpretations of the requirements in the court system. Large organizations may have to spend large sums defending themselves against alleged violations of the law. Since legal interpretations may change over time as a reflection of economic, social or political trends, the verdicts on these court battles are not always easy to predict. It is safe to say that the legal profession will have a place in American corporations for a long time to come.

Organizational Strategy and Human Resources Management

We mentioned at the beginning of this chapter the importance of aligning HR management with organizational strategy. In fact, an important part of developing a strategy is human resources planning. This helps ensure that the organization has capable and motivated people to implement its chosen strategy. Part of HR planning involves figuring out how to make sure the supply of employees with various skills matches various organizational demands, as defined by the strategic plan. Based on this understanding of strategy, human resources planners can forecast the future needs or demands of the organization for people with specific skills and experience. To complete the human resources planning process, managers must also analyze the future availability or supply of human resources. They then determine what the organization must do to meet the forecasted need.

One source of information about the availability of human resources is a **human resources audit,** which *evaluates the current human resources of the organization.* If future needs are similar to current needs, in terms of skill levels and number of people, then the job of human resources planning is easier. The manager must simply maintain the current pool of employees and place them into future positions as needed. But managers seldom face such a simple scenario. In dynamic environments, with new markets emerging, new technologies, new products, and new processes, HR managers are constantly dealing with gaps in future human resources needs that they must help the organization close. To do this, they must either plan to develop the current group of employees to meet future needs or plan to bring in new people when needed. In other words, they must have a **human resources strategy,** *a plan for providing capable and motivated people to fulfill the mission of the organization.*

Once a strategy is put in place, managers must continue to assess current needs for human resources to make sure that the organization has the people it needs to meet its strategic objectives. When people leave a position through retirement, transfers, promotions, demotions, or some type of termination, this usually creates needs for human resources to execute the current strategy. So, managers must put in place processes that ensure the continued availability of human resources to fill the needs of the organization. In the remainder of the chapter we discuss the various human resources management activities that help ensure the organization has a capable and motivated work force. The *A Look at Managers in Action* box on page 314 provides an example of parts of Xerox's HR strategy for the future.

Job Analysis

Before managers can know what human resources are needed, they must understand the jobs or positions that the people will fill in the organization. **Job analysis** is *the process and procedures used to collect and classify information about tasks the organization needs done.* Job analysis helps the manager understand the work activities required in a process and thus helps to define jobs and their interrelationships, along with the knowledge, skills, abilities, and other characteristics (KSAOCs) needed to fulfill those requirements. Job analysis in traditional organizations has been a means to many ends. The results can be used for writing job descriptions, evaluating and classifying jobs, restructuring jobs, appraising performance, training and development, designing recruitment and selection systems, and other aspects of human resources planning. Further, Supreme Court actions emphasize the importance of conducting thorough job analyses.

We should note that while job analysis is important in managing human resources, it can also be a source of problems when applied rigidly to who does what. TQM, with its emphasis on processes, cooperation, and adding value, requires flexibility in job definition, so employees can pitch in and do whatever is required to complete a process. An article in *Fortune* warns managers:

Human resources audit A process for evaluating the current human resources of the organization.

Human resources strategy A plan for providing capable and motivated people to fulfill the mission of the organization.

Job analysis The process and procedures used to collect and classify information about tasks the organization needs done.

A LOOK AT

MANAGERS
IN ACTION

HUMAN RESOURCES MANAGEMENT AT XEROX

The Xerox Corporation is a leader in the implementation of Total Quality Management. It pervades all their planning and decision making. To maintain their leadership in what they call the document business, top managers have developed the Xerox 2000 strategy that takes the company into the next century. Edward J. Leroux, Human Resources Vice President, Office Products Division, shares these parts of the strategy pertaining to human resources:

Foundation: The Xerox 2000 Quality strategy embraces the values of teamwork, empowerment, diversity, and continuous learning.

Strategy Overview: All Human Resources processes must align and support the challenges of Xerox 2000.

Strategy Elements:

- *Selection and Recruitment*—External hiring processes and internal selection processes must focus on knowledge, skills, and attributes contained within the leadership attributes and defined by the core competencies within the business unit.
- *People Development*—Each employee has a primary responsibility to be a continuous learner and acquire needed skills. Managers have a primary role in the development of their people.
- *Management Roles and Selection*—Management roles will be defined by selecting the most appropriate leadership attributes for each position and matching individuals to positions through management assessment against those same attributes.
- *Reward and Recognition*—The principles of reward systems must provide closer linkage between the customer and our business performance, team performance, and individual contribution.
- *Employee Involvement*—Increased employee involvement is an important foundation of empowerment and is an enabler for continuous work and process improvement. The ultimate goal is structural empowerment—the establishment of high-performing, self-managed work groups as the pervasive mode of both employee involvement and leadership processes.
- *Work Environment*—The work environment should be an enabler for empowered work groups, productivity improvement, and work force diversity, while adhering to Xerox health, welfare, and safety standards.
- *Valuing Diversity*—Work force diversity is a priority at Xerox and adds value to our business. Diversity of our work force requires an openness by all employees in respect to age, race, gender, and thought.

When you read these items they sound both abstract and idealistic. Yet Xerox managers are passionate about putting them into practice. This is because they know these points are the foundation of the company's continued success.

*Today's hierarchical systems designed to control workers and break down pro-
duction into its smallest component tasks are obsolete. They are steadily giving
way to looser, more decentralized arrangements that give workers more autonomy and responsibility in the hope of enlisting their pride, judgment, and creativity. The aim: to get them to think constantly about how the job they know best
could be done better; to have them be flexible, so they can do more than one part
of the process, when needed; and to care about the quality of the job they do.*[4]

This does not negate the importance of job analysis, but it does suggest that
HR planning take a closer look at processes and understanding jobs in relation to
one another rather than as independent entities. HR managers have an important
role to play in working with line managers and employees to undertake this
analysis, which includes the following general steps.

Information Gathering.   As in the development of strategy or decision making, the
first step in job analysis is gathering information. HR managers can gather information on jobs and processes from various sources, including: current, past, and future
job occupants; superiors and subordinates; peers; and other job experts. They can
even find information from documents such as background records (such as organization charts), training materials, performance appraisal materials, and standard
operating procedures, and from the Dictionary of Occupational Titles (a compendi-
um describing various occupations). The methods used to gather information for
job analysis are very diverse. They include interviewing, diary keeping, self-reports
by job incumbents, having job analysts actually perform the job, direct observation
by experts, surveys, analysis of critical incidents, checklists, and questionnaires.

They also include analysis and mapping of work processes to understand the
important steps and what is involved in executing them. Some approaches to job
analysis have been standardized to provide managers with a very structured
approach to job analysis. For example, the Position Analysis Questionnaire (PAQ)
has been in widespread use for decades.[5] The PAQ consists of 194 items or job
elements that are used to rate a job in terms of information input, mental
processes, work output, relationships with other persons and job context.

Documenting the Job Analysis.   Once the manager has analyzed a job, the information must be documented in a form that is useful for subsequent HR activities.
Work-oriented information that describes the job itself is documented in a *job
description*. A typical job description might contain information on the

- job duties and responsibilities
- machinery, tools and materials used
- supervision
- working conditions, hazards, and social environment
- work schedules
- performance standards
- relationships with other jobs

A job description for a managerial job at a company that we will call AIS, a German company with operations in Knoxville, Tennessee, is shown in Exhibit 9-1.

EXHIBIT 9-1 Position Brief for Manager of Business Development in the Manufacturing Engineering Department of the Operations Division of AIS, Inc.

Position Brief

TITLE: Manager, Business Development   CODE: ME-05

DIVISION: AIS, Operations   DEPARTMENT: Manufacturing
                                                      Engineering

APPROVED: _____   DATE: November 15, 1992
             (Signature of Supervisor)

SUMMARY STATEMENT

The Business Development position is a function that is chartered to quote and initiate the manufacture of AIS products at the AIS facility in Knoxville, Tennessee.

REPORTS TO: Director, Manufacturing Engineering

SUPERVISES: One Administrative Assistant

PRIMARY RESPONSIBILITIES:

The detailed job assignments include:

- Plan and help implement manufacturing proposals (Domestic and International).
- Act as the liaison between customer and operations.
- Quote/Proposal cycle time reduction.
- Execute a standard process for cost estimates.
- Develop subordinate skills through organizing and executing a development plan for each.
- Participate in corrective actions as requested by other departments. Also perform corrective actions as documented in the procedures manual.
- Set-up spare parts to meet customer/marketing needs.

PRINCIPLE WORKING RELATIONSHIPS/CONTACTS:

For AIS in the USA and International, strong relationships with Product Engineering, Purchasing, Finance, and Manufacturing in order to develop assumptions used in cost analysis, start-up production, and transfer of information between groups. Also, important relationship with customers for manufacturing services in terms of support and manufacturing start-up.

AIS refers to the job description as a position brief. The position brief shown in Exhibit 9-1 describes the job of the Manager of Business Development. This position brief was developed as a requirement in the ISO-9000 program, an international set of quality standards which requires extensive documentation of all work processes. The facility in Knoxville, Tennessee was the first AIS facility in the world to receive ISO-9000 certification.

Worker-oriented information that describes the qualifications and personal requirements that an individual needs to do the job is documented in a *job specification*. A typical job specification might contain information on such personal characteristics as:

- education level
- technical knowledge
- work experiences
- physical skills and abilities
- interpersonal and communication skills
- analytical skills and judgment
- creative abilities

Exhibit 9-2 on page 318 shows the position specification for the job of Manager of Business Development at AIS.

It is not possible for job descriptions and specifications to capture all the dynamics of a particular job. Most job descriptions and specifications will thus be incomplete. However, they do provide a good basis for subsequent human resources planning. Job descriptions and specifications provide information about the kind of people to hire, the training and development needed, and how to structure compensation. It is good business sense to make job-related decisions (such as hiring, training, and improving) on the basis of solid information about a particular job.

In addition, legal requirements dictate that job analysis be conducted when an organization seeks to prove that its selection devices, such as intelligence tests and physical abilities tests, are useful predictors of job performance. This legal requirement is based on the Supreme Court ruling in *Albemarle Paper Co. v. Moody* (1975) and the Federal Uniform Guidelines on Employee Selection Procedures (1978). Further, employment practices that are discriminatory, for example, those that exclude a disproportionate number of protected classes such as blacks or females, must be shown to be job related (*Griggs vs. Duke Power,* 1971).

Job Analysis and Total Quality Management

In an organization practicing continuous improvement, the job analysis should be viewed as another activity in making improvements to systems and processes. As the work of the organization is changed to improve quality, for example, people's jobs will change. This means job analysis information must be continuously updated for it to be relevant. Further, job analysis is not something that staff experts in a personnel or human resources department will do alone. Line managers must be involved in human resources management. After all, human resources are a critical input to the systems and processes that managers are responsible for improving.

EXHIBIT 9-2 Position Specification for Manager of Business Development in the Manufacturing Engineering Department of the Operations Division of AIS, Inc.

Position Specification

TITLE: Manager, Business Development   CODE: ME-05

DIVISION: AIS, Operations   DEPARTMENT: Manufacturing
                                                             Engineering

APPROVED: _____   DATE: November 15, 1992
                    (Signature of Supervisor)

EDUCATION:
B.S. in Mechanical, Electrical, or Industrial Engineering.

SPECIAL KNOWLEDGE OF SKILLS:
Strong business orientation regarding cost accounting, knowledge of AIS products, manufacturing processes, and financial standards.

PRIOR EXPERIENCE DESIRABLE:
Minimum 5 years in various manufacturing and/or engineering roles that offer exposure to products, manufacturing processes, information systems, and finance.

OTHER QUALIFICATIONS OR REQUIREMENTS:
Strong organizational skills, communication skills, and self disipline in time management. Some leadership skills needed, but can be developed. Must be professional in appearance and willing to travel internationally. Requires good negotiation skills and diplomacy with customers.

One of the imperatives in Total Quality Management is educating and developing a flexible and adaptable work force. For example, firms that are improving the responsiveness of their manufacturing processes often require workers to move from one job to another as needed. This requires workers to have multiple skills and an ability to learn and adapt. For managers in a total quality environment, job analysis will also indicate a need for people who are flexible and able to continue learning and adapting.

? **THINKING CRITICALLY**

1. Why is there such an intimate relationship between human resources planning and the successful execution of organizational strategy? Use Scitor, the company described at the beginning of this chapter, as an example in your answer.

2. In a company that practices TQM and encourages flexibility among workers, what is the value of doing a job analysis and having detailed job descriptions?

STAFFING THE ORGANIZATION

Once managers understand the organization's strategy and the processes involved in executing that strategy, they then have a better sense of the type of people the organization needs to move ahead. Finding and attracting those people is the human resources activity called **staffing,** which includes *two multifaceted steps: recruitment and selection.*

> **Staffing** A process that includes two multifaceted steps: recruitment and selection.

Recruitment

To fill the vacant job positions in an organization, the manager must attract potential employees to the job. **Recruitment** is *a process of attracting the best qualified people to apply for the job.* There is usually a large pool of potential applicants, but not all of them fit the job specifications, and those who do fit may not be aware or interested in the job. Through internal and external recruitment, human resources managers, often working with line managers, make potential applicants aware of the job, inform them about the personal requirements needed, and motivate them to apply for the job.

> **Recruitment** A process of attracting the best qualified people to apply for the job.

Internal Recruitment.   Companies that hire-from-within must engage in **internal recruitment,** *a process for attracting applications for jobs from people who already work for the company.* Internal recruitment is often done through job posting. Vacant positions can be posted on bulletin boards, listed in company papers or newsletters, or included in interoffice memos. Job postings usually list a brief job description and specification to allow the potential applicants to determine whether the job matches their interests and capabilities.

> **Internal recruitment** A process for attracting applications for jobs from people who already work for the company.

Job posting is really a form of general advertisement to attract potential applicants without a specific person in mind. Internal recruitment may also be more directed at specific individuals. For example, potential candidates for a position may be identified in a human resources database that lists employees and their job experiences and personal characteristics. The manager may directly contact these individuals to encourage them to apply for the job.

Often managers do not have to do an extensive search to fill a position because they have a specific candidate in mind as soon as the job comes open. For example, there may be an established succession plan or career path in an organization that allows the assistant manager to step into a vacant position for a manager when that occurs. Many companies have a **fast track,** *a development path that should quickly lead selected individuals into positions of more and more responsibility.* These programs give these individuals diverse experiences they need to move eventually into upper management positions. For example, for over 30 years, AT&T and many of the Bell Companies have used assessment centers for the early identification of managerial talent.[6]

> **Fast track** A development path that should quickly lead selected individuals into positions of more and more responsibility.

So, when a management position comes open, there may be a fast track manager waiting to take it. In these cases, recruitment activities are not formally carried out. Companies that rely heavily on internal recruitment, like IBM, also tend to heavily emphasize career development and ongoing education to cultivate their internal pool of human resources.

There are several advantages of hiring people from within the organization. It provides motivation for people who aspire to develop their skills and careers. If a company never hired from within, many people already in the company would be demoralized by the prospects of a stagnant career and no opportunity for new or increased responsibilities. Hiring from within is also less costly than hiring people from outside the company. This is because it takes less time, there are no employment agency or advertising costs, there is less screening involved, and the company does not have to spend as much on orientation and training as for external recruits. Managers can easily obtain and review the work history of the employee. The major disadvantage of hiring from within is that it can close the organization off from fresh perspectives and ideas brought in by outsiders. These ideas help challenge the status quo and can help improve the organization. For example, boards of directors often bring a new CEO in from the outside for that very reason. Another disadvantage is that the selection of internal people is more likely to be affected by political agendas in the organization, which focuses more on who a person doing the hiring knows and likes than on the candidate's performance. A goal of a company like Xerox's HR strategy is to enhance hiring from within while minimizing the internal politics of doing this.

Ultimately, a growing organization must bring in people from the outside. Natural attrition, due to retirements and resignations, means there will be job vacancies. Unless the organization is downsizing, people have to be brought in from the outside to replace those that leave. Organizations may also be forced to do external recruiting because of mandated affirmative action programs. The Equal Employment Opportunity Commission often requires companies to establish plans to correct imbalances in the number of minorities and women represented in the work force to be considered for government contracts. If minorities and women are underrepresented in the work force, for example, managers may undertake external recruitment to bring them into the organization.

External recruitment The process of attracting qualified candidates for jobs from outside the organization.

External Recruitment. Just like the internal recruitment process, **external recruitment** is *the process of attracting qualified candidates for jobs from outside the organization.* There are many ways to go about this. Most companies and industries will use the indirect approach of general advertising to identify potential employees. These ads list vacant positions, with brief job descriptions and qualifications required in professional journals and newspapers.

Rather than incur the costs of professional assistance in recruiting, some companies encourage their employees to refer their friends for jobs. Many companies also rely on their reputation or word-of-mouth communications to encourage walk-ins to file applications at the personnel office. The applications from walk-ins and employee referrals may be kept on file along with those of other past job applicants. This database provides the company another source of information that can be used to directly recruit potential applicants whose personal characteristics match the job specifications. Research shows that such informal methods of recruiting will likely lead to longer job tenure than more formal approaches such as newspaper ads.[7]

Other forms of external recruitment are more directed to specific sources. Many recruiters visit vocational/technical schools, and colleges and universities on carefully planned recruiting trips. The company may work closely with the placement office of the educational institution to set up workshops, collect applications, and initiate the selection process. Companies also rely on public and private employment agencies, managerial search firms or "head-hunters," and unions to identify potential applicants.

External recruitment can be quite costly. However, the cost of not recruiting externally can be even higher. Organizations can fall behind competitors in terms of the levels of skill, knowledge, and motivation of the work force if they are not seeking out the best qualified applicants for vacant jobs. An organization needs a steady stream of new employees to replace those that retire or leave for other reasons.

Realistic Job Previews.   Organizations should always provide applicants with realistic job previews (RJPs). By providing applicants with an objective description of the job and its requirements, they will have more realistic expectations and can subsequently choose to self-select out of the process. Research suggests that using RJPs reduces employee turnover and produces employees who can better cope with the jobs.[8]

Selection

Once there is a pool of applicants available for a job, the next step is to decide which one to hire. The **selection process** is *a series of steps from initial screening of applicants to finally hiring the new employee.* The goal of the selection process is to choose the applicant which best fits the job specifications and the culture of the organization. There is no way to know for sure which applicant will ultimately perform best. However, there are a number of predictors that managers can use throughout the selection process to help them gain an understanding of which person is most likely to succeed.

When designing a selection process, managers need to keep in mind the legal issues associated with their process. For example, in Connecticut vs. Teal (1982), the Supreme Court ruled that the "job relatedness" argument must be applied to all steps of a multiple hurdle selection procedure. At each point in the process where a decision is made to keep/drop an applicant, the manager must make sure that the criteria used are job related.

Initial Screening.   Application forms or resumes are generally the starting point for managers seeking information about job applicants. Companies like Procter & Gamble receive thousands of applications and resumes each year. Managers must weed through all the paper and identify those applicants who are potentially qualified for the available jobs. This step is often performed by employees in the HR department, based on their understanding of the job requirements. In this first step of the selection process, the company screens out those who are not qualified. For example, *initial screening* eliminates from consideration those people who lack the experience, educational background, or requisite KSAOCs that are listed in the job specifications.

Initial screening usually does not rank the candidates who are chosen for further consideration. It simply reduces the pool of applicants to a smaller set of individuals. Then the manager can concentrate on this smaller set of individuals and devote more time and resources to assessing their capabilities through more extensive evaluations.

Selection process A series of steps from initial screening of applicants to finally hiring the new employee.

Interviews.   One of the most frequently used steps in the selection process is the interview. The job applicant meets with a person or group of people from the company to discuss job-relevant issues that will help the company make selection decisions. Job interviews may be held off site, away from the company, or on site. Off-site interviews are often used for initial screening purposes, such as when recruiters visit college campuses to interview applicants. However, interviews are mostly used to further assess the job candidates at later stages of the selection process. This is because interviews are time-consuming and expensive, especially if the interviewee is from out of town. Thus, companies only go to this stage after screening out all but the most qualified candidates.

To ensure compliance with legal concerns and to maximize the benefits of interviews, the manager should focus on those motivational and interpersonal skill dimensions (e.g., oral communication, sensitivity, etc.) that are necessary for successful performance (based on job analysis results). They should avoid discussion of traits that can be measured by more valid selection tools, such as intelligence, aptitudes, and specific job skills.[9] Most importantly, the interview affords managers an opportunity to assess personally the candidate's "fit" with the organization's needs. One way they do this is by comparing the candidate's values, beliefs, and attitudes with those of the organizational culture. These values may include, for example, receptivity to learning and team orientation. Interviewers must be careful, though, not to ask illegal questions. For example, it is illegal to ask about a candidate's history of medical problems. It is also illegal to ask if the candidate has ever been arrested for a crime, although it is all right to ask if a person has ever been convicted of a crime if he or she may be required to handle money or other valuables. Some people may go through several rounds of interviews with a number of different people before finally being hired (or rejected).

In addition to assessing the job candidate, interviews are also an opportunity for the manager to sell the candidate on the company. After all, highly qualified candidates may be shopping around and looking for the best organization to work for. So, many job interviews are indeed a two-way street, with both the job candidate and the manager selling to and evaluating the other party.

Testing.   One of the mainstays of the selection process is testing to objectively and accurately measure job-relevant characteristics of candidates. Many tests are available to managers for assessing different human characteristics. These include cognitive abilities, personality tests, and performance tests.

Cognitive ability tests are broadly used to evaluate people for all types of jobs. These are typically paper-and-pencil tests intended to assess how well candidates learn and apply knowledge. They also measure a candidate's problem-solving ability. Jobs vary in the type of thinking that is required. Accordingly, there are different tests to measure cognitive ability in various areas such as clerical, mechanical, sensory, and general mental capabilities.

These tests have been around for decades. In fact, intelligence testing, as many people refer to it, was initiated by the military early in this century as a means of identifying people with potential to be leaders and officers. In industry, the Wonderlic Personnel Test is often used as a means of assessing general mental abilities. Wonderlic tests people on mathematics, vocabulary, spatial relations, perceptual speed, and analogies. Other examples include the Watson Glaser Critical Thinking Appraisal and the Employee Aptitude Survey.

Such cognitive abilities tests should be used carefully, however, because they can have adverse impact on minorities. **Adverse impact** means *that the test or other employment hurdle eliminates a greater percentage of minorities than should be expected*. If the test is not valid, that is, not related to the content of the job or not related to some important criterion that measures success on the job, it could be illegal to use it. The 1971 Supreme Court decision *Griggs vs. Duke Power Company* ruled that the Wonderlic Personnel Test was unconstitutional because Duke Power was unable to show that the test was related to the job. Use of the test was excluding minorities from equal opportunity to jobs for which they may have been qualified.

Adverse impact The judgment that a test or other employment hurdle eliminates a greater percentage of minorities than should be expected.

Personality tests like the California Personality Inventory (CPI) offer a standardized approach to evaluating individual personalities. The CPI has 480 items that require answers of "true" or "false." These tests are often used just to identify people who may be mentally ill or inclined to have emotional problems and thus cause problems on the job.

Personality tests are not intended only to measure whether a person is likeable or sociable, which is a common meaning for the term personality. They evaluate other dimensions of personality. For example, the CPI assesses dominance, sociability, social presence, self-acceptance, responsibility, socialization, self-control, tolerance, achievement via conformance, achievement via independence, intellectual efficiency, and flexibility.

Although paper and pencil tests have many advantages, for example they are easy to administer, are cost effective, and are valid, they also have some disadvantages. For instance, many candidates are resistant to such tests since they do not see any relationship between the test taken and job requirements. It is important, therefore, to make sure that such tests have a demonstrable connection to assessing the candidate's job abilities. Situational tests, which involve a sample of actual job behavior, are usually perceived as more relevant and valid for all concerned.

Performance tests or work samples are often used to test physical abilities. For example, Levi Strauss uses a performance test to select maintenance and repair people who will keep the sewing machines in working order. One of the performance tests is quite simple. The test administrator gives job candidates a sewing machine subassembly and asks them to disassemble it into its component parts and then reassemble it. The amount of time taken to perform this task is used as a measure of the person's aptitude for the job.

No one test is perfect as a selection device. Errors in measurement may occur, for example when a person has an "off" day in an interview. And even when the measurement is highly accurate, the characteristic that is measured may not be perfectly related to job performance. For example, a sales job requires some verbal ability. However, a masters degree in English and perfect command of the language may not be required. Other factors like persistence, empathy, and determination may be more important in predicting the success of a salesperson.

To overcome the deficiencies of any one test, managers typically use a battery of tests, each of which is related to the job in some way. For example, organizations such as the Tennessee Valley Authority and Alliant Health Care Systems use a battery of tools including assessment centers, Watson Glaser Critical Thinking Appraisal, the CPI, and others. In selecting managers, companies often use an assessment center to evaluate candidates.

An *assessment center* may engage the job candidate in one to three full days of various tests, simulations, role plays, and interviews. The assessment center is

A LOOK AT

THE GLOBAL
ENVIRONMENT

SELECTION AND HIRING AT TOYOTA MOTOR MANUFACTURING, U.S.A., INC.

Toyota Motor Company of Japan (TMC) has established a reputation for building high-quality, low-cost, and highly reliable automobiles. In the 1980s, TMC decided to prove that its renowned Toyota Production System could produce the same results in America, with American workers. As a part of a global strategy to produce in every major market in which it sells, the Japanese automobile producer established a company, Toyota Motor Manufacturing, U.S.A., Inc. (TMM), in the heartland of America, Georgetown, Kentucky.

TMM has developed a selection and hiring process to build a team with the ability and commitment to achieve Toyota's goal to produce America's number one quality automobile. Since it was announced in 1985 that Toyota would build an automobile manufacturing plant, the Kentucky Department for Employment Services has recorded inquiries from over 200,000 people. Through the selection and hiring process shown in Exhibit 9-3, Toyota completed its first shift hiring in December 1988. Hiring for the second shift was completed in May 1989. Employment reached approximately 5000 people when the expansion facility began operation in late 1993. Annual payroll, as of November 1991, exceeded $150 million.

Toyota had objectives for the selection and hiring process beyond just building a team of people capable of realizing its market strategy. These objectives include the following:

- *Accuracy.* Selecting the most qualified candidates is top priority. Candidates are selected for their potential to perform, their desire and ability to learn, and their interpersonal skills.
- *Residential Commitment.* A preference is given to Kentucky residents.
- *Fairness.* Every candidate must have maximum and equal opportunities to demonstrate their skills to assure selection based on relevant criteria.
- *Efficiency.* The hiring process has to be efficient to effectively process the large number of applicants.
- *Applicant Convenience.* Applicants are processed through the 27 Kentucky Employment Services Offices located throughout the state.

Exhibit 9-3 on page 325 outlines how Toyota has sought to meet these objectives.

supposed to provide the company with a complete view of the person by evaluating his or her performance in a variety of situations. Diamond Star Motors used an assessment center to simulate an assembly plant setting that required close teamwork and continuous improvement methods. For years, companies like Kodak's Colorado Division has used diagnostic assessment centers for facilitating career planning and development activities.

When a company moves to a total quality approach to management, the assessment center can be especially helpful in identifying candidates who will fit in and add the most value to the organization. These assessments can focus on finding people who work well in groups and at problem solving and improvement. For example, Motorola uses video tapes of problem-solving groups in action and asks candidates how they would respond to various quality-related issues.[10] Indeed, the whole assessment process becomes more important in a

EXHIBIT 9-3 The Selection and Hiring Process at Toyota Motor Manufacturing, U.S.A., Inc.

Phase I Orientation/Application

Fill out an application and view a video of the Toyota work environment and selection system process (1 hour).

> Objective: To explain the job and collect information about work experiences and skills.
> Conducted: Kentucky Department of Employment Services.

Phase II Technical Skills Assessment

Pencil/Paper tests
• General knowledge test (2 hours)
• Tool & Die or general maintenance test (6 hours) (For skilled trades only).

> Objective: To assess technical knowledge and potential.
> Conducted: Kentucky Department of Employment Services.

Phase III Interpersonal Skills Assessment

• Group and individual problem-solving activities (4 hours).
• Production assembly simulation (5 hours) (For production only).

> Objective: To assess interpersonal and decision-making skills.
> Conducted: Toyota Motor Manufacturing, Georgetown, Kentucky.

Phase IV Toyota Assessment

Group interview and evaluation (1 hour).

> Objective: To discuss achievements and accomplishments.
> Conducted: Toyota Motor Manufacturing, Georgetown, Kentucky.

Phase V Health Assessment

Physical exam and drug/alcohol tests (2.5 hours).

> Objective: To determine physical fitness.
> Conducted: Scott County General Hospital and University of Kentucky Medical Center.

Phase VI On-The-Job Observation

Observation and coaching on the job after being hired (6 months).

> Objective: To assess job performance and develop skills.
> Conducted: Toyota Motor Manufacturing, Georgetown, Kentucky.

TQM-directed company as employees are considered the company's most important resources, and this allows the company to get a better idea of how someone may fit in and perform if hired.

Background Investigation.   After completing the foregoing steps in the selection process, and the pool of candidates is whittled down to a few, the organization may do a background investigation. The investigation can serve several purposes. It can help the manager gather more information on the candidate. For example, former superiors and colleagues can offer insights on what it is like to work with the candidate over extended periods of time. Background investigations can also confirm that candidates have truthfully reported their job histories.

Sometimes background investigations are quite simple, as when the manager checks the references listed on a resume. It may involve only a ten-minute phone conversation with the candidate's previous employer. However, the background investigation can be an extensive and costly venture, as when a defense contractor requires a security clearance.

Hiring.   The final step in the selection process is making the decision to hire a candidate. Often a group of managers will make this decision, including both line and staff people. There are many ways to make the hiring decision. They may pick the person who seems most qualified for the job. This person might be the one who scored the highest on the various measures used during the selection process. Alternatively, they may narrow the list to a few candidates who acceptably meet requirements on all of the selection measures and then make the final decision based on other criteria. For example, if they want to increase diversity in the organization, they may choose a minority candidate who meets requirements and should be able to perform satisfactorily.

Once the manager decides which candidate to hire, the company makes a formal job offer. At this point a negotiating process may ensue. If the candidate has other job options, he or she may be in a position to dicker over the level of salary and benefits. Little if any bargaining takes place for new hires such as college graduates. However, some new employees, particularly for managerial and professional jobs, are able to negotiate for signing bonuses or reimbursement for moving expenses. Until the company and the candidate agree on these terms of employment, the hiring process is not complete. (The company may also require a medical exam to make sure the candidate is physically and mentally fit for the job, although such requirements can be discriminatory if shown not to be relevant to performance.)

The hiring process is not over until the person actually starts working. Even then, the new employee may be placed on a probation period for 90 days to determine whether he or she will be kept permanently. Once on the job, the organization typically offers orientation and training programs to kick off the new employee's career with the company.

THINKING CRITICALLY

1. If you were a manager and had to fill a position, would you rather hire internally or externally? Why? What difference does it make?
2. Is the use of racial or gender hiring quotas a good practice?
3. From a TQM perspective, what do you think are some of the most important characteristics and skills a company should look for in a job candidate?

TRAINING AND DEVELOPMENT

Training A process for helping employees gain particular job skills and techniques that help them contribute to achieving the organization's strategy.

Once new employees enter an organization there is often (though not always) a training program for them. The term **training** refers *to helping employees gain particular job skills and techniques that help them contribute to achieving the organization's strategy.* Training is intended to improve a person's ability to perform various tasks involved with their particular jobs. Besides training, organizations also seek to develop employee skills and abilities on a long-term basis. The term **development** involves *on-going education to help prepare employees for future jobs*. It involves more than just learning a skill. Development focuses on skills such as problem analysis, creativity, team-building, and leadership.

Development On-going education to help prepare employees for future jobs.

Training helps the organization make sure that employees are properly prepared to execute the work for which they were hired. Development provides employees with the capabilities needed to adapt to future job demands. The learning that employees do within an organization usually begins with an orientation just after they have been hired.

Orientation

Orientation *introduces the new employee to the company's policies and culture*. Some companies, particularly those with less than 50 employees, may not conduct an extensive orientation for new employees. They may informally have the supervisor or co-workers provide the new employee with a tour of the facility to show them the parking, the cafeteria, the bathroom, and the work environment. On the tour, the new employee may get introduced to co-workers. However, new employees may be left to learn the ropes largely by themselves.

Orientation A process for introducing new employee to the company's policies and culture.

Orientations are more common in large companies. These programs usually will take up the first few days of employment. A formal orientation program allows the company to systematically introduce the new employee to the company and to the job. It does not leave the indoctrination to chance. The orientation program usually provides an overview of the company's policies, procedures, and safety guidelines. The orientation program may also be used to provide initial training on job responsibilities, requirements, and levels of performance expected. The orientation program also gives the company a chance to introduce new employees to its culture, values, beliefs, and norms of behavior. These programs facilitate employees' entry into the company, helping them adapt more quickly to the company's way of operating. They help both new employees and the company feel comfortable with each other faster. While orientation programs are more common in large companies, this is not to suggest that small companies would not benefit from formally orienting employees, as well. Any program that gets a new person up to speed quickly makes sense for an organization, regardless of size.

On-The-Job Training

Introduction to the company and to the job does not end with the formal orientation program. It often continues through on-the-job training. **On-the-job training** means that *new employees are given job instruction while they are actually performing the job, on the actual work site*. For example, Walt Disney World in Orlando, Florida uses on-the-job training as a part of their orientation program. After a couple of days in the formal orientation program, the new employee is assigned to a buddy who is an experienced employee. The buddy stays with the new employee for two days to two weeks, depending on the job. Buddies show new employees the job duties and give feedback on their performance while they are learning how to perform their jobs.

On-the-job training Job instruction given new employees while they are actually performing the job, on the actual work site.

Ongoing Training and Development

In a changing environment, with the organization continuing to introduce new strategies, new technologies, and new work processes, the employees must continue learning. They must acquire new skills, and they must continue to improve how they think about business. Companies often devote ample resources to developing managers for the future. They select promising candidates fresh out of college or MBA programs and place them on the fast track. The fast trackers get rotated through a number of positions to broadly expose them to the company's diverse operations. This job rotation is also accompanied by focused training and development courses to support their on-the-job learning.

Some companies rely on consultants and universities to deliver their training and development courses. Others use outsiders only to supplement their own internal capabilities. Xerox has a campus in Leesburg Virginia that it uses for a variety of training and development activities. These activities range from technical training for repair technicians to management development seminars for executives. Courses are taught there by Xerox experts and by external trainers. GE has its own highly regarded training facility, the General Electric Management Development Institute.

Training and development is important for accomplishing the mission and vision that leaders choose for an organization. For example, in the 1980s Westinghouse decided that it needed an entirely new model of management to be globally competitive. With leadership from its chairman, Westinghouse established a Productivity and Quality Center in the 1980s to develop and apply techniques and technology to help Westinghouse become more competitive in the global marketplace. As another example, to support its strategy for globalization, Procter and Gamble has developed a college which emphasizes language and intercultural skills for managers.

Training in TQM Companies. Companies that are adopting Total Quality Management often use training and education as a basis for stimulating change. They do more than just put a few standout employees on the fast track. They provide training and education for all of the work force. These companies realize that transforming the organization requires the involvement of all of the human resources.

In fact, training is a central part of the culture of companies that actively put TQM into practice. The initial implementation of TQM requires training in new skills, such as teamwork and statistical process control. Then, because TQM recognizes the importance of continuous improvement to remain competitive, this means committing to continuously upgrading employee skills through training. This subject matter of this training might include relevant job skills, human relations skills, writing skills, management skills, financial skills, computer skills, and so on. In companies such as IBM, Motorola, Westinghouse, and thousands of others, top management understands that training is not a cost but an investment central to the organization's long-term survival.

THINKING CRITICALLY

1. Reflect on your own experience in a particular job. Did you have formal training or were you expected to learn informally for other employees? Which form of training do you think is preferable? Why?

2. Think of yourself as an employee in an organization that does not have ongoing training. Develop an argument to convince your boss to support such training.

PERFORMANCE APPRAISAL

Many organizations use **performance appraisal** as *a way to evaluate how well employees have met expected levels of accomplishment compared to some standards or goals.* The evaluation is usually conducted by a superior, although peers and even subordinates may be involved. It is typically recorded on a special form that breaks performance into a variety of categories and is then discussed with the employee. The appraisal becomes a part of the employee's permanent record and often influences human resources decisions on such issues as pay, promotion, and training and development. When performance appraisal is used in such decisions, the manager must be careful to document the appraisal and be sure that the appraisal system meets legal requirements for being job related. The best way to do that is to base the appraisal on a job analysis.

Performance appraisal A way to evaluate how well employees have met expected levels of accomplishment compared to some standards or goals.

Methods of Appraisal

Appraisals are typically conducted every six months or once a year to review and summarize the individual's performance for that period. There are a variety of methods available for managers to use in the appraisal process, depending upon the standards and criteria selected to evaluate the employee's performance. The appraisal may focus on outcome measures, such as levels of quality, productivity, or financial performance. Objective measures of these outcomes are typically available in company records, such as those held in the quality control or the accounting departments. For outcome measures, the appraisal may simply involve comparing the actual outcomes with goals or objectives for the employee, accompanied with an explanation for deviations.

The appraisal may also focus on behavioral measures. Evaluating behavioral performance is somewhat more subjective, requiring more judgment, than the comparison of outcome measures to goals and objectives. Various formats for recording a performance appraisal might be used. Some companies have the evaluator simply write a paragraph or two to describe the employee's performance. This approach does not direct the evaluator to consider specific dimensions of performance, as do checklists and graphic rating scales.

A checklist is a simple method that allows the evaluator to check the behaviors or accomplishments that were displayed during the evaluation period. A graphic rating scale, such as the ones shown in Exhibit 9-4 on page 330, allows the evaluator to rate the employee on various dimensions of performance, such as quality, meeting deadlines, teamwork, communication with superiors, and technical skills. In addition to ratings on various dimensions of performance, an overall rating may also be done to summarize the evaluator's overall judgment of the employee's performance.

One problem with graphic rating scales is that they require subjective judgments by the evaluator about what is good and what is bad performance. To make evaluation a less difficult task, some companies use *Behaviorally Anchored*

EXHIBIT 9-4 Examples of Graphic Rating Scales

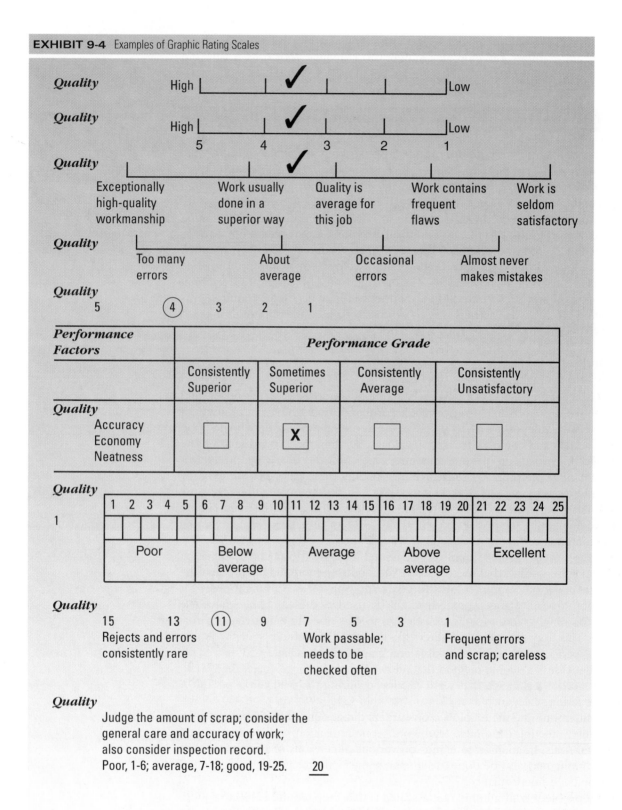

Source: R.M. Guion. *Personnel Testing.* New York: McGraw-Hill, 1984, p. 98. Reprinted with permission.

Rating Scales (BARS) that provide behavioral descriptions along the scale. BARS provide the evaluator and the employee with a better understanding of what the rating scale actually means. Exhibit 9-5 on page 332 shows a BARS scale.

Purpose of Appraisal

Traditional performance appraisal is primarily used as a control mechanism focused on individual behavior or accomplishments. It provides a superior the opportunity to give a subordinate feedback on his or her performance, to recognize and reward good performance, and to propose corrective action for bad performance. The recognition of good performance may be as simple as praise and a handshake. Some managers refer to this as an "ATTABOY," or "ATTAGIRL." The recognition may even be monetary, such as a bonus equal to 30 percent of the employee's salary. The corrective action may be to refer the employee for more training if the cause of the bad performance seems to be lack of skills. It might be as severe as dismissal from work for a few days without pay if the cause of the problem seems to be the willful neglect or rebellious attitude of the worker.

Depending on the nature of the performance consequences (recognition, reward, punishment, or corrective action) that a company typically uses, the performance appraisal has the potential to be a very emotionally charged event. Whatever the recognition or corrective action might be, the performance appraisal used as a control mechanism is supposed to provide the employee motivation and direction for doing a good job. Unfortunately this is not always the case.

Problems with Performance Appraisal

There are obvious problems with the validity (or objectivity) of the measures recorded during performance appraisals. Objective measures like productivity and quality may reflect a team's performance more than that of an individual. The records may be inaccurate or misleading. Subjective measures requiring judgmental ratings are also problematic. If done from memory at the end of six months, the evaluator may introduce bias into the measurements. The evaluator may only remember recent events, or recall only one or two critical incidents that stick out in memory, and forget all the other days of performance. Additionally, a superior is rarely able to observe all of the behaviors of the employee, so there are inevitably errors of measurement introduced in the appraisal process. For these reasons, many companies try to use a combination of methods and many sources of information to overcome the weaknesses of each one alone. For example, peers and subordinates may provide ratings as additional sources of information.

Even when the measurement system is relatively good, poorly administered performance appraisals can undermine an employee's motivational purpose. For example, an office worker in a division of Provident Insurance Company was demoralized and angered by her performance appraisal. She was a diligent and capable worker. Her superior gave her "Excellent" scores on all specific dimensions of the graphic rating scale used to document the performance appraisal. However, her overall rating was "Average." When she asked why she received an "Average" overall rating, the superior explained that the performance appraisal

EXHIBIT 9-5   A Behaviorally Anchored Rating Scale for College Professors

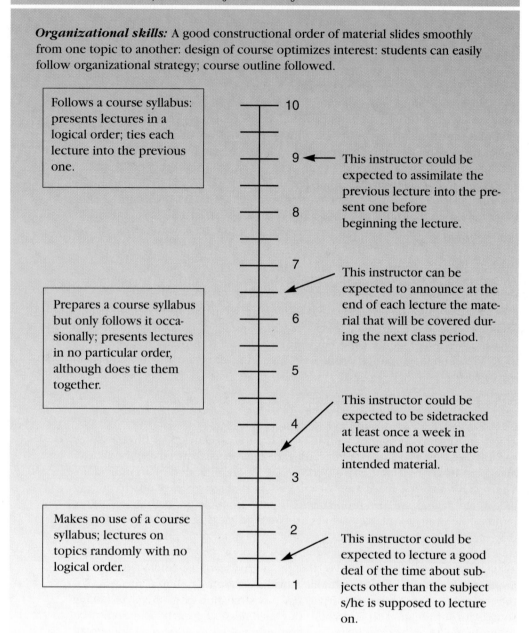

Organizational skills: A good constructional order of material slides smoothly from one topic to another: design of course optimizes interest: students can easily follow organizational strategy; course outline followed.

Follows a course syllabus: presents lectures in a logical order; ties each lecture into the previous one.

— 10

9 ← This instructor could be expected to assimilate the previous lecture into the present one before beginning the lecture.

8

7   This instructor can be expected to announce at the end of each lecture the material that will be covered during the next class period.

Prepares a course syllabus but only follows it occasionally; presents lectures in no particular order, although does tie them together.

6

5

This instructor could be expected to be sidetracked at least once a week in lecture and not cover the intended material.

4

3

Makes no use of a course syllabus; lectures on topics randomly with no logical order.

2   This instructor could be expected to lecture a good deal of the time about subjects other than the subject s/he is supposed to lecture on.

1

Source: Bernardin (1977a). Bernardin, H.J. Behavioral expectation scales versus summated scales: A fairer comparison. Journal of Applied Psych., 1977, 62, 422–427.

was tied to merit pay raises. Overall ratings above "Average" would earn the worker corresponding pay increases. Since the budget was tight this year, the department could not afford to give her a raise. So, the superior had to give her an "Average" rating.

Another problem with the formal performance appraisal is that it is really not an adequate tool for providing feedback. Subordinates need feedback more frequently than just once or twice a year. In fact, managers who are seeking to improve the systems and processes of the organization should be in frequent contact with the people working within the system. In this total quality context, performance feedback should be ongoing, not just to individuals, but to the team as a whole.

Further, performance appraisals tend to focus on the individual and ignore other factors in the system. This leads the superior to look at the individual for the causes of poor performance. As discussed in earlier chapters, from a systems perspective, the causes of poor performance are spread throughout the processes of the organization. This situation produces two types of negative consequences. First, these processes are the responsibility of managers, not employees working within the system. If managers are focused on blaming workers for their personal inadequacies, they may not attend to the other factors that cause poor performance, including the machines, materials, work methods, measurements, and other inputs and impediments provided by employees and processes in other areas.

Second, when employees feel blamed for poor performance and they could not really control the causes of the performance, the trust and respect between the superior and subordinates is undermined. Resentment and apathy can result from the feelings of helplessness. The performance appraisal process can create divisiveness and destroy the personal relationships that are the basis of teamwork within the company. Playing the role of a judge in evaluating a subordinate's performance may interfere with the superior's ability to be a counselor and coach. This is a difficult challenge for superiors conducting appraisals.[11]

Some companies are deciding that traditional performance appraisals do more harm than good. They are doing away with the evaluative component and emphasizing the role of the superior in counseling and coaching the individual for improvement. The companies that are doing this are typically the ones who are practicing Total Quality Management and taking responsibility for developing human resources as a critical input to the systems and processes of the organization. They are continuously improving the human resources of the organization, and not just trying to control them to meet predetermined standards. For example, managers at Cadillac have decided that traditional performance appraisals do not fit their future strategy and culture.

Total Quality Management Alternatives to Performance Appraisal

While most organizations are unwilling to completely abandon individual performance appraisals, flawed though they are, managers can make changes that make them more useful. Rather than focusing on various specific goals, which can invite manipulation of the system for individual gain, appraisals can focus on improvement of skills that will help the employee add more value to the organization. Further, peers can become involved in the process with the goal of evaluating and improving team cooperation.[12]

A useful way to think about performance appraisals from a TQM perspective is as being the Check step of the PDCA improvement cycle. It is the step that allows individuals, their teammates, and managers to look at how well they are working together and how they might improve in their individual and mutual areas of responsibility to improve the organization's processes.

Managers seeking to implement Total Quality Management need to move away as much as possible from a focus on individuals when developing a performance appraisal procedure. There are no objective schemes for doing this, but Exhibit 9-6 contrasts areas managers should emphasize in an effective performance appraisal program with those of a more traditional program. The point here is that those programs that reward or punish individuals are less likely to succeed in facilitating improved performance of the entire organization. They may in fact undermine that performance over the long run as individuals seek to look out for themselves rather than their team and the organization as a whole.

❓ THINKING CRITICALLY

1. If you were an employee, on what criteria would you like your manager to appraise your performance? Do you think these criteria would allow for an objective appraisal?
2. If you were a manager, do you think you could be objective in appraising your employees' performance? Why or why not? What are the implications of your answer for judging the validity of performance appraisals?
3. Do you think the TQM argument against performance appraisals is valid? Why or why not?

COMPENSATION, REWARDS, AND RECOGNITION

No one offers their services to an organization for free. Compensation, rewards, and recognition have to do with understanding how the organization values the contribution of employees with specialized skills who help the organization achieve its mission and purpose in the marketplace. Compensation provides employees with the funds they need to purchase from other specialists all the goods and services they need to support their lifestyle. Rewards and recognition go beyond compensation to indicate the special value the organization places on specific behaviors.

EXHIBIT 9-6 TQM and Traditional Performance Appraisal

The left column represents values and methods consistent with Total Quality Management. The right column represents values and methods consistent with traditional management practice. The TQM values and methods are more likely to facilitate the long-term success of the organization.

TQM Values and Methods in PA	Traditional Values and Methods in PA
• Give direction to the work force	• Direct individuals
• Control processes	• Control people
• Feedback based on needs of customers and key indicators of process success	• Feedback based on personal characteristics not relevant to the work
• Feedback from parts of the system that receive one's work	• Feed-down from the next layer in the heirarchy
• Feedback useful for improvement	• Feedback used for ratings, rewards, and sanctions
• Supprt employees' inherent motivation	• Motivating or de-motivating employees

Source: Adapted from Peter R. Scholtes, "Total Quality Management or Performance Appraisal: Choose One, "*National Productivity Review*, Summer 1993, Vol. 12, No. 3, p. 354.

TRANSFORMING PERFORMANCE APPRAISAL AT CADILLAC[13]

The Cadillac division of General Motors is a recipient of the Malcolm Baldrige National Quality Award. In moving to a total quality approach to managing this division, Cadillac executives have put a heavy emphasis on cross-functional teamwork. This has helped them in the development of new products, especially the adoption of simultaneous engineering. This is a process of involving all functional groups right from the start in designing new products. In this way everyone, from the design team to engineering to materials management to assembly to marketing, can contribute to the process. This minimizes rework and helps everyone anticipate potential problems and eliminate them before they occur.

This has brought about a profound culture change at the company. People throughout Cadillac are engaged in teamwork more than ever before. In this new culture, Cadillac has discovered that its traditional performance appraisal undermined the teamwork that was becoming so important to its culture. The old appraisal system involved a ranking system to evaluate employee performance. These appraisals were always conducted by an employee's functional superior. For example, a design manager evaluated the performance of designers, and a materials management manager judged employees involved in this area.

This approach created a conflict with the goals of cross-functional teamwork and simultaneous engineering. People reasoned "If my superior is ranking my performance, then my first allegiance is to the functionally focused goals established by that superior, not the goal of cross-functional teamwork or simultaneous engineering." To eliminate this conflict, Cadillac replaced the traditional performance appraisal with what they call the "Personal Development Process," which emphasizes gathering feedback from superiors and peers on perceived training needs. Correspondingly, employee compensation is now based on job knowledge and personal development rather than traditional performance appraisals.

When the performance appraisal was changed to emphasize the development of human resources, the tone of the relationship between the superiors and subordinates at Cadillac became more positive. The two people were able to focus on identifying opportunities for improvement rather than casting blame and bickering over the ratings. Their relationship became more collaborative and allowed both parties to work together to make improvements. The change in the appraisal system also shifted the superior and subordinates away from an adversarial relationship and provided a basis for the teamwork that is needed to accomplish continuous improvement. In this context, the actions of people at Cadillac can be proactively focused on the needs of the future and not focused on assigning blame and evaluating the events of the past.

TQM IN ACTION

Cadillac: Baldrige Award Winner

Compensation

Compensation *is a payment from the organization to employees for their services.* Basic compensation is made up of wages, salary, benefits, and perquisites.

Wages and Salary. *For employees paid on a hourly basis or on the amount of measurable work performed, monetary compensation comes in the form of* **wages.** For example, employees on an assembly line may earn from eight to 15 dollars per hour. Or members of a farm crew may earn 50 cents per bushel for harvesting produce. For professional and managerial workers, monetary

Compensation A payment from the organization to employees for their services.

Wages Payment made to employees for their services; computed on an hourly basis or on the amount of measurable work performed.

Salary An annual amount of money paid to for the services of an employee that does not depend upon hours worked or productivity.

Benefits Compensation consisting of different types of personal and family insurance and other additional services paid for by the employer.

compensation most often comes in the form of **salary,** *an annual amount of money paid for employee services that does not depend upon hours worked or productivity.*

Benefits.   In addition to monetary pay, compensation often includes a package of various **benefits** *consisting of different types of personal and family insurance and other additional services paid for by the employer.* Legally required benefits include workers compensation to cover job related injuries, social security for retirement, and unemployment compensation for when employees are laid off or terminated. As basic compensation the company may also offer additional benefits such as medical insurance, life insurance, paid vacation time, pension funds, and day care. These benefits are not required by law, but increasingly competitive labor markets are leading employees to expect such benefits. These benefits are often standardized for certain levels or grades of employees. For example, wage earners may not get paid vacation time, but they get all other benefits the same as the salaried people.

Each company varies in how it structures benefits for its employees. Some companies allow their employees to structure their own benefits through a *cafeteria plan of flexible benefits.* In this plan, the organization puts together a set of benefits that employees can choose from, depending on their individual needs. These plans include different types of medical and dental insurance, life insurance, and disability insurance. For example, a dual-career couple, with each spouse working for a different company, does not need two different medical insurance policies covering the family. Through a cafeteria system, one of the spouses may choose to give up medical coverage for additional life insurance. While benefitting the employee, the cafeteria system can be cost efficient for the company by only providing what the employee really needs and wants.

Perquisites (or "perks") A variety of extra company-paid-for goods and services that go beyond standard compensation and benefits.

Perquisites.   In addition to benefits, many companies offer **perquisites** (or "perks") to its managers and professionals. These include *a variety of extra company-paid-for goods and services that go beyond standard compensation and benefits.* Executives may receive country club or health club memberships, a company car, special parking privileges in the staff parking lot, first-class air travel, and executive dining room privileges as well as generous expense accounts.

Some companies, though, avoid making distinctions among the work force with benefits and perks. They have come to see that when promoting a team atmosphere and cooperation, special perks create stratification, separation, and resentment among employees. It thus makes sense to strive for a more egalitarian atmosphere. Nucor Corporation, a successful steel company that has implemented TQM, for example, has sought to eliminate all special forms of compensation between management and other employees. Some of the specific ways the company has done this include the adoption of the following policies:

- Everyone has the same group insurance.
- Everyone has the same holidays.
- Everyone is entitled to the same amount of vacation time.
- Everyone wears the same color hard hat in the plant.
- There are no reserved parking places.
- There are no company cars.

- There is no executive dining room.
- There is no company airplane or boats.
- There is no company hunting lodge.
- Everyone travels economy class.

This approach not only helps to hold down costs for Nucor, it also establishes a culture of teamwork and commitment to the company. It avoids using perks as status symbols, an approach that can create divisiveness within a company. Nucor also offers an unusual benefit. For every child of every employee in the company, the company pays $2,000 per year for four years of college or four years of vocational training past high school.

Equity of Compensation.   One of the biggest concerns for managers administering compensation systems is ensuring that the levels of compensation are equitable, or perceived to be fair. To ensure perceptions of fairness, managers must make internal and external comparisons. Through a structured approach to job evaluation they must compare jobs within the company. Through market studies, they must compare the compensation levels of the company's employees with that of comparable jobs in other companies. Pay grades or levels are established based on these studies. To ensure fairness across time, companies may also offer cost-of-living increases adjusted to account for inflation. Many professional organizations, such as the American Society for Training and Development, regularly prepare and publish salary studies for practitioners in their area. Consulting companies also collect and sell such information for use in determining salary levels as well.

Rewards

Beyond standard compensation and benefits, many organizations also make additional payments of money or premiums (such as trips or various products) to reward employees for their contributions to the company's performance. There may also be special forms of recognition for the same purpose.

Contingent Pay and Incentives.   To reward and direct employees to behave in certain ways or accomplish specific outcomes, companies often use contingent pay and other incentives. This additional pay comes in the form of bonuses, lump sum payments at the end of a quarter or end of a fiscal year. The bonus may be contingent upon meeting a personal or unit goal for something like productivity, efficiency, quality improvement, cost reduction, sales volume, or profitability. Bonuses can be quite large for higher-level managers. Sometimes they are as high as 50 to 100 percent of a manager's base salary, and for top managers, they can be two or three times or more as much as their base pay.

A problem with contingent pay or bonuses and the use of premiums is that they are often aimed at rewarding the achievement of specific goals by an individual, such as a sales increase or higher productivity. This encourages doing anything possible to reach such goals within a certain time frame, such as manipulating sales numbers by making special deals. While these actions may make an employee look good, they may not contribute to the overall performance of an entire team or the efficient operation of cross-functional processes or be in the best interest of the entire company.

As an alternative to rewards that focus on short-term performance, an organization may use incentives such as stock options to encourage employees to think about the long-term performance of the company. A stock option is an opportunity to buy company stock at a reduced price at some point in the future. If the company performs well, the stock will go up, and the employee can make money on the purchase of the stock. Profit sharing is another incentive that companies use to make sure employees do what is good for the whole company and not just for themselves. In profit sharing, a certain percentage of the profit is shared with the employees, perhaps as a function of employee wage or salary level.

Recognition and Appreciation

In addition to formal compensation and contingent payments, companies can use other means to reward people. Recognition and appreciation can be given through informal means, such as a genuine expression of "Thanks for a job well done." For example, employees of the month might be recognized by displaying their pictures on the wall. Material tokens of appreciation may also be given. For example, a manager at Xerox Corporation explains how he uses these:

One of the fellows from the warehouse did some work for us and I gave him a dinner certificate for two, not very much, $25, and said sincerely "Thanks a lot. We really appreciate your help." That guy would kill for me now, because no one ever did that for him before. Another time we gave pizza for the whole group. Sometimes it's just a pat on the back. Sometimes I don't go directly to the person to say thank you. It's a lot nicer when I go to the boss or write to the boss, and the boss passes it along. Or I may thank the guy in front of the boss. People like to be told that they did a good job, if you tell them sincerely. If you just pass these things out, it loses its significance.[14]

Companies often hold formal ceremonies to recognize and appreciate the special contributions of their employees. A retirement ceremony is often used to recognize the long-term service of an outgoing employee. Other types of ceremonies include sharing sessions wherein teams of employees share with others the results of their continuous improvement activities. With top management represented in the audience, these sharing sessions can be not only a source of information and learning but also personally rewarding for the team members who get a chance to tell about their efforts and their successes. Sometimes it gives them a chance to reveal their problems as well and get the support of top management to help solve them.

Motorola holds a world-wide competition called the Total Customer Satisfaction Team Competition. Thousands of teams participate each year. The contestants share what they have done in the previous year to improve quality. For example, some of the team accomplishments included:

Motorola: Total Customer Satisfaction Team Competition Overview

- removed bottleneck in testing pagers
- designed and delivered a new chip for Apple Computer in six months
- eliminated component alignment defects in pagers
- developed quality system for design of Iridium satellites
- cut training program from 5 years to 2 with better results
- cut production time and defect rate on new battery part
- cut response time on tooling orders from 23 to four days

- improved efficiency of boiler operations
- cut product development time in half to win IBM contract
- eliminated resin seepage in semiconductor assembly

Such changes save over $2 billion for Motorola each year. Finalists in the competition compete for trophies that are presented by Motorola executives at corporate headquarters in Schaumburg, Illinois.[15]

Promotion and Transfer

A **promotion** is *a move upward in the hierarchy of command within the organization.* The move typically involves an increase in pay, responsibility, and authority. The promoted individual may have to manage a bigger budget, a larger staff, or a more important activity. A **transfer** is *a lateral movement to a different organizational job with about the same level of pay, responsibility, and authority.* Promotions and transfers are one way managers fill vacant positions in an organization. However, for the individual receiving the promotion or transfer, it can be a reward and recognition for outstanding performance. The transfer offers the individual diversity, job challenge, and an opportunity to broaden their base of experience. In the long term, this can lead to promotions and more responsibility. The promotion offers both better compensation and more job challenge.

Some companies explicitly use promotions and transfers as a way to reward excellent performance in a company. Some companies base promotions on seniority, particularly for wage earners. Emphasizing seniority rewards people for being stable, long-term performers, not necessarily excellent performers. Other companies do not use promotions and transfers as rewards at all. They simply look for the person that best fits the vacant position. Excellent performers in one job may not be considered excellent candidates in another job. For example, the top salesperson may not make the best sales team manager. So, managers must be careful not to use promotions and transfers simply for the purpose of reward. They must also consider the impact on the company.

Promotion A move upward in the hierarchy of command within the organization.

Transfer A lateral movement to a different organizational job with about the same level of pay, responsibility, and authority.

Team Versus Individual Rewards

One important issue in rewarding performance is whether to reward individuals or teams of people. A company implementing Total Quality Management may find that team rewards are more appropriate than individual rewards. Managers must know that they usually get the behavior and the outcomes that they reward. If they reward individuals for personal accomplishments, they will typically get these at the expense of team accomplishments. Individual rewards based on personally defined goals and objectives can interfere with teamwork because individuals become more concerned with their own performance than with that of the team as a whole. Consider an analogy: individualized rewards lead individuals to be concerned about how big a slice of the pie they will get. Team rewards lead individuals to be concerned with how to make the pie bigger for everyone.

This principle applies not only to individuals but also to units within the company. For example, one manufacturer decided to introduce some "healthy competition" between shifts by establishing a contest to see which shift could outproduce the other. Neither of the two shift foremen would shut the equipment down for preventive maintenance. Ultimately, the plant had to be closed for costly repairs that could have been avoided.[16]

TQM IN ACTION

PAYING FOR QUALITY[17]

Mark Graham Brown is a consultant in TQM and a Baldrige Award examiner. He has reflected on the relationship of compensation and the practice of Total Quality Management. He has sought to find answers to how organizations can use pay to improve productivity, cooperation, quality, and customer satisfaction. Here are some of his ideas:

Gainsharing. This is an approach that emphasizes higher levels of performance across organizational processes through the involvement and participation of employees. As performance improves, employees share financially in the gain. To make gainsharing work, Brown recommends that:

1. Design the plan with employee input—otherwise they won't feel ownership and commitment to it.
2. Make sure the size and frequency of payments are often enough and large enough to make a difference to employees. Otherwise, they will lose interest.
3. Tie payments to individual and team performance. This allows the company to recognize the extraordinary efforts of individuals as well as the effort of the entire team.
4. Make sure the performance measures are those that employees can influence or control. If employees, by their efforts, cannot control performance improvements, then the plan will not motivate improvements.

Skill-Based Pay. Another plan often touted is tying pay increases and bonuses to the number of job-related skills an employee has mastered. In using this type of plan to encourage skill acquisition, it is important that employees can use the skills promoted to bring about measurable gains in productivity, customer satisfaction, and the achievement of organizational goals. Otherwise, though it is desirable for all employees to improve their skills, it is problematic to pay employees for gaining skills that may or may not allow them to add more value to the organization.

Pay Based on Customer Satisfaction. This is the plan Brown favors the most. He cites companies like FedEx that tie quarterly employee bonuses to how much their personal work and the work of their team contributes to customer satisfaction, as measured by the company. Executive bonuses are based on financial performance, but actual payment depends on how well their leadership is rated by their employees and by levels of customer satisfaction they have influence over. Brown believes that a large portion of compensation, 25 percent or more, should be "at risk" and payable upon measurable improvements in quality and customer satisfaction. This means that base pay is put at a just-acceptable level but with high incentive pay tied to quality issues.

Such programs as mentioned here all have the goal of encouraging individuals and teams to figure out what is necessary to maximize their added value to the organization, work together to achieve this, and then tie it all to the organization's purpose of serving customers.

RESULTS AT SCITOR

Roger Meade's human resources investments seem to be paying off. The company has had 13 years of profitable growth. However, Meade sees this success not as the result of setting some numerical goals and working hard to achieve them. Rather he refuses to set goals for growth or profitability. He explains, "Profits and growth are a byproduct of doing the job right and focusing on customer satisfaction. Satisfy the customers and make them successful, and *we'll* be successful."

Meade believes that the way to do this is to make life on the job as agreeable and easy to handle as possible. He wants to create an environment where his employees are not distracted from this goal of customer satisfaction. Not only has his approach brought about continued success in the marketplace, it has also held down turnover to 2.1 percent in an area where average turnover in software engineers is 16.5 percent. This means that Scitor does not have to spend lots of money recruiting and training new employees. Instead, it can invest this money in enhancing the skills of its already highly experienced work force.

The bottom line: The Scitor investment in its employees is yielding big dividends. It is an approach that takes a strong leader who is willing to buck the conventional wisdom and bet on his employees. But it is also a dramatic example of what happens when a such a leader makes that bet and wins. If Scitor did not offer products and services that its customers valued, it would not matter how well or poorly Meade treated employees. However, when a company does have a strong offering for customers, a Scitor-style human resources approach helps them build on that in ways that will continuously enhance the company's success, year after year.

Perhaps a more significant issue is whether superiors are even able to separately assess an individual's contribution to the performance of a system. The work outcomes of a group of individuals within a system are highly interdependent. Poor performance may result from factors outside the control of any one employee, despite the level of skill, education, enthusiasm, and effort that person exhibits. If individuals are rewarded or punished for events outside their control, their morale will certainly be diminished. To avoid these problems, many companies are basing rewards on team performance and not individual performance. The *A Look at TQM in Action* box on page 340, *Paying for Quality,* describes some suggestions for tying compensation programs to quality principles.

❓ THINKING CRITICALLY

1. If you were a top executive, would you want the perks that often go with the job, such as reserved parking, first-class air travel, and country club memberships? Why or why not?

2. Assume you are a manager of a company that has adopted TQM. Make an argument for paying special bonuses to individuals, even though they are members of a team. Make an argument for paying comparable bonuses to all team members and not giving special payments to any individuals. Which approach do you think is more equitable? Why?

SUMMARY

Human Resources Planning

- Sound human resources planning is aimed at aligning organizational strategy with skilled and knowledgeable employees who can execute that strategy.

- There are a variety of environmental factors that influence human resources planning, including globalization, competitiveness, technology, labor market trends, legal requirements, and technological advances.

- An important part of human resources planning involves figuring out how to make sure the supply of employees with various skills matches various organizational demands.

  —One way HR managers can do this is by undertaking job analyses to classify the tasks the organization needs done. From these analyses, HR managers provide line managers with the information they need to organize and train people to accomplish strategic goals.

- While it is important to classify jobs, TQM also reminds us of the importance of developing a flexible work force that can quickly respond to new challenges and opportunities.

Staffing the Organzation

- Staffing includes two involved steps: recruiting and selecting.

  —Recruitment consists of identifying and attracting qualified candidates for organizational jobs.

  —Selection involves screening, interviewing, testing, and hiring new employees

Training and Development

- The goal of training is to improve employees' ability to perform various tasks associated with their jobs.

- Development involves the on-going education of employees to help prepare them for future jobs in the organization.

Performance Appraisal

- Performance appraisals are formally instituted sessions where managers evaluate levels of employee accomplishment against some standard or expectation.

- Performance appraisals provide managers with an opportunity to recognize good performance and take corrective action for poor performance.

- There are several problems with performance appraisals that center around lack of objective standards and the idea that individual performance is really dependent on system performance.

- Total Quality Management suggests ways to alleviate some performance appraisal problems by focusing on issues involving teamwork, process improvement, and customer satisfaction.

Compensation, Rewards, and Recognition

- Compensation consists of wages and salaries paid to employees for their services as well as company-paid benefits and perquisites.

- Rewards include various bonuses for special performance.

- TQM suggests that compensation and bonuses should be tied to measurable improvements in quality and customer satisfaction.

KEY TERMS

Adverse impact 323

Benefits 336

Compensation 335

Development 327

External recruitment 320

Fast track 319

Human resources audit 313

Human resources planning 310

Human resources strategy 313

Internal recruitment 319

Job analysis 313

On-the-job training 327

Orientation 327

Performance appraisal 329

Perquisites (or "perks") 336

Promotion 339

Recruitment 319

Salary 336

Selection process 321

Staffing 319

Training 326

Transfer 339

Wages 335

REVIEW QUESTIONS

1. How does globalization affect human resources planning? How does diversity affect this planning?
2. What is the purpose of a human resources audit?
3. How does a job analysis contribute to understanding what human resources an organization needs?
4. What is the difference between a job description and a job specification?
5. What are the advantages of hiring from within? What are the disadvantages?
6. What are the advantages of hiring outside the company? What are the disadvantages?
7. What are the steps in the selection process and what is the importance of each?
8. What is the difference between training and development, and why is each important?
9. What is the difference between performance appraisal in a traditionally managed organization and in a TQM organization?
10. In a TQM organization, why are perquisites for senior managers not a good idea?

EXPERIENTIAL EXERCISE

Break into groups of 4 to 6 people and address the following issue: The traditional approach to management and quality control can be contrasted with a Total Quality Management approach that emphasizes processes, teams, and continuous improvement as follows:

Traditional Quality Control	Total Quality Management
Inspection oriented	Management oriented
Results oriented	Means oriented
Screens out defects	Builds in quality
Police	Coach
Minimally acceptable	On target
Just within specification	Reduced variation
Maintains current standards	Continuously challenges standards

Based on this contrast, develop a set of Human Resources Principles that would serve as the basis for an effective human resources strategy in support of Total Quality Management. Describe the implications for each stage of human resources recruiting and selection, training and development, appraisal, and compensation.

CASE ANALYSIS AND APPLICATION
XEL Communications Becomes Competitive[18]

XEL Communications is a telecommunications equipment company that supplies custom circuit boards to companies such as GTE. In the mid-1980s, Bill Sanko purchased the corporation from GTE. The company was making money, but it was still struggling. Sanko realized he had to do something to differentiate XEL from its competitors, Northern Telecom and AT&T. He determined XEL would have to focus on speedy response with close attention to cost. At the time, XEL took eight weeks to turn around an order. The management structure at XEL was characterized by a lengthy chain of command. Line workers reported to supervisors who reported to unit or departmental managers on up the ladder to Sanko.

Sanko began a transformation at XEL by first developing a new vision statement that positioned the company as far more responsive to its customers. Then he redesigned the production flows in the plant to create work cells and established self-managing teams throughout the plant. Colored banners hang from the ceiling to mark each team's work area. Charts are posted on important performance variables like attendance and on-time deliveries. The teams have posted responsibility charts to indicate who is responsible for tasks such as scheduling. Each week the schedulers meet with the vice-president of manufacturing to review what needs to be built that week. The teams meet daily to plan their daily agenda. Additional team meetings may be called to discuss topics such as vacation planning or recurring production problems. Once a quarter each team formally presents its accomplishments to management and establishes goals for further improvement.

Since Sanko established these teams, support staff and supervisory staff have been reduced by 30%, the cost of assembly reduced by 25%, and inventory cut in half. Most importantly XEL's time for turning orders around is four days. Accomplishing these changes required XEL managers to change their mindsets dramatically. In particular, they had to be willing to give up a great deal of control to the work teams.

Discussion Questions

1. What changes do you think were necessary in XEL's approach to human resources management to support its new strategy?

2. What impediments may have come up during XEL's transformation which could have been addressed or overcome by enlightened human resources practices?

VIDEO CASE: COMBINING QUALITY MANAGEMENT
AND SOCIAL RESPONSIBILITY
Julia Stasch

Historically, men have held 98 percent of the jobs in the construction industry—high-paying jobs with exceptional benefits. Julia M. Stasch, as president and chief operating officer of Stein & Company, a Chicago-based commercial real estate services firm, has helped change this situation by creating the Female Employment Initiative (FEI), a program that increases the number of tradeswomen on job sites.

Rising from secretary to executive at Stein & Company, Stasch realized that she could use the power of her position to advance the cause of equal opportunity. In 1984, she began taking affirmative action on behalf of minority-owned businesses that sought construction project contracts. In 1989 she decided to assist female construction workers as well.

Stasch's approach is unique—and successful—because it is collaborative and comprehensive. She brings together as a unified coalition the owner/developer, prime contractor, subcontractors, affirmative action consultants, unions, women's advocacy groups and community-based organizations. While emphasizing creative cooperation, Stasch is nonetheless pressing for measurable results every step of the way.

FEI is distinctive because Stein & Company requires its contractors to share its commitment to an equal opportunity workplace. Stein also works with women's advocacy groups and community-based organizations to actively recruit women of all skill levels, and to facilitate access to union apprenticeships and job referrals. FEI representatives monitor hiring practices and act as advocates for women once they are on the job site, and frequent meetings are held so that all parties are in a continual dialogue regarding problems and opportunities.

Women constituted approximately 7 percent of the total work force on the first construction project to use FEI, in contrast to the norm of less than 2 percent. In 1990, Stein & Company received the Exemplary Voluntary Efforts Award from the U.S. Department of Labor's Office of Federal Contract Compliance Programs for its efforts. Since then, the program has been replicated on several Stein & Company projects as well as other projects around the country. FEI was used as the model program for congressional legislation, passed in 1992, to assist women in the pursuit of "non-traditional" occupations.

Stasch's efforts have benefited not only tradeswomen but also her own firm. Stasch helped her firm become a major force in the construction industry by differentiating Stein & Company as a creative, socially concerned enterprise in a highly competitive market.

Video Case Questions

1. Explain how Julia Stasch improved various aspects of the human resources management system in her company and other companies.
2. What contribution has Julia Stasch made to society?

10. ORGANIZATIONAL CULTURE

LEARNING OBJECTIVES

When you finish this chapter you should be able to:

1. Explain how culture is related to the behavior of employees and the performance of organizations.

2. Define organizational culture and explain the three levels that make up culture.

3. Explain two human needs that help us understand why and how culture develops.

4. Describe why the role of managers is important in forming and changing an organizational culture.

5. Describe the benefits and problems of a strong culture.

6. Explain how TQM helps an organization build a strong, yet flexible, culture.

SOUTHWEST AIRLINES IS A FUNNY COMPANY[1]

Southwest Airlines is unique. The Dallas-based carrier makes money in the airline business when all its larger rivals are losing money. Southwest turns its planes around in 15 to 20 minutes at its gates while other airlines average an hour. Its planes make about 10 flights per day versus an industry average of five flights. It is a regional airline, and most of its flights are about an hour long. They operate out of secondary airports such as Love Field in Dallas and Midway in Chicago, with no assigned seats and no food *and* with cheap prices. It seems to be a formula for success, but it wouldn't happen without an extraordinary CEO and dedicated employees all working together in a unique can-do but have-fun culture. A Harvard business school case study on Southwest said the airline had succeeded in "differentiating itself through its focus on service, operations, cost control, marketing, its people, and its corporate culture."

The company is run by Herb Kelleher, a person some business observers feel is the best, and one of the most unusual, CEOs in America. Southwest reflects Kelleher's personality and values, which include equal doses of humor, enthusiasm, and working together to get things done. One Wall Street analyst tells the story of having lunch in the Southwest cafeteria when Kelleher, across the room eating with several female employees, jumped to his feet, kissed one of the women, and then began leading everyone in the room in cheers. Why? He had just successfully negotiated a new contract with the company's flight attendants.

Unlike other airlines, Kelleher has created a culture where his union people identify personally with the company, making labor negotiations go much more smoothly. People also work together with less worry about who should do what. For example, if things start to back up, a pilot may work the boarding gate or ticket agents may load luggage. And if elderly passengers need special help, employees go out of their way to make sure they are properly cared for at their destinations.

Kelleher has always sought to create a culture characterized by what he calls "an insouciance, an effervescence." Southwest's passengers are not only not surprised by how Southwest employees go out of their way to startle and amuse, they have come to expect it. If a plane is a little late, the ticket agents might award a prize to the passenger with the biggest hole in his or her sock. Or they might be greeted (surprised might be a better word) by a flight attendant popping out of an overhead luggage bin. Announcements over the intercom often kid as well as inform: "Good morning ladies and gentlemen. Those

of you who smoke will please file out to our lounge on the wing where you can enjoy our feature film, *Gone With the Wind*."

When hiring, Kelleher says, "What we are looking for first and foremost is a sense of humor. Then we are looking for people who have to excel to satisfy themselves and who work well in a collegial environment. We don't care that much about education and expertise, because we can train people to do whatever they have to do. We hire attitudes."

The company seeks people who will be a part of the Southwest family in the full meaning of that word. Alan S. Boyd, retired chairman of Airbus North America, who has long watched the U.S. airline industry says of Kelleher and Southwest: "At other places, managers say that people are their most important resource, but nobody acts on it. At Southwest, they have never lost sight of the fact."

The culture at Southwest Airlines reflects the personality of its leader, Herb Kelleher. It is a culture that emphasizes people and getting the job done. We might compare the Southwest approach with that of Frank Lorenzo and the now defunct Texas Air Corporation, which had a history of constant battling with its employees for changes in work rules and lower salaries. This is the Frank Lorenzo who bought Eastern Airlines and under whose management it went out of business and under whose leadership Continental Airlines ended up in bankruptcy, twice, fighting off salary demands of unionized employees. This is also the same Frank Lorenzo whose most recent attempt to start a new regional airline was turned down because of poor safety practices at Texas Air. We will look further at Kelleher's contrasting approach and the culture he has established at Southwest at the end of this chapter. We will answer the question: Can this attitude of caring translate to the bottom line?

WHAT IS ORGANIZATIONAL CULTURE?

If personality is a reflection of the values, beliefs, experience, talents, and behaviors of a person, then culture is a way to define the personality of an organization. One way to understand individual personality is as our individual sense of what it means to be a person and how we behave in light of that understanding. There are broad categories of personalities: aggressive, kind, humble, egocentric, formal, informal, political, loner, and lots more, usually found in combinations, with certain traits dominating. These categories imply how people with these personalities will behave under various circumstances. Thinking about yourself and how you would categorize your personality helps you to understand your behavior in different situations.

The same is true of organizations and their culture. The culture really is an image of how the leaders and the employees define their organization and how it should behave as an entity in the marketplace and as a member of society. It is part of the glue that holds the pieces of the organization together as a whole. Managers, especially top managers, can have a strong influence on the culture of an organization, which likewise can have a profound influence on its success. In this chapter we will delve into this idea of organizational culture: its formation and its management. And if you keep the idea of individual personality and behavior as a metaphor for organizational culture and behavior, it should help you better understand all the material that follows.

Paradigm Shifts

In 1991, Stanley Gault, age 65, had just retired as Chairman and CEO from Rubbermaid, a company often high on Fortune's list of the best American companies.[2] He was drafted shortly thereafter by the board of Goodyear, the last major American-owned tire company, which was, at that time, losing money and mired in debt. After about 30 days at Goodyear, he wrote out what he called "The 12 Objectives for Managing Goodyear Successfully in the 90s." These objectives included leadership in keeping costs low, in quality, in customer service, and in innovation. Using videos and personal presentations, he communicated his ideas to Goodyear people around the world.

Part of his message was that the company would stop using the word "employee." From then on the correct word would be "associate." The goal was to eliminate hierarchies and emphasize responsibility and working together as "associates" of Goodyear. Gault tells the story of being at a company gathering when four black associates came up to him and one asked hesitantly, "Does the word 'associate' refer to me?" He then continues, "Well, I tell you, that really grabs you doesn't it, when this guy with 35 years of service—and that's how long he had—comes up and says that. He wanted to know, because he was black and worked down in the mill, if the word 'associate' applied to him. Well, I told him very quickly where we stood on this word 'associate' applying to everybody, his job and my job alike. I made it a point within the next month to go down in the area where he was working to see my new associate down there. With a grapevine like Goodyear has, that was around the world in the next 60 seconds with electronic mail." Stanley Gault was making a point, and the culture of Goodyear was changing. Within 18 months after he joined the company, it had paid off its $1.7 billion debt, was making a profit and increasing market share, and morale in the company was much higher.

What happened at Goodyear? The turnaround could be described in different terms: refocused goals, increased efficiency, better strategic planning, improved technologies, and better communication. These changes all took place, but the fundamental causes of these changes were underlying changes in perceptions, values, beliefs, and assumptions about how employees in a company can work together to serve the needs of customers. All of these changes can be referred to as "culture change." Managers often refer to such a radical change as a "paradigm shift." We will talk more about paradigms and how cultures change later in the chapter. For now think of paradigm as a way of viewing and understanding the world and interacting with it. The more realistic your paradigm, the more successful your interactions are likely to be.

To understand how to change a culture, managers must first understand what culture is. One of the goals of this chapter is to learn about organizational cultures, how they arise, and how important a culture is in affecting the behavior of employees (or associates). Some people may be tempted to argue that the word "culture" is just a fancy term used to explain changes, such as those at Goodyear. Does it really explain anything about how the changes came about? It depends on how you define the concept of culture. Managers must understand human behavior and how it relates to culture if they are to help the members of an organization (including themselves) shift their paradigm of the world, and thus how they interact with each other and with outsiders.

Different Definitions of Culture

We often hear the word culture used to describe or explain the behaviors, thoughts, and traditions of a nation or region of the world. However, we rarely hear a precise meaning of the term. There are many definitions of culture, but there is no single correct one. The differences result from the fact that culture is a concept, an idea, an abstract notion. Writers arbitrarily define the concept to suit their own needs and preferences for understanding reality.[3] The various definitions simply focus on different slices of reality. In this chapter we apply the concept of culture to organizations. National, regional, or ethnic differences influence the cultures of business organizations, but an organizational culture takes on a life of its own once it is established as an entity separate from the broader host culture. The concept of culture is an important one for managers to understand because it helps us understand the basis of employee and business behavior in general and the specific behaviors of individual organizations and their members.

As a manager, how you define a concept determines what you focus on, think about, and act upon.[4] Our definition of culture is useful to managers since it does not serve just as a label for behavior or business practices. Instead, it helps explain the causes of behavior. Seeing culture as the cause of business behavior helps managers deal with the challenges they face in managing behavior.

Defining Culture

Culture A pattern of artifacts, behaviors, values, beliefs, and underlying assumptions that is developed by a given group of people as they learn to cope with internal and external problems of survival and prosperity.

We define **culture** as: *a pattern of artifacts, behaviors, values, beliefs, and underlying assumptions that is developed by a given group of people as they learn to cope with internal and external problems of survival and prosperity.* This definition of culture has several elements and we have based it on commonalities among many accepted definitions.[5]

Let's look in more detail at the key phrases in this definition to help explain it more fully.

1. *developed by a given group of people:* This phrase means that culture does not exist without the people—those who develop it and share it. For example, Southwest Airlines' culture reflects the common values and beliefs of its employees.
2. *a pattern of artifacts, behaviors, values, beliefs and underlying assumptions:* This phrase implies that the elements of culture are not random, but are naturally interrelated in logical patterns that have worked to help the company succeed. Again, we can look at Southwest Airlines and see a specific pattern in the values, beliefs and assumptions that guide the behaviors of employees.
3. *as they learn to cope with internal and external problems of survival and prosperity:* This phrase means culture arises through learning, adaptation, and change, and it helps people make sense of events, helps provide solutions to guide behavior, and helps people achieve the organization's purposes. Southwest's culture is one in which all employees help one another thus prospering in an industry where profits have disappeared for most companies.

As explained above, our definition of culture suggests how culture arises in organizations, what purpose it serves, how it perpetuates itself, and how it changes. It implies that culture guides employees in what behaviors the organization approves and disapproves. In so doing, culture is an organizing device that helps remove uncertainty for employees, thereby providing a context for getting work done. It is useful to understand that an organizational culture can be dysfunctional in the same way that a family can be dysfunctional. A dysfunctional organizational culture, such as that at Texas Air, undermines the company's ability to compete in the long run. In the remainder of this chapter, we will elaborate on these ideas and apply them to understanding how culture contributes to managerial and organizational success or the lack of it.

Managers and Organizational Culture

Culture—the values, beliefs, and underlying assumptions that give meaning to the organization's way of doing things—is thus of deep importance to managers. It can either be limiting or facilitating. Many of the problems in today's companies are at least partially related to cultures that have inhibited a company's ability to adapt and deal with new problems and opportunities in a fast-changing world. Since all organizations have cultures, it is incumbent on managers to make sure the cultures they operate within and help shape allow employees to work together well to achieve objectives.

This is easier said than done, however. Traditional managers tend to focus on results, formal roles, technologies, and combinations of these elements.[6] They often ignore culture or take it as a given, though it provides part of the context for bringing together these elements. Managers have been taught that all they need to do is establish goals, clarify employee roles to fulfill the goals, give employees the required technologies, and reward their performance. And this is correct, except there are all kinds of idiosyncratic assumptions that affect just how managers implement these things.

By understanding their organizations from a cultural view, managers can and must strive to create a culture that facilitates rather than hinders success. Managers do not fully control the development of their organization's cultures. However, managers, especially top managers, do have the most influence. It is their values, beliefs, and assumptions about how organizations can successfully adapt to and serve the larger environment in which they exist from which the culture evolves. Employees, based on their experiences and understanding, adapt to the tone set by top managers. This interaction between managers and employees, through time and learning, ultimately results in *culture*. To the degree the organization succeeds, the culture grows and prospers.

Though top managers influence corporate culture, they cannot arbitrarily dictate culture. Because if the culture and the resultant behaviors do not help the company succeed in the marketplace, the top managers will be gone. Then new managers appear who often drastically change the company's culture along with its strategy and deployment of people and resources. Such is the case at IBM under CEO Lou Gerstner and what happened at Goodyear under Stanley Gault. Sometimes there will be a culture that over a long period of time has proven itself in the marketplace. An example would be 3M Corporation, which is known for promoting innovation and the continuous flow of new products. The role of top management in this kind of company is to perpetuate this culture rather than change it.[7]

A Cultural View of Organizations

Cultural view of organizations A view that recognizes two sides or parts to organizational life: one side is outwardly visible and the other side is hidden from view and resides in people's minds.

A **cultural view of organizations** *recognizes two sides or parts to organizational life: one side is outwardly visible and the other side is hidden from view and resides in people's minds.*[8] The outward side of culture is directly observable.[9] It includes tangible achievements such as artifacts (see Exhibit 10-1), patterns of behavior, speech, formal laws, technical know-how, and the use and production of physical objects and products. Traditional managers usually address only these outward manifestations of culture, often not really appreciating the hidden side of culture in the minds of employees, which guides their behavior. For example, in 1991 Fortune ran a poll that showed that a majority of 212 CEOs believed that morale was good in their companies, especially among middle managers. At the same time, other middle manager polls showed drops in morale were driven by downsizing and the beliefs that top managers did not want to know what middle managers had to say. Whether that is true or not is not the issue. Middle managers believe it, and this will not change until those at the top do something, often dramatic, to change those beliefs.[10]

The hidden side of culture is shared in the minds of the members of a group.[11] It includes the mental frameworks, ideas, beliefs, values, attitudes, and ways of perceiving the environment. It stresses the internal process through which behavior is learned and the implicit (often unstated) rules through which behavior is governed.

These two sides of culture are easily distinguished, but impossible to separate. In reality, they blend together. Each reflects and reinforces the other. The hidden side of culture usually can be inferred by observing the behavior of organizational members, especially those at the top. For example, managers reserve the seat at the end of the conference table for the CEO because it symbolizes a position of leadership. The seating arrangement also reinforces the practice of directing most of the conversation to the CEO, which in turn reinforces the belief that the CEO is in charge. A CEO who wanted to change that belief, for example, has to decline that seat and that role in the meeting. The CEO also may assign someone else to facilitate discussion simply to take part as another member of the team.

If managers only focus on the outward side of culture, they will not fully understand the human behavior they are trying to manage. For example, if top managers focus only on numbers and results and employees believe that bad numbers will reflect badly on them, they come to believe "If I give them accurate numbers, they will use those against me." This suggests manipulating the system to deliver "good" numbers whether they are accurate or not. Meanwhile the top managers, looking only at results, may never figure out what is going on until it is too late, and the company is in trouble.[12]

As stated earlier, people and their behaviors ultimately determine all activities in an organization. In today's competitive environment, managers cannot afford to ignore important forces that shape people's behaviors. The following framework provides the basis for understanding how and why culture develops.

Three Levels of Culture

It is useful to think of culture as consisting of three levels as illustrated in Exhibit 10-1: (1) Artifacts and Behaviors, (2) Values and Beliefs, and (3) Basic Underlying Assumptions.[13] Level 1 corresponds to the outward side of culture that exists in the open for everyone to see. Levels 2 and 3 correspond to the inward side of culture that collectively resides in the minds of the people in the organization.

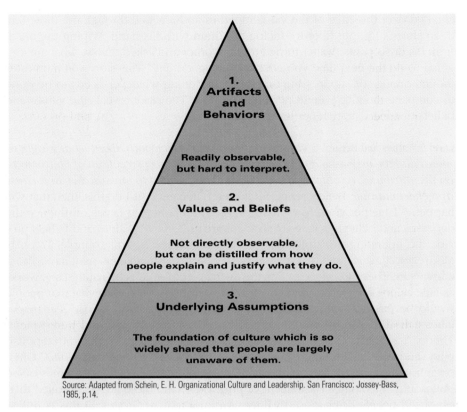

EXHIBIT 10-1
Three Levels of Organizational Culture

Source: Adapted from Schein, E. H. Organizational Culture and Leadership. San Francisco: Jossey-Bass, 1985, p.14.

Levels 2 and 3 are deeper than Level 1, first, because they deal with issues that reside in people's minds. People may even be totally unaware of basic underlying assumptions at Level 3. Second, these deeper levels of values and beliefs are underlying forces that guide behaviors. There are dynamic relationships among these levels that continuously undergo reconstruction by the people who make up the organization.[14]

Level 1: Artifacts and Behaviors. **Behaviors** are *the actions that people take in the organization.* Behaviors are frequently described with words like customs, habits, patterns, practices, rituals, traditions, and styles. **Artifacts** *result from people's behaviors.* Any product of human behavior can be described as a cultural artifact, including written and spoken language, dress, material objects, and plant and furniture arrangements. All these are perceivable symbols of culture.

Other terms used to describe Level 1 include: rites, celebrations, ceremonies, heroes, jargon, myths, and stories. These surface level manifestations of culture are easily observed and documented. However, such descriptions are not useful unless they are understood as symbols of the deeper levels of culture.[15] For example, stories and legends about company heroes express underlying values and beliefs about what makes a hero in this company. The incident Stanley Gault related that reinforced the idea of associates is a good example of a story that will influence the entire culture of Goodyear.

Here is another story: Workers and managers at U.S. Paper Mills Corporation for years have told the following story about its founder and principal stockholder, Walter Cloud. Walking through a mill one morning, Walter noticed a worker trying to unclog the drain of a blending vat using an extension pole. Walter

Behaviors The actions that people take in the organization.

Artifacts Aspects of culture that result from people's behavior.

climbed over the edge of the vat, jumped in and reached through the three feet deep slurry of paper fiber to unclog the drain with his hand. Wiping the muck from his dress pants, Walter turned to the worker and asked, "Now, what are you going to do the next time you need to unclog a drain?" This story communicates the importance of suppressing one's ego and doing whatever needs to be done to complete the job, even at personal sacrifice. The story reveals the values and beliefs that exist at a deeper level of culture.

Level 2: Values and Beliefs.   **Values** represent *our convictions about what is right or moral and the way we ought to behave*. **Beliefs** are *our perceptions of how objects, events, attributes, or outcomes are associated or related to one another in a cause and effect manner*. Beliefs represent if-then statements. "If I do this, then that will happen." Together, these underlying values and beliefs at Level 2 influence the decisions and behaviors that manifest culture at Level 1.[16] Values and beliefs provide the operating principles that guide daily behavior. For example, Douglas McGregor suggests two divergent sets of beliefs that managers may have about employees: Theory X suggests that the average employee is by nature lazy, works as little as possible, lacks ambition and shuns responsibility. Believing that people would be passive without pressure from management, the theory X manager takes action to control people through persuasion, rewards, and punishment. Theory Y suggests that employees are motivated, creative, and want responsibility, and such beliefs suggest an alternate set of management behaviors.[17] Often organizations have formal statements of their values and beliefs (sometimes called philosophy, ideology, or statement of principles), and these are often called their espoused beliefs or espoused values. An important aspect of all this is unless employees and outsiders see consistency between management behavior and the espoused values and beliefs, any formal statements will be ignored. Behaviors always reflect actual values and beliefs regardless of what is written or said.

Level 3: Basic Underlying Assumptions.   Often, formal values and beliefs do not coincide with what people actually do in the organization.[18] People often say one thing and do another. For example, in the early stages of implementing quality improvement programs, managers are often guilty of setting forth slogans such as *Quality First* and *Zero Defects*. Then they make decisions that undermine the slogan. For example, they purchase raw materials based on lowest cost with no concern for quality; they chastise people who make mistakes experimenting with new methods; they cut training for skills improvement; and they berate subordinates for making problems public with data charts. Such actions undermine any slogans to the contrary.

Although it may seem they are simply lying or deliberately misleading people, there are other explanations for the inconsistency between what is said and what is done. Formal statements may reflect management's aspirations and dreams for the future—which they recognize are different from current realities. Alternatively, managers may even be unaware of the inconsistency between the theory they espouse and the theory they actually use. They may unconsciously act based on a different set of deeply held values and beliefs and just use the pronouncements to put up a good front. They may actually believe that such pronouncements are what they are supposed to say regardless of what they do.

It is this deepest level of culture, the basic underlying assumptions, that really drive much of the behaviors in organizations. **Assumptions** are *values and beliefs that are so deeply ingrained in the minds of people in the organization,*

Values Convictions about what is right or moral and the way people ought to behave.

Beliefs Our perceptions of how objects, events, attributes or outcomes are associated or related to one another in a cause and effect manner.

Assumptions Values and beliefs that are so deeply ingrained in the minds of people in the organization, they are taken for granted or assumed to be unquestionably true.

TOM PETERS' BONKERS BAROMETER

Tom Peters relentlessly pounds managers with the idea that flexibility and fast response are vital to the survival of today's and tomorrow's organizations. He devised the following "Bonkers Barometer" for managers to do a brief analysis of their companies' culture stands on these issues. While it is somewhat tongue in cheek, it is still useful and thought-provoking.

A LOOK AT

TQM IN ACTION

Forget It						Get with It
Lifetime employment	1	2	3	4	5	Network/career as a portfolio of jobs
Following instructions	1	2	3	4	5	Create your own projects
Waltz	1	2	3	4	5	Street rap
Mass market	1	2	3	4	5	Niche market
Wingtips	1	2	3	4	5	Nikes
Business suit	1	2	3	4	5	Levis
Corporate tower	1	2	3	4	5	Open campus
Market research	1	2	3	4	5	Try it
Worker as "pair of hands"	1	2	3	4	5	Worker as source of curiosity
Staffer/worker	1	2	3	4	5	Business person/entrepreneur
Months	1	2	3	4	5	Nanoseconds
Patience	1	2	3	4	5	Impatience
Yes, sir	1	2	3	4	5	Up yours
Stick to your knitting	1	2	3	4	5	Unravel it before a competitor does
Hide your mistakes	1	2	3	4	5	To err is glorious
Memorization	1	2	3	4	5	Imagination
The flawless resume	1	2	3	4	5	Unexplained gaps
Jimmy Stewart	1	2	3	4	5	Madonna
Foreign competitors don't play fair	1	2	3	4	5	The more competitors the merrier

Source: Reprinted from *Tom Peters On Achieving Excellence*, June 1993, The Liberation Management Workshop. © 1993 TPG/Communications. Used with permission.

The higher the score the better from Peters' perspective. He suggests using the scale to determine where managers see their organizations and where they want to be. Then he says, "If most of your marks are not on the Get with It side of the scale, well, forget it!"

they are taken for granted or assumed to be unquestionably true. Assumptions represent our nearly unquestioned understanding of how things are. Since these assumptions are generally shared by people in an organization, they are not frequently discussed. They serve as an "automatic pilot" to guide decision making and behaviors without demanding fully conscious attention.[19]

People may feel threatened when these assumptions are challenged. For example, a newly hired employee challenged a management team that was attempting to diagnose their culture. The employee noted that people tended to assume that only people who had been with the company a long time could understand how it really operated and, as a result, recently arrived employees wanting to contribute were not taken seriously by other employees. The senior person in the group turned on the youngster and said angrily, "How can you sit there and make a statement about the [company's] culture when you have been here barely one year? You are completely wrong. We accept the ideas of new employees."[20] Unwittingly, the senior person's reaction actually proved the new employee's point.

Since these basic underlying assumptions are held as incontrovertible truths, largely beneath conscious awareness, that are socially shared by group members, they are not often challenged. They are also likely to be the most stable and enduring part of culture, and may be the most difficult part to change. However, this deepest level of culture is perhaps the most important part to change when there are problems because it continues to drive the whole culture. When Stanley Gault joined Goodyear, he had to go to work changing assumptions about status and responsibility; he demonstrated such by making sure his actions were consistent with his words.

Because the various levels and elements of culture are dynamically related, any efforts to make changes in a culture must address more than one level. A manager can try to change goals, formal roles, technologies, and other surface aspects of culture to redirect an organization. However, without changes in the values, beliefs, and assumptions out of which the current culture evolved, such surface changes are likely to make little difference in performance.

How do these three levels of culture emerge? What causes culture to develop? What purpose does culture serve? We have hinted at some of the answers to these questions. We will now explore these questions in more depth. Our goal is to provide a sense of how managers can shape and change an organizational culture to improve performance.

THINKING CRITICALLY

1. If you worked at Goodyear and Stanley Gault had just reinforced that you and he are associates, each with your role to play, how would that make you feel? How do you think it might affect how you go about your job?
2. Have you ever been involved in an organization where the espoused values and beliefs and the actions taken by leaders were inconsistent with one another? Whether yes or no, how do you think this would affect your understanding of what you are supposed to do and believe in the organization?

HOW AND WHY AN ORGANIZATIONAL CULTURE DEVELOPS

When people join an organization they carry with them the values, beliefs, and behavioral habits developed over a lifetime of experiences with family life, formal education, friendships, work organizations, and society at large. Such experiences provide a sense of order in our lives and a context for interpreting words, actions, and our place in the scheme of things. All of the social experiences of organization members provide background and input for the development of an organizational culture.

However, once a group of people form an organization, the culture emerges and evolves as the members of the organization adapt to and interact with their managers, themselves, and the organization's environment—all with the purpose of achieving some goals. Through time, employees come to share common practices, behaviors, symbols, meanings, understandings, values, beliefs, and assumptions.

Two driving forces cause a group of people to develop shared culture: (1) the human need to seek order and stability, and (2) the pragmatic need to solve the problems of social organizations. As you will read below, these two forces are really interrelated.

The Human Need to Seek Order and Stability

Each of us is driven to make sense of our experiences and understand how we relate to and should act to succeed in the world. Instinctively, we impose our personal meanings on whatever we encounter. These meanings are always subjective and based on our experiences and understanding. Our judgments of others and their behaviors are based on our experiences and understanding of what is right and wrong, what is impressive and unimpressive, and the myriad of categories we use to determine what the behavior of others means to us. Everyone's experiences are different and the judgments we make based on our experiences are likewise different from one another.

We also know that by working together, we can combine our talents and resources to create goods and services, as well as experiences, that would not happen if everyone worked independently. Organizational culture evolves as we attempt to adapt to each other and lessen the differences in how we make sense of each other and the rest of the world. For example, if you were to visit a country in Africa, it would take a while for you to grasp an African people's view of the world and how they interpret various events and actions. If you wanted to fit

Organizational culture evolves as individuals attempt to adapt to each other and lessen the differences in how each makes sense of one another and the rest of the world.

in, you would need to learn their ways. The same is true of people working together. Through time people develop shared understandings that allow them to imbue stability and some certainty to their relationships and expected behaviors.

An important aspect of this development of culture is the role of the organization head. Because the top manager has authority over the organization's allocation of resources, as well as rewards and punishments, other members take their behavioral cues and sense of responsibility from this person. In a manner of speaking, the top manager has significant influence over the creation of the environment to which everyone else adapts. Over time a stability emerges among the members, including the top managers, from which expectations about one another are derived. This stability helps them get along and work together. However, if the patterns of interaction members have developed through this process are inefficient and directed at internal goals, such as maintaining turf or competing for the boss's favors, rather than continuously improving the quality of their processes and outputs, the company could be in trouble. Enlightened top managers understand their important cultural influences and consciously work to create the kinds of values, beliefs, and assumptions that will lead to continued organizational success.

Sometimes organizations have processes that do not facilitate its survival, yet members tend to resist making changes. Why? One reason is that people do not like to admit that what they have built themselves may no longer be functional. People have projects, systems, or procedures that they created and developed and that are tied to their egos and self-images. These issues have members' names on them. They have personal meaning. These members view it as a personal assault when someone wants to change things.

People also preserve the status quo for security and predictability in their lives. They seek certainty in an uncertain world, and when they have that, they do not want to give it up. As creatures of habit, people become comfortable with the ease of their current methods. When their expectations are threatened by proposed changes, they instinctively defend the old way. They may fail to see that the changes will actually enhance their security over the long run. In today's competitive and changing environments, organizations cannot afford to sit still and be content with the status quo. Ironically, this tendency to protect and preserve the status quo can defeat that which it intends to ensure, namely, the survival and prosperity of the organization.

Thus culture provides people in an organization with stability and predictability and also provides reinforcement that the work they are doing is purposeful and worthwhile.

The Social Organization's Need to Solve Problems

Businesses and organizations are social entities that involve human interactions to accomplish their missions or purposes. Any time there is human interaction, there are certain social issues that must be addressed to ensure harmony and continuity of the group. These social issues are called problems of internal integration.

Solving Problems of Internal Integration.   Organization members constantly face problems of building and maintaining human relationships. As the organization matures, the members learn cultural solutions for these problems. Some of these solutions for successfully interacting and fulfilling a common purpose include: a shared language, specified group boundaries and criteria for inclusion and

CHANGING CORPORATE CULTURE AT FLORIDA POWER AND LIGHT COMPANY

A LOOK AT

MANAGERS IN ACTION

Beth Hauser is the area manager for commercial/industrial customer service in the West Palm/Treasure Coast territory at Florida Power & Light (FPL). FPL recognized a change in the business environment for electric utilities. Beth describes the process FPL went through in moving from a traditional utility corporate culture to one that will facilitate success in a more competitive environment.

Around 1988, FPL's top management started to anticipate a major change in the electric utility business. Since this is a stable business, people in this industry have been complacent for about 50 years. Many had difficulty imagining any changes from their standard operating procedures as a regulated monopoly. To deal with this new future, it had become apparent to management that we had to look at how we did business and who our customers are. We needed to answer four key questions: (1) What business are we in? (2) What will the environment be? (3) What are the critical success factors? (4) What are our strengths and weaknesses? We knew we would have to become more responsive and flexible. We needed to look at and adapt the corporate culture to new realities.

The first step was to form several employee teams to answer these questions and look at possible changes suggested by the answers. We reviewed technology, financial needs, resource needs, customer demographics, and the regulatory environment. Then we tried to anticipate future changes. The answer was almost everything—and drastically. In particular, we saw a tremendous possibility for the opening of the electric utility business to competition and found we were not ready for that. We did not know our customers, their needs, and their criteria for choosing a utility. We did not know what we would do to ensure they remained our customers and were not sure we were responsive enough to meet those needs once we became aware of them.

The next step toward changing our culture was to create a vision for the company. This, too, was done by bringing together a group of employees to determine what it was we wanted to be. Our answer was: "To be the preferred provider of safe, reliable, and cost-effective products and services that satisfy the electricity-related needs of all customer segments." This said two things to our employees. One, we anticipate that our customers will have choices and we must make sure they choose us; and second, we were in the electric service business. FPL had a strategy of diversification into other industries during the previous five years and this vision told us that we needed to get back to basics.

The next step was to take a look at the organization. In many cases, we had seven-to-nine layers of management, decision making was slow and cumbersome. Top management asked me and 11 other employees to start with a blank piece of paper and develop an effective FPL organization as if it were a new company. We split into several teams, each looking at different parts of the business. The teams reviewed processes involved in different parts of the business and designed an organization structure to optimize those processes. On the customer side, for instance, we took a look at our different customer segments and designed the organization around the different needs of commercial/industrial and residential customers.

We also greatly reduced the layers of management. Like the children's telephone game, trying to get customers' voices through seven to nine layers of management brought a garbled message to decision makers. The business unit that serves our largest commercial/industrial customer now has three people between the customer and the president of the company. If the customer has a message for management, it gets there with no interpretation.

The role of the manager in this new organization was also changed. The reduction in layers of management resulted in a greatly increased span of control. One of the overriding changes in culture for this new organization was to be the empowerment of employees. With spans of control averaging 12 to 15 employees per manager, the employees must be able to make some of their own decisions. A manager cannot stay involved in everyone's work decisions with so many subordinates. Hence, the manager's role is to "translate" corporate strategies and objectives, communicate expectations, and ensure appropriate resources are available.

To further emphasize changes in relationships between employees and managers, we also modified our performance appraisal system. At the beginning of each year, the employees and managers sit down and establish key responsibilities and competencies required for that year, as well as ways to measure success. They also agree to formally review those key responsibilities and competencies at least once during the year and at the end of the year. Performance appraisals do not include long numerical responses, but a discussion of accomplishments versus the key responsibilities and competencies. This takes much of the fear out of performance appraisal and enhances communication between employee and manager.

We continuously review all policies and processes to ensure that they continue to help us meet our vision. Our new organization and culture allowed us to react exceptionally well in the face of a recent hurricane. We found that increased employee empowerment made us more flexible and responsive even in an emergency.

exclusion, the resolution of issues involving power and status, friendship, rewards and punishments, and the development of an organizational ideology or belief system. These solutions allow members to interact and behave comfortably without being preoccupied with their individual positions and identities. Once they have learned the rules of the game, they can predict and understand events in the organization. This allows them to focus on adapting to the external environment without distraction of internal uncertainties. This external adaptation offers another set of problems organizational culture helps members solve.

Solving Problems of External Adaptation. An organization is an open system, and it has a role to play in the larger environment in which it exists. Indeed, the nature of the organization can reflect the role it plays. Sports organizations, for example, depending on the quality of coaching, develop team-oriented, can-do cultures. This reflects the team's roles as symbols of a city or state and as entertainers who need to win games. Often, small entrepreneurial companies adopt an informal culture reflected in casual dress, lack of titles, and the need for everyone to pitch in to achieve goals and serve the market.

As the culture matures, people learn joint solutions for the problems of external adaptation. The members develop a sense of mission, goals for fulfilling that mission, means for accomplishing the goals, measurements to assess how well they are doing, and procedures for making course corrections.

Internal integration and external adaptation are interdependent. The successful development of an internal culture appears in how well the company handles external challenges. While an organization may have a coherent internal culture, if this culture does not help it deal with the environment in which the organization exists, the organization will not last long. The culture of a company does not prescribe exactly how people will adapt to the external environment. Like TQM which has deep implications for culture, culture provides a context for doing this, precluding certain actions and suggesting others. Again, if we refer to Southwest Airlines, its culture suggests how employees interact to keep customers happy—often with humor.

How does culture actually develop in an organization? Below we discuss and expand on earlier ideas about (1) the role of founders and leaders, and (2) the role of the learning process in providing and developing cultural solutions.

The Role of Founders and Leaders in Establishing Organizational Culture

IBM Rochester: Baldrige Award Winner

At the beginning of an organization, the *founder* assembles a group of people for specific purposes, either to serve societal needs, such as by a social or charitable organization, or to serve commercial needs for products and services. The founder, perhaps with a few key personnel, usually establishes the mission, vision, and goals that give the organization direction. Founders and their key people serve as the first leaders of the organization.

The leaders not only set the mission and vision for the organization, but also how members will accomplish it. In doing this, the leaders offer their own favorite solutions for the internal and external problems faced by the organization. When Tom Watson Sr. founded IBM in 1914, he incorporated his personal values and beliefs into the company's culture including *respect for the individual, the best customer service, and pursuit of excellence.*[21]

Watson believed:

1. A company must respect individual employees and help them respect themselves, rather than psychologically abuse them. Companies should let the employees know they make a difference, reward superior performance, promote from within, and create a democratic environment (e.g., no titles on doors, and no executive washrooms).
2. The customer must be given the best possible service. Companies must let customers know how important they are and satisfy their requirements. To give the best possible service, every employee's job description must be related to this goal and every employee must receive appropriate training and education on how to reach it.
3. Excellence and superior performance must be pursued. A company must strive to avoid defects in products and services. To do so it must hire motivated individuals and then provide the necessary training and environment conducive to excellence.

These principles are supposed to provide the foundation for all of IBM's business activities. Although these have withstood time and remained on their lips, IBM has slipped in its ability to live up to them in the modern, competitive marketplace. Several years ago the leader of one of IBM's "big" customers told the chairman of the board that "you don't listen to us, you're not doing a good job." This kind of feedback opened the eyes of IBM's executives. In fact the long-term troubles that prompted the IBM board to recruit Lou Gerstner have caused him to revise these principles as he seeks to recast the company and its culture. In fact, these three principles have been replaced with eight goals, with heavy emphasis on serving the customer and becoming more efficient. Principle 1, respect for the individual, is now Principle 8 on Gerstner's revised list.[22]

Leadership may come from people throughout the organization—not just top managers. However, leaders must have the power and influence to make the mission or vision a reality. Given their positions of authority, founders and top managers are often able to impose their own wills on the organization. But leaders do not inspire commitment to a vision simply by exercising authority. They must draw on other sources of power and influence.

In addition to formal authority, leaders often rely on a quality called *charisma* to clearly and vividly communicate a vision and embed it in people's thinking. Charisma springs from such diversities as the leader's self-confidence, conviction, interpersonal skills, creativity, perspective, and energy. A person who has charisma has the ability to inspire confidence in others as well and bring out their personal best. Leaders may use both formal authority and charisma through a variety of concrete mechanisms to influence the culture of their organization.

The most powerful of these mechanisms include:
- what leaders pay attention to, measure, and control
- leader reactions to critical incidents and organizational crises
- deliberate role modeling, teaching, and coaching by leaders
- leaders' criteria for allocation of rewards and status
- leaders' criteria for recruitment, selection, promotion, retirement, and excommunication

The use of each of these mechanisms influences the behavior of others in the organization. As time goes by, these behaviors become ingrained as patterns, and the culture takes shape.

For example, Dick Brooks, the founder and CEO of a $40-million chemical manufacturing business, ChemDesign Corp., makes no bones about where he stands on environmental issues. He prints it right on his business card: "chief environmental officer." Brooks estimates he spends 40% of his time staying two steps ahead of environmental regulations with heavy capital investments in environmental controls and cleaning up old plants that his company purchases. "It also makes a statement to my employees," says Brooks. "While working at this company you either subscribe to pro-environmental policy or you don't work here."[23]

Some secondary mechanisms that will work if they are consistent with the primary mechanisms include:
- the organization's design and structure
- organizational systems and procedures
- design of physical space, facades, and buildings
- stories, legends, myths, and parables about important events and people
- formal statements of organizational philosophy, creeds, and charters[24]

For example, the arrangement of open offices, with no walls and doors separating people, promotes open communication and social interaction among workers. At a company like Intel, even Andy Grove, the CEO, occupies an open cubicle as do all other employees. The purpose: to emphasize leanness and not extravagant spending and to downplay status and upgrade performance.[25]

The Importance of Cultural Consistency

Cultural consistency The extent to which all elements of culture fit together and are mutually supportive.

Managers must realize that it is important to achieve **cultural consistency,** or *the extent to which all elements of culture fit together and are mutually supportive.* For example, the leader's reactions to critical incidents should be consistent

CULTURAL WORK OUT AT GE[26]

TQM IN ACTION

One of the most admired corporate leaders in the U.S. is Jack Welch, Chairman and CEO of General Electric Corporation, a company that sells among other things, 50-cent light bulbs, billion dollar power plants, jet engines, financial services, refrigerators, and owns the NBC network. With revenues of more than $60 billion and such a large number of businesses with more than 300,000 employees, Welch has a tremendous challenge to keep this company growing, profitable, and responsive to its customers.

Welch is well aware that GE could become so big and so laden with overhead that it simply could not sustain itself in today's competitive world. He is not about to let that happen. He says it's his responsibility to make sure the culture facilitates "speed, simplicity, and self-confidence." He emphasizes that the company must "take out the boss element." He knows that he has to create a culture where people can maximize their contributions to the company. "We're going to win on our ideas, not whips and chains," he asserts.

With the top management of the company, Welch created a wide-open style in shirt-sleeve meetings where executives could freely exchange ideas and challenge Welch's thinking. However, this was not happening further down in the company's divisions—bureaucracy and inefficiency were common. After thinking about this, Welch worked with James Baughman, the head of the GE Management Development Institute, to develop a program called Work Out to begin changing the company's culture and enhancing the voice and authority of employees at all levels. Work Out is both a process and a place. It takes place as an off-site forum where participants can (1) get a mental work out, (2) take unnecessary work out of their jobs, and (3) work out problems together. It was started in March 1989, and by 1991 over 40,000 employees had participated in a least one Work Out.

A Work Out is three sessions of 40 to 100 people selected from all functional areas and levels in a division. The meeting begins with an introduction by the boss, who spells out a rough agenda, usually emphasizing how to simplify forms, processes, approvals—any work that does not add value to final outputs. Then the boss leaves. An outside facilitator helps run the meeting. Typically, the group will break into five or six teams, with each team problem-solving one of the agenda items. For one-and-a-half days they attack the problem, analyze it, devise ideas, and finally prepare a plan of action and a presentation for the final day. On that day the boss returns to listen to each team's suggestions. The rules of Work Out call for the boss to do one of three things as each suggestion is made: agree on the spot to implement, say no, or ask for further information which must be delivered and acted on by a certain date.

One boss, Armand Lauzon of the Lynn, Massachusetts, aircraft engine facility characterizes the response of GE managers in a Work Out session: "I was wringing wet within a half an hour. They had 108 proposals, I had about a minute to say yes or no to each one, and I couldn't make eye contact with my boss, which would show everyone in the room I was chicken." Eventually Lauzon said yes to all but eight of the ideas. The message of Work Out throughout the organization: We want your ideas for improvement, and we are going to implement them.

It has made a difference. People like to be heard and want to contribute. In a meeting with officials of the International Union of Electrical Workers, which represents the Lynn aircraft engine plant employees, Welch said, "Why do you guys poke your finger in my eye every three years [referring to wage negotiations]?" The response: "We had the feeling you were trying to phase us out. Now at least we have an avenue to make a pitch for our jobs." By bringing more and more employees into the process, not only is GE improving itself, it is also saving jobs that would be long gone in the old, bureaucratic version of the company.

Work Out is just one part of Welch's actions for transforming the company, but it serves as a good example of how a leader-created cultural change can affect performance.

with the values and beliefs present in the organizational myths. Consistency ensures that people do not get mixed messages about what the culture expects of them. A strong culture may develop when all signals and mechanisms of leaders are consistently conveying the same values, beliefs, and assumptions.

When an organization is young or small, one or a few leaders may dominate the culture. As the culture develops, it will be less likely that one or a few leaders will dominate the development of the culture. Leadership will become more dispersed. Over time, the social learning that takes place among the employees will have a greater influence on how the culture develops. At this point, it is possible for cultural inconsistencies to develop.

Inconsistencies that seem insignificant or minor may be ignored. Employees take their cues from leader actions more so than from formal statements, designs, and procedures. A policy statement may be totally ignored if it is inconsistent with past or current practices. Inconsistencies may be a constant source of confusion and conflict when managers act inconsistently from one occasion to another. To develop a strong culture requires a lot of attention by leaders to ensure cultural consistency. If they do not act consistently, no one else will see this as important either.

The Role of the Learning Process

Once an organization has been founded, individual members interact socially to coordinate their actions and accomplish their missions. As the organization grows, cultural learning takes place as members and managers work out which solutions and techniques work best for dealing with internal problems and interacting with the external environment including suppliers, customers, and the community. The following are the three types of learning processes: learning from consequences, avoidance learning, and socialization.

Learning from conse-
quences Learning that
results from successful or
unsuccessful experiences.

Learning from Consequences. **Learning from consequences** means that *people learn which solutions work based on their failures and successes.* When a solution accomplishes a goal, removes a felt need, or earns a certain reward, the members of the organization are more likely to try it again. If it works repeatedly, members come to share a belief in its effectiveness. If it does not work, or if it causes punishment, then they develop beliefs about its ineffectiveness.

Over time, with repetition of the same results, the belief may be taken for granted and unquestioned. As this happens, the solution is on its way to becoming a part of the cultural assumptions providing the foundation for much of the behavior in the organization.[27] When employees learn there are no consequences for failing to behave in ways consistent with cultural expectations, this affects and contributes to the creation of a dysfunctional culture. It may also serve as a signal that certain cultural behaviors have outlived their usefulness.

Symbolic or abstract
learning Learning that
takes place through the use
of language and other
abstract symbols, which
communicate the ideas and
experiences of others that
affect behavior.

Symbolic or Abstract Learning. In **symbolic or abstract learning,** people learn through *the use of language and other abstract symbols, which communicate the ideas and experiences of others that affect behavior.*[28] Symbolic learning takes place in a variety of ways, such as by reading, listening, observing, and inferring. This form of learning is called symbolic or abstract because it is a type of learning that happens without direct experience by the learner. It also deals with theories and principles that allow people to classify experiences so they have a better sense of how to deal with them. This learning is mainly symbolic. You

McJOBS FOR A STRONG CORPORATE CULTURE[29]

A LOOK AT

DIVERSITY

When Ray Kroc put up the first set of arches (red arches then) in 1955 in Des Plaines, Illinois, he did so with the hope of one day being able to help those individuals who did not fit the stereotypical American lifestyle. Kroc, a high school dropout himself, went about building a restaurant chain that recognized its role as a food provider for all segments of society and sought the same diversity in its workforce. Today, McDonald's is a global corporation consisting of approximately 11,000 stores worldwide. The 8,000 stores in the United States employ over 480,000 people.

Recognizing that social and ethnic differences do exist is the first step in melding this diversity into a single corporate culture. The next step is training and educating—a huge task for such a big and widespread organization. McDonald's has the largest training program in the United States (even larger than that of the U.S. Army). The program teaches people that there are some things that can be done to establish a common ground for all of its people. McDonald's Hamburger University, located near Chicago, serves as the national training facility. Training also takes place around the world at other Hamburger Colleges, where ideas such as personal hygiene, appearance, and responsibility are taught. Later in life, when former employees are asked what they remember from their training at McDonald's, teamwork and personal responsibility are usually at the top of the list.

To maximize diversity in its labor force, McDonald's has played an active role in training and hiring disabled people through its program called McJobs. Instituted in 1981, McJobs, besides looking for ethnic diversity, also encourages searching out and employing some of the millions of disabled citizens and giving them a chance at self-sufficiency. The U.S. Bureau of Labor reports that of the 43 million disabled people in the U.S., 8.5 million are classified as "unemployed but employable." Each year 350,000 disabled people graduate from various special education programs around the country, but only 35% find jobs. The remaining 65% of the graduates go home and do not work. McDonald's targets this segment and attempts to integrate them into mainstream America.

The McJobs program is a win-win situation for both McDonald's and society. Since 1981, McDonald's has put more than 10,000 physically disabled individuals through the program. In an industry marked by high turnover rates, the retention rate of 80% for McJobs is a welcomed success. Pat Brophy, McJobs program director, reflects the corporate sentiments: "Sure, it's good business to employ disabled people, but it's also the right thing to do." This view of mutual benefits is instilled in the minds of top executives down all the way to every crew member. Each year about 1,000 disabled persons graduate from the program and make it into the workforce.

McDonald's management realized that it is simply not enough to train handicapped personnel on how to perform the day-to-day tasks and how to fit into McDonald's work systems. They must also train the co-workers. In an effort to make the crew aware of what their new associates are going through, simulations are set up to show the crew what it feels like not being able to see, hear, speak, or even move around easily. Crew members are blindfolded, wear oversized gloves, or whatever it takes to give some insight as to what the disabled person feels like every day. While sensitivity training may instill a sense of empathy, it is primarily designed to help crew members understand the *abilities* of the disabled.

In a program called McMasters, elderly people are sought out to return to the workforce and work directly with the younger generations on the front lines. By mixing older and younger associates there is a sense of family at the restaurant which has been noticed by customers. Values such as courtesy, pride, and responsibility are finding their way back into the work place. McDonald's management feels that the morale of its work crews has improved as a result of these programs.

learn a lot about what goes on in organizations without actually having to do things yourself. You learn from reading this and other books as well from lectures and discussions with others.

One thing that makes human beings unique is our ability to learn through the use of language and thought without actual experience. Of course, experience will reinforce or modify what we learn symbolically. In organizations, new employees will learn much about the culture from being told about it by others, by watching and interpreting what others do, and from reading documents such as policies and correspondence. In groups, people help each other interpret events and understand meaning through the process of socialization.

Socialization Learning that comes from people figuring out how to behave appropriately through their social interaction with other people.

Socialization Learning.   The process of **socialization** and the learning associated can be simply summed up as "learning the ropes." *People figure out how to behave appropriately through their social interaction with other people.* Socialization formally begins the day a person joins an organization. Introductory orientation and training programs start the process. However, people continue to learn what is expected of them every day, in every type of job interaction. People influence each other's thinking through formal communications such as memos and announcements, through informal communications such as a chat by the water fountain, through nonverbal communications such as a pat on the back or an icy stare, and through other symbols, such as rituals, ceremonies, stories, heroes, logos, and decor.[30]

Role models Informal leaders and people whose behavior is particularly liked, respected, and emulated.

Social cues are also given through the actions of **role models** or *informal leaders and people whose behavior is particularly liked, respected, and emulated.* Other people infer appropriate behaviors, thoughts, and feelings from the actions of role models. Role models have an even greater impact on others when rationale and explanations are also provided to justify their actions. Herb Kelleher is the role model at Southwest Airlines. His antics, along with his caring about employees and customers, influences the other employees and affects their behavior. The same is true for leaders like Jack Welch and Stanley Gault.

❓ THINKING CRITICALLY

1. In your own experience, how do you think our human need for order and stability has influenced the culture of some organization you have been part of, either at work, at church, at a club or some other type of organized group?
2. If you were starting an organization, how do you think your values, beliefs, and behaviors would influence the culture? What are some attributes you would instill that might help ensure the success of your organization?
3. How do you think the McJobs program contributes to the success of McDonald's?

CULTURAL, INDIVIDUAL, AND ORGANIZATIONAL BEHAVIOR

Behavior is an element of culture that both causes and results from other elements of culture. For example, managerial decisions and actions influence the values and beliefs of others, which in turn, affect decisions and actions. It is a never-ending process. As mentioned earlier, consistency among cultural elements tends to reinforce behaviors that are in sync with shared values and beliefs. However, cultural elements are not always consistent. People do not always behave, think, and feel as expected. Values and beliefs are not always unanimously shared. This *variation in behavior by individuals or groups of individuals who deviate from what the culture prescribes* is called **cultural nonconformity.**

Cultural Nonconformity

It is important for a manager to understand the sources of nonconformity, as this can either help or hinder the organization's ability to meet its goals and objectives. We will review two sources of cultural nonconformity; they are: (1) the diverse personal backgrounds of individuals, and (2) the isolation of subgroups that develop cultures of their own.

Diverse Personal Backgrounds and Individual Nonconformity.   One source of nonconformity is the diversity of members' personal backgrounds. Each person brings values and beliefs from prior experiences with families, communities, churches, schools, and other organizations. While the socialization process can help a person learn to fit into a new organization, it certainly cannot cleanse people of all prior cultural influences. Organizational members are likely to retain some vestiges of their prior cultural heritage. An organizational culture results from the many cultural influences brought into it by the members.[31] Each person brings something different to the organization. For example, an engineer who spent the first ten years of his career in an organization that encourages a team approach to product design will likely try to practice a team approach at the next organization he joins, even if that is not its way of operating.

When people think and act differently, the rest of the organization often notices. The framework shown in Exhibit 10-2 on page 368 is useful for characterizing individual nonconformity.[32] The framework is formed by responses to two questions: (1) to what extent does the individual behave as prescribed by the culture? and (2) to what extent does the individual hold the beliefs and values of the culture? The answers to these questions can range from "a great deal" to "not at all," to position an individual on the two-dimensional framework.

Four cells of the framework are labeled *maverick, good soldier, adapter, and rebel* as caricatures or stereotypes. The further an individual gets from the good soldier position, the harder it is to maintain social standing and perform effectively in the group. For example, rebels have to be imaginative to remain effective and accepted in the group. It may be easier for mavericks since they at least may be perceived as committed to the same beliefs and values.

Nonconformists can be quite successful in the organization, but they have to have resources and support. They may gain the freedom to be nonconformists because of support from powerful others, particularly powerful good soldiers. This support gives the nonconformists a sort of cultural insurance.

They may also gain the freedom to be nonconformists because of their own track record, personal power, and credibility. This reservoir of social credits may be cashed in to buy the right to be a nonconformist. To sustain this strategy, social credits must be replenished by successful performance or social repayment. Whether they rely on cultural insurance or social credits, individual nonconformists can get reputations as people who get away with murder, but also are respected for their contributions.[33]

Subgroup Nonconformity.   As suggested in our definition, culture develops within social groups of people. Since organizations often have many subgroups (divisions, functional groups, departments, or work teams), subcultures will likely

EXHIBIT 10-2
Culture Caricatures: Analytical Scheme for Studying Cultural Nonconformity

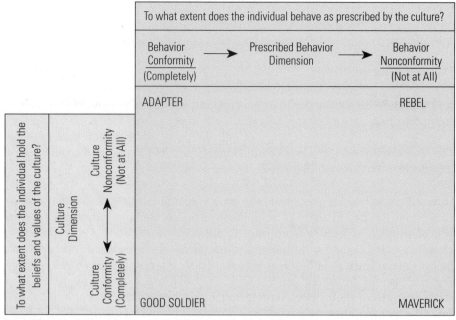

Subculture A specific culture that develops within an organizational subgroup that shares some common characteristics.

develop. A **subculture** is *the specific culture that develops within an organizational subgroup that shares some common characteristics.* The subculture may have unique symbols, jargon, interpretations, norms, values, and beliefs that set them apart in some way. It develops because of the relatively intense interactions required among the people within the subgroup and helps them get along and do their work. For example, functional subcultures often develop within marketing and manufacturing. As another example, conflicts among unions and management may be viewed as subcultural disagreements.

The more different the subcultures are, the more difficult it is for them to communicate and integrate their actions. Each may have different values, priorities, and goals. Each may have different beliefs about how to get work done. Having separate cultures can further reinforce isolation. They may develop stereotypes of each other and even seek to further differentiate and isolate themselves. TQM, with its focus of integrating work on processes across functions, helps people break down these divisions for the purpose of delivering more value to customers.

Strong culture A culture characterized by a high level of uniformity or consensus among all members of an organization.

The Benefits of a Strong Culture

Paradigm A model consisting of the organizational patterns (such as values, beliefs, traditional practices, methods, tools, etc.) that members of a group construct to integrate and give order to the thoughts and actions of the group.

As a culture matures and becomes stronger, it controls the members' behaviors more and more. Shared understandings and meanings, common expectations, values, and beliefs combine to strongly influence behavior. The term **strong culture** implies *uniformity or consensus among all members of an organization.* Individual and group nonconformity are minimal.

A strong culture might be referred to as a paradigm.[34] We mentioned this term earlier in the chapter, and it is popular in management circles today. It is often referred to when managers talk about changing from traditional management to Total Quality Management. For managers, **paradigm** *consists of the* *organizational realities, (such as values, beliefs, traditional practices, methods, tools, etc.) that members of a social group construct to integrate and give order to the thoughts and actions of the group.* A paradigm provides a sense of what works and does not work, how components of the organization are connected to one another, and what the purpose of the organization is. It suggests patterns of relationships and behaviors. To put it simply, a **managerial paradigm** consists of *the context and sense of order people bring to the act of conducting a business.*[35]

There are benefits to a strong culture. Since members have shared understandings, they communicate easier. The mutual understanding and dedication to the same values and beliefs leads to more cooperation. It helps people make good decisions in unusual or ambiguous situations, when there is no time to consult others, or when there appears to be no written rule to follow.

A strong culture provides an efficient alternative to bureaucratic rules and autocratic controls.[36] When all people in the organization are dedicated to the same values and beliefs, it is easier for them to act in unison. In a strong culture, managers need not legislate rules to cover every possible scenario, but managers should be consistent in reinforcing common values and beliefs, which in turn, become the intrinsic guides for role perceptions, behaviors, and accomplishments. People will rely more on their common values and beliefs to guide their decisions and actions. TQM and the systems view is a particularly good managerial paradigm on which to build a strong culture. It encompasses a broad range of behaviors, practices, and techniques to optimize organizational processes and the work of managers and employees.

Managers should be proactive in doing all that is within their power to develop the kind of cultures needed to survive and prosper. They should not leave them to chance. They should make conscious attempts to bridge the gaps between internal subcultures, to build a sense of common purpose and consensus on how to achieve that purpose. Certainly, managers cannot control everything, but they can set the general patterns of culture. Again, TQM and the systems approach provides a foundation and direction for doing this in a realistic and humane fashion.

One way to think of building such a culture is in terms of the concept of leverage. Leverage means getting the most return for the effort expended. It means focusing on those actions that will generate the most *bang for the buck.* For example, Jack Welch focuses on the Work Out process with the goal that such meetings will translate into many improvements. Good managers always look for leverage points when minor actions bring great results. Such points bring everyone together and good things happen. Conversely, managers who do not appreciate leverage will expend energy on lots of ideas and actions that bring little return. Exhibit 10-3 on page 370 illustrates the concept of leverage and the return for aligning people and processes to create a culture where goals are more easily achieved, and what happens when this is not the case.

Managerial paradigm
The context and sense of order people bring to the act of conducting a business.

The Problems of a Strong Culture

There are certainly benefits to strong culture. However, there are also problems.[37] Strong culture can lead to stagnation, since there are strong forces making people conform to the accepted cultural paradigm. It may encourage narrow-mindedness and the *not invented here* syndrome when employees are not interested

EXHIBIT 10-3
Leverage when culture and
processes are aligned and when
they are not

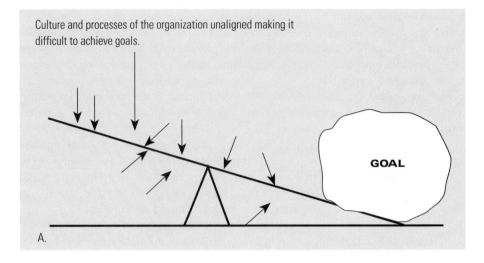

Culture and processes of the organization unaligned making it
difficult to achieve goals.

GOAL

A.

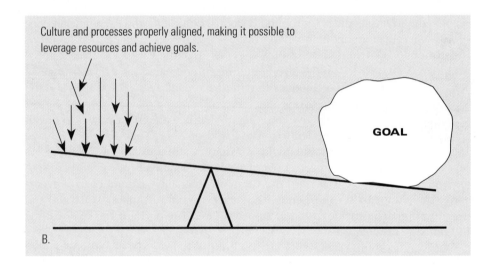

Culture and processes properly aligned, making it possible to
leverage resources and achieve goals.

GOAL

B.

in ideas from the outside. It makes it difficult for people to perceive new opportunities for change. Nonconformity is suppressed, yet it is what can lead to improvement. If the demands of the environment change, and the strong culture keeps people from responding, it can spell the demise of the organization.

Even when people think of new ideas, the strong culture may keep them from making any changes. For example, a company we will call GEO hired a facilitator named Pete to help them implement a Total Quality Management program, which is now required by many government contracts in the defense industry. GEO managers intended to only meet minimal requirements so they could argue that the terms of the contract were met. Pete helped put a program in place, but he also attempted to actually change the way GEO was managed.

Unfortunately, GEO managers had no intention of changing. Pete incessantly pushed his agenda and frequently chastised managers. Ultimately, Pete was rejected by the organization and laid off. The GEO Total Quality Management program continued to exist only on paper. Managers never really changed. Pete thrashed and kicked the whole way, but he never diverted the path of the GEO organization. Pete was doomed by GEO's strong culture from the beginning, but it does not have to be this way in every strong culture.

Making the Best of a Strong Culture

The secret to making the best of a strong culture is to make the cultural values and beliefs consistent with actions that are most likely to ensure an organization's long-term survival and prosperity. For example, many organizations are establishing a Total Quality strategy focused on improving customer value. The concept of organizational culture can help managers implement Total Quality Management by facilitating two important features: (1) teamwork for integrated efforts to improve customer value, and (2) the practice of continuous improvement throughout the organization.

Teamwork for Integration.   A Total Quality culture provides everyone in the organization with a common focus—the customer. The concept of culture can help managers understand how to accomplish this integration. The key is to establish a shared understanding that cuts across all functions, divisions, and levels of the organization.

While managers should not set out to destroy subcultures, they should seek to develop shared beliefs, values, and assumptions. All subgroups within the organization should understand the big picture and how they fit into it; share common goals and have consensus on how to accomplish those goals; and perceive the compatibility of everybody's roles in helping the organization achieve its mission. With this mutual understanding, subgroups will more easily integrate their efforts for Total Quality.

The Practice of Continuous Improvement.   The values of a Total Quality culture insist on continuous improvement and challenging the status quo. It builds in a self-corrective mechanism to continuously improve the culture along with its processes and outputs. It ensures that the culture evolves to match the organization's strategy for serving customers.

A Total Quality culture recognizes that a certain amount of nonconformity can be beneficial. Creative thought, sharing of diverse opinions, and change are valued as means to achieve improvement. Nonconformists, such as mavericks and rebels, can give the organization unique perspectives and visions. They can help avoid certain blindspots, unforeseen threats, and opportunities.[38] In a culture based on TQM, managers must achieve a balance with enough nonconformity to avoid stagnation and enough conformity to ensure harmony and continuity in social relationships.

TQM and Continuous Cultural Change.   With the values of continuous improvement and challenging the status quo, a TQM culture overcomes the tendency for stagnation inherent to a strong culture. In this sense, having a strong TQM culture would seem to be a contradiction, because culture, itself, is a force for stability. If a culture has a core value that encourages instability by challenging the status quo, it would seem self-defeating. Indeed, this is the irony of a Total Quality culture. It is designed to continuously remake itself, to maintain relevance to the changing demands of the environment, particularly customers.

Delight '94

Strong Culture and Total Quality Management

The values of a TQM culture emphasize the importance of trust, open communication, willingness to confront problems, openness to change, and adaptability. Further, in a TQM culture, these values are directed toward the strategic purpose of aligning people, processes, and resources to create value for customers. With Total Quality, strong culture becomes an asset. It inspires and demands continuous improvement for strategic purposes.

A strong Total Quality culture also provides a customer-focused vision with which people more readily identify. It is more compatible with people's general value systems. People throughout the organization become much more enthusiastic about improving for customers than they do about improving to please the boss, or to enhance productivity, reduce costs, or improve financial performance—all internally focused goals that do not necessarily benefit the organization in the long run. In fact, campaigns to squeeze out more productivity or reduce costs often turn off workers. Workers often see these campaigns as manipulations by management to achieve self-serving purposes like bonuses or promotions or to please Wall Street analysts, who do not care about employees.

One of the most admired and successful companies in the U.S. is Wal-Mart. Sam Walton established what he called his ten rules of business, though he always favored those who followed rule ten, which, if interpreted in the right spirit suggests breaking the rules. Though it is important to point out that the way any company sets up a culture based on the principles of TQM is special to them, Sam Walton's ten rules[39] are a good example of the values of a TQM company.

Rule 1:   *Commit to your business.* Believe in it more than anybody else. Passion and commitment can make all the difference.

Rule 2:   *Share your profits with all your associates and treat them as partners.* In turn, they will treat you as a partner and together you will perform beyond your wildest dreams.

Rule 3:   *Motivate your partners.* Constantly, day by day, think of new ways to challenge your partners. Set high goals. Keep everybody guessing about your next trick. Keep them involved.

Rule 4:   *Communicate everything you possibly can to your partners.* The more they know, the more they'll understand. The more they understand, the more they'll care. Once they care, there is no stopping them.

Rule 5:   *Appreciate everything your associates do for the business.* A paycheck and stock option are one kind of appreciation, but nothing works so well as a few well-chosen, well-timed sincere words of praise. They're absolutely free and worth a fortune.

Rule 6:   *Celebrate your successes; find humor in your failures.* Don't take yourself so seriously. Have fun, show enthusiasm—always.

Rule 7:   *Listen to everyone in your company and figure out ways to get them talking.* The folks on the front lines—the ones who actually talk to the customer—are the only ones who really know what's going on out there.

Rule 8:   *Exceed your customers' expectations.* If you do, they'll come back over and over. Give them what they want—and a little more.

SOUTHWEST AIRLINES: PRODUCTIVITY, PROFITS, AND A GREAT PLACE TO WORK

How well is Southwestern doing in the airline business? At the beginning of the chapter we said that it was profitable when all the other airlines were losing money. Part of the reason for this success is that Southwest, with its no frills but low prices approach to serving customers and its fast turnaround of planes, is far more productive than any of the five largest airlines in the U.S. Exhibit 10-4 shows the dramatic difference between Southwest and other airlines. In every category, Southwest is operating more efficiently and has lower costs than its rivals.

Southwest is entering new markets and making acquisitions. In the case of acquisitions, employees bend over backwards to welcome new employees to the family and make sure they are treated fairly. When Southwest acquired Morris Air (based in Salt Lake City) in 1993, hundreds of Southwest employees sent candy, cards, and company T-shirts to Morris employees welcoming them to the fold.

Because its fares are so low, it attracts passengers who would not normally fly and this expands the market for its services. For example, the company started a new service in 1993, between Louisville and Chicago at a time when only about 8,000 people per week were making this trip. After Southwest entered the market, with its low fares and frequent service, this number jumped to 26,000. Similar growth happened when Southwest started a $49 one-way fare between St. Louis and Kansas City which TWA was serving with a fare of $250.

Not only does Southwest lead the industry in profitability and productivity, in 1992 and 1993, it also won the Department of Transportation's Triple Crown—most on-time flights, best baggage handling, and highest customer satisfaction. How this happens and the difference between Southwest and other airlines, notes a Wall Street analyst "is the effort Herb gets out of the people who work for him. That is very hard to duplicate." What this analyst should have noted is that these people do not work *for* Kelleher, they work *with* him to create enjoyable jobs, an exciting workplace, and continuously improve their ability to deliver value to their customers.

EXHIBIT 10-4 Productivity at Southwest						
	American	**Delta**	**Northwest**	**Southwest**	**United**	**USAir**
Cost per available seat mile	8.9 cents	9.4 cents	9.1 cents	7.0 cents	9.6 cents	10.8 cents
Passengers per employee	840	1,114	919	2,443	798	1,118
Employees per aircraft	152	134	127	81	157	111

Source: Adapted from Kenneth Labich, "Is Herb Kelleher the Best CEO in America?" *Fortune*, May 2, 1994, p.50.

Rule 9: *Control your expenses better than your competition.* This is where you can always find competitive advantage. For 25 years Wal-Mart has been No. 1 for the lowest ratio of expenses to sales. This can cover a lot of other mistakes.

Rule 10: *Swim upstream.* Go the other way. Ignore conventional wisdom. If everybody else is doing it one way, there's a good chance you can find your niche by going in exactly the opposite direction.

Wal-Mart has taken these values to heart and created a culture that keeps value to customers high, expenses low, and associates committed. In so doing, this company with headquarters in Bentonville, Arkansas, has also become the leading retailer in the U.S.

THINKING CRITICALLY

1. How would you label yourself as a member of an organization—a maverick, a good soldier, an adapter, or a rebel? Whichever category you select, how do you think this will help you contribute to your company's cultural development and its ability to serve customers?

2. Why do you think the values espoused by TQM—focus on customers, process-orientation, use data to make decisions, and focus on teams—might be a good basis for an organizational culture. How do you think Herb Kelleher's Southwest Airlines reflects these values?

3. Give three specific potential examples of how Sam Walton's ten rules would influence the decisions of a Wal-Mart manager, for example in dealing with suppliers or compensating associates.

SUMMARY

What is Organizational Culture?
- Organizational culture is analogous to individual personality and provides cues for guiding and understanding behavior.
- Culture is an organizing device that helps remove uncertainty for employees and provides a context for doing the company's work.
- Employees, based on their experience and understanding, adapt to the tone set by top managers, and through time and learning this interaction results in culture.
- Culture has a visible part, the physical artifacts and the behaviors, and a hidden part, the values, beliefs, and assumptions. The latter is more important than the former for understanding and changing a culture.

How and Why an Organizational Culture Develops
- Cultures develop because of the human need for order and stability and as the means to work together to solve problems as a group.

- Founders and organizational leaders have the most influence on the values and beliefs of an organization, but they must be consistent in adhering to them and must be willing to change them when they do not facilitate responsiveness to customer needs.

- Cultural learning and change also take place through (1) learning from consequences, (2) avoidance learning, and (3) socialization learning.

Culture, Individual, and Organizational Behavior

- While culture provides a context for employee behavior, there will also be diversity and nonconformity, which can either be a negative or positive for the organization.

- A strong culture, or a managerial paradigm, facilitates interaction and decision-making, and dealing with diverse problems in a consistent manner. However, it can also promote close-mindedness and the *not invented here* syndrome.

- TQM provides a sound basis for the development of a strong culture that is open to change and improvement.

KEY TERMS

Artifacts 353	Managerial paradigm 369
Assumptions 354	Paradigm 368
Behaviors 353	Role models 366
Beliefs 354	Socialization 366
Cultural consistency 362	Strong culture 368
Cultural nonconformity 367	Symbolic or abstract learning 364
Cultural view of organizations 352	Subculture 368
Culture 350	Values 354
Learning from consequences 364	

REVIEW QUESTIONS

1. What is the relation between culture and behavior in an organization?
2. Why is it important for managers to be aware of the values, beliefs, and assumptions that underlie organizational culture?
3. What are the three levels of organizational culture and how they are related?
4. How does the human need for stability and order contribute to the development of organizational culture?
5. What is the relation between the organization's need to solve problems and its culture?
6. Why are founders and top managers so central in the development and change of an organization's culture?

7. What are the three ways individuals learn in an organization? How does this learning influence the development and change of culture?
8. How does cultural nonconformity influence cultural change?
9. How do the values of TQM help create a culture that is open, stable, yet constantly changing?

EXPERIENTIAL EXERCISE

Assemble into teams of five or six people. Assume that you are the founders of a new business organization. (For the purposes of this exercise, also assume that it does not matter what type of business.) Your task is to articulate the values (convictions about what is right and moral, e.g., you do not hurt others to achieve goals), beliefs (how the components of the organizations are related to one another to create order and bring about action, e.g., if we behave ethically, this is good business), and assumptions (ingrained and unquestioned beliefs about how the world works, e.g., profitability is necessary to survive) that will form a sound basis for working together inside the organization and succeeding in the marketplace.

In doing this, start with separate sheets of paper for values, beliefs, and assumptions and come to an agreement on each category. You probably should not have more than three or four items listed for each one. If there are disagreements, try to resolve them among yourselves using the criteria that only those values, beliefs, and assumptions that are likely to perpetuate the long-term survival and prosperity of the organization should be retained.

Compare your final lists with the ideas of Total Quality Management, which call for focus on delivering customer value, align and manage processes rather than people, use data to make decisions, continuously improve, work in teams, and train and empower people so they can maximize their contributions. Answer the following questions:

1. How are your listed values, beliefs, and assumptions compatible or not compatible with the principles of TQM?
2. What might cause you to compromise your values, beliefs, and assumptions to achieve some business purpose? Why would it be a good idea to make such compromises, or would it?
3. Most lists of values, beliefs, and assumptions will seem idealistic. Are yours? If you find them compatible with TQM, what does that tell you about the relationship between doing things right and being successful?

Each team should choose one person to present their findings to the class.

CASE ANALYSIS AND APPLICATION
A Strategy for Service—Disney Style[40]

The Walt Disney World Resort, located a few miles southwest of Orlando, Florida, includes the Magic Kingdom Park, EPCOT Center, the Disney-MGM Studios Theme Park, resorts, and recreational facilities. Guests at the Walt Disney World Resort typically comment on three main aspects of the quality of service: the cleanliness of the place, the show itself, and the friendliness of the employees. These reactions are compiled through comments, surveys, focus groups, and letters. If you visit the resort, you might be prompted to ask, "How does Disney get over 32,000 employees (called cast members) to perform more than 1,400 different jobs (called roles) and deliver quality service with a smile? How do they do this for millions of guests, 365 days a year, often in 98 degree heat and 100% humidity? How do they maintain a quality service standard that many say is unmatched anywhere?"

The compliments that Walt Disney World Resort receives from its guests reflect the original business philosophy of Walt Disney, who summed it up by saying:

- Quality will win out!
- Give the people everything you can give them;
- Keep the place as clean as you can keep it;
- Keep it friendly;
- Make it a fun place to be.

The Disney organization believes that if the guests are happy, they'll return. Repeat visitation is the name of the game. In fact, most of the guests who visit the resort most years have visited before. Many people travel great distances to spend time there. Disney understands that it cannot disappoint a guest, even once; if it does, the guest may never return. Each cast member serves each guest in a series of *magic moments* that add up to the overall experience. It is this understanding that defines Disney's service as *guest-driven*.

Rick Johnson, manager of Business Programs for Walt Disney World Seminar Productions, states, "The answer to how Disney does it, is the corporate culture." Disney defines quality service as a series of behaviors exhibited by cast members in the presence of guests. These behaviors include smiling, making eye contact, using pleasant phrases, performing their role functions, and implementing the many other details that add up to the personal touch in the eyes of guests. At the core of this approach is the Disney philosophy that people (both guests and cast members) are products of their environments. To the degree that an environment can be controlled, the appropriate reactions of people within that environment can be predicted. Disney, therefore, strives to control, within good business sense, as much of the environment at the resort as possible.

Discussion Questions

1. What Disney values and beliefs about its business does this case illustrate?
2. Do you think Disney's attempt to control the environment and the responses of its cast members to guests is smart business practice? If the park remained just the same, but service was just average, how do think this would affect the success of the Disney World Resort?
3. Identify a service organization you have recently patronized, such as a restaurant, bank, or government agency. Do you think the quality of service you received was based on a similar philosophy to Disney? Why or why not? What does that tell you about the culture and values of that business?

VIDEO CASE: COMBINING QUALITY MANAGEMENT AND SOCIAL RESPONSIBILITY
Jack Stack

Jack Stack, president and chief executive officer of Springfield ReManufacturing Corporation (SRC), Springfield, Missouri, has pioneered a highly effective and democratic management system that requires all employees to learn and use SRC's monthly financial statements to improve the company's performance. Through *open book management* and worker participation, Stack has elicited huge productivity gains and turned around a failing manufacturing plant in an intensely competitive industry. The system has not only made SRC highly competitive and responsive to changing market conditions, but has also built a highly motivated workforce and an exceptionally open and robust corporate culture.

This remarkable system of running a company—dubbed "The Great Game of Business" by Stack—grew out of an attempt to save 119 jobs at a troubled engine remanufacturing plant then owned by International Harvester. In 1983, rather than accepting a likely shutdown or sale of the factory, Stack led 12 fellow managers in negotiating a leveraged buyout of the plant. Even though worker morale was low and the factory purchase required an unprecedented debt-to-equity ratio of 89 to 1, Stack and his colleagues were convinced that they could become profitable. Their strategy: revamp the production process. Teach everyone, from executive to shop floor worker, how their individual work performances affected key financial results. Forge an open and cooperative work culture. And give workers a substantial equity stake in the company.

Over the past ten years, the company has wildly exceeded all of these goals. SRC's annual revenues have grown from $16 million to over $70 million. Its workforce has grown from 119 to 439 employees, and another 300 jobs have been added as nine new subsidiaries were created. SRC's highly innovative management system has been so successful that hundreds of business people travel to Springfield each year to participate in the company's seminars. Stack's book about SRC's management philosophy and practice, *The Great Game of Business* (1992), has sold more than 50,000 copies.

The SRC management philosophy illustrates how managers can elicit the resourcefulness and higher aspirations of every employee, boosting business performance in the process. It has also demonstrated how an open corporate culture built around genuine communication, trust, worker empowerment and clear standards of accountability can greatly enhance a company's competitiveness and long-term growth.

Video Case Questions

1. Describe the nature of the changes in SRC's organizational culture.
2. How did the leaders at SRC accomplish these changes?
3. What were the positive outcomes of these changes for the various SRC stakeholders?

ALLIANT HEALTH SYSTEM: CULTURAL AND STRUCTURAL CHANGE

Alliant Health System is a not-for-profit healthcare corporation located in Louisville, Kentucky. In 1989, three organizations (Norton Hospital, Methodist Evangelical Hospital, and Kosair Children's Hospital) merged to form the Alliant Health System. The oldest of the three hospitals, Norton Hospital, opened in 1886, and is composed of several units, including coronary and intensive care units, a psychiatric unit, a hematology-oncology unit, rheumatory care, cardiovascular surgery, and a Women's Pavillion with a wide range of women's programs. Methodist Evangelical Hospital provides an array of adult and ambulatory healthcare services, such as orthopedics, urology, opthalmology, diabetes, and toxicology. Kosair Children's Hospital provides acute care for children. Alliant now serves more than 32,00 inpatients and 140,000 outpatients each year.

In the wake of rising healthcare costs and increased societal and legislative pressures for reform, many healthcare providers are trying to change the way they do business. Alliant has led these efforts in the healthcare industry. The foundation for its current efforts were established in 1986, before the merger of the three hospitals that formed Alliant. Led by President and CEO Rodney Wolford, Norton Hospital became one of the nation's first healthcare organizations to implement TQM to improve the quality, appropriateness, and effectiveness of its healthcare. Norton Hospital decided to base its TQM effort on an extensive benchmarking effort to learn from the country's TQM leaders, including IBM, Hewlett Packard, General Electric, L. L. Bean, Johnson & Johnson, McDonalds, and the Ford Motor Company. After visiting these companies, the leaders at Norton identified several principles they thought would be important in succeeding with Total Quality. These principles, listed here, are still an important part of Alliant's TQM philosophy.

1. **Meeting Customer Requirements.** Quality is meeting defined requirements of the customer, whether "quality in fact "(based on technical, functional, or professional standards), or "quality in perception" (based on customers' perceptions).

2. **Continuous Improvement.** Errors are contrary to quality requirements, and may relate to structure, process, or outcomes. Errors and their correction cost money. Quality improvement must center around the reduction of errors, through an attitude that no level of error is acceptable.

3. **Management by Prevention.** Rather than being reactionary in nature and simply focusing on a "quick fix," we must anticipate errors and take whatever steps are necessary to avoid them. When errors occur, root causes must be identified and eliminated to prevent recurrence.

4. **Performance Measures.** All types of quality can be measured. Measurement is required if we are to improve. Quality in healthcare can be measured across six components:
   a. Competency (professional and/or organization)
   b. Appropriateness/accessibility
   c. Resource utilization (efficiency)
   d. Effectiveness (desired outcome)
   e. Safety/risk management
   f. Customer satisfaction

5. **Action for Improvement.** A systematic process must exist for defining the error, identifying the root cause, determining the action to eliminate the root cause, implementing the action, and measuring the effectiveness of the action taken.

6. **Ownership.** For quality improvement to achieve its potential, all employees must feel a sense of ownership (e.g., responsibility, pride,

---

This case was prepared by Jeff Kudish, Rick Carter, and Greg Bounds.

and involvement). *A culture of ownership requires management to:* (1) support innovation; (2) recognize and reward quality improvement; (3) communicate owner information; and (4) remove barriers to quality (e.g., those system defenses which keep employees from achieving error-free work).

Cultural Changes to Realize the Principles

Over the years Alliant has done a number of things to bring these principles to life in its culture. Alliant leaders have developed formal statements of the organization's mission and vision for the future. Managers are required to develop specific action plans for improvement at all levels of the organization. Alliant established an infrastructure to support TQM. It included a policy-setting and planning steering committee, as well as committees and employee teams to recommend policy changes, involve people in quality improvement, and promote decision making at the lowest possible level. Realizing that the success of TQM depended on linking the skills, abilities, and commitment of its people, Alliant provided extensive training on the quality, philosophy, goals, systems, and improvement processes. Alliant also offers staff experts to help managers with one-to-one or small group facilitation, and to assist in developing survey instruments to gather information from internal and external customers. These and other feedback mechanisms allow customers and employees to identify opportunities for improvement.

As another key component, Alliant also developed a quality review process that would measure and monitor quality for all areas of the hospital. Each department defined its scope of service, its customers, quality indicators, requirements, and monitoring processes for each key aspect of service. Alliant redesigned both the management and employee performance appraisal systems to ensure that individuals' performance expectations are directly linked to the corporate values and the TQM philosophy.

Alliant put in place Quality Improvement Teams (QITs) to allow employee participation (at all levels) in structured problem-solving processes. Today, after being provided with the necessary skills and abilities (e.g., focusing on managing by fact, identifying root causes, etc.), QIT members are empowered to identify, attack, and solve organizational problems. If a quality improvement plan (QIP) affects several different parts of the organization, each of the effected departments contribute a member to the QIT. For example, in response to findings from a customer survey, Alliant officials decided to examine its billing process, with the objective being twofold: (1) to reduce cycle time (e.g., increase the promptness of billings) and (2) to increase the readability of bills (e.g., make bills more understandable and clear). The cross-functional QIT that addressed these issues included representatives from the finance, medical records, customer service, admitting, and various other clinical departments. Medical staff also work together to develop consensus on ideal treatment processes.

Alliant also developed systems for improving the measurement of clinical quality by taking into account the relative illness severity of patients, providing comparative data, and focusing on the long-term outcomes of treatment processes. Alliant also decided to improve its planning process by developing annual and long-term corporate goals that will be supported by the operations and capital budgets.

Self-Directed Work Teams

Up until 1990, Alliant's employee involvement strategy allowed employees to participate in problem identification, problem solving, and decision making through vehicles such as QITs. However, individual jobs were not changed, nor were managerial roles changed dramatically. However, in 1990, jobs changed to allow more variety, autonomy, feedback, and personal growth as self-directed teams/work groups were allowed to take over certain management functions. Interestingly, however, the evolution of self-directed teams occurred somewhat unexpectedly.

In 1990, several of Alliant's second- and third-shift medical laboratories began losing supervisors. In the absence of replacement supervisors, employees began to manage things by themselves. Even more fascinating was that the employees, like the laboratory personnel on the third-shift at Kosairs Children Hospital, were functioning more happily and productively without a supervisor. Alliant executives were so impressed with this finding that they listed creation of at least nine more self-directed work groups as a corporate goal for 1991. Hence, the teams that accidentally sprouted by supervisory attrition now found themselves as role models.

Bill Newkirk of Alliant's Education and Development department was charged to help establish these self-managed teams. After a careful study, Newkirk and his colleagues designed a list of requirements for shared-direction, including a formal process of unit readiness surveys, steering committee deliberation, just-in-time training and education, tracking, and evaluation. As a result of these efforts, ten self-directed teams were formed (Weber, 1993). In 1992, the Alliant goal statement increased the goal to 25 teams. Again the quota was met. In fact, the goal was exceeded—34 teams were in place by the end of 1992. Indeed, the outlook was bright for 1993.

Unfortunately, Alliant's goal of establishing more self-directed teams never materialized. Instead, in the absence of essential support systems (e.g., there were no group-level incentives or reward systems to reinforce the team concept; no mechanisms for team or peer reviews; insufficient team training, relaxed standards, etc.), many of the existing teams found it difficult to sustain themselves. In addition, the move toward self-directed teams acted as a disincentive for those managers who feared that such structures would ultimately displace their jobs. Overall, as support unraveled, Alliant was forced to reduce the number of self-directed work teams to 19 in 1993.

Restructuring Toward Patient Care Centers (PCCs)

Despite the problems Alliant encountered with its self-directed work teams, there were good things happening on the horizon. From the inception of Alliant's quest for excellence in 1986, to early 1993, the culture of the organization and the design of jobs was altered; however, the organizational structure did not change. This began to change in 1993. In an effort to better meet their customers' needs, Alliant had been examining the idea of moving from traditional, functionally designed organizations/departments (e.g., nursing, patient registration, finance, food, and nutrition services) to product-centered business units. By shifting resources and moving to product-centered, decentralized, *patient care centers* (PCCs), Alliant believed it could better organize its work and better meet the needs of patients. While centralized functions (e.g., nursing) would not be eliminated totally, under the PCC design, they would be dramatically reduced in size. The shift to PCCs represented a radical restructuring for Alliant, unlike anything the organization had ever experienced. While the self-directed work teams had been applied at the lowest levels of the organization, the changes associated with the PCCs would reach to the top of the management hierarchy.

In March of 1993, Alliant had reached a milestone—its executive committee approved recommendations (generated by three functional design teams) on the deployment of services to PCCs. These recommendations included how various jobs should be done in the patient centers, covering everything from patient registration to the purchase of supplies. The recommendations also outlined what kinds of work should be done by a central department and what should be relocated/redeployed to the patient care center.

The clinical services that were recommended for redeployment included phlebotomy, common lab test, basic respiratory care, and simple X-ray procedures for adults. Service functions that were redeployed included patient room cleaning, patient transportation, the ordering and delivery of meals, and inventory management (e.g., the ordering and distribution of supplies). Administrative functions include patient registration, chart analysis and abstraction, and concurrent coding, an activity needed for reimbursement of third-party payers.

Under the new structure, each PPC is managed by an executive manager who reports to an executive team led by a senior vice-president/administrator. The executive manager is accountable for: (1) employee selection, development, and involvement; (2) quality management (e.g., responsible for supporting and facilitating the QI process through employee teams, self-managed groups, the employee suggestions system, and physician committees); (3) planning and service development (e.g., market analysis and planning of the short- and long-term objectives of the PCC); (4) fiscal management (e.g., maintaining the profitability of the center); and (5) operational leadership (e.g., promoting the vision and operating requirements of the business unit).

Reporting to the executive manager is a clinical manager, as well as a host of team leaders from a variety of functional areas. The composition of teams in each PCC depends on the structure of the PCC. For example, a Pediatric Ambulatory PCC team might include members from functional areas such as Patient and Family Services, Respiratory Therapy, Children's X-rays, Environmental Services, and Nursing Services, among others. Under the PCC design, all other associates (team members) are classified as either a service, administrative, or clinical associates. Overall, each PCC has a total of three organizational layers.

Status of Alliant's Restructuring Efforts

Despite the 1993 goal to implement at least two PCCs, Alliant was only able to fully operationalize one by the end of the year, namely the Women's Pavillion Patient Care Center. Nevertheless, efforts are currently underway to operationalize several other PCCs during 1994, including the Psychiatry Patient Care Center and the Pediatric Ambulatory Care Center. Overall, Alliant's goal is to eventually have eleven PCCs in place. Early on, Alliant executives realized that the move to PCCs would be cost neutral for the first five years. In fact, some even predicted that Alliant would initially lose money on their investments because construction costs could off-set any short-term gains in reduced personnel expenses or overhead. For example, new admitting areas would have to be built for ten of the eleven PCCs. Just as important as the financial results were the reactions of the people who have to work within the PCCs.

Initial Perceptions. In April 1993, prior to the operationalization of the first PCC, Alliant decided to assess employees' reactions to the proposed PCC restructuring. Alliant used a 65 item survey to assess employees' attitudes toward several issues, including: (1) the move toward PCCs; (2) the status of work teams; (3) perceptions of the characteristics associated with employees' jobs; and (4) overall job satisfaction. A total of 1738 employees responded to the survey. The results suggested that there were great differences between the perceptions of managers and non-managers with regard to the PCC-oriented questions. While managers generally agreed that they understood and supported the transition toward PCCs, employees were markedly less optimistic and supportive of the new strategic direction. For example, while there was a general perception that a change in healthcare was necessary, employees did not believe that the transition to PCCs would likely result in improved patient care. This may have been due to the fact that they also reported that they didn't understand the reasoning behind the restructuring. Overall, while there was strong support from the top of the agency, it was clear that top management was faced with a dilemma. If the move toward a PCC infrastructure was to be successful, Alliant had to do a better job of communicating the corporate vision to employees.

Reactions to Implementation. Three of the nine team leaders of the Women's Pavillion PCC resigned their leader roles after six months. They cited several reasons for stepping down. For example, most team leaders suffered from role overload and role ambiguity. Because the PCC structure was a new concept to Alliant, making it work meant devoting a lot of extra effort and time to the cause. Further, it meant not just managing others, but also getting one's hands dirty in daily issues. Being part of a PCC also meant having to negotiate extensively with centralized functional areas. According to some team leaders, there was simply too much time spent negotiating for goods and services. Alliant's flatter structure also impacted the size of each of the functional teams within the PCC. Team leaders now found themselves facilitating large groups of individuals. This larger composition of team members (e.g., direct reports) increased the complexity and difficulty of team leaders' roles. Taken together, the team leader role was just too stressful and demanding for some individuals.

Moreover, many team leaders felt that they had an insufficient understanding of *both* their roles and team members' roles. This was partly due to the limited amount of training provided by Alliant's Education and Development Department. Although team leaders went through several days of training, the training content focused on theoretical issues (e.g., gaining an awareness of PCC roles/behaviors), rather than providing team leaders with experiential learning/skills training. Since the concept of PCCs was so new the Education and Development staff was not

sure of the specific, requisite skills needed to successfully manage a PCC. Instead, they could only talk broadly with regard to team leaders' roles.

Finally, some team leaders felt that top management had let them down. For example, some leaders felt that there was too little support from upper management. Many also perceived that their hopes/expectations were not being met. Despite being told at the outset that they would be empowered to make many critical decisions, the truth was they were given too little discretion to take action. In short, top management was not "walking its talk."

Under the PCC structure, functions such as the transportation of people/goods and dietary services were supposed to be managed by the PCC's executive manager. This meant that an executive manager could pull resources from centralized functions as needed. Unfortunately, Alliant executives had grossly underestimated the amount of support needed by each of the PCCs. What resulted was a potential fiasco. Using this deployment strategy (pulling personnel from centralized functions as needed and placing them into a PCC), the Women's Pavillion nearly stripped the centralized departments of all their employees. To make matters worse, they tended to take the organization stars, leaving the centralized department with a skeleton staff of weaker performers.

Not surprisingly, Alliant executives had to step back and modify their

deployment strategy. Rather than taking a functional unit-by-unit approach when starting up their PCCs (e.g., deploying folks as needed each time a PCC becomes operational), they decided to allocate personnel to various areas, even if those areas weren't targeted for PCCs. By doing so, these areas would not be greatly effected each time a PCC became operational.

Promising Results

There is no question that Alliant's management team sees the shift to TQM as a never-ending quest, one driven by quality, continuous improvement, and customer delight. So far, Alliant has improved quality, contained costs, and decreased charges, thereby improving the value of the services they provide. For example, by examining critical paths at their Norton Psychiatric clinic, they claim to have reduced the average length of a patient's stay by 3.6 days, resulting in an average savings of $1577.00 per case. Similarly, a study of critical paths at their Methodist Evangelical Hospital resulted in the reduction of a patients stay (involving joint replacements) by 2.6 days, resulting in a savings of $2,136.00 per case.

While Alliant has celebrated several successes, they continue to deal with a variety of challenges. For example, in April 1993, it was announced that Rodney Wolford, the leader behind the agency's TQM initiative and the move toward patient-centered care, resigned from his position as president and CEO.

As the search for a new CEO got underway, many employees at Alliant were fearful that progress to date could be delayed, if not jeopardized, if Alliant executives hired a candidate from outside the organization. To the delight of almost everyone, the selection came from within the organization. Moreover, Wolford's successor was no stranger to the TQM philosophy. Rather, CEO Steve Williams was the chief operating officer under Wolford, as well as Alliant's first Director of TQM. The message was clear—in order to continue the journey, Alliant had to have a leader who was a staunch supporter of TQM and patient-centered care (PCCs).

? CASE QUESTIONS

1. Explain how restructuring around PCCs *helps* Alliant accomplish its plan to implement TQM principles throughout the organization. Do you see any problems with the restructuring that might *hinder* Alliant's TQM efforts?

2. Alliant is a good example of an organization that sees TQM as a way of life that requires cultural and structural change. They also realize that these changes (e.g., self-managed teams, PCCs) are not simple, overnight, quick-fixes. However, despite these convictions, managers do not always make the right decisions about how to make the changes succeed. Imagine that you were the new CEO, Steve Williams. What would you do to ensure that the restructuring of Alliant around PCCs will succeed? Develop an action plan that explains how you would support and reinforce the new structure.

SOCIAL AND CULTURAL PROCESSES

11. LEADERSHIP

LEARNING OBJECTIVES

When you finish this chapter you should be able to:

1. Describe the importance of leadership in successful management practice.

2. List and explain five bases for management power in an organization.

3. Describe the main components of the following theories of leadership and explain how they guide leadership behavior:
   —trait theory
   —Ohio State studies
   —Managerial Grid
   —Fiedler's contingency model
   —situational leadership theory
   —path-goal theory
   —Vroom-Yetton model

4. Distinguish between transactional and transformational leadership and explain how to become a transformational leader.

5. Explain how TQM provides insights into and direction for successful leadership behaviors.

GE: THE COMPANY THAT JACK BUILT[1]

Jack Welch had proven himself to be an ambitious man and a fierce competitor long before joining forces with General Electric (GE). His classmates described him as "relentless," "very competitive," a man who was "always looking one step ahead" and having "a desire to win." He received a Ph.D. in engineering from the University of Illinois in 1960, and earned the distinction of being the first student to complete his doctoral studies in only three years. The same year, Welch embarked on his life-long career with GE, having accepted a position with the company's plastics division in Pittsfield, Massachusetts. The company recognized his talent, and he progressed through a series of managerial positions with more and more responsibility until he assumed the helm of General Electric on April Fool's Day of 1981.

Welch was not impressed with the goal that had guided GE since the 1960s—to be a successful competitor in all of its businesses. Being a successful competitor was not enough for Welch, and he promptly upped the ante by setting a new company-wide goal: he had ambitions for each of GE's businesses to be a leader in its industry, ranking either number one or number two in the global market. He demanded quality, he envisioned unparalleled excellence, and he communicated his expectation in simple terms: "To me, quality and excellence mean being better than the best."

GE employees quickly realized that Welch was dedicated to the goal he had set. He introduced the "three circle concept" which divided GE's businesses into the areas of (1) core, (2) high technology, and (3) service. Listed within each circle were the businesses that were leaders in their markets; listed outside the circles were the businesses that had not yet succeeded in becoming number one or number

two. The message to the managers of those businesses outside the circle was clear: for their businesses to remain operative and justify the investment required, they had to find a way to move their enterprises into the circle. If they could not put themselves in the circle, GE would divest these businesses. There was little doubt among employees that Welch would fulfill his promise; by 1983, he had sold 118 businesses and product lines, freeing up $3.5 billion for investment in market-leading companies.

One of Welch's quality initiatives was to push authority for decision making down to the level of the operating units. In addition, he worked to increase the number of employees reporting to each manager. He stated that: "I firmly believe that an overburdened, overstretched executive is the best executive, because he or she doesn't have time to meddle, to deal in trivia, or to bother people. This way you have no choice but to let people flex their muscles, to let them grow and mature."

Welch continued to find ways to break GE of its bureaucratic tendencies. He initiated a 360 degree feedback program which provides managers with performance feedback from not only their supervisors, but from their subordinates, as well. Welch considered subordinates' evaluations to be a rich source of feedback, and he encouraged

managers to take them seriously. "If they don't improve, they have to go." Welch also created a program of town meetings designed to elicit employees' candid reviews and evaluations of management practices in their organizations. (See *A Look At TQM in Action* box in Chapter 10 on *Work Outs at GE*.) Welch ensured that employee input was given consideration and treated with respect as a valuable tool for maintaining quality business practices.

Welch did not believe that employees needed to create something new to gain recognition. "Parochialism—'not invented here'—is dead at GE," he proclaimed in his report to shareholders. "We don't claim to be the global fountainhead of management thought, but we may be the world's thirstiest pursuer of big ideas—from whatever their source—and we're not shy about adopting or adapting them." Welch is proud of the programs they have discovered and adopted from other companies. The implementation and success of adopted programs is the result of the "best practices" program he initiated. The early best practices program targeted about ten companies that showed higher productivity growth than GE could claim. A team of 10 or more GE managers visited the organizations and studied and questioned their methods. The result was that the managers returned to GE and implemented the "best of the best." GE is extolling the virtues of customer service as conceptualized at American Express, quality improvement as it is envisioned at Hewlett Packard, quick response cycle time reduction techniques gained from a company in New Zealand, Quick Market Intelligence as it is implemented at Wal-Mart. To become a world-class competitor, Welch saw the need to learn from the global market leaders.

Despite having increased GE's market value by $67.6 billion, Welch is still dreaming of a better GE. He has set goals for leaders throughout the company that include creating a customer-focused vision, gaining the self-confidence to empower other employees, developing "global brains and global sensitivity," embracing and welcoming change, and having boundless energy to inspire others. And while most Welch-watchers would marvel at the speed with which he inspired and transformed the General Electric company, Welch himself is still not content. "GE would be better off if I had acted faster." Will there ever be a ceiling on the GE legacy that Jack built?

Perhaps no area in management is considered as important or has been more thoroughly investigated than leadership. The term "leadership" provokes images of individuals like John F. Kennedy, Margaret Thatcher, Norman Schwarzkopf, Lee Iacocca, and Jack Welch. The importance of leadership is echoed in the fact that organizations pump millions of dollars per year into leadership training for managers and executives.

With all of this, many organizations are drifting because of poor leadership. Being a leader requires empowering people and taking risks, but the environment of many organizations discourages sharing power or trying new things. The message is to go along with the program, and employees end up aspiring to high-level positions in their functional area, such as human resources, marketing, or finance where they have input but are not directly responsible (or accountable) for making the major decisions that influence the organization's future. And pundits cite lack of leadership and political courage as primary reasons for our inability to deal with a runaway national debt and the health care crisis.[2]

We will begin this chapter by defining leadership and differentiating it from management and supervision. Then we will focus on the importance of leadership, especially in quality-driven organizations and review four major theoretical orientations. Finally we will integrate the various frameworks and provide you with some insight on the connection between TQM and leadership.

MEANING OF LEADERSHIP

Leadership can be a difficult term to define. Nearly every researcher in the field has their own definition. For this book, we will take the best of those and define **leadership** as *a process of influencing the activities of individuals or groups toward achieving a goal*. There are several important aspects of this definition:

- Leadership can occur only when two or more individuals work together; leadership cannot exist in isolation—there must a leader and a follower.

- Leadership involves a change in the individual being led. This change is typically both cognitive and behavioral. That is, leaders change others' perceptions of problems and their subsequent behavior. Moreover, subordinates follow a leader willingly.

- Leadership is an influence process. Leaders are effective at changing the behavior of others. For example, think back to the leadership of General Electric's Jack Welch in the opening case. His leadership transformed the manner in which employees performed their jobs at GE and resulted in a more participative, less bureaucratic culture.

Leadership A process of influencing the activities of individuals or groups toward achieving a goal.

Why is Leadership Important?

Simply put, leadership is probably the most important determinant of an organization's success. This can be seen very easily by examining the turnaround stories of several companies. One of the most dramatic turnarounds in the U.S. auto industry occurred at the General Motors plant in Fremont, California. In 1982, the plant was on the verge of closing. As Exhibit 11-1 shows, costs were high, productivity was low, and labor problems were rampant. The company was drifting without any direction. Employees were not motivated to move toward a common goal since no such goal had been articulated. Management-labor relations were terrible, and grievances were common. In this environment, individual and organizational performance deteriorated and was continuing to do so.

In 1984, the management of the plant changed. The New United Motors Manufacturing Incorporated (NUMMI) was formed as a partnership between GM and Toyota. The management of the plant was turned over to Toyota. The work force remained the same. The Toyota management team brought leadership to the plant. Instead of managing solely by the numbers, treating

EXHIBIT 11-1 Selected performance measures at the GM Plant in Fremont, California before and after NUMMI

MEASURE	1982	1985
Absenteeism	20%	2%
Grievances	2000	2
Strikes	3	0
Employees	5000	2500
Productivity	Lowest of GM Plants	Highest of GM Plants
Quality	Lowest of GM Plants	Highest of GM Plants
Costs	130% of GM Standard	100% of GM Standard

employees as machines, and having a short-term orientation, they lead an effort based on the long-term goal of creating customer satisfaction and taking full advantage of employees and their abilities. They moved the plant toward teams and provided extensive training to all employees. They created an environment based on mutual trust and high expectations. Today, NUMMI is thriving, having recently added production of Toyota pickup trucks to its successful Corolla, Prizm, and Nova lines of compact cars. Furthermore, the turnaround occurred very quickly.[3]

There are numerous other examples demonstrating the importance of leadership. Think about the turn-arounds (and those companies that have never had to turn themselves around) that you read about in papers and magazines. Leaders such as Lee Iacocca of Chrysler, David Kearns at Xerox, Fred Smith of FedEx, John Young at Hewlett Packard, and Robert Galvin at Motorola are a few notable examples. Leadership is also critical outside of the business world. Look at the effect that Mikhail Gorbachev had on the former Soviet Union, Vince Lombardi on the profession of football, and Martin Luther King, Jr. on the Civil Rights movement. Leadership is also critical for communities, towns, social clubs, churches, sports teams, and the successful operation of all organizations. Without leadership, the best ideas and plans are doomed to fail. In managing, no matter how competent you are as a decision maker or how creative you are as an individual, *your ultimate success will depend upon whether you are able to lead others*. The best ideas often end up in the board room trash can because there was inadequate leadership pushing for their adoption and implementation.

Leadership is critically important in organizations that consciously practice Total Quality Management. As we emphasized several times previously, TQM requires that employees focus on continuous improvement and deliver unparalleled customer value. There is no way that you can force someone to have a customer orientation. Similarly, you cannot make employees create innovative suggestions for improving organizational processes. Instead, you must be able to lead so as to bring about changes in their perceptions and attitudes about their jobs and responsibilities. And that is part of what a leader does.

Leadership Versus Management

Students often confuse leadership and management. In fact, many executives may not understand the difference. We can distinguish between them in terms of attitudes and behaviors. While leadership is the process of guiding others toward goal accomplishment, we can define management as the rational assessment of a situation, the development of goals and strategies to respond to the situation, and the design, organization, direction, and control of the activities required to attain the goals.[4] Thus, while leadership involves vision, motivation, and empathy, management is more detached and analytic. Good management brings order and consistency to key dimensions like processes and costs. Leadership involves setting a direction and inspiring people, and driving change within the organization. Exhibit 11-2 presents some differences between leaders and managers.[5] It is not a coincidence, by the way, that these differences are similar to those we presented in Chapter 3 showing the difference between a process manager and a traditional manager (see Exhibit 3-4, p. 87). TQM fosters leadership because it values actions that bring out the best in everyone for working together to deliver value to customers.

EXHIBIT 11-2   Some differences between leaders and managers

LEADERS	MANAGERS
• Innovate	• Administer
• Develop	• Maintain
• Inspire	• Control
• Long-term Oriented	• Short-term Oriented
• Originate	• Imitate
• Do the Right Thing	• Do Things Right
• Change the Status Quo	• Accept the Status Quo

An individual can be a great leader, and at the same time be a terrible manager, or conversely, he or she might be a terrible leader but a fantastic manager. In essence, management and leadership are conceptually independent of each other. Many start-up companies have strong leadership but eventually fail because they are poorly managed. For example, consider Steve Jobs (whom we introduced in Chapter 6) when he was head of Apple Computer. He had a vision for Apple, and his vision captured the minds, hearts, and imaginations of his employees and customers. However, as the company grew, it needed more attention focused on management of its processes to make sure it continued to effectively and efficiently deliver products customers will value—not just gee-whiz technology that Steve Jobs liked. The company needed to develop standardized policies and implement processes to contain costs. Jobs did not provide such management and, more importantly, was unwilling to delegate responsibility to others who were more equipped with management skills to do these things. As a result, he was forced out as CEO at Apple Computer, the company he co-founded. The same story is true of Rod Canion, co-founder of Compaq Computer. He too was forced out as his ability to manage the company in the face of increased competition and lower prices was found wanting.

The fact is both leadership and management are critical for organizational effectiveness. All managers of an organization need leadership skills, not just those at the top. Many organizations are restructuring and have pushed decision making down to the lowest level possible. These restructurings bring great changes in culture and values, along with new job roles and responsibilities for all employees. To carry off these kinds of changes requires leadership at all levels of the organization. Even a first-level supervisor must lead employees to take more responsibility for their work, to inspect their own work, to actively participate in continuous improvement groups, and to focus on customer needs. In essence, in today's work environment, leadership and management are *complementary*. A successful manager must be effective at leading *and* managing.

Several researchers have proposed that one of the major reasons why the U.S. has lost some competitive advantages in the global marketplace is that most organizations have become overmanaged and underled.[6] Consider the business curriculum at your school. If your program is like most, you will spend a lot of time in courses designed to help you develop strong analytical skills and make sound business decisions. For example, in finance you will learn about multiple methods to reduce the cost of capital. However, typically less than one course is devoted to leadership or developing leadership skills. This probably explains why most organizations spend huge sums of money providing leadership training for their managers. This is not unlike a medical school education that focuses on the technicalities of the human body and disease but teaches hardly anything on how to relate to patients, who must work with the doctor to heal themselves. An important goal of this chapter is to help you gain a greater appreciation for the role of leadership so you will be a more successful manager.

Leader Emergence Versus Leader Effectiveness

Leadership research has focused on both leader emergence and the effectiveness of appointed leaders. Leader emergence and effectiveness represent two different processes. **Leader emergence** requires that *peers recognize the leadership potential of a group member and allow that person to influence their futures.* (Notice here we are not talking about *manager* emergence, though there may be overlap.) For example, the president of a fraternity is an emergent leader. This individual emerged into leadership because he was supported by his fraternity members. Four major factors appear to be associated with leader emergence:[7]

1. **Participation Rates:** Group members who participate at a higher rate have a higher probability of emerging as leaders.
2. **Expertise/Problem Solving:** Individuals who contribute more to solving the group's problems have a higher probability of emerging as a leader.
3. **Social Skills:** Individuals who are tactful, quickly able to establish relationships with others, and sympathetic to others' needs and problems have a higher probability of emerging as a leader.
4. **Power Motive:** Individuals who enjoy power and like being in positions of responsibility have a higher probability of emerging as a leader.

Most organizations do not select employees to managerial positions based upon the emergence of a leader through time. For example, when there is an opening for a group manager, most companies usually will not allow the group to function without a manager for several months to see who emerges as the group's leader. They will typically advertise the position and then select, either from within the company or from outside, the individual whom they believe is best suited for the position. In this context, leadership emergence is not as important because the organization has already appointed the leader.

Given this standard way of operating, it becomes important for organizations to figure out why some appointed leaders are effective and others are ineffective. Since most leadership research is funded and supported by organizations, it is not surprising that there are many more studies identifying factors that will predict the **leader effectiveness** of appointed managers than identifying factors that predict the emergence of leaders. Typically, leader effectiveness is *the acknowledged ability of a manager to guide a group toward goal accomplishment.* In fact, as you will soon see, all of the theories we will discuss are designed to predict and facilitate the leadership effectiveness of individuals already in place.

Bases of Power for Leaders

There are several bases of power through which leaders may influence employees.[8] To understand these bases, first consider the idea of influence and what it entails. What it means is that managers create the context for employee beliefs and understandings about what they are supposed to do and that give direction to their

---

Leader emergence A process where peers recognize the leadership potential of a group member and allow that person to influence their futures.

Leader effectiveness The acknowledged ability of a manager to guide a group toward goal accomplishment.

actions. But at a deeper level, the way managers influence suggests to employees what is important in the organization in terms of its values and how people are to be treated to achieve organizational goals. The idea of influence suggests that it is managers who shape the environment to which employees will adapt.

In Chapter 5 on ethics, we suggested that the Golden Rule was a good model for ethical behavior, but with the understanding that people learn how they should treat others by how they are treated. If managers rule by fiat and expect employees to be subservient and not question their authority, that mindset is what employees learn to value. But in an ironic way, they also come to mirror that behavior back to their managers. By not listening, managers are telling their employees that not listening is a positive value, and it often happens that such employees will not listen to their managers, doing the minimum to keep their jobs. They will not work hard for a manager (or pseudo-leader) who does not work for them. The same is also true in a more positive environment. When managers seek to make things go well for employees and establish an environment for accomplishment, where they listen to employees and give them the information and resources they need to do their jobs, the employees will likewise mirror this behavior. They will listen, share information, and want to maximize their performance. Creating this kind of environment is an important part of the influencing nature of leadership. It is an idea consistent with and part of the total quality approach to managing.

Let's return to the research about power and influence. Traditionally, leaders have relied on the formal power given to them by the organization. These bases of power are inherent in most managerial positions. They include: (1) reward power, (2) coercive power, (3) legitimate power, (4) expert power, (5) referent power. Let's review each of these.

Reward power operates *when the employees believe that their manager will reward them for compliance and performing various tasks.* Reward power is only useful when the organization provides the manager with rewards to control behavior. Such rewards might include a large budget for salary increases or the opportunity to promote employees.

> **Reward power** Influence based on employees' belief that the manager will reward them for compliance and performing various tasks.

Coercive power is based upon *the employees' beliefs that a manager can deliver punishments when they do not conform to directives.* Coercive power is becoming much less important in our society. Most organizations greatly restrict a manager's ability to punish a subordinate. Furthermore, while coercive power may have short-term benefits, it will not foster the development of good relationships with subordinates. In fact, subordinates will look for a way to "get even" with a manager who relies upon coercive power. As Dwight D. Eisenhower once said, "You do not lead by hitting people over the head—that's assault, not leadership." Many of the fragging incidents in Vietnam (officers being shot by their own soldiers) can be traced back to a high use of coercive power. This goes back to the idea that these managers have taught their subordinates how to treat them by how they have treated their subordinates.

> **Coercive power** Influence on employees based on their belief that a manager can deliver punishments for noncompliance with directives.

The third base of power provided by the organization is **legitimate power.** A manager has legitimate power because *employees believe that a managerial position automatically affords the manager certain rights and authority.* Legitimate power has the potential to be very dangerous for an organization. Its very existence means that ideas are given more attention simply because of the position from which they originated. (In the military, it means "salute the uniform not the person.")

> **Legitimate power** Influence that arises because employees believe that a manager's position automatically affords the manager certain rights and authority.

In many organizations, legitimate power has meant that the boss is always right, and this can result in many poor decisions and actions. For example, at

General Motors during the 1970s and 1980s, showing deference to authority had come to be a very important value, considered more important than actual performance. Middle managers were expected to meet out-of-town superiors at the airport, carry their bags, and chauffeur them around day and night. One group of Chevrolet sales executives had a refrigerator put in the hotel room of a visiting senior executive after they had heard that he liked to have a few cold beers before going to bed. Since the refrigerator would not fit through the door, they actually hired a crane to bring the refrigerator through the windows of the suite.[9] Such distorted perspectives on what legitimate power is and entails prevented information (especially negative information) from flowing up to the top management team and contributed to many of the current problems at General Motors.

Successful managers practice leadership by relying less on organizationally provided bases of power and more on their own personal style to influence subordinates. **Expert power** is based upon *the employees' belief that the manager has specialized knowledge, skills, or experiences to accomplish goals and objectives.* Hence, they listen to the manager and are willing to accommodate the manager's requests. For example, imagine that you were going sky-diving for the first time. Your instructor would have expert power. Because of your instructor's special expertise, you would be very attentive and follow every direction.

Referent power is based upon *the degree to which employees identify with and respect a manager.* They follow directives because they trust the manager. They believe that the manager would not ask them to do something that is not in their best interest and because they want the manager to like them. An example of referent power would be employees agreeing to work late without giving it a second thought, simply because their manager asked them to. They know that if their manager asked them to work late, it must be important and that the manager will, if at all possible, be working late with them.

While reward, coercive, and legitimate powers are inherent in managerial positions, expert and referent powers must be earned. The organization cannot force your employees to perceive you as an expert or as a trustworthy and high-integrity manager. You can gain expert and referent powers only through your actions, including demonstrating effective problem solving and treating employees with dignity and respect. Moreover, as organizations move to cross-functional teams, managers are frequently being asked to influence individuals over whom they have little formal authority. To be effective in such an environment, managers must finely hone their interpersonal and problem-solving skills and be able to influence employees through expert and referent powers. Exhibit 11-3 tells the story of one person's understanding of leadership based on referent power.

Expert power Influence on employees based on their belief that the manager has specialized knowledge, skills, or experiences to accomplish tasks.

Referent power Influence on employees based on the degree to which they identify with and respect a manager.

THINKING CRITICALLY

1. Who is the most effective *leader* that you have ever known personally? Why was this individual so effective?
2. Who is the most effective *manager* that you have ever known personally? Why was this individual so effective? Do you think the skills of managing and leading overlap for you? In considering these two questions, think about the differences in how you relate to a manager and a leader.
3. What basis of power do you use in your interactions with others? How could you move more toward referent and expert powers?

EXHIBIT 11-3   Knowing a Leader When You Follow One

John Cowan is a priest and writer who has written a book of essays called *Small Decencies: Reflections and Meditations on Being Human at Work.* A subject like leadership can be described in terms of science and theory, but in the end it boils down to performance and relationships among those being lead and the person leading. In his essay, "On Leadership," Cowan captures this point. The following is excerpted from that essay:

. . . Olson stood next to a pile of industrial pipe three times the diameter of anything I had ever handled. "You guys go see what you think. Cowan, go with 'em."

We descended the back stairs, worked our way through a crawlspace to the front wall, then back out to the street, swinging the metal finder to locate the main. Then they reported in. "Gotta hand-carry the bleeping pipe into the bleeping basement, no way to get a crane on it."

"Gotta weld the bleeping pipe down in that crawl hole; one bleeping mistake and the bleeping hotel burns up."

"Can't use the bleeping ditcher, gotta hand tunnel out from the bleeping basement."

"That's what I thought," said Olson with satisfaction. And all five of them were smiling back at him as if they had been granted a month's vacation. "So, let's do it." And we did it. With speed and joy and precision. After two days of constant sweat the only sign of our presence was six inches of capped pipe sticking into the basement and a square of fresh asphalt in the street.

It was a simple conspiracy. We were the small main and industrial crew. If it was tough to do, and it had to be done by hand, it was assigned to us. And we could do what nobody else could do, at least that is what Olson had us convinced was true.

. . . Cowan then asks and answers the question, What made Olson a leader?

1. He was always a step or three ahead of the game. Unlike other crews, we never waited for stuff, it was there.
2. He had a vision of what he wanted and he shared it and held us to it.
3. His values showed in every bead of sweat he generated.
4. We decided what to do; he corrected seldom, only when needed.
5. He understood himself better than most people do. "Don't know I should take it," he told me when he was offered a promotion to superintendent. "Like using my hands too much."

It's Richard E. Byrd's [the admiral and explorer of the North and South Poles] theory of leadership I have used in analyzing Olson, but with all due respect to behavioral science, if the theory and Olson had not matched, I'd question the theory. I know a leader when I have followed one.

Source: Selected excerpt from "On Leadership" from *Small Decencies* by John Cowan. Copyright © 1992 by John Cowan. Reprinted by permission of HarperCollins Publishers, Inc.

THEORETICAL APPROACHES TO LEADERSHIP

Several theoretical approaches have been developed to predict the effectiveness of leaders. These approaches focus on: (1) the traits of the leader, (2) the behaviors of the leader, (3) the combination of the situation and leader traits/behaviors, and (4) leading change in organizations and people. We now turn our attention to these major theoretical approaches.

Trait Approach to Leadership

The **trait approach** to leadership can be stated simply: *effective leaders have specific personality traits that make them successful.* This theory is often referred to as the "Great Man Theory" and assumes that effective leaders are born, not

Trait approach The assertion that effective leaders have specific personality traits that make them successful.

made. The trait approach to leadership is seen in Field Marshal Montgomery's description of an effective leader:

The leader must have infectious optimism, and the determination to persevere in the face of difficulties. He must also radiate confidence, relying on moral and spiritual principles and resources to work out rightly even when he himself is not too certain of the material outcome. He must be able to see his problems truly and whole. Self-control is a vital component of his make-up.[10]

It is clear that Montgomery believes that effective leaders have certain characteristics that ineffective leaders do not have. Based on his success, we must also suspect that Jack Welch of GE has such traits.

Researchers conducted approximately 100 studies on leader traits during the first half of the 20th century. The typical study tested the hypothesis that the effective leader has more of some attribute than the ineffective leader. As the attribute increased, leadership effectiveness was thought to increase. Traits frequently studied are presented in Exhibit 11-4. Perhaps one of the most controversial traits on the list is that of gender. Some interesting results of this research are presented in *A Look At Diversity* box on page 397.

A number of traits were found to differentiate leaders from non-leaders. Some of the most important leadership traits are described below.[11]

1. **Drive:** Successful leaders exert high levels of effort. They are ambitious, tenacious, and proactive.
2. **Leadership Motivation:** Successful leaders have a strong desire to lead and to influence others in support of an organization's vision.
3. **Honesty and Integrity:** Successful leaders are trustworthy in all dealings with others, and their actions are consistent with their words.

EXHIBIT 11-4 Leadership Traits Frequently Studied

Age	Height
Weight	Physique
Appearance	Fluency of Speech
Talkativeness	Intelligence
Knowledge	Originality
Adaptability	Extroversion
Dominance	Persistence
Ambition	Integrity
Self-Confidence	Self-Control
Independence	Gender
Diplomacy	Masculinity
Authoritarianism	Motivation
Perceptiveness	Empathy
Persistence	

THE MALE LEADERSHIP MYTH[12]

A large percentage of the population believes that men are more effective leaders than women. Stereotypes of females suggest that they are illogical, inconsistent, softhearted, and emotionally unstable. Consistent with this view, very few women have gained top management positions. Nevertheless, recent studies have found that women and men are equally effective in leading but use different leadership styles. Women often adopt a more participative, democratic leadership style, whereas men tend to adopt directive, autocratic styles. This difference in styles may prove advantageous to women, especially for those who lead Total Quality Management organizations. The "give and take" inherent within the participative management style may enable women to be better negotiators; it may also help them empower people through shared responsibility. Their willingness to share information and responsibility may result in higher performance. If men are unwilling or unable to adopt participative approaches, women may actually be more effective as leaders in the future.

A LOOK AT

DIVERSITY

4. **Self-Confidence:** Successful leaders are confident in their abilities and decisions and project this confidence when dealing with others.
5. **Intelligence:** Successful leaders have keen minds and the ability to gather, integrate, and interpret enormous amounts of information.
6. **Knowledge:** Successful leaders have a good understanding of the organization, its industry, and larger societal changes that may affect the organization's future.

While these are traits that distinguish leaders, you probably see that they are traits most of us would admire in others and ourselves, whether in a leadership position or not. Individuals exhibiting these traits usually are able to bring out the best in themselves and by so doing help bring out the best in others as well.

Personal Implications of the Trait Approach

The trait approach provides several suggestions for how you can enhance your leadership effectiveness. First, *know your strengths and weaknesses.* This means that you need to spend time reflecting on how you perform various tasks and how you respond to various situations. Furthermore, collect feedback from others and benchmark or compare your performance by observing how others respond to similar situations. Second, *use your skills to maximize your ability to contribute.* In other words, rely upon your strengths and try to avoid your weaknesses. As an example suppose that, when playing on a basketball team, you quickly learn that your strength is shooting the 17-foot jumper, and not driving to the basket. This understanding would dramatically enhance the quality of your play and of your team's performance. Third, *try to develop skills that you lack.* In other words, do not avoid difficult challenges; actively seek them. Always try to improve. Read about leadership, management, and interpersonal topics. Seek additional training whenever possible. Finally, *emphasize integrity in all your dealings with people.* Researchers have found this is probably the most critical leadership characteristic. The values of successful leaders indicate how important they believe in these types of behaviors. They are honest, ethical, and trustworthy. (Recall our discussion of the integrity approach to ethics in Chapter 5.) In fact, lack of integrity was the most common cause of failure among managers.[13] Without integrity, your probability of success as a leader will be dramatically reduced.

? THINKING CRITICALLY

1. Based on your experience, do you think you can identify a leader by personality traits? Why or why not?
2. Why is integrity potentially such an important trait for a leader?

BEHAVIORAL/SITUATIONAL APPROACHES TO LEADERSHIP

Despite the identification of some leadership traits, most of the findings of these studies were not very conclusive, and situational factors appeared to be more important, at least for studying leadership in a concrete manner. For example, the traits needed for leadership effectiveness on the debating team are different than the traits needed for leadership effectiveness on the football team. Similarly, the traits needed to be a successful leader at a small, start-up advertising agency are different than the traits needed to be an effective leader at a mature chemical company. These findings prompted many leadership researchers to discount the trait approach to leadership and instead focus on leader behavior. The essence of the **behavioral approach** is that *a leader's actual behavior, not traits, predicts leader effectiveness.*

For example, consider an individual who is fairly reserved and introverted. You would probably think that this individual would have difficulty being effective as a leader, given the social interactions required in leadership positions. However, even though the individual is naturally reserved, he or she may behave gregariously at work. This person may recognize the need to speak with employees, superiors, and peers and may warmly express appreciation for jobs well done. In essence, although this person does not have an outgoing personality, he or she is able to exhibit extroverted behaviors when needed at work. The point of this example is that our behaviors at work are often inconsistent with our basic traits. The behavioral approach to leadership shifts the focus from traits to actual behavior in leadership positions.

What are the behaviors that result in leadership effectiveness? Two major behavioral approaches have been proposed. We will examine these in the sections below.

Ohio State Leadership Studies

A large project to examine the behaviors of effective leaders was started at Ohio State University in the 1950s. This research interviewed over one thousand leaders and subordinates to identify the behaviors that are important for leader success. Research indicated that "consideration" and "initiating structure" are the two most important types of leader behavior.[14]

Consideration refers to *behavior indicating mutual trust, respect, and a certain warmth between managers and employees.* Examples of consideration behavior are asking about an employee's family, providing support during a challenging assignment, finding time to listen to subordinates' problems and give help when requested, allowing and encouraging subordinates to participate in decision making, and encouraging honest and forthright communication.

Initiating structure is *the degree to which a manager defines, structures, and organizes the roles of employees and implements standardized procedures to ensure goal accomplishment.* Examples of initiating structure include assigning employees to tasks, redirecting discussion toward processes and improvement, providing

---

Behavioral approach to leadership An approach that says the leader's actual behavior, not traits, predicts leader effectiveness.

Consideration Leader behavior indicating mutual trust, respect, and a certain warmth between managers and employees.

Initiating structure The degree to which a manager defines, structures and organizes the roles of employees and implements standardized procedures to ensure goal accomplishment.

guidance and instruction for tasks, sharing information, and working with employees to establish and maintain performance standards. We should note that the consideration and initiating structure behaviors are fully consistent with and the logical outgrowth from a systems view of organizations. Yet from a traditional hierarchical approach they may be considered special and not necessarily consistent or logical. The point: The systems view and TQM encourage managerial behaviors that have been found through research to drive success in organizations.

Initiating structure and consideration are relatively independent of one another. One way of describing leaders is by examining their combination of initiating structure and consideration behaviors in a matrix as show in Exhibit 11-5.

Further research focused on determining the effects of initiating structure and consideration on leader effectiveness. Early research supported the "high-high" hypothesis, which proposed that effective leaders were high on both initiating structure and consideration, and ineffective leaders were low on either initiating structure and/or consideration. For example, "high-high" leaders tend to have higher employee performance, less employee turnover, and fewer employee grievances than "high-low," "low-high," or "low-low" leaders.[15] This is not surprising as these behaviors say to the employee, "I care about you personally, and I care about supporting you in all the ways I can in your work." These behaviors are likely to elicit a strong performance in response.

Leadership Grid

A second behavioral approach is the **Leadership Grid,** formerly known as the Managerial Grid, developed by Blake and McCanse.[16] *This approach proposes various leadership behaviors differ in terms of concern for people and concern for production.* Using a two dimensional matrix, the grid classifies five basic behavioral styles: country club, impoverished, authority-compliance, middle of the road, and team. When the grid was developed the idea was to identify different types of leadership styles. However, if we are consistent with our definition of leadership as the

Leadership Grid Model developed by Blake and McCanse that proposes various leadership behaviors differ in terms of concern for people and concern for production.

EXHIBIT 11-5
Four leadership styles based on the Ohio State studies

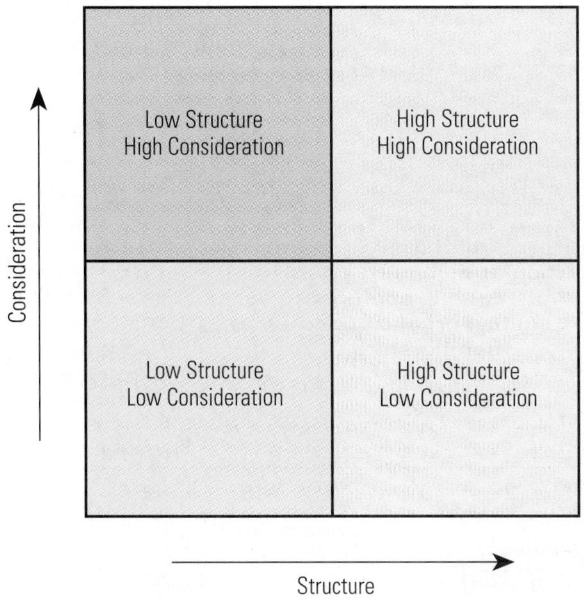

Low Structure High Consideration	High Structure High Consideration
Low Structure Low Consideration	High Structure Low Consideration

Consideration (vertical axis) — Structure (horizontal axis)

ability to influence people toward the achievement of goals, then what the grid actually identifies are behavioral styles that work well or not so well to achieve leadership. We can use the grid to better understand why some managers exhibit stronger leadership and successfully guide employees to goal achievement while others are not successful at this. Exhibit 11-6 illustrates the leadership grid.

A manager who focuses solely upon developing good social relations among workers and not upon the productivity of the work unit demonstrates *country club behavioral style*. Managers who try to lead this way ignore the need for task accomplishment and strive instead for social harmony. In essence, they believe that it is critical to create a work environment where people enjoy work and have important social needs met. This behavioral style is unlikely to be successful since employees will not be concerned about task accomplishment. In addition, the performance of task-oriented and achievement-oriented employees will also suffer since the rewards delivered by this type of manager will not be related to the accomplishment of goals and objectives. Many newly appointed managers are concerned about offending their employees and, as a result, they adopt a country club behavioral style.

At the other extreme is *authority-compliance*. Under this style, the person believes that leadership means emphasizing production with minimal concern for

EXHIBIT 11-6
The Leadership Grid

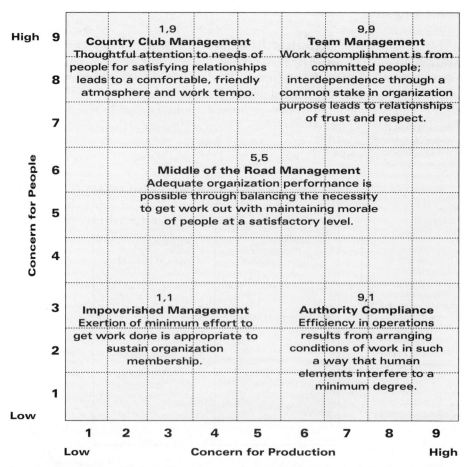

Source: From Robert A. Blake and Anne Adams McCanse, *Leadership Dilemmas—Grid Solutions* (Houston: Gulf Publishing Co. 1991), p. 29. Copyright ©1991 by Scientific Methods, Inc. Reproduced by permission of the owners.

people. Managers with this style would have little concern for employees' personal welfare. They mostly treat employees as pieces of equipment whose work is to be planned, controlled, and directed. They have little or no concern for the personal feelings of employees, and the social climate of the work group suffers because of this. While authority-compliance behavioral style often results in short-term accomplishment, it also causes resentment, and serious morale problems can develop. Lack of concern for the feelings and needs of others is one of the major factors that derails promising managerial careers.[17]

One way of trying to deal with the apparent conflict between a concern only with people and a concern only for production is to use a *middle of the road* behavioral style. The basic assumption with this approach is that being a leader means emphasizing moderate levels of concern for both people and production. In essence, this leadership approach emphasizes productivity—but not to the extent that morale will suffer—and emphasizes concern for people, but not to the extent that performance will suffer. The middle of the road behavioral style is striving for a happy medium in addressing both concern for people and concern for production. While such a behavioral style is "safe" in that it tends to avoid serious problems, it also results in only a mediocre level of performance. Most organizations are unable to tolerate mediocre performance in the competitive global marketplace.

An idea underlying all of the above leadership positions on the grid is that a concern for people and a concern for production somehow are not compatible. However, the team behavioral style, which consists of a high concern for people and production, exposes this misunderstanding. It shows through research that these two orientations do, in fact, go together. With the team style there is a realistic understanding that being sensitive to the needs of people and wanting to maximize output support one another. The phrase "mission first, people always" is another way of describing team behavioral style of leadership. In fact, of the various behavioral styles, only the team approach is actually consistent with our definition of leadership. Managers who practice team-oriented behaviors are those most likely to lead their employees in the harmonious and successful achievement of organizational goals.

While the team approach is the most successful behavioral style, it is also the most difficult to implement. It requires managers to integrate the inputs of members of the work group so that the production effort represents shared responsibility on the part of each employee. The manager must utilize each individual's talents to achieve task-related goals. A team leader should:

1. Obtain input from group members when setting goals and planning.
2. Know employees well enough to capitalize on each one's strengths.
3. Insure that individual goals can be accomplished while achieving outstanding performance for the organization.
4. Continually train employees so that their career opportunities improve while their performance on the job also improves.

The Leadership Grid is a very popular theory for understanding successful leadership behaviors. Many organizations send their managers to Leadership Grid training. Such training begins with an assessment of behavioral style. For example, you may have a 1,9 behavioral style (high concern for people and low concern for production). Training focuses on moving you to a 9,9 behavioral style, one who exhibits a high level of concern for both people and production.

We should not be surprised that the most successful behavioral style for a manager is the team approach nor should we be surprised that this is consistent with TQM, which emphasizes teams, training, and continuous improvement of work processes. The findings of those who promote the Leadership Grid once again affirm the idea that an organization is a system, and that behaviors which facilitate the successful management of a system are most likely to drive success.

Implications of the Behavioral Approaches

It is interesting to consider the implications of the Ohio State Studies and Leadership Grid for leadership effectiveness. Both of these approaches make very similar predictions. Specifically, they indicate that effective leadership requires both a concern for people (consideration) and a concern for productivity (initiating structure). To be effective as a leader, you must *simultaneously* be concerned for your employees and task accomplishment. Many new managers tend to rely more on concern for people or concern for production, but not both. Implementing a "high-high" leadership style is not an easy task. It requires the ability to deal sensitively with performance problems and appreciate the ideas of others. A manager must be able to disagree with others and provide them with feedback that will redirect the behavior, but in a manner that does not alienate them. Human relations skills, including oral communication, awareness of the needs of others, and social perceptiveness, are critical.

While it is clear that successful managers use different behaviors than unsuccessful ones, the situation also influences the appropriateness of various managerial behaviors. For example, a plant manager leading steel mill employees may need to exhibit different behaviors than a plant manager leading employees at an Apple Computer factory. Similarly, a manager of blue collar employees needs to use different behaviors to lead than a manager of an engineering group. Thus, contrary to the predictions of the Ohio State Studies and Leadership Grid, there does not appear to be a universal behavior pattern associated with effective leadership. In other words, the appropriate way to exhibit consideration varies with the job situation. These observations resulted in the development of several contingency (meaning behavior changes given different situations) theories of leadership. We will now examine this perspective.

Fiedler's Contingency Model

Given that high concern for production and high concern for people seems the most desirable combination of attitudes and behaviors for successfully leading people and organizations, we might wonder why the endless discussion on the subject. Researcher Fred Fiedler[18] has developed some ideas to help us answer this question. He does not believe that managers can show equal concern for both the task and the people in the work group. He suggests that the personality of managers is a major determinant of whether they will have a production orientation or people orientation. In other words, personality, in conjunction with experience and knowledge, strongly affects how people behave as managers and how well they lead.

Fiedler proposes that people have one of two motivational orientations: task orientation or relationship orientation. A manager who is task-oriented has a tendency to push for task accomplishment even if such behavior alienates employees. A manager who is relationship-oriented tends to value good interpersonal relationships even when they interfere with task accomplishment. Fiedler views a leader's motivational orientation as a relatively stable personality trait that is difficult to change.

We should emphasize that task-oriented individuals are also concerned about relationships. However, whenever they are under pressure, they have a tendency to focus strongly on the task to the exclusion of relationships. Similarly, a relationship-oriented individual may be task-oriented in some situations. When experiencing stress, however, relationship-oriented individuals revert back to their natural tendencies and focus on forming and maintaining relationships. For example, suppose that you are leading a group project and that, according to this theory, you have a very strong task orientation. You recognize a need to focus on relationships in the group, and so you do. However, if you fall behind schedule and miss deadlines on the group project, you will have a tendency to become very task-oriented, and you will find that you no longer have time for conversation or other "distracting" interactions. In essence, falling behind produces some stress, and you respond to stress by reverting back to your natural style.

Situational Favorability.   The behavioral orientation of managers does not predict their success as leaders. Instead, Fiedler proposed that the *success of a work group can be maximized when there is a good match between the leader and particular situational characteristics in the organization*. Thus, in addition to your behavioral orientation (task- or relationship-oriented), your success in leading others depends upon situational factors. Fiedler classified leadership situations according to their **situational favorability.** Three factors influence situational favorability:

Situation favorability The idea that the success of a work group can be maximized when there is a good match between the leader, task structure, and position power.

1. **Leader-Member Relationships:** Interpersonal relationships that exist between the manager and subordinates.
2. **Task Structure:** The degree to which task requirements are clearly defined.
3. **Position Power of the Leader:** The amount of power the organization confers upon the manager.

Favorable situations exist when the manager is accepted and trusted by the group (high manager-member relationships), the group's tasks are clearly defined (high task structure), and the manager has the ability to dispense rewards and punishments (high position power). In this type of situation, the manager has the relationships and resources to act successfully in situations with these parameters. Unfavorable situations exist when the manager is not trusted or accepted (low manager-member relations), the group's tasks are poorly defined or undefined (low task structure), and the manager has limited ability to administer rewards and punishments (low position power). It is clear that leading would be easier in the favorable situation than in the unfavorable situation. Exhibit 11-7 on page 404 shows the favorability of various leadership situations.

Fiedler conducted numerous studies in which he measured the motivational orientation of the leader and the favorableness of the situation. The summary of his findings are also presented in Exhibit 11-7. As the exhibit shows, certain situations logically call for a manager who is more task-oriented and some logically call for one who is more relationship-oriented. In general, if a manager has good relationships with employees, then task-orientation will make more sense. This is true except where the manager power position is low, and thus will require working more closely with employees to get things done. When the manager has

Manager-Member Relations	Good				Poor			
Task Structure	Structured		Unstructured		Structured		Unstructured	
Manager power position	High	Low	High	Low	High	Low	High	Low
Most effective leading behavior	Task-Oriented	Task-Oriented	Task-Oriented	Relation-ship-Oriented	Relation ship-Oriented	Relation-ship-Oriented	Task-Oriented	Relation-ship-Oriented
Octant	1	2	3	4	5	6	7	8

OVERALL SITUATION FAVORABILITY

Favorable for Manager   Unfavorable for Manager

EXHIBIT 11-7 Situational favorability and the contingency model of leading behavior

poor relationships with employees, but the task is highly structured, then relationship orientation makes sense. Finally, if the manager has poor relationships with employees, and the task is not well structured, the situation will still favor a task orientation. By carefully reviewing this exhibit, you can determine the logic of its recommendations for yourself.

Implications of Fiedler's Contingency Model.   One implication of Fiedler's contingency model is that organizations need to place managers in situations where their leadership skills can be used to best advantage. For example, if you are relationship-oriented, your organization should place you in a moderately favorable situation where you can best take advantage of this orientation. If you are task-oriented, your organization should place you in either a very favorable or unfavorable situation. Thus, selection of managers with different aptitudes and skills to handle different situations is very critical from Fiedler's perspective.

Fiedler's theory is provocative in that it proposes that successful leadership is not just a function of the manager or of the situation, but of a combination of the two. While Fiedler's contingency model has not been strongly supported,[19] parts of it have important implications for leadership success. The model points out that each individual has a personal bias toward either a task-oriented or relationship-oriented style of leading. Moreover, the bias toward one style or the other will be most obvious when managers are under stress. For example, when an organization is restructuring or there is a new boss, some managers may become stressed and hence predisposed to be task- or relationship-oriented. In fact, their behaviors may become somewhat inflexible in such situations, preventing them from dealing effectively with problems. Hence, they need to monitor their behaviors and guard against such tendencies.

TQM and Fiedler's Contingency View of Leadership.   Fiedler's ideas suggest that managers with different orientations will more likely succeed in situations that favor their orientations. Intuitively this makes sense. It is important to consider, though, that Fiedler's underlying assumption in this research was that organizations are hierarchies, and it is the boss's job to organize and control the behaviors of subordinates. Given different situations, bosses with different personality orientations have the probability of doing better if the situation matches their orientations.

The situation in a TQM organization, though, is nearly always one that favors good manager-member relationships (with a heavy emphasis on teamwork), a structured set of tasks (clearly defined processes), with a deemphasis on the use of power. This suggests that the most effective style of leadership will be one that brings a balance between task- and relationship-orientations. While Fiedler suggests that when managers get into stressful situations they will revert to one style or the other, such reversion is not common in TQM organizations. The culture of a TQM organization should be strong enough that managers, rather than reverting, will seek to use the tools and techniques of TQM to discover problem causes and address these in a sensible and rational fashion. Indeed, an important aspect of TQM is transcending organizational problems that can be identified as the personality quirks of managers. The idea is to replace this kind of instability with a constancy of purpose and way of operating that ensures the organization's long-term survival. Here is what Arend Sandblute, CEO of Minnesota Power, says about what happens when an organization moves away from managers and bosses and toward quality and leadership:

If managers ask, "When can I get back to my regular work?" the answer you must give them is that improving our corporate culture is your regular work—that it is a never-ending process of improvement, not a quick-fix program with a finite time frame. . . . Now maybe I haven't always been successful in my efforts to avoid reverting back to my old management behavior. But I'm determined to develop an awareness, an internal voice that tells me when I should back off and let employees solve a problem. And I'm finding that often employees can come up with better solutions than I could, since they know their jobs much better than I do.[20]

Situational Leadership® Model

Paul Hersey and Kenneth Blanchard's[21] Situational Leadership® theory (SL) is another contingency approach for understanding leadership. It is one of the most commonly used strategies for leadership training. SL has been used in training and development programs in many of the Fortune 500 companies, and it is widely accepted in the military as well as in small entrepreneurial companies. Some of the companies that use SL include BankAmerica, Caterpillar, IBM, Mobil Oil, and Xerox.

The basic premise of SL is that managers need to provide different leadership styles during the cycle of employee development. Think about how you felt on the first day of your most recent job. You probably had little understanding of the major tasks that you were expected to perform. You wanted (and expected) direction from your supervisor or others. Without such direction you felt lost. Later, when you are a high-performing and competent employee who understands the details of your job and take responsibility for your performance, you do not need much direction. Instead, you would likely prefer someone who understands that leadership is providing employees with the direction, resources, and responsibilities they need at different points in their careers. You would probably like to make decisions concerning day-to-day problems and ask for assistance only when it is needed. This scenario demonstrates the basic premise of **Situational Leadership®**: *Managers who seek to be leaders must change their leadership styles depending upon the management needs of their followers and the tasks in which they are involved.*

Situational Leadership®
An approach that asserts that managers who seek to be leaders must change their leadership styles depending on the needs of their followers and their tasks.

Types of Situational Leadership® Styles. Hersey and Blanchard have delineated four behavioral styles that managers may use to successfully lead in different situations. These four styles, along with the situations in which they are used most successfully, are described below. Note that the situations generally have to do with the *readiness* of the follower.

1. **Telling:** Some situations require a leadership characterized by telling—giving specific instructions and closely supervising performance. This style works best when a follower is new or involved in new situations. It is not a style that will work over the long run to facilitate success, and the astute leader understands when to use telling and when not to.

2. **Selling:** Some organizational situations require leadership characterized by selling, where leaders explain their decisions, are open to questions, and provide opportunity for clarification. This style emerges in situations where followers know their jobs, but managers bring expertise and special responsibility to achieve goals and understand they must work with others to do this.

3. **Participating:** Many situations require a leadership where managers share ideas and facilitate group decision making. This style works when followers have mastered the technical aspects of the job but do not yet feel confident to act without direction.

4. **Delegating:** Leading by delegating emerges when managers understand that followers, when given the authority, training, and resources they need to do their jobs, are often in a better position to make decisions about the area over which they have control than anyone else. It is a form of leadership that says managers respect employees and their judgment, and it fosters respect for managers in return.

Exhibit 11-8 captures these ideas in graphic form.

Implications of Situational Leadership®. Many start-up companies train their managers to use Situational Leadership®. For example, when Saturn opened their plant in Springhill, Tennessee, they provided their team leaders with Situational Leadership® training. As team members became more competent and confident, the team leader provided less direction and allowed the team to be more involved in the decisions. Eventually, when the team was ready, the leader turned over to the team responsibility for the day-to-day operations. The managers could then spend their time analyzing processes and attempting to better meet customer needs.

Situational Leadership® is intuitively appealing and has been used in a number of organizations. However, the empirical research supporting the theory is sparse and some initial studies have not been very supportive.[22] In defense of the approach, it is relatively new and has not been as thoroughly examined as many of the other leadership theories we have discussed.

There are several major points that you should retain for Situational Leadership®. First, you need to recognize the differences in the readiness levels of the followers you will lead. In the typical work group, you will have some employees who are very mature and who will require limited direction. Others will require close direction and guidance. You must recognize these differences in readiness levels. Second, you must use a different leadership style with followers at the various readiness levels. You should not try to treat all followers in the same manner. Instead, recognize that your followers will have different leadership needs based upon their readiness levels. Some will need close direction, some will need

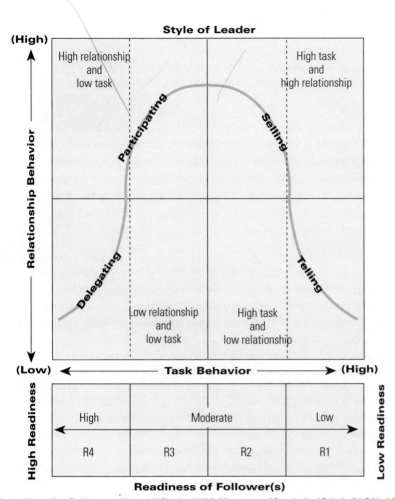

EXHIBIT 11-8
The Situational Leadership®
Model

Source: Adopted from Paul Hersey and Kenneth H. Blanchard (1993). *Management of Organizational Behavior* (6th Edition). Englewood Cliffs, NJ: Prentice Hall, p. 186. Situational Leadership® is a registered trademark of the Center for Leadership Studies. Reprinted with permission. All rights reserved.

a person to share their fears about failing, and some will need little from you. Third, Situational Leadership® points out that you must be able to delegate authority to competent employees and allow them to perform their jobs without meddling.

As was noted in the opening Case in Point, Jack Welch believes that managers must give employees the freedom to "flex their muscles, to let them grow and mature." We have watched many promising young managers fail because they were unable to release tasks to competent followers. An important part of learning to lead is to recognize that just as you seek help when you have a problem and want the authority to make your own decisions when you know what you are doing, this is also true of others. Managers who somehow forget this about themselves are those that will have trouble with others.

Path-Goal Theory of Leadership

The path-goal theory of leadership is based upon the expectancy theory of motivation. As we will discuss in detail in the next chapter, expectancy theory proposes that individuals choose behavior that maximizes their outcomes while minimizing their efforts. If you can obtain a salary increase by simply coming to work and performing at the minimum level, you will probably engage in the minimum behavior, especially if performing at a higher level does not result in a subsequent increase in rewards or at least feedback that indicates that higher levels of performance are appropriate.

Let's consider some basic aspects of path-goal theory. First, goals are defined as *outcomes which subordinates value.* Examples of goals include pay, job security, self-esteem, pats on the back or recognition, more flexible job assignments, overtime, and other pay opportunities. Goals tend to vary from employee to employee. Some employees will attach great significance to salary, whereas others will attach more significance to recognition. Second, a *path is the means by which the subordinate may fulfill personal goals.* Examples of paths include extra effort on the job, education, and training. For example, if an employee's major goal is to have fun at work, then establishing friendships with co-workers would be one path to this goal. The third aspect of path-goal theory is that *the path to the goal may be blocked,* thus preventing the employee from achieving a goal. Examples of blocking factors might include an ambiguous task, poor direction from superiors, poor relationships with peers, and lack of supplies necessary to perform the job.

It is the responsibility of the manager to lead so that paths are clear and barriers are removed. Path-goal theory proposes that managers can lead so as to provide direction to subordinates' motivation by making the paths to goals easier to travel by clarifying them and reducing roadblocks.[23]

Assume that you are manager of an employee who desires to become a team leader in your organization. Your job is to clarify the path to the goal (e.g., let the employee know that exceptional work performance, two years of experience, and an associate's degree in a technical field are required to be promoted to team leader) and then remove roadblocks in the path. For example, the employee may need constructive feedback on certain aspects of job performance. In addition, you may need to coordinate communications with human resources so that the employee can receive educational assistance benefits. Furthermore, if the employee has difficulty working with others, you will need to help him or her develop effective team-building skills. The consequence of your behavior is that the employee's goal of becoming a team leader, and the organization's goals of high performance, can be *simultaneously accomplished.*

Environmental and Personal Characteristics. Path-goal theory is a contingency theory in that it identifies two factors that influence the extent to which the manager must lead so as to clarify paths to goals. These two contingency factors are *characteristics of the environment* and *characteristics of the employee.* Exhibit 11-9 schematically depicts the relationship of these two factors. Characteristics of the environment are situational characteristics that may impact goals or the perceived probability of accomplishing goals.

Perhaps the most common environmental characteristic is the role clarity of the subordinate's job. If the task is unclear, the subordinate will need to have the paths clarified. A manager can clear paths by providing instruction and training, and by emphasizing the importance of various aspects of the job. Such behavior will illuminate the paths through which employees can accomplish their goals. This also will help to increase their motivation to do so. For example, assume that you are preparing a business plan as a class project. This is an ambiguous task and requires that you consider potential markets, plant locations, cost of financing, and a multitude of other factors. In this situation, you will want direction and guidance from the instructor. Such guidance clarifies the path to the goal (successful project) and increases the probability that you will receive a good grade in the course.

Characteristics of the person constitute the second contingency factor in path-goal theory. Individuals differ in the extent to which they clearly perceive the paths to goals and in the extent to which they believe that road blocks must be removed for them. For example, assume that you have an individual working for you who has a low level of self-confidence. This person is likely to believe that there will be many obstacles in the way of achieving particular goals and receiving desired rewards. In fact, the person may use every little difficulty that arises on the job as a reason to stop working at the task. As a direction for leading behavior, the path-goal theory suggests that you should counsel that the employee possesses the skills necessary to accomplish goals and objectives. In essence, your job is to demonstrate belief in employees' abilities so they begin to believe in themselves as well. Acting as a leader means clarifying employees' paths to goals, helping them enhance their convictions that they can accomplish job-related goals, and, thus, contribute to the performance of the entire work group.

A large number of employee and environmental characteristics have been identified in path-goal theory. Some of these are presented in Exhibit 11-9. Each of these factors has the possibility of influencing employees' perceptions of paths and goals. For example, if the job is dangerous, employees will want strong direction from the leader. If employees are inexperienced, they may need paths frequently clarified by training or instructions from the leader.

Implications of Path-Goal Theory.   Path-goal theory has several direct applications for managers. First, to succeed in leading, you should know your employees very well. You need to have a good idea about what they are thinking. That way, if employees feel that they are going to fail or a path is blocked, you can give them special attention. Such a style will increase the motivation of your team members.

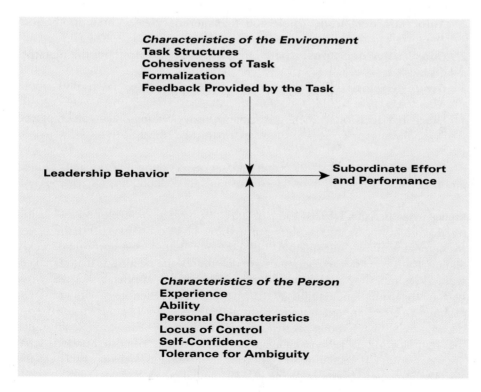

EXHIBIT 11-9
The Path-Goal Model of Leadership

A second implication of path-goal theory is that in leading, flexibility is a virtue. You need to be attentive to a wide variety of situational and employee factors and be willing to act appropriately given different situations. In complex and ambiguous situations or with inexperienced or low self-esteem employees, you will need to provide guidance and direction. In routine and structured situations or with experienced and self-confident employees, you should provide less direction and guidance. Many managers have difficulty responding flexibly to such a wide variety of contexts.

TQM and the Path-Goal Theory.   This theory of leadership makes explicit in an organizational setting that sound human relations skills—being empathetic to individuals and the situations in which they find themselves—will result in successful outcomes. From a systems management-TQM perspective, this focus on relationships is consistent with an emphasis on teamwork and processes. TQM recognizes that work gets done through people working together well. The path-goal theory simply suggests ways that managers can help people interact more successfully. W. Edwards Deming has proposed 14 points for managing. Point seven reads, in part, as follows: "Institute leadership. The aim of leadership should be to help people and machines and gadgets to do a better job."[24]

Vroom-Yetton Model for Leadership Decision Making

The final contingency leadership theory that we will discuss is the Vroom-Yetton model of decision making.[25] The Vroom-Yetton model lays out a methodology for analyzing various situations and what type of decision to make to lead successfully in light of this analysis. The point of the theory is that different situations will require decisions that range from

1. **Autocratic decisions,** where the manager decides without input from employees.
2. **Consultative decisions,** where employees provide input but the manager decides.
3. **Group decisions,** where the manager and group arrive at a consensus about what to do.
4. **Delegated decisions,** where the manager turns over authority to an employee or employees to decide what to do in a particular situation.

Vroom and Yetton classify decision making on a continuum from autocratic to group decision making. Exhibit 11-10 illustrates this continuum.

Vroom-Yetton Decision Tree.   Vroom and Yetton have also developed a decision tree for analyzing situations (shown in Exhibit 11-11 on page 412) that enables managers to follow the principles behind each of eight decision rules quickly and easily. The answer to each question determines the next track that managers will follow until they are left with the decision-making approach that will work best in that situation. Exhibit 11-12 on page 413 describes a situation that requires a certain approach to decision making to solve. Use the Vroom-Yetton decision tree to figure out what that approach should be. This example illustrates that by following these steps, managers can figure out in most situations what approach to decisions will reflect appropriate leadership behaviors to help the organization and its members achieve their mutual goals.

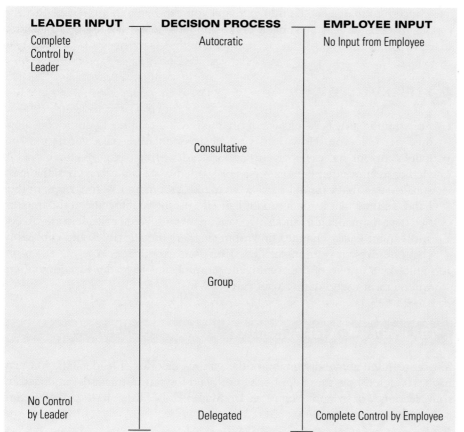

LEADER INPUT	DECISION PROCESS	EMPLOYEE INPUT
Complete Control by Leader	Autocratic	No Input from Employee
	Consultative	
	Group	
No Control by Leader	Delegated	Complete Control by Employee

EXHIBIT 11-10
Employee and leader input into the various decision-making processes

TQM and Contingency Theories

All four of the contingency theories propose that successful leadership is a function of understanding helping people deal with the organizational situations in which they find themselves. Exhibit 11-13 on page 414 provides a summary of the four contingency theories [These theories demonstrate that leadership is a complex phenomenon, and you must be sensitive to the needs of employees and to situational factors in order to be a good leader. Such an outward focus is consistent with the TQM approach of thinking of employees as internal customers and managers as suppliers to these customers. Just as organizations must understand their roles as serving their external customers, so this idea suggests that managers should likewise view their employees as customers for services that facilitate employees successfully doing their jobs. The idea is that if as a manager you adopt this orientation, you will be attentive to situational contingencies that affect job performance and will modify your behavior accordingly]

In addition to thinking about leadership in terms of serving internal customers, it is also important to consider (as we have often pointed out) that in a TQM organization, a manager's job is to focus on processes. This includes human relations processes so as to continuously improve the firm's ability to serve its customers. Contingency theories simply provide a context and some methods for figuring out how to do this. One of the values of TQM and the systems view of organizations is that it reminds us that these are issues that are of real concern to managers. Further, perhaps you can begin to appreciate that the various theories we have just been discussing have real use outside of filling up space in a college textbook and lecture time in the classroom.

? THINKING CRITICALLY

1. Are you primarily task- or person-oriented? Ask a couple of your friends how they perceive you? How does your basic orientation (task versus person) influence your success in groups and in leadership positions?
2. Fiedler assumes that person versus task orientation is a relatively stable personality trait that cannot be easily changed. Vroom and Yetton, on the other hand, assume that leaders can and should use both autocratic and participative decision-making methods. Do you agree with Fiedler (leaders are "fixed" and cannot easily change) or Vroom (leaders are "flexible" and can easily change)? Explain your answer based on your experience.
3. Which one or two of the contingency approaches to leadership do you feel will be most useful during your career? Why?

Ames Rubber: Baldrige Award Winner

THE LEADER AS A CHANGE AGENT

As you read the above discussion of the various theories of leadership, you may have wondered how these approaches explain the transformations produced by some leaders. For example, consider Dr. Martin Luther King, Jr. Clearly, Dr. King

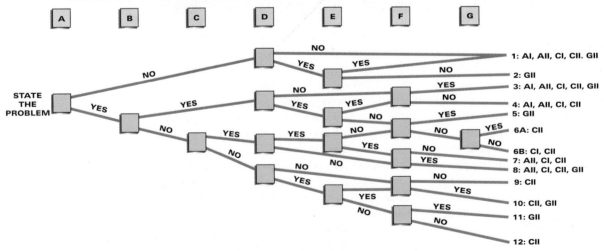

A. DOES THE PROBLEM POSSESS A QUALITY REQUIREMENT?
B. DO YOU HAVE SUFFICIENT INFORMATION TO MAKE A HIGH-QUALITY DECISION?
C. IS THE PROBLEM STRUCTURED?
D. IS ACCEPTANCE OF DECISION BY SUBORDINATES IMPORTANT FOR EFFECTIVE IMPLEMENTATION?
E. IF YOU WERE TO MAKE THE DECISION BY YOURSELF, IS IT REASONABLY CERTAIN THAT IT WOULD BE ACCEPTED BY YOUR SUBORDINATES?
F. DO SUBORDINATES SHARE THE ORGANIZATIONAL GOALS TO BE ATTAINED IN SOLVING THIS PROBLEM?
G. IS CONFLICT AMONG SUBORDINATES OVER PREFERRED SOLUTIONS LIKELY?

Source: Reprinted from *Leadership and Decision Making,* by Victor H. Vroom and Philip W. Yetton, by permission of the University of Pittsburgh Press. © 1973 by University of Pittsburgh Press.

EXHIBIT 11-11   The Vroom-Yetton Decision Tree

EXHIBIT 11-12 Decision-making Case

Assume that you are the manufacturing manager in a large electronics plant. The company has been searching for ways of increasing efficiency and recently installed new machines. But to the surprise of everybody, the expected increase in productivity was not realized and, in fact, production has begun to drop and quality has fallen off. You do not believe that there is anything wrong with the machines. You have had representatives from the firm that built the machines go over them, and they report that the machines are operating at peak efficiency.

You suspect that a design change in the product may be responsible for the problem, but this view is not widely shared among your immediate subordinates, who are four first-level supervisors. The drop in production has been attributed to poor training of the operators, lack of an adequate system of financial incentives, and poor morale. Clearly this is an issue about which there is considerable depth of feeling within individuals and potential disagreement among your subordinates.

This morning you received a phone call from your division manager. She had just received your production figures for the last six months and was calling to express her concern. She indicated that the problem was yours to solve, but she would like to know within a week what steps you plan to take. You share your division manager's concern with the falling productivity. You know that your people are also concerned. Which of the following decision-making processes would you use (circle your answer):

AI: You solve the problem yourself using the information available at the present time.

AII: You obtain any necessary information from subordinates and then make the decision yourself. You may or may not tell the subordinate the purpose of your questioning. Your subordinates' roles are simply to provide you with information.

CI: You share the problem with your subordinates individually, getting their ideas and suggestions without bringing them together as a group. Then you make the decision, which may or may not reflect your subordinates' ideas.

CII: You share the problem with your subordinates in a group meeting. In this meeting, you obtain their ideas and suggestions. Then you make the decision, which may or may not reflect your subordinates' ideas.

GII: You share the problem with your subordinates as a group. Together you generate alternatives and attempt to reach consensus on the best solution. Your role is much like a chairman of a meeting. You are willing to accept and implement any solution that has the support of the entire work group.

Source: Adopted from V. H. Vroom and A. G. Yago, *The New Leadership: Managing participation in organizations.* Englewood Cliffs, NJ: Prentice Hall, pg 43.

was a great leader and helped American society change its ideas concerning civil rights. Can you explain the effectiveness of his leadership based upon situational leadership theory? Fiedler's contingency theory? Vroom-Yetton's model of decision making? Path-goal theory? These theories focus on interacting with and leading employees on a day-to-day basis but do not consider leadership characteristics such as vision, inspiration, and charisma. An effective leader must possess these three characteristics in order to effect widespread organizational change.

Transactional Versus Transformational Leadership

Bernie Bass[26] proposed that leadership can be divided into two types of processes. A **transactional leader** is effective because *followers' needs are met when they meet the leaders' expectations.* Transactional leadership focuses on the daily

Transactional leader
A person who influences employees by meeting their expectations and delivering rewards for accomplishing goals.

EXHIBIT 11-13   Summary of contingency models

THEORY	LEADER BEHAVIOR/TRAITS	SITUATIONAL FACTORS
Fiedler's Contingency Model	Task vs. Relationship	Situational Favorability
Situational Leadership	Telling, Selling, Participating, Delegating	Readiness of Employee
Path-Goal Theory	Behavior Clarifies Goals and Removes Roadblocks	Environmentental and Employee Characteristics
Vroom-Yetton Model of Decision Making	Autocratic, Consultative Group, and Delegated Decision Making	Situational Factors Measured in Decision Tree

interactions that occur between leaders and their employees and colleagues. The theories we have been reviewing in this chapter fall into this category, and most theories of leadership focus on transactional leadership. When implemented appropriately, transactional leadership results in performance that meets expectations. That is, employees will fulfill the requests of leaders because they identify their welfare with doing what they are supposed to do.

Bass indicated that truly exceptional leaders are able to get employees to perform "beyond expectations" by engaging in transformational leadership. A **transformational leader** *influences change through vision, inspiration, and an intense and honest concern for employee welfare.* Followers are motivated to accomplish goals and objectives that transcend immediate self-interests through transformational leadership. A transformational leader gets employees excited about the organization's goals and gets them to consider new ways of accomplishing these goals. Transformational leadership causes employees to become truly committed to the goals of the organization—and take them on as their own.

Perhaps one way to understand the difference between transactional and transformational leadership is to consider your study behavior in various courses. In many of these courses, you are likely studying the material because the course is required, and you will be tested on it. Your test performance will affect your grade point average, and this can ultimately influence the quality of employment opportunities. This is how employees feel when they are led by a transactional leader. Under a transactional leader, motivation is extrinsic, that is, employees feel motivated to perform to receive rewards controlled by the organization and its managers. However, in a few of your courses, you may be studying the material because the ideas are of deep personal interest to you. The fact that you are tested or given credit for the course is of secondary importance. Even if you were not in one of these courses, you might still be studying the material.

This typifies the way employees feel when they are influenced by transformational leadership. Transformational leaders help to bring out the intrinsic motivation inside each of us. Performance takes on personal meaning beyond any rewards employees receive for their contribution to the company. They understand the vision of the organization as articulated by the transformational leader and share this vision and want to see it succeed.

Some can even become extreme in their commitment to a transformational leader's vision, as illustrated by the Branch Davidians profiled in *A Look At Ethics* box. This example demonstrates that transformational leadership requires a high-

Transformational leader
A person who influences change through vision, inspiration, and an intense and honest concern for employee welfare.

THE DARK SIDE OF TRANSFORMATIONAL LEADERSHIP[27]

ETHICS

He was born Vernon Howell, but Americans will always remember him as David Koresh, the militant cult leader who held federal agents at bay for weeks before his Waco, Texas, compound exploded into a fiery inferno, ending the standoff and killing nearly one hundred "Branch Davidians." Koresh, the self-proclaimed "sinful incarnation of Christ," was an abused child born to an unwed teenage mother, a person with a learning disability, a high school drop-out, a reject from several church congregations, a rock musician wanna-be who grew to personify the evil face of transformational leadership. Although he was never able to hold a job, he was able to capture the minds—and the lives—of nearly a hundred followers who were willing to die at his command.

Former Branch Davidians described the twisted life he created for his followers. They relinquished all of their earnings and material possessions. They ate military ready-to-eat type meals. They were trained in military combat. Children were corporally punished for "intolerable" transgressions, and under the mandate of Koresh's "new light" declaration, men surrendered their wives and daughters for Koresh's exclusive sexual gratification and the procreation of his children. He had such a powerful hold over his followers that one woman denied medical treatment, saying that she would rather cut off her injured finger than leave the Waco compound. Ultimately, his followers gave their lives to affirm his prophecies. What put them so strongly in his control?

There is little doubt that Koresh was a transformational leader—but an unethical one. He was said to have had a "folksy way of making listeners feel that he was genuinely concerned about their spiritual well-being," but at the same time it was said that he "treated the lives under his command like poker chips." He was charismatic, radiating energy as he preached his interpretation of the gospel. He used his expert knowledge of the Bible—which he is said to have memorized by age 12—to intimidate followers into believing that his was the true interpretation, that he was a divinely ordained prophet. He officially rejected those followers who challenged his teachings or voiced independent or divergent views; his decisions were not to be questioned. He manipulated followers to fulfill the fate he proclaimed for himself a decade earlier: he would die a martyr. In their minds, they all did.

---

ly ethical set of values be held by leaders. If not, the leading behavior of such individuals becomes manipulative of their followers, who want to believe but do not have the experience or understanding to see through the manipulation. Cults and political extremist groups often are lead by transformational leaders whose ethics and motives are subject to question.

Behaviors of Transformational Leaders

There are four behavioral patterns that are typical of transformational leaders. First, transformational leaders are *charismatic*. They have a vision and a sense of mission and, by showing a concern for others, are able to get them to take on this vision and mission as their own. They are able to gain the respect, trust, and confidence of employees. Transformational leaders are also *inspirational*. They give pep talks and are optimistic and enthusiastic about the future, and communicate their vision with excitement. Transformational leaders use *intellectual stimulation*, especially when correcting poor performance or considering the future. They actively encourage a new look at old methods, foster creativity, and stress the use of intelligence and problem solving. Instead of telling employees what to do, they ask probing questions that prompt rethinking and the reexamination of basic assumptions. Transformational leaders engage in *individualized consideration*. They give personal attention to all employees, making each individual feel valued. More than that, they care about their employees and coach, advise, and provide feedback in ways that are easy for each group member to accept, understand, and use for personal development.

An excerpt from the famous "I Have a Dream" speech given by Dr. Martin Luther King, Jr. is presented in Exhibit 11-14. Is it transformational? Can you see a vision? Does it cause you to look at problems differently? Is it optimistic? Does it show a concern for people? Undoubtedly the answer is yes to each of these questions, which is why Dr. King was a successful transformational leader.

Becoming a Transformational Leader

As you read the above description of transformational leadership, you may have thought that only a few such individuals exist in the world at any one time. Clearly, certain individuals are born with a greater capability to be a transformational leader than are others. However, recent research is emerging that demonstrates that transformational leadership can also be developed with training.[28] There are several practices that you can use to enhance your transformational leadership. To be charismatic you need to have a vision, a sense of what and where you want your organization to be in the future. Researchers are constantly amazed at how few managers have a vision for their work groups. And most managers who do have visions have failed to share them with others in their organizations.

Where do visions come from? If you do not think about the future, you can be assured that you will not have a vision. Once you have constructed a vision, you should articulate your vision as frequently as possible. Transformational leaders use analogies and powerful metaphors to illustrate their points. Often a simple vision can transform an organization (e.g., Ford: "Quality is Job One"; Lexus: "The Relentless Pursuit of Perfection").

In addition to articulating vision, you should try to influence subordinates through questioning whenever possible. When a subordinate brings you an idea that would have negative ramifications for customers, don't simply point out the problems with the suggestion. Instead, ask questions to encourage the subordinate to evaluate the idea in terms of your vision (e.g., "That's a good idea, but how can we improve on it further to make sure it increases the value of our offerings to our customers?").

EXHIBIT 11-14   "I Have a Dream" by Dr. Martin King, Jr.

"So let freedom ring from the prodigious hilltops of New Hampshire. Let freedom ring from the mighty mountains of New York. Let freedom ring from the snow capped Rockies of Colorado. . . . But not only that. Let freedom ring from Stone Mountain of Georgia. Let freedom ring from Lookout Mountain of Tennessee. Let freedom ring from every hill and molehill of Mississippi, from every mountainside, let freedom ring. And when we allow freedom to ring, when we let it ring from every village and hamlet, from every state and city, we will be able to speed up that day when all God's children—black men and white men, Jews and Gentiles, Catholics and Protestants—will be able to join hands and to sing in the words of the old Negro spiritual: 'Free at last, free at last, thank God Almighty, we are free at last.'"

You must also be optimistic at all times. After all, if you are not excited about your vision of the future, how do you expect your employees to be excited about it? Some managers feel that it is unprofessional to walk around with the purpose of trying to inspire people. As one manager suggested to a researcher, "I'm not being paid to be a cheerleader." That shows just how much some managers misunderstand their roles.

You also need to care about your employees—this cannot be faked. If you are truly concerned about your people, they will perceive your concern as genuine and will be much more likely to join you. You are asking your employees to change. Change is always uncomfortable and often involves risks. If your employees do not believe that you are concerned about their welfare, they will be hesitant to work toward the vision.

You must also be willing to empower your employees. In other words, give them the flexibility and freedom to translate your vision within their day-to-day tasks. Give them the flexibility to be innovative and to find new and creative ways to alter their work processes to accomplish goals and objectives. If you can sell the vision to your employees, you will be amazed at the work changes that will be suggested and implemented by employees. The Saturn Division of General Motors estimates that employee-generated work changes saved $85 million in 1993.

The final tip for transformational leadership, and perhaps the most difficult, is that *you must be willing to take risks*. Your employees will watch your actions carefully to see if you really believe in the vision. If you retreat the first time that you encounter resistance, your employees will become skeptical of your commitment to your vision. Leaders in many organizations fail to take risks because their culture supports a "safety-first" attitude. That is, the way to be promoted and rewarded is to avoid critical mistakes and failures. Playing it safe is a sure-fire way of not being innovative. Some organizations have actually started to reward failure to encourage risk-taking. They have implemented failure award programs. These awards consist of a substantial cash bonus that is received for FAILING. How do you receive a failure award? You take an idea and push it as far as it can go but fail. Identifying and celebrating these failures encourages other leaders to take risks. For example, at NuCor Steel, it is widely accepted that 40 percent of new initiatives will fail. Without these failures, NuCor could not remain the low-cost producer of steel in the U.S. In addition, some organizations have started to send leaders to Outward Bound leadership training programs.[29] Many of these programs involve high-risk physical activities such as rapelling, climbing, and swinging across gorges. These programs are designed to encourage risk taking and to show managers that risks are a part of daily living. It will be impossible for you to sell a vision centering on customer satisfaction to your work group if you are unwilling to take risks.

? THINKING CRITICALLY

1. What leadership traits do you believe are important for transformational leadership?
2. Think of two people you have considered to be leaders in your life. Were they transformational? Why or why not?
3. Why do you think it is so hard for most people to be transformational leaders?

WHY IS JACK WELCH A SUCCESSFUL LEADER?

Jack Welch has been very successful as a corporate leader. Why? Leadership research suggests that his success can be traced to his transformational leadership style and his focus on quality.

Welch exhibits many characteristics of a transformational leader. First, he has vision for General Electric. His vision is relatively simple but powerfully stated. He demanded quality, he envisioned unparalleled excellence, and he communicated his expectation in simple terms: "To me, quality and excellence mean being better than the best." Quality has also been the centerpiece of his vision. He is driving GE so that "customers' vision of their needs and the company's view become identical, and every effort of every man and woman in the company is focused on satisfying those needs."

Jack Welch is also a risk taker. He espoused a "lean and agile" company philosophy, which he attained by reducing GE's work force from 402,000 in 1980 to 330,000 in 1984 to 298,000 in 1990. GE was downsizing well before it became popular in corporate America. But the goal was to become more efficient, not cut bodies because that was the most expedient way to cut costs. These reductions in the work force made Welch unpopular with GE employees for a while, and the press actually gave him the nickname "Neutron Jack." This derives its meaning from the effect of the neutron bomb, which eliminates people while leaving buildings intact. Jack Welch was willing to be a media target and be disliked by some employees because he was building the future of GE.

Jack Welch also believed in his employees. He empowered employees to use their skills to enhance organizational productivity. He turned to employees for ideas and asked employees to evaluate the effectiveness of his management team. He always indicated that he wanted to let the people who knew the business the best, the employees, be involved in as many decisions as possible. He did this not because he wanted employees to feel good, but because he knew this is simply smart and good business practice.

Finally, Jack Welch is constantly seeking improvement. He will never be satisfied with the status quo. His vision of GE, a boundaryless company, is based upon constant expansion, refinement of processes, and changing work roles. The only thing that Welch knows for sure is that GE will always have the customer at the center of every change.

LEADERSHIP IN A TOTAL QUALITY ORGANIZATION

Leadership is vital in all organizations, but it is especially important in those seeking to implement Total Quality Management. In fact, TQM not only requires leadership, part of what it is about is creating an environment where leadership blossoms. TQM demands what for many will be an entirely new way of understanding what an organization is, their work, and their roles in the organization. We have pointed out at various points in this chapter the fact that successful leadership behaviors are consistent with the teachings of TQM and that TQM, in fact, builds a culture that fosters leadership in employees across the organization. This is because it emphasizes teamwork and the empowerment of all employees as the organization seeks to deliver quality to customers.

Whereas many traditional ideas about management focus on how to be a "boss," this is neither what leadership is about nor is this consistent with managing an organization when it is understood as a system. Being a boss is about constraining behavior. Being a leader is about helping employees take full advantage of their skills and

TQM IN ACTION

LEADING TO QUALITY[30]

Sometimes it takes a crisis to bring out leadership. For example, at Rice Aircraft, a $15 million a year parts supplier to aircraft manufacturers, the owner of the company, Bruce Rice, made the mistake of giving kickbacks to employees of some customers and ended up in prison. Before he left, he recruited his wife, Paula De Long Rice, a high school history teacher to run the company in his absence. He was able to train her in the basics and then she was on her own. Because of this incident, the company had lost much of its business.

Paula Rice decided the only way to turn things around was to commit to total quality. She instituted training in statistical process control, time management, and human relations skills, the last to improve communication among employees. The company sought and gained ISO 9002 certification, which is an international standard for quality. Paula called on the company's quality assurance manager to sell the new company to its former customers, such as Boeing and Grumman. They were impressed with the changes and with the quality of the company's products, and started buying again. Paula Rice could only achieve this by getting all employees on board, giving them the authority, support, resources, and training they needed to work together. These actions typify the behaviors of a successful leader and they typify the approach of TQM to addressing such situations as Rice Aircraft faced.

experience to achieve organizational goals. What TQM points out is that being a boss undermines quality and the efficiency and effectiveness of organizational processes.

Leaders create the environment to which all employees will adapt, be that a positive, can-do environment such as Jack Welch is working on at GE or the self-destructive environment of the Branch Davidians. TQM requires dedicated leadership by top managers to change the environment and culture to one where all employees view their jobs in terms of their roles in processes that ultimately result in satisfying customers and other stakeholders. The theories in this chapter provide managers with an understanding of how to do this. The theories suggest which types of behavior managers should exhibit in various situations to help employees take full advantage of skills and experience to add value to the organization's efforts. When used wisely, these theories can help managers make the changes required to create a total quality organization.

The characteristics of a total quality organization include customer focus, process management, working in teams, data-based decisions, and continuous improvement of all aspects of the operation. Driving the efforts to make these things happen in an organization requires leaders, not bosses. All employees must be involved and committed, and that can only happen when they believe in the company and its *leaders,* in the best sense of that term.

❓ THINKING CRITICALLY

1. Based on your experience in school and in other organizations, have you encountered individuals who have exhibited strong leadership behaviors? If yes, what characteristics did these people exhibit to make you feel this way? If no, why do you think these individuals lacked leadership skills?

2. Based on your understanding, explain why quality fosters leadership behaviors and why those who seek to lead in the best sense of that term would likely embrace TQM.

SUMMARY

Meaning of Leadership

- Organizational leaders are the ones who set the direction of the organization and create the environment to which all employees ultimately must adapt. They thus profoundly affect the organization's ability to achieve its goals to satisfy customers and other stakeholders.

- While management has to do with the abstractions of running an organization (strategy creation, structure, finance), leadership has to do with the concrete pulling together of people and exerting influence to achieve goals.

- Most theories of leadership deal with identifying effective leadership skills and behaviors and their appropriate application rather than how leaders emerge in organizations.

- There are five bases of power for leaders: reward, coercive, legitimate, expert, and referent powers.

Theoretical Approaches to Leadership

- There are several theories to explain and understand leadership. These include (1) trait theories, (2) behavioral theories, and (3) contingency theories that look at behaviors and situations.
  —Trait theories try to associate leadership behaviors with specific personality traits of those people identified as leaders.

Behavioral/Situational Approaches to Leadership

- Behavioral theories emphasize that it is not traits but the behavior of a person in a leadership position. The Ohio State studies looked at consideration and initiating structures. The Leadership Grid examined a combination of concern for people and concern for production.

- Contingency models include (1) Fiedler's task vs. relationship orientation, (2) Hersey and Blanchard's situational leadership theory, (3) the Path-Goal theory, and (4) the Vroom-Yetton model for analyzing situations.

The Leader as a Change Agent

- Whereas transactional leadership looks at day-to-day behaviors of leaders, transformational leadership studies how those who lead bring people together to make major organizational or social changes.

Leadership in a Total Quality Organization

- TQM both requires and fosters the development of leadership in organizations. This is because TQM, like successful leadership, is about building productive organizations that align people and processes so all employees maximize their contributions to achieving organizational goals.

KEY TERMS

Behavioral approach to leadership 398

Consideration 398

Coercive power 393

Expert power 394

Initiating structure 398

Leadership 389

REVIEW QUESTIONS

1. What is the relationship between leadership and organizational success?
2. What is the difference between management and leadership and why do people confuse the two?
3. What are the five bases of power for a manager, and what is the source of each of these types of power?
4. What are the most important traits that researchers have identified? What is the weakness of the trait approach to understanding leadership?
5. What is the relationship between consideration and initiating structure in successfully leading?
6. What is the misunderstanding that people have about the ideas in the Leadership Grid (concern for people and concern for production). How does TQM help managers clear up this misunderstanding?
7. Why is the orientation of a person (relation or task) so important in Fiedler's contingency model? How does TQM question Fiedler's view of leadership?
8. What is the relationhip of employee readiness and leadership behaviors in the situational leadership theory?
9. How does a leader operate when following the path-goal theory?
10. How does the Vroom-Yetton model help managers understand what type of leadership to practice in various situations?
11. What is the difference between transaction leadership and transformational leadership? What distinguishes a transformational leader?
12. What is the relationship between the practice of TQM and leadership?

EXPERIENTIAL EXERCISE

Exercise 1. This is an exercise for interviewing and analyzing a variety of people and their leadership behaviors. Here are the steps to follow in this exercise:

1. Form a series of groups of five or six students each. Each group should focus upon a different industry or sector in the economy, e.g., government, finance, manufacturing, service companies, fast food.
2. Each group should interview managers from one of the segments. Some possible questions to ask include:
   a. How do you define leadership?
   b. How do you define management?
   c. What is the major difference between management and leadership?
   d. What is the most important advice for a leader in your industry/position?
   e. What is the worst mistake that you have made as a leader?
   f. What makes an effective leader?

3. Be prepared to discuss the interviews. Your instructor will lead a discussion focusing on common themes and issues.

Exercise 2. Presented below are a series of statements. Answer each one and see what type of leader you are. If you have not been employed in a leadership position, answer each question from a student leadership position (e.g., leader of a group project, leader in high school; leader in sorority or fraternity). Rate each item on the following scale:

1 = Never
2 = Seldom
3 = Occasionally
4 = Often
5 = Always

1 2 3 4 5	1. I let employees or group members know what is expected of them
1 2 3 4 5	2. I am friendly and approachable
1 2 3 4 5	3. I encourage the use of uniform procedures or policies
1 2 3 4 5	4. I do things to make it pleasant to be a member of my group
1 2 3 4 5	5. I provide suggestions and ideas to the group
1 2 3 4 5	6. I listen to the suggestions of others
1 2 3 4 5	7. I make my positions clear to the group
1 2 3 4 5	8. I treat group members as equals
1 2 3 4 5	9. I decide what shall be done and how it shall be done
1 2 3 4 5	10. I look out for the welfare of each group member
1 2 3 4 5	11. I assign individuals to specific tasks
1 2 3 4 5	12. I explain my actions to the group
1 2 3 4 5	13. I schedule the work to be done
1 2 3 4 5	14. I consult with the group before making decisions

Scoring: Sum your responses to the odd number items. Then sum your responses to the even number items. You should have a score between 7 and 35 for each scale. Your responses to the odd-numbered questions provide a measure of task-oriented behavior or initiating structure. Your responses to the even-numbered questions provide a measure of relationship-oriented behavior or consideration. Use the following chart to interpret your score:

Leadership Behavior	7-21	22-28	29-35
Initiating Structure	Low	Average	High
Consideration	Low	Average	High

Think back about the content in this chapter and answer the following questions:

1. What are the implications for your leadership style?
2. In what situations will you be an effective leader?

3. How can you increase your initiating structure or consideration behavior? How might the principles of TQM give direction in this process?

CASE ANALYSIS AND APPLICATION
The Culture of Leadership at 3M[31]

Minnesota Mining and Manufacturing (3M) is one of the most successful companies in the U.S. It is consistently in the top 10 of various lists of most-admired corporations. 3M has adapted successfully to a global environment with sales of $15 billion in 1994. 3M has 85,000 employees on payroll.

William L. McKnight is the former and long-term CEO of 3M. After graduating from Duluth Business College, he was hired by 3M as an assistant bookkeeper. He quickly rose to national sales director. His strategy in sales was to go directly to the users of 3M's products, such as sandpaper, rather than talking to managers who were removed from everyday problems. He encouraged the salespeople to visit shop floors and see how 3M's products were actually used every day. The company took this information seriously, and the salespeople provided regular feedback to 3M's factories about quality problems and customer concerns. He believed that the production department would be innovative if they understood the customers' use of their products.

Once McKnight became CEO, he was able to stamp his personal beliefs on 3M's culture. His remarks in 1948 provided a vision for the company to this day: "As our business grows, it becomes increasingly necessary to delegate responsibility and to encourage men and women to exercise initiative. Mistakes will be made, but if the person is essentially right, the mistakes he or she makes are not as serious in the long run as the mistakes management will make if it is dictatorial and undertakes to tell those under its authority exactly how they must do their job. Management that is destructively critical when mistakes are made kills initiative, and it's essential that we have many people with initiative if we're to continue to grow."

McKnight had a trust in 3M employees. He defined the role of management as establishing direction and creating an environment supportive of growth and skill development. He argued that all individuals have creativity and the organization needs to encourage creativity to blossom on the job. McKnight also had a keen awareness that workers should be encouraged in their efforts. He spent Saturday mornings having breakfast with the employees that he admired. He spent time listening to their ideas and sharing problems at 3M with them. 3Mers who took part in these breakfasts still talk about them today.

McKnight once reflected on his 65-year relationship with 3M. He indicated that 3M and, indeed, American industry, needs to have a "healthy appreciation of those who exercise the free man's option for excellence, permitting the creation of something for all of us, enriching lives with new ideas and products."

Today 3M has a culture that highly values innovation. It encourages employees to "work outside of the boxes" of their jobs to facilitate the development of new products. The word "lawlessness" is used since ideas can bubble up from the rank and file and risk taking is openly encouraged.

3M is one of the most innovative companies in the world. It has a corporate goal that 25 percent of sales come from products introduced in the last five years. During 1993, 30 percent of sales came from products introduced in the last four years. 3M currently sells over 60,000 products in markets such as electronics, health care, adhesives, data cartridges and diskettes, recording media, plastics, information imaging, and perhaps its most ubiquitous product, the "Post-It Note."

Discussion Questions

1. Why was William McKnight an effective leader? What leadership theory or theories might you use to explain his style?
2. If William McKnight had been CEO of General Motors during the 1970s and 1980s when Japan was getting its foothold in the American market, how might the company be different today? Why?

VIDEO CASE: COMBINING QUALITY MANAGEMENT AND SOCIAL RESPONSIBILITY
J. Irwin Miller-Lifetime Achievement Award

J. Irwin Miller was honored with The Business Enterprise Lifetime Achievement Award for his commitment to responsible management and his concern for all those touched by his enterprises.

Miller was born in 1909 in Columbus, Indiana. His family was both wealthy and religious, two attributes that later influenced his thoughts and actions as a business leader. The family fortune had been made in banking, but increased when Miller's great-uncle invested in a fledgling diesel engine business. An outstanding student, Miller graduated from Yale University in 1931. He went on to study politics at Oxford University, where he received a masters of arts degree. He returned to Columbus in 1934 as General Manager of Cummins Engine. At that point, the company had yet to make a profit, and employed just 60 people.

By focusing on diesel engine technology, manufacturing quality and cost-cutting, Miller helped turn the company around. By 1937, Cummins was profitable, and remained so throughout Miller's long stewardship. When he stepped down as chief executive in 1977, Cummins was a billion dollar company with nearly 50 percent of the U.S. market for diesel truck engines and a 12 percent return on equity for all but seven of the prior thirty years. In addition, Miller charted a model philosophy of corporate responsibility and, as an individual, set a standard for community, national and civic involvement.

Cummins is particularly well known for its commitment to the community. Miller instituted a policy for corporate giving under which 5 percent of pretax profits were donated to charitable concerns. The Cummins Engine Foundation provided the funds for many community projects, and also paid world-renowned architects to design schools, churches and other public buildings for the city, establishing the town as a midwestern architectural mecca.

Religion played a dominant role in Miller's life. From 1960 to 1963, he led the National Council of Churches in the U.S. as its first lay president. His religious views undoubtedly helped form his belief—that business has a responsibility to the future of the nation as a whole. He argued that business should cooperate with government, and appealed to corporations to take a leadership role, citing government's inability to single-handedly solve such complex national problems as population explosion, urban congestion and poverty, unequal educational opportunities, and pollution.

J. Irwin Miller was especially concerned with business' role in righting racial inequities. A vocal supporter of the civil rights movement, he worked actively to promote it, helping organize the original March on Washington. He personally helped to desegregate Columbus, and recruited approximately 100 minority managers and trainees to Cummins between 1965 and 1973. Dr. Martin Luther King, Jr. once called Miller "the most progressive businessman in America."

Video Case Questions

1. If you had to define leadership based solely on the actions of J. Irwin Miller, what would that definition be?
2. Do you think a person like J. Irwin Miller will be a leader in every group or organizational setting he enters? Explain.
3. What might keep Miller from being a leader in other settings?

12. MOTIVATION AND WORK PERFORMANCE

CARING ABOUT THE COMPANY BY CARING ABOUT ASSOCIATES[1]

Rosenbluth International is a $1.5 billion travel agency with 750 U.S. offices. Hal Rosenbluth, owner and CEO, is not a conventional thinker, especially when it comes to his employees. He is co-author of the book entitled *The Customer Comes Second*. His philosophy is that when a company looks out for its employees, they will likewise look out for customers.

In 1989, Rosenbluth decided to locate a data-entry operation for the company in the town of Linton, North Dakota, which had been suffering from the effects of an eight-year drought. The company originally advertised for 20 data processors, and they received 80 applicants. So Rosenbluth decided to hire 40 people part time, to spread the wealth. Originally this work had been handled by temps and employees on overtime. The Linton operation was an experiment, but one that has turned out extremely well for the company. From the initial 40 part-time employees, the office has grown to 180 employees that handle data entry, accounting, ticketing, reservations, expense management, and customer service. Rosenbluth soon found that employees in a rural community like Linton could be paid less (living expenses are lower) and, at the same time, turnover and absenteeism are much lower.

To orient the new associates (as all Rosenbluth employees are known) to the company's way of doing business, they were all sent to a two-day orientation in Philadelphia where, among other activities, they were treated to high tea, served by Hal Rosenbluth and another high-level executive. The idea was for employees to experience first class service as well as demonstrate that the principles of service applied to Rosenbluth as well as everyone else. Associate Missy Kilde states, "You really feel you matter and are part of the company, not like you were just stuck out in some office."

The company values training and has found that having peers lead the training works best. It goes back to the idea that you learn the most when you have to teach something. The company offers off-hour seminars on topics like personal finance and health. Any associate can volunteer to be a seminar leader on a topic related to company affairs. When this happens the person is flown to company headquarters to learn teaching techniques. For example, Associate Sheila Horner trained her peers on how to build customer profiles for a large client. She comments, "Training others helps you understand the entire work process, and you have ownership and can take charge of the project."

Teamwork and communication are valued highly in this company. Rosenbluth holds informal question and answer sessions whenever he is in town (at least once a quarter). There are also team meetings about every

two weeks, where team leaders present their work plans for an upcoming period. Supervisors ask questions and make suggestions, but the plan comes from the team.

To keep employees challenged and make work interesting, the Linton managers instituted cross-training with the goal of every associate knowing how to do at least three different tasks and 20 percent will know all the jobs in the office. This has allowed associates to cover for one another as well as facilitated movement among jobs and promotions. The company also shares all financial and other pertinent information with associates so they know where the company stands. To help associates appreciate the value of this information, managers instituted a contest to see which team could lower its supply costs the most.

One other thing the company does is allow employees to set their own schedules as much as possible. The idea is to get the work done and meet deadlines but not tie people to their offices for a certain set of hours everyday. For example, data entry employees can work weekends if they choose.

There is a real sense of family in this Linton, ND, office of a large national company. They are all willing to pitch in and help one another and have a strong belief that the company cares about them and this is reciprocated. Hal Rosenbluth has found that "rural America is a great place to do business." Sure that's true, but what's also true is that great places to do business also happen because of great business practices.

Motivation is a key to an organization's survival and prosperity. Managers must have people who are motivated to do the work that accomplishes the organization's mission. It sounds quite simple, but managers are often baffled by the challenge of motivating the workforce to enact its strategy. There is nothing so complex as the inner workings of the human mind, which is the wellspring for human motivation. There is no way to completely cover this important topic in one chapter. However, we present some key theories about *what* motivates people and *how* people are motivated. We also discuss implications for managerial practice. In thinking about the ideas presented in this chapter, you will find it useful and insightful to relate them to those in chapter 11 on leadership. Being motivated to behave in certain ways in an organization is a function of the relationship between employees and their managers. An important part of leading is a manager's ability to successfully direct employee motivation toward the accomplishment of organizational goals.

MOTIVATION: THE HIDDEN CAUSE OF BEHAVIOR

Companies that are trying to succeed in an ever more competitive world can do so only when all its people have the information, skills, training, *and* motivation to make it succeed. To lead people and get them to behave in desired ways, managers must understand what causes behavior. As we have noted frequently in this text, it is by understanding causes that managers can take appropriate actions to achieve the results they want.

The hidden cause of behavior is the often misunderstood concept called motivation. It is hidden because motivation resides in our minds. It gives us directions as we encounter and seek to understand situations. In organizations, managers have much influence over the shaping of those situations so that employees will be motivated to behave in ways that are good for themselves and the organization. Like it or not, the managers' behaviors strongly affect the direction of employees' motivations. Managers influence whether employees will identify their welfare with that of the organization (or not) and want to act in ways that take full advantage of their skills and experience.

Here's an initial assumption for our study: People *are* motivated, and they always behave in ways they believe to be in their best interests to attain some goal or fulfill some need. In an organization, managers have the challenge and responsibility to bring about the convergence of individual goals and best interests with those of the organization. By studying motivation, we can begin to understand how people figure out what is in their best interests and learn how they may come to converge their self interest with the needs of the organization. Exhibit 12-1 graphically illustrates this managerial challenge.

Managers provide direction for individual motivation and the convergence of individual and organizational goals through the human resources practices, culture and communication, organizational design and structure, strategies, and work processes they put in place. In some organizations people may seem motivated to do little. However, when we explore why this is the case, we usually see that they somehow do not identify their interests with those of the organization. They either feel constrained by the structures and practices of the organization or they do not have sufficient information about their role or they lack the the tools and authority to perform beyond some minimum level. In this case, what we usually find are employees motivated to simply follow rules. And, among themselves, they are probably motivated to complain about management and the way they are being treated.

Managers have the authority, responsibility, and obligation to create and maintain organizations that (1) do not unreasonably constrain employees and (2) provide an environment that brings out the best in all employees as they come to see how their needs and goals are fulfilled by contributing their time and talents to the organization. To do this, it is useful to review what we have learned about motivation and its role in successful organization action.

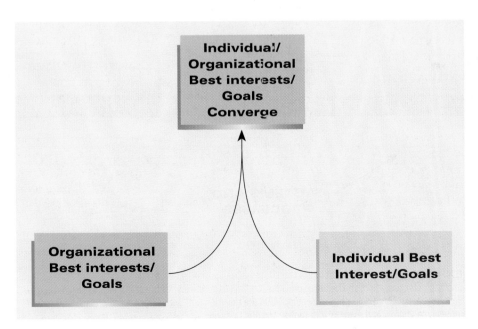

EXHIBIT 12-1
The managerial challenge: to bring convergence of organizational and individual best interests and goals

Motivation Defined

Motivation An inner state of mind that is responsible for energizing, directing, or sustaining goal-oriented behaviors.

Let's start with a definition. **Motivation** is *an inner state of mind that is responsible for energizing, directing, or sustaining goal-oriented behaviors.* Other words might be chosen to describe motivation, such as force, stimulus, drive, or sense of purpose. What is common to all of these terms is the notion that motivation gives direction to purposeful behaviors.

A general model of motivation might be described as in Exhibit 12-2. The model indicates that we can understand motivation in terms of goal-oriented behaviors in some environment that supplies the tools, information, processes, and feedback that then motivate individuals' behaviors in subsequent similar situations. People bring with them certain knowledge, skills, abilities, needs, interests, and energy levels that can affect their motivation to act in particular ways in particular situations.

When employees act the way the organization feels is appropriate to achieve its goals, employees are said to be *motivated.* However, this is not the best way to characterize behaviors. It is not whether employees are motivated or not. It is whether they are motivated to do what the organization wants. What is more accurate to say is that when employees are doing a good job, this means they understand and identify with their role in helping the organization achieve its purpose and have the support necessary to make their contributions in that process. Managers of the organization have a responsibility to make sure that is the case.

The organizational environment incorporates certain goals and objectives, job design, task demands, social arrangements, and physical realities that affect

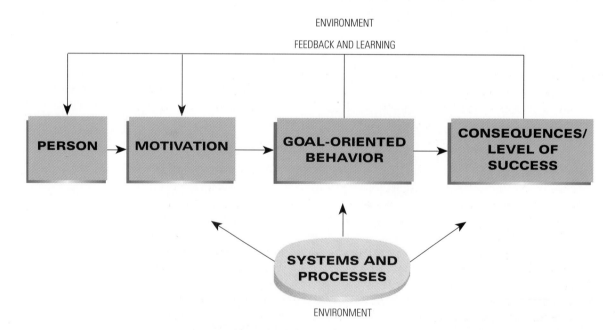

EXHIBIT 12-2 A model of motavation. Internal motivation generates behavior toward achievement of a goal. The success of the behavior provides learning experiences, which affect motivation and subsequent behavior. The whole process occurs within the environment, with systems and processes, which influence and provide the context for motivation and behavior.

motivation. Some particularly important aspects of the work environment that have been discussed in prior chapters include organizational roles and processes and the leader's vision. This combination of person and environment affects how motivated employees will feel about contributing to the organization versus just putting in their time. It is worth remembering that TQM is well aware of this point. An important part of TQM is creating a relationship between employees and the work environment that energizes their motivation to contribute to the organization.

Too often when managers think about motivation, they wrongly consider it a process that is centered in the individual. Motivation to achieve organizational goals is determined by the *relationship* between employees and their managers. In an organization, the manager is the one who has the most influence over how these relationships work. That's another reason why it is useful to explore what motivation is and how managers can take advantage of the motivation that is within each of us to coordinate action and successfully achieve organizational goals.

While most motivation theories look at the individual, it is important to understand that motivation is also a social phenomenon. We can best understand it in the context of topics discussed in some of the other chapters of this book, particularly organizational culture, leadership, and group dynamics and teambuilding. People do not operate in a vacuum. Behavior deals with how people adapt and relate to their environments to achieve goals. In considering the theories we will cover in this chapter, think about them, in terms of how these ideas explain how individuals relate to the larger environments in which they exist and identify their best interests with those of the environment. As we have noted in Chapter 11 on leadership, managers, by creating the environment to which employees adapt, greatly influence what they are motivated to do and with what enthusiasm they go about their work.

Motivation for Total Quality Behaviors

Any management practice obviously affects the behaviors of employees. How managers act, their values, and the ways they relate to employees provide the cues and information employees use to do their jobs. In Chapter 11 we saw how some GM managers thought they needed to install a refrigerator in a hotel room for a senior manager. Given their understanding of their responsibilities and the GM culture and environment at the time, that is what they were motivated to do. Since TQM is about creating a particular culture and suggests certain managerial behaviors, TQM practices likewise will affect what employees are motivated to do.

Total quality behaviors include (1) working in teams to design and execute work processes, (2) using data to improve work processes, and (3) acting to maximize the value of individual input and minimize rework and waste in whatever a particular job entails (with the final goal of delivering quality to customers). Managers have the responsibility of creating an environment in which employees direct their motivations and behaviors toward doing these things. Putting the principles of TQM into practice lets managers develop this kind of environment. As we have stated often, the ideas of TQM that we have explored throughout this book are about providing employees the information, training, tools, and the authority to act so that quality products and services are the results. In other words, the practices of TQM recognize that it takes a particular kind of environment and set of managerial actions to give direction to employee motivation and successful accomplishment of goals.

Managers who successfully practice TQM establish relationships with employees and create appropriate environments that motivate them to achieve goals.

We may compare the kind of direction successfully-implemented TQM gives to motivation with that of more traditional management practices. In the latter, employees often are not given either enough information or authority to do their jobs beyond some narrow constraints. There is less focus on working together (though it is by working together that final outputs are delivered to customers). They are often not sure how their jobs contribute to accomplishing the organization's goals. In these situations, what we find is that employees lack direction for their motivations. They do not have a good sense of their purpose, of what their role is in accomplishing organizational goals. Because motivation on the job is related to successful *goal-oriented* behavior, the level of motivation to accomplish organizational goals in these kinds of companies may be found lacking. However, what is actually lacking are employees' understandings of where they fit in to accomplish these goals. They do not have a clear sense of purpose. The principles of TQM take this into account. That is why we find suggestions for how managers may create an environment that facilitates teamwork, process improvement, and the goal of delivering value to customers.

Theory X and Theory Y

Theory X An assumption that people are lazy and inherently dislike work and avoid it whenever possible; employees must be coerced and controlled to get them to put forth enough effort to accomplish organization goals.

Several decades ago, Douglas McGregor summed up a continuum of human motivation with two ends that he called Theory X and Theory Y.[2] McGregor suggested that managers at the **Theory X** end of the continuum *assume that the average human being is lazy and inherently dislikes work and avoids it whenever possible. These managers believe that they must coerce and control employees to get them to put forth enough effort to accomplish the organization's goals. They believe that employees have little ambition and try to avoid responsibility*. By contrast, managers at the **Theory Y** end of the continuum *assume that the average human being naturally enjoys expending physical and mental energy in work. They believe that employees become committed to work when they understand their roles in achieving goals and that they exercise self-direction and seek responsibility. Finally, they assume employees will exhibit creativity and ingenuity on the job when given the chance to do so.*

Theory X and Theory Y are supposed to describe different ways employees as individuals are motivated. The theories represent basic assumptions about how people behave in organizations and go about working with others to achieve goals. Theory X suggests that people in an organization have no sense of purpose and are not interested in knowing how they fit into the scheme of things. Theory Y assumes the opposite, affirming that individuals want to be involved and will take personal responsibility for doing well.

The problem with this approach to motivation is that it ignores the relationship between managers and employees. It fails to consider that the assumptions managers make about employees affect how managers interact with these employees. Remember, it is the responsibility of managers to create environments that give direction to employee motivation. Managers who believe Theory X will create Theory X environments. They will provide detailed direction for how to do work with little tolerance for differences of opinion. In such an environment, employees will likely resent management, do only what is asked of them, and, in general, behave in ways that will confirm what the manager expects. All the while, neither managers nor employees are aware that by their assumptions and behaviors, they are making Theory X come true.

The same is true of Theory Y. Managers who assume this is true will create empowering environments (ones that may take on many of the attributes of TQM) that allow employees to take full advantage of their abilities to contribute to their organizations. Employees, experiencing this kind of situation, are likely to respond positively and behave in ways that also confirm managers' beliefs about Theory Y.

As a whole the automobile industry in America treated workers with a Theory X mentality until the 1980s when the challenge of global competition forced it to change. Labor relations used to be adversarial, worker attitudes were sour, and a lot of human potential was wasted. Now the American companies are acting more like their Japanese competitors. Consider how Fujio Cho, the CEO of Toyota Motor Manufacturing, U.S.A., describes his philosophy of respecting human dignity:

- Do not make people do work they do not find meaningful.
- *Muda,* or work that does not add value to the product, is a typical example of this. We must eliminate *muda.*
- People use machines, and not the other way around.
- Take measures so that problems are apparent to everyone and encourage team members to correct them.
- Always leave room for people to make decisions in their work.

Recently, the UAW has earned its workers special rights to participate in decisions. For example, workers in auto assembly plants are dealing directly with car buyers, and following up on problems with dealers and suppliers. Workers have won the right to shut down machines that are producing defective parts, and to

Theory Y An assumption that people naturally enjoy expending physical and mental energy in work and that employees become committed to work when they understand their roles in achieving goals and that they exercise self-direction and seek responsibility.

file official complaints about poor quality. At Saturn there is no personnel department since team members determine how many people are needed on the team and make hiring decisions. UAW President Owen Bieber explains what this approach to management can mean to employees and their organizations: "Work becomes safer and more satisfying. Quality and productivity go up, making customers happier and keeping workers' jobs and incomes secure."[3]

Of course, managers encounter variation in motivation across individual workers; some have a higher energy level than others. However, there is also variation within the same person over time and across different situations; a normally high-energy person may occasionally be less energized. They may not understand how doing some action will contribute to achieving a goal. Think about your own life: There are some activities that inspire you to find enormous energy, while others provoke no interest. Some people may generally have a higher energy level than others, and human resource systems should be designed to select these individuals as employees. However, every person has the potential to fit both the Theory X and Theory Y descriptions at different times and circumstances (including managers). Managers need to realize this, and deal with people such that managers give each person what he or she needs to succeed.

In the past there has been a lot of controversy about whether Theory X or Theory Y is true, with little appreciation of the managers' roles in making one or the other of these ideas a reality in any organization. Because we can only understand motivations and behaviors within the contexts in which they take place, including the contexts created by the behavior of managers, the real value of Theories X and Y today are to remind of us of this.

Scholars have developed many theories to explain motivation and the drive to achieve various goals. These theories can help managers better understand what motivates employees and how they can take advantage of that to the benefit of individuals and the organization. We will look at several of these. The first set of theories we will review are called content theories because they identify the various drives and needs that motivate people. Then we will discuss some process theories that describe how people are motivated.

? THINKING CRITICALLY

1. Does our definition of motivation coincide with your own sense of what gives direction to your behavior? Why or why not?
2. Are you more likely to be motivated to work hard on a project because you feel it has personal value to you in some way or other or because you want to please someone else? Explain.
3. Explain why TQM best fits with Theory Y.

Content theories Theories that suggest people have certain needs that compel them to take actions to fulfill those needs.

Need A felt lack of something useful, required, or desired.

CONTENT THEORIES OF MOTIVATION

Content theories describe the felt needs that motivate people. The basic idea of **content theories** is that *people have certain needs that compel them to take actions to fulfill those needs*. A **need** is *a felt lack of something useful, required, or desired*. Unfulfilled needs create tension within individuals and stimulate behavior to get what they lack.

People often use the word need to refer to motivational forces when other words might be more appropriate. For example, the words goal, need, and want each have different nuances. In a restricted sense of the word, need may indicate a lack of something useful or required ("I *must* have it"). We have physiological needs, such as for food and water, and psychological needs, such as for social acceptance, love, and security. *Want* indicates a lack of something desired or wished for, but not required ("I *would like* to have it"). Wants include desires for intellectual stimulation, entertainment, or happiness. A *goal* represents an unfulfilled aspiration ("I intend to achieve it by next month"). Common personal goals are those for prosperity, health and fitness, social status, and career accomplishments. The need or desire that people have to preserve their self-images also motivates them to behave in ways that are consistent with that self-image. For example, if people believe themselves to be loving, caring, brave, or even macho, these can act as strong motivational forces for particular behaviors. Self-images can drive people to only fulfill their needs with products or services that are compatible with how they view themselves (such as a car, clothes, etc.).

No matter what term is used to describe the underlying needs, content theories explain how managers can provide direction for employees' motivations by helping them meet their needs. The challenge for managers is to determine how to link job behaviors with the satisfaction of individuals' needs. This is a challenge because different individuals may have different needs, and these needs may change over time. The following reviews several content theories of motivation that emphasize different sets of human needs.

Maslow's Hierarchy of Needs

Abraham Maslow, a psychologist, suggested a range of needs that drive human behavior. Maslow arranged these needs in a *hierarchy of importance,* called **Maslow's Hierarchy of Needs,** which includes: *physiological, safety/security, love, esteem, cognitive, aesthetic, and self-actualization needs.*[4] Maslow's hierarchy of needs might be partitioned into higher order and lower order needs as suggested in Exhibit 12-3 on page 436. The following describes each of these needs.

Maslow's Hierarchy of Needs The physiological, safety/security, love, esteem, cognitive, aesthetic, and self-actualization needs said to motivate human behavior.

1. **Physiological Needs.** Chemical needs of the body, including sexual desire, hunger, thirst, sleep, activity needs, desired sensory satisfactions.
2. **Safety or Security Needs.** The need to be free of danger, such as the motivation to avoid wild animals, extremes of temperature, assault, disease, or any type of threat to well-being.
3. **Love Needs.** Desire for affiliation and belongingness, to give and receive, such as with friends, spouse, children, parents, group members.
4. **Esteem Needs.** Fulfillment of esteem needs can be derived internally through feelings of strength, achievement, adequacy, confidence, independence, and freedom; or externally through reputation, prestige, recognition, attention, importance, and appreciation from others.
5. **Cognitive Needs.** Desire to know and understand. These include the desire to know or be aware of reality, get facts and satisfy curiosity, and a related need to understand or explain, systematize, organize, analyze, and seek out relationships and meanings.
6. **Aesthetic Needs.** A craving for beauty in one's surroundings and, when ugliness prevails, provoking a real sense of deprivation, even sickness.

EXHIBIT 12-3
Maslow's Hierarchy of Needs

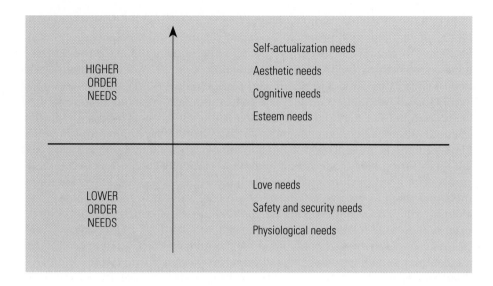

7. **Self-Actualization.** The desire to realize or actualize one's full potential; a growth need, which continues to get stronger later in life and is never fully satisfied.

Maslow's notion of a hierarchy implies that some needs are more basic, and the drive to fulfill them takes precedence over the drive to fulfill other needs. For example, an unfulfilled physiological drive like hunger takes priority over an unfulfilled need for love. Maslow also suggests that people progress up the hierarchy of needs one step at a time. Once the basic needs like hunger are fulfilled, they lose their primary importance in our lives, and we feel drives to fulfill needs at the next higher level of the hierarchy. According to Maslow, an individual progresses up the hierarchy until a lower order need resurfaces and takes priority.

Maslow's ideas about a hierarchy of needs are difficult to prove or disprove. However, they have a powerful intuitive appeal, and have proven popular with anyone interested in human motivation. They provide some useful insights for managers into understanding how to direct employee motivation to help achieve organizational goals. Maslow's hierarchy suggests that for people to concentrate their energies on these higher pursuits, they should not be distracted by more basic drives, such as needs for safety and security. Managers can help employees fulfill these needs by providing job security, adequate compensation, and clean, healthy work environments. Once freed from worrying about these needs, employees can turn their attentions to dealing with the fulfillment of needs that appear at the higher level of the hierarchy. Managers then have the responsibility of providing challenges that engage these higher levels. These might include special projects or promotions that fulfill the needs for recognition and esteem or the challenges and authority to make important decisions that fulfill the need for self-actualization. The point to remember is that managers can use Maslow's ideas to bring about the convergence and fulfillment of individual needs and organizational needs simultaneously.

Maslow's hierarchy also reminds managers of the range of human needs that people seek to fulfill. If these needs are not fulfilled at work, people will likely seek other avenues. For example, if a person's work is basically mindless and repetitive, they will seek to fulfill their higher level needs outside the organization through hobbies, membership in voluntary organizations, or other social activities that have nothing to do with the organization. Of course, people will do this anyway, but to not take advantage of employees' inborn motivations to use their talents to help the organization is a wasted opportunity. For example, a factory worker we will call Joe Smith was asked to perform repetitive tasks that required little thought during the work day. At night, Joe designed and built guitars and mandolins that were genuine works of art. Not creating a situation where Joe could use these talents on the job represents a squandering of human resources.

It is easy to think of examples that appear to contradict Maslow's hierarchy. For example, the so-called "starving artist" pursues needs for aesthetics and self-actualization despite apparent deficiencies in fulfilling physiological and security needs because of the lack of a good income. This example seems to be a compelling contradiction; however, it may be that the artist has simply learned to cope with hunger and deprivation of other social amenities. Furthermore, each individual may be able to tolerate different levels of deprivation, in effect, to suppress the potency of the need. People develop many such coping strategies as they mature. So, if you view Maslow's Hierarchy of Needs as a lifestage model of personal development, such contradictions are easily explained.

Alderfer's ERG Theory

Clayton Alderfer refined Maslow's theory and suggested three broad categories of needs: existence needs, relatedness needs, and growth needs. The initials of these three categories of needs give the acronym ERG, by which the theory is known.[5] Existence needs include physiological and safety needs that are satisfied by physical material. Relatedness needs are security, love, and esteem needs that are satisfied by other people. Growth needs include self-esteem and self-actualization needs. Alderfer did not emphasize the step-wise progression of an individual through a hierarchy, but suggested that an individual may be influenced by many types of needs simultaneously. Alderfer's ideas are easily illustrated in companies that are competing in global markets.

Enormous energy can be unleashed when managers are faced with a crisis that threatens the existence of the organization. Such a situation can arouse a number of needs to motivate people to take action. For example, Harley-Davidson saw its market share for large motorcycles shrink over a couple of decades from a high of around 77 percent to a low of 22 percent by the early 1980s. Foreign competitors, such as Honda, Yamaha, and Kawasaki from Japan, offered higher quality, lower priced motorcycles and helped put Harley-Davidson on the verge of bankruptcy. This company transformed its approach to management based on the principles of Total Quality Management, reversed the market-share trend and made the company profitable again.

With their security and esteem threatened, Harley-Davidson managers were extremely motivated to learn new ways of behaving and to bring about the changes needed to make them competitive once again. According to Maslow and Alderfer, they had to engage in creative thinking and learning behaviors that were motivated by higher order needs.

It is difficult to tell if the principles of Maslow's hiearchy have been violated. Did Harley-Davidson managers use higher order cognitive needs to serve the lower order security needs? Does this example confirm or disconfirm Maslow's hierarchy? Does it illustrate Alderfer's idea that there can be many needs motivating behavior? Answers to such theoretical questions are interesting, but difficult to prove or disprove. For managers like those at Harley-Davidson, the only thing that matters is that the people are motivated to fulfill the missions of their organizations. To this end, Maslow and Alderfer offer some useful ideas about how to think about and motivate desired behaviors.

McClelland's Acquired Needs Theory

Acquired Needs Theory
A theory that suggests that people learn certain needs as they mature.

Maslow and Alderfer imply that all humans are equipped with a particular set of needs when they are born, as if these needs were human instincts. By contrast, McClelland's **Acquired Needs Theory** suggests that *people develop or learn certain needs as they mature*. David McClelland has identified three needs that are important to understanding the behavior of people in organizations: needs for achievement, affiliation, and power.[6]

- **Need for Achievement.**   People with high need for achievement show a strong desire to assume personal responsibility for finding solutions to problems; they are goal-oriented and preoccupied with task accomplishments; they prefer moderate challenges and take calculated risks, and they seek concrete feedback on their performances.

- **Need for Affiliation.**   People with high need for affiliation are attracted to other people to get approval and feel reassurance; they tend to conform to people whose friendship they value, and they show interest in others' feelings.

- **Need for Power.**   People with high need for power usually attempt to control or influence others or their environment, and they often have good leadership abilities.

The implications and challenges for management are to try to identify the needs of employees and match the job demands with their needs. For example, it is a waste of potential human energy to place a person with high need for achievement in a job with routine or non-challenging demands. This person would not feel challenged and would probably not excel. People high in need for affiliation are likely to perform better in jobs that demand a high amount of interpersonal contact and that offer a lot of personal support and approval tied to their performances. People high in need for power are likely to excel in management positions where they can influence others.

Personal Values

Personal values General beliefs about what is personally important

People may decide how to direct their energy depending on how a specific behavior contributes to and detracts from the fulfillment of the types of needs suggested by Maslow, Alderfer, and McClelland. However, other theorists have suggested additional sources of motivation that managers might consider including **personal values** that are *general beliefs about what is personally important*.

Milton Rokeach has identified a number of broad personal values that endure over time and guide many aspects of a person's life. These include, for example, the importance of being cheerful, forgiving, helpful, loving, clean, obedient, polite, responsible, self-controlled, broadminded, capable, courageous, imaginative, independent, and intellectual.[7] Another researcher, Lynn Kahle, includes the following items in a list of personal values: sense of belonging, security, fun-enjoyment-excitement, being well respected, sense of fulfilment, warm relationships with others, self-fulfillment, and sense of accomplishment. These types of personal values guide a person's beliefs about "what should be," and how to judge particular behaviors as (in)appropriate or (un)desirable.[8] In addition to broad values, people might hold values that are particular to different domains of their life. For example, they might have beliefs that pertain to their religion, family, or work.[9]

People are more likely to be motivated to work hard for a purpose that matches their personal values. As discussed in the earlier chapters on organizational culture and leadership, one of the key roles of a leader in motivating people is to give them a vision that they can relate to. The alienation and detachment of factory work is often attributed to the boring nature of the work itself. However, workers can find meaning in even the most boring tasks when they see that they are contributing to something worthy of their efforts.

For example, a Total Quality philosophy helps give people an important focus, namely, adding value to the quality of outputs delivered to customers. People are more likely to work to achieve improved quality and productivity when they see the direct connection of what they do to improving service for a customer. They are not as likely to get excited about another productivity program that is intended to reduce costs and enhance profits for the company. No matter what theory of motivation you apply, leadership is always an important component in achieving motivation among employees.

People have a host of needs, goals, wants, self-image perceptions, and personal values that determine their motivation for a particular behavior. Next, we will examine the processes whereby a person matches needs with certain behavioral options.

❓ THINKING CRITICALLY

1. Maslow suggested that Abraham Lincoln and Thomas Jefferson were two historic people who had reached the level of self-actualization. List the names of some contemporary people you think have reached the level of self-actualization and provide evidence to support your choices.
2. How do the ideas of Total Quality Management relate to fulfilling needs and achieving organizational goals as suggested by the various content theories of motivation?

PROCESS THEORIES

Content theories emphasize the internal forces, needs, values or self-concepts that motivate people to behave in certain ways. **Process theories** *emphasize how individuals choose behaviors to fulfill their needs and accomplish various goals.* Process theories focus on what people actually do to achieve their purposes and how they reason out what they are going to do. For example, one process theory focuses on reinforcement and emphasizes the reinforcing effect that behavioral consequences have on an individual's choice of subsequent behavior. The other process theories that we discuss expand upon reinforcement theory. However, they also describe the cognitive processes going on in people's minds as they go about understanding situations and deciding how much effort to exert on particular behaviors.

Process theories Theories that emphasize how individuals choose behaviors to fulfill their needs and accomplish various goals.

Reinforcement Theory

Reinforcement theory A theory that suggests behavior is determined by its consequences.

Reinforcement theory suggests that *behavior is determined by its consequences*. Reinforcement theory does not encourage managers to focus on the needs within a person. It encourages managers to create an environment that motivates particular behaviors. It assumes that people look out for themselves, and that they always ask the question, "what's in it for me" or, said another way, they behave in ways that are consistent with their subjective sense of their personal best interests. Reinforcement Theory suggests that people get some type of personal satisfaction from every action they take.

Operant conditioning A theory that suggests that people learn to exhibit behaviors that bring them pleasurable outcomes and to avoid behaviors which bring them painful outcomes.

Operant Conditioning. Reinforcement theory holds that through **operant conditioning** *people learn to exhibit behaviors which bring them pleasurable outcomes and to avoid behaviors that bring them painful outcomes.* One of the most famous theorists of operant conditioning, B.F. Skinner, suggests that there is no need to study the inner workings of the human mind.[10] To condition behavior, Skinner would argue that managers must simply understand the relationships between behaviors and their consequences, and then arrange contingencies that reinforce desirable behaviors and discourage undesirable behaviors. There are four basic ways that managers might arrange these contingencies and modify the behavior of individuals: positive reinforcement, avoidance learning, extinction, and punishment.[11]

- **Positive reinforcement.** This is the application of a pleasurable or valued consequence. For example, a manager might use praise, bonuses, promotions, paid vacations, or some other form of recognition to encourage a particular behavior.

- **Avoidance learning.** This is the withholding or removal of an unpleasurable consequence. For example, a manager might eliminate an unenjoyable weekly performance review because the employee is behaving as desired.

- **Extinction.** This is the withdrawal or failure to provide a pleasurable consequence. With lack of reinforcement, the employee may eventually cease engaging in the behavior. Extinction can be used to reduce the probability of undesirable behavior, such as when a manager stops giving attention to the antics of an employee. If they are not careful, however, managers can also inadvertently extinguish desirable behavior, such as when a manager fails to show appreciation for good work.

- **Punishment.** This is the application of an unpleasurable or painful consequence. For example, a manager might use demotions, dismissals, reprimands, or poor performance evaluations to punish undesirable behavior.

Organizational Behavior (OB) modification The application of reinforcement theory to modify employee behavior and help an organization accomplish its goals.

Organizational Behavior Modification. **Organizational behavior (OB) modification** *involves the application of reinforcement theory to modify employee behavior and help an organization accomplish its goals.* In OB modification, managers use extinction and punishment to eliminate undesired behavior, and they use positive reinforcement and avoidance learning to elicit the desired behavior. Conducting OB modification can require extensive work by the manager to identify performance-related behaviors, establish baseline measurements, identify existing contingencies of reinforcement, carry out the intervention, and evaluate the performance results.[12] OB modification can be used for such diverse perfor-

This motivated employee finds her job satisfying while participating in the electric company's goal of delivering quality services to customers.

mance objectives as to increase quality, productivity, safety, attendance, and customer service, or to reduce employee theft or organizational costs.

Reinforcement can have a powerful effect on behavior; however, there are several drawbacks to OB modification. First, managers may resist administering a complex program of OB modification. There are so many behaviors required to run a successful organization, it can be overwhelming for managers to have to analyze and modify each of them. Second, employees can resent the control and manipulation that is involved in OB modification. Employee resentment can be particularly acute when managers rely heavily on punishment to modify behavior. Resentment can undermine the teamwork that is so important in Total Quality (or any) organizations. Finally, reinforcement theory does not fully explain how people are motivated. It ignores the mental processes that are so important in determining motivation. Humans beings are thinkers. The key to understanding motivation rests with understanding the mental processes that provide a rationale for our behaviors. For these reasons, few companies rely exclusively on behavior modification. Instead, they may use the principles of reinforcement in conjunction with other approaches to managing employee motivation.

Expectancy Theory

The expectancy theory of motivation was first introduced by Victor Vroom in 1964.[13] Like reinforcement theory, expectancy theory emphasizes the role of valued consequences in determining behavior. However, **expectancy theory** *emphasizes the role of individual perceptions and feelings (i.e., expectations of particular results) in determining motivation and behavior*. It tries to explain how people rationalize and make choices about the direction and intensity of their behaviors based on their expectations. Expectancy theory suggests that rationalizations, and thus motivation, for choosing one behavior over another are

Expectancy theory A theory that emphasizes the role of individual perceptions and feelings (expectations of particular results) in determining motivation and behavior.

based on a person's beliefs that certain outcomes will result from doing one thing instead of another.

The best way to remember the tenets of expectancy theory is with the acronym VIE, which stands for its three basic components: Valence, Instrumentality, and Expectancy.

- **Valence.**   The value or anticipated satisfaction that an individual attaches to an outcome.
- **Instrumentality.**   The likelihood that successful performance will yield the valued outcome.
- **Expectancy.**   The likelihood that a certain level of effort will result in successful behavioral performance.

According to expectancy theory, the motivational force to engage in a particular behavior can be expressed as a formula:

Motivational Force = Valence × Instrumentality × Expectancy

Expectancy theory suggests that motivational force is determined according to the mathematics of this equation. If any of these three components is low, then the force to engage in the behavior is low. For example, the general manager of an industrial wood products plant requested that his production department managers use statistical process control (SPC) to improve quality. The general manager even promised a bonus for a five percent improvement in quality in the next quarter. The department managers wanted the bonus (high valence), and they believed they would get it if they met the improvement objective (high instrumentality). However, they were not confident in their ability to successfully use statistical process control (low expectancy), since they had only received a two-day overview instructing them on the theory of SPC. As a result, their motivation for using SPC was low, so they did not implement it. They decided to use more traditional methods of increased inspection and tighter supervision to achieve the quality goals. The traditional approach was more costly and potentially less effective at improving quality than SPC. However, the department managers felt extremely confident in their ability to execute it (very high expectancy) and thus were motivated to go in that direction rather than with SPC.

Expectancy theory gives very clear implications for managers about how to increase employee motivation to behave in ways that are consistent with organizational goals. First, managers must work to develop a shared understanding with employees of the value of the outcomes of various behaviors. Employees must be able to see the value of jobs in contributing to the organization's goals of delivering products and services to customers, for example. This requires open communication and a clear sense of purpose by both managers and employees.

Some people believe that it is the manager's responsibility to identify what particular employees value so the organization can provide appropriate rewards for behaving in particular ways. This suggests an individualized approach to motivation, which can fragment the organization and downplay the importance of teamwork and effective and efficient management of processes. A more productive approach is to use communication and culture to develop a shared sense of what is important so everyone works together and the successful accomplishment of a goal has high valence in and of itself.

Second, managers should set up feedback processes that allow employees to know how well they are doing. They need to perceive a clear connection between what they are doing and the accomplishment of organizational goals. This idea plugs into the notion of instrumentality in expectancy theory. If employees do not see a relationship between their efforts and expected results, their motivation to expend these efforts will be diminished. Finally, managers must ensure that employees have confidence in their capability to perform the behavioral requirements that are desired. This self-confidence can be built through training and development activities to give employees the knowledge and skills they need to perform. If people do not believe they can do something, they will very likely avoid it.[14]

In everyday life, few of us think through every behavior based on some calculated sense of the outcomes depending on what we do. Much of our interaction with others, for example, is based on our personal sense of what is right. That is based on our experience, and we seldom stop to question it (though that might be a good idea at times). Thus, while expectancy theory seems to suggest that people continuously weigh outcomes, it is questionable whether that takes place. Nevertheless, expectancy theory does give us a way to think about the reasons people do what they do and provides managers with some techniques for more successfully bringing individual and organizational goals together.

Intrinsic Versus Extrinsic Motivation.   One of the deficiencies of expectancy theory is that it leads managers to think that all behavior is motivated by *extrinsic* rewards, the delivery of which are in the hands of other people. This suggests the idea of **extrinsic motivation,** that is that *our behavior is designed to please others rather than ourselves to get these rewards.* But this is clearly not always the case. People are often motivated by *intrinsic* rewards, the ones associated with doing the behavior itself. *The process of being motivated based on the satisfaction derived from the behavior itself* is called **intrinsic motivation.** For example, many people are motivated to come to work in the morning and work late because they like what they do. If you are involved in some activity, for example, sports or writing poetry or programming computers, you likely do it because it is personally satisfying, that is for intrinsic reasons. Exhibit 12-4 summarizes the difference between extrinsic and intrinsic motivation.

Extrinsic motivation
Suggests that our behavior is designed to please others rather than ourselves to get certain rewards.

Intrinsic motivation The process of being motivated based on the satisfaction derived from the behavior itself.

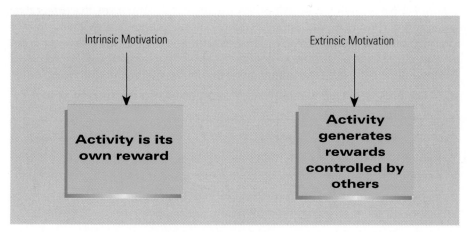

EXHIBIT 12-4
Intrinsic vs. extrinsic motivation

In applying expectancy theory, it is important for managers to recognize the difference between intrinsic motivation and extrinsic motivation.[15] It is actually possible that the introduction of extrinsic motivators like pay or recognition may reduce a person's intrinsic motivation.[16] For example, researchers discovered in an experimental setting that paying someone to solve puzzles may dampen their intrinsic motivation. The people paid to solve puzzles do not persist in the behavior once they are given some free time. Those not paid often continue solving the puzzles despite the fact that the experiment is declared complete. They find it challenging and interesting and want to continue.

However, in most organizational settings, high intrinsic motivation levels are not likely to be dampened by extrinsic factors such as a bonus, praise, or some other form of recognition.[17] In fact, many Total Quality organizations such as Xerox and Motorola use extrinsic rewards, like a gift of money or a dinner certificate, to recognize the contributions of their improvement teams. Toyota even gives rewards as a part of its suggestion system to encourage participation. These rewards appear to generate enthusiasm for the program. Though they are usually modest in size, they effectively serve as the feedback and recognition people need to know if their efforts are adding value to the organization.

Perhaps the most important reason to recognize the difference between intrinsic and extrinsic motivation is that managers need to look for ways to make the job or work behaviors more intrinsically interesting. We will discuss this topic more thoroughly in a later section on job design.

Goal Setting Theory

Xerox: Baldrige Award Winner

We understand a goal as a desired standard of accomplishment, an aspiration, or a performance aim. Having goals helps focus our energies and builds commitments to the tasks required to accomplish the goals.[18] As we have suggested throughout this chapter, we make sense of behavior in light of goals and the fulfillment of needs. Our behaviors have purposes. In fact, when we see someone behaving in a way we do not understand, we do not know the purpose of his or her behavior. People are generally not motivated to perform a task unless they know what purpose it will accomplish.

Anyone in the organization can set goals and the form goals take can vary tremendously. In the most general terms, goals can be deadlines, targets for productivity or quality measures, quotas for units produced, career aspirations, and so on. People working in organizations usually have many goals that affect their motivations to undertake various activities. For example, Joe Williams, a vice president and division manager of a manufacturing firm, has the following goals:

- to be the president of the company when his boss retires in five years.
- to achieve a 10 percent improvement in profitability over the next year.
- to increase sales by 5 percent in the next quarter.
- to increase customer satisfaction levels to 95 percent in the next quarter.
- to reduce scrap and rework rates by 10 percent in the next quarter.
- to complete a business proposal by the end of the month.
- to prepare a financial analysis for a Tuesday morning management meeting before the close of business on Monday.

These goals provide Joe with a means to regulate and evaluate his performance during his work day. He will direct his energy to specific tasks according to what he feels he needs to do in order to accomplish these goals.

Increasing the Motivational Force of Goals. *Parkinson's Law* indicates that work expands to fill the time available for its completion.[19] In other words, people adjust their effort level to fit their perception of the amount of time allowed to do the task. If they perceive the task to be more difficult, they will work harder to complete it in the alloted time. You have probably experienced this in your own life as a student. If you know a paper is due in two weeks, it is likely to take that long to complete it regardless of the difficulty. If it is a tough assignment, you will probably work hard and devote more of your time to the paper during those two weeks than if it was less demanding. The implication for goal setting is for managers to work with employees to set goals that are more challenging though achievable because they provide greater motivational forces than those that are easy to attain.

For goals to motivate people, they must be perceived as attainable. A salesperson may have no motivation to pursue a goal to increase sales by 5 percent in the next quarter if he or she believes that it is impossible to accomplish the goal. This requirement for attainability makes sense in terms of expectancy theory (low expectancy or low self-confidence produces low motivational force). It also means that managers must find a balance between providing goals that are difficult enough to provide the employee challenge, but not so difficult as to be discouraging.

Goals are also more motivational if they are specific, quantifiable, measurable, and clearly related to overall organizational purpose. Specific goals provide more motivation than general statements that lack specificity. For example, a general goal to increase sales, does not provide as much information as a specific goal to increase sales by 5 percent in the next quarter. The general goal could mean a one percent increase or a 10 percent increase. The specific information helps to prioritize a sales person's behaviors. He or she is likely to devote more energy to achieve a 10 percent increase than one percent. If the goal is also measurable, the specific information allows individuals to monitor their progress toward the goal.

Another way to improve the motivational force of a goal is to involve employees in setting goals that pertain to their work as AT&T does in its performance management process. Using a traditional command and control approach to management, managers may be inclined to dictate goals, without employee participation. This directive approach can produce goals that are unrealistic, particularly when managers are not intimately familiar with the work of their subordinates. Employees are more inclined to accept and be committed to goals that they help to define. Further, in terms of the organization as a whole, it is important to appreciate that goals that focus on the improvement of processes and enhancing teamwork and quality are far more effective than specific numerical goals, which may or may not be attainable given a system's current capabilities.

Management By Objectives. Many companies have a formalized goal setting theory as a fundamental approach to management. For example, in **Management By Objectives,** *employees at all levels of the organization agree to measurable numerical goals that are interlinked.* The goals at higher levels of the organization pertain to the whole organization, such as profitability or return on investment, and these are supported by more specific goals at the next level down, such as cost containment and sales revenue in a division. At the lowest level,

Management By Objectives (MBO) A program where employees at all levels of the organization agree to measurable numerical goals that are interlinked.

a worker might have productivity goals, such as to produce 200 units a day. The theory behind an MBO program is that if all the subordinates accomplish their numerical goals at the lower levels, then the organizational goals will be accomplished. Unfortunately, the theory has not worked in reality.

There are many problems with MBO, as it is usually implemented, that cause people to question its value in any organization. For example, it encourages game playing by employees. Individuals will often try to negotiate for easily attainable goals so they can be assured of looking good at appraisal time. Managers end up spending too much energy playing the game and administering the paperwork. Also, people can become obsessed with accomplishing the measured goals, particularly when progress toward the goals is used in performance appraisals and compensation decisions.

Goals, MBO, and Total Quality.   A major problem with MBO and its focus on numerical goals for individuals is that it is based on managing people rather than processes. It assumes that individuals are responsible for their successes independent of the system and its processes. Because we know that organizations are systems, where the success of any one person is dependent on the work of many other people, any goals program that does not recognize this will have problems. Employees will be assessed as if they had total responsibility for their success when this is not the case.

Further, it causes people to focus on making their personal goals, perhaps to the detriment of other employees and the system as a whole. Imagine, for example, a basketball team in which every player had a goal to make a certain number of points. This would mean that they all would be taking more shots rather than assisting those in a better position to score. Basketball teams, as well as teams in any organization, work best when all members see their roles in terms of the entire team and the system they are part of. MBO does not account for this.

Being highly focused on goals can be good for organizations if they have the right goals—those that focus on continuous improvement of processes and the quality of the goods and services delivered to customers. Kodak produced the poster shown in Exhibit 12-5 to communicate their obsession with Total Quality. Such mottos can be inspirational. However, they only have meaning when backed up with real long-term commitments to creating a system where the mottos become the reality.

W. Edwards Deming warned against using mottos and exhortations to get people to work harder and improve. He writes of slogans like "Do it right the first time":

A lofty ring it has. But how could a man make it right the first time when the incoming material is off-gauge, off-color, otherwise defective, or if his machine is not in good order, or the measuring instruments not trustworthy? This is just another meaningless slogan.[20]

Deming had more to say about MBO and the problems with setting numerical goals as described in the *A Look at TQM in Action* box on p. 448.

Social Comparison and Equity Theory

People in social work environments will compare their behaviors and performances with that of others. Such social comparisons help people learn the norms of the organizational culture to help them adapt to their organiza-

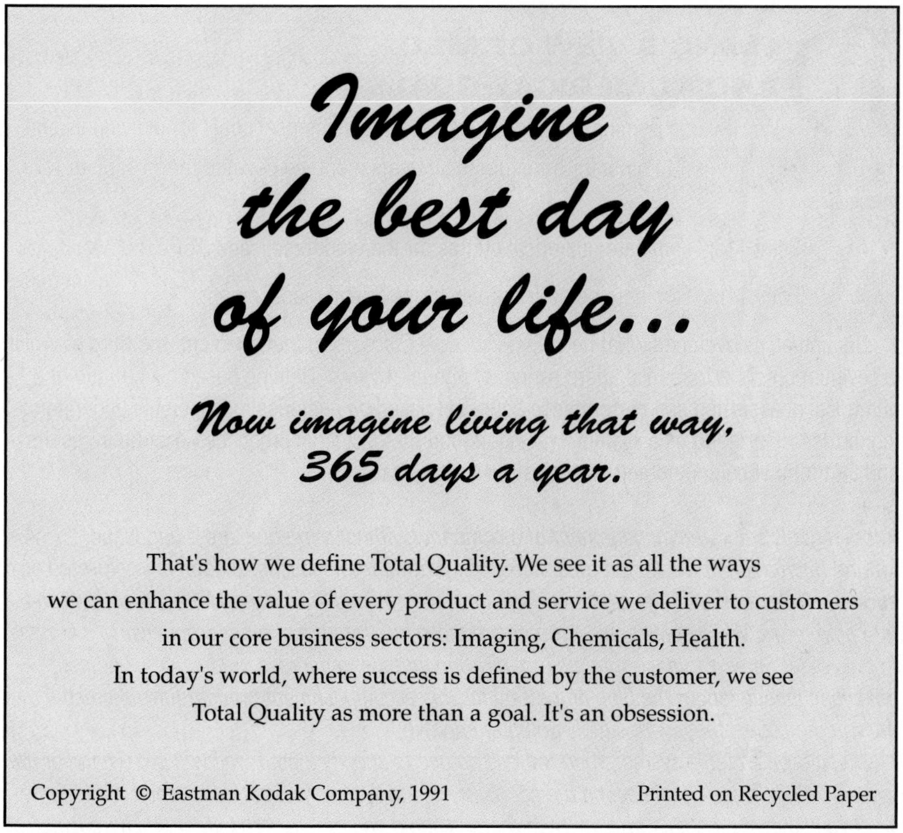

EXHIBIT 12-5
Eastman Kodak's poster for inspiring an obsession with total quality

tional environments. People look for role models to determine the appropriate ways to behave. Social comparisons influence employees' aspirations and serve as a basis for feelings of self-satisfaction over their own behaviors. People also make social comparisons on the consequences of their behaviors. They look for consistency in how people are treated in terms of work behaviors, fairness, rewards, and discipline. **Equity theory** addresses these ideas and is concerned with *how fairly or equitably people feel they have been treated*. As discussed earlier, a person's work behaviors bring on certain consequences or outcomes. People judge how fairly they have been treated by looking at their *inputs* (such as energy, time, knowledge, skills, or other contributions) and the *outcomes and feedback* (such as bonuses, praise, promotions, and disciplinary action).

Equity theory suggests that people do not look just at their own inputs and outcomes, they make social comparisons with the inputs and outcomes of other people as well.[21] They are concerned with how they relate to others. This is because individuals can only make sense of what happens to them by comparing their circumstances with those of others. They may make comparisons with co-workers, superiors, subordinates, or others within the organization. They may even make comparisons directly with others outside the organization, such as a friend who works at another company or indirectly with data on industry averages, for example on pay levels.

Equity theory A theory concerned with how fairly or equitably people feel they have been treated.

A LOOK AT

TQM IN ACTION

DEMING'S VIEW OF MBO AND NUMERICAL GOALS[22]

W. Edwards Deming strongly opposed setting numerical goals for individuals and the use of MBO. In his 14 Points for transforming management, he devoted the 11th point to this issue:

Point 11a: "Eliminate numerical quotas for the workforce," and

Point 11b: "Eliminate numerical goals for people in management."

Deming also developed what he called *7 Deadly Diseases* of management, the third of which is "evaluation of performance, merit rating, or annual review." Deming based his critique of numerical goal setting and performance appraisal based on numerical goals on his understanding of the organization as a system. He understood that a system produces variation in results and that it must be understood statistically. He explains:

Internal goals set in the management of a company, without a method, are a burlesque. . . . A natural fluctuation in the right direction (usually plotted from inaccurate data) is interpreted as success. A fluctuation in the opposite direction sends everyone scurrying for explanations and into bold forays whose only achievements are more frustration and more problems. . . . A man in the Postal Service told me that his organization intends to improve productivity 3 percent next year. Enquiry about the plan or method for this accomplishment brought forth the usual answer: no plan—they were simply going to improve.

If you have a stable system, then there is no use to specify a goal. You will get whatever the system will deliver. A goal beyond the capability of the system will not be reached.

If you have not a stable system, then there is again no point in setting a goal. There is no way to know what the system will produce: it has no capability.

To manage, one must lead. To lead, one must understand the work that one's subordinates are responsible for. Who is the customer (the next stage), and how can we serve better the customer?

To improve the use of goal setting, managers should recognize that simply setting goals does not ensure that people will be motivated to accomplish them. Further, goals must be oriented toward the improvement of processes and not at some arbitrary numerical targets that the system may or may not be capable of. Managers must have a plan for improving the system to accomplish their goals. Without a system-wide plan, neither the managers nor other employees can take the goals seriously. Managers bear the responsibility to improve all aspects of the system, including the factors that directly determine an employee's motivation (e.g., education, skill, self-confidence, value of rewards).

In essence, people compare their own outcomes/inputs versus others' outcomes/inputs. If these two comparison ratios are about equal, the person will perceive that they have been treated fairly, a situation that leads to satisfaction with the job situation. In other words, equity theory suggests that people make social comparisons with others to see if they received what they deserved compared with what others get for similar efforts. Equity theory treats fairness in terms of equitable ratios of inputs to outputs. This means that people receive, for example, pay equal to the value of their inputs in an organization's processes in ratio to the value of other people's inputs. People who do similar jobs should be paid similar salaries.

If ratios are not equal, then employees will perceive unfairness or *inequity*. Inequity leads to either guilt, because individuals feel they are getting more than deserved, or anger, because people feel they are getting less than deserved. Either situation is dissatisfying. This dissatisfaction creates a tension that motivates the individual to take action to correct the inequity. There are several actions a person can take to correct a perceived inequity:

- **Alter the Outcomes.**   Since people generally want to maximize valued outcomes, this may be the first place they attempt to make a change. Most often this comes into play when a person feels angry over getting less than deserved. For example, a person might ask for a raise, a bonus, or other benefits to correct an imbalance in compensation. In extreme cases, individuals may even steal from the company to make up for the compensation not rightfully received. Occasionally they may attempt to change the outcomes of others by complaining about inequitable compensation rates.

- **Alter the Inputs.**   This might mean either changing your own level of effort or the time devoted to work. For example, a person who is not being recognized for their workplace improvements as much as a colleague may simply stop making improvements. It might also be done by altering the inputs of others. For instance, people sometimes use peer pressure to get a "rate buster" to slack off on his or her high productivity rates because it is making others look bad. Peers may even harass the person out of the job.

- **Self-Deception.**   Rather than actually altering the inputs and oucomes, a person may deceive themselves by distorting these results in their minds For example, if Bob is feeling guilty about earning more money than someone else for the same job, he may weigh more heavily the importance of his higher level of education to justify his higher pay.

- **Changing the Reference Source.**   A person may shift just to a new reference source to reduce inequity. This may be difficult to do when the previous reference source is one's peers in the same organization with whom one has constant contact. However, it might be a more viable strategy for a person who previously compared himself to other similar professionals nationally to shift to a more local comparison, namely, similar professionals within his own company.

- **Leaving the Situation.**   Another way of dealing with inequity is to reduce or entirely eliminate it by leaving the situation altogether, either through transfer or quitting. Leaving is an extreme solution that is usually only done when the magnitude of inequity exceeds that which can be corrected through less drastic means. At lower levels of inequity, a person may simply engage in absenteeism.

Managers should be sensitive to employee feelings about equity because it can lead them to engage in unproductive behaviors that undermine the harmony of the organization. All of the actions listed above to restore equity are short-term approaches by the individual feeling the inequity. They do not involve the efforts of managers to understand the underlying problem that causes such feelings. Many of these actions to restore equity can disrupt teamwork in even the most cohesive organization. It is almost always better for managers to deal directly with inequities by searching for the root causes of the problem and dealing with them in a permanent manner.

Equity Theory and TQM

The principles of TQM are consistent with equity theory and can help managers understand how and why to treat employees fairly. The systems view requires that managers focus on how to help people work together to execute organizational processes and to have communication programs that maximize the amount of information available to employees. In this way, employees know their roles in organizations, how they fit in with others, and this, by definition, requires that treatment for everyone is equitable and that compensation be proportionate to the value added in the organizations' processes. For example, Hewlett-Packard sets aside 12 percent of its pre-tax earnings for a profit-sharing bonus. Every HP employee gets a check that represents the same percentage of their salary, whether he or she is a materials handler or a senior executive.

One of the reasons equity becomes an issue in traditionally managed organizations is that managers do not understand the systems view. They do not understand that their organizations are systems nor do they understand the implications of this for treating employees equitably. Managers may believe that the way they treat one person is not related to how they treat others. Nevertheless, that is not usually the case. Perceived inequities cause the system to function poorly and result in the behaviors listed previously, which serve to further exacerbate the problems. TQM and the systems view serves to remind managers that equitable treatment of employees makes the most sense to ensure the organization operates smoothly, successfully, and ultimately achieves its purpose.

 **THINKING CRITICALLY**

1. Do you agree or disagree that desire for high grades and the avoidance of low grades are a good way to motivate class performance? Explain.
2. Explain Deming's problem with numerical goals. Do you agree or disagree with Deming? Why?

We Are Graniterock

Employee involvement
A process for empowering employees to participate in managerial decision making and improvement activities appropriate to their levels in the organization.

MOTIVATION BY EMPLOYEE INVOLVEMENT

Employee involvement is *a process for empowering employees to participate in managerial decision making and improvement activities appropriate to their levels in the organization.* Since McGregor's Theory Y first brought to managers the idea of a participative management style, employee involvement has taken many forms, including the job design approaches and special activities such as quality of work life (QWL) programs.

As the previous review of motivation theories suggests, there are several ways to understand the behavioral motivation of people working in organizations. These ideas consider both intrinsic and extrinsic factors. One of the primary sources of intrinsic motivation is the job itself. Managers must attend to job design to make sure that people like doing the job enough to motivate the appropriate behaviors.

WHO TO LAY OFF WHEN RECESSION HITS: ROBOTS OR WORKERS?[24]

A LOOK AT

ETHICS

In the late 1980s and early 1990s, Japan was trying to cope with a severe labor shortage. Many small Japanese businesses popped up in rural areas where the business owners could find workers. These small businesses often do work that is farmed out by big manufacturers like Sony and Nikon. This trend has transformed much of rural Japan from its agricultural economy—mainly silkworm, apple, grape, and rose growing—to an industrial economy that makes products for export. Even in these rural factories, however, the owners were using robots to help ease the labor shortage and to do jobs that were tedious or difficult for human beings. Mr. Hiroshi Ito's small manufacturing company, Sagamiya, in Sakaki, Japan, is just such a small business. Sagamiya has three large robots that cost as much as $153,000 each that are used to produce things such as plastic camera parts. He also has nine smaller robots that help his workers do repetitive tasks like shaping metal parts.

The robots helped Sagamiya satisfy demand when times were good. However, Sagamiya, has faced hard times during the Japanese recession. Demand for Sagamiya's plastic and metal fittings fell 40 percent to about $900,000 in 1992. Meanwhile, his prime contractors asked him to slash production costs by 10 percent.

Despite having to pay their salaries, Mr. Ito has shut down the robots rather than give pink slips to the workers. It would have been tempting for Mr. Ito to cut his labor costs by laying off workers. However, there are several reasons that he took the robots off the line instead of the people—among those reasons are his conviction that human workers are more valuable when the work slows down and his communal responsibilities.

The 20 workers at Mr. Ito's factory worked overtime nearly every day during the boom period a few years earlier. Now they go home after a standard eight hours and alternate taking weekends off. But at least all of his workers still have jobs. And Mr. Ito's commitment to their welfare reinforces their loyalty and their motivation to work hard for the company.

Herzberg's Two Factor Theory

Frederick Herzberg suggests that the keys to motivating people are to understand job designs and to recognize that satisfaction and dissatisfaction are two different events.[23] Herzberg's **Two Factor Theory** suggests that *there are two different sets of factors that determine job dissatisfaction versus satisfaction, and ultimately, job motivation,* as shown in Exhibit 12-6 on page 453. The first set of factors he labeled *motivators* or *satisfiers,* because these factors are what really lead to job satisfaction and motivation. If these are absent, the person in the job will not likely be satisfied or highly motivated. They include the chance for responsibility, growth, and special challenges.

The second set of factors he labeled *hygienes or dissatisfiers,* because they do not lead to satisfaction and do not motivate people to work. Hygiene factors are simply aspects of a job that keep a person from being dissatisfied. They are necessary, but not sufficient to keep people satisfied or highly motivated. For example, poor working conditions can make a person dissatisfied. However, good

Two Factor Theory A theory that suggests that there are two different sets of factors that determine job dissatisfaction versus satisfaction, and ultimately, job motivation.

KEEPING MOTIVATED AT DELTA

Danica M. Taurosa is a project manager in Personnel Assessment at Delta Airlines. She explains her approach to motivation.

With my current responsibilities, I have been involved in many discussions about what motivates individuals to do their jobs. Delta, like many organizations, is going through a period of tremendous change, and what seemed to motivate our employees in the past seems no longer appropriate. Since Delta was founded in 1929, we have viewed ourselves, our customers, and our shareholders as family. Our greatest challenge as an organization, and my personal challenge as a manager in this company, concerns redefining what it means to be part of "The Delta Family."

How do you keep employees motivated when everything they have been taught to believe as good about the "family"—unconditional lifetime employment, promotion strictly from within, and so on—are no longer appropriate motivators in this fiercely competitive industry. There is unrelenting pressure to control costs while providing excellent, high value service. Our established ways of doing business, which served us well in the past, will not sustain in the future.

We have launched a series of initiatives to deal with these new realities to develop new ways to sustain the motivation of everyone at Delta. Our goals are to expand the responsibility, authority, and accountability of Delta employees, empowering them to act quickly and decisively in their jobs. We believe that we must redefine what it means to be a part of the Delta family. We will continue to value our people as we have always done. The motivators, however, must now change.

My role as a manager is key in this process. I will no longer be evaluated on the accomplishment of my tasks as an individual. I am now being evaluated on how well I develop my people to meet the challenges that are ahead of us. I am, for the first time, asked to set specific objectives that are aligned with our corporate strategy. Once I have done this, it is my responsibility to keep my staff motivated to assist me in accomplishing these goals.

For example, my most recent project was to develop a new management performance appraisal. My team was composed of individuals on temporary assignment from several divisions. None of these people have backgrounds in human resources. The first thing I did was clearly explain what our goals were and the strict deadlines we were under. We discussed the resources that were available to us and discussed what our thoughts were about performance appraisals. I allowed the team to set their own objectives and time line. We agreed on specific roles and responsibilities for each team member. Then we set out to implement our action plan.

At the beginning there was a need to meet frequently and make several team decisions. As those decisions were made, the need to meet as a team was less frequent, but still necessary through the entire process. I continuously made myself available to the team and to individuals to discuss progress and to assist in removing obstacles. I also was able to provide them resources they would not necessarily have had access to. It was difficult for me to not jump in and take over when the staff hit some rough spots.

The team worked long hours, pushed themselves to continuously learn, held each other accountable to deadlines, and met the objectives. The team created a motivating environment, and I supported that environment by changing my role from the typical manager role to coach and counselor. It is not an easy change to make, and I feel like I need additional training to improve the skills necessary for my new role. But this is where the motivation comes full circle; I have seen the results, I have had a victory, and now I am personally motivated to improve my skills so that I can lead my team in making a positive impact on our company.

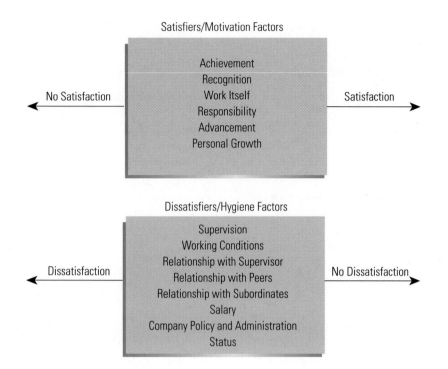

Source: Adapted from Frederick Herzberg, "One More Time: How Do You Motivate Employees?" *Harvard Business Review,* January–February 1987, pp. 109–120.

working conditions tend to be taken for granted. In this case, good working conditions are a hygiene factor.

If you study the list of motivators and hygienes, you will notice, for the most part, the motivators are directly associated with the design of the job. For example, the work itself, responsibility, and achievement are motivators. By contrast, the hygienes, such as interpersonal relations, status, and job security, are not associated with job design.

Herzberg's Two Factor Theory is not universally accepted. It is uncertain that the job aspects that satisfy and the job aspects that dissatisfy are two separate dimensions. However, he does remind managers of the importance of **job design,** which is *the determination of the tasks, responsibilities, and authority associated with a particular position or job.*

Job design The determination of the tasks, responsibilities, and authority associated with a particular position or job.

Job Characteristics Model

Richard Hackman and Ed Lawler originally developed the *Job Characteristics Model* of job design that focuses on the psychological effects of work on the individual worker.[25] Hackman and Lawler based their job design model on expectancy and need theories of motivation. The basic propositions of their model are as follows:

- To the extent that people believe they can obtain a valued outcome by engaging in some particular behavior, they are more likely to do so.

EXHIBIT 12-7
The Job Characteristics Theory

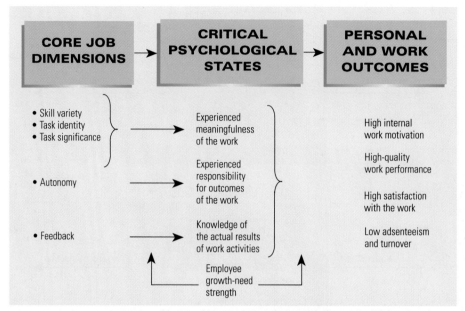

Source: From J.R. Hackman and G.R. Oldham, "Motivation Through the Design of Work: Test of a Theory," *Organizational Behavior and Human Performance,* vol. 16. Copyright © 1976 by Academic Press, Inc. Reprinted by permission of Academic Press, Inc.

- Outcomes are valued by people to the extent that they help satisfy their physiological or psychological needs.

- To the extent that conditions at work can be arranged so that employees can satisfy their own needs best by working effectively toward organizational goals, employees will tend to work hard toward these goals.

- Most lower level needs are reasonably well satisfied for people in contemporary society, therefore, these will not serve as motivational incentives except under unusual circumstances. This is not true, however, for certain higher order needs, such as needs for personal growth and development or feelings of worthwhile accomplishment.

- People who desire higher order need satisfaction are more likely to obtain them when they work successfully in meaningful jobs that adequately provide feedback on how they are doing.

Understanding the propositions of this model, managers can incorporate them into designing jobs that employees are more likely to be motivated to perform. Hackman and another researcher, Greg Oldham, later expanded the Job Characteristics Model to the form shown in Exhibit 12-7. The model suggests that five factors are associated with the motivational potential of a job. The more these five core job dimensions can be designed into a job, the higher the workers' motivation and job performance.[26]

1. **Skill variety** refers to the number of activities in a job and the number of skills used in the performance of the job. For example, a standardized, specialized manufacturing job based upon division of labor, such as installing the left side mirror, is low in skill variety.

DESIGNING JOBS TO BETTER SERVE CUSTOMERS AT MUTUAL BENEFIT LIFE[27]

TQM IN ACTION

Mutual Benefit Life (MBL) reengineered its processing of insurance applications so that it can better serve customers. The changes described below involved transforming the work process from one that flowed across several organizational boundaries to a simplified process that is captured in one redesigned job.

[Before reengineering] the long, multistep process involved credit checking, quoting, rating, underwriting, and so on. An application would have to go through as many as 30 discrete steps, spanning 5 departments and involving 19 people. At the very best, MBL could process an application in 24 hours, but more typical turnarounds ranged from 5 to 25 days—most of the time spent passing information from one department to the next.

MBL's rigid, sequential process led to many complications. For instance, when a customer wanted to cash in an existing policy and purchase a new one, the old business department first had to authorize the treasury department to issue a check made payable to MBL. The check would then accompany the paperwork to the new business department.

The president of MBL, intent on improving customer service, decided that this nonsense had to stop and demanded a 60% improvement in productivity. It was clear that such an ambitious goal would require more than tinkering with the existing process. . . . The team realized that shared databases and computer networks could make many different kinds of information available to a single person, while expert systems could help people with limited experience make sound decisions.

MBL swept away existing job definitions and departmental boundaries and created a new position called a case manager. Case managers have total responsibility for an application from the time it is received to the time a policy is issued. Unlike clerks, who performed a fixed task repeatedly under the watchful gaze of a supervisor, case managers work autonomously. No more handoffs of files and responsibility, no more shuffling of customer inquiries. . . . MBL can now complete an application in as little as four hours, and average turnaround takes only two to five days.

Such changes not only simplify the work of the organization, they create jobs that enlarge an employee's responsibility and sense of accomplishment, thus plugging into factors likely to motivate better and more enthusiastic performance.

2. **Task identity** refers to the extent to which the employee performs the total job with a definable beginning and a definable end. The employee who installs the left side mirror has low task identity compared with assembling the entire car.
3. **Task significance** refers to the extent to which employees perceive that their jobs have importance and impact on the company or its customers. Installing the side mirror may have low task significance unless the employee understands the importance of proper installment on customer satisfaction and sales for the firm.
4. **Autonomy** refers to the extent to which the worker has discretion in the performance of the job. An individual employee on an assembly line may have little autonomy, but the team that plans the work and decides how to assemble the car has considerable autonomy.

5. **Feedback** is the extent to which employees learn about the outcomes of their performances. Providing auto assemblers with customer satisfaction data is an example of feedback.

The Job Characteristics Model states that the five job dimensions combine to yield three Critical Psychological States, which are intermediate positions leading to enhanced work performance. These states include:

1. **Experienced meaningfulness of the work** refers to how satisfying the work is, a result that is primarily determined by the skill variety, task identity, and task significance.
2. **Experienced responsibility for outcomes of the work** is associated with the amount of autonomy people perceive themselves to have.
3. **Knowledge of the actual results of work activities** is associated with the feedback.

One variable that moderates all the above relationships is Employee Growth-Need Strength. It means that different workers have different needs to grow and develop. Those with low needs do not respond well to applications of this model. In other words, trying to develop job designs that enhance a person's skills and responsibilities will not work to motivate him or her. Workers with a high growth-need strength respond well to the application of the Job Characteristics Model.

Job Enlargement, Enrichment, and Rotation

Frederick Taylor's approach to Scientific Management and Henry Ford's assembly line approach encouraged managers to pursue specialization and division of labor. Their prescriptions for job design are to simplify and break jobs into small, repetitive tasks that are easily mastered and do not require skilled labor. This approach to job design can be efficient. However, it often produces alienation, boredom, and dissatisfaction, a set of undesirable human outcomes that are characteristic of assembly line work. These are also outcomes that undermine employee motivation to engage in these tasks. This suggests that managers need to find a way to balance their concerns for efficiency and for human motivation. There are a number of ways to design a job to achieve the motivational effects suggested by the job characteristics model. Three general approaches to job design include enlargement, enrichment, and rotation.

Job enlargement An approach to job design which involves broadening the scope of a job by adding more tasks to the job.

Job Enlargement. **Job enlargement** is *a general approach to job design that involves broadening the scope of a job by adding more tasks to the job.* For example, a sales clerk's job may be enlarged by adding responsibilities to check and order inventory as needed. Some of the advantages of job enlargement include a greater skill variety. In factory work this increased variation in skill requirements allows the worker to use different muscle groups that create less fatigue and avoid muscle damage. Employees may also get a greater sense of accomplishment because they complete a larger part of the task.

Job Enrichment. Job enrichment is widely used among Fortune 1000 companies that are practicing Total Quality Management.[28] While job enlargement makes a job broader, **job enrichment** is *a general approach to job design that makes a job deeper by adding some managerial decision-making autonomy and authority to the job.* A job may be enriched by building in (1) direct feedback to aid decision making, (2) opportunity for continuous learning, (3) responsibility to schedule one's own work, and (4) control over the resources needed to improve and execute work. For example, the sales clerk may be given some authority in the decision of what cash registers to buy and how to lay out merchandise to appeal to customers.

Sometimes managers may use job enrichment simply for humanitarian reasons, on the premise that everyone deserves to have some mental challenge and opportunity for self-determination. In other instances, job enrichment is a natural part of the organization's strategy for delivering value to customers. For example, a FedEx driver does not just pick up and deliver packages. He or she represents the company and must be empowered to make decisions in unanticipated situations. However, job enrichment is not always appropriate. For example, not everyone wants to assume managerial responsibility, and some people will react negatively when it is forced upon them. In general, though, it is important to appreciate that while job enrichment works to increase employee motivation on the job, it is also smart business practice. It affirms that those doing the work are those who best understand the implications of decisions that affect their work and thus should make those decisions with the sanction and blessing of their managers. Making sure employees have this authority is an important part of TQM.

Job Rotation.   **Job rotation** refers to *moving employees from one job to another,* a practice now common in many companies. If rotation occurs frequently, such as at the Saturn plant in Spring Hill, Tennessee, which allows workers to rotate jobs among a team of workers several times a day, job rotation can achieve some of the same skill variety benefits as job enlargement. It can help avoid boredom, muscle fatigue, and it can allow the worker to feel a greater sense of accomplishment.

Combining Approaches to Job Design.   It is not unusual to see more than one of these job design strategies employed at once. A good example of enlargement can be found at Ford's Walton Hills stamping plant outside of Cleveland. Jobs that were narrowly drawn have been broadened. Some job descriptions have been merged with other job descriptions to create fewer job classes. Many of the production workers now perform their own maintenance. In the past, maintenance was done by a separate group of workers. Examples of enrichment can also be found at this plant. Plant managers gave more autonomy to the workers. For example, Bob Kubec and his partner, Mark Asta, now run a transfer press, a highly technical press that stamps sheets of metal, with little direct supervision. In fact, both men were involved in buying and setting up the press.[29]

Some companies use a combination of job enlargement, enrichment, and rotation as a managerial strategy. For example, Rohm & Haas Bayport, a producer of specialty chemicals in LaPorte, Texas, designed the jobs of its 67 employees so that everyone has a management role. There are only three levels in the reporting structure, with 46 process technicians and 15 engineers and

Job enrichment An approach to job design that makes a job deeper by adding some managerial decision-making autonomy and authority to the job.

Job rotation A practice of moving employees from one job to another.

chemists reporting to one of the two manufacturing unit managers, who in turn report to the executive team. The technicians work in self-managing teams of four-to-seven people. Team members rotate jobs within the team every 4-to-12 weeks. The team makes all operating decisions and also perform routine maintenance and repairs of equipment in their area of the plant. They even conduct performance appraisals for each other and make hiring decisions for jobs within their team.[30] Such activities seem to enhance motivation and performance on the job.

Quality of Work Life (QWL) Programs

Quality of Work Life (QWL) Programs with the general intention to make organizations better places to work and to enhance the dignity of all workers.

Quality of Work Life (QWL) programs are diverse in their emphases, but *their general intention is to make organizations better places to work and to enhance the dignity of all workers.*[31] QWL programs intend to make the workplace more safe, trusting, equitable, comfortable, challenging, and satisfying. QWL programs fall into the following categories according to their objectives[32]

- Safe and healthy work environments
- Adequate and fair compensation
- Development of human capabilities
- Opportunity for growth and security
- Opportunity for social integration to achieve self-esteem
- Protection of constitutional rights
- A balance of work, leisure, and family time
- Social relevance and social responsibility

QWL programs pursue these objectives in a number of ways, including employee surveys, suggestion systems, and task forces. They take these actions to gather input, make decisions about courses of action, and implement the improvement plans. For example, a flextime work schedule allows employees to accomplish a balance of work, leisure, and family time.

These QWL objectives are important because they appeal to a number of the bases for human motivation. They are also important to creating employee satisfaction. Managers should be concerned with employee satisfaction, because dissatisfied employees are likely to be motivated to engage in various kinds of undesirable behaviors, including: turnover, absenteeism, grievances, lawsuits, strikes, stealing, sabotage, and vandalism. They are also more likely to exhibit lower mental and physical health and lower corporate citizenship.[33]

There has been a tendency to view QWL programs as opposed to the competitive needs of the organization for efficiency and effectiveness. However, companies that have adopted Total Quality Management should see QWL objectives as consistent with their efforts for continuous improvement. Managers and employees should work together to identify and remove obstacles in the workplace which frustrate workers. The results of such improvement will always be greater trust and commitment among employees, two outcomes that are central to any continuous improvement effort. Managers should beware, however, participative management is not a panacea. It does not always result in improved levels of motivation, higher productivity, and quality.[34] Just like

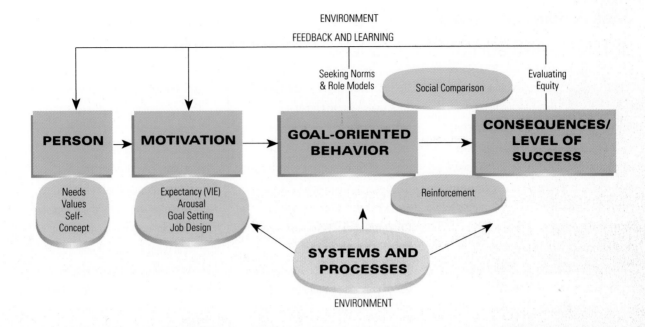

EXHIBIT 12-8   A model of motivation integrating various theories

any other managerial tool, technique, or style it has to be used appropriately and for the right purpose in order to achieve significant improvement.

Putting It All Together

Now that you have studied the specifics of various theories of motivation, it should be useful to review how these ideas all fit together. The general model of motivation shown in Exhibit 12-2 is reproduced in Exhibit 12-8 with each of the major ideas about motivation also represented on the model. As a review, the model suggests that motivation arises from the combination of a person and an environment. The environment presents the person with certain tasks specified in the job design, as discussed in this chapter. The social organization also imposes certain role requirements or expected behaviors, values, and beliefs. The management of the organization provides the larger system within which the individual works. Finally, the leadership of the organization provides the vision and sense of purpose that inspires meaning in the work. Each person brings to the situation a lifetime of experiences, personal needs, values, and self-perceptions, which are the personal ends that people are generally motivated to accomplish.

The process of motivation occurs when people either openly or subconsciously evaluate their behavioral choices, perhaps according to expectancy theory or valence/instrumentality/expectancy (VIE) analysis. People will attempt to accomplish their desired ends, and they will set goals that will allow them to do so. Once people choose the aim of their behaviors and levels of desired performances, they will take actions. The process of motivation is

LISTENING AND SUPPORTING ASSOCIATES AT ROSENBLUTH[35]

Hal Rosenbluth knows that keeping his company prosperous means keeping his employees happy and motivated. He wants to know their concerns and how the company can do better. Some items he has instituted to keep in touch are the following.

- **Associate Hotline.** All associates have direct access to Rosenbluth through his 800 number voice mail. Associates leave an average of seven messages a day, with suggestions for improvements, problems, requests, or praise. They are free to make the call annonymous or ask for a direct response.

- **Up Interviewing.** Quality assurance teams consisting of nonmanagers travel to branch offices asking associates to review the performance of their managers, then ask these managers to review their managers and so on up the line.

- **Crayon Caper.** This is a unique exercise where Rosenbluth sends 100 randomly selected associates a box of crayons and requests pictures of what the company means to them. The responses reveal feelings not always found in surveys.

- **Happiness Barometer.** Twice a year, Rosenbluth spends a day with 18 associates chosen at random, who have completed surveys. At these meetings they discuss staff morale and how they can work together to improve it.

The work environment at Rosenbluth International is not perfect, but associates know that the company and its top management care about them and want to make it possible for them to perform well and enjoy their work life. Hal Rosenbluth is constantly trying to make improvements to make sure that happens. The result is a company full of committed and motivated associates.

---

dynamic. Motivation levels can change in a moment. For example, a person may embark on a course of action, but may immediately perceive that his or her goals are not attainable. Rather than stick to the original decision, that person's motivation level drops and then stops.

Once they engage in behaviors, they experience a connection between what they do and its consequences, as explained by reinforcement theory. People also make social comparisons of their behaviors and their consequences. All of these experiences and comparisons offer the individual important information that can be used in subsequent choices and goal setting. Finally, their accomplishments may actually make changes in their environments in some way, for example, as when the behavior is directed toward the improvement of a system. Changes in either the environment or the person can immediately affect an individual's motivation level. Motivation is indeed a dynamic process. By understanding it, managers have a better chance of taking the right actions to direct and improve it. Based on these theories, various approaches to employee involvement may be used to motivate people, such as job design and quality of work life (QWL) programs.

Finally, we should note that the concern with and implementation of theories covered in this chapter are consistent with the systems view and TQM. This is because TQM is fundamentally about finding the best ways to bring people into organizations to work together for their mutual benefits and the benefits of customers and stakeholders. Using what we understand about motivation is one way to do that.

❓ THINKING CRITICALLY

1. In your school or work life, identify those aspects that you would consider *hygiene factors* and those that you would consider motivators. Explain your rationale for each.
2. Look at the five factors for enhancing motivation suggested by the job characteristics model. Based on your experience, explain why each of these factors would or would not motivate you on the job.
3. What theories of motivation do you think Hal Rosenbluth employs to keep associates at Rosenbluth International happy and motivated to contribute?

SUMMARY

Motivation: The Hidden Cause of Behavior

- Motivation explores what drives people to behave in certain ways and how managers can use the theories of motivation to help people identify personal drives and needs with high level performances in an organization.

- An important thing to remember about motivation in an organization is that it is shaped and directed by the *relationship* between managers and employees.

- TQM helps to create an environment where positive relationships exist between managers and employees and people feel motivated to do their best.

- Theory X and Theory Y are two assumptions about employee motivation and behavior that help us think about how managerial assumptions affect managers' behavior and how these assumptions affect employee behavior.

Content Theories of Motivation

- Content theories deal with ideas about human needs and how behaviors that fulfill these needs motivate actions.

- Maslow's Hierarchy of Needs categorizes human needs from those basic for life to those that motivate us to fully express our humanity. Managers can use this to understand how to more fully take advantage of employee talents and experience.

- Alderfer's ERG (existence, relatedness, and growth-needs) theory is another way to classify human needs, similar to the ideas of Maslow, except that it does away with the idea of a hierarchy.

- McClelland's Acquired Needs Theory suggest that people acquire various needs through learning as they mature and that not all people in an organization have acquired the same needs. Managers must be sensitive to this as they match jobs and responsibilities with the needs of different employees.

- Personal values or beliefs motivate people to behave in ways consistent with those values.

Process Theories

- Process theories are concerned with how people choose behaviors to fulfill their needs and accomplish goals.
- Reinforcement theory suggests that people choose behaviors based on consequences they believe to be good for themselves, but that are shaped or controlled by others.
- Expectancy theory suggests that when people value a result, have the means, and are likely to succeed in their efforts, they will be motivated toward particular behaviors.
- Goal setting theory is based on the assumption that goals motivate people when they believe they are attainable. The problem with some goals, especially numerical goals, is that they are not process-oriented and can motivate people in ways that undermine cooperation.
- Equity theory suggests that people are motivated to behave in particular ways by perceptions of how fairly or unfairly they are being treated.

Motivation by Employee Involvement

- Employee involvement approaches aim at enhancing responsibility, increasing authority, and making jobs challenging and interesting to employees, based on their abilities and the needs of the organization.
- Herzberg's Two Factor Theory suggests that there are (1) hygiene factors that are necessary, but not sufficient to motivate employees and (2) motivators which are necessary to drive performance.
- The job characteristics model suggests that there are several aspects of job design that affect motivation and managers need to make sure these factors are present.
- Job enlargement, enrichment, and rotation are three ways to create variety and make work more meaningful.
- Quality of work life programs are aimed at making the workplace more safe, trusting, equitable, comfortable, challenging, and satisfying.

KEY TERMS

Acquired needs theory 438

Content theories 434

Employee involvement 450

Equity theory 447

Expectancy theory 441

Extrinsic motivation 443

Intrinsic motivation 443

Job design 453

Job enlargement 456

Job enrichment 457

Job rotation 457

Management by Objectives 445

Maslow's Hierarchy of Needs 435

Motivation 430

Need 434

Operant conditioning 440

Organizational behavior (OB)
   modification 440

Personal values 438

Process theories 439

Quality of work life (QWL) 458

Reinforcement theory 440

Theory X 432

Theory Y 433

Two Factor Theory 451

REVIEW QUESTIONS

1. What is motivation and why should managers be concerned with motivation theories?
2. How will the effective implementation of TQM affect employee motivation and why?
3. What is the relation between Theory X and Theory Y and the behavior of managers?
4. What do the content theories of motivation tell us about the causes of human behavior?
5. What is the difference between Maslow's Hierarchy of Needs theory and Alderfer's ERG theory?
6. What distinguishes McClelland's Acquired Needs theory from other content theories?
7. What is the difference between content theories and process theories of motivation?
8. What are the implications of reinforcement theory for management action?
9. What is the relationship of valence, instrumentality, and expectancy in the expectancy theory of motivation?
10. How can managers use goals to enhance employee motivation?
11. What is the relation of equity theory to motivation on the job?
12. Why should managers pay attention to the characteristics of a job?
13. How do job enlargement, enrichment, and rotation affect employee motivation?

EXPERIENTIAL EXERCISE

To practice the management of motivation using what you have learned in this chapter, execute the following three steps.

1. Identify a recent behavior that was important to your life, either as a student or an employee in an organization.
2. Use each of the theories discussed in this chapter to identify all of the motivational forces that influenced the behavior. List the forces that were motivating (encouraging or attractive) as well as demotivating (discouraging or distractive).
3. If this behavior is desirable in the future, describe what you would do as a manager to develop an even stronger motivational force for it.

CASE ANALYSIS AND APPLICATION
Reinventing the Occupational Health and Safety Administration (OSHA)

The Occupational Safety and Health Administration (OSHA) was established within the Department of Labor as a result of the Occupational Safety and Health Act of 1970. At that time, there was a need to improve the health and safety conditions of American jobs. The 1970 Act extends OSHA coverage to all employers and their employees in all fifty states, the District of Columbia, Puerto Rico, and all other territories under the federal government's jurisdiction. Coverage is provided either directly or through an OSHA approved state program. OSHA's mission can be summed up in terms of the following goals.

- Encourage employers and employees to reduce workplace hazards and to implement new or improved existing safety and health programs.
- Provide for research in occupational safety and health to develop innovative ways of dealing with occupational safety and health problems.
- Establish responsibilities and rights for employers and employees for the achievement of better safety and health conditions.
- Maintain a reporting and recordkeeping system to monitor job-related injuries and illnesses.
- Establish training programs to increase the number and competence of occupational safety and health personnel.
- Develop mandatory job safety and health standards and enforce them effectively.
- Provide for the development, analysis, evaluation, and approval of state occupational safety and health programs.

OSHA's original approach to fulfilling its mission was to ensure that work sites have specific guidance on programs, conditions, and methods of worker protection. OSHA guidelines were intended to ensure that employees were not injured as a result of easily foreseeable unsafe behavior.

Through the years OSHA's mission has remained constant, but the standards and the practices have not been consistently applied over time and across all regions of the country. OSHA officials and inspectors often arbitrarily changed their priorities and the guidelines they use in conducting their work. For example, they have been accused of reacting to the "hazard of the month," refocusing their attention on the most recently publicised tragedies or hot topics in the public media. Further, OSHA has not been creative in devising new approaches to fulfill its mission. Many people have felt that OSHA has not been able to fulfill its mission lately. Former head of OSHA during the Reagan administration explains some of the problems that OSHA now faces:

I cringe at reports that list the cause of the incident as "unsafe act by the employee" and list as the corrective action "counselled employee to work more safely." I know this sounds harsh, but I think the vast majority of case reports like that are just garbage designed to cover up the failure of the program or the people who are supposed to make the program work.

We know that people are going to be careless some of the time. It's not enough to tell employees to be careful and not to put their fingers in a punch press. Instead, you need to fix the problems so that the press's safeguards prevent the operator from reaching into it. We put safety belts and air bags in automobiles for the same reason. People aren't perfect and they are always going to make mistakes.

Once you accept that premise, then the question really becomes: How safe is safe? (Or, how far should you go to protect employees from unsafe behavior?) To me, specific standards are necessary to ensure that question is answered uniformly in all worksites. Safety is a basic value, and everyone should be entitled to the same level of protection.

Once you reach that point, then the question becomes: How do you ensure compliance so that the level of safety is uniform? The U.S. approach for 20 years has been to inspect employers to ensure that the standards are met and to issue citations and penalties the first time an employer is found not in compliance. The U.S. government issues penalties for the first violation because it can't inspect every workplace and therefore wants to encourage compliance before the inspection.

I think the U.S. approach has been successful, but clearly it hasn't solved all of the problems. We need to do more. Some say that more rigorous enforcement is needed, and the penalty should be higher for employers who don't comply. Some say that we need more inspections.

But these options may not be realistic given today's climate and resources. Business is slowly crawling out of the recession, and higher penalties may draw some political heat. Since government's budget is in a cutback (not an expansion) mode, the likelihood of more OSHA officers and inspections is slim.[36]

Under increased legislative pressure and with new leadership from Joseph Dear, the current administrator, OSHA has started the process of reform to revamp its standards and practices. Some of these initiatives are listed below.

- Promotion of worker-management cooperation in safety and health programs.
- Require companies to establish safety-and-health committees composed of both employee and manager representatives.
- Give additional authority to compliance officers and perhaps even allow them to issue certain citations on-site at the time of an inspection (rather than going through a complex review process first).
- Revamp OSHA's inspection scheduling process to give more attention to the worst worksites and focus first on the most flagrant offenders of its guidelines.
- More effective enforcement and increased criminal penalties for violations of OSHA rules.
- Extend responsibility for safe workplaces from company executives down to the managers who may order employees to work under dangerous conditions.
- A streamlined standard-setting process within OSHA.

- Establish priorities on standards that will endure over time and not change from month-to-month in a fadish way.
- The use of an independent third party to audit and assess OSHA's fulfillment of its obligations.[37]

Discussion Questions

1. Identify incidents, initiatives, or other elements of this case that reflect underlying (perhaps unstated) assumptions about human motivation on the job. Describe these assumptions from the perspective of the company employees and managers in private industry, as well as from the perspective of OSHA officials.
2. Discuss the pros and cons of the proposed new OSHA initiatives in terms of what you learned about motivation in this chapter.
3. What advice would you give to OSHA officials in their efforts to transform their organization so that it better fulfills its mission?

VIDEO CASE: COMBINING QUALITY MANAGEMENT AND SOCIAL RESPONSIBILITY
Daka International Inc.

The AIDS epidemic, long recognized as a medical problem, has become a significant business concern. Individuals most affected are between 25 and 45 years of age, a prime segment of the nation's workforce. The disease is also spreading to women, youths, and minorities, whose roles in the labor force are steadily growing. As people with AIDS live longer, making the illness a chronic disease, business also faces new complications in managing the workplace, crafting employee policies, and determining benefits. How can a company manage a workforce and maintain productivity in the face of this stigmatizing, tragic disease?

The Business Enterprise Trust is honoring DAKA International, Inc., a restaurant and food service business based in Danvers, Massachusetts, for its courage in implementing an aggressive AIDS education program in an industry highly vulnerable to public fears and misconceptions about the disease.

Every public health authority has concluded that the AIDS virus is not transmittable through food, and no known cases of AIDS have been transmitted in this way. Notwithstanding the scientific consensus, fear about AIDS has resulted in work stoppages and disruptions, sales declines, negative publicity, and unlawful firings and litigation in dozens of businesses around the country. In the restaurant/food service business, some customers worry about becoming infected by employees with HIV or AIDS. Many workers still believe, erroneously, that sharing a work space or bathroom with HIV-infected people may be dangerous. Other companies fear that showing sensitivity to HIV-infected employees identifies the company with the disease.

Since 1987, instead of ignoring the facts and the growing magnitude of the AIDS crisis, DAKA has pioneered a series of progressive AIDS programs and policies for its 8,000 employees. First begun under President Allen R. Maxwell, DAKA's program now consists of an AIDS counseling office, a company hotline, a flexible sick leave and disability policy, a supportive benefits package, and AIDS education for all employees. DAKA's campaign against AIDS makes it the only major food service or restaurant company to address the epidemic openly and aggressively. DAKA Chairman and CEO William Baumhauer is one of the few CEOs in the nation to become personally active in the fight against AIDS—through speeches, articles, and participation in the National Leadership Coalition on AIDS.

The company has not only shown great moral leadership by taking a highly visible stand against AIDS, but has also improved its business operations by minimizing the soaring business costs of the disease. By attracting and retaining loyal, motivated employees, DAKA has helped reduce its workforce turnover, a major cost in the food service and restaurant industries.

The program has also enhanced DAKA's reputation as a progressive, caring employer.

Video Case Questions

1. Using the concepts discussed in this chapter, explain how DAKA affected the motivation of its employees.
2. What are the positive benefits of DAKA's educational initiatives for its business and for society?

13. COMMUNICATION

COMMUNICATING FOR PRODUCTIVITY AT GOODYEAR[1]

The Goodyear Tire and Rubber Plant in Lawton, Oklahoma, is the most productive of the company's 84 factories. The head of this plant, John Loulan, says that their success comes from a comprehensive communication program that keeps all employees in the loop. Loulan comments, "We make an effort to give associates a sense of ownership in their pieces of the business. For them to buy in, they need good information." He stands by these words. Every employee at the Lawton plant has more information available than managers formerly had even a few years ago. They have created several ways to deliver information to employees. These include:

- Giving all employees computer access to production information on themselves, their department, and the plant as a whole.
- Each shift tracks its productivity on marker boards on the plant floor. In the stock prep area, for example, they update the board every two hours with information on average output per hour, total output per shift versus the shift's target, and the rate of scrap.
- There is a factory-wide video network that delivers daily announcements, training programs, and videotaped interviews between Loulan and employees. One show, for example, dealt with the unpopular shutdown of the plant for one week. Loulan says, "We used television to bring things into the open and lay to rest rumors of layoffs or other cutbacks."
- Each of the plant's five business centers includes a conference room for twice-monthly work team meetings during which they discuss issues like safety and improvement projects.
- There is a weekly plant newsletter sent to each employee's home—its goal is to involve employee families in the company's business. Loulan also regularly sends letters to employees' homes with information about plant milestones, social events, and benefits news.

THE IMPORTANCE OF COMMUNICATION

Communication is how people tell others what they expect and discover what others expect of them. In organizations clear, correct, and complete communication is vital to ensure that everyone understands what is happening and what their roles are in executing organizational processes. The managers of Goodyear are well aware that communication is the lubricant that keeps their company running smoothly and continuously improving. They understand that well-informed employees can do their jobs better and that their employees have much to contribute. This means they must create a culture and a means to facilitate as much communication as possible from bottom up, top down, and among peers. When employees know what is going on, they can work more intelligently and with a clear sense of purpose. As we noted in Chapter 12, a sense of purpose is at the heart of feeling motivated. This chapter focuses on developing methods of communication that keep an organization well lubricated.

Think about the managerial tasks and activities that have been covered so far in this book. Communication underlies every one of these activities. A healthy organization culture is characterized by open communication. Honest, thoughtful communication is at the heart of leadership behaviors. Ethical behavior assumes this kind of communication as well. As a manager, you will be unable to solve problems if you cannot collect accurate and complete information from employees. Your ideas, no matter how brilliant, will have little effect on the organization if the culture of the organization does not value and create channels for communicating ideas, regardless of their sources. Similarly, decisions that you make will not be effectively implemented if the culture does not facilitate honest communication and dialogue. You cannot form a supportive interpersonal relationship with subordinates without forthright communication. In essence, a manager's number-one challenge can be summed up in one word: *communication.*

Communication is critical for organizational effectiveness. Good communication is a key attribute of successful companies. Just like Goodyear, the best companies in America "encourage open communication, informing people of new developments, and encouraging them to offer suggestions and complaints."[2] Communication is even more critical in a total quality management organization. In a traditional organization, the focus of communication has been internal and hierarchical; employees communicate with their immediate superiors and subordinates—chain of command communication. In a total quality management organization, on the other hand, the emphasis is on setting up methods for complete and honest communication among everyone involved in processes. There is less concern for the formalities of hierarchical relationships, which seldom do much to contribute to productivity and quality. Communicating clearly and completely is a learned skill that allows employees to enhance their contributions to the organization. We can best see the value of these skills when something goes wrong because of poor communication, as in the anecdote described in Exhibit 13-1, for example.

There is substantial research indicating that communication is critical for an organization's effectiveness and for success as managers.[3] We will begin by describing a model of the communication process. This model identifies leverage points that facilitate successful communication and or undermine it. We then turn our attention to the manner in which organizational structures facilitate or impede communication. We conclude by discussing implications of communication for total quality management.

EXHIBIT 13-1   Miscommunication of Simple Ideas

A motorist was driving on the Merritt Parkway outside of New York City when his engine stalled. He quickly determined that his battery was dead and managed to stop another driver who consented to push his car to get it started.

"My car has automatic transmission," he explained, "so you'll have to get up to thirty or thirty-five miles an hour to get me started."

The second motorist nodded and walked back to his own car. The first motorist climbed back into his car and waited for the good Samaritan to pull up behind him. He waited and waited. Finally, he turned around to see what was wrong.

There was the good Samaritan—coming up behind his car at about 35 miles an hour!

The damage amounted to $3800.

Source: Adapted from David A. Whetten and Kim S. Cameron, *Developing Management Skills,* (New York: HarperCollins, 1991)

Communication can be considered as either a one-way or a two-way process. **Two-way communication** occurs when *two or more parties exchange informa-tion and share meaning.*[4] It is a two-way process in that both parties express ideas and listen to each others' reactions. For example, think about your most recent telephone conversation. That conversation consisted of two-way commu-nication because you listened to the other individual and used the information provided to clarify your ideas as necessary. For example, you may have said, "Our next game is Thursday." Your team-mate may have responded, "Today?", to which you replied, "No, next Thursday." Two-way communication is necessary for understanding because it allows both parties to clarify the content of the communication.

One-way communication occurs when *one person simply disseminates information to others.* For example, think about what happens when you watch the evening news. You simply listen to the broadcast without being able to request clarification. The broadcaster cannot change the vocabulary or the pace of presentation to clarify the news. You also use one-way communication when you leave a message on an answering machine. Our writing in this book is one-way communication, and we are responsible for clearly writing ideas and exam-ples to make sure they are as understandable as possible. Although one-way communication may be effective for conveying a large amount of information, the inability to clarify messages often results in misunderstandings. In fact, some researchers argue that the primary reason for misunderstanding is the lack of two-way clarification among parties.

Two-way communication
Communication that occurs when two or more parties exchange information and share meaning.

One-way communication
Communication that occurs when one person simply disseminates information to others.

THINKING CRITICALLY

1. Would you say that having good communication skills is more important, of the same importance, or less important than other technical skills in perform-ing effectively? Explain your answer.

A MODEL OF EFFECTIVE COMMUNICATION

The basic communication model is presented in Exhibit 13-2 on page 472. As shown, information passes between the sender and the receiver. Communication is successful when the receiver understands the message as the sender intended. A primary cause of misunderstanding is the improper interpretation of the

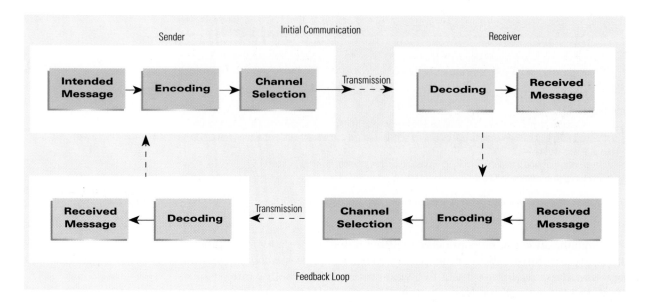

EXHIBIT 13-2 A model of communication

message sent. If you reflect on your experiences, you probably can remember several examples of misunderstanding for this reason. You probably also can appreciate how important it is to minimize such misunderstandings in managing an organization. Ensuring the message intended is the message received is more likely when communication is a two-way process.

Two-way communication allows the sender to get feedback from the receiver and to compare the feedback with the intended message to determine whether the message has been communicated clearly. The communication model incorporates that point. Let's look at it in more detail.

Sender The individual conveying the message.

Receiver The individual to whom the message is transmitted.

Intended message The information that the sender would like to communicate.

Channel The path or paths of communication used to send a message to others.

- **Sender and Receiver.** The **sender** is *the individual conveying the message* and the **receiver** is *the individual to whom the message is transmitted.* When, as a manager you explain a task to your employees, you are the sender, and they are the receivers. When one of your employees is explaining a customer's problem to you, the employee is the sender, and you are the receiver.

- **Intended Message and Encoding.** The **intended message** is *the information that the sender would like to communicate.* It represents the ideas the sender is trying to convey to a receiver. This entails encoding or translating the ideas into symbols, such as a series of words that stand for the points being made. Translating your ideas into a memo, letter, fax, in-person or on the phone constitutes encoding.

- **Channel Selection and Transmission.** The **channel** is *the path or paths of communication used to send a message to others.* The intended message can be encoded into one of several possible channels. These channels include: face-to-face communication, telephone conversation, letter, memorandum, video conferencing, fax, electronic mail, and so on. As you will find out through experience, some channels are more appropriate for certain situations than are others. Additionally, the sender's choice of channels provides a signal or message to the receiver. For example, telephoning a business client sends a different message than sending a formal letter even when the words are essentially the same. Likewise, an unannounced visit to a sales district sends a different message to employees than does a planned visit to the district.

Consider the manner in which the president of a small medical supply company strategically selected the channel to make an impression. This company had experienced a sharp downturn in sales, introduced a new product line, and established higher sales targets. The company president could have informed sales representatives about these changes by letter or through the district managers. Instead, he flew 143 sales representatives into Chicago for a 90-minute meeting at an airport hotel. Most sales representatives arrived by 11:00 A.M. and flew out by 3:00 P.M. The travel costs to the organization were over $40,000 for this one day. Why did the president choose a personal face-to-face channel instead of a letter? He wanted to emphasize the importance of the company's problem and make sure employees recognized that the company's entire future hung in the balance. He also wanted individuals to know that there would be no second chances. Although he selected an expensive channel, it sent a strong message to his sales force and probably saved his company.

Once a channel has been selected, the message can be transmitted to the receiver. Transmission is the process through which the intended message is sent via the selected channel to the receiver. Transmission may occur by voice (telephone call), visual (a letter), or both voice and visual (face-to-face interactions).

- **Decoding the Received Message.** Once the message is transmitted, it must be received and then decoded. **Decoding** is *the process by which the recipient translates the message back to ideas.* The receiver uses personal knowledge and experience to interpret the transmitted message. Since the sender and receiver often have different backgrounds, skills, and experiences, the receiver may decode the message differently than the sender intended. By comparing the receiver's interpretation of the transmission with the sender's intended message, the effectiveness of the communication can be evaluated.

  Decoding The process by which the recipient translates the message back to ideas.

- **Communication fidelity** is *the degree to which there is agreement between the message intended by the sender and the message received by the source.* High communication fidelity occurs when the received message is exactly the same as the intended message. Often the received message and intended message can differ dramatically. For example, you may provide frequent performance feedback ("that was a really good job") to an employee. You may intend your communication to mean "I appreciate the excellent job that you are doing." However, your employee may interpret your communication to mean that "my supervisor does not trust me and feels that she must constantly monitor my performance." What you intended to be a compliment was actually perceived negatively by your employee.

  Communication fidelity The degree to which there is agreement between the message intended by the sender and the message received by the source.

- **Feedback Loop.** The **feedback loop** *allows the receiver to acknowledge the received message or to ask the sender to clarify the intended message.* With the feedback loop, the receiver and the sender exchange roles; the receiver becomes the sender, and the sender becomes the receiver. For example, after decoding the message, the receiver may respond with a question. The question provides the original sender with knowledge that the message has

  Feedback loop Method that allows the receiver to acknowledge the received message or ask the sender to clarify the intended message.

been received. On the other hand, the question may suggest that the receiver did not understand the sender's intended message. In the previous example concerning the misinterpreted compliment, the supervisor may be able to recognize that the receiver reacted negatively to the compliment. The supervisor may be able to glean such a negative reaction by observing the employee's eye or facial expressions. Armed with this additional information, the sender can attempt to clarify the intended message ("You are really doing a good job. I appreciate your effort and ability to work without close supervision.")

As can be seen in the model, communication is a complex process. Communication requires a large number of handoffs, any one of which can be fumbled. To some extent, communication is only as effective as the weakest link. That is, as a sender, you may do an excellent job of encoding your intended message but select an inappropriate channel. As a result of your poor channel selection, the receiver may inaccurately decode your message and communication will be ineffective.

❓ THINKING CRITICALLY

1. Reflecting on your own experience, identify someone you think is a great communicator. Why is this person so effective?
2. Describe the worst miscommunication that you have ever been involved in. Using the model to describe the situation, where did the breakdown occur and why?
3. Given the importance of communication, why would you say many managers still have difficulty communicating effectively?

CHANNELS OF COMMUNICATION

There are a number of channels through which information and ideas may be communicated. In this section, we will focus on characteristics of several communication channels.

Verbal Versus Nonverbal Communication

Verbal communication
The words used to share ideas.

Channels differ in their abilities to effectively transmit complex and emotional information. One major difference among channels is that some provide for only verbal communication while others provide both verbal and nonverbal communication. **Verbal communication** consists strictly of *the words used to share ideas*. If a student calls a friend this afternoon to discuss this class, they are using verbal communication. Writing a letter to relatives constitutes another example of verbal communication.

Nonverbal communication All aspects of the message transmitted through means other than words, such as tone of voice, facial expressions, body language, format of documents, channel chosen, and other such actions.

However, more than half of any message is expressed nonverbally. **Nonverbal communication** consists of *all other aspects of the message transmitted through means other than words, such as tone of voice, facial expressions, body language, format of documents, channel chosen, and other such actions.* For example, articulation of the phrase, "I don't think that the project is a good idea" could take on multiple meanings depending upon the nonverbal communication that accompanies it. It could mean "I believe that the project is a terrible mistake and I will not participate in it." Such a message would be delivered with tremendous emotion, e.g., hand gestures to emphasize points, facial grimaces, and loud vocalization. Or, it might mean, "Although I believe that the project is a mistake, I'm really not too sure of my position, and I will do whatever you think is best." The only way to discern the differences in meaning between these two positions is by paying close attention to nonverbal cues. For example, the volume of the presentation, eye contact, body position, and intonation of speech all provide some cues about the intended message of the sender. Research has indicated that over 70 percent of the information transmitted in communication comes from nonverbal sources.[5]

Information Richness

Some channels of communication can carry tremendous amounts of information whereas others can carry limited information. **Information richness** is *the potential information-carrying capacity of the channel.*[6] Richness is influenced by several characteristics. First, channels that allow verbal *and* nonverbal communication are richer than those that provide only verbal communication. Hence, a face-to-face meeting would be richer than a telephone conversation. Second, richness increases as the opportunity for feedback increases. Though all channels provide some opportunity for feedback, the speed of feedback varies dramatically. For example, with face-to-face communication, feedback is immediate. The sender can observe the facial expressions and other non-verbal and verbal responses of the receiver. With an article placed in the company newsletter, feedback is much slower. Feedback occurs only when employees write letters to complain about the content of an article. This feedback process may take several weeks.

What type of information richness is most appropriate for different messages? Exhibit 13-3 on page 476 shows the relationship between complexity of problems and the appropriate channels for communicating about them. When a problem is simple, such as asking employees to name a beneficiary for a company life insurance policy, a communication channel low in richness would be most appropriate. Hence, a form letter could be sent to all employees.

When the problem is complex or difficult, face-to-face communication is needed. For example, assume as a manager that you are trying to determine whether you should expand your plant's manufacturing capacity. This is a complex and unstructured situation, and a poor decision would have dire consequences. Senior managers would want to talk with knowledgeable individuals one-on-one to collect as much information as possible. With a one-on-one conversation, participants can probe to insure that each individual's thoughts on the topic are understood. Also, because of the quick feedback provided in one-on-one communication, it is less likely misinterpretation of their statements will occur.

One could also collect the same information with a less-rich channel, such as sending employees a letter requesting their thoughts on the matter. However, important information may be left out of their responses. And, because of the slow response to formal written communications, managers may not have

Information richness
The potential information-carrying capacity of a communication channel.

EXHIBIT 13-3
Most appropriate communication channel as a function of problem complexity

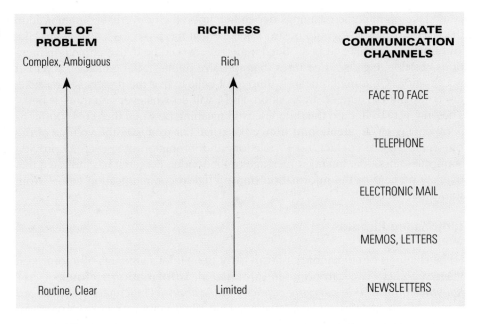

TYPE OF PROBLEM	RICHNESS	APPROPRIATE COMMUNICATION CHANNELS
Complex, Ambiguous ↑	Rich ↑	FACE TO FACE
		TELEPHONE
		ELECTRONIC MAIL
		MEMOS, LETTERS
Routine, Clear	Limited	NEWSLETTERS

time to collect their input. In addition, since there would be only verbal communication from them, there is a higher probability of misinterpretation of their intended meanings.

Telephone conversations have a moderate level of richness and thus are appropriate when dealing with moderately difficult or ambiguous problems. For example, assume that a regional manager had failed to complete a report by the due date. A phone call to clarify the status of the project would be an appropriate channel of communication. It provides immediate feedback and clarifies most miscommunications.

There are a large number of channels that have been developed to help the hearing- or visually-impaired communicate. Sign language, lip reading, and Braille are a few of these channels. More recently, technological advances have been developed to improve the communication of those with disabilities. For example, Telecommunication Devices for the Deaf (TDDs) allow telephone communication between deaf and hearing individuals. Speech is translated into written format on a terminal display, and deaf individuals type their responses. The typed responses are translated back into speech for hearing individuals. The use of nontraditional channels is allowing hearing- and visually-impaired individuals to perform successfully in almost all jobs. The *A Look At Diversity* box on page 477 discusses some common communication myths concerning hearing impaired individuals.

❓ THINKING CRITICALLY

1. Think about when you felt there was some ambiguity between the verbal message and nonverbal message you received from someone. How did that make you feel? What does that tell you about the importance of nonverbal language?

COMMUNICATING WITH THE HEARING IMPAIRED[7]

Position:	Editor-in-Chief of a university town newspaper serving 25,000.
Responsibilities:	Coordinate and supervise the activities of an editorial staff consisting of 5-to-8 journalists.
Qualifications:	Masters Degree with a minimum of two years relevant experience
Candidate:	Ron Smedly, hearing-impaired individual with Masters Degree in Fine Arts and five years of relevant journalistic experience
Decision:	Hired.

A LOOK AT

DIVERSITY

Prior to the development of communication technology, hearing- impaired individuals would have had difficulty serving as an editor-in-chief of a newspaper. Such technology, combined with the enactment of the Americans with Disabilities Act (ADA), gives qualified applicants such as Mr. Smedly opportunities to make valuable contributions to various organizations. The ADA legally prohibits employment discrimination toward *qualified* individuals with disabilities. With the development of new communication technologies, there are not many jobs that hearing-impaired individuals cannot perform. The following are some of the myths about the communication of hearing-impaired.

MYTHS	REALITIES
Deaf cannot use the telephone	Telecommunication Devices for the deaf allow telephone communication between deaf and hearing-impaired individuals. Cost: $200
I would not be able to call a coworker who is deaf.	Relay centers permit deaf-hearing phone conversations. Either the deaf or the hearing employee calls the relay center. Relay centers are mandatory in all states. Cost: $0, toll free number
A hearing-impaired employee could not hear the phone ring.	A light signaling system can be installed to activate when the phone rings. Cost: $10
Certain jobs require too much talking to be performed by the deaf.	Simple job restructuring involves the changing of duties. Also, the hearing-impaired are excellent communicators using sign language and lip reading.
People who are deaf cannot participate in multiple-person meetings or conferences.	Voice-simulators, interpreters, and computer conferences enable hearing-impaired employees to successfully participate in multiple-person interactions.

A LOOK AT

TECHNOLOGY

E-MAIL—TOO MUCH OF A GOOD THING[8]

Electronic mail is great technology that gives people throughout an organization ready access to information and the ability to connect with other employees quickly and easily. As with all good things, though, there is this natural tendency within us to take advantage of it, and this seems to be the case with e-mail as reported in an article in *The Wall Street Journal.* The ease of sending messages to anyone, anytime is a great temptation for some people.

For example, Charles Wang, chairman of Computer Associates International, a company that sells e-mail software, no longer sends or reads e-mail. He also shuts down the company's e-mail system five hours a day so employees won't be distracted by it. He says, "As a leader in a company, you have to go to an extreme to demonstrate a point." He finds subordinates have begun to copy their bosses on everything they write. "It's become a CYA tool."

Gary Chapman, an advocate for the development of the information highway states, "I totally wasted a third of my life this way," as he was receiving upwards of 80 messages a day. When he found himself without an e-mail address and thus no messages, he started to get things done without having his daily agenda diverted.

While e-mail technology facilitates communication, it also gives everyone the ability to type a message one time and have it delivered to all other employees with a couple of keystrokes. This is both its strength and its weakness. It is just as easy to send trivial messages as it is those that are useful to employees. Mitch Kertzman, chairman of Powersoft Corporation, receives hundreds of messages per week, including such messages as one from an employee trying to sell a dog. He expresses his frustration saying that if not for the advice of lawyers and psychologists, the company's e-mail abusers "would've been caned a long time ago."

2. If you were a highly placed manager in a company that was going through downsizing and had to lay off 100 employees, what channel and method would you choose to tell them and why? For example, would you use a form letter, personal face-to-face meetings, personal letters, a group meeting?

DIRECTION OF COMMUNICATION

Communication is often categorized based upon its direction. Communication can occur downward (manager to employee), upward (employee to manager) and horizontally (employee to employee). The following reviews each of these types of communication.

Downward Communication

Downward communication Communication that occurs when information is being transmitted from manager to employee.

Downward communication occurs *when information is being transmitted from manager to employee.* Downward communication provides the direction and guidance needed by employees to perform job-related tasks. Moreover, it insures that the work completed by various employees is coordinated and complementary. Without downward communication, different groups of employees often work toward different goals. Providing information on performance expectations, promotional opportunities, training, and benefit plans are all examples of downward communication. Without downward communication, it is impossible to coordinate the activities of employees. Such communication often happens via memo or other written documents, such as booklets with company policies, benefit plans, or information relevant to groups of employees.

Upward Communication

Upward communication occurs *when information flows from employees to managers.* Good upward communication helps managers to become aware of employees' feelings and ideas. It also suggests to employees a readiness to listen, which makes listening a positive value in the culture and thus encourages them likewise to listen to managers. Since employees can provide managers with valuable information, it is critical that they tap into employee knowledge and suggestions. Moreover, employees quite often are the first to recognize problems and can bring important information to the attention of the management team. Unfortunately, many employees shy away from such behavior because they fear retaliation or retribution. Upward communication will occur only if employees believe management is responsive to their ideas. That is one reason it is so important to create an environment that eliminates fear and encourages openness.

An example of what can happen when upward communication breaks down can be seen at Westinghouse Electric. This powerful company, with holdings in power generation, environmental services, and the defense industry, lost over $6 billion in 1992-1993. CEO Michael Jordan, hired in 1993, attributed many of the organization's problems to poor communication. He noted that little information flowed from the factories and plants to the top management team. As a result, numerous problems remained undetected and uncovered for many years. (We should note that the problems at Westinghouse were in divisions of the company other than Nuclear Fuels division, which we profiled in Chapter 6 on decision making.)

Many organizations are working to establish effective upward communication links. For example, status differences between managers and employees are minimized. Many organizations also have a formal **open door policy**. Most open door policies state that *employees have the right to meet with management about any issue, whenever they desire such a meeting.* Suggestion boxes are also a good way to encourage upward communication. Some organizations have begun to implement **subordinate evaluation systems** in which *employees evaluate the effectiveness of the management team.* All of these arrangements are designed to provide formal mechanisms through which employees can express their ideas or opinions without threat of retribution.

The Case in Point on Rosenbluth International in Chapter 12 is an example of a company that values upward communication as is CSX Transportation. CSX managers are required to hold frequent "town meetings" with their employees. Employees are free to talk about any issue that they would like to discuss. These meetings have forced CSX's management team to be more responsive to employee needs and suggestions.

Horizontal Communication

Horizontal communication occurs *when information is exchanged between individuals at the same level of the organization.* Although horizontal communication occurs effectively in most organizations *within* a work group, it often is

Upward communication Communication that occurs when information flows from employees to managers.

Open door policy A statement that employees have the right to meet with management about any issue, whenever they desire such a meeting.

Subordinate evaluation systems Programs in which employees evaluate the effectiveness of the management team.

Horizontal communcation Communication that occurs when information is exchanged between individuals at the same level of the organization.

ineffective *across* work group boundaries. That is, employees are able to communicate effectively with their peers within their work groups, but communication with employees in different work groups is often infrequent and ineffective.

There are several reasons for the difficulty of horizontal communication across work groups. First, employees often feel responsible only to their own supervisors and are unwilling to spend the time and energy necessary to effectively communicate with employees in different work groups. In essence, they do not believe that communicating with employees in another work group is a critical part of their jobs. Second, employees from the various functional areas often have different backgrounds and educational experiences. These differences in experience make communication difficult.

For example, employees in purchasing have a language all their own (e.g., purchase orders, encumbrances) that may make communication with a marketing employee difficult. More problematic, however, is the fact that most organizations are hierarchically organized and some even openly discourage communication across departments. Some organizations have an organizational policy that indicates that certain types of information (e.g., requests for job interviews) must flow entirely through the chain-of-command. Hence, managers cannot simply call an employee directly; rather, they must inform their bosses, who then passes the information along to their bosses, and so forth until the message is transmitted to the receiver. Of course, the more people the message flows through, the more opportunity there is for misunderstanding.

Horizontal communications are critical in total quality management organizations. One of the major thrusts of total quality management is the implementation of cross-functional teams, with each team focusing on a different process or service. For example, a team may be formed to reduce water use during a manufacturing operation. This team will have representation from all functional departments (e.g., engineering, design, manufacturing, accounting). The effectiveness of the team will depend upon the ability of team members to communicate horizontally with each other.

? THINKING CRITICALLY

1. If you worked in an organization where downward communication was most valued, what would that tell you about its culture and what top management thought of employees? Why is that an unhealthy approach?
2. Think about organizations you have joined. Was upward communication common? Why or why not? Assume that it was common. How would that make you feel about the organization and your commitment to it? Why?
3. What channels of communication are most appropriate for upward, downward, and horizontal communication, and why?

BARRIERS TO EFFECTIVE COMMUNICATION

Given the importance of communication, you may have wondered why every manager is not effective at it. Effective communication requires quite a bit of skill and effort. In this section, we will focus on the factors that prevent effective communication and discuss ways in which you can improve communication.

COMMUNICATION AT HALLMARK CARDS

Dave Seifert is the Internal Communications Manager at Kansas City-based Hallmark Cards, Inc. The following explains his company's approach to facilitating communication among all employees.

Communication is a priority at Hallmark and our managers are on the front line when it comes to advancing employee communication. Employees are part-owners of this privately owned company through a profit-sharing plan, and management sees employees as Hallmark's most important asset. They directly affect all aspects of the company's performance, and they have a right and a need to be informed and to have a forum for raising ideas, suggestions, and concerns. Employees want:

- To know about the business the company is in and how their jobs fit that business
- Informed supervisors who can and will communicate
- Face-to-face communication

Information has an impact on performance in all companies. At Hallmark, our formal communications strategy is based on the goal of building the level of knowledge among employees so they will be able to understand how effectively each segment of the company is performing. Understanding this information helps build a foundation for reasonable expectations about the overall performance of the company.

Communication is encouraged right from the top at Hallmark. The company's senior managers have established open, honest, and proactive communications as an important priority and encourages all levels of managers to be supportive of specific communications efforts. Managers at all levels are given access to a broad range of information and are given the authority and responsibility to share that information with employees.

To help managers in this communication role, Hallmark's Internal Communications department creates and distributes a variety of communications vehicles. One of the most valuable of these is a newsletter designed to provide managers with background information to discuss with employees. This newsletter is published "as needed" when important information needs to be disseminated.

Hallmark managers also receive periodic "communication packets" for use in further cultivating two-way communication in meetings with employees. Communication packets provide the means for supervisors to share information, as well as a structured way to encourage employees to offer ideas, suggestions, and questions.

Using these packets successfully requires that our managers learn to listen to employees with empathy. We want to do everything possible to encourage two-way communication between managers and employees. We work with managers to help them overcome the natural tendency to judge, to evaluate, or to approve or disapprove the statements of other persons or groups. We know, for example, if managers show that they don't want to hear bad news, there will be no bad news. Neither will there be two-way communication between managers and subordinates.

Good communication is difficult to define but is easy to recognize. We all know when someone has communicated well or badly. Effective communication is sometimes seen as too time consuming or even as an obstacle to getting things done. In reality, however, we know that effective communication enables companies like Hallmark to get things done.

Communication also helps employees keep their sense of direction and helps instill willingness to commit to company goals and priorities. All of that adds up to employee commitment—and employee commitment is ultimately a reward that managers earn or lose—based on their communication skills.

Selective Attention and Overload

Information overload
A situation in which managers receive more information than they can handle.

One of the biggest barriers to effective communication is **information overload**, *a situation in which managers receive more information than they can handle*. Most managers are bombarded by a constant onslaught of information. They receive numerous phone calls, letters, memos, faxes, E-mail messages, and voice-mail messages daily. With this much information coming in, it is possible that some information will be lost, ignored, or misinterpreted.

Selective attention
Attention given only to those messages that a person believes are important and ignoring all the rest.

How do managers deal with information overload? One of the most common ways is the use of **selective attention.** They end up *attending only to those messages that they believe are important, ignoring all the rest*. A powerful example of selective attention is the cocktail party phenomenon. This phenomenon refers to the fact that one can overhear one's name in a conversation at a noisy party even if the conversation is across the room. In essence, despite the information overload at the party, one selectively focuses on and attends to one's name because the communication may be a particularly important one. Similarly, managers have a tendency to selectively attend to the parts of information that they believe are important to them. Unfortunately, this causes problems in that what the receiver believes is important may lead to discounting other messages and information that is equally if not more deserving of managers' attentions.

The problem of communication overload is exacerbated by the swift and dramatic advancements in technology, including electronic-mail, voice-mail, faxes, cellular phones, and beepers. Although such systems reduce the costs of paper, postage, and distribution, they result in a proliferation of correspondence and messages of all sorts. For example, once a letter is typed in the computer—with one key stroke—it can be sent to all members of the organization. The obvious advantage of E-mail is that it is distributed instantaneously. The letter is transferred by telephone wires to other computers. The disadvantage is that a tremendous amount of trivial correspondence is sent contributing to information overload.

Exception principle
A communication guideline that states that only significant deviations from policies and procedures are communicated to others.

Many organizations are trying to control the barrage of information and have established communication guidelines. For example, trivial messages are not allowed to be sent through the organization's E-mail systems. Some organizations now base communications on the **exception principle**.[9] The exception principle states that *only significant deviations from policies and procedures are communicated to others*. However, it is likely that this will have little effect on the problem of information overload. It cannot really be handled by policy. It is best handled by managers as they become aware of the problem and seek to prioritize tasks and the information required to carry them out.

Frame of Reference Differences

Frame of reference
A combination of your educational, developmental, intellectual, cultural, and work-related experiences.

We all have frames of reference that we use to interpret incoming information. For example, if you and another person were asked to evaluate a colleague for promotion, it is possible, based on your experience with that person, that your evaluation could be enthusiastic while someone else might be only lukewarm toward this individual. The way each of us interprets information or offers judgments and opinions depends on our experience and knowledge. The same is true for every receiver and sender of information.

Your **frame of reference** is *a combination of your educational, developmental, intellectual, cultural, and work-related experiences* and will never completely overlap with that of anyone else. These differences can create difficulty in communication as individuals interpret messages based on their frames of reference. As communicators, we need to know that if our receivers do not understand our messages, it is not their faults, it is ours. When sending messages we must strive to be aware of the experiences, knowledge, cultures, and educational levels that make up the frames of reference of our receivers. Understanding that we are more likely to compose messages in ways that receivers will correctly interpret and understand. Two of the most important factors are differences in culture and in experience and educational backgrounds.

Cultural Differences.   One common frame-of-reference problem is produced by culture. We all are influenced to some extent by our cultural assumptions. Cultures differ on four major dimensions:[10]

1. Valuing individual accomplishment versus valuing group accomplishment
2. Valuing logical argument versus valuing emotion
3. Valuing strong social order versus toleration of disorder
4. Short-term versus long-term orientation

The importance of cultural differences for communication can be seen when Japanese and North American managers interact. Due to cultural barriers, even the most basic forms of communication can present a challenge. One of the most confusing aspects of communication between the two cultures lies in recognizing how each side conveys a yes or no response. Many North Americans find that their Japanese counterparts are reluctant to provide simple yes or no answers. The differences go beyond words. A Japanese manager will frequently nod his head and say "yes, yes." While North Americans usually view such behavior as a signal of comprehension, to the Japanese, it merely means "I'm listening, please continue." Further, they may answer yes to a question that in the U.S. would elicit a no. For example, the statement "this isn't going to work, is it?" would elicit a response of "yes" from the Japanese, meaning, "yes, it isn't going to work." The American response to that question would be "no," if we wanted to indicate that it would not work.

Although differences between the two styles can lead to confusion, both Japanese and North Americans often admire each other's communication styles. North Americans appreciate how the Japanese style, with its emphasis on observing formal relationships and group harmony, strengthens the organization. On the other hand, although the Japanese often find the manners of North Americans aggressive and blunt, they admit that the North Americans' willingness to express opinions clearly and frankly can help clarify issues and facilitate moving ahead.[11]

Ethnocentrism is the belief that one's culture is superior to others. It is typically not a conscious belief of superiority, but instead an implicit assumption that one's culture should generalize to all others. We Americans (and others) tend to act based on our own cultural norms, and consequently, we often offend those from other cultures.

Consider this situation, for example, of a meeting between American and Japanese managers: The meeting started with the traditional exchanging of business cards. A business card is perceived as an extension of the individual by Japanese, and thus quite a bit of time is spent presenting and receiving cards. After the exchanging of business cards and during the meeting, one young American manager pulled out the business card of one of the Japanese managers and made a note on it. The Japanese managers were appalled. It was as if someone took a prize possession and defiled it right in front of their eyes. This single act communicated disrespect for the Japanese manager. The manager's offensive actions were not due to malicious intent but to ignorance and ethnocentrism. The manager assumed that what was acceptable in the U.S. culture was acceptable in other cultures.

Many organizations have programs that train their managers prior to sending them on international visits or assignments. These programs are designed to encourage employees' recognition of other cultural values and assumptions so that they will be able to communicate more effectively. Typically, these training programs involve roleplays and help managers recognize their cultural assumptions before communication efforts have been seriously compromised.

Educational and Experience Differences.   Differences in experience and education can result in significantly different frames of reference. Many managers (and college professors) have difficulty explaining information so that it is understandable for a less experienced or less educated employee. For example, imagine a plumber who writes to the Environmental Protection Agency to inquire whether it is safe to use hydrochloric acid to clean pipes. The response from the EPA could read: "The efficacy of hydrochloric acid is indisputable, but the corrosive residue is incompatible with metallic permanence."[12] The plumber may decode this response to mean "hydrochloric acid can be used to clean pipes," whereas the intended message was "hydrochloric acid eats holes in pipes."

Managers need to be aware of experiences and educational levels when communicating with others. For example, when writing a letter, managers should be careful that they are not writing at a level higher than the receiver can understand. Many word processors now contain grammar-checkers that determine the reading level of letters or memos. This chapter has a reading level of 14, which connotes sophomore college level. Hence, it would not be appropriate for a high school business book.

Jargon Technical words or phrases that have special meaning to an occupation and specialized job.

Jargon.   Jargon often interferes with effective communication. **Jargon** refers to *technical words or phrases that have special meaning to an occupation and specialized job.* Though jargon is common in most organizations, it can interfere with effective communication when the sender and receiver do not share the same frame of reference. For example, in a project with the U.S. Army, some researchers had to conduct a large number of interviews with soldiers and officers. Despite the researchers' high educational levels, they still had difficulty understanding the Army organization. Answers to questions were filled with jargon (e.g., ARTEPS, NCO, PM), and researchers experienced difficulty decoding the intended messages of the speakers. They needed to understand the jargon before communicating effectively in this context.

Most listeners will not spend the time to understand jargon. They will expect managers to be able to take the business's complex ideas and translate them into content listeners can understand, and it is managers' responsibility to do so if they want to be understood. This means managers must be sensitive to receivers' backgrounds and skill levels, and encode the message accordingly.

Sender empathy The ability of the sender to appreciate the perspectives of others.

Sender Empathy.   It is important that a sender be able to take into account a receiver's frame of reference. **Sender empathy** is *the ability of the sender to*

INTERNATIONAL BLUNDERS[13]

International business has brought with it a modern-day "Tower of Babel Business." A questionnaire completed on the subject of international communications indicated that 80 percent of business travelers reported difficulties conducting business with foreigners because of the latters' misunderstanding of American English. The frequent use of idioms (e.g., flying by the seat of your pants), jargon (e.g., downtime), and various dialects (e.g., y'all) by Americans confounds even those who are well-versed in standard English. Misunderstandings also flow in the other direction. For example, when an Englishman states that a project will be finished "at the end of the day," he simply means that it will be done when it's done—which could take six months. Be careful how you try and say embarrassment in Spanish—*estoy embarazado* means "I am pregnant." Likewise, don't be offended if a Frenchman "demands something." The French verb for ask is "demander."

Americans conducting business in Japan can get into trouble using the word "you." The Japanese do not think in terms of self but of the company. The company is important, not the individual. Moreover, Japanese businessmen at the highest levels do not expect to be addressed directly or even looked at directly. Finally, there is no real word for "no" in the Japanese language. Instead, the Japanese may reply with a sad-faced, "it is very difficult."

Nonverbal gestures also can cause problems for those doing international business. The widely accepted fingers circle "okay" sign in America is considered vulgar in Brazil, signifies money in Japan, and means "zero" or "worthless" in southern France. Giving the thumbs up to an Australian is considered rude, whereas waving to a Greek will be taken as a serious insult. Additionally, nodding the head to indicate "yes" signifies "no" in Bulgaria and Greece.

There have been some great blunders in advertising produced by ethnocentrism. Coca Cola ran an advertisement in Asian markets using their theme "Coke adds life." The advertisement was interpreted to mean that "Coke brings you back from the dead." The name of one of General Motors' automobile models, Nova, translates into "No Go" in Spanish. Needless to say, the car did not sell well in Mexico.

A LOOK AT THE GLOBAL ENVIRONMENT

appreciate others' perspectives. Obviously, most senders are sensitive to some extent to others' backgrounds. For example, if the receiver only speaks French, the sender would not attempt to communicate in English. On the other hand, there are subtle differences that are often overlooked by most communicators. For example, "participative management" means something dramatically different to employees at Saturn than it means to employees at Toyota's plant in Georgetown, Kentucky. At Saturn, participation means that teams make most decisions, including the hiring and firing of their own team members. At Toyota, it means that employees participate in continuous improvement teams and make recommendations to management; the work process and workflow are controlled by management. Thus the same term, "participative management," has different meanings depending on the work environment.

Empathetic senders take into account receivers' frames of reference when communicating. They study their audiences and learn as much about them as possible. For example, when making a sales call to a new client, an empathetic communicator would look for evidence concerning the background of the client (e.g., where is she from? did she go to college? what are her hobbies? how long has she worked for this company? what other companies has she worked for? what type of car does she drive?). This information can be used to develop a bond and common frame of reference that facilitates communication between them.

Status Differences

Status differences can also influence the effectiveness of communication. Status differences are often perceived as a threat to individuals with lower status, and they may be less willing to engage in two-way communication with those perceived to be of higher-status in the organization. For example, a nurse may be unwilling to question a physician. Moreover, lower-status employees may be nervous when communicating with higher-status managers, and their nervousness may interfere with clear and direct communication, whether in face-to-face settings or in writing.

To enhance the accuracy of communication, managers need to down-play status differences when communicating with employees. Conversations in their offices or at neutral sites (e.g., the cafeteria) will minimize status differences. Managers can also minimize status differences in the office by being sure that their desks are not between themselves and their employees as they converse. For example, as can be seen in Exhibit 13-4, managers are much better to use sitting arrangements b and c than a.

Many organizations have attempted to minimize status differences between employees to encourage more open communication. For example, at Honda Motors plant in Marysville, Ohio, visible status differences have been eliminated. All employees eat in the same cafeteria and park in the same parking lot. There are no reserved parking spaces for the management team or individual offices for anyone. Instead, managers work in a large area right along with other employees. The consequences of these procedures are that status differences are reduced and communication is enhanced.

Poor Listening Skills

Communication in many organizations suffers because managers have weak listening skills. Part of the reason for this is that many managers *listen to respond, rather than listen to understand.* That is, they are searching for information that will allow them to handle problems in the fastest way possible. What happens is that they pick up a few cues from the discussion, integrate those into their experiences, and provide responses consistent with their viewpoints while discounting the viewpoints of the speakers. This type of listening sends the unspoken message that managers only value their own ideas and not those of their employees. With more careful listening, managers might hear the message actually intended, seek to understand it from the sender's perspective, and take a different action.

Although listening skills are critical, most managers take them for granted. Effective listening is an active process and requires a lot of work. **Active listening** is *a process of spending time and energy to accurately understand the sender's intended message.* Active listeners do not interrupt senders or pay attention to only parts of the senders' messages. They are attentive to nonverbal behaviors as well, and they use this information to decode the intended messages of the speakers. Active listeners encourage senders to be open by demonstrating nonverbally that they are paying attention to them. They nod in

Active listening A process of spending time and energy to accurately understand the sender's intended message.

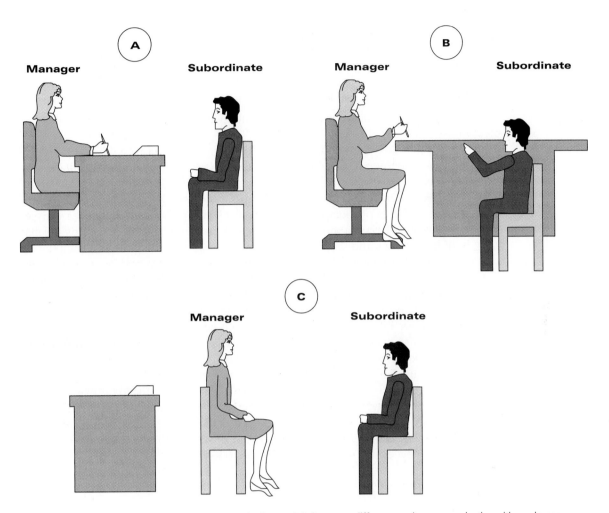

EXHIBIT 13-4   Seating arrangements can emphasize or minimize status differences when communicating with employees

response to speakers, maintain eye contact with speakers, and don't work on other tasks while senders are speaking. An active listener also continuously interprets the senders' messages and looks for the meaning behind the senders' words. Active listeners try not to jump to conclusions, but instead attempt to listen carefully to speakers.[14]

Active listeners also paraphrase senders' messages to insure that they understand it. By putting the senders' ideas in their own words, they provide tests that they have accurately decoded the messages. Consider the following exchange:[15]

Sarah: Jim should never have become a teacher.

Fred: You mean he doesn't like working with kids or is he too impatient?

Sarah: No, neither of those two things. I just think that his tastes are too expensive and he's going to be frustrated on a teacher's salary.

Note that Fred attempted to paraphrase Sara's intended meaning, but he was inaccurate with his paraphrasing. Without paraphrasing, the miscommunication never would have been identified.

Active listeners also encourage speakers to express their ideas. Open-ended probes are questions that allow speakers to explain their positions in more detail. For example, consider the following exchange.

Employee: I think that it was a mistake to give the Smith account to Thompson.

Manager: Tell me your concerns about giving the account to Thompson.

Note that this open-ended probe encourages the employee to elaborate. Furthermore, open-ended probes show that listeners are not defensive and are willing to consider alternative positions.

Active listeners also *close conversations with a summary statement.* This provides a synopsis of the speaker's main ideas and provides the speaker with an opportunity to clarify the intended message. Summary statements insure that both the speaker and the listener are on the same wave length. An example of a summary statement is, "Thank you for bringing your concerns about quality control to me. It sounds like your main concern is that quality control does not communicate with the first line supervisors and actually is working to turn employees against first line supervisors." A summary statement gives the sender an opportunity to clarify his or her intended message, if necessary.

Active listeners also *find time to listen.* That is, they have a good **talk-listen ratio**. Talk-listen ratio is *the percentage of time that one talks during a conversation.* If managers are talking more than 50 percent of the time, they are probably not adequately listening to employees. Managers will be amazed at how employees respond when managers do not dominate conversations. They may be surprised at first, but eventually they will talk up a storm. Remember that effectiveness as a manager will be influenced by the ability to obtain information from employees. Be sure to take the time to listen.

Talk-listen ratio The percentage of time that one talks during a conversation.

? THINKING CRITICALLY

1. If you were asked to make a presentation to the president or chancellor of your school, what frame-of-reference problems may exist? How would you attempt to avoid them?
2. What is the most serious frame-of-reference problem that you have ever experienced? What was the consequence of this difference?
3. Why do you think many people are poor listeners? What nonverbal messages does poor listening send to those doing the speaking?
4. Which barriers to communication are most likely to occur in downward communication? Upward communication? Horizontal communication? Why?

COMMUNICATION AND ORGANIZATIONAL STRUCTURE

Communication effectiveness can be affected greatly by organizational structure. Some organizational structures encourage the flow of information between employees and supervisors, whereas other organizational structures dampen that flow. In this section, we will focus on the influences of organizational structure on various communication patterns.

Communication in Hierarchical Organizational Structures

Exhibit 13-5 illustrates a typical hierarchical organization. Vertical communication is the norm in hierarchical organizations. That is, employees communicate primarily with their immediate supervisors. If one employee needs to communicate with another employee in a different group, the employee informs the supervisor, who informs the supervisor of the other employee, who finally informs the employee that communication needs to happen. Obviously, this route for passing information prevents an organization from responding quickly to meet customer needs or internal problems. It is orderly, but inefficient and stifling.

There are two types of hierarchical organizations. The first type is a *tall organization* (Exhibit 13-5a). A tall organization has a large number of layers between top managers and employees, and each supervisor tends to have a small span of control. Most bureaucratic organizations, such as government agencies, are tall. Given the number of layers through which information must pass in tall organizational structures, the intended message is often distorted multiple times by the frames of reference of the various senders and receivers. Furthermore, the communication process is slow in tall organizations, so that often competitive advantages or opportunities to provide valuable services to customers is missed.

Most of us have had more than enough experiences with tall organizations (for example, calling to request a policy change on car insurance). Such a simple modification may require talking with three of four different individuals. Moreover, if it is a special request, the caller will not receive an immediate decision. Instead, the customer file might have to be read and approved by two or three

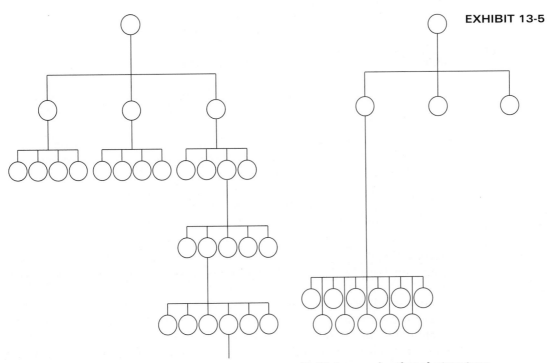

EXHIBIT 13-5

A. Tall organizational structure   **B. Flat organizational structure**

supervisors. Then a letter may be received in two weeks indicating that the request has been granted, only to find out that they changed the wrong part of the policy. As the request flowed up the organizational hierarchy, some information was lost or confused.

There is, however, a benefit of tall organizations. Communication between the managers and direct reports tends to be good due to the small span-of-control. That is, since most managers are responsible for only a few employees in a tall organization, they know their employees well and can spend a lot of time ensuring that their intended messages have been accurately received. Furthermore, tall organizations tend to have good communication between employees within the same work group since most work groups are small and specialized in tall organizations.

Many organizations have recently opted for fewer management levels. Such delayering has resulted in *flatter organizations* (see Exhibit 13-5b). There are fewer management levels, but each manager has a larger span-of-control. Speed of vertical communication is faster in these organizations since information goes through fewer levels. Moreover, less distortion should occur because fewer translations of the information are required. For example, if employees have ideas for a new customer service, they can tell their manager, who can inform the vice president. In a tall organization, the suggestion might need to be passed through two or three additional managers before it reaches the vice president. While flat organizations should result in more accurate communications than tall organizations, the thrust is still on vertical communication. That is, communication occurs through the chain-of-command. Hence, communication across work groups is still limited.

NuCor Steel, the sixth largest steel company in the U.S., is a good example of a flat organization. It has only three levels between the president and the steel worker. This results in a rapid flow of information throughout the organization, which enables NuCor to act quickly to meet customers' needs. For example, the plant manager at a facility can call the CEO directly and recommend a new technology without the idea being filtered through numerous managerial levels.

Communication in Horizontal Organizations

In contrast to the hierarchical organizational structure, *horizontal organizations* facilitate communication across functional areas. Sample horizontal organizational structures are presented in Exhibit 13-6. Most organizations maintain the functional hierarchical structure, but assign employees to specific project teams. These project teams are cross-functional. That is, while members have functional supervisors, their primary responsibilities are to support the projects to which they are assigned. Hence, a cross-functional team is established for a given product (e.g., design of an economy car). In essence, they work cross-functionally to provide a service or to create a product. Communication is not constrained by the chain-of-command in cross-functional teams. Instead, daily interactions occur across functional lines. Chrysler's recently introduced Neon was designed using a cross-functional, team-based organizational structure. The car was brought to market in half the time of other automobiles, due to the excellent cross-functional communication.

The engineering division of Philips Consumer Electronics is an example of an organization that has recently changed from a hierarchical organizational structure to one characterized by cross-functional platform teams. Philips manufactures Magnavox televisions. Employees from various functional areas have been

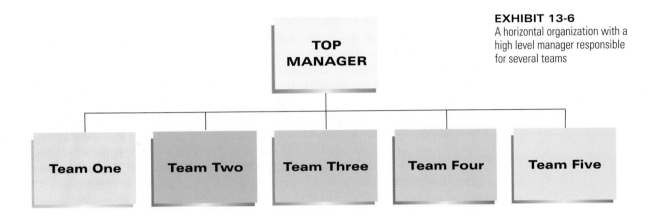

EXHIBIT 13-6
A horizontal organization with a high level manager responsible for several teams

assigned to support the development of different product lines. Thus, there is constant interaction between manufacturing, engineering, and marketing. The increased communication across the various functional areas should result in higher quality designs that better meet customers' needs and that can be more efficiently and more reliably manufactured. This happens because each functional specialty works more closely with the others, and this helps to eliminate one group optimizing at the expense of another group.

Although cross-functional teams result in greatly enhanced horizontal communications, they are not easily implemented. Most employees prefer to communicate within their own functional groups since employees within the same function share a similar frames of reference. With cross-functional groups, various perspectives are represented in the group. This means that employees must work harder to prevent miscommunicating. The benefits of such work are higher quality products and more responsiveness to customers' needs.

Formal and Informal Communications

Regardless of the formal pattern of communication in the organization, there also will be an informal communication chain, or a **grapevine.** The grapevine, or rumor mill, is *an informal communication network established by employees to provide them with an alternative source of information than that offered by management.* Grapevines tend to be cross-functional and cut across organizational levels. They are not based upon organizational positions or job descriptions, but instead are based on personal friendships.

The grapevine can either assist or prevent managers from being effective. Grapevines provide a second source of information, so they may prevent managers from distorting information to influence employees. For example, if managers are planning a restructuring, but inform employees that they are not making any changes, their real plans may be revealed through the grapevine and undermine their credibility. Information enters the grapevine from many sources including friends, secretaries, employees, and faxes that are read by unintended individuals.

There is often an amazing amount of information transmitted through the grapevine. Employees often know about major decisions even before many managers have been officially notified. The grapevine carries various types of information including which employees might be looking for other jobs, compensation paid to individual employees, and information concerning sexual harassment or

Grapevine An informal communication network established by employees to provide them with an alternative source of information than that offered by management.

union organizing efforts. The grapevine will also likely contain information about managers' leadership styles, the quality of decisions, and managers' integrity.

Information passed through the grapevine often gets exaggerated as it travels from employee to employee. This is particularly true for organizations that fail to openly distribute information. In essence, given the absence of open and honest information from management, employees try to fill the vacuum by providing bits of information to each other, even if this includes speculation rather than facts.

Some employees may be inclined to exaggerate the truth, and a dangerous rumor may arise. For example, at one organization, the grapevine contained information that a manufacturing facility was being closed. This rumor may have started because an employee overheard that the human resources department was conducting an extensive study of the local job market. Employee morale suffered, and some employees even started to look for other jobs, based on the rumor. In reality, this organization was thinking about *expanding* their operations at the facility. This suggests that keeping employees informed makes more sense for the welfare of the organization than confidentiality.

The pervasiveness of the grapevine has two major implications for managing. First, managers need to recognize that their organizations will have a grapevine, and use it to their benefits. If they are able to gain the trust of employees, employees will share the information on the grapevine. This will provide managers with access to the basic attitudes and thoughts of the workforce. Think of the grapevine as one pulse of the organization. If managers can monitor it, they will be able to identify problem areas and aggressively counteract inaccurate rumors before the rumors adversely affect employees' morale or performance.

Managers should also work to minimize the importance of, or the need for, the grapevine. Grapevines exist to provide employees with information that they believe is more accurate than the information provided by management. In fact, when there is constant chit-chat via the grapevine talking about problems within the organization and complaints about management, that is a strong indication that the internal health of the organization is suffering, and management needs to make some serious changes. If employees trust their managers, and managers share with them as much information as possible, the grapevine will gradually lose its influence. Moreover, managers should encourage employees to contact them directly and ask about any questions they have, rather than rely upon the grapevine. If managers are candid and honest with employees, they will be that way back, and the grapevine will gradually lose its impact, a sign of a healthy organization.

Communication at United Parcel Service (UPS) is a good example of this principle. Management at UPS communicates directly and frequently with employees. Whenever management meetings are held, minutes are transcribed and circulated to all districts. A prework communication meeting is held at the start of every work day to discuss either specific questions about work or larger issues involving strategic direction. The outcome of this process is that employees feel they are receiving and will always receive important information and hence are not overly reliant upon the grapevine.

❓ THINKING CRITICALLY

1. If you were a manager in an organization, do you think that the advantage of preserving order by using vertical communication via the chain of command would be more important than encouraging communication among people

who are most related to a problem even when this does not flow through the chain of command? Why or why not?

2. Do you think a manager needs to know business matters that go on among employees? Why or why not?

3. Do you think the grapevine would be more important in a tall or flat organization? Why?

COMMUNICATION AND TECHNOLOGY

Rapid technological advances are changing the face of communication. Think about all the new channels for communicating that were unavailable ten years ago. Fax machines are now commonplace as are cellular phones. People can communicate with colleagues around the world with electronic mail. Video telephones are now available and will become more prevalent in the future. Video- and teleconferencing allows meetings to be held across the world without incurring travel expenses for participants. These modern technologies mean that work can occur at any location since information can flow directly to employees, whether they are in their cars, their home offices, or on vacation.

A good example of how technology is changing communication can be seen with voice mail. **Voice mail** systems use *computer software to digitally record, store, and play back voice messages.* Most large organizations and a growing percent of medium and small businesses now have voice mail systems. Unlike the 9-to-5 secretary, voice mail works 24-hours a day. Moreover, people can leave complex messages by voice mail, and not waste time playing telephone tag.

Voice mail Computer software used to digitally record, store, and play back voice messages.

Initial research suggests that voice mail enhances productivity. While the typical phone conversation lasts between four and five minutes, the typical voice mail message is less than one minute in length. Moreover, voice mail messages appear to be concise, and they can be replayed if receivers are having difficulty understanding messages. Individuals can also call and check for messages from any location. Since the system is controlled with personalized identification numbers, confidentially is also assured.

While voice mail is efficient, it can also be impersonal. The overuse of voice mail is not an effective technique to cultivate relationships between managers and employees. It has its place, but the personal warmth, spontaneity, and interaction of conversation is lost with voice mail. Moreover, while some individuals like the efficiency of voice mail, others despise its impersonal nature, especially when they call the company's main number and get a machine rather than a real person to direct their calls.

Advanced communication technology has allowed managers to have a wider range of responsibility and simultaneously direct more projects. Consider the managers of Fluor, a large engineering and construction company in California with revenues of $8 billion in 1993. The organization has recently restructured and relies heavily on technology to communicate. Before the reorganization, each local office operated autonomously, with its own management, and its own marketing and purchasing departments. Besides adding overhead cost, this structure prevented the various offices from cooperating. For example, since each office was independent, one office would hire additional engineers to finish a project while engineers at another facility were idle. Today, one team of mobile managers runs all Fluor facilities. These managers communicate constantly via fax, E-mail, and phone. Moreover, employees share work electronically. For example, engineers in New Orleans

Advanced technology in communications is changing the way in which people communicate and work, since information can flow to and from any location via the electronic highways.

are preparing drawings for a copper mine on an Indonesian island. Plans and drawings are constantly being shipped back and forth between the site and New Orleans through a computerized network. This allows work to be distributed evenly throughout the local offices, irrespective of the actual construction site.[16] Thus, high technology communication is providing the organization with great flexibility. Moreover, work can be reassigned to avoid bottle-necks in project schedules.

In multinational companies, it is now possible to work on projects 24-hours a day. For example, engineers, using computer-aided design programs, can work on a project from 8:00 A.M. to 5:00 P.M. eastern standard time in New York City. Their plans can then be electronically shipped to Japan, where a second set of engineers can begin working on the designs at the start of their work days. After a day of work in Japan, the plans can be electronically shipped back to New York by the beginning of the next work day. Work flows around the world, following the sun, which allows the project to advance rapidly. It also allows companies to distribute more evenly workloads across international locations.

It is clear that technology is changing the way in which individuals communicate. Despite these technological changes, effective communication still depends on the appropriateness of the intended messages, decoding, channel selections, transmissions, and clarifications of the communication based on feedback from the receiver. Thus, the basic model of communication must still hold regardless of technological sophistication.

❓ THINKING CRITICALLY

1. If you have used E-mail, what is your experience with it? Based on your experience, what do you think its strengths are as a business communication channel? What do you think some of its weaknesses might be? How might people abuse E-mail?

2. Overall, do you think communication technology facilitates work processes or unnecessarily complicates them? In answering this question, think about ideas like information overload, time, availability of information, and proper use of technology.

PERFORMANCE FEEDBACK

Some of the most important information communicated to employees is feedback on their performances. **Performance feedback** *tells employees what aspects of their performances are valued (or not valued) and why.* Performance feedback, when communicated correctly, has a positive effect on employees. It provides them with the information needed to improve their performances. It is difficult (and sometimes impossible) to improve performances without feedback.

Effectively communicated feedback that focuses on behaviors also motivates employees to improve and perform at higher and higher levels. On the other hand, when performance feedback is poorly communicated and seems aimed at employees personally rather than on specifics of behavior, it can have a devastating effect on them. Employees will become defensive and block out any other information that might help them make appropriate alterations. They will think that the feedback is unfair and that their supervisors do not understand them or their jobs.

For this and other reasons, many managers are unwilling to provide employees with negative feedback unless their performances are extremely poor. They tend to believe the old adage that "If you can't say anything nice about someone, then you shouldn't say anything at all." What this means is that they do not understand the purpose of such feedback (to inhibit unproductive behaviors) or how to deliver it.

Unfortunately, without negative feedback, many employees continue to perform at marginal levels despite the fact that they have the potential to be outstanding performers. Employees want feedback, both positive and negative. Positive feedback lets them know what they are doing right. Negative feedback suggests which behaviors are not productive and should be eliminated or modified. Negative feedback can result in enhanced motivation as long as it is specific and sensitively delivered. The best way to think about this is to eliminate the notions of positive and negative and just focus on the idea of feedback itself. Managers need to give employees the direct information they need to understand how well they are performing and how they can improve.

Further, it is important to think about feedback as an ongoing activity. Managers often think of this idea in terms of annual or semi-annual performance appraisals. There is some question of the usefulness of these, as suggested in Chapter 9 on human resources. What is much more valuable are ongoing dialogues between managers and employees about the best ways to get jobs done, problems, ways to solve these problems, and ways to improve processes. We should also note that such feedback should be both up and down. Managers, with the role of supporting and facilitating the work of their employees, also need feedback on how they are doing. The most healthy organizations are those where this two-way feedback on performance is part of the culture. Certainly, this is an important aspect of TQM.

Performance feedback
Communication that tells employees what aspects of their performances are valued (or not valued) and why.

THINKING CRITICALLY

1. If you were seeking to improve your performance in writing papers for class, what kinds of feedback would you want to do this? Why would the types

you choose help you improve? If you were told the reason your papers get poor grades is because you are a lousy writer, how would you feel? Would that help you improve? Why or why not?

2. Are you comfortable providing negative feedback to others? Describe a recent example where you provided negative feedback to another individual. Was your feedback specific, timely, and sensitively delivered? Did the person appreciate it? Why or why not?

COMMUNICATION AND TOTAL QUALITY MANAGEMENT

Organizations where TQM is practiced have cultures that promote open and complete sharing of information among all employees. This is because the systems view *requires* such openness. When people have information spelling out what is going on, this eliminates rumors and speculation, and provides the details needed for people to identify with the company to have a common purpose and to work well together. Three of Deming's 14 Points for Management that we have referred to regularly in this book directly address issues involving communication: **Point 1**: Create constancy of purpose toward improvement of products and services; **Point 8**: Drive out fear, so that everyone may work effectively for the organization; and **Point 9**: Break down barriers between departments.[17] Implementing each of these ideas depends on effective communication. Let's discuss each one in more detail.

- *Create constancy of purpose.* Employees and managers can work best together when they have constancy of purpose that they all understand and when they know their roles in making that happen. The purpose in organizations where managers understand TQM is to serve customers and continuously improve their ability to do this. A culture that values and facilitates open communication helps managers maintain constancy of purpose in a dynamic world that is constantly changing.

- *Drive out fear.* The source of fear for most people is uncertainty about their roles or what is going on in their environments. When people understand their roles and have the information they need to perform well in contributing to organizational processes, this helps to eliminate uncertainty. Further, open sharing of information about individual, department, business unit, and organizational performances, be that good or bad, eliminates uncertainty on which fear is based and helps give employees direction for their behaviors.

- *Break down barriers between departments.* Barriers arise in organizations when one group of people does not know what another is doing or exactly how what that group does is going to affect them. Clearly, open communication about processes and activities throughout the company and the interrelationship among departments to execute organizational strategies is an important method for breaking down such barriers.

Communication and the Principles of TQM

In Chapter 3 we reviewed several principles of TQM. These principles all assume that an organization has well-developed methods for discovering and sharing organizational information with all employees. Some of those principles in which communication plays an important role include: (1) the management of process-es; (2) customer focus; (3) continuous improvement; (4) teams and teamwork; (5) empowerment of employees; and (6) databased decision making. The fol-lowing reviews the role of communication in implementing these principles.

1. *The management of processes.* We have noted often that work gets done by employees making their individual contributions to execute organization processes. This means that these processes must be well-documented and that people know their roles vis-a-vis each other and how work is progress-ing. All of this happens through regular communication, both formal and informal. It requires a culture that stresses that what every employee does affects and is dependent on what others do. The only way that happens is by communication that lets people know how well things are going and what the problems are, so they can work together to solve them.

2. *Customer focus.* Processes work best when employees understand how what they do adds value for customers in the final output. An important goal in any organization is to keep reducing work that does not add such value. Thus, managers must (a) make sure they regularly and assertively communi-cate with customers to understand their needs and how well the organiza-tion is doing at fulfilling these needs, and (b) make sure all employees have this information so they can judge their performances by this criterion of customer satisfaction and devise ideas for improvement. Doing this requires formal and informal collection of customer information as well as methods for its dissemination throughout the company in ways employees can use. Further, it requires methods that make it possible for employees to suggest improvements in product or service quality and the processes by which these are created.

3. *Continuous improvement.* An important part of any organization's efforts in the practice of TQM involves the continuous improvement of work processes and the goods and services offered to customers. Fundamentally continuous improvement means that employees, alone and in teams, are constantly going to be experimenting with new ideas to see which work and which may have unintended consequences. This requires regular for-mal and informal communication and interaction among everyone involved with the constant reevaluation of how things are going and what they will try next.

4. *Teams and teamwork.* Teamwork clearly requires regular and honest inter-changes among team members. Otherwise cooperation breaks down. In fact, teamwork requires regular meetings to discuss team assignments, progress, problems, and future goals. Skilled communication is at the heart of making meetings work, as members listen, contribute, and decide among themselves what actions they will take. Finally, it is not unusual for there to be disputes among team members, and it is only through the use of communication tech-niques that members can resolve disputes.

5. *Empowerment of employees.* Giving employees decision-making authority over their work processes can only work in an environment that values open communication among employees and management. Employees need detailed information about work processes to do their jobs. Further, empow-erment suggests that they are managing themselves, and thus must use com-munication skills to keep their interactions with others smooth.

Regular communication lets people know how well work is going and can identify problems so they can work together to solve them.

6. *Databased decision making.* Decisions in traditional organizations are often made on the impressions or prejudices of managers. Organizations that have adopted TQM base decisions, as much as possible, on data that accurately reflect the measurement of work processes. This requires both the collection and sharing of information among employees and managers.

We could go on with this approach. The point is that managers, who understand that their organizations are systems and that have implemented TQM, know that communication and complete dissemination of business information among all employees simply makes systems work better. People act in accordance with their understandings of situations. When they lack information, they are more likely to misunderstand the situation. This will negatively affect their actions and will reverberate throughout the system. Open and complete sharing of business information helps make sure that employees have accurate understandings of their organizations. This helps ensure that their actions will most likely add value to the processes involved in delivering quality to customers.

Communication with Suppliers

The points above are about communication within the organization and with customers. Another situation in which communications play an important role in the TQM organization is in relations with suppliers. Communication with suppliers takes on increased importance in a total quality organization. Traditionally managed companies view suppliers with suspicion and attempt to "low ball" them into providing services and products for as low a price as possible. Information is not shared since it could be used for competitive advantage in negotiations. Companies work with multiple suppliers and tend to play them against each other.

When managers take the systems view, they see suppliers as *part of their systems* and as partners in the process of delivering products and services to customers. TQM companies reduce the number of suppliers and work as teams with the remaining ones. They realize this is the smartest way to ensure quality, timeliness, and reliability of the commodities, components, products, and services they need to do their work. This allows suppliers to better plan and be able to meet their customers' needs, while reducing costs and improving quality. In other words, this is a smart way to do business for both parties.

For supplier-company strategic alliances to be successful, managers must be able to communicate openly and honestly with the representatives of their supplier companies. Many companies actually have employees of suppliers working on their premises. This enables suppliers to better understand the company's needs and design better products and services. To better meet their needs, many companies actually provide suppliers with proprietary information.

Throughout this chapter, we have emphasized the importance of communication for managerial and organizational effectiveness, especially in a total quality management organization. In the final section of this chapter, we will make a few suggestions for developing personal communication skills. Practicing these skills will help you become a more valuable and productive member of whatever organization you join.

THINKING CRITICALLY

1. Have you ever been in an organization where employees were afraid to speak out or where there was an adversarial relationship between management and employees? How do you think this affects performance?
2. Based on what we have said throughout this book, why would you say that communication is vital to implementing TQM?

DEVELOP YOUR COMMUNICATION SKILLS

There are a number of areas to focus on and actions to take to develop your business communication skills. We review those here.

Speaking

A good communicator always speaks clearly and with authority. There are a number of ways to improve speaking skills. First, speakers should *never ramble.* Formal presentations and informal conversations should be concise and well organized. This happens when speakers know what they are talking about. Speakers should develop a habit of making mental outlines about what needs to be said and follow them. Second, speakers should *monitor and eliminate any annoying habits that occur while speaking.* Many people display nervous habits such as tapping a pencil or playing with a paperclip while speaking. Or they use annoying phrases, such as "you know." These habits distract listeners from focusing on messages and nonverbally create poor impressions of ideas. Third, speakers should constantly *maintain eye contact with their audiences.* People like to be looked at when they are being spoken to. It shows respect and demonstrates that the speaker is interested in their audiences' reactions to comments. Moreover, speakers are more likely to recognize frame-of-reference differences if they are maintaining eye contact. Fourth, speakers should seek to *vary the volume and pitch of their voices, and should show enthusiasm when speaking.* If their ideas are presented in monotones and with limited enthusiasm, many listeners will tune out the speakers and not listen to their ideas. After all, if speakers are not excited about their own ideas, how good can they be? In summary, speakers should know what they want to say, should respect their listeners, and should speak in a way that will engage their audiences.

Fostering Open Communication

A good communicator shares information with employees and superiors and is receptive to their ideas and inputs. There are a number of things that managers can do to encourage open communication. First, *communicate regularly and formally with other employees.* For example, establish a departmental bulletin board or hold weekly team meetings. Second, *hold occasional informal meetings* without an agenda or objectives. For example, arrange monthly departmental lunches at which the staff determines the topics of discussion. Third, be *receptive to negative information.* Since managers want employees to feel free to approach them with both bad and good news, managers need to make sure that they do not "shoot the messenger" who delivers bad news. If employees inform managers of impending problems with suppliers, managers shouldn't scream and yell at employees. Instead, managers should recognize that employees help by bringing problems to managers' attentions. Fourth, always *encourage others to express contrary viewpoints.* Some managers find it useful to appoint a formal "devil's advocate" in group meetings. This employee's role is to constantly challenge and offer alternative ideas to the group. Fifth, *take responsibility for keeping managers informed* by ensuring they receive copies of all important correspondences. Some managers have encouraged their superiors to meet with them weekly so that communication lines stay open and surprises are avoided.

Active Listening

Listening skills are also critical for effective communication. We must make sure that we spend the time and energy necessary to be good listeners. For example, *managers should not continue working while meeting with an employee.* The work will be distracting and will prevent the listener from focusing on the intended message of the sender. Listeners should also *pay close attention to nonverbal cues.* They should show speakers that they are interested in the speakers' ideas by leaning toward them, smiling, and nodding in a natural way. Listeners should also pay close attention to the nonverbal behaviors of speakers and attempt to determine their emotional states (e.g., are they angry, hurt, indifferent,

KEEPING COMMUNICATIONS FRESH AT GOODYEAR[18]

While all the programs we covered at the beginning of the chapter work well, they all can be improved as well. Loulan has established an employee Communications Council to monitor these programs. All employees, including Loulan, are accountable for specific communications, goals, and results. Managers, for example, must document meeting effectiveness by supplying councils with minutes, outcomes, and logs of who led each session. Work teams, for instance, can be judged on the quality of their bulletin boards—there should be no notices over ten days old.

These audits have helped the Lawton plant improve several of its communication practices, such as assuring that all questions raised at meetings are answered either at the meeting or later. This careful audit and documentation of communication techniques has helped Goodyear transfer these programs to other plants.

Jerry Putt, manager of the plant's component prep business center, says he uses all the company's programs. However, he also notes, "the most effective communication tool we have is the ability to walk up to people on the floor and talk to them without a lot of finger pointing."

---

or enthusiastic). Listeners should also use *probes and paraphrases to clarify the senders' intended messages.* One effective procedure is to rephrase the received message and seek verification that it matches the intended message.

Writing

Writing skills are also important for effective communication, especially since organizations are asking many managers to use their own personal computers to prepare correspondence and memos. One should recognize that *correct grammar, spelling, and punctuation are critical.* With the technology currently available, everyone can use correct grammar and spelling, and the failure to do so shows limited attention to detail. If managers are prone to making spelling errors, they should use a spell-checking program on a word processor. After the document is input, the computer program's spell-checker feature identifies misspelled words. Writers should note recurring mistakes, watch for them, and eliminate them in the future. Managers need to *write simply and avoid unnecessary details.* Most individuals will not read long letters or reports, so writing should be direct and to the point. *Visual aids should also be used in reports.* Charts and graphs are powerful tools and can concisely express complex ideas.

Recognize Frame of Reference Differences

Effective communicators are also flexible and alter their communications based on the needs of the receivers. As we noted earlier, individuals differ in terms of education, skills, experiences, and cultural values. Effective communicators actively attempt to *understand their audiences and alter their communications to match the needs of listeners.* It is the communicators' job to make sure their intended ideas are meaningful for their listeners. In some situations, this may mean that communicators need to speak slowly and with a low-level vocabulary. In another context, for example, it may be necessary for communicators to avoid mathematical phrases. Remember that it is the communicators' responsibility to alter their communications to match the listeners' frames of reference.

? THINKING CRITICALLY

1. Which communication skill—speaking, listening, or writing—do you think you will need to work hardest on as a manager? Why?
2. As a manager, which communication skill do you think is most important? Why? Of the guidelines presented in this part of the chapter, which will be most useful to you? Why?

SUMMARY

The Importance of Communication
- Communication underlies nearly every management task and responsibility, and open and honest communication is at the heart of healthy and productive corporate cultures.

A Model of Effective Communication
- The model of communication includes the following elements:
  - —Sender and receiver
  - —Intended message and its encoding
  - —Channel selection and transmission
  - —Decoding the received message
  - —Feedback loop

Channels of Communication
- Channels of communication vary in their abilities to transmit verbal and nonverbal parts of a message. This is important because the nonverbal aspect of our communications transmits up to 70 percent of meaning.

Direction of Communication
- Communication can be downward, from management to employees; upward, from employees to management; or horizontal, among peers in the same group or in different groups.
- It is the responsibility of managers to foster upward communication. This is necessary to keep in touch with the problems and progress of the company by hearing, in an honest way, from those doing the work.

- Horizontal communication is becoming more and more important as companies practicing TQM create cross-functional teams to plan and execute work processes.

Barriers to Effective Communication

- Information overload happens when managers receive more information than they can handle. In that situation, they attend to that which they feel is directly relevant to them and their work.

- Frames of reference are the filters through which information passes on the way to its interpretation. Managers must be sensitive to different frames of reference to make sure messages are correctly understood by their target audiences.

- Other barriers to communication include educational and experience differences, the use of jargon, status differences, and poor listening skills.

Communication and Organizational Structure

- Vertical communication is the norm in hierarchical organizations, where all communications, upward and downward, are supposed to go through the chain of command. This can stifle or slow down communication and cause messages to be misinterpreted.

- Horizontal organizations, characterized by flat structures and teams, make communication across functions a priority. Thus, employees from different areas understand their interdependence and optimize their performances together.

- Regardless of structure, every organization has a grapevine, through which information is informally communicated among employees. Healthy organizations, characterized by open and extensive communication through many channels, are less likely to be burdened by grapevines and the rumors they invite.

Communication and Technology

- The new electronic communication technologies are adding new channels for communication and enhancing accessibility of employees to one another. Such channels provide the ability to immediately share information with anyone who needs it.

Performance Feedback

- Managers need to understand how to provide feedback about individuals' and teams' performances in ways that will allow people to improve their contributions to organizations and remain motivated and committed to their companies.

Communication and Total Quality Management

- Nearly everything associated with TQM has to do with facilitating cooperation and successful interaction among employees. Communication skills help make this happen.

Developing Communication Skills

- There are a number of actions we can take to improve our communication skills in speaking, listening, writing, fostering an environment for the open exchange of ideas, and being sensitive to and valuing different frames of reference.

KEY TERMS

Active listening 486	Nonverbal communication 474
Channel 472	One-way communication 471
Communication fidelity 473	Open door policy 479
Decoding 473	Performance feedback 495
Downward communication 478	Receiver 472
Exception principle 482	Selective attention 482
Feedback loop 473	Sender 472
Frame of reference 482	Sender empathy 484
Grapevine 491	Subordinate evaluation systems 479
Horizontal communication 479	Talk-listen ratio 488
Information overload 482	Two-way communication 471
Information richness 475	Upward communication 479
Intended message 472	Verbal communication 474
Jargon 484	Voice mail 493

REVIEW QUESTIONS

1. What is the relationship between successful management practice and communication skills?
2. What are the elements of the communication model and how does each one affect communication?
3. What happens when nonverbal and verbal aspects of a message are not in agreement?
4. What kinds of messages are best sent in form letters or similar impersonal media? What kinds of situations are best handled with face-to-face communication?
5. Why is it a good idea for managers to cultivate upward communication? What special measures can a manager take to do this?
6. What organizational problem can occur when managers experience information overload?
7. Why is it important to be sensitive to frames of reference?
8. Why is active listening a valuable management skill?
9. What effect does organizational structure have on communications between managers and employees?

10. Why does an active grapevine indicate problems in an organization?
11. What aspects of communication in organizations is helped by technology? What problems does communication technology introduce into managing?
12. What kinds of feedback can help employees improve their performance? What type of feedback is unlikely to bring about improvement?
13. Why is open and complete communication of information so important in organizations that practice TQM?

EXPERIENTIAL EXERCISES

1. Identify individuals who will be giving speeches or talks at your school or in your community. These could be government leaders, industry leaders, ministers, student government leaders, etc. Carefully observe one of the presentations, paying particular attention to the quality of the communication. Specifically, be sure to consider the following issues:
   a. Did the speaker effectively use nonverbal behavior (e.g., eye contact, hand movements)?
   b. Did the presentation take into account the frame-of-reference of the audience? How?
   c. Did the speaker show enthusiasm in the presentation? How?
   d. Was the presentation targeted to the appropriate educational level?
   e. Were the ideas clearly organized?
   f. How could the presentation have been improved?
2. Presented below are a series of statements. Answer each one and see how effective a communicator you are. Rate each item on the following five-point scale.

1 = Never
2 = Seldom
3 = Occasionally
4 = Often
5 = Always

1 2 3 4 5	1. I express my ideas concisely.
1 2 3 4 5	2. I enunciate words very clearly.
1 2 3 4 5	3. I make eye contact when speaking.
1 2 3 4 5	4. I use proper grammar.
1 2 3 4 5	5. I use voice inflection to emphasize points.
1 2 3 4 5	6. I use hand movements to emphasize points.
1 2 3 4 5	7. I nod to show the speaker that I'm listening.
1 2 3 4 5	8. I outline in my mind what I'm trying to say and then stick to it.
1 2 3 4 5	9. I use the correct tenses of verbs while speaking.
1 2 3 4 5	10. I keep my speech very simple and avoid words with technical meanings.

1	2	3	4	5	11. I speak in short, concise sentences.
1	2	3	4	5	12. I use powerful action verbs for emphasis.
1	2	3	4	5	13. I encourage others to express their ideas to me.
1	2	3	4	5	14. I give my undivided attention to others when listening.
1	2	3	4	5	15. I am patient when others are speaking.
1	2	3	4	5	16. I pay attention to others' nonverbal behaviors.
1	2	3	4	5	17. I paraphrase others' communications to insure that I understand them.
1	2	3	4	5	18. Prior to making presentations, I anticipate the audience's needs.
1	2	3	4	5	19. I use visual aids effectively when making formal presentations.
1	2	3	4	5	20. I outline written correspondence before I write it

Scoring: Sum your responses to all items. If you scored 80 or higher, your communication should be effective. If you score between 60 and 79, your communication should be moderately effective and needs some improvement. If you scored below 60, you need to focus on improving your communication skills, as this lack of skill could be a problem when joining an organization.

CASE ANALYSIS AND APPLICATION
Communication at Honeywell's Automation and Control Plant[19]

Honeywell's Automation and Control plant, located in Phoenix, Arizona, makes industrial controllers that enable refineries, chemical plants, and paper mills around the globe to achieve world-class process control capabilities. In the late 1980s, the managers of this plant recognized that they were not going to be competitive in the future if they did not make some changes. They created and implemented a three-year plan designed to decrease defect rates, decrease the time from order of products to shipment, and decrease material costs. The goals of this plan included slashing defects tenfold and decreasing cycle times by a factor of five.

To be successful, this program needed the support of all 700 employees at the plant. On April 4, 1990, Gayle Pincus, vice president of manufacturing, closed the plant for a day and required all employees to attend an offsite meeting. While closing a plant was radical, and considered by some an extreme measure, she wanted every employee at this meeting. She spent six hours "trying to articulate the need for change—and then explaining what the change would be." She indicated that "the challenge was to make people feel good about their past success, and yet explain that, if we didn't change the way we manufacture, we won't deserve to be in business at some future time." The change she had in mind was called the world-class manufacturing (WCM) program. The kick off of this program was this one-day meeting.

Several changes were made in the plant after the meeting. The plant converted from an hourly to an all-salaried workforce. Employees were organized into teams and given the responsibility and authority for quality and continuous improvement their areas of the plant. Employees received training in group processes and communication methods. These empowered work teams took their responsibilities seriously, and, after a period of adjustment, they dramatically enhanced the quality and value of products.

Several problems occurred during the implementation of these teams. Cycle time did not decrease as expected. Teams made their areas run as well as possible but did not have broader views of the relations between their work and that of other teams or of the relations between their work and customers' needs. In other words, communication and cooperation was good within teams, but communication *between* teams was poor. Randy Harris, director of manufacturing, took three team leaders aside and said, "The three of you are going to be measured on how you perform as a product line, not as an individual team." Harris wanted to these leaders to understand that only when all teams saw their work in relation to what the other teams were doing could the company make real progress with this new approach. This meeting with Harris raised the consciousness of these leaders to the fact that there were problems and that communication and coordination among their teams was vital. After this meeting, the teams began to work better together, and cycle times for delivering finished products began to come down substantially.

Phoenix plant managers also recognized that they needed better communication with customers. They formed strong "Customer Alliance" partnerships and worked extensively with customers to figure out how their products were being used. They also asked their suppliers to understand their production processes and material needs. They benchmarked their processes against other leading companies in the world and borrowed the best management and work practices from these other companies. They even did "book reports" on popular business books and shared the information with each other.

A globally-oriented customer satisfaction organization (CSO) was also formed. It serves as a customer advocate and as a change agent. The CSO ensures that Honeywell's Phoenix operations will stay in touch with the needs of customers.

How successful have these changes been? Internal defect rates have been reduced by 70 percent. Customer rejects are down 57 percent. Investment in materials was trimmed 46 percent. Warranty costs have been reduced 30 percent. Manufacturing cycle time for products has been reduced by 89 percent. It is clear that the WCM program has been successful.

Discussion Questions

1. List all the places where effective communication techniques played a role in making these changes happen at Honeywell. In doing this, think about the company as a system that starts with suppliers delivering components that the company must then transform and deliver to customers.
2. Gayle Pincus could have communicated the changes she was looking for by memo, by company newsletter, or by small group discussions. These actions would have prevented closing the plant for a day. Why did she choose to hold a one-day meeting? How would the received message have differed through various communication channels she might have chosen?

3. Why do you think the teams failed to coordinate activities among themselves in order to achieve the goals of WCM without outside intervention?
4. What did shifting to an all-salaried workforce communicate to employees? What effect might this have had on communication among all employees in the company?

VIDEO CASE: COMBINING QUALITY MANAGEMENT AND SOCIAL RESPONSIBILITY
Inland Steel Industries Affirmative Action Focus Group

Five employees of Chicago's Inland Steel Industries were jointly honored for their creativity and initiative in promoting greater sensitivity to workplace diversity and multiculturalism and creating broader opportunities for minorities within their corporation.

When Steven Bowsher, an 18-year veteran of Inland Steel, was named general manager of sales for the Inland Steel Flat Products Co. in 1987, he was approached by a group of four middle-managers—Tyrone Banks, Vivian Cosey, Robert Hudson, and Scharlene Hurston—who related to him the difficulties minorities and women still faced in business and at Inland Steel. Bowsher met with the group and listened closely. He then embarked upon a process of self-education and reflection and attended an intensive workshop on race relations which acted as a true "conversion experience." Bowsher and the four employees together, as the Affirmative Action Focus Group, worked to initiate significant change in gender and race relations within Inland's sales operation.

Bowsher also took it upon himself to push for more substantive change throughout the organization. He required all 100 of his staff to attend the race relations workshop, and convinced Inland President Robert Darnall to attend as well. Darnall, also moved by the experience requested that other executives at Inland develop action plans for improving the utilization and development of their diverse workforce. In conjunction with Darnall's directive and the continuing influence of the Affirmative Action Focus Group, other Inland employees began to take courageous steps, as the original group had done, to communicate with supervisors and one another. Hispanic and women employees' focus groups formed to discuss and address needed action, and hundreds of management-level personnel from other departments began attending diversity workshops. A growing cultural momentum now engenders diversity and its benefits to the company.

The recruitment and promotion of women and minorities has become a significant priority within the organization, and non-management employees have begun participating in diversity training workshops. Over 800 Inland executives and employees have now attended. Thanks to Bowsher, Banks, Cosey, Hudson, and Hurston, Inland Steel Industries, though a company long committed to equal employment, has been energized to take increasingly aggressive action to improve opportunities for minorities and women.

Video Case Question

1. Describe what you perceive to be the deficiencies of the communication processes at Inland Steel prior to its use of focus groups.
2. Using the concepts presented in this chapter, discuss how these deficiencies were overcome.
3. What else would you do to improve communications and promote diversity at Inland Steel?

14. GROUP DYNAMICS AND TEAMBUILDING

"QUALITY TOGETHER" TEAMS AT METHODIST MEDICAL CENTER OF OAK RIDGE[1]

Methodist Medical Center of Oak Ridge, Tennessee began as a military hospital when it was established to serve the scientists and workers of the top secret Manhattan Project during World War II. In the 1950s, the hospital came under civilian control and began to serve several rural counties in eastern Tennessee. Methodist Medical Center is now a fully accredited, non-profit organization that has grown into a 301-bed facility, with 24 specialty departments, 140 physicians, 1,284 employees, and 200 volunteers.

Around 1986, as the health care market became increasingly competitive, Methodist Medical Center began to focus on a goal that it called "completing the circle of care." This goal called for providing all the health care services that are available in nearby Knoxville at an equal or greater level of quality. Four critical areas that Methodist Medical Center did not handle at the time were cardio-vascular surgery, neurosurgery, plastic surgery, and radiation oncology. Within two years of adopting its goal, the hospital had developed these departments. Because of a growing population in its five-county target market, the center is now seeking to increase its capacity to serve this population.

While growing and expanding, the management team at Methodist

Medical Center has tried a variety of methods to meet their objectives for delivering quality health care, including industrial engineering and quality circles. These efforts yielded disappointing results. However, once President and CEO Marshall Whisnant began to view his facility as a system with interrelated processes with the purpose of serving a variety of stakeholders, he undertook some new initiatives. His efforts focused on employee involvement, long-term thinking, pride of workmanship, and an emphasis on teamwork to get things done.

With the support of the board of directors and with professional assistance from QualPro, a local consulting firm, Methodist Medical Center launched an initiative called "Quality Together." This initiative was founded on the following four principles:

1. Traditional hospital quality assurance includes oversight committees who monitor the outcome of policies and sometimes procedures long after the events have taken place. By contrast, "Quality Together" moves assessment closer to those actually performing the procedures by forming teams of employees who use statistics to monitor work processes and make improvements on a continuous basis.

2. The number one rule is to satisfy customers, whether they be patients, physicians, corporate clients, or third-party payors. Measurements should be customer focused.

3. All events that affect customers should be regarded as outcomes of a system. Improvement opportunities exist in making the overall

system and its processes function better and *not* in the management of individuals or discrete events.

4. Managers are responsible for reducing inherent variation in the system, and local supervisors and the workforce are responsible for reducing variation caused by special events or problems that deviate from the normal system.

To bring these principles to life in "Quality Together," QualPro consultants led Methodist Medical Center through the following phases of implementation: Commitment, Initial Success, Implementation, and Self-Sufficiency.

- **Phase I: Commitment.** The consultants conducted a needs assessment of the organization using methods such as a survey of employee attitudes and perceptions. They then developed a plan for implementation and conducted training for the top management team. Finally, the managers selected several process improvement projects that met the criteria of being significant, doable, and relatable. *Significant* meant the results of the project must affect the company's bottom line or the level of customer satisfaction. *Doable* implied that success could be achieved within six months. *Relatable* meant the effects of the project would affect the employees and their work in a positive manner.

- **Phase II: Initial Success.** Teams of managers and other employees were assembled to work on the projects selected in Phase I. Team members attended workshops where QualPro personnel assisted them in applying an improvement process to these projects. The dramatic results achieved during this phase lent credibility to the process and provided a strong base for future improvement efforts.

- **Phase III: Implementation.** Quality improvement efforts then began to spread throughout the organization. All remaining managers and selected members of the workforce received training. The focus of this phase was on building teams. Improvement projects in Phase III were primarily interdepartmental.

- **Phase IV: Self-Sufficiency.** During Phase IV, the consultants of QualPro began to let go of the process. Methodist Medical Center employees took over the training responsibilities. Quality improvement and teamwork became more fully integrated throughout the organization.

The Quality Together initiative emphasizes the involvement of all employees throughout Methodist Medical Center. Department quality improvement teams are now the norm, and the center uses interdepartmental teams to work on short-term improvement projects.

Teamwork is key to running any organization. To effectively use teams, managers must understand the social dynamics that occur in groups of people. With this understanding, managers will be more capable of using methods and strategies for improving a team's effectiveness. This chapter reviews group dynamics and how to effectively use teams to accomplish the goals of the organization.

TEAMS IN ORGANIZATIONS

The word "teamwork" is becoming more common in business vocabulary as managers realize that it is only by employees conscientiously cooperating with one another that organizations can efficiently and effectively meet its goals. Methodist Medical Center has discovered that teams are very useful in accomplishing its goals to continuously improve the quality of its service to customers. However, there are many kinds of teams that an organization might use and many purposes that these teams might serve. Below we define what we mean by teams and discuss why it is important to study teams.

What Is a Team?

The popularity of teams has produced an outbreak of new terms and applications. There are several different types of teams, such as quality circles, quality improvement teams, process action teams, semiautonomous teams, self-directed teams, and so on. Each of these have different functions; however, there are general principles about group dynamics and teambuilding that apply to all of them.

First let's make a distinction between a group and a team. A **group** is *a number of people gathered together to form a recognizable unit or band.* For example, professional associations are groups, formed to represent their interests. The word team implies something more than just a group. It suggests that the people in the group work together in a coordinated fashion. Back in Chapter 3, we defined **team** as *a small group of people with complementary skills who are committed to a common purpose, set of performance goals, and approach, for which they hold themselves mutually accountable.*[2] A team is like a mini-organization within the larger company. It is small enough for each of its members to interact and communicate with all other members. At the General Motors Saturn plant, for example, cooperation and joint problem solving are an integral part of that division's philosophy. They implement these concepts throughout Saturn with every employee being part of a team. Through these teams, employees have opportunities for self-determination and participation in decision making. New Saturn employees are hired based in part on how well they will function in a team-based work environment.

The word **teamwork** refers to *the collaborative efforts of people to accomplish common objectives.* Teams are often composed of people from the same work group or unit, but they can come from several groups or departments, with the purpose of solving a problem or accomplishing a goal that affects all of the groups from which team members come. For example, Joe in the distribution department and Sandy in manufacturing may work together with others to reconfigure their production scheduling and shipping information systems. Joe and Sandy's efforts represent organizational teamwork in action. Teamwork is a necessity in any organization.

Let's review these terms again. A group is a collection of people recognized as a unit. Teamwork means collaboration among people to accomplish common objectives. A team puts these two ideas together as a group of people engaged in teamwork. So, a team is a specific application of the general concept of a group. (This means all teams are groups, but not all groups are teams). Finally, teams are a formal part of the organization, separate and distinct from any informal groups or teamwork that might exist in the organization.

The Role of Teams

The members of a **formal group** or a team *interact with one another in ways prescribed or authorized by the organization.* Teams are intentionally brought together to perform specific activities that contribute to transforming inputs (e.g., raw materials, parts, or ideas) into some output (e.g., a finished product or service). An early recognition of the value of teams came from Rensis Likert. In 1961 he described **hierarchical teams** *as groups composed of managers and their direct subordinates.*[3] Likert suggested that middle managers serve as linking pins in the organization by simultaneously being members of teams at two different levels of the hierarchy, as one of several subordinates in one team, and as a

Group A number of people gathered together to form a recognizable unit or band.

Teamwork The collaborative efforts of people to accomplish common objectives.

Formal group A group in which interaction among members takes place in ways prescribed or authorized by the organization.

Hierarchical teams Groups composed of managers and their direct subordinates.

superior in another team. As linking pins, these middle managers help to translate strategy (from the top of the organization) into operations (at the bottom of the organization). Exhibit 14-1 shows the linking pin function within the hierarchical organization. The three roles played by middle managers in these teams, as superior, peer, and subordinate, each have their own communication demands and power implications. It is a demanding position.

Likert argues that the work groups, shown within the triangles at each level, must function as a team, with lateral relations among all team members and not just vertical relations between superiors and subordinates. (For simplicity only three subordinates are indicated in the hierarchy). Likert asserts that in regular staff meetings, held by the group leader to solve problems and make decisions: "Any member of his staff can propose problems for consideration, but each problem is viewed from a company-wide [or group-wide] point of view. It is virtually impossible for one department to force a decision beneficial to it but detrimental to other departments if the group, as a whole, makes the decisions."

Unfortunately, the linking pin role of middle managers does not necessarily ensure that these hierarchical teams actually engage in teamwork and cooperatively work toward common objectives.[4] The reasons for the inadequacy of hierarchical management have been discussed in previous chapters, for example, in the chapters on organizational structure and design and organizational culture. In a nutshell, the problem is that specialized functions or departments tend to focus on their own work and ignore the horizontal flow of work systems and processes that serve customers. In other words, they act only as a for-

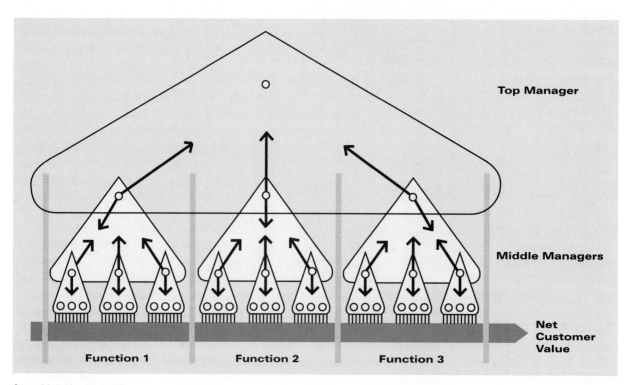

Source: Adapted from Likert, 1949

EXHIBIT 14-1   The hierarchy and traditional linking pin function of middle managers

mal work group and do not really function as a team, with a focus on cooperation across functions to deliver the best final output.

To remedy the deficiency of hierarchical teams, managers often put in place special roles for individuals, like an expeditor or coordinator. The role of these individuals is to solve problems that occur because of breakdowns in cooperation among groups (breakdowns that would be lessened with the implementation of formal teams). Managers sometimes even redesign the organization, for example, by introducing a matrix design, with special product or project managers who have responsibilities that cut across the functional and departmental boundaries. The problem with these approaches is that they are attempts to retain hierarchies and functional autonomy and still facilitate cooperation across functions. These two goals are fundamentally at odds with each other.

One of the soundest approaches for dealing with the deficiencies of hierarchical teams is to flatten organizational structures and focus on cross-functional cooperation, specifically with the establishment of teams. These teams will operate in both functional areas and cross-functionally to execute processes and achieve goals. Notice that Likert's idea of teams involves only superiors and their subordinates within their functional areas, which is only three ranks deep from top to bottom (the managers, their subordinates, their peers, and their superiors). By contrast, many companies today, like Ford and Motorola, are establishing teams which take a vertical slice of several ranks and different departments. They may include people from the assembly line with top managers and others from departments like engineering, design, and finance. The idea resonates with common sense: bring together the specific people from across the organization needed to accomplish a mission or purpose and give them the authority and resources they need to do this work.

One type of cross-functional team is a **committee,** *a relatively permanent team whose purpose is to deal with recurring problems or long-standing issues.* Another type of cross-functional team is a **task force,** *a team set up with a specific problem to solve or a project to complete* (see Chapter 3). Task forces usually disband after their purpose has been fulfilled. However, sometimes task forces are designed as permanent parts of an organization, such as when the task force is assigned ownership for a work process or system of the organization. For example, the *A Look at TQM in Action* box on page 518 describes how the simultaneous engineering teams at Cadillac work on decreasing the time needed to develop new designs and produce a high-quality car. We will discuss more about these specific applications of teams later in the chapter. For now, let's focus on the general roles played by teams in an organization.

Teams usually exist to perform one of three broad functions or roles in an organization: (1) production and service, (2) advice and involvement, and (3) projects and development.[5] We review each of these below. Exhibit 14-2 on page 516 summarizes the functions of each of these teams.

Production and Service. **Production and service teams** are what most people think of when they hear the term team. Such teams usually *consist of line employees working together to generate a product or service.* Examples include production crews, surgery teams, musical groups, and aircraft flight crews. Companies are finding that by giving workers more autonomy for managing themselves in teams they can yield positive business results. Levi Strauss & Company,

Committee A relatively permanent team whose purpose is to deal with recurring problems or long standing issues.

Production and service teams Teams consisting of line employees working together to generate a product or service.

EXHIBIT 14-2 Different types of organizational teams and their work

for example, discontinued its individual piece-rate system where employees were paid for sewing a piece of a pair of jeans (e.g., pocket or hem) and adopted an innovative manufacturing system in which teams of employees produce nearly the entire garment. The change has been slow and costly (all 880 employees each have undergone 75 hours of training), but it has affected the bottom line. It used to take 40 days to get an order from the shelves to the retailer; now it takes only 15 days.[6]

Production and service teams have also been used successfully at many other companies. One of the oldest team-based facilities in the United States is the Gaines Pet Food plant in Topeka, Kansas. Since its opening over 22 years ago, this plant has been managed by its employees. Under three different owners, Topeka has been first in labor productivity compared with other pet food plants within the company.[7] At Tektronix Inc., self-directed teams can produce as many products in three days as it once took an assembly line two weeks to produce. Productivity at Procter and Gamble's team-based plants average 30-40% higher than productivity at conventional plants. Similarly, Xerox Corporation's team-based plants perform about 30% above its non team-based plants.[8]

Advice and involvement teams Groups used to give employees an opportunity to contribute suggestions and participate in decision making.

Advice and Involvement. **Advice and involvement teams,** such as quality circles, are *used to give employees an opportunity to contribute suggestions and participate in decision making.* During the 1980s, these quality circles became popular and were used as vehicles to increase employee motivation and productivity. These teams are often composed of volunteers. Typically, they meet to identify ways to improve production processes or customer service. For example, at Shaklee Corporation's plant in Norman, Oklahoma, suggestions from quality circles have enabled employees to achieve the same volume of production at 40% of previous labor costs.[9] However, these teams can be ineffective if they are not given adequate time to meet and discuss ideas or if the scope of their activity is overly restricted.[10]

Projects and Development.   Most organizations have some activities or projects that require group cooperation across functional lines. **Project and development teams** *are formed to work on a specific project.* Once the project is complete, the team members return to their routine work activities or go to another project group. When a special production problem or project comes up at Harley-Davidson, for example, specific employees may be asked to join a project team. These teams work on solutions to major problems and disband when the project is completed or the problem solved.

The experimental division of Lockheed known as the "skunk works" is another excellent example of a project and development group. This group was first formed in 1943 to design, build, and prove the first jet fighter in the United States. After handpicking the best person in each functional skill, the group set out on its task. A scant 143 days after they began, a new jet-powered aircraft was flying. Over the years the skunk works has developed a reputation as a group that can tackle seemingly impossible projects. Since developing America's first jet, the skunk works have been used to jump-start the design and production of such aircraft as the high flying U-2 spy plane, the SR-71 (the world's fastest aircraft), and the stealth fighter.

Project and development teams Teams formed to work on a specific project.

Why Study Teams and Teamwork?

The history of American industry is filled with personal success stories—individuals who started with nothing and diligently created a very successful organization. John D. Rockefeller and Andrew Carnegie, for example, rose from low paying jobs to become two of the world's most influential men. Henry Ford made automobiles affordable for the masses with mass production of the Model T automobile. His production process made him a national hero. Today, the exploits of industrial heroes still captivate us. Steve Jobs built Apple Computer Company in his garage and became a multimillionaire before he turned thirty. After dropping out of college, Bill Gates created Microsoft, one of the most successful computer software companies, while becoming one of the richest people in America. Lee Iacocca, the son of immigrant parents, worked his way up to the presidency of Ford Motor Company, and then went on to become a business legend as chairman of Chrysler in the 1980s.

The accomplishments of these individuals, and many others, have inspired a countless number of entrepreneurs. They perpetuate the belief that hard work, self-reliance, and a strong desire to accomplish something is all that is needed to succeed. However, individual accomplishment is not sufficient in the business world. Even the heroes discussed above had to build effective teams within their organizations to achieve their goals.

Recent developments in the business environment make teamwork even more important. The globalization of product and service markets, the rapid introduction and equally rapid obsolescence of new technologies, changing demographic characteristics of the U.S. workforce, the availability of less expensive labor in developing countries, and the changing demands of consumers worldwide have altered the way businesses must operate to survive. To compete in such a globally competitive business environment companies will need powerful and determined leaders to inspire and lead employees toward a common vision and goals through teamwork.

Today's companies need to unleash the talents and creativity of all employees, not just a handful of clever entrepreneurs or charismatic CEOs. Competitive

TQM IN ACTION

SIMULTANEOUS ENGINEERING TEAMS AT CADILLAC

Simultaneous engineering means that people from throughout the organization are involved in all stages of engineering a new product. Engineers and designers do not create new models without getting input from the manufacturing people who must build it and the purchasing people who must buy the parts for it. Rather, they all work together to design and produce new products that will satisfy customers. Since Cadillac is always working on developing new car models and improved production processes, these teams continue indefinitely, although their membership and the focus of their work may change over time. Cadillac uses teams to integrate cross-functionally at several levels of their vehicle development efforts:

- *Vehicle Teams,* such as for the Eldorado,
- *Vehicle System Management Teams,* such as for the electrical system within the vehicles, and
- *Product Development and Improvement Teams,* such as for a particular switch within the electrical system.

Simultaneous Engineering teams help managers anticipate how changes in one functional area will affect the others, making it easier to prevent problems and bottlenecks, to determine in advance how to monitor and control production processes, and to identify opportunities for quality improvement. Cadillac also uses a steering committee to monitor and manage the Simultaneous Engineering process. In the early stages of its development, the steering committee served as liaison to communicate the process to the total organization. The steering committee's major responsibilities include:

- Review progress and provide leadership to continuously improve the Simultaneous Engineering process.
- Plan and implement Simultaneous Engineering policy and direction.
- Allocate resources to the product development process while balancing the total of all vehicle program requirements with the organization's capacity.
- Provide leadership for the development of effective communication processes between Simultaneous Engineering teams.
- Establish consistency in the processes and tools used by the Simultaneous Engineering teams where it is considered appropriate.
- Work with the vehicle teams and vehicle system management teams to identify and eliminate waste in the product program development process.

Simulaneous Engineering has been embraced at Cadillac because they have found it a more productive way to create new products. It is a dramatic change from their old ways of operating, but it also symbolizes how a team-based customer-focused approach can make big differences.

advantage will come from the continuous, incremental improvement of basic business processes. Organizations need to take advantage of the skills of employees at every level and in every kind of job. In this sense, companies of the future will grow or die based on their cultivation of the creativity and flexibility of all employees. However, companies cannot simply expect that the aggregation of a lot of individual accomplishments will make them successful. They must bring these accomplishments together so that *a team of employees working together can accomplish more than they could working separately,* a result known as **synergy.**

There has been much speculation about the virtues of teams—how important they are for organizations to compete with foreign competition, how organizations should make teams the basic organizational building block, how teams will be the salvation of American industry, and so on. Unfortunately, the words "teamwork" and "teams" are thrown about rather loosely, and they are in danger of becoming little more than management buzzwords. Many managers have no idea of what teams can do for an organization, and do not understand how to make them work.

Why should managers study the issues of group dynamics and teamwork? If understood and used correctly, teams can be a powerful tool for accomplishing an organization's goals, particularly those focusing on continuous improvement of processes and quality. If misunderstood or used incorrectly, teams can detract from the accomplishment of these goals. Not only can teams fail to achieve synergy, they can fail to live up to the potential that the individual members working alone should be able to achieve. These losses are due to poor social processes, lack of motivation, and lack of coordination.[11] Managers clearly have a lot to gain by improving their understanding of these critical issues.

Synergy The idea that a team of employees working together can accomplish more than they could working separately.

Levels of Autonomy in Teams

One concern managers have about teams is how much autonomy or self-direction they should have. **Autonomy** refers to *the amount of authority team members have to decide what to do and how to do it and the amount of responsibility group members have for group outcomes.* What is the best level of autonomy for teams? The answer is that there is no one best level. It depends on what the organization would like to accomplish and what the people are capable of doing. Below we describe three general levels of autonomy for teams.

Autonomy The amount of authority team members have to decide what to do and how to do it and the amount of responsibility group members have for group outcomes.

Management-Directed Teams.   At lower levels of autonomy, groups exist simply to share information. In a **management-directed team,** *the leader (usually a manager or supervisor) makes all of the important decisions, informs employees about the decisions made, and then clarifies what is required and responds to employee questions.* This type of interaction encourages conformance to organizational policies, procedures, and standards. It is best used in situations where work is standardized and requires little creativity. Conformance may be important, but it is constraining. It does not free team members up to engage in creative problem solving needed to come up with the innovations and improvements necessary to remain competitive in today's business world.

Management-directed team A team in which the leader (usually a manager or supervisor) makes all of the important decisions, informs employees about the decisions made, and then clarifies what is required and responds to employee questions.

Semi-Autonomous Teams.   The amount of autonomy increases with an increase in the use of joint problem-solving groups and more opportunity for self-direction. A **semi-autonomous team** is *somewhat on its own, but with management*

Semi-autonomous team A team somewhat on its own but with management retaining some control over team activities.

retaining some control over team activities. Managers may solicit team member suggestions for solving a problem or the team members may approach their managers with a problem and suggestions. This type of team is best characterized by two-way communication between team members and management. Managers may empower the team to make decisions and take action affecting important issues as long as the team keeps management informed as to what it is doing. Or the team may check with managers before taking action. This may be an intermediate step on the way to self-managed teams. Semi-autonomous teams foster cooperation between team members and management, commitment to the objectives and goals of the organization, and increasing accountability on the part of team members.

Self-Managed Teams. At the highest level of autonomy, a **self-managed team** *is given responsibility for planning, controlling, and improving a whole process and the authority to take appropriate measures to do so* (see Chapter 3). Team members are expected to manage their own processes, from receiving, through production, to shipping. As such, they have the authority to determine priorities, establish schedules, and control the quantity and quality of their work. Self-managed teams may also prepare their own budgets, keep their own records, solve minor technical problems, select their own new members, and even appraise their own performance, administer discipline when needed, and handle compensation. In essence, the team members perform many or all of the functions usually handled by managers or supervisors. Self-managed teams foster complete ownership of a process, product, or service, thereby increasing team member commitment and contribution to the team, cooperation with each other, and full accountability for team decisions and actions.

Self-managed teams do not guarantee business success. Like any other activities in an organization, this must be done so as to enhance the organization's ability to achieve its goals. Self-managed teams can be made more successful by adhering to the following suggestions:

- *Select Team Players.* Selection of team members must be fair and efficient. The selection system should be able to identify the candidates who are most likely to succeed in a team setting, however, the candidates should also feel that the system assessed them accurately. This can be accomplished through the use of simulations, activities that closely resemble the actual job procedures. Realistic job previews can also discourage employees who decide that a team environment is not for them.

- *Train for Success.* Team members should be multiskilled to allow for flexibility in job rotation. Heavy emphasis in technical training is important. Team members may spend as much as 20% of their time in training during the first year of team operation. Training is essential to improve job skills, social interaction skills, and quality improvement skills.

- *Initiate Leadership Transitions.* Since traditional managers often fear that introducing self-managing teams will eliminate their positions, they may interfere with the transition. It must be made clear what a manager's new role will be. It is up to the organization to determine these new roles. Often, a manager will serve as a contact person with customers and suppliers, help gain access to resources, or even fill in when team members are absent.

TQM IN ACTION

EDY'S GRAND ICE CREAM AND SELF-MANAGED TEAMS[12]

"To continually reach the level of customer delight that keeps the company on top in this fiercely competitive industry," writes the author of a profile on this company, "every Edy's associate manages—and is held accountable for—short-term, bottom line business results." In fact, the Fort Wayne, Indiana company is completely run by self-managed teams. One associate, Wanda Dabe, explains the cross-functional team responsibility this way: "We have the teams set up so that members can identify with their product from the minute that it comes from raw receiving and made into mix, all the way until it ships out the back door." A typical "business unit" team consists of four or five people who are responsible for making certain types of ice cream and are responsible for everything from sanitation checks to meeting individual business goals to internal scheduling to training and career development.

Kirk Raymond, the plant manager, mainly sees his role as a boundary protector between the various business units and as a facilitator of the teams. While he has an overall budget, it is the teams who decide how it will be allocated, even to the determination of pay rates. The understanding at the plant is that team members will set fair rates that will allow the company to be profitable and thrive, thus ensuring their jobs well into the future.

There is great emphasis on continuous improvement of processes by all teams as well as the maintenance of careful performance measures so everyone always knows how well they are doing and where the opportunities to improve productivity might be. One of the company's management "Grooves" (or philosophies) is that "mistakes are opportunities for organizational learning." They call this "failing forward." Another emphasis is on training, and the average annual training days per employee is 18. They have developed a pay for skills compensation system that rewards employees for improving their skills and their abilities to add value to the company.

The company was not always managed this way. However, once the parent company, Dreyers, adopted the TQM approach, teams just evolved at Edy's to the point where team associates know what needs to be done, and they do it.

- *Reward Team Performance.* Team members should be paid for job depth, the amount of job knowledge and skill in a specific area, and job breadth, knowledge and skill in a lot of different areas. Bonus programs should reward team performance. The bonus may be divided equally among the team members or they may decide how to distribute the bonus.[13]

? THINKING CRITICALLY

1. Have you ever been a member of a hierarchical team? Did you feel a sense of teamwork, or was the emphasis on individual performance? Do you think a focus on individual performance is the best way to optimize the contributions of employees? Why or why not?
2. Based on what you have read here and your experience, what is the difference between a hierarchical team and a cross-functional team? Which type of team makes the most sense to you to get work done and why?

3. What would you say is the relationship between technology for delivering information throughout an organization and the development of self-managed teams?

4. Why do you think motivation increased at Edy's Ice Cream with the implementation of self-managed teams?

AT&T Transmission Systems: A Journey Well Begun

IMPLEMENTING TEAMS

Implementing teams is difficult because there is no objective how-to book to follow. No two teams are alike, and what may work for one, may not work for another. Similarly, what works well in one organization may be a disaster in another. Despite the difficulty in implementing teams, there are a number of general lessons that have been distilled from the successful and unsuccessful efforts of many companies.

General Lessons on Implementing Teams

Each of these lessons tells us something that is necessary, but not sufficient for implementing teams, and nothing can guarantee their success. The actions of managers before and after a change to a team-based work system are just as important as the formation of the team itself. Managers must take actions to address the following factors: culture, honesty, open communication, and tolerance. In reviewing these ideas, note that they are not unique to teams and organizations. Similar points were discussed in Chapter 11 on leadership, and these factors play a role in all successful human endeavors.

- *Culture.* One very important lesson is for management to create the appropriate culture before teams are even attempted. Like Cadillac and Edy's Ice Cream, employees must not only be encouraged to join teams, they must also be encouraged to participate in the design and implementation of teams. Employees must feel that they can make a contribution to the organization by being a member of a team. They must also feel that their suggestions and ideas will be heard, valued, and acted upon.

- *Honesty.* Teams should be implemented to help employees improve the quality of the organization's products and services. Teams should *not* be used for hidden purposes, such as downsizing or to lay off employees, under the guise of quality improvement. If downsizing is an objective, then managers must be up front about it. The employees should not end up blaming the teamwork approach for the loss of jobs. Ideally, no employees should lose their jobs because of a shift to a team-based approach. This is likely to be a tough issue in overgrown bureaucratic organizations that are streamlining and changing to a team-based approach.

- *Open Communication.* The management of an organization in the process of implementing teams must do everything possible to open downward and upward lines of communication. There must be a continuous stream of information flowing to the employees from management and to management from employees. This communication must be open and honest and must be present every step of the way. People should not fear reprisal for any facts or opinions that are revealed. If fear exists, people will repress valuable information. When it began to implement teams, the Chevron Chemical Company moved to alleviate the concerns of supervisors by getting them involved in defining their roles in the new organization. The supervisors wrote up a list of duties they wanted to keep performing and this information was used in the design and implementation of the teams. The worst mistake Chevron could have made would have been to use that information as a way to eliminate supervisors' jobs without providing alternate work. If a layoff is unavoidable, the company is better off to do it before implementing teams, then provide job security to remaining employees and engage them in crafting a new team-based approach for the future.

- *Tolerance:* In addition, it is important not to focus on mistakes. It is human nature to want to point fingers and assign blame, but managers and employees should encourage each other to learn from mistakes (many of which will occur during the process) and keep looking forward. The practice of TQM, of which teams and teamwork are an important part, teaches us not to blame people but processes, and then work to fix processes, including those processes involved in forming teams in the first place.

Individualism Versus Teamwork

Many companies are trying to use teams to achieve synergy. But, unfortunately, many of these companies are still geared around the individual as the primary unit of interest. They are looking for stars, and human resources systems are often designed to identify and reward those individuals. Selection systems, for example, are designed to identify personal qualities in individuals that predict performance on a particular job or setting. Training programs are developed to provide employees with the specific knowledge, skills, and abilities necessary for effective job performance. The tradition of annually evaluating individual job performance assumes that performance is mostly determined by differences among employees, and that these differences can be accurately measured. In addition, compensation systems often rely on individual merit (usually identified in the annual performance evaluation) as the basis for salary and promotion decisions.

Recently, the assumptions underlying these individually based approaches have been challenged by the systems view and Total Quality Management. TQM requires managers to attend to the influence of factors that are beyond the control of any individual employee. As discussed in Chapter 3 on the principles of TQM, system factors such as equipment, materials, and work processes account for much of the variation in individual performance. If a company wants to improve performance of employees who are part of the system, managers must pay attention to many different things that influence how well the system with all its components functions as a unit to deliver output.

The move to teams is an acknowledgment of the systems view of organizations. It is the recognition that management approaches that focus on individuals undermine the productivity of the entire system. Such programs reward people for optimizing their own performances regardless of whether what any individual does is in the best interest of the entire company. For example, companies often push salespeople to write orders even when the company is not able to deliver what the salesperson promises. Nevertheless, if these salespeople make their goals or quotas, they are rewarded. In the meantime, the company does not deliver, causing problems with the customer and lost business in the future.

The move to teams and process management creates an environment and an approach to working together that seeks to optimize the performance of all parts of the system. When sales and marketing are part of the team with manufacturing and engineering, salespeople do not promise what cannot be delivered, and manufacturing and engineering better appreciate what they need to do to satisfy customers. There is synergy to the benefit of all. However, before managers and employees working together can design and implement teams, they must first understand the characteristics of an organization's technical and social systems.

Implementing Teams: Understanding Organizational Needs

To make best use of teams to execute processes, managers must understand their organization, its potential capabilities, and the environment in which it operates. From studying and analyzing the organization, managers and employees working together can come up with a plan for the best way to use and implement teams to get work done. This study and analysis is a three step process best undertaken by a team of managers and employees rather than a team of managers working apart from employees. When employees are involved right from the beginning, they gain ownership of the adopted plan and have a personal commitment to its success.

The first step is to conduct an organizational/environmental analysis. After this, managers should conduct a task/technical system analysis, followed by a person/social system analysis. Once they have gathered and analyzed this information, they can determine the feasibility and type of teams needed. If teams are feasible, their design and implementation can follow. Everyone in the organization should have the opportunity to review the data at each step of the process, discuss the data, and make recommendations.

Organization/environment analysis A process for undertaking a system-wide examination of components that determine where and when a team-based approach will produce the desired effect in the organization.

Organization/Environment Analysis.   The purpose of the **organization/environment analysis** is *to examine system-wide components that determine where and when a team-based approach will produce the desired effect in the organization.* This level of analysis is concerned with factors within the organization as well as factors in the organization's environment that may affect team functioning. The goal is to understand the strategic direction of the organization and the various forces acting on it. The organization/environment analysis should provide information regarding the organization's mission, fundamental processes, input and output, boundary definitions and conditions, any existing problems within the organization or with suppliers or customers, and an in-depth stakeholder analysis.

Task/technical system analysis A process for identifying the tasks being performed by employees and the equipment and machinery they are using to accomplish their tasks.

Task/Technical System Analysis.   The **task/technical system analysis** is concerned with *identifying the tasks being performed by employees and the equipment and machinery they are using to accomplish their tasks.* This level of analysis identifies not only the types of work activities performed by employees, but also the conditions under which these jobs are performed. Information collected in this phase includes: what types of tasks do employees perform on a regular basis; what tasks do employees perform infrequently or in an emergency situation; to what extent do employees rely on machinery to perform work; what type of equipment do employees have to be familiar with; what type of skills are required to perform a particular job or operate a piece of machinery, and similar issues. This analysis is also concerned with identifying anticipated technological advances that may alter the manner in which work is performed.

TEAMS AND TURNAROUND AT CHRYSLER

Robert J. Dika is manager of platform quality and reliability planning at Chrysler Corporation. He writes about changes at Chrysler that have allowed the company to become the lowest price producer of cars in the U.S.:

A LOOK AT

MANAGERS IN ACTION

After Lee Iacocca turned Chrysler around in the early 1980s with a focus on cost cutting and strong decision making, helped also by the success of the minivan it created, the company faced another slump in the late 1980s. Corporate profits were starting to erode as was the confidence of Wall Street. The company's products were starting to age, and the strong top-down management approach that served the company well during the earlier crisis seemed to have reached a barrier. The company wasn't continuing to improve at a rate necessary to compete with increasingly fierce competition and the fast strengthening domestics. Some viewed the nature of the company as too structured, inflexible, and even bureaucratic. There seemed to be limits to further improving the way the company worked.

Then the company changed the rules again. Two principal events fueled this change: the reorganization into platform teams and the opening of the new Chrysler Technology Center (CTC in Auburn Hills, Michigan). These two events became the drivers for a cultural shift within the company from functional control to cross-functional teamwork.

Chrysler divided itself into four smaller, more nimble operating groups: Small Car, Large Car, Minivan, and Jeep/Truck. Along with this came a new process for designing and developing new cars. Each platform was free to establish new rules and more effective relationships. Because they were smaller, communication was easier. In the team environment, people were able to understand the ways and requirements of their counterparts in other functions resulting in more cooperation and better, faster decisions.

Within each platform, small teams became the norm. Teams were formed around product systems, manufacturing technologies, and business practices. People were meeting often, and those with the technical expertise had the responsibility and authority to make decisions that in the past had been made by top management. Since these were good decisions, top brass learned not to interfere, but to negotiate with working-level teams. The genie was let out of the bottle, and people were encouraged to be creative and were able to see their ideas become reality.

On the first day people moved into CTC, the effect of co-location of people serving on cross-functional platform teams was felt throughout the company. The new facility brought about a radical improvement in the quality of people's worklives and boosted employees' sense of pride in working for Chrysler. It allowed people who formerly rarely saw one another to have to see each other all the time and work closely together. People started just dropping in to ask a question or work out a problem. Since prototype-building operations and a pilot manufacturing plant were on-site, people from all disciplines could easily walk down to the shop to see what was going on, and problems that before took a long time to be resolved were taken care of quickly. Working at CTC showed people who understood the principle of teamwork just how powerful it was.

Today at Chrysler, leaders are assuming the role of coach as well as champion. Managers are reevaluating themselves and their relationship to the teams that they sponsor. We are working to find better ways of bringing out the best in our teams and our people, and trust that this will thrust the company into the future. Chrysler believes in teams. We are seeing the results of operating in a team mode, and there is no turning back.

Person/social systems analysis A process to critically analyze the characteristics of the workforce within the organization.

Person/Social Systems Analysis. The purpose of the **person/social systems analysis** is to *critically analyze the characteristics of the workforce*. The emphasis should not be used in determining what tasks employees are performing but rather in assessing the social interactions, norms, and patterns of behavior in the organization. One way of approaching this analysis is to interview all employees in the organization or, if that is impossible, to interview focus groups of individuals who are representative of the employee population. Information the team should collect in this phase includes details about the degree to which employees are in contact with their supervisors, who makes important decisions, who makes routine decisions, who is responsible for obtaining resources for employees, how self-reliant are the individual employees, and so on. The idea is to understand relationships among employees and managers, communications, and, in general, how people get along and work together in the organization.

The information generated in this study and analysis provides managers and all employees with a background for figuring out what kinds of teams are needed to do the company's work and how they can best implement teams. It helps them understand what changes need to happen culturally and structurally. It helps them understand what training may be necessary. Reorganizing around teams is not easy, but it is necessary if organizations want to become more efficient and effective in executing the processes by which organizational work gets done.

Team Design and Implementation

An organization structure based on teams is generally designed and centered around processes, for example logistics or product development or order generation and fulfillment, and have key goals such as reducing cycle time or costs or both.[14] Exhibit 14-3 illustrates a team-based structure. When moving to teams, planners must identify key processes, who is involved in their execution, how these processes contribute to delivery of final output, and what are the indicators of successful performance. Then changes in organizational structure, perhaps culture, support systems, compensation, and training need to happen to get the team approach underway.

Moving to teams is a major endeavor for any organization. Implementing teams is a part of adopting TQM, and it is not something a company simply tries while maintaining its traditional hierarchy and chain of command. TQM is about the efficient and effective management of systems. Traditional hierarchical management is about maintaining order and structure and doling out information and resources as members of the hierarchy feel is appropriate. Organizations cannot move to TQM with its emphasis on teams and process management while maintaining a traditional hierarchy. The two are not compatible with one another. When a company goes to TQM and teams, it changes everything else at the same time. In fact, it reduces the role of the hierarchy. When teams have access to information as needed and the authority to do what is necessary to meet their goals for executing their processes, the traditional hierarchy loses much of its purpose.

In making the move to a structure based on teams, most companies have to take it slow and give employees plenty of opportunity to shape the new teams. Issues to be resolved include: how many people will be on a team, how will these employees be selected, what training will team members receive, where in the organization should teams be implemented first, how much autonomy will

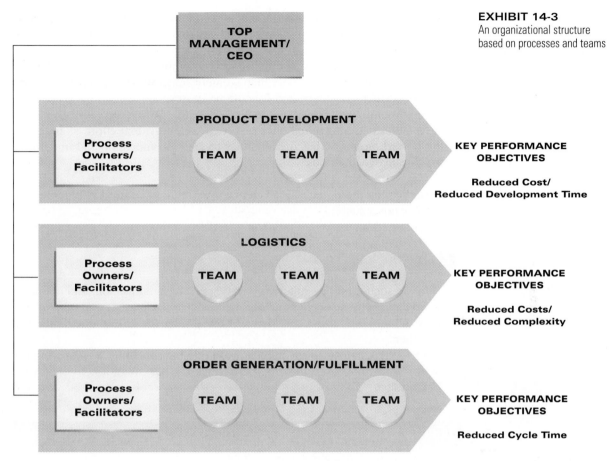

EXHIBIT 14-3
An organizational structure based on processes and teams

Source: Adapted from Thomas A. Stewart, "The Search for the Organization of Tomorrow," Fortune, May 18, 1992, p. 94.

team members have, how will the teams be compensated, how will team performance be measured, and who will provide guidance and direction for production scheduling and day-to-day operational issues? Once these issues are resolved, teams should be implemented slowly and carefully, allowing for the "bugs" and problems to be resolved before any more teams are implemented.

There are many different ways to design and implement a team-based organization. However, there are several key issues to address in doing this:

1. Managers should involve employees in developing the approach from the very beginning of the process. Employees should be encouraged to offer their suggestions regarding how to go about team design and implementation, and they should be allowed to express their opinions and concerns about the teams once the teams are in place.
2. Frequent, honest communication from everybody involved is mandatory. Management should not try to hide any relevant information from employees. The same is true for employees, they should not hide any reservations about the impending change.
3. Teams should be organized around processes rather than functions, such as those mentioned earlier—product development, materials processing, and

order/delivery. The reason for this is simple: It is by processes that input moves through the organization on the way to transformation and delivery as output to customers.

4. There has to be substantial training to help employees make the transition, including training on process management, meeting skills, and how teams work together to manage and execute processes.

5. Compensation programs have to reward skills improvement and team success rather than individual efforts. A focus on individual effort, as indicated by reward programs, has the tendency to create competition and undermine cooperative team efforts.

By addressing these issues, managers are more likely to make the implementation of teams a success.

? THINKING CRITICALLY

1. Why do such things as culture, honesty, open communication, and tolerance keep coming up again and again as necessary to facilitate organizational success? What is the relationship between these values and people working well together?

2. Do you think individualism and teamwork are incompatible? Why or why not?

3. Why did the move to teamwork seem to play an important role in the revival of Chrysler?

GROUP DYNAMICS

To make teams effective, managers must understand the way they work. There are many social processes managers need to understand because these processes can interfere with the ability of the team to properly complete its tasks. Behavioral scientists have studied the topic of group dynamics for many years and have learned ways to make teams more effective. Below we discuss some general principles about group dynamics that apply to almost every type of group, including formal teams and informal groups.

Group Development and Maturity

Once a group forms, its members must resolve a variety of issues before it can function effectively. Members must work out personal differences, find strengths on which to build, balance other work and non-work commitments, and learn how to improve business processes. Dealing with these internal group needs is important for accomplishing the group's task. Yet too often group members underestimate the need for developing themselves as teams and end up spending most of their time struggling through group meetings that seem to lead nowhere or bungling their way through group projects. Having an understanding of the typical ways in which groups evolve and the time and effort required to reach effective maturity can aid members in dealing with their frustrations.

Research on group development suggests there are four *stages of group development:* forming, storming, norming, and performing.[15] In the *forming* stage, group members orient themselves to the group and explore the boundaries of acceptable group behavior. For most people, it takes time to adjust from focusing just on their own tasks to being a member of a team where members have mutual responsibility for task completion. During this time, very little work is accomplished because team members are distracted by the excitement, anticipation, and optimism of doing something new. However, members may also feel tentative, suspicious, and anxious about the job ahead and what is required of them.

The second stage, *storming,* is usually the most difficult stage for a developing group. As the members begin to understand the task, they may realize that it is very different and much more difficult than they imagined. At this point, it is normal for members to become blameful and testy. Some members may even panic. When this uncertainty about the group creeps in, members typically fall back on their personal and professional experiences and try to solve the problems as individuals, resisting any collaboration with other team members. Again, these pressures on the group may cause the members to make little progress towards its objective, but they are beginning to understand one another.

In the *norming* stage, group members reconcile differences among themselves and finally get used to working together. They accept each other, their roles and group rules or norms. As this happens, the group member's initial resistance fades away and competitive relationships become more cooperative, with members beginning to help each other. Because members can now concentrate on the group's objective, significant progress is made.

By the *performing* stage, the group members have reconciled most of their differences and expectations. As they become more comfortable with each other, they discover and accept each other's strengths and weaknesses. And as they better understand the objective and what is expected of them, they are better able to work in concert as an effective work unit. You can tell a group has reached this stage because it starts to get a lot of work done, quickly and efficiently, without expending too much time addressing social issues.

The duration and intensity of these stages vary from group to group. Sometimes the first three stages can be achieved in one or two meetings with very little effort. Other times it may take several months and excruciating effort. The speed with which a group matures depends on the personalities and experiences of the members, as well as their social compatibility and the level of support received from the organization. Leadership in guiding the group through its development is also important.

Another view of group development suggests that rather than progressing through a universal series of stages, each group may go through a unique sequence of activities to accomplish a task.[16] According to this view, groups begin by establishing their own framework to follow, a kind of roadmap developed by the group to keep them on track toward the objective. Further, most groups do not make much progress on their task until the middle of their lives, at which time groups undergo a "transition." Similar in some ways to a midlife crisis, these midpoint transitions are characterized by a maturity and mutual understanding by members and a clear sense of their roles and how to work together. They understand how to use resources, take advantage of new technology and information, and at this point make dramatic strides in the execution of their work. After the midpoint transitions, the group remains focused on the completion of its tasks. These views of group development can help managers understand some of the perplexing events that often occur in group dynamics. The important point is that managers should be aware of this and be patient, knowing that these social processes are quite natural and not uncommon.

TQM IN ACTION

XEL LEARNS TEAMWORK REQUIRES WORK[17]

XEL Communications is a small firm with 180 employees that supplies circuit boards to companies like its former parent GTE as well as several of the Baby Bell companies. To succeed against large competitors like Northern Telecom and AT&T, owner and CEO Bill Sanko decided his company needed to have quick turnaround on orders and be more responsive to customers. Stated Sanko: "We needed everybody in the building thinking and contributing about how we could better satisfy our customers, how we could improve quality, how we could reduce costs."

Sanko developed a vision statement to help bring this about. Part of that statement included the phrase, "we will be an organization where each of us is a self-manager." From this goal, VP of manufacturing, John Puckett, designed the plan for cellular production, with each cell staffed by teams who could manufacture several different circuit boards. That was in 1988.

By 1993, the company had completely rebuilt itself around teams and was being cited as a role model by dozens of other companies and was featured in a video on team-based management produced by the Association for Manufacturing Excellence. Visitors at the plant would see charts on the wall tracking attendance, on-time deliveries, and other measures of team performance. After five years of self-managed teams, cost of assembly has dropped 25 percent, inventory has been cut by half, and quality level has improved by 30 percent. And the all-important cycle time, the amount of time from start of production to delivery of final product, had dropped from eight weeks to four days. Still, XEL has learned that team-based structures also make special demands on a company and its management, and they have learned several lessons that any company going in this direction should be aware of. These include:

- *Hiring and training new people is more difficult in a team-based environment.* The problem is that team members want to have a say in who gets hired, and yet they have little time to do the interviewing. The company also needs to find people not only with technical abilities but who also feel comfortable working on a team rather than on their own. It also takes a while for a new person to bond with other team members and learn his or her role. Because a team's success depends on everyone performing, there can be extra pressure on new people.

- *Teambuilding does not flow neatly from one stage to the next.* While the forming, storming, etc. model is useful, it does not always hold true. Sometimes teams slip back, and this can have consequences throughout the company. At XEL, a stockroom team broke down. Puckett received complaints from customers and other teams, and he found out certain members were cheating on their time cards. Puckett had to intervene and actually disbanded teams in this part of the company, bringing in a supervisor to take over. His goal, though, was to work himself out of job by reestablishing the best practices demonstrated by another successful manufacturing team.

- *Managers need skills no MBA program ever taught them.* With self-managing teams, managers must know when to intervene and when to back off, as shown by performance indicators. Three skills Puckett has discovered are what he calls (1) *diplomacy,* the job of managing relations among teams, which can get sticky sometimes; (2) *monkey managing,* the fine art of not allowing someone else's monkey, or problem, to jump onto your back; and (3) *innovation triage,* which means that managers must encourage and reward innovation but make sure teams don't go too far and adversely affect other parts of the plant.

- *Employees need skills they never had before.* Employees need to learn skills such as statistical process control, as well as learn how to do several of the team's jobs, so they can fill in for one another and make sure there is no breakdown in production. Employees also need a kind of attitude that makes them care about the quality of their work and the motivation to set their own priorities rather than waiting for someone else to do it for them.

- *Compensation and performance reviews have to change.* Pay can no longer be based on individual performance. XEL created a reward program based on the acquisition of skills, the performance of the team and profit sharing. The company also went to a peer review program where team members evaluate one another in terms of their contribution to the team's performance.

The move to teams at XEL has affected how all employees and managers think about their jobs. One team member sums it up this way: "Some of the new hires, it blows their minds when they come in. Most people are used to these structured deals, where you do your little piece and you send it on, and you don't care what happens to it after that. Here you're involved in the whole picture. You have the mind-set: OK, this is the flow—and this is what we have to do to accomplish that."

Factors Influencing Group Effectiveness

To discuss factors that influence group effectiveness, one must first define what it means for a group to be effective. For purposes of this chapter, we will define effectiveness in terms of group performance and group viability.[18] **Performance** refers to *acceptability of output (e.g., products, services, information, or decisions) to customers within or outside the organization.* **Viability** refers to *the group members' satisfaction with the group, their active participation in its activities, and their desire to continue functioning as a group.*

By considering both performance and viability, this definition goes beyond the typical criteria of effectiveness that focus exclusively on output (such as quality and quantity of output) or member reactions to the group (such as satisfaction). By itself, the criteria of performance fails to consider the possibility that while a group may be producing a high-quality output, conflict or interpersonal problems may be preventing group members from wanting to continue working together, and this may eventually have a detrimental effect on performance.

As team members interact with one another and acquire knowledge of and experience in team processes, the team develops a set of characteristics that enable it to function more effectively as a group. Some of these characteristics (e.g., individual roles) are properties of the individual team members. The others (e.g., norms, cohesiveness, goals) are properties of the team itself.

Individual Roles.   As defined in Chapter 1, a role is a pattern or set of behaviors expected to be performed by someone occupying a particular position. There are formal roles prescribed by the official content of a job description, and there are informal roles, the expected behaviors that are not necessarily documented or measured. Everyone has both formal and informal roles to play in an organization.

In addition to their organizational roles, group members also have roles within their groups. In organizations that are organized around processes and teams, these group roles and organization roles tend to meld together. Every group needs a leader to facilitate group activity, organize resources, and direct group

Performance Acceptability of output (e.g., products, services, information, or decisions) to customers within or outside the organization.

Viability A term describing the group members' satisfaction with the group, their active participation in its activities, and their desire to continue functioning as a group.

efforts. Without a leader the group may not have the focus to accomplish its objective. It does not really matter who plays this role, as long as it gets fulfilled by someone. In fact, the role of leadership often rotates from one group member to another as the team moves from one task to another. Groups may also need a devil's advocate to challenge prevailing thinking and to encourage creative thinking and problem solving. In meetings and in the execution of specific projects, groups may need a timekeeper—someone to keep the group aware of time constraints or deadlines. There are many other roles group members can play. Group effectiveness will depend on the degree to which every group member understands their roles. The most effective groups are those that are able to assign roles that take advantage of each member's talents and abilities.

Group Norms.   Underlying all human behavior are the expectations people in a group have of each other. A **norm** is *an unwritten standard of behavior expected of group members; it explains what behaviors are appropriate and inappropriate.* These expectations guide behavior. Consider a college graduate just hired by an organization as a manager. Not only must this individual perform the multitude of roles normally performed by someone in this position, but he or she may also be pressured to dress, talk, and act like other managers in the organization. If managers in the organization dress formally, the manager who fails to do so may not be fulfilling the expected norm.

Norms develop over time through the interaction of group members and the reinforcement of behaviors by the group. For example, group members may act to encourage certain behaviors (e.g., production standards) by reinforcing a specific level of production. Group members may also discourage certain behaviors (e.g., arriving late for work) by responding negatively to their occurrences.

Norms are pervasive and cover many areas of work life (e.g., attendance, performance, innovation, interpersonal relations, dress, and loyalty). Ideally, a group will reinforce norms that facilitate its survival, help predict the behavior of group members, prevent embarrassing interpersonal problems from arising, express the group's central values, and clarify the group's identity.[19] Groups will be effective to the extent that such norms are agreed on by all members.

Group Cohesiveness.   **Cohesion** is *the degree of attraction members have for the group and for each other.* Cohesiveness is identified by friendliness, congeniality, loyalty to the group, a feeling of responsibility for group efforts, and a willingness to defend the group against attack. Cohesive work groups are powerful entities, but they can be a double-edged sword—they can be greatly helpful or devastating. A highly cohesive work group whose goals are in agreement with organizational objectives can use its strength to increase productivity. However, cohesive groups can make stupid mistakes that have catastrophic results through a process called *groupthink,* which is discussed below. Consider some examples from history. Commanders in Hawaii ignored information that could have helped them anticipate the Japanese attack on Pearl Harbor, which devastated the United States' Pacific fleet. President Kennedy's advisors were reluctant to express misgivings about the Bay of Pigs invasion of Cuba, which ended in a fiasco. NASA officials discounted information that could have aborted the fatal launch of the space shuttle Challenger in January, 1986. In all three cases, the people in charge were aware of the potential dangers. However, their highly cohesive

Norm An unwritten standard of behavior expected of group members; it explains what behaviors are appropriate and inappropriate.

Cohesion The degree of attraction members have for the group and for each other.

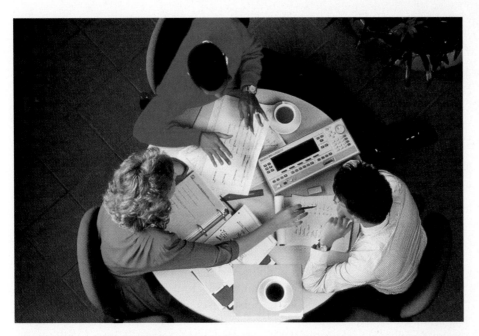

Small group size encourages friendliness, commitment, and responsibility for group success while ensuring that each member's view will be discussed.

groups exhibited a variety of dysfunctional decision-making symptoms that served to protect an apparent consensus, which resulted in the failure to prevent or stop poor decisions from being implemented.

Several factors influence the degree of cohesiveness group members have for each other and the group itself:

1. All things being equal, small groups are generally more cohesive than larger groups. Members of small groups are more likely to see and interact with each other than are members of larger groups.
2. Homogeneous groups are likely to be more cohesive than heterogeneous groups. That is, workers of the same gender, age, or race, and workers with similar attitudes are usually more cohesive than are mixed groups.
3. External pressures or threats often develop cohesiveness in groups. Such threats may cause the group members to band together in opposition.
4. Rewards for team performance are likely to increase group cohesiveness as members become more dependent on each other for their pay.

Group Size.   Members of small groups can interact more frequently, and smaller is generally considered to be better than large groups. However, when groups get too small, problems arise. For example, in a two person group (known as a dyad), if a decision is required and there is no consensus, one group member may believe he or she has lost. Much research has sought to determine the optimal size for groups. This research has led to the following conclusions:

- When consensus in a conflict situation is important, the use of three to five members with no formal leader will ensure that each member's view will be discussed.

- When the quality of a complex group decision is important, the use of seven to twelve members under a formal leader is most appropriate.
- When both quality and consensus are important, five to seven members seems optimal.
- There tends to be greater group conflict in even-sized groups, and there is more conflict in groups of two and four members than there is in groups of six members.[20]

These research findings offer some guidelines; however, there is no one right answer to the question of the "right" size of a group. Other factors such as technology and the specific type of group task should also be considered. For example, advanced information technology can be used to pull together large groups of people to gather input, analyze data, and make decisions.

Group Leadership.   As discussed in Chapter 11 on leadership, the importance of having a good leader is vital in building and managing a successful organization. The group leader is the person everyone looks to for guidance in achieving the group's objectives. He or she is the person everyone can depend on in times of crisis. In groups, the roles of leadership may often be spread throughout the group. One person may attend to the internal problems of cohesion, while another person focuses on developing strategies for fulfilling the group's task, while another person attends to monitoring progress toward goals and time deadlines, and so on. One of the drawbacks of shared leadership, however, is that the tasks of leadership may fall through the cracks as everyone assumes that someone else will do them. When this happens, the group may want to specifically assign roles for various leaders to play. The roles might be rotated over time.

There are several ways group leaders can come to power. First, group leaders may be formally designated by management. Second, leaders may be formally chosen by the group members. Third, leaders may gradually and informally assume their positions through the day to day actions of their groups.

Goals and Objectives.   Every group needs to have some objective or purpose to guide its members. Goals and objectives help explain why groups exist and what they hope to accomplish. Group goals will often be defined by the creation of the group itself—to streamline business processes, to identify what the organization's customers desire, to identify and correct problem areas, to manage and improve specific processes. For the group to be effective, each member must clearly understand the group's purpose and goals. They should also agree that the purpose and goals are workable, and understand the purpose of individual steps, meetings, discussions, and decisions.

Problems In Groups

Social loafing The tendency for people to exert less effort when they pool their efforts toward a common goal than when they are individually accountable.

Every group has its problems, and some groups have more than others. Managers need to recognize when there is a problem and deal with it in a timely manner. The following section describes some common problems in work groups.

Social Loafing.   **Social loafing** is *the tendency for people to exert less effort when they pool their efforts toward a common goal than when they are individually* *accountable.* Social loafing can be reduced or eliminated when the task is challenging or appealing, when people feel that they can make a unique and indispensable contribution to their group, and when the other group members are believed to be trying as hard as possible.[21]

Group Polarization.   **Group polarization** is *the tendency of decision-making groups to shift toward the dominant point of view that was initially expressed.*[22] Polarization leads the group to either make more risky decisions or more cautious decisions than any individual member would make. In other words, the average inclination of group members before discussion is generally strengthened by discussion. Leaders can help the group avoid group polarization by encouraging the expression of diverse opinions as soon as possible.

Group polarization The tendency of decision-making groups to shift toward the dominant point of view that was initially expressed.

Groupthink.   **Groupthink** refers to *the tendency of cohesive groups to ignore more realistic alternatives so they maintain agreement and avoid causing conflict within the group.*[23]   The cabinet of President John F. Kennedy engaged in groupthink when it made the decision to support the Bay of Pigs invasion of Cuba, which turned out to be a disaster. There are several symptoms of groupthink team members should be conscious of:

Groupthink The tendency of cohesive groups to ignore more realistic alternatives so they maintain agreement and avoid causing conflict within the group.

- An illusion of invulnerability or belief that nothing can harm the group.
- Discounting challenges to their past decisions by collectively justifying or rationalizing them.
- An unquestioned belief in the group's morality.
- A stereotyped view of opponents as too evil to negotiate with or too weak and unintelligent to possibly defend themselves.
- Pressure to conform to the group's assumptions and plans.
- Failure of group members to speak honestly about their feelings and misgivings.
- An illusion of unanimity caused by self-censorship and conformity pressure.
- The presence of individual members who act to protect the group from evidence or information that would dispute the effectiveness or morality of its decision.

To prevent groupthink, the group leader can make group members aware of the phenomenon, instruct everyone to critically evaluate any plans or decisions, assign one or more members the role of devil's advocate, allow members to express remaining doubts, and have each group member tell about the group's deliberations with a trusted associate and report their reactions. The key to avoiding groupthink is to get the group to accept alternative suggestions from outside the group and to be less protective of the group's own ideas. Had President Kennedy done this, he could have avoided international embarrassment.

Interpersonal Conflict.   When personal disagreements between group members become more of an issue than accomplishing the group objective, the group has a real problem. In such cases, the people in disagreement will often go to war during group meetings, preventing anything from getting accomplished. This type of behavior also makes the other group members feel like spectators at a boxing match and fearful that if they get involved, they will be dragged into the contest on one side or the other.

The best way to deal with interpersonal conflict is to prevent it from happening by carefully selecting group members. If this is not possible, the leader must lay down some ground rules or set an agenda about what will and will not be discussed at the meeting and get the two parties to discuss the problem on their own time. Be careful, however. A conflict of ideas should be encouraged when it is necessary to achieve a better group product. It is the conflict due to personal agendas and petty squabbling that should be suppressed.

? THINKING CRITICALLY

1. In your experience in being a member of a group, did the stages of forming, storming, norming, performing stages coincide with your experience? Why do you think groups go through such stages?
2. Why do you think implementing teams, as illustrated by the XEL company example, is so demanding on managers and the company as a whole? Given that it is so demanding, why is it still a good thing to do?
3. Based on your experience and the ideas presented here, what do you think the most important factors are for influencing the successful performance of groups or teams?

TEAMBUILDING PROCESSES

Teambuilding Any effort to improve team functioning, effectiveness, viability, and performance.

Teambuilding might generally be defined as *any effort to improve team functioning, effectiveness, viability, and performance.* It is the process of getting a group of people to operate as a team, collaboratively working together to accomplish common objectives. Researchers and practitioners have devised a variety of teambuilding interventions that are aimed at improving group communication, problem solving, and interpersonal relations. However, teambuilding is not a well-defined concept, and organizations employ many types of teambuilding activities as the team's problems change or as specific situations arise that require a team solution. The implicit assumption behind these activities is that teams become more effective as they develop the ability to solve their own problems. The most popular teambuilding interventions focus on improving one or more of the following: interpersonal processes, goal-setting, role definition, and problem solving.

Interpersonal Processes

These types of interventions assume that teams operate best when there is mutual trust and open communication among team members. Such interventions involve candid discussions of expectations, relationships, and conflicts among team members. These approaches attempt to help team members speak with honesty, clarity, and directness, improve active listening skills, and build group cohesion. Teambuilding helps reduce losses due to poor social processes.

One interpersonal process intervention that is becoming more popular is outdoor training. Although it can take many forms, this type of training typically involves taking an intact team to a remote location free from the distractions of the office (e.g., mountains, white water river) where the members are presented with problems or challenges and asked to solve them on their own. For example, a group of 10 people may have to build a raft out of two canoes and some boards, which would then be used to carry the entire group across a river or lake. The assumption behind such exercises is that, by actively engaging in problem solving, team members can gain self-reliance and confidence as well as develop a bond with their teammates.

This approach is being used by companies such as Centel, Digital Equipment Corp., Honeywell, Southern Bell, TCI West, and Toshiba America Medical Systems, Inc. However, the problem with such training is that it is difficult to link the lessons learned in the wild to the problems of operating teams.[24] The leaders or trainers who are conducting the learning exercise should devote time to making these connections so that the team skills and learning will transfer back to the organization.

Goal Setting

This approach, based on goal-setting theory, attempts to identify the team's long-term goals and specific objectives, often by defining subtasks and establishing timetables. Goal setting is often combined with performance measurement and feedback from a manager. It ensures that the team has a specific focus for their efforts. Otherwise, the team may waste time and resources on activities that are not related to its purpose. Many TQM companies set team goals for improvement in quality or customer satisfaction to make sure that the team is connected to the strategy of the organization.

Role Clarification

This intervention entails clarifying individual role expectations and shared responsibility of team participants. **Responsibility charting** *is one method that can be used to clarify what roles and accomplishments are required of team members.*[25] The first step in responsibility charting is to construct a grid; the types of decisions and classes of actions that need to be taken are listed along the left-hand side of the grid, and the team members who might have to take action or play some part in the action are identified across the top of the grid. Then the grid is filled in by assigning a behavior to each of the actors opposite each of the issues. There are four classes of behavior:

Responsibility charting
A method used to clarify what roles and accomplishments are required of team members.

1. **Responsibility (R).** The responsibility to initiate action to ensure that the decision is carried out.
2. **Approval Required, or the Right to Veto (A-V).** The particlar item must be reviewed by the particular role occupant, and this person has the option of either vetoing or approving it.
3. **Support (S).** Responsibility for providing logistical support and resources for the particular item.
4. **Inform (I).** Member must be informed and, by inference, cannot influence the decision or actions.

Exhibit 14-4 on page 538 shows such a grid filled in for a team responsible for the development of software documentation.

EXHIBIT 14-4
Responsibility chart for a team developing software documentation

ACTION / ACTORS	Ron	Melinda	Jose	LaVanna	Michael
Write documentation	R	R	S	I	I
Create illustrations	A-V	I	I	I	R
Check for accuracy	I	I	I	R	I
Create design	A-V	S	R	I	S
Prepare pages for printing	A-V	S	R	R	S

Many companies use responsibility charting to clarify roles. For example, the project owners of Xerox's Central Logistics and Asset Management, described in the Case in Point in Chapter 2, used this technique to clarify the interdependencies among their projects.

Group Decision-making Techniques

Without a process in place, group decision making can be frustrating for people working in teams. Groups often bargain, compromise, and/or vote, resulting in a final decision that is a potpourri that no member fully understands or believes in. And without the understanding and commitment of all group members, most such decisions will not work. However, when group members are equipped with tools that help them explore ideas and make decisions, they can operate more like a team.

What follows are several techniques often used to help teams reach decisions that reflect group consensus. In considering these techniques, we need to appreciate the importance of team members having mutual respect for each other. Everyone needs to have bought into working together the understanding that each member brings skills and knowledge necessary for the team to accomplish its goals. TQM suggests working in teams because teams bring people, whose jobs are interdependent, together in a more efficient and effective manner. It allows everyone to align themselves better as they execute organization processes and work to improve them.

There are four techniques for group decision making we will explore here. Each is designed to help members fully explore a problem or opportunity and come to a consensus understanding about its implications and what to do next. The idea of **consensus** means *finding a solution or proposal acceptable enough to all members that no member will oppose it*.[26] In group or team decision making, achieving consensus will usually result in the best decision for all concerned and for the organization. Exhibit 14-5 illustrates the overall quality of team decisions (in terms of participation, commitment, and maximizing the talents of the entire team) as we move from a team leader making the decision to majority rule to consensus.

Three techniques for reaching consensus understanding and action are brainstorming with multivoting, nominal group technique, and the Delphi technique.

Brainstorming with Multivoting. **Brainstorming** is *a technique for generating many different ideas for dealing with a situation in a short amount of time*. A successful brainstorming session should be very free wheeling, with no constraints

Consensus An idea that suggests finding a solution or proposal acceptable enough to all members that no member will oppose it.

Brainstorming A technique for generating many different ideas for dealing with a situation in a short amount of time.

on what members suggest and no member being allowed to criticize the suggestions of other members. Here are some basic guidelines for brainstorming:[27]

- One person records all ideas in each speaker's own words on a flip chart, giving each idea a number.
- No criticisms or judgments about ideas allowed.
- Members can either take turns giving ideas or call them out as they come up with them.
- Go for volume of ideas and forget feasibility.
- Build on ideas from each other.
- No discussion of ideas during their generation.

This kind of session often will spark ideas in all members that they probably would not have working alone. Not only does brainstorming work to generate a lot of ideas, it also encourages creativity as members piggy back on each other.

Once the ideas are collected, the next step is to pare down the list to a few that seem most useful and that everyone can agree on. Then their task is to select one or two that best capture the team's understanding of what action they could take that would be most fruitful. A useful method for doing this **multivoting,** *a process for selecting the most important or popular items with limited discussion and difficulty.* Here is how it works:

1. Number all items on the list. If two or more ideas are similar, combine them, but only if all members agree.
2. Each team member writes down on a slip of paper the numbers of the items they prefer from the entire list. For example, if there are 50 ideas, each member might write the numbers of 15 to 20 of these. Members should agree ahead of time on what amount of items each member will select. Normally the number would be about one-third as many as on the entire list.
3. Tally the votes for each item on the list. On a team of eight members, some items may have eight votes, some may have none or anywhere in between. After tallying the list, eliminate those with the fewest votes. For example, in a team of eight members, eliminate those with three or fewer votes.
4. Go through the procedure again until the team has narrowed the list to a small number of items.

Multivoting A group decision-making technique for choosing among the most important or popular possible solutions or actions with limited discussion and difficulty.

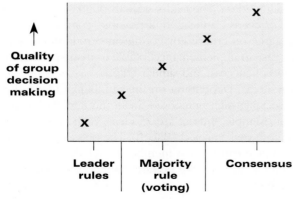

EXHIBIT 14-5
The relative quality of team decisions

Source: Adapted from William Lareau, *American Samurai* (New York: Warner Books, 1991) p. 289.

5. The team leader then leads a discussion that will bring the team to consensus on their course of action, which may include some combination of the final items.

This procedure for generating ideas and voting on them is not meant to be rigid. Sometimes members will not be able to come to a consensus decision in one meeting or even two meetings because they need to collect more information. However, they can still use this procedure to come up with a final set of ideas from which they can make their final consensus choice.

Despite its popularity and widespread use, several problems exist with brainstorming. First, asking group members to generate as many ideas as possible does not produce better ideas than simply asking group members to come up with high-quality ideas in the first place. In addition, because there is no evaluation or ranking of ideas, the group may lack a sense of closure on the problem-solving process, which may leave some members dissatisfied. Other techniques discussed below can be used to accomplish closure. There is also evidence that indicates the quality of ideas may be more closely related to the characteristics of the group members than the brainstorming process. This suggests that the selection of group members may be more important than the process they are following.

Nominal group tech-nique (NGT) A structured process to give everyone in a group an equal voice in helping a group decide on a course of action.

Nominal Group Technique. **Nominal group technique (NGT)** is *a structured process to give everyone in a group an equal voice in helping a group decide on a course of action.* It is especially useful in situations where some members might seem to dominate in the group or when team members are new to each other. An advantage of NGT is that it allows a large number of issues to be pared down quickly. A potential disadvantage is that it discourages a lot of discussion. Here are the steps for NGT:[28]

1. Define the problem or opportunity so that everyone agrees on it and understands it. Write it on a flip chart in the front of the room.
2. Generate ideas. Each person individually and silently writes down all their ideas on a sheet of paper that address the problem or opportunity. There should be a set amount of time for this, approximately five to seven minutes. These ideas should be written as short phrases.
3. Record ideas on a flip chart. The leader goes around the room taking one idea from each person, continuing until all ideas are recorded. Number each item listed.
4. Discuss and clarify ideas. The leader goes through each idea, asking if anyone has questions or needs clarification. If possible, combine ideas that are similar.
5. Discuss and agree on criteria for voting on certain items. For example, the idea must be easy to implement, acceptable to management, low cost, have a high likelihood of success, and similar criteria.
6. Rank vote the items. Depending on the number of ideas, the members are directed to select a smaller number of these and rank their preference for their selections. For example, if there are 25 ideas, each member selects 5. If there are 50 items, each person selects 8 to 10. The process for voting is as follows:
   • On three by five cards, each member writes down one selected idea on the middle of a card and the number of the idea chosen in the upper left corner of the card.

- After selecting the agreed-on number of ideas, each member then ranks these from most preferred to least preferred. If there are eight items selected, the one most preferred is ranked as 8 and so on to the least preferred, which is ranked 1. The figure just below shows what a card should look like:

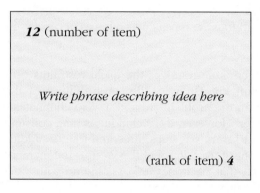

12 (number of item)

Write phrase describing idea here

(rank of item) *4*

7. Collect the cards and tally the vote. The leader goes through and places the numbers showing the rankings for each idea. The final tally might look like this if there were 24 items:

1. 4-6-1	9. 6-1-5	17. 5-7
2. 3-8	10. 5-3-8-1	18. 7-2-3
3. 8	11.	19. 1-3-6
4.	12. 7-2-4	20.
5. 4-8-7-3-2	13.	21. 2-5-6
6.	14. 2-5-1	22.
7.	15.	23. 6-4-2
8.	16. 4-7-8-3	24.

8. Add the rankings for each item together, and the one with the highest total is the group's choice. In the list above, idea 5 has the highest total with 24. If the vote is close, select the two or three highest vote getters and through discussion come to a consensus about the idea that best meets the group's criteria for acceptance.

While the nominal group technique is a little bit involved, it is a fair and impartial way to arrive at a decision on a problem or opportunity with a minimum of disagreement among members.

Delphi Technique.   The **Delphi technique** was developed at the Rand Corporation to help groups confront novel or unusual problems. The technique is *aimed at providing group members with each other's idea's and evaluative feedback while avoiding the inefficiency and inhibitors characteristic of face-to-face groups.* In the Delphi method, it is unnecessary for group members to ever meet face-to-face. Rather, the following steps are taken:

1. Each group member independently and anonymously writes down ideas, comments, and solutions to the problem confronting the group.

Delphi technique A group decision-making technique aimed at providing group members with each other's ideas and evaluative feedback while avoiding the inefficiency and inhibitors characteristic of face-to-face groups.

2. All comments are sent to a central location where they are complied and reproduced.
3. Each group member is sent the written comments of all other members.
4. Each member provides feedback on the others comments, writes down new ideas or suggestions stimulated by their comments, and forwards these to the central location.
5. Steps three and four are repeated as often as necessary until the group reaches consensus.

The Delphi technique removes the usual restraints on communication and allows for the full knowledge, skills, and abilities of the participants to be brought to bear on the problem at hand. It also eliminates the costs of bringing the group together. However, the technique is time consuming and may require substantial effort to carry out steps three and four. In addition, the nature of the process takes it out of the control of the group—the members may procrastinate, go off on tangents that are irrelevant, or come up with a decision that goes outside group or organizational constraints.

Problems in Group Decision Making.   In the U.S., with our great emphasis on individualism, we sometimes have a hard time working together, and team decision making can break down. Teams and groups have problems when members do not check their egos at the door and do not appreciate the value each person adds to the group and its work. Exhibit 14-6 lists 10 problems teams often have while trying to come to an understanding about a problem or opportunity and what to do about them.

EXHIBIT 14-6   Ten Common Problems and What to Do About Them

1. Floundering
Definition: This happens when team members don't know what to do next. This usually happens because the team is unclear about its task or how to tackle it.
Dealing with It: Handle this by clarifying the team's goal or addressing specific issues that seem to be holding the team up, such as lack of data, knowledge, bad feelings, or lack of method.

2. Overbearing Participants
Definition: This happens when one or more members seem to wield a disproportionate amount of influence. These participants may discourage discussion in their area of authority or expertise or they may discount proposals by stating that in their experience, these proposals won't work.
Dealing with It: Leader should remind members that no area is sacred from discussion. Talk to the overbearing person outside the meeting, emphasizing the disruptive nature of this behavior.

3. Dominating Participants
Definition: This happens when some members take up a disproportionate amount of time in discussions, whether they know much about the topic or not. Their talk inhibits the group from making progress.
Dealing with It: In planning discussions with team members, list "balanced participation" as a goal. Have leader practice gate-keeping: "We've heard from you on this, Tom; let's hear what others think."

4. Reluctant Participants
Definition: This happens because most groups have participants who would rather listen than talk. This is natural but becomes a problem when there is no mechanism to get these members to participate more.
Dealing with It: As with dominating participants, make balanced participation a goal. When possible divide up tasks into individual assignments. Leader, acting as gatekeeper, should invite the comments of reluctant participants.

5. Unquestioned Acceptance of Opinions as Facts
Definition: This happens when team members express personal beliefs with such confidence that they are taken as facts. This can lead to faulty assumptions in coming to a decision.
Dealing with It: The team leader should ask the person, "Is that a fact or an opinion?" or "What data do you have to back that up?" Have the group agree on the importance of data-based assumptions and decisions.

6. Rush to Accomplishment
Definition: This happens when one or more members are eager to "do something" before the team has completed its deliberations. Too much of this pressure can lead teams to make decisions in an unstructured manner, which can then cause further problems for the team or organization.
Dealing with It: Leader should remind team of its commitment to data-based decisions. The leader might also use contructive feedback with these members, using examples of past problems when other teams rushed to accomplishment.

7. Attribution
Definition: This happens when a member attributes motives for another's behavior designed to undermine that person's credibility, for example, "He's just trying to take the easy way out."
Dealing with It: The leader and team should affirm their commitment to a data-based approach. Ask the person accused to explain motives so as to dispel the attributed motive.

8. Discounts and "Plops"
Definition: Discounts happen when one member ignores or ridicules the values or ideas of another member. "Plops" happen when someone makes a suggestion or comment, and no one acknowledges it and the discussion immediately moves on to another subject.
Dealing with It: Team leaders should support discounted persons by asking them to talk more about their comments. The team should understand and practice active listening so plops don't happen.

9. Wanderlust: Digression and Tangents
Definition: This happens when meetings are not focused, and one member starts telling a story that reminds another member of a related story and off the meeting goes with no special goal or purpose.
Dealing with It: A written agenda with time limits for discussions can help members keep on track. The leader should also be conscious of this problem and lead the group back to the main topic.

10. Feuding Team Members
Definition: Sometimes participants argue because of past differences or dislike for each other. Such differences usually predate the group or team.
Dealing with It: The leader should work to get adversaries to discuss their differences outside the meeting and leave them outside. The leader can also seek to have these members make some contract about their behavior ("If Pam does . . . , I will agree to . . . .")

Source: Peter R. Scholtes, *The Team Handbook* (Madison, WI: Joiner Associates, 1988) pp. 6-36 to 6-45.

QUALITY TOGETHER TEAMS AT METHODIST MEDICAL CENTER

One of the keys to the success of Quality Together teams at Methodist Medical Center is that the roles and responsibilities of the participants have been clarified and understood. For example, department managers identify problems to be solved, and they have the authority to initiate projects within their own departments. However, proposals for projects that involve other departments must be submitted to the steering committee for approval. These proposals indicate the purpose and scope of the project and identify the employees who will serve as team members, facilitators, leaders, and sponsors. The committee meets monthly to fulfill the following responsibilities:

- Review and approve project topics
- Provide feedback regarding scope and team composition
- Prioritize the implementation of team projects
- Attend team presentations
- Plan and direct other QT activities

The roles of individuals who participate in the QT teams include the following:

- **Manager.** Managers are encouraged to lead QT efforts in their own departments. They may also recommend projects regarding interdepartmental concerns to the steering committee for approval. Managers remain abreast of team progress by visiting team meetings. They support improvement efforts by providing necessary resources, by communicating progress to the department, and by aiding in the implementation of team solutions.
- **Leader.** The role of the leader is to plan and conduct team meetings and to maintain well-organized records of team activities. Leadership also encompasses the training and coaching of team members. Leaders act as liaisons between the team and MMC management.
- **Facilitator.** Facilitators are specially trained in all aspects of the QT process. They act as resource persons for department managers in addition to serving on QT teams. Facilitators keep team meetings focused. They also provide technical support by aiding in the selection of key measures and measurement tools. Facilitators assist team members as they prepare their final presentations for the steering committee.
- **Team Members.** Team members are expected to coordinate their team responsibilities with their work activities. They collaborate and contribute at each stage of the improvement process. Members are responsible for the collection and documentation of necessary data, and for assisting with the implementation of proposed solutions. They are reminded that during the QT process only systems should be criticized, not people.

Because everyone understands the system and their roles, this removes ambiguity and allows all players to focus on what they need to do: continuously improve in the delivery of quality service to all their stakeholders.

Teams are just one possible solution to the competitive challenges that companies face in today's global markets. It is important to remember that teams are a means to an end, not an end in themselves. For some organizations, the purpose of using teams may be to improve business processes for even better quality of products or services. For others, teams may be a last ditch effort to prevent the organization from going out of business. Some organizations want teams to transform the entire company. Others want teams to improve one small part of the company. Whatever the case, teams represent the potential to increase the involvement of a large number of employees throughout the organization in improving its competitiveness.

 **THINKING CRITICALLY**

1. Have you ever been a member of a group or team where there was some ambiguity about who was going to do what? Do you think a responsibility chart would have helped you? Why or why not?
2. Have you ever been in a group where the group had problems coming to an agreement? What were the circumstances? How might the methods described here for team decision making have helped?
3. If you have been a member of a group or team where things went well, what characterized that team and its interactions? How did you make decisions that everyone could agree on?

SUMMARY

TEAMS IN ORGANIZATIONS
- Teams are intentionally brought together to perform specific activities that contribute to transforming input into output to satisfy customers.
- Managers can use teams for many purposes; teams usually exist to perform one of three broad functions in an organization: (1) production and service, (2) advice and involvement for management, (3) projects and development.
- If managers understand and use teams correctly, they can be a powerful tool for engendering cooperation and the effective and efficient achievement of organizational goals.
- There are three levels of autonomy for teams: (1) those directed by management, (2) semi-autonomous teams, which are on their own but check in with management, and (3) self-managed teams, those responsible for themselves with minimum input from management.

IMPLEMENTING TEAMS
- To successfully implement teams, managers must be concerned with developing a team-oriented culture, honesty and open communication, and tolerance for different opinions and mistakes.
- The move to teams emerges from an understanding of organizations as systems rather than as individuals coming together to optimize their individual performances.
- In understanding an organization's need for teams, a manager should undertake (1) an organization/environment analysis, (2) a task/technical system analysis, and (3) a person/social systems analysis of the organization.
- Organizations cannot move to TQM and teams without letting go of the traditional hierarchical structure. There is less need for a strong hierarchy when teams have access to the information they need and have the authority to execute the processes they are responsible for.

GROUP DYNAMICS
- There are several general principles about group dynamics that can help managers more successfully implement teams.

- Factors that affect group performance and effectiveness include: roles, group norms, cohesiveness, size, and leadership.
- Typical problems in groups include social loafing, group polarization, group-think, and interpersonal conflict.

TEAMBUILDING PROCESSES

- Teambuilding is the general process of getting a group of people to operate as a team, collaboratively working together to accomplish common objectives.
- Some processes to address in teambuilding include (1) interpersonal relationships, (2) goal setting, (3) role clarification.
- Some common group decision-making techniques include brainstorming with multivoting, nominal group technique, and the Delphi technique.

KEY TERMS

Advice and involvement teams 516	Norm 532
Autonomy 519	Organization/environment analysis 524
Brainstorming 538	Performance 531
Cohesion 532	Person/social systems analysis 526
Committee 515	Production and service teams 515
Consensus 538	Project and development teams 517
Delphi technique 541	Responsibility charting 537
Formal group 513	Semi-autonomous team 519
Group 513	Social loafing 534
Group polarization 535	Synergy 519
Groupthink 535	Task/technical system analysis 524
Hierarchical teams 513	Teambuilding 536
Management-directed team 519	Teamwork 513
Multivoting 539	Viability 531
Nominal group technique (NGT) 540	

REVIEW QUESTIONS

1. What is the difference between a group and a team? From a management perspective, what is the significance of this difference?
2. What is a hierarchical team? Why are hierarchical teams not usually as efficient and effective as cross-functional teams?
3. What are three roles performed by teams in organizations and what is the difference among these roles?
4. Why is teamwork becoming so important in today's organizations when in the past a focus on individuals and charismatic leaders was sufficient?
5. What are the three levels of autonomy for teams and what is the best use of each level?

6. What are four areas managers must address in implementing teams in an organization?
7. What are three types of analysis an organization should undertake as a prelude to implementing teams?
8. How does the implementation of teams change organizational structure and what types of activities employees focus on?
9. What are the four stages groups go through as they develop and what are the characteristics of these four stages?
10. What are five factors that affect group performance and describe the influence of each of these factors?
11. What is the relationship between interpersonal processes, goal setting, and role clarification and group effectiveness?
12. What are three ways to make decisions in groups and how does each work?

EXPERIENTIAL EXERCISES

1. A Problem with a Team Member

You are a member of a five-person self-managing team responsible for the production of office furniture (e.g., desks, chairs, file drawers, etc.). The team does many things in the production of the office furniture and has the obligation to meet goals set by management for quality and quantity. When all team members are working together the team can easily surpass their goals and thus be eligible for a generous productivity bonus. When any team member does not pull his or her weight, team productivity falls to minimally acceptable levels. At these lower levels the team does not get into trouble with top management because the team is meeting minimum production goals; however, the team is not eligible for any bonus in pay. Recently one of the team members has been neglecting his duties. For the previous two pay periods the team has not received any bonus. Other team members have talked to this person, but their concerns seem to have gone unheard. It looks like your team will not receive a bonus for the present pay period. What initiatives might you and your fellow team members take to solve this problem?

2. Making a Recommendation to Top Management

Divide the class into teams of 6 to 8 people each. Each team should then consider itself on staff at a large company that wants to get into restaurant franchising by starting a new chain. Using the nominal group technique, have each team develop ideas defining market opportunities here. The team should come up with ideas for themes, target market segments, and other information related to starting such a chain. For example, the team might vote to recommend a Chinese-Mexican theme restaurant serving moderately priced ethnic food to families. The goal is to come up with two ideas to recommend to top management, with the reasoning behind them.

In doing this exercise, each group should first choose a team leader, who will coordinate the NGT process as described on page 540. Have flip charts to record ideas and 3 by 5 cards available to do the voting. After your team has finished voting and made its selection, discuss what you thought of the process and if you found it a useful way to come up with and select ideas on which to work further.

CASE ANALYSIS AND APPLICATION
Hallmark's Journey[29]

The outside of Hallmark Cards Inc.'s headquarters, in the Crown Center complex in Kansas City, Missouri, remains just as it has for years: orderly and unchanged. But inside the building a revolution is playing out. Expectations are going up, walls are coming down, and time is of the essence. Hallmark is being transformed by a new management system based on TQM. Hallmark calls it "the Journey" to emphasize that the entire company—all 22,000 of its employees—has embarked in a new direction. One of the key characteristics of the new management system is the use of teams and the flattening of the organization by eliminating levels of middle managers.

There are fewer middle managers in many of Hallmark's departments, but displaced workers have, for the most part, been reassigned. Because of these types of changes, many employees enjoy making more decisions. Quality has improved, and the time it takes to complete a job has been reduced significantly. Wayne Herran, vice president of Hallmark's graphic arts division, states that "Jobs that used to take 80 days now take eight days . . . with an improvement in quality." Employees in Herran's division take the picture from the artist's easel and the words from the writer's pad and put them together into a greeting card ready for the printer. The typical greeting card once needed 40 days to go through the six different specialties that the graphic arts department handled. Harran's goal now is to zip a card through the graphic arts department in no more than three days.

The main way to get such dramatic reductions in cycle time is to attack the biggest time eater in almost any organization: "queue time," or the wasted time that a piece of work waits in line. For example, imagine a piece of work that has been finished in one specialty department and is passed to the next specialty. It may wait in an "in" basket for days before the worker picks it up. If the worker is confused about something or needs even a simple clarification, he or she is likely to craft a memo and send it, along with the piece of work, back to the first specialty, where it will wait for a couple of days more in an "in" basket. Sometimes the question or clarification is routed through a supervisor. Following this sequence, a piece of work could take weeks to drag through the half dozen or so specialties.

Hallmark's solution to this problem is to break apart the silos of specialties and form new teams composed of one or two members of each of the six specialties. Now, if employees have questions, the person who can help them is usually nearby for immediate discussion. Hallmark even took down the walls in the graphic arts department and replaced them with cubicles that are open above chest level. Now workers can get questions answered literally without leaving their seats. There are no more memos stacked up in "in" baskets. With these changes, the team concept is working for Hallmark.

Discussion Questions

1. How does breaking into teams help eliminate "queue time"?
2. How would you suggest that Hallmark use empowerment to ensure these teams are successful?
3. What do you think the new role of middle managers should be in this new team-based approach?

VIDEO CASE: COMBINING QUALITY MANAGEMENT AND SOCIAL RESPONSIBILITY
GE Plastics

GE Plastics routinely sponsored employee golf and tennis matches and other physical competitions as a means of fostering teamwork and improving morale. But in 1988, the company's general desire for teambuilding gained a new urgency. GE acquired Borg-Warner Chemicals, which meant the integration of 5,000 new employees with GE's existing 9,000—two groups which had been arch-rivals for decades. How could GE Plastics cultivate trust and loyalty among former Borg-Warner Chemical employees, "re-recruit" its own existing employees, and deal with the emotional trauma of staff layoffs and restructuring resulting from the acquisition?

The Business Enterprise Trust Award recognizes GE Plastics for devising a remarkably simple but creative plan to combine employee teambuilding with community service. The sales, marketing, technology, and manufacturing departments of GE Plastics took a day out of their 1989 national meetings to renovate needy community facilities in San Diego, California. This program, called "Share to Gain," proved exceptionally successful at fostering team spirit while leaving something meaningful behind for the people of San Diego.

Joel Hutt, GE Plastics' manager of marketing communications, first proposed the "Share to Gain" concept. With the enthusiastic encouragement of GE Management, Hutt and a small team spent several months planning renovation projects near the national meeting site. Extensive planning was necessary to select suitable projects and to ensure that hundreds of GE employees could simply walk onto the sites and be effective. At the national meetings, employees were divided into work groups and asked to attend short "skills sessions" to get some basic training in painting, tile-laying, etc. Hutt received tremendous response: about 99 percent of the workforce participated. In total, the four GE Plastics departments renovated five San Diego community facilities including three YMCA buildings, a boys' & girls' club, and a shelter for the homeless. Over the two weeks of meetings, 3,200 gallons of paint were applied, 2,000 windows installed, and over 40,000 square feet of vinyl and carpet laid.

In addition to making a profound impact on the community centers, GE Plastics gives glowing reports on the teambuilding effects of "Share to Gain." Prior to the San Diego meetings, many managers from Borg-Warner still considered GE Plastics to be "the competition." After a day of pounding nails, painting walls, and planting shrubs, they were teammates. The success of the experiment has led GE to replicate the project elsewhere within the company and to promote the concept to other organizations.

Discussion Questions

1. Why was it important to foster teamwork and improve morale at GE?
2. Explain why GE's approach to teambuilding was so effective in promoting teamwork.

15. ORGANIZATIONAL CHANGE AND LEARNING

LEARNING OBJECTIVES

When you finish this chapter you should be able to:

1. List and explain the external and internal forces for change.

2. Describe Lewin's three stage model of change and its implications for managers.

3. List and describe six types of planned change.

4. List different types of interventions by managers and others to bring about organizational change.

5. Explain the relationship between culture and change.

6. List several reasons why people resist change and what managers can do to minimize resistance.

7. Explain what a learning organization is and how it relates to Total Quality Management.

ANALOG DEVICES COPES WITH CHANGE THROUGH ORGANIZATIONAL LEARNING[1]

Analog Devices, Inc. produces semiconductor integrated circuits that measure and control real world phenomena such as temperature, pressure, and velocity. The circuits are used in microprocessors and computers by equipment manufacturers in diverse markets, including military and aerospace, industrial automation, and the automotive and transportation industries. Analog Devices is a world leader in producing these integrated circuits. In about 75 percent of its product lines, the company has the largest market share. Analog Devices has repeatedly been recognized by industry experts as the best midsize semiconductor company in the United States, and it is highly regarded by its customers.

Analog Devices is a sound business, but it has experienced some fierce pressures for change in its brief history. Chairman and CEO Ray Stata explains,

"We have noted some sobering trends. For the first twenty-five years of our existence, right up to 1984, we grew at an average rate of 25 percent per year. Since 1984 there has been a noticeable flattening of the slope of that growth curve. We are not alone; our experience mirrors a pervasive slowdown in the growth of the electronics industry." The industry is entering what it calls the era of very-large-scale integration. The chips for integrated circuits have gotten smaller and grown more complex. Some of Analog Devices chips have a half million transistors on them. At the same time, prices are dropping dramatically, but the necessity to invest in research and development is increasing.

The market is also changing, as Stata describes: "For a long time, our business was driven by military, industrial, medical, and instrumentation applications, where high performance in modest quantities was key. Today,

however, peace prevails, and the military market is on the skids. . . . Suddenly, we have to look for new places to grow." To meet the market demands that will come from new applications in consumer products, computer peripherals, and communication systems, Analog Devices must be able to shift gears in terms of technology, markets, customers, and its whole approach to doing business. Stata explains how demands on management have risen:

What's happening at Analog Devices is happening to a lot of companies around the world, particularly in the United States. In my view, the underlying drive behind what has come to be called the management paradigm shift is the fact that the rate of change in technology and markets is exponential. Future shock has arrived, and we're living it every day. That changes a great deal of what management is all about. At the same time, the standard for what constitutes successful performance in world markets has gone up by orders of magnitude.

I know this from our own experience. We used to think we were terrific managers and we had a wonderful company. We were considered to be world-class in what we were doing. But as I look back to 10 or 15 years ago, I see that our capabilities were pedestrian compared with what it will take to survive in the 1990s.

551

Performance standards have escalated so enormously in the last decade largely because of developments in Japan. . . . Japan was the first industrial nation to rise to international power not on the basis of traditional technology innovation (as had the United States, England, France, and Germany) but through management innovation. For whatever reasons, the Japanese have been and continue to be extraordinary innovators in the management of complex organizations. And now we're all scrambling to understand what they've done.

In the last analysis, the challenge is to accelerate our rate of learning. I look at improvement and learning as two sides of the same coin. Back in the 1980s, we thought we were making reasonable progress in learning and improvement. But as I look ahead, it is clear that we must accelerate our rate of improvement significantly in comparison with the past. . . .

What it takes to satisfy customers changes rapidly these days as a result of rapid changes in society. To me, "market in" is an elegant and powerful way to express what the management revolution is all about. ["Market in" means that the real purpose of work is customer satisfaction. It is externally oriented, as opposed to the "product out" approach, which is internally oriented (see Exhibit 15-1).] And so, for ADI, a primary concern is changing the culture to get employees to take customer satisfaction seriously. Employees must be willing and able to change rapidly in response to customers' changing needs.

For more than 20 years, Analog Devices enjoyed a virtual monopoly in many of its product lines. We called the shots, and our customers danced to our tune. To tell you the truth, we liked that arrangement. A lot of our people got used to it—and many don't want to change. It's hard for a company like Analog to accept the reality that we don't call the shots any more. You can say the words, you can draw the pictures, and you can talk about the concept, but actually making the cultural transition is a struggle. To do it, you must do a lot of learning.

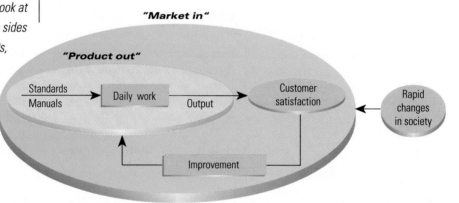

Source: "Market In" vs. "Product Out" Concept of Work, from Ray Stata, "Organizational learning: The key to success in the 1990s." *Prism*, Fourth Quarter, published by Arthur D. Little, 1992, p. 93. Reprinted by permission.

EXHIBIT 15-1   "Market In" vs. "Product Out" concept of work

In recent decades, many businesses have experienced an increasing number of problems. Productivity falls short of what it could be, the safety of their workers and/or customers is compromised, or the quality of products and services fails to meet rising customer expectations. At the same time, managers are finding great opportunities to develop new strategies to serve new markets and transform their organizations in creative ways. Carefully managing change to address these problems and opportunities helps organizations cope and succeed in an increasingly competitive business environment. In this chapter we examine many aspects of organizational change, including forces for change, areas of change, the importance of continuous learning, and dealing with resistance to change.

Managing change brings together many of the ideas we have covered up to this point in the book, including culture, human resources policies, leadership, motivation, communication, and teams. The challenge is to manage business systems so they have the capacity not only to successfully adapt to changes, but to be drivers of change as well. The success of the Japanese that Ray Stata talks about in the Case in Point has come from the initiation of change and continuous improvement in the way they manage their businesses.

Systems are always changing. Because TQM is about the management of systems, we should not be surprised with its focus on managing change, on learning, and on continuously improving organizational systems. Even companies as successful as Analog Devices will soon be history if they do not keep up with and, indeed, help create change. As we proceed through this chapter, you will see a reiteration of principles that have cropped up in other chapters, such as open communication, empowerment, cooperative effort, focus on the customer and others. That's because managing change is the successful application of these ideas. So keep that in mind as you read on.

CONSTANT PRESSURES FOR CHANGE

If there is one constant to life, it is change. The world around us is constantly changing and so are we as a part of that world. Our success as individuals often is directly related to our ability to adapt to changes in the world we are part of. The same is true of organizations, which also must adapt to a changing world. A problem is that many times managers are unaware of the pace of change until it nearly overwhelms them. As with Analog Devices, companies perceive the need to change only when they notice certain tell-tale signs—sales are down, product development cycle times are uncompetitive, employee morale is low, customers are complaining. Only then do they start to respond, sometimes too late. The point is that since change is a part of our world, it makes more sense to anticipate it and even help create it than to sit back and let it destroy you.

For example, hindsight for Analog Devices indicated that the loss of competitive edge was a ten- to fifteen-year-old problem. Had they recognized the indicators a little earlier, Analog Devices may have been able to respond more quickly and avoid some of the pain they went through in moving to new markets. It sounds very simple, but studying all of the forces that drive the need for organizational change is not easy. Nevertheless, managers need to monitor these forces and use their understanding to improve the quality of their decisions.

External Forces

There are many external environmental forces that affect organizations and to which they must adapt. This process of adaptation often means changes in the organization. We cannot discuss all of the possible forces and their effects here, but some of them are listed below.

- **Government regulations** are a frequent impetus for change. Laws passed since 1990 are already having a profound impact on businesses. The 1991 Civil Rights Act, for example, promises to make recruiting and hiring of minority employees more important. The Americans with Disabilities Act took effect

Technological advances in audio CD development and production have made vinyl disk records obsolete in one decade.

in 1992 to protect people who are physically disadvantaged by requiring businesses to make their buildings more accessible to handicapped people (both employees and customers).

- **Economic forces** affect almost all organizations in some way. The high cost of operating a business in many big cities has prompted a number of firms to relocate or expand to more rural areas. Toyota Motor Company USA, for example, opened their multi-million dollar production facility in Georgetown, Kentucky; and General Motors built its Saturn plant in Spring Hill, Tennessee. The state of the economy also has an impact on organizations. The recession of the early 1990s has forced many organizations to cut costs and lay off thousands of employees.

- As open systems, organizations depend on the *marketplace* as an outlet for their products and services. If an organization loses touch with its market (customers), it may find itself offering products or services nobody wants to buy or not offering products or services that could be highly profitable. For example, Pizza Hut had the capability to provide home delivery, however it stayed with its strategy of offering only "dine-in" or "carry-out" for many years. Pizza Hut was ignoring a market need. When it finally started making home deliveries, Pizza Hut was successful in taking some of that lucrative market away from entrenched competitors like Domino's.

- *Technology* also creates the need for change in both products and production processes, and organizational structure and culture. Technological advances in compact-disc technology made the phonographic record obsolete in the last decade. Similar advances in high-definition television and flat-screen technology could revolutionize the TV industry. As robotic and automated manufacturing advances are made, assembly lines in many industries are changing dramatically as technologically advanced machinery replaces human labor.

- *Labor market fluctuations* are another force for change. The current shortage of registered occupational therapists has forced hospitals to redesign jobs and improve their reward and benefit packages to attract and retain these therapists.

Obviously, these are but a few of the factors in the external environment that are forces for change. We have discussed many of the others in earlier chapters, such as changing standards for ethics, the emergence of new markets around the world, and the complexities of politics. A casual glance through the daily paper will reveal all of these forces for change and many others. Managers who do not pay attention to these forces can expect problems in their companies as a result.

Internal Forces

Forces within the organization can also stimulate the need for change. These forces can result from the impact of external changes or from the operations of the organization itself. For example, if management redefines or modifies its *strategy*, it often introduces a host of changes. General Electric undertook significant strategy changes in the 1980s. In 1981, GE was competing in almost sixty product and service areas. Recognizing that this uncoordinated diversity of products and services could be harmful to the company, its new CEO put everyone on notice to either become the dominant player in their area or be sold or closed. GE sold off unprofitable divisions and concentrated management talent and financial resources on its best performers. By 1990, ten of GE's fourteen businesses led their markets, and two were number two in their markets.

An organization's *workforce* is another powerful force for change. Rarely is an organization's workforce static. It usually changes in terms of age, education, gender, and so forth. Jobs may need to be restructured to attract new employees and to satisfy the career needs of those who occupy the lower ranks. The compensation and benefits systems might also need to be redesigned to reflect the needs of an older work force. The importance, therefore, of continually training and developing employees cannot be overstated. Many an organization has learned that employees are the competitive weapon that can help it prosper, and if the company takes care of its people, the people will take care of the company. Companies practicing TQM have found employees to be great generators of change. Once managers get employees focused on customer needs and empower them to respond, lots of ideas for change and improvement, large and small, start to come in.

The introduction of new *equipment* represents another internal force for change. Jobs may need to be restructured to accommodate the changes in equipment, or the plant or office may need to be redesigned. In addition, employees may need to receive training to operate the new equipment, or be required to establish new interaction patterns within their formal teams.

Evolutionary Change Versus Framebreaking Change

Organizations are constantly changing in response to pressures like those listed above. Managers and employees make minor changes to procedures, work methods, and rules. Employees come and go as members of the organization, which constantly alters the workforce composition. Employees receive training and develop new skills and behaviors, which can impact the company. The company discontinues old products and develops and introduces new ones, often using new procedures that have the goal of making the company more efficient and effective. Managers create new departments and eliminate, combine, or reconfigure old ones under a new label.

Over time all of these changes accumulate to make the organization different than before. However, because of the evolutionary nature of these changes, most people in the organization are not upset by them. They only notice the dramatic effect on the organization when, after many years, they look back at old documents or pictures to see how things used to be. Such *evolutionary changes* do not threaten the existing culture, because they do not usually call into question more than a few beliefs, values or behaviors at any one time.[2]

However, in today's competitive environment organizations are finding it necessary to radically change over short periods of time. *Revolutionary changes of an organization*, as opposed to incremental changes, might be referred to as **framebreaking change**. *It reshapes the entire nature of the organization by altering critical elements such as strategy, structure, systems, people and processes.*[3] For many organizations, for example, the move to Total Quality Management is a framebreaking change that requires redoing almost everything about the way an organization functions to achieve its goals. Such radical change may meet with resistance from employees who have a vested interest in the old ways. Being a framebreaker requires a great deal of planning and commitment of time and resources by everyone. But when organizations complete these changes, they are almost always better off.

Boeing is in the midst of framebreaking change. In the middle of the worst airline slump in history, and having to cut its workforce by 28,000, Boeing realized that the existence of the company was at stake. Facing tough competition in the commercial airline business, with Lockheed, McDonnell Douglas, and Airbus, Boeing is preparing itself for another powerful adversary, Toyota. Toyota Motor Corporation says: "We're in the transportation business. It is our destiny to be in the airplane business." With such a challenging future before them, Boeing is leaving no stone unturned in its efforts to reinvent itself.

Boeing used to keep its manufacturing process top secret, but in an effort to better anticipate customers' needs and to cut down on redesigns, it now offers office space to key clients. Boeing wants to make manufacturing faster, cheaper, and more efficient. One way it is trying to do this is by moving toward a just-in-time inventory system. Boeing plans to reduce the 737 model production time from 13 to six months, and cut costs by 25% or more by the year 2000. Boeing's newest project, the 777, has been developed from the start with customer input. Boeing is also making changes in other areas. For example, inventory was not carefully accounted for so managers never knew the cost of what they had in stock. By going to a just-in-time system and involving their suppliers in the process, Boeing and the suppliers can better account for inventory and reduce its costs. As another example, the new wing assembly plant is being laid out for efficiency and flow times have been reduced from 100 to 15 days.

To initiate change at Boeing, Chairman Frank Shrontz sent 100 top executives on a tour of world-class companies. These 100 executives then started a trickle-down training program that would train all 43,000 workers within a year. Boeing is trying to teach its employees to embrace change, and look forward to the future.[4]

Framebreaking change
Change that reshapes the entire nature of the organization by altering critical elements such as strategy, structure, systems, people and processes.

❓ THINKING CRITICALLY

1. In most colleges and universities budgets are being tightened with less funding for most activities. What kinds of changes has this brought about for you and others at your school?
2. Have you ever been a part of an organization undergoing a framebreaking change? What was it like? Whether you have or not, why do you think TQM would be a framebreaking change for most companies? What kinds of changes do you think implementing TQM would require?

THE PROCESS OF PLANNED CHANGE

Planned change is *the deliberate design and implementation of structural, procedural, technological, cultural, or personnel changes directed at increasing an organization's effectiveness.*[5] Planned change is directed at preparing the organization to more readily solve problems, to adapt to changes in the environment, and to create changes within the organization and in the larger world that help ensure its vitality. Planned changes are seldom easy, inexpensive, or painless, and employees are often asked to surrender familiar work habits for new procedures, policies, and expectations. Nevertheless, planned change is a more intelligent approach than change forced onto the organization because it didn't plan. In undertaking change initiatives, it is helpful for managers to understand how change takes place in an organization. We will look at that next.

Planned change The deliberate design and implementation of structural, procedural, technological, cultural, or personnel changes directed at increasing an organization's effectiveness.

Lewin's Three Stage Model of Change

Researchers have sought to understand planned change by developing models that describe the different stages a changing organization goes through. These models describe how managers may successfully implement change, including the timing and methods to help employees become a part of the process. There are many such models in existence. One very popular model is Kurt Lewin's change model.[6] This model applies to organizations, groups, or individuals. It views change as a modification of the forces acting to keep a system's behavior stable. (See Exhibit 15-2 on page 558.) Specifically, there are two sets of forces acting on people's behavior—those forces striving to maintain the status quo and those pushing for change. If both forces are exerting equal force, current levels of behavior are maintained in what Lewin called "quasi-stationary equilibrium." To change that state, one can either increase the forces pushing for change or decrease the forces acting to maintain stability. Lewin suggests that reducing the forces that maintain the status quo produces less stress than increasing the forces for change. In other words, when maintaining the status quo seems like it is going to cause problems for people, they are more willing to make changes.

Lewin viewed the change as a three step process. First, the forces maintaining the organization's present level of performance must be *unfrozen*, or prepared for change. Unfreezing causes people to become aware of the weakness in their current conditions and motivates them to look for better ways to behave. This can be accomplished in several ways. The most common way is to provide information that demonstrates a failure of the current organizational systems to produce the desired results.

EXHIBIT 15-2
Lewin's Model of Change. Change happens when the forces for the status quo weaken. TQM helps us to understand that the third stage is no longer valid. Today's organizations remain in stage 2 permanently (as indicated by the darker outline of the box).

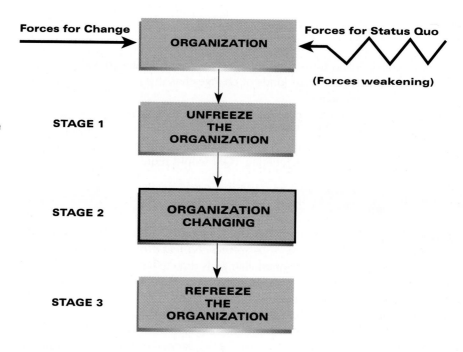

For example, an organization's financial performance is a good indicator of the success of the current system. Losing money for the past six years is a good indication that some sort of change is probably necessary. Consistently poor product quality, high turnover and absenteeism rates, habitually low morale, and low productivity are other symptoms of problems that suggest that organizational systems need to be changed. Examining this type of discrepant information should make employees ready and willing to learn new behaviors. Managers should be creative in getting employees to perceive the need for change. Fellowes Manufacturing Co., a small family-owned business in Itasca, Illinois, produces office-organization products ranging from corrugated record-storage boxes to computer-diskette trays. While searching for ways to decrease setup time on its injection-molding presses, Fellowes managers videotaped the existing process of changing over molds in a press. Employees watched the videotape to spot inefficiencies and come up with improvements. They reduced setup time to one third of its original time.[7]

The second step in this process is known as *moving* or *changing*. Moving occurs when changes are made to some part of the organization such as its strategy, technology, structure, systems, or work methods, or some combination of areas. Ideally, these changes will help employees develop new values and attitudes toward the organization and its products or services and new, more productive behaviors.

The third step in this process is *refreezing*. Refreezing refers to the process by which the new organizational values, beliefs, goals, behaviors, etc. are tested for fit. If it is not clearly more desirable than the old state, people usually revert to their old ways. If it seems to fit or is better than the old state, it is locked into place by means of supporting or reinforcing mechanisms, so that they become the new norm. This can be accomplished by redesigning organizational systems such as performance appraisal, career development, and pay to support and reinforce the changes. For example, an organization changing to a team-based approach should also make the necessary changes to its pay system so that people will be paid, at least in part, on their team's performance. When managers put in place these support programs, they tell everyone that they are serious about making the changes work, which will be instrumental in refreezing the new behaviors.

Lewin's model of change is still useful, for example, in helping managers think about how to transform their organizations and shift to Total Quality Management. Every so often managers will need to make dramatic changes of course, to implement a radical new approach or methods for work. However, there is one caveat that applies in today's dynamic marketplace, and particularly to TQM. Organizations implementing TQM never really go into a refreezing stage. Rather, managers do not have the luxury of settling into another long period of stability after refreezing. They understand the need to continuously pursue change and improvement.

Part of the value of TQM is the creation of a climate that promotes openness to change and the development of capabilities to bring it about in proactive fashion. TQM reminds managers that in addition to radical changes, or discontinuous change, they must be prepared to pursue continuous improvements by constantly adjusting and modifying the organization to the rapid changes in the environment. Dr. Barry Bebb, former Vice President of Reprographics, Xerox Corporation describes the rates of change that successful organizations must now deal with:

The world's best corporations are reducing costs by factors of two, reducing product development schedules by factors of two and improving quality by factors of ten every five to ten years. Such rapid rates of improvements require very rapid rates of changes in how businesses operate. The cultural comforts provided by stability in an enterprise environment are not viable in today's rapidly changing global village. Successful corporations learn how to drive enormous amounts of change through an entire infrastructure with frightening speed.[8]

Planning the Change Effort

Plans for change can come from organization members or outside consultants. Outsiders have several advantages over insiders. They will usually not be distracted by day-to-day operating responsibilities, and they may have more credibility because of their perceived expertise in organizational change. Also, the outsider may be more objective than someone working for the organization. On the other hand, outsiders may not be able to fully understand the organization in a short period of time. Furthermore, they do not have to stick around to deal with the mess that their proposed changes may create. To ensure that the proposed changes are appropriate, it is probably best to pair an outsider (when needed) with an insider who can provide key insights about the organization's culture and political environment. Such insights can determine the success or failure of a planned change.

Proactive Versus Reactive Change

Change usually results when influential people within the organization (usually top managers or the board of directors) decide the organization needs to go in a new direction. For example, corporate boards of directors are beginning to exert

Proactive change
Managerial decisions to try new things in anticipation of changes in the environment.

Reactive change A decision to make changes in response to events in the environment that affect the company.

influence over the strategic direction of the company. The General Motors Board of Directors forced Robert Stempel out of his job as CEO in an effort to bring in new leadership and turn the company around. Radical changes are sometimes initiated by bringing in new leaders. However, this is not always the case. For example, David Kearns remained as CEO of Xerox in the 1980s as that company launched a major initiative to transform the company and shift to Total Quality Management.

Proactive change happens when *managers make decisions to try new things in anticipation of changes in the environment. They understand they must be ahead of the curve to take advantage of these changes.* Proactive change is often goal oriented or driven by a leader's vision for the future. Alternatively, **reactive change** is *a decision to make changes in response to events in the environment that affect the company.* Reactive change is driven by the need to fend off a particular threat or deal with a pressing problem. For example, the makers of carbon paper were forced to drastically change their strategy after Xerox introduced photocopiers (they got into a new line of work!). Later, Xerox was forced into reactive change in the 1980s when determined Japanese competitors started taking its market share with higher quality and lower cost copiers.

Of course, organizations must be able to react to changes in their environment, like Xerox had to do in the 1980s. However, a better strategy would be for the organization to anticipate changes, or better yet, proactively institute such changes themselves as part of a policy to continually improve their products and services to customers. There are many examples (successful and unsuccessful) of both proactive and reactive organizational changes. The *A Look At TQM in Action* box on page 561 provides two examples.

? THINKING CRITICALLY

1. Does Lewin's model of change make sense to you? Describe an experience where the status quo became untenable and forced some changes in your life.
2. Do you think Lewin's model can work to explain proactive as well as reactive change? Explain your answer.
3. Do you agree that organizations (and individuals) need to be prepared for continuous change? Does this mean organizational (and personal) stability will be lost? Why or why not?

TYPES OF PLANNED CHANGE

Getting planned change efforts underway is a difficult undertaking. It usually involves months of hard work, intensive planning, and the coordinated efforts of many people throughout the organization. The change process itself is guided, to a large degree, by the specific types of changes that are going to be made. In bringing change about, there are five areas managers can affect: strategy, technology, structure, personnel, and culture. Changes in any one of these areas will potentially affect all the others.

Strategic Change

An organization's strategy outlines its overall purpose and objectives as well as how they are to be achieved. In other words, a strategy defines the organization's role in its environment. It details what types of products or services they will sell, what mar-

PROACTIVE BRYCE AND REACTIVE UPS

A LOOK AT

TQM IN ACTION

The Bryce Corporation in Memphis, Tennessee, is an excellent example of an organization making proactive changes to its strategy, structure, and culture to remain a world class manufacturing organization. Ever since its opening, Bryce Corporation has pursued one goal: to become the world's foremost supplier of flexible packaging (e.g., plastic bags). As Bryce Corporation has grown, it has managed to retain the informality and personal relationships characteristic of smaller, family-owned companies. Bryce has also earned a reputation as a reliable and dependable source of plastic bags to companies such as Frito-Lay and M&M Mars. In fact, for the past three years, Bryce has been named Frito-Lay's supplier of the year. But, in the tradition of continuous improvement fostered by the high-involvement culture, the employees are not satisfied with such accolades. They want to be even better. They have come to realize that being rated best is relative—and fleeting—as competitors improve their capabilities and customers change their expectations.

To improve the productive capacity of its employees, Bryce has continually updated its plants with the latest manufacturing innovations. Supporting their state-of-the-art facilities is an aggressive employee training and development system developed to ensure that Bryce employees have the knowledge and skills to fully exploit the available technology. This training includes everything from basic information about the company (a program known as Bryce University) to training on process improvement interventions such as just-in-time inventory control and high-tech training on new equipment. Bryce has also unleashed employee creativity and innovation by fostering participation at every level. Employees are encouraged to offer suggestions for improving operations, and are generously rewarded if their suggestions are adopted. Bryce is also developing its international business by expanding its partnership with Toga, a Brazilian firm. With one joint-venture plant already operational, a second plant is planned to open in late 1994.

As a company, Bryce Corporation never sits still. The corporate philosophy has always been to constantly monitor the environment for cues that might help the company adapt. Because of this, employees are constantly looking forward in an attempt to develop new products that will exceed customers' expectations.

Strategy change may also be reactive. An example of a successful reactive change is United Parcel Service. UPS was recently forced into the high-tech era by competitors such as FedEx, which have automated package tracking systems. With this system, FedEx could keep up with every shipment to make sure that it fulfilled its next-day-delivery promise to customers. It was also able to tell any customer where his or her package was at any point in time. UPS employees are now using on-board computers to provide quicker pickup and delivery service than they have ever provided before.

kets they will compete in, as well as how to relate to their environment. Strategy also guides the actions taken by an organization. **Strategic change** *involves changing the strategic direction of an organization in terms of, for example, products, services, markets, and/or distribution.* Such changes are often necessary for survival.

For example, PepsiCo's strategic foundation has long been "to do only what we do best." Because of this strategy, PepsiCo is no longer in the transportation or sporting goods business, which it once was, because it turned out to be not very good at strategically managing those businesses. The company is now one-third beverage business (Pepsi-Cola, Slice, Seven-Up, Mountain Dew), one-third snack business (Frito-Lay), and one-third restaurants (Pizza Hut, Kentucky Fried Chicken, Taco Bell)—and it leads its markets in each of these categories.

Strategic change Change involving the strategic direction of an organization in terms of, for example, products, services, markets, and/or distribution.

Another example of strategy change comes from the Will-Burt Company, a mid-sized manufacturing firm in Orrville, Ohio. Will-Burt changed its strategy because of the potential for lawsuits resulting from some of its products. The company stopped making parts for ladders, scaffolds, and aircraft—anything that could create liability problems—and instead focused their energies on producing metal parts (everything from engine shields to meat-grinding tubes) for their customers.

Technological Change

Technological change

Change that involves altering the organization's equipment, engineering processes, research techniques, or production methods.

Technological developments can have great impact on a business. As a result of technological advances, more than half of all existing jobs will be changed within the next decade and an estimated 30% will be completely eliminated.[9] **Technological change** *involves altering the organization's equipment, engineering processes, research techniques, or production methods.* Technological innovations are perhaps the biggest reason for organizational change today.

Factories have been changed dramatically through the infusion of new technology and the better matching of the technical system with the social system. The once familiar scene of blue-collar workers with grease-stained clothes standing on an assembly line performing one small job is rapidly becoming a part of history. Now, robots and computer-controlled machines do some of the repetitive mechanical work in manufacturing, while technicians sit in darkened, climate controlled "nerve centers" monitoring these computers.

Employees who do work on assembly lines are often cross-trained and capable of performing many jobs on the line. So they may often rotate across jobs several times a week or even several times a day. Many also perform routine maintenance on equipment. Assembly-line workers are also often trained to perform managerial duties, such as planning work activities, and collecting and analyzing production data.

The General Motors Saturn plant in Spring Hill, Tennessee provides an excellent example of high-tech changes in manufacturing. At Saturn, cars ride through computer-controlled assembly lines on hydraulic lifts called skillets, which workers can raise or lower to their own height. Workers are also able to "ride" the platform along with the cars, which allows them to finish their work more quickly and with less muscle fatigue. Saturn was able to increase production without increasing the line's speed by moving cars through the assembly sideways instead of bumper to bumper. In addition to these high-tech innovations, Saturn employed some low-tech solutions to common problems. For instance, workers use battery-operated tools to minimize repetitive strain injuries, and stand on soft birch-wood floors instead of concrete.

High technology transformation is not only affecting industrial settings, modern office suites are beginning to look very different from their 1970s and 1980s counterparts. Because of advances in computer chip design and manufacturing, desktop computers are capable of running hundreds of business software packages, and network systems allow computers to communicate with each other. In addition, computer software is becoming so user-friendly that people barely realize they're using computers. Service industries such as banking are also being transformed by new technologies. Automated teller machines have introduced a new level of automated customer service to an industry not traditionally noted for its concern for customers.

Structural Change

An organization's structure is defined in terms of how people and tasks are grouped together, reporting relationships, information flows, and how authority is distributed. **Structural change** *focuses on increasing organizational effectiveness through modifications to the existing organizational structure.* This process can take several forms such as carefully defining job responsibilities, creating the appropriate divisions of labor, or modifying the flow of work. One of the most significant trends is decentralizing the organization—creating a flat, lean structure, organized around processes and teams.

Wal-Mart is a good example of the trend toward decentralization. At Wal-Mart, the distance between employees (known as "associates") and managers is short. Top executives have plain offices on the ground floor of the company's Bentonville, Arkansas, headquarters. They often spend four days a week visiting stores to listen to employees and customers for ideas and suggestions about improving operations. Portraying employees as associates is more than window dressing. Wal-Mart stresses participation, and it is not unusual to see a store manager or department head cleaning up a spill or removing fingerprints from the store's glass doors. In addition, store managers have great freedom to stock whatever items that are selling in their geographic area, within broad boundaries. Although Wal-Mart emphasizes individual initiative and autonomy, it also stresses accountability. Every store manager is responsible for tracking financial information about the store and (with the help of district managers) continually reducing expenses.

Structural change Change that focuses on increasing organizational effectiveness through modifications to the existing organizational structure.

Personnel Change

Personnel change *focuses on increasing organizational effectiveness by upgrading the skills and knowledge of employees.* Ultimately every change in the organization changes the personnel in some way or another. But when an organization stresses regular training and pushes for continuous learning and improvements based on that learning, it means employees become the drivers of change. This is a very important way to make change and improvement a positive and vital force in organizations. It is central to companies practicing TQM. TQM requires training initially in the practical implications of ideas like customer focus, continuous improvement, statistical process control, and teamwork. Then it requires the continuous updating of skills and knowledge. When employees put their new skills to work, this continues to drive change and improvement in a never-ending cycle.

Personnel change Change that focuses on increasing organizational effectiveness by upgrading the skills and knowledge of employees.

Cultural Change

Cultural change refers to *changing the set of shared values, attitudes, beliefs, and assumptions that serve to shape the behaviors and guide the actions of all employees.* Cultural change is an important part of any organizational change because culture defines the organizational environment to which all employees adapt. If an organization attempts to change some part of its operation without addressing how its culture should change along with it, the effort is likely to fail.

The process of changing an organization's culture can take several forms depending on the level of culture one seeks to change. At the individual level, sensitivity

Cultural change Changes in the set of shared values, attitudes, beliefs, and assumptions that serve to shape the behaviors and guide the actions of all employees.

TQM IN ACTION

THE U.S. AIR FORCE RECONCEIVES ITSELF AS A SYSTEM[10]

The U.S. Air Force is facing tremendous pressures for change: force reductions put troop strength in constant flux, planners struggle with budgetary uncertainty, and missions are realigned among units. As the Air Force redesigns its forces to fit real-world constraints and continue meeting mission requirements, it is important that its leaders seriously consider how they envision the organization. It is doubtful whether the traditional, pyramidal organizational structure and corresponding managerial approaches will continue to meet their needs. Air Force personnel today are better educated and more aware of their rights than were previous generations, and their desire for personal and professional fulfillment requires that the Air Force take this into account in their plans.

If a well-educated and self-aware workforce is to excel, it needs something more than directions and instructions. If air crews, officers, and civilians are to continue accomplishing the Air Force mission in an outstanding manner, knowing what to do and even how to do it is not enough. They also need to know why—that is, how their jobs affect the mission. Only when people accept the importance of the mission itself and the importance of their duties in accomplishing that mission will they be able to excel in their duties. To this end, Air Force leaders are reconceiving their organization in terms of a system, based on Deming's flow chart of production as a system (see Exhibit 15-3). Notice how the elements of the organization are arranged in a horizontal flow with input, processes, and output that serves the mission rather than in the form of a hierarchy, which suggests that people serve the next highest rung in that structure.

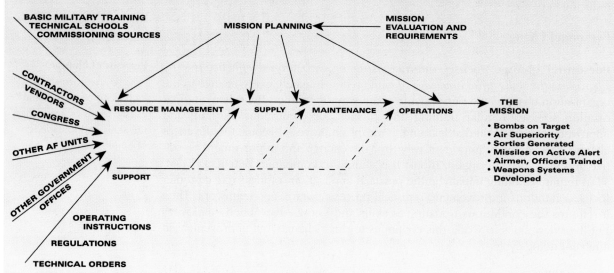

Source: Graham W. Rhinehart, "A New Paradigm for Organizational Structure," *Airpower Journal*, Spring 1992, pp. 49-50. Courtesy of *Airpower Journal*, Airpower Research Institute.

EXHIBIT 15-3 Expanded system flowchart with Air Force-related applications

The mission, the ultimate organizational purpose of the unit, may be strategic or tactical, involving everything from nuclear alerts in support of deterrence to close-air support in Operation Desert Storm. Captain Graham W. Rhinehart, USAF, describes what this new organizational approach might mean for Air Force personnel:

The commander is charged with accomplishing the mission of the unit—for example, the airlifting of cargo and troops by a Military Airlift Command wing. Working backward on the flowchart from the mission (the right number of troops and equipment in the right place at the right time), we first find the aircraft and aircrews who actually perform the mission. Right behind them we find the crew chiefs and maintenance personnel who keep the aircraft airworthy. If we look carefully, we will probably find instructors and standardization/evaluation officers who keep the aircrews trained, as well as air traffic controllers who keep the operations smooth. Working backward even further, we find the supply squadron that provides the proper tools, parts, and individual equipment; mission planners and schedulers; aerospace medicine and life-support functions; and technical-order libraries and contractor support personnel. If we enlarge our vision enough, we find safety technicians, on-the-job training monitors, civil engineering facilities crews, and transportation services. The further back we go through the flowchart, the more we see of what goes into accomplishing the mission.

The systems view and TQM are helping the Air Force maintain its ability to achieve its mission in the face of cutbacks. TQM allows this branch of the military to make more efficient use of all its resources—an important outcome and reason for the adoption of TQM in the first place in any organization.

training has been a widely used technique. At the group or team level, process consultation and teambuilding have been used with some success. At the organization level, survey feedback is frequently used to assess the total organization's functioning. The idea is to involve people in understanding that the values that underlie an organizational culture, how those affect behavior, and how changes in behavior, especially by top management, will eventually bring about new cultural values.

Interdependence of Changes

Because organizations are open systems composed of interacting, interdependent elements, any planned change effort will be more likely to succeed if it acknowledges this interaction and tries to change the system as a whole. Efforts to change one segment (e.g., culture, technology, structure) and graft it back onto the whole will likely meet with failure. In fact, the number of elements that need to be involved in the change increases with the magnitude of change desired. Consider, for example, an organization changing from an individual-based approach to a team-based approach. Not only will the organization have to wrestle with the issues concerning how the teams will accomplish their work (e.g., job design, work layout, etc.), the organization will also have to change performance appraisal, rewards, training, and career development to be consistent with and to support the team approach.

On the other hand, it is also true that some organizational changes are so comprehensive (involving many types of change) that it may be necessary to choose an aspect of the organization and just get started in increments. Change in one part of the organization will bring with it reactions to and changes in the other parts. Realistically, the "master plan" for change will probably have stages. Perhaps in such comprehensive changes, managers begin with strategic and technological changes, followed by structural and personnel changes, and cultural change will probably be the slowest of all.

❓ THINKING CRITICALLY

1. If you were a manager, what aspects of the organization would you try to influence first to bring about changes that will make the company more efficient and effective? Would you make changes in strategy? How about technology or in training for employees? Explain your approach.
2. Why is the systems view a good foundation for beginning major organizational change, especially toward TQM?

ORGANIZATIONAL DEVELOPMENT INTERVENTIONS

As a manager, it is important to appreciate that there is no best way to bring about change in an organization. Sometimes managers and employees will be able to plan, implement, and monitor the entire change effort themselves. In other cases, they will hire a consultant to assist with the planning and execution of the change process. In either case, there are a number of interventions that can be used to aid the change effort. **Intervention** is a term meaning *special actions aimed at bringing about specific changes.* Many of the organization development interventions used today are grounded in the theories of leadership, motivation, teamwork, and communication that were discussed in earlier chapters. A good organization development effort should integrate various types of interventions into a planned change effort. Some of these interventions are discussed below.

Intervention Special actions aimed at bringing about specific changes.

Surveys

This technique involves the use of standardized *surveys* or *questionnaires* to systematically collect and measure employee attitudes about different aspects of the organization. For example, the questionnaire could contain items about employee satisfaction with various aspects of work: job, the organization itself, co-workers, supervisor, working conditions, and so on. It may also ask employees to identify the organization's strengths as well as areas that need improvement. In short, the questionnaire should ask about any aspects of the company that may help identify if and where changes should occur. In addition, the questionnaire may even go so far as to ask for employee suggestions about needed changes.

Typically, a consultant or a human resources manager will distribute questionnaires to all employees, who are asked to complete and return them (usually anonymously) within a certain time period. The HR management will then analyze employee responses and managers will use them to understand what direction change might take and how to bring it about. These surveys might suggest the need of training or new technology, for example. Some organizations use these instruments on a regular basis and measure differences across time.

A problem can arise with the use of surveys. Unless managers plan to use the results to make concrete changes, their use can reinforce a sense of cynicism by employees. They tell their managers what is on their minds, and then nothing happens. This is all too frequently the case with surveys. As a manager, if you take a survey, share its results with employees, tell them what changes you are going to make, and then make those changes.

Teambuilding

As discussed in Chapter 14, teambuilding is a conscious effort to develop effective work teams throughout the organization. This approach analyzes the activities, resource allocations, and relationships of a team (or group or committee) to improve its unity and effectiveness. Most teambuilding activities focus on identifying and reducing barriers to effective team performance as well as improving relationships between team members. Such interventions may also attempt to improve team communication, problem solving, and decision-making processes.[11]

Job Enrichment

Another intervention is job enrichment, which involves basic changes in the content and level of responsibility of a job so as to provide greater challenge to the employee. By expanding the employee's responsibilities, such changes provide an opportunity for employees to derive a feeling of achievement, recognition, responsibility, and personal growth in performing the job, and perhaps increase the motivating potential of the job. Job enrichment helps to influence cultural change because it redefines job responsibilities and expectations for behavior.

Process Consultation

Process consultation focuses on interpersonal relations and group dynamics occurring in work teams. Usually, a process consultant helps group members diagnose problems in team functioning (such as poor communication, ineffective decision-making techniques) and develop appropriate solutions to these problems. The objective is to help team members gain the skills and abilities necessary to identify and solve problems by themselves.

Teamwork Training

This is related to process consultation, but it involves special training offsite to help team members gain confidence in themselves and their teammates. Teamwork training is a kind of Outward Bound type experience where people must depend on each other to get through various obstacles, such as climbing cliffs, whitewater rafting, and similar demanding activities.

Sensitivity Training

Sensitivity training is an organizational development technique that uses discussion groups to develop an awareness of and sensitivity to interpersonal relationships. The objectives of such training are to increase: (1) a person's openness with others, (2) concern for the needs of others, (3) tolerance for individual differences, and (4) listening skills, and similar skills and attributes. Sensitivity training peaked in popularity in the 1970s, although some companies still use it today. Managers typically have trouble transferring the skills learned in sensitivity training back to the organization.

Most people do not feel it is appropriate to always be open about your emotions and feelings in a work environment. Over the years, sensitivity training has

DIVERSITY

GAINING SENSITIVITY TO WOMEN AND TEAMWORK AT FORD[12]

Research at Ford Motor Company has determined that women buy about 49 percent of all cars and influence nearly 80 percent of all buying decisions. To win back consumers from the Japanese, domestic auto makers must keep women's priorities in mind when designing vehicles. However, traditionally, few women have gone into the field of automotive design. This was true at Ford Motor Company, maker of the Probe, a vehicle targeted at women. Mimi Vandermolen became the first woman to completely supervise the creation of a Ford vehicle when she was put in charge of redesigning the 1993 Probe. Mimi made Ford's designers aware of women's special needs, so the new probe includes such features as a fingernail-proof glove compartment and seats that won't snag pantyhose.

Vandermolen earned the job when she made a suggestion that Ford change the design process. Formerly, the car's interior- and exterior-design teams reported to different managers. The two departments operated as separate entities. That meant that the people who designed the hood, fenders, doors and windshield worked in one area and those who designed the seats, dash, steering wheel, and rearview mirror worked in another. Since she came to Ford as a young designer in 1970, Vandermolen often asked why Ford should not put everyone in one big room and have them all report to one person? In 1987, having gained the experience to make her a credible participant and observer, Mimi Vandermolen finally submitted a proposal to her boss, Fritz Mayhew, a director of the luxury car division.

She spelled out her plan's advantages. A united, flexible team would allow Ford to avoid making mistakes in exterior design that would ultimately cause problems in interior design. For example, if the shape of the roof is already set in stone when you get ready to do the interior, you may have to sacrifice passenger space. But if you plan the interior and exterior together, you can create harmony between the two. Vandermolen further explains, "Of course, the key to any good proposal is the bottom line. I pointed out that combining the teams would allow us to reduce head count, save on labor costs by cutting down on overtime and even reduce spending on materials. I was able to demonstrate that changing to this system could save the company about 20 percent on the cost of design." When Mayhew was promoted later that year, he made Vandermolen a design executive and gave her the go-ahead on her proposal. She headed up the first combined team at Ford, which redesigned the Probe, and helped initiate what became a significant shift in Ford's corporate culture. Vandermolen gives the following advice about accelerating change:

- Study the current system.
- Write up a proposal stressing how your plan will be more cost- and staff-efficient. Acknowledge any problems with the plan and offer solutions.
- If you're given the chance to make the presentation to top management, go for it, but don't insist. While everyone should know it's your idea, it also pays to let your boss shine.
- When you get the green light, immediately request everything you'll need to succeed. Top management is likelier to go the extra mile at the outset of the project.

become associated with psychotherapy rather than proper business training, so it is not widely used as an organizational development technique today. However, it has recently been revived in the form of programs aimed at promoting multicultural awareness or dealing with gender issues, or ethic and racial diversity in the workplace.

These are only a few of the many organizational development interventions. The techniques just described primarily deal with issues concerning human process and job structure issues. However, other interventions exist to help organization members become more effective in dealing with strategy and technology issues.

Choosing the appropriate organizational development intervention(s) requires careful attention to the needs of the people involved in the change situation. Attention must also be given to team dynamics, skills of the practitioner, and applicability of the intervention to the desired change.

THINKING CRITICALLY

1. Have you ever filled out a survey in an organization? Did it result in any significant changes taking place?
2. Do you think interventions would work better if initiated by organization management or with the use of outside consultants? Explain your answer.

CULTURE AND CHANGE

Organizational culture refers to the shared values, attitudes, beliefs, and assumptions that are gained or transmitted through group experience and that serve to shape behavior and guide action. Culture is important because it is so pervasive—it shapes employee attitudes and influences the way the organization interacts with its environment. A strong, widely accepted culture can contribute to the success (or downfall) of an organization because it provides people with common understandings, values, and beliefs. These are the basis for cooperation and teamwork. Conversely, culture can also be the source of intense internal competition and divisiveness in an organization, diverting employee attention from their purpose, serving customers and all stakeholders.

It is important that an organization's culture be appropriately focused. Cultures that are focused externally—that is, centered on service to the customer—are usually more sensitive to environmental changes and better able to adapt quickly than companies without such cultures and the values they include.[13] However, just as there is no one best personality type, there is no one best culture. According to the contingency approach, managers should try to nurture a culture that fits the organization's strategy and industry. The only fiat is that continuous improvement of the organization's ability to deliver quality to customers should be its core value.

Microsoft, a company that dominates the worldwide computer software market, maintains the informality and personal relationships characteristic of smaller companies. This not only attracts new computer programmers but helps keep the current employees satisfied. Companies like 3M, Hewlett-Packard, Johnson & Johnson, Cray Research, Merck & Co., and Milliken gear their cultures to encourage and support creativity and innovation; while organizations such as Nucor, Andersen Corporation, and Steelcase emphasize cultures of employee-centered incentives.

Companies trying to implement Total Quality Management often mistakenly believe that they can implement TQM by duplicating programs and approaches that have been successfully used elsewhere. Well-informed managers avoid this approach. They understand, first, that TQM is not a program, and second, that each company is unique and will implement it in ways consistent with their industry, history, size, customer needs, and other factors that make each company different from others.

Cultural Diversity But Common Values

Westinghouse: Baldrige Award Winner

Westinghouse's Productivity and Quality Center provides training, education, and consulting support for the implementation of TQM in all its divisions. However, Westinghouse guards against the tendency to homogeneity by not mandating a single approach to quality throughout the company. Instead, the company has developed a general philosophy with guiding principles, called "The 12 Conditions of Excellence for Total Quality" as shown in Exhibit 15-4. Each division is expected to create programs that reflect this philosophy, but that are also unique to its own operations and needs. Each of the 12 Conditions of Excellence is briefly defined and discussed below.

1. **Customer Orientation**. Satisfying customers through meeting their requirements and value expectation is the primary task of every employee.
2. **Participation**. All employees participate in establishing and achieving Total Quality improvement goals.
3. **Development**. People are recognized as key strategic resources. Development opportunities are provided to assure that each employee understands, supports and contributes to achieving Total Quality.
4. **Motivation**. Employees are motivated to achieve Total Quality through trust, respect and recognition.
5. **Products and Services**. Products and services are appropriately innovative and are reviewed, verified, produced, and controlled to meet customer requirements.
6. **Processes and Procedures**. Processes and procedures used to create and deliver products and services are developed as an integrated, verified and controlled system using appropriate technology and tools.
7. **Information**. Required information is clear, complete, accurate, timely, useful, accessible and integrated with products, services, processes, and procedures.
8. **Suppliers**. Suppliers are considered partners that are selected, measured, controlled and recognized based on their potential and actual value contributions to meeting requirements for Total Quality.
9. **Culture**. Management has established a value system in which individual and group actions reflect a "Total Quality First" and appropriately innovative attitude and direction to meet established world-class requirements.
10. **Planning**. Strategic business and financial planning recognize Total Quality as a primary business objective.
11. **Communications**. Verbal and nonverbal communications are two-way, clear, consistent and forceful.
12. **Accountability**. Accountability measures for Total Quality are established, reported, analyzed and effectively used.

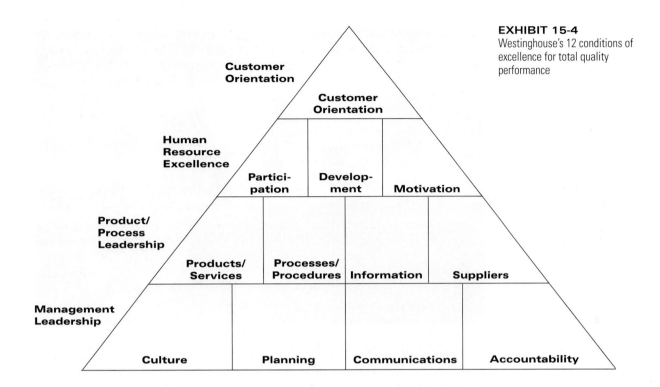

EXHIBIT 15-4
Westinghouse's 12 conditions of
excellence for total quality
performance

Factors Influencing Cultural Change

A Job Well Begun

Since culture emerges from the actions of employees that have been programmed over a long period of time, employees tend to get acclimated to particular ways of doing things and resist change. This is natural as most people prefer
the known to the unknown. This can make changing a culture difficult. Under
the most favorable conditions, cultural changes have to be measured in years,
not weeks or months. However, certain situational factors may facilitate cultural
change or inhibit it. Let's review some of these:

- *Environmental or internal disruption.* This can be any shock—such as a major
  technical breakthrough by a competitor, a dramatic financial loss for the period,
  or the loss of an important customer—that undermines the status quo or calls
  into question the relevance of the current culture. (This is consistent with
  Lewin's model that we discussed earlier.) The situation at IBM that brought
  about the resignation of former chairman John Akers and the hiring of Lou Gerstner from outside the company is one such crisis. A competitive challenge can
  disrupt the complacency of an organization and create a motivation for change.
  Unfortunately, when leaders wait for a crisis to goad them into action, they have
  sometimes waited too long. To avoid this problem, leaders may create competitive challenges or perceptions of crisis to get people motivated for change.[14]

- *The quest for the Malcolm Baldrige National Quality Award.* Quests for this
  award and others can motivate profound cultural changes as the company
  seeks to use the award criteria to remake itself. While not everyone would
  agree that the Baldrige Award provides the best model for guiding planned
  change, many leaders advocate it. For example, Robert Galvin, Chairman of

Competitive challenge and financial loss disrupted the complacency at IBM resulting in the hiring of outsider Lou Gerstner. Even though he had no computer background, he was hired because he also had no IBM corporate cultural bias to hinder his radical changes.

Motorola's Executive Committee, has frequently stated that the Baldrige Award is "the most important catalyst for transforming American business." Some companies use benchmarking of world class companies to disrupt the complacency of people in the company by showing them the "possibilities."

- *Change in leadership.* This usually implies that a new chief executive and other senior managers have been brought on, and with them will usually come many changes that affect culture. For example, Stanley Gault, who was brought in as CEO of Goodyear after retiring from Rubbermaid, has greatly affected the culture of his new company, creating openness, informality (he requests that all employees address him by his first name), and sharing of information that was not there before. A change in leadership often goes hand in hand with organizational disruptions arising from events like lost market share and declining profitability. Under the proper circumstances, new top leadership can provide alternative ways of organizing and behaving and may be perceived as more capable of responding to the organization's needs.

  We mentioned that the board of directors at IBM hired Lou Gerstner, the former chairman and CEO of RJR Nabisco Holdings Corporation, to reverse the eight-year slide of the once dominant computer maker. Although Gerstner has no experience working in a high tech industry, he was brought in from "outside" because he has no prejudices about IBM or the computer industry to prevent him from making whatever radical changes are necessary.

- *Age of the organization.* In general, and all other things being equal, the younger the organization, the easier it will be to change its culture. In younger organizations, the existing culture may not be as solidified or entrenched as the cultures of older organizations. In addition, younger organizations tend to be smaller, allowing management to communicate their new vision and values to employees more easily. Apple Computer was formed in 1976 by Steve Jobs and Steve Wozniak after they had built one of the first PCs in their garage. As the company grew, it became known for its unique informal culture as well as for its innovative, user-friendly products. For example, employees would always dress casually for work. A suit and tie would have stood out like a sore thumb at Apple. This culture continued until 1989 when John Sculley reorganized the company and it became less laid back, and somewhat less casual. Concerned about the future prosperity of the company, he hired several conservative, authoritative managers for key positions. These changes did not go over well with the employees, but the fact remains that such dramatic changes would not have been as easy at a more mature company such as IBM or General Motors.[15]

- *Strength of culture.* In general, the more widely held are culture's values, beliefs, and assumptions among employees, the more difficult it will be to change. In contrast, a weaker culture without strong values and widespread support is more amenable to change. For example, in 1994, a proposed merger between Southwestern Bell and TCI Cable company came unraveled. One of the reasons given for this was culture conflict. The informal atmosphere of Colorado-based TCI clashed with the button-down world of Southwestern Bell. When parts of the deal also became troublesome, this diversity of culture contributed to their not being able to work out the problems.

It is difficult to separate out cultural change from other changes in an organization, because it is so pervasive and influences how managers and employees interpret situations and make decisions. However, by the same token we are not meant to be slaves to our culture. We create it, we can understand it, and we can change and make improvements in it. However, this does not happen by decree of management. It happens when managers and everyone openly address company problems, make decisions about changes that solve these problems, and then, most importantly, "walk the talk." When top management behaves in ways consistent with cultural values it seeks to implement, employees will get the message. This is not a quick process, but over time the new values that enhance productivity will become the norm.

❓ THINKING CRITICALLY

1. If you have ever been a member of an organization, such as a fraternity or sorority or some other social, professional, or service group, did you find it had an entrenched culture? If you were leading that organization and felt the need for a culture change, how do you think you would bring that about?
2. What actions did Glen Hiner take that helped Owens Corning change its culture? Why do you think he succeeded?

RESISTANCE TO CHANGE

As a manager it is part of your responsibility to implement change. We often hear that people resist change. However, this is not exactly true. What is true is that people resist doing things they do not understand, that make them uncertain, and that they do not see to be in their best interest.[17] This is perfectly natural. This does not mean though that people resist all change. In fact, all of us are

A LOOK AT

ETHICS

OWENS-CORNING REJUVENATES UNDER NEW LEADERSHIP[16]

Owens-Corning Fiberglas Company has been having some rough times lately. To save itself from a takeover, the company had to do a leveraged buyout on itself, borrowing about $2 billion to pay shareholders a dividend of $81 a share. The new debt made the company an unattractive takeover target but forced management to sell off businesses and cut their funds for research and development (R&D), which had been an important company strength for many years. With the retirement of its CEO and business slowdowns due to economic conditions (low residential construction and cut back on boat production), and asbestos lawsuits, the company had to make some serious changes.

The Owens-Corning board hired a new CEO, Glen Hiner, who walked into an unpleasant situation with enthusiasm. He began to transform the company by shifting more R&D budget into product development and away from cutting processing costs. Along with this, he emphasized creating new markets for products made of fiberglas. For example, to expand its already strong presence in the roofing business, Owens-Corning developed fiberglas roof tiles that look like terra-cotta clay but are lighter and easier to install. This meant that the tiles could be sold in the replacement market, too, for roofs that could not support heavy tiles. In similar fashion, Owens Corning has entered the house window business with glass fiber window frames, patio doors and skylights.

Hiner pounds away at building a better company. "One of my jobs is to convince people that the good old days aren't coming back," he says. "Sure there will be early retirement options, and cost-cutting. We have 40 plants—why does every plant need its own payroll department? We don't do a very good job of leveraging our purchasing or information systems. So there's plenty to do. This is a different world, and it challenges everything we do. Can we do it better? Because if we don't, someone else in the world will take it away. Restructuring is a way of life."

Hiner shies away from the image of a ruthless cost-cutter. "I'm from West Virginia. Dad worked in a coal mine all his life. I come with a certain amount of humility. I didn't come here to tear down the company. The role of dignity and respect in this company would be special to me, from day one." Hiner takes part in get-together-with-the-boss programs, tours plants with the union leaders, attends family nights at baseball games, hockey, and the symphony with employees. Restructuring and cost-cutting don't have to mean relentlessly firing people and playing hardball with everyone inside and outside. In the best organizations, it means getting more efficient, taking better advantage of employee talents, and, most importantly, delivering quality products to customers that will bring back the business.

often making changes, small and sometimes large, in our lives that we believe will benefit us in one way or another. As a student for example, you may change your study habits as you discover different techniques to make you more efficient. This might include how you take notes or prepare for a test. On the job, you might discover a better way to perform some task and adopt it over what you had been doing previously.

In general people do not resist change, but they may resist being changed by others, especially when that change seems mainly to have a payoff for someone else. Understanding how people react to change can help you as a manager more successfully implement change in any organization of which you might be a member.

There are a number of reasons employees tend to believe that proposed changes will not be in their best interest. They often provoke anxiety and uncertainty, feelings we all like to avoid. However, by understanding how employees might come to be uncertain about how changes will benefit them, managers can take steps to make sure that employees have a good answer for the WIIFM (what's in it for me) question. Exhibit 15-5 summarizes several sources of resistance to change, and these are described below.

Insecurity

Once people have worked in a particular culture for a period of time, they begin to feel comfortable; they know where things are, who the people are, and what to expect on a day to day basis—even when that culture is not open and supportive. People adjust to whatever circumstances they find themselves in. Change brings with it uncertainty, insecurity, and sometimes fear. When people are unsure of what is going to happen to them, they resist making changes. When managers start discussing reorganization and redesigning people's jobs or the possibility of reporting to a new boss, employees are naturally going to become anxious. In addition, feelings of insecurity can be exacerbated if employees who share the same fears and self-interests band together. In proposing such changes as described above or any change, managers need to be aware of and sensitive to these feelings in their employees.

Disturbance of Established Social Systems

Change may result in a disruption of social and professional relationships. Once employees understand their relationships with others, they are going to resist changes that threaten these relationships. For example, changes in job, tasks, or

EXHIBIT 15-5
Sources of resistance to change

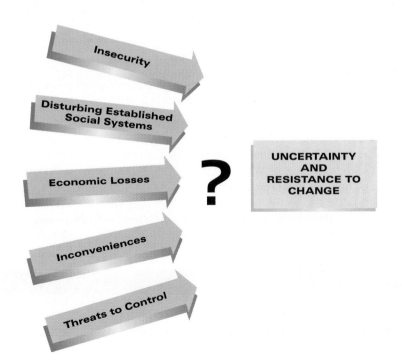

responsibilities may require people to work in a different area of the company, or with different co-workers and may prevent an individual from maintaining contact with previous friends. This not only disrupts formal work patterns and hierarchy, it also changes the informal work group.

Economic Losses

Employees may come to believe that a proposed change in the organization represents a threat to them economically. They may begin to worry about whether they will retain their jobs and what effect the change will have on their careers. Further, they may begin to worry about money issues and the need to have an income to support their lifestyles. Although such worries may be completely unfounded, they will still be there, causing resistance.

Inconveniences

Change can produce a variety of inconveniences for people who are accustomed to their routines. Sometimes a person will remain employed but be transferred to a new job where they may have a reduction in pay, power, influence, and, perhaps, self-esteem. Similarly, the potential obsolescence of a person's knowledge, skills, and contacts may become more apparent when major changes are eminent. Even if organizational changes do not result in a disruption of social relationships or a reduction in income, new procedures and techniques often have to be learned, and old habits have to be unlearned. Unlearning is painful for most people and requires time and energy for new learning.

Threats to Control

Sometimes, organizational changes may reduce the power base of an individual or group. As an individual or group gives up part of its stake in the organization, or as its stake changes, the individual or group's influence in the system is diminished. Changes may even cause some people to feel that their own destiny is being controlled by someone else, which may result in resentment.

? **THINKING CRITICALLY**

1. Have you ever been presented with proposed changes that you were unsure were in your best interest? What did that do to your motivation to participate? Did the changes come to pass or did a lack of support cause the initiative to dissolve?
2. If you were a manager, how do you think you would help employees understand that a proposed change was in their best interest?

OVERCOMING RESISTANCE TO CHANGE

As noted above, people are going to resist changes that they do not see as being clearly in their best interest. There are several steps managers can take to help employees see the personal gain in going along with a change. In general, these

EXHIBIT 15-6
Techniques for overcoming employee resistance to change by demonstrating payoff to employee for making change

steps aim at bringing employees into the process early and valuing their input. Exhibit 15-6 briefly captures these steps, which are described in more detail above.

Communication/Involvement

Managers should involve employees in the planning and execution of change efforts, especially if those employees will be affected by the change. Employees should be involved from the very first step, helping to identify the reasons or necessity for change, the nature of the change, the timing of the change, and its possible effects on the organization and its members. It is difficult for an individual to resist a change decision in which they participated. But for this to happen, there must be open and honest two-way communication between all levels in the organization. Withholding information from employees is only going to result in opposition to the planned change. Similarly, any surprises for employees will usually be greeted with suspicion and resistance.

Understanding

Only when all organization members fully understand a proposed change can it be effective. They need to understand the purpose of the change in terms they can relate to, how the change is going to happen, when, and who will be involved and affected in the change. This understanding helps generate support for the change by focusing attention on the personal and organizational benefits that will result from it. Certain questions will invariably be asked by employees, and managers should be prepared to answer them before moving ahead. These questions include: Will I lose my job? Will my knowledge, skills, and abilities become obsolete? Am I capable of operating effectively under the changes? How will my power and prestige be changed? Will I have to work longer or different hours?

Education and Retraining

Employees may resist change if they believe (correctly or incorrectly) that they will not have the necessary skills to perform effectively under the changes. To combat this resistance, managers should assure employees that they will receive training in any new skills and knowledge they need to perform and that they have an important role to play after the change is implemented. For example, an organization's secretarial staff should be assured they will receive training in new software programs and other skills they may need when a company moves to flatten its organizational structure.

Make Only Necessary Changes

Changes should only be made when the situation demands that they be made, not because of a whim on the part of management. Change for the sake of change is wasteful and is likely to be met with considerable opposition. Any change in the organization must be carefully thought out, with the purpose of improving employees' capabilities for adding value to organizational processes.

Pilot Test

Resistance to change can also be reduced by starting first on a small scale in one part of the organization. A pilot test of a proposed change will allow organization members to spend some time working under the change and provide feedback so adjustments can be made before the change effort is implemented across the organization. The pilot test can also illustrate the potential benefits of the change and show that the drawbacks of change really aren't all that painful.

Positive Attitude

A powerful, but often overlooked tool for reducing resistance to change is a positive attitude about change. Managers across the organization should consciously project this attitude. Optimism must pervade the ranks of management and "infect" the employees. Successful change efforts usually have at least one person who champions the change; an individual who stands behind the change at all times and who will accept nothing else. The key to instilling a proper attitude is to address all of the other issues discussed above. But it must be done through effective leadership.

Managers will have a good foundation for promoting change once they acknowledge that their performance will increasingly depend on higher quality products, flawless service to customers, and continuous improvement of every organizational system and product. They must be willing to make necessary

AN ENVIRONMENT FOR CHANGE

Louise Goeser is vice president for quality at the Whirlpool Corporation in Benton Harbor, Michigan. She is a former judge for the Malcolm Baldrige National Quality Award. She writes of change in organizations and her experience at Whirlpool.

Change is one of those things that look pretty simple on paper and turns out to be a lot more complicated in reality. I've either seen or participated in quite a few corporate change processes—as an employee and as a Baldrige examiner—and I'm always struck by the fact that it takes so much planning and work to gain the initial momentum for change, no matter how necessary and desirable the change might be.

The reason for this is that corporate organizations have a lot of inertia, which is also momentum, of course, but it's a kind of momentum that uses its energy to keep things the way they are. There are some time-honored procedures for carrying out key functions, traditional measurements, longstanding customs and conventions for handling routine decisions. All of these tend to resist change even if employees are generally supportive of management's desire to find new ways of doing things.

That's why understanding how to harness employee motivation in the process is so essential in successful change efforts. It's not so much that you need to break down employee resistance; it's that you need to battle the organization's inertia to make change happen in spite of all that work to keep things the same. You have to recognize that you're forging an alliance, which means the employees have to understand *why* as well as *what* changes are necessary.

Some companies are effective at forging such alliances. Many aren't. The one's that aren't are generally the ones in which management thinks employees are obstacles rather than partners in change. The ones who are effective realize that there's more to change than making decrees and expecting employees to simply go along. Those good at change realize they have to be extremely good in five areas.

The first is *leadership.* This is a term to toss around, but I have a favorite definition that captures what I mean: Leadership is the ability to make people believe they can accomplish things they never thought possible. An example of leadership of this kind is Whirlpool CEO David Whitwam. Five years ago, he took the helm of a $4 billion domestic appliance manufacturer. Since then, he has not only convinced our workforce that their company can be a global leader in their industry, he has inspired them to do exactly that. Today, Whirlpool is a $7.5 billion company operating in North America, Latin America, Europe, and Asia. This represents a huge change, and it's one that couldn't have been achieved without the kind of leadership that is capable of developing a clear vision that is shared with the entire workforce.

Sharing the vision obviously implies extensive *communication.* This the second key characteristic of companies that know how to change successfully. The *what* and the *why* and the *how* of change have to be communicated, even to the point of overkill, throughout the organization. Only this kind of communication can bring about the laser-like focus that's needed to change exactly the right things. Certainly it's a lot easier to talk in general terms about "improving everything," but nothing ever really improves unless your people know precisely which priorities are at the top of the list. Whirlpool, for example, develops a list of between five and seven clear priorities for each business year, and these are the focus of company communications—and accountabilities—throughout the year.

But leadership and communication aren't sufficient by themselves. That's because the *how* of change usually involved acquiring new skills, new ways of solving problems, new business perspectives. These are capabilities that can only be acquired through *education and training.* Companies that are serious about their change plans are the ones who prove it by investing in the courseware and time needed to learn new skills and ideas.

A LOOK AT

MANAGERS IN ACTION

The fourth key factor may seem obvious, but it's surprising how many companies overlook the need for *measurement of results*. Unless you know how to gauge the amount of changes you've accomplished, in terms that relate change to improved results in the market, any seeming successes by internal measures will be delusions.

The final characteristic is hard to capture with a label, but it's as important as the others. It has to do with *the overall environment* and whether it is one that openly encourages new and different ideas. This requires allowing, or even seeking out, differences of opinion, opportunities for the kind of learning that occurs when ideas are tested by means of debate and experimentation. Clearly, this is an environment that can't exist without leadership, communication, and training, but it's not an automatic by-product of these either. In fact, it's the real difference between companies that lead their markets and those that are just trying to keep up.

changes in strategy, structure, technology, personnel, and culture in order to better cope in a globally competitive business environment. Once managers adopt this attitude, then they will be in a position to develop a workforce with committed, flexible, multi-skilled, constantly retrained employees who work together as a team.

 THINKING CRITICALLY

1. In reviewing the techniques managers can use to overcome resistance to change, how do you think each of these techniques helps to reduce uncertainty in employees? Why does reducing uncertainty reduce resistance to change?
2. If major changes were planned in organization you were part of, how do you think you would feel about them if you were consulted early on and kept informed throughout the planning? Why?

LEARNING ORGANIZATIONS

Over the past few years a concept called "the learning organization" has developed out of the systems view of organizations. The systems view is an inclusive sense of an organization, which is designed to raise management and employee consciousness that "we are all in this together." This implies that whether managers like it or not or understand it or not, the efficiency and effectiveness of the organization is, to a large degree, dependent on how well everyone works together to achieve objectives.

A learning organization is one in which everyone understands that the world is changing rapidly, that they must be aware of these changes, adapt to them, and more importantly, be a force for change. Since change is so predominant, it is important to be aware of it and to do everything possible to lead change (and improve) rather than be trampled by it. Here is a more complete definition of **learning organization:** *"It is an organization that has woven a continuous and enhanced capacity to learn, adapt, and change into its culture."* The learning results in continuous improvement in areas such as work processes, products, and services, the structure and function of individual jobs, and effective management practices."[18]

Learning organization
An organization that has woven a continuous and enhanced capacity to learn, adapt, and change into its culture.

So a learning organization is one in which change and improvement is institutionalized, not for the sake of change but to help the company more effectively and efficiently meet its purpose of delivering quality to customers and satisfying its other stakeholders. This is an organization where employees are constantly aware of what their experience is telling them about performance, learning from their experience, and learning from the experience of others. As a whole these organizations also make it a policy to train employees in new skills and knowledge to help them improve their abilities to contribute.

There are 12 factors that help define what a successful learning organization is like. These derive from an extensive study of organizations that are widely recognized as valuing learning and change and that are very successful in their markets and industries. The following briefly reviews these 12 factors. As you read them, reflect on how they help to describe what is going on in companies like Whirlpool as described in the *A Look At Managers in Action* box on page 579.

1. **Clearly Understood Strategy and Vision.**   A vision and broad strategy that everyone understands and shares provide direction and focus for learning by organizational members. Further, the vision and strategy must incorporate the ideas that learning and improvement are going to take place. Achieving the shared vision, thus, requires that learning take place. Companies such as GE, Corning, Motorola, and Johnsonville Foods all have strategies based on the idea that continuous learning will help ensure the achievement of these strategies.

2. **Supportive Executive Practices.**   Top managers support the idea of continuous learning and serve as inspiration to employees in its practice. As an example of what this means, consider this statement to top managers from Alan Mulally, a vice president of Boeing Corporation: "Keep asking yourself every day, 'What is the biggest contribution I can make to establish a creative learning environment, an environment where everyone is contributing to the business plan?'"

3. **Supportive Managerial Practices.**   For the learning organization to work, those who manage and supervise employees must support and make its practice a reality. When employees know their supervisors are behind individual and group learning to improve, they believe it and act on it. These managers help employees integrate what they have learned to improve their performance. They act more as coaches than supervisors. In companies like Johnsonville Foods, for example, they have eliminated the term "manager" and use instead the term "coordinator," which they believe better describes what a manager does.

4. **A Climate of Openness and Trust.**   This incorporates the organization's overall values and attitudes about how people are supposed to act and go about their jobs. It is about the same as the idea of culture. In a learning organization, there is a climate or openness and trust, where employees are not afraid to say what's on their minds and people listen to each other.

5. **Supportive Organization/Job Structure.**   In learning organizations there is flexibility in structure and job descriptions. This flexibility facilitates rather than constrains the people working together and doing what's necessary to achieve goals. The idea is to eliminate bureaucracy and get people working together cross-functionally to more efficiently and effectively achieve goals. At Hallmark, for example, the company redesigned jobs around holiday-

related products, eliminating the old functional department. This has greatly reduced the amount of time to get cards on the market.

6. **Ready Access to Information.** Companies that value learning and improvement take advantage of technology to obtain and distribute information. They have systems in place that allow employees to gain quick access to information they need to do their jobs. Wal-Mart, with its own satellite communication system connected to every store and vendor, gives store managers (among others) immediate access to financial and inventory information to enhance their decision making.

7. **Experience Sharing Between Individuals and Teams.** Learning organizations have methods set up that allow individuals and teams to share their experiences with others so everyone benefits by learning from mistakes as well as successes. In learning organizations, no one is looking to blame anyone for making a mistake. They simply see this as another opportunity to better understand what works well and what works poorly. At the Palo Alto Research Center of Xerox, for example, the company found that technicians learned more about repairing machines from sharing experiences with each other than from reading manuals.

8. **Work Processes that Value Continuous Learning and Improvement.** While a company can give lip service to learning and even have communication and other systems in place to support it, the test is whether they encourage it in the everyday work habits on employees. Does it support the use of systematic problem-solving methods or the use of benchmarking (learning from the best practitioners within or outside the company)? Xerox, for example, has trained all its employees in a six-step process for understanding and creatively solving problems.

9. **Regular Feedback.** In learning organizations, managers provide employees with regular feedback on how they are doing. There is a continuous dialog between managers and employees so employees know that what they learn and are trying to apply is improving their performance. Without regular feedback built into the learning process, it would lack direction. At Bell Atlantic, for example, CEO Raymond Smith has made it a priority to give employees regular information on the company's goals and strategies and regular feedback on each department and even each individual is contributing to achieving those goals. Further, these organizations actively seek out feedback, especially complaints, from customers as information they need to improve.

10. **Value Training and Education.** Learning organizations make formal training and education an important part of their culture and practices. These training programs help employees learn from each other as well help employees at every level gain new skills. At Corning, for example, employees each average 92 hours of training per year and many of the instructors are the employees themselves. This is based on the idea that you learn most when you have to teach. As employees at Corning gain new skills, their pay increases.

11. **Empowered Individuals and Teams.** Managers of learning organizations understand that when employees and teams have the responsibility to learn, they must also have the authority to adapt that learning in their daily work. This reinforces with individuals and teams how much the company values learning and management wants them to use what they learn to improve. At Polaroid, for example, empowered teams developed the Helios medical imaging technology in less than half the time taken for other products. Comments

TRANSFORMING MANAGERS INTO LEADERS AT ANALOG DEVICES, INC.

Chairman and CEO Ray Stata explains what he calls "the biggest challenge of all" in accomplishing change, that is, transforming managers into leaders.

"The first time I heard of quality management was back in the early 1980s, when Analog was doing wonderfully. My motivation for learning TQM was the thought, 'We're great, but we can do even better.' This is a hard sell if your goal is to create revolutionary change. Also, my approach to managing change was naive—'Here are the books; you're smart guys, go read them and make it better. Quality's free; just do it!'

"Three years after the speeches and slogans, of course, nothing had happened. So I said to myself, well, maybe we're missing something here. Maybe we need a vice president of quality. So we went out and got a very good one, Art Schneiderman. Art arrived in the mid-1980s, when things weren't looking quite so good and the environment was a bit more receptive to change. Art knew what he was talking about and, at the time, I didn't. So I said, 'Hey, Art,

would you please come in here and get this damn place on the road to quality?' The way I saw it, my role was occasionally to cheerlead, give more speeches, and say how important this quality stuff was. Making it happen was Art's job.

"Between 1986 and 1990, Art made incredible progress in convincing the organization of the value of TQM methods. This was what's called, in the language of Joseph Juran of the Juran Institute in Wilton, Connecticut, the period of 'picking the low-hanging fruit.' There were so many problems out there that you could do almost anything and make progress.

"Then, in 1990, we began to hit the wall again. This time our motivation was fear and humiliation—far more powerful than earlier motivators. At this time I came to understand . . . that making it happen was my job, not Art's. So I had to become knowledgeable enough and skilled enough to lead the process. This challenge started with me but would have to cascade down through every manager in the company. We all had to transform ourselves into leaders of the change process.

"There are many dimensions to this transformation. The new knowledge and skills required to be an effective leader in the 1990s can be pretty daunting. The leader of the 1990s will be a facilitator of change—a learner and teacher, a coach and counselor, a role model, a diagnostician, a designer of new systems and organizational structures, and a master of conversation.

"A special role for the leader at the top of the organization is to be an iconoclast. The biggest impediment to change is your assumptions and beliefs; nothing fails like success. You have to identify the beliefs and assumptions that used to work but are now getting in your way. In companies with strong cultures, that's a hard knot to unravel. The leader must demonstrate through words and deeds that throwing out things that were once held sacred is not only OK but necessary.

"I'm excited and challenged by how much I have to learn to provide the leadership Analog Devices needs. Every day I learn a little bit more, and every day I learn just how much more I have yet to learn."[19]

CEO I. MacAllister Booth, "Our researchers are not any smarter, but by working together they get the value of each other's intelligence almost instantaneously." When teams value learning and openly share what they learn with others and feel empowered to use it, the organization gets better faster.

12. **Reward and Recognition Programs.** Reward and recognition programs are really highly visible forms of feedback. They reinforce what the company

values in a public manner. In the case of the learning organization, rewards, from raises and bonuses to a lunchtime recognition ceremony, this tells employees that learning and improvement is the heart of the organization and an important part of their jobs. Sometimes this may even mean rewarding employees when they make mistakes as that helps the company learn.

All of these factors overlap one another. They are all consistent with an approach that recognizes that change and improvement are vital to any organization's prosperity. You will also note that these ideas are consistent with those we have introduced throughout the book. When you view an organization as an open system, you begin to appreciate its dynamic nature and the importance of change and improvement to remain a part of that world. Companies that have failed have been those whose managers misunderstood the importance of learning and adaptation to change.

Finally we should also note that the ideas surrounding a learning organization are completely consistent with the principles of Total Quality Management. TQM is about managing system processes to serve customers and continuously improve a company's ability to do that. This implies learning and change. As a manager responsible for some part of your organization's success, you should be aware of what it takes to create a learning organization. They represent the attributes of those managers and organizations most likely to survive, grow, and prosper over the long haul.

 **THINKING CRITICALLY**

1. What is your reaction to the characteristics that describe a learning organization? Do they describe an organization you would like to work for? What does that tell you about implementing these characteristics as a manager?
2. Have you ever worked for an organization that could be described as a learning organization? If yes, what was it like? If not, did you feel frustrated in your position or at least uninspired beyond putting in your hours?

SUMMARY

CONSTANT PRESSURES FOR CHANGE
- Change is a constant in life within and outside of organizations.
- Some factors outside the organization that bring about change include government regulations, economic forces, marketplace changes, technology, and labor market fluctuations.
- Internal forces for change include such things as strategy, workforce composition, and new equipment.

THE PROCESS OF PLANNED CHANGE
- Lewin's three stage model of change includes (1) an unfreezing stage, (2) a change and movement stage, and (3) a refreezing stage. TQM suggests that healthy organizations stay mainly in stage two.
- Managers may successfully initiate change proactively in anticipation of opportunities or reactively in response to various market and other pressures.

TYPES OF PLANNED CHANGE

- There are several types of planned changes a manager can suggest, including changes involving strategy, technology, organization structure, personnel, and culture. All of these are interdependent, where a change in one area affects all the others.

ORGANIZATIONAL DEVELOPMENT INTERVENTIONS

- There are a variety of ways managers can intervene to bring about changes. This include surveys, team building exercises, job enrichment, process consultation, teamwork training, and sensitivity training.

CULTURE AND CHANGE

- Organizational culture plays a key role in whether it will be easy or difficult for management to bring about change.
- Some factors influencing cultural change include disruptions from outside the organization that shock it into change, the quest for the Baldrige Award, changes in leadership, the organization's age, and how rigid the culture is.

RESISTANCE TO CHANGE

- Employees resist change when they are uncertain about any personal payoffs for making a change.

OVERCOMING RESISTANCE TO CHANGE

- Managers, by bringing employees into the change process early and demonstrating how change is in their best interest, can successfully deal with resistance to change.

LEARNING ORGANIZATIONS

- A learning organization gives change and improvement primacy in its culture.

KEY TERMS

Cultural change 563	Proactive change 560
Framebreaking change 556	Reactive change 560
Intervention 566	Strategic change 561
Learning organization 580	Structural change 563
Personnel change 563	Technological change 562
Planned change 557	

REVIEW QUESTIONS

1. Especially today, why is a concern with change and improvement so important to everyone in an organization?
2. What are the three stages of Lewin's model of change? Why is the third stage no longer completely accurate?

3. What is the difference between proactive and reactive change? Is one more effective than the other? Why or why not?
4. What are six types of planned changes and how are they interrelated?
5. What is an organizational development intervention, and what is its relationship to managing change?
6. What is the relation of culture to organizational change?
7. How would the quest for the Baldrige Award affect organizational culture?
8. Why do employees and people in general seem to resist change?
9. In general, how can managers overcome employee resistance to change?
10. What is the relationship between a learning organization and Total Quality Management?

EXPERIENTIAL EXERCISE

Identify an incident that required you to make a dramatic change in your life, either as a member of a student organization, a work organization, a volunteer organization, or your family. Draw a force field diagram that shows the forces that encouraged you to resist the change, and the forces that encouraged you to go along with the change. Based on what you learned in this chapter, develop a plan for intervening in this situation (with suggested intervention techniques and sequence of implementation) to modify the status quo and move toward changes that would improve the situation. Relate this plan to how a manager would plan an intervention to bring about change in an organization.

CASE ANALYSIS AND APPLICATION
The Role of Education and Lifelong Learning in Cultural Transformation at Honeywell-Canada[20]

In 1987, Minneapolis-based Honeywell launched a corporate-wide effort to refocus the organization. Every Honeywell plant analyzed the products it was producing, figured out which ones it was best at and could sell. The objective was for each plant to focus on building a narrow range of product lines and to become the very best manufacturer of its chosen products.

As part of this effort, the managers at Honeywell's factory in Scarborough, Ontario, wanted to accomplish three objectives: (1) break down the traditional factory culture, (2) design a new team-based approach, and (3) continue to provide high value to customers. To reinvent the factory, managers realized they had to change the factory's culture. They also recognized that the major barrier to such change would be employee resistance. Employees who were used to working at one area and constantly being told what to do by a supervisor would naturally be resistant when asked to operate independently in self-directed work teams.

Honeywell managers recognized that employee education was the only way to make this endeavor succeed. They realized that the renewal effort was dependent on the workforce and its ability to be creative and flexible, and to operate effectively in the new environment. So Honeywell-Scarborough began a quiet revolution in the job training and education its employees received. Formally known as the "Learning for Life" initiative (named to signify that learning is a never-ending process), it was nothing less than a plant-wide effort to upgrade employees' knowledge, skills, and abilities so they would be capable of meeting the challenges in the factory of the future.

The Learning for Life initiative began in 1991 (in partnership with the local board of education and several local labor agencies) by offering courses in basic adult education such as literacy, numeracy, and computer literacy. These early courses were free, voluntary, and on-site, but employees attended classes on their own time.

To provide more advanced knowledge and skills, a partnership was formed with a nearby community college. Through this partnership, employees were able to earn college diplomas and certificates. These classes focused on production and inventory management as well as workplace interpersonal skills. Like the earlier classes, these courses were free, voluntary and on-site, but employees attended classes immediately after work hours.

In addition to the after-work educational opportunities, mandatory job-related training was also provided. This on-the-job training emphasizes skills important to specific jobs such as just-in-time inventory control systems, team effectiveness, interpersonal communication skills, problem solving, and similar courses.

The emphasis on employee education and training paved the way for needed changes in the factory systems, and the results of this tremendous change effort are clear. Between 1987 and 1992, productivity at the Scarborough factory rose 40%, work-in-process inventory went down 60%, the cycle-time from customer order to delivery of the final product dropped 50%, and scrap and rework rates went down 50%. In addition, employees now work in self-directed teams and are more committed than ever to the philosophy of continuous education and improvement.

The transformation of Honeywell's culture was not easy and did not happen overnight. It took time, patience, energy, and understanding on the part of everyone involved. Results like those at Honeywell depend on a workforce with greater knowledge, skills, and abilities. These, in turn, lead to increased creativity, adaptability, and flexibility—attributes that are essential for competing (and surviving!) in today's global marketplace.

Discussion Questions

1. Why did Honeywell need to change?
2. Evaluate Honeywell's efforts to change in terms of the concepts discussed in this chapter.
3. How could Honeywell have better used "customer focus" in its efforts to transform its culture?
4. Do you think Honeywell is a good example of a learning organization? Why or why not?

SERVICE QUALITY AT FEDEX

FedEx is a leader in the transportation industry and a model of how to use the principles of Total Quality Management to provide superior services to customers and enhance its success as the leader in overnight shipping. FedEx's front line employees (couriers who pick up and deliver packages, customer service representatives who handle customer queries, and the staff of mini-center shipping offices) are the ones who interact the most with customers. Since these "service providers" have the greatest opportunity to understand customer needs, FedEx gathers their input to develop new and improved services and to identify opportunities for continuously improving existing services.

These employees are also the key to ensuring that their customers are satisfied with the company's services. For these reasons, FedEx devotes a lot of attention to motivating employees to attend to their customers needs, communicate this information to managers, and to continuously improve the service they provide to customers. FedEx even empowers the service providers to waive the charges if a package is delivered late or if the customer is not satisfied with some other aspect of the service. All of these efforts are part of FedEx's overall strategy to develop a customer-focused culture.

FedEx has these service providers help the company in administering 2,100 customer interviews per quarter to gather information on the company's quality of service and customer satisfaction. Information gathered through these surveys helped FedEx to establish programs such as real-time tracking with 1-800 telephone service, expedited customs clearance, volume discounts, and customized rate programs.

FedEx also publishes a magazine called *Via* and offers subscriptions to secretaries and other administrators at most of the organizations that use their services. *Via* has articles relating to the jobs that these clerical workers perform, such as shorthand, grammar, dictation, memos, office ergonomics, and desk exercises. Since the magazine targets the person primarily responsible for deciding on shipping services, it helps to create a bond with the company and a preference for FedEx's services. FedEx couriers are also able to procure customer surveys that are included in *Via*.

Besides engaging their service providers in helping the company better understand customer needs, FedEx clearly communicates the company's goals and standards to all employees and evaluates progress in meeting these goals and standards. Fred Smith, FedEx's founder and CEO, has frequently stated that the company's objective is to provide 100% customer satisfaction. Service delivery performance is evaluated through FedEx's Service Quality Indicator (SQI) program. SQI data is obtained from the customer by a FedEx service provider, usually a courier. The twelve components that comprise the SQI are weighted differently depending upon its importance to customer satisfaction. For example, a weight of one is given for a package that is delivered on the right day but later than was promised, while a 10 is allocated for a forgotten or missed pick-up. Management meets daily to discuss the day's SQI results and compare them to weekly, monthly, and annual trends.

FedEx also attends to the human needs of its employees in accordance

The authors thank Dave Freeman for contributing to the development of this case. Information taken from G. Bounds, "Federal Express: The Vision Made Real," in G. Bounds, L. Yorks, M. Adams, and G. Ranney, *Beyond Total Quality Management* (New York: McGraw-Hill, 1994) p. 520; additional sources for the case include: J.P. Cananess and G.H. Manoocheri, "Building Quality into Services," *SAM Advanced Management Journal,* Winter 1993, pp. 4–8; K. Denton, "Behind the Curve," *Business Horizons,* July-August 1993, pp. 1–4; R. Jacob, "TQM: More than a Dying Fad?" *Fortune,* October 18, 1993, pp. 66–72; P. Palvia, S. Sullivan, and S. Zeltman, "PRISM Profile: An Employee Oriented System," *HR Focus,* June 1993; B. Smith, "FedEx's Key to Success," *Management Review,* July 1993, pp. 23–24.

with its policy of "putting the employee first." For example, FedEx gathers employee opinions and attitudes through its Survey, Feedback, Action (SFA) program. The annual survey gives people an opportunity to express attitudes about the company, management, pay and benefits, and the company's service. FedEx uses employee responses to the first ten items to compute a "leadership index," which determines a manager's annual bonus. A quick look at these items reveals how FedEx defines the term leadership. These ten items do not evaluate how closely managers supervise their people, nor how well managers control their budgets. Instead, the leadership index reveals how well managers support their people and how well they empower them to perform. While the responses to SFA are kept confidential, overall results are passed on to all managers, who must then meet with their workgroups to develop an action plan for resolving any problem that arises. To help ensure that this part of the SFA process really works, item 29 on the survey asks employees whether or not "The concerns identified by my workgroup in last year's survey feedback have been addressed."

FedEx also has a Guaranteed Fair Treatment (GFT) process to ensure that employees feel that they are treated fairly. Anyone who has a grievance or concern about their job or who feels that they have been mistreated (for

whatever reason) can have these concerns addressed through the management chain. If an employee does not get satisfaction at one level, they can take their concerns to progressively higher levels of management until they do. In fact, CEO Fred Smith joins the chief personnel officer and two senior vice presidents each week to review GFT cases that have progressed to the final stage of the appeals board. In addition to the GFT process, FedEx has what it calls the FX TU telephone system to provide any employee with a direct line to top management to express concerns about service quality or customer satisfaction.

To ensure that FedEx employees have the knowledge and skills to live up to customers' high expectations, the company provides extensive training and ongoing education. All service providers receive extensive training before they assume their jobs. For example, the call center agents are given six weeks of intensive classroom and hands-on training before taking their first call. FedEx wants every customer inquiry to be handled by the first person the customer talks to rather than have them experience the frustration of being passed around a company for an answer. FedEx also provides employees with self-directed training programs. For example, employees have the opportunity to learn quality techniques through the use of the PRISM human resources system, which provides access to 4000 courses. The

company has more than 25,000 on-line terminals that allow employees to register for courses, take the course through interactive video, and then be tested on what they learned at their own convenience. Every six months couriers, service agents, and customer service agents participate in job-knowledge testing. Approximately 1250 job-knowledge tests are administered and scored by PRISM each week, and the results of the tests are available to employees on the same day they take the test. This recurrent training has been part of FedEx's pilots FAA requirement for years. And just as the FAA requires pilots who fail the tests to be taken off the line until they can pass, so are FedEx's couriers and customer agents. Pass or fail, each person receives a personalized "prescription" that targets areas needing improvement. The prescription recommends resources, training materials, and interactive video lessons to help them get back up to speed.

In addition to detecting and correcting deficiencies, FedEx attempts to catch people doing things right and reward them for it. For example, the "Circle of Excellence" award is presented monthly to the best performing FedEx station to recognize and encourage effective teamwork. The winning station has its group photo placed in the lobby of corporate headquarters. The "Golden Falcon" award goes to employees who go above and beyond the call of duty. For example,

Stephanie Flores, in southern Louisiana, hiked through flood water up to her knees to deliver one company's payroll. Maurice Jant scanned all of the packages he was picking up on the ninth floor of an office building in San Francisco during an earthquake. Then he carried them nine floors down a rubble-strewn staircase to get to the airport on time. The "Bravo Zulu" (a Navy term for "well done") program allows managers to give a dinner, theater tickets, or cash to any employee who has done a particularly outstanding job. These rewards and recognitions are important to FedEx employees, but they are not the most important aspect of its culture. As CEO Fred Smith states: "What is becoming increasingly more obvious to us is that, for most employees, the job itself is the reward—the autonomy and empowerment to make on-the-spot decisions to meet our customers' needs, the opportunity to design one's job."

? CASE QUESTIONS

1. Identify all of the ways that FedEx managed the social and cultural processes of the organization. Explain the importance of each to its strategy.

2. What other opportunities for improvement of FedEx's social and cultural processes would you suggest? Explain each.

METHODS FOR CONTROL AND IMPROVEMENT

16. STATISTICAL QUALITY CONTROL FOR CUSTOMER VALUE

LEARNING OBJECTIVES

When you finish this chapter you should be able to:

1. Explain what a standard is and how managers use standards to manage performance.

2. Identify and explain the four steps in the traditional management control process.

3. Explain the fundamental weakness of the traditional management control process.

4. Define statistical process control and describe the relationship between the systems view of organizations and the value of statistical process control.

5. Describe how statistical process control charts help managers control and improve organizational processes.

6. Describe the appropriate managerial reaction to common cause and special cause variation.

7. Explain the TQM approach to preliminary, concurrent, rework, and damage control.

VARIATION IN THE LIFE OF A MANAGER

Scott Ehrenfried, the production manager at Treco Products in Newport News, Virginia, recently took a course in time management. A few weeks after completing the course, Scott sat through a one-day overview of a course offered by a local consultant on statistical methods and **variation,** or *the change and fluctuation of outcomes over time.* The consultant stressed the importance of reducing variation in business outcomes, like quality and delivery times, because of the negative impact it has on the company and customers. Scott reflected on how he feels as a consumer when he gets a product that deviates from what he expects. For example, he was frustrated when he went to a local hardware store and found that two items he wanted were out of stock. Certainly, some of Scott's customers have felt that same sense of frustration over variation in the quality of his own products and their availability.

The courses on time management and statistics encouraged Scott to become conscious of how he used his time by keeping a diary of some of his activities. He collected data on how long it took him to do mundane things like shower, shave, eat breakfast, drive to work, and stand in the lunch line. What he noticed in the data was a pervasive inconsistency, or *variation,* in how long it took to do the same thing on different days. For example, one day

it would take 15 minutes to drive to work, and another day it would take 20 minutes. He was not surprised at the variation because daily changes in traffic conditions are to be expected from day to day.

Scott also noticed variation in outcomes that occur under much the same conditions from day to day. For example, Scott goes to the local gym each evening and stays in good physical condition. But his performance varies from day to day on time to run a mile, pounds benchpressed, and racquetball games won against the same opponent. Despite these variations, Scott also noticed that his performance overall seemed remarkably consistent over time. The variation in his time to run a mile fluctuated by only a few seconds

around what he considered to be his personal average. In running, weight lifting, and racquetball, he could identify clear patterns in the variations in his performance.

Scott finds the most vivid example of this tendency toward patterned variation in his dart game. On many Saturday evenings, down at the local hangout, Scott and his friends throw darts competitively, with a few wagers on the side. Scott is an average dart player, so his tosses land darts all over the board. Most of them land in the inner circles, but it is not uncommon for him to land several out toward the edge of the board. He rarely misses the board, though. So the edge of the dart board defines the limits of what Scott should expect: it defines his

capability. Scott's friend Ted is much better. The vast majority of his darts land in the inner circles, although there is still some variation.

In thinking over the data from his company's internal reports, memos, and measures, and his personal experiences, Scott realizes that the events in his company show variation, much like those of his personal life. There is variation in the time it takes to conduct the morning production meeting, in the monthly departmental expenses, in quantities of product defects on Quality Control reports, in the number of customer complaints each week, and in the response time to computer inquiries sent to the accounting department.

One point that the statistical consultant made about variation during the recent course stuck in Scott's mind: "The way managers react to variation determines how much of it there will be in the future." For days after hearing these words, Scott pondered how managers in his organization responded to variation. He realized that sometimes it was rather unpredictable. Sometimes they ignore a deviation from a target, and other times they get into an uproar. It is not always clear what constitutes a significant departure or when managers really should be alarmed. This whole issue raised a number of questions in Scott's mind.

Scott has observed that sometimes changes are introduced that alter the variation that he sees. For example, Scott suspected that the response time from the accounting department depended on who was responding. Things seemed to get better after he had heard Joe was let go. Response time variation seemed less. Was it really?

Scott also has questions about how much variation his company can afford to live with. When should variation be tolerated, and when should it be attacked because it is affecting performance? And what can be done about it, if anything? In the past, Scott's company has tolerated a lot of variation because they had enough sales income with a high enough markup to cover mistakes and waste that comes from variation. Their prices were set up to cover waste in their processes, just like allowing for an extra 30 minutes to get to the airport in case you encounter a problem.

If a Treco customer wanted just-in-time delivery, Scott would build enough to stockpile it in a warehouse and ensure that Treco always had products available for shipment. But that added cost. With increased competition, Scott's company felt pressure to hold prices down, so it became more difficult to cover the cost of waste and variation in their processes. And top management is getting stressed out about deviations from targets. How does Scott's company deal with the existence of variation under these circumstances?

Controlling The managerial role concerned with ensuring that the organization uses its resources properly over time to achieve goals.

Answering that question is what this chapter is about. Decreasing variation and waste in business processes helps a company do two things: increase quality and decrease costs, both very desirable from a business standpoint. From a traditional management perspective, the issues of reducing waste and controlling costs to make sure the organization achieves its goals fall into the category of "control." *The important managerial role of ensuring that the organization uses its resources properly over time to achieve goals* is called **controlling.** In this chapter we discuss two different approaches to controlling. First, the *traditional approach*, which focuses on maintaining a set course of action to ensure the organization performs as planned. This approach treats variation in performance more as isolated incidents that should be suppressed. Second, the *TQM approach*, which focuses on learning about the causes of variation in performance and addressing those causes to bring about improvement. As you will see, the second approach, which is based on a systems view of organizations, is the one most likely to reduce variation and improve the efficiency and effectiveness of the organization to the benefit of all its stakeholders.

TRADITIONAL CONTROL TO MAINTAIN CURRENT COURSE

The role of controlling has been described in management literature for decades.[1] As illustrated in Exhibit 16-1, there are four basic steps to the traditional controlling process:

1. Set predetermined standards, plans, or objectives.
2. Measure and monitor performance.
3. Compare performance to the predetermined standards.
4. Make a decision and take corrective action.

Step 1: Setting Standards

A **standard** generally represents *a desired level of performance; it might be expressed in many specific forms: a plan, objectives, a target, or a range of acceptability.* Organizations typically have standards for performance throughout the organization, at all levels of management. Standards for an entire organization include strategic objectives for market share, sales volume, profitability, returns to investors, and target dates for launching a new product. Standards for groups of people in departments, like engineering, marketing, production, accounting, and personnel, might include targets for overhead cost reduction, defect levels, or financial budgets. Standards for individuals might include not only those for outcomes, such as sales and production quotas, but also those for behavior, such as safety practices, absenteeism, and ethical conduct. Standards for products and services include the specifications that describe their physical characteristics (length, width, density, color), performance levels (strength, durability, fuel efficiency), and timeliness (how long it takes to deliver, install, and repair).

Some standards prescribe a range of acceptable performance. For example, product specifications often consist of a range around a target value. The fill weight in jars of coffee might be specified as 16.5 ± .5 ounces. So, any jar filled to at least 16 ounces but not more than 17 ounces meets the standard. Other standards may specify only a minimum or a maximum value, such as a target for

Standard A desired level of performance; it might be expressed in many specific forms: a plan, objectives, a target, or a range of acceptability.

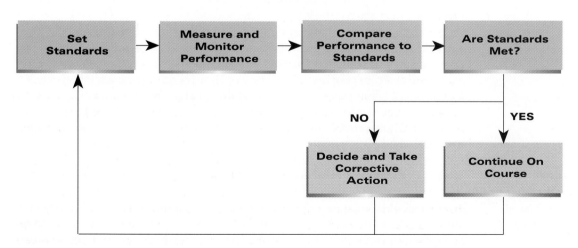

EXHIBIT 16-1   Traditional control process

cost of materials in a production department. Some standards may simply set a target, such as the due date for a new product design from the engineering department. Some are derived from customer preferences and needs, such as those for product characteristics. Other standards come from demands by other stakeholders, such as profitability goals wanted by owners, stockholders, and investors. Some are based on historical averages, such as estimates of overhead costs. Still others are based on aspirations for the future, ideal levels of performance used as goals to motivate improvement.

No matter how they are derived, standards become targets for performance and are the measures of success. If managers meet their standards, they are judged to be successful. Ideally, the standards throughout the company are interrelated and directed toward a common purpose or strategy. For example, gaining share in the tire replacement market means coming up with new tires that are safer and inexpensive requires that the engineering department delivers designs on time, the production department manufactures them at a certain cost and within a set time frame, and the marketing department gets a set number of dealers to carry the product. In theory, when all employees and departments do their part and perform to standards laid out by management, the coordinated action allows the organization to achieve its purposes. As you may suspect, this is difficult to do. Simply laying out standards and then judging people on whether or not they make them does not give managers much direction for figuring out what to do when standards are not met—a very common occurrence.

Step 2: Measuring and Monitoring Performance

Once agreed on, managers then must monitor performance, based on how well employees and departments are adhering to their standards. Ideally, each standard of performance should have at least one measurement attached to it that will provide data for managers, such as quarterly financial performance, market share percent, variance from target budget, defect rates, and sales volume. Measurements produce quantifiable results that managers must monitor or review on a daily, weekly, monthly, quarterly, or annual basis. The frequency of monitoring depends on the type of data and the purpose of its use. For example, data used to control production operations may be monitored daily, while profitability is measured quarterly.

Monitoring does not have to be limited to reviewing numerical reports. Managers often like to see for themselves what goes on in an organization. They may do so to verify the numbers they get through reports, with non-quantitative information gathered in conversation with people or by directly observing events. Or they may just want to get a feel for what the numbers mean and make sure they do not become detached from the work of the organization. Nevertheless, what drives the whole process are the standards and the measures of results compared to the standards.

Step 3: Comparing Performance to Standards

Managing by exceptions Managers pay little attention to the numbers that conform to a standard, noting only significant deviations from expectations.

To evaluate performance, managers compare it against the standards identified in Step 1. In the traditional approach to control, managers use the rule of **managing by exceptions,** which means *managers pay little attention to the numbers that conform to a standard, noting only significant deviations from expectations.*

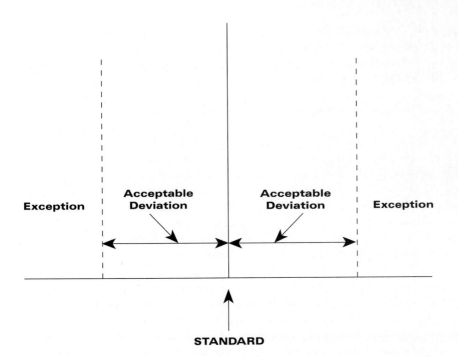

EXHIBIT 16-2
Managers often have zones of acceptable deviation from standard and only consider it an exception when performance exceeds these zones.

It is natural to attend only to the numbers that deviate from standard because they are easy to spot. This also saves time because managers only need spend time on problem areas and not worry about those aspects of the business that are meeting or exceeding standards.

In identifying exceptions, managers must decide what constitutes a significant deviation from standard. Given the inevitability of variation, managers should not expect performance to be the same time after time. If the engineering department deviates by one day from the targeted due date for a design, how does the manager react? What if costs exceed the maximum standard by 10 percent one month? Is this significant? Does it require an investigation? Strictly interpreted, the traditional control process says that managers should look into all deviations from standard. In reality, this may not happen. Sometimes managers grow indifferent to deviations that are not excessive. Managers may have a zone of acceptability just outside the standard. They may grow indifferent to variation because they do not understand its impact on the business of a certain amount of deviation, by experience, comes to be accepted. In this, they may follow the customs established by managers before them. Exhibit 16-2 illustrates this idea of zone of acceptability.

There is often a lot of subjectivity in deciding how to react to deviations. Different managers may react differently to the same deviation. The same manager may even vary over time in reaction to the same deviation, seemingly based on whim. This inconsistency can be frustrating for employees who are never sure whether the deviation is OK or if the manager will become upset by it. Of course the traditional approach is not supposed to encourage such subjectivity, but because it does not provide any objective way to figure out what level of deviation is acceptable, managers vary from time to time depending on what pressures they are feeling from their superiors. The TQM approach, discussed later in this chapter, gives managers a means for deciding what constitutes an acceptable or unacceptable deviation using some basic statistical tools. It also provides direction for understanding why this happens and for reducing deviation (or variation) from standards.

Step 4: Making a Decision and Taking Corrective Action

After managers decide that a deviation is significant (by whatever subjective method they choose), they must decide what to do about it. Do they ignore it and hope it was a fluke or take corrective action to fix it? This final step in the traditional control process, taking corrective action, is where the actual controlling takes place. The success or failure of the controlling process hinges on the actions taken by the manager to correct the deviation.

To understand the typical approach to taking corrective action, consider this anecdote from management consultant Daniel R. Tobin:[2]

When I first became a manager I attended a week-long training course. At one point, the instructor asked the participants to take out a paper and pen. "Think back to when you were 6 years old. What did you want to be when you grew up?" After a few minutes, she asked, "How many of you wrote down 'manager?'" When no one else responded, I raised my hand. The instructor looked at me in astonishment. "At 6 years old you knew you wanted to be a manager? You knew what a manager was?" "No," I replied, "but I came pretty close. I wrote down 'firefighter.'"

Crisis management Managerial action that involves eliminating the immediate trouble or minimizing the bad consequences of a deviation from standard.

This story points out what many managers spend most of their time doing—putting out business fires, otherwise known as crisis management and problem solving. **Crisis management,** also referred to as firefighting, *involves eliminating the immediate trouble or minimizing the bad consequences of a deviation from standard.* Controlling in this sense means putting out the fire, but allowing the embers that caused it to remain burning. Put another way, it is an approach that deals with eliminating problem symptoms rather than causes. In fact, firefighting and crisis management have been the conventional ways of operating in many corporations and emerge from the traditional approach to control. However, this is changing as managers begin to realize that they need to permanently solve problems when they arise and that an approach that emphasizes problem prevention makes the most sense. **Problem solving** addresses *the underlying causes of the deviation to help make sure that the same problem does not recur in the future.* The next section looks at this approach to control, which emerges from understanding organizations as systems.

Problem solving Managerial action that addresses the underlying causes of the deviation to help make sure that the same problem does not recur in the future.

❓ THINKING CRITICALLY

1. When you read about the traditional steps to controlling performance, do they make sense to you? Why or why not?
2. Do you think a psychologist working on an experiment can test one rat in one situation and draw any conclusions from observations taken? Why not? What does that tell you about understanding organizational processes and capabilities?

HOW TO IMPROVE THE TRADITIONAL CONTROL PROCESS

The four steps of the traditional control process have the purpose of helping managers maintain a steady course toward the organization's objectives. The problems with this approach, though, are that it does not take into account that an organization is a system with interrelated processes nor that variation in the outputs of processes will naturally occur through time. It provides managers with no sound way to understand the relationships among organizational parts and how those relationships bring about variation around a standard. Further, the traditional approach often sets standards in an arbitrary fashion that has more to do with wishful thinking than with an understanding of organizational capability. Finally, such standards may even hold the organization back as managers become more concerned with achieving specific goals and standards when, with a different emphasis, the company could exceed them. We can contrast this with the Total Quality Management approach to control. It has less to do with maintaining a particular standard than it does on understanding process capability and working on continuous improvement.

Knowledge about Causes

The key to successful control is *knowledge of the causes* of deviations. Managers should view deviations as a part of a pattern of variation over time that they can study, using statistical analysis to understand the causes of these patterns. In this context, measuring variation that takes place over time provides us with clues about how the system is performing. And by studying patterns of variation, we can learn about their causes. **Statistics,** which is *the study of variation in data*, is an important tool we use to discover causes. This is not the only way to develop knowledge, but using statistics helps managers make sure that their decisions are grounded in empirical evidence, not opinion.

Statistics The study of variation in data.

Control as Emphasis on Continuous Improvement

The traditional approach to control does not necessarily encourage continuous improvement or improvement of any kind. This approach encourages adherence to specific numerical standards and doing whatever is necessary to hit those standards. Sure, standards can be raised to new levels. But, once the standards are set, the traditional control approach offers little help on how to actually meet the current or higher standards other than go out and do it. This approach does not take into account that meeting standards of any kind is a function of how well the system and its processes operate. If the goal is to meet higher standards and the system has not been improved, if there has not been an intelligent effort to make processes operate more efficiently, then higher standards will not really mean much.

The TQM approach to control, conversely, which is based on statistical methods to understand processes, helps managers figure out how to improve process efficiency and thus be able to meet higher standards and even go beyond them. It does this by helping them discover the causes of current system performance. The TQM approach also encourages managers to go beyond minimum requirements of fixed standards. Whereas the traditional approach is set up to get people to conform to some arbitrary norm, TQM is about figuring out system capability so you can make it work better and better. TQM goes beyond the "if it ain't broke, don't fix it" mentality. TQM does not assume that a system is broken or not broken. It does assume that at any time it is working as well as it can and that its operations can be continuously improved. Then it provides the tools for doing that.

Problems with Managing toward Standards

The traditional control process, with an emphasis on managing through the use of standards, sounds straightforward enough. However, just telling people what to do through standards does not ensure they will (or even can) do it. As we suggested above, there may be many reasons why people, as individuals and as groups, might not be able to meet standards. The traditional approach is based on a flawed assumption, that individuals have personal control over their performance independent of the system that is the organization. The flaw is that they are not independent. In reality we can only begin to understand individual performance in relation to and as part of the whole system in which individuals operate. The work of any one person affects that of many others and vice versa. Only by examining the whole system and the ways people executing processes interact with one another can we begin to understand performance, variations in performance, and how to bring about improvements.

Here is a typical situation: in a traditional organization, the standards in one area might contradict those in another area. For example, the standards for low-cost bidding imposed on the purchasing department may attract inferior suppliers and

In order to make performance improvements, the individual worker must be considered in relation to the whole system. On an assembly line, any one person's work affects that of many others further on in the process.

interfere with the production department's ability to meet standards for quality. However, not seeing the organization as a system makes managers downplay such interdependencies with the result that performance of the system is compromised.

Two standards for the same individual or department might even be in conflict. For example, an employee may be given a quota that requires him to produce 50 units a day, with a defect level that does not exceed 5 percent. However, when he works fast enough to achieve the production quota, the employee tends to make mistakes and produce 7 to 8 percent defectives. Every other employee has the same problem, but management insists on the quotas, particularly the production quotas. What the system is telling us, unbeknownst to these managers, is that without other improvements, the system is incapable of achieving this standard. It is very frustrating for the workers who must try to comply.

Disgusted with their negative impact, W. Edwards Deming has exhorted managers to eliminate quotas, work objectives, and numerical standards altogether. He did so because he realized that numerical goals do not contribute to improvement. When employees are rewarded on whether they achieve an arbitrary standard, they will do anything they can to meet it. Usually this will involve manipulating the system in one way or another to look good. For example, salespeople may take orders they know the company cannot fulfill. Or a warehouse manager may reduce parts inventory to lower costs even though this affects those working on machinery in a negative fashion. In both of these cases, these individuals are "making their numbers," but these actions hurt other parts of the organization. Deming, among many others, saw the folly in this and regularly railed against it.

Another problem with standards and numerical goals, according to Deming, is that they encourage complacency, because employees are satisfied with just meeting a standard and not going any further. Deming would have managers eliminate standards and just pursue continuous improvement. In this way, managers focus on the current capabilities of the system and continually make refinements that improve the efficiency of processes and the quality of outputs.

There are different ideas about how to accomplishment this improvement. In contrast to Deming, other quality gurus include the use of standards in their approaches to improvement. For example, Kaoru Ishikawa, one of the leaders of the quality revolution in Japan, suggests: "Standards and regulations are imperfect. They must be reviewed and revised constantly. If newly established standards and regulations are not revised in six months, it is proof that no one is seriously using them."[3]

Ishikawa suggests that managers can achieve improvement by regularly setting new standards. The idea is to provide managers with targets for their improvement efforts, but these targets are never fixed. Setting new standards is one thing. Meeting them is another. As both Deming and Ishikawa suggest, managers must address the *means* of accomplishing improvement to meet higher standards. This is what the TQM approach to control does by directing attention toward the means of improvement.

? THINKING CRITICALLY

1. Intuitively, do you think it makes more sense to do everything possible to meet a certain standard set out by the boss in an organization or does it make more sense to continuously improve performance? Explain your answer.
2. Why would you say that numerical goals and quotas are counter to a systems view of organizations?

TQM IN ACTION

VARIATION AND STANDARDS AT NORTHWEST AIRLINES

Many companies have telephone service centers or help lines for customers to call. Company representatives provide answers to inquiries, product information, and instructions on filling out forms, redressing problems, and obtaining services. Travel agencies and airlines conduct most of their business transactions over the phone. So, the telephone conversation is an integral part of providing customer service.

Have you ever been treated rudely by an operator who seemed very eager to terminate the phone conversation? Why would an operator behave that way? After all, the sole reason for their job is to help customers. It might be because of the standards of performance used to control the operator's behavior.

Under deregulation the airline industry has become increasingly competitive. Airlines must do everything they can to attract and keep customers, and their efforts begin with the first phone call. Consider how Northwest uses service standards for phone calls. Northwest Airlines has standards for their representatives on such activities as the number of calls handled per day, time taken per call, and reservations booked.

For example, representatives are supposed to handle domestic reservations and flight inquiries in one minute and forty seconds on the average. Northwest managers recognize and expect variation in these phone conversations. For example, flight information can be given in a few seconds, whereas it can take some time to book a flight for a customer considering several departure and route options.

Although a representative can eventually be fired for persistently exceeding the standard, Northwest managers do not overreact to minor deviations from standard. Rather, they look for patterns and long term trends. Overreacting by managers might cause the representatives to be rude to customers or cut them off prematurely just to meet the standard (as often happens in different industries that apply standards to judge performance). Representatives are not just employed to process reservations quickly. They must also establish a congenial relationship with the customer. If the customer does not enjoy transacting business with the company, they may choose another airline for future traveling.

Most importantly, Northwest managers do not hold individual representatives accountable without providing them the means to perform. Northwest managers recognize that the performance of an individual representative is a function of the larger system they operate in. The efficiency and effectiveness of this system is the responsibility of managers. To ensure the representatives are capable of meeting the standard, Northwest begins by testing job applicants on job-relevant abilities, such as keyboard usage.

New representatives go through four weeks of training on the computer system, work processes, and code abbreviations. Refresher courses are frequently offered during the work day in 15-minute to one-hour sessions. If a representative persistently and excessively deviates from the standard, Northwest offers counseling and follow-up training to correct the problem. Dismissal is a last resort. This approach has allowed Northwest to wisely use its resources, without wasting time, but also improve its service to customers.

STATISTICS, VARIATION, AND MANAGING IMPROVEMENT

Imagine you are a mechanic and are trying to improve the mileage on your car. You realize that an automobile engine is a complex device and that to maximize performance all its components must be optimized to work in concert with one another. To start your project, you first have to find out what the current mileage is. Understanding that mileage varies given driving habits and type of driving, you take several measures, which all fall between a range of 23.4 and 19.3 miles per gallon before you determine that your car averages 21.8 miles per gallon. Given the current state of the engine, that is its capability.

Now, before we explore how you might improve your mileage, let's interrupt this scenario for a moment. This situation of variation in a system (in this case an automobile, its engine, and a driver) is similar to variation in organizations, which we also know are systems. The traditional management approach to improving the mileage would be to tell you to keep your mileage at 22 miles per gallon with no more than a half-mile deviation. You know that the variations you experienced are inherent in the way your car operates, and you cannot meet this standard, but your manager is not interested in that. Unless you fudge your figures, you are unlikely to accomplish what your manager requests. Nevertheless, this approach to improvement is very common today in organizations today, and many managers find themselves forced to fudge their figures and hope for the best. In reality, it is counterproductive to actually making improvements because it does not focus on solving the problems that hold back performance.

If you really want to improve your mileage on a permanent basis, you can start doing things like using synthetic oil, making sure the car is properly tuned, use high performance spark plugs, make sure your tires are always properly inflated, and use a light foot on the accelerator. In each case, you can take measurements to determine if these changes are working and eventually you will discover a combination of actions that will help reduce the variation in mileage while also improving the average mileage you get.

This approach is called statistical process control. It is a realistic technique to controlling processes and bringing about improvement. It approaches the problem of understanding variation and improvement from the perspective of *systems management* using quantitative tools that allow a person to collect facts and make decisions based on those facts.

Variation, Change, and Stability

Managers must be concerned with both change *and* stability to provide superior customer value over the long term. Facilitating continuous change for improved performance allows managers to keep up with changing market demands. A concern with stability allows managers to consistently deliver products and services which currently match customer needs. By studying variation using statistics, managers can learn how to maintain stable production of goods and services and how to accomplish change and improvement.

The presence of variation sometimes makes it difficult to notice when a significant change has occurred. In the example with the car just above, a good mileage day is not necessarily indicative that a sustained improvement has taken place. Using statistics allows managers to know how confident they should be in drawing conclusions from their observations of variation. There are several statistical tools for tracking and analyzing process variation. The most simple tool is a histogram, and it provides a good example of how such tools help managers gather and begin to understand system processes.

Histograms

Managers can collect various types of data to understand how well an organization is operating. For example, they can collect data that reveal process outcomes. These may be collected on a daily, weekly, monthly, or some other time period basis. The data may show such outcomes as the percentage of defective outputs in factory work, on-time delivery performance in transportation, absenteeism, sales volume, and so on. Managers can then summarize this data in a histogram. A **histogram** is *a chart that depicts the frequency of occurrence of various numerical values.* The histogram also reveals the amount of dispersion, or the extent of variation in the numbers. The next section on The Folger Coffee Company provides a concrete example of what a histogram is and how managers can use it to characterize the performance of a production process.

> **Histogram** A chart that depicts the frequency of occurrence of various numerical values.

A histogram is useful, but it only gives a historical summary of what happened in a given period of time. It does not give the manager enough clues about the causes of variation. It does not reveal what happened during the interval of time, or the time order of the data, which reveals patterns. Studying data over time through process control charts is the key to learning about the causes of variation. We will look at those after we review what was going on at the Folgers coffee plant.

Using Histograms: Folgers Seeks to Reduce
Variation in Filling Coffee Jars

The managers of The Folger Coffee Company were experiencing a conflict among their standards (Note: the numbers below are realistic but altered). One of the two standards that were in conflict was a quality control requirement, and the other was a cost reduction target imposed by top managers. Every producer of packaged food products is required by law to ensure that the contents match what is on the label. By law a product labeled as a 16 ounce jar of coffee should contain at least 16 ounces of coffee. Quite pragmatically, the government also recognizes the existence of variation. So they tolerate it if up to two percent of the jars inspected are slightly below the weight stated on the label. If a company violates the law, the government may impose sanctions and fines, and customer satisfaction may be jeopardized.

To meet this government regulation, the managers of the production line have learned that they have to set the machine that fills the jars at some level greater than 16 ounces (which is the QC Specification or Spec). After all, deviations happen, and nobody and no machine is perfect. The filler machine has 10 rotating heads that fill the jars as they move underneath on a belt.

After considerable trial and error, the managers have determined that if they set the fill weights to 16.5 ounces they will rarely get a jar that contains less than 16 ounces of coffee. The variation in fill weights is shown in the first *histogram* shown in Exhibit 16-3. The histogram graphically illustrates the frequency with which each fill weight occurs. The average is 16.5 and the variation ranges from

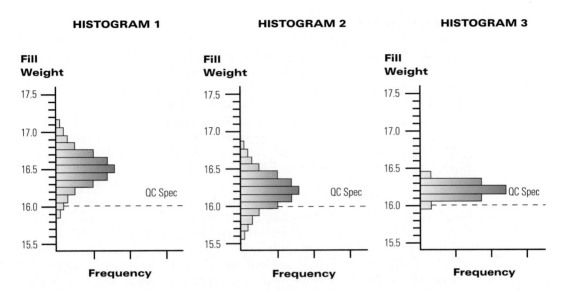

EXHIBIT 16-3   Histograms showing frequencies of fill weight for 100 jars with wide variations

16 ounces to 17 ounces. Notice that none of the fill weights in this sample of 100 jars was less than the QC Spec of 16 ounces.

On the average the department is overfilling each jar by half an ounce. Since the coffee costs money, this overfill represents waste. In the span of a year, the department overfills more than 4 million jars by half an ounce on the average. That adds up to around 125,000 pounds of coffee and a lot of money. The cost reduction target imposed by top managers for the production department is to reduce material costs by two percent. This two percent target represents an estimate of how much the costs need to be reduced to keep the price competitive, yet remain profitable. In fact, saving the 125,000 pounds of extra coffee packaged in the 4 million jars would yield a savings of over three percent in the cost of the coffee itself, so improving the ability to regulate the amount of coffee going into each jar is a sound idea.

To accomplish this target of 2 percent reduction in materials costs, the manager would have to reduce the average fill weight from 16.5 to 16.2 ounces per jar. Look at the second histogram shown in Exhibit 16-3, and you see that if you shift the distribution down to where the average fill weight equals 16.2, you will have a significantly larger number of jars below the legal limit. Not only will the company incur the wrath of the government inspectors, but some customers will undoubtedly notice the extra empty space in their jars. Many customers might switch brands if Folgers seemed to be regularly skimping on the product. The managers seem to be in a real bind, with one target requiring them to reduce the fill weights to remain profitable, and another target demanding that they keep the fill weights up to remain legal and attractive to customers.

The best option for Folgers' managers in this situation is to reduce the variation. A tighter distribution, like the third histogram shown in Exhibit 16-3, would allow the settings for the average fill weight on the machines to be shifted down closer to the legal limit without going over it. The way to reduce variation in the machine's capability is to study it, learn what causes it, and then act on what you have learned to make improvements.

Statistical Process Control

Statistical analysis informs managers about the probability of certain outcomes and lends scientific credence to their decisions about how to control and improve performance. This is because it allows them to make decisions based on facts rather than impressions. The kind of statistical analysis we are referring to helps managers gain an insight into the causes of variations in a process. Only by understanding these causes can managers learn how to control and improve outputs of a process. Statistics also help managers distinguish between a deviation from standard that is unusual from one that is to be expected.

When managers use the traditional approach, they will do things such as review accounting reports for the past month to discover if a department is over budget for expenses. If it is, they may request written explanations and a plan for bringing the department back in line with the budget. They may do this without considering how the immediate past month's expenses compare to those in preceding months. What such an analysis might show is that rather than being unique, this overbudget figure could have been a normal variation, within expected boundaries, and not really due to any special or unusual circumstances. Recall the random variation in Scott Ehrenfried's life events such as dart throwing. Similarly, business results will always either be on target or above or below it, and the deviations from target may just be random due to circumstances in the system that no one can predict exactly.

Statistical Process Control Charts. The **statistical process control (SPC) chart** shown in Exhibit 16-4 illustrates how statistics can be used to identify unusual deviations. The SPC chart is *a graphic display of data that is listed in time order, with a process average and upper and lower control limits computed based on that data.* A **control limit** is *a line on a control chart that indicates the extent of variation you should expect above or below an average line based on statistical probability.* The placement of the lower and upper control limits on an SPC chart are found by performing calculations with a fairly simple statistical formula. A **data point,** that is *a single measurement,* that exceeds either the upper or lower control limit is unusual because it exceeds what you might expect to see. In other words, except for this one occurrence, the data seems stable, with random variation of data points within the statistical limits. Going back to our mileage example, if you suddenly got only 15 miles per gallon, this would likely fall outside the lower control limit, and you would probably note that this occurred because you were driving in the mountains with a heavy load, an unusual situation. When a data point falls outside the control limits, this indicates an unusual event brought about by some identifiable circumstances. In more general terms, we note that this is a **special cause variation,** which is *an extreme variation brought about by an identifiable event.*

As another example, imagine that the measurement being plotted on the chart is the percentage of defects per day. On one day there are more defects than normal. When management does its analysis, they find that this one occurrence happened because an employee was sick, and a temporary employee had filled in. Lacking training and experience, the temp was responsible for a higher-than-normal level of defects. Understanding that this was a special cause variation, management took measures to have an experienced employee from another area available to fill in when someone is sick. In other words, because the manager

Statistical process control (SPC) chart A graphic display of data that is listed in time order, with a process average and upper and lower control limits developed from that data.

Control limit A line on a control chart that indicates the extent of variation you should expect above or below an average line based on statistical probability.

Data point A single measurement.

Special cause variation An extreme variation brought about by an identifiable event.

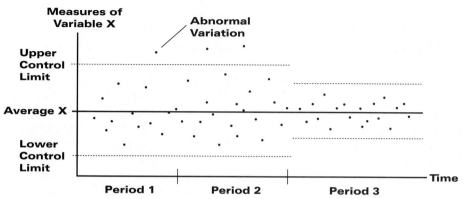

EXHIBIT 16-4
A Example of a Statistical
Process Control Chart

had a statistical control chart indicating expected from unexpected performance in this process, she could immediately identify when an unusual event had happened and take care of it right then. Without this analysis it would have been difficult to identify whether this was any different from other deviations in performance and that it needed special attention. After addressing the problem indicated by the special cause variation, we see in time period 2 on Exhibit 16-4 that the process returned to a state of statistical control.

Common Cause Variation.   When all data points fall within the control limits, this indicates there are no unusual events occurring and that the variation is just part of the way the system functions. We call this **common cause variation,** which is *variation due to factors inherent in the process itself.* For example if you drive between home and school, it may take you an average of between 13 minutes per day with a variation of 2 minutes more or less than 13 minutes. This variation is brought about by common causes inherent in the process of driving, such as traffic, stop lights, weather, and similar everyday factors that affect how quickly you are able to drive between two locations. In an office situation, common cause variation would explain why, for example, a word processing center would average 12.5 percent of letters typed per day needing to be redone because of errors, with a variation of about 3 percent on either side of this average. These errors happen for a variety of reasons, such as poor handwriting by the originator, interruptions, fatigue, and so on. Given the current working situation, this is simply to be expected.

The Importance of Special Cause and Common Cause Variation.   There are two important things to remember about special cause and common cause variation: (1) common cause variation will exist in every system—this is just the way the world works; you can do things to reduce it, but you can never completely eliminate it, and (2) you cannot make any judgments about whether variation is due to common or special causes without taking several measurements and creating a statistical process control chart. A single measurement tells you very little about a process.

   Say the word processing department one day ends up needing to retype nine percent of the letters completed. You cannot make any generalizations about this department's processes or capabilities based on this single measurement. Only after taking several measurements and developing an SPC chart can you begin to figure out what is usual performance and what would be unusual. As we noted

Common cause variation
Variation due to factors
inherent in the process
itself.

MANAGERS IN ACTION

SPC AT THE WATERVLIET ARSENAL

Greg Conway is the chief of statistical methods at the Watervliet Arsenal in Watervliet, New York. He talks about managers and managing at this company:

The best managers at Watervliet Arsenal are the ones who know what is going on. Those are the managers who can either direct or conduct analysis efforts that assess performance at the micro level (what is the primary cause of defective output on operation #330?) as well as the macro level (what future product lines are most likely to result in long term profits?). Unsuccessful managers are those who are quick to give an opinion and don't have the facts.

Future managers are evaluated for important promotions during meetings and discussions that occur in day-to-day business. Those who really change things for the better are those who can gather and analyze data and present the facts with a minimum of personal opinion. In the old days a manager could be successful by collecting a minimum of facts and presenting an opinion with much force and emotion. The new managers will get all the facts possible, present them clearly and objectively, without emotion. The detail and accuracy of an objective analysis radiates a compelling force of truth that eliminates the need for emotional admonition. Improving quality on the shop floor is a process that requires facts and a knowledge of the reality of manufacturing.

A *reality check* lets us know what is really going on. From time to time, a reality check gets us back in line with the facts, with truth. The problem is that managers are almost never aware that their beliefs about the quality of an operation are not accurate. In other words, managers often don't know that they don't know the facts. What do managers do for a reality check? Managers in action at Watervliet Arsenal use SPC as one type of reality check. Our managers would like to believe that our people are joyful in their work, our machines are not making any defective products and that since our customers keep coming back, they must still like our products. Is this reality?, we ask ourselves.

In the real world, managers usually know that there are some defective products being made or that customers are not entirely happy, despite what they would like to believe. However, managers can get used to unsatisfactory conditions. It's like walking around with a rock in your shoe. At some point you get used to it and don't even notice. Then a new employee, usually fresh out of college, asks, "Why is everyone walking around with rocks in their shoes?" Of course, only after having this pointed out do the managers start to understand that they don't have to be so uncomfortable.

At Watervliet Arsenal, we have had situations like this. And when problems have occurred on the shop floor, we have had as many opinions on how to fix them as people involved in the situation. What is the answer to this way of solving problems? Statistical process control has been the great "reality check" for us. When we run into a problem or a defective process (that will result in a defective product eventually), the most powerful tool we use to tackle the situation is collecting objective data and facts.

We use data and facts about the process as the *key* information needed to determine what's really going on, to the get the *reality* of the situation. This dramatically accelerates our coming up with a lasting solution and avoids a lot of unnecessary heated debate. Opinions can be valuable when they are based on an analysis of the facts. We have found that managers in some companies jump to a conclusion about the cause of a problem because of the pressure to have a quick answer, a quick fix, a quick solution. We have found a better approach in the new Watervliet manager, who is more likely to say, "Let me check the control chart, and get my facts straight before I propose a solution."

earlier, such determinations are not possible based on a single data point. The problem with traditional control is that this is exactly what it suggests managers do—make decisions based on single events.

By collecting data on processes and developing control charts, you will see that any unusual deviation will be due to a special (and often identifiable) cause, while normal deviations are caused by normal operating conditions (common causes) that are always present. This means the process is in **statistical control,** that is, *the level of variation in the process is predictable and stable* (for example, the word processing department consistently having to redo between 9.5 and 15.5 percent of its letters daily).

When a process is in statistical control, the data points on the chart will fluctuate around a stable average or centerline, with a tendency to hug the centerline, but not too closely. The points may scatter out to the boundaries indicated by the upper and lower control limits, but they will not exceed these limits. The variation is generally constant over time. You cannot reduce the variation in a system that is in statistical control without addressing how the system itself functions and doing something to make the system work more efficiently. In the case of the word processing department, by instituting training and upgrading computers, we affect the way this system functions and reduce the average percent of letters needing to be redone to, perhaps, 5 percent with a variation of 1.5 percent on either side of this. Such reduction represents a 5+ percent increase in productivity, making it well worth pursuing.

The statistical theory underlying control charts is not important to understand at this point. The computations are relatively easy and can be found in many industrial statistics texts. Mastering the computations is not as important as understanding how to interpret the control charts to learn what the variation tells you about the causes of performance.

One of the most important messages from statistical theory is that managers should react differently to variations in processes due to special causes versus those due to common causes. Specifically, managers should not go in search of special causes when none may exist. For example, the data points on Exhibit 16-4 that come very close to the upper control limit, but do not exceed it, may tempt managers to go in search of special causes (like an untrained worker or a broken machine) that may have led to the apparent increase in defects. This search may prove frustrating and fruitless, because the fluctuation is to be expected given the way the current system operates (it is within the control limits), and any changes they make because they believe they are dealing with a special cause problem will not result in improvement.

Statistical control The level of variation in the process is predictable and stable.

How To Reduce Common Cause Variation

After developing a control chart that shows how the system is operating, with its expected levels of variation, the next step for managers is to figure out how to reduce variation. In doing this, managers can increase the possibility that outputs will be free of defects and work to match the standard of quality the company and customers expect. SPC charts give managers direction for figuring out how to do that.

Using SPC charts, managers can first easily spot and address problems that are due to special causes. Then they can start dealing with variation due to common causes in the system itself. Such improvement can result in reduced variation, as illustrated in time period 3 in Exhibit 16-4. The study of variation is fundamental to control, whether it be for maintenance or improvement, and understanding these ideas is central to the successful management of organizations as systems that we have been emphasizing throughout this text.

The chart in Exhibit 16-5 illustrates a pattern of data patterns from a process which is in statistical control. To reduce variation and improve the outputs in a system like this that has no special causes, managers need to study the data and the process which generated it and then use this information to formulate changes to improve the system's processes. We earlier discussed the *Plan-Do-Check-Act improvement cycle* in Chapter 6 on decision making. Applying this idea of PDCA, here specifically is what a manager does to reduce variation due to common causes:

1. Take the process apart step by step and look for weaknesses and opportunities for improvement (PLAN).
2. Implement those improvements (DO).
3. Collect data on process operation to determine how well the improvements are working (CHECK).
4. Make any necessary adjustments to the improvements based on the check step and make them permanent (ACT).
5. Do it all over again and again.

W. Edwards Deming quotes this example from a newspaper clipping demonstrating how using this method can result in an improvement.[4]

REVOLUTION IN MANAGEMENT

London (AP)—London's famous red buses scored a big productivity increase in the last six months, and officials say that a "revolution in management" is the reason.

London Transport, which runs the publicly owned system, attributes the improvement to the end of central control. The 5500 buses on 300 routes were split into eight districts, each responsible for finances, repairs and complaints.

Scheduled mileage–the number of miles covered by buses on the road–increased by 10 percent.

Waiting time at bus stops has been slashed, and the number of buses off the road and waiting for repairs was cut from more than 500 to 150.

In this transportation system, the buses could not have improved as long as administration remained centralized. However, with the decentralization, they were able to utilize the buses and personnel more efficiently to make these gains in performance. The *A Look At TQM in Action* box on page 612 on promotions at Campbell Soup illustrates another lesson for successful management control using SPC charts.

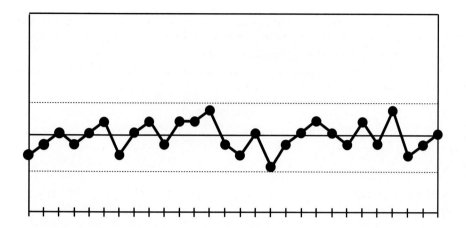

EXHIBIT 16-5
An SPC chart showing a process in statistical control

The Fallacy of Reactive Control

The traditional approach to control suggests that managers should react to deviations from standard and take corrective action. However, if managers fail to understand the theory of variation, they can spend a lot of time overreacting to deviations. The control chart in Exhibit 16-6 illustrates why. The points plotted in Exhibit 16-6 represent measures of sulfur content in sheets of steel. The upper and lower specifications (standards) are drawn on the chart. These fall inside the computed upper and lower control limits for this process. As you can see, a number of points exceed these standards. According to traditional control theory, the manager (or whoever is in charge) should investigate to determine what caused each of these deviations and take corrective action.

By contrast, the statistical control limits indicate that only one point exceeds the control limits and therefore merits special investigation. The remaining points, all of which are within the statistical control limits, are simply due to the common causes that are always present in the system. A manager who investigates to find a special cause for a measurement that exceeds specification, but does not exceed the statistical control limits, would most likely come up empty-handed.

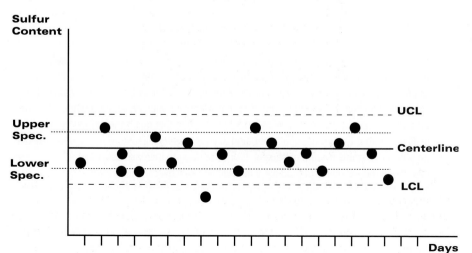

EXHIBIT 16-6
An SPC Chart showing the difference between being "out of spec" and "out of statistical control."

TQM IN ACTION

MARKETING PROMOTIONS IN A STABLE SYSTEM OF DEMAND FOR CAMPBELL SOUP[5]

Managers often measure sales volume to gauge their success in the marketplace. The marketing managers who are in charge of promoting specific products may even be given bonuses for reaching sales targets for these products. One of the devices that marketing managers use to boost the sales of a product is the promotional campaign, which immediately increases demand for the product. For example, the manufacturer may offer the consumer coupons for 50 cents off the purchase of a can of soup. Since consumers are always looking for a deal, such promotions usually accomplish the intended objective for the marketing manager, an immediate upswing in sales volume. The sales upswings caused by promotions can come in handy for marketing managers at the end of a quarter. They can ensure that these managers make their quarterly sales quota if projected sales are lagging behind a sales goal or standard.

The usefulness of sales promotions might be gauged from another vantage point, however. Let's consider the impact of the sales promotion within a broader context. The control chart in Exhibit 16-7 shows approximately what happened to the sales for a Campbell Soup product when the company staged promotional campaigns. In between the promotional campaigns, the sales are stable, with some variation week to week. Sales volume varied from week to week for a number of different reasons, but the demand for the product was very predictable. Campbell Soup knew what the orders would be, within a given range, for the coming weeks.

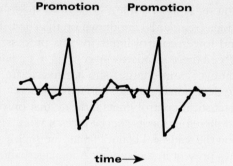

Source: Kim I. Melton *Intro to Stat. for Process Studies* (McGraw-Hill, 1993).

EXHIBIT 16-7 Different signals from specification limits and statistical control limits

Then along comes a promotional campaign which yields a big spike in demand. The companies ordering the product would "stock up" (just like individuals) when the price was reduced for bulk orders. Then the sales would drop off in the subsequent weeks and gradually rise to the normal level. What is most disturbing about this data is that the sales volume immediately after the promotion would drop below the centerline, that is, below the normal level of demand. The companies that had stocked up did not need to make any more purchases for a while. Over the long term, the net gain in sales volume was negligible. From this result the marketing managers have to conclude that the promotional campaign acts as a special cause which temporarily disturbs an otherwise stable system of causes. It does nothing to increase sales overall.

While the promotion does not produce a net gain in sales over the long term, it does create avoidable costs for Campbell Soup. The most obvious costs are that of the promotion itself, and the lost revenues from the discounts. The promotion also helped to raise production costs, though marketing managers, with their own concerns, paid little attention to these. During the stable periods of demand between promotions, Campbell Soup production operations ran smoothly. Plants could regularly order ingredients and supplies, schedule personnel and equipment, and maintain a fairly steady work flow without incurring high inventories. However, the promotional campaigns disrupted their production operations and those of their suppliers. Plants had to pay workers extra to work overtime during the promotions, and then they would sit idle in the coming weeks. Procurement of ingredients was made more difficult, which added further to the costs of production.

As the Campbell Soup managers learned more about the theory of variation that distinguishes special causes from common causes of variation, they rethought this managerial practice. They realized that their promotional campaign was just a special cause that only disrupts an otherwise stable system. It does not achieve a lasting effect on the level of customer demand. It just incurs a lot of costs in other parts of the system, which cuts into the profit margin for the product or gets passed on to customers in higher prices after the promotion is over. Campbell Soup managers decided they should look for other ways to increase customer demand over the long term. As a result of this enlightened understanding of the system of demand, Campbell Soup, and other food products manufacturers like Procter and Gamble, have curbed the use of promotional campaigns and reduced the number of consumer coupons offered. Their efforts are more narrowly focused and intended to attract new customers who would not otherwise purchase the product.

The manager would not find a special event, like a machine malfunction or operator error, as he or she may for the measurement that exceeds the statistical control limits.

In traditionally managed organizations, the standards imposed are often unrelated to the capability of the system to meet the standards. A system may inherently produce variation that exceeds standards, as the one shown in Exhibit 16-6, and the employees actually executing the process may be able to do very little about it. Under these circumstances, managers would be overreacting if they attempted to "control" and take corrective action for each point that exceeds the specification.

Overreaction can be not only time consuming and frustrating for both employees and managers, it can even make matters worse. In the example above, the manager might have instructed operators to make machine adjustments to "correct" a deviation that exceeded the upper specification limit. The adjustments could cause the process to swing back to the other extreme and eventually exceed the lower specification limit. More adjustment could cause yet another swing to the other extreme. This type of overreaction, called **tampering,** which is *"making continual adjustments to a stable system, result by result, hoping to make things better."*[6] Because the person doing the tampering is reacting to events with no understanding of whether the system is in statistical control or not, there is no way this can create improvements that will have any lasting effect. In fact, tampering may produce more variation than the system would produce if left alone.

Managers throughout traditional organizations, not just those in production departments, are guilty of tampering. The most insidious form of tampering

Tampering Making continual adjustments to a stable system, result by result, hoping to make things better.

comes when managers compare performance to a running average. So, one month performance is above average, and everyone celebrates and enjoys accolades. The next month performance dips below average, and the consternation and disapproval of managers leads to a frenzied search for the causes of the supposed decline.

Peter Senge described the mentality that underlies the traditional approach in his book *The Fifth Discipline*:

We are conditioned to see life as a series of events, and for every event, we think there is one obvious cause. Conversations in organizations are dominated by concern with events: last month's sales, the new budget cuts, last quarter's earnings, who just got promoted or fired, the new product our competitors just announced, the delay that just was announced in our new product, and so on. The media reinforces an emphasis on short-term events—after all, if it's more than two days old it's no longer "news." Focusing on events leads to "event" explanations: "The Dow Jones average dropped sixteen points today," announces the newspaper, "because low fourth-quarter profits were announced yesterday." Such explanations may be true as far as they go, but they distract us from seeing the longer-term patterns of change that lie behind the events and from understanding the causes of those patterns.[7]

Unfortunately, managers may think they need to try to control what is the natural random variation found in the system without understanding that it is natural in the first place. All this usually does is make the variation worse. For example, the "corrective action" taken in response to deviation may always be followed by a return to normal. But this does not mean managers doing this have really controlled the situation. Check a sequence of points in Exhibit 16-7. An extreme point, outside the specifications (but inside the control limits), is almost always followed by a point within the specification limits. You should expect this in a stable system. However, when it fluctuates back into the center line, the manager may falsely believe that his or her actions were responsible for correcting the problem. This perception may lead them to do the same thing next time. Over the long term, the deviations return over and over. And managers build a false sense of confidence that they know how to handle the problem, because it always goes away.

Real improvement and reduction of variation only comes from knowledge about the system. With an understanding of TQM and statistics, the manager knows when to engage in problem solving (to eliminate special causes and achieve statistical control) and when to engage in improvement (to address common causes and reduce variation). Without this understanding, managers are prone to overreact, tamper, and do nothing to make things better.

You should by now start to see that trying to control business processes as if any fluctuation from a standard were to be immediately addressed and fixed is not going to generate long term success. Exhibit 16-8 lists contrasts the traditional with the TQM approach to control. You will see similarities between this and Exhibit 3-4 which listed differences between the concerns of a traditional manager and a process manager.

As you read the following description of a TQM approach to control and improvement, these differences will become even more clear.

EXHIBIT 16-8 Contrasting the traditional and TQM approaches to understanding
the principles of control

Traditional Approach	TQM Approach
Reactive	Proactive
Blame the person	Blame the process
Maintain	Improve
Handle discrete events	Manage patterns over time
Suppress deviation	Study variation and learn
Manage crises	Reduce variation
"If it ain't broke, don't fix it."	"It's OK, but you can make it better"

THINKING CRITICALLY

1. Think of a situation in which you engage regularly, such as exercise. In terms of your performance, do you find it varies from day to day within certain limits? Has there ever been a day when your performance was altered significantly? What do these experiences tell you about the usefulness of understanding common cause and special cause variation? Can you make assumptions about your general performance based on a special cause variation? Why or why not?
2. Have you ever had a manager that asked you to meet standards beyond the capabilities of the system you were part of? What was that like? If the manager had known about SPC, how could he or she have made improvements that would have allowed you to meet these standards?

TQM'S CONTROL AND IMPROVEMENT PROCESS

Using what we have learned up to now about focusing on systems, variation, and improvement, there is a process managers can apply to better control and improve any systems they are managing. This process incorporates some elements of the traditional control process with the statistical study of variation and its causes.[8] To understand how control works in a TQM organization, let's first review two basic models: (1) the organization as a system and (2) the learning process.

The Organization as a System

Exhibit 16-9 on page 616 depicts an **organization as a system.** It shows the four steps that describe *the macro processes of any system: inputs, transformation process, outputs, all aimed at the satisfaction of customers or other stakeholders.* A manager's primary responsibility is to make this system work as well as possible and keep improving. All the topics in this book provide direction and examples for doing this. Once managers have a system up and operating, it is through control, as discussed in this chapter, that managers can assess how well the system is functioning and how to make it better.

Organization as a system
The macro processes of any system: inputs, transformation process, outputs, all aimed at the satisfaction of customers or other stakeholders.

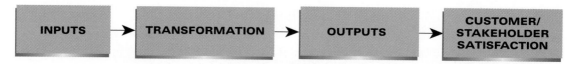

EXHIBIT 16-9   The Performance Process. This depicts the basic steps by which a system delivers outputs to satisfy customers and other stakeholders.

The best way to understand this model is start on the right with customers. Serving customer is what gives meaning to what the organization does. They expect a certain level of quality in the products and services they buy, and it is up to the organization to deliver that. Moving to the left, then, the outputs of the organization must meet certain customer-specified criteria, or they will fail in the market. These criteria include performance of the outputs in their intended use (delicious food at an expensive restaurant, winning football by your favorite team, trouble-free operation from your computer, fabricated parts that meet specifications for use as components by a manufacturer, and so on). These criteria also include a monetary value, beyond which the customer will not pay.

To deliver these outputs, managers must make sure their processes operate as efficiently and effectively as possible, minimizing waste and maximizing quality. Part of successfully managing the transformation process is having high-quality inputs, including components from outside suppliers, and also a well-developed strategy, an organizational structure that facilitates people working together, product designs, machinery, plant layout, policies, work procedures, and rules for conduct that do not constrain performance, and well-selected and trained human resources. All of these have to be in place before the organization can begin to transform inputs into outputs for customers. Successful managing ultimately involves aligning the inputs, transformation processes, and outputs with customer needs. This allows the system to create the mutually beneficial relationships between customers and company that keep it profitable and in business. Managing the organization to get better and better at that is the central idea of the TQM approach to control.

Statistical Process Control as a Learning Process

The statistical approach to understanding variation we have been reviewing in this chapter is really a learning process for managers. It involves the steps managers must go through to discover how the processes of their organization function and what is necessary to improve them. The basic elements of this **learning process,** which we can define as *the way managers use scientific thinking to develop knowledge about the causes of outcomes,* include the following four steps, which are represented in the circles on Exhibit 16-10. This learning process is somewhat like the PDCA cycle. Here is a description of each step:

Learning process The way managers use scientific thinking to develop knowledge about the causes of outcomes.

1. *Set Standards for Control and Improvement.* This is similar to the Plan step of PDCA. The standards referred to here involve eliminating waste and complacency. Whereas traditional product or service specification often tolerate a range of variation around a target standard (such as plus or minus five minutes for a commuter train), TQM encourages continuously reducing variation so the company almost always hits the target (no more than 30 seconds off

schedule for the train, for example). It also requires managers to keep raising targets to keep up with evolving customer needs and the competition.

Managers will not set arbitrary standards and quotas for employees that may be beyond system capability and would be harmful to employees and the organization. Rather, they are realistic and based upon feedback about current performance capabilities. Further, they will provide employees with a vision that inspires action and improvement. Managers will only establish quantitative goals and objectives when they also know employees have the means of achieving these goals. These standards are not used as yardsticks to evaluate and judge individuals. Rather, they are used to communicate the vision of what is possible as they work together to improve the system and its processes. Furthermore, standards are not set as lofty objectives independent of what the current system is capable of producing.

2. *Measure.* Similar to step 2 in the traditional control process, here managers develop appropriate scales of measurement (such as time to execute a process or number of defective parts in lot sizes of 1000) for analyzing system and process capabilities. Then they use these scales to collect data by measuring outputs to assess system performance.

3. *Study.* In this step managers analyze the data they have collected. They use statistical methods and other tools and techniques to understand the causes of variation. This is a significantly different step in the control process compared to the traditional activity of "Compare Performance to Predetermined Standards." The study step places a priority on learning about the system rather than evaluating and assigning blame for deviations. It uses organizational results as feedback for understanding system operation. Furthermore, it does not assume, like the traditional approach to control, that managers already know what the causes of deviations are.

4. *Act.* This step means making improvements or corrections based on the knowledge developed through the study of information about system performance. Depending on the situation, corrective action may mean dealing quickly to relieve a symptom (crisis management) solving a problem brought about by a special cause or improving the system by reducing common causes of variation.

EXHIBIT 16-10
The learning process

Now, let's combine the model of the organization as a system with this learning process model, as shown in Exhibit 16-11. You should study this exhibit and return to it frequently while reading below. It is important that you see how all of its elements fit together to create a realistic model of control and improvement.

Managers should establish standards and corresponding measures at points corresponding to each of the four steps that describe a system's processes and communicate these to everyone who needs to know throughout the organization. For example, to ensure high quality inputs, managers need to establish standards for suppliers before placing orders. Then they need to measure specific characteristics of products shipped from suppliers to check that these items are meeting their standards. Product specifications standards tell employees what output they are supposed to deliver, and in-process and end-of-line inspections reveal whether or not they are meeting those specifications. Finally, standards describe how the product should perform after customers put it into use. To make sure they are meeting these standards, managers may conduct customer satisfaction surveys to see the company's products are satisfying customers.

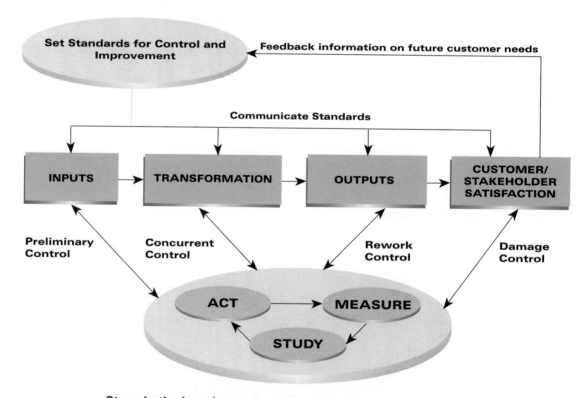

Steps in the learning process for controlling and making improvements at any stage: (1) collect feedback on current performance, (2) study relationships among measures of performance throughout the system, (3) take action to improve.

Source: Bounds, Yorks, Adams and Ranney, *Beyond Total Quality Management* (New York: Mc Graw-Hill, 1994). Reprinted by permission of McGraw-Hill.

EXHIBIT 16-11 A TQM approach to control and improvement based on the study of variation.

The control and improvement process, as shown in Exhibit 16-11, looks at the same three steps for each of the four stages describing system operation. These steps describe how managers learn from the process or situation they are dealing with and use this learning to improve in the future. They are depicted in the oval at the bottom of Exhibit 16-11 and include:

1. **Measure.** Collect feedback on current performance based on appropriate measurements that let the manager know how well the process is functioning at this stage. For example, is the company, at the customer satisfaction stage, missing promised delivery dates consistently by two or three days? This is the measure part of the control process.
2. **Study.** Analyze measurements using statistical methods to figure out what part of the system is causing the problem. Propose changes that will address the problem, such as the missed delivery dates.
3. **Act.** Implement the proposed changes. For example, by improving the assembly process for a product and minimizing rework, a company can improve its ability to deliver products on time to customers.

Application of the Measure-Study-Act sequence at each of the four stages shown in the model constitutes the four different types of control of system performance: (1) *Preliminary Control* applied at the inputs stage, (2) *Concurrent Control* at the transformation stage, (3) *Rework Control* at the outputs, and (4) *Damage Control* at the customer satisfaction stage. These approaches to control are listed in order of their effectiveness in achieving control and improvement. Generally, the earlier in the system managers can apply control, the more long lasting it will be. Preliminary control is most long lasting and will have most beneficial effect on the system, and damage control deals with a single situation and has little effect beyond that situation, except perhaps to wake managers up that they need to apply some preliminary control. Control at each of these stages will always involve the learning process discussed above, with the goal of learning the cause of the problems or deviations from standard and learning ways to make sure they do not happen in the future.

Preliminary Control

Managers achieve **preliminary control** by *making projections about the future, anticipating needed changes, and taking appropriate action*. Preliminary control is both *preventive*, to avoid undesirable outcomes, and *proactive*, to achieve desired outcomes. The most important part of preliminary control is the job of reducing common cause variation and thus improving the quality of outputs. It is here that managers attack the root causes of problems. By monitoring and improving inputs, managers exert a great deal of control over the performance of subsequent or "downstream" events, including transformation, output, and customer satisfaction.

An important managerial responsibility is to improve the materials, machinery, manpower, methods and measures used to produce outputs for customers. Sometimes employees may identify opportunities for improvements they can make to inputs while they are doing the work of transforming inputs into outputs. With control charts to document the result of their actions, employees can work

Preliminary control Managerial action that involves making projections about the future, anticipating needed changes, and taking appropriate action early in a process to prevent problems downstream.

autonomously to make limited changes and incremental improvements to the system in which they work. However, managers are the ones who put most system inputs in place and are responsible for their overall operation and improvement.

The Campbell Soup Company, for example, has developed a program to improve its suppliers. One of the first in the food products industry, the program is called the Select Supplier Program. It requires that suppliers use statistical methods to improve the quality, cost, and delivery characteristics of their products and services if they want to do business with Campbell. This same principle of proactive system improvement applies to all other inputs, including human resources, which must be selected, placed, trained, and developed on an ongoing basis, and engineering designs, which must be delivered on time, be producible, cost effective, and also match customer needs.

Concurrent Control

Concurrent control

Action taken on a real time basis, as workers execute the tasks to transform inputs into outputs, to ensure standards are met.

Concurrent Control is *action taken on a real time basis, as workers execute the tasks to transform inputs into outputs, to ensure standards are met.* Concurrent control is also known as operational control or steering control. A good analogy is driving a car. When behind the wheel, the driver attentively monitors road and traffic conditions and makes adjustments to ensure safe arrival at his or her destination. Similarly, a great deal of concurrent control in industrial organizations is the responsibility of employees doing work on the line.

Concurrent control is often based upon process measurements, or data collected at one of the steps in transforming inputs into outputs. For example, employees at the paint room of a car manufacturer may monitor pressure gauges to ensure the smooth flow of paint to the sprayers. Statistical control charts provide a useful tool for employees to accomplish self-control by helping them to spot and react to special cause problems. The charts also help employees understand process capability and what suggestions they might make to improve the overall operation of the process.

Concurrent control consists of fine tuning and making course corrections that help make sure that the work is executed according to the designs, procedures, and steps determined at the inputs stage. Corrective actions may involve making adjustments to machine settings, redistributing time and energy, or changing behavior. Significant advances have been made in achieving concurrent control with advancements in computer controls and automated measurement devices that monitor and make adjustments to minimize variation. Automated control is particularly important in the complex manufacturing processes of products like chemicals at DuPont, oil and gasoline at Exxon, and paper at Georgia-Pacific.

Because concurrent control focuses on controlling processes while they are happening, it can occasionally require that managers or employees take action to avoid an eminent crisis. For example, sometimes employees have to compensate for the inadequacy of inputs that come from the larger system. Poor quality raw materials will require increased vigilance and adjustments to work procedures and machine settings to ensure that quality of outputs is not compromised. While concurrent control is essential to good performance, it has its limits. This is because most variation in a process is caused by variation in inputs. If managers can successfully implement preliminary controls to eliminate problems caused by poor inputs, concurrent controls will work fine to make sure the transformation process works as designed.

USING HIGH SPEED VIDEO IN PRELIMINARY CONTROL[9]

A LOOK AT

TECHNOLOGY

Imagine a paper manufacturing machine as long as a football field that operates 24 hours a day rolling out a half-ton of newsprint per minute. There is a factory in Longview, Washington along the Columbia River that has three such machines. It is jointly owned by the Weyerhaeuser Company and Nippon Paper Company. The internal operations of the machines themselves are monitored by computers, a form of concurrent control. As the finished paper comes out of the machine, it is captured on a reel which, when full, is lifted away by a crane. The reels fill up quickly, and there is a special procedure of cutting the paper ending on one reel and starting a new reel. If there are any glitches in this process, a ton or more of finished newsprint is quickly spilled out onto the factory floor.

With one machine, this started happening on three out of 10 runs. This was costing the company $350,000 per year in lost production. The company can recycle the lost paper, but this represents waste and rework. To figure out what was going wrong, managers decided to use a high-speed video camera to record exactly what happened in the transfer from full to empty reels. This camera allows investigators to record up to 1000 frames per second. They can then review the video, looking at the process frame by frame to figure out what was going wrong.

They recorded more than 100 transfers, and the carefully scrutinized images revealed that the problem wasn't one single event but a series of subtle sequences within the process. The videotape showed that the problem was happening during the transfer process, when the tail of the paper was attaching to the new reel. This takes place in two to three-tenths of a second. Investigators found that if the machine was run at speeds faster than this, it would cause a failure. They also discovered slight differences in the ways individual operators handled the transfers and how this led to inconsistencies in the process. Using this information, they were able to fine tune the process and improve efficiency so that 9 out 10 transfers were successful.

What this technology revealed was a problem that appeared to be a special cause variation but when reviewed more carefully was a variation inherent in the process itself. By carefully modifying the process, the company was able to reduce variation and improve the efficiency of the process by two-thirds. Of course, this is not satisfactory, and by continuing to refine their methods, they will be able to reduce this variation even more.

This is just one example of technology now being used to monitor and control manufacturing processes. In magazines like *Quality, Quality Progress,* and many others you will find whole sections devoted to devices designed to measure processes on an ongoing basis and automate the development of SPC charts.

Rework Control

Rework control is *action taken to redo a job*. It is necessary when the previous two forms of control, preliminary and concurrent control, have failed. Generally rework comes as the result of inspectors finding defective or off-target outputs that cannot be sold without first being repaired. Consider some examples. A too-long shaft must be reground to meet the specification for length before it can be included in a subassembly. A financial report must be rewritten before it is presented to the board of directors because its calculations were based upon some faulty numbers. Sometimes rework is not even possible. The output may have to be discarded or sold for salvage. In some cases, managers just have to accept the output and make the best of it. For example, financial results, like sales volume

Rework control Action taken to redo a job.

and profitability, which are outputs for the company that allow it to continue in business, are difficult to rework, despite the determined efforts of many creative accountants.

Managers should not rely on rework control because it is more costly to do things twice than it is to do it right the first time by executing effective preliminary and concurrent control. Relying on rework to control performance means wasted resources, unpredictable delivery schedules, and extra inventory as safety stock. And too often, defective products slip through inspection undetected and get into the marketplace to customers. This is particularly problematic with services, such as a manicure, a haircut, or an oil change, which are delivered as they are produced. The solution to this: prevent the defects from ever happening in the first place by applying SPC techniques at every step, minimizing variation and maximizing quality.

Damage Control

Damage control Actions taken to minimize the negative impact of a defect or some other variation on customers.

If defective or off-target output does get into the hands of customers (or other stakeholders), then managers have to engage in **damage control,** or *take action to minimize the negative impact of a defect or some other variation on customers.* There are many ways they might do this, including apologizing, refunding money, replacing the product, performing the service again (a form of rework), and promising to do better in the future. The 5 year/50,000 mile warranty on new automobiles represents a form of damage control necessitated by quality control problems in the past. However, if automobile manufacturers can eliminate defects, then they minimize warranty costs while increasing customer satisfaction—everyone wins.

Other forms of damage control seek to minimize the perception of damage by the customer, which might be referred to as image management. For example, a young couple buying their first car, a Mazda minivan, from a used car dealer, notice that the car smoked more than it should. The car salesman insists "It's not a Mazda if it doesn't smoke a little." Like political "spin doctors" who attempt to manipulate potentially damaging news about their candidate by putting a positive "spin" on it, salespeople and customer services representatives are often placed in this role of damage control. When the president of a company stands up before the board of directors, he or she may engage in damage control to soften the impact of the "bad" financial numbers in the quarterly report. Glance through an annual report of a Fortune 500 company on the downslide, and you will find all kinds of damage control. While this may work temporarily, unless the company addresses the causes of the problems that require damage control in the first place, it will be in for serious problems.

The most important point about damage control is that it happens when all the previous approaches to control, including preliminary, concurrent, and rework control, have failed. The damage has taken place, and all managers can do is hope to try to make things good for customers and hope they will not lose future business because of the problem. To prevent this from happening in the future, managers must take action upstream in the system. The further upstream they can go in taking action, the better. At times, all four approaches to control are necessary. However, if managers devote more time and effort to preliminary control, less time, effort, and cost will be required downstream in the other forms of control. It is important to note here that employees engaged in rework and

WORKING IN THE SYSTEM[10]

ETHICS

Managers often reward and praise subordinates who meet their standards, and punish and berate those who fail. Managers who use this approach ignore two important principles: (1) it is the manager's responsibility to put in place the system that enables subordinates to perform well, and (2) every system inherently produces variation that may or may not be controlled by the people who work within it. Managers who ignore these principles can produce stressful work conditions for subordinates. Consider the following example.

A variety of automotive after-market products were produced in a plant. The plant manager made a practice of holding a weekly management meeting in which area managers was praised or criticized, depending on whether they had met the previous week's production schedule for their area. An annual physical inventory turned up a large disparity between the physical count of one type of product and the amount shown in the computerized inventory record. The physical count was short. The plant manager decided that thieves from the surrounding town must be stealing parts from the warehouse. He had a fence built around the company's property to prevent any more stealing.

A physical count a few weeks later showed another shortage. The plant manager decided that employees must be stealing from the warehouse, so he had a fence built around the warehouse and gates installed that could be locked. After this, another physical count showed that the problem still existed. The plant manager hired a detective to catch the thieves. During the night, the manager of the area that produced the product that was stored in the warehouse and two of his employees were observed hoisting boxes of the product over the warehouse fence and taking them back to the production area.

For several months, the area manager had shown consistently good performance meeting his weekly production goals. He did this by coming up with a method that made his performance look good, so that he didn't have to endure embarrassment and criticism in the weekly production meetings. When production problems occurred and the area manager saw he wouldn't be able to meet his schedule, he would "borrow" material from the warehouse, bringing it back to the production area. Then the material handlers, who also logged production figures into the computer inventory record, would move the material back into the warehouse. The area manager had thought he would somehow be able to make up the discrepancies before a physical count revealed them, but production problems continued to crop up.

After he had begun his new method of "manufacturing" product, he found it difficult to stop, because he couldn't figure out a way to explain the sudden deterioration in performance that would occur if he stopped. This manager had learned at some point that making his numbers was all management cared about. He figured out a way to do this. Given what you have learned about TQM's approach to control and improvement, would you recommend that the area manager be dismissed for dishonest practices? What about his boss, the plant manager? Was he also unethical by putting in place standards without providing a system capable of meeting the standards?

damage control add costs, not value, to the organization's processes. They are repairing mistakes that should not have happened. Depending on this kind of control is one reason many American businesses have lost their competitive edge to the Japanese, who, through their preliminary control techniques, deliver higher-quality products at lower prices than Americans have been able to do.

Feedback Information

Feedback information
Data gathered on the performance process that is fed back to managers.

**Globe Metallurgical:
Baldrige Award Winner**

Feedback information, or *data gathered on the performance process that is fed back to managers,* is critical to control and improvement. It does not change what has been done in the past, but it does inform people about past performance and future customer needs. If studied, feedback information can lead to learning on how to improve future performance. Feedback on customer needs gathered during product design can help ensure that the right standards are set in the first place. Then feedback on performance reveals whether those needs were met.

Notice in Exhibit 16-11 that feedback flows in both directions, upstream and downstream, through the Measure-Study-Act sequence. This two-way flow ensures that corrective actions are taken based on feedback information from both upstream and downstream measures. For example, with downstream feedback, the engineers designing a new manufacturing process as an input will study the impact of the new process on workers in the transformation process, the quality of products and services output, and the satisfaction of customers who acquire and use these outputs. Engineers provide upstream feedback when they notify workers of process changes and inform them about how best to conduct concurrent control during the transformation process.

The two-way flow of feedback information also implies that managers study the relationships between measurements at the various stages of the performance process. Statistical methods are available for investigating these relationships. Consider some examples. Cadillac division of General Motors, like all other automobile producers, conducts market tests of various prototype designs (input stage) to see what customers value. Engineers study the effect of computer control algorithms (transformation stage) on the physical characteristics of chemical products (output stage) at DuPont. Georgia-Pacific salespeople study the impact of variations in thickness and surface characteristics of particle board (output stage) when it is used by their customers, furniture manufacturers, as a base for lamination (customer satisfaction stage).

When managers take this approach to control, they use information to guide corrective actions. Their top priority is to control and improve the inputs that the system uses because all subsequent performance depends upon how well they do this job.

"Winging It" Without Statistical Analysis

Do managers have to use statistics in every case to make improvements? The answer is no. For example, one manager at Hughes Aircraft tells about an employee 15-minute-a-week meeting that he established, where the only topic was quality. The employees cut workmanship errors 85 percent and improved productivity in excess of 30 percent in such areas as circuit card manufacturing. The gains did not come through applying statistics, but by thoughtful analysis of practices and personal values. Such gains are often possible when there are big opportunities for improvement. Sometimes in TQM, this is called gathering the

CRISIS MANAGEMENT AND PROBLEM SOLVING AT TRECO

As we have seen throughout this chapter, the way a manager reacts to deviations determines whether or not variation in performance is reduced over time. The following experiences of Scott Ehrenfried, the production manager at Treco Products, illustrates the difference between crisis management and problem solving, two very different ways to react to variation.

One afternoon a machine broke down on the production line of Treco. Unexpectedly, the machine parts needed for repair were not in the stock room. Scott had to expedite the delivery of repair parts to get the machine fixed and get the production line going again. To keep the employees busy during the shutdown, and to get a promised delivery out to customers, Scott had some of the workers attempt to recover defective product from the scrap bin. They reworked the defective products with hand tools, and substituted them for those not being produced by the broken machine.

Four hours later, the machine parts arrived by special delivery, they repaired the machine, and production proceeded as normal. The flames of crisis had temporarily been snuffed. The standard for downtime at Treco is a target of less than 2 hours a week. Because no machines broke down the following week this standard was met,

so the manager must have done his job in controlling operations. Right? Unfortunately, the same scenario was repeated with a different machine the next month. The problem was not really solved, but only temporarily suppressed, not permanently controlled.

Problem solving is not always simple, because there are so many angles to take. In the case of Treco Products, Scott could avoid the crisis in a number of ways.

1. He could stockpile finished material in the warehouse to protect against breakdowns. This would ensure customers would be served, but it is a costly way to do busines.

2. He could stock up on repair parts to allow quick repairs, so instead of being down four or five hours the line would only be down for 30 minutes. This would help, but it would be costly to carry repair parts to cover every possible breakdown.

3. He could establish faster procedures for expediting parts from suppliers, perhaps cutting the time required in half. This way he would avoid carrying the inventory, but he would still have to endure some downtime.

These solutions are not really satisfactory because they do not get at the root cause of the problem. The company really has no procedure for maintaining its machines nor any sense of how often they should receive routine maintenance. They just run them until some-

thing goes wrong, and then they fix it. What would be a better way? One way might be to develop a control chart that tracks machine performance. They could have learned by taking measurements of machine outputs through time that when the outputs of the machine start becoming consistently out of spec, this indicates wear on the machine and preventive maintenance is due. From then on, they would have eliminated the crisis management approach to control.

So why hadn't this happened for a long time at this company? It seems that top management thought it would cost more money to hire more maintenance people to do the preventive maintenance than to repair machines when they finally broke down. Their general philosophy was "If it ain't broke don't fix it."

Scott eventually convinced these managers to invest in preventive maintenance. He dedicated a maintenance man to such tasks as regularly lubricating machines, checking parts for wear, and making repairs during scheduled downtimes to replace parts before they break down. The investment paid off. Machine breakdowns were virtually eliminated. Downtime standards are now easily met. Other benefits also resulted. The costs of expediting were eliminated, safety stocks of finished goods were reduced, and customer service levels were maintained.

"low-hanging fruit." These are easy-to-achieve improvements, brought about because there has been so much room for improvement in many companies.

When American automobile producers started to seriously improve quality in the early 1980s, for example, they easily made many big and immediate gains because there were so many obvious problems. Some managers have reported that defect rates were higher than 40 percent in some plants. Under these circumstances, any attention to quality can yield improvements. After initial successes, achieving continuous improvement becomes more difficult. It is here that the study of variation can contribute to further learning.

Even if managers do not personally use statistical methods, the theory of variation and the thinking associated with it is vital. It gives managers a deep insight into how organizations function as systems with processes and how performance can be improved. In brief, employees are stuck with the systems that managers provide them. Under these circumstances, the traditional approach to control, where managers blame the employee for poor performance is not only unfair, it is based on deep misunderstandings about what causes performance, good or bad. Further, this approach does not help improve poor performance that may be blamed on employees, and it could make performance worse by creating a hostile relationship between employees and management.

Sometimes collecting the numbers and conducting formal statistical analyses may be burdensome and even unnecessary. A manager who is well trained statistically and educated (with knowledge of common cause and special cause variation), can often decipher the solution very quickly. However, the manager should exercise caution in jumping to conclusions. It is often hard to tell the difference between a situation where you can intuit the right answer and one where you only think you have the right answer. Doing the statistical analysis using a control chart can help provide added insight needed to get the right answer. And engaging in structured analysis with a group of employees or peers can provide a consensual validation of the thinking.

❓ THINKING CRITICALLY

1. Have you ever been an employee at a company where rework and damage control were common? What was it about the company's operations that made this common?
2. Have you had to ask a company to take care of a problem on a product you bought because it had defects? What costs do you think were associated with the problem of defects for the company whose product this was? How do you think this company could have avoided this problem?
3. How do you think ignorance of statistical process control might hamper a manager trying to practice preliminary control?

SUMMARY

TRADITIONAL CONTROL TO MAINTAIN CURRENT COURSE

*   Traditional management practice looks on control as a way to enforce adherence to standards defined by management. The traditional approach includes four steps:

–Set predetermined standards, plans, or objectives.

–Measure and monitor performance.

–Compare performance to the predetermined standards.

–Make a decision and take corrective action.

HOW TO IMPROVE THE TRADITIONAL CONTROL PROCESS

- The traditional approach does not take into account that an organization is a system with interrelated processes nor that variation in the outputs of processes will naturally occur through time.

- TQM suggests that understanding variation, its causes, and how to deal with these causes to improve performance is at the heart of successful managerial control.

STATISTICS, VARIATION, AND MANAGING IMPROVEMENT

- The way to understand process variation is through the use of statistical process control charts, which can help managers identify common cause and special cause variation. With this information, managers can then make suggestions for reducing variation and improving performance.

- Managers address variation due to special causes by taking measures to make sure these do not recur.

- Common cause variation requires managers to carefully use the PDCA improvement cycle to reduce variation and improve process efficiency and quality of outputs.

- Managers may try to get employees to meet specifications which are beyond the capacity of the system's processes.

- Managers may try to make adjustments (called "tampering") when performance falls outside specifications, which can make the organization perform even more erratically.

TQM'S CONTROL AND IMPROVEMENT PROCESS

- The TQM approach to control brings together the model of an organization with its four parts: inputs, transformation processes, outputs, and the satisfaction of customers with a model for organizational learning with its four steps: set standards for control and improvement, measure, study, and act.

- The combination of these two models creates a model for understanding TQM control as a learning process that emphasizes control and prevention of problems as early as possible in any process. Doing this includes the regular taking of measurements, development of statistical process control charts, and the reduction of common cause variation.

- Control can be applied at any of the parts of the process: preliminary control is concerned with inputs, concurrent control focuses on transformation processes, rework control is concerned with outputs, and damage control deals with customer satisfaction.

- While it may be possible to make improvements without the use of SPC charts, this mainly takes care of the "low-hanging fruit," the easy improvements. Continuous improvement requires the consistent gathering of data, its analysis, and the use of the PDCA improvement cycle.

KEY TERMS

Common cause variation 607

Concurrent control 620

Control limit 606

Controlling 594

Crisis management 598

Damage control 622

Data point 606

Feedback information 624

Histogram 604

Learning process 616

Managing by exceptions 596

Organization as a system 615

Preliminary control 619

Problem solving 598

Rework control 621

Special cause variation 606

Standard 595

Statistical control 609

Statistical process control (SPC) chart 606

Statistics 599

Tampering 613

Variation 593

REVIEW QUESTIONS

1. What are the four steps in the traditional management control process? How do managers apply these steps to controlling organizational and individual performance?
2. Why is it a problem to use numerical goals and standards to control organizational performance?
3. Why is a knowledge of causes vital to realistically controlling and improving organizational performance?
4. What tool can managers use to understand the causes behind organizational performance and how does it work?
5. What is a histogram and how can managers use it to understand organizational processes?
6. How should a manager go about reducing variation due to common causes?
7. What is likely to happen if a manager places specification limits inside the upper and lower control limits on an SPC chart?
8. What are the four types of control in TQM and what is the timing of each one?
9. Which type of control is most effective in reducing variation, costs, and improving quality? Why? Which type of control is least effective and most costly? Why?

EXPERIENTIAL EXERCISE

Break into groups of five or six students each. Find a copy of the *Wall Street Journal* one of the popular business magazines like *Business Week* or *Fortune*. Find an article describing a business having problems of one sort or another. Working together, discuss the problem and its seeming causes. Then answer the questions:

1. Does the article blame a person for the problems? What does it say this person did?
2. Does the article explain how the problem evolved? In thinking about this situation, do you think the problem was more the fault of a single person or the poor control of the company's processes?
3. How might the rigorous application of statistical process control have helped to prevent this problem?

Now, find an article describing a successful company and in your group discuss the nature of the company's successes and why you think these are happening. Then answer the following the questions:

1. Does the article suggest a single person is mainly responsible for this success? What does it say this person did singlehandedly to bring this about?
2. In thinking about this success, do you think it was due to the actions of one person or because the company's processes were operating well and were aligned with customer needs?
3. Does this company provide a good example of the use of statistical process control at work? If yes, how was it applied? If no, explain why the application of SPC would help the company do even better.

Choose one of your articles and report your conclusions about this company and its use of SPC to the class.

CASE ANALYSIS AND APPLICATION
Measuring Performance at the Air Mobility Command (AMC)[11]

The Air Mobility Command (AMC) supports the U.S. armed forces by providing airlift, aerial refueling, aeromedical evacuation, and combat rescue during wartime and peacetime. AMC also supports humanitarian efforts during natural and man-made disasters. The AMC has experienced pressure from its customers to do a better job. Under the leadership of General Hansford T. Johnson, AMC developed programs for improving its people, mission, facilities, and equipment starting in September 1989. However, this approach seemed inadequate, as Johnson explains, "Each program was independent from the others. . . . About that time, total quality management was catching on in the military. I came to the conclusion that quality was a unifying approach."

With the help of an outside facilitator, Johnson launched a new approach to improvement. The first task was to develop a vision for the organization, or an ideal state that AMC would like to reach. AMC summed up its vision as one of providing "support America can always count on." AMC's vision is grounded in the vision of the U.S. Air Force: "Air Force people building the world's most respected air and space force—global power and reach for America." AMC leaders realized that having a vision without a means of accomplishing it does not amount to much, so they developed an infrastructure of goals, objectives, and performance indicators, as well as a quality improvement plan to help realize the vision. AMC's infrastructure in built upon six longterm (10-year) goals:

- *Quality support to people.* Develop a passion for delivering quality support to AMC personnel and motivate them to provide the same level of quality service to their customers.
- *Readiness.* Ensure all elements of the command are ready to meet the current and future needs of the United States.
- *Environment.* Focus on environmental excellence that propels the command from correction and prevention to leadership in improving its living and working environment.
- *Patient Airlift.* Provide a responsive system that melds top-quality medical care with sensitivity and efficiency in customer service.
- *Passenger Airlift.* Provide quality passenger service that makes AMC travel an enthusiastic choice for its customers' missions and individual needs.
- *Cargo Airlift.* Make AMC the most efficient and effective cargo service from the customers' point of view.

To help AMC personnel really understand what these long term goals mean, AMC developed short-range (two- to three-year) objectives for the goals. Each goal has at least two objectives, for a total of 17 objectives. For example, the objectives for the goal of cargo airlift are:

1. Provide an airlift system responsive to customer needs by delivering cargo on time and undamaged.
2. Minimize cost to the customer by improving the efficiency of the system.
3. Develop and field a system capable of providing in-transit visibility from receipt to delivery.

To measure progress in achieving these objectives, AMC developed a measurement system that contains more than 70 *performance indicators* that were designed to measure the entire process. For example, the indicators for the first objective listed above are:

- Timeliness of cargo deliveries
- Discrepancy reports on damaged and lost cargo
- Results of satisfaction surveys of outbound shippers and inbound receivers.

Discussion Questions

1. To assess AMC's progress toward its strategic goals, AMC needs to develop a plan that addresses:

    - who is to collect the data,
    - when data is to be collected,
    - how data will be collected and analyzed, and
    - how the data will be used to promote improvement.

Discuss the major issues that AMC should consider in making decisions about each of these important dimensions of their assessment plan.

2. Describe how AMC should forge a connection between measurement and data analysis and the other important elements of management through a quality improvement plan. Elements that should be addressed include:

   - Empowerment
   - Teamwork
   - Structure
   - Training
   - Recognition
   - Commitment

List and describe connections with other elements as you see fit.

17. OPERATIONS MANAGEMENT FOR CONTROL AND IMPROVEMENT

LEARNING OBJECTIVES

After you finish this chapter, you should be able to:

1. Define operations management and explain the role it plays in guiding organization success.

2. List and explain the issues involved in selecting a facility site.

3. List and explain the issues involved in facility layout.

4. Explain the issues surrounding capacity utilization and production scheduling for meeting organizational output goals.

5. Define inventory and explain the importance of inventory management to control costs and facilitate operations.

6. Explain how to plan and prioritize activities to maximize output and customer satisfaction and minimize costs.

7. Define push and pull systems and just-in-time inventory control.

8. Explain the relationship between pull systems, just-in-time inventory control and Total Quality Management.

TOYOTA SUPPLIERS FOCUS ON QUALITY OPERATIONS

Supplier Development Outreach Program

When Toyota (and many other Japanese manufacturers) began operating production facilities in the U.S., a key ingredient of the "world class" system they had developed at home seemed to be missing—reliable and efficient component parts suppliers. If their U.S. facilities were to function properly, this weak link in the chain had to be strengthened. Without the consistent delivery of small batches of high-quality components, their system could not work.

Toyota, like most automobile (and many other large durable item) manufacturers, does not make every component that goes into its final product. It uses a myriad of "specialist" organizations to make and sometimes partially assemble various portions of the vehicle. Since Toyota will ultimately be held responsible for the performance of the final product, it takes the quality of components very seriously. It also takes the selection of component suppliers very seriously. Once selected, the relationship between Toyota and a supplier is considered a partnership, and considerable effort is made to ensure the success of the supplier organization. This is in Toyota's best interest as well as the supplier's. Each one's success depends on the other's.

Flex-n-Gate, Inc. (FNG) of Danville, Illinois and Continental Metal Specialties, Inc. (CMS) of Richmond, Kentucky are two such suppliers that, with the help of Toyota's Supplier Outreach Program, are on their way to "world class" in their own operations. In addition to the benefits to Toyota, these improvements have made each of them more competitive in their other markets. They have even become "teachers" to some of their other customers.

George Hommel, CEO of CMS explained it as "paying attention to the details." On a tour of one of the four facilities operated by CMS in Eastern Kentucky, Mr. Hommel described some of the changes. "Look at all this space on the shop floor. You can see all the machines and workers now. A year or so ago there was hardly enough room for the fork-lift to maneuver the materials from one machine to the next. Now, we've freed up enough space that used to hold work-in-process that we can move most of the quality management activities on the plant floor where they need to be. We've cut press changeovers from two hours to 45 minutes, with improvements still being made. We had to. Toyota has to have multiple shipments weekly, and they only take what they will use until the next shipment. We can't afford long changeovers." Roy Coleman, Flex-n-Gate's general manager for manufacturing, echoed the improvements made with Toyota's guidance. "It was almost chaos around here before!"

FNG makes bumpers for Toyota trucks. CMS makes structural members such as door frame braces. Each also does some assembling of the parts it makes, primarily welding pieces into sub-assemblies. If they are to keep Toyota as a customer, they must make almost daily shipments to the assembly plant. Each shipment will be installed

in a finished vehicle within a day or two of its shipment. Each piece must be "on the mark" in quality, and the shipments must arrive within a narrow time window.

Toyota's responsibility to its suppliers is to provide firm schedules as to the specific components desired far enough in advance for FNG or CMS to plan and execute their manufacture. Toyota can't change the order once the "point-of-no-return" is reached. Toyota also provides free consultation and training to the suppliers as they work to achieve even greater efficiencies. These suppliers have focused on improving the "manufacturing operations" function of their businesses. For them, this is the critical element to their continued success.

OPERATIONS AND ORGANIZATIONS

Operations The organizational function in which the combination and transformation of inputs into outputs occurs.

Operations management The process of planning, implementing, and controlling operations.

As systems, we can understand what organizations do in terms of three basic functions: organizations *obtain* resources from society, they *combine* or *change* these resources in many possible ways and *provide* the newly created output back to society. **Operations** is *the function in which the combination and transformation of inputs into outputs occurs*. **Operations management** is *the process of planning, implementing, and controlling operations*. Another, more graphic, description of operations management might be that "it's where the rubber meets the road." It includes a variety of techniques managers can use to minimize waste, reduce cycle time (the amount of time it takes to complete a process), and deliver quality outputs customers will value.

Most of the ideas that underlie the principles of TQM were born in the operations function. What has happened is that people have begun to wake up to the fact that everything an organization does is an operation of one sort or another. For example, the accounting department takes in order and accounts payable data and transforms it into reports that will help management understand how the company is doing and how it might improve. Every activity involves taking some inputs, transforming them in some way, and creating outputs with the ultimate purpose of helping the company serve customers and other stakeholders. TQM, as we have regularly suggested throughout this book, provides the methods for doing this best.

While the use of statistical process control methods in manufacturing is almost as old as the mass production methods of the early 20th century, until recently few manufacturing businesses really understood their value. Businesses have begun to see that SPC techniques and the management approach behind them may not be just the latest management fad but the key to survival. They realize that they must take these now expanded managerial concepts as their *modus operandi,* or they will be beaten up by those that do.

Supply chain A schematic of the flow of materials, and the transformations occurring during that flow, from basic raw materials to a finished product delivered to the final consumer.

The importance of operations in our everyday lives is perhaps best illustrated by a concept called the **supply chain.** This concept is depicted in Exhibit 17-1[1], a schematic of *the flow of materials, and the transformations occurring during that flow, from basic raw materials to a finished product delivered to the final consumer.* Note also that along the chain, each conversion processor is a customer of the process that precedes it. The conversions at each stage along the chain and the movement between stages are all *operations* that require planning, execution, and control—in other words, management.

634

A Historical Perspective

There is ancient evidence that operations, and thus operations management, pre-date written history. The earliest bands of humans, recognizing various tasks necessary for their society's success, managed their resources—primarily the different skills of the members of the group—to enhance the total output achieved. This mainly involved dividing up their labor, and managing their activities to find inputs and transform them into desired outputs.

Some of the classical examples that come to mind: (1) the construction of the pyramids and other ancient structures, the Egyptians, Mayans, Incas, Aztecs, and others were able to develop methods, obtain resources, and utilize them to attain certain outputs and goals. While we may question the social benefit resulting from that utilization of resources, and the way they obtained some inputs (such as slave labor), there is no question that these efforts required significant management of "operations." Unfortunately, much of what was known of their methods was lost as those political and economic powers were replaced by others.

Operations management, as a subject for scholarly examination, begins with the Industrial Revolution. Inter-organizational competitiveness in market-based economies encouraged the development of techniques to better utilize all the inputs in the transformation process. New machinery and sources of energy to drive them came with increasing speed. But human labor remained the primary, and most costly, resource, and management efforts most often focused on getting more output from each unit of labor input. The focus of study was on those organizations whose outputs were "goods," rather than services. In the nineteenth and early twentieth centuries, the number of people involved in the creation of goods, relative to other activities, grew almost exponentially. Populations grew rapidly, but improved agricultural practices, including mechanization,

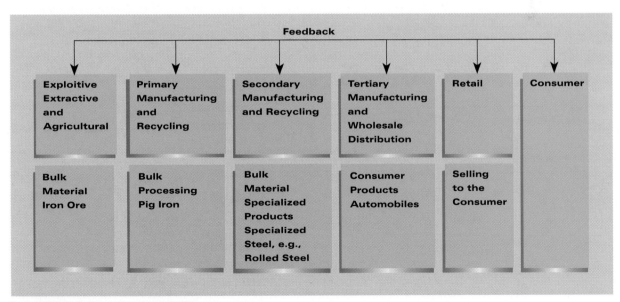

Source: *APICS–The Performance Advantage,* April 1994

EXHIBIT 17-1   The total supply chain

required fewer and fewer workers. Farm workers became factory workers as demand for industrial output grew, and the number and size of industrial organizations grew to meet it.

In the last forty years or so, the impact of "mechanization"—replacing human labor with machines—has seen a trend like that of a century or so earlier in the movement of workers from farms to factories. The number of workers needed to create the "goods" demanded by society today is a decreasing portion of the workforce. The "services" component of demand has become relatively larger. Exhibit 17-2[2] illustrates these trends. Increasing competition for markets and greater emphasis on value by these consumers continue to create a need for new ideas for improving the management of operations.

Manufacturing and Non-Manufacturing in Perspective

Organizations that create and deliver services have an "operations" component just as do organizations that produce goods. In many ways the operating decisions in the service industry are more complex than those in a goods producing organization. And in many organizations, it is difficult to make a clear distinction, since they provide both goods and services.

Exhibit 17-3 gives a few examples of this. It may be useful to distinguish between organizations (or individuals) that are creating "intangible" services—for example, advice from an attorney or office cleaning, and a service associated with obtaining goods—for example, a retail grocery store. There are some significant distinctions between service and manufacturing organizations (or service activities within a goods producing organization) that require different approaches to decisions. The major difference is that goods can be stored for a period of time. These stored goods can be used for, among other things, a smoother, perhaps more efficient, use of manufacturing capacity. We will discuss this issue in

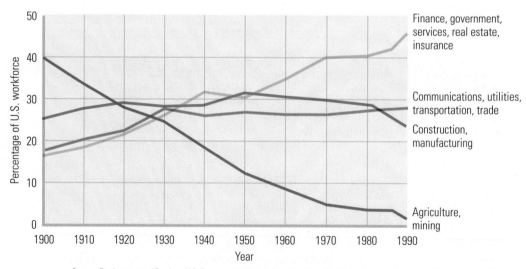

Source: *Employment and Earnings,* U.S. Department of Labor, Bureau of Labor Statistics, January 1982, p. 167; January 1985, p. 183; and January 1991, p. 193; *Long-Term Economic Growth,* 1860–1970, U.S. Department of Commerce, Bureau of Economic Analysis, June 1973, p. 76; and *People and Jobs,* U.S. Department of Labor, Bureau of Labor Statistics, April 1975, pp. 12–13.

EXHIBIT 17-2 Percentage of the Workforce in Four Sectors of the U.S. Economy, 1900–1990

EXHIBIT 17-3 Examples of services with significant product component	
Service	**Some Product Components**
Physician's office	Diagnostic equipment, supplies (swabs, bandages, medicines)
Restaurant	Inventory of food supplies, dishes, utensils
Airplane trip	Fuel inventory, repair parts, equipment
Package delivery	Vehicles, repair parts, packaging materials

EXHIBIT 17-3
Examples of services with significant product component

some detail later in the chapter. In service industries, though, capacity to provide service when none is needed cannot, in most cases, be saved to add to capacity in periods of high requirements. Some obvious examples include empty seats on a departing aircraft, a bank teller with no customer to serve, or fresh food in a restaurant without enough diners.

In the sections that follow, we will introduce the major types of problems faced by operations managers, and provide an overview of the various models that have been developed to help in solving these problems. In reviewing these models, try to keep in mind that they each emerge from understanding the organization as a system. They will help you start to understand how the systems view informs managerial decisions about operations. We will point out those models—and associated issues—that are considered "state of the art" and most helpful to managers in attaining excellence, and why.

Some types of decisions must be made quite often, such as daily assignments to employees. Others are made much less frequently, such as adding an additional machine to those already available. Both, however, are part of operations management. As we saw in Exhibit 17-2, the number of workers in manufacturing and agriculture has declined since the 1950s, while service industries (including government) have grown substantially. This change in numbers of workers should not be confused with a decline in importance of manufacturing to our global competitive position.

The ability of developed (often called "industrialized") and developing nations to improve their standards of living is closely tied to their ability to provide manufactured goods that meet the needs of consumers around the globe. Japan provides an example of a country that has become very good at this. Their manufacturing management models have created higher-quality, lower-cost cars, electronics, and myriad other products than competitors, including the U.S. They captured markets by exporting these products, and thereby raised the standard of living in their nation. U.S. companies have only in the past decade come to see the value of techniques mastered (though not necessarily discovered) by the Japanese.

Changing political and economic environments have created a global marketplace and global competition. International commerce is largely based on the transfer of goods—the output of manufacturing operations, rather than services. It will continue to be critically important that U.S. manufacturing operations become, and remain, more competitive in the global economic environment. The creation of goods is the basic economic activity that creates societal wealth.

EXHIBIT 17-4 Typical Products from Major Operations Categories Defined by Customer Involvement

Category	Example Products
Make-to -stock	Canned vegetables
	Microwave ovens
	Textbooks
	Fax machines
Make-to-order	Family portrait
	Yacht
	Custom drapes for your home
Assemble-to-order	Most automobiles
	Standard drapes for your home
	Mainframe computer systems

Classifying Operations

To better understand the variety and complexity faced by operations managers, it is helpful to look at various types of operations within the two major categories: manufacturing and non-manufacturing. Recognize that these are general descriptions. Many organizations may have units of different types, and many units will not fit one of our types exactly.

Manufacturing Operations

There are several ways to categorize manufacturing operations. What follows is a review of some of the common approaches for doing this.

Customer Involvement.   One way to separate manufacturing operations is to look at the nature of their involvement with the *customer* of their operation. Using customer involvement, there are three categories of operations: make-to-stock (MTS), make-to-order (MTO), and assemble-to-order (ATO). Exhibit 17-4 above shows example outputs of each type.

Make-to-stock (MTS) operations *produce items in anticipation of demand with a common design and price.* Most products that we see in retail stores are from this type of operation. They are designed for consumers in general rather than being customized for individuals in any way. Individual customers have low involvement with make-to-stock items. They take in most of the goods we buy as consumers. The facilities dedicated to the manufacture or processing of these products have limited flexibility to change the general characteristics of the product. Customers accept them as is or choose a competitor's version.

Make-to-order (MTO) operations *produce only after receipt of an order from a customer.* In an extreme case, the product would be a one of a kind. Thus, in make-to-order, there is a high level of customer involvement. Like MTS, however, a facility is generally dedicated to a relatively narrow range of product types—the equipment and expertise available limit customization or development of a wide range of products. Many of the issues faced in the MTS environment are avoided. For example, forecasting future demand is much less complex, as are issues associated with stocks of goods awaiting sale or shipment to distribution

Make-to-stock (MTS) Operations that produce items in anticipation of demand with a common design and price.

Make-to-order (MTO) Operations that produce goods only after receipt of an order from a customer.

points. Except in extreme cases, these companies maintain a stock of basic materials from which to work. A small industrial steel fabricator would be an example of a make-to-order operation. Such companies have a capability to manufacture and deliver a limited range of parts for construction or other uses, made to customers' specifications.

Assemble-to-order (ATO) operations allow *a degree of customization by designing a product that has a number of standard characteristics, but there are others that can be varied depending on the desires of the customer.* Here there is a moderate amount of customer involvement. ATO has some of the advantages of MTO, particularly in having the ability to more closely match the specific desires of an individual customer. For the "standard" portions of the item, however, it is more like the MTS operation. Furniture manufacturers would be an example of an assemble-to-order operation. When people purchase furniture, they often make a choice at a furniture retail showroom, including specific fabrics, and then receive the freshly assembled item several weeks later.

Volume and Variety.   Another way to categorize the operations function is on the basis of flexibility, that is, the variety of different products that might be created by the operation. This classification also looks at the volume or rate at which output can be delivered. Exhibit 17-5[3] depicts this category in terms of size and potential flexibility of different operations. The overlap in boxes indicates that some operations do not fit easily into one classification.

Continuous process manufacturing is *an operation in which the output is not in discrete units.* Chemical production, pulp and paper making, and oil refineries are examples of this category. The technology of the process is the primary determinant of the facility design and physical arrangement. The technology may also limit the discretion of the manager in controlling the rate of output. For example, there is a very narrow range of speed at which a paper-making machine will operate when making a specific type of paper.

Repetitive manufacturing is similar to the continuous production system described above. *This is basically the assembly line type operations for the manufacture of all kinds of consumer and industrial goods* from air conditioners to

Assemble-to-order (ATO)
Operations that allow a degree of customization by designing a product that has a number of standard characteristics, but there are others that can be varied depending on the desires of the customer.

Continuous process manufacturing An operation in which the output is not in discrete units.

Repetitive manufacturing The assembly line type operations for the manufacture of all kinds of consumer and industrial goods.

EXHIBIT 17-5
Classification of Manufacturing Types

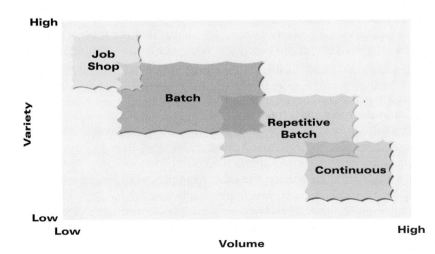

automobiles to tableware. There is a high volume of similar units. Production capacity, in the form of labor and equipment is quite specialized, both in terms of function and location. Each unit of output follows the same path through the labor and equipment.

There is some flexibility in the characteristics of the units. For example, either an automatic or manual transmission in an automobile could be installed at the same point on the assembly line. Like the continuous process, the system is designed to work as a large single unit. The nature of the products and the target rate of output determine the technology employed. The higher the output, the more likely the operation is mechanized. Managers are concerned with fine tuning the rates, insuring proper flow of input materials, and, of course, improvement of processes.

Batch manufacturing
Operations that create a number of different items with intermediate volume requirements.

In **batch manufacturing** we find *operations that create a number of different items with intermediate volume requirements*. The equipment used has considerable flexibility, and is relatively easy to convert from one item to another. An example in this category might be a manufacturer of wooden household furniture. The volume of any one piece or style may not justify the investment required to dedicate labor or equipment solely to that product. So they make a batch of a certain style and a batch of another style. At one extreme, this type of manufacturing begins to merge with the "repetitive" system; at its other extreme, it merges with a system we call a *job shop*, described below. Where a particular operation falls among these categories depends on the variety and volume of the individual products off the line.

Batch manufacturing poses some special managerial challenges in controlling the flow of batches through the processes. Since each product differs somewhat from the others being made, the "route" or path each batch follows is different. This variable path creates the potential for conflicts on the assignment of a particular machine to a specific product at a given time. There are also concerns about the size of the batches and the buildup of partially finished batches hung up between machine operations.

Job shops Manufacturing organizations that operate in the low-volume, high-variety, custom-order market.

Manufacturing organizations that operate in the low-volume, high-variety, custom-order market are called **job shops.** They are characterized by general-purpose equipment and a labor force with a variety of skills. The volumes are often very small—even just one, and the designs are also often unique, and well may never be produced again. A steel fabrication shop that manufactures customized steel parts is an example of a job shop.

The managerial issues for job shops are quite similar to those for batch manufacturing. The decision about the batch size is generally not so difficult, since production is based on an order for a specific quantity. The potential for scheduling conflicts still exists, as do the problems of managing the stock of materials that might accumulate.

Project manufacturing
Construction of goods that are not only low in volume but also require a relatively long period of time to complete each unit.

Project manufacturing involves *constructing goods that are not only low in volume but also require a relatively long period of time to complete each unit*. Such goods are projects with each unit managed almost as an independent business. The most common examples are in the construction industry—a high-rise building or a single family residence, but other examples would include building an oil tanker or a super-computer, which are usually managed as projects. Often with projects, labor, equipment, and materials must be moved to the location of the project rather than building the item in a factory. Projects require a special set approach to managing them as operations.

Service Operations

There are several ways to categorize service operations, based on common management issues for each type. This category includes:

- **Variety-volume,** which have to do with how many different services are offered and the volume or size of the operation. For example, a hotel offers rooms, restaurant meals, meeting services, and catering.
- **Tangible versus intangible.** Tangible services would include airline flights or retail operations and intangible services would include legal or business advice.
- **Customer involvement** is based on the amount of interaction required with the customers. High involvement services would include a physical exam or the services of a barber. Low involvement activities would include car repair. Moderate involvement services would include tax preparation.

Managerial Issues in Service Operations

There are four major differences between manufacturing and service operations. As we next take up decision models, keep these differences in mind.

1. Productivity is more difficult to measure in service operations when there is a less tangible output.
2. Quality standards are more difficult to create and monitor in some service operations than in manufacturing operations. Intangible services, such as advice from an attorney or physician, are particularly difficult to measure as to quality.
3. The customer's contact with the provider of service is usually closer than with the provider (manufacturer) of goods.
4. Manufacturing operations can, in many cases, store the output of their activities in the form of inventory to meet future requirements. Unused service capacity, in general, is lost.

THINKING CRITICALLY

1. Why would you say organizations have been more quick to apply statistical process control and other quality management techniques to operations such as manufacturing than to activities like sales, accounting, or human resources?
2. Based on what you have read here and elsewhere in the book, how much of Japanese success is attributable to how well they manage operations? Explain your answer.
3. Have you noticed differences in the quality delivered among different service businesses you have dealt with? How much of that difference would you say is due to how the operation is managed? What advice would you give to a manager of a service firm you have dealt with to improve the quality of its service?

DESIGNING OPERATIONS

To understand operations management, it is useful to start from scratch and look at how managers go about designing the operations of a system that will take inputs and transform them into outputs customers will value. Doing this requires that managers go through a series of decisions that help them figure out how a system can work best for their organization's purpose. In looking at the design activities we assume that key strategic decisions have already been made, such as the general type of product or service to be provided, a rough measure of the total market, and organizational goals for market share. We will build from there, since those decisions become the foundation upon which operation design decisions are made.

System Design Issues

The success of the system depends upon the interaction of two elements: (1) the *process* (how machines, workers, input materials, technology, information, etc. come together) and the *product,* the formal output of the process. No matter how efficient the process, if the product has no value to customers then it is a failure. Conversely, if the product is valued by consumers but the processes to create it are inefficient, then the product may be too costly and fail. Consumers will not purchase it in sufficient numbers to make its manufacture worthwhile. From this point on, the term "product" will mean output of goods or services.

There is a close relationship between the company's strategy, the product's design, and the process designed to create the product. If the company's strategy is to deliver a low-price detergent to compete with budget brands, developers must work to keep the cost of the product's formulation and the processes for its manufacture low. For this reason, it is important to keep this linkage in mind to make sure the operations involved in manufacturing do not undermine the company's strategy.

Process Design Issues

Assume that an organization has determined its product and that it has reliable estimates for demand, including who wants it, and where and when demand is likely to occur. Managers can then go about designing and implementing the operations involved in its manufacture. In an ongoing business, we might call this activity *process redesign* since, for most organizations, the product line and the market are constantly changing. Thus the process is also always in some state of re-design. Our approach to studying these issues is to start with those design factors that tend to have the longest cycle between changes. Those generally have to do with the establishment of the facility itself and its purpose.

Facility Decisions

Facility The physical infrastructure put in place by the organization to support its operations.

A **facility** is *the physical infrastructure put in place by the organization to support its operations.* All operations require a place where the activities occur. A doctor's office, a factory, an airport, and a retail outlet are all facilities. In deciding on a facility, managers need to deal with a variety of issues, such as location and layout of the facility as well as its capacity or planned maximum output. The last issue involves the market size, the complexity of the product (complex items need larger outputs to achieve economies of scale), and the capital available. Let's look in more detail at location and layout issues.

Facility Location.   There are several factors to take into consideration in deciding where to locate a facility. The nature of the operation makes the importance of each of the factors vary in different situations. Let's review some of these factors:

- **Cost.**   This includes the cost of land, the cost of labor to build the facility and staff it, and operating costs such as utilities, taxes, and insurance.

- **Access to raw materials and suppliers.**   Generally industrial facilities need to be close to raw materials, suppliers, and transportation. It is not an accident that General Mills and Pillsbury are both located in Minneapolis, giving them ready access to grains from Midwestern farmers for processing into flour and many other products. Nor is it unusual that one of Procter & Gamble's major paper products plants is located near Green Bay, Wisconsin, a state with many paper mills.

- **Proximity to customers.**   It only makes sense to choose a location that gives your customers easy access to your offerings. Retail malls are usually located near major suburbs. Automobile parts manufacturers are usually clustered around assembly plants, wherever they are located. Fast food restaurants are on major thoroughfares.

- **Transportation.**   This includes access to rail and truck transportation for transporting outputs to markets. It also includes whether employees can easily find their way to the facility via car, bus, or other public transport.

Concentrating retail stores and restaurants into one location enables a large number of businesses to share construction and operating costs.

- **Community interest.**   Often different communities will vie for new facilities, and the various incentives they offer can be a consideration in making a location decision. The location of various foreign automobile plants in Southern states comes as a result of such incentives.
- **Access to labor.**   The availability of skilled labor can be an important consideration.
- **Quality of life issues.**   These include quality of local schools, the availability of recreational and cultural facilities, and an overall community environment that will contribute to the organization's ability to attract and retain high-caliber employees, especially managers.

Choosing a site to locate a facility always involves a combination of these factors, and there are always compromises to make. The goal is to find a balance that will help an organization best meet its goals for efficiently and effectively serving its customers and other stakeholders.

Facility Layout

Layout The spatial arrangement of operations units relative to each other.

Layout means *the spatial arrangement of operations units relative to each other.* Different types of facilities require different types of layouts to operate most efficiently. The "best" layout is highly dependent on the type of operation—manufacturing, distribution, tangible, or intangible service. In terms of layout, services and manufacturing have some things in common, but there are also some significant differences. A key factor in layout is the volume-variability mix. As a way to understand layout in helping a company achieve its objectives, think about three different types of restaurants:

1. A *fast-food restaurant* (such as Burger King, McDonald's, Wendy's, Taco Bell) would be classified as high-volume, low variety, make-to-stock or assemble-to-order. Kitchen, buffer (extra stock ready to go when needed) storage, serving and payment facilities are arranged to support the objectives of these facilities. Travel distances for the counter personnel are minimized, allowing each employee to serve more customers per hour.
2. *Cafeterias* are high volume, moderate variety, assemble-to-order, batch production operations. Counter personnel are more specialized; they assemble your main dishes on your plate, you serve yourself salad, bread, dessert, and beverage. Buffer stock storage units are close to serving locations. For example, the salad keeper is directly behind the salad serving shelves. The kitchen facilities use relatively large ovens, baking dishes, etc., and multiple servings of a particular item are prepared at one time, for example 100 rolls baked in a batch.
3. An *elegant restaurant* is a low-volume, high-variety, make-to-order operation. The layout is designed to support a different strategy—to create an experience, not just a meal. Food preparation and assembly are away from the point of service to change the ambience of the dining area. Kitchen operations are arranged to support the high-variety, low-volume nature of demand, but with consideration of the need to move about and have adequate work space for numerous orders-in-process. There is probably little need for buffer storage space or finished elements, but, perhaps relatively more space for raw materials because of the variety required.

These same types of considerations work in the layout of any facility. There are four general classifications for facility layout. The one selected depends on the company's goals, its size, and the nature of the product. These four are product, process, fixed position, and cell.

Product Layout.   This is usually used in situations with *high volume and low variability* in the output. The spatial relationship between successive production units is designed around the sequence of operations required to create large numbers of very similar output units. Each output unit follows the same path through the production units, and receives essentially the same activity at each station. This is the traditional assembly line where products flow from one area to the next and are assembled in a sequential fashion. The product layout is equally applicable to services where a client flows from one area to another, such as in air travel—check in area, boarding area, airplane, departing area, luggage pickup, and ground transportation.

Product layout Assembly line layout designed around a sequence of operations to deliver products in high quantity with low variability.

Process Layout.   This is also known as a *functional layout.* This is typical of job shops or other businesses *where products move from function to function depending on requirements.* Each functional area may include several stations or individuals who perform the same task or process. Process layouts work best with *high variability* and *low volume* in particular outputs. Most offices are set up functionally, with administration, marketing, finance, accounting, legal, and human resources all having their assigned areas. In the case of offices, outputs of the various functional areas are the reports and support services needed to coordinate the processes by which the company delivers final products to customers.

Process layout Functional layout where products move from function (or process) to function.

A job shop that takes on specialized projects for clients that require different types of work, not always the same, would likely have a process layout. Another example would be a clinic or hospital where the patient will be directed to the functional areas required to deliver different services, such as internal medicine, laboratory, physical therapy, and pharmacy.

Fixed Position Layout.   In this layout *the product is fixed and workers come to it.* This is most common in building ships and airplanes, and in construction. Here the idea is to create a layout that makes different areas of the item being built as accessible as possible, which means the steps in construction must be carefully planned.

Fixed position layout A layout in which the position of the product is fixed and workers come to it.

Cellular Layout.   This arrangement facilitates the use of cross-functional teams, where *all the activities involved in the creation of a product or service are located near one another.* This arrangement makes it easy for employees with different skills to work together to deliver the final product. There are usually several cells with each devoted to certain products. Cellular layouts are often implemented when the company has a variety of products, each of which is best created by a multifunctional group working together. This approach also facilitates the use of self-managed teams. The Edy's Ice Cream plant discussed in Chapter 14 is an example of a cellular layout.

Cellular layout A layout in which all the activities involved in the creation of a specific product or service are located near one another.

The Best Layout.   In manufacturing, the assumption is that the best layout is the one that reduces the cost and time of moving products between the various stations. It is also usually assumed that the cost of movement is directly proportional to volume and distance. The obvious solution is to put those activities that have a large volume of interaction close together. Materials receiving or shipping operations are

TQM IN ACTION

IMPROVING LAYOUT IMPROVES PRODUCTIVITY AT CRITIKON[4]

Critikon is a Johnson & Johnson company that manufactures intravenous catheters for use in hospitals. The company has adopted a TQM approach to managing, with an emphasis on *kaizen* or continuous improvement. The plant is organized around cells that manufacture these products. The most critical operation for product performance is forming the tip of the intravenous catheter. A malleable plastic material must be held to a .0005 tolerance or else the "ouch" factor (customer dissatisfaction) in catheter use goes up.

One of the areas in the plant is responsible for the Trim and Form (TAF) process. This process includes a conveyor that moves products from position to position. As an exercise in kaizen, the company sought to reduce the time involved in delivering finished products from this process while maintaining tip tolerances. The work team responsible for this process did a time and motion analysis. They determined that it took an average of 4.5 seconds to pick a component assembly created by one machine out of a container, pick another one created by a separate machine out of another container, connect them and place them back on the conveyor belt. They then discovered that if they rearranged the machines, moving a machine called the Instron tensile tester and the catheter assembly machine closer to the conveyor, walk time would be reduced.

Working with the facilities people in the plant, they experimented with different positions for a few hours until they found one that optimized motions and time. With this new configuration, they found that the entire cell could operate with seven operators instead of nine, and they improved productivity by 22 percent! Exhibit 17-6 illustrates the before and after layouts of this cell.

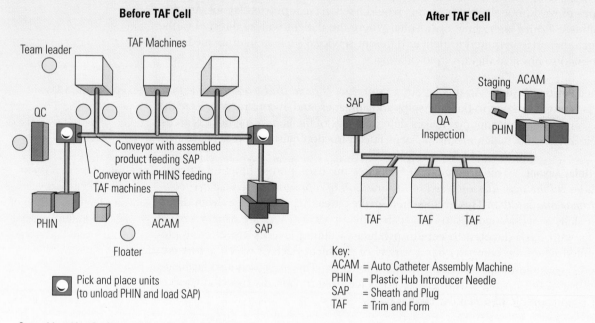

Source: Adapted from Ray Cheser and Cheryl Tanner, "Critikon Declares War on Waste, Launches Kaizen Drive," *Target*, July/August 1993, p. 19.

EXHIBIT 17-6 A kaizen improvement model

This example may seem mundane, but it represents the kind of issues that go on every day in manufacturing organizations and shows the importance of layout to productivity. It also shows the importance of reconsidering layout as a way to make gains in productivity. In many plants, the current layouts may have been set up years ago, and no one ever thinks to question them. TQM reminds managers that continuous improvement requires that everyone regularly look for ways to enhance efficiency and productivity as an important aspect of maintaining competitive edge.

on the outside edge of the building because of their interaction with the transport activity. Unfortunately, the best location for many of the other activities is not so easy to determine. Cost is not the only consideration. Safety, process interference, and environmental concerns might override movement cost factors. For example, the painting process would probably not be located near a welding unit, even though most of the welded pieces are painted just after welding. Because of the complexity of layout design in large manufacturing facilities, computer programs have been developed to help optimize layouts for more complex processes.

People as Workers

The last facet of the operation design section focuses on the work done by the people in the system—those whose cumulative efforts convert the inputs into the outputs. Job design, defined in Chapter 12, determines the activities required of a position. The objective of the job design activity is to create a feasible set of tasks that an organization might reasonably expect from an employee. There are three aspects to the feasibility:

1. **Technical/physical.** These include the physical or mental skills required to perform the assigned tasks. These vary substantially across different organizational requirements. Some are more mental (for example, a computer programmer); others are more physical (for example, a logger).
2. **Economic.** The value of the output of the workers' efforts should be greater (or at least equal to) the cost to the organization. This is usually rather a straightforward analysis for physical work, for example, how many trees were harvested by the loggers this week. However, this is more difficult to calculate for jobs that carry greater levels of responsibility, such as managers, physicians, or any kind of "knowledge workers." The output of their work is not always immediately apparent.
3. **Behavioral.** This has to do with the potential impact that the tasks required have on the social and psychological perceptions of the job holder. It includes whether employees will be intrinsically motivated to do the work and whether compensation for performance of the tasks will be sufficient to attract competent people.

Correctly designed jobs consider the needs of the job holder and the organization. Many jobs are in a regular state of redesign. New technology in the workplace requires employees continuously revise their work and take on new or different tasks and skills.

Whether in services or manufacturing, the employee-machine interface becomes a critical element in job redesign. As an example, think about the differences in the job of a typist when the technology was a manual typewriter versus electric typewriter versus the word processing software on today's desktop computer. The goal is to develop machines that can successfully do work that machines can do well—repetitive mechanical tasks and to design work that human beings do well—problem solving, decision making and improvement.

❓ THINKING CRITICALLY

1. If a retail operation were to locate itself in an out of the way part of town, what would that say about its strategy? What do you think the layout of such a store might be like?
2. Would you say it always makes sense to try to replace people with machines? Why or why not?

MANAGING OPERATIONS

We now turn our attention from operations systems design to managing the operations once they are in place.

Planning and Control

The manager's challenge is to ensure that the right resources are brought together and processed so that the right output is available at the right place and time to meet the needs of customers. Doing this involves a variety of decisions that form a cycle—some recurring quite frequently (even minute to minute, perhaps), others much less often (perhaps only annually). The sequence for planning and control that we suggest is framed in a manufacturing context, but the relationship to activities for non-manufacturing is generally easy to see. We will define the decisions, then discuss the appropriate models.

Sequence of Decisions in Planning and Controlling Operations

Forecasts Estimates of near term requirements for units of output.

The first decision or concern of an operations manager concerns **forecasts** or *estimates of near term requirements for units of output*. This might be stated in actual units, or in some other aggregated measure of output, depending on the industry. For example, for textbooks, it would be the actual number of units. For airlines, it would be available seat miles. For a steel plant, it would be tons of steel.

Capacity utilization plan The high level plan that determines the degree of utilization of design capacity, and the source of resources to attain that utilization.

The next decision for an operations manager deals with the development of a **capacity utilization plan,** also called the aggregate schedule. This is *the high level plan that determines the degree of utilization of design capacity, and the source of resources to attain that utilization.* Since the output of a manufacturing system often requires longer planning horizons and may involve building up an inventory of inputs and spare parts, the complexity of the decision is often greater than for a service system. For example, a bank office is designed and built with a fixed number of teller windows. This is the design capacity. The decision as to how many of the windows will be open during different hours and the source of the tellers (such as overtime or part-time workers) is the capacity utilization plan.

Next comes a **master production schedule,** which is *the breakdown of the capacity utilization plan into a time-phased set of steps for producing a specific output of units consistent with the forecast.* In a service system, this schedule and the capacity utilization plan may be synonymous.

The next concern of a manager is the **resource requirements plan,** which is *the planned allocation of operating resources (specific materials and plant capacity) to the creation of the output specified by the master production schedule.* Again, the application of these specific decisions to a manufacturing system is easy to see. If you want to build 200 bicycles this week, you must have made or purchased 200 frames, 400 wheels, tires, tubes, and other parts. Making 200 frames requires specific capacity on certain equipment within a relatively narrow time frame.

In general, managers initially have to figure out the quantity of input materials required to deliver a certain output since that will dictate the allocation of production capacity to process those materials into final products. The materials requirement leads to a concern for inventory control decisions. In other words, managers need to be sure they have enough inventory of input materials to meet their plan but not more than they need as that ties up cash that could be used for other things. The application of these ideas in the service industry for materials is quite similar. The master production schedule for a specific airline flight generates the materials requirements for fuel, in-flight food and beverages, utensils, and other supplies and it specifies the capacity needed in terms of available flight crew, baggage handling, and counter capacities, and an available aircraft of proper configuration. Flights to Hawaii are usually on Boeing 747s with large capacity to handle the number of vacationers going there in peak periods. Boeing 737s are more appropriate for shorter flights to mid-sized cities around the country.

Finally managers must be concerned with the development of **detail or work schedules,** which comprise *the assignment of specific tasks to specific capacity units at specific times.* This may mean furloughing employees, such as in times of weak automobile demand when plants are shut down for a week or two. Or it may mean adding overtime to meet the output specified by the master production schedule.

Models for Operations Planning

People in the profession of operations management have developed a variety of models or tools for dealing with the types of planning problems we have just been reviewing. We are next going to look at some of these models. As we go through them, you should recognize that the decisions made in earlier stages of the planning sequence become inputs that facilitate or put constraints on succeeding decisions and actions. You should also recognize that planning is a process subject to continuous revision. For example, a proposed master production schedule, when put into the resource requirements plan may prove infeasible because it overloads a specific capacity resource, such as one kind of machine. If the company cannot obtain additional capacity, either elsewhere in the company or by contracting with outsiders, managers should consider a different master production schedule.

Master production schedule The breakdown of the capacity utilization plan into a time-phased set of steps for producing a specific output of units consistent with the forecast.

Resource requirements plan The planned allocation of operating resources (specific materials and plant capacity) to the creation of the output specified by the master production schedule.

Detail or work schedules The assignment of specific tasks to specific capacity units at specific times.

Models for Forecasting Demand. There are two basic types of forecasting models, (1) historic and (2) causal. They both work well and often some combination of the two provides the best forecast of demand.

Causal models *try to identify the underlying causes of demand for a company's products or services.* They work by determining the relationship between certain causal factors and the demand for the company's output. Once data is collected, causal models work by applying certain statistical calculations, such as multiple regression. The advantage of causal models is that it helps companies quickly identify changes in the causes of demand so they can respond without delay to these changes. For example, a government report on the health benefits of a particular food can increase the demand for that food. Using causal models can help a company determine how much increase in its demand such a report might generate.

There are two disadvantages to causal models: (1) the cost to develop and maintain the model may be relatively high and (2) information on the values for the causal factors may be difficult to figure out in time to take action.

Historic models *analyze data from the past for patterns and project those patterns into the future.* This model uses simpler statistical techniques, such as moving averages or exponential smoothing. The advantages of this approach are that data is readily available, and the models are easy to maintain. The disadvantage is that substantial changes in underlying causes for demand change may not be recognized quickly by the model.

Even with the disadvantages, historic type models are widely used for operational forecasting. The underlying causal factors for most products and services do not change rapidly. Historic patterns are likely to continue. Thus, if managers do not need to forecast too far into the future, and they place some appropriate "flags" on the control system (for example, flags that call attention to errors of significant magnitude, or consistently in the same direction), historic models are quite useful.

Capacity Utilization and Master Production Schedule Models. We develop models for these two steps together because of the high degree of coordination between the results. The master production schedule for outputs over time depends on the capacity available for production. We assume that the capacity a plant is designed for is greater than the aggregate demand for at least some period of the planning horizon. In other words, an assumption behind these models is that a plant has excess capacity to meet increasing demand.

Interaction between a master production schedule and a capacity utilization plan is largely a function of the variability of specific master production schedule items from those of the "average" output unit used for the aggregate capacity plan. If all specific outputs are similar in material and capacity requirements, there is little likelihood of a conflict between the master production schedule and the aggregate schedule. If the output units have variable requirements, it is possible that a master production schedule could create requirements above those allowed for in the aggregate capacity plan. Managers must resolve these conflicts if they are to maintain efficient operation.

There are two basic approaches to this problem.

1. **Constant output rate.** In this approach, managers estimate the total requirement for the planning horizon, compute the average for an operational horizon, and set capacity to create output at that rate. For example, if

estimated requirements for the year were 12,000 units, managers could set our capacity utilization to create 1000 units per month. The items created in the months when demand is lower than 1000 units are stored to meet the demand in months when demand exceeds the unit output.
2. **Variable output rate.**   In this approach managers constantly change the rate of output to match the demand. They change this output by using more or less of the design capacity in each period. This plan approach avoids the costs of holding the goods from their creation in the low-demand periods until their use in the high-demand periods. Unfortunately, there are additional costs associated with changing the rate of output, such as adding or subtracting workers, using overtime, and coordinating inventory from suppliers.

There are many variations between the extreme plans described above. Which is best? Several mathematical models have been applied with varying degrees of success to figure this out. At least two important factors limit the applicability of these models.

1. Good estimates of the cost functions are difficult to determine and may not behave to fit the model requirements.
2. Estimates of demand for a long planning horizon may not be reliable.

As with most models, if you have good data, they work well. When such data is not readily available, more managerial judgment is required, and mistakes will be made.

Materials Management

Managing and controlling inventory used or created in operations is an important responsibility of an operations manager. **Inventory** is defined as *a stock of material held for future use*. It is also an idle resource. In many organizations the cost of materials, not just their purchase, but their movement, storage, and control, is the single major cost item. The 1982 Census of Manufacturers[5] reported that in large manufacturing firms, almost 60 percent of cost was due to materials, with only 17 percent in labor, and the remaining 23 percent in other overhead, such as administration, marketing, rent, and utilities. Clearly the decisions that determine the flow of materials through the operation are among the most important. The objective of materials management is to have the correct amount of material available at the time it is needed, where it is needed, while minimizing the total cost.

Changing Understanding of Materials and Inventory Management.   The focus of inventory management during the early part of the industrial revolution was on the utilization of labor. That was generally the most expensive of the inputs. The philosophy of materials management was to always have plenty on hand. The cost to keep this stock of material or inventory on hand was relatively low, or so it was believed. Space was usually not an issue. Models focused on minimizing apparent costs within this basic philosophy. This attitude prevailed well past World War II in the U.S. The changing mix of cost factors and a better understanding of the true cost of large stocks of idle materials has altered the focus of materials management. The goal now is to increase the *rate of flow* of material through the system rather than on having large stocks of items needed in a manufacturing process. Because

Inventory A stock of material held for future use.

Having just enough raw materials in inventory just in time to manufacture copper wire maximizes the flow and reduces all the costs in the system.

large stocks of inventory are costly because they tie up funds that could be used for other purposes, organizations want to minimize these costs by focusing on making sure supplies are available when needed but not before. The objectives have not changed—the correct material when and where it is needed—but the focus is now on just enough, and just in time. This maximizes the flow and reduces all the costs in the system.

Types of Inventory.   Accounting systems developed for manufacturing systems generally categorize inventory by its degree of completion or its readiness for sale. The three standard categories of inventory are:

Finished goods Inventory in which all processing is done; these goods are available for shipment.

Work-in-process Material that has had some, but not all of its transformation completed.

Raw material Material that has been received but has not been transformed in any way.

- **Finished goods:**   *All processing is done, and these goods are available for shipment.*
- **Work-in-process:**   *Material that has had some but not all of its transformation completed.*
- **Raw material:** *Material that has been received but has not been transformed in any way.*

This classification is useful as we look at inventory within a manufacturing organization, but it has little meaning for distribution and other types of service organizations. Almost all of the material there would be considered finished goods for sale.

The Importance of Managing Inventory.   In 1990, the U.S. Department of Commerce[6] reported that the value of inventory held in the manufacturing sector averaged 13.4 percent of sales. The same report indicated that manufacturing profits averaged 5.4 percent of sales. Look at these data another way. About two and a half years of profits are invested in inventory. If a company can lower inventory costs, it goes straight to the bottom line. Why do organizations invest so much in idle resources? Maintaining inventories helps managers and customers in a number of ways, such as:

1. Facilitating immediate delivery of goods to customers.
2. Smoothing out production schedules.
3. Providing protection from disruption of material flow.
4. Providing protection from mis-forecasting demand.
5. Reduce purchase price by buying in larger quantities.
6. Reduce manufacturing costs by producing larger quantities at a time.

In the complex manufacturing-distribution system of a modern economy, we should also recognize the existence and need for **pipeline inventory,** *material in transit from one processing point to another.* This relates to the important idea of **just-in-time (JIT) inventory control.** This approach to inventory means that *companies work closely with their suppliers to make sure that parts and raw materials needed to keep the plant functioning arrive within 24 to 48 hours of the time they are needed.*

Just-in-time inventory requires open communication and a long-term relationship between companies and suppliers. It substantially reduces inventory costs but also helps guarantee supplies will be there when needed. Just-in-time inventory is an important aspect of Japanese operations management and is being implemented in many American companies, especially those that have adopted TQM. *Lean manufacturing* is another term used to describe a system that seeks to operate with no idle inventory. As most operations are working to reduce the amount of inventory they hold, it is important to understand the models developed to manage those assets and the applications and limitations of these models.

Managing Different Types of Inventory.   The appropriate tools for managing inventory differ for raw material, work-in-process, and finished goods. The differences are due to the ways the models address certainty or uncertainty in the timing and quantity of requirements. Let's review the causes of uncertainty and how these influence inventory management and control.

- **Independent demand.** *The timing and quantity of organizational outputs are controlled by the consumer of the output and not by the organization producing the inventory.* There is considerable uncertainty about those requirements, and the managers must take these uncertainties into account when making decisions. Here, we are talking about the uncertainty of demand by final customers.
- **Dependent demand.**   *The timing and quantity of requirements for various goods is dependent on decisions of the organization holding the materials.* Once a company makes decisions about what it is going to manufacture, there is much less uncertainty about the inventory it will need. For example, once Apple computer managers decide on a master production schedule that they will manufacture 15,000 units of one model of a Macintosh computer per month, the demand for all component parts building those computers is set. This means that the demand for components is dependent on the demand for

Pipeline inventory Material in transit from one processing point to another.

Just-in-time (JIT) inventory control An approach in which companies work closely with their suppliers to make sure that parts and raw materials needed to keep the plant functioning arrive shortly before the time they are needed.

Independent demand Demand in which the timing and quantity of organizational outputs are controlled by the consumer of the output and not by the organization producing the inventory.

Dependent demand Demand in which the timing and quantity of an output is dependent on decisions of the organization holding the materials.

Macintosh computers as determined by Apple managers. Similar examples can be drawn from the service industry. The requirements for specific instruments and supplies in a hospital operating room depend on the type of operations scheduled. Once scheduled, the demand is set.

Inventory Management Models

Once managers have determined that it is desirable or necessary to have a stock of material available, they must answer two questions: (1) When should an order to obtain more of an item be placed? and (2) How much should be ordered? Other decisions about inventory, in general, have to do with its control after it is received.

Independent Demand—Timing.   Developing an answer for the first question above can be complicated for independent demand items. There is uncertainty about the rate of use of the existing stock by customers as well as how long it might take from the placing of the order until its receipt. The impact of each type of uncertainty differs from situation to situation.

For example, a retail grocery store that has scheduled weekly delivery of soft drinks from a local bottling operation has very little uncertainty about how long it will be before the next shipment arrives, but there is somewhat more uncertainty about how many soft drinks customers will demand before the next delivery. Managers need to understand how to make a decision on the quantity to maintain in inventory to cover this uncertainty.

There are two basic models and one hybrid model for making these decisions.

1.   **Time-based model.**   This is the simplest approach and is widely used in distribution systems that have a very large number of items. The stock of each item is reviewed on a regular cycle (for example, weekly), and managers place an order for the difference between the quantity on hand and a specified target number. In this approach, managers need to make decisions about the frequency of the review and the specified target number. The primary advantage of this system is the low cost of inventory control. Disadvantages include the larger amount of inventory required to protect against sudden high levels of demand and the large number of small quantity orders that might be generated. Managers can address the small order difficulty in at least two ways. First, all items received from a particular supplier might be on the same cycle. Second, adjust the model from a purely time-based reorder to one that better matches the time period to exhaust current stock.

2.   **Time- and quantity-based (min-max) model.**   Like the previous approach, managers review inventory on a periodic cycle. Each review does not necessarily result in an order, however. This approach calls for figuring out two target numbers: a minimum, which serves as the trigger for an order. If the quantity on hand is less than the minimum, the manager places an order for the difference. If the number on hand is above the minimum, no order is placed. This model reduces the number and cost of ordering and of inventory monitoring, but requires greater stock to protect against stock outs that might occur before the next review and order receipt.

3.   **Quantity-based, or perpetual control models.** This is a hybrid between the two approaches just listed. The manager establishes *a target minimum number that triggers a replenishment order,* often called the **reorder point (ROP).**

Reorder point (ROP)

A target minimum number that triggers a replenishment order.

Every item transaction is recorded, and as soon as the ROP is reached, an order for additional stock is placed. The advantage of this model is that companies can maintain the minimum amount of stock for uncertainty since there is no time lag between reaching the ROP and placing the order. There are additional costs in this approach, though, for the perpetual monitoring of inventory.

As the speed, power, and utility of computer systems have increased, and costs have declined, the cost advantages of inventory monitoring attributed to the time-based models have disappeared. Even retail outlets with thousands of items have the capability to maintain perpetual inventory records at modest cost. Usage is recorded automatically by computers connected to the checkout scanners. The availability of such information does not always mean that a pure quantity-based system will provide lower costs, so fixed-interval ordering systems are still quite common.

Regardless of the systems used, the basic considerations of when to trigger a new order are an effort to minimize costs. There are three basic cost factors to be considered:

1. The cost to hold the material until it is required (sold or used in further processing). These costs include space, protection and insurance, damage or obsolescence, the managerial control system, and the investment or opportunity costs. Opportunity costs, often the most important, are often difficult to determine, as are the intangible impacts on flexibility and process improvement.
2. The cost to obtain the material in addition to the cost of material itself. These are usually referred to as *ordering costs,* and include all the administrative costs of creating, tracking, and paying for an order. Other costs we might also include are those associated with finding a source of the materials, agreeing on specifications, and negotiating terms. These are usually called set-up costs and can be quite significant in batch-repetitive or job-shop environments.
3. The costs incurred when a required item is not on hand. These are generally referred to as stockout costs and include:
    a. lost profit from missed sale
    b. loss of goodwill, affecting future sales potential
    c. cost of rescheduling associated activities
    d. cost of expediting (speeding up) operations to maintain other schedules or requirements

Costs *a* and *b* predominate in wholesale and retail distribution systems. Costs *c* and *d* are more likely in a manufacturing environment.

Unfortunately, the decisions that reduce one or two of these costs tend to raise the others. The objective is to find the balance that minimizes the total of all the costs. It is important to remember that we are still dealing with uncertainty in several aspects of the system, and that uncertainty increases cost. For example, assume there is a constant requirement for item X of 100 units per week. It always takes exactly three weeks for an order to arrive. If we placed an order when the quantity on hand was 300 (100 units per week × 3 weeks), it would arrive just as the last unit on hand was being used up. There would be no stock-out costs to worry about, and we could focus on minimizing the other two costs by changing the size of each order (fewer orders, but larger quantities or vice versa).

We know, though, that rate of use and the timing of deliveries are not constant. How, then, do we adjust the decision to minimize the impact of this uncertainty? The stock of goods we maintain to reduce the severity of stock out costs is called safety stock. The decision of how much safety stock a company should maintain tries to balance the additional holding cost associated with this stock against the reduced costs of stock-outs. Larger safety stocks reduce the likelihood of a shortage, but increase holding cost, since they are not required on every cycle. Exhibit 17-7 depicts the situation. Increasing the safety stock would reduce the probability of a stockout, but the average amount of stock on-hand and associated holding costs over all the cycles would be increased.

Independent Demand—Quantity. When a company is dealing with an independent demand situation, that is, it does not have control over demand for its outputs, managers need to figure out how much safety stock to keep on hand. They can maintain a low stock and have frequent reorders, or they can maintain a higher stock with few reorders. Frequent reorders have higher ordering costs and lower holding costs associated with them. Fewer reorders have lower ordering costs but higher holding costs.

One widely recognized model to determine the best quantity of safety stock is called the **economic order quantity (EOQ) model.** The equation we present here is for information and does not include the derivation. Most specialized texts on operations management or logistics will present a detailed explanation of it and its several variations.

Economic order quantity (EOQ) model A widely recognized model to determine the best quantity to order when each reorder is placed.

$$Q = \sqrt{\frac{2DS}{H}}$$

where D = total requirement over the planning horizon
S = cost to prepare one order (or setup)
H = cost to hold one unit for the planning horizon
Q = the order quantity that minimizes these costs

EXHIBIT 17-7
Typical Inventory Status

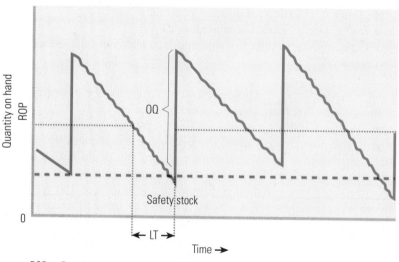

ROP = Reorder point
OQ = Order quantity
LT = Lead time

If we were to fill in this formula for a professional book on business, it might look like this:

$$D = 20,000 \text{ units over life of book (3 years)}$$
$$S = \$2000 \text{ (cost to set up for printing book)}$$
$$H = \$3.00 \text{ (cost to hold one unit for planning horizon—3 years)}$$

$$Q = \sqrt{\frac{2\,(20,000)(2000)}{3.00}}$$

The approximate quantity to be ordered would be 5,165 units, which would likely be rounded to 5,000 units.

To the extent that the values of D, S, and H are correct, the model provides an appropriate answer for what an economically sound quantity should be. One problem with this approach is that it is dependent on a manager's ability to predict demand. As with any such model, therefore, care must be exercised in its use. With its mathematical foundation, this approach to inventory decisions can lull managers into not paying attention to what composes the costs that are used to do the calculation. They apply the formula and make decisions based on the answers they get.

What they should be concerned with continuously, however, is how to lower the costs that are plugged into the formula. We should also recognize the difficulty of correctly estimating these costs, particularly the costs represented by H (holding costs). The true costs of larger order quantities are usually much higher than many managers realize. This is because holding large quantities of inventory in any form that the company must use up reduces its flexibility to improve quality to meet changing customer requirements.

Materials Requirements Planning

A technique developed to manage dependent-demand inventories (inventories that come from components or raw materials to support scheduled production of finished goods), primarily work-in-process and raw materials, is called **materials requirements planning,** better known by its initials MRP. It was developed in the late 1960s and early 1970s with considerable support from IBM. The data storage and manipulation, as well as the report generating capabilities require a computer for operations of any significant size. This may explain IBM's early interest in the applications.

Exhibit 17-8 depicts the basic MRP calculation report format for three components needed in the manufacture of a particular product. The idea here is fairly simple. The successful execution of MRP requires that you know how many of a particular component you need, when you need it, and how long it will take to deliver it either from those who produce these parts in the company or from a supplier. You then set up some tables that you use to track your inventory of each item, how much you will need in various time periods, and when orders need to be placed. The example in Exhibit 17-8 is relatively straightforward. It shows that to complete 100 units of a product, the company needs 200 A components, 300 C components, and 300 R components. However, this process can get very complicated when a company is trying to track many different components and parts that go into a final product with many different lead times. That is why successful MRP requires the complex computer program mentioned above to process data, generate orders, and keep track of current inventory.

Materials requirements planning A technique developed to manage dependent-demand inventories.

EXHIBIT 17-8
MRP Computation Model

Master schedule "X"	0	0	0	50	100	0	50

Component "A"   Lead Time – 1 Week

Time period	0	1	2	3	4	5	6
Gross requirement				100	200		100
Projected on-hand	50	50	50	–50	–250		–350
Net requirement				50	200		100
Planned order release				50	200		100	

Component "C"   Lead Time – 2 Weeks

Time period	0	1	2	3	4	5	6
Gross requirement				150	300		150
Projected on-hand	0	0	0	–150	–450	–450	600
Net requirement				150	300		150
Planned order release		150	300		150		

Material "R"   Lead Time – 2 Weeks

Time period	0	1	2	3	4	5	6
Gross requirement		300	600		300		
Projected on-hand	900	600	0	0	–300	–300	–300
Net requirement					300		
Planned order release			300				

Here is a breakdown of each the categories for tracking inventory of various components (refer to Exhibit 17-8 as we go through this):

- **Gross requirements.**   This is the required amount of a component you will need for any time period. For component A, the company will need 100 of these in time period 3, 200 in time period 4, and so on. The company knows this because it has already set up a master production schedule for what it expects to produce.

- **Projected on-hand.**   This is a running balance in which the company notes the current balance of a component it has in inventory and from which it deducts when the on-hand component is used. For component A, the company has 50 units in stock and uses these up in time period 3. Since it needs 100, there is a –50 in this row for that period. This suggests that the company needs to place an order a week earlier (because it needs a one week lead time) for 50 more of this component.

- **Net requirements.**   These show the timing and quantity of requirements that have not been ordered. Since the projected-on-hand is a cumulative value, it becomes a larger and larger negative value as additional gross requirements appear. The net requirements show the amount that needs to be ordered to meet the needs of that time period. For component A, this shows that the company needs to order 50 of these in time period 2 for use in time period 3.

- **Planned order release.** This row shows when an order must be made if the component needed is to be available at the time the requirement occurs. In the case of component A, it is one week, and the order thus goes out one week before the component is needed. The difference in the time of the requirement and the time for the order to be placed is called *lead-time offset*.

Activity Planning and Control Decisions

MRP suggests that a company knows how much of each component it needs to assemble a final product. For those components the company manufactures itself, for example fenders for a car that it stamps from sheet metal, it needs to determine specific capacity requirements for creating these components when needed. As an analogy, think of an elaborate dinner party with several courses. To bring it off well, you have to figure out when to prepare the various dishes ahead of time so they all come together for the dinner. And you have to make sure your kitchen has the capacity to prepare the food planned. You would not plan a dish for which you did not have the capacity, that is, the ingredients or equipment, needed to prepare it. Manufacturers have to think about their tasks in the same way and have to schedule their capacity to produce component parts so they are ready when needed on the assembly line. Doing that is called activity planning and control.

Capacity Requirements Planning.   Following the example developed above, component C (Exhibit 17-7) has a two-week lead time. During the two weeks before delivery, the item ordered, say a fender, will move through several machines in a specified sequence. Since managers know how long each process takes (remember the work on time standards), and the quantity of the order, they have a good estimate of the *load* they are placing on each machine's capacity. Accumulating this information from all the planned orders allows them to generate a *load profile* for each resource. If there are significant imbalances in the required versus available capacities, they will have to do some replanning, perhaps all the way back to the master production schedule. Or, they might find additional capacity by using overtime, or perhaps an alternate routing for some of the orders.

At the end of the planning sequence, managers make a specific assignment of resources needed, such as material, equipment, and labor, to a specific task or job. They also specify when the task is to be started and completed. Then, at the completion of each task, the resources become available for the next specific assignment. (When you finish baking one dish for your dinner party, the oven becomes available for another.) *The constant updating, evaluating, and reordering of the remaining jobs* is called **priority control.**

Priority Control.   The nature of the operations processes determines the difficulty of priority control decisions. Continuous and repetitive type operations with low variety, make priority determination a relatively easy task. In batch-repetitive or job-shop operations, priority control becomes complex, on-going, and critical

Priority control The constant updating, evaluating, and reordering that determines the order in which jobs will be undertaken.

to efficient operations. The difficulty of figuring out the priority for various jobs and making sequencing decisions for the work comes from the conflicting objectives of the manager. These include:

1. Meeting planned completion date of job.
2. Utilizing resources efficiently, minimizing excessive idle time for resources.
3. Minimizing the amount of material in the system and the accumulation of excess work-in-process inventory.

These objectives conflict because completing one job on time may mean taking employees from another job where they are needed as well, or it may mean having many projects going at the same time in various stages of completion. You can never get rid of this problem, but you can figure out how to balance these objectives to minimize waste and maximize on-time delivery.

Because of the number of decisions of this type, and their complexity, the operations management field has developed different models, or priority rules, to help managers. There usually is not time to analyze all possible alternatives at every decision point, but following these rules helps assure a good outcome. Remember, an output unit may require processing through many operations, and numerous orders for output are moving through the system at the same time, all contributing to complexity that these rules help managers to handle. These rules include:

1. **First Come–First Served.** Here jobs are sequenced in the order they were received. This is very common in service organizations.
2. **Earliest Due Date.** Do the job that is promised soonest first.
3. **Shortest Operating Time.** Do the job that takes the least time first.

There are many other more complex possibilities. They are usually combinations or variations on the simple ones listed. The decision is difficult because each of the rules performs differently on the several objectives listed above. No one rule performs best on all dimensions. The rule used depends on the relative importance of the conflicting objectives. Unfortunately, it can also lead to suboptimal systems performance, because managers may be evaluated on only one of the criteria, for example, utilization of equipment or labor. This can lead them to hold excessive inventories, so there will always be work to do, but excessive inventory increases holding costs and may reduce customer service by missing due dates. (This is an example of the abuse of management by objectives, leading to behaviors that allow the individual to meet his or her goals but that are detrimental to the system as a whole.)

Push and Pull Systems. Regardless of the approach used to generate the schedule or the sequence, the resulting movement of materials through the system is described as a **push system.** In a push system, *as employees finish an order, they pass it on (or push it) to the next station, whether this station is ready for it or not.* At the time indicated by the schedule, the order is released from planning to operations. The sequencing rule determines what order goes first at the work center. As each order is completed, it is pushed to the next work center by the processing plan (routing), where it will, in turn, receive the next step in its fabrication. Eventually, the order is pushed to completion.

Push system As employees finish an order, they pass it on (or push it) to the next station, whether this station is ready for it or not.

An alternative approach that has become popular in recent years is the **pull system.** It is derived from a TQM approach to operations management and is sometimes called just-in-time (JIT), that we introduced earlier. The basic idea is that *processes nearer the completed product (downstream), reach back and pull the required materials through the operations as needed.* An upstream process operates only when its downstream customer requests additional material by drawing down the relatively small amount of work-in-process (WIP) inventory allowed between the processes.

Pull system An approach in which processes nearer the completed product (downstream), reach back and pull the required materials through the operations as needed.

There is strict control of the amount of work-in-process between supplier and user work centers. The movement of this WIP is the trigger for the supplier station to make one more batch of the item just used. Each movement starts a chain reaction back through the system, pulling the required items from finished product back to raw material. The system also includes external supplier firms, who do not deliver goods until needed, sometimes just 24 hours before.

TQM and JIT

Throughout this book, we have stressed the broad managerial behavioral and leadership issues involved in implementing Total Quality Management. These issues are often expressed in the *operations* function as the *just-in-time philosophy*. There is no doubt that this philosophy was greatly enhanced by a number of Japanese manufacturing companies, Toyota being the most often cited.

The comprehensive philosophy of JIT is sometimes referred to as the productivity triad. The three components of this triad are:

1. People involvement
2. Total quality control
3. JIT (or coordinated) flow of material

The first includes an emphasis on teamwork, open communication, and leadership. The second includes the use of data-based decisions using statistical process control. These ideas have been covered in earlier chapters, but let's look closer at the third item on the list.

Although all the ideas of TQM are applicable in all types of operations, the specifics of JIT flow better fit repetitive operations, with their supporting batch operations, than they do for make-to-order operations. The following characteristics typify the most successful JIT operations.

1. There is a uniform production rate.
2. They use a pull method coordination of work centers.
3. There are fast and inexpensive machine changeovers.
4. There are multi-skilled workers and flexible facilities.
5. They have highly reliable equipment and output.
6. They have a commitment to and from a limited set of suppliers.
7. There are short and stable supply lead times.

These characteristics are not inherent in any manufacturing operation. They happen because managers make them happen. These managers understand that this approach is the one that will make operations run most efficiently and effectively to deliver goods and services to customers. This is the approach that minimizes waste and maximizes resources. It is also an approach that emphasizes continuous improvement in all seven areas. The *A Look At Technology* box on page 663 shows what one industry is doing to use the JIT philosophy to turn itself around.

Service Scheduling Models

We have been looking at the manufacturing side of operations. Now let's turn to services. As noted earlier, capacity to provide services cannot, in general, be accumulated (inventoried) during slack periods to offset requirements in later periods. Airplanes, for example, have a fixed number of seats per day, and those unoccupied today cannot be used for future flights. The greater the degree of customer involvement in the service, the more difficult the problem. This means that this is less of a problem in the car service repair business, for example, where you can more efficiently schedule employees to deliver services, than in the barbering business, where the customer has to be there. The degree of customer contact, the need for customization rather than standardization, and the lack of an inventoriable product make achieving high efficiency in service operations a formidable task.

There are ways to improve efficiency in service operations, though. What follows describes some possible actions used in service operations to increase productivity. Some of these become, in effect, business strategies, since they tend to define who the target customers will be, and which needs will be served. These actions include:

1. Standardize services and limit the degree of customer choice to a small set of standard transactions, for example a limited menu in a fast food restaurant or focusing only on oil changes rather than full service auto repair.
2. Uncouple the customer from all aspects of the service package that do not require the direct involvement of the customer, that is, a "back-office," without direct customer contact, and a "front-office" that provides the customer interface. This is common in repair facilities of all types.
3. Use one or more activities to "manage," or influence the demand pattern. Some possible actions include:
   a. Create a fixed schedule, for example, airline flights.
   b. Create an appointment system, for example, a dentist's office.
   c. Delay delivery, that is, create a waiting line of customers, e.g. appliance repair.
   d. Incentivize to smooth demand, e.g. reduce fare for late night flight, or long-distance phone service on weekends.

Despite these efforts, there will still be fluctuating demand for services, and managers must figure out how to minimize resources in times of low demand and have them available during periods of high demand. Some actions service providers can take to deal with this problem to gain efficiency include:

1. Stagger work-shifts. Vary the start and stop times of service personnel so that maximum capacity is available at periods of highest demand, for example, more police officers scheduled at night in a high crime area.
2. Part time on-call staff. Match capacity more closely with requirements by use of a workforce available as called. These are sometimes called "snap" workers, that is they come at the snap of a finger. Temporary employees often fill this role.

THE LATEST FASHION, JUST IN TIME[7]

A LOOK AT

TECHNOLOGY

The textile and apparel industry in the U.S. has been hard hit by imports. Between 1980 and 1992, 420,000 jobs were lost because Americans were buying lower- priced imported textiles and clothing. Part of the problem has been the incredibly inefficient operations both in the manufacture of textiles and the manufacture of finished clothing. Studies indicate that it takes 66 weeks beginning with textile manufacture through sales in a retail outlet for a piece of clothing to find its way to the final consumer. Of that 66 weeks, a 1985 industry study showed that for 55 of those weeks, the materials were simply sitting in inventory somewhere in the value chain. This same study identified waste of about $25 billion in the system, resulting from excess inventory-carrying costs, lost sales, and clearance markdowns. Industry leaders know that reducing these costs is vital to rejuvenating this industry in the U.S.

An industry group started in 1979, [TC]², short for Textile/Clothing Technology Corporation, is trying to do something about this problem. Their goal is to substantially reduce the amount of time to deliver a finished garment to a customer, what they call "quick response manufacturing techniques," and technology is their tool for doing this.

They have developed a teaching factory, which incorporates such machines as a computer numerical control cutter. This factory produces T-shirts, skirts, and women's slacks on a flexible, quick replenishment basis for a 52-outlet chain of clothing stores. Using technology, the factory manufactures and ships orders within a week. The production is triggered by point-of-sale data (taken from scanning merchandise as it is sold) relayed by a computer network to the factory. When a customer makes a purchase, this initiates an electronic purchase order to replenish the item sold.

This is essentially a pull system, what they call demand-activated manufacturing (DAM), where sales to consumers generate demand for garments to replace sold goods. The idea is for this demand to be transmitted all the way back in the value chain, creating integration among fiber, textile, and apparel manufacturers, and retailers. This approach will allow apparel makers and retailers to quickly respond to consumer demand for off-size garments without having to stock excessive amounts of inventory in all sizes. A retailer could stock just a few very small or very large sizes with the confidence that when they sell these, the data will be transmitted back to factories, where new replacement garments will be sewn and shipped within days.

One of the most intriguing ideas to come out of [TC]² is the possibility of retailers of men's and women's tailored clothing to have electronic body scanners on the premises. In connection with other technology, these devices would allow a company to sell custom-tailored suits, for example, at ready-to-wear prices. When a customer enters the store looking for a suit, he is escorted to a booth where his body is scanned.

After selecting the style and fabric, this information along with 3D body measurements result in the output of a 2D pattern from a computer for the finished suit. This pattern would be transmitted via modem to an apparel manufacturer where it is matched to a pattern in an existing computer database. After making adjustments to customize the garment to the customer, the pattern is transmitted electronically to a high-speed laser cutter. This automatically cuts out the pieces of material for the suit, which then go to a flexible team-based manufacturing cell for sewing together. They package the garment for express shipment, and the customer has his tailor-made suit within days. And because it was manufactured using ready-to-wear techniques, it costs no more than any good suit would.

While this may sound too good to be true, this kind of sophisticated use of technology to improve operations is happening in many industries to eliminate waste and improve customer responsiveness. It is an example of how a quality and customer-oriented, continuous improvement approach to operations can mean the difference between success or failure.

3. Flexible skilled floaters. These are especially helpful in providing specialty services, such as health care. Floaters are assigned to units where abnormally high loads occur.

Again, the idea here, as in manufacturing, is to align availability with demand with a minimum amount of waste.

Project Management

As defined earlier, a project is an operation with a small output volume, and, often, nonroutine tasks. The output of the project might be a product, for example, a bridge or a software package, or a service, for example, an advertising campaign or even something as large as the Olympic Games. Projects also differ from other operations because of their finite life. Some organizations have projects as their only product line, such as construction companies or lawyers who handle individual cases for clients. In many other cases, projects occur within organizations whose primary output are other goods and/or services, for example, a major maintenance project on a paper machine. It is beyond our scope to cover all the special aspects of project management here, but an overview of the basic approach to planning and control of projects is appropriate.

Network A graphical representation of the activities required to complete a project.

Network Techniques. We define a **network**, when used in operations management, as *a graphical representation of the activities required to complete a project.* The primary function of a network is to depict the precedence relationships

EXHIBIT 17-9
A Simple Project Network Diagram

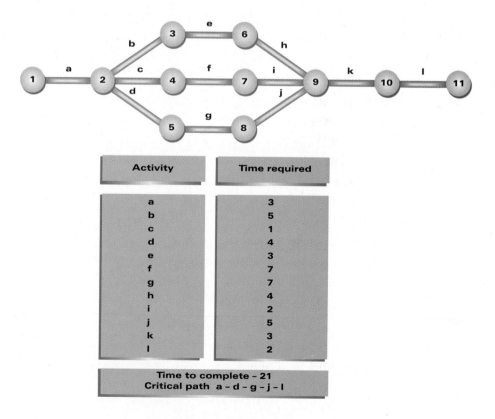

Activity	Time required
a	3
b	5
c	1
d	4
e	3
f	7
g	7
h	4
i	2
j	5
k	3
l	2

Time to complete – 21
Critical path a – d – g – j – l

among the various activities. Precedence relationships mean what activities must happen in what order. These relationships, along with time estimates of the individual activities, can be used to plan and schedule resources and monitor progress of the project. Exhibit 17-9 depicts a simple project in network form, and defines some common terms associated with this method.

We can trace the uses of networks in project management to two different origins, both occurring in the late 1950s. Although they have much in common, they were developed independently, for different purposes.

The critical path method, better known by its acronym, CPM, was developed by E.I. duPont de Nemours and Company and the Rand Corporation. The **critical path** *tracks those activities that are at the center of a project and that must be completed in a set sequence*. For example, the critical path in the building of a house would track laying the foundation, building the frame, installing wiring and plumbing, putting up drywall, and so on through painting and laying the carpet. Each of these activities must happen in a sequence, and this is the critical path for completing the project. It was developed to improve scheduling, and thus performance, in major maintenance activities in DuPont's chemical production facilities. Shut down and start-up of these facilities is very expensive, and the opportunity cost from lost output due to unnecessary delays is significant.

The Program Evaluation and Review Technique, PERT, was created about the same time by Booz, Allen, Hamilton and the U.S. Navy to manage the Polaris submarine development and construction. It was later required in most Department of Defense development contracts.

The only significant conceptual difference in these methods is in their approach to estimating the time each activity might require. CPM, coming from an environment with significant historical data about the activities, makes one *most likely* time estimate for each activity, and assumes it deterministic for subsequent use in planning. PERT, however, was developed to plan and control essentially *never-done-before* activities. It was felt that some way to evaluate the probabilistic nature of the estimates would be useful, thus PERT uses a series of estimates, generally called *optimistic time* (everything goes very well), *pessimistic time* (everything goes poorly), and *most likely time* (some go well, others poorly, and so on). The most likely time is probably not the simple average of optimistic and pessimistic times. The graphical representation is the same in both activities.

The critical path, that is, the sequential set of activities that require the longest time to complete, provides the key to these models. This determines the shortest time in which the project can be completed. This idea may cause some confusion. The longest path and the shortest completion time seem contradictory at first glance. But remember, every activity must be completed, and a succeeding activity cannot be started until all its preceding activities have been completed.

For example, suppose you and two friends who live in different cities are going on an automobile trip together. You plan to meet in yet another city before proceeding together. Even if you all depart your hometowns at the same time, the one with the longest time to the meeting place determines when the next leg can begin, and the completion time of the trip. The computations are actually not complicated, but they can be somewhat tedious for large projects. Computer software, such as Microsoft Project, is widely used for these computations and developing graphical representations of the critical path.

Critical path A method that tracks those activities that are at the center of a project and that must be completed in a set sequence. It is the path requiring the longest time to complete.

TQM IS MAKING A DIFFERENCE IN CMS AND FNG OPERATIONS

CMS's strategy to use the TQM concepts with its suppliers and to encourage some of its other customers to adopt them has begun to show results. Exhibit 17-10 illustrates their idea of how to get to world-class in their operations. This plan was developed by Mr. Hommel and his staff after receiving some training on the Toyota system. You should notice the Deming philosophy throughout. It is explicitly shown in the PDCA cycles on the schematic. The Japanese idea of kaizen is also prominently displayed. It is now part of the American vocabulary in TQM organizations.

Look at the titles in the blocks identified as "System Concept." These are the key areas that must be addressed in a manufacturing system if is to become a customer- driven, TQM enterprise. Built-in quality, for instance, implies a system that works on the design of the products and processes as well as the production operation. For instance, they have developed a new procedure for the creation of the stamping dies that ensures proper alignment of die and stock. This allows for more rapid changeovers and eliminates the scrap created while fine-tuning the die installation. Meeting Toyota's small quantity shipping schedule requires the ability to make these changeovers easily. Improvements in each of the other areas has provided similiar productivity gains, such as better cus-

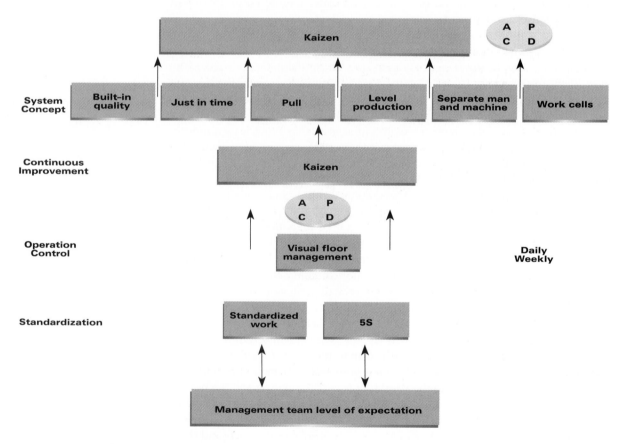

EXHIBIT 17-10 CMS, Inc. Improvement Model

tomer service, higher machine utilization, greater employee morale and improved profitability.

As CMS has improved its processes, it has become an active advocate for its suppliers and other customers to adopt these principles. They recognize that all parties will be better off when they are all using the same management approach. Most of CMS's other customers are also component suppliers to other manufacturers. As all successful manufacturers continue their journey toward TQM, each unit in the supply chain will be fully integrated, conceptually, with all the others.

Flex-n-Gate has had similar improvements in important measures of business success. Shahid Kahn, president, noted these important results. "Flow time has been reduced by 70%, quality is up 85%, and profits . . . Profits are much better, too."

In network terminology an *activity* requires time and other resources to complete. To figure out how much time it will take for each activity, we compute:

1. Early start or finish time (ES, EF), the soonest, after the project begins that an activity can start and finish.
2. Late finish or start time (LF, LS), the latest time, start or finish, for an activity without delaying the completion of the project.
3. Slack time, the difference between the ES and LS, or EF and LF for an activity, or sub-set of connected activities. The path with the minimum amount of slack is the critical path.

Having this information, managers can more wisely allocate resources to correct activities, with primary attention to those on the critical path, or with very little slack. As work proceeds, managers monitor the completion of activities against the plan, and revise the schedule if required. On very long projects, it is quite possible for a new critical path to develop. This is because managers discover things that are critical to complete the project they may not have anticipated or known about when the project started. This may require reallocation of resources to minimize additional costs or time in completing the project. These network methods greatly improve the manager's ability to make the correct re-allocations

❓ THINKING CRITICALLY

1. Think about a situation in which you have some responsibility for executing certain activities, perhaps in a club or a job. Explain how the concepts *master production schedule, resource requirements plan,* and *detail schedules* might help you plan how to successfully complete these activities.
2. In terms of your own experience, do you think it makes more sense to have a store of goods you can use in your various activities, even if you have to invest in those goods before you need them, or does it make more sense to purchase what you need when you need it? Explain your answer. What does this tell you about just-in-time inventory control?
3. In terms of planning completion of your assignments in school, especially papers for various classes, which priority control would you use and why? (Rules: First come-first served, earliest due date, and shortest operating time.) Explain your answer.

SUMMARY

OPERATIONS AND ORGANIZATIONS

- The purpose of operations management is to efficiently and effectively plan, implement, and control the work involved in transforming inputs into outputs (either goods or services) that customers will value.

- A major difference between manufacturers and service companies is that the manufactured goods can be stored for use later on. Services must be consumed when needed and cannot be stored.

- Manufacturing operations can be classified in terms of customer involvement with the development of the product or in terms of volume and variety of outputs.

- Service operations can be classified in terms of variety and volume of services offered, tangible versus intangible services, and the level of customer involvement when the service is delivered.

DESIGNING OPERATIONS

- The first major decision for managers in designing operations concerns facilities, the physical plant where the work is done. Decisions about facilities include location and layout.

- To make sure the facility runs smoothly, managers must also think in terms of job design, making sure employees have work that takes advantage of their skills.

MANAGING OPERATIONS

- Managing operations includes a sequence of ongoing decisions managers need to make. There are various models to assist managers in making these decisions. The decisions include:

  —*forecasting* demand for outputs

  —developing *capacity utilization plans* to use the facility efficiently

  —developing a *master production schedule* to match capacity with demand for outputs

  —developing a *resources requirements plan* to line up resources needed to deliver planned outputs.

  —developing *work schedules* for employees to execute the master production schedule

- The various models to assist managers in making decisions about these issues include:

  —Forecasting: *causal models* and *historic models* assist in these decisions

  —Capacity utilization and master production schedule: Managers can use an approach that emphasizes a *constant output rate or a variable output rate* to meet expected demand.

- Materials management and inventory control are important concerns of an operations manager. Goods held in inventory for inappropriate periods of time tie up cash, waste resources, and undermine profitability.

- There are three types of inventory: finished goods, work-in-process, and raw materials.

- When managers are unsure of the demand for their outputs, i.e., demand is independent of their control, there are time and quantity-based models they can use to figure out how much inventory to have on hand to meet potential demand and when to reorder. These models include the *economic order quantity model,* and *materials resources planning.*

- In controlling inventory, there are three basic costs managers must be concerned with: *storage costs, ordering costs,* and *stockout costs.* An additional cost, more difficult to calculate, is *opportunity cost.*

- Managers must also make sure they have the capacity available to produce components and finished goods. They can do this by gaining *load profiles* of resources needed and combining this with demand and then use this information to *prioritize* the work to be done.

- Just-in-time (JIT) inventory control is a new approach to minimizing inventory costs while ensuring goods are available when needed.

- JIT is related to the pull system of operations management, where those downstream in a process accept outputs of an upstream process only when they need them. In this way, no unfinished inventory accumulates before it is needed for a process.

- JIT is an important part of the operations management component of TQM. It helps organizations better align resources with demand and minimize waste in processes.

- JIT is harder to implement in services, yet there are a number of actions managers can take to align resources with the times services are demanded. These include:

  —standardizing services and limiting choice

  —uncouple customer from timing of service

  —create schedules to influence demand pattern

- Because projects are one-of-a-kind outputs, various network techniques have been developed to manage timing of steps in production and utilization of resources.

KEY TERMS

Assemble-to-order (ATO) 639

Batch manufacturing 640

Capacity utilization plan 648

Causal models 650

Cellular layout 645

Continuous process manufacturing 639

Critical path 665

Dependent demand 653

Detail or work schedules 649

Economic order quantity (EOC) model 656

Facility 642

Finished goods 652

Fixed position layout 645

Forecasts 648

Historic models 650

Independent demand 653

Inventory 651

REVIEW QUESTIONS

1. How does the idea of operations as traditionally defined apply to other activities not traditionally seen in operations terms, such as accounting, finance, and marketing?
2. How does a supply chain help managers to understand operations and their management?
3. What is a fundamental difference between manufacturing operations and service operations?
4. How do levels of customer involvement and volume and variety of output help managers categorize manufacturing operations?
5. What are the three ways we can categorize service operations?
6. What are the factors that influence the location of a facility?
7. What are four types of layout for a facility and what factors influence the choice of layout?
8. What is the relationship between forecasting, capacity utilization, and a master production schedule?
9. What is inventory, and why is its management so important?
10. What is the difference between independent demand and dependent demand, and what is the relationship of these ideas to operations management and inventory control?
11. What is the difference between a push system and a pull system?
12. What is the relationship between a pull system and just-in-time inventory control?

EXPERIENTIAL EXERCISE
Operating a Tape Duplication Business

Divide into groups of five or six students each. Imagine you are starting a videotape duplication business to make tape copies of movies, instructional videos, and so on. Using the information in this chapter, respond to the following questions involved in creating an operations plan for this business:

- What category of operation is this business?
- Where should the business be located and why?
- What kind of layout do you think would work best for the operations (tape duplicating) part of the business? Why?
- What special concerns should you have about capacity to deliver duplicated tapes and anticipated demand?
- How will you decide how much inventory of blank tapes to keep on hand? Should you order blank tapes from a supplier on a per job basis? Why or why not?
- How will you set your priorities for starting jobs when you have several to do?
- What other operations concerns should you consider to make sure things run smoothly?

Have each group write up their findings and prepare a 10 minute report to the class. Discuss differences and similarities among the ideas of the different groups.

CASE ANALYSIS AND APPLICATION
Increasing Productivity and Customer Satisfaction at Tibor Machine Products[8]

Tibor Machine Products is a metal parts fabricator founded in 1968 and located in Chicago Ridge, Illinois. By 1993, the company had grown to 150 employees by paying attention to the basics and looking out for its customers. To achieve this growth, in the early 1990s the company's management had begun to explore new markets. Up until then, its major product was turned hydraulic components sold to just one customer, a large manufacturer of earth moving and construction equipment. While this simplified manufacturing operations—the shop made the same parts over and over with consistent lead times—it left the company vulnerable should that customer go away. Further, it limited the company's growth.

The company's marketing department started looking for new customers, and soon the company had a variety of jobs. These new customers presented a series of problems to the manufacturing operations at Tibor. Each new customer had unique requirements. Writes Joseph Corso, master scheduler at Tibor:

Product routings became longer and more complex and, for the first time, Tibor's staff had to manage significant production sent outside for processing. Also, the new and varied customer base no longer placed orders in stable patterns. There were peaks and valleys in the demands placed on Tibor's plant. The new customers were often not content with Tibor's standard lead times and wanted product more quickly than the company was used to providing.

The company's management realized that they had scheduling problems and that they had to do something about this if their plans for growth were to succeed. They had to figure out how to meet the varying needs of many different customers, delivering finished products when these customers wanted them.

For a job shop like Tibor, this is complicated. Different products require many different inputs and amounts of time to fabricate. The company already had a materials resources planning program running on its computer, but this did not help them schedule jobs. The company talked to various vendors and purchased a new program to deal with "finite capacity scheduling" (translation: scheduling for small capacity shops). Of course, buying software that is supposed to solve your problems and then having that happen are two separate things.

The managers at Tibor knew that getting this new program up and running would take time, and they were willing to invest that time. The company has the goal of being a "world class" competitor in their field. To them this means being extremely responsive to customers while driving costs to their absolute minimum. With this as their motivation they developed a strategy for bringing this new program on line.

Before the software was delivered, the master scheduler and the materials handler formulated a vision of what they wanted out of the software, which included its ability to work in concert with their MRP program. They then got the data processing department involved in addressing system integration issues. They next brought all involved parties together, including employees from the shop floor, to draw up a blueprint for how the new scheduling system would work. This was a flexible document. It was clear they would have to improve the system once it was in place. They were aware that no one ever gets it right the first time, and continuously getting new business calls for continuously refining operations.

After they developed an initial plan for use of the system, including the keying in of data that the program would use to develop work schedules, they moved to the implementation phase. At this point, the scheduling staff received five days of training on using the new software. The company set up a pilot test to see how well it would work. They chose the "chucker department," an area where the manager was enthusiastic, and they had long run sizes and consistent orders, thus making it easiest to schedule.

By running a pilot, they could learn the capabilities of the program and how to use it to their advantage. They discovered that though they had data for this area, it was not precise enough for the new system to give them accurate work schedules. Joseph Corso explains, though, that:

After eight weeks of part time effort by the master scheduler, the data had been cleaned up, and the system was generating highly accurate schedules for the chucker department. Once it had been proven in the chucker department, we began to spread the use of the scheduling system throughout the plant.

One other problem was the acceptance of the new schedules by employees on the floor. They were naturally skeptical that a computer program could generate accurate schedules and were concerned that management would hold them to unrealistic time lines. Management emphasized that people, not machines, make decisions at Tibor. Further they pointed out the system was only a tool to help make the company's goals easier to achieve, and managers wanted to work with shop employees to refine the data so the program would work well. Employees began making suggestions, and they soon saw that the program could help them.

Once the system was up and running, the company found it gained several benefits. In the past, the scheduling staff spent a lot of time maintaining the status quo, often making inaccurate schedules because of incomplete information. Now, with more accurate information and software to help in its analysis, they are doing a much better job of scheduling.

Because they can schedule better and finish jobs on time, they have much less work-in-process inventory that comes from moving from one job before another is completed. The system has helped them identify and reduce bottlenecks in fabrication processes, and reduce overtime costs. The company is also moving more toward just-in-time inventory control because they know better when they need materials from outside suppliers.

Using the software has impacted the company's relationship with customers. It can now make delivery date promises to customers that it can keep, building the trust and confidence necessary to maintain that business. Corso reports, "Finally, and maybe most importantly, installation and operation of the scheduling system has helped Tibor embark on new directions and realize the strategic vision of its management."

Discussion Questions

1. What is the relationship between Tibor's strategy to grow with new customers and getting the management of its operations under control?
2. Trace the impact of better scheduling to the company's achievement of its goals. In doing this, consider the utilization of capacity, better inventory control, the reduction of costs, and improved ability to meet delivery dates.
3. What is the relationship between successful operations management and teamwork, as demonstrated by this case?

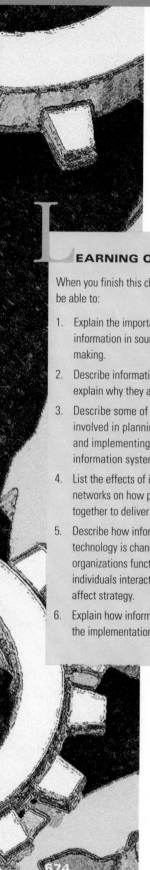

18. MANAGEMENT INFORMATION SYSTEMS

LEARNING OBJECTIVES

When you finish this chapter you should be able to:

1. Explain the importance of information in sound decision making.

2. Describe information systems and explain why they are important.

3. Describe some of the steps involved in planning, developing, and implementing effective information systems.

4. List the effects of information networks on how people work together to deliver customer value.

5. Describe how information technology is changing the way organizations function, how individuals interact, and how it can affect strategy.

6. Explain how information facilitates the implementation of TQM.

HEALTH CARE: HEAL THYSELF[1]

Tory Andrews is an 8-year-old cancer patient. Under normal health-care procedures, he would be spending a lot of time in the hospital. However, the New England Medical Center has made changes that allow Tory to be at home with his parents. In Tory's home is a computer with an interactive program that instructs his parents on how to change dressings and administer a blood test. If the results show a blood count that has reached a dangerous level, the system automatically alerts his doctor. This system saves nearly all the costs of having Tory stay in the hospital, and it makes life less traumatic for the little boy because he is at home with his parents. This is just one example of how computerized information systems are beginning to make a big difference in the delivery of health care in the U.S.

Arthur D. Little Inc., a consulting company, has estimated that the annual U.S. health-care bill could be cut by as much as $36 billion by the more efficient management of information using computers and networks connecting them. Up until recently, nearly all records for patients have been compiled in paper folders that follow patients around when they go for care. Information can get lost in these folders, doctors miss items because they don't have time to read them completely. This is symptomatic of an approach to information management in health-care institutions that nearly defines inefficiency. But who cares? In the past no one did because costs were picked up by insurance companies without many questions.

That is all changing now. With heath-care reform, and the pinch on costs, hospitals and all types of health-care facilities are looking to take advantage of information technology to control costs and improve the quality of their services to patients. The use of this technology for these purposes is already widespread in other industries, but health care is only now catching up.

One new but obvious use of computers is for maintaining records of patient health histories and treatments. Such records can keep better track of medications that patients are allergic to, for example. Then if the doctor prescribes one of these medicines, an alarm will go off. At the Latter Day Saints Hospital in Salt Lake City, such a system had a catch rate 60 times higher than when doctors used paper records. These systems also make it much easier for doctors to share information and consult on various cases from locations across the country or even around the world.

As reported in *Business Week,* here are some specific suggestions for the use of information technology to start realizing billions of dollars in savings:

- **Bedside Terminals.** Patient records would be kept on computers located in each room, replacing thick hard-to-decipher paper files.

Using a local-area network, doctors could order lab tests and medicines. The computer could alert the doctor to any special conditions of the patient or allergies to medicines.

- **Videoconferencing.** CAT scans and other images could be reviewed by specialists thousands of miles away from each other. Teams of doctors scattered throughout a region could consult on a difficult case without having to move the patient.

- **Home Health Terminals.** Patients could consult on-line with doctors, key in results of self-administered tests for physicians to monitor, and call up information on their illnesses.

- **Diagnostic Systems.** Software programs would advise doctors on the likely diagnosis and preferred treatment of a particular set of symptoms, including a cost/benefit analysis.

The point of all this, as you will see as you proceed in this chapter, is to learn how to use technology to manage information better. This technology is far more efficient at storing, accessing, and updating information than processes involving paper. It also can make a big difference in the quality and speed of delivery of health services. At the end of the chapter we will see how one hospital has "reengineered" itself using information technology.

MANAGERS AND INFORMATION

Throughout the earlier chapters we have stressed the idea of the organization as a system—composed of numerous subsystems, such as an operations subsystem, a distribution subsystem, a human resources subsystem, and others—all interacting with, influencing, and supporting each other. When well managed, the results of this interaction are positive for the organization, and when poorly managed, the results are not so positive.

Information subsystem
The subsystem that consists of the processes for gathering data, interpreting, and turning it into information and then distributing it throughout the organization.

The subsystem that connects all these others together and the internal organization to its environment is the **information subsystem.** The information subsystem consists of *the processes for gathering data, interpreting, and turning it into information and then distributing it throughout the organization.* This information lets employees and managers know where things stand and helps guide their decisions. In one way, we might compare the information to the central nervous system in the human body. Through our senses we gather sensory data, which our brains interpret and turn into information, which we use to guide our behavior.

Data Unorganized facts, measurements, or statistics about events, time, behaviors, attitudes, or anything people care to observe and/or measure.

The distinction between data and information is important to note here. **Data** are *unorganized facts, measurements, or statistics about events, time, behaviors, attitudes, or anything people care to observe and/or measure.* Data are the raw materials used to create information. This happens through grouping, ordering, comparing, and organizing the data to discover useful patterns. **Information** is *data ordered to see patterns that are useful in making decisions and guiding behavior.* Data might come from surveys, grocery store scanners, sales reports, interviews, focus groups, measuring devices, population studies, and myriad other sources. Through the application of statistical, financial and other tools, we interpret, quantify, find relationships, and order this data (literally, put it "in formation") to detect trends and patterns that let us know what seems to be going on during any period of time. The success of subsequent behaviors often

Information Data ordered to see patterns that are useful in making decisions and guiding behavior.

The authors thank Kyle Lundby for his contributions in writing this chapter.

depends on how accurate our data is and how we interpret it. Think of your own experiences. When something has gone wrong, it is usually because you have misinterpreted data in some way to create faulty information that you acted on.

Sound information is the basis of all management and employee efforts to improve the efficiency of internal operations and enhance the value of organizational offerings to customers. The questions for most organizations, though, are what kind of data, how is it to be interpreted, and what actions do they take? In traditional organizations, there is often a tendency to take small amounts of data, use personal experience (rather than scientific analysis) to interpret it, and draw conclusions (often looking for someone to blame) that may or may not help the organization. The problem here is that sound information only comes from looking at data over time and using it not to blame a person but understand the system, its capabilities, and how it can be improved. This is the TQM approach.

For example, at Northern Telecom, a telecommunications giant operating in the global marketplace, actionable data are transformed into information that becomes a tool used at all levels for strategic planning, education, and continuous improvement. As a result the information becomes part of a continuous loop that enables change. Telecom's Assistant Vice President of Quality explains,

It's how we handle information that's important. Information is part of the operation that you never see. We will take you through our operations, and all you see is white clean floors, white clean walls, well-dressed people, and lots of equipment. You don't see the strategic nature of how information is used. Information gives us a competitive advantage in global operations.[2]

Northern Telecom believes that information is the power that enables them to build and maintain a superior competitive advantage in the global market. Again, Telecom's Assistant V.P. of Quality explains,

Here at Northern Telecom we see two major forces going on all over the world that are going to shape us. First, it won't be long before we will all feel the force of global competitors. Even if you are a small business in Knoxville, Tennessee, you can bet that eventually the global competitor will be there pushing hard to take over your business. The second force we are all going to have to deal with is information technology. Information technology is the key to white-collar productivity. Today, it is not the factory worker we should be concerned with, it is the white-collar worker. We know how to design manufacturing processes to be effective. However, it is the effectiveness of business processes we need to be concerned with, and they involve the need for productive white-collar workers. If we are going to compete with the global competitors, we are going to have to make major strides in white-collar productivity.[3]

In the following sections, we discuss several aspects of the information subsystem. The rapid technological advances in this area create many opportunities for significant improvements in the way managers, and employees, approach their work. However, organizations that fail to keep up with these technological advances will face stiffer competition in the future, particularly from those who embrace the new technology and its intelligent use.

Management, Information, and Technology

No one can dispute that our lives, and society in general, have become more complex. Technology, especially "information" technology, is partially responsible for that. Transmission of audio or video images of events as they occur to a global audience is one obvious example. Businesses use electronic technology to disperse information to managers and employees, literally at the speed of light. A businessperson in Madison, Wisconsin can, for example, call the FedEx 800 number in Memphis, Tennessee and may have a FedEx van arrive 10 minutes later to pick up a package. The information for the pickup is sent from the home office to the appropriate delivery person via computer and satellite, and it shows up on a screen in the truck.

Improvements in computer speed and capability, and corresponding declines in costs have made them almost as common in businesses as telephones, which, often in new high-tech versions, are also an integral part of information technology. Today, many companies send sales representatives into the field armed with laptop computers that communicate directly with their headquarters through phone lines. This technology allows salespeople to access price quotes and place orders instantly.[4] Technology is clearly changing the way many companies do business, and some of these can be seen in Exhibit 18-1.

Today, the quantity and quality of information available to managers and workers is much greater than was available in the past. Technology alone, however, is not a panacea. With greater quantities of information comes the risk of too much information. Thus, the modern manager must be able to sift through the excess to determine what is useful and what is not. One organizational

---

EXHIBIT 18-1 How Information Technology is Changing Business

The advance of electronic information technology is having a dramatic impact on businesses, their employees, and the suppliers and customers who trade with them. Here's a sampling of how:

Organization — New electronic systems are breaking down old corporate barriers, allowing critical information to be shared instantly across functional departments or product groups—and even with employees on the factory floor.

Operations — Manufacturers are using information technology to shrink cycle times, reduce defects, and waste. Likewise, service firms are using electronic data interchange to streamline ordering and communication with suppliers and customers.

Staffing — New information systems and processes have eliminated the need for layers of management and reduced the number of people needed to get work done. Meanwhile, companies are using less costly computers, telephones, and fax machines to create "virtual offices" giving employees working in far-flung locations instant access to each other.

New Products — The information "feedback loop" is collapsing development cycles. Companies are electronically feeding customer and marketing comments to product-development teams so that they can rejuvenate product lines and target specific customers.

Customer Service — No longer simply an order entry job, customer-service representatives are tapping into company-wide databases to solve caller's problems instantly, from simple changes of address to billing adjustments.

Source: Adapted from Ira Sager, "The Great Equalizer," *Business Week*, 1994 Special Edition, p. 101.

expert, Robert Moskowitz, suggests that the key to doing this is to think strategically about your goals. As a consultant he tries to get executives thinking about four or five goals they want to accomplish over the next year and then organize their time around accomplishing those goals. By doing that managers eliminate about 50 percent of the information that may cross their desks as irrelevant.[5]

Characteristics of Useful Information

Although managers require a great deal of information to perform their duties efficiently and effectively, more information isn't always better information. There are several characteristics that distinguish good from bad information: accuracy, value, currency, and frequency.[6]

Accuracy.   Information is accurate to the extent that it describes your data in a precise manner. Your score on an exam, for example, is accurate to the extent that the number of points assigned by your professor is a true reflection of the number of items you answered correctly. For information to be useful it must be accurate. For example, if a manager schedules fewer employees for the winter holiday than are necessary, based on inaccurate information about business during this period, the organization may be understaffed and may compromise customer relations.

Value.   Information must have some value if it is to be useful to managers. Many managers are inundated with stacks of computer printouts, memos, letters, newsletters, E-mail, and so on, much of which offers redundant or unnecessary information. To have value for managers, information must be relevant to their objectives and concerns and add value to efforts to achieve these objectives.

Currency.   Information should generally be current or up to date if it is to have utility. The same manager preparing for the coming holidays will have little use for projections into the next decade. Similarly, the manager will have no use whatsoever for last year's projections that arrive too late.

Frequency.   How frequently a manager needs information will depend on the manager and the type of organization. In general, however, information should be available with a frequency that will enable the manager to respond promptly to problems and opportunities. In the computer industry, technology is constantly changing as new ideas surface; thus managers require frequent and up-to-date information to stay ahead of the competition.

   In sum, information should be accurate, valuable, current, and frequent. Information that has utility for one manager, however, may not have utility for another. The next section examines how information needs may differ for people with different types of responsibilities.

Information Needs for Different Types of Decisions

Managers at different organizational levels have different decision-making responsibilities. Upper-level managers, for example, must concern themselves with long-term strategic issues. Middle- and lower-level managers focus more on day-to-day tactical and operational activities, such as assisting and coaching employees in handling different problems, scheduling employees and production runs, purchasing raw materials, and maintaining equipment in proper working order. We should note here that in implementing TQM, with its flattened hierarchies, we no longer specifically associate tactical and operational decisions with only lower management levels. In those companies with self-managed teams, for example, the tactical and operational decisions are made by the teams rather than managers. Nevertheless, it is helpful to think of these in terms of management levels of responsibility as this is the case in many organizations today. Exhibit 18-2 depicts these different types of decisions for different levels of management responsibility.

Upper-level managers are likely to require information that will aid them in making strategic decisions. Strategic decisions focus on top-level, long-range decisions. They determine the future direction of the organization and broadly determine resource allocation policies. Information and the systems to support these decisions must be able to:

- Access internal and external information sources
- Provide feedback on organizational performance
- Help with nonprogrammed decisions

Decisions at this level are more complex than those at the lower operational level. Problems are not well-structured, and outcomes of particular actions are not certain. External information becomes more important to good decisions. Systems that allow a "what-if" capability become increasingly valuable as decision aids. For example, an upper-level manager at General Motors may be involved in gathering information to aid in planning a new production facility. Of interest to this manager may be information such as the quality of local freeways, tax incentives for new industry, and the availability of qualified workers.

In contrast, managers and employees with lower levels of responsibility require information that allows them to make more immediate tactical decisions. Tactical decisions focus on intermediate range decisions that direct allocation of resources to support the plans of the organization. Developing next

EXHIBIT 18-2
Levels of Decision Making. Each requires different types of information.

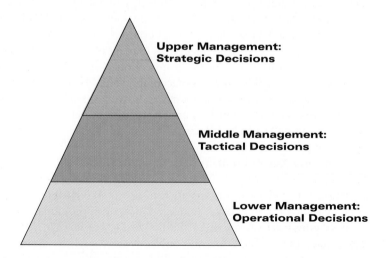

quarter's divisional budget is an example of a tactical decision. Information systems to support these decisions must be able to:

- Support intermediate-range planning
- Provide feedback on division or department performance
- Help with semi-programmed decisions

Tactical decisions require information that assists those making the decisions to ensure the implementation of operational objectives. For example, lower-level managers may be interested in how a flu epidemic may affect immediate performance levels. They may also be interested in evaluating which of the temporary replacement employees might be qualified and/or interested in positions at the new production facility. To do this, they need information to better understand these situations and make an informed choice about what actions to take.

? THINKING CRITICALLY

1. In your own opinion, why is information so important for managers and employees?
2. Think about a job you have had in the past and the kind of information you needed to perform effectively. What happened when that information was unavailable or inaccurate?

INFORMATION SYSTEMS

To understand information systems in organizations better let's go back to the human body as a metaphor. This time think of an information system as being similar to the digestive system, which, after food is ingested, processes it in a way that yields energy and converts energy into action through the skeletal and muscular systems. The organization's information system operates in a similar fashion. It facilitates the capture and storage of data, which, using various software programs, it interprets or transforms into meaningful information, and allows for the transmission of this information to users on demand in a manner that helps them guide the organization toward its various goals and objectives.

Consistent with the principles of TQM, an information system should be designed to clearly add value to the ability of managers and employees to deliver higher-quality goods and services to customers. One way companies are using information systems to add value in this way is through the use of high-speed computer networks that link companies to suppliers and customers via digital technology. These networks transmit valuable information to and from companies allowing them to tap directly into what the customers want. Easy access such as this will enable companies to react quickly to customer needs, thereby ensuring product value. These kinds of systems are now being used in some large retailers like Wal-Mart. Data from cash registers trigger orders with suppliers to make sure the store keeps well-stocked. We will discuss more about these networks later in the chapter.

Often, managers must gather large amounts of data before they can derive meaningful information. It is unlikely, for example, that you would be willing to base a semester grade on a single-item exam. Instead, you would want multiple items. What single-item exams may gain in terms of speed, they also lose in terms of accuracy. Thus, instructors use multiple-item exams because they can cover a broader range of relevant course material and students will be in a better position to demonstrate their knowledge.

In a similar way, managers require sufficient information to make sound decisions. If one automobile comes off an assembly line with a scratch on its fender, there may be several plausible reasons. It may be a problem with the process, but it is also possible that the vehicle had been bumped by a worker or a piece of machinery. A supervisor can determine little from this single piece of data. However, if most cars coming down the line have similar scratches, the supervisor is in a better position to figure out the cause and suggest a course of action to eliminate similar mishaps in the future.

Information Systems and Data Processing

Modern information systems cannot be separated from the computer technology. Prior to the computer revolution, the output of management information systems often were not available in time to allow managers to make immediate decisions and affect outcomes. At best, they provided some indication of good or bad managerial decisions, and thus direction for improvements. Some examples of outputs of information systems which pre-date the computer include traditional financial accounting reports like balance sheets, profit and loss statements, and budget variance reports. Without the speed of the computer to convert the data inputs into information in a timely manner, such reports, while useful for some purposes, do not allow managers to keep as current with organization performance and problems as with the electronic networks.

In general, an information system should encompass one or more of the following:

- It must embrace sensors of all types necessary to capture data on internal and external conditions related to situations that confront the organization (or may confront it in the future). This suggests that companies must have a variety of means for collecting the data needed to develop useful information.

- It must provide communication channels from the sensors to the decision-making centers (people, groups of people, and machines controlled by people). This means that the company needs to have good ways to distribute data and information to those who need it.

- It must include storage facilities for data not immediately required or that may be required to be used more than once. This now means keeping information stored on computers for easy access by those who need it.

- It must have facilities for aggregating and collecting data to convert them into information bearing on the decision processes necessary to the organization. Generally in larger organizations this includes a specific department devoted to information management and dispersion. It may also happen in specific departments, such as marketing (for customer and market research data) or accounting and finance (for financial information).

- It must provide channels of communication from the decision centers to the persons responsible for carrying out the necessary activities. This means the system must include good feedback loops so those collecting the data can refine their activities to create information that is truly useful.
- It must provide output information in a readily comprehensible form to those persons and machines involved in the activities of the organization.[7]

Transaction Processing

Transaction processing is an important use of information technology in most organizations. The earliest uses of computers in businesses were not directly related to management enhancement. They were used to replace manual, or semi-mechanized, routine repetitive clerical functions. We'll refer to these applications *transaction processing systems* or, as they were originally called, *data processing*. Exhibit 18-3 shows some modern examples of transactions common to many organizations. Data obtained from the transaction processing system provide a basis for creating managerially useful information. Because processes are interrelated, each transaction may create a series of others within the organization. From several of the transactions noted in Exhibit 18-3, you can easily imagine a series of subsequent transactions, basically driving what others in the organization do.

Transaction processing systems are usually designed for a narrow range of activities. For example, the computer terminal operated by a travel agent can access flight schedules and determine availability, reserve a seat for a specific flight, create (directly or indirectly) flight documents, invoices or credit card documents. The agent must use specific procedures to accomplish these transactions. The procedures cannot be changed by the user, nor can the computer perform other functions. Transaction information gives managers what they need to understand the current financial status of the organization, what is selling, where it is selling, current work-in-process, accounts receivable, accounts payable, and similar information related to any company operations.

EXHIBIT 18-3 Examples of transactions captured by transaction processing systems

Type of Organization	Transaction
Bank	Process checks and deposits
Stock brokerage	Update client records for sale and purchase of securities
Airline or travel agent	Make flight reservations
Mail-order retailer	Enter a customer order Create a shipping order
University	Register for class Enter grades for student records
Supermarket	Record product and price of customer purchases
Almost all organizations	Process payrolls Post to accounting ledgers Generate invoices, statements, etc.

Management Information Systems

Transaction processing systems are not "information systems." They may provide a major source of data for a **management information system (MIS).** MIS is *a system that organizes, summarizes, and presents information helpful to managers for making decisions.* Data processing, even to the extent of summarizing and reporting results of a series of transactions may not help in making some kinds of decisions, especially those involving strategy. Other data, perhaps collected from sources external to the organization, need to be included if useful information is to be provided to a manager. A management information system has the responsibility for collecting the right data and developing such information for management use and decision making. One type of management information system that we reviewed in Chapter 17 deals with materials requirements planning and scheduling. This system helps operations managers coordinate operating processes to minimize waste and maximize output. Another type of system is designed to help executives make decisions.

Executive Information System

A relatively recent innovation within MIS is the executive information system (EIS). An **executive information system** is *a computerized system that provides executives with easy access to internal and external information relevant to the factors they consider critical to organizational success.*[8] These systems are designed to provide top managers with key information necessary to keep up-to-date on critical organizational factors. The EIS can help executives track key indicators demonstrating how well the organization is operating. These indicators are often very industry specific.

They might include sales, sales per square foot, sales per employee, sales per product line, sales per division, monthly inventory costs, general and administrative costs, and similar information from internal sources. The EIS may also provide information on industry sales for different products to different market segments, recent industry cost data, and other such information. This may be available from specific companies designed to collect it or from an internal information department that collects and analyzes such data.

It is important to remember that these kinds of numbers, when they only indicate information for one or two time periods, are not valuable for making decisions. Numbers regarding internal and external performance indicators can only have value to executives as they track this data over time, creating SPC charts to note system capability and performance.

Managers may make serious mistakes basing decisions on short-term data. For example, in traditional management approaches, if sales drop one month, they want to find out what is wrong and who is to blame. TQM and statistical process control teaches us that a drop in sales in any one month might just be a common cause variation in the system and no one person is to blame.

Robert Kidder, CEO of Duracell, used his company's EIS to compare U.S. and European sales staff productivity over time. What he discovered was higher performance by the U.S. staff than the Europeans. Then, by exploring information also available from the EIS, he found that the German salespeople were calling on too many small stores that generated small revenues for the company. This information about the process of selling in Germany allowed Duracell to make an improvement by licensing distributors to service the small shops instead of having salespeople call on them.[9]

The EIS also has the function of gathering information for developing organizational strategy. It facilitates bringing together data on the environment, emerging technologies, the competition, company research and development, and other information gathered through data collected on the strengths, weaknesses, opportunities, and threats (SWOT) analysis we discussed in Chapter 7 on strategy. The EIS brings this information together in ways that allow managers to see relationships, develop scenarios, and figure out what strategic directions make the most sense for the company. Of course, the quality of these decisions is ultimately dependent on the quality of the data input into the system.

Information, Decisions, and Models

In the earlier sections of this chapter we referred to the importance of information in decision making at all organizational levels. Information about numerous aspects of a decision situation can provide the greatest advantage when it is considered in a orderly way. The tools that help in this process are often called Decision Support Systems (DSS). **Decision support systems** utilize *decision rules, decision models, a comprehensive database, and the decision maker's own insights in an interactive computer-based process to assist in making specific decisions.*[10] The DSS interacts with the MIS by applying specified mathematical and/or statistical operations to the information available in the MIS. These tools allow managers to evaluate the possible effects of alternative decisions in a more structured manner. Some tools are easy to use and understand. They have been employed as decision aids longer than computers have been available. Break-even analysis, for instance, is an example of a simple tool that might be included in a DSS. More complex models, such as multiple regression, time series analysis, and mathematical programming are commonly available.

Decision support systems Information systems that use decision rules, decision models, a comprehensive database, and the decision maker's own insights in an interactive computer-based process to assist in making specific decisions.

MIS-DSS in Practice

Landa, Inc. is the leading manufacturer of pressure washers in North America. In 1993, it had over $25 million in sales in the $300 million pressure washer business. Landa's customer, and thus Landa itself, are facing an increasingly restrictive set of regulations about waste water from all sources. For example, the owner of the do-it-yourself car wash must comply with federal, state and local regulations as to their discharge into either a sewer system or into a natural runoff. Landa developed a new product, the Water Maze, to clean the water before discharge. This brought about more sales, but it also brought a much more complex ordering, designing, manufacturing, installing, and servicing system.

To deal with this increased complexity, Landa put in place a concept called enterprise resource planning (ERP). ERP goes beyond the traditional focuses of a manufacturing organization support for manufacturing process and financial statements. Landa's ERP addresses all aspects including engineering, customer support and sales projecting. It is built with an ultimate customer service orientation, including quality, delivery, service, and price. The importance of the computerized MIS in this organization is summed up by CEO Larry Linton: "The things we're doing with ERP now are putting a foundation in place to keep up

A LOOK AT

TECHNOLOGY

THE LAPTOP AND THE SALESPERSON[11]

When the 20 salespeople from Nordstrom Valve, Inc. of Sulphur Springs, Texas, call on customers, they are far more productive than they used to be thanks to their laptop computers. Nordstrom manufactures valves used in the production, transportation, and distribution of oil and gas. Before the computers and the automation they have brought to the sales process, each call consumed far more time and resources than now. In an article in *Industry Week* magazine, Sheri Caudron describes the old way of doing things:

The company's 20 salespeople would visit with customers—who were most likely engineers—and gather data to help calculate the flow rate of the oil or gas distribution network. The salesperson would then cross-reference this information in product binders and perform a series of complex calculations to determine the types and sizes of valves needed. The salesperson's recommendations would then be sent to Nordstrom's engineers, who, when they got around to it, would verify the calculations and check to see that the recommended valve was the correct one for the customer's particular application.

Now, using laptop computers with special programs, Caudron explains the new way of selling:

While sitting with their customers, they instantaneously determine the appropriate valve for the project in question. After inputting all specifications, the computer performs the necessary calculations. This has shortened the time to design a valve system tenfold. The computerized system also provides printouts of the calculations so customers can check their accuracy after placing an order.

The amount of information needed to determine what would work best for a customer has not been reduced by this new system. What has been reduced is the amount of time and effort needed to gather and organize this information. Taking advantage of information technology thus allows the company to save time and money and serve its customers better. Everyone is a winner.

This same story is repeating itself in many industries. For example *Business Week* reports on the before and after laptop 200-person sales force of Ascom Timeplex, a manufacturer to telecommunications equipment:

Before "reengineering," sales reps would spend days getting quotes and proposals typed up and faxed to customers. "The salesperson was continually on the phone," says Peter Cammick, director of sales. Incoming orders triggered a paper chase that lasted as long as 10 days before manufacturing of a custom system could begin. Now, with laptop computers handling much of the process, price quotes are available in two hours, not two weeks. Orders have 25 percent fewer errors and take just four days to process.

In any transaction between salespeople and customers involving information, from identifying sales potential among potential customers to configuring products to their needs to processing orders, laptop computers can make the process go faster, smoother, and more beneficial for all parties. Exhibit 18-4 depicts the changes that have taken place with the introduction of the laptop to automate sales.

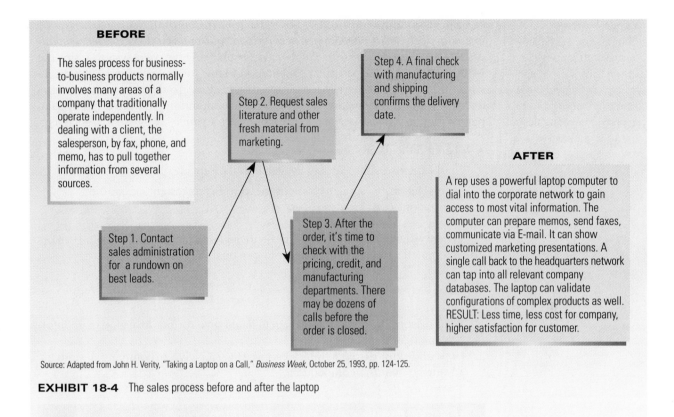

BEFORE

The sales process for business-to-business products normally involves many areas of a company that traditionally operate independently. In dealing with a client, the salesperson, by fax, phone, and memo, has to pull together information from several sources.

Step 1. Contact sales administration for a rundown on best leads.

Step 2. Request sales literature and other fresh material from marketing.

Step 3. After the order, it's time to check with the pricing, credit, and manufacturing departments. There may be dozens of calls before the order is closed.

Step 4. A final check with manufacturing and shipping confirms the delivery date.

AFTER

A rep uses a powerful laptop computer to dial into the corporate network to gain access to most vital information. The computer can prepare memos, send faxes, communicate via E-mail. It can show customized marketing presentations. A single call back to the headquarters network can tap into all relevant company databases. The laptop can validate configurations of complex products as well. RESULT: Less time, less cost for company, higher satisfaction for customer.

Source: Adapted from John H. Verity, "Taking a Laptop on a Call," *Business Week*, October 25, 1993, pp. 124-125.

EXHIBIT 18-4   The sales process before and after the laptop

Over the next few years, companies will literally be investing billions of dollars on this technology. If you plan a career in sales, and this is an entry level position in many different businesses, you should be prepared to work with laptops.

with the tremendous sales volume we anticipate in the future. The problem has been shifted from one of being able to access the data to knowing what to do with the data. It takes training at all levels of the organization. That's our challenge at Landa."[12]

MIS Extensions

Expert Systems and Artificial Intelligence are two extensions or enhancements to computer information systems. They might be considered variations on a DSS, since they do include decisions in their constructs, yet they vary from a traditional DSS in their use of models.

Artificial intelligence is *"the study of ideas which enable computers to do the things that make people seem intelligent."*[13] Artificial intelligence tries to make the computer emulate the human reasoning process by incorporating qualitative as well as quantitative information. It allows the user to inject "fuzzy" logic—or intuition—into the simulation model provided by the computer. These techniques have found business applications in robotics, and in designing expert systems.

Artificial intelligence The study of ideas which enable computers to do the things that make people seem intelligent.

Expert systems
Computerized programs designed to preserve and disseminate scarce expertise by encoding the relevant experience of an expert and making this experience available as a resource to the less experienced person.

Expert systems are used *"to preserve and disseminate scarce expertise by encoding the relevant experience of an expert and making this experience available as a resource to the less experienced person."*[14] The expert system stores the wisdom of experts for particular situations, and the computer provides the mechanism whereby a non-expert can access this wisdom. To develop such a system, the expert's decision-making process is evaluated and incorporated into a computer program. Expert systems are useful under a variety of situations, such as:

- When a difficult problem recurs regularly.
- When expertise is not widely available in the organization.
- When solutions to similar problems need to be consistent across the organization.

Expert systems have been used in financial audits, as an aid to help bankers make commercial loans, and to assist in personal financial planning.

 THINKING CRITICALLY

1. What reasons do you think managers might give for not investing in an information system?
2. How and why do you think a good MIS can give a company a strategic advantage over the competition?

MIS DEVELOPMENT AND IMPLEMENTATION

Different business situations call for different types of management information systems. The information needs of General Motors, for example, will be quite different from Ben and Jerry's Ice Cream, a comparatively smaller and more centralized organization. Factors such as size, variety of locations, and complexity of an organization will influence the type of system that will best meet management needs.

Management information systems that work successfully are the result of sound planning, design, programming, and implementation by systems developers.[15]

System Planning

Careful planning is a critical element in MIS development. The first step in planning is a thorough assessment of the organization's objectives with an emphasis on the system's role in helping the organization achieve those objectives. Without an initial assessment, managers run the risk of investing much time and money on a system that does not deliver what they want.

Management should ask itself questions, such as what they hope to achieve by implementing the MIS system, that is, what are the short-term and long-term objectives of the system. Determining system objectives up front will provide the criteria necessary to evaluate the system's effectiveness later on. Management also needs to consider how the system will help in planning, controlling, problem solving, and decision making. That is, how will the system help managers fulfill their responsibilities? Finally, management should compare the system's probable cost to its anticipated benefits. Are the anticipated benefits worth the investment?

Planning may be greatly simplified if the company chooses an off-the-shelf program. Several computer software packages are currently available costing much less than custom-designed programs for those who choose this approach. However, what many off-the-shelf systems offer in terms of convenience, they lose in fit to the organization's particular needs. For this reason, many company's choose to build customized information systems, particularly in larger and more complex organizations. However, the sophistication of off-the-shelf programs is growing, and it is likely in the future that organizations will use more such programs, many of which they can customize to their own use.

Whatever approach a company chooses, either off-the-shelf or customized systems, the first step must be a thorough needs assessment. This will ensure that the company avoids wasting time and money on a system that is too simple or too complex for their particular needs.

Conceptual Design

This phase of system development is similar the conceptual stage of a new automobile, in which sketches are drawn, prototypes are developed, and plans are made for how to proceed. Four sub-phases should take place at this stage of system development: development of performance specifications, systems analysis, feasibility analysis, and selection of a conceptual design from among the alternatives.

1. **Development of performance specifications.**   At this first phase, managers should specify what they expect to gain from the system. For example, are they looking for gross sales, sales by product line, by division, by salesperson? How do they want to track overhead? How might the system capture and organize customer complaints and compliments? When do they need this information, and how often and how quickly? How should it be available—in printouts or on-line or both? Should it construct charts and graphs to summarize information?

   In other words, what information are managers looking for to help them make decisions? What kind of information will give them the most realistic picture of their performance and what is going on in the marketplace? And how can it be presented in a manner that managers can find what they are looking for quickly and easily? Managers have to think about these issues and provide direction to designers. Skilled designers will also be able to give managers many ideas for how systems can deliver information, so this step is very much a collaborative process. Many times, managers will not be able to tell a designer every type of information they may need. New needs emerge over time, and systems will be refined and even completely redesigned to meet new information needs.

2. **Systems analysis.**   In this step, developers begin to figure out how a system might operate to deliver the information managers are looking for. If a system is already in place, they will do a detailed analysis of what data it takes in, the sources of that data, and what kinds of reports the system generates. The goal here is to look at inputs, processes, and outputs on the system in terms of management needs.

3. **Feasibility analysis.**   At this stage, developers begin to look at whether they can develop a system that will deliver what management wants, how

much it will cost, and what its features might be. It will likely include a cost/benefit analysis to determine how much return on investment the system will deliver.

4. **Selection of a design from among the alternatives developed.** Finally, developers present their ideas to management, and after reviewing various alternatives, they choose the one that is best suited to their needs and budget.

The next stage, detailed design, looks at how to most efficiently and effectively incorporate the goals of the conceptual design.

Detailed Design

At the detailed design stage, developers may first reassess information gathered in the planning stage, but in greater detail. They will begin to analyze objectives and cost/benefit tradeoffs more thoroughly. They will examine information needs of managers in detail and map out system capabilities for delivering this information. Developers will consider the type of reports the system should generate along with the capabilities the system should have to deliver this information.

Next, the developers will review the hardware, software, and database requirements of the system. A good question to ask here is, why look at database requirements? The reason is that much of the information that will be of interest to managers is data configured in particular ways. In the example we noted above for Duracell batteries salespeople, just the fact that sales figures per person were lower in Germany would not be enough to make a decision. Only when Robert Kidder had information about sales per call—two pieces of data combined into a single report—could he then make a decision. Database programs have the unique capability of, upon request, combining and relating different types of data into single reports that help managers gain a good picture of what is going on.

An important element of the database design includes how data is to be input, and the design of forms used to capture this data. One type of form is the standardized scansheet, often used for testing. Respondents fill in circles on the scansheet, which is then fed into a computer that records and tallies individual responses. Other ways to input data include barcodes of various types that are scanned using special windows or handheld readers.

Following the planning and design stages, comes programming stage, in which the design is turned into the software needed to achieve goals. This is a demanding, time-consuming and expensive process, but if the system delivers the goods, it is worth the investment. After programming comes the critical test—implementation.

Implementation

Implementation occurs when all of the earlier preparations are put into action. Often, organizations will need to train system users and identify one or several people who will be responsible for information monitoring and system maintenance. Organizations often designate chief information officers (CIO) to fill this position. Universities who operate mainframe computer systems often have similar positions as well as phone-in help lines.

MIS implementation requires continuous training in the use of the system as the needs of the organization change and technology improves.

System maintenance is an ongoing process. As time passes, unanticipated problems are likely to arise and will need to be addressed. Also, as the organization changes, so will its particular needs and the system should undergo similar changes to keep pace. Otherwise, the entire system will become obsolete. This is true for two reasons: changing needs and improving technology. As organizations make internal changes in terms of structure, personnel, and strategy, the information system needs to be updated to handle these changes. Also, with the increasing pace of technology improvement, organizations need to be aware of how this technology might help them. Indeed, besides the enhanced capabilities of new technology, it also is often less expensive, providing companies with the opportunity to lower costs by its use.

Necessary Precautions

As organizations profit from the benefits of information technology, they must be wary of potential risks associated with information technology. The vulnerability of an organization's information system to misuse or loss is of particular concern to managers. Security of databases from unauthorized access becomes more complex as the information system is more widely used—and access is required by more and more employees or managers. Procedural safeguards, such as limited access, passwords, and the routine back-up of data and applications, offer a first line of security. In addition, MIS personnel should be selected, trained, and monitored carefully.

Information Systems Problems

Sometimes, despite the best of intentions, information systems do not work as expected and managers fail to use them. Some reasons for this include lack of buy-in, lack of knowledge or understanding of the system, and fear of change.

These problems can be largely avoided, however, if managers take time to communicate the potential value of the system, listen for employee and staff concerns, and make sure everyone is properly trained in using the system.

Lack of Buy-in.   In previous chapters, we have emphasized the importance of empowerment and its role in company effectiveness and efficiency. Information systems are no different. Employees must be given an active role in the system development. Employees will be able to offer valuable insights and their participation will encourage commitment to the system.

Lack of knowledge.   By the same token, employee participation in development will ensure that they possess the requisite knowledge to use the system effectively. As system changes occur, employee skills must be updated as well through formal training.

Fear of change.   People are often fearful of what they do not understand, particularly when it comes to computers and technology. Fear can be minimized, however, if employees participate in development, are taught how to use the system properly, and are re-trained as system changes occur.

Another concern employees often have, and with good reason, is that technology will eventually encroach upon and eliminate the need for their jobs. While this has been true in some cases, managers can help by noting how technology can be beneficial. With the aid of technology, employees may perform at higher levels, thereby ensuring themselves an important place in the organization. Employees should also be encouraged to seek additional training and knowledge that will keep them current and in a strong competitive position.

? THINKING CRITICALLY

1. If you have bought a computer and software or are planning on it, explain how the four steps in the development of an MIS might help you in this purchase, appropriately modified for your purchasing process.
2. What are some of the precautions that organizations can take to see that sensitive information is available to only those who should have access? What are some of the issues or information that organizations may want to limit employee access to?
3. Why do you think some people resist using computers? How do you think you could overcome that resistance as a manager—both before and after the system is in place?

Network The connecting up by computer of employees throughout an organization, regardless of location, with each other, with internal information databases, with suppliers, with customers, and with outside sources of information.

THE INFORMATION NETWORKS REVOLUTION

Everything we have covered up to now in this chapter is really background on what traditional information systems are about. Now we are going to talk about the real impact of the new information technology and the revolution it is promoting in organizations across the country and across the world. There is one word that captures this revolution better than any other: **network.** Network, as used in communication technology, means *the connecting up by*

MIS AND TQM AT IBM

Raul Cosio is a Director of Manufacturing at the marketing and service unit of IBM Latin America. He writes about the use of MIS in the work he is involved with.

Management information systems play a central role in IBM's Total Quality Management system. Information systems are used to support complex business processes, including product development, manufacturing, and the customer order and delivery processes. Timely and accurate information is crucial to improving customer satisfaction through defect prevention and cycle time reduction. The following example typifies how information systems are an integral part of improvement at IBM.

Within the marketing and services business unit of IBM Latin America, there exists an organization responsible for product demand planning, scheduling, and distribution. Their mission is to support shipments from multiple IBM manufacturing plants around the world to the 17 countries in the Latin America market. As responsiveness to an order and on-time delivery contribute greatly to customer satisfaction, this organization continuously seeks ways of improving related business processes.

A key objective of this organization is to reduce the overall cycle time from when an order is placed through delivery and installation at a customer's location. Through MIS applications, which are part of IBM's Latin America Order Management and Distribution Systems, employee process improvement teams are able to monitor order status as well as the physical flows of products through the global distribution network.

The employee teams are responsible for defining cycle time objectives and a corresponding process improvement plan. The information provided by the MIS applications is used for identifying opportunities for process simplification, cycle time reduction, and defect prevention. In addition, the information allows for monitoring progress toward the defined objectives and for conducting root cause analysis of defects such as delays in delivery time.

All members of the team have the ability to access information throughout the supply and delivery chain. The analysis of this information may result in action to correct a delay and prevent dissatisfaction for a specific customer. Pareto Charts (see appendix to Chapter 18) are developed by teams for all products, which are then used to validate previously implemented process improvements or to identify new opportunities for improvement. As a result of this approach, cycle times were reduced by close to 30 percent from the prior year.

Timely and accurate information is essential to driving quality improvement. As such MIS will continue to be a critical success factor in achieving desired results throughout IBM.

A LOOK AT

MANAGERS IN ACTION

computer of employees throughout an organization, regardless of location, with each other, with internal information databases, with suppliers, with customers, and with outside sources of information.

These networks give everyone in an organization direct access to each other and to the information they need to do their work. They allow for daily inputs into databases from which managers, salespeople, engineers, or anyone can pull ideas for product improvements, new strategic direction, and, in general do their jobs in a more informed and efficient manner. They allow people to communicate with each other, sharing information and ideas to help the company meet its goals and respond to customers.

For the general public, there are CompuServe, America On Line, Prodigy, the Internet, and similar services that give anyone, for a small fee, access to information in virtually any field in which they have an interest and the ability to communicate with anyone else also on the system. Now imagine such services dedicated to delivering information of value to those on the job. That is what organizations of every size are now developing. And the installation of these systems is having profound effects on the way managers manage and employees work. Let's review some of the changes this technology has wrought.

Eliminating Hierarchies

We have stated throughout this book that the traditional command and control, chain of command, hierarchical style of managing is inefficient and incompatible with a systems view of organizations. Still, it has been around for a long time as middle managers acted as conduits and summarizers of information up and down the hierarchy. They preserved a certain orderliness to work and assumed responsibility for the performance of their employees. But they also slowed things down as information and messages passed through several pairs of hands on the way from senders to recipients. Networks make such work superfluous. These actions no longer add value in a networked organization.

Why is this?, you might ask. Consider this. In the days before networks, information was stored on paper documents in various filing cabinets throughout the organization. If employees needed information located in those files, they might check with their manager or supervisor, who gives them permission to get the file. Then they go to the file room and check it out, as if from the library, and take it back to their desk for use. Since this is the only copy of this information, it is important that someone take responsibility for where it is and who is using it—the middle manager. And the employee needs to be careful to return the information to the file cabinet from which it was taken. If employees need additional information, they either get it from other files or from their manager. Since there is no mechanism for querying other employees other than through memos or phone, both time-consuming activities, there is much less sharing of information or talking about problems, especially among employees in different locations.

With the introduction of networks, employees have direct access to the information they need without ever looking at a piece of paper or leaving their office to get permission. They can also check with others throughout the organization to gain additional information. As you can see, the middle manager's role as a kind of "middleman" in the distribution and coordination of information loses its utility.

In an article in *Fortune* magazine, Thomas Stewart writes, "Networks connect people to people and people to data. They allow information that once flowed through hierarchies—from me up to my boss and then hers, then down to your boss and to you—to pass directly between us. And, information being power, that can greatly hurry the process cutting slices from the old wedding-cake bureaucracy."[16] Melvyn E. Bernstein, president of Technology Solutions echoes this: "People who don't add value are going to be in trouble. If your job is just passing orders along, you could be lost in the shuffle.[17]

What happens via networks is that employees become empowered whether managers like it or not. They gain access to the information they need to do their jobs with a minimum amount of direction. Indeed, the system allows people to go directly to the person they need to talk to quickly without worrying about chain of command, which can get in the way of clear and quick communication.

Networks bring the people involved in a project or problem together regardless of their locations so they can share their expertise, information, and come to a consensus on-line. It lets those most directly involved deal with problems faster and more efficiently. In fact, Helen Runtagh, CEO of GE Information Services warns, "The worst of all worlds is clinging to hierarchical behavior while bringing in network-based communications. You are in for chaos, frustration, and poor financial results." She then goes on to say, "Communications in a network are absolutely incompatible with a strict, parochial hierarchy."[18]

TQM has always urged the dismantling of hierarchies, which interfere with the efficient operation of processes to deliver quality to customers. TQM organizations are characterized by, among other things, the establishment of cross-functional teams, empowered employees, open communication, and sharing of information. Networked information systems simply facilitate all this. They force managers to see that the old command and control approaches will not work in the networked organization and that to hang on to those approaches is a bad career move.

This does not mean that you will not find a traditional organization chart in networked organizations with their apparent hierarchies. However, what you will see is completely new roles for these managers as members of the teams that make things happen. They are coordinators and facilitators, not bosses. Being a boss suggests controlling information and doling it out, along with approval or disapproval, as he or she sees fit. When everyone has access to the information as needed, with nearly instantaneous feedback on the results of their actions, then the traditional boss role loses value and even undermines productivity.

Increased Productivity

A significant outcome of the new networks is increased productivity. This means that by using the new networked information technology, fewer employees taking less time and resources are doing the same work that in the past took more people more time with more resources.

Example: A few years ago Aetna Life & Casualty Company had 22 business centers with over 3,000 employees to process policy applications. It took about 15 days to do this processing, with about 60 different employees handling an application—checking, approving, passing on for more checking and approving until the process was completed. Now there are only 700 employees in four centers, and it takes only five days to process an application, with each application handled by a single employee. The secret: The work is all done by a representative using a PC networked to all the necessary databases, such as actuarial information, so the rep can gather all the information needed for quick approval.[19]

Example: At Lotus Development, the company uses its own bestselling Notes program (software that sets up electronic mail systems) to link up its programmers around the world so they have instantaneous access to each other's work. Now when the company releases an English language version of a product, it can have a Japanese language version available within three or four weeks. It used to take three or four months.[20]

Much of the waste in many processes comes from the time it takes for a piece of work to move through the pipeline from employee to employee, each of whom must do something to this work. Networks speed up how quickly work and the information needed to do the work flows through the pipeline and helps eliminate stops along the way, as the Aetna example shows.

Networks and Teamwork

Another component of TQM, which we have talked about at several points in this book, is teamwork. In today's fast-paced business environment, rapid response to the competition and quickly getting new products and services on the market is vital. This requires cross-functional cooperation and teamwork. Networking not only helps people work in teams, it literally creates teams on the spot as people dealing with the same or similar problem come together over the network to help one another. And for those employees working in teams on specific projects, the computer network keeps them in regular contact with one another, sharing information and progress as needed. Such communication helps team members reduce redundancy and deal with problems earlier than if they waited for regular meetings.

Networks and Dealing with Customers

Networks facilitate faster response to customer problems and needs. When a customer calls or a salesperson reports a customer problem, networks allow a single person to gain access to the information or person who can help solve that problem. At Hewlett-Packard, for example, when a customer calls with a technical problem, it is routed to one of four engineering hubs around the world, depending on the time of day—in this way customers have 24-hour access to help. As one group works on the problem, they enter data into the system keeping it constantly up to date about this problem and this customer. If they cannot solve the problem quickly, it is routed to the next office just starting their business day somewhere around the globe. They not only take care of the problem, they have information that will help them solve the same or similar problems from other customers and, indeed, make changes that will eliminate it in future product releases.[21]

Lotus Development receives more than 4 million calls a year from customers with questions and problems. Before networking, technical support reps collected and catalogued data for use by marketing and software development. However, this was a slow and irregular process. Now that the company is networked, the information goes directly into a database, filed under the appropriate category and is immediately available to anyone who needs it. Those noting certain kinds of problems brought up by this information spontaneously form cross-functional teams to help one another solve them. Why does this happen? When people have access to information about problems and who shares those problems, it is just natural to come together to work on them. In the old style hierarchical organization, such information is seldom available to all the people who could use it. Thus, responding to customer problems does not happen as quickly as it does in networked companies. And, indeed, a customer problem may not be solved at all because the company cannot find the right person to handle it.

Networks and Working with Suppliers

In Chapter 17 on page 663, we included a technology box on the use of networks in the apparel industry to deliver the right finished products to retailers when and where they want them. This technology is already in wide use in

STRATEGIC ADVANTAGE FROM CUSTOMER SERVICE INFORMATION[22]

TQM IN ACTION

Before Otis Elevator faced competitive pressures from Japanese elevator companies and independent service providers, it had local answering services take customer calls for repairs in each of 360 service centers. With the new competitors, Otis's management decided to make some changes. They developed the OtisLine center, which now fields about 1.2 million calls per year from customers with questions and problems about such things as broken escalators and stuck elevators.

When customer service representatives receive a call, they start by punching in to a computer console the customer's number, which immediately identifies the building that houses the Otis equipment and its repair history. Within minutes, an Otis repair person has been dispatched to the problem, informed by a radio dispatch received via a wireless data terminal. Responsive? Yes. But this is only part of the story.

After the repair person completes the job, he or she reports back a full summary of the problem and its correction. At that point, a full-time 20-member engineering team reviews that and similar problems to see if there is a pattern to the breakdowns. The goal is to use this information to help in the redesign of products or possibly change maintenance procedures. Using this approach, Maria Gallo, manager of Otis customer service center, says "We've seen dramatic reductions in callbacks and entrapments (stuck elevators)."

The same information, now stored and available on the computer information system, is used to plan weekly maintenance rounds by Otis mechanics. With the glut of office buildings, the demand for new elevators has dropped off, and Otis makes most of its revenue from maintenance services. This use of information systems to improve its service and maintenance work has resulted in more reliable products and higher levels of satisfied customers, helping Otis maintain its competitive edge in this market.

More and more companies like Otis are discovering that investing in sophisticated computers to capture and use customer service data can pay tremendous returns. In 1993, consultants at Computer Sciences Corporation found that 70 percent of 782 large U.S. and European companies indicated that customer service was the main focus of their investments in new technology. And all the large suppliers, Hewlett-Packard, Sun Microsystems, and IBM have important products for this market.

The idea is to able to collect, analyze, and use data derived from customer complaints, problems, and comments to continuously improve the quality of products and services offered to customers. Companies are finding that information taken from customer-service transactions can contribute to every part of the business. It can help hold down field-service costs, cultivate better relationships with customers, provide ideas for product development, and actually help produce new sources of revenue.

For example, Whirlpool Corporation now uses customer service information not just to find washer problems, but to help lower spare parts inventories (the company knows the areas in which problems are most likely to occur) and to drive harder bargains with its suppliers of various components. If a particular part seems to break down more than it should, Whirlpool can use that information to gain better warranties from the supplier of that part.

Information used this way simply allows companies to be more efficient and effective in achieving the purpose of delivering quality and value to customers. Many of them are also discovering that if they do not take advantage of this information, their competitors most assuredly will.

Scanning the bar codes on items as they are sold in this auto supply store triggers new orders for products from suppliers.

Electronic data interchange (EDI) Networked connections among companies and their supplers that allow for the instant transfer of information about current inventories and automatic placement of orders for new goods as needed.

many industries, including the clothing industry. *Networked connections among companies and their suppliers allow for the instant transfer of information about current inventories and automatic placement of orders for new goods as needed.* This type of network is called **electronic data interchange (EDI).** Wal-Mart uses this type of system to feed in information about sales of every item at every store via satellite to the company headquarters, which transfers this information to its suppliers in the form of orders. By this system, which Wal-Mart has perfected to a science, the company almost always has the right amount of an item on hand in its stores—and not more or less than it needs. This is a primary reason why Wal-Mart's prices are consistently low, and the company seldom offers special sales. It doesn't have to. It usually does not have excess inventory to move via clearance sales.[23]

John W. Fitzgerald, vice president of information services at McKesson Corporation, the U.S.'s largest distributor of health and beauty aid products, predicts that there will be systems that seamlessly connect customers, retailers, distributors, and manufacturers. Sales data, collected via scanners, will be transmitted from retailer to distributor to manufacturer, with automated ordering of replacement goods only as needed as if the entire group were one large system (which, in fact, they are). Fitzgerald says, "We're going to have a seamless network. It will be transparent to everybody, and all without paper." For many companies this is already happening. Strawbridge & Clothier, a Philadelphia retailer, has been eliminating suppliers not tied into its point-of-sale system. The reason: they can't compete in terms of price and delivery with those suppliers that are.[24]

All kinds of manufacturers are now bar coding parts, scanning them as used, which sends information back to suppliers, triggering new orders of those parts from suppliers. These systems are also working at completely eliminating paperwork, with all information transferred and stored electronically. *A Business Week* article reports on DuPont: "With about 5 percent of its suppliers, the chemical giant doesn't even bother with purchase orders. Outside vendors are linked electronically with DuPont's internal inventory system. When the suppliers see that DuPont is running short on an item, they simply deliver replacement goods."[25]

Networking and the Virtual Office

The **virtual office** is a term that suggests *people work as if they were all in a single office when they are spread about in many locations.* With networks, E-mail, fax machines, telephones, video conferencing, and centralized voice mail systems in place, "knowledge workers" can live anywhere. (Knowledge workers, as defined by Peter Drucker, are managers or employees who "do not produce a physical product—a ditch, a pair of shoes, a machine part. They produce knowledge, ideas, information. By themselves, these 'products' are useless. Somebody else, another person of knowledge, has to take them as his input and convert them into his output before they have any reality."[26]) Information networks are making everyone in the organization a knowledge worker.

In the past and still today, knowledge workers usually all congregate in a single location to do their work. This work consists of taking data and information and creating knowledge about customers, finance, marketing, and so on that will guide the organization's delivery of outputs customers will value. With networks in place, these employees no longer have to be all in one place. They can become **telecommuters,** suggesting employees who *work in the home or other remote locations and transmit and receive required data or information to and from other employees and locations.*

There is a trend underway for more and more people to work in this manner, coming to the central office only for special purposes. Such arrangements save the organization and individual employees time and money that would be taken up in office space, commuting, clothing, going out to lunch, and myriad other expenses necessary when employees and managers have to be all in one place. The full realization of telecommuting is probably a long way off, but you should not be surprised if someday you find yourself working as a telecommuter.

> **Virtual office** A term that describes people who work as if they were all in a single office when they are spread about in many locations.

> **Telecommuters** Employees who work in the home or other remote locations and transmit and receive required data or information to and from other employees and locations.

Some Management Implications of the Information Network

The networks linking employees, customers, suppliers, and information are not just tools to simplify managerial work. They are redefining what managers do and how they do it.

Create a Climate of Trust.   First of all a climate of trust becomes more important. Because the network inevitably flattens hierarchies and makes employees less dependent on their managers, organizations have to develop a culture where trust and responsibility are important values. When employees have equal access to information with top executives, managers have to trust that employees will use this information wisely. Building a culture of trust and responsibility means, basically, that managers must trust employees. When employees feel trusted, they behave in trustworthy ways. Further, management must make it clear that it expects people to take full advantage of these systems and provide training as appropriate.

Use the System.   Some top managers install networks and then never learn about or use them—leaving that to the rest of the employees. They do this because (1) they think technology is not really important to their decision making or (2) the organization will run itself once the technology is installed. Both of these are fallacies. In the first, if technology does not help, why invest all that money installing it? And in the second, if the organization will run itself, what does it need with top managers? So managers must learn it and use it to better understand what is going on in and outside the company and better drive the strategic and operational direction of the organization. Otherwise they will be out of the loop.

Encourage and Reward Teamwork.   Networks facilitate teamwork but do not guarantee the success of teams. Managers must encourage the use of teams. If people are networked together as teams using their mutual and individual skills and expertise to solve problems and work on projects, the reward structure needs to be set up to recognize these behaviors. People need acknowledgement for their successes as team members. Further, when individual members of cross-functional teams are recognized, it is important their department heads also get appropriate rewards. This reinforces the importance of encouraging employees to work with people from other parts of the organization.

? THINKING CRITICALLY

1. If you have used the network at your college or university, do you find that it facilitates communication and access to information more efficiently? How might easy access to information and people help you be a better student?
2. Explain in your own words, perhaps with personal experience, how you think a network helps break down hierarchies.
3. Can you imagine working in a virtual office? Would you like to be a telecommuter? Why or why not?

INFORMATION, TECHNOLOGY, AND TQM

The ideas we have been discussing about networks and the effect they have on organizations should sound familiar to you. Networks are making it easier for organizations to implement Total Quality Management. They make it easier for people to work together to execute organization processes. They help make processes operate more efficiently and effectively with less waste.

Eliminating Waste

Waste comes into processes when there is uncertainty and "sloppiness" in the system. This happens when different employees are not exactly sure what or when to expect inputs from those who precede them in a process or how their work affects others in the organization. In these situations, there is poor control of inventory, lots of uncompleted work-in-process, mistakes that require nonvalue-added rework to fix, and dissatisfaction among customers who do not get what they want when they want it.

BEAVER MEDICAL CENTER REENGINEERS ITSELF[27]

Beaver Medical Center in Beaver County, Pennsylvania serves patients in Aliquippa and nearby Youngstown, Ohio, both steel towns. Noting the demise of the steel industry in these areas due to lack of flexibility and slow response to customers, the center decided to learn from these mistakes. Robert N. Gibson, president of Beaver Medical Center hired Andersen Consulting to come in and make recommendations. He also took nurses, doctors, and administrators on a tour of a reorganized Westinghouse Electric plant, a company that practices TQM. After studying how the current system operates and gaining a better understanding of customer needs, the hospital is well into its $30 million makeover. Using information technology and computers, here are some of the changes they have instituted:

- Cellular phones and beepers connect doctors and nurses with the hospital's new computer and communication center.
- They have done away with nursing stations, bells, and droning loudspeakers. In their place, doctors and nurses have pagers that alert them when patients press a button. When help arrives an infrared eye detects their presence and turns on a color-coded light outside to indicate to others whether there is a nurse or technician inside.
- Procedures are immediately recorded on in-room terminals, which give doctors and nurses quick access to patient records.
- They have installed automatic drug dispensers that look like an automatic teller machine, to maintain better inventory control of drugs.

Besides the use of technology, the hospital has reorganized each ward into a kind of mini-hospital, with its own administration, pharmacy, lab, and X-Ray departments. These are staffed by multiskilled teams. The idea is to reduce the time it takes to deliver and coordinate action among care givers. In the traditional hospital, patients move from department to department, each with its own agenda and problems. This slows service and raises costs. Beaver Medical Center is not done yet. There are still more areas it needs to improve, but it has taken the first step down a road that will inevitably lead to a more efficient and effective system for delivering health care.

Another source of waste in many organizations is the processing and storing of paper documents. An important goal of information networks in many organizations is to minimize or even get rid of paper altogether. We already talked about electronic data interchanges, which is part of this drive to minimize paper. The idea is to use machines to take care of the mechanics of accessing and storing information and leaving to people the responsibility of making best use of that information. Again, as we have mentioned before, the idea is to let machines do what they can do best and let people do what they do best.

Aligning People and Processes

Ready access to information and the ability to link up all the parties in a process will makes systems operate much more efficiently and effectively. A primary responsibility of Total Quality Management is the alignment of all parts of a system to deliver the goods and services customers need, want, and will value. Technology, such as the materials requirements planning and scheduling programs we discussed in Chapter 17 in use at Tibor Machine Products, plays a role in this alignment. Information networks that allow point-of-sale data to move from retailer to wholesaler to manufacturer to raw materials supplier in a seamless flow also play an important role in this alignment. Giving employees access to internal and external databases further strengthens the alignment. Finally, the ability to share information and communicate with employees, customers, representatives of suppliers, and representatives of distributors also helps keep the system in alignment.

Continuous Improvement

An important part of TQM is making decisions based on facts, not guesswork. When managers and employees have facts readily available to them, they will make better decisions. Networked information systems help eliminate the uncertainties that encourage guesswork. However, they do not eliminate uncertainty. People, organizations, and the world are always changing. Uncertainty, thus, is a fact of life. However, organizations can either be swept along by change or help lead it. In the former circumstance, they are likely to be overwhelmed by change; in the latter they profit from it.

Quest for Excellence

Another important principle of TQM, continuous improvement, suggests that the best managers are constantly looking for how to get better, to be a leader in change. Again, information networks have a role to play here. Networks facilitate quick feedback on how satisfied customers are, what problems they are encountering, what the competition is doing, and allow for the more rapid dispersion of information to deal with different situations.

TQM also emphasizes training to help employees improve, and over the next decade or so, we will see more interactive, multimedia training materials that make it possible for employees to use computers to learn new skills and techniques. Training in this manner can take place at the manager or employee's convenience rather than bringing people to some central location. They may take the training individually or in groups as appropriate.

The growth of networks and information technology in general is not an accident. They add real value to systems, making them operate better. This growth affirms the assertion that we have made throughout this book about organizations being systems. Networks simply make it easier for people to work together.

If organizations were merely the sum of their parts, with the quality of outputs being the result of lots of individuals working hard to meet their individual goals, networks and information technology would play a far smaller role in organizations. However, organizations are not the just the sum of their parts, they are separate wholes, and the quality of outputs depends on *how well all the parts work together.* TQM recognizes this, and it forms the foundation of TQM's approach to managing. It also explains the explosion in information technology.

 THINKING CRITICALLY

1. Based on what you have read throughout this book, why do you think the development of information systems and networks are such a boon to the practice of Total Quality Management?
2. Would you say that the extensive investment in information networks affirms the systems view of organization? Why or why not?

SUMMARY

MANAGEMENT AND INFORMATION

- Managers require information to make the decisions necessary to build value into products.

- Not all information is useful. Information should be accurate, valuable, current, and frequent.

- Information needs are not the same for managers at different organizational levels.

INFORMATION SYSTEMS

- Information systems should add value to the organization's goods or services.

- Information systems transform data into information which can be used by managers and employees.

- Computers have improved our ability to process data dramatically.

- Management information systems (MIS) summarize and present information in a form that is helpful to managers.

- Expert systems and decision support systems can guide managers in specific instances modeling the decision situation.

- Expert systems contain the knowledge of experts and suggest courses of action the experts would take.

SYSTEM DEVELOPMENT AND IMPLEMENTATION

- System effectiveness will be determined largely by the actions that take place up front.

- While the steps that are taken will be shaped largely by the organization and its specific needs, system development should include planning, conceptual and specific design, and implementation.

- Following these steps will not guarantee that the system will work, but failing to do so will surely guarantee failure.

- Security precautions, such as limited access, passwords, and routing back-up, offer safeguards for the organization.

- Systems can fail if there is a lack of buy-in, lack of knowledge, or when employees are fearful of change.

THE INFORMATION NETWORKS REVOLUTION

- The installation of networks in organizations of all sizes is profoundly changing the way people work and managers manage.

- Networks hasten the elimination of hierarchies in organizations that add complexity but not value to getting work done.

- Networks make it easy for teams to form to solve short or long term problems and for formal and informal teams to work together.

- Networks facilitate gathering information about customers and responding more quickly to their needs.

- Networks help create a seamless bond between organizations, their suppliers, their distributors, and customers.
- Networks make employees working from any location nearly as efficient as those working in a home office.

INFORMATION, TECHNOLOGY, AND TQM

- Information systems and networks greatly contribute to the elimination of waste in processes brought about uncertainty, an important goal of TQM.
- Information systems facilitate the alignment of everyone in and out of the organization with its purpose of serving customers.
- Information systems contribute to an organization to better understand processes and work toward continuous improvement.

KEY TERMS

Artificial intelligence 687

Data 676

Decision support systems
 (DSS) 685

Electronic data interchange (EDI) 698

Executive information system 684

Expert systems 688

Information 676

Information subsystem 676

Management information system
 (MIS) 684

Network 692

Telecommuters 699

Virtual office 699

REVIEW QUESTIONS

1. Why is information so important for managers and how does useful information relate to customer value?
2. What are the characteristics that make information useful? Why is information with these characteristics useful?
3. What are the information needs of managers with different levels of responsibility in the organization?
4. What is the difference between data and information? Give an example of each.
5. Do you think information systems could ever replace human decision making entirely? Why or why not?
6. What are the stages that should be followed in developing an information system?
7. How do information networks help eliminate levels of management in an organization?
8. What is the relationship between information networks and increased productivity? Give an example of how networks enhance productivity.
9. What is a virtual office and how does networking make it possible?
10. How does a well-planned information system help eliminate waste in an organization?
11. What is the relationship between information systems and continuous improvement?

EXPERIENTIAL EXERCISES

Exercise 1.

Have the class reflect upon the types of information systems in place at your university. As a group, discuss the type of information communication that occurs between faculty and students, departments within the university, and with other universities or agencies, both domestic and international. Try to develop a list of the information systems that would be appropriate in each of these situations. For instance, video conferencing and fax transmissions can aid communication with other universities in the United States and abroad. Many professors routinely transmit data and information via Internet to their colleagues at other institutions. These are some of the possibilities that should come up. How might these information systems be different in the future and how could they be improved today.

Exercise 2.

In early March, 1993, a severe winter storm with record-breaking snow moved across the southeastern U.S. Strong winds accompanied the snow, causing widespread power outages and road and airport closings. Airplanes and crews were "snowed in" at some places, and others were "snowed out." Airports not directly affected by the weather could not risk getting equipment stuck in those that were. As the storm moved, some airports cleared and opened, others were closed down.

Define the information needed by operational managers to create new schedules for passengers, crews and aircraft to minimize the unavoidable disruptions. Could any reasonable solution be reached without a sophisticated, computerized information system.

CASE ANALYSIS AND APPLICATION
Calling All Customers: Ericsson Collects on the Cellular Market[28]

Ericsson is a Swedish telecommunications equipment maker founded in 1876. Since its inception, Ericsson's core product has been wire-based public phone network equipment; however, that is about to change. Lars Ramqvist, L.M. Ericsson's president, is positioning his company to take the lead in the booming cellular market. Ramqvist hopes to introduce his company into every aspect of the growing wireless market, from cordless office phones to entire cellular networks. And for the first time in its history, the primarily wire-based company is switching to cellular communication as its leading product.

Despite the booming cellular market, Ericsson's push into cellular technology is not an easy one. Ericsson has been squaring off against other cellular companies that are just as interested in the market. At the same time, sales two of Ericsson's product lines crashed, and it appeared that Ericsson would lose its biggest cellular customer to AT&T.

While all of this was going on, Ramqvist convinced hesitant directors to accept a 50 percent increase in the R&D budget. It was at that point that one of Ericsson's largest customers pulled out sending stock crashing. Against the advice of associates, Ramqvist persisted with his R&D drive. To help the company survive, he cut overhead and jobs, and cut the number of factories by one half.

Ramqvist's gamble paid off. If he had taken the advice of others to cut R&D, Chief Financial Officer Carl Wilhelm Ros predicted that the company would soon be out of business. Instead, Ericsson is expanding into new markets in Canada, Taiwan, and Japan. Ericsson has beat out competitors like Motorola and Finland's Nokia by developing a hand-held cellular phone that weighs in at 12 ounces less than the closest competitor. Before long, Ramqvist anticipates phone sales to double to $650 million.

Ramqvist is also thinking strategically. Ericsson is taking aim at the general public by making cellular phones available at prices that would be affordable for everyone. If successful, Ericsson would cash in on a market that would quintuple from its current 22 million subscribers by the end of the century.

Now is not the time to rest, however. Market researchers predict that cellular growth will stall by 1996. Ericsson already has plans to drive forward into multimedia switches, an area where it has been lagging thus far. By looking forward and positioning itself today, Ericsson should be prepared to face what comes its way tomorrow.

Discussion Questions

1. If Ericsson wanted to expand its stake in the information technology market, what are some other products that they, as a high-tech company might be able to work on?
2. What parallels do you see between Ramqvist's actions and TQM's philosophy of continuous improvement?

VIDEO CASE: COMBINING QUALITY MANAGEMENT AND SOCIAL RESPONSIBILITY
Louis Krouse

Nearly 25 percent of Americans today do not have bank accounts. In low-income neighborhoods, the rate can approach 60 percent. For these citizens, paying the monthly utility bill can mean the purchase of expensive money orders month after month, or bus treks across town to pay bills in person. Moreover, because low-income people often must pay their bills at the last minute, it is not uncommon for their phone or electric service to be cut off—later requiring expensive charges to restore service.

This pervasive problem troubled Louis Krouse, a long-time employee and management trouble-shooter for New York Telephone. As an expert in electronic information systems, Krouse saw great potential in devising an electronic funds transfer system to meet the payment needs of low-income people. Risking his job security, his entire savings, and all the credit card debt he could muster, Krouse left NYNEX to found National Payments Network (now known as Easy Pay). Krouse's unique system provides rapid, convenient, and inexpensive bill processing—all at no cost to the consumer. Consumers pay their utility bills with cash directly to merchants in their neighborhoods. The money is then electronically transferred to the utility company, allowing consumers' accounts to be credited within a day and utilities to receive payments within four days. In exchange for this administrative convenience, utilities pay between 45 and 55 cents per transaction, of which retailers receive 10 to 30 cents, depending upon their volume.

This elegant system benefits everyone: customers pay bills easily, without writing checks and without any transaction fees. Retailers earn transaction fees and attract a large number of potential customers to their stores. Utilities gain interest otherwise lost in delayed transactions, as well as fewer service cutoffs due to late payments.

Within three years the system was handling over 4 million transactions per month, and reaping annual revenues in excess of $26 million. Western Union purchased the entire business in July 1989 for nearly $30 million. This spectacular growth demonstrates the potential social and financial rewards of serving traditionally underserved low-income consumers in creative new ways.

Video Case Questions

1. Describe the information system that Louis Krouse devised and explain how it was integrated into the operations of other companies.
2. Discuss the dimensions of customer value that were improved by Krouse's information system.

Chapter 18 Appendix

TQM TOOLS FOR GATHERING AND CONVEYING INFORMATION

An important part of Total Quality Management is making decisions based on sound facts and information. TQM recognizes that any decision is going to have repercussions throughout the system and that decisions should, therefore, be based on a clear understanding of how the system is working internally, and in relations with its supplers and customers. Deming and other proponents of TQM recognize the critical nature of information in delivering value to customers. TQM has developed a number of tools to assist managers in gathering data and information for use in making decisions that will affect organizational systems positively. In this appendix, we will review some of the information-gathering tools that are commonly associated with TQM.

TQM has developed several tools for gathering information that will help individual managers and teams to understand situations and make better decisions. Though many of these tools are fairly simple, their use can yield big dividends by helping managers and team members gather, understand, and visualize organizational processes and their results. They facilitate collecting data and information in an orderly fashion and have proven themselves over time. Some, such as checksheets, have been around for a long time, but managers have often not appreciated their full value. These tools are usually used in conjunction with each other to develop information that will help managers pinpoint problems and propose solutions. The goal in their use is to eliminate guesswork as much as is possible and to gain a *realistic* picture of how well or poorly the organization's processes are functioning.

Sometimes managers have thought that if they start using these tools, that is the solution to all their problems. They cannot help but improve. While these tools are valuable, they work best only when managers have fully appreciated the systems view of their organization and focus on developing a strategy for improving the system's ability to deliver value to customers. What follows is only a sampling of tools available to managers. The four tools discussed below are meant to give you a flavor of how managers practicing TQM go about collecting specific types of data and analyzing it to make sound decisions.

The basic tools of quality improvement reviewed are: (1) flow charts, (2) cause-and-effect diagrams (which we introduced in Chapter 3), (3) checksheets, and (4) Pareto charts. Another important tool is the statistical control chart (which we discussed in Chapter 16). By using these tools, managers can gain powerful insights into how their companies operate and substantially upgrade the quality of their decision making.

Flow Charts

Flow chart A chart that provides a picture of all the steps in a process or sequence of events.

A **flow chart** provides *a picture of all the steps in a process or sequence of events*. For example, the flow chart in Exhibit 18A-1 shows the steps for changing oil in a car. This is a simple chart of a simple process. The charts for many business processes, especially those in manufacturing are often much more complex. However, this one works well to convey what the charts are like.

The flow chart is useful for making sure that a manager or the members of a team understand the steps of a particular process that might be either part of a problem or be affected by a problem or opportunity. Flow charts are also helpful

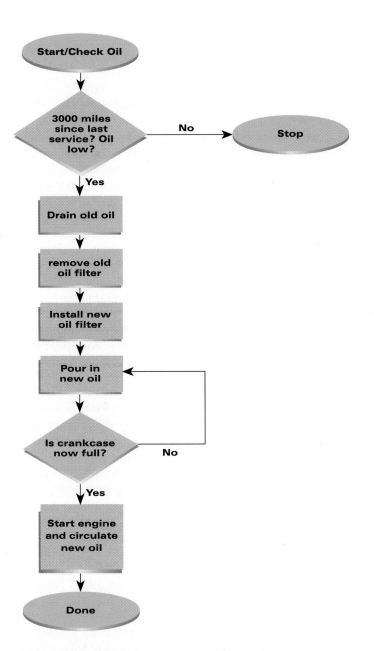

EXHIBIT 18A-1
A simple flow chart showing the
steps in changing oil in a car

for understanding a process in the first place. One of the goals of continuous improvement is to make sure processes work as efficiently as possible. To do so, we first determine the steps we are dealing with.

Steps for Constructing a Flow Chart.   The first step in constructing a flow chart is to define the boundaries of the process. The boundaries of the flow chart in Exhibit 18A-1 start with checking the oil, end with starting the engine to circulate the new oil, and the chart follows the process through each step. Once managers determine the boundaries, they can construct a flow chart in many different ways. A popular way is to use an oval to indicate the starting and stopping positions, a rectangle to indicate a process step, a diamond to indicate a decision point, and a line to indicate the flow or sequence of these activities (as in Exhibit 18A-1). There should be only one output arrow out of a process step and at least two options out of a decision diamond.

Use of Flow Charts.   Managers and teams use flow charts in many ways. For example, they may be a first step for the members of a team to collectively document their understanding or beliefs about a process. The chart ensures that everyone has a common understanding. In some cases there may be disagreements. These can be cleared up when the team goes out and verifies the actual process by seeing first hand what the flow of steps in the process really is. For example, managers are often surprised at the number of rework loops a product has to go through to finally meet product specifications. The rework step in Exhibit 18A-1 checks to see whether the crankcase is full and says to add more oil if it is not. Rework wastes time and resources, and figuring out how to eliminate problems associated with rework is one area about which managers must make decisions. Flow charts help managers gather information about processes so they can learn where rework steps are.

Creating an ideal process to compare with an actual process is another use of flow charts. This comparison reveals opportunities for improvement by eliminating wasteful steps and revamping the process to be more like the ideal flow. Managers can also use the flow chart to identify places in the process where measurements of quality or productivity might be taken.

Cause-and-Effect Diagrams

Cause-and-effect diagram
A pictorial technique that managers use to help them identify problems or their causes and how they might be dealt with.

We introduced cause-and-effect diagrams in Chapter 3. The **cause-and-effect diagram** is another *pictorial technique that managers use to help them identify problems or their causes and how they might be dealt with*. Kaoru Ishikawa, a Japanese quality control pioneer, developed this diagram, called an "Ishikawa" or fishbone diagram (the latter because of its appearance). Managers use the cause-and-effect diagram to represent the relationship between some effect and all the possible causes that influence it. The cause-and-effect diagram in Exhibit 18A-2 illustrates how the effect, hard cookies, results from a combination of various causes having to do with ingredients, methods, understanding of baking, and other related problems.

Steps for Constructing a Cause-and-Effect Diagram.   After clearly defining the effect or problem, the potential causes may be generated through brainstorming or through observation of events leading up to the effect. First, place the effect on the main arrow, or the spine of the fishbone. Next, group the major possible causes into such categories as materials (or raw materials), machines (any kind of equipment or tools), method (techniques and steps), and manpower (human resources). These are not the only major causes, but they are common categories for many different problems. Each of these groups forms a branch of the main arrow. Onto each of these branches, write in the detailed causes like twigs on a branch. These causes should answer the question "Why did this happen?" Include as many twigs as possible. As managers or team members develop more knowledge about cause-and-effect relationships, they can record these on the chart, so that it evolves over time. The diagram in Exhibit 18A-2 records answers to these questions:

1. How did the cooking methods contribute to hard cookies? They were cooked for too long. The ingredients were improperly blended because no electric mixer was available.

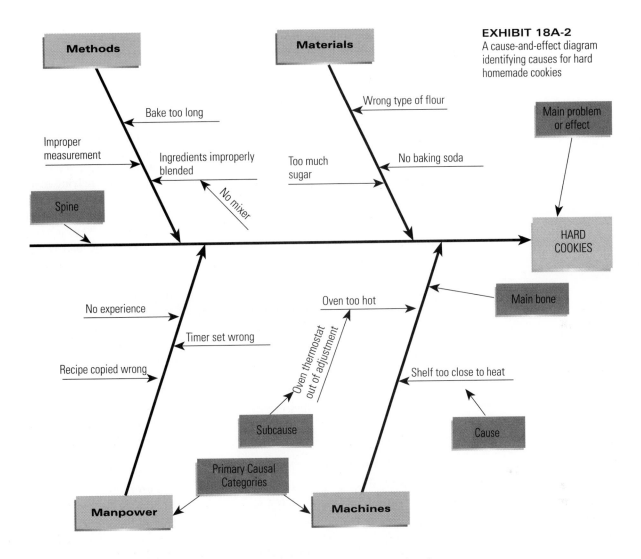

EXHIBIT 18A-2
A cause-and-effect diagram identifying causes for hard homemade cookies

2. How did the oven contribute to the problem? The oven was too hot because the thermostat was not in proper adjustment. The oven shelf was too close to the heat source.
3. How did the person doing the work contribute to the problem? He copied the recipe incorrectly and had little cooking experience.
4. How did materials used help cause the problem? The person used too much sugar, the wrong type of flour, and forgot baking soda.

All of these causes contributed to the problem. In developing this kind of chart and examining the various causes, we can sometimes (but not always) get at a root cause to which all other causes are related. In this case, the inexperience of a cook has much to do with all other aspects of the problem. This suggests training would be appropriate to eliminate this problem in the future.

Uses of the Cause-and-Effect Diagram.   The cause-and-effect diagram captures the knowledge of a manager or managers or a team and puts it into a form that is easily communicated and understood. It can help managers or a team decide where to focus their investigative efforts. And it serves as a means of documenting the knowledge that people develop about cause-and-effect relationships. When problems arise in the future, it is a source of information about how to resolve the problem.

Checksheets

Checksheets A document used to record the measurements or counts of actual events.

The techniques discussed so far may be used to document the opinions of team members or factual knowledge. **Checksheets,** however, are used only *to record the measurements or counts of actual events.* The checksheet provides a format for a manager or worker to record observations by simply checking or tallying marks on a special form. For example, the checksheet shown in Exhibit 18A-3 was used to record the types of problems a small car repair shop dealt with during one week.

Steps for Constructing a Checksheet. The steps for constructing a checksheet vary with its purpose. In general, the team should agree on the event being observed. The people collecting the data should be looking for the same things. The checksheet should specify the time period during which the data were collected so it can be used to analyze possible causes during that specific time period. The checksheet should be usable, easy to understand, and contain enough space to enter the data.

Uses of Checksheets. A checksheet can be used for a number of purposes. Some popular applications are:
- Keep counts of events of various types.
- Record measures of production process outcomes, like the length of a shaft after a grinding operation.
- Record the types of defects.
- Record the location of defects on a product with a sketch of the product used as a checksheet.
- Record suspected causes of defects.

EXHIBIT 18A-3
An example of a checksheet to collect data for later analysis

Car Repairs Problems Checksheet

PROBLEMS	MON	TUES	WED	THUR	FRI	TOTALS
Clutch Slippage	I	II	I	III	III	9
Brakes	IIII IIII I	IIII III	IIII IIII III	IIII IIII II	IIII IIII	54
Radiator Leaks	II	II	III	II	—	9
Faulty Fuel Injectors	II	I	III	I	I	8
Air Conditioner Problems	I	—	II	IIII	III	10
Alignment	—	I	II	I	II	6
Oil Leaks	IIII III	IIII IIII I	IIII II	IIII III	IIII	39
Other	I	—	II	II	—	5

YARD & SHOP
DAMAGE REPORT

VIN

Date _____
Reported by _____
Port _____

DAMAGE DISCOVERY
(Place an "X" in Appropriate Box)

FOUND AT: FP   CW   SH ____   CA   LL   OT _____

FPR   CAR WASH   SHOP (LIST) FCA   LOAD LINES   OTHER (LIST)

EXTERIOR   INTERIOR

DAMAGE DESCRIPTION

NO.	DAMAGED PART	CONDITION	NO.	DAMAGED PART	CONDITION	NO.	DAMAGED PART	CONDITION	NO.
01	Left Fender		09	Hood		17	Glass		25
02	Right Fender		10	Roof		18	Mldg's. Finish Panels		26
03	Left Front Door		11	Deck Lid		19	Wheels, Tires		27
04	Right Front Door		12	Front Bumper		20	Seats, Carpet, Dash		28
05	Left Rear Door		13	Rear Bumper		21	Interior Trim Panels		29
06	Right Rear Door		14	Truck Bed-Left		22	Engine Compartment		30
07	Left Quarter Panel		15	Truck Bed-Right		23	Luggage Area		31
08	Right Rear Quarter Panel		16	Tailgate		24	Other		32

CONDITION CODES: DT = Dent, SC = Scratched,   PC = Chipped,   SN= Stained, Soiled, CR = Cracked, Broken, OT = Other
(Record code along Damaged Part)

YD   SH   BW   RR

CLASS: YARD   SHOP   SEVERITY: BTU/WPO   REP/REF

DAMAGE CAUSE

PROBABLE   IN   CW   PI   VM   VS   OP   EQ   UK
CAUSE
                INCOMING CAR   PIO   VEHICLE   VEHICLE   OPERATOR EQUIPMENT UNKNOWN
                          WASH   INSTL.   MOVEMENT STAGING

INVESTIGATION: _____

COUNTER MEASURE: _____

OPERATIONS MANAGER SIGNATURE: _____

EXHIBIT 18A-4   Toyota's Damage Report Form

Exhibit 18A-4 shows the elaborate Yard and Shop Damage Report used by Toyota. It combines several variations of a checksheet on one form to describe vehicle damage, where the damage occurred, and the probable cause of damage.

Pareto Charts

A **Pareto Chart** is a way *to graphically depict data in terms of the frequency of occurrence of various types of events*. The term Pareto originated with a 19th century Italian economist, Vilfredo Pareto, who noticed that 80 percent of the

Pareto Chart A chart that depicts data in terms of the frequency of occurrence of various types of events.

Pareto Principle A principle which states that 20 percent of the elements involved in any situation cause 80 percent of the effects.

wealth in a region was concentrated in less than 20 percent of the population. Dr. Joseph Juran later formulated what he called the **Pareto Principle,** which states that *20 percent of the elements involved in any situation cause 80 percent of the effects*. This is sometimes called the "80-20 rule." Juran called the 20 percent of elements that cause most effects, the "vital few" and the 80 percent of elements to which 20 percent of effects could be attributed, the "trivial many."[1] While the breakdown when doing a Pareto analysis is not always 80-20, you will generally find that a majority of effects are due to a minority of causes.

Steps for Constructing a Pareto Chart. A Pareto Chart takes the form of a vertical or horizontal bar graph. A Pareto Chart like that shown in exhibit 18A-5 can be constructed from information gathered through a checksheet, or by some other means, such as automated data collection. In this case, we show the results of the data collected on the checksheet for an auto repair shop. This Pareto Chart was constructed by converting each count of repairs to a percentage with each representing different car problems. Cumulative percentages are drawn above showing how much each category contributes to the total. In this case, brake problems and oil leaks are the two main problems the shop dealt with during that week, making up 67 percent of all the problems. These figures can help a shop manager better prepare for handling the most common problems by stocking more parts to deal with brake repairs and oil leaks.

Uses of Pareto Charts. Managers can use the Pareto Chart, for example, to graphically illustrate where most problems reside, what types of products are most frequently ordered, or what types of injuries occur most often on the job. Basically, it can be used to track any type of activity or events for frequency. Managers usually employ the Pareto Chart to determine what problems or activities deserve attention. The Pareto Principle would advise managers to deal with those situations that either cause the vital few problems or present significant opportunities. In general, managers gain more by first attacking the tallest bars in the Pareto

EXHIBIT 18A-5
An example of a Pareto Chart

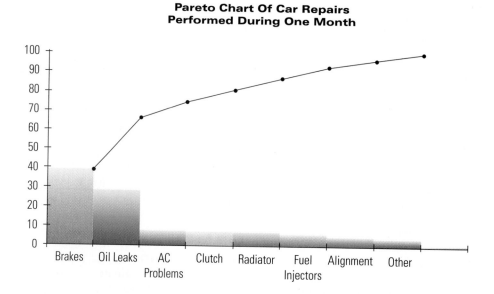

**Pareto Chart Of Car Repairs
Performed During One Month**

Chart. This may not always be true, however, the smallest bar may occur less frequently but be the most costly to the manager if it represents a catastrophic event. For example, infrequent failure of the brakes on a new car can be much more costly than frequent failure of an interior dome light.

Toyota used Pareto Charts to keep track of defects on automobiles coming off their assembly line and discovered that three of the top four categories of initial quality problems for a new car were exterior paint/molding, interior defects, and body defects. Toyota learned that quality problems like these often occur during the delivery of the vehicle to the dealer. This finding prompted Toyota to initiate a Delivery Quality Improvement program to reduce defects caused during vehicle delivery.

SHOP FLOOR MANAGEMENT AT NISSAN

In 1989 Nissan Motor Manufacturing Corporation, USA announced the launch of a new automobile called the Altima, a four door passenger car that would compete in the lower middle class of the U.S. automobile market. Producing the Altima would require some capital investments and an additional 2000 employees at the Smyrna, Tennessee facility. When the new project was initiated, NMMC management had two major concerns:

1. Maintaining the superior levels of quality that had been achieved on the Sentra and truck models built by the company since 1983, and

2. Improving quality levels to meet and exceed the ever increasing quality demands of the American car consumer.

To address these concerns, NMMC launched a campaign that it calls Shop Floor Management, or Genba Kanri in Japanese. Shop Floor Management not only enables NMMC to maintain existing levels of quality, it enables the company to continuously improve quality. As a result, the Altima, Sentra and truck models built at the plant in Smyrna, Tennessee are among the highest quality automobiles in their class.

NMMC's Shop Floor Management program involves everyone at NMMC and continues to grow and expand. The key to Shop Floor Management is to identify the causes of problems and install countermeasures to eliminate them forever. Some of the major elements of Shop Floor Management are listed below.

- **QCDS Tracking.** A measurement and tracking system focused on key business outcomes, including Quality, Cost, Delivery, and Safety (QCDS).

- **Extensive Training.** Starting with management, everyone at NMMC was trained in areas such as problem solving (Plan, Do, Check, Act cycle), interpersonal skills, group dynamics, industrial engineering, and ergonomics.

- **Daily Activities.** Area managers and inspectors observe the operations and perform quality checks during the day to monitor quality and adherence to work standards. They also conduct audits to assess cleanliness and orderliness.

- **Off-Line Vehicle Evaluation System (VES).** Finished vehicles are taken to a specially constructed booth with flourescent lighting and rigorously inspected for surface quality, adherence to dimensional standards, and weld integrity. Data provides input for immediate countermeasures and for monitoring trends over time.

- **Quick Response Quality Control (QRQC).** Every morning area management teams assemble to discuss quality concerns revealed by Off-Line VES and to propose counter-

measures. Additional meetings are held later in the day to assess progress on countermeasures. Each week the NMMC executives meet to discuss the countermeasures and address other quality concerns.

- **IMProvement ACTivity (IMPACT).** At the heart of the Shop Floor Management program is NMMC's version of kaizen called Improvement Activity (IMPACT). An IMPACT is a group effort focused on one operation or process to achieve immediate improvements. IMPACTs are targeted at improving measures on the QCDS tracking system. Consider the following example of an IMPACT.

In one area in the plant, management selected the "sill outer" assembly operation as a target for a two-day IMPACT. A "sill outer" is the external body panel directly below the door on a passenger car. The IMPACT was led by an industrial engineer and the IMPACT team consisted of two maintenance engineers, a day shift and night shift technician, a representative from material handling and the area manager. The leader began the first day with a quick description of the IMPACT process and a review of the general comments for IMPACTs which are

The authors thank Nissan Motor Manufacturing Corporation and particularly Vince Sorgi, Frank Gallina, and Mike Steck, for contributing time and resources to this case. We also thank Bob Wilson for contributing to the development of this case.

GENERAL COMMENTS FOR IMPACTS

SEVEN COMMON WASTES IN MANUFACTURING
1) OVER PRODUCTION
2) WAIT TIME (FOR MATERIAL OR MACHINE)
3) UNNECESSARY TRANSPORTATION (PARTS HANDLING)
4) UNNECESSARY OPERATION
5) UNNECESSARY STOCK (SPACE)
6) UNNECESSARY MOTION
7) WORK CAUSED BY DEFECTS

RULES OF MOTION ECONOMY
1) REDUCE THE NUMBER OF MOTIONS
2) PERFORM MOTIONS SIMULTANEOUSLY
3) SHORTEN DISTANCES
4) MAKE MOTIONS EASIER

ITEMS TO CONSIDER
1) MAN
2) MACHINE
3) MATERIAL
4) METHOD

REMEMBER TO ASK THE QUESTION: "WHY?"

FIGURE 1

listed in Figure 1. Next the IMPACT team went out to observe the operations and identify concerns. Then they regrouped and brainstormed on the concerns to develop an extensive list of problems in the sill outer assembly operation.

After brainstorming on the concerns, the group returned to the operation to collect data through pace analysis, work sampling, walk pattern analysis, and ergonomic analysis. These analysis techniques give the IMPACT team an idea of how long the operation takes, the number of steps the technician must take, the layout of the operation, and the distribution of the technicians activities. After data collection, the impact team prioritized their concerns and set targets and goals for the IMPACT. The team then developed countermeasures to address each concern and assigned people to initiate the countermeasures. For instance, putting a repeat trigger on one of the welding guns was assigned to the maintenance engineer. The remainder of the first day was spent preparing for countermeasure implementation and communicating to the night shift the IMPACT events. For example, the team had to write work orders and line up maintenance workers to assist with the changes. Some of the changes in the sill outer operation were actually initiated on the afternoon of day one.

The leader began day two by meeting with the night shift area personnel to discuss the IMPACT activities and gather their feedback. Next the leader and the day shift area manager met with day shift personnel to discuss night shift feedback and plans for additional countermeasures during the day.

After all immediate countermeasures were implemented, the team collected data again to assess the impact of the countermeasures. Standard operation sheets were updated to reflect the new procedures. New concerns were listed along with possible countermeasures. Costs and savings were tallied for the IMPACT using the QCDS tracking system. Finally, the IMPACT team presented the results to the top managers of the plant.

Currently, NMMC conducts 50 of these two-day IMPACTs per month. During the early stages of the IMPACT program, management became concerned about the success of these efforts.

IMPACTs were initially accepted with skepticism because early IMPACTs were stand-alone projects lacking the collective support of all other shop floor management programs. However, since it has been combined with NMMC's overall approach to Shop floor management, the IMPACT has been well received by almost everyone in the plant. NMMC employees are directly involved in the IMPACTs along with managers and engineers. Working together, the IMPACT team follows through to implement countermeasures. It has proven quite useful in achieving employee involvement and continuous improvement in Quality, Costs, Delivery and Safety.

? CASE QUESTIONS

1. How does shop floor management attack each of the seven common wastes in manufacturing?

2. Explain how each these seven common wastes might be found in other organizational activities (besides manufacturing) such as administration and the provision of services.

3. Write a list of principles that you think explain why Shop Floor Management is successful at Nissan.

4. Make suggestions for improving Nissan's approach to Shop Floor Management based on what you learned from Chapters 16, 17, and 18.

ENDNOTES

CHAPTER 1

1. Paul Froiland, "Quality in a Box," *Training,* February, 1994, pp. 62–66.
2. Henri Fayol, *General and Industrial Management* (New York: Pitman, 1949).
3. Henry Mintzberg, "The Manager's Job: Folklore and Fact," *Harvard Business Review*, 53 (4) 1975, pp. 49–61.
4. Henry Mintzberg, "Structured Observation as a Method of Studying Managerial Work," 1970, *Journal of Management Studies*, (7) pp. 87–104; *The Nature of Managerial Work* (New York: Harper & Row, 1973); "The Manager's Job: Folklore and Fact," *Harvard Business Review*, 53 (4) pp. 49–61.
5. Michael Porter, "Capital Disadvantage: America's Failing Capital Investment System," *Harvard Business Review*, September–October 1992, pp. 65–83.
6. W. Band, *Creating Value for Customers: Designing and Implementing a Total Corporate Strategy* (New York: John Wiley and Sons, 1991).
7. G.M. Bounds and G.H. Dobbins, "The Manager's Job: A Paradigm Shift to a New Agenda," in M.J. Stahl and G.M. Bounds (Eds.), *Competing Globally Through Customer Value* (Westport, CT: Quorum Books, 1991) pp. 117–145.
8. John H. Sheridan, "Jack Croushore: From Tough Guy to 'Cream Puff,'" *Industry Week*, December 6, 1993, pp. 11–16.
9. Peter M. Senge, *The Fifth Discipline: The Art and Practice of the Learning Organization* (New York: Doubleday Currency, 1990) p. 68.
10. W. Edwards Deming, from the Foreword to the book, John O. Whitney, *The Trust Factor* (New York: McGraw-Hill, Inc., 1994), pp. vii–viii.
11. Peter F. Drucker, *Management: Tasks, Responsibilities, Practices* (New York: Harper & Row, Publishers, Inc., 1973) p. 45.
12. Drucker (1973) pp. 60 and 61.
13. Armand V. Feigenbaum, *Total Quality Control, Third Edition, Revised* (New York: McGraw-Hill, Inc., 1991) p. 7.
14. William H. Miller, "Boeing Gives Credence to Clearwater's Revival," *Industry Week*, January 17, 1994, pp. 40–42.
15. For more on this point, see Tim Smart, et al., "GE's Brave New World," *Business Week,* November 8, 1993, pp. 64–70.
16. Many of the points in this section adapted from Andrew W. Singer, "Can a Company Be Too Ethical?" *Across the Board*, April 1993, pp. 17–22.
17. For more on this idea, see Bill Roth, "Is It Quality Improves Ethics or Ethics Improves Quality?" *Journal or Quality and Participation*, September, 1993, pp. 6–9.
18. Howard Gleckman, et al., "The Technology Payoff," *Business Week*, June 14, 1993, pp. 56–68.
19. The examples in this section taken from Michelle Galen, et al., "Work and Family," *Business Week*, June 28, 1993, pp. 80–88.
20. Information for this section came from Michele Galen "White, Male, and Worried," *Business Week*, January 31, 1994, pp. 50–55 and Cresencio Torres, and Mary Bruxelles, "Capitalizing on Global Diversity," *HRMagazine*, December 1992, pp. 30–33 and Michele Galen, et al., "Work and Family," *Business Week*, June 28, 1993, pp. 80–88.
21. G. Bounds, L. Yorks, M. Adams, and G. Ranney, *Beyond Total Quality Management* (New York: McGraw-Hill, Inc., 1994).
22. Catherine Ramano, "Report Card on TQM," *Management Review*, January 1994, p. 22.
23. Froiland, *Training*, February 1994.

CHAPTER 2

1. David T. Kearns and David A. Nadler, *Prophets in the Dark* (New York: HarperBusiness, 1992) pp. 121–122.
2. M.J. Stahl and G.M. Bounds (Eds.), *Competing Globally Through Customer Value* (Wesport, CT: Quorum Books, 1991) Foreword.

3. Exodus 18: 17–22, *Good News Bible, Today's English Version.*

4. For more on this point, see A. Chandler, *The Visible Hand* (Cambridge, MA: Harvard University Press, 1977).

5. V.A. Thompson, *Modern Organization* (New York: John Wiley & Sons, 1964). This book includes a discussion of the problem "bureaupathology."

6. Henri Fayol, *General and Industrial Management* (New York: Pitman, 1949).

7. Vice President Al Gore, *Creating a Government that Works* (Washington, DC: The Government Printing Office, 1993) pp. 3–4.

8. Hugo Munsterberg, *Psychology and Industrial Efficiency* (Boston: Houghton Mifflin, 1913). This book outlines Munsterberg's ideas.

9. Chester Barnard, *The Functions of the Executive* (Cambridge, MA: Harvard University Press, 1938).

10. Mary Parker Follett, *The New State: Group Organization the Solution of Popular Government* (London: Longmans, Green, & Co., 1918).

11. Elton Mayo, *The Human Problems of an Industrial Civilization* (New York: Macmillan, 1933) and Fritz J. Roethlisberger and William J. Dickson, *Management and the Worker* (Cambridge, MA: Harvard University Press, 1939).

12. Abraham Maslow, *Motivation and Personality*, 2nd Ed. (New York: Harper & Row, 1970).

13. Douglas McGregor, *The Human Side of Enterprise* (New York: McGraw-Hill, 1960).

14. P. Mirvis and Edward. E. Lawler III, "Measuring the Financial Impact of Employee Attitudes," *Journal of Applied Psychology*, 62, 1977, pp. 1–8.

15. Edward E. Lawler III and Lyman W. Porter, "The Effect of Performance on Job Satisfaction," *Industrial Relations*, October 1967, pp. 466–80.

16. Howard J. Weiss and Mark E. Gershon, *Production and Operations Management*, 2nd Edition (Needham Heights, MA: Allyn & Bacon, 1993) p. 133.

17. Information for this case came from the following sources: R. Rose, "Vrooming Back," *Wall Street Journal* (August 31, 1990): p. A1; Vaughn L. Beals, "Quality and Productivity: The Harley-Davidson Experience," *Survey of Business*, Spring 1986, pp. 9–11; Susan Caminiti, "The Payoff from a Good Reputation," *Fortune*, February 10, 1992, pp. 74–77; "Learning from Japan," *Business Week*, January 27, 1992, pp. 52–60; and personal conversations with Harley-Davidson representatives.

18. Ludwig von Bertalanffy, "Problems of General System Theory," *Human Biology*, 23, 1951, pp. 302–312 and Ludwig von Bertalanffy, *General System Theory* (New York: George Braziller, 1968).

19. Russell L. Ackoff, *Creating the Corporate Future* (New York: John Wiley & Sons, 1981); Russell L. Ackoff, & Emery, F. E., *On Purposeful Systems* (Chicago: Aldine-Atherton, 1972); G. Morgan, *Images of Organization* (Beverly Hills, CA: Sage, 1986).

20. E.H. Schein, *Organizational Psychology*, Second Edition (Englewood Cliffs, NJ: Prentice-Hall, 1970).

21. F. Kast and J. Rosenzweig, *Organization and Management*, 4th Edition (New York: McGraw-Hill, 1985); D. Katz and R.L. Kahn, *The Social Psychology of Organizations* (New York: John Wiley & Sons, 1978).

22. "The Virtual Corporation," *Business Week*, Feb. 8, 1993, p. 98–103.

23. J. Rampey and H. Roberts, "Perspectives on Total Quality," *Proceedings of Total Quality Forum IV*, November 1992, p. 4. Also included in the 1992 Procter & Gamble sponsored *Report of the Total Quality Leadership and Steering Committee and Working Councils.*

24. Oscar Guris, "Competitors Blinded by Chrysler's Neon," *The Wall Street Journal*, January 10, 1994, p. B1.

25. *Harvard Business Review*, November-December, 1991.

26. Quoted from "Report Card on TQM," *Management Review*, January 1994, p. 23.

27. G. Bounds, L. Yorks, M. Adams, and G. Ranney, *Beyond Total Quality Management*, New York: McGraw-Hill, 1994.

28. Ackoff, 1981, pp. 16–17.

29. "Zebco Saves Time to Stay on Top," *Nation's Business*, November, 1991, p. 12.

CHAPTER 3

1. Information for this case derived from James M. Carman, "Continuous Quality Improvement as a Survival Strategy: The Southern Pacific Experience," *California Management Review*, Spring, 1993, pp. 118–132.

2. Brian Dumaine, "Payoff from the New Management," *Fortune*, December 13, 1993, pp. 103–110.

3. Theodore Levitt, "Marketing Myopia," *Harvard Business Review*, July-August, 1960, pp. 45–56.

4. Robert Chapman Wood, "A Lesson Learned and A Lesson Forgotten," *Forbes*, February 6, 1989, pp. 70–78.

5. For more on this idea, see Brian L. Joiner, *Fourth Generation Management: The New Business Consciousness* (New York: McGraw-Hill, 1994) pp. 22–24.

6. Kaoru Ishikawa and D. Lu, *What is Total Quality Control? The Japanese Way*, Englewood Cliffs, NJ: Prentice-Hall, 1985, p. 45.

7. Liz Wilson, "The Quality Measure is Customer Opinion," *Journal for Quality and Participation*, Oct/Nov 1993, pp. 12–14.

8. Ishikawa and Lu (1985) pp. 55–56.

9. Howard S. Gitlow and Shelley J. Gitlow, *The Deming Guide to Quality and Competitive Position*, (Englewood Cliffs, NJ: Prentice-Hall, Inc., 1987), p. 32.

10. Karen Lowry Miller, "Overhaul in Japan," *Business Week*, December 21, 1992, pp. 80–86.

11. This material taken from discussion of Juran's work in Brian L. Joiner (1994) pp. 33–34.

12. W. Edwards Deming, *Out of the Crisis* (Cambridge, MA: MIT Center for Applied Engineering Study, 1986) pp. 4–5.

13. Joiner (1994) p. 27. The video is a eight part training course called "Fundamentals of Fourth Generation Management," available through Films Inc., 5547 N. Ravenswood Ave., Chicago, IL 60640.

14. Henry Mintzberg, *The Nature of Managerial Work* (New York: Harper & Row, Publishers, 1973) p. 31.

15. Ishikawa and Lu (1985) p. 63.

16. Masaaki Imai, *Kaizen* (New York: McGraw-Hill, Inc., 1986) p. 50.

17. Taiichi Ohno, *Toyota Production System: Beyond Large-Scale Production* (Cambridge, MA: Productivity Press, 1988) p. 17.

18. Ishikawa and Lu (1985) p. 63.

19. "Dr. Deming: His Last Interview," *Industry Week*, January 17, 1994, pp. 21–28.

20. "Get Real: Teach Life Skills, Not Customer Service," *Tom Peters' On Achieving Excellence*, November 1992, p. 5.

21. Malcolm Baldrige National Quality Award, *1994 Award Criteria* (Washington, DC: National Institute of Standards and Technology, 1994), p. 21.

22. Kevin Kelly, "Motorola: Training for the Millenium," *Business Week*, March 28, 1994, pp. 158–162.

23. Ishikawa and Lu (1985) p. 126.

24. From the book *SchoolWorks*, by Bill Northdurft. Described in Martha E. Mangelsdorf, "Ground-Zero Training," *Inc.* February, 1993, pp. 82–93.

25. Cheri Henderson, "Putting on the Ritz," *The TQM Magazine*, November/December 1992, pp. 292–296.

26. Bob Flipczak, "Ericsson General Electric: The Evolution of Empowerment," *Training*, September 1993, pp. 21–27.

27. Adapted from George L. Miller and LaRue L. Krumm, *The Whats, Whys, and Hows of Quality Improvement* (Milwaukee: ASQC Quality Press, 1992) p. 30. G.M. Bounds and H.G. Carothers, "The Role of Middle Management in Improving Competitiveness," in M. Stahl and G. Bounds, *Competing Globally Through Customer Value,* New York: Quorum, 1991.

28. Jon R. Katzenbach and Douglas K. Smith, "The Discipline of Teams," *Harvard Business Review*, March-April 1993, p. 112.

29. H. James Harrington, *The Improvement Process* (New York: McGraw-Hill, Inc., 1987) p. 101.

30. Adapted from Theodore B. Kinnl, "John Crane Belfab," *Industry Week*, October 18, 1993, pp. 37–39.

CHAPTER 4

1. Information for this case taken from: Barbara Rudolph, "Monsieur Mickey," *Time*, March 21, 1991, pp. 48–49; Anne B. Fisher, "Lessons from Europe's Currency Crisis," *Fortune*, October 19, 1992, p. 12; Stewart Toy, "Is Disney Headed for the Euro-Trash Heap?," *Business Week*, January 24, 1994, p. 52; Peter Gumbel, "Euro Disney Calls in Mary Poppins to Tidy Up Mess at Resort in France," *The Wall Street Journal*, February 22, 1994, p. A13; Peter Gumbel and Richard Turner, "Fans Like Euro Disney But Its Parent's Goofs Weigh the Park Down," *The Wall Street Journal*, March 10, 1994, p. A1.

2. Kevin Kelly, "The Rumble Heard Round the World: Harleys," *Business Week*, May 24, 1993, pp. 58–60.

3. Amy Borrus, "The Stateless Corporation, *Business Week*, May 14, 1990, p. 103.

4. Otto Friedrich, "Freed from Greed?" *Time*, January 1, 1990, p. 76.

5. The authors thank Al Cole, Senior Logistics Officer of the CIA, for contributing this material on maquiladoras.

6. Laurence Hecht and Peter Morici, "Managing Risks in Mexico," *Harvard Business Review,* July-August 1993, pp. 32–40.

7. Secretary of Labor Robert Reich during his confirmation hearings before the Senate Labor and Human Resources Committee.

8. Smart, Tim, et al., "GE's Brave New World," *Business Week*, November 8, 1993, pp. 64–70.

9. Harris, Philip R. and Moran, Robert T., *Managing Cultural Differences, Third Edition* (Houston: Gulf Publishing Co., 1991).

10. Kenichi Ohmae, "The Global Logic of Strategic Alliances," *Harvard Business Review*, March-April 1989, pp. 143–154.

11. Richard A. Melcher, "Anheuser-Busch says *Skoal, Salud, Prosit,*" *Business Week*, September 20, 1993, pp. 76–77.

12. Joyce Barnathan, "China: The Emerging Powerhouse of the 21st Century," *Business Week*, May 17, 1993, pp. 54–69.

13. Lester Thurow, *Head to Head: The Coming Economic Battle Among Japan, Europe, and America* (New York: William Morrow and Company, Inc., 1992) p. 12.

14. L.B. Forker, "Quality: American, Japanese, and Soviet Perspectives," *Academy of Management Executive*, 1991, Vol. 5, No. 4, pp. 63–74.

15. "Super-Industrialism and The New Japan," *TOKYO Business Today*, March, 1989.

16. Lester Thurow (1992).

17. B. Bowonder and T. Miyake, "Technology Development and Japanese Industrial Competitiveness," *Futures*, 1990.
18. Nill Gross, "The New World Lasers are Conquering," *Business Week*, July 16, 1990, pp. 160–162.
19. Keith Ferrell, "Forum," *Omni*, April, 1991; Frederic Paul, "E-Mail Comes of Age," *Omni*, April, 1991.
20. Robert C. Maddox, *Cross-Cultural Problems in International Business* (Westport, CT: Quorum, 1993) p. 21.
21. Adapted from David Vogel, "Is U.S. Business Obsessed with Ethics?," *Across the Board*, November/December 1993, pp. 31–33.
22. Martin Rosch, "Communications: Focal Point of Culture," *Management International Review*, Vol. 27, No. 4, 1987.
23. Robert Maddox (1993).
24. Robert C. Maddox (1993) see above; D.A. Ondrack, "International Human-Resource Management in European and North-American Firms," *International Studies of Management & Organization*, Summer 1985, pp. 6–32.
25. Karen Lowry Miller, "The Man Who's Selling Japan on Jeeps," *Business Week*, July 19, 1993, pp. 56–57.
26. Shari Caudron, "The Myth of the European Consumer," *Industry Week*, February 21, 1994, pp. 28–36.
27. Noted in Shlomo Maital, "When in Rome . . . ," *Across the Board*, April 1993, pp. 53–54.
28. See note 1. The article, by Peter Gumbel and Richard Turner, "Fans Like Euro Disney But Its Parent's Goofs Weigh the Park Down," *The Wall Street Journal*, March 10, 1994, p. A1, is an especially good summary of the situation at Euro Disney.
29. Adapted from Robert A. Mamis, "You Had to Be There," *Inc.*, January 1994, pp. 69–70.

CHAPTER 5

1. W.S. Frederick, K. Davis, and J.E. Post, *Business and Society*, 6th ed. (New York: McGraw-Hill, 1988) pp. 549–560.
2. LaRue T. Hosmer, *The Ethics of Management*, 2nd edition, (Homewood, IL: Irwin, 1991) p. 1.
3. Hosmer (1991).
4. John A. Rawls, *A Theory of Justice* (Cambridge, MA: Harvard University Press, 1971).
5. Richard T. DeGeorge, "The Status of Business Ethics: Past and Future," *Journal of Business Ethics*, 6, April 1987, pp. 201–11.
6. O.C. Ferrell and J. Fraedrich, *Business Ethics: Ethical Decision Making and Cases* (Boston: Houghton Mifflin Co., 1991).
7. Roger Bennett, "Profile of Harry Crown, Founder of General Dynamics, Inc.," *New York Times*, June 16, 1985, p. 26F.

8. Peter Waldman, "Insurers, Long Free of Antitrust Curbs, Face Rising Challenges," *The Wall Street Journal*, July 8, 1988, p. 1A.
9. Ferrell and Fraedrich (1991); Hosmer (1991).
10. Archie B. Carroll, "A Three-Dimensional Conceptual Model of Corporate Performance," *Academy of Management Review*, 1979, Vol. 4, No. 4, pp. 497–505.
11. Peter F. Drucker, "The New Meaning of Corporate Social Responsibility," *California Management Review*, Winter 1984, pp. 53–63.
12. Milton Friedman, *Capitalism and Freedom* (Chicago: University of Chicago Press, 1962).
13. Lynn Sharp Paine, "Managing for Organizational Integrity," *Harvard Business Review*, March-April 1994, pp. 106–117, quote from p. 111.
14. Adapted from a memorandum outlining a research agenda on the relationship between quality and ethics, provided by Gary Edwards and Jason Lundby of the Ethics Resource Center, Inc. in Washington, DC.
15. Bruce Nash, and Allen Zullo, *The Misfortune 500* (New York: Pocket Books, 1988).
16. Ida M. Tarbell, *The History of the Standard Oil Company* (Gloucester, MA: Peter Smith, 1963) Vol. 1, p. 102.
17. Ferrell and Fraedrich (1991).
18. Ferrell and Fraedrich (1991).
19. Deborah L. Jacobs, "Are You Guilty of Electronic Trespassing?" *Management Review*, April 1994, pp. 21–25.
20. Annual Report of Johnson & Johnson, 1992, p. 2.
21. The authors thank Joanne Wingard for her contribution to the development of this case. Sources for this case include: Kathleen Deveny, "R.J. Reynolds Battles the AMA, Defending Joe Camel Cartoon Ad," *The Wall Street Journal*, February 5, 1992; Lisa Bannon and Maureen Kline, "Camel Lawsuit Advances," *The Wall Street Journal*, July 16, 1993, p. B5; Paul Farhi, "Push to Ban Joe Camel May Run Out of Breath," *The Washington Post*, December 4, 1993, p. C1; Eben Shapiro, "FTC Staff Recommends Ban of Joe Camel Campaign," *The Wall Street Journal*, August 11, 1993, p. B1; Wanda Coleman, "Say It Ain't Cool, Joe," *Los Angeles Times*, October 18, 1992, p. MAG6; "Old Joe Camel Ads Defended," *Los Angeles Times*, May 7, 1992, p. D2; Joanne Lipman, "Surgeon General Says It's High Time Joe Camel Quit," *The Wall Street Journal*, March 10, 1992, p. B1.

CHAPTER 6

1. Adapted from Laxmi Nakarmi and Robert Neff, "Samsung's Radical Shakeup," *Business Week*, February 28, 1994, pp. 74–76 and G. Pascal Zachary and Ken Yamada, "Steve Jobs' Vision, So On Target at Apple, Now Is Falling Short," *The Wall Street Journal*, May 25, 1993, p. A1.

2. The authors thank Althea Washington for contributing to the development of this box. The information sources for this case include: "Toward Diversity with Carrots and Sticks," *Across the Board,* January/February 1993, p. 50; "Diverse by Design," *Business Week,* Special Issue: Reinventing America, 1992, p. 72; "Levi's Haas Moves on 3 Fronts," *Daily News Record,* November 17, 1993, pp. 1–4; "The Payoff From A Good Reputation," *Fortune,* February 10, 1992, pp. 49–61; "Robert Haas' Vision Scores 20/20," *Industry Week,* April 2, 1990, pp. 19–23; "Levi's Corporate AIDS Program," *Long Range Planning,* December 1990, pp. 31–34; Jennifer Laabs, "HR's Vital Role at Levi Strauss," *Personnel Journal,* December 1992, pp. 34–46.

3. Saul W. Gellerman, "Why 'Good' Managers Make Bad Ethical Choices," *Harvard Business Review,* July-August, 1986, pp. 85–90.

4. Rahul Jacob, "Thriving in a Lame Economy," *Fortune,* October 5, 1992, pp. 44–54.

5. Kevin Kelly, "Caterpillar's Don Fites: Why He Didn't Blink," *Business Week,* August 10, 1992, pp. 56–57.

6. Kevin Kelly, *Business Week,* August 10, 1992, p. 57.

7. Dori Jones and Michael Oneal, "Can Nike Just Do It?," *Business Week,* April 18, 1994, pp. 86–90.

8. Richard S. Teitelbaum, "The new race for intelligence," *Fortune,* November 2, 1992, pp. 104–107.

9. Julie Tilsner, "You Were Expecting Maybe John Grisham?" *Business Week,* April 25, 1994, p. 40.

10. A. Tversky and D. Kahneman, "Judgment under Uncertainty: Heuristics and Biases," *Science* 185, 1974, pp. 453–463.

11. B.M. Staw, "Knee-Deep in the Big Muddy: A Study of Escalating Commitment to a Chosen Course of Action," *Organizational Behavior and Human Performance,* 16, 1976, pp. 27–44.

12. Adapted from V. Daniel Hunt, *Quality in America* (Homewood, IL: Business One Irwin, 1992) pp. 135–138.

13. Alan Farnham, "It's a Bird!, It's a Plane! It's a Flop!" *Fortune,* May 2, 1994, pp. 108–110.

14. Farnham, p. 109.

15. J.G. March and H.A. Simon, *Organizations* (New York: John Wiley & Sons, 1958) and H.A. Simon, *Administrative Behavior,* New York: Macmillan, 1957.

16. Marj Charlier, "Yuengling Brews Up a Transformation," *The Wall Street Journal,* August 26, 1993, p. B1.

17. C.E. Lindblom, "The Science of 'Muddling Through,'" *Public Administration Review,* Spring 1959, pp. 79–88.

18. J.B. Quinn, *Strategies for Change: Logical Incrementalism* (Homewood, IL: Irwin, 1980).

19. M.D. Cohen, J.G. March, and J.P. Olsen, "A Garbage Can Model of Organizational Choice," *Administrative Science Quarterly,* 1972, 17, pp. 1–25.

20. Adapted from Gary Samuels, "CD-ROM's First Big Victim," *Forbes,* February 28, 1994, pp. 42–44.

CHAPTER 7

1. John Saxton, and William B. Locander, "A Systems View of Strategic Planning At Procter and Gamble," In M.J. Stahl and G.M. Bounds, *Competing Globally Through Customer Value: The Management of Strategic Suprasystems* (New York: Quorum Books, 1991).

2. Kenichi Ohmae, *The Mind of the Strategist* (New York: McGraw-Hill, 1982), pp. 91–92.

3. Alfred Chandler, *Strategy and Structure* (Cambridge, MA: The M.I.T. Press, 1962), p. 16.

4. G. Bounds, L. Yorks, M. Adams, and G. Ranney, *Beyond Total Quality Management* (New York: McGraw-Hill, 1994).

5. F. Gluck, S. Kaufman, and A.S. Wallach, "The Four Phases of Strategic Management," *Journal of Business Strategy,* Vol. 2, Winter 1982, pp. 9–21.

6. G. Hamel and C.K. Prahalad, "Strategic Intent," *Harvard Business Review,* May-June 1989, pp. 63–76.

7. A.A. Thompson, Jr. and A.J. Strickland, III, *Strategic Management: Concepts and Cases* (Homewood, IL: Irwin, 1990).

8. A.E. Pearson, "Corporate Redemption and the Seven Deadly Sins," *Harvard Business Review,* May-June, 1992, pp. 65–75.

9. K.R. Andrews, *The Concept of Corporate Strategy* 3rd ed., (Homewood, IL: Irwin, 1987); H.I. Ansoff, *Corporate Strategy* (New York: McGraw-Hill, 1965); C.W. Hofer and D. Schendel, *Strategy Formulation: Analytical Concepts* (St. Paul, MN: West, 1978).

10. Dess and Miller (1993) p. 11.

11. Judith H. Dobrzynski, "Rethinking IBM," *Business Week,* October 4, 1993, pp. 86–97; Ira Sager, "Lou Gerstner Unveils His Battle Plan," *Business Week,* April 4, 1994, pp. 96–98.

12. Michael Porter, "How Competitive Forces Shape Strategy," *Harvard Business Review,* March-April 1979, pp. 137–145; Michael Porter, *Competitive Strategy; Techniques for Analyzing Industries and Competitors* (New York: The Free Press, 1980).

13. A.A. Lappen, "Battling for a Beachhead," *Forbes,* November 28, 1988, p. 138; M. Shao, "A Bright Idea that Clorox Wishes It Never Had," *Business Week,* June 24, 1991, pp. 118–119.

14. Kaoru Ishikawa and D. Lu, *What is Total Quality Control? The Japanese Way* (Englewood Cliffs, NJ: Prentice-Hall, 1985).

15. Judith K. Dobrzynski (October 4, 1993) p. 89.

16. For a complete listing of these awards, see James W. Cortada and John A. Woods, *The Quality Yearbook* (New York: McGraw-Hill, published annually).

17. James W. Cortada and John A. Woods, *The Quality Yearbook 1994* (New York: McGraw-Hill, 1994) p. 622.
18. *Business Week*, "Quality," November 30, 1992, pp. 66–75.
19. Richard P. Rumelt, "Evaluation of Strategy: Theory and Models," in D.E. Schendel and C.W. Hofer, Eds., *Strategic Management: A New View of Business Policy and Planning*, (Boston: Little-Brown, 1979).
20. R.E. Miles and C.C. Snow, *Organizational Strategy, Structure, and Process* (New York: McGraw-Hill, 1978).
21. Richard Brandt, "Microsoft Hits the Gas," *Business Week*, March 21, 1994, pp. 34–35.
22. Richard Brandt (March 21, 1994) p. 35.
23. For a comparison of these various portfolio management techniques, see D.F. Abell, and J.S. Hammond, *Strategic Market Planning* (Englewood Cliffs, NJ: Prentice-Hall, 1989).
24. George S. Day, "Diagnosing the Product Portfolio," *Journal of Marketing*, Vol. 41, April 1977, pp. 29–38.
25. D.C. Hambrick, I.C. Macmillan, and D.L. Day, "Strategic Attributes and Performance on the BCG Matrix: A PIMS-Based Analysis of Industrial Product Businesses," *Academy of Management Journal*, Vol. 25, No. 3, September 1982, pp. 510–531.
26. John A. Pearce, "Selecting Among Alternative Grand Strategies," *California Management Review*, Spring 1982, pp. 23–31.
27. H.I. Ansoff, *Corporate Strategy* (New York: McGraw-Hill, 1965).
28. Porter (1980).
29. Kenichi Ohmae, *The Borderless World: Power and Strategy in the Interlinked Economy* (New York: Harper Business, 1990).
30. Kenichi Ohmae, "Getting Back to Strategy," *Harvard Business Review*, November-December, 1988, pp. 149–156.
31. Saxton and Locander (1991).
32. Adapted from Richard Knee, "Mattel's Romper Room," *American Shipper*, October, 1993, pp. 40–41; Kevin G. Hall, "Mattel's Import Transactions Go Paperless on West Coast," *Journal of Commerce*, August 17, 1992, p. 38; Joyce Anne Oliver, "Mattel Chief Followed Her Instincts and Found Success," *Marketing News*, March 16, 1992, p. 15; Kevin G. Hall, "California Businesses Step Up Pitch for NAFTA Amid Job Concerns," *Journal of Commerce*, September 8, 1993, p. 3A.

CHAPTER 8

1. Helen L. Schneider, Christopher Schneider, and Deal Riley, "Clearing a Hurdle to Quality," *Quality Progress*, September 1991, pp. 39–41.

2. Tom Peters, *Thriving on Chaos* (New York: Knopf, 1987). p. 355.
3. Michael Hammer and James Champy, "The Promise of Reengineering, *Fortune*, May 3, 1993, pp. 95–96.
4. Harold Koontz, "Making Theory Operational: The Span of Management," *Journal of Management Studies*, October, 1966, pp. 229–43.
5. Peters (1987), p. 360.
6. Runyon, Marvin. "Delivering Customer Satisfaction," *Vital Speeches of the Day*, January 15, 1993, pp. 198–200.
7. Bill Arnold, "TQM Champion," *Healthcare Financial Management*, September 1992, p. 20.
8. "Blueprints for Service Quality: The Federal Express Approach," *AMA Management Briefing* (New York: AMA Membership Publications Division, 1991).
9. "How Motorola Took Asia By the Tail," *Business Week*, November 11, 1991, p. 68.
10. Gregory G. Dess and Alex Miller, *Strategic Management* (New York: McGraw-Hill, 1993).
11. John Child, "The Shape of Organization-Grouping Activities," in *Organizations: A Guide to Problems and Practice* (London: Harper and Row, 1977) p. 72–94; J. Galbraith, *Organization Design* (Reading, MA: Addison Wesley, 1973); J. Galbraith, "Matrix Organization Designs: How to Combine Functional and Project Forms," in R.E. Hill and B.J. White (Eds.), *Matrix Organization & Project Management* (Ann Arbor, MI: Michigan Business Papers, Number 64, 1979) pp. 43–59.
12. K.L. Kelley, "Are two bosses better than one?" *Machine Design*, January 12, 1984, pp. 73–76.
13. C.E. Kur, "Making matrix management work," *Supervisory Management*, 27, 1982, pp. 37–43.
14. Christopher A. Bartlett and Ghoshal Sumantra "Top Level Managers Losing Control of their Companies," *Harvard Business Review*, July-August, 1990.
15. Floris A. Maljers, "Inside Unilever: The Evolving Transnational Company," *Harvard Business Review*, September-October, 1992, p. 51.
16. Greg Bounds, Lyle Yorks, Mel Adams, and Gipsie Ranney, *Beyond Total Quality Management: Toward the Emerging Paradigm* (New York: McGraw-Hill, 1994) p. 776.
17. Michael Meyer, "Here's a 'Virtual Model' for America's Industrial Giants," *Newsweek*, August 23, 1993, p. 40.
18. J.B. Miner, *Theories of Organizational Structure and Process* (New York: The Dryden Press, 1982).
19. Alfred Chandler, *Strategy and Structure* (Cambridge, MA: The MIT Press, 1962).
20. J.R. Galbraith, and Robert K. Kazanjian, *Strategy Implementation: Structure, Systems, and Process*, 2nd ed. (St. Paul, MN: West Publishing, 1986); R. Miles and C.C. Snow, *Organizational Strategy, Structure, and Process* (New York: McGraw-Hill, 1978).

21. Miles & Snow (1978).
22. Miner (1982).
23. Bernard Baumohl, "When Downsizing Becomes Dumbsizing," *Time*, March 15, 1993, p. 55.
24. Michael Hammer and James Champy, *Reengineering the Corporation*, (New York: HarperBusiness, 1993) p. 46.
25. John A. Byrne, "Congratulations. You're Moving to a New Pepperoni," *Business Week*, September 20, 1993, pp. 80–81.
26. Hammer and Champy (1993) pp. 32–36.
27. Hammer and Champy (1993) pp. 39–44.
28. Schneider, et al. (1991), p. 41.
29. The authors thank Tom Morris for his contribution to the development of this case.
30. "Our Competitive Advantage," *Forbes*, April 12, 1993, 59–62; "Penney Plans to Open Stores in Mexico," *The New York Times*, January 29, 1993, p. D3; "J.C. Penney," *Value Line*, November 26, 1993, No. 1645; "Penney Pushes Abroad in Unusually Big Way as It Pursues Growth," *The Wall Street Journal*, February 1, 1994, p. A1.

CHAPTER 9

1. Adapted from Michael A. Verespej, "Roger Meade: Running on People Power," *Industry Week*, October 18, 1993, pp. 13–18.
2. O. Shenkar and Y. Zeira, "Human Resource Management in International Joint Ventures: Directions for Research," *Academy of Management Review*, 12, 1987, pp. 546–557.
3. J.J. Hallett, *Worklife Visions* (Alexandria, VA: American Society for Personnel Administration, 1987).
4. Myron Magnet, "The Truth About the American Worker," *Fortune*, May 4, 1992, pp. 48–65; quote taken from p. 58.
5. E.J. McCormick, P.R. Jeaneret, and R.C. Mecham, "A Study of Job Characteristics and Job Dimensions as Based on the Position Analysis Questionnaire (PAQ)." *Journal of Applied Psychology*, 1972, 56, pp. 347–368.
6. G.C. Thornton III and W.C. Byham, *Assessment Centers and Managerial Performance* (New York: Academic Press, 1982); G.C. Thorton III, *Assessment Centers in Human Resource Management* (Reading, MA: Addison-Wesley, 1992).
7. J.A. Breaugh, "Relationships Between Recruiting Sources and Employee Performance, Absenteeism, and Work Attitudes," *Academy of Management Journal*, 24, 1981, pp. 142–147.
8. S.L. Premack and J.P. Wanous, "A Meta-Analysis of Realistic Job Preview Experiments," *Journal of Applied Psychology*, 70, 1985, pp. 706–719; R.A. Dean, and J.P. Wanous, "The Effects of Realistic Job Pre-

views on Hiring Bank Tellers," *Journal of Applied Psychology*, 69, 1984, pp. 61–68.
9. H. John Bernardin, Russell Bernardin, and E.A. Joyce, *Human Resource Management* (New York: McGraw-Hill, 1993).
10. David E. Bowen and Edward E. Lawler III, "Total Quality-Oriented Human Resource Management," *Organizational Dynamics*, Spring 1992, pp. 29–41.
11. H.H. Meyer, E. Kay, and J.R.P. French, Jr., "Split Roles in Performance Appraisal," *Harvard Business Review*, 1964, 43, pp. 123–129.
12. Bowen and Lawler (1992), p. 37.
13. Greg M. Bounds, unpublished case study, 1994.
14. Greg Bounds, Lyle York, Mel Adams, and Gipsie Ranney, *Beyond Total Quality Management* (New York: McGraw-Hill, 1994), p. 766.
15. Barnaby J. Feder, "At Motorola, Quality Is a Team Sport," *New York Times*, January 21, 1993.
16. Greg M. Bounds and L.A. Pace, "Human Resource Management for Competitive Capability," in *Competing Globally Through Customer Value: The Management of Strategic Suprasystems* (Westport, CT: Greenwood Press, 1991).
17. Mark Graham Brown, "Paying for Quality," *The Journal for Quality and Participation*, September 1992, pp. 38–43.
18. John Case, "What the Experts Forgot to Mention," *Inc.*, September 1993, pp. 66–77.

CHAPTER 10

1. Kenneth Labich, "Is Herb Kelleher America's Best CEO?" *Fortune*, May 2, 1994, pp. 44–52.
2. This example adapted from "Leaders of Corporate Change (No One Excluded: Stanley Gault)" *Fortune*, December 14, 1992, pp. 104–105.
3. R.H. Brown, "Social Theory as Metaphor," *Theory and Society*, 1976, 3, pp. 169–197; T.E. Deal and A.A. Kennedy, *Corporate Cultures* (Reading, MA: Addison-Wesley, 1982); G. Morgan, "Paradigms, Metaphors, and Puzzle-Solving in Organization Theory," *Administrative Science Quarterly*, 1980, 25, pp. 605–622; J.S. Ott, *The Organizational Culture Perspective* (Pacific Grove, CA: Brooks/Cole Publishing Co., 1989). For the origins of these definitions see Ott's list and review.
4. L. Smircich, "Concepts of Culture and Organizational Analysis," *Administrative Science Quarterly*, 1983, 28, pp. 339–358.
5. A.F. Buono, J.L. Bowditch, and J.W. Lewis, III, "When Cultures Collide: The Anatomy of a Merger," *Human Relations*, 38 (5), 1985, pp. 477–500; J.S. Ott, (1989); E.H. Schein, "Coming to a New Awareness of Organizational Culture," *Sloan Management Review*, Winter, 1984, pp. 3–16; E.H. Schein, *Organizational Culture*

and Leadership (San Francisco: Jossey-Bass, 1985).

6. C. Perrow, *Complex Organizations* (Palo Alto: Scott Freeman, 1979); W.R. Scott, *Organizations: Rational, Natural and Open Systems* (Englewood Cliffs, NJ: Prentice-Hall, 1981); J.D. Thompson, *Organizations in Action* (New York: McGraw-Hill, 1967).

7. Tom Brown, "On the Edge with Jim Collins," *Industry Week*, October 5, 1992, pp. 12–20.

8. A.F. Buono, et al. (1985); V. Sathe, "Implications of Corporate Culture: A Manager's Guide to Action," *Organizational Dynamics*, Autumn, 1983, pp. 5–23; H.M. Trice and J.M. Beyer, "Studying Organizational Cultures through Rites and Ceremonials," *Academy of Management Review*, 9, 1984, pp. 653–669.

9. V. Barnouw, *Culture and Personality*, (Homewood, IL: Dorsey Press, 1979); A.L. Kroeber and C. Kluckhohn, *Culture: A Critical Review of Concepts and Definitions* (New York: Vintage Books, 1952—Kroeber and Kluckhohn identified 164 different definitions of culture in their search of the literature); J.P. Spradley and D.W. McCurdy, *Anthropology: The Cultural Perspective*. New York: Wiley, 1975).

10. Anne B. Fisher, "CEOs Think that Morale is Dandy," *Fortune*, September 18, 1991, pp. 83–84.

11. R. Linton, *The Study of Man* (New York: Appleton-Century-Crofts, 1936); T. Parsons, *The Social System* (Glencoe, IL: The Free Press, 1951); A.R. Radcliffe-Brown, *A Natural Science of Society* (Glencoe, IL: The Free Press, 1957); H.D. Triandis, V. Vassilou, G. Vassilou, Y. Tanka, and A.V. Shanmugan, *The Analysis of Subjective Culture* (New York: Wiley-Interscience, 1972).

12. Marshall Sashkin and Kenneth J. Kiser, *Putting Total Quality Management to Work* (San Francisco: Barrett-Koehler Publishers, 1993) pp. 73–74.

13. J. Martin and C. Siehl, "Organizational Culture and Counterculture: An Uneasy Symbiosis," *Organizational Dynamics*, Autumn, 1983, pp. 52–64; J.S. Ott (1989); E.H. Schein (1985).

14. J.S. Ott (1989).

15. J.S. Ott (1989); V. Sathe, *Culture and Related Corporate Realities* (Homewood, IL: Irwin, 1985).

16. M. Fishbein, and I. Ajzen, *Belief, Attitude, Intention and Behavior: An Introduction to Theory and Research* (Reading, MA: Addison-Wesley, 1975).

17. Douglas McGregor, *The Human Side of Enterprise* (New York: McGraw-Hill, 1960).

18. Chris Argyris, "Theories of Action That Inhibit Individual Learning," *American Psychologist*, 31, 1976, pp. 638–654.

19. Chris Argyris, (1976); A.L. Wilkins, "The Culture Audit: A Tool for Understanding Organizations," *Organizational Dynamics*, Autumn 1983, pp. 24–38.

20. E.H. Schein (1985), pp. 23–24.

21. For more information, see the book by Watson, T.J., Jr. *A Business and Its Beliefs: The Ideas That Helped Build IBM* (New York: McGraw Hill, 1963).

22. Laurie Hays, "Gerstner is Struggling as He Tries to Change Ingrained IBM Culture," *The Wall Street Journal*, May 13, 1994, p. A1.

23. "Green Card," *Inc.*, August 1990, p. 108.

24. E.H. Schein (1985).

25. Robert D. Hof, "Inside Intel," *Business Week*, June 1, 1992, pp. 86–94.

26. Thomas A. Stewart, "GE Keeps Those Ideas Coming," *Fortune*, August 12, 1991, pp. 40–49.

27. E.H. Schein (1985).

28. B. Clark, "The Organizational Saga in Higher Education," in J. Baldridge and T. Deal (Eds.), *Managing Change in Educational Organizations* (Berkeley: McCutchan, 1975); E.H. Schein, (1985); H.S. Schwartz, "The Usefulness of Myth and the Myth of Usefulness: A Dilemma for the Applied Organizational Scientist," *Journal of Management,* 1985, vol. 11 (1), pp. 31–42.

29. The authors thank Lisa McWherter for her contribution to the development of this case. Sources include: Michael DeLuca, "Independence Day," *Restaurant Hospitality*, August 1990, p. 135; Scott Pendleton, "Giving Golden Arches Global Span," *The Christian Science Monitor*, May 21, 1991, p. 8; Edwin M. Reingold, "America's Hamburger Helper," *Time*, June 19, 1992, pp. 66–67; "Training Serves Up Success at McDonald's," *Hotels*, April 1990, pp. 36–45; Ben Wildavsky, "McJobs," *Reader's Digest*, January 1990, pp. 126–130.

30. V. Sathe (1983).

31. Erving Goffman, "The Characteristics of Total Institutions," in Amatai Etzioni (Ed.), *A Sociological Reader on Complex Organizations*, 2nd Ed., pp. 312–338 (New York: Holt, Rinehart & Winston, 1961); K.L. Gregory, "Native-View Paradigms: Multiple Cultures and Culture Conflicts in Organizations," *Administrative Science Quarterly*, 1983, 28, pp. 359–376.

32. V. Sathe (1983 and 1985).

33. E.P. Hollander, *Leadership Dynamics: A Practical Guide to Effective Relationship* (New York: The Free Press, 1978); V. Sathe (1983).

34. Thomas S. Kuhn, *The Structure of Scientific Revolutions,* (Chicago: The University of Chicago Press, 1962).

35. G. Bounds, L. Yorks, M. Adams, and G. Ranney, *Beyond Total Quality Management,* (New York: McGraw-Hill, 1994).

36. W.G. Ouchi, "Markets, Bureaucracies, and Clans," *Administrative Science Quarterly*, 1980, 25, pp. 129–141; A.M. Pettigrew, "On Studying Organizational Cultures," *Administrative Science Quarterly*, 1979, 24, pp. 570–581.

37. V. Sathe (1983).

38. V. Sathe (1983).

39. "Sam Walton in His Own Words," *Fortune*, June 29, 1992, pp. 98–106.

40. Rick Johnson, "A Strategy for Service—Disney Style," *The Journal of Business Strategy*, September/October 1991, pp. 38–43.

CHAPTER 11

1. This case was written by Lauren Bauman based upon materials drawn from *General Electric: Jack Welch's Second Wave* (Harvard Business School), *General Electric Company Report*, 1993; "A Master Class in Radical Change," *Fortune*, December 13, 1993; Noel Tichy and Ram Charn, "Speed, Simplicity, Self-Confidence: An Interview With Jack Welch," *Harvard Business Review*, September-October 1989, pp. 112–120.

2. Warren G. Bennis, *On Becoming a Leader* (Reading, MA: Addison-Wesley, 1989); Abraham Zaleznik, "The Leadership Gap," *Academy of Management Executive*, 1990, 4, p. 1.

3. The turnaround at NUMMI is dramatically told in the book *The Machine that Changed the World* by James P. Womack, Daniel T. Jones, and Daniel Roos (New York: Harper Perennial, 1990).

4. Theodore Levitt, "Management and the Post Industrial Society," *The Public Interest*, Summer, 1976, p. 73, quoted in Abraham Zalenik, "Managers and Leaders: Are They Different?" *Harvard Business Review*, May-June 1977, pp. 67–78.

5. Warren G. Bennis, (1989); Abraham Zalenik, (1977).

6. Abraham Zaleznik (1990).

7. B.M. Bass, *Bass and Stogdill's Handbook of Leadership* (New York: The Free Press, 1990).

8. J.R.P. French and B.H. Raven, "The Bases of Social Power," in D. Cartwright (Ed.), *Studies of Social Power*, (Ann Arbor, MI: Institute for Social Research, 1959) pp. 150–167.

9. J. Martin, and C. Siehl, "Organizational Culture and Counterculture: An Uneasy Symbiosis," *Organizational Dynamics*, Vol. 11 No. 2, 1983, pp. 52–64.

10. Bernard L. Montgomery, *The Memoirs of Field Marshall Montgomery of Alamein* (New York: World Publishing Co., 1958).

11. S.A. Kirkpatrick and E.A. Locke, "Leadership: Do Traits Matter?" *Academy of Management Executive*, Vol. 5 No. 2, 1991, pp. 48–60.

12. For a review of leadership differences among men and women, see A.H. Eagly and B.T. Johnson, "Gender and Leadership Style: A Meta-Analysis," *Psychological Bulletin*, 108, 1990, pp. 233–256; A.H. Eagly, M.G. Makhijani, and B.C. Klonsky, "Gender and the Evaluation of Leaders: A Meta-Analysis," *Psychological Bulletin*, 111, 1992, pp. 3–22; G.H. Dobbins and S.

Platz, "Sex Differences in Leadership: How Real Are They?" *Academy of Management Review*, 11, 1986, pp. 118–127.

13. J.M. Kouzes and B.Z. Posner, *The Leadership Challenge: How To Get Extraordinary Things Done in Organizations* (San Francisco: Jossey-Bass, 1987).

14. E.A. Fleishman, "The Description of Supervisory Behavior," *Personnel Psychology*, 37, 1953, pp. 1–6.

15. E.A. Fleishman and E.F. Harris, (1962) "Patterns of Leadership Behavior Related to Employee Grievances and Turnover," *Personnel Psychology*, 15, 1962, pp. 43–56.

16. R.R. Blake and J.S. Mouton, *The Managerial Grid* (Houston: Gulf Publishing, 1985); R.R. Blake and A.A. McCanse, *Leadership Dilemmas-Grid Solutions* (Houston: Gulf Publishing Company, 1991).

17. M.W. McCall, Jr. and M.M. Lombardo, "Off the Track: Why and How Successful Executives Get Derailed," *Technical Report No. 21* (Greensboro, NC: Center for Creative Leadership, 1983).

18. Fred E. Fiedler, *A Theory of Leadership Effectiveness* (New York: McGraw-Hill, 1967); Fred E. Fiedler, "Validation and Extension of the Contingency Model of Leadership Effectiveness: A Review of Empirical Findings," *Psychological Bulletin*, 76, 1971, pp. 128–148.

19. C.A. Schriesheim and S. Kerr, "Theories and Measures of Leadership: A Critical Appraisal," In J.G. Hunt and L.L. Larson (Eds.), *Leadership: The Cutting Edge* (Carbondale, IL: Southern Illinois University Press, 1977) pp. 9–45; R.W. Rice, "Construct Validity of the Least Preferred Coworker Score," *Psychological Bulletin*, 85, 1978, pp. 1199–1237.

20. Arend Sandblute, "Lead, Don't Manage," *Industry Week*, November 1, 1993, pp. 16–17.

21. Paul Hersey, and Kenneth P. Blanchard, *Management of Organizational Behavior* 6th Edition (Englewood Cliffs, NJ: Prentice Hall, 1993).

22. R.P. Vecchio, "Situational Leadership Theory: An Examination of a Prescriptive Theory," *Journal of Applied Psychology*, 72, 1987, pp. 444–452; W. Blank, J.R. Weitzel, and S.G. Green, "A Test of the Situational Leadership Theory," *Personnel Psychology*, 43, 1990, pp. 579–597.

23. R.J. House, "A Path-goal Theory of Leader Effectiveness," *Administrative Science Quarterly*, 16, 1971, pp. 321–339.

24. W. Edwards Deming, *Out of the Crisis* (Cambridge, MA: MIT Center for Advanced Engineering Study, 1986) p. 23.

25. V.H. Vroom and A.G. Jago, *The New Leadership: Managing Participation in Organizations* (Englewood Cliffs, NJ: Prentice-Hall, 1988); V.H. Vroom and P.W. Yetton, *Leadership and Decision Making* (Pittsburgh: University of Pittsburgh Press, 1973).

26. For more information on transformational leadership,

see B. Bass, B. Avolio, and L. Goodhein, "Biography and the Assessment of Transformation Leadership at the World Class Level," *Journal of Management*, 13, 1987, pp. 7–19; J.J. Hater and B.B. Bass, "Superiors' Evaluations and Subordinates' Perceptions of Transformation and Transactional Leadership," *Journal of Applied Psychology*, 73, 1988, pp. 695–702; B. Bass, "From Transactional to Transformational Leadership: Learning to Share the Vision," *Organizational Dynamics*, 1991, pp. 19–31.

27. Barbara Kantrowitz, et al., "The Messiah of Waco," *Newsweek*, March 15, 1993, pp. 56–58; Barbara Kantrowitz, et al., "Day of Judgment," *Newsweek*, May 3, 1993, pp. 18–27; Richard Lacayo, "Cult of Death," *Time*, March 15, 1993, pp. 36–39; Nancy Gibbs, "Tragedy in Waco," *Time*, May 3, 1993, pp. 28–43.

28. B. Bass, "From Transactional to Transformational Leadership: Learning to Share the Vision," *Organizational Dynamics*, 1991, pp. 19–31.

29. J.A. Conger, *Learning to Lead: The Art of Transforming Managers Into Leaders* (San Francisco: Jossey-Bass Publishers, 1993).

30. Terence P. Pare, "Rebuilding a Lost Reputation," *Fortune*, May 30, 1994, p. 176.

31. Adapted from C. Manz and H. Sims, *Superleadership: Leading Others to Lead Themselves* (Englewood Cliffs, NJ: Prentice-Hall, 1989) and 3M Corporation *1992 Annual Report for Minnesota Mining and Manufacturing*, St. Paul, Minnesota.

CHAPTER 12

1. Michele Moreno, "Travel, Tea, Training, For Top Customer Service, Treat Support Staff Like Royalty," *Tom Peters on Achieving Excellence*, October 1993, pp. 2–4.

2. Douglas McGregor, *The Human Side of Enterprise* (New York: McGraw-Hill, 1960).

3. G. Bounds, L. Yorks, M. Adams, and G. Ranney, *Beyond Total Quality Management* (New York: McGraw-Hill, 1994) pp. 457–463.

4. Abraham Maslow, *Motivation and Personality,* 2nd Ed. (New York: Harper & Row, 1970).

5. Clayton P. Alderfer, *Existence, Relatedness, and Growth: Human Needs in Organizational Settings* (New York: The Free Press, 1972).

6. David C. McClelland, *The Achieving Society* (New York: Van Nostrand, 1961).

7. Milton Rokeach, *Beliefs, Attitudes, and Values* (San Francisco: Jossey Bass, 1968); Milton Rokeach, *The Nature of Human Values* (New York: The Free Press, 1973).

8. Lynn Kahle, *Social Values and Social Change: Adaptation to Life in America* (New York: Praeger, 1983).

9. J.E. Scott and L.M. Lamont, "Relating Consumer Values to Consumer Behavior: A Model and Method for Investigation," in *Increasing Marketing Productivity* (Chicago: American Marketing Association, 1973) pp. 283–288; D.E. Vinson, J.E. Scott, and L.M. Lamont, "The Role of Personal Values in Marketing and Consumer Behavior," *Journal of Marketing*, 1977, Vol. 41, pp. 44–50.

10. B.F. Skinner, *Science and Human Behavior* (New York: Macmillan, 1953).

11. H. Rachlin, *Modern Behaviorism* (New York: W.H. Freeman and Co., 1970).

12. F. Luthans and R. Kreitner, *Organizational Behavior Modification* (Glenview, IL: Scott-Foresman, 1975).

13. V.H. Vroom, *Work and Motivation* (New York: John Wiley & Sons, 1964).

14. A. Bandura, "Self-Efficacy: Toward a Unifying Theory of Bahavioral Change," *Psychological Review*, 84, 1987, pp. 191–215.

15. J. Galbraith and L.L. Cummings, "An Empirical Investigation of the Motivational Determinants of Task Performance: Interactive Effects between Instrumentality-Valence and Motivation-Ability" *Organizational Behavior and Human Performance*, Vol. 2, 1967, pp. 237–257.

16. R. deCharms, *Personal Causation: The Internal Affective Determinants of Behavior* (New York: Academic Press, 1968); E.L. Deci, *Intrinsic Motivation* (New York: Plenum, 1975); E.L. Deci, "The Hidden Costs of Rewards," *Organizational Dynamics*, Vol. 4, No. 3, 1976, pp. 61–72.

17. H.J. Arnold, "Effects of Performance Feedback and Extrinsic Reward upon High Intrinsic Motivation," *Organizational Behavior and Human Performance*, Vol. 17, 1976, pp. 275–288.

18. E.A. Locke, "Toward a Theory of Task Motivation and Incentives," *Organizational Behavior and Human Performance*, Vol. 3, 1968, pp. 157–189.

19. C.N. Parkinson, *Parkinson's Law and Other Studies in Administration* (Boston: Houghton-Mifflin, 1957).

20. W. Edwards Deming, *Out of the Crisis* (Cambridge, MA: MIT Center for Advanced Engineering, 1986) p. 66.

21. J.S. Adams, "Toward an Understanding of Inequity," *Journal of Abnormal and Social Psychology*, Vol. 67, No. 5, 1963, pp. 422–436; J.S. Adams, "Inequity in Social Exchange," In Leonard Berkowitz (Ed.), *Advances in Experimental Social Psychology*, Vol. 2, New York: Academic Press, 1965, pp. 267–299.

22. W. Edwards Deming (1986) pp. 75–76.

23. F. Herzberg, "One More Time: How Do You Motivate Employees?" *Harvard Business Review* January-February, 1987, pp. 109–120.

24. Koza Mizoguchi, "Robots, Not Workers, are Laid Off

as Japan Grapples With Recession," Associated Press, *The Knoxville News-Sentinel*, Sunday, April 25, 1993, p. D6.

25. J.R. Hackman and E.E. Lawler, "Employee Reactions to Job Characteristics," *Journal of Applied Psychology*, Vol. 55, 1971, pp. 259–286.

26. J.R. Hackman and G.R. Oldham, "Motivation Through the Design of Work: Test of a Theory," *Organizational Behavior and Human Performance*, Vol. 16, 1976, pp. 250–279; J.R. Hackman and G.R. Oldham *Work Redesign* (Reading, MA: Addison-Wesley, 1980).

27. Michael Hammer, "Reengineering Work: Don't Automate, Obliterate," *Harvard Business Review*, July-August, 1990, pp. 106–107.

28. E.E. Lawler, S. Mohrman, and G.E. Ledford, Jr., *Employee Involvement and Total Quality Management* (San Francisco, CA: Jossey-Bass, 1992).

29. "Team Spirit: A Decisive Response to Crisis Brought Ford Enhanced Productivity," *Wall Street Journal*, Dec. 15, 1992.

30. D. Nichols, "Taking Participative Management to the Limit," *Management Review*, August 1987, pp. 28–32.

31. R.E. Kopelman, "Job Redesign and Productivity: A Review of the Evidence," *National Productivity Review*, Summer 1985.

32. R.E. Walton, "Quality of Work Life: What Is It?" *Sloan Management Review*, 15, 1973, pp. 11–21.

33. D. Henne and E. Locke, "Job Dissatisfaction: What are the Consequences?" *International Journal of Psychology*, 20, 1985, pp. 221–240.

34. E.A. Locke, D.M. Schweiger and G.P. Latham, "Participation in Decision Making: When Should It Be Used?" *Organizational Dynamics*, Winter 1986, pp. 62–75.

35. Michele Moreno (1993), p.2.

36. Patrick R. Tyson, "Is Europe a Model for OSHA Reform?" *Safety & Health*, Vol. 148, p. 29.

37. The authors thank Althea Washington for her contribution to the development of this case. Sources for this case include: *All About OSHA* (Washington, DC: U.S. Department of Labor, 1992); Teresa Barker, "OSHA Compliance: Is Good-Enough Enough?" *Safety & Health,* July 1993, p. 48; J. David Hanson, "Occupational Safety and Health Administration Reform Stranded" *Chemical and Engineering News,* Nov. 15, 1993, p. 52; "Reich Backs OSHA Reform Bill, *Engineering News Record,* Dec. 13, 1993, p. 5; Patrick R. Tyson, "OSHA Did Some Summer (and Fall) Cleaning," *Safety & Health,* January 1994, p. 27.

CHAPTER 13

1. Adapted from "Communication is Strategy—Audit Your Results," *Tom Peters on Acheiving Excellence,* October 1991, p. 5.

2. R. Levering, M. Moskowitz, and M. Katz, (1984). *The 100 Best Companies to Work for in America* (Reading, MA: Addison-Wesley, 1984) p. 9.

3. E.R. Alexander, M.M. Helms, and R.D. Wilkins, "The Relationship Between Supervisory Communication and Subordinate Performance Among Professionals," *Public Personnel Management*, 1989, pp. 415–429.

4. C.A. O'Reilly and L.R. Pondy (1979) "Organizational communication. In Steven Kerr (Ed.), *Organizational Behavior*, (Columbus, OH: Grid, 1979).

5. A. Mehrabian, *Silent Messages* (Belmont, CA: Wadsworth, 1971).

6. R.L. Daft and R.I. Lengel, "Information Richness: A New Approach to Managerial Behavior and Organization Design," in Barry M. Staw and L.L. Cummings (Eds.), *Research in Organizational Behavior (Vol. 6)* (Greenwich, CT: JAI Press, 1984).

7. The authors would like to thank DeAnna Putney for contributing this box.

8. G. Pascal Zachary, "It's a Mail Thing: Electronic Messaging Gets a Rating—Ex," *The Wall Srreet Journal,* June 22, 1994, p. A1.

9. J.L. Gibson, J.M. Ivancevich, and J.H. Donnelly, *Organizations: Behavior, Structure, Processes* (Homewood, IL: Irwin, 1991).

10. G. Hofstede, *Culture's Consequences: International Differences in Work-Related Values* (Newbury Park, CA: Sage Publications, 1984).

11. William C. Byham and George Dixon, *Shogun Management: How North Americans Can Thrive in Japanese Companies* (New York: HarperBusiness, 1993).

12. G.B. Northcraft and M.A. Neale, *Organizational Behavior: A Management Challenge* (Hinsdale, IL: The Dryden Press, 1990).

13. Written by Tammy Allen based upon R.E. Axtell, *Do's and Taboos Around the World* (New York: John Wiley & Sons, 1990).

14. B.L. Davis, C.J. Skube, L.W. Hallervik, S.H. Gebelein, and J.L. Sheard, (1992) *Successful Manager's Handbook: Development Suggestions For Today's Managers* (Minneapolis, MN: Personnel Decisions, Inc, 1992).

15. R.L. Hughes, R.C. Ginnett, and G.J. Curphy, *Leadership: Enhancing the Lessons of Experience* (Homewood, IL: Irwin, 1992).

16. Nancy J. Perry, "How to Mine Human Resources," *Fortune*, February 24, 1994, p. 96.

17. Cited in George L. Miller and LaRue L. Krumm, *The Whats, Whys, and Hows of Quality Improvement* (Milwaukee, WI: ASQC Quality Press, 1992) p. 25.

18. *Tom Peters on Achieving Excellence*, October 1991, p. 5.

19. Adapted from John H. Sheridan, "Honeywell, Inc., Phoenix" *Industry Week*, October 18, 1993, pp. 26–28.

CHAPTER 14

1. The authors thank Sue Anderson, Michael Canon, and Marshall Whisnant for providing the information contained in this case.

2. Jon R. Katzenbach and Douglas K. Smith, "The Discipline of Teams," *Harvard Business Review*, March-April, 1993, p. 112.

3. Rensis Likert, *New Patterns of Management* (New York: McGraw-Hill, 1961).

4. G.M. Bounds and G.H. Carothers, "The Role of Middle Management in Improving Competitiveness," in *Competing Globally Through Customer Value: The Management of Strategic Suprasystems* (Westport, CT: Greenwood Press, 1991).

5. E. Sundstrom, K.P. De Meuse, and D. Futrell, "Teams: Applications and Effectiveness," *American Psychologist*, 45, 2, 1990, pp. 120–133.

6. A. Geisel, "Labor, Management Eye Teamwork," *The Knoxville News-Sentinel*, November 22, 1992, p. D1.

7. R.W. Walton, "Work Innovation at Topeka: After Six Years," *Journal of Applied Behavioral Science*, 13, 1977, pp. 422–433; Thomas A. Stewart, "The Search for the Organization of Tomorrow," *Fortune*, May 18, 1992, pp. 92–98.

8. J. Hoerr, M.A. Pollock, and D.E. Whiteside, "Management Discovers the Human Side of Automation," *Business Week*, September 29, 1986, pp. 70–76.

9. "The Workers Know Best," *Time*, January 28, 1980.

10. P.C. Thompson, "Quality Circles at Martin Marietta Corporation, Denver Aerospace/Michoud Division," in R. Zager and M. Rosow (Eds.), *The Inovative Organization* (New York: Pergamon, 1982) pp. 3–20.

11. I.D. Steiner, *Group Process and Productivity* (Orlando, FL: Academic Press, 1972).

12. Adapted from Tracy Benson Kirker, "Edy's Grand Ice Cream," *Industry Week*, October 18, 1993, pp. 29–32.

13. Richard S. Wellins, "Building a Self-Directed Work Team," *Training and Development*, December 1992, pp. 24–28.

14. Thomas A. Stewart, *Fortune* (May 18, 1992), p. 94.

15. Bruce W. Tuckman, "Developmental Sequence in Small Groups," *Psychological Bulletin*, 63, 1965, pp. 384–389.

16. C.J.G. Gersick, "Time and Transition in Teams: Toward a New Model of Group Development," *Academy of Management Journal*, 31, 1988, pp. 9–41.

17. John Case, "What the Experts Forgot to Mention," *Inc.* September 1993, pp. 66–77.

18. Sundstrom, et al., (1990).

19. D.C. Feldman, "The Development and Enforcement of Group Norms," *Academy of Management Review*, 9, 1984, pp. 47–53.

20. L.L. Cummings, G.P. Huber, and E. Arendt, "Effects of Size and Spatial Arrangements in Group Decision Making," *Academy of Management Journal*, 17, 1974, pp. 470–485.

21. N.L. Kerr, "Motivation Losses in Small Groups: A Social Dilemma Analysis," *Journal of Personality and Social Psychology*, 45, 1983, pp. 819–828; J. Jackson and K.D. Williams, "Social Loafing on Difficult Tasks: Working Collectively Can Improve Performance, *Journal of Personality and Social Psychology*, 49, 1985, pp. 937–942.

22. S. Moscovici, and M. Zavalloni, "The Group as a Polarizer of Attitudes," *Journal of Personality and Social Psychology*, 12, 1969, pp. 125–135.

23. I.L. Janis, *Victims of Groupthink* (Boston: Houghton Mifflin, 1972).

24. R. Broderick, "Learning the Ropes," *Training*, October 1989, pp. 78–86; J.J. Laabs, "Team Training Goes Outdoors," *Personnel Journal*, June 1991, pp. 56–63; B.B. Thompson, "Training in the Great Outdoors," *Training*, May 1991, pp. 46–52.

25. R. Beckhard and T. Harris, *Organizational Transactions: Managing Complex Change* (Reading, MA: Addison-Wesley Publishing, 1977).

26. Peter R. Scholtes, *The Team Handbook* (Madison, WI: Joiner Associates, 1988), p. 2–40.

27. This section on brainstorming and multivoting adapted from Peter Scholtes, *The Team Handbook* (Madison, WI: Joiner Associates, 1988) pp. 22–37 to 2–41; Peter Capezio and Debra Morehouse, *Total Quality Management* (Shawnee Mission, KS: National Press Publications, 1992) pp. 168–169; William Lareau, *American Samurai* (New York: Warner Books, 1991) pp. 294–295.

28. Adapted from Scholtes (1988) pp. 2–41 to 2–44; *Total Quality Transformation: Improvement Tools* (Miamisburg, OH: PQ Systems, 1994) section on NGT; Lareau (1991) pp. 295–296.

29. Charles R. T. Crumpley, "Hallmark's Journey." *Kansas City Star*, December 13, 1992, p. A1.

CHAPTER 15

1. Ray Stata, "Organizational Learning: The Key to Success in the 1990s," *Prism*, Fourth Quarter 1992, pp. 87–94.

2. E.H. Schein, "Coming to a New Awareness of Organizational Culture," *Sloan Management Review*, 23, 1984, pp. 55–68; E.H. Schein, *Organizational Culture and Leadership* (San Francisco: Jossey-Bass, 1985).

3. M.L. Tushman, W.H. Newman, and D.A. Nadler, "Executive Leadership and Organizational Evolution: Managing Incremental and Discontinuous Change," in

R.H. Kilmann, T.J. Covin & Associates, *Corporate Transformation: Revitalizing Organizations for a Competitive World* (San Francisco, CA.: Jossey-Bass, 1988) pp. 102–130.

4. Dori Jones Yang and Andrea Rothman, "Reinventing Boeing," *Business Week*, March 1, 1993, pp. 60–63.

5. T.G. Cummings and E.F. Huse, *Organizational Development and Change* (St. Paul, MN: West Publishing Company, 1989).

6. Kurt Lewin, *Field Theory in Social Sciences* (New York: Harper & Row, 1951).

7. Sharon Nelton, "The Benefits that Flow from Quality," *Nation's Business*, March 1993, pp. 71–72.

8. G.M. Bounds and L.A. Pace, "Human Resource Management for Competitive Capability," in *Competing Globally Through Customer Value: The Management of Strategic Suprasystems* (Westport, CT: Greenwood Press, 1991) p. 649.

9. E.G. Flamholtz, Y. Randle, and S. Sackmann, "Personnel Management: The Tenor of Today," *Personnel Journal*, June 1987, p. 64.

10. Graham W. Rhinehart, "A New Paradigm for Organizational Structure," *Airpower Journal*, Spring 1992, pp. 49–50.

11. Cummings and Huse (1989).

12. Mimi Vandermolen, "Shifting the Corporate Culture," *Working Woman*, November 1992, pp. 25–28.

13. Thomas J. Peters and Robert H. Waterman, *In Search of Excellence: Lessons from America's Best-Run Companies* (New York: Harper & Row, 1981).

14. M. Beer, R.A. Eisenstadt, and B. Spector, *The Critical Path to Corporate Renewal* (Boston: Harvard Business School Press, 1990).

15. B. O'Reilly, "Apple Computer's Risky Evolution," *Fortune*, May 8, 1989, pp. 75–83.

16. Jerry Flint, "These are the Good Old Days," *Forbes*, January 4, 1993, pp. 60–61.

17. Clay Carr, "7 Keys to Successful Change," *Training*, February 1994, pp. 55–60.

18. This quote and other material on the learning organization adapted from Joan Kremer Bennet and Michael J. O'Brien, "The Building Blocks of the Learning Organization," *Training*, June 1994, pp. 41–49. The person most responsible for the idea of a learning organization is Peter M. Senge in his book *The Fifth Discipline: The Art and Science of the Learning Organization* (New York: Doubleday Currency, 1992). This book is highly recommended. Also see Fred Kofman and Peter M. Senge, "Communities of Commitment: The Heart of Learning Organizations," *Organizational Dynamics*, Autumn 1993, pp. 5–23.

19. Stata (1992), pp. 103–104.

20. N.S. Nopper. "Reinventing the Factory with Lifelong Learning," *Training*, May 1993, pp. 55–58.

CHAPTER 16

1. Henri Fayol, *General and Industrial Management* (New York: Pitman, 1949); R.J. Mockler, Editor, *Readings in Management Control* (New York: Appleton-Century-Crofts, 1970) p. 14.

2. Daniel R. Tobin, "The Manager as Firefighter," *Training*, May 1994, p. 14.

3. Kaoru Ishikawa, *What is Total Quality Control? The Japanese Way* (Englewood Cliffs, NJ: Prentice-Hall, 1985) p. 65.

4. W. Edwards Deming, *Out of the Crisis* (Cambridge, MA: MIT Center for Advanced Engineering Study, 1986) pp. 365–366.

5. Information for this box adapted from Kim I. Melton, *Introduction to Statistics for Process Studies, 2nd Ed.* (New York: McGraw-Hill, 1993).

6. Brian L. Joiner, *Fourth Generation Management: The New Business Consciousness* (New York: McGraw-Hill, 1994) p. 125.

7. Peter M. Senge, *The Fifth Discipline* (New York: Doubleday Currency, 1990) p. 21.

8. G. Bounds, L. Yorks, M. Adams, and G. Ranney, *Beyond Total Quality Management* (New York: McGraw-Hill, 1994).

9. "Paper Snags Cut by Two-Thirds," *PI Quality*, March/April 1994, pp. 57–59.

10. G. Bounds, et al. (1994).

11. Karen Bemowski, "Quality in Flight," *Quality Progress*, July 1992, pp. 27–32.

CHAPTER 17

1. Adam Bartkowski, "Challenge of Competitiveness—Today's Industrial Sector Marketplace," *APICS-The Performance Advantage*, April 1994, p. 47.

2. James B. Dilworth, *Operations Management: Design, Planning, and Control for Manufacturing and Services* (New York: McGraw-Hill, 1992) p. 8.

3. Dilworth (1992) p. 10.

4. Ray Cheser and Cheryl Tanner, "Critikon Declares War on Waste, Launches Kaizen Drive," *Target*, July/August 1993, pp. 12–22.

5. Dilworth (1992) p. 342.

6. Dilworth (1992) p. 349.

7. John H. Sheridan, "A Vision of Agility, *Industry Week*, March 21, 1994, pp. 43–46.

8. Joseph Corso, "Challenging Old Assumptions with Finite Scheduling," *APICS-the Performance Advantage*, November 1993, pp. 50–53.

CHAPTER 18

1. Catherine Arnst, "Hospitals Attack a Crippler: Paper," *Business Week*, February 21, 1994, pp. 104–106.
2. Greg Bounds, *Cases and Profiles in Quality* (Burr Ridge, IL: Irwin, 1995).
3. Greg Bounds (1995).
4. John W. Verity, "Taking a Laptop on a Call," *Business Week*, October 25, 1993, pp. 124–125.
5. Rick Tetzeli, "Surviving Information Overload," *Fortune*, July 11, 1994, pp. 60–64.
6. Robert Murdock, *MIS Concepts and Design* (New Jersey: Prentice Hall, 1986) pp. 143–147.
7. K.J. Radford, *Information Systems in Management* (Reston, VA: Reston Publishing Co., 1973).
8. Hugh Watson, R. Kelly Rainer, and George Houdeshel, *Executive Information Systems* (New York: John Wiley & Sons, Inc., 1972) pp. 82–83.
9. Jack B. Rochester, *Computers: Tools for Knowledge Workers* (Burr Ridge, IL: Irwin, 1993), p. 480.
10. Bartow Hodge, Robert A. Fleck, Jr., and C. Brian Honess, *Management Information Systems* (Reston, VA: Reston Publishing Co., 1984) p. 193.
11. Shari Caudron, "High Touch *Plus* High Tech," *Industry Week*, May 2, 1994, pp. 21–25; John W. Verity, "Taking a Laptop on a Call," *Business Week*, October 25, 1993, pp. 124–125.
12. Andy Gale, "When the Pressure's On . . . ERP Clears Away Major Roadblocks,"*APICS-The Performance Advantage*, July 1993, pp. 41–43.
13. T.H. Winton, *Artificial Intelligence* (Reading, MA: Addison-Wesley, 1984) p. 1.

14. D.G. Schwartz and G.J. Klir, "Fuzzy Logic Flowers in Japan," *IEEE Spectrum*, July 1992, pp. 32–35.
15. Robert Murdock, *MIS Concepts and Design* (New Jersey: Prentice Hall, 1986) pp. 406–616.
16. Thomas A. Stewart, "Managing in a Wired Company," *Fortune*, July 11, 1994, pp. 44–56.
17. Howard Gleckman, et al., "The Technology Payoff," *Business Week*, June 14, 1993, pp. 57–68. Quote taken from p. 58.
18. Thomas A. Stewart (July 11, 1994), p. 47, p. 49.
19. Howard Gleckman (June 14, 1993), p. 60.
20. Thomas A. Stewart (July 11, 1994), p. 47.
21. Thomas A. Stewart (July 11, 1994), p. 46.
22. John W. Verity, "The Gold Mine of Data in Customer Service," *Business Week*, March 21, 1994, pp. 113–114.
23. Howard W. Gleckman et al. (June 14, 1993), p. 60.
24. Both examples from Howard W. Gleckman et al. (June 14, 1993) p. 64.
25. Howard W. Gleckman (June 14, 1993) p. 59.
26. Peter F. Drucker, *The Effective Executive* (New York: Harper & Row, 1967), pp. 4–5.
27. Stephen Baker, "How One Medical Center is Healing Itself," *Business Week*, February 21, 1994, p. 106.
28. Adapted from Greg Girard, "Plugged into the Wireless World, *Business Week*, October 4, 1993, pp. 106–107.

CHAPTER 18 APPENDIX

1. J.M. Juran, *Managerial Breakthrough* (New York: McGraw-Hill, 1964) pp. 43–54.

GLOSSARY

Acquired Needs Theory A theory that suggests that people learn certain needs as they mature.

Active listening A process of spending time and energy to accurately understand the sender's intended message.

Adaptive model An approach that describes a strategy that changes and adapts to changes in the external environment.

Administrative theories Management theories that attempt to develop ideal models of how to manage large organizations.

Adverse impact The judgment that a test or other employment hurdle eliminates a greater percentage of minorities than should be expected.

Advice and involvement teams Groups used to give employees an opportunity to contribute suggestions and participate in decision making.

Artifacts Aspects of culture that result from people's behavior.

Artificial intelligence The study of ideas which enable computers to do the things that make people seem intelligent.

Assemble-to-order (ATO) Operations that allow a degree of customization by designing a product that has a number of standard characteristics, but there are others that can be varied depending on the desires of the customer.

Assumptions Values and beliefs that are so deeply engrained in the minds of people in the organization, they are taken for granted or assumed to be unquestionably true.

Autonomy The amount of authority team members have to decide what to do and how to do it and the amount of responsibility group members have for group outcomes.

Batch manufacturing Operations that create a number of different items with intermediate volume requirements.

BCG matrix A four-cell form used to categorize a business according to whether it is high or low on the two dimensions of market share and market growth.

Behavioral approach to leadership An approach that says the leader's actual behavior, not traits, predicts leader effectiveness.

Behavioral school An approach that emphasizes the importance of understanding human behaviors, needs, emotions, and attitudes in the workplace, as well as social interactions and group processes.

Behavioral sciences An attempt to overcome the deficiencies of previous theories of management by developing theories about human behavior based on scientific methods.

Behaviors The actions that people take in the organization.

Beliefs Our perceptions of how objects, events, attributes or outcomes are associated or related to one another in a cause and effect manner.

Benefits Compensation consisting of different types of personal and family insurance and other additional services paid for by the employer.

Bounded rationality Limitations on the human ability to be rational.

Brainstorming A technique for generating many different ideas for dealing with a situation in a short amount of time.

Bureaucracy An idealized model of an efficient organization which includes a blueprint of structure, authority, activities, and relationships.

Business environment The context for the system's operation that provides its inputs and accepts its outputs.

Business ethics The moral principles and standards that guide behavior in the world of business.

Business level strategy A level of strategy that focuses on understanding and meeting customer needs, and market positioning of products and services relative to competitors.

Capacity utilization plan The high level plan that determines the degree of utilization of design capacity, and the source of resources to attain that utilization.

Causal models Models that seek to identify the underlying causes of demand for a company's products or services.

Cause-and-effect diagram A pictorial technique that managers use to help them identify problems or their causes and how they might be dealt with.

Cellular layout A layout in which all the activities involved in the creation of a specific product or service are located near one another.

Chain of command The hierarchical reporting relationships between superiors and subordinates.

Channel The path or paths of communication used to send a message to others.

Checksheets A document used to record the measurements or counts of actual events.

Classical school The first significant effort to develop formal theories of management for modern industrial organizations. These theorists emphasized specialization, division of labor, and the application of scientific principles to increase efficiency.

Coercive power Influence on employees based on their belief that a manager can deliver punishments for non-compliance with directives.

Cohesion The degree of attraction members have for the group and for each other.

Committee A relatively permanent team whose purpose is to deal with recurring problems or long-standing issues.

Common cause Variation variation due to factors inherent in the process itself.

Communication fidelity The degree to which there is agreement between the message intended by the sender and the message received by the source.

Compensation A payment from the organization to employees for their services.

Compliance approach An approach to ethics in which firms have a policy of telling employees what not to do—do not break the law, but there is no direction for what to do beyond that.

Concurrent control Action taken on a real time basis, as workers execute the tasks to transform inputs into outputs, to ensure standards are met.

Consensus An idea that suggests finding a solution or proposal acceptable enough to all members that no member will oppose it.

Consideration Leader behavior indicating mutual trust, respect, and a certain warmth between managers and employees.

Content theories Theories that suggest people have certain needs that compel them to take actions to fulfill those needs.

Contingency view An approach that suggests that the decisions managers make and methods they use should depend on the situation.

Continuous process manufacturing An operation in which the output is not in discrete units.

Control limit A line on a control chart that indicates the extent of variation you should expect above or below an average line based on statistical probability.

Controlling The managerial role concerned with ensuring that the organization uses its resources properly over time to achieve goals.

Coordination The alignment of the work of employees into efficient and effective processes to achieve a common purpose.

Corporate level strategy A level of strategic management that large corporations use when operating in more than one business area and how they allocate resources among them.

Cost leadership strategy A strategy that creates customer value by producing goods at low cost and competing on price to gain market share.

Crisis management Managerial action that involves eliminating the immediate trouble or minimizing the bad consequences of a deviation from standard.

Critical path A method that tracks those activities that are at the center of a project and that must be completed in a set sequence. It is the path requiring the longest time to complete.

Cultural change Changes in the set of shared values, attitudes, beliefs, and assumptions that serve to shape the behaviors and guide the actions of all employees.

Cultural consistency The extent to which all elements of culture fit together and are mutually supportive.

Cultural nonconformity Variation in behavior by individuals or groups of individuals who deviate from what the culture prescribes.

Cultural view of organizations A view that recognizes two sides or parts to organizational life: one side is outwardly visible and the other side is hidden from view and resides in people's minds.

Culture A pattern of artifacts, behaviors, values, beliefs, and underlying assumptions that is developed by a given group of people as they learn to cope with internal and external problems of survival and prosperity.

Culture An integrated set of values, beliefs, and practices that are accepted by a society or group of people.

Customer value The combination of benefits received and costs paid by a user of a product or service.

Damage control Actions taken to minimize the negative impact of a defect or some other variation on customers.

Data point A single measurement.

Data Unorganized facts, measurements, or statistics about events, time, behaviors, attitudes, or anything people care to observe and/or measure.

Decision making A process for developing and selecting a course of action to address problems or opportunities.

Decision support systems Information systems that use decision rules, decision models, a comprehensive database, and the decision maker's own insights in an interactive computer-based process to assist in making specific decisions.

Decoding The process by which the recipient translates the message back to ideas.

Delphi technique A group decision-making technique aimed at providing group members with each other's ideas and evaluative feedback while avoiding the inefficiency and inhibitors characteristic of face-to-face groups.

Departmentalization The organization of work groups according to some commonality, such as function or product group.

Dependent demand Demand in which the timing and quantity of an output is dependent on decisions of the organization holding the materials.

Detail or work schedules The assignment of specific tasks to specific capacity units at specific times.

Development On-going education to help prepare employees for future jobs.

Differentiation strategy A strategy that creates customer value by offering products or services that are somehow perceived as different from other alternatives by customers.

Discretionary responsibilities Those responsibilities left to the judgment and choice of the organization, in which it voluntarily contributes to society beyond its economic, legal, and ethical responsibilities.

Distributive justice An approach that requires managers not be arbitrary and use only relevant characteristics or evidence in deciding how to treat people.

Division of labor The dividing up of work into individual tasks that, when brought together in a coordinated fashion, help the organization achieve its overall goals.

Divisional structure A structure which groups employees into work units that contain all of the functions necessary to conduct business.

Domestic firms Firms that produce and sell goods and services in only one country.

Downsizing Restructuring that involves reducing organization size by laying off large numbers of employees to cut costs.

Downward communication Communication that occurs when information is being transmitted from manager to employee.

Economic man A view of human nature that suggests people will work harder only for personal rewards.

Economic order quantity (EOQ) model A widely recognized model to determine the best quantity to order when each reorder is placed.

Economic responsibilities Responsibilities that require the organization to provide valued goods and services to customers and profitable returns to owners or shareholders.

Effective The delivery of outputs that customers and others in the external environment will desire, value, and accept.

Efficient Minimizing waste in transforming inputs into outputs and in delivering them to customers.

Electronic data interchange (EDI) Networked connections among companies and their supplers that allow for the instant transfer of information about current inventories and automatic placement of orders for new goods as needed.

Employee involvement A process for empowering employees to participate in managerial decision making and improvement activities appropriate to their levels in the organization.

Empowerment Ensures that employees know their roles in implementing the organization's mission and have the resources, information, and skills, and gives the decision-making authority for those roles.

Equity theory A theory concerned with how fairly or equitably people feel they have been treated.

Escalation A situation where a manager continues to commit to a previous decision when a "rational" decision maker would withdraw.

Ethical relativism A suggestion that the definition of what is right and wrong varies relative to cultural or regional standards.

Ethical responsibilities Requirements that the organization meet societal expectations for doing what is right, beyond meeting the minimal requirements of law.

Ethnocentric An approach to management that assumes that one's own culture is superior to that of other nations where a company has operations.

Evolution Steady progress to alter a situation, often through small and undramatic changes.

Exception principle A communication guideline that states that only significant deviations from policies and procedures are communicated to others.

Executive information system A computerized system that provides executives with easy access to internal and external information that is relevant to the factors they consider critical to organizational success.

Expectancy theory A theory that emphasizes the role of individual perceptions and feelings (expectations of particular results) in determining motivation and behavior.

Expert power Influence on employees based on their belief that the manager has specialized knowledge, skills, or experiences to accomplish tasks.

Expert systems Computerized programs designed to preserve and disseminate scarce expertise by encoding the relevant experience of an expert and making this experience available as a resource to the less experienced person.

Exporting Selling domestically-created goods to customers in other countries.

External recruitment The process of attacting qualified candidates for jobs from outside the organization.

Extrinsic motivation Suggests that our behavior is designed to please others rather than ourselves to get certain rewards.

Facility The physical infrastructure put in place by the organization to support its operations.

Fast track A development path that should quickly lead them into positions of more and more responsibility.

Feedback information Data gathered on the performance process that is fed back to managers.

Feedback loop Method that allows the receiver to acknowledge the received message or ask the sender to clarify the intended message.

Finished goods Inventory in which all processing is done; these goods are available for shipment.

First-line manager The management level that facilitates the work of non-managerial people such as workers, laborers, operators, service representatives, technical representatives, sales personnel, technical specialists, or staff professionals.

Fixed position layout A layout in which the position of the product is fixed and workers come to it.

Flat organization A structure in which managers have wider spans of control and therefore fewer levels in the chain of command from top to bottom.

Flow chart A chart that provides a picture of all the steps in a process or sequence of events.

Focus strategy A strategy that creates customer value by targeting products or services toward a particular market segment.

Forecasts Estimates of near term requirements for units of output.

Formal authority The official right to make decisions and take actions that go with a certain formal position in the organizational hierarchy.

Formal group A group in which interaction among members takes place in ways prescribed or authorized by the organization.

Formal structure An illustration of how the organization looks as planned out on paper, with specified relationships among employees.

Frame of reference A combination of your educational, developmental, intellectual, culturual, and work-related experiences.

Framebreaking change Change that reshapes the entire nature of the organization by altering critical elements such as strategy, structure, systems, people and processes.

Franchise A form of licensing in which the parent company offers a combination of trademark, equipment, materials, managerial guidelines, consulting advice, and cooperative advertising for a fee and a percentage of revenues.

Fully-owned subsidiary An international investment approach where the multinational corporation directly invests capital and personnel by building a new operation abroad or by purchasing operating facilities from a foreign company.

Functional level strategy A level of strategy that deals with integrating functional department goals with those of the entire business.

Functional manager A classification for managers who take responsibility for one type of specialized activity or function, such as marketing, finance, research and development, manufacturing, or distribution.

Functional structure A structure with groups of employees involved in similar or related functional activities or who belong to the same professional or occupational group.

Garbage can model The decision-making process in an organization best described as "organized anarchy" that verges on randomness when dealing with nonprogrammed decision situations.

General manager The classification for managers who take responsibility for all or part of the organization, such as a division, a plant, a subsidiary, a hospital, or a government agency and have top authority for most specialized activities or functions.

Geocentric An approach to management that appreciates cultural differences but takes an integrative international viewpoint.

Goals Aspirations defining various aspects of future business performance.

Grand strategy An overall approach to taking action at the corporate level.

Grapevine An informal communication network established by employees to provide them with an alternative source of information than that offered by management.

Group A number of people gathered together to form a recognizable unit or band.

Group polarization The tendency of decision-making groups to shift toward the dominant point of view that was initially expressed.

Groupthink The tendency of cohesive groups to ignore more realistic alternatives so they maintain agreement and avoid causing conflict within the group.

Growth strategy A strategic approach that seeks to increase an organization's overall size, by increasing its volume, market share, or number of markets served.

Hawthorne effect The extra employee motivation that results from managers paying attention to them.

Hierarchical teams Groups composed of managers and their direct subordinates.

Hierarchy The structure of superior and subordinate reporting relationships in an organization.

Histogram A chart that depicts the frequency of occurrence of various numerical values.

Historic models Forecasting models that analyze quantity data from the past for patterns and project those patterns into the future.

Holding company structure A structure in which the corporation manages unrelated businesses as autonomous profit centers.

Horizontal communcation Communication that occurs when information is exchanged between individuals at the same level of the organization.

Horizontal corporation People primarily concerned with how their work fits into a process flow across specialized functions to serve customers.

Human potential movement A view of the employee as a "self-actualizing being" who seeks to reach fully his or her potential.

Human relations movement An approach that assumes people are basically good and that they would make a positive contribution if treated with decency and respect.

Human resources strategy A plan for providing capable and motivated people to fulfill the mission of the organization.

Human resources audit A process for evaluating the current human resources of the organization.

Human resources planning A process for developing alignment between the organization's strategy and the people it employs to execute this strategy.

Hybrid structure A combination of divisional, functional, and matrix structures.

Independent demand Demand in which the timing and quantity of organizational outputs are controlled by the consumer of the output and not by the organization producing the inventory.

Industrial statistics The study of variation in measured characteristics, to analyze and improve business results.

Informal structure The patterns of relationships and communications that evolve as people interact to do their work on a daily basis.

Information Data ordered to see patterns that are useful in making decisions and guiding behavior.

Information overload A situation in which managers receive more information than they can handle.

Information richness The potential information-carrying capacity of a communication channel.

Information subsystem The subsystem that consists of the processes for gathering data, interpreting, and turning it into information and then distributing it throughout the organization.

Initiating structure The degree to which a manager defines structures and organizes the roles of employees and implements standardized procedures to ensure goal accomplishment.

Integrity approach An approach in which firms proactively develop policies that direct employees to do what is legal, right, ethical, and socially responsible for all stakeholders.

Intended message The information that the sender would like to communicate.

Internal recruitment A process for attracting applications for jobs from people who already work for the company.

International management The efficient and effective managing of organizational (or system) processes and resources across national borders to serve one or more customer groups.

Intervention Special actions aimed at bringing about specific changes.

Intrinsic motivation The process of being motivated based on the satisfaction derived from the behavior itself.

Inventory A stock of material held for future use.

Jargon Technical words or phrases that have special meaning to an occupation and specialized job.

Job analysis The process and procedures used to collect and classify information about tasks the organization needs done.

Job design The determination of the tasks, responsibilities, and authority associated with a particular position or job.

Job enlargement An approach to job design which involves broadening the scope of a job by adding more tasks to the job.

Job enrichment An approach to job design that makes a job deeper by adding some managerial decision-making autonomy and authority to the job.

Job rotation A practice of moving employees from one job to another.

Job shops Manufacturing organizations that operate in the low-volume, high-variety, custom-order market.

Job specialization The breaking of work into smaller tasks that require less skill to perform.

Joint venture A partnership to pursue mutual business objectives.

Just-in-time (JIT) inventory control An approach in which companies work closely with their suppliers to make sure that parts and raw materials needed to keep the plant functioning arrive shortly before the time they are needed.

Justice approach An approach that emphasizes the equitable treatment of people and relies on concepts of equity, fairness and impartiality.

Law of comparative advantage An economic concept that reminds us it is to our advantage for work of various types to be done by those who do it best for the least price.

Layout The spatial arrangement of operations units relative to each other.

Leader effectiveness The acknowledged ability of a manager to guide a group toward goal accomplishment.

Leader emergence A process where peers recognize the leadership potential of a group member and allow that person to influence their futures.

Leadership A process of influencing the activities of individuals or groups toward achieving a goal.

Leadership Grid Model developed by Blake and McCanse that proposes various leadership behaviors differ in terms of concern for people and concern for production.

Learning from consequences Learning that results from successful or unsuccessful experiences.

Learning organization An organization that has woven a continuous and enhanced capacity to learn, adapt, and change into its culture.

Learning process The way managers use scientific thinking to develop knowledge about the causes of outcomes.

Legal process The laws and procedures for enforcing laws and regulating behavior.

Legal responsibilities Requirements that the organization operate within the framework of laws and regulations.

Legitimate power Influence that arises because employees believe that a manager's position automatically affords the manager certain rights and authority.

Licensing The selling of rights to manufacture or market brand name products or product specifications or to use copyrighted materials, patented production processes, or other assets, usually granted to a company for a fee or royalty based on sales.

Logical incrementalism A term describing individual decision processes as streaming together in a piecemeal fashion over time to form an overall strategy for the organization without necessarily having a strong sense of direction ahead of time.

Make-to-order (MTO) Operations that produce goods only after receipt of an order from a customer.

Make-to-stock (MTS) Operations that produce items in anticipation of demand with a common design and price.

Management By Objectives (MBO) A program where employees at all levels of the organization agree to measurable numerical goals that are interlinked.

Management information system (MIS) A system that organizes, summarizes, and presents information helpful to managers for making decisions.

Management science The development of sophisticated techniques and mathematical models to understand complex situations.

Management The organization that embraces the decisions and actions involved in bringing people and other resources together to achieve some purpose.

Management-directed team A team in which the leader (usually a manager or supervisor) makes all of the important decisions, informs employees about the decisions made, and then clarifies what is required and responds to employee questions.

Managerial paradigm The context and sense of order people bring to the act of conducting a business.

Managing by exceptions Managers pay little attention to the numbers that conform to a standard, noting only significant deviations from expectations.

Maslow's Hierarchy of Needs The physiological, safety/security, love, esteem, cognitive, aesthetic, and self-actualization needs said to motivate human behavior.

Master production schedule The breakdown of the capacity utilization plan into a time-phased set of steps for producing a specific output of units consistent with the forecast.

Materials requirements planning A technique developed to manage dependent-demand inventories.

Matrix structure A structure that leaves the functional hierarchy in place but superimposes a horizontal structure based on products or projects to achieve some coordination and integration across the functional departments.

Middle manager The level of management primarily responsible for implementing the strategies and policies devised by their superiors.

Mission statement A statement that identifies the organization's purpose and answers the question, "What business are we in?"

Moral rights approach An approach that emphasizes the importance of preserving an individual's rights and liberties.

Motivation An inner state of mind that is responsible for energizing, directing, or sustaining goal-oriented behaviors.

Muddling through A method where managers find their way and develop a sense of direction as they undertake a sequence of of individual decisions.

Multinational corporation (MNC) A company that maintains significant operations in more than one country.

Multivoting A group decision-making technique for choosing among the most important or popular possible solutions or actions with limited discussion and difficulty.

Need A felt lack of something useful, required, or desired.

Network 1. As used in operations management, a graphical representation of the activities required to complete a project. 2. As used in communication technology, the connecting up by computer of employees throughout an organization, regardless of location, with each other, with internal information databases, with suppliers, with customers, and with outside sources of information.

Network structure A temporary network of independent companies linked by information technology to share skills, costs, and access to one another's markets.

Nominal group technique (NGT) A structured process to give everyone in a group an equal voice in helping a group decide on a course of action.

Nonprogrammed decision situations New, novel, or poorly defined situations that require special analysis and actions to deal with.

Nonverbal communication All aspects of the message transmitted through means other than words, such tone of voice, facial expressions, body language, format of documents, channel chosen, and other such actions.

Norm An unwritten standard of behavior expected of group members; it explains what behaviors are appropriate and inappropriate.

On-the-job training Job instruction given new employees while they are actually performing the job, on the actual work site.

One-way communication Communication that occurs when one person simply disseminates information to others.

Open door policy A statement that employees have the right to meet with management about any issue, whenever they desire such a meeting.

Open systems model An approach that assumes an organization is open to its environment as it turns inputs (labor, energy, capital, raw materials) into outputs (products and services), through a series of transformation processes.

Operant conditioning A theory that suggests that people learn to exhibit behaviors that bring them pleasurable outcomes and to avoid behaviors which bring them painful outcomes.

Operations management The process of planning, implementing, and controlling operations.

Operations research The application of management science to real managerial problems.

Operations The organizational function in which the combination and transformation of inputs into outputs occurs.

Opportunity An occasion to make an improvement or to create new possibilities.

Organization A collection of people working together to achieve a common purpose.

Organization as a system The macro processes of any system inputs, transformation process, outputs, all aimed at the satisfaction of customers or other stakeholders.

Organization/environment analysis A process for undertaking a system-wide examination of components that determine where and when a team-based approach will produce the desired effect in the organization.

Organizational Behavior (OB) modification The application of reinforcement theory to modify employee behavior and help an organization accomplish its goals.

Organizational design The process of creating a structure that best fits a particular strategy and environment.

Organizational structure The specific working relationships among people and their jobs to efficiently and effectively achieve organizational purpose.

Orientation A process for introducing new employee to the company's policies and culture.

Paradigm A model consisting of the organizational patterns, (such as values, beliefs, traditional practices, methods, tools, etc.) that members of a group construct to integrate and give order to the thoughts and actions of the group.

Pareto Chart A chart that depicts data in terms of the frequency of occurrence of various types of events.

Pareto Principle A principle which states that 20 percent of the elements involved in any situation cause 80 percent of the effects.

PDCA cycle An approach to improving decision making that includes four elements: plan, do, check, and act.

Performance Acceptability of output (e.g., products, services, information, or decisions) to customers within or outside the organization.

Performance appraisal A way to evaluate how well employees have met expected levels of accomplishment compared to some standards or goals.

Performance feedback Communication that tells employees what aspects of their performances are valued (or not valued) and why.

Perquisites (or "perks") A variety of extra company-paid-for goods and services that go beyond standard compensation and benefits.

Person/social systems analysis A process to critically analyze the characteristics of the workforce within the organization.

Personal values General beliefs about what is personally important

Personnel change Change that focuses on increasing organizational effectiveness by upgrading the skills and knowledge of employees.

Pipeline inventory Material in transit from one processing point to another.

Planned change The deliberate design and implementation of structural, procedural, technological, cultural, or personnel changes directed at increasing an organization's effectiveness.

Policy Guidelines to influence thinking and requiring the use of judgment.

Political stablity A concept suggesting the likelihood that a nation's political system or policies will remain in place.

Polycentric An approach to management that sees each country's culture and operating environment as unique and difficult to handle from the perspective of the home culture.

Portfolio management A strategy approach used by managers of diversified corporations to evaluate each business and define that business's roles and goals within the corporation.

Preliminary control Managerial action that involves making projections about the future, anticipating needed changes, and taking appropriate action early in a process to prevent problems downstream.

Priority control The constant updating, evaluating, and reordering that determines the order in which jobs will be undertaken.

Proactive change Managerial decisions to try new things in anticipation of changes in the environment.

Problem A situation that exists when actual conditions differ from what is desired or when people need an answer to a question.

Problem solving Managerial action that addresses the underlying causes of the deviation to help make sure that the same problem does not recur in the future.

Procedural justice An approach that requires managers to clearly state and consistently administer the rules and established procedures of the organization, and not to bend the rules to serve their own interests or to show favoritism.

Procedure A definite approach or sequence of steps to resolve a problem.

Process layout Functional layout where products move from function (or process) to function.

Process theories Theories that emphasize how individuals choose behaviors to fulfill their needs and accomplish various goals.

Product layout Assembly line layout designed around a sequence of operations to deliver products in high quantity with low variability.

Production and service teams Teams consisting of line employees working together to generate a product or service.

Programmed decision situations Familiar situations for which standard decisions and actions have been developed.

Project and development teams Teams formed to work on a specific project.

Project manufacturing Construction of goods that are not only low in volume but also require a relatively long period of time to complete each unit.

Promotion A move upward in the hierarchy of command within the organization.

Pull system An approach in which processes nearer the completed product (downstream), reach back and pull the required materials through the operations as needed.

Push system As employees finish an order, they pass it on (or push it) to the next station, whether this station is ready for it or not.

Quality circle An on-going voluntary membership team, often with people all from the same department, with the responsibility to develop specific suggestions for how to improve a process.

Quality of Work Life (QWL) Programs with the general intention to make organizations better places to work and to enhance the dignity of all workers.

Quality or process improvement team A team charged with improving a process, improving the quality of a process's output, decreasing waste, or improving productivity in a process that crosses departmental lines.

Quantitative school An approach that advocates the use of quantifiable data and scientific methods to improve the decision making of managers.

Quota Limit on the quantity or monetary value of imported goods.

Rational The use of sound procedures, carefully collected data, and sound analysis, all directed toward achieving established organizational goals and objectives.

Raw material Material that has been received but has not been transformed in any way.

Reactive change A decision to make changes in response to events in the environment that affect the company.

Receiver The individual to whom the message is transmitted.

Recruitment A process of attracting the best qualified people to apply for the job.

Reengineering The fundamental rethinking and radical redesign of business processes to achieve dramatic improvements in critical contemporary measures of performance such as cost, quality, service, and speed.

Referent power Influence on employees based on the degree to which they identify with and respect a manager.

Reinforcement theory A theory that suggests behavior is determined by its consequences.

Reorder point (ROP) A target minimum number that triggers a replenishment order.

Repetitive manufacturing The assembly line type operations for the manufacture of all kinds of consumer and industrial goods.

Resource requirements plan The planned allocation of operating resources (specific materials and plant capacity) to the creation of the output specified by the master production schedule.

Responsibility assignments The specific work tasks different managers oversee and coordinate in a department.

Responsibility charting A method used to clarify what roles and accomplishments are required of team members.

Retrenchment An attempt to turn around a poorly performing company by reducing the size or number of operations.

Revolution A disruptive turn of events that results in a dramatically different situation.

Reward power Influence based on employees' belief that the manager will reward them for compliance and performing various tasks.

Rework control Action taken to redo a job.

Role models Informal leaders and people whose behavior is particularly liked, respected, and emulated.

Roles The expected behaviors and performance results associated with a particular position.

Root cause The initial flaw deep in a process that causes problems later in a process, often manifesting itself far down the line.

Rule A proven solution or prescription for what a manager should or should not do.

Salary An annual amount of money paid to for the services of an employee that does not depend upon hours worked or productivity.

Satisfice A solution to a problem that involves settling for an alternative that is acceptable or reasonable to all stakeholders.

Scientific management The application of scientific methods of observation, data collection and data analysis to improve managerial practice and worker productivity.

Selection process A series of steps from initial screening of applicants to finally hiring the new employee.

Selective attention Attention given only to those messages that a person believes are important and ignoring all the rest.

Self-managed team A team given responsibility for planning, controlling, and improving a whole process and the authority to take appropriate measures to do so.

Semi-autonomous team A team somewhat on its own but with management retaining some control over team activities.

Sender empathy The ability of the sender to appreciate the perspectives of others.

Sender The individual conveying the message.

Servant leader A structure in which managers perceive their roles as primarily to support their employees and help them perform the work that provides value to customers.

Simple structure A type of formal structure in which the owner/manager makes or approves most of the business decisions, provides coordination by directly overseeing work tasks, and performs many tasks that would be delegated to specialists in a larger organization.

Situation favorability The idea that the success of a work group can be maximized when there is a good match between the leader, task structure, and position power.

Situational Leadership® An approach that asserts that managers who seek to be leaders must change their leadership styles depending on the needs of their followers and their tasks.

Social loafing The tendency for people to exert less effort when they pool their efforts toward a common goal than when they are individually accountable.

Social responsibility The obligation a business assumes to increase its positive effect and reduce its negative effect on society as a whole.

Socialization Learning that comes from people figuring out how to behave appropriately through their social interaction with other people.

Span of control The number of people that report directly to a manager.

Special cause variation An extreme variation brought about by an identifiable event.

Specialization The act of specifying work tasks when the organization puts into practice division of labor.

Stability An attempt to maintain the status quo, to neither gain position nor retrench.

Staffing A process that includes two multifaceted steps recruitment and selection.

Stakeholders The individuals and organizations who have an interest in the performance of the organization.

Standard A desired level of performance; it might be expressed in many specific forms a plan, objectives, a target, or a range of acceptability.

Statistical control The level of variation in the process is predictable and stable.

Statistical process control (SPC) chart A graphic display of data that is listed in time order, with a process average and upper and lower control limits developed from that data.

Statistics The study of variation in data.

Strategic alliance A partnership to pursue mutual business objectives.

Strategic business unit A structure which combines related divisions in a large corporation into homogeneous groups.

Strategic change Change involving the strategic direction of an organization in terms of, for example, products, services, markets, and/or distribution.

Strategic intent An expression of a desired leadership position and the criterion by which the organization will chart its progress.

Strategic management A systematic process of choosing a mission, conducting external and internal analyses, forming improvement plans, and taking action to achieve the organization's mission.

Strategy The organization's plan for achieving its mission and goals in the business environment.

Strength Any resource or ability to which the organization has access to take advantage of opportunities or to fight off threats.

Strong culture A culture characterized by a high level of uniformity or consensus among all members of an organization.

Structural change Change that focuses on increasing organizational effectiveness through modifications to the existing organizational structure.

Subculture A specific culture that develops within an organizational subgroup that shares some common characteristics.

Subordinate evaluation systems Programs in which employees evaluate the effectiveness of the management team.

Supply chain A schematic of the flow of materials, and the transformations occurring during that flow, from basic raw materials to a finished product delivered to the final consumer.

SWOT analysis A review of the organization's strengths, weaknesses, opportunities and threats.

Symbolic or abstract learning Learning that takes place through the use of language and other abstract symbols, which communicate the ideas and experiences of others that affect behavior.

Synergy The idea that a team of employees working together can accomplish more than they could working separately.

System A way of understanding an organization (or anything) as a set of interacting components working together to sustain themselves and achieve various goals.

Systems school A conception of management that focuses on the relationship of the organization to the larger environment.

Talk-listen ratio The percentage of time that one talks during a conversation.

Tall organization A structure in which managers have narrow spans of control and therefore more levels in the chain of command from top to bottom.

Tampering Making continual adjustments to a stable system, result by result, hoping to make things better.

Tariff A tax that a company must pay in order to bring its goods into another country.

Task force or project team A team set up with a specific problem to solve or a project to complete.

Task/technical system analysis A process for identifying the tasks being performed by employees and the equipment and machinery they are using to accomplish their tasks.

Team A small group of people with complementary skills who are committed to a common purpose, set of performance goals, and approach for which they hold themselves mutually accountable.

Teambuilding Any effort to improve team functioning, effectiveness, viability, and performance.

Teams The grouping of employees to allow them to work more closely and communicate with one another, and use their individual and mutual talents to solve problems, improve processes, and keep work moving ahead.

Teamwork The collaborative efforts of people to accomplish common objectives.

Technological change Change that involves altering the organization's equipment, engineering processes, research techniques, or production methods.

Telecommuters Employees who work in the home or other remote locations and transmit and receive required data or information to and from other employees and locations.

Theory A set of beliefs about the relationship between observable events.

Theory X An assumption that people are lazy and inherently dislike work and avoid it whenever possible; employees must be coerced and controlled to get them to put forth enough effort to accomplish organization goals.

Theory Y An assumption that people naturally enjoy expending physical and mental energy in work and that employees become committed to work when they understand their roles in achieving goals and that they exercise self-direction and seek responsibility.

Threat Anything, internally or externally, that might hurt the organization's ability to profitably serve customers.

Top managers The management group that includes the chairman, president, CEO and COO as well as other senior executives who have responsibility for overall organizational performance.

Total Quality Management An approach to management that looks at processes—the interactions among people and organizational resources—and their continuous improvement to serve the needs of customers.

Training A process for helping employees gain particular job skills and techniques that help them contribute to achieving the organization's strategy.

Trait approach The assertion that effective leaders have specific personality traits that make them successful.

Transactional leader A person who influences employees by meeting their expectations and delivering rewards for accomplishing goals.

Transfer A lateral movement to a different organizational job with about the same level of pay, responsibility, and authority.

Transformational leader A person who influences change through vision, inspiration, and an intense and honest concern for employee welfare.

Two Factor Theory A theory that suggests that there are two different sets of factors that determine job dissatisfaction versus satisfaction, and ultimately, job motivation.

Two-way communication Communication that occurs when two or more parties exchange information and share meaning.

Upward communication Communication that occurs when information flows from employees to managers.

Utilitarian approach An approach that suggests managers should strive to provide the greatest degree of benefits (or utility) for the largest number of people for the least costs.

Values Convictions about what is right or moral and the way people ought to behave.

Variation The change and fluctuation of outcomes over time.

Verbal communication The words used to share ideas.

Viability A term describing the group members' satisfaction with the group, their active participation in its activities, and their desire to continue functioning as a group.

Virtual office A term that describes people who work as if they were all in a single office when they are spread about in many locations.

Vision An ability and imagination to see the future of an organization and guide it to achieve this future.

Voice mail Computer software used to digitally record, store, and play back voice messages.

Wages Payment made to employees for their services; computed on an hourly basis or on the amount of measurable work performed.

Weakness Any deficiency in the organization's resources and processes that make it vulnerable in the marketplace.

Work-in-process Material that has had some, but not all of its transformation completed.

PHOTO CREDITS

NAME INDEX

SUBJECT INDEX